Double (Non-)Taxation and EU Law

EUCOTAX Series on European Taxation

VOLUME 57

Series Editors

Introduction

EUCOTAX (European Universities Cooperating on Taxes) is a network of tax institutes currently consisting of eleven universities: WU (Vienna University of Economics and Business) in Austria, Katholieke Universiteit Leuven in Belgium, Corvinus University of Budapest, Hungary, Université Paris-I Panthéon-Sorbonne in France, Universität Osnabrück in Germany, Libera, Università Internazionale di Studi Sociali in Rome (and Università degli Studi di Bologna for the research part), in Italy, Fiscaal Instituut Tilburg at Tilburg University in the Netherlands, Universidad de Barcelona in Spain, Uppsala University in Sweden, Queen Mary and Westfield College at the University of London in the United Kingdom, and Georgetown University in Washington DC, United States of America. The network aims at initiating and coordinating both comparative education in taxation, through the organization of activities such as winter courses and guest lectures, and comparative research in the field, by means of joint research projects, international conferences and exchange of researchers between various countries.

Contents/Subjects

The EUCOTAX series covers a wide range of topics in European tax law. For example tax treaties, EC case law, tax planning, exchange of information and VAT. The series is well-known for its high-quality research and practical solutions.

Objective

The series aims to provide insights on new developments in European taxation.

Readership

Practitioners and academics dealing with European tax law.

Frequency of Publication

2-3 new volumes published each year.

The titles published in this series are listed at the end of this volume.

Double (Non-)Taxation and EU Law

Christoph Marchgraber

Wolters Kluwer

Published by:
Kluwer Law International B.V.
PO Box 316
2400 AH Alphen aan den Rijn
The Netherlands
Website: www.wolterskluwerlr.com

Sold and distributed in North, Central and South America by:
Wolters Kluwer Legal & Regulatory U.S.
7201 McKinney Circle
Frederick, MD 21704
United States of America
Email: customer.service@wolterskluwer.com

Sold and distributed in all other countries by:
Quadrant
Rockwood House
Haywards Heath
West Sussex
RH16 3DH
United Kingdom
Email: international-customerservice@wolterskluwer.com

ISBN 978-90-411-9410-7

e-Book: ISBN 978-90-411-9411-4
web-PDF: ISBN 978-90-411-9412-1

Table of Contents

Preface ix

List of Abbreviations and Acronyms xi

CHAPTER 1
Double (Non-)Taxation: Two Legal Phenomena 1
1 Political and Economic Background 1
2 The Phenomena of Double Taxation and Double Non-Taxation from an EU Law Perspective 7
2.1 BEPS, Double Non-Taxation and EU Law 7
2.2 The Phenomenon of Double Taxation from an EU Law Perspective 14
2.3 The Phenomenon of Double Non-Taxation from an EU Law Perspective 22
3 The Fundamental Freedoms and the State Aid Rules as Legal Means to Tackle Double Taxation and Double Non-Taxation 25

CHAPTER 2
Double (Non-)Taxation and EU Tax Policy 31
1 Double (Non-)Taxation and the Member States' Direct Tax Systems 31
1.1 Changes in EU Direct Tax Policy 31
1.2 Double Taxation in the Tax Policy Debate on Direct Taxes 41
1.2.1 Juridical Double Taxation 41
1.2.2 Economic Double Taxation 44
1.3 Double Non-Taxation in the Tax Policy Debate on Direct Taxes 49
1.3.1 Double Non-Taxation and Exit Taxation 49
1.3.2 The Code of Conduct Group's Work on Cross-Border Tax Arbitrage 51
1.3.3 The European Commission's Work on Double Non-Taxation 53
2 Double (Non-)Taxation and the European VAT System 57

2.1 The Continuing Development of the European VAT System 57
2.2 Double (Non-)Taxation in the European VAT System 60

CHAPTER 3
The EU Primary Law Framework in Tax Matters 65
1 The Legal Concept of the Internal Market 65
1.1 Free Movement and Undistorted Competition as Characteristics of the Internal Market Concept 65
1.2 The Legal Means to Implement the Internal Market Concept 68
2 The Scope of Protection of the Fundamental Freedoms 71
2.1 The Relevance of the Fundamental Freedoms in Tax Law 71
2.2 The Convergence and the Limits of Applying the Fundamental Freedoms 75
2.3 The Different Kinds of Obstacles to Free Movement 88
2.3.1 The Discrimination of Cross-Border Economic Transactions 88
2.3.2 The Restriction of Cross-Border Economic Transactions 94
2.3.2.1 "Double Burdens" and "Double Hurdles" 94
2.3.2.2 "Neutral Rules" and "Even-Handed Rules" 100
2.3.3 The Impediments for Free Movement Resulting from Disparities 104
2.4 Comparability 108
2.4.1 The Function of the Comparability Analysis in the ECJ's Tax Jurisprudence 108
2.4.2 The Spectrum of Comparability 119
2.4.3 The Influence of the Legal Situation in Other Member States 130
2.5 Justification Grounds 136
2.5.1 Written and Unwritten Justification Grounds 136
2.5.2 Justification Grounds in the ECJ's Tax Jurisprudence 138
2.5.3 The Blurred Boundaries Between the Principle of Territoriality, the Balanced Allocation of Taxing Powers and the Concept of Fiscal Cohesion 142
2.6 Proportionality 155
3 The Scope of Protection of the State Aid Provisions 160
3.1 The Relevance of the State Aid Provisions in Tax Law 160
3.2 Tax Benefits as Obstacles to Undistorted Competition 169
3.2.1 Aid in Any Form Whatsoever 169
3.2.2 Granting by a Member State or Through State Resources 172
3.2.3 Distortions of Competition and Adverse Effects on Trade Between Member States 175
3.3 Comparability 178
3.3.1 Different Treatment 178
3.3.2 Preferential Treatment 191

3.3.3 Selective Treatment 195
3.4 Exceptions and Justification Grounds 200
3.4.1 *De Jure* Exceptions and Discretionary Exceptions 200
3.4.2 Justification by Means of the Mechanisms Inherent in the Tax System 202
3.4.3 Justification by Means of Objectives Extrinsic to the Tax System 204
3.5 Proportionality 209
4 The Convergence of the ECJ's Approaches with Regard to the Fundamental Freedoms and the State Aid Provisions 211

CHAPTER 4
The Impact of EU Law on Double (Non-)Taxation 223
1 Double Taxation in the Light of EU Law 223
1.1 The Challenge of Tackling Double Taxation by Means of Primary EU Law 223
1.2 Double Taxation and Positive Integration 227
1.2.1 Secondary EU Law as a Tool to Legally Enforce the Primary EU Law's Aim of Avoiding Double Taxation 227
1.2.2 The Lindfors Decision: Has the ECJ Changed Its Position on Double Taxation with Regard to Non-harmonized Taxes? 232
1.3 Double Taxation and the Fundamental Freedoms 235
1.3.1 Juridical Double Taxation 235
1.3.1.1 The ECJ's Dilemma and Suggested Solutions 235
1.3.1.2 Tax Treaty Override, Juridical Double Taxation and Primary EU Law 250
1.3.1.3 The Fundamental Freedom's Impact on Double Taxation Conventions 261
1.3.1.4 The Compensation for Discriminatory Effects by Means of a Double Taxation Convention 271
1.3.2 Economic Double Taxation 278
1.3.2.1 The (Apparent) Resemblance of Economic and Juridical Double Taxation from an EU Law Perspective 278
1.3.2.2 The Obligation of the Shareholder's Member State of Residence to Avoid Bilaterally-Caused Economic Double Taxation 280
1.3.2.3 The Obligation of the Distributing Company's Member State of Residence to Avoid Unilaterally-Caused Economic Double Taxation 290
1.3.2.4 The Avoidance of Double Non-Taxation Through Linking the Member States' (Dividend) Taxation Systems 294

1.4 Double Taxation and the Limits of the Fundamental Freedoms 304
2 Double Non-Taxation in the Light of EU Law 313
2.1 The Challenge of Tackling Double Non-Taxation by Means of Primary EU Law 313
2.2 Double Non-Taxation and Positive Integration 318
2.2.1 Specific Provisions Aimed at Avoiding Double Non-Taxation 318
2.2.1.1 Double Non-Taxation and the VAT Directive 318
2.2.1.2 Double Non-Taxation and the Parent-Subsidiary Directive 324
2.2.2 The Avoidance of Double (Non-)Taxation by Means of Secondary EU Law 333
2.3 Double Non-Taxation and the State Aid Rules 340
2.3.1 The Unilaterally-Directed Effect of the State Aid Rules 340
2.3.2 Thoughts on the State Aid Law Compatibility of Selected Measures Commonly Associated with Double Non-Taxation 344
2.3.2.1 Relief from Juridical Double Taxation and State Aid Law 344
2.3.2.2 Transfer Pricing Adjustments and State Aid Law 355
2.3.2.3 Participation Exemption Regimes and State Aid Law 367
2.4 Double Non-Taxation and the Limits of the State Aid Rules 371

CHAPTER 5
Concluding and Summarizing Remarks 381

Bibliography 391

Index 441

Preface

Writing the preface for the monography that has kept me busy for years is, on the one hand, a big relief. It means that the time of agonizing about abstract and sophisticated problems which are more or less all connected with one and the same issue has come to an – at least preliminary – end. On the other hand, however, it demands to once again visualize the whole process of the project: the first thoughts about a suitable topic, the overwhelming number of problems that seemed to be connected therewith, the tentative attempts to structure all questions that should be answered (and also to identify the questions that need not to be addressed), the numerous hours that were spent on the analysis, the many written pages that were deleted, and especially the intensive discussions, conversations and sometimes monologues that were held.

Although there were, without doubt, tough times as well, going through these memories once again makes me aware how fortunate I have been. Having academic promoters who constantly challenge you and thereby foster your scientific and professional development is not a matter of course. During my time as a research associate at the Institute of Austrian and International Tax Law of the WU in Vienna, I had the privilege of being supported by great scholars who have taught me very valuable lessons (not only) about becoming an academic. I, therefore, owe a debt of gratitude to Prof. Michael Lang, Prof. Josef Schuch and Prof. Claus Staringer who have put a lot of effort into fostering my scientific career. As this was certainly not always easy, I am all the more grateful that they never lost their optimism. They have influenced me in so many ways, but still managed to let me find my own way. Certainly, it is to a large extent thanks to their efforts that I have been able to finish this book.

Since he has joined the Institute as a professor in 2014, Prof. Alexander Rust has also greatly contributed to my today's understanding of research and teaching, especially by his inspirational talent and constant efforts to explain complex problems in an easy and understandable way. Moreover, I owe a debt of gratitude to Prof. Alexander Rust – and also to Prof. Georg Kofler – for having taken over the task of reviewing the manuscript of this book during my habilitation process.

I did not only benefit from the knowledge, experience and support of professors. There are also many things I have learned from my former colleagues at the Institute.

Anyone who knows the Institute of Austrian and International Tax Law a little bit can understand that it is almost impossible to name all the great people I had the privilege to meet and work with during my time as a research associate. However, I hope that all unmentioned colleagues will forgive me that I especially want to thank Daniel Blum, Veronika Daurer, Kasper Dziurdź, Thomas Ecker, Martina Gruber, Daniela Hohenwarter-Mayr, Eline Huisman, Ina Kerschner, Elke Pfeiffer, Sebastian Pfeiffer, Birgit Rohm, Markus Seiler, Nicole Skala, Karoline Spies, Karin Spindler-Simader and Elisabeth Titz-Frühmann for the great time we had as colleagues and still have together as friends.

Despite all the support I have received from professors and other colleagues, without the love and constant encouragement of my family and friends I would have never been able to write this book. It is not possible to put into words how thankful I am to my parents Monika and Walter, to my brother Jürgen, to my grandparents (especially to my grandmother Christina) and to all other members of my family who have not only closely witnessed but also shaped my personal as well as professional development. I also want to thank all my friends for not only being lenient but also supportive towards my academic ambitions.

Last but not least I want to stress that during the process of writing this book I met a girl who has by now not only become the most important person in my life. From the very beginning, Nicole has rather also been truly appreciative and supportive with regard to my academic and professional efforts. Irrespective of how diffuse and puzzled my thoughts were, she always listened to them and not only once helped me to put them in order. However, it is not so much due to her contribution to this book, but rather because of the perspective of having her by my side in the future as well that I want to dedicate this monography to her: Nicole, this book is for you!

Vienna, July 2017

List of Abbreviations and Acronyms

1. General Abbreviations

AEUV	Vertrag über die Arbeitsweise der Europäischen Union (*see* TFEU)
AG	Advocate General
arg.	argument
ass.	assistant
BEPS	Base Erosion and Profit Shifting
BFH	Bundesfinanzhof (Federal Fiscal Court of Germany)
BVerfG	Bundesverfassungsgericht (Federal Constitutional Court of Germany)
C	Information and Notices Series (the acronym C stems from the French title "Communications et Information")
CCCTB	Common Consolidated Corporate Tax Base
CDFI	Cahiers de Droit Fiscal International
cf.	Latin: *conferre* (typically read as "compare")
CFC	controlled coreign corporation/company
CFE	Confédération Fiscale Européenne
CFSP	Common Foreign and Security Policy
CIT	Corporate Income Tax
CJEU	Court of Justice of the European Union
DBA	Doppelbesteuerungsabkommen (double taxation convention)
DISC	Domestic International Sales Corporation
Doc.	Document

DStJG	Deutsche Steuerjuristische Gesellschaft (German Tax Lawyers Association)
DTC	double taxation convention
e.g.	exempli gratia (for example)
EAEC	European Atomic Energy Community
EC	European Community/Communities
ECHR	European Convention of Human Rights
ECJ	(European) Court of Justice
ECOFIN	Economic and Financial Affairs Council
ECSC	European Coal and Steel Community
ed.	editor
EDC	European Defense Committee
eds.	editors
EEA	European Economic Area
EEC	European Economic Community
EESC	European Economic and Social Committee
EFTA	European Free Trade Association
EG	Europäische Gemeinschaft (European Community)
EGC	(European) General Court
EStG	Einkommensteuergesetz (Income Tax Act)
et seq.	et sequens (and the following)
ETI	extraterritorial income
EU	European Union
EUR	Euro
EUV	Vertrag über die Europäische Union (*see* TEU)
FN	footnote
FS	Festschrift
GAAR	general anti-avoidance rule/s
GATS	General Agreement on Trade and Services
GATT	General Agreement on Tariffs and Trade
GST	Goods and Services Tax
HMRC	Her Majesty's Revenue and Customs
i.e.	id est (that is)
IBFD	International Bureau of Fiscal Documentation
ICC	International Chamber of Commerce
IDW	Institut der Wirtschaftsprüfer
IFA	International Fiscal Association

IFSt	Institut Finanzen und Steuern (Institute Finances and Taxes)
Intl.	International
J.	Journal
JHA	Justice and Home Affairs
L	Legislation Series
LL.M.	Legum Magister/Magistra
LOB	limitation of benefits
m.no.	marginal number/s
MFN	most-favored nation
MN	marginal number/s
MNE	multinational enterprise/s
No.	number/s
NWV	Neuer Wissenschaftlicher Verlag
OECD	Organisation for Economic Co-operation and Development
OECD MC	OECD Model Tax Convention on Income and on Capital
OEEC	Organisation for European Economic Co-operation
OJ	Official Journal of the European Union
ÖJT	Österreichischer Juristentag
ÖZW	Österreichische Zeitschrift für Wirtschaftsrecht
p.	page
para.	paragraph/s
pp.	pages
Rev.	Review
s./ss.	Section/Sections
SA	Société Anonyme
SCM	Subsidies and Countervailing Measures
SDU	Staatsdrukkerij en Uitgeverij
TAXUD	Directorate-General for Taxation and Customs Union of the European Commission
TEU	Treaty on the European Union
TF	Task Force
TFEU	Treaty on the Functioning of the European Union
U.N.T.S.	United Nations Treaty Series
UK	United Kingdom
UN	United Nations

UN MC	UN Model Double Taxation Convention between Developed and Developing Countries
US	United States of America
VAT	Value Added Tax
VCLT	Vienna Convention on the Law of Treaties
VfGH	Verfassungsgerichtshof (Supreme Administrative Court of Austria)
Vol.	Volume
VwGH	Verwaltungsgerichtshof (Constitutional Court of Austria)
WTO	World Trade Organization

2. Acronyms for Documents of the EU Institutions

C	documents relating to official instruments for which the European Commission has sole responsibility; some are transmitted to the Council or the European Parliament for information
COM	proposed legislation and other Commission communications to the Council and/or the other institutions, and their preparatory papers; commission documents for the other institutions (legislative proposals, communications, reports, etc.)
IP	forms part of the document number of a European Commission's press release
SEC	documents of the European Commission which cannot be classified in any of the other series
SWD	European Commission staff working document

3. Abbreviations of Cited Journals

Am. U. J. Intl. L. Pol.	American University Journal of International Law and Policy
AnwBl	Anwaltsblatt
BB	Betriebs-Berater
Bost. Coll. L. Rev.	Boston College Law Review
Bull. Intl. Taxn.	Bulletin for International Taxation
Colum. J. Eur. L.	Columbia Journal of European Law

Colum. J. Tax L.	Columbia Journal of Tax Law
Colum. J. Transnatl. L.	Comlubia Journal of Transnational Law
Common Market L. Rev.	Common Market Law Review
DB	Der Betrieb
Denning L. J.	Denning Law Journal
DÖV	Die Öffentliche Verwaltung
DStR	Deutsches Steuerrecht
DStZ	Deutsche Steuer-Zeitung
EuR	Zeitschrift Europarecht
Eur. Bus. Org. L. Rev.	European Business Organization Law Review
Eur. L. Rev.	European Law Review
Eur. St. Aid L. Q.	European State Aid Law Quarterly
Eur. Taxn.	European Taxation
EuZW	Europäische Zeitschrift für Wirtschaftsrecht
EWS	Europäisches Wirtschafts- und Steuerrecht
FJ	Finanz Journal
Fla. J. Intl. L.	Florida Journal of International Law
Fordham Intl. L. J.	Fordham International Law Journal
FR	Finanz-Rundschau
German L. J.	German Law Journal
GES	Zeitschrift für Gesellschaftsrecht und angrenzendes Steuerrecht
GmbH	Gesellschaft mit beschränkter Haftung
GmbHR	GmbH-Rundschau
H&I	Highlights and Insights on European Taxation
Harv. Intl. L. J.	Harvard International Law Journal
Harv. L. Rev.	Harvard Law Review
Hous. Bus. & Tax L. J.	Houston Business and Tax Law Journal
Intl. & Comp. L. Q.	International and Comparative Law Quarterly
Intl. Tax J.	International Tax Journal
ISR	Internationale Steuer-Rundschau
IStR	Internationales Steuerrecht
IWB	Internationale Wirtschaftsbriefe
JBl	Juristische Blätter
JCMS	Journal of Common Market Studies
JZ	Juristenzeitung
Mich. L. Rev.	Michigan Law Review
Notre Dame L. Rev.	Notre Dame Law Review

NZG	Neue Zeitschrift für Gesellschaftsrecht
ÖStZ	Österreichische Steuer-Zeitung
RdW	Recht der Wirtschaft
RIW	Recht der Internationalen Wirtschaft
RWZ	Zeitschrift für Recht und Rechnungswesen
StuW	Steuer und Wirtschaft
SWI	Steuer und Wirtschaft International
SWK	Steuer- und WirtschaftsKartei
Tax L. Rev.	Tax Law Review
Tax Mgt. Intl. J.	Tax Management International Journal
Ubg	Die Unternehmensbesteuerung
Virginia L. Rev.	Virginia Law Review
World J. of VAT/GST L.	World Journal of VAT/GST Law
Yale L. J.	Yale Law Journal
ZaöRV	Zeitschrift für ausländisches öffentliches Recht und Völkerrecht

CHAPTER 1

Double (Non-)Taxation: Two Legal Phenomena

1 POLITICAL AND ECONOMIC BACKGROUND

Anyone doing business abroad is confronted with different legal requirements in various countries. It is a challenge to be in line with all these statutory provisions and to keep pace with new developments in the different jurisdictions. When it comes to taxation, complying with all the legal rules is not enough to avoid an additional economic burden resulting from cross-border activities. Since there is neither an explicit nor a customary international law prohibition of double taxation,[1] the same event may be taxed in two or even more states. Of course, if two or more states do subject the same income to taxation, this could pose a considerable threat to cross-border economic activities.[2] In order to overcome this obstacle states entered into bilateral international tax conventions from as early as the end of the nineteenth century.[3] For more than 100 years, concluding new and further developing existing double taxation conventions has been the principal theme in the international direct tax arena. However, the increasing importance of cross-border business activities has revealed that international taxation not only entails pitfalls for taxpayers, but for the states levying the taxes as well.

1. See K. Vogel, *Der räumliche Anwendungsbereich der Verwaltungsrechtsnorm* (Alfred Metzner Verlag, 1965), at pp. 351-352; K. Vogel, Doppelbesteuerungsabkommen und ihre Auslegung (I), 59 *StuW* 2 (1982), p. 111 (at p. 112); K. Vogel/A. Rust in E. Reimer/A. Rust (eds.), *Klaus Vogel on Double Taxation Conventions, Fourth Edition* (Kluwer, 2015), Introduction, at MN 9.
2. See, for example, Opinion of AG Colomer in *D.*, C-376/03, EU:C:2005:424, at point 85: "*[T]he fact that a taxable event might be taxed twice is the most serious obstacle there can be to people and their capital crossing [...] borders.*"
3. See K. Vogel/A. Rust in E. Reimer/A. Rust (eds.) *Klaus Vogel on Double Taxation Conventions, Fourth Edition* (Kluwer, 2015), Introduction, at MN 20 et seq.

For a long time, states have used tax incentives to attract foreign investments.[4] By the early 1980s, though, the increasing number of states attracting investors through favourable tax systems forced developed economies to also compete for investment through lowering taxes.[5] Although tax competition is not per se problematic,[6] concerns may be raised if it leads to an imbalance between tax revenues and public expenditures.[7] Therefore, the OECD[8] and the European Commission[9] have attempted to discourage the spread of tax havens and harmful practices. Although these initiatives have been quite successful,[10] preventing harmful tax competition is still an issue.[11] However, not only states have discovered how to benefit from increasing cross-border commerce. As business activities have become more mobile, multinational corporations have also adapted to the globalized business environment and continuously improved international tax planning. Traditionally, countries around the world treated tax planning as a legitimate practice, unless the borders to abusive behaviour have been crossed. However, over time, business structures have become more sophisticated and tax authorities have become involved in keeping pace with the continuous

4. The earliest example of a tax incentive mentioned in the literature dates back to 1160, when wool weavers were granted tax concessions to locate in the upper town of Biella in the Pietmont region of Northern Italy. See, for example, R. Mudambi, The Role of Duration in Multinational Investment Strategies, 29 *J. Intl. Bus. Stud.* 2 (1998), p. 239 (at p. 241).
5. See, for example, R.S. Avi-Yonah, Globalization, Tax Competition, and the Fiscal Crisis of the Welfare State, 113 *Harv. L. Rev.* 7 (2000), p. 1573 (at pp. 1573 et seq.); B.J. Kiekebeld, *Harmful Tax Competition in the European Union* (Kluwer, 2004), p. 3 (at pp. 3 et seq.); A.P. Morriss/L. Moberg, Cartelizing Taxes: Understanding the OECD's Campaign Against "Harmful Tax Competition," 4 *Colum. J. Tax L.* 1 (2012), p. 1 (at pp. 33 et seq).
6. See B.J. Kiekebeld, *Harmful Tax Competition in the European Union* (Kluwer, 2004), at p. 20; on the issue of "fair" versus "harmful" tax competition see, for example, C. Pinto, *Tax Competition and EU Law* (Kluwer, 2003), at pp. 10-12; W. Schön, Tax Competition in Europe – General Report, in W. Schön (ed.), *Tax Competition in Europe* (IBFD, 2003), p. 1 (at pp. 4-8).
7. See, for example, W.J. Bos, The Changing World of European Tax Policy, 40 *Eur. Taxn.* 9 (2000), p. 409 (at p. 410); W. Schön, Der "Wettbewerb" der europäischen Steuerordnungen als Rechtsproblem, in J. Pelka (ed.), *Europa- und verfassungsrechtliche Grenzen der Unternehmensbesteuerung*, DStJG 23 (Dr Otto Schmidt, 2000), p. 191 (at pp. 200-203); W. Schön, Tax competition in Europe - the legal perspective, 9 *EC Tax Rev.* 2 (2000), p. 89 (at pp. 93-95).
8. See, for example, OECD, *Harmful Tax Competition An Emerging Global Issue* (OECD, 1998); OECD, *Towards Global Cooperation: Progress in Identifying and Eliminating Harmful Tax Practices* (OECD, 2000); OECD, *Guidance in Applying the 1998 Report to Preferential Tax Regimes (Consolidated Application Note)* (OECD, 2004).
9. See, for example, Communication from the Commission, *Towards Tax Co-ordination in the European Union: A Package to Tackle Harmful Tax Competition*, COM(97) 495 final (1 Oct. 1997); Communication from the Commission, *A Package to Tackle Harmful Tax Competition in the European Union*, COM(97) 564 final (5 Nov. 1997); Conclusions of the ECOFIN Council Meeting on 1 Dec. 1997 concerning tax policy, *OJ* C 2 (6 Jan. 1998), at pp. 1 et seq.
10. On the progress of the OECD's work on harmful tax competition see e.g. OECD, *The OECD's Project on Harmful Tax Practices: The 2001 Progress Report* (OECD, 2001); OECD, *The OECD's Project on Harmful Tax Practices: The 2004 Progress Report* (OECD, 2004); OECD, *The OECD's Project on Harmful Tax Practices: 2006 Update on Progress in Member Countries* (OECD, 2006); on the progress within the EU see e.g., Doc. 13563/00 FISC 193 (20 Nov. 2000); Doc. 8789/01 FISC 83 (18 May 2001); Doc. 14467/01 FISC 249 (27 Nov. 2001); Doc. 8848/02 FISC 129 (14 May 2002); Doc. 7018/1/03 FISC 31 (6 Mar. 2003); Doc. 14361/03 FISC 173 (17 Nov. 2003).
11. See, for example, OECD, *Countering Harmful Tax Practices More Effectively, Taking into Account Transparency and Substance, Action 5: 2014 Deliverable* (OECD, 2014); also cf. J. Englisch/A. Yevgenyeva, The "Upgraded" Strategy Against Harmful Tax Practices Under the BEPS Action Plan, 58 *British Tax Rev.* 5 (2013), p. 620 (at pp. 620-637).

refinements in international tax planning. The interaction of domestic tax systems, including rules adopted in accordance with international standards to relieve double taxation, can lead to gaps that provide opportunities to eliminate or significantly reduce taxation on income. In the past decades, more and more taxpayers have started to exploit these inconsistencies. By engaging in such complex cross-border tax structures, global corporations in particular have been able to significantly reduce their worldwide tax burden. This is not a new phenomenon. In fact, it was already red-flagged by US President J.F. Kennedy in 1961.[12] Still, for a long time tax policy had focussed on other issues.

This changed dramatically after the beginning of the global financial crisis in 2007. The ensuing economic slowdown put enormous pressure on countries' budgets and the resultant increase in the tax burden of ordinary individuals led to a public sensitization with regard to the tax system as a whole.[13] Since the media and non-governmental organizations have increasingly unmasked the tax planning schemes used by multinational corporations to reduce taxation on income,[14] political steps have become inevitable.[15] It was realized that *"too little attention has been paid*

12. J.F. Kennedy, Special Message to the Congress on Taxation (20 Apr. 1961) ("*Recently more and more enterprises organized abroad by American firms have arranged their corporate structures – aided by artificial arrangements between parent and subsidiary regarding intercompany pricing, the transfer of patent licensing rights, the shifting of management fees, and similar practices which maximize the accumulation of profits in the tax haven – so as to exploit the multiplicity of foreign tax systems and international agreements in order to reduce sharply or eliminate completely their tax liabilities both at home and abroad.*").
13. See H. Ault, Some Reflections on the OECD and The Sources of International Tax Principles, 70 *Tax Notes Intl.* 12 (2013), p. 1195 (at p. 1196); M. Plowgian, BEPS: The Shifting International Tax Landscape and What Companies Should Be Doing Now, 65 *The Tax Executive* 4 (2013), p. 255 (at p. 255).
14. See, for example, B. Barrow, Amazon Faces Probes after "not paying a penny in company tax in Britain for two years," *The Daily Mail* (5 Apr. 2012); T. Bergin, Special Report: How Starbucks Avoids UK taxes, *Reuters* (15 Oct. 2012); T. Bergin, Fast Food, Tax Lite, *Reuters* (15 Oct. 2012); P. Campbell, Facebook's UK Tax Bill Was Less than It Pays Its Average Worker: Company Paid Just £238,000 to the Taxman in 2011 Despite UK Revenue Being £175million, *The Daily Mail* (10 Oct. 2012); C. Duhigg/D. Kocieniewski, How Apples Sidesteps Billions in Taxes, *The New York Times* (28 Apr. 2012); J. Drucker, Google 2.4% Rate Shows How $60 Billion Is Lost to Tax Loopholes, *Bloomberg* (21 Oct. 2010); J. Drucker, Dodging Repatriation Tax Lets U.S. Companies Bring Home Cash, *Bloomberg* (29 Dec. 2010); J. Drucker, Google Revenues Sheltered in No-Tax Bermuda Soar to $10 Billion, *Bloomberg* (10 Dec. 2012); D. Egan, Does a Company's Responsibility to Society Start with Paying Its Taxes?, *The Guardian* (9 Sep. 2011); S. Pfeifer, He Put a Dent in Tax Evasion, *Los Angeles Times* (26 Oct. 2009); R. Sutherland, Amazon, Google, and the Sordid Reality of Tax Avoidance, *The Daily Mail* (6 Apr. 2012); R. Sutherland, Apple "made £6bn" in UK ... But Paid Only £10m in Tax, *The Daily Mail* (8 Apr. 2012); M. Warman, Google Pays Just £6m UK Tax, *The Telegraph* (8 Aug. 2012); R. Waters, Microsoft's Foreign Tax Planning under Scrutiny, *Financial Times* (7 Jun. 2011). See also David Kocieniewski's series called "But Nobody Pays That" in *The New York Times*, for which he was awarded a Pulitzer Price for explanatory journalism in 2013; similar series are "Tax Gap" in *The Guardian* and "The Great Corporate Tax Dodge" in *Bloomberg*.
15. See H. Ault, 70 *Tax Notes Intl.* 12 (2013), at p. 1196; Y. Brauner, BEPS: An Interim Evaluation, 6 *World Tax J.* 1 (2014), p. 10 (at p. 10); Y. Brauner, What the BEPS?, 16 *Florida Tax Rev.* 2 (2014), p. 55 (at pp. 57-58); P. Essers, International Tax Justice Between Machiavelli and Habermas, 68 *Bull. Intl. Taxn.* 2 (2014), p. 54 (at pp. 55-56); A. de Graaf/P. de Haan/M. de Wilde, Fundamental Change in Countries' Corporate Tax Framework Needed to Properly Address BEPS, 42 *Intertax* 5 (2014), p. 306 (at pp. 312-314); M. Herksen, The BEPS Action Plan

to the problems of double non-taxation or inappropriate low taxation on MNEs, which can be just as distortive to international trade and investment as double taxation."[16]

Until now, states have in particular relied on general anti-avoidance rules in order to limit the possibilities for undesirable tax planning. However, a key characteristic of many of the practices in question is that they are conceptually different from tax avoidance schemes since they strictly comply with the legal requirements.[17] Although general anti-avoidance rules may be an effective tool, they do not provide a comprehensive response to "aggressive" tax planning structures.[18,19] Hence, it became obvious that domestic tax systems and the widely recognized principles of international taxation have not fully kept pace with economic developments.[20] In order to properly address the issue of "aggressive" tax planning, the OECD[21] and the European

- A Story of the Turtle and the Hare?, 14 *Transfer Pricing Intl. J.* 8 (2013), p. 4 (at p. 4); M. Plowgian, 65 *The Tax Executive* 4 (2013), at p. 255.

16. H.J. Ault, 70 *Tax Notes Intl.* 12 (2013), at p. 1199.
17. See M. Boyle, Cross-Border Tax Arbitrage – Policy Choices and Political Motivations, 50 *British Tax Rev.* 5 (2005), p. 527 (at p. 528); T. Ehrke-Rabel/G. Kofler, Gratwanderungen – Das Niemandsland zwischen aggressiver Steuerplanung, Missbrauch und Abgabenhinterziehung, 22 *ÖStZ* 19 (2009), p. 456 (at pp. 470 et seq.); G. Kofler, Steuergestaltung im Europäischen und Internationalen Recht, in R. Hüttemann (ed.), *Gestaltungsfreiheit und Gestaltungsmissbrauch im Steuerrecht,* DStJG 34 (Dr Otto Schmidt, 2010), p. 213 (at p. 232); G. Kofler/H. Kofler, Internationale Steuerarbitrage, in G. Brähler/C. Lösel (eds.), *Deutsches und internationales Steuerrecht – Gegenwart und Zukunft, Festschrift Djanani* (Gabler, 2008), p. 381 (at pp. 382-383); D. Rosenbloom, International Tax Arbitrage and the "International Tax System," 53 *Tax L. Rev.* 137 (2000), p. 137 (at p. 143). see also OECD, *Action Plan on Base Erosion and Profit Shifting* (OECD 2013), at p. 15.
18. See OECD, *Hybrid Mismatch Arrangements: Tax Policy and Compliance Issues* (OECD 2012) p. 13; see also Commission Recommendation of 6 Dec. 2012 on aggressive tax planning, C(2012) 8806 final (6 Dec. 2012), at p. 2; European Commission Press Release, *State aid: Commission investigates transfer pricing arrangements on corporate taxation of Apple (Ireland) Starbucks (Netherlands) and Fiat Finance and Trade (Luxembourg),* IP/14/663 (11 Jun. 2014), at p. 2; European Commission, *Statement by Vice President Alumnia on opening of three investigations on transfer pricing arrangements on corporate taxation by Apple (Ireland), Starbucks (Netherlands) and Fiat Finance and Trade (Luxembourg),* Statement/14/190 (11 Jun. 2014), at p. 1; also see P. Pistone/R. Szudoczy, The Coordination of Tax Policies in the EU, in M. Lang/P. Pistone/J. Schuch/C. Staringer (eds.), *Introduction to European Tax Law on Direct Taxation*[4] (Linde, 2015), p. 27 (at p. 46).
19. On the vague meaning of the term "aggressive tax planning" see M. Lang, "Aggressive Steuerplanung" – eine Analyse der Empfehlung der Europäischen Kommission, 23 *SWI* 2 (2013), p. 62 (at pp. 62-64 and 68).
20. See OECD, *Addressing Base Erosion and Profit Shifting* (OECD, 2013), at pp. 5, 7, 13 and 47; OECD, *Action Plan on Base Erosion and Profit Shifting* (OECD, 2013), at pp. 9-11; cf. J. Owens in V. Houlder, The tax avoidance story as a morality tale, *Financial Times* (22 Nov. 2004): "*Tax is where the environment was 10 years ago*"; also cf. D. Tillinghast, The Impact of the Internet on the Taxation of International Transactions, 50 *Bull. Intl. Taxn.* 11/12 (1996), p. 524 (at pp. 524 et seq.).
21. In 2010, the OECD created the Aggressive Tax Planning Steering Group in order to "*strengthen international co-operation on countering aggressive tax planning amongst tax administrations and tax policy makers so as to improve the design and implementation of tax laws in an international context*" (OECD, *Directory of Bodies* (OECD, 2012), at p. 276). Based, *inter alia,* on the work of this steering group, the OECD published several reports dealing with various aspects of aggressive tax planning (OECD, *Addressing Tax Risks Involving Bank Losses* (OECD, 2010); OECD, *Corporate Loss Utilisation Through Aggressive Tax Planning* (OECD, 2011); OECD, *Tackling Aggressive Tax Planning Through Improved Transparency and Disclosure* (OECD, 2011); OECD, *Hybrid Mismatch Arrangements: Tax Policy and Compliance Issues* (OECD, 2012);

Commission[22] have launched similar initiatives. These initiatives are commonly discussed under the heading "Base Erosion and Profit Shifting" or its abbreviation "BEPS." Considering the attention these initiatives get in the media, and from politicians, scholars and society as a whole, one is tempted to expect the beginning of a new era in international tax law. Unsurprisingly, "BEPS" is hence the most common acronym in the current international tax law debate.[23]

Due to the topic's current prominence, there is an intense political and temporal pressure to rapidly reform the international tax regime. The danger associated with this is that the BEPS movement will not lead to a comprehensive, systematic and principled development of the current tax system, but rather result in "*popular, ad-hoc partial solutions based on an already existing arsenal of measures.*"[24] Within an EU context, this is particularly worrisome, because all envisaged changes to the Member States'

OECD, *Aggressive Tax Planning Based on After-Tax Hedging* (OECD, 2013)). The political mandate to intensify these efforts in the framework of the BEPS project was given to the OECD by the G20 in 2012 (G20 Leaders Declaration (19 Jun. 2012), at para. 48 ("*We reiterate the need to prevent base erosion and profit shifting and we will follow with attention the ongoing work of the OECD in this area.*"); G20 Final Communiqué, Meeting of Finance Ministers and Central Bank Governors (4-5 Nov. 2012), at para. 21 ("*We also welcome the work that the OECD is undertaking into the problem of base erosion and profit shifting and look forward to a report about progress of the work at our next meeting.*")), and by the G8 in 2013 (G8 Communiqué (18 Jun. 2013), at p. 1 and paras 23-29; also see G8 Lough Erne Declaration (18 Jun. 2013)). In the first BEPS report on "Addressing Base Erosion and Profit Shifting," the OECD delimited the topic by: (1) describing various studies and data on the existence and magnitude of BEPS, (2) giving an overview of the economic developments that have had an impact on global business models, as well as (3) depicting the key principles that underlie the taxation of cross-border activities and the resultant BEPS opportunities. The report concluded that BEPS is a fundamental policy issue that has to be addressed in a comprehensive, coordinated and collaborative manner (OECD, *Addressing Base Erosion and Profit Shifting* [OECD, 2013], at pp. 47-50). To this end, the OECD developed a global and comprehensive action plan with a view to elaborate concrete proposals to realign international standards with the current global business environment (OECD, *Action Plan on Base Erosion and Profit Shifting* (OECD, 2013)). Fifteen actions were introduced the OECD intended to work on and to deliver results within a very ambitious time frame. Numerous action items reflect issues the OECD has already addressed – to varying degrees – in the past (see J. Scott Wilkie, Policy Forum: BEPS One Year In – Taking Stock, 62 *Canadian Tax J.* 2 (2014), p. 458 (at p. 460)), such as the impact of the digital economy on international taxation (Action Item 1), CFC legislation (Action Item 3), rules that limit excessive interest deductions (Action Item 4), harmful tax competition (Action Item 5), abuse of tax treaties (Action Item 6), the PE concept in the OECD MC (Action Item 7), transfer pricing (Action Items 8, 9, 10 and 13), and dispute resolution (Action Item 14). The other actions on hybrid mismatch arrangements (Action Item 2), on methodologies to collect and analyse data on BEPS (Action Item 11), on mandatory disclosure rules for tax planning arrangements (Action Item 12) and on the development of multilateral instruments in international taxation (Action Item 15) have hitherto not been dealt with by the OECD itself, but were addressed in the literature in one way or another. Accordingly, the Action Plan on BEPS consolidates the previous efforts of the OECD to limit tax planning opportunities, supplemented by related issues that have not been addressed by the OECD so far and peppered with a few elements – such as Action Item 14 – to avoid that the BEPS project inadvertently leads to a supererogatory imposition for businesses. Cf. J. Scott Wilkie, 62 *Canadian Tax J.* 2 (2014), at p. 458 ("*The catchy BEPS acronym may be unique, but the undercurrents of base erosion and profit shifting have been present, for those who would notice, for quite some time.*").

22. See Chapter 2.
23. See C. Staringer, BEPS – Was kommt jetzt auf uns zu?, 25 *SWI* 12 (2015), p. 575 (at p. 575).
24. Y. Brauner, 6 *World Tax J.* 1 (2014), at p. 11; Y. Brauner, 16 *Florida Tax Rev.* 2 (2014), at p. 60.

domestic or double tax treaty law have to be in line with EU law.[25] Although aware of this issue,[26] the OECD and the European Commission have hitherto only given little thought as to whether the various actions and provisions already suggested meet the requirements of primary and secondary EU law.[27] This is remarkable, because their compatibility – especially with the fundamental freedoms – is by no means obvious.[28]

25. See E.C.C.M. Kemmeren, Where is EU Law in the OECD BEPS Discussion?, 23 *EC Tax Rev.* 4 (2014), p. 190 (at pp. 190-191); C. HJI Panayi, The Compatibility of the OECD/G20 Base Erosion and Profit Shifting Proposals with EU Law, 70 *Bull. Intl. Taxn.* (2016), p. 95 (at p. 96).
26. See OECD, *Designing Effective Controlled Foreign Company Rules, Action 3: 2015 Final Report* (OECD, 2015), at p. 10 ("*In particular, this report recognises that the recommendations must be sufficiently adaptable to comply with EU law, and it sets out possible design options that could be implemented by EU Member States.*"); OECD, *Preventing the Granting of Treaty Benefits in Inappropriate Circumstances*, Action 6: 2015 Final Report (OECD, 2015), at pp. 14 ("*some countries may have [...] concerns based on EU law that prevent them from adopting the exact wording of the model provisions that are recommended in this report*"), 19 ("*It is also recognised that the LOB rule will need to be adapted to reflect certain constraints or policy choices concerning other aspects of a bilateral tax treaty between two Contracting States (e.g. constitutional restrictions or concerns based on EU law or policy choices concerning the treatment of collective investment vehicles)*").
27. See OECD, *Designing Effective Controlled Foreign Company Rules, Action 3: 2015 Final Report* (OECD, 2015), at pp. 17-18; OECD, *Limiting Base Erosion Involving Interest Deductions and Other Financial Payments, Action 4: 2015 Final Report* (OECD, 2015), at pp. 85-86; Proposal for a Council Directive laying down rules against tax avoidance practices that directly affect the functioning of the internal market, COM(2016) 26 final (28 Jan. 2016), at pp. 8 and 13; Communication from the Commission to the European Parliament and the Council, A Fair and Efficient Corporate Tax System in the European Union: 5 Key Areas for Action, COM(2015) 302 final (17 Jun. 2015), at p. 6.
28. See P. Baker, The BEPS Action Plan in the Light of EU Law: Treaty Abuse, 61 *British Tax Rev.* 3 (2015), p. 408 (at pp. 408-416); J. Bates/D.M. Berman/R. Gani/D. Gutmann/T. Imamura/G. Klugman/A. Rust, Limitation on Benefits Articles in Income Tax Treaties: The Current State of Play, 41 *Intertax* 6/7 (2013), p. 395 (at pp. 403-404); P. Benéitez Régli, BEPS Actions 2, 3 and 4 and the Fundamental Freedoms: Is There a Way Out?, 56 *Eur. Taxn.* 6 (2016), p. 230 (at pp. 230-245); F. Debelva/D. Scornos/J. Van den Berghen/P. Van Braband, LOB Clauses and EU-Law Compatibility: A Debate Revived by BEPS?, 24 *EC Tax Rev.* 3 (2015), p. 132 (at pp. 132-143); R. de Bour/O. Marres, BEPS Action 2: Neutralizing the Effects on Hybrid Mismatch Arrangements, 43 *Intertax* 1 (2015), p. 14 (at pp. 33-35); E.C.C.M. Kemmeren, 23 *EC Tax Rev.* 4 (2014), at pp. 191-193; S. Douma, Limitations on Interest Deduction: an EU Law Perspective, 61 *British Tax Rev.* 3 (2015), p. 364 (at pp. 370-377); A.P. Dourado, Aggressive Tax Planning in EU Law and in the Light of BEPS: The EC Recommendation on Aggressive Tax Planning and BEPS Actions 2 and 6, 43 *Intertax* 1 (2015), p. 42 (at pp. 54-56); J. Englisch, BEPS Action 1: Digital Economy – EU Law Implications, 61 *British Tax Rev.* 3 (2015), p. 280 (at pp. 285-307); M. Helminen, EU Law Compatibility of BEPS Action 2: Neutralising the Effects of Hybrid Mismatch Arrangements, 61 *British Tax Rev.* 3 (2015), p. 325 (at pp. 325-339); C. HJI Panayi, 70 *Bull. Intl. Taxn.* (2016), at pp. 96-112; C. Marchgraber, Tackling Deduction and Non-Inclusion Schemes – The Proposal of the European Commission, 54 *Eur. Taxn.* 4 (2014), p. 133 (at pp. 139-141); E. Pinetz, Use of a Principal Purpose Test to Prevent Treaty Abuse, in M. Lang/P. Pistone/A. Rust/J. Schuch/C. Staringer (eds.), *Base Erosion and Profit Shifting* (Linde, 2016), p. 271 (at pp. 294-296); P. Pistone/R. Julien/F. Cannas, Can the Derivative Benefits Provision and Competent Authority Discretionary Relief Provision Render the OECD-Proposed Limitation on Benefits Clause Compatible with EU Fundamental Freedoms?, in M. Lang/P. Pistone/A. Rust/J. Schuch/C. Staringer (eds.), *Base Erosion and Profit Shifting* (Linde, 2016), p. 165 (at pp. 166-210); A. Rust, BEPS Action 2: 2014 Deliverable – Neutralising the Effects of Hybrid Mismatch Arrangements and Its Compatibility with the Non-discrimination Provisions in Tax Treaties and the Treaty on the Functioning of the European Union, 61 *British Tax Rev.* 3 (2015), p. 308 (at pp. 308-324); A. Rust, Der BEPS Aktionspunkt 2 zur Neutralisierung der Effekte hybrider Gestaltungen und seine Vereinbarkeit mit den Diskriminierungsverboten der Doppelbesteuerungsabkommen und des

It is hence indeed "*time to broaden the OECD discussions on BEPS with the EU law perspective.*"[29]

2 THE PHENOMENA OF DOUBLE TAXATION AND DOUBLE NON-TAXATION FROM AN EU LAW PERSPECTIVE

2.1 BEPS, Double Non-Taxation and EU Law

Among the main issues the BEPS project intends to address is the phenomenon of "double non-taxation."[30] It is a term that is used quite frequently

AEUV, in W. Schön/C. Heber (eds.), Grundfragen des Europäischen Steuerrechts (Springer, 2015), p. 89 (at pp. 89-106); W. Schön, Transfer Pricing Issues of BEPS in the Light of EU Law, 61 *British Tax Rev.* 3 (2015), p. 417 (at pp. 420-428); R. Streinz, Multilateral Instrument and EU Competence, 61 *British Tax Rev.* 3 (2015), p. 429 (at pp. 429-442); R. Szudoczky/P. Koch, Limiation on Benefits: "Qualified Person" – Article X(1) and (2) of the OECD Model, in M. Lang/P. Pistone/A. Rust/J. Schuch/C. Staringer (eds.), *Base Erosion and Profit Shifting* (Linde, 2016), p. 219 (at pp. 239-244); E. Traversa, Interest Deductibility and the BEPS Action Plan: *nihil novi sub sole?*, 58 *British Tax Rev.* 5 (2013), p. 607 (at pp. 615-619); A. Zalasiński, Conclusion of the BEPS Multilateral Instrument and Distribution of Competences Between the EU and Its Member States, 61 *British Tax Rev.* 3 (2015), p. 444 (at pp. 444-448).

29. E.C.C.M. Kemmeren, 23 *EC Tax Rev.* 4 (2014), at p. 193.
30. See OECD, *Addressing Base Erosion and Profit Shifting* (OECD, 2013), at p. 34 ("*The interaction of domestic tax systems sometimes leads to an overlap, which means that an item of income can be taxed by more than one jurisdiction thus resulting in double taxation. The interaction can also leave gaps, which result in an item of income not being taxed anywhere thus resulting in so called 'double non-taxation'.*"); OECD, *Action Plan on Base Erosion and Profit Shifting* (OECD, 2013), at p. 10 ("*BEPS relates chiefly to instances where the interaction of different tax rules leads to double non-taxation or less than single taxation.*"); OECD, *OECD/G20 Base Erosion and Profit Shifting Project, Explanatory Statement, 2014 Deliverables* (OECD, 2014), at p. 3 ("*Beyond securing revenues by realigning taxation with economic activities and value creation, the OECD/G20 BEPS Project aims to create a single set of consensus-based international tax rules to address BEPS, and hence to protect tax bases while offering increased certainty and predictability to taxpayers. A key focus of this work is to eliminate double non-taxation.*"); OECD, *OECD/G20 Base Erosion and Profit Shifting Project, Explanatory Statement, 2015 Final Reports* (OECD, 2014), at para. 3 ("*BEPS can result in double non-taxation but addressing BEPS should not result in double taxation.*"); OECD, *OECD/G20 Base Erosion and Profit Shifting Project, Preventing the Granting of Treaty Benefits in Inappropriate Circumstances,* Action 6: 2015 Final Report (OECD, 2015), at pp. 10, 13 and 91 ("*tax treaties are not intended to be used to generate double non-taxation*"); also see with regard to the European Commission using this term Staff working paper, The internal market: factual examples of double non-taxation cases, Consultation document, TAXUD D1 D(2012) (29 Feb. 2012); Summary report of the responses received on the public consultation on factual examples and possible ways to tackle double non-taxation cases, TAXUD D1 D(2012) (5 Jul. 2012); Commission Recommendation of 6 Dec. 2012 on aggressive tax planning, C(2012) 8806 final (6 Dec. 2012), at pp. 2 and 3; Communication from the Commission to the European Parliament and the Council, A Fair and Efficient Corporate Tax System in the European Union: 5 Key Areas for Action, COM(2015) 302 final (17 Jun. 2015), at p. 9; Commission Recommendation of 28 Jan. 2016 on the implementation of measures against tax treaty abuse, COM(2016) 271 final (28 Jan. 2016), at p. 2; M. Vestager in European Commission Press Release, *State aid: Commission opens formal investigation into Luxembourg's tax treatment of McDonald's*, IP/15/6221 (3 Dec. 2015), at p. 1; European Commission Press Release, *State aid: Commission concludes Belgian "Excess Profit" tax scheme illegal; around €700 million to be recovered from 35 multinational companies*, IP/16/42 (11 Jan. 2016), at p. 2; also see U.S. Department of the Treasure White Paper, The European Commission's Recent State Aid

nowadays.[31] Its increasing prominence is insofar remarkable as there is essentially no satisfying internationally accepted circumscription of this phenomenon.[32] Most commonly, double non-taxation is considered to be an (allegedly) inadvertent result of the application of double taxation conventions.[33] Indeed, such a treaty may, for example, prevent one of the contracting states from taxing a certain item of income, but may not provide for a corresponding obligation for the other contracting state to tax this item of income domestically.[34] This could lead to an item of income remaining untaxed,

---

Investigations of Transfer Pricing Rulings (24 Aug. 2016), at p. 24 ("*In light of the increase in double* non-*taxation, the international community embarked on the BEPS project to reform the existing international tax architecture.*").

31. See, for example, L. De Broe, At Last, Some Output on the Fight against Double Non-taxation, 23 *EC Tax Rev.* 6 (2014), p. 310 (at pp. 310 et seq.); M. Helminen, The Problem of Double Non-Taxation in the European Union – To What Extent Could This Be Resolved through a Multilateral EU Tax Treaty Based on the Nordic Convention?, 53 *Eur. Taxn.* 7 (2013), p. 306 (at pp. 306 et seq.); C. Kahlenberg, Prevention of Double Non-taxation: An Analysis of Cross-Border Financing from a German Perspective, 43 *Intertax* 3 (2015), p. 218 (at pp. 218 et seq.); C. Marchgraber, The Avoidance of Double Non-taxation in Double Tax Treaty Law: A Critical Analysis of the Subject-To-Tax Clause Recommended by the European Commission, 23 *EC Tax Rev.* 5 (2014), p. 293 (at pp. 293 et seq.); P. Rossi-Maccanico, Fiscal Aid, Tax Competition, and BEPS, 75 *Tax Notes Intl.* 10 (8 Sep. 2014), p. 857 (at pp. 862-867); D.S. Smit, International Juridical Double Non-taxation and State Aid, 25 *EC Tax Rev.* 2 (2016), p. 109 (at pp. 109-112); A. Ting, iTax – Apple's International Tax Structure and the Double Non-Taxation Issue, 59 *British Tax Rev.* 1 (2014), p. 40 (at pp. 40 et seq.); A. Van de Vijver, International Double (Non-)taxation: Comparative Guidance from European Legal Principles, 24 *EC Tax Rev.* 5 (2015), p. 240 (at pp. 240 et seq.); also see M. Lang, Dreifache Nichtbesteuerung als Ergebnis der Anwendung von Doppelbesteuerungsabkommen, 25 *SWI* 5 (2015), p. 198 (at pp. 198 et seq.), who even uses the term "triple non-taxation."
32. Cf. H. Hahn, Generalthema I des 58. IFA-Kongresses 2004 in Wien: Double-Non-Taxation Überblick über den deutschen Nationalbericht, 12 *IStR* 13 (2003), p. 446 (at pp. 446-448); I. Jankowiak, *Doppelte Nichtbesteuerung im Internationalen Steuerrecht* (C.H. Beck, 2009), at pp. 32-33; M. Schilcher, *Subject-to-tax-Klauseln in der österreichischen Abkommenspraxis* (Linde 2004), at p. 17; J. Rogers-Glabush, *IBFD International Tax Glossary*[7] (IBFD, 2015), at p. 157 ("*A term used to describe the situation that results when income is not taxed either in the state of source or in the state of the recipient's residence.*").
33. Cf. G. Frotscher, *Internationales Steuerrecht*[4] (C.H. Beck, 2015), at p. 7, at § 1 MN 19; F. Haase, *Internationales und Europäisches Steuerrecht*[4] (C.F. Müller, 2014), at p. 16, at § 1 para. 37; V. Kluge, *Das Internationale Steuerrecht*[4] (C.H. Beck, 2000), at p. 929, at S.334; E. Traversa/C. Helleputte, Double (Non-)Taxation in VAT and Direct Taxes: How to Achieve Some Convergence within a *Summa Divisio*? A European Perspective, in M. Lang/P. Melz/E. Kristoffersson (eds.), T. Ecker (ass. ed.), *Value Added Tax and Direct Taxation* (IBFD, 2009), p. 339 (at p. 340); U. Wolff, Generalthema I: Doppelte Nicht-Besteuerung, 13 *IStR* 16 (2004), p. 542 (at p. 542); also cf. M. Lang, 25 *SWI* 5 (2015), at pp. 198 et seq.
34. See M. Lang, Die Vermeidung der Doppelbesteuerung und der doppelten Nichtbesteuerung als DBA-Auslegungsmaxime?, 11 *IStR* 18 (2002), p. 609 (at pp. 611-612); M. Lang, *General Report*, in IFA (ed.), *Double Non-Taxation*, CDFI 89a (SDU, 2004), p. 73 (at p. 83); M. Lang, Vermeidung der Doppelbesteuerung und der doppelten Nichtbesteuerung als Auslegungsmaxime für Doppelbesteuerungsabkommen?, in W. Haarmann (ed.), *Auslegung und Anwendung von Doppelbesteuerungsabkommen* (Dr Otto Schmidt, 2004), p. 83 (at p. 92).

because one contracting state is restricted from taxing it by the double taxation convention, while the other contracting state does not exercise the taxing right assigned to it by the very same double taxation convention domestically.[35]

Moreover, according to the prevailing assumption, double taxation conventions may also lead to an item of income remaining untaxed even if it is taxable according to both contracting states' domestic tax laws. After all, the courts or the competent authorities of the contracting states may come to different conclusions when applying and interpreting the double taxation convention. According to the OECD, this may be due to: (1) a varying evaluation of the facts of the case, (2) a diverging interpretation of the rules of the double taxation convention, or (3) the disparities between the domestic tax systems of the contracting states.[36] Such a situation is considered to result in double taxation if the competent authorities of both contracting states infer a taxing

35. This may be the result, for example, if an Austrian resident sells real estate situated in Germany that has been held in a private portfolio for more than ten years (see C. Marchgraber, 23 *EC Tax Rev.* 5 [2014], at pp. 297-298). Under German domestic tax law, the alienation of immovable property held in the private portfolio is taxable, unless the acquisition took place more than ten years ago (see ss. 49(1)(8)(a), 22(2) and 23(1)(1) German Income Tax Act). In Austria, on the contrary, capital gains derived from the disposal of real estate are subject to a flat tax rate of 30%, irrespective of the holding period (see ss. 30, 30a, 30b and 30c Austrian Income Tax Act). According to Article 13(1) of the double taxation convention between Austria and Germany (DTC Austria-Germany), such capital gains may be taxed in the contracting state where the immovable property is situated. According to Article 23 DTC Austria-Germany, both contracting states apply the exemption method in order to avoid double taxation of such capital gains. Therefore, Austria would be obliged to refrain from taxing the alienation of the real estate, because it is situated in Germany, while Germany would not levy any income taxes either, because the acquisition took place more than ten years ago.

36. See OECD, *The Application of the OECD Model Tax Convention to Partnerships*, Issues in International Taxation No. 6 (OECD, 1999), at MN 94 et seq.; also see H. Loukota, *Die Vermeidung von Besteuerungskonflikten für das international tätige Unternehmen*, in W. Gassner/M. Lang (eds.), *Besteuerung und Bilanzierung international tätiger Unternehmen*, 30 Jahre Steuerrecht an der Wirtschaftsuniversität Wien (Orac, 1998), p. 265 (at p. 269); H. Loukota, *Der Einfluss des österreichischen Ertragsteuerrechtes auf die Auslegung von Doppelbesteuerungsabkommen*, in R. Beiser/S. Kirchmayr/G. Mayr/N. Zorn (eds.), *Ertragsteuern in Wissenschaft und Praxis*, Festschrift für Werner Doralt (LexisNexis, 2007), p. 263 (at pp. 280 et seq.); H. Loukota, Lösung internationaler Qualifikationskonflikte, 9 *SWI* 2 (1999), p. 70 (at pp. 70 et seq.); J. Schuch/J. Bauer, Die Überlegungen des OECD-Steuerausschusses zur Lösung von Qualifikationskonflikten, in W. Gassner/M. Lang/E. Lechner (eds.), *Personengesellschaften im Recht der Doppelbesteuerungsabkommen* (Linde, 2000), p. 27 (at p. 31).

right from the double taxation convention,[37] or double non-taxation if both contracting states conclude that the double taxation convention does not allow them to tax.[38]

37. This may, *inter alia*, be due to disparities between the domestic tax systems of the contracting states. Generally, the attribution of income is not a matter of double tax treaty law, but exclusively contingent upon domestic law (see, for example, M. Lehner in K. Vogel/M. Lehner (eds.), *Doppelbesteuerungsabkommen*[6] (C.H. Beck, 2015), Grundlagen at paras 113e, 152g and 181b; A. Rust in E. Reimer/A. Rust (eds.), *Klaus Vogel on Double Taxation Conventions*[4] (Kluwer, 2015), at Article 1 MN 16). Therefore, the same item of income may be attributed to different taxpayers if the contracting states' domestic income attribution principles deviate from one another. Such a conflict of income attribution may also result in a diverging exercise of the double taxation convention by the contracting states and, hence, lead to double taxation or double non-taxation. The former is illustrated in the OECD Partnership Report, *inter alia*, by the following example (OECD, *The Application of the OECD Model Tax Convention to Partnerships*, Issues in International Taxation No. 6 (OECD, 1999), at p. 42): "*Example 14: Partner A, a resident of State R, sells his interest in P to D, a resident of State P, for an amount that exceeds A's adjusted basis in the interest. Under State R's domestic law, State R treats P as a company and would regard the gain as a capital gain of a resident of State R. Under State P's domestic law, State P treats P as fiscally transparent and would regard the gain as attributable to a State P permanent establishment.*

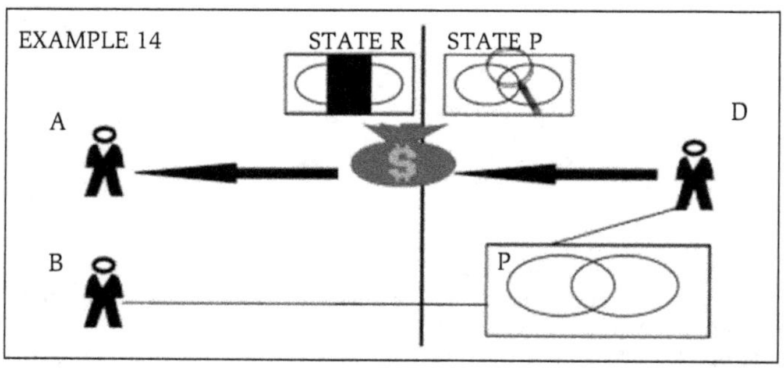

"

If one follows the reasoning of the OECD (for a different approach, see M. Lang, *The Application of the OECD Model Tax Convention to Partnerships – A Critical Analysis of the Report Prepared by the OECD Committee on Fiscal Affairs* (Linde, 2000), at p. 86), State R's domestic qualification of the partnership as an opaque company leads to the conclusion that the capital gain received by A may only be taxed in State R in accordance with the provisions of Article 13(5) OECD MC, whereas State P's domestic qualification of the partnership as a transparent entity leads to the conclusion that it may also be taxed in State P due to Article 13(1) or (2) OECD MC (OECD, *The Application of the OECD Model Tax Convention to Partnerships*, Issues in International Taxation No. 6 (OECD, 1999), at para. 107).

38. According to Article 3(2) OECD MC, for example, when a contracting state applies a double taxation convention, "*any term not defined therein shall, unless the context otherwise requires, have the meaning that it has at that time under the law of that State for the purposes of the taxes to which the Convention applies, any meaning under the applicable tax laws of that State prevailing over a meaning given to the term under other laws of that State.*" If the meaning of an undefined treaty term has to be determined by reverting to the domestic law definition, it is possible that the contracting states ultimately apply the double taxation convention differently. After all, the definitions of the contracting states' domestic laws do not necessarily coincide. This may, *inter alia*, lead to double non-taxation, which can be illustrated by the following example from the OECD Partnership Report (OECD, *The Application of the OECD Model Tax Convention to Partnerships*, Issues in International Taxation No. 6 (OECD, 1999), at p. 39): "*Example 13: Partner A makes a loan to partnership P, which has been established in State P where it carries on*

However, although double taxation conventions may be involved, the phenomenon of double non-taxation is apparently considered to be much more sophisticated. The OECD, for example, also refers to this term in its 2012 report on hybrid mismatch arrangements. Such tax planning structures are supposed to exploit "*differences in the tax treatment of instruments, entities or transfers between two or more countries*" and "*often lead to "double non-taxation" that may not be intended by either country.*"[39] Thus, the term double non-taxation is also used to describe situations where no double taxation convention is applicable. Financial instruments, for example, are traditionally divided into equity and debt. A wide variety of instruments, however, incorporate elements of both equity and debt, and are therefore referred to as hybrid financial

---

a business through a permanent establishment. P pays interest to A. State P recognizes loans between partners and partnerships; under its domestic legislation State P allows P a tax deduction for the interest. State R does not recognize loans between partners and partnerships under its domestic law. Both States treat partnerships as transparent entities and apply Article 7 to the income of P, but State P applies Article 11 to the interest payment and State R does not.

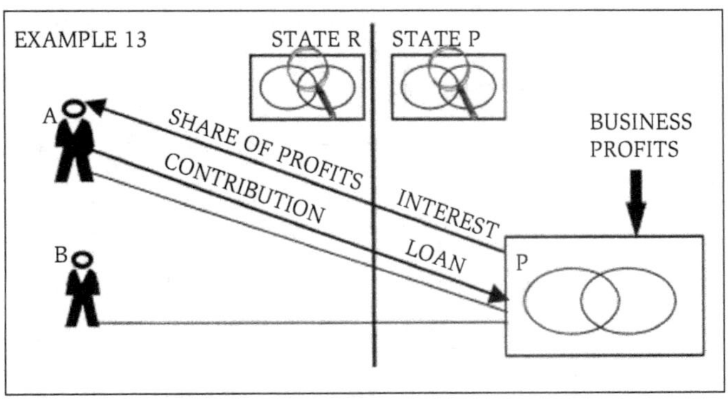

"

According to the OECD Partnership Report (OECD, *The Application of the OECD Model Tax Convention to Partnerships*, Issues in International Taxation No. 6 (OECD, 1999), at paras 96 et seq.; for a different approach see M. Lang, *The Application of the OECD Model Tax Convention to Partnerships – A Critical Analysis of the Report Prepared by the OECD Committee on Fiscal Affairs* (Linde, 2000), at p. 86), the term "*debt-claims of every kind,*" which is included in Article 11(3) OECD MC, requires a recourse to domestic law according to Article 3(2) OECD MC. If the payment received by A from P is treated as a debt-claim under State P's domestic law, Article 11 OECD MC is applicable, i.e., State P's tax must not exceed a certain rate or its taxing right is even entirely removed, if the respective provision of the R-P convention, in contrast to Article 11 OECD MC, does not provide for any source taxation right. If according to State R's domestic law the payment is, on the other hand, not considered to be a debt-claim, but forms part of the partnership's business profits which is attributable to a permanent establishment situated in State P, the taxing right of State P would not be restricted at all due to Article 7 OECD MC. If State R thus exempted the payment from taxation according to Article 23 A(1) OECD MC, it would either partially (if Article 11 OECD MC provides for a limited source taxing right) or entirely (if Article 11 OECD MC does not provide for a source taxing right) remain untaxed (OECD, *The Application of the OECD Model Tax Convention to Partnerships*, Issues in International Taxation No. 6 (OECD, 1999), at para. 99).

39. OECD, *Hybrid Mismatch Arrangements: Tax Policy and Compliance Issues* (OECD, 2012), at para. 3.

instruments.[40] As such instruments usually cannot be clearly classified as either equity or debt the classification may vary in different jurisdictions. From a tax planning perspective, this mismatch in treatment can be exploited by using a hybrid instrument that is treated as debt in the source state and as equity in the residence state. Thereby, it is possible to obtain a double tax benefit,[41] since the amount paid by the debtor is deductible as interest in the source state and might be exempt as a dividend at the level of the creditor in the residence state due to a dividend exemption system (see Example 1):[42]

Example 1

Member State A, where the parent company is resident, treats a hybrid loan as equity and received payments as exempt "dividends." Member State B, where the subsidiary is resident, treats the same hybrid loan as debt and payments on it as deductible "interest."[43]

Diagram: Cross-border tax arbitrage using a hybrid instrument

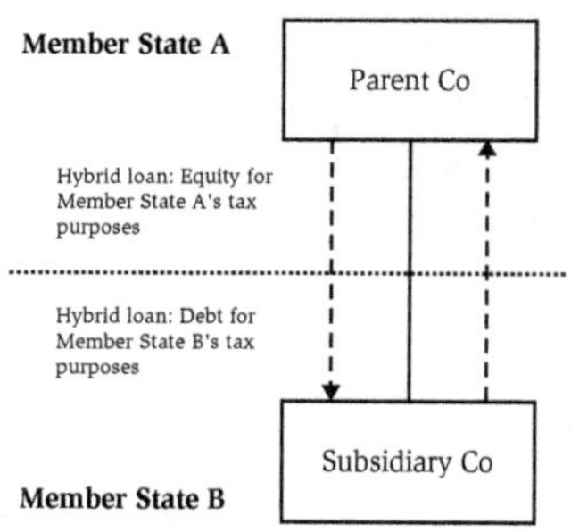

40. See, for example, J.A. Duncan, General Report, in IFA (ed.), *Tax Treatment of Hybrid Financial Instruments in Cross-Border Transactions*, CDFI 85a (SDU, 2000), p. 24 (at pp. 24 et seq.); M. Helminen, *The Dividend Concept in International Tax Law* (Kluwer, 1999), p. 251 (at pp. 251 et seq.); M. Helminen, Classification of Cross-Border Payments on Hybrid Instruments, 58 *Bull. Intl. Taxn.* 2 (2004), p. 56 (at pp. 56 et seq.).
41. Some scholars also refer to "double dip" in this context (see, for example, S. Bendlinger, *Steueroasen und Offshore-Strukturen* [Linde, 2013], at pp. 230-231; T. Polivanova-Rosenauer, AbgÄG 2014: Abzugsverbot für Zinsen und Lizenzgebühren, 10 *taxlex* 3 [2014], p. 105 (at p. 108); W. Wiesner, Abgabenänderungsgesetz im BBG 2011 – Unternehmensbesteuerung, 21 *RWZ* 1 (2011), p. 3 (at p. 4); see also J. Bundgaard, Classification and Treatment of Hybrid Financial Instruments and Income Derived Therefrom under EU Corporate Tax Directives – Part 2, 50 *Eur. Taxn.* 11 (2010), p. 490 (at p. 490), who distinguishes, though, between "*real double-dip structures and deduction/non-inclusion structures*").
42. See C. Marchgraber, 54 *Eur. Taxn.* 4 (2014), at pp. 134-135; C. Marchgraber, Cross-Border Tax Arbitrage, the Parent-Subsidiary Directive (2011/96) and Double Tax Treaty Law, 70 *Bull. Intl. Taxn.* 3 (2016), p. 123 (at p. 124).
43. See Commission Staff Working Document, Impact Assessment, SWD (2013) 474 final (25 Nov. 2013), at p. 11.

However, not all situations where something remains untaxed are necessarily problematic. As, for example, neither Austria nor Germany levy an income tax on lottery winnings,[44] a German citizen who wins in the Austrian lottery does not have to pay taxes in either state. Although the lottery winnings could thus be regarded as double non-taxed, it is doubtful that such an outcome would trouble the tax administrations involved. But even with regard to those scenarios of alleged double non-taxation that are considered to be problematic from a tax policy perspective, referring to the phenomenon of double non-taxation is not in itself sufficient to prove that there is a legal problem. Neither the provisions of the OECD MC nor the European Treaties explicitly refer to this term.[45] Hence, the term double non-taxation seems to be legally inexistent.[46,47] Still, the European Commission considers double non-taxation to be as

44. For Austria see, for example, M. Laudacher in S. Kanduth-Kristen/M. Laudacher/C. Lenneis/E. Marschner/M. Vock (eds.), *Jakom Einkommensteuergesetz*[9] (Linde, 2016), at § 2 para. 20; for Germany see, for example, P. Fischer in P. Kirchhof (ed.), *EStG*[15] (Dr Otto Schmidt, 2016), at § 22 para. 71.
45. Within the OECD/G20 BEPS project, however, it has been considered necessary to clarify "*that tax treaties are not intended to be used to generate double non-taxation*" (OECD, *Action Plan on Base Erosion and Profit Shifting* (OECD, 2013), at p. 19; OECD, *Preventing the Granting of Treaty Benefits in Inappropriate Circumstances*, Action 6: 2014 Deliverable (OECD, 2014), at p. 98; OECD, *Preventing the Granting of Treaty Benefits in Inappropriate Circumstances*, Action 6: 2015 Final Report (OECD, 2015), at p. 13). To this end, it is planned to change the preamble of the OECD MC in order to clarify that a double taxation convention aims at "*the elimination of double taxation with respect to taxes on income and on capital without creating opportunities for non-taxation or reduced taxation through tax evasion or avoidance (including through treaty-shopping arrangements aimed at obtaining reliefs provided in this Convention for the indirect benefit of residents of third States)*" (OECD, *Preventing the Granting of Treaty Benefits in Inappropriate Circumstances*, Action 6: 2015 Final Report (OECD, 2015), at p. 92). However, this proposal does not address double non-taxation in general, but is specifically limited to double non-taxation and reduced taxation resulting from tax evasion or avoidance. Moreover, although the terms double taxation and double non-taxation should thus both be included in the preamble of the OECD MC, they are still not referred to in any provision.
46. It would hence be inept inopportune to criticize the general report on the first of the two main subjects of the 2004 IFA congress, which was held in Vienna, for not providing for a definition of double non-taxation. See M. Lang in IFA (ed.), *Double Non-Taxation*, CDFI 89a (SDU, 2004), at pp. 73 et seq.
47. The term "double taxation," on the other hand, had been included in Article 293 second indent EC Treaty (ex-Article 220 second indent EEC Treaty). At least in the past, it was thus not fully correct to label this term as "legally negligible" (see J. Englisch, *Wettbewerbsgleichheit im grenzüberschreitenden Handel* [Mohr Siebeck, 2008], at p. 762) or "legally inexistent" (see J.M. Mössner, Die Methoden zur Vermeidung der Doppelbesteuerung – Vorzüge, Nachteile, aktuelle Probleme, in K. Vogel [ed.], *Grundfragen des Internationalen Steuerrechts* [Dr Otto Schmidt, 1985], p. 135 [at p. 137]; F. Wassermeyer in F. Wassermeyer/C. Kaeser/M. Schwenke [eds.], *Doppelbesteuerung*[132] [C.H. Beck, 2016], at Vor Art. 1 para. 1). According to this provision, the "*Member States shall, so far as is necessary, enter into negotiations with each other with a view to securing for the benefit of their nationals [...] the abolition of double taxation within the Community.*" Although this provision was repealed in 2007 (Treaty of Lisbon amending the Treaty on European Union and the Treaty establishing the European Community, *OJ* C 306 (17 Dec. 2007), at p. 130), it is argued that abolishing double taxation is still one of the Treaties' objectives (before Article 293 second indent EC Treaty was repealed, the ECJ repeatedly pointed out that it is up to the Member States to provide for "*the abolition of double taxation within the Community,*" which "*is [...] included among the objectives of the Treaty*"; see Judgment in *Gilly*, C-336/96, EU:C:1998:221, at para. 16; also see Judgment in *Bouanich*, C-265/04, EU:C:2006:51, at para. 49; Judgment in *Damseaux*, C-128/08, EU:C:2009:471, at para. 28; Order in *Levy and Sebbag*, C-540/11, EU:C:2012:581, at para. 27), because double taxation is detrimental to the

incompatible with the internal market as double taxation.[48] From an EU law perspective, this raises the question whether there are legal arguments supporting such a view.

2.2 The Phenomenon of Double Taxation from an EU Law Perspective

With regard to double taxation, it is argued that the imposition of comparable taxes in two (or more) Member States on the same business activity is a severe obstacle for the free movement requirement of the internal market concept.[49] The Treaties aim at eliminating the compartmentalizing effect of the Member States' legal systems.[50] This objective is reflected by various provisions; first and foremost - especially in tax matters - by the fundamental freedoms.[51] In the past, the ECJ considered the abolition

---

establishment of the internal market (see G. Kofler, *Doppelbesteuerungsabkommen und Europäisches Gemeinschaftsrecht* (Linde, 2007), at pp. 369-370; E.C.C.M. Kemmeren, After repeal of Article 293 EC Treaty under the Lisbon Treaty: the EU objective of eliminating double taxation can be applied more widely, 17 *EC Tax Rev.* 4 (2008), p. 156 [at pp. 157-158]; also cf. Opinion of AG Colomer in *D*, C-376/03, EU:C:2004:663, at point 78). This is hence convincing as the internal market aims at the abolition of obstacles to the free movement of goods, persons, services and capital (see Chapter 3.1), and "*the fact that a taxable event might be taxed twice is the most serious obstacle there can be to people and their capital crossing [...] borders*" (Opinion of AG Colomer in *D*, C-376/03, EU:C:2004:663, at point 85). Thus, albeit the term double taxation is no longer mentioned in the Treaties, it at least was a legal phenomenon under EU law.

48. See Taxation in the European Union, SEC(96) 487 final (20 Mar. 1996), at p. 13 ("*[t]he Single Market is clearly not compatible with either double taxation of the same taxable base or no taxation at all*"); Opinion of the Economic and Social Committee on Taxation in the European Union, Report on the development of tax systems (SEC[96] 487 final and COM[96] 546 final), *OJ* C 296 (29 Sep. 1997), p. 37 (at p. 43: "*[d]ouble taxation or the absence of taxation is incompatible with the internal market*"); Tax co-ordination in the European Union, Working Paper, Economic Affairs Series, ECON 125 EN (European Parliament, 2000), at p. 22 ("*The Single Market has several particular implications for the taxation of employment incomes. [...] Incomes should not escape tax altogether, or be taxed at discriminatorily low rates, as a result of cross-border tax arbitrage, avoidance or evasion.*"); Commission Recommendation of 6 Dec. 2012 on aggressive tax planning, C(2012) 8806 final (6 Dec. 2012), at p. 2 ("*[t]he Single Market is clearly not compatible with either double taxation [...] or no taxation at all*").
49. Answer given by Mr Bolkestein on behalf of the Commission in order to answer the written question E-2287/99 by Karin Riis-Jørgensen (ELDR) to the Commission regarding "Right to freedom of movement and Danish tax rules," *OJ* C 225 E (8 Aug. 2000), p. 87 (at p. 88 "*the [...] Member States are bound by the EC Treaty principle of free movement within the Community to avoid and eliminate double taxation*"); for further references see G. Kofler, *Doppelbesteuerungsabkommen und Europäisches Gemeinschaftsrecht* (Linde, 2007), at pp. 160-162.
50. See, for example, A. Cordewener, *Europäische Grundfreiheiten und nationales Steuerrecht* (Dr Otto Schmidt, 2002), at p. 352; G. Kofler, *Doppelbesteuerungsabkommen und Europäisches Gemeinschaftsrecht* (Linde, 2007), at p. 51; B. Strassburger, *Die Dogmatik der EU-Grundfreiheiten* (Mohr Siebeck, 2012), at p. 10.
51. The designation "fundamental freedoms" is not a legal term, but rather a prevalent collective name for (1) the free movement of goods (Article 28 TFEU) which, *inter alia*, comprises the prohibition of customs duties and charges having equivalent effect (Article 30 TFEU), the prohibition of quantitative restrictions and measures having equivalent effect on imports (Article 34 TFEU) and exports (Article 35 TFEU), (2) the free movement of persons that compounds the free movement of workers (Article 45 TFEU) and the freedom of establishment (Article 49 TFEU), (3) the freedom to provide services (Article 56 TFEU), and (4) the free movement of capital and payments (Article 63 TFEU) (see A. Cordewener, *Europäische Grundfreiheiten und nationales Steuerrecht* [Dr Otto Schmidt, 2002], at p. 15; T. Kingreen, *Die Struktur der Grundfreiheiten des Europäischen Gemeinschaftsrechts* (Duncker & Humblot, 1999),

of double taxation to also be included among the objectives of EU law.[52] However, from an EU law perspective, it is still unclear what the meaning of the term double taxation actually is. This may seem surprising, because there is a vast consensus that by using this term reference is either to *"the imposition of comparable taxes in two (or more) States on the same taxpayer in respect of the same subject matter and for identical periods"*[53] (juridical double taxation) or to *"taxation of the same income in the hands of different persons"*[54] (economic double taxation). These definitions have been used by the OECD since the first version of its model convention for the avoidance of double taxation with respect to taxes on income and on capital was published in 1963.[55] However, double taxation is not only a legally relevant term used in the preamble of double taxation conventions. It also used to be a legal term of EU law.[56] According to Article 293 second indent EC Treaty (ex-Article 220 second indent EEC Treaty), the *"Member States shall, so far as is necessary, enter into negotiations with each other with a view to securing for the benefit of their nationals [...] the abolition of double taxation within the Community."* Thus, the question arises whether the EC Treaty's understanding of the term double taxation corresponds with the content attached to this term by the OECD.

---

at p. 20; T. Kingreen, Fundamental Freedoms, in A. von Bogdandy/J. Bast (eds.), *Principles of European Constitutional Law²* (Hart Publishing, 2009), p. 515 [at pp. 515-516]; R. Szudoczky, *The Sources of EU law and Their Relationships: Lessons for the Field of Taxation* (IBFD, 2014), at pp. 136-138). The fundamental freedoms are supplemented by the general prohibition of discrimination on grounds of nationality (Article 18 TFEU) and the right of Union citizens to move and reside freely within the EU (Article 21(1) TFEU) (see A. Cordewener, *Europäische Grundfreiheiten und nationales Steuerrecht* [Dr Otto Schmidt, 2002], at p. 16).

52. Judgment in *Gilly*, C-336/96, EU:C:1998:221, at para. 16; also see Judgment in *Bouanich*, C-265/04, EU:C:2006:51, at para. 49; Judgment in *Damseaux*, C-128/08, EU:C:2009:471, at para. 28; Order in *Levy and Sebbag*, C-540/11, EU:C:2012:581, at para. 27.
53. Commentary on the 1992-2014 OECD MC, Introduction para. 1; see also Commentary on the 1963-1977 OECD MC, Article 23(A) and 23(B) para. 1.
54. Commentary on the 1977-2014 OECD MC, Article 9 para. 5; see also Commentary on the 1963 OECD MC, Article 23(A) and 23(B) para. 2.
55. The commentary on the first "Draft Convention for the Avoidance of Double Taxation with respect to Taxes on Income and on Capital," which was published in 1963 (C(63) 113 (19 Nov. 1963)), described juridical double taxation as a situation *"where the same income or capital is taxable in the hands of the same person by more than one State"* (see Commentary on the 1963 OECD MC, Article 23(A) and 23(B) para. 1) and economic double taxation as *"taxation of the same income or capital in the hands of two different persons both chargeable to tax"* (see Commentary on the 1963 OECD MC, Article 23(A) and 23(B) para. 2). Similar descriptions of double taxation had already been used in prior documents of the OEEC (see Press/A(56) 19 (25 May 1956); FC(58) 2 (13 Feb. 1958), at p. 4; FC(58) 2 (1st Revision) Part I (19 Apr. 1958), at p. 3; C(58) 118 Part I (28 May 1958), at p. 3). However, no discussions seem to have taken place within the Fiscal Committee regarding this understanding of double taxation.
56. Considering the currently envisaged presidency compromise on the European Commission's Proposal for a Council Directive on Double Taxation Dispute Resolution Mechanisms in the European Union (COM[2016] 686 final (25. Oct. 2016)), the term double taxation may have a revival as an offical legal term in (secondary) EU law. According to Article 2(1)(c) of this proposal, double taxation should be defined as *"the imposition of taxes covered by an agreement or convention referred to in Article 1 by two (or more) Member States in respect of the same taxable income or capital when it gives rise to either (i) additional tax charge, (ii) increase in tax liabilities or (iii) cancellation or reduction of losses, which could be used to offset taxable profits"* (Doc. 9420/17 LIMITE FISC 111 ECOFIN 429 (19 May 2017), at p. 7).

For various reasons, it is questionable whether the OECD's understanding of double taxation also formed the basis of Article 293 second indent EC Treaty (ex-Article 220 second indent EEC Treaty). First, double taxation is not – and has never been – an exclusive problem of income taxes. The OECD, for example, has also developed a model tax convention for the avoidance of double taxation with respect to taxes on estates, inheritances and gifts.[57] Moreover, due to the spread of VAT/GST, double taxation issues are also increasingly discussed in connection with indirect taxes.[58] With regard to secondary EU law, for example, the relevance of a double imposition of VAT has already been reflected in Articles 8(1)(a) and 9(3) of the Sixth VAT Directive, which explicitly refer to "*double taxation.*"[59] Since the wording of Article 293 second indent EC Treaty (ex-Article 220 second indent EEC Treaty) is not restricted to a certain type of taxes, the term double taxation used therein may hence also include situations of, for

57. Recommendation of the Council concerning the Avoidance of Double Taxation with respect to Taxes on Estates and Inheritances and on Gifts, C(82) 64/FINAL (3 Jun. 1982).
58. Cf., for example, G. Bizioli, Comparative Analysis of the Causes of Double (Non-)Taxation in the Income and VAT/GST Contexts, in M. Lang/P. Melz/E. Kristoffersson (eds.), T. Ecker (ass. ed.), *Value Added Tax and Direct Taxation* (IBFD, 2009), p. 383 (at pp. 383 et seq.); T. Ecker, *A VAT/GST Model Convention* (IBFD, 2013), at pp. 27-47; T. Ecker, Tax Treaties – A Solution to VAT/GST Double Taxation, in M. Lang/P. Melz/E. Kristoffersson (eds.), T. Ecker (ass. ed.), *Value Added Tax and Direct Taxation* (IBFD, 2009), p. 1269 (at pp. 1269 et seq.); T. Ecker/E. Variychuk, VAT treaties: the Russian Federation, 2 *World Tax J.* 2 (2013), p. 81 (at pp. 81 et seq.); J. Englisch, *Wettbewerbsgleichheit im grenzüberschreitenden Handel* (Mohr Siebeck, 2008), at pp. 763-769; N. Eriksen/K. Haydl, Avoidance of VAT/GST Double (Non-)Taxation: Recommendations and Other Types of Soft Law v. Legally Binding Instruments to Allocate Taxing Rights Between States (e.g. Bilateral Tax Treaties), in M. Lang/P. Melz/E. Kristoffersson (eds.), T. Ecker (ass. ed.), *Value Added Tax and Direct Taxation* (IBFD, 2009), p. 1145 (at pp. 1145 et seq.); M. Lang, Umsatzsteuer und Doppelbesteuerung, in M. Achatz/M. Tumpel (eds.), *Umsatzsteuer und Internationales Steuerrecht* (Linde, 2012), p. 19 (at pp. 19-32); R. Millar, Cross-border Services: A Survey of the Issues, in R. Krever/D. White (eds.), *GST in Retrospect and Prospect* (Thomson Reuters, 2007), p. 317 (at pp. 317-347); R. Millar, *Sources of Conflict in Cross-Border Services Rules for VAT*, Sydney Law School Research Paper No. 08/14 (2008); R. Millar, Intentional and Unintentional Double Non-Taxation, in M. Lang/P. Melz/E. Kristoffersson (eds.), T. Ecker (ass. ed.), *Value Added Tax and Direct Taxation* (IBFD, 2009), p. 409 (at pp. 409-442); P. Pistone, Soft Tax Coordination: A Suitable Path for the OECD and the European Union to Address the Challenges of International Double (Non-)Taxation in VAT/GST Systems, in M. Lang/P. Melz/E. Kristoffersson (eds.), T. Ecker (ass. ed.), *Value Added Tax and Direct Taxation* (IBFD, 2009), p. 1161 (at pp. 1161 et seq.); P. Rendahl, Unilateral Measures to Avoid International Double (Non-)Taxation: VAT/GST v. Direct Taxation, in M. Lang/P. Melz/E. Kristoffersson (eds.), T. Ecker (ass. ed.), *Value Added Tax and Direct Taxation* (IBFD, 2009), p. 1119 (at pp. 1119 et seq.); H.G. Ruppe, General Report, in IFA (ed.), *International Problems in the Field of General Sales Taxes on Sales of Goods and Services, CDFI 68b* (IBFD, 1983), p. 109 (at pp. 121-144); Traversa E./Helleputte C., Double (Non-)Taxation in VAT and Direct Taxes: How to Achieve Some Convergence within a *Summa Divisio*? A European Perspective, in Lang M./Melz P./Kristoffersson E. (eds.), Ecker T. (ass. ed.), *Value Added Tax and Direct Taxation* (IBFD, 2009), p. 339 (at pp. 339 et seq.); A.A. Verstraeten, Double (non-)taxation in VAT and Direct Taxes: Which Tax is Better for Developing Countries?, in M. Lang/P. Melz/E. Kristoffersson (eds.), T. Ecker (ass. ed.), *Value Added Tax and Direct Taxation* (IBFD, 2009), p. 369 (at pp. 369 et seq.).
59. Sixth Council Directive of 17 May 1977 on the harmonization of the laws of the Member States relating to turnover taxes – Common system of value added tax: uniform basis of assessment (77/388/EEC), *OJ* L 145 (13 Jun. 1977), p. 1 (at pp. 5 and 6).

example, multiple indirect tax burdens.[60] The ECJ has in fact already confirmed that "*double taxation*" may also arise in the area of inheritance taxes,[61] VAT,[62] special payroll levies,[63] excise duties[64] and parafiscal charges.[65]

Second, Article 293 second indent EC Treaty was already included in the EEC Treaty of 1957, whereas the definition of double taxation that is commonly referred to nowadays was not agreed upon until 1963.[66] Before, the precise definition of double taxation had been much more disputed.[67] In 1946, the League of Nations, for example, still used a very different definition. Thus, "*[i]nternational double or multiple taxation arises when the taxes of two or more countries overlap in such a manner that persons*

60. See I.E. Schwartz/W. Mölls in H. van der Groeben/J. Schwarze (eds.), *Kommentar zum Vertrag über die Europäische Union und zur Gründung der Europäischen Gemeinschaft*[6] (Nomos, 2004), at Artikel 293 EG para. 80.
61. Judgment in *Block*, C-67/08, EU:C:2009:92.
62. Judgment in *Schul I*, 15/81, EU:C:1982:135; Judgment in *Schul II*, 47/84, EU:C:1985:216; Judgment in *Ministère public / Profant*, 249/84, EU:C:1985:393, at para. 25; Judgment in *Bergeres-Becque*, 39/85, EU:C:1986:36; Judgment in *Drexl*, 299/86, EU:C:1988:103; Judgment in *ORO Amsterdam Beheer en Concerto*, 165/88, EU:C:1989:608, at para. 22; Judgment in *Commission/Italy*, 120/88, EU:C:1991:74; Judgment in *Commission/Spain*, C-119/89, EU:C:1991:75; Judgment in *Commission/Greece*, C-159/89, EU:C:1991:77; on double taxation being contrary to the principle of fiscal neutrality inherent in the VAT system see Judgment in *Kühne / Finanzamt München III*, 50/88, EU:C:1989:262, at para. 10; Judgment in *Commission / France*, C-68/92, EU:C:1993:888, at para. 14; Judgment in *Cookies World*, C-155/01, EU:C:2003:449; Judgment in *Finanzamt München III / Mohsche*, C-193/91, EU:C:1993:203, at para. 9; Judgment in *Bakcsi*, C-415/98, EU:C:2001:136, at para. 46; Judgment in *Fischer and Brandenstein*, C-322/99 and C-323/99, EU:C:2001:280, at para. 76; Judgment in *Teleos and others*, C-409/04, EU:C:2007:548, at para. 25; Judgment in *Collée*, C-146/05, EU:C:2007:549, at para. 23; Judgment in *Puffer*, C-460/07, EU:C:2009:254, at para. 46; Judgment in *Swiss Re Germany Holding*, C-242/08, EU:C:2009:647, at para. 32; Judgment in *Klub*, C-153/11, EU:C:2012:163, at para. 42; Judgment in *X*, C-334/10, EU:C:2012:473, at para. 33; Judgment in *Fonderie 2A*, C-446/13, EU:C:2014:2252, at para. 31; Judgment in *NLB Leasing*, C-209/14, EU:C:2015:440, at para. 40.
63. Judgment in *CIBA*, C-96/08, EU:C:2010:185.
64. Judgment in *Alevizos*, C-392/05, EU:C:2007:251, at para. 38; Judgment in *Scandic Distilleries*, C-663/11, EU:C:2013:347, at para. 23.
65. Judgment in *Statens Kontrol*, 142/77, EU:C:1978:144, at paras 32-34; Judgment in *Nygård*, C-234/99, EU:C:2002:244, at paras 37-38; also cf. Judgment in *Scharbatke*, C-72/92, EU:C:1993:858.
66. The commentary on the first "Draft Convention for the Avoidance of Double Taxation with respect to Taxes on Income and on Capital," which was published in 1963 (C(63) 113 (19 Nov. 1963)), described juridical double taxation as a situation "*where the same income or capital is taxable in the hands of the same person by more than one State*" (see Commentary on the 1963 OECD MC, Article 23(A) and 23(B) para. 1) and economic double taxation as "*taxation of the same income or capital in the hands of two different persons both chargeable to tax*" (see Commentary on the 1963 OECD MC, Article 23(A) and 23(B) para. 2). Similar descriptions of double taxation had already been used in prior documents of the OEEC (see Press/A(56) 19 (25 May 1956); FC(58) 2 (13 Feb. 1958), at p. 4; FC(58) 2 (1st Revision) Part I (19 Apr. 1958), at p. 3; C(58) 118 Part I (28 May 1958), at p. 3). However, no discussions seem to have taken place within the Fiscal Committee regarding this understanding of double taxation.
67. See also with further references, K. Ebling, *Unilaterale Maßnahmen gegen die internationale Doppelbesteuerung bei den Steuern vom Ertrag* (Dissertation Johannes Gutenberg Universität Mainz, 1970), at pp. 13-17; B. Lornsen, *Unilaterale Maßnahmen der Bundesrepublik Deutschland zur Ausschaltung der internationalen Doppelbesteuerung bei der Einkommen- und Körperschaftsteuer* (Peter Lang, 1987), at pp. 8-21; M. Pires, *International Juridical Double Taxation of Income* (Kluwer, 1989), at pp. 11-29.

liable to tax in more than one country bear a higher tax burden than if they were subject to one tax jurisdiction only. The additional burden so incurred must, of course, be due not merely to differences in tax rates for the countries concerned, but to the fact that two or more jurisdictions concurrently impose taxes having the same bases and incidence without regard to the claims of other tax jurisdictions."[68] From an internal market perspective this definition seems more suitable than today's general understanding of double taxation. If Article 293 second indent EC Treaty (ex-Article 220 second indent EEC Treaty) had been based on the OECD's current definition of juridical double taxation, the Member States' obligation to enter, "*so far as necessary, [...] into negotiations with each other with a view to securing for the benefit of their nationals [...] the abolition of double taxation within the Community*" would have implied that (a) multi-[69] or bilateral[70] convention(s),[71] which should have been the result of such

68. League of Nations, Fiscal Committee, London and Mexico Model Tax Conventions, Commentary and Text, Official No.: C.88.M.88.1946.II.A. (League of Nations, 1946), at p. 7.
69. See A. de Graaf, Avoidance of International Double Taxation: Community or Joint Policy?, 7 *EC Tax Rev.* 4 (1998), p. 258 (at p. 270); J. Englisch, Meistbegünstigung im EG-Steuerrecht: Der Weg ins Chaos, in A. Cordewener/S. Enchelmaier/C.P. Schindler (eds.), *Meistbegünstigung im Steuerrecht der EU-Staaten* (C.H. Beck, 2006), p. 163 (at p. 175, FN 83); L. Hinnekens, Different Interpretations of the European Tax Arbitration Convention, 7 *EC Tax Rev.* 4 (1998), p. 247 (at p. 250); H. Krabbe, EG-Schiedsverfahren bei Berichtigung von Verrechnungspreisen im Konzern, 28 *RIW* 4 (1982), p. 269 (at p. 270); U. Eyles, *Das Niederlassungsrecht der Kapitalgesellschaften in der Europäischen Gemeinschaft* (Nomos, 1990), at pp. 264-265; A. Musil, *Deutsches Treaty Overriding und seine Vereinbarkeit mit Europäischem Gemeinschaftsrecht* (Duncker & Humblot, 2000), at pp. 101-103; P. Pistone, *The Impact of Community Law on Tax Treaties* (Kluwer, 2002), at pp. 71-72; T.B. Scherer in D. Birk (ed.), *Handbuch des Europäischen Steuer- und Abgabenrechts* (NWB, 1995), at § 31 para. 102; T.B. Scherer, *Doppelbesteuerung und Europäisches Gemeinschaftsrecht* (C.H. Beck, 1995), at pp. 79-87; S. van Thiel, *Free Movement of Persons and Income Tax Law: The European Court in Search of Principles* (IBFD, 2002), at pp. 130-131; C. Vedder, Einwirkungen des Europarechts auf das innerstaatliche Recht und auf internationale Verträge der Mitgliedstaaten: die Regelung der Doppelbesteuerung, in M. Lehner/O. Thömmes/C. Vedder/A. Wiedow, *Europarecht und Internationales Steuerrecht* (C.H. Beck, 1994), p. 1 (at p. 9); D. Weber, Most-Favoured Nation Treatment under Tax Treaties Rejected in the European Community: Background and Analysis of the *D* case, 33 *Intertax* 10 (2005), p. 429 (at p. 436).
70. See J.F. Avery Jones, Flows of capital Between the EU and Third Countries and the Consequences of Disharmony in European International Tax Law, 7 *EC Tax Rev.* 2 (1998), p. 95 (at p. 96); A. Cordewener/E. Reimer, The Future of Most-Favoured-Nation Treatment in EC Tax Law - Did the ECJ Pull the Emergency Brake Without Real Need? - Part 2, 46 *Eur. Taxn.* 7 (2006), p. 291 (at p. 300, FN 160); M. Lehner, *Möglichkeiten zur Verbesserung des Verständigungsverfahrens auf der Grundlage des EWG-Vertrags* (C.H. Beck, 1982), at p. 142; N. Dautzenberg, Doppelbesteuerung und EG-Vertrag: Die Anrechnungsmethode als gemeinschaftsrechtlicher Mindeststandard?, 47 *DB* 31 (1994), p. 1542 (at p. 1543); H. Doyle, Is Article 26 of the Netherlands-United States Tax Treaty Compatible with EC Law?, 35 *Eur. Taxn.* 1 (1995), p. 14 (at p. 16); H. Schaumburg, Problemfelder im internationalen Erbschaftsteuerrecht, 47 *RIW* 3 (2001), p. 161 (at p. 169); J. Schuch, EC law requires multilateral tax treaty, 7 *EC Tax Rev.* 1 (1998), p. 29 (at p. 36); F. Vanistendael, The Limits to the New Community Tax Order, 31 *Common Market L. Rev.* 2 (1994), p. 293 (at p. 295); P.J. Wattel, Corporate Tax Jurisdiction in the EU with Respect to Branches and Subsidiaries; Dislocation Distinguished from Discrimination and Disparity; a Plea for Territoriality, 12 *EC Tax Rev.* 4 (2003), p. 194 (at p. 199); P.J. Wattel, Red Herrings in Direct Tax Cases Before the ECJ, 31 *Legal Issues of Economic Integration* 2 (2004), p. 81 (at p. 87).
71. See W. Schön, Die beschränkte Steuerpflicht zwischen europäischem Gemeinschaftsrecht und deutschem Verfassungsrecht, 4 *IStR* 3 (1995), p. 119 (at p. 119); I.E. Schwartz/W. Mölls in H.

negotiations, always had to entirely restrict at least one Member State's taxing right. With regard to direct taxes, for example, it would not be sufficient that the residence state "*allow[s] [...] as a deduction from the tax on the income of that resident, an amount equal to the income tax paid in [the other contracting state].*"[72] This is due to the fact that the same taxpayer would still be subject to "*comparable taxes in two [...] states in respect of the same subject matter and for identical periods,*"[73] if the amount of tax levied by the residence state was higher than the amount of tax levied by the other contracting state.[74] Such an understanding would conflict with the widely accepted assumption that juridical double taxation of income is avoided if the residence state applies the credit method.

From an internal market perspective, the main shortcoming of today's commonly used definition of double taxation is that the overall tax burden is disregarded.[75] Whether a cross-border situation is unduly burdened so that the internal market's objective of free movement is restricted can only be determined if the taxation of the cross-border situation is contrasted with the taxation of a comparable domestic situation,[76] unless taxation per se is considered to impede the establishment of the internal market.[77] However, it is unclear which state's tax burden is to be used for

von der Groeben/J. Schwarze (eds.), *Kommentar zum Vertrag über die Europäische Union und zur Gründung der Europäischen Gemeinschaft*[6] (Nomos, 2004), at Artikel 293 EG para. 85.

72. See Article 23 B para. 1 OECD MC.
73. Thus, some scholars suggest distinguishing "double taxation" from "overlapping taxation." See R. Mason, Made in America for European Tax: The Internal Consistency Test, 49 *Bost. Coll. L. Rev.* 4 (2008), p. 1277 (at pp. 1287-1289).
74. See G. Frotscher, *Internationales Steuerrecht*[3] (C.H. Beck, 2009); V. Kluge, *Das Internationale Steuerrecht*[4] (C.H. Beck, 2000) at p. 29; B. Lornsen, *Unilaterale Maßnahmen der Bundesrepublik Deutschland zur Ausschaltung der internationalen Doppelbesteuerung bei der Einkommen- und Körperschaftsteuer* (Peter Lang, 1987), at pp. 17-57; K. Vogel, 85 *DStZ* 9 (1997), at p. 277.
75. See B. Lornsen, *Unilaterale Maßnahmen der Bundesrepublik Deutschland zur Ausschaltung der internationalen Doppelbesteuerung bei der Einkommen- und Körperschaftsteuer* (Peter Lang, 1987), at pp. 17-19; L. Fischer/P. Warneke, *Grundlagen der Internationalen Betriebswirtschaftlichen Steuerlehre*[2] (Erich Schmidt Verlag, 1974), at p. 41; A. Philipp, *Befreiungssystem mit Progressionsvorbehalt und Anrechnungsverfahren* (Orac, 1971), at pp. 8-10; K. Vogel, Internationales Steuerrecht, 85 *DStZ* 9 (1997), p. 269 (at p. 277).
76. See J. Englisch, The European Treaties' Implications for Direct Taxes, 33 *Intertax* 8-9 (2005), p. 310 (at p. 325); B. Lornsen, *Unilaterale Maßnahmen der Bundesrepublik Deutschland zur Ausschaltung der internationalen Doppelbesteuerung bei der Einkommen- und Körperschaftsteuer* (Peter Lang, 1987), at p. 20; E. Reimer, Die Auswirkungen der Grundfreiheiten auf das Ertragsteuerrecht der Bundesrepublik Deutschland - Eine Bestandsaufnahme, in M. Lehner (ed.), *Grundfreiheiten im Steuerrecht der EU-Staaten* (C.H. Beck, 2000), p. 39 (at p. 57); also cf. W. Schön, Freie Wahl zwischen Zweigniederlassung und Tochtergesellschaft - ein Grundsatz des Europäischen Unternehmensrechts, 11 *EWS* 7 (2000), p. 281 (at p. 290); J. Englisch, *Dividendenbesteuerung* (Dr Otto Schmidt, 2005), at pp. 253-254; M. Lehner, Avoidance of Double Taxation Within the European Union: Is There an Obligation under EC Law?, in M. Lang/J. Schuch/C. Staringer (eds.), *Tax Treaty Law and EC Law* (Linde, 2007), p. 11 (at p. 16).
77. Cf. A. Cordewener, *Europäische Grundfreiheiten und nationales Steuerrecht* (Dr Otto Schmidt, 2002), at p. 289; P. Farmer/R. Lyal, *EC Tax Law* (Clarendon Press, 1994), at p. 328; G. Kofler, *Doppelbesteuerungsabkommen und Europäisches Gemeinschaftsrecht* (Linde, 2007), at p. 122; E. Reimer in H. Schaumburg/J. Englisch (eds.), *Europäisches Steuerrecht* (Dr Otto Schmidt, 2015), at MN 7.191; B.J.M. Terra/P.J. Wattel, *European Tax Law*[6] (Kluwer, 2012), at pp. 56 and 84; see also Opinion of AG Kokott in *X*, C-686/13, EU:C:2015:31, at point 40.

determining whether the cross-border situation is treated less beneficially.[78] According to settled case law, the "*Treaty offers no guarantee to a citizen of the Union that transferring his residence to a Member State other than that in which he previously resided will be neutral as regards taxation. Given the disparities in the tax legislation of the Member States, such a transfer may be to the citizen's advantage or not, according to circumstances.*"[79] Thus, different tax policy decisions of the Member States have to be accepted even in the internal market. Insofar as harmonizing measures have not been taken,[80] the Member States are free to take choices of economic policy irrespective of other Member States' decisions,[81] unless these choices conflict with EU law. If, for example, a taxpayer moved to another Member State, free movement would not be restricted by the Member State where the taxpayer moved to simply because the former residence state has a lower tax rate.[82] Neither would the establishment of the internal market be impeded if the cross-border relocation leads to a lower tax burden than previously due to the different tax rates applied in the Member States involved. From an internal market perspective, it is hence only problematic if the taxes of two or more states overlap in such a manner that the cross-border situation bears a higher tax burden than a comparable domestic situation would have to face in the tax jurisdiction

78. See also with further references, M. Pires, *International Juridical Double Taxation of Income* (Kluwer, 1989), at pp. 21-22.
79. Judgment in *Block*, C-67/08, EU:C:2009:92, at para. 35; see also Judgment in *Hervein*, C-393/99 and C-394/99, EU:C:2002:182, at para. 51; Judgment in *Weigel*, C-387/01, EU:C:2004:256, at para. 55; Judgment in *Lindfors*, C-365/02, EU:C:2004:449, at para. 34; Judgment in *Schempp*, C-403/03, EU:C:2005:446, at para. 45; Judgment in *Alevizos*, C-392/05, EU:C:2007:251, at para. 76; Judgment in *Renneberg*, C-527/06, EU:C:2008:566, at para. 40; Judgment in *Schulz-Delzers and Schulz*, C-240/10, EU:C:2011:591, at para. 42; Judgment in *National Grid Indus*, C-371/10, EU:C:2011:785, at para. 62.
80. Opinion of AG Geelhoed in *Test Claimants in Class IV of the ACT Group Litigation*, C-374/04, EU:C:2006:139, at point 47.
81. Judgment in *Columbus Container Services*, C-298/05, EU:C:2007:754, at para. 51; Judgment in *Block*, C-67/08, EU:C:2009:92, at para. 31; Judgment in *CIBA*, C-96/08, EU:C:2010:185, at para. 28; Judgment in *Commission/Hungary*, C-253/09, EU:C:2011:795, at para. 83; Judgment in *Banco Bilbao Vizcaya Argentaria*, C-157/10, EU:C:2011:813, at para. 39; Judgment in *X*, C-302/12, EU:C:2013:756, at para. 29.
82. See Judgment in *Gilly*, C-336/96, EU:C:1998:221, at para. 47; Judgment in *de Groot*, C-385/00, EU:C:2002:750, at para. 86; also cf. M. Gammie, The Role of the European Court of Justice in the Development of Direct Taxation in the European Union, 57 *Bull. Intl. Taxn.* 3 (2003), p. 86 (at p. 89); J. Englisch in A. Cordewener/S. Enchelmaier/C.P. Schindler (eds.), *Meistbegünstigung im Steuerrecht der EU-Staaten* (C.H. Beck, 2006), at p. 176; G. Kofler, *Doppelbesteuerungsabkommen und Europäisches Gemeinschaftsrecht* (Linde, 2007), at p. 234; also cf. M. Tumpel, Europarechtliche Besteuerungsmaßstäbe für die grenzüberschreitende Organisation und Finanzierung von Unternehmen, in J. Pelka (ed.), *Europa- und verfassungsrechtliche Grenzen der Unternehmensbesteuerung*, DStJG 30 (Dr Otto Schmidt, 2000), p. 321 (at p. 345).

that has the highest tax burden of all tax jurisdictions involved.[83,84] From an EU law perspective, double taxation should hence be perceived as a situational and relative phenomenon.[85] Whether a cross-border situation is subject to double taxation depends on the tax burden the respective comparable domestic situation would have to face in the individual Member States which are involved.[86]

83. With regard to direct taxation see G. Kofler, *Doppelbesteuerungsabkommen und Europäisches Gemeinschaftsrecht* (Linde, 2007), at p. 235; J. Englisch, 33 *Intertax* 8-9 (2005), at p. 325 (FN 151); J. Englisch in A. Cordewener/S. Enchelmaier/C.P. Schindler (eds.), *Meistbegünstigung im Steuerrecht der EU-Staaten* (C.H. Beck, 2006), at p. 176; L. Fischer/P. Warneke, *Grundlagen der Internationalen Betriebswirtschaftlichen Steuerlehre*[2] (Erich Schmidt Verlag, 1974), at p. 41; E. Reimer in M. Lehner (ed.), *Grundfreiheiten im Steuerrecht der EU-Staaten* (C.H. Beck, 2000), at pp. 57-58; J. Schönfeld in H. Flick/F. Wassemeyer/H. Baumhoff/J. Schönfeld (eds.), *Außensteuerrecht*[57] (Dr Otto Schmidt, 2005), Vor § 34c EStG at m.no 2; J. Schönfeld, Doppelbesteuerung und EG-Recht, 83 *StuW* 1 (2006), p. 79 (at pp. 80-82); Y. Brauner, An International Tax Regime in Crystallization, 56 *Tax L. Rev.* 2 (2002), p. 259 (at pp. 309-310: "*Ideally, no item of income should avoid any country's claim for taxation, and no item of income should be subject to taxation at a level (rate) higher than that of either of the competing countries (what is normally called 'double taxation'). […] [T]he tax […] ideally should not amount in total to a rate higher than the highest of the rates, but not more than that.*"); with regard to indirect taxation see J. Englisch, *Wettbewerbsgleichheit im grenzüberschreitenden Handel* (Mohr Siebeck, 2008), at p. 788.
84. It could be argued that such an understanding would ignore the fact that, for example, the overall tax burden of the cross-border situation could be higher than the tax burden a comparable domestic situation would have to face in the tax jurisdiction that has the lowest tax burden of all tax jurisdictions involved, but could nevertheless be lower than what a comparable domestic situation would have to face in the tax jurisdiction that has the highest tax burden of all tax jurisdictions involved. This could happen, for example, if the cross-border situation is subjected by the Member State with the lower tax rate to an additional tax in the amount of the difference between its own tax rate and the higher tax rate of the other Member State. If the other Member State provides for a tax exemption in order to avoid double taxation, the resultant tax burden of the cross-border situation would still not exceed the tax burden a comparable domestic situation would have to face in the tax jurisdiction that has the highest tax burden of all tax jurisdictions involved. However, in such a situation, the alleged problem does not primarily result from overlapping tax systems, but rather from the fact that the Member State which levies an additional tax on cross-border situations treats cross-border situations less beneficially than purely domestic situations. If such a different treatment constituted an infringement of the fundamental freedoms, the responsible Member State would be obliged to stop levying the additional tax in order not to violate EU law. Hence, the additional tax levied on cross-border situations would not be a question of (bilaterally-caused) double taxation, but of (unilaterally-caused) discrimination. If, by contrast, there was no infringement of the fundamental freedoms, this would mean that the respective Member State is allowed to subject cross-border situations to a higher tax burden than purely domestic situations. It would thus make no sense to compare the overall *tax burden of the cross-border situation* with the *tax burden of the comparable domestic situation* in the respective Member State. As this Member State is allowed to levy a higher tax burden on the cross-border situation, the *overall* tax burden of the cross-border situation should rather be compared with this Member State's *domestic* tax levied on cross-border situations.
85. Cf. R.A. Musgrave, *The Theory of Public Finance* (McGraw-Hill, 1959), at p. 163 ("*The only meaningful way in which the terms* double taxation *or* under-taxation *can be used in connection with equity is to indicate discrimination for or against particular taxpayers in terms of a given index of equality.*").
86. The definition of double taxation as included in the currently envisaged presidency compromise on the European Commission's Proposal for a Council Directive on Double Taxation Dispute Resolution Mechanisms in the European Union (COM[2016] 686 final (25 Oct. 2016) also suggests such an understanding. After all, whether "*the imposition of taxes covered by an agreement or convention referred to in Article 1 by two (or more) Member States in respect of the*

2.3 The Phenomenon of Double Non-Taxation from an EU Law Perspective

This understanding is insofar plausible as free movement is impaired if a cross-border transaction sustains a higher tax burden than a comparable domestic transaction. However, if the result is the other way around, i.e., a cross-border transaction sustains a lesser tax burden than a comparable domestic transaction, the internal market's free movement requirement is obviously not infringed. On the contrary, as every form of taxation hinders economic activity in one way or another,[87] there is nothing better for free movement than a taxpayer, a certain item of income, a transaction or an activity remaining untaxed. If this is true, why does the European Commission consider double non-taxation to be as incompatible with the internal market as double taxation?[88]

The explanation is unintentionally given by the OECD, according to which double non-taxation may lead to "*a reduction of the overall tax paid by all parties involved as a whole, which harms competition, economic efficiency, transparency and fairness.*"[89] From an internal market perspective, the first two aspects in particular are legally remarkable, because the EU is based on the economic policy perception of "*an open market economy with free competition, favouring an efficient allocation of resources.*"[90,91] To foster this policy objective, the free movement dimension of the internal market concept aims at eliminating the compartmentalizing effect of the

---

same taxable income or capital [...] gives rise to either (i) additional tax charge, (ii) increase in tax liabilities or (iii) cancellation or reduction of losses, which could be used to offset taxable profits" (Doc. 9420/17 LIMITE FISC 111 ECOFIN 429 [19 May 2017], at p. 7) can only be verified by making a comparison. Determining whether there is an "additional" tax charge or an "increase" in tax liabilities, for example, requires to know what the "original" tax charge or tax liability was.

87. See B.J.M. Terra/P.J. Wattel, *European Tax Law*[6] (Kluwer, 2012), at p. 84.
88. See Taxation in the European Union, SEC(96) 487 final (20 Mar. 1996), at p. 13 ("*[t]he Single Market is clearly not compatible with either double taxation of the same taxable base or no taxation at all*"); Opinion of the Economic and Social Committee on Taxation in the European Union, Report on the development of tax systems (SEC[96] 487 final and COM[96] 546 final), *OJ* C 296 (29 Sep. 1997), p. 37 (at p. 43: "*[d]ouble taxation or the absence of taxation is incompatible with the internal market*"); Tax co-ordination in the European Union, Working Paper, Economic Affairs Series, ECON 125 EN (European Parliament, 2000), at p. 22 ("*The Single Market has several particular implications for the taxation of employment incomes. [...] Incomes should not escape tax altogether, or be taxed at discriminatorily low rates, as a result of cross-border tax arbitrage, avoidance or evasion.*"); Commission Recommendation of 6 Dec. 2012 on aggressive tax planning, C(2012) 8806 final (6 Dec. 2012), at p. 2 ("*[t]he Single Market is clearly not compatible with either double taxation [...] or no taxation at all*").
89. OECD, *Action Plan on Base Erosion and Profit Shifting* (OECD, 2013), at p. 15.
90. Article 120 TFEU.
91. See, for example, D. Hanf, Legal Concept and Meaning of the Internal Market, in J. Pelkmans/D. Hanf/M. Chang (eds.), *The EU Internal Market in Comparative Perspective* (Peter Lang, 2008), p. 77 (at p. 77); W. Schön, Der "Wettbewerb" der europäischen Steuerordnungen als Rechtsproblem, in J. Pelka (ed.), *Europa- und verfassungsrechtliche Grenzen der Unternehmensbesteuerung*, DStJG 30 (Dr Otto Schmidt, 2000), p. 191 (at pp. 191-195); W. Schön, 9 *EC Tax Rev.* 2 (2000), at p. 91; W. Schön, Transfer Pricing, the Arm's Length Standard and European Union Law, in I. Richelle/W. Schön/E. Traversa (eds.), *Allocating Taxing Powers Within the European Union* (Springer, 2013), p. 73 (at p. 93); J. Schönfeld, *Hinzurechnungsbesteuerung und Europäisches Gemeinschaftsrecht* (Dr Otto Schmidt, 2005), at pp. 16-18; J.H.H. Weiler, The Transformation of Europe, 100 *Yale L. J.* 8 (1991), p. 2403 (at pp. 2477-2478); B. Strassburger, *Die Dogmatik der EU-Grundfreiheiten* (Mohr Siebeck, 2012), at p. 8.

Member States' legal systems.[92] However, to ensure an efficient allocation of resources a level playing field within the internal market also has to be provided for.[93] Therefore, the TFEU contains provisions aimed at avoiding distortions of competition induced by the market participants,[94] by the Member States,[95] or by differences between the Member States' legal systems.[96] Since the Treaty of Lisbon, the importance of undistorted competition is also emphasized in a protocol annexed to the Treaties which clarifies that the *"internal market [...] includes a system ensuring that competition is not distorted."*[97] If it is hence correct that competition and economic efficiency may be harmed[98] by a cross-border transaction sustaining a lesser tax burden than a comparable domestic transaction, the question arises whether the Treaties' provisions dealing with undistorted competition prohibit such a preferential treatment of cross-border situations.[99]

From a tax perspective, the State aid rules of Articles 107-109 TFEU are the most relevant means to implement the competition aspect of the internal market concept.[100] Thus, tax measures favouring certain undertakings or the production of certain goods are, in so far as trade between Member States is affected, incompatible with the internal market if competition is thereby distorted or threatened to be distorted. The most important criterion of the State aid rules for tax matters is whether a domestic measure causes a selective advantage.[101] According to the ECJ's more recent jurisprudence, this is the case if a tax measure leads to a preferential treatment of certain economic operators which are in a comparable situation with non-privileged economic

92. See, for example, A. Cordewener, *Europäische Grundfreiheiten und nationales Steuerrecht* (Dr Otto Schmidt, 2002), at p. 352; G. Kofler, *Doppelbesteuerungsabkommen und Europäisches Gemeinschaftsrecht* (Linde, 2007), at p. 51; B. Strassburger, *Die Dogmatik der EU-Grundfreiheiten* (Mohr Siebeck, 2012), at p. 10.
93. Cf. J. Pelkmans/P. Robson, The Aspirations of the White Paper, 26 *JCMS* 3 (1987), p. 181 (at p. 183); W. Schön in J. Pelka (ed.), *Europa- und verfassungsrechtliche Grenzen der Unternehmensbesteuerung*, DStJG 30 (Dr Otto Schmidt, 2000), at p. 194.
94. Articles 101-102.
95. Articles 106-107.
96. Article 116.
97. Protocol (No 27) on the Internal Market and Competition, *OJ* C 326 (26 Oct. 2012), p. 47 (at p. 309).
98. OECD, *Action Plan on Base Erosion and Profit Shifting* (OECD, 2013), at p. 15.
99. Cf. W. Haslehner, Double Taxation Relief, Transfer Pricing Adjustments and State Aid Law, in I. Richelle/W. Schön/E. Traversa (eds.), *State Aid Law and Business Taxation* (Springer, 2016), 133 (134-160); R. Luja, EU State Aid Rules and Their Limits, 76 *Tax Notes Intl.* 4 (27 Oct. 2014), p. 353 (at pp. 353-356); R. Luja, EU State Aid Law and National Tax Rulings: In-Depth Analysis for the TAXE Special Committee, IP/A/TAXE/2015-02, PE 563.453 (October 2015), at pp. 14-15; R. Luja, Will the EU's State Aid Regime Survive BEPS?, 60 *British Tax Rev.* 3 (2015), p. 379 (at pp. 379-390); P. Rossi-Maccanico, 75 *Tax Notes Intl.* 10 (8 Sep. 2014), at pp. 857-868; P. Rossi-Maccanico, Fiscal State Aids, Tax Base Erosion and Profit Shifting, 24 *EC Tax Rev.* 2 (2015), p. 63 (at pp. 63-77); D.S. Smit, 25 *EC Tax Rev.* 2 (2016), at pp. 110-112; R. Szudoczky, Double Taxation Relief, Transfer Pricing Adjustments and State Aid Law: Comments, in I. Richelle/W. Schön/E. Traversa (eds.), *State Aid Law and Business Taxation* (Springer, 2016), 163 (163-183); A. Taferner/J.W. Kuipers, Tax Rulings: In Line With OECD Transfer Pricing Guidelines, but Contrary to EU State Aid Rules?, 56 *Eur. Taxn.* 4 (2016), p. 134 (at pp. 142-143).
100. See P. Pistone/R. Szudoczy in M. Lang/P. Pistone/J. Schuch/C. Staringer (eds.), *Introduction to European Tax Law on Direct Taxation*[4] (Linde, 2015), at p. 28.
101. See Chapter 3.3.3.3.

operators.[102] The Court's State aid analysis is thus based on a comparison. In order to determine whether a cross-border situation is unduly privileged so that the internal market's objective of undistorted competition is harmed, the taxation of the cross-border situation should hence be contrasted with the taxation of a comparable domestic situation.[103] Against this background, when referring to double non-taxation, the European Commission seemingly refers to a situation in which a cross-border transaction sustains a lesser tax burden than a comparable domestic transaction.

According to such an understanding, double non-taxation does not necessarily mean that a taxpayer, a certain item of income, a transaction or an activity remains untaxed. Although neither Austria nor Germany levy an income tax on a German citizen who wins in the Austrian lottery, the resultant non-taxation of the lottery winnings would be in line with the internal market concept, even if the tax laws of other Member States subjected lottery winnings to income tax. From an internal market perspective, such an outcome is not a cause for concern insofar as the Member States are free to deliberately decide that a property gain should not be taxed.[104] For the same reason, the establishment of the internal market would not be impeded if a taxpayer moved to another Member State that does not levy an income tax on capital gains, while the former Member State of residence only taxes capital gains of taxpayers subject to unlimited tax liability. If such a taxpayer alienated, for example, shares in a company located in the former Member State of residence, the resultant capital gain would remain untaxed, at least to the extent the increase in value took place after the cross-border relocation. Unless the policy choice of the particular Member State not to tax such capital gains is in conflict with EU law, such an outcome is in line with the internal market concept. From an internal market perspective, it is hence only problematic if the tax systems of two or more states overlap in such a manner that the cross-border situation bears a lesser tax burden than a comparable domestic situation would have to face in the tax jurisdiction that has the lowest tax burden of all tax

102. Judgment in *Adria-Wien Pipeline and Wietersdorfer & Peggauer Zementwerke*, C-143/99, EU:C:2001:598, at para. 38; Judgment in *GIL Insurance and others*, C-308/01, EU:C:2004:252, at para. 68; Judgment in *Spain/Commission*, C-409/00, EU:C:2003:92, at para. 47; Judgment in *Heiser*, C-172/03, EU:C:2005:130, at para. 40; Judgment in *Portugal/Commission*, C-88/03, EU:C:2006:511, at para. 54; Judgment in *Unión General de Trabajadores de la Rioja*, C-428/06 to C-434/06, EU:C:2008:488, at para. 46; Judgment in *British Aggregates/Commission*, C-487/06 P, EU:C:2008:757, at para. 82; Judgment in *Presidente del Consiglio dei Ministri*, C-169/08, EU:C:2009:709, at para. 61; Judgment in *Paint Graphos and others*, C-78/08 to C-80/08, EU:C:2011:550, at para. 49; Judgment in *P*, C-6/12, EU:C:2013:525, at para. 19; Judgment in *Ministerio de Defensa and Navantia*, C-522/13, EU:C:2014:2262, at para. 35.

103. With regard to the VAT principle of fiscal neutrality cf. Judgment in *Eurodenthal*, C-240/05, EU:C:2006:763, at paras 46-47.

104. See W. Schön, Tax Legislation and the Notion of Fiscal Aid – A Review of Five Years of European Jurisprudence –, *Max Planck Institute for Tax Law and Public Finance Working Paper 2015-14* (December 2015), at pp. 2-3 and W. Schön, Tax Legislation and the Notion of Fiscal Aid: A Review of 5 Years of European Jurisprudence, in I. Richelle/W. Schön/E. Traversa (eds.), *State Aid Law and Business Taxation* (Springer, 2016), p. 3 (at p. 5: "*Non-taxation of economic behaviour as such is not an issue under European law*"); also cf. P.J. Wattel, Stateless Income, State Aid and the (Which?) Arm's Length Principle, 44 *Intertax* 11 (2016), p. 791 (at p. 797: "*[T]he Commission correctly does not consider double non-taxation in itself as State aid*").

jurisdictions involved.[105] Just as double taxation, double non-taxation should hence be perceived as a situational and relative phenomenon for purposes of EU law. Whether a cross-border situation leads to double non-taxation depends on the tax burden the respective comparable domestic situation would trigger in the individual Member States which are involved.[106]

3 THE FUNDAMENTAL FREEDOMS AND THE STATE AID RULES AS LEGAL MEANS TO TACKLE DOUBLE TAXATION AND DOUBLE NON-TAXATION

If both double taxation and double non-taxation are perceived as relative and situational phenomena, the Member States, by independently and autonomously taking tax policy decisions that are per se compatible with EU law, not only create their domestic tax environment, but also draw the limits for the internal market-compliant taxation of cross-border situations. If the tax burden on the cross-border situation does not fall within the "tax corridor"[107] that is established by the EU law-compliant tax

105. There might also be situations where the overall tax burden of the cross-border situation is lower than the tax burden a comparable domestic situation would have to face in the tax jurisdiction that has the highest tax burden of all tax jurisdictions involved, but nevertheless is higher than the tax burden a comparable domestic situation would have to face in the tax jurisdiction that has the lowest tax burden of all tax jurisdictions involved. This could, for example, happen, if a double taxation convention provides for a "tax sparing credit" or a "tax matching credit," i.e., the amount of foreign taxes that is credited by the residence state is higher than the amount actually levied by the other contracting state (see M. Lang, *Introduction to the Law of Double Taxation Conventions*[2] [Linde, 2013], at p. 139). However, in such a situation, the alleged problem does not primarily result from overlapping tax systems, but rather from the fact that the residence state treats cross-border situations more beneficially than purely domestic situations. After all, by granting a matching credit, not only the domestic, but also the overall tax burden of the cross-border situation is reduced compared to the domestic tax burden of a comparable domestic situation. There are discussions in the literature whether such a different treatment is in line with Article 107(1) TFEU or not (see R. Luja, Tax Treaties and State Aid: Some Thoughts, 44 *Eur. Taxn.* 4 (2004), p. 234 (at p. 236); F.P. Sutter, Die DBA-Freistellungsmethode als unzulässige Beihilfe i. S. d. Art. 87 EG?, 14 *SWI* 1 (2004), p. 4 (at p. 9, FN 31); F.P. Sutter, Die abkommensrechtliche Verteilung der Besteuerungsrechte zwischen Ansässigkeits- und Quellenstaat aus beihilfenrechtlicher Sicht, in M. Lang/J. Schuch/C. Staringer [eds.], *Die abkommensrechtliche Verteilung der Besteuerungsrechte zwischen Ansässigkeits- und Quellenstaat* (Linde, 2005), p. 83 (at pp. 114-115)). If not, the residence state would be obliged to stop granting a matching credit in order not to violate EU law. Hence, the matching credit would not be a question of (bilaterally-caused) double non-taxation, but of (unilaterally-caused) State aid. If, by contrast, there was no infringement of the State aid rules, it would make no sense to compare the overall *tax burden of the cross-border situation* with the *tax burden of the comparable domestic situation* in the respective Member State. As this Member State consciously levies a lower tax on the cross-border situation, this should be kept in mind when making the comparison.
106. Cf. Y. Brauner, 16 *Florida Tax Rev.* 2 (2014), at p. 79 ("*'double non-taxation', that is, taxation of circumstances of transactions at a level that is lower than they would have faced in a purely domestic setting*").
107. Cf. J. Englisch, *Wettbewerbsgleichheit im grenzüberschreitenden Handel* (Mohr Siebeck, 2008), at pp. 269 and 789.

systems of the Member States involved, either double taxation or double non-taxation is at hand. This can be illustrated by the following example: Member State A provides for an income tax rate of 15% on employment income. The corresponding income tax rate in Member State B is 10%. If a resident of Member State A works in Member State B due to a cross-border secondment, the effective tax rate on this taxpayer's employment income should be neither above 15% (double taxation) nor below 10% (double non-taxation):[108]

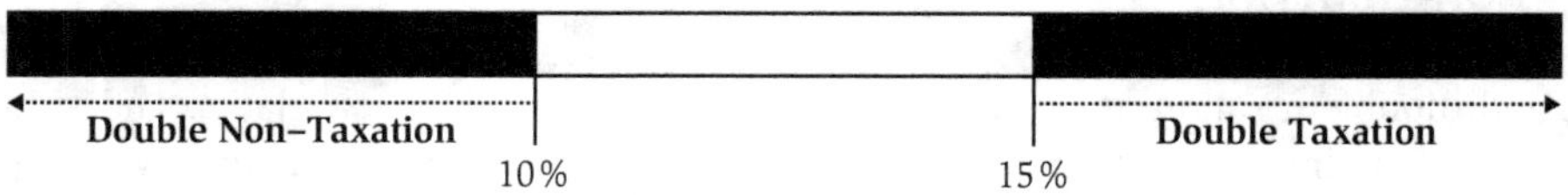

Admittedly, it may be confusing to refer to double *non*-taxation if the effective tax burden is higher than zero. After all, the income does not remain *un*taxed. However, although commonly accepted, the term *double* taxation is likewise misleading. According to the OECD MC, juridical double taxation can be avoided by the residence state through granting a tax credit.[109] However, if the residence state's tax rate was higher than the other contracting state's tax rate,[110] such a credit would not change the fact that the same taxpayer is still subject to "*comparable taxes in two [...] states in respect of the same subject matter and for identical periods.*"[111] Apparently, double taxation hence does not mean that a taxpayer is taxed by *two* different Member States. Neither does it mean that the tax burden in a cross-border situation is *twice* as much as it would be in a purely domestic situation. If the tax rates of the states involved do not coincide, the result of being taxed by two different states may be lower or higher than the doubled tax burden in each single state. From an internal market perspective, the terms double taxation and double non-taxation should thus be understood to mean that the tax burden on a cross-border situation is higher (double taxation) or lower (double non-taxation) than in the relevant comparable domestic situation.

According to such an understanding,[112] double taxation and double non-taxation are phenomena exclusively emerging in a cross-border context.[113] From an EU law

108. This example is based on the assumption that the tax base is calculated in both Member States in the same way.
109. See Article 23 B para. 1 OECD MC.
110. See G. Frotscher, *Internationales Steuerrecht*[3] (C.H. Beck, 2009); V. Kluge, *Das Internationale Steuerrecht*[4] (C.H. Beck, 2000) at p. 29; B. Lornsen, *Unilaterale Maßnahmen der Bundesrepublik Deutschland zur Ausschaltung der internationalen Doppelbesteuerung bei der Einkommen- und Körperschaftsteuer* (Peter Lang, 1987), at pp. 17-57; K. Vogel, 85 *DStZ* 9 (1997), at p. 277.
111. Thus, some scholars suggest distinguishing "double taxation" from "overlapping taxation." See R. Mason, 49 *Bost. Coll. L. Rev.* 4 (2008), at pp. 1287-1289.
112. If double taxation and double non-taxation are generally perceived as relative and situational phenomena (cf. R.A. Musgrave, *The Theory of Public Finance* (McGraw-Hill, 1959), at p. 163), they may not only arise in an international, but also in another context. However, the comparison that is needed to determine whether double taxation or double non-taxation occurs may not always be the same. Whether a taxpayer, a certain item of income, a transaction or an activity is subject to double taxation would depend on the tax burden suffered by a comparable taxpayer, a comparable item of income, a comparable transaction or a comparable activity.

perspective, this raises the question whether the consequences of over- or under-taxing cross-border situations are legally problematic. Thereby it is undisputed that double

Many Member States, for example, provide for an integration of corporate and shareholder income tax in order to avoid economic double taxation resulting from the taxation of profits earned by a corporation and distributed to a shareholder (see Chapter 2.1.2.2). Income derived by a corporation is initially subject to corporate income tax. If the after-tax profit is subsequently distributed, it is again taxed at the level of the shareholder as a dividend. This is generally considered to result in economic double taxation, the avoidance of which is typically considered to be desirable. Within the EU, the most frequently used relief methods are schedular systems that provide for a reduced tax rate or a diminished tax base in the case of dividend income (see J. Englisch, Shareholder Relief and EC Treaty Law – Supranational "Aims and Effects"?, 33 *Intertax* 5 (2005), p. 200 (at p. 200); G. Kofler, *Doppelbesteuerungsabkommen und Europäisches Gemeinschaftsrecht* (Linde, 2007), at pp. 938-940). Such relief mechanisms do not change the fact that profits are first taxed at the level of the corporation and – after being distributed – again taxed at the level of the shareholder. But if it is not about the same profits being taxed twice (see R.A. Musgrave, *The Theory of Public Finance* (McGraw-Hill, 1959), at p. 163 ("*the concept of double taxation as taxing a thing more than once is fallacious*")), what is the reason to speak about economic double taxation? The most plausible explanation is that the term economic double taxation involves a comparison of the tax burdens resulting from the use of different legal forms when organizing a business (Cf. H.G. Ruppe, *Die Steuerliche Doppelbelastung der Körperschaftsgewinne* (Jupiter-Verlag, 1967), pp. 139-140). Without an integration of corporate and shareholder income taxes, it would make a huge difference whether a business is organized as an individual enterprise, a partnership or a corporation, because direct tax systems are typically affected by a dualism of business taxation. Thus, profits earned via an individual enterprise or a partnership are directly attributable to the individual acting as a sole proprietor or a partner within a partnership. The effective tax burden of such profits hence results from the effective tax rate of the individual. By contrast, profits earned by corporations are initially subject to corporate income tax. If the after-tax profit is subsequently distributed, it is again taxed at the level of the shareholder as a dividend. Without a relief mechanism, the effective tax burden of profits earned via a corporation would be composed of the effective tax burden of the corporate profits plus the effective tax burden of the distributed (after-tax) profits. The different legal form cannot justify such a different treatment of business profits per se (see J. Lang, Prinzipien und Systeme der Besteuerung von Einkommen, in I. Ebling (ed.), *Besteuerung von Einkommen,* DStJG 24 (Dr Otto Schmidt, 2001), p. 49 (at pp. 98-100); J. Hennrichs, Dualismus der Unternehmensbesteuerung aus gesellschaftsrechtlicher und steuersystematischer Sicht, 79 *StuW* 3 (2002), p. 201 (at p. 202); J. Hennrichs/U. Lehmann, Rechtsformneutralität der Unternehmensbesteuerung, 84 *StuW* 1 (2007), p. 16 (at p. 17); J. Hey, Besteuerung von Unternehmensgewinnen und Rechtsformneutralität, in I. Ebling (ed.), *Besteuerung von Einkommen,* DStJG 24 (Dr Otto Schmidt, 2001), p. 155 (at pp. 166-167); M. Jachmann, *Steuergesetzgebung zwischen Gleichheit und wirtschaftlicher Freiheit* (Boorberg, 2000), at pp. 60-66). The integration of corporate and shareholder income taxes is hence meant to at least mitigate the different tax burdens resulting from the dualism of business taxation (see M. Desens in J. Hey/M. Wendt (eds.), *C. Herrmann/G. Heuer/A. Raupach, Einkommensteuer- und Körperschaftsteuergesetz, Kommentar*[265] (Dr Otto Schmidt, 2014), at Einf. KSt para. 31; J. Hey in in I. Ebling (ed.), *Besteuerung von Einkommen,* DStJG 24 (Dr Otto Schmidt, 2001), at pp. 157-181; M. Jachmann, *Steuergesetzgebung zwischen Gleichheit und wirtschaftlicher Freiheit* (Boorberg, 2000), at pp. 61-66; M. Jachmann, Besteuerung von Unternehmen als Gleichheitsproblem, in J. Pelka (ed.), *Europa- und verfassungsrechtliche Grenzen der Unternehmensbesteuerung,* DStJG 23 (Dr Otto Schmidt, 2000), p. 9 (at pp. 17-22); W. Schön, Zum Entwurf eines Steuersenkungsgesetzes, 77 *StuW* 2 (2000), p. 151 (at p. 152); S. Sieker, Möglichkeiten rechtsformneutraler Besteuerung von Einkommen, in S.F. Seeger (ed.), *Perspektiven der Unternehmensbesteuerung,* DStJG 25 (Dr Otto Schmidt, 2002), p. 145 (at p. 176); also cf. J. Englisch, *Dividendenbesteuerung* (Dr Otto Schmidt, 2005), at pp. 130-131; J. Heinrich, Die Rechtsformneutralität der Besteuerung – rechtspolitisches Ziel oder rechtliches Gebot?, in M. Achatz/T. Ehrke-Rabel/J. Heinrich/R. Leitner/O. Taucher (eds.), *Steuerrecht Verfassungsrecht*

taxation runs counter to the internal market's free movement dimension.[114] This is convincing, because after all the internal market aims at the abolition of obstacles to the free movement of goods, persons, services and capital[115] and "*the fact that a taxable event might be taxed twice is the most serious obstacle there can be to people and their capital crossing [...] borders.*"[116] It is hence not surprising that many scholars have examined whether the fundamental freedoms can be relied upon by taxpayers in order to get relief from double taxation.[117] By contrast, the impact of EU law on the phenomenon of double non-taxation has not yet attracted a lot of attention within the scientific community. But if it is true that competition and economic efficiency are harmed by a cross-border transaction sustaining a lesser tax burden than a comparable domestic transaction,[118] it should be examined whether double non-taxation conflicts with the competition aspect of the internal market concept. Since the resultant distortions of competition are primarily induced by the Member States' unharmonized tax systems, the question arises whether the State aid rules of the TFEU prohibit such a preferential treatment of cross-border businesses.[119]

The above considerations already suggest the structure of this book, which particularly aims at analysing the EU law's impact on the phenomenon of double non-taxation and at the same time taking account of the discussions regarding the compatibility of double taxation with the fundamental freedoms. The *second section* will illustrate the political efforts undertaken within the EU in order to address double

Europarecht, Festschrift für Hans Georg Ruppe (Facultas, 2007), p. 203 (at pp. 203-211); J. Lang in S. Widmann (ed.), *Besteuerung der GmbH und ihrer Gesellschafter*, DStJG 20 (Dr Otto Schmidt, 1997), p. 69 (at pp. 70-71)).

113. With regard to double taxation cf. J. Englisch, The European Treaties' Implications for Direct Taxes, 33 *Intertax* 8/9 (2005), p. 310 (at p. 323); M. Lehner in M. Lang/J. Schuch/C. Staringer (eds.), *Tax Treaty Law and EC Law* (Linde, 2007), at p. 16; G. Kofler, *Doppelbesteuerungsabkommen und Europäisches Gemeinschaftsrecht* (Linde, 2007), at p. 155; G. Kofler, Double Taxation and European Union Law: Analysis of the Jurisprudence, in A. Rust (ed.), *Double Taxation Within the European Union* (Kluwer, 2011), p. 97 (at p. 106); W. Schön, 11 *EWS* 7 (2000), at p. 290.
114. See G. Kofler, *Doppelbesteuerungsabkommen und Europäisches Gemeinschaftsrecht* (Linde, 2007), at pp. 369-370; E.C.C.M. Kemmeren, 17 *EC Tax Rev.* 4 (2008), at pp. 157-158; also cf. Opinion of AG Colomer in *D*, C-376/03, EU:C:2004:663, at point 78; E.C.C.M. Kemmeren, The termination of the "most favoured nation clause" Dispute in Tax Trea Law and the Necessity of a Euro Model Tax Convention, 6 *EC Tax. Rev.* 3 (1997), p. 146 (at p. 147).
115. See Chapter 3.1.
116. Opinion of AG Colomer in *D*, C-376/03, EU:C:2004:663, at point 85.
117. In the literature, it is emphasized that this question "*is nearly as old as the EC Treaty itself*" (G. Kofler in A. Rust (ed.), *Double Taxation Within the European Union* (Kluwer, 2011), at p. 104; also see G. Kofler, *Doppelbesteuerungsabkommen und Europäisches Gemeinschaftsrecht* (Linde, 2007), at p. 154).
118. OECD, *Action Plan on Base Erosion and Profit Shifting* (OECD, 2013), at p. 15.
119. Cf. W. Haslehner in I. Richelle/W. Schön/E. Traversa (eds.), *State Aid Law and Business Taxation* (Springer, 2016), 134-160; R. Luja, 76 *Tax Notes Intl.* 4 (27 Oct. 2014), at pp. 353-356; R. Luja, EU State Aid Law and National Tax Rulings: In-Depth Analysis for the TAXE Special Committee, IP/A/TAXE/2015-02, PE 563.453 (October 2015), at pp. 14-15; R. Luja, 60 *British Tax Rev.* 3 (2015), at pp. 379-390; P. Rossi-Maccanico, 75 *Tax Notes Intl.* 10 (8 Sep. 2014), at pp. 857-868; P. Rossi-Maccanico, 24 *EC Tax Rev.* 2 (2015), at pp. 63-77; D.S. Smit, 25 *EC Tax Rev.* 2 (2016), at pp. 110-112; R. Szudoczky in I. Richelle/W. Schön/E. Traversa (eds.), *State Aid Law and Business Taxation* (Springer, 2016), 163-183; A. Taferner/J.W. Kuipers, 56 *Eur. Taxn.* 4 (2016), at pp. 142-143.

taxation and double non-taxation. Thereby it is possible to identify the underlying policy concerns on which a legal analysis should be based. The *third section* is dedicated to the EU primary law framework in tax matters which is of course also relevant when analysing the impact of EU law on the phenomena of double taxation and double non-taxation. Constraints to the Member States' sovereignty not only result from harmonizing measures, such as regulations or directives, but from negative integration as well. The most prominent means to implement the internal market concept in tax law are the fundamental freedoms and the State aid rules. Therefore, their scope of protection as well as the development of the ECJ's jurisprudence are thoroughly analysed in order to be able to apply, in the *fourth section*, these set of rules to the specific problem of double taxation and double non-taxation. First, the impact of the fundamental freedoms on double taxation is examined. Numerous scholars as well as the ECJ have already dealt with this issue in the past. Still, not only will the various views and opinions be given account of but it will also be analysed whether it has been sufficiently borne in mind that double taxation is a situational and relative phenomena. Second, many proposals have been made how double taxation should be "solved" by means of the fundamental freedoms. Since no in-depth research exists on the question whether similar thoughts can be made with regard to the State aid rules' impact on double non-taxation, the second part of the fourth section will focus on this issue. Based on these considerations, the *fifth section* will provide some conclusions and an outlook on possible developments in the future.

CHAPTER 2
Double (Non-)Taxation and EU Tax Policy

1 DOUBLE (NON-)TAXATION AND THE MEMBER STATES' DIRECT TAX SYSTEMS

1.1 Changes in EU Direct Tax Policy

From a direct tax perspective, the EU is characterized by the fact that Member States' direct tax systems have always differed to one extent or another. It was already noted in the *Neumark* Report of 1962 that such disparities cause obstacles for the establishment and functioning of the internal market.[120] In order to ensure that competition is not impeded or distorted,[121] an extensive harmonization of taxation was recommended by the Fiscal and Financial Committee of the EEC.[122] In the *Segré* Report of 1966, a group of independent experts entrusted by the European Commission with a study of the problems confronting the capital markets of the Community advocated attempts at harmonization, especially of the tax treatment of dividend and interest payments.[123]

120. Report of The Fiscal and Financial Committee, in *The EEC Reports on Tax Harmonization, The Report of the Fiscal Committee and The Reports of The Sub-Groups A, B and C, An Unofficial Translation prepared by Dr. H. Thurston* (IBFD, 1963) (hereinafter: *Neumark* Report), p. 93 (at pp. 100 et seq.).
121. *Neumark* Report, at p. 104.
122. For an overview of the suggestions see, for example, A.J.M. Jiménez, *Towards Corporate Tax Harmonization in the European Community* (Kluwer, 1999), at pp. 107-109; C. HJI Panayi, *European Union Corporate Tax Law* (Cambridge University Press, 2013), at pp. 9 et seq.; H.P.A.M. van Arendonk, Citizens and Taxation in the EU: Fifty Years after the Neumark Report, 21 *EC Tax Review* 3 (2012), p. 144 (at pp. 144-145).
123. *The Development of a European Capital Market, Report of a Group of experts appointed by the EEC Commission* (1966) (hereinafter: *Segré* Report), at p. 312 ("*At present there are many disparities between member countries in their fiscal treatment of dividend and interest paid to non-residents or to persons not making a tax return. Here taxation and supervision systems should be harmonized.*"). See also *Report to the Council and the Commission on the realization by stages of Economic and Monetary Union in the Community*, Supplement to Bulletin 11-1970 of the European Communities (8 Oct. 1970), at p. 20 (hereinafter: *Werner* Report) ("*In the field*

Following these conclusions, the European Commission held that *"there is a need for certain approximation of the systems of direct taxation."*[124] As a long-term objective the European Commission envisaged: (1) an approximation of the structure as well as the methods of assessment and rates of direct taxes on company profits, and (2) a single comprehensive personal income tax *"which admittedly may differ from one member country to the other for a long time to come."*[125]

While the attempts at harmonizing indirect taxes were quite successful,[126] the Member States were reluctant to forfeit parts of their sovereignty in the area of direct taxation as well.[127] The *Van den Tempel* Report of 1970[128] indicated that the corporate tax systems within the Community were very different and unanimous agreement on a uniform system was unlikely, in particular because the recommendations of the *Neumark* Report,[129] the *Segré* Report[130] and the *Van den Tempel* Report[131] were not consistent.[132] Moreover, it was suspected that such an extensive harmonization of corporate taxation would also affect the varying incentives offered to holding companies by the Member States and, hence, *"inevitably touch off a flight of capital to tax havens outside the Community and would therefore fail to put an end to the tax evasion that is the authorities' main concern in this matter."*[133] Despite these concerns, the European Commission introduced a proposal for a corporate tax harmonization in 1975.[134] While the Committee on Budgets supported this attempt,[135] the European

of direct taxes, it will be necessary to standardize certain types of tax which are likely to have a direct influence on the movement of capital within the Community. In practice it is mainly a question of the harmonization of the fiscal regime applied to interest payments on fixed interest securities and dividends. It will also be necessary to initiate and actively promote the harmonization of the structure of taxes on corporations.").

124. Tax harmonization programme, Programme for the harmonization of direct taxes, Supplement to Bulletin No. 8-1867 of the European Economic Community (1967), p. 7.
125. See *Tax harmonization programme*, Supplement to Bulletin No. 8-1867 of the EEC, p. 8; see also *Werner* Report, pp. 19-21.
126. See Chapter 2.2.
127. See, for example, C.M. Harris, The European Community's Parent-Subsidiary Directive, 9 *Fla. J. Intl. L.* 123 (1994), p. 111 (at pp. 120 et seq.); A.J.M. Jiménez, *Towards Corporate Tax Harmonization in the European Community* (Kluwer, 1999), at p. 115; H. Kogels, Unity Divided, 21 *EC Tax Review* 3 (2012), p. 117 (at p. 120).
128. Corporation Tax and Individual Income Tax in the European Communities, Doc. 14138/XIV/69-N (1970) (hereinafter: *Van den Tempel* Report).
129. See *Neumark* Report, pp. 139 et seq.
130. See *Segré* Report, pp. 298 et seq.
131. See *Van den Tempel* Report, pp. 76 et seq.
132. See C.M. Harris, 9 *Fla. J. Intl. L.* 123 (1994), at. p. 123; see also European Parliament, Tax Co-ordination in the EU – the Latest Position, ECON 128 EN (2001) at p. 20; C. HJI Panayi, *European Union Corporate Tax Law* (Cambridge University Press, 2013), at pp. 12 and 14.
133. Report on the Tax Arrangements Applying to Holding Companies, COM(73) 1008 final (18 Jun. 1973), p. 8.
134. Proposed Directive Concerning the Common System of Taxation Applicable in the Case of Parent Corporations and Subsidiaries of Different Member States, *OJ* C 39 (22 Mar. 1969), p. 7 (at pp. 7 et seq.).
135. Report drawn up on behalf of the Committee on Budgets on the proposal from the Commission of the European Communities to the Council (Doc. 228/75) for a directive concerning the harmonization of systems of company taxation and of withholding taxes on dividends, Doc. 291/77 (28 Oct. 1977).

Parliament opposed the proposal due to a lack of any provisions for harmonization of taxable bases.[136] Notwithstanding the political resistance, it took until 1990 for this proposal to be finally withdrawn.[137]

Although there was obviously a strong resistance, the European Commission continued to promote tax harmonization,[138] but it gradually also accepted political reality. [139] In the White Paper of 1985, it was stressed that the European Commission "*will urge the Council to complete ongoing work on a group of proposals which aim at removing obstacles to cooperation between European firms [...] and to give high priority to harmonizing indirect taxes on transactions and securities*" until a general framework for the taxation of enterprises in the Community is elaborated.[140] In fact, beside the

136. Resolution on the harmonization of systems of company taxation and of withholding taxes on dividends, *OJ* C 140 (5 Jun. 1979), p. 19 (at pp. 19-20); see also the Interim Report drawn up on behalf of the Committee on Economic and Monetary Affairs on the harmonization of company taxation and of withholding taxes on dividends, Doc. 104/79 (2 May 1979) (hereinafter: *Nyborg* Interim Report), at p. 5; Resolution on the harmonization of taxation in the Community, *OJ* C 342 (19 Dec. 1983), p. 73 (at p. 76: "*[...] it would be a mistake to attempt to harmonize corporation tax rates without at the same time harmonizing the bases of assessment*").
137. See Commission Communication to Parliament and the Council, Guidelines on company taxation, SEC(90)601 final (20 Apr. 1990), at p. 10. In 1988, the European Commission developed another (unpublished) proposal on harmonized rules for the determination of the bases of assessment for taxes on company profits (see Tax harmonization programme, Supplement to Bulletin No. 8-1867 of the EEC, p. 8). However, since a realization had little prospect of being successful, the proposal was not even transferred to the Council. See, for example, E. Haug-Adrion, Die Harmonisierung der direkten Unternehmensbesteuerung in der EG, in P. Eisele/R. Zimmermann (eds.), *Steuerrecht im Wandel* (Stuttgart: Schäffer Verlag, 1989), p. 267 (at pp. 293 et seq.); G. Kofler, *Mutter-Tochter-Richtlinie* (LexisNexis, 2011), at p. 52; R. Kreile, Zum Vorentwurt einer EG-Richtlinie über die Harmonisierung der steuerrechtlichen Gewinnermittlungsvorschriften, Supplement 18/88 to 41 *Der Betrieb* 45 (1988); J. Meerpohl, *Die Mutter-/Tochter-Richtlinie der Europäischen Gemeinschaft und ihre Umsetzung in das Recht der Mitgliedstaaten* (Peter Lang, 1998), at p. 15; see also European Parliament, Tax co-ordination in the EU – the latest position, ECON 128 EN (2001), at pp. 20-21.
138. Action Programme for Taxation, COM(75) 391 final (23 Jul. 1975), at p. 1 ("*Despite the disappointments of the first stage, achievement of economic and monetary union remains the priority objective in the work of building the new Europe. The union cannot be attained without a number of measures with regard to taxation.*"); The approximation of European tax systems, *European File* 9 (1986), at p. 10 ("*The creation of a large unified market on a European scale requires that capital be able to circulate freely, that industrial cooperation be facilitated, and that conditions of competition become less unequal. It is for that reason that there must be some approximation of the tax burden on businesses [...].*").
139. See, for example, Report from the Commission to the Council on Scope for Convergence of Tax Systems in the Community, COM(80) 139 final (27 Mar. 1980), at p. 7 ("*[...] such approximation will be possible only at a much more advanced stage of economic integration. Then, however, it will be absolutely necessary, since the harmonization of structures and bases of assessment will no longer be sufficient.*"); see also *Nyborg* Interim Report, at p. 10 ("*Really uniform taxation of companies' earnings in the Member States can only be achieved over a longer period. [...] The first stage must consist of harmonization of the systems so that common guidelines are laid down to help investors to assess the tax implications of investing in different Member States and end the practice of some Member States of discriminating between resident and non-resident shareholders.*"); Information Report of the Section for Economic and Financial Questions of the Economic and Social Committee on Tax Harmonization, 6 *Intertax* 10 (1978), p. 384 (at p. 462: "*Sooner or later corporation tax will have to be harmonized.*").
140. Completing the Internal Market, White Paper from the Commission to the European Council, COM(85) 310 final (14 Jun. 1985), at p. 38.

ambitious attempts for a far-reaching harmonization of direct taxes, the European Commission was anxious to remove tax obstacles which had already been detrimental to the competitiveness of European enterprises in the past.[141] This led to a preliminary draft for a "EC Multilateral Tax Convention on Income and Capital" in 1968[142] as well as proposals for a "Directive concerning the Common System of Taxation applicable in the case of Parent Corporations and Subsidiaries of different Member States"[143] and a "Directive on the Common System of Taxation applicable to Mergers, Divisions and Transfers of Assets concerning Companies of different Member States"[144] in 1969. Although these proposals were developed merely as part of the much larger programme of direct tax harmonization, this package can be seen as the foundation of a more focused tax policy strategy.[145]

141. See Tax harmonization programme, Supplement to Bulletin No. 8-1867 of the EEC, p. 7 ("*Any tax obstacles to the amalgamations which will be needed if enterprises are to adjust themselves to the scale of the Common Market and if the firms of the Community are to hold their own against competition on the world market [...] must therefore be eliminated.*"); see also U. Anschütz, Harmonization of Direct Taxes in the European Economic Community, 13 *Harv. Intl. L. J.* 1 (1972), p. 1 (at p. 17); F.C. de Hosson, The Parent-Subsidiary Directive, 18 *Intertax* 10 (1990), p. 414 (at p. 416); O. Thömmes/K. Nakhai, Parent-Subsidiary Directive, in O. Thömmes/E. Fuks (eds.), *EC Corporate Tax Law* (IBFD, 2007), at Article 2 para. 51.

142. Preliminary Draft EC Multilateral Tax Convention on Income and Capital, Doc. 11.414/XIV/68-N (1 Jul. 1968).

143. Proposed Directive Concerning The Common System Of Taxation Applicable In The Case Of Parent Corporations And Subsidiaries Of Different Member States (Submitted by the Commission to the Council), COM(69) 6 final, *OJ* C 39 (22 Mar. 1969), at pp. 7 et seq. (hereinafter: Parent-Subsidiary Directive) Supplement to *Eur. Taxn.* No 7 (Unofficial translation by the International Bureau of Fiscal Documentation, based on the official text in French).

144. Vorschlag einer Richtlinie des Rates über das gemeinsame Steuersystem für Fusionen, Spaltungen und die Einbringung von Unternehmensteilen, die Gesellschaften verschiedener Mitgliedstaaten betreffen, COM(69) 5 final, *OJ* C 39 (22 Mar. 1969), at pp. 1 et seq. (hereinafter: Merger Directive).

145. Other steps towards a more specific approach were taken with regard to problems of international tax evasion and avoidance (see Report on the Tax Arrangements Applying to Holding Companies, COM[73] 1008 final [18 Jun. 1973], at p. 9; Problems of International Tax Evasion and Avoidance, COM[74] 1971 [20 Nov. 1974]; Council Resolution of 10 Feb. 1975 on the measures to be taken by the Community in order to combat international tax evasion and avoidance, *OJ* C 35 [14 Feb. 1975], at pp. 1 et seq.). In order to strengthen the collaboration between tax administrations within the Community through an efficient exchange of information, a "Directive concerning mutual assistance by the competent authorities of the Member States in the field of direct taxation" was adopted in 1977 (Council Directive 77/799/EEC of 19 Dec. 1977 concerning mutual assistance by the competent authorities of the Member States in the field of direct taxation (hereinafter: Exchange of Information Directive), *OJ* L 336 [27 Dec. 1977], at pp. 15 et seq.). Furthermore, in 1988, the Council called upon the European Commission "*to submit to the Council, by 31 December 1988, proposals aimed at eliminating or reducing risks of distortion, tax evasion and tax avoidance linked to the diversity of national systems for the taxation of savings and of controlling the application of these systems.*" (See Article 6 para. 5 of the Council Directive 88/361/EEC of 24 Jun. 1988 for the implementation of Article 67 of the Treaty, *OJ* L 178 [8 Jul. 1988], at p. 5). The following proposal of the European Commission was based on a common system of withholding tax at source on payments of interest income in order to "*ensure that a minimum level of taxation is applied to all investment income arising within the Community*" (see Tax Measures to be adopted by the Community in connection with the liberalization of Capital Movements, COM[89] 60 final/3 [12 May 1989], at p. 14). Other remarkable attempts at partial harmonization were the proposal for a "Directive on the Elimination of Double Taxation in Connection with the Adjustment of Transfers of Profits between Associated Enterprises (Arbitration Procedure)" in 1976 (see COM[76] 611

Since extensive harmonization of direct taxes turned out not to be promising – at least in the short or medium term[146] –, a more nuanced strategy was embarked on by the European Commission in 1990, *"particularly in view of the principle of subsidiarity."*[147] Thus, a harmonization of direct taxation should only be considered if it was essential for completing the internal market.[148] Concerning direct taxes, the European Commission wanted to focus on the removal of obstacles to cross-border activities of companies and especially on the problem of double taxation.[149] In order to evaluate which harmonization measures are necessary to remove or mitigate distortions in the internal market due to differences in company taxation, a Committee of independent experts was set up. In 1992, the findings of this Committee were published in the *Ruding* Report.[150] In that report, it was recommended to concentrate, *inter alia*, on *"removing those discriminatory and distortionary features of countries' tax*

final, *OJ* C 301 [21 Dec. 1976], at pp. 4 et seq.), the proposal for a "Directive on the application to collective investment institutions of the Council Directive concerning the harmonization of systems of company taxation and of withholding taxes on dividends" in 1978 (see COM[78] 340 final, OJ C 184 [2 Aug. 1978], at pp. 8 et seq.), the proposal for a "Directive concerning the harmonization of income taxation provisions with respect to freedom of movement for workers within the Community" in 1980 (see COM[79] 737 final, *OJ* C 21 [26 Jan. 1980], at pp. 6 et seq.), the proposal for a "Directive of the Council on the harmonization of the laws of the Member States relating to tax arrangements for the carry-over of losses of undertakings" in 1984 (see COM[84] 404 final, *OJ* C 253 [20 Sep. 1984], at pp. 5 et seq.), which was the outcome of a previous communication of the European Commission (Tax and Financial Measures in Favour of Investment, COM[83] 218 final [28 Apr. 1983], at pp. 6, 7 and 12), and the proposal for a "Directive concerning arrangements for the taking into account by enterprises of the losses of their permanent establishments and subsidiaries in other Member States" in 1991 [see COM[90] 595 final, *OJ* C 53 [28 Feb. 1991], at pp. 30 et seq.).

146. See, for example, The Economic Consequences of Fiscal Harmonization in Europe, National Parliaments Series No 10 (1990), at p. 6 (*"In the long term, the experts envisaged that the tax on investment income of households, corporation tax, in full or in part, and taxes on pollution will become Community own resources."*).
147. Guidelines on company taxation, SEC(90)601 final (20 Apr. 1990), at p. 2. Although the principle of subsidiarity formally was already introduced by the Single European Act of 1987 (*OJ* L 169 [29 Jun. 1987], at pp. 1 et seq.), it only concerned actions by the Community relating to the environment (Article 130r(4) Single European Act: *"The Community shall take action relating to the environment to the extent to which the objectives referred to in paragraph 1 can be attained better at Community level than at the level of the individual Member States."*). However, in 1989 the European Commission generally considered the principle of subsidiarity to be *"[a]n essential element in defining the appropriate balance of power within the Community"* (Report on economic and monetary union in the European Community [hereinafter: *Delors* Report] [17 Apr. 1989], at p. 14). Since the Single European Act and the *Delors* Report also defined *"a new approach to economic integration,"* the European Commission wanted to give priority *"to the coordination and approximation of policies rather than to systematic use of harmonization. [...] In the tax field, priority has been given to removing tax barriers to completion of the internal market and, in particular, to abolishing all forms of double taxation between now and 1993."* See Guidelines on company taxation, SEC(90)601 final (20 Apr. 1990), at p. 10.
148. Guidelines on company taxation, SEC(90)601 final (20 Apr. 1990), at p. 2; see also Taxation in the Single Market, Periodical 6/1990, at pp. 25 et seq.
149. See Guidelines on company taxation, SEC(90)601 final (20 Apr. 1990), at p. 10; Removal of tax obstacles to the cross-frontier activities of companies, Supplement 4/91 to Bulletin of the European Communities (1991), at pp. 8 and 11.
150. Conclusions and Recommendations of the Committee of Independent Experts on Company Taxation (Office for Official Publications of the European Communities, 1992) (hereinafter: *Ruding* Report).

arrangements that impede cross-border business investment and shareholding."[151] The *Ruding* Report also included several concrete proposals in this respect.[152] Since the Committee was aware that the consequent removal of fiscal barriers to cross-border activities associated with the creation of a single market may create "*opportunities for international tax arbitrage and 'treaty shopping' that arise as a consequence of differences in the tax treatment of various investors and alternative investors,*"[153] it also dealt with various issues related to tax planning.[154] The Committee was mainly concerned by the "*problem of revenue loss*" resulting from the potentially increasing opportunities for tax planning, but also had objections concerning the "*fairness of tax laws*" and the "*undesirable*" results tax arbitrage might produce "*from an economic efficiency standpoint.*"[155] Although the question was raised "*whether there should be Community-wide rules that limit the opportunities [of international tax planning],*"[156] the *Ruding* Report does not include any concrete proposals in this respect. However, it has to be kept in mind that the Committee recommended introducing "*a minimum level for statutory corporation tax rates and also common rules for a minimum tax base, so as to limit excessive tax competition between Member States intended to attract mobile investment or taxable profits of multinational firms, either of which tend to erode the tax base in the Community as a whole.*"[157] Since the *Ruding* Report concluded that "*any narrowing of the differences in tax bases and statutory tax rates between Member States would obviously reduce the potential for tax arbitrage activities,*"[158] separate concrete measures to curtail opportunities for international tax planning were probably not deemed to be necessary.

The European Commission's response to the *Ruding* Report was ambivalent.[159] Whereas the recommendations on elimination of double taxation (mainly via the extension of the Parent-Subsidiary Directive,[160] the ratification of the Arbitration Convention,[161] which were both adopted – together with the Merger Directive[162] – by

---

151. *Ruding* Report, at p. 13.
152. For an overview see, for example, A.J.M. Jiménez, *Towards Corporate Tax Harmonization in the European Community* (Kluwer, 1999), at pp. 132-133; M. Tumpel, *Harmonisierung der direkten Unternehmensbesteuerung in der EU* (Verlag Österreich, 1994), at pp. 77 et seq.; F. Vanistendael, *The Future of Corporate Income Harmonisation in the E. C. after Ruding and Maastricht* (ZEW, 1992), at pp. 14 et seq.
153. *Ruding* Report, at p. 39 (see also p. 209).
154. *Ruding* Report, Ch. 6.
155. *Ruding* Report, at p. 39.
156. *Ruding* Report, at p. 140.
157. *Ruding* Report, at p. 13.
158. *Ruding* Report, at p. 40.
159. See also A.J.M. Jiménez, *Towards Corporate Tax Harmonization in the European Community* (Kluwer, 1999), at p. 135; C. HJI Panayi, *European Union Corporate Tax Law* (Cambridge University Press, 2013), at p. 19.
160. Council Directive 90/435/EEC of 23 Jul. 1990 on the common system of taxation applicable in the case of parent companies and subsidiaries of different Member States, *OJ* L 225 (20 Aug. 1990), at pp. 6 et seq.
161. Convention 90/463/EEC on the elimination of double taxation in connection with the adjustment of profits associated enterprises, *OJ* L 225 (20 Aug. 1990), at pp. 10 et seq.
162. Council Directive 90/434/EEC of 23 Jul. 1990 on the common system of taxation applicable to mergers, divisions, transfers of assets and exchanges of shares concerning companies of different Member States, *OJ* L 225 (20 Aug. 1990), at pp. 1 et seq.

the Council in 1990, and further work on transfer pricing and thin capitalization)[163] were embraced,[164] the European Commission was sceptical[165] concerning the proposals regarding a statutory margin of the corporate tax rate and a set of minimum standards for the tax base.[166] The Council's assessment was in line with the European Commission's conclusions,[167] but it additionally emphasized *"the importance of ensuring adequate and effective taxation at least once."*[168] Subsequently, the European Commission also pointed out that *"[t]he guiding principle of Community policy in the field of direct taxation is to eliminate the double taxation of cross-border activities whilst ensuring taxation at least once."*[169]

The *Ruding* Report led to a change of the European Commission's tax policy. Albeit the long-term objective of a harmonization of direct taxation was not given up, the main focus was to abolish national tax measures that constitute an obstacle for cross-border activities within the Community. At the same time, the European Commission wanted to ensure that taxpayers do not unduly benefit from the developing internal market.[170] The Economic and Social Committee even suggested amending the

163. *Ruding* Report, at pp. 203 et seq.
164. Commission Communication to the Council and to Parliament subsequent to the conclusions of the Ruding Committee indicating guidelines on company taxation linked to the further development of the internal market, SEC(92) 1118 final (26 Jun. 1992), at pp. 10 et seq.
165. Commission Communication to the Council and to Parliament subsequent to the conclusions of the Ruding Committee indicating guidelines on company taxation linked to the further development of the internal market, SEC(92) 1118 final (26 Jun. 1992), at pp. 19 et seq.
166. See *Ruding* Report, at pp. 207 et seq.
167. Council Conclusions on Guidelines on Company Taxation Linked to the further Development of the Internal Market, 1008/92 (Presse 216) (23 Nov. 1992); see also Opinion of the Economic and Social Committee on the Conclusions and Recommendations of the Ruding Committee of Independent Experts on Company Taxation, and the Commission Communication to the Council and to Parliament subsequent to the Conclusions of the Ruding Committee indicating Guidelines on Company Taxation Linked to the Further Development of the Internal Market, *OJ* C 19 (25 Jan. 1993), at pp. 65 et seq.; Resolution of the Parliament on the Commission communication to the Council and to Parliament subsequent to the conclusions of the Ruding Committee indicating guidelines on company taxation linked to the further development of the internal market, *OJ* C 128 (9 May 1994), at pp. 92 et seq.
168. Council Conclusions on Guidelines on Company Taxation Linked to the further Development of the Internal Market, 1008/92 (Presse 216) (23 Nov. 1992), at pp. 10-11.
169. Communication from the Commission to the Council, "Making the Most of the Internal Market": Strategic Programme, COM(93) 632 final (22 Dec. 1993), at p. 35.
170. Taxation in the European Union, Report on the developments of tax systems, COM(96) 546 final (22 Oct. 1996), at p. 3 ("*Tax systems must allow cross-border economic activity to develop within the Union. However, at the same time, there is a need to ensure that the increased opportunities for cross-border trade and investment do not lead to an unacceptable loss of tax revenues through tax arbitrage, avoidance or fraud. Just as it is necessary to prevent the double taxation of cross-border income flows, transactions within the Union should not be able to escape tax altogether.*" See also Taxation in the European Union, SEC[96] 487 final [20 Mar. 1996], at p. 6: "*The completion, application and fully effective functioning of the Single Market remains an overriding priority. Removing the tax obstacles will bring economic and welfare benefits for citizens and for business, whilst, at the same time, preventing non-taxation within the Single Market as a result of cross-border tax arbitrage, avoidance or evasion.*"); Commission Staff Working Paper, The 1996 Single Market Review, SEC(96) 2378 (16 Dec. 1996), at p. 50 ("*The central concern which underpins all these problem areas must be the elimination of double taxation on, and other possible tax obstacles to, cross-border income flows, while at the same time ensuring taxation at least once in the EU.*") and at p. 54 ("*The central objective must be to create a policy framework to eliminate all forms of double taxation on, and other possible*

EC Treaty in order to explicitly emphasize that "*[d]ouble taxation or the absence of taxation is incompatible with the internal market.*"[171] Although this proposal was not implemented, it is in line with the opinion of the European Commission, according to which "*[t]he Single Market is clearly not compatible with either double taxation of the same taxable base or no taxation at all.*"[172]

Although both double taxation and double non-taxation were declared incompatible with the internal market, a holistic approach to tackling these issues was missing. For the time being, the European Commission concentrated on a related problem that emerged due to the progressing development of the internal market and the increased integration of the world economy: In the *Ruding* Report, concerns were expressed "*about the tendency of Member States to introduce special tax regimes designed to attract internationally mobile business. [...] [T]here is a danger that such schemes will lead to tax atrophy in particular sectors.*"[173] This point was picked up by the European Commission in 1996[174] and led to an initiative that aimed to tackle harmful tax competition within the EU.[175] As a result of this initiative, the "Code of

obstacles to, cross-border income flows. The framework should also prevent tax losses within the single market as a result of cross-border arbitrage, avoidance or evasion."); Communication from the Commission to the Council, the European Parliament and the Economic and Social Committee, Tax Policy in the European Union – Priorities for the years ahead, COM(2001) 260 final (23 May 2001), *OJ* C 284 (10 Oct. 2001), p. 6 (at pp. 24-25: "*Double taxation due simply to the cross-border nature of economic activity cannot be accepted, but its elimination should not create opportunities for tax avoidance and evasion. Neither should any greater co-ordination of Member States' tax systems give rise to unintentional non-taxation.*"). A specific example of the European Commission's policy can already be found in the "Commission Recommendation of 21 Dec. 1993 on the taxation of certain items of income received by non-residents in a Member State other than that in which they are resident (94/79/EC)" (*OJ* L 39 [10 Feb. 1994], p. 22 [at p. 28: "*The aim of this recommendation is to ensure that individuals receiving certain types of income in a Member State in which they are not resident are taxed on a fair and non-discriminatory basis. It is also necessary to ensure, however, that non-residents do not benefit from more favourable tax treatment than other taxpayers. This could happen if they were to benefit, in the Member State of residence, from the same deductions of other tax reliefs which they had already been granted in the Member State of activity.*"]).

171. Opinion of the Economic and Social Committee on Taxation in the European Union, Report on the development of tax systems (SEC[96] 487 final and COM[96] 546 final), *OJ* C 296 (29 Sep. 1997), p. 37 (at p. 43).
172. Taxation in the European Union, SEC(96) 487 final (20 Mar. 1996), at p. 13; see also Tax co-ordination in the European Union, Working Paper, Economic Affairs Series, ECON 125 EN (European Parliament, 2000), at p. 22 ("*The Single Market has several particular implications for the taxation of employment incomes. [First,] Incomes should not escape tax altogether, or be taxed at discriminatorily low rates, as a result of cross-border tax arbitrage, avoidance or evasion.*").
173. *Ruding* Report, at p. 201.
174. Taxation in the European Union, SEC(96) 487 final (20 Mar. 1996); see also Taxation in the European Union, Report on the development of tax systems, COM(96) 546 final (22 Oct. 1996), at pp. 5-6 and 9-10.
175. Communication from the Commission to the Council, Towards tax co-operation in the European Union, COM(97) 495 final (1 Oct. 1997); Communication from the Commission to the Council and the European Parliament, A package to tackle harmful tax competition in the European Union, COM(97) 564 final (5 Nov. 1997).

conduct for business taxation" was adopted by the Council in 1998,[176] which is a non-binding political declaration of the Member States to eliminate domestic tax measures and refrain from introducing new provisions that are to be considered harmful.[177] Thereby, the European Commission wanted to induce the Member States to a further approximation of their tax systems. Whereas the attempts at legislative harmonization were considered a reduction of the Member States' sovereignty, the coordination of national tax policies through a soft law approach was presented as "*a more effective defence than hitherto against the loss of national fiscal sovereignty in favour of the markets experienced by Member States.*"[178]

The Code of Conduct already indicated the new strategy of the European Commission.[179] Since it is still of the opinion that a comprehensive approach is needed in order to meet the challenges of company taxation within the EU, the long-term project of a Common Consolidated Corporate Tax Base (CCCTB) has been introduced in 2001.[180] However, given that a legislative harmonization of direct taxes has proved to be difficult, other methods were to be found in order "*to achieve progress in removing tax obstacles and distortions to the Internal Market, which taxpayers have a right to expect.*"[181] According to the European Commission, "*only a two-track strategy provides a realistic prospect of removing the obstacles and hence ensuring that the full potential of the Internal Market is realised.*"[182] From a short- and medium-term perspective, the European Commission, since then, especially relies on: (1) the enhanced use of infringement procedures in case Member States' tax rules are suspected of being in

176. Resolution of the Council and the representatives of the Governments of the Member States, meeting within the Council of 1 Dec. 1997 on a code of conduct for business taxation (hereinafter: Code of Conduct), *OJ* C 2 (6 Jan. 1998), at pp. 2 et seq.
177. For the content and the impact of the Code of Conduct see, for example, J. Mössner, Der Code of Conduct for Business Taxation vom 1 Dec. 1997, in M. Lang/J. Schuch/C. Staringer (eds.), *Soft Law in der Praxis* (Linde, 2005), p. 136 (at pp. 136-144).
178. Taxation in the European Union, Report on the development of tax systems, COM(96) 546 final (22 Oct. 1996), at p. 9. See W. Schön, Neue Wege im Europäischen Steuerrecht, 9 *EuZW* 5/6 (1998), p. 129 (at p. 129); W. Schön, 9 *EC Tax Rev.* 2 (2000), at p. 96; W. Schön in J. Pelka (ed.), *Europa- und verfassungsrechtliche Grenzen der Unternehmensbesteuerung*, DStJG 23 (Dr Otto Schmidt, 2000), at p. 206.
179. See M. Monti, The Single Market and beyond: challenges for tax policy in the European Union, 6 *EC Tax Rev.* 1 (1997), p. 2 (at pp. 2-3); M. Monti, The climate is changing, 7 *EC Tax Rev.* 1 (1998), p. 2 (at pp. 2-3).
180. Communication from the Commission to the Council, the European Parliament and the Economic and Social Committee, Towards an Internal Market without tax obstacles, COM (2001) 582 final (23 Oct. 2001), at pp. 15 et seq.; for the later developments see, for example, P. Pistone/R. Szudoczy in M. Lang/P. Pistone/J. Schuch/C. Staringer (eds.), *Introduction to European Tax Law on Direct Taxation*[4] (Linde, 2015), at pp. 37-38.
181. Communication from the Commission to the Council, the European Parliament and the Economic and Social Committee, Tax Policy in the European Union – Priorities for the years ahead, COM(2001) 260 final (23 May 2001), *OJ* C 284 (10 Oct. 2001), p. 6 (at p. 22).
182. Communication from the Commission to the Council, the European Parliament and the Economic and Social Committee, Towards an Internal Market without tax obstacles, COM (2001) 582 final (23 Oct. 2001), at p. 11; see also Commission Staff Working Paper, Company Taxation in the Internal Market, SEC(2001) 1681 (23 Oct. 2001).

conflict with EU law;[183] (2) the implementation of non-legislative or soft law approaches comparable to the Code of Conduct, such as communications, recommendations, guidelines or interpretative notices;[184] (3) the possibility of enhanced cooperation between sub-groups of like-minded Member States;[185] (4) the strict application of the State aid provisions of the TFEU in order to reduce distortions of competition in the internal market;[186] and (5) an extension and improvement of those legislative measures that already have been adopted.[187]

183. Communication from the Commission to the Council, the European Parliament and the Economic and Social Committee, Tax Policy in the European Union – Priorities for the years ahead, COM(2001) 260 final (23 May 2001), *OJ* C 284 (10 Oct. 2001), p. 6 (at pp. 22-23).
184. Communication from the Commission to the Council, the European Parliament and the Economic and Social Committee, Tax Policy in the European Union – Priorities for the years ahead, COM(2001) 260 final (23 May 2001), *OJ* C 284 (10 Oct. 2001), at pp. 23-24.
185. Communication from the Commission to the Council, the European Parliament and the Economic and Social Committee, Tax Policy in the European Union – Priorities for the years ahead, COM(2001) 260 final (23 May 2001), *OJ* C 284 (10 Oct. 2001), at p. 24.
186. Commission notice on the application of the State aid rules to measures relating to direct business taxation (98/C 384/03), *OJ* C 384/3 (10 Dec. 1998).
187. Communication from the Commission to the Council, the European Parliament and the Economic and Social Committee, Towards an Internal Market without tax obstacles, COM (2001) 582 final (23 Oct. 2001), at p. 12. At that time, the Parent-Subsidiary Directive (Council Directive 90/435/EEC of 23 Jul. 1990 on the common system of taxation applicable in the case of parent companies and subsidiaries of different Member States, *OJ* L 225 [20 Aug. 1990], at pp. 6 et seq.), the Merger Directive (Council Directive 90/434/EEC of 23 Jul. 1990 on the common system of taxation applicable to mergers, divisions, transfers of assets and exchanges of shares concerning companies of different Member States, *OJ* L 225 [20 Aug. 1990], at pp. 1 et seq.), the Exchange of Information Directive (Council Directive 77/799/EEC of 19 Dec. 1977 concerning mutual assistance by the competent authorities of the Member States in the field of direct taxation, *OJ* L 336 [27 Dec. 1977], at pp. 15 et seq.; see also Council Directive of 6 Dec. 1979 amending Directive 77/799/EEC concerning mutual assistance by the competent authorities of the Member States in the field of direct taxation [79/1070/EEC], *OJ* L 331 [27 Dec. 1979], at pp. 8 et seq.; Council Directive 92/12/EEC of 25 Feb. 1992 on the general arrangement for products subject to excise duty and on the holding, movement and monitoring of such products, *OJ* L 76 [23 Mar. 1992], at pp. 1 et seq.) and the Arbitration Convention (Convention on the elimination of double taxation in connection with the adjustment of profits of associated enterprises [90/463/EEC], *OJ* L 225 [20 Aug. 1990], at pp. 10 et seq.; see also Convention on the accession of the Republic Austria, the Republic of Finland and the Kingdom of Sweden to the Convention on the elimination of double taxation in connection with the adjustment of profits of associated enterprises [96/C 26/01], *OJ* C 26 [31 Jan. 1996], at pp. 1 et seq.; Protocol amending the Convention of 23 Jul. 1990 on the elimination of double taxation in connection with the adjustment of profits of associated enterprises [1999/C 202/01], *OJ* C 202 [16 Jul. 1999], at pp. 1 et seq.) have already been adopted. Besides, the European Commission has made proposals for a "Directive to ensure minimum of effective taxation of savings income in the form of interest payments within the Community" (see COM[1998] 295 final [20 May 1998], *OJ* C 212 [8 Jul. 1998] [hereinafter: Savings Directive], at pp. 13 et seq.) as well as a "Directive on a common system of taxation applicable to interest and royalty payments made between associated companies of different Member States" (see COM[1998] 67 final [4 Mar. 1998], *OJ* C 123 [22 Apr. 1998] [hereinafter: Interest and Royalty Directive], at pp. 9 et seq.) in 1998, which were both adopted in 2003 (Council Directive 2003/49/EC of 3 Jun. 2003 on a common system of taxation applicable to interest and royalty payments made between associated companies of different Member States, *OJ* L 157 [26 Jun. 2003], at pp. 49 et seq.; Council Directive 2003/48/EC of 3 Jun. 2003 on taxation of savings income in the form of interest payments, *OJ* L 157 [26 Jun. 2003]).

1.2 Double Taxation in the Tax Policy Debate on Direct Taxes

1.2.1 Juridical Double Taxation

The phenomenon of juridical double taxation is one of the main issues which have shaped EU direct tax policy since its very beginning. It was already stressed in the *Neumark* Report of 1962 that due to a lack of harmonization in the area of direct taxes situations of juridical double taxation should be avoided by replacing "*the existing network of bilateral conventions [...], as soon as possible, by a multilateral convention.*"[188] A few years later, the *Segré* Report emphasized that since "*the work in progress in this field may take some time to produce results, it might be wise in the iterim to look for an at least temporary solution of the double taxation problem within the bilateral framework, i.e. by adding to and improving the current principles and techniques.*" However, it was also pointed out that "*[t]he ideal way of eliminating the remaining cases of double taxation between Member States would undoubtedly be by conclusion of a multilateral convention between them.*"[189] Considering these statements, it is no surprise that the European Commission developed a preliminary draft for a European Double Taxation Convention in 1968.[190] However, the project did not turn out to be successful, mainly due to the "*the major legal discrepancies between tax systems at the time.*"[191]

Although this attempt of introducing a multilateral solution to the problem of juridical double taxation turned out to be ineffective, the European Commission's work was (at least partly) further - directly or indirectly - dedicated to juridical double taxation. Some of the proposals became and (at least partly) still are part of secondary EU law, such as the Parent-Subsidiary Directive,[192] the Merger Directive,[193] the Interest

188. *Neumark* Report, at p. 143.
189. *Segré* Report, at p. 296.
190. Vorentwurf 1968 zu einem Europäischen Doppelbesteuerungsabkommen (Multilaterales Abkommen der Mitgliedstaaten der Europäischen Gemeinscahften zur Vermeidung der Doppelbesteuerung des Einkommens und des Vermögens und über gegenseitige Amtshilfe auf dem Gebiet der direkten Steuern), EG-DOK 11.414/XIV/68-D (1 Jul. 1968); for further references regarding this preliminary draft see G. Kofler, *Doppelbesteuerungsabkommen und Europäisches Gemeinschaftsrecht* (Linde, 2007), at p. 135 (FN 24).
191. EC Law and Tax Treaties, Workshop of Experts, TAXUD E1/FR DOC (05) 2306 (9 Jun. 2005), at m.no. 32 (FN 44).
192. Council Directive 2011/96/EU of 30 Nov. 2011 on the common system of taxation applicable in the case of parent companies and subsidiaries of different Member States, *OJ* L 345 (29 Dec. 2011), p. 8 (at pp. 8-16), as amended by (1) Council Directive 2013/13/EU of 13 May 2013 adapting certain directives in the field of taxation, by reason of the accession of the Republic of Croatia, *OJ* L 141 (28 May 2013), p. 30 (at pp. 30-31), (2) Council Directive 2014/86/EU of 8 Jul. 2014 amending Directive 2011/96/EU on the common system of taxation applicable in the case of parent companies and subsidiaries of different Member States, *OJ* L 219 (25 Jul. 2014), p. 40 (at pp. 40-41) and (3) Council Directive (EU) 2015/121 of 27 Jan. 2015 amending Directive 2011/96/EU on the common system of taxation applicable in the case of parent companies and subsidiaries of different Member States, OJ L 21 (28 Jan. 2015), p. 1 (at pp. 1-3).
193. Council Directive 2009/133/EC of 19 Oct. 2009 on the common system of taxation applicable to mergers, divisions, partial divisions, transfers of assets and exchanges of shares concerning companies of different Member States and to the transfer of the registered office of an SE or SCE between Member States, *OJ* L 310 (25 Nov. 2009), p. 34 (at pp. 34-46), as amended by (1)

and Royalty Directive[194] and the Savings Directive.[195] Others, in contrast, like the Proposal for a Council Directive Concerning the Harmonization of Systems of Company Taxation and of Withholding Taxes on Dividends[196] or the Proposal for a Council Directive Concerning the Harmonization of Income Taxation Provisions with Respect to Freedom of Movement of Workers within the Community,[197] were less successful. Still, over the years, the European Commission has maintained its motivation "*to abolishing all forms of double taxation.*"[198]

However, in the *Ruding* Report of 1992 it was observed that the coverage of bilateral double taxation conventions concluded between Member States themselves and also with third countries was still limited. It was, therefore, recommended to define "*a common attitude with regard to policy on double taxation agreements.*"[199] The European Commission was apparently willing to consult with the Member States about "*defining a common policy towards double taxation agreements within the Community and with non-member countries.*"[200] Only several years later, the European Commission had to admit that "*[a]lthough the intra-EU network of double taxation treaties is*

Council Directive 2013/13/EU of 13 May 2013 adapting certain directives in the field of taxation, by reason of the accession of the Republic of Croatia, *OJ* L 141 (28 May 2013), p. 30 (at pp. 30-31).

194. Council Directive 2003/49/EC of 3 Jun. 2003 on a common system of taxation applicable to interest and royalty payments made between associated companies of different Member States, *OJ* L 157 (26 Jun. 2003), p. 49 (at pp. 49-54), as amended by (1) Council Directive 2004/66/EC of 26 Apr. 2004 adapting Directives 1999/45/EC, 2002/83/EC, 2003/37/EC and 2003/59/EC of the European Parliament and of the Council and Council Directives 77/388/EEC, 91/414/EEC, 96/26/EC, 2003/48/EC and 2003/49/EC, in the fields of free movement of goods, freedom to provide services, agriculture, transport policy and taxation, by reason of the accession of the Czech Republic, Estonia, Cyprus, Latvia, Lithuania, Hungary, Malta, Poland, Slovenia and Slovakia, OJ L 168 (1 May 2004), p. 35 (at p. 35), (2) Council Directive 2004/76/EC of 29.4.2004 amending Directive 2003/49/EC as regards the possibility for certain Member States to apply transitional periods for the application of a common system of taxation applicable to interest and royalty payments made between associated companies of different Member States, OJ L 157 (30 Apr. 2004), p. 106 (at pp. 106-113) and (3) Council Directive 2013/13/EU of 13 May 2013 adapting certain directives in the field of taxation, by reason of the accession of the Republic of Croatia, *OJ* L 141 (28 May 2013), p. 30 (at pp. 30-31).
195. Council Directive 2003/48/EC of 3 Jun. 2003 on taxation of savings income in the form of interest payments, *OJ* L 157 (26 Jun. 2003), p. 38 (at pp. 38-48), repealed by Council Directive (EU) 2015/2060 of 10 Nov. 2015 repealing Directive 2003/48/EC on taxation of savings income in the form of interest payments, *OJ* L 301 (2015), p. 1 (at pp. 1-4).
196. Proposal for a Council Directive concerning the harmonization of systems of company taxation and of withholding taxes on dividends, COM (75) 392 final (23 Jul. 1975), *Bulletin of the European Communities*, Supplement 10/75, p. 23 (at pp. 23 et seq.)
197. Proposal for a Council Directive concerning the Harmonization of Income Taxation Provisions with Respect to Freedom of Movement of Workers within the Community, *OJ* C 21 (26 Jan. 1980), p. 6 (at pp. 6 et seq.).
198. See Commission Communication to Parliament and the Council, Guidelines on company taxation, SEC(90)601 final (20 Apr. 1990), at p. 10.
199. *Ruding* Report, at p. 32 and 206.
200. Answer given by Mrs Scrivener on behalf of the Commission to the written question No. 647/92 by Mrs Christa Randzio-Plath (S) & Mrs Karla Peils (PPE) to the Commission of the European Communities (93/C 40/18), *OJ* C 40 (15 Feb. 1993), at p. 13.

largely complete, there nevertheless remain some gaps"[201] and hence wanted to start, *inter alia*,[202] a new attempt for a "*conclusion of [...] a multilateral convention between all EU Member States.*"[203]

Until now, neither does such a multilateral convention exist nor does it seem that the European Commission is seriously furthering the conclusion of such a convention anymore (or - considering the historical development - for now). In order to tackle the still existing problems with regard to juridical double taxation, the European Commission's idea rather is to strengthen existing instruments (e.g., through recasting the Interest and Royalty Directive),[204] to extend the coverage and scope of double taxation conventions by encouraging the dialogue between the Member States, to support Member States in consistently interpreting and applying the provisions of exiting double taxation conventions and to accelerate dispute resolution within the EU.[205] Since the beginning of the BEPS project, the European Commission has especially focussed on the last issue - dispute resolution.

The idea of dispute resolution is not new to EU tax policy. In fact, the European Commission had already published a Proposal for a Council Directive on the Elimination of Double Taxation in Connection with the Adjustment of Transfer of Profits between Associated Enterprises in 1976.[206] After long negotiations in the Council, this proposal was rejected (mainly due to sovereignty reasons)[207] and instead transformed from a directive into an inter-governmental Convention which was signed on 23 July 1990.[208] Although it is part of the *acquis communautaire*, this Convention is not part of EU law and hence the ECJ has no jurisdiction over its interpretation. Moreover, its direct effect depends on the individual Member States' domestic constitutional law.[209]

Due to these and other shortcomings that were identified by the European Commission, a Proposal for a Council Directive on Double Taxation Dispute Resolution Mechanisms in the European Union was presented in 2016, which "*builds on the*

201. Commission Staff Working Paper, Company Taxation in the Internal Market, SEC (2001) 1681 (23 Oct. 2001), at p. 11.
202. See G. Kofler, *Doppelbesteuerungsabkommen und Europäisches Gemeinschaftsrecht* (Linde, 2007), at pp. 145-150.
203. Communication from the Commission to the Council, the European Parliament and the Economic and Social Committee, An Internal Market without company tax obstacles COM(2003) 726 final (24 Nov. 2003), at p. 11; also see Communication from the Commission to the Council, the European Parliament and the Economic and Social Committee, Towards an Internal Market without tax obstacles, COM (2001) 582 final (23 Oct. 2001), at p. 21.
204. Proposal for a Council Directive on a common system of taxation applicable to interest and royalty payments made between associated companies of different Member States, COM(2011) 714 final (11 Nov. 2011).
205. Communication from the Commission to the European Parliament, the Council and the European Economic and Social Committee, Double Taxation in the Internal Market, COM(2011) 712 final (11 Nov. 2011), at pp. 9-10.
206. Proposal for a Council Directive on the Elimination of Double Taxation in Connection with the Adjustment of Transfer of Profits between Associated Enterprises, *OJ* C 301 (21 Dec. 1976), p. 3 (at pp. 3 et seq.).
207. For further references see G. Kofler in E. Reimer/A. Rust (eds.), *Klaus Vogel on Double Taxation Conventions, Fourth Edition* (Kluwer, 2015), Article 9 at m.no. 132 (FN 905).
208. Convention 90/436/EEC on the elimination of double taxation in connection with the adjustment of profits of associated enterprises, *OJ* L 225 (20 Aug. 1990), p. 10 (at pp. 10 et seq.).
209. See, for example, B.J.M. Terra/P.J. Wattel, *European Tax Law*^{6} (Kluwer, 2012), at pp. 709-711.

existing Union Arbitration Convention, [...] but broadens its scope to areas which are not currently covered and adds targeted enforcement blocks to address the main identified shortcomings, as regards enforcement and effectiveness of this mechanism."[210] However, according to the latest Presidency compromise on the European Commission's proposal, this directive would not end juridical double taxation in the EU. It would rather only "*ensure the effective resolution of disputes concerning the interpretation and application of such bilateral tax treaties and the Union Arbitration Convention, in particular disputes leading to double taxation.*"[211] Hence, if a situation of juridical double taxation was not triggered by disputes about the interpretation and application of agreements and conventions that provide for the elimination of double taxation of income and, where applicable, capital, the presently envisaged compromise text would not provide for relief. Juridical double taxation will, therefore, most probably remain one of the biggest "construction areas" of EU tax policy.

1.2.2 Economic Double Taxation

Whereas juridical double taxation is a phenomenon that generally arises only in a cross-border context, economic double taxation frequently also occurs in a purely domestic situation.[212] Probably, the most illustrative example arises when profits are earned by a company and subsequently distributed to its shareholders. Typically, the

---

210. Proposal for a Council Directive on Double Taxation Dispute Resolution Mechanisms in the European Union, COM (2016) 686 final (25 Oct. 2016), at p. 3; for an analysis of this proposal see L. Cerioni, The Commission's Proposal for a Directive on Double Taxation Dispute Resolution Mechanisms: Overcoming the Final Hurdle of Juridical Double Taxation within the European Union, 57 *Eur. Taxn.* 5 (2017), p. 182 (at pp. 182-191); F. Debelva/J. Luts, The European Commission's Proposal for Double Taxation Dispute Resolution: Turning the Tide?, 71 *Bull. Intl. Taxn.* 5 (2017), forthcoming; CFE, Opinion Statement FC 4/2017 on the Proposed Directive on Double Taxation Dispute Resolution Mechanisms in the European Union, 57 *Eur. Taxn.* 8 (2017), forthcoming; S. Govind/L. Turcan, The Changing Contours of Dispute Resolution in the International Tax World: Comparing the OECD Multilateral Instrument and the Proposed EU Arbitration Directive, 71 *Bull. Intl. Taxn.* 3/4 (2017), forthcoming.
211. Doc. 9420 LIMITE FISC 111 ECOFIN 429 (19 May 2017), at p. 3.
212. See G. Kofler, *Doppelbesteuerungsabkommen und Europäisches Gemeinschaftsrecht* (Linde, 2007), at p. 155; G. Kofler in A. Rust (ed.), *Double Taxation Within the European Union* (Kluwer, 2011), at p. 106; W. Hellerstein/G. Kofler/R. Mason, 62 *Tax L. Rev.* 1 (2008), at p. 7; V. Heydt in W. Haslehner/G. Kofler/A. Rust (eds.), *Landmark Decisions of the ECJ in Direct Taxation* (Kluwer, 2015), at p. 181; also cf. J. Englisch, 33 *Intertax* 8/9 (2005), at p. 323; but see B.J.M. Terra/P.J. Wattel, *European Tax Law*[6] (Kluwer, 2012), at p. 1046; E. Traversa/C. Helleputte in M. Lang/P. Melz/E. Kristoffersson (eds.), *Value Added Tax and Direct Taxation* (IBFD, 2009), at p. 340 ("*juridical double taxation is rare in the national context*"); P. Wattel, Taxation of Intercompany Dividends and EU Law: Three Surprising Aspects of the Recent Case Law of the European Court, in G. Maisto (ed.), *Taxation of Intercompany Dividends under Tax Treaties and EU Law* (IBFD, 2012), who argues that "*for some reason many people think that juridical double taxation does not exist domestically. That is only the case, precisely,* because *it is invariably prevented in internal situations*" (at p. 44). Admittedly, unless there are constitutional restraints, there is nothing that prevents a Member State from imposing comparable taxes on the same taxpayer in respect of the same subject matter and for identical periods. However, it seems artificial to argue that a Member State "avoids" juridical double taxation by, for example, not levying a withholding tax of 25% on dividends and additionally requiring the receiving shareholder to pay another 25% tax within the tax assessment, but instead obliging taxpayers to pay a tax of 50% on all dividends received.

taxation of corporations and their shareholders is based on the principle of separation.[213] Income derived by a corporation is initially subject to corporate income tax. If the after-tax profit is subsequently distributed, it is again taxed at the level of the shareholder as a dividend. Due to the thereby connected distorting effects of income being subjected to tax twice, the integration of corporate and shareholder income taxes has been a subject of debate ever since.[214]

While some scholars prefer a classical system that does not provide for any relief from economic double taxation,[215] the majority considers the avoidance of double taxation to be desirable. There are various possibilities to achieve this. Economic double taxation can be avoided by granting relief to either the corporation or the shareholders. At the level of the corporation, this is typically done by granting a deduction for dividend distributions or by refunding the corporate tax underlying the distributed profits.[216] In essence, the corporate income tax thereby merely serves as a tax on retained earnings. However, in practice, it is much more common to grant relief to the shareholders. In order to provide full or partial relief from economic double taxation, imputation systems enable shareholders to credit all or part of the corporation tax attributable to the profits out of which the dividend was paid against their income tax.[217] Of course, full relief also can be achieved by exempting dividends from income taxation altogether. However, such systems are typically limited to corporate shareholders.[218] Within the EU, the most frequently used relief method is a schedular system that generally provides for a reduced tax rate or a diminished tax base in the case of dividend income.[219] However, such systems do not provide an accurate, but only an approximate, relief from economic double taxation.[220]

The debate on how to integrate corporate and shareholder income taxation has also affected the EU. In as early as 1962, the different approaches taken by the Member States were identified as "*unfortunate.*" Although the proposed introduction of a

213. For Austria see, for example, K. Uebelhoer/S. Pfeiffer/E. Huisman/E. Schaffer, *Introduction to Austrian Tax Law* (Facultas, 2014), at MN 98.
214. For a US perspective see, for example, The US Department of Treasury's Report on Ingetration of The Individual and Corporate Tax Systems (1992); for a European perspective see, for example, U. Ilhi/K. Malmer/P. Schonewille/I. Tuominen, Dividend Taxation in the European Union, in IFA (ed.), *Trends in Company Shareholder Taxation: Single or Double Taxation?*, CDFI 88a (Kluwer, 2003), p. 71 (at pp. 74-78); G. Kofler, *Mutter-Tochter-Richtlinie* (LexisNexis, 2011), Einleitung at paras 30-62.
215. For a positive view concerning such systems see, for example, R.S. Avi-Yonah, Corporations, Society, and the State: A Defense of the Corporate Tax, 90 *Virginia L. Rev.* 5 (2004), p. 1193 (at pp. 1253-1254); H.J. Schlunk, How I Learned to Stop Worrying and Love Double Taxation, 79 *Notre Dame L. Rev.* 1 (2003), p. 127 (at pp. 127 et seq.).
216. See J. Englisch, *Dividendenbesteuerung* (Dr Otto Schmidt, 2005), at p. 89; B.J.M. Terra/P.J. Wattel, *European Tax Law*[6] (Kluwer, 2012), at p. 226.
217. See J. Englisch, *Dividendenbesteuerung* (Dr Otto Schmidt, 2005), at p. 88; B.J.M. Terra/P.J. Wattel, *European Tax Law*[6] (Kluwer, 2012), at pp. 227-228.
218. But see G. Kofler, *Doppelbesteuerungsabkommen und Europäisches Gemeinschaftsrecht* (Linde, 2007), at pp. 939, who mentions Cyprus, Estonia, Greece and Latvia as exemplary tax systems which also provide for a dividend exemption for individuals.
219. See J. Englisch, 33 *Intertax* 5 (2005), at p. 200; G. Kofler, *Doppelbesteuerungsabkommen und Europäisches Gemeinschaftsrecht* (Linde, 2007), at pp. 938-940.
220. See J. Englisch, *Dividendenbesteuerung* (Dr Otto Schmidt, 2005), at p. 89; B.J.M. Terra/P.J. Wattel, *European Tax Law*[6] (Kluwer, 2012), at pp. 224-226.

harmonized "*special tax on companies*"[221] was in principle taken up by the European Commission,[222] it did not turn out to be successful due to the Member States' absent political will. Still, the different effects of the various relief mechanisms applied by the Member States on domestic and cross-border dividend distributions were not lost sight of.[223] Beginning in 1967, due to the increasing integration of companies into groups, the European Commission had pushed for a systematic and cross-border application of "*tax arrangements governing the transfer of profits from one company to another [...] so as to make it impossible for the same profits to be taxed successively in two or more companies.*"[224] To this end, it was proposed to adopt a directive concerning the common system of taxation applicable in the case of parent companies and subsidiaries of different Member States.[225]

For a continuing lack of political willingness, initially, this proposal received only little attention.[226] Thanks to the European Commission's tenacity,[227] it was still not buried in oblivion. Although it took more than twenty years, the Parent-Subsidiary Directive was ultimately adopted in 1990.[228] Since then, this directive has shaped the taxation of cross-border profit distributions between EU-resident companies. With regard to economic double taxation, it obliges the Member State of the parent company and the Member State of its permanent establishment to either refrain from taxing profits distributed by a company of another Member State or to grant an indirect tax credit. However, the Parent-Subsidiary Directive only applies if certain conditions are fulfilled. It is, for example, required that the receiving as well as the distributing

221. *Neumark* Report, at p. 122.
222. See Proposal for a Council Directive concerning the harmonization of systems of company taxation and of withholding taxes on dividends, *OJ* C 253 (5 Nov. 1975), p. 2 (at pp. 2 et seq.).
223. See *Segré* Report, at p. 301.
224. See *Tax Harmonization Programme*, Supplement to Bulletin No. 8-1867 of the EEC, p. 18.
225. Proposed Directive Concerning the Common System of Taxation Applicable in the Case of Parent Corporations and Subsidiaries of Different Member States, *OJ* C 39 (22 Mar. 1969), p. 7 (at pp. 7 et seq.).
226. See F.C. de Hosson, 18 *Intertax* 10 (1990), at p. 417; also see C. M. Harris, 9 *Fla. J. Int'l L.* 123 (1994), at pp. 122-123.
227. See Communication from the Commission to the Council, Action Programme for Taxation, COM(75) 391 Final (23 Jul. 1975), at p. 7 ("*The Commission recalls [...] that [...] it put forward in January 1969 two proposals for directives concerning the common tax arrangements applying to mergers, divisions and contributions of assets between companies in different Member States and the common tax arrangements applying to parent companies and subsidiaries in different Member States.*"); Report from the Commission to the Council on Scope of Convergence of Tax Systems in the Community, COM(80) 139 final (27 Mar. 1980), at p. 14 ("*The 1969 proposals for Directives on cross-frontier company mergers and the tax treatment of parent companies and subsidiaries from different Member States [...] have still not been adopted, something which at long last should be done*"); Communication of Mr Tugendhat to the Council, Fiscal Measures aimed at the Encouragement of Cooperation Between Undertakings of Different Member States, SEC(84) 77 (17 Jan. 1984), at pp. 1-2 and 4; Communication from the Commission to the Council, Fiscal Measures aimed at Encouraging Cooperation Between Undertakings of Different Member States, COM(85) 360 final (5 Jul. 1985), at pp. 1-3; Commission Communication to Parliament and the Council, Guidelines on company taxation, SEC(90)601 final (20 Apr. 1990), at p. 7; also see G. Kofler, *Mutter-Tochter-Richtlinie* (LexisNexis, 2011), Einleitung at paras 42-48.
228. Council Directive 90/435/EEC of 23 Jul. 1990 on the common system of taxation applicable in the case of parent companies and subsidiaries of different Member States, *OJ* L 225 (20 Aug. 1990), p. 6 (at pp. 6-9).

company take one of the forms listed in the directive's annex[229] and that there is a minimum holding of 10% in the capital of the other company.[230] If these or other requirements of the Parent-Subsidiary Directive are not met, "*it is for the Member States to determine whether, and to what extent, economic double taxation of distributed profits is to be avoided and, for that purpose, to establish, either unilaterally or by conventions concluded with other Member States, procedures intended to prevent or mitigate such economic double taxation.*"[231]

This does not mean that "*any difference in treatment in relations between parent and subsidiary companies established in different Member States should be attributed solely to the co-existence of different tax regimes.*"[232] After all, the limited scope of the Parent-Subsidiary Directive does not prevent the ECJ from reproaching the Member States that they are not "*entitled to impose measures that contravene the freedoms of movement guaranteed by the Treaty.*"[233] Consequently, "*in structuring their tax system and, in particular, when they establish a mechanism for preventing or mitigating the imposition of a series of charges to tax or economic double taxation, Member States must comply with the requirements of Community law and especially those imposed by the Treaty provisions on free movement.*"[234] This is insofar important as, traditionally, many Member States granted relief from economic double taxation only in the case of purely domestic dividend distributions.[235] Due to this limitation's inherent discrimination of cross-border situations, the *Ruding* report of 1992 already emphasized that "*the manner in which Member States currently provide relief for the double taxation of*

229. See B.J.M. Terra/P.J. Wattel, *European Tax Law*[6] (Kluwer, 2012), at pp. 605-607; G. Kofler, *Mutter-Tochter-Richtlinie* (LexisNexis, 2011), Artikel 2 at paras 17-22; G. Kofler, Mutter-Tochter-Richtlinie, in H. Schaumburg/J. Englisch (eds.), *Europäisches Steuerrecht* (Dr Otto Schmidt, 2015), p. 581 (at pp. 603-604, at MN 14.16-14.17).

230. See B.J.M. Terra/P.J. Wattel, *European Tax Law*[6] (Kluwer, 2012), at pp. 612-613; G. Kofler, *Mutter-Tochter-Richtlinie* (LexisNexis, 2011), Artikel 3 at paras 29-30; G. Kofler in H. Schaumburg/J. Englisch (eds.), *Europäisches Steuerrecht* (Dr Otto Schmidt, 2015), at pp. 618-619, at MN 14.34.

231. Judgment in *Amurta*, C-379/05, EU:C:2007:655, at para. 24; Judgment in *Aberdeen Property Fininvest Alpha*, C-303/07, EU:C:2009:377, at para. 28; Judgment in *Gaz de France - Berliner Investissement*, C-247/08, EU:C:2009:600, at para. 60; Judgment in *Commission/Italy*, C-540/07, EU:C:2009:717, at para. 31; also see Judgment in *Les Vergers du Vieux Tauves*, C-48/07, EU:C:2008:758, at para. 46; Order in *Tate & Lyle Investments*, C-384/11, EU:C:2012:463, at para. 20.

232. Opinion of AG Mengozzi in *Amurta*, C-379/05, EU:C:2007:323, at point 27 (FN 10); also see Judgment in *Amurta*, C-379/05, EU:C:2007:655, at paras 21-23.

233. Judgment in *Test Claimants in Class IV of the ACT Group Litigation*, C-374/04, EU:C:2006:773, at para. 54; Judgment in *Commission/Spain*, C-487/08, EU:C:2010:310, at para. 40; also see Judgment in *Amurta*, C-379/05, EU:C:2007:655, at para. 24; Judgment in *Les Vergers du Vieux Tauves*, C-48/07, EU:C:2008:758, at para. 46; Judgment in *Commission/Netherlands*, C-521/07, EU:C:2009:360, at para. 35; Judgment in *Commission/Italy*, C-540/07, EU:C:2009:717, at para. 31; Judgment in *Commission/Germany*, C-284/09, EU:C:2011:670, at para. 48.

234. Judgment in *Test Claimants in the FII Group Litigation*, C-446/04, EU:C:2006:774, at para. 45; also see Judgment in *Accor*, C-310/09, EU:C:2011:581, at para. 43; Judgment in *Les Vergers du Vieux Tauves*, C-48/07, EU:C:2008:758, at paras 45-47.

235. See H.J. Ault, Corporate Integration, Tax Treaties and the Division of the International Tax Base: Principles and Practices, 47 *Tax L. Rev.* 2 (1992), p. 565 (at p. 579); P. Farmer/R. Lyal, *EC Tax Law* (Clarendon Press, 1994), at pp. 251-252; G. Kofler, *Doppelbesteuerungsabkommen und Europäisches Gemeinschaftsrecht* (Linde, 2007), at pp. 941 and 971; O.H. Jacobs, Corporation Income Tax Systems in the European Union – An Analysis of their Effects on Competition

corporate profits distributed to individual shareholder in the form of dividends constitutes a source of discrimination against cross-border investment flows."[236] It was hence concluded that "*Member States with various forms of tax relief for dividends received by domestic shareholders from domestic companies should be obliged, on a reciprocal basis, to provide equivalent relief for dividends received by domestic shareholders directly from companies in other Member States."*[237]

Over the years, it had indeed been increasingly questioned whether domestically-aligned relief mechanisms for dividend distributions are in line with the fundamental freedoms.[238] In fact – and in contrast to its jurisprudence on juridical double taxation[239] – the ECJ's case law turned out to be quite effective in tackling economic double taxation within the EU.[240] Therefore, not only the Parent-Subsidiary Directive but also the ECJ's case law regarding the fundamental freedoms have dramatically influenced the Member States' tax treatment of cross-border dividends and hence the EU's approach with regard to economic double taxation. This might be the reason why nowadays the tax policy discussions rather focus on the (from an EU law perspective) unresolved issue of juridical than on economic double taxation. After all, the latter has been dealt with by primary and secondary EU law to a much more intense extent.

---

and Reform Proposals, 27 *Intertax* 8/9 (1999), p. 264 (at pp. 271-272); S. Lodin, The Imputation Systems and Cross-Border Dividends – the Need for New Solutions, 7 *EC Tax Rev.* 4 (1998), p. 229 (at p. 229).

236. Commission of the European Communities, *Report of the Committee of Independent Experts on Company Taxation* (1992), at p. 207.
237. *Ruding* Report, at p. 33.
238. See, for example, N. Dautzenberg, Die Ertragsbesteuerung des Kapitaleinkommens in der EU: Zur Bedeutung des Begriffs „Kapitalanlageort" in Art. 73 d EGV, 8 *EWS* 11 (1997), p. 379 (at p. 383); B. Knobbe-Keuk, Ist das deutsche Körperschaftsteueranrechnungsverfahren zu halten?, in P. Kirchhof/K. Offerhaus/H. Schöberle (eds.), *Steuerrecht Verfassungsrecht Finanzpolitik*, Festschrift für Franz Klein (Dr Otto Schmidt, 1994), p. 347 (at pp. 351-352); H. Liede/L. Hintsanen, 43 *Eur. Taxn.* 1 (2003), at pp. 31-35; S. Lodin, 7 *EC Tax Rev.* 4 (1998), at pp. 220-238; K. Ståhl, Dividend Taxation in a Free Capital Market, 6 *EC Tax Rev.* 4 (1997), p. 227 (at pp. 227-236); C. Staringer, Auslandsdividenden und Kapitalverkehrsfreiheit, 13 *ÖStZ* 2 (2000), p. 26 (pp. 27-31); C. Staringer, Dividendenbesteuerung und Kapitalverkehrsfreiheit, in E. Lechner/C. Staringer/M. Tumpel (eds.), *Kapitalverkehrsfreiheit und Steuerrecht* (Linde, 2000), p. 93 (at pp. 99-112); W. Schön in W. Schön (ed.), *Gedächtnisschrift für Brigitte Knobbe-Keuk* (Dr Otto Schmidt, 1997), at pp. 774-776; M. Tumpel in J. Pelka (ed.), *Europa- und verfassungsrechtliche Grenzen der Unternehmensbesteuerung*, DStJG 30 (Dr Otto Schmidt, 2000), at pp. 358-361; G. Toifl, Besteuerung ausländischer Dividendeneinkünfte und Kapitalverkehrsfreiheit, 12 *SWI* 10 (2002), p. 458 (at pp. 458-466); M. Tumpel, Zweifel des Verwaltungsgerichtshofes an der Vereinbarkeit der Dividenden-besteuerung in Österreich mit der Kapitalverkehrsfreiheit, 12 *SWI* 10 (2002), p. 454 (at pp. 454-457); K. van Raad, The Impact of the EC Treaty's Fundamental Freedoms Provisions on EC Member States' Taxation in Border-Crossing Situations Current State of Affairs, 4 *EC Tax Rev.* 4 (1995), p. 190 (at pp. 200-201); G. Toifl, Verstößt die Beschränkung der Endbesteuerung auf inländische Kapitalerträge gegen die Kapitalverkehrsfreiheit nach Art. 73b EGV?, 9 *SWI* 6 (1999), p. 255 (at pp. 255-257).
239. For an analysis of this case law see Chapter 4.1.3.1.
240. For an analysis of this case law see Chapter 4.1.3.2.

1.3 Double Non-Taxation in the Tax Policy Debate on Direct Taxes

1.3.1 Double Non-Taxation and Exit Taxation

Since the publication of the *Ruding* Report, the European Commission has repeatedly emphasized that it is not in line with the internal market concept that certain income might remain untaxed accidentally.[241] However, it was not until 2006 that the first tentative attempt has been made to provide some guidance for the Member States on how this issue could be dealt with.[242] The ECJ's decisions in the *De Lasteyrie* case[243] and in the *N.* case[244] were decisive in this respect. In these cases, the Court had to deal with the taxation of individuals who moved from one Member State to another Member State. In the Member State from which the individuals departed, the transfer of residence triggered taxation on the unrealized increase in value of certain assets held by the individuals. The ECJ concluded that it is legitimate for a Member State to reserve the right to tax the portion of income which originated while the individual was a resident in that Member State.[245] However, in order to be proportional effective

241. Communication from the Commission to the Council, "Making the Most of the Internal Market": Strategic Programme, COM(93) 632 final (22 Dec. 1993), at p. 35; Taxation in the European Union, Report on the developments of tax systems, COM(96) 546 final (22 Oct. 1996), at p. 3; Taxation in the European Union, SEC(96) 487 final (20 Mar. 1996), at p. 6; Commission Staff Working Paper, The 1996 Single Market Review, SEC(96) 2378 (16 Dec. 1996), at p. 50 and at p. 54; Tax Co-ordination in the European Union, Working Paper, Economic Affairs Series, ECON 125 EN (European Parliament, 2000), at p. 22; Communication from the Commission to the Council, the European Parliament and the Economic and Social Committee, Tax Policy in the European Union – Priorities for the years ahead, COM(2001) 260 final (23 May 2001), *OJ* C 284 (10 Oct. 2001), at pp. 24-25; Communication from the Commission to the Council, the European Parliament and the Economic and Social Committee, Co-ordinating Member States' direct tax systems in the Internal Market, COM(2006) 823 final (19 Dec. 2006), at p. 4 and at p. 6; Communication from the Commission to the Council, the European Parliament and the Economic and Social Committee, The application of anti-abuse measures in the area of direct taxation – within the EU and in relation to third countries, COM(2007) 785 final (10 Dec. 2007), at p. 6; see also Opinion of the European Economic and Social Committee on the Impact of the territoriality of tax law on industrial change (2008/C 120/14), *OJ* C 120 (16 May 2008), at p. 51; Annex Growth-Friendly Tax Policies in Member States and better Tax Coordination in the EU to the Communication from the Commission to the Council, the European Parliament, the Economic and Social Committee and the Committee of Regions, Annual Growth Survey 2012, COM(2011) 815 final, Vol. 5/5 – Annex IV (23 Nov. 2011), at pp. 9-11; Staff working paper, The internal market: factual examples of double non-taxation cases, Consultation document, TAXUD D1 D(2012) (29 Feb. 2012), at p. 4; Summary report of the responses received on the public consultation on factual examples and possible ways to tackle double non-taxation cases, TAXUD D1 D(2012) (5 Jul. 2012), at p. 2.
242. Communication from the Commission to the Council, the European Parliament and the Economic and Social Committee, Exit taxation and the need for co-ordination of Member States' tax policies, COM(2006) 825 final (19 Dec. 2006); also see Communication from the Commission to the Council, the European Parliament and the Economic and Social Committee, Co-ordinating Member States' direct tax systems in the Internal Market, COM(2006) 823 final (19 Dec. 2006).
243. Judgment in *De Lasteyrie du Saillant*, C-9/02, EU:C:2004:138.
244. Judgment in *N.*, C-470/04, EU:C:2006:525.
245. Judgment in *N.*, C-470/04, EU:C:2006:525, paras 44-46; see also Judgment in *National Grid Indus*, C-371/10, EU:C:2011:785, para. 46; Opinion of AG Kokott in *N*, C-470/04, EU:C:2006:217, at points 91-99.

taxation has to be deferred until the increase in value was realized without any further conditions to be met by the emigrating individual. In addition, full account has to be taken of reductions in value capable of arising after the transfer of residence by the taxpayer concerned, unless such reductions have already been taken into account in the new residence state.[246]

In order to resolve mismatches between the Member States' tax systems, which could lead to double taxation and double non-taxation, the European Commission published a communication on the implications of the ECJ's jurisprudence on "exit taxes."[247] Assuming that the principles developed by the Court in the decisions in *De Lasteyrie* and in *N.* also apply to cross-border transfers of assets by companies,[248] the European Commission pointed out, *inter alia*, that a transfer of assets to a PE in another Member State can lead to unintentional double non-taxation if either "*an asset is transferred from a [Member State] which allows transfer at book value to a [Member State] which values the transferred asset at market value*" or "*the [Member State] to which the asset is transferred attributes a higher value to the asset, thus allowing for a higher depreciation of the asset against the taxable profits of the PE and taxing a lower amount of gains on any possible subsequent disposal of the asset.*"[249] However, apart from one minor consideration,[250] the communication does not contain specific approaches on how to tackle these issues.[251] The European Commission rather called upon the Member States to take appropriate measures to avoid double non-taxation resulting from cross-border transfers of assets within the EU. For the time being, the main objective was to provide "*a prime example of an area where [Member States]*

246. Judgment in *N.*, C-470/04, EU:C:2006:525, paras 48-55.
247. Communication from the Commission to the Council, the European Parliament and the Economic and Social Committee, Exit taxation and the need for co-ordination of Member States' tax policies, COM(2006) 825 final (19 Dec. 2006).
248. Communication from the Commission to the Council, the European Parliament and the Economic and Social Committee, Exit taxation and the need for co-ordination of Member States' tax policies, COM(2006) 825 final (19 Dec. 2006), at pp. 5-7.
249. Communication from the Commission to the Council, the European Parliament and the Economic and Social Committee, Exit taxation and the need for co-ordination of Member States' tax policies, COM(2006) 825 final (19 Dec. 2006), at p. 7.
250. Communication from the Commission to the Council, the European Parliament and the Economic and Social Committee, Exit taxation and the need for co-ordination of Member States' tax policies, COM(2006) 825 final (19 Dec. 2006), at p. 8 ("*Where an asset is transferred from a MS which allows transfer at book value to a MS which would usually value the transferred asset at market value, MSs should take appropriate measures to avoid double non-taxation of the difference between the book value of the asset and its market value at the moment of transfer. One way to do this would be for the MS to which the asset is transferred to use the other MS's book value as the starting value for tax purposes. In these circumstances, an approach based on mutual recognition would appear the obvious solution.*").
251. But see Council Resolution of 2 Dec. 2008 on coordinating exit taxation (2008/C 323/01), *OJ* C 323 (18 Dec. 2003), at p. 1.

could benefit from co-ordination at EU level."[252] In order to determine the scope for possible coordinating measures, it was intended "*to discuss these issues with [Member States] in more detail.*"[253]

1.3.2 *The Code of Conduct Group's Work on Cross-Border Tax Arbitrage*

Partly, these discussions have been taken place within the Code of Conduct Group, which was established by the Council in 1998.[254] In order to also address the issue of double non-taxation, a sub-group was set up in 2009.[255] Although some Member States were of the opinion that "*discuss[ing] measures on tax coordination aimed at resolving mismatches resulting from disparities [...] falls outside the mandate of the Code of Conduct Group,*"[256] it was intended to provide guidelines on how to avoid double non-taxation resulting from: (1) profits distributed from a company resident outside the EU to a company resident within the EU (inbound profit transfers), (2) profits distributed by a company resident within the EU to a company resident outside the EU (outbound profit distributions), and (3) mismatches resulting from disparities of the Member States' tax systems, in particular hybrid entities and profit-participating loans.[257]

252. Communication from the Commission to the Council, the European Parliament and the Economic and Social Committee, Exit taxation and the need for co-ordination of Member States' tax policies, COM(2006) 825 final (19 Dec. 2006), at p. 10.
253. Communication from the Commission to the Council, the European Parliament and the Economic and Social Committee, The application of anti-abuse measures in the area of direct taxation – within the EU and in relation to third countries, COM(2007) 785 final (10 Dec. 2007), at p. 6; see also Communication from the Commission to the Council, the European Parliament and the Economic and Social Committee, Double Taxation in the Single Market, COM(2011) 712 final (11 Nov. 2011), at p. 3 (FN 2), at p. 8 and at p. 11.
254. Council Conclusions of 9 Mar. 1998 concerning the establishment of the Code of Conduct Group (business taxation) (98/C 99/01), *OJ* C 99 (1 Apr. 1998), at pp. 1 et seq.
255. At first, the Code of Conduct Group's work was limited to monitoring the Member States' commitment to refrain from introducing any new harmful tax measures (standstill) and to amend any laws or practices that are deemed to be harmful in respect of the principles of the Code of Conduct (rollback). After some discussions within the Code of Conduct Group (see Doc. 9047/07 FISC 62 [26 Apr. 2007], at pp. 6 et seq.; Doc. 16084/08 FISC 166 [20 Nov. 2008], at pp. 5 et seq.) the mandate of the Group was extended to other areas as well, in particular anti-abuse (see Doc. 16410/08 FISC 174 [26 Nov. 2008]; Doc. 16319/08 PTS A 61 [1 Dec. 2008], at p. 2). The Code of Conduct Group agreed "*that anti - abuse examination should also include inbound and outbound profit transfer and mismatches, in particular hybrid entities and profit participating loans, and that in order to assist this work of the Group a sub-group should be established*" (see Doc. 10200/1/09 REV 1 FISC 69 [29 Jun. 2009], at p. 8). After the Council agreed to the establishment of this sub-group (see Doc. 11967/09 FISC 96 [20 Jul. 2009]; Doc. 12270/09 PTS A 35 [24 Jul. 2009]), the first meeting was held on 23 Sep. 2009 (see Doc. 16233/09 FISC 163 [18 Nov. 2009], at p. 5).
256. Doc. 10857/11 FISC 75 (27 May 2011), at p. 7 (FN 1).
257. Doc. 9779/10 FISC 43 (12 May 2010); Doc. 10033/10 FISC 47 (25 May 2010), at pp. 8-9; Doc. 16766/10 FISC 139 (22 Nov. 2010), at pp. 6-7; see also Doc. 17081/11 FISC 144 (21 Nov. 2011), at p. 5; Doc. 17081/1/11 REV 1 FISC 144 (13 Dec. 2011), at p. 5; Doc. 10903/12 FISC 77 (11 Jun. 2012), at p. 6; Doc. 16488/12 FISC 173 (23 Nov 2012), at pp. 4-5; Doc. 10242/13 FISC 112 (13 Jun. 2013), at p. 6; Doc. 11465/13 FISC 134 (21 Jun. 2013), at p. 5; Doc. 16656/13 FISC 226 (29 Nov. 2013), at p. 5.

The Code of Conduct Group as well as its sub-group emphasized that inbound profit transfers can result in double non-taxation if the income of the distributing company "*has not been taxed or it has been subject to tax at source at a low tax rate. There is a risk of abuse in this case, since the subsidiary resident in a third country will be able to avoid inbound taxation by using the most convenient Double Taxation Agreement (DTA). That income will afterwards freely flow within the EU with no withholding tax (under the Parent-Subsidiary Directive), arriving untaxed at final destination.*"[258] Based on the proposal of the sub-group,[259] the Code of Conduct Group agreed that "*Member States which operate a participation exemption should either ensure that the profits which give rise to foreign source dividends are subject to effective anti-abuse or countermeasures, or apply switch-over provisions targeted at ensuring effective taxation. The first could be achieved through a Member State having CFC-legislation or other anti-abuse provisions which ensure that profits artificially diverted from that Member State which may give rise to foreign source dividends are appropriately taxed.*"[260]

Some Member States expressed the concern that outbound profit distributions may also give rise to double non-taxation if the residence state of the distributing company was a Member State that "*wishes to apply a withholding tax. It could be that by channelling the dividends through another Member State which does not apply such a withholding tax, the profit distribution remains untaxed, as under the Parent-Subsidiary Directive it can be transferred untaxed to the specific Member State, from which it can flow untaxed to a third country.*"[261] In order to avoid double non-taxation in such situations, the sub-group suggested: (1) the "*[a]pproximation of rates and renegotiations of [double taxation conventions],*" and (2) the "*[d]evelopment of anti-abuse rules.*"[262] Since most Member States were anxious that these suggestions might be difficult to apply, "*it was not possible to find a satisfactory solution within the framework of the Code of Conduct.*"[263] Therefore, this issue is still discussed within the sub-group.[264]

Another problem identified by the sub-group arises in the area of company finance.[265] Financial instruments are traditionally divided into equity and debt. A wide variety of instruments, however, incorporate elements of both equity and debt and are,

258. Doc. 9779/10 FISC 43 (12 May 2010), at p. 2; Doc. 10033/10 FISC 47 (25 May 2010), at p. 8; Doc. 16766/10 FISC 139 (22 Nov. 2010), at p. 6.
259. Doc. 9779/10 FISC 43 (12 May 2010), at pp. 2-3.
260. Doc. 16766/10 FISC 139 (22 Nov 2010), at p. 6.
261. Doc. 10033/10 FISC 47 (25 May 2010), at p. 9; Doc. 9779/10 FISC 43 (12 May 2010), at p. 5.
262. Doc. 9779/10 FISC 43 (12 May 2010), at p. 5.
263. Doc. 9779/10 FISC 43 (12 May 2010), at p. 5; Doc. 10033/10 FISC 47 (25 May 2010), at p. 9.
264. Doc. 16488/12 FISC 173 (23 Nov. 2012), at p. 4.
265. But see the transcript of the presentation of Eamonn O'Dea (vice-chairman of the EU Code of Conduct Group and the Assistant Secretary for Corporate Business & International, Irish Tax and Customs of the Republic of Ireland) published in R.A. de Boer/M.F. Nouwen (eds.), *The European Union's Struggle with Mismatches and Aggressive Tax Planning* (Eleven International Publishing, 2013), at pp. 105 et seq.

therefore, referred to as hybrid instruments or mezzanine capital.[266] As such instruments usually cannot be clearly classified as either equity or debt, the classification may vary from jurisdiction to jurisdiction. From a tax perspective, a mismatch in treatment can lead to double non-taxation when the hybrid instrument is treated as debt in the source state and as equity in the residence state of the recipient, since the amount paid by the debtor is deductible as interest in the source state and might be exempt as a dividend at the level of the creditor in the residence state.[267] The sub-group concluded that double non-taxation resulting from profit-participating loans can either be avoided by the source state denying the payor to deduct the payment or by the residence state denying the payee to exempt the payment.[268] The Code of Conduct Group agreed on the second option and suggested that *"[in] as far as payments under a hybrid loan arrangement are qualified as a tax deductible expense for the debtor in the arrangement, Member States shall not exempt such payments as profit distributions under a participation exemption."*[269]

In the meantime, the Code of Conduct Group has already started to monitor whether the previously agreed guidance on inbound profit transfers is implemented by the Member States.[270] However, the issue of double non-taxation resulting from mismatches is still subject to discussion.[271]

1.3.3 *The European Commission's Work on Double Non-Taxation*

The European Commission not only welcomed the work of the Code of Conduct Group in the area of mismatches.[272] Since it was called upon to rapidly develop concrete ways to improve the fight against tax fraud, including in relation to third countries,[273] the European Commission also reinforced its own efforts to tackle double non-taxation. To

266. See, for example, J.A. Duncan in IFA (ed.) *Tax Treatment of Hybrid Financial Instruments in Cross-Border Transactions*, CDFI 85a (IBFD, 2000), at pp. 24 et seq.; M. Helminen, *The Dividend Concept in International Tax Law* (Kluwer, 1999), at pp. 251 et seq.; M. Helminen, 58 *Bull. Intl. Taxn.* 2 (2004), at pp. 56 et seq.
267. Doc. 9779/10 FISC 43 (12 May 2010), at p. 5.
268. Doc. 9779/10 FISC 43 (12 May 2010), at p. 6.
269. The respective paragraph of the report of the Code of Conduct Group is not publicly available (Doc 10033/10 FISC 47 [25 May 2010], at p. 9 [para. 31]; see also Doc. 9779/10 FISC 43 [12 May 2010], at p. 6 [para. 13]; Doc. 16766/10 FISC 139 [22 Nov. 2010], at p. 7 [para. 17]). However, it was quoted by the European Commission in its proposal for a council directive amending the Parent-Subsidiary Directive (Proposal for a Council Directive amending Directive 2011/96/EU on the common system of taxation applicable in the case of parent companies and subsidiaries in different Member States, COM[2013] 814 final, at p. 2 [FN 5]).
270. Doc. 16488/12 FISC 173 (23 Nov. 2012), at p. 5; Doc. 11465/13 FISC 134 (21 Jun. 2013), at p. 5; Doc. 16656/13 FISC 226 (29 Nov. 2013), at p. 5.
271. Doc. 16488/12 FISC 173 (23 Nov 2012), at p. 4; Doc. 11465/13 FISC 134 (21 Jun. 2013), at p. 5; Doc. 11507/13 FISC 138 ECOFIN 636 CO EUR-PREP 31 (25 Jun. 2013), at p. 23; Doc. 16656/13 FISC 226 (29 Nov. 2013), at p. 5; Doc. CM 2488/14 FISC ECOFIN (15 Apr. 2014), at p. 1; Doc. 11227/14 FISC 102 ECOFIN 701 CO EUR-PREP 23 (23 Jun. 2014), at p. 14.
272. Annex Growth-Friendly Tax Policies in Member States and Better Tax Coordination in the EU to the Communication from the Commission to the European Parliament, the Council, the European Economic and Social Committee and the Committee of Regions, Annual Growth Survey 2012, COM(2011) 815 final, Vol. 5/5 – Annex IV (23 Nov. 2011), at pp. 10-11.
273. Doc. EUCO 4/2/12 REV 2 CO EUR 2 CONCL 1 (26 Apr. 2012), at p. 3.

this end, in 2012, a public consultation was launched *"in order to establish evidence concerning double non-taxation within the EU and in relation with Third Countries."*[274] The European Commission's intention was to get an overview and a better understanding of the phenomenon of double non-taxation in order to be able to decide on how to respond to it.[275] After the acknowledgements of various stakeholders had been analysed,[276] it was announced that concrete policy responses were to be expected as early as the end of 2012.[277] Indeed, the European Commission introduced a strategy to improve the fight against tax fraud and tax evasion in due time.[278] Besides emphasizing the instruments and proposals that already existed back then,[279] a series of new initiatives was presented[280] and an outlook on the short-, medium- and long-term plans was provided.[281]

As a first step to effectively tackle double non-taxation within the EU, a recommendation on aggressive tax planning was introduced. The European Commission thereby focussed on two specific issues: First, it concentrated on double non-taxation resulting from the interaction of uncoordinated domestic tax systems and double taxation conventions. Usually, contracting states simply bind themselves not to raise any taxes with respect to taxing rights that are given to the other contracting state under the double taxation convention. However, since there is no corresponding obligation for the other contracting state to exercise a taxing right domestically, it is possible that certain income remains untaxed.[282] In order to avoid such unintended double non-taxation the European Commission encourages the Member States to

274. Staff working paper, The Internal Market: Factual Examples of Double Non-taxation Cases, Consultation Document, TAXUD D1 D(2012) (29 Feb. 2012), at p. 3.
275. Staff working paper, The Internal Market: Factual Examples of Double Non-taxation Cases, Consultation Document, TAXUD D1 D(2012) (29 Feb. 2012), at p. 4 ("*Our aim is to obtain a better picture of the real problem and, if possible, of its financial impact.*") and at p. 15 ("*[T]he Commission will [...] carefully analyse the information provided in order to identify and develop the appropriate policy response.*").
276. Summary report of the responses received on the public consultation on factual examples and possible ways to tackle double non-taxation cases, TAXUD D1 D(2012) (5 Jul. 2012).
277. Communication from the Commission to the European Parliament and the Council on concrete ways to reinforce the fight against tax fraud and tax evasion including in relation to third countries, COM(2012) 351 final (27 Jun. 2012), at p. 13.
278. Communication from the Commission to the European Parliament and the Council, An Action Plan to strengthen the fight against tax fraud and tax evasion, COM(2012) 722 final (6 Dec. 2012).
279. Communication from the Commission to the European Parliament and the Council, An Action Plan to strengthen the fight against tax fraud and tax evasion, COM(2012) 722 final (6 Dec. 2012), at pp. 3-5 and at pp. 7-8.
280. Communication from the Commission to the European Parliament and the Council, An Action Plan to strengthen the fight against tax fraud and tax evasion, COM(2012) 722 final (6 Dec. 2012), at pp. 5-8; see also Commission Recommendation regarding measures intended to encourage third countries to apply minimum standards of good governance in tax matters, C(2012) 8805 final (6 Dec. 2012); Commission Recommendation of 6 Dec. 2012 on aggressive tax planning, C(2012) 8806 final (6 Dec. 2012).
281. Communication from the Commission to the European Parliament and the Council, An Action Plan to strengthen the fight against tax fraud and tax evasion, COM(2012) 722 final (6 Dec. 2012), at p. 7 and at pp. 9-15.
282. See M. Lang, 11 *IStR* 18 (2002), at pp. 611-612; M. Lang in W. Haarmann (ed.), *Auslegung und Anwendung von Doppelbesteuerungsabkommen* (Dr Otto Schmidt, 2004), at p. 92.

include a subject-to-tax clause in their bilateral double taxation conventions,[283] according to which the taxing right of a contracting state may be restricted by the double taxation convention only if the other contracting state domestically exercises the taxing right assigned to it.[284] Second, the Member States are invited to domestically introduce a general anti-abuse rule in order "*[t]o counteract aggressive tax planning practices which fall outside the scope of their specific anti-avoidance rules.*" The European Commission not only provides a recommendation on how to draft such a provision, but also illustrates the requirements that have to be fulfilled in order for the general anti-abuse rule to apply.[285] However, based on the findings of the public consultation on double non-taxation carried out before, the European Commission emphasized that "*[a]ggressive tax planning can take a multitude of forms.*" Thus, the Member States' approaches towards tax planning structures that take "*advantage of the technicalities of a tax system or of mismatches between two or more tax systems for the purpose of reducing tax liability*" need to be coordinated.[286] Insofar, the recommendation should only be perceived as a first attempt to address very specific issues that have come up as a result of the public consultation launched in 2012.[287]

Apparently, the EU institutions are well aware that the phenomenon of double non-taxation requires a comprehensive approach. In 2013, for example, the "Commission Expert Group to be known as the Platform for Tax Good Governance, Aggressive Tax Planning and Double Taxation" was set up in order to allow for a broader dialogue "*in which experience and expertise are exchanged and the views of all stakeholders are heard.*"[288] Not least due to the work of this platform, the European Commission has come to the conclusion that "*[a] new approach is [...] needed to ensure that corporate taxation can be growth-friendly, fair and transparent. To this end, the corporate tax framework in the EU needs to be significantly reviewed. There is a strong case for reforming the corporate tax framework in Europe and reviewing how national tax systems interact.*"[289] Upon invitation of the European Council,[290] an "Anti Tax

283. Commission Recommendation of 6 Dec. 2012 on aggressive tax planning, C(2012) 8806 final (6 Dec. 2012), at p. 4.
284. For a critical analysis of this proposal see C. Marchgraber, 23 *EC Tax Rev.* 5 (2014), at pp. 293-302.
285. Commission Recommendation of 6 Dec. 2012 on aggressive tax planning, C(2012) 8806 final (6 Dec. 2012), at pp. 4-5.
286. Commission Recommendation of 6 Dec. 2012 on aggressive tax planning, C(2012) 8806 final (6 Dec. 2012), at p. 2. For critical remarks on this proposal, see M. Lang, 23 *SWI* 2 (2013), at pp. 62 et seq.; M. Lang, Direkte Steuern und EU-Steuerpolitik – Wo bleiben die Visionen?, 22 *IStR* 10 (2013), p. 365 (at pp. 365 et seq.).
287. Commission Recommendation of 6 Dec. 2012 on aggressive tax planning, C(2012) 8806 final (6 Dec. 2012), at p. 2; see also the Opinion Statement FC 3/2014 of the CFE on the Recommendation C(2012)8806 on aggressive tax planning, an EU GAAR and double non-taxation (available at http://www.cfe-eutax.org).
288. Commission Decision on setting up a Commission Expert Group to be known as the Platform for Tax Good Governance, Aggressive Tax Planning and Double Taxation, C(2013) 2236 final (23 Apr. 2013), at p. 3; Commission Decision of 17 Jun. 2015 establishing the Commission Expert Group "Platform for Tax Good Governance, Aggressive Tax Planning and Double Taxation" and replacing Decision C(2013)2236, C(2015) 4095 final (17 Jun. 2015), at p. 3.
289. Communication from the Commission to the European Parliament and the Council, A Fair and Efficient Corporate Tax System in the European Union: 5 Key Areas for Action, COM(2015) 302 final (17 Jun. 2015), at p. 6.

Avoidance Package" was hence presented in 2016,[291] which aims at protecting *"the Single Market, and create a coherent and coordinated EU approach to corporate taxation."*[292] Among the key elements of this package was a proposal for an anti-tax avoidance directive[293] - which was later on adopted by the Council[294] and is by now commonly referred to as the Anti-Tax Avoidance Directive (ATAD) -, a recommendation on how to reinforce tax treaties against abuse by aggressive tax planners[295] and a study on the Member States' corporate tax rules that can facilitate aggressive tax planning and key structures used by companies to avoid taxation.[296] All these documents show a strong link to the BEPS project of the OECD.[297] However, in contrast to the various documents developed within the BEPS project, they in particular take into account *"the unique elements of the Single Market."*[298] To a certain extent, the European Commission has hence responded to the request of broadening *"the OECD discussions on BEPS with the EU law perspective."*[299] However, the anti-tax avoidance package is primarily about implementing the results of the BEPS project and other associated features in an EU-law compliant way. Despite the various efforts to tackle

290. Doc. 15150/15 FISC 185, ECOFIN 965 (8 Dec. 2015).
291. For a first analysis see A.P. Dourado, The EU Anti Tax Avoidance Package: Moving Ahead of BEPS?, 44 *Intertax* 6/7 (2016), p. 440 (at pp. 440-446).
292. Communication from the Commission to the European Parliament and the Council, Anti-Tax Avoidance Package: Next steps towards delivering effective taxation and greater tax transparency in the EU, COM(2016), 23 final (18 Jan. 2016), at p. 9.
293. Proposal for a Council Directive laying down rules against tax avoidance practices that directly affect the functioning of the internal market, COM(2016) 26 final (28 Jan. 2016); for an analysis, see S. Benz/J. Böhmer, Das Anti Tax Avoidance Package (ATA-Paket) der Kommission zur Umsetzung der BEPS-Maßnahmen in der EU, 69 *DB* 6 (2016), p. 307 (at pp. 307-314); C. Kahlenberg, Die Anti-BEPS-Richtlinie als wesentlicher Bestandteil des EU Anti Tax Avoidance Package, 26 *SWI* 4 (2016), p. 206 (at pp. 206-215); J. Lüdicke/F. Oppel, Der Vorschlag der EU-Kommission einer Anti-BEPS-Richtlinie - ein erster Überblick, 71 *BB* 6 (2016), p. 351 (at pp. 351-356); A. Navarro/L. Parada/P. Schwarz, The Proposal for an EU Anti-avoidance Directive: Some Preliminary Thoughts, 25 *EC Tax Rev.* 3 (2016), p. 117 (at pp. 117-131); CFE, Opinion Statement FC 3/2016 on the European Commission's proposal for an Anti-Tax Avoidance Directive of 28 Jan. 2016 (2016).
294. After some amendments (Doc. 9520/16 FISC 87 ECOFIN 512 [26 May 2016]; Doc. 10426/16 FISC 104 ECOFIN 628 [17 Jun. 2016]; Doc. 10539/16 FISC 110 ECOFIN 648 [7 Jul. 2016]), the proposal was adopted by the Council on 12 Jul. 2016 (Doc. 11171/16 VOTE 45 INF 129 PUBLIC 48 [13 Jul. 2016]) and published in the Official Journal on 19 Jul. 2016 (Council Directive (EU) 2016/1164 of 12 Jul. 2016 laying down rules against tax avoidance practices that directly affect the functioning of the internal market, *OJ* L 193 [19 Jul. 2016], p. 1 [at pp. 1-14]).
295. Commission Recommendation of 28 Jan. 2016 on the implementation of measures against tax treaty abuse, C(2016) 271 final (28 Jan. 2016).
296. Study on Structures of Aggressive Tax Planning and Indicators, Taxation Papers, Working Paper n. 61-2015 (European Union, 2016).
297. See Commission Staff Working Document Accompanying the document Communication from the Commission to the European Parliament and the Council - Anti Tax Avoidance Package: Next Steps towards delivering effective taxation and greater tax transparency in the EU, SWD(2016) 6 final (28 Jan. 2016), at pp. 48-50.
298. Communication from the Commission to the European Parliament and the Council, A Fair and Efficient Corporate Tax System in the European Union: 5 Key Areas for Action, COM(2015) 302 final (17 Jun. 2015), at p. 6.
299. E.C.C.M. Kemmeren, 23 *EC Tax Rev.* 4 (2014), at p. 193; also see A.P. Dourado, 44 *Intertax* 6/7 (2016), at p. 440.

double non-taxation, the question still remains unanswered whether there is a legal reasoning to support the view that this phenomenon is incompatible with the internal market.[300]

2 DOUBLE (NON-)TAXATION AND THE EUROPEAN VAT SYSTEM

2.1 The Continuing Development of the European VAT System

Double taxation and double non-taxation are predominantly associated with direct taxes and - albeit to a much lower extent - estate, inheritance and gift taxes.[301] However, both phenomena may also arise in the area of indirect taxes. Given the expansion of VAT/GST, it is not surprising that there is an increasing debate on how to avoid unintended double taxation and double non-taxation in the area of VAT/GST.[302] With regard to intra-EU transactions, however, this issue is considered to be less

300. See Taxation in the European Union, SEC(96) 487 final (20 Mar. 1996), at p. 13 ("*[t]he Single Market is clearly not compatible with either double taxation of the same taxable base or no taxation at all*"); Opinion of the Economic and Social Committee on Taxation in the European Union, Report on the development of tax systems (SEC[96] 487 final and COM[96] 546 final), *OJ* C 296 (29 Sep. 1997), p. 37 (at p. 43: "*[d]ouble taxation or the absence of taxation is incompatible with the internal market*"); Tax co-ordination in the European Union, Working Paper, Economic Affairs Series, ECON 125 EN (European Parliament, 2000), at p. 22 ("*The Single Market has several particular implications for the taxation of employment incomes. [...] Incomes should not escape tax altogether, or be taxed at discriminatorily low rates, as a result of cross-border tax arbitrage, avoidance or evasion.*"); Commission Recommendation of 6 Dec. 2012 on aggressive tax planning, C(2012) 8806 final (6 Dec. 2012), at p. 2 ("*[t]he Single Market is clearly not compatible with either double taxation [...] or no taxation at all*").

301. See J. Englisch, *Wettbewerbsgleichheit im grenzüberschreitenden Handel* (Mohr Siebeck, 2008), at p. 763.

302. See G. Bizioli in M. Lang/P. Melz/E. Kristoffersson (eds.), T. Ecker (ass. ed.), *Value Added Tax and Direct Taxation* (IBFD, 2009), at pp. 383-408; T. Ecker, *A VAT/GST Model Convention* (IBFD, 2013), at pp. 27-47; T. Ecker in M. Lang/P. Melz/E. Kristoffersson (eds.), T. Ecker (ass. ed.), *Value Added Tax and Direct Taxation* (IBFD, 2009), at pp. 1269-1284; T. Ecker/E. Variychuk, 2 *World Tax J.* 2 (2013), at pp. 81 et seq.; J. Englisch, *Wettbewerbsgleichheit im grenzüberschreitenden Handel* (Mohr Siebeck, 2008), at pp. 762-800; N. Eriksen/K. Haydl M. Lang/P. Melz/E. Kristoffersson (eds.), T. Ecker (ass. ed.), *Value Added Tax and Direct Taxation* (IBFD, 2009), at pp. 1145 et seq.; M. Lang in M. Achatz/M. Tumpel (eds.), *Umsatzsteuer und Internationales Steuerrecht* (Linde, 2012), at pp. 19-32; R. Millar in R. Krever/D. White (eds.), *GST in Retrospect and Prospect* (Thomson Reuters, 2007), at pp. 317-347; R. Millar, Sydney Law School Research Paper No. 08/14 (2008); R. Millar in M. Lang/P. Melz/E. Kristoffersson (eds.), T. Ecker (ass. ed.), *Value Added Tax and Direct Taxation* (IBFD, 2009), at pp. 409-442; P. Pistone, in M. Lang/P. Melz/E. Kristoffersson (eds.), T. Ecker (ass. ed.), *Value Added Tax and Direct Taxation* (IBFD, 2009), at pp. 1161 et seq.; F. Rendahl in M. Lang/P. Melz/E. Kristoffersson (eds.), T. Ecker (ass. ed.), *Value Added Tax and Direct Taxation* (IBFD, 2009), at pp. 1119 et seq.; H.G. Ruppe in IFA (ed.), *International Problems in the Field of General Sales Taxes on Sales of Goods and Services, CDFI 68b* (IBFD, 1983), at pp. 121-144; E. Traversa/C. Helleputte in M. Lang/P. Melz/E. Kristoffersson (eds.), T. Ecker (ass. ed.), *Value Added Tax and Direct Taxation* (IBFD, 2009), at pp. 339 et seq.; A.A. Verstraeten, in M. Lang/P. Melz/E. Kristoffersson (eds.), T. Ecker (ass. ed.), *Value Added Tax and Direct Taxation* (IBFD, 2009), at pp. 369 et seq.; also see OECD, *International VAT/GST Guidelines* (OECD, 2015), at p. 9, para. 1.

problematic, because VAT is widely harmonized within Europe.[303] The first steps towards harmonization were already taken in 1967 through adoption of the first two VAT directives.[304] Whereas France only had to amend its existing domestic VAT system, the other Member States had to replace their cumulative turnover tax systems by the beginning of 1970 at the latest.[305] However, the implementing legislation of the Member States derogated to a variable extent from the basic framework laid down by the VAT directives. Moreover, a number of issues were left entirely open. The Member States were hence granted broad discretionary leeway. Despite the efforts to harmonize turnover taxes, these deficiencies led to the result that "*there really existed nine separate and different systems of VAT, rather than a single Community system.*"[306]

In order to overcome – at least partly – the teething troubles of VAT harmonization within the EU, the Sixth VAT Directive was approved in 1977, which repealed and replaced the former VAT directives.[307] However, it took until 1988 for all of the former Member States to more or less implement this directive.[308] Henceforth, the European VAT system was characterized by a steady advancement. Numerous changes were made to the Sixth VAT Directive.[309] This led to a complex and hardly straightforward system. For reasons of clarity and rationalization, it was considered necessary to recast this directive. Since 2006, the main rules of the European VAT system can thus be found in the (Recast) VAT Directive.[310] Despite its new format, the EU legislator has still been "*hyper active in the field of VAT.*"[311] Not only has the VAT Directive been changed several times[312] but it has also been supplemented by various other

303. See T. Ecker, *A VAT/GST Model Convention* (IBFD, 2013), at p. 46; T. Ecker in M. Lang/P. Melz/E. Kristoffersson (eds.), T. Ecker (ass. ed.), *Value Added Tax and Direct Taxation* (IBFD, 2009), at p. 1270; E. Traversa/C. Helleputte in M. Lang/P. Melz/E. Kristoffersson (eds.), T. Ecker (ass. ed.), *Value Added Tax and Direct Taxation* (IBFD, 2009), at pp. 348-354.
304. First Council Directive of 11 Apr. 1967 on the harmonization of legislation of Member States concerning turnover taxes (67/227/EEC), 10 *OJ* 71 (14 Apr. 1967), p. 1301 (at pp. 1301-1303); Second Council Directive of 11 Apr. 1967 on the harmonization of legislation of Member States concerning turnover taxes – Structure and procedures for application of the common system of value added tax (67/228/EEC), 10 *OJ* 71 (14 Apr. 1967), p. 1303 (at pp. 1303-1312).
305. See R. de la Feria, *The EU VAT System and the Internal Market* (IBFD, 2009), at p. 52; A.J. Easson, *Taxation in the European Community* (The Athlone Press, 1993), at pp. 100-101.
306. A.J. Easson, *Taxation in the European Community* (The Athlone Press, 1993), at p. 101; also cf. R. de la Feria, *The EU VAT System and the Internal Market* (IBFD, 2009), at pp. 53-54.
307. Sixth Council Directive of 17 May 1977 on the harmonization of the laws of the Member States relating to turnover taxes – Common system of value added tax: uniform basis of assessment (77/388/EEC), *OJ* L 145 (13 Jun. 1977).
308. See A.J. Easson, *Taxation in the European Community* (The Athlone Press, 1993), at pp. 103-104.
309. For an overview see B.J.M. Terra/P.J. Wattel, *European Tax Law*[6] [Kluwer, 2012], at pp. 175-176.
310. Council Directive 2006/112/EC of 28 Nov. 2006 on the common system of value added tax, *OJ* L 347 (11 Dec. 2006).
311. B. Terra/J. Kajus, *Introduction to European VAT* (IBFD, 2016), at Ch. 8.2.
312. Council Directive 2006/138/EC of 19 Dec. 2006 amending Directive 2006/112/EC on the common system of value added tax as regards the period of application of the value added tax arrangements applicable to radio and television broadcasting services and certain electronically supplied services, *OJ* L 384 (29 Dec. 2006), p. 92 (at pp. 92-93); Council Directive 2007/75/EC of 20 Dec. 2007 amending Directive 2006/112/EC with regard to certain temporary provisions concerning rates of value added tax, *OJ* L 346 (29 Dec. 2007), p. 13 (at pp. 13-14); Council Directive 2008/8/EC of 12 Feb. 2008 amending Directive 2006/112/EC as regards the

directives[313] and regulations.[314] Although by now *"the common system of VAT has [hence] become a truly European tax,"*[315] the VAT integration process is still ongoing.

place of supply of services, *OJ* L 44 (20 Feb. 2008), p. 11 (at pp. 11-22); Council Directive 2008/117/EC of 16 Dec. 2008 amending Directive 2006/112/EC on the common system of value added tax to combat tax evasion connected with intra-Community transactions, *OJ* L 14 (20 Jan. 2009), p. 7 (at pp. 7-9); Council Directive 2009/47/EC of 5 May 2009 amending Directive 2006/112/EC as regards reduced rates of value added tax, *OJ* L 116 (9 May 2009), p. 18 (at pp. 18-20); Council Directive 2009/69/EC of 25 Jun. 2009 amending Directive 2006/112/EC on the common system of value added tax as regards tax evasion linked to imports, *OJ* L 175 (4 Jul. 2009), p. 12 (at pp. 12-13); Council Directive 2009/162/EU of 22 Dec. 2009 amending various provisions of Directive 2006/112/EC on the common system of value added tax, *OJ* L 10 (15 Jan. 2010), p. 14 (at pp. 14-18); Council Directive 2010/23/EU of 16 Mar. 2010 amending Directive 2006/112/EC on the common system of value added tax, as regards an optional and temporary application of the reverse charge mechanism in relation to supplies of certain services susceptible to fraud, *OJ* L 72 (20 Mar. 2010), p. 1 (at pp. 1-2); Council Directive 2010/45/EU of 13 Jul. 2010 amending Directive 2006/112/EC on the common system of value added tax as regards the rules on invoicing, OJ L 189 (22 Jul. 2010), p. 1 (at pp. 1-8); Council Directive 2010/88/EU of 7 Dec. 2010 amending Directive 2006/112/EC on the common system of value added tax, with regard to the duration of the obligation to respect a minimum standard rate, *OJ* L 326 (10 Dec. 2010), p. 1 (at pp. 1-2); Council Directive 2013/42/EU of 22 Jul. 2013 amending Directive 2006/112/EC on the common system of value added tax, as regards a Quick Reaction Mechanism against VAT fraud, *OJ* L 201 (26 Jul. 2013; p. 1 (at pp. 1-3); Council Directive 2013/43/EU of 22 Jul. 2013 amending Directive 2006/112/EC on the common system of value added tax, as regards an optional and temporary application of the reverse charge mechanism in relation to supplies of certain goods and services susceptible to fraud, *OJ* L 201 (26 Jul. 2013), p. 4 (at pp. 4-6); Council Directive 2013/61/EU of 17 Dec. 2013 amending Directives 2006/112/EC and 2008/118/EC as regards the French outermost regions and Mayotte in particular, *OJ* L 353 (28 Dec. 2013), p. 5 (at pp. 5-6).

313. Thirteenth Council Directive 86/560/EEC of 17 Nov. 1986 on the harmonization of the laws of the Member States relating to turnover taxes Arrangements for the refund of value added tax to taxable persons not established in Community territory, *OJ* L 326 (21 Nov. 1986), p. 40 (at pp. 40-41); Council Directive 2008/9/EC of 12 Feb. 2008 laying down detailed rules for the refund of value added tax, provided for in Directive 2006/112/EC, to taxable persons not established in the Member State of refund but established in another Member State, *OJ* L 44 (20 Feb. 2008), p. 23 (at pp. 23-28); Council Directive 2009/132/EC of 19 Oct. 2009 determining the scope of Article 143(b) and (c) of Directive 2006/112/EC as regards exemption from value added tax on the final importation of certain goods, *OJ* L 292 (10 Nov. 2009), p. 5 (at pp. 5-30); Council Directive 2006/79/EC of 5 Oct. 2006 on the exemption from taxes of imports of small consignments of goods of a non-commercial character from third countries, *OJ* L 286 (17 Oct. 2006), p. 15 (at pp. 15-18); Council Directive 2007/74/EC of 20 Dec. 2007 on the exemption from value added tax and excise duty of goods imported by persons travelling from third countries, *OJ* L 346 (29 Dec. 2007), p. 6 (at pp. 6-12).

314. Council Implementation Regulation (EU) No. 282/2011 of 15 Mar. 2011 laying down implementing measures for Directive 2006/112/EC on the common system of value added tax, *OJ* L 77 (23 Mar. 2011), p. 1 (at pp. 1-22); Council Implementation Regulation (EU) No. 967/2012 of 9 Oct. 2012 amending Implementing Regulation (EU) No. 282/2011 as regards the special schemes for non- established taxable persons supplying telecommunications services, broadcasting services or electronic services to non-taxable persons, *OJ* L 290 (20 Oct. 2012), p. 1 (at pp. 1-7); Council Implementation Regulation (EU) No. 1042/2013 of 7 Oct. 2013 amending Implementing Regulation (EU) No. 282/2011 as regards the place of supply of services, *OJ* L 284 (26 Oct. 2013), p. 1 (at pp. 1-9).

315. J. Englisch, Development of the EU VAT System, in M. Lang/C. Staringer/J. Schuch/P. Pistone/D. Raponi (eds.), *ECJ – Recent Developments in Value Added Tax* (Linde, 2014), p. 21 (at p. 22).

2.2 Double (Non-)Taxation in the European VAT System

Given the vast harmonization of VAT within the EU, one might be tempted to assume that situations of double taxation and double non-taxation are fully taken care of in the European VAT system.[316] However, there are various reasons why double taxation and double non-taxation may arise despite the high degree of harmonization within the EU. Most obviously, such situations can occur if a third country is involved in a cross-border transaction.[317] Non-Member States are not bound to follow the rules of secondary EU law and may hence, for example, apply different place-of-supply rules.[318] In order to avoid double taxation, non-taxation and distortions of competition resulting from the application of deviating place-of-supply rules by a Member State and a third country, Article 59a VAT Directive grants the Member States the option to unilaterally deviate from the standard place-of-supply rules laid down by the VAT Directive and to instead tax services at the place where they are effectively used and enjoyed.[319] However, a thorough analysis of this provision shows that its potential to avoid double taxation, non-taxation or a distortion of competition is more limited than one might expect at first glance.[320]

Moreover, double taxation and double non-taxation may not only arise if a third country is involved. Even within the EU, such results cannot be completely excluded. In the *RBS Deutschland Holding* case, for example, double non-taxation resulted from two Member States implementing the secondary EU law provisions differently.[321] Under UK domestic VAT law, lease transactions were treated as supplies of services.

316. Cf. J. Englisch, *Wettbewerbsgleichheit im grenzüberschreitenden Handel* (Mohr Siebeck, 2008), at p. 771 ("*Im harmonisierten Verbrauchsteuerrecht der Europäischen Gemeinschaft dürften Doppelbesteuerungseffekte infolge abweichender nationaler Steuerbestimmungen eigentlich nicht vorkommen.*").
317. See E. Traversa/C. Helleputte in M. Lang/P. Melz/E. Kristoffersson (eds.), T. Ecker (ass. ed.), *Value Added Tax and Direct Taxation* (IBFD, 2009), at pp. 355-356.
318. With regard to VAT, the application of different proxies to establish the place of consumption is a typical reason for double taxation or non-taxation. See T. Ecker in M. Lang/P. Melz/E. Kristoffersson (eds.), T. Ecker (ass. ed.), *Value Added Tax and Direct Taxation* (IBFD, 2009), at p. 1270; T. Ecker, *A VAT/GST Model Convention* (IBFD, 2013), at p. 40; N.P. Eriksen, Should Tax Treaties Play a Role for Consumption Taxes?, 33 *Intertax* 4 (2005), p. 166 (at p. 168); R. Millar in R. Krever/D. White (eds.), *GST in Retrospect and Prospect* (Thomson Reuters, 2007), at p. 325; R. Millar in M. Lang/P. Melz/E. Kristoffersson (eds.), T. Ecker (ass. ed.), *Value Added Tax and Direct Taxation* (IBFD, 2009), at p. 430; also see OECD, *The Application of Consumption Taxes to the International Trade in Services and Intangibles, Progress Report and Draft Principles* (OECD, 2005), at p. 3; Consultation paper Introduction of a mechanism for eliminating double imposition of VAT in individual cases, Taxud/D1/ ... (5 Jan. 2007), at pp. 2-3; also cf. H.G. Ruppe in IFA (ed.), *International Problems in the Field of General Sales Taxes on Sales of Goods and Services, CDFI 68b* (IBFD, 1983), at p. 121.
319. See B. Terra/J. Kajus/O. Henkow in B. Terra/J. Kajus (eds.), *A Guide to the Recast VAT Directive* (IBFD, 2015), at Ch. 5.7.4., citing the VAT Committee's Working Paper No. 633.
320. See Chapter 4.2.2.1.1.
321. Judgment in *RBS Deutschland Holding*, C-277/09, EU:C:2010:810; also see European Commission, Consultation paper, Introduction of a mechanism for eliminating double imposition of VAT in individual cases, TAXUD/D1/ ... (5 Jan. 2007), at pp. 2-3; also cf. J. Englisch, *Wettbewerbsgleichheit im grenzüberschreitenden Handel* (Mohr Siebeck, 2008), at pp. 772-774; H. Stadie in G. Rau/E. Dürrwächter (eds.), *Umsatzsteuergesetz*[154] (Dr Otto Schmidt, 2013), at Einf. paras 750-753 and 763.

The place of supply was hence deemed to be where the supplier's business was established. According to German domestic VAT law, however, lease transactions were treated as supplies of goods. The place of supply was thus deemed to be where the goods were located when the supplies took place. Consequently, a lease transaction between a UK lessee and a German lessor resulted in double non-taxation. From an EU tax policy perspective, such situations should - at least theoretically - only be a temporary problem. With regard to *RBS Deutschland Holding*, for example, it is obvious that either the UK's or Germany's interpretation of the EU VAT system is erroneous. It would hence be up to the ECJ to decide whether the lease transactions at stake constituted a supply of goods - as supposed by Germany - or a supply of services - as supposed by the UK - under the rules of the Sixth VAT Directive.[322] But since this question has "*not been raised*" by the referring court, the ECJ has not enlarged upon this issue.[323]

In contrast to a different understanding of the secondary EU law rules, double taxation and double non-taxation resulting from a deviating assessment of the facts of the case or the legal description cannot be curtailed by the ECJ.[324] Such a situation could, for example, occur if "*[t]wo Member States both consider that leasing is a supply of services under Article 43 of the VAT Directive but one of them considers that the contract between Mr X and company Y is a leasing contract while the other Member State regards it as a sale of the vehicle (by instalments) falling under the provisions on the supply of goods.*"[325] In order to avoid such a result, the European Commission has proposed to implement a "*[m]echanism for eliminating double taxation in individual*

322. Cf. G. Bizioli in M. Lang/P. Melz/E. Kristoffersson (eds.), T. Ecker (ass. ed.), *Value Added Tax and Direct Taxation* (IBFD, 2009), at p. 400; T. Ecker, *A VAT/GST Model Convention* (IBFD, 2013), at p. 46; T. Ecker in M. Lang/P. Melz/E. Kristoffersson (eds.), T. Ecker (ass. ed.), *Value Added Tax and Direct Taxation* (IBFD, 2009), at p. 1270; H. Grambeck, Outsourcing in the EU Financial Sector – Where Are We Heading?, 20 *Intl. VAT Monitor* 6 (2009), p. 462 (at p. 469); H. Stadie in G. Rau/E. Dürrwächter (eds.), *Umsatzsteuergesetz*[154] (Dr Otto Schmidt, 2013), at Einf. para. 752; also cf. European Commission, Report on the outcome of the consultation on "Introduction of a mechanism for eliminating double imposition of VAT in individual cases," TAXUD/D1/EWS/mav D(2007) 15925 (24 Oct. 2007), at p. 2; also cf. Judgment in *Faaborg-Gelting Linien / Finanzamt Flensburg*, C-231/94, EU:C:1996:184.
323. Opinion of AG Mazák in *RBS Deutschland Holding*, C-277/09, EU:C:2010:566, at point 32-33; also see M. Lang in M. Achatz/M. Tumpel (eds.), *Umsatzsteuer und Internationales Steuerrecht* (Linde, 2012), at pp. 24-25; S. Pfeiffer, *VAT Grouping from a European Perspective* (IBFD, 2015), at p. 190 (FN 961); K. Spies, The CJEU's Approach in Direct Tax and VAT Law: Consistencies and Divergences, in M. Lang/P. Pistone/A. Rust/J. Schuch/C. Staringer/D. Raponi (eds.), *CJEU – Recent Developments in Value Added Tax 2015* (Linde, 2016), p. 135 (at p. 158, FN 135); C. Wächter, Rechtsmissbrauch und Qualifikationskonflikt im Umsatzsteuerrecht, 49 *DStR* 2 (2011), p. 49 (at p. 51).
324. European Commission, Consultation paper, Introduction of a mechanism for eliminating double imposition of VAT in individual cases, TAXUD/D1/.... (5 Jan. 2007), at p. 4; also see P. Rendahl, EU VAT and Double Taxation: A Fine Line Between Interpretation and Application, 41 *Intertax* 8/9 (2013), p. 450 (at p. 456); H. Stadie in G. Rau/E. Dürrwächter (eds.), *Umsatzsteuergesetz*[154] (Dr Otto Schmidt, 2013), at Einf. paras 754-757.
325. European Commission, Consultation paper, Introduction of a mechanism for eliminating double imposition of VAT in individual cases, TAXUD/D1/ ... (5 Jan. 2007), at p. 3.

cases"[326] that should be based on "*a mutual agreement procedure, followed if necessary by an arbitration procedure if attempts at a mutually agreed solution failed.*"[327] However, so far, the European Commission has not taken any further steps to introduce such a procedure. Double taxation and double non-taxation may hence still arise due to a deviating assessment of the facts of the case or the legal description.

Not only a different interpretation of the same provision, a deviating appraisal of the same situation or a divergent assessment of the legal description may result in double taxation or double non-taxation. The European VAT system also contains rules that give leeway to the Member States on how to develop their domestic VAT system. Such a "*discretionary domestic normative power retained according to the VAT Directive, in particular in order to define the place of supply and/or the subjective and objective elements of the transaction,*"[328] entails the risk that it results in double taxation or double non-taxation. According to Article 11 VAT Directive, for example, each Member State may independently decide to "*regard as a single taxable person any persons established in the territory of that Member State who, while legally independent, are closely bound to one another by financial, economic and organisational links.*" If it is assumed that the fundamental freedoms require Member States that exercise this option to extend the scope of the domestically implemented VAT grouping mechanism to persons established in the territory of another Member State as well,[329] it would be possible that one Member State regards two companies as a single taxable person, whereas the other Member State considers them to be separate taxable persons. If an intra-group service took place between two companies and the service recipient provides tax-exempt transactions, the fact that only one of the two Member States involved opted for a domestic VAT grouping regime would lead to double taxation or double non-taxation:[330]

326. Communication from the Commission to the Council, the European Parliament and the European Economic and Social Committee, Review and update of VAT strategy priorities, COM(2003) 614 final (20 Oct. 2003), at p. 8.

327. European Commission, Consultation paper, Introduction of a mechanism for eliminating double imposition of VAT in individual cases, TAXUD/D1/ ... (5 Jan. 2007), at p. 10.

328. G. Bizioli in M. Lang/P. Melz/E. Kristoffersson (eds.), T. Ecker (ass. ed.), *Value Added Tax and Direct Taxation* (IBFD, 2009), at p. 400.

329. See C.B. Eskildsen, VAT Grouping versus Freedom of Establishment, 20 *EC Tax Rev.* 3 (2011), p. 114 (at pp. 114-120); J. Mühlehner, Umsatzsteuerliche Organschaft und Niederlassungsfreiheit, 16 *SWI* 7 (2006), p. 300 (at pp. 300-306); S. Pfeiffer, *VAT Grouping from a European Perspective* (IBFD, 2015), at pp. 63-115; A. van Doesum/H. van Kesteren/G. van Norden, The Internal Market and VAT: Intra-group Transactions of Branches, Subsidiaries and VAT Groups, 16 *EC Tax Rev.* 1 (2007), p. 34 (at pp. 37-41); K. Vyncke, VAT Grouping in the European Union: Purposes, Possibilities and Limitations, 18 *Intl. VAT Monitor* 4 (2007), p. 250 (at pp. 256-257). R. Zuidgeest, Cross-Border VAT Grouping, 21 *Intl. VAT* Monitor 1 (2010), p. 25 (at pp. 27-30); also cf. T. Ehrke-Rable, VAT Grouping: the Relevance of the Territorial Restriction in Article 11 VAT Directive, 1 *World J. of VAT/GST L.* 1 (2012), p. 61 (at pp. 70-78).

330. See S. Pfeiffer, *VAT Grouping from a European Perspective* (IBFD, 2015), at pp. 86-87 and 224-226; A. van Doesum/H. van Kesteren/G. van Norden, 16 *EC Tax Rev.* 1 (2007), at pp. 38-39; for other possibilities to use VAT grouping in order to reduce the VAT burden on cross-border transactions see J. Swinkels, VAT-Saving Concepts and Interpretations, 16 *Intl. VAT Monitor* 6 (2005), p. 417 (at pp. 423-425); J. Swinkels, VAT-Saving Solutions and Abuse of Law, 18 *Intl. VAT Monitor* 5 (2007), p. 331 (at p. 340); J. Swinkels, The Phenomenon of VAT Groups under EU Law and Their VAT-Saving Aspects, 21 *Intl. VAT Monitor* 1 (2010), p. 36 (at

Example 2

Parent Co is a company resident in Member State A, which provides tax exempt services in this Member State. It holds 100% of the shares in Subsidiary Co, which is a company resident in Member State B. Subsidiary Co provides intra-group services to Parent Co. To this end, input transactions are bought in Member State B.

Diagram: Input Tax Deduction and Cross-Border VAT Groups

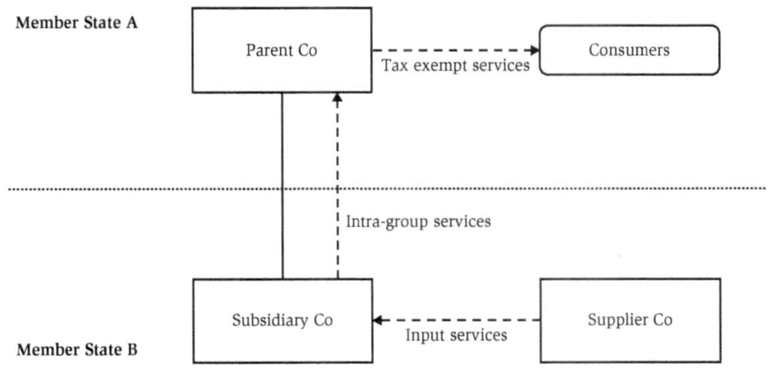

Double non-taxation may arise if it is assumed that Member State A exercised the option to implement VAT grouping, which allows Parent Co and Subsidiary Co to be treated as a single taxable person. Member State A would hence not levy VAT on the intra-group supplies. Unless Member State B accepted the consequences of the VAT group in Member State A, it would treat the intra-group transaction as taxable and thus grant an input tax deduction for Subsidiary Co's input supplies. However, in the end, Member State B would also refrain from taxing the intra-group service. Since it is a business-to-business transaction, Article 44 VAT Directive stipulates that the place of supply is the place where the service recipient (Parent Co) has established its business (Member State A).

By contrast, if it is assumed that Member State B exercised the option to implement VAT grouping, whereas Member State A did not, this would lead to double taxation. If Member State B treated Parent Co and Subsidiary Co as a single taxable person, Subsidiary Co would not be granted relief for the input transactions acquired in Member State A. Unless Member State A accepted the consequences of the VAT group in Member State B, the intra-group supply would be subject to VAT due to Article 44 VAT Directive. Due to its tax-exempt output transactions, Parent Co would not be able to redeem these input taxes.

Within the widely harmonized European VAT system, double taxation and double non-taxation could thus arise more often than one might expect. The question

pp. 39-41); for another example of double non-taxation see M. Achatz, Der Handel mit Zahnersatz im Binnenmarkt, in P. Kirchhof/H. Nieskens (eds.), *Festschrift für Wolfram Reiss zum 65. Geburtstag* (Dr Otto Schmidt, 2008), p. 169 (at p. 180).

whether these phenomena are in line with primary EU law is, therefore, not limited to direct taxes. Still, the vast harmonization and the different character of VAT as compared to direct taxes may lead to different challenges. There are, for example, only a few decisions of the ECJ that deal with the impact of the fundamental freedoms on the European VAT system.[331] Applying the State aid rules to indirect taxes also raises different questions as compared to the area of direct taxes.[332] However, these challenges should not result in turning a blind eye to indirect taxes. If double taxation and double non-taxation are considered to be incompatible with the internal market,[333] it should not make a difference whether such results arise due to the levy of a direct or an indirect tax.

331. Judgment in *Schul* (hereinafter: *Schul I*), 15/81, EU:C:1982:135; Judgment in *Schul* (hereinafter: *Schul II*), 47/84, EU:C:1985:216; Judgment in *Lease Plan*, C-390/96, EU:C:1998:206; Judgment in *Société générale des grandes sources d'eaux minérales françaises*, C-361/96, EU:C:1998:282; Judgment in *Kieffer and Thill*, C-114/96, EU:C:1997:316; Judgment in *Schmelz*, C-97/09 EU:C:2010:632; Judgment in *Crédit Lyonnais*, C-388/11, EU:C:2013:541.

332. See J. Englisch, EU State Aid Rules Applied to Indirect Tax Measures, 22 *EC Tax Rev.* 1 (2013), p. 9 (at pp. 9-18); J. Englisch, Indirect Taxation, in A. Rust/C. Micheau (eds.), *State Aid and Tax Law* (Kluwer, 2013), p. 69 (at pp. 69-85).

333. See Taxation in the European Union, SEC(96) 487 final (20 Mar. 1996), at p. 13 ("*[t]he Single Market is clearly not compatible with either double taxation of the same taxable base or no taxation at all*"); Opinion of the Economic and Social Committee on Taxation in the European Union, Report on the development of tax systems (SEC[96] 487 final and COM[96] 546 final), *OJ* C 296 (29 Sep. 1997), p. 37 (at p. 43: "*[d]ouble taxation or the absence of taxation is incompatible with the internal market*"); Tax co-ordination in the European Union, Working Paper, Economic Affairs Series, ECON 125 EN (European Parliament, 2000), at p. 22 ("*The Single Market has several particular implications for the taxation of employment incomes. [...] Incomes should not escape tax altogether, or be taxed at discriminatorily low rates, as a result of cross-border tax arbitrage, avoidance or evasion.*"); Commission Recommendation of 6 Dec. 2012 on aggressive tax planning, C(2012) 8806 final (6 Dec. 2012), at p. 2 ("*[t]he Single Market is clearly not compatible with either double taxation [...] or no taxation at all*").

CHAPTER 3

The EU Primary Law Framework in Tax Matters

1 THE LEGAL CONCEPT OF THE INTERNAL MARKET

1.1 Free Movement and Undistorted Competition as Characteristics of the Internal Market Concept

Since the beginning of the European integration process,[334] the legal concept of the internal market is an integral part of the Treaties. Until 1987, only the term "common

334. The origin of the EU can be traced back to the 1950s. Based on the ideas conceived by, *inter alia*, Jean Monnet (for details on the "Monnet Plan" see, for example, F.M.B. Lynch, Resolving the Paradox of the Monnet Plan: National and International Planning in French Reconstruction, 37 *Econ. Hist. Rev.* 2 [1984], at pp. 229-243) and Robert Schumann (*The Schumann Declaration* [9 May 1950]) the Treaty establishing the European Coal and Steel Community (ECSC) was signed by Belgium, France, Germany, Italy, Luxembourg and the Netherlands in 1951 (Treaty establishing the European Coal and Steel Community [18 Apr. 1951], 261 U.N.T.S. 140). The ECSC Member States agreed to transfer the administration of the coal and steel industry to an independent supranational institution, which was, *inter alia*, empowered to take decisions binding on Member States as well as on certain undertakings in order to establish a common market for coal and steel. Despite the failure to form a pan-European defence force – the European Defence Community (for further details on the EDC see, for example, E. Furdson, *The European Defence Community: A History* [Macmillan, 1980]) –, the governments of the ECSC Member States agreed on taking a further step towards a united Europe (*The Messina Declaration* [3 Jun. 1955]). As a result, a preparatory committee responsible for drafting a report on the creation of a European common market was established in 1955 (Resolution adopted by the Foreign Ministers of the Member States of the ECSC at their Meeting at Messina [1-3 Jun. 1955]). The committee's work on the creation of a general common market and on the establishment of an atomic energy community led to a report which was approved by the ECSC Member States in 1956 (Comité Intergouvernemental, *Rapport Des Chefs de Délégation aux Ministres des Affaires Etrangéres* [21 Apr. 1956]). Based on this so-called *Spaak* Report, the Treaties establishing the European Economic Community (EEC Treaty: Treaty establishing the European Economic Community [25 Mar. 1957], 298 *U.N.T.S.* 11) and the European Atomic Energy Community (EAEC Treaty: Treaty establishing the European Atomic Energy

market" was used.[335] Although there was no explicit definition, the characteristics of the common market concept could be inferred from various provisions. Article 3 EEC Treaty, for example, called for, *inter alia*, "*(a) the elimination, as between Member States, of customs duties and of quantitative restrictions on the import and export of goods, and of all other measures having equivalent effect; (b) the establishment of a common customs tariff and of a common commercial policy towards third countries; [and] (c) the abolition, as between Member States, of obstacles to freedom of movement for persons, services and capital.*" Thus,[336] the ECJ concluded that "*the concept of a common market [...] involves the elimination of all obstacles to intra-Community trade in order to merge the national markets into a single market bringing about conditions as close as possible to those of a genuine internal market.*"[337] Moreover, according to Article 3 (f) EEC Treaty, a "*system ensuring that competition in the common market is not distorted*" shall be instituted "*in order to arrive at 'establishing a Common Market' which is one of the fundamental objectives set out in Article 2 [EEC Treaty].*"[338] Overall,

Community [25 Mar. 1957], 298 *U.N.T.S.* 167) were negotiated at an intergovernmental conference in Brussels. After the signing one year later in Rome, both treaties entered into force in 1958. In 1993, the EEC was renamed EC by the Treaty of Maastricht (Article G(A)(1) of the Treaty on European Union, *OJ* C 191 [29 Jul. 1992], at pp. 4 et seq.). Moreover, the EU was established on the basis of the European Communities [the ECSC, the EAEC and the EC] through Articles G, H, I of the Treaty of Maastricht, supplemented by the Common Foreign and Security Policy [CFSP] and the Justice and Home Affairs (JHA) through Articles J and K of the Treaty of Maastricht. In 2003, the JHA was renamed Police and Judicial Co-Operation in Criminal Matters (Treaty of Amsterdam amending the Treaty on European Union, the Treaties establishing the European Communities and certain related acts, *OJ* C 340 [10 Nov. 1997], at pp. 16 et seq.). In 2007, the Treaty of Lisbon merged these three pillars of the EU and renamed the EC Treaty the Treaty on the Functioning of the European Union (TFEU: Treaty of Lisbon amending the Treaty on European Union and the Treaty establishing the European Community, *OJ* C 306 [17 Dec. 2007]). The institutional structure of the European Communities has thereby been maintained to a large extent, albeit the importance of the individual institutions has changed over time (see C.W.A. Timmermans, Genesis and Development of the European Communities, in P.J.G. Kapteyn/A.M. McDonnell/K.J.M. Mortelmans/C.W.A. Timmermans/ L.A. Geelhoed [eds.], *The Law of the European Union and the European Communities*[4] [Kluwer, 2008], p. 1 [at pp. 24 et seq.]). From a tax perspective, the most important institutions of the EU are the Council, the European Parliament, the European Commission and the Court of Justice of the European Union (CJEU). Within this quadripartite structure the Council serves as a platform for the Member States' governments to defend their own country's national interests, the European citizens are represented in the European Parliament, the interests of the EU as a whole are promoted by the European Commission and the CJEU upholds the rule of European law (see K. Good, Institutional Reform under the Single European Act, 3 *Am. U. J. Intl. L. Pol.* 1 [1988], p. 299 [at p. 303]).

335. See, *inter alia*, Articles 1-4 ECSC Treaty and Articles 2-3 EEC Treaty.
336. Judgment in *Commission/Italy*, 159/78, EU:C:1979:243, at para. 7; Judgment in *Polydor and others/Harlequin and others*, 270/80, EU:C:1982:43, at para. 16.
337. Judgment in *Schul*, 15/81, EU:C:1982:135, at para. 33; also see Judgment in *Metro/Commission*, 26/76, EU:C:1977:167, at para. 20; Judgment in *Commission/United Kingdom*, 207/83, EU:C:1985:161, at para. 17; Judgment in *Ryborg*, C-297/89, EU:C:1991:160, at para. 14; Judgment in *France/Commission*, C-41/93, EU:C:1994:196, at para. 19; Judgment in *Klattner/ Elliniko Dimosio*, C-389/95, EU:C:1997:258, at para. 25.
338. Judgment in *Italy/Council of the EEC and Commission of the EEC*, 32/65, EU:C:1966:42, at para. 12.

the common market concept of the EEC Treaty was thus characterized by the free movement of goods, persons, services and capital as well as a system of undistorted competition.[339]

Through the Single European Act,[340] the notion of common market was supplemented by the notion of internal market, which was defined as *"an area without internal frontiers in which the free movement of goods, persons, services and capital is ensured in accordance with the provisions of this Treaty."*[341] This led to a debate on the possible difference between both expressions. Based on, *inter alia*, the case law of the ECJ, it was argued that the common market is only a preliminary stage of an internal market.[342] Another part of the literature held the converse view that the internal market is a mere subset of the common market, which does not include certain policy areas, such as competition, agriculture, transport and taxation.[343] Other scholars were, on the other hand, of the opinion that the internal and the common market coincide.[344] After the ECJ clarified that the internal market concept also aims at the elimination of distortions of competition,[345] the potential differences between the concepts of a

339. Judgment in *Cullet/Leclerc*, 231/83, EU:C:1985:29, at para. 11; Judgment in *Perfili*, C-177/94, EU:C:1996:24, at para. 11.
340. Single European Act, *OJ* L 169 (29 Jun. 1987), p. 1 (at pp. 1-28).
341. See Article 8a EEC Treaty as amended by the Single European Act, Article 7a EC Treaty as amended by the Treaty of Maastricht and Article 14 EC Treaty as amended by the Treaty of Amsterdam.
342. See, for example, M.A. Dauses, Die rechtliche Dimension des Binnenmarktes, 1 *EuZW* 1 (1990), p. 8 (at p. 10); M.R. Deckert/N.O. Lilienthal, Die Rechtsetzungskompetenzen der EG im Privatrecht, 10 *EWS* 4 (1999), p. 121 (at pp. 125-126); P. Müller-Graff, Die Rechtsangleichung zur Verwirklichung des Binnenmarktes, 24 *EuR* 2 (1989), p. 107 (at pp. 123-126).
343. See, for example, Y. Bock, *Rechtsangleichung und Regulierung im Binnenmarkt* (Nomos, 2004), at pp. 23-25; A. Epiney, Gemeinschaftsrechtlicher Umweltschutz und Verwirklichung des Binnenmarktes – "Harmonisierung" auch der Rechtsgrundlagen?, 47 *JZ* 11 (1992), p. 564 (at p. 567); P. Pescatore, Die "Einheitliche Europäische Akte" – Eine ernste Gefahr für den Gemeinsamen Markt, 21 *EuR* 2 (1986), p. 153 (at p. 157); K. Lenaerts/P. Van Nuffel, *Constitutional Law of the European Union*[2] (Sweet & Maxwell, 2005), at p. 143; P. VerLoren van Themaat, The Contributions to the Establishment of the Internal Market by the Case-Law of the Court of Justice of the European Communities, in R. Bieber/R. Dehousse/J. Pinder/J.H.H. Weiler (eds.), *1992: One European Market?* (Nomos, 1988), p. 109 (at p. 110); N. Zorn, Rechtsangleichungskompetenzen des Rates der Europäischen Gemeinschaften für die Besteuerung von Unternehmen, in J. Pelka (ed.), *Europa- und verfassungsrechtliche Grenzen der Unternehmensbesteuerung*, DStJG 30 (Dr Otto Schmidt, 2000), p. 227 (at pp. 230-231).
344. See, for example, R. Barents, The Internal Market Unlimited: Some Observations on the Legal Basis of Community Legislation, 30 *Common Market L. Rev.* 1 (1993), p. 85 (at pp. 104-105); M. Kotzur in R. Geiger/D. Khan/M. Kotzur (eds.), *EUV/AEUV*[5] (C.H. Beck), at Artikel 26 AEUV para. 4.
345. Judgment in *Commission/Parliament* (commonly referred to as *Titanium Dioxide*), C-300/89, EU:C:1991:244, at paras 14-16 and para. 23; also see Judgment in *British American Tobacco (Investments) and Imperial Tobacco*, C-491/01, EU:C:2002:741, at para. 179; Judgment in *SGL Carbon*, C-308/04 P, EU:C:2006:433, at para. 31; Judgment in *Germany and others/Kronofrance*, C-75/05 P and C-80/05 P, EU:C:2008:482, at para. 66; Judgment in *Commission/Greece*, C-369/07, EU:C:2009:428, at para. 119.

common market and an internal market were considered to be more blurry than ever.[346] Therefore, it was suggested to replace the term "common market" by the term "internal market."[347]

Since the Treaty of Lisbon, the TEU as well as the TFEU solely refer to the internal market concept. The term "common market" was completely abandoned.[348] While the definition of the internal market has not changed,[349] a protocol has been annexed to the Treaties that clarifies that the "*internal market [...] includes a system ensuring that competition is not distorted.*"[350] Considering the previous case law of the ECJ, it is thus reasonable to conclude that the internal market concept is (still) characterized by the objectives of: (1) abolishing obstacles (such as double taxation) to the free movement of goods, persons, services and capital, and (2) ensuring that competition is not distorted (by, e.g., situations of double non-taxation).[351,352]

1.2 The Legal Means to Implement the Internal Market Concept

The internal market concept reflects the EU economic policy perception of "*an open market economy with free competition, favouring an efficient allocation of resources.*"[353,354] To foster this policy objective, the free movement dimension of the internal market concept aims at eliminating the compartmentalizing effect of the

346. See Doc. CONV 325/2/02 REV 2 CONTRIB 111 (7 Mar. 2003), at p. 32 ("*The use of the two terms in the current Treaty is determined more by chance than by logic.*").
347. See Doc. CONV 325/2/02 REV 2 CONTRIB 111 (7 Mar. 2003), at p. 32.
348. See Article 2(2)(g) Treaty of Lisbon.
349. See Article 26(2) TFEU.
350. Protocol (No. 27) on the Internal Market and Competition, *OJ* C 326 (26 Oct. 2012), p. 47 (at p. 309). On the background and objectives of this protocol see, for example, P. Behrens, Der Wettbewerb im Vertrag von Lissabon, 19 *EuZW* 7 (2008), p. 193 (at p. 193); C. Nowak, Binnenmarktziel und Wirtschaftsverfassung der Europäischen Union vor und nach dem Reformvertrag von Lissabon, 44 *Europarecht* Beiheft 1 (2009), p. 129 (at pp. 188-190).
351. See J. Bast in E. Grabitz/M. Hilf/M. Nettesheim (eds.), *Das Recht der Europäischen Union*[42] (C.H. Beck, 2010), Art. 26 AEUV at para. 12; J. Englisch, *Wettbewerbsgleichheit im grenzüberschreitenden Handel* (Mohr Siebeck, 2008), at pp. 219-229; A. Hatje in J. Schwarze (ed.) *EU-Kommentar*[3] (Nomos, 2012), Artikel 26 AEUV at paras 10-14; K. Lenaerts/P. Van Nuffel, *Constitutional Law of the European Union*[2] (Sweet & Maxwell, 2005), at p. 147; P. Oliver/W. Roth, The Internal Market and the Four Freedoms, 41 *Common Market L. Rev.* 2 (2004), p. 407 (at p. 413); J. Schönfeld, *Hinzurechnungsbesteuerung und Europäisches Gemeinschaftsrecht* (Dr Otto Schmidt, 2005), at pp. 21-33.
352. Since the Treaty of Lisbon, the wording of Article 113 TFEU distinguishes between the requirement "*to ensure the establishment and the functioning of the internal market*" and "*to avoid distortion of competition.*" It would, therefore, be possible to argue that the avoidance of undistorted competition is not included in the internal market concept. However, considering the protocol on the internal market and competition (Protocol (No. 27) on the Internal Market and Competition, *OJ* C 326 [26 Oct. 2012], p. 47), such an interpretation would not be convincing.
353. Article 120 TFEU.
354. See D. Hanf in J. Pelkmans/D. Hanf/M. Chang (eds.), *The EU Internal Market in Comparative Perspective* (Peter Lang, 2008), at p. 77; W. Schön in J. Pelka (ed.), *Europa- und verfassungsrechtliche Grenzen der Unternehmensbesteuerung*, DStJG 30 (Dr Otto Schmidt, 2000), at pp. 191-195; W. Schön, 9 *EC Tax Rev.* 2 (2000), at p. 91; W. Schön in I. Richelle/W. Schön/E. Traversa (eds.), *Allocating Taxing Powers Within the European Union* (Springer, 2013), at p. 93; J. Schönfeld, *Hinzurechnungsbesteuerung und Europäisches Gemeinschaftsrecht* (Dr Otto

Member States' legal systems.[355] This is reflected by various provisions of the Treaties, first and foremost - especially in tax matters - by the fundamental freedoms: The designation "fundamental freedoms" is not a legal term, but rather a prevalent collective name for: (1) the free movement of goods (Article 28 TFEU) which, among other things, comprises the prohibition of customs duties and charges having equivalent effect (Article 30 TFEU), the prohibition of quantitative restrictions and measures having equivalent effect on imports (Article 34 TFEU) and exports (Article 35 TFEU), (2) the free movement of persons that compounds the free movement of workers (Article 45 TFEU) and the freedom of establishment (Article 49 TFEU), (3) the freedom to provide services (Article 56 TFEU), and (4) the free movement of capital and payments (Article 63 TFEU).[356] These fundamental freedoms are supplemented by the general prohibition of discrimination on grounds of nationality (Article 18 TFEU) and the right of Union citizens to move and reside freely within the EU (Article 21(1) TFEU).[357]

The fundamental freedoms as well as the free movement right of EU citizens prevent Member States from enacting or maintaining laws or administrative practices that impede free movement within the internal market.[358] However, to ensure an efficient allocation of resources, a level playing field within the internal market has to be provided for as well.[359] Therefore, the competition aspect of the internal market concept intends to avoid distortions induced by the market participants,[360] by the Member States,[361] or by differences between the Member States' legal systems.[362] From a tax perspective, the State aid rules (Article 107 TFEU) are the most relevant means to implement this aspect of the internal market.[363] Thus, tax measures favouring certain

Schmidt, 2005), at pp. 16-18; J.H.H. Weiler, 100 *Yale L. J.* 8 (1991), at pp. 2477-2478; B. Strassburger, *Die Dogmatik der EU-Grundfreiheiten* (Mohr Siebeck, 2012), at p. 8.

355. See, for example, A. Cordewener, *Europäische Grundfreiheiten und nationales Steuerrecht* (Dr Otto Schmidt, 2002), at p. 352; G. Kofler, *Doppelbesteuerungsabkommen und Europäisches Gemeinschaftsrecht* (Linde, 2007), at p. 51; B. Strassburger, *Die Dogmatik der EU-Grundfreiheiten* (Mohr Siebeck, 2012), at p. 10.
356. See A. Cordewener, *Europäische Grundfreiheiten und nationales Steuerrecht* (Dr Otto Schmidt, 2002), at p. 15; T. Kingreen, *Die Struktur der Grundfreiheiten des Europäischen Gemeinschaftsrechts* (Duncker & Humblot, 1999), at p. 20; T. Kingreen, Fundamental Freedoms, in A. von Bogdandy/J. Bast (eds.), *Principles of European Constitutional Law*[2] (Hart Publishing, 2009), p. 515 (at p. 515); R. Szudoczky, *The Sources of EU Law and Their Relationships: Lessons for the Field of Taxation* (IBFD, 2014), at pp. 136-138.
357. See A. Cordewener, *Europäische Grundfreiheiten und nationales Steuerrecht* (Dr Otto Schmidt, 2002), at p. 16.
358. See B.J.M. Terra/P.J. Wattel, *European Tax Law*[6] (Kluwer, 2012), at p. 36; concerning the question whether the fundamental freedoms also bind EU legislation see, with further references, R. Szudoczky, *The Sources of EU Law and Their Relationships: Lessons for the Field of Taxation* (IBFD, 2014), at pp. 154-161.
359. Cf. J. Pelkmans/P. Robson, 26 *JCMS* 3 (1987), at p. 183; W. Schön in J. Pelka (ed.), *Europa- und verfassungsrechtliche Grenzen der Unternehmensbesteuerung*, DStJG 30 (Dr Otto Schmidt, 2000), at p. 194.
360. Articles 101-102 TFEU.
361. Articles 106-107 TFEU.
362. Article 116 TFEU.
363. See P. Pistone/R. Szudoczy in M. Lang/P. Pistone/J. Schuch/C. Staringer (eds.), *Introduction to European Tax Law on Direct Taxation*[4] (Linde, 2015), at p. 28.

undertakings or the production of certain goods are, in so far as trade between Member States is affected, incompatible with the internal market, if competition is thereby distorted or threatens to be distorted.

The fundamental freedoms and the State aid rules are, as a means of negative integration,[364] influential factors in promoting the implementation of the internal market concept in the area of taxes. However, the degree of integration that can be accomplished by these principles is limited.[365] Anyway, the Treaties also allow for harmonization or approximation of the Member States' different laws as a means of implementing the internal market concept via positive integration. Several provisions of the TFEU provide for this possibility by specifically referring to the establishment and functioning of the internal market[366] and/or the distortion of competition caused by differences between the Member States' domestic laws.[367] But not every legal aspect that somehow relates to the internal market provides a basis for harmonization or approximation of laws. The TFEU rather requires that, thereby, the conditions for the establishment and functioning of the internal market be improved[368] – for example, by abolishing obstacles to the free movement of goods, persons, services or capital[369] – or distortions of the conditions of competition in the internal market be eliminated.[370] Moreover, with regard to the internal market, the EU shares competence with the Member States,[371] i.e., that harmonization or approximation of laws in this principal area: (1) is premised on the fact that "*the objectives of the proposed action cannot be sufficiently achieved by the Member States, either at central level or at regional and local level, but can rather, by reason of the scale or effects of the proposed action, be better achieved at Union level,*"[372] and (2) "*shall not exceed what is necessary to achieve the objectives of the Treaties.*"[373]

With regard to direct taxes, only a few steps towards positive integration have been taken so far.[374] It is hence no surprise that double taxation and double non-taxation may arise quite frequently, particularly due to the varying tax systems of the Member States. However, the example of VAT shows that even an advanced stage of

364. Opinion 1/91, EU:C:1991:490, at para. 18.
365. See G. Kofler, *Doppelbesteuerungsabkommen und Europäisches Gemeinschaftsrecht* (Linde, 2007), at pp. 122-130; also see A. Schnitger, *Die Grenzen der Einwirkungen der Grundfreiheiten des EG-Vertrages auf das Ertragsteuerrecht* (IDW, 2006).
366. Articles 81(2), 113-115, 118 TFEU.
367. Articles 113, 116-117 TFEU.
368. With regard to Article 114 TFEU see, for example, Judgment in *Germany/Parliament and Council*, C-376/98; EU:C:2000:181, at para. 83.
369. Judgment in *Spain/Council*, C-350/92, EU:C:1995:237, at para. 33; Judgment in *Germany/Parliament and Council*, C-233/94, EU:C:1997:231, at para. 19.
370. Judgment in *Commission/Council*, C-300/89, EU:C:1991:244, at para. 15; Judgment in *Spain/Council*, C-350/92, EU:C:1995:237, at para. 32.
371. Article 4(2)(a) TFEU.
372. Article 5(3) TEU; also see Protocol (No. 2) on the Application of the Principles of Subsidiarity and Proportionality, *OJ* C 326 (26 Oct. 2012), at pp. 206-209.
373. Article 5(4) TEU; also see Protocol (No. 2) on the Application of the Principles of Subsidiarity and Proportionality, *OJ* C 326 (26 Oct. 2012), at pp. 206-209.
374. For an overview see Ł. Adamczyk/A. Majdańska, The Sources of EU Law Relevant for Direct Taxation, M. Lang/P. Pistone/J. Schuch/C. Staringer (eds.), *Introduction to European Tax Law on Direct Taxation*[4] (Linde, 2015), p. 1 (at pp. 19-22).

harmonization cannot avert situations of double taxation and double non-taxation.[375] However, if these phenomena are considered to be incompatible with the internal market,[376] a remedy may still be found through negative integration.

2 THE SCOPE OF PROTECTION OF THE FUNDAMENTAL FREEDOMS

2.1 The Relevance of the Fundamental Freedoms in Tax Law

The power to tax is an essential requirement to guarantee the internal sovereignty and external independence of a state.[377] Without the ability to dispose over public funds generated through the imposition of taxes, modern western states' governments would not be able to achieve their political and economic objectives.[378] It is, therefore, unsurprising that the limitation of the national power of taxation by EU law is a sensitive subject for Member States. With regard to indirect taxation, it has nevertheless been possible to achieve extensive harmonization through positive integration.[379] This is mainly due to the immediate repercussions of indirect taxes, especially customs duties and excises, on cross-border movement and trade.[380] Taking the internal market concept seriously means, therefore, accepting harmonization in this respect.[381] Concerning VAT, it also has to be kept in mind that the first steps towards harmonization were taken at a time when the importance of this kind of tax for Member States'

375. See Chapter 2.2.
376. See Taxation in the European Union, SEC(96) 487 final (20 Mar. 1996), at p. 13 ("*[t]he Single Market is clearly not compatible with either double taxation of the same taxable base or no taxation at all*"); Opinion of the Economic and Social Committee on Taxation in the European Union, Report on the development of tax systems (SEC[96] 487 final and COM[96] 546 final), *OJ* C 296 (29 Sep. 1997), p. 37 (at p. 43: "*[d]ouble taxation or the absence of taxation is incompatible with the internal market*"); Tax co-ordination in the European Union, Working Paper, Economic Affairs Series, ECON 125 EN (European Parliament, 2000), at p. 22 ("*The Single Market has several particular implications for the taxation of employment incomes. [...] Incomes should not escape tax altogether, or be taxed at discriminatorily low rates, as a result of cross-border tax arbitrage, avoidance or evasion.*"); Commission Recommendation of 6 Dec. 2012 on aggressive tax planning, C(2012) 8806 final (6 Dec. 2012), at p. 2 ("*[t]he Single Market is clearly not compatible with either double taxation [...] or no taxation at all*").
377. See M. Lehner, Limitation of the National Power of Taxation by the Fundamental Freedoms and Non-discrimination Clauses of the EC Treaty, 9 *EC Tax Rev.* 1 (2000), p. 5 (at p. 5); M. Lehner in M. Lang/J. Schuch/C. Staringer (eds.), *Tax Treaty Law and EC Law* (Linde, 2007), at p. 21; F. Vanistendael, The European Tax Paradox: How Less Begets More, 50 *Bull. Intl. Taxn.* 11/12 (1996), p. 531 (at p. 531).
378. See C. Seiler, Das Steuerrecht unter dem Einfluss der Marktfreiheiten, 82 *StuW* 1 (2005), p. 25 (at p. 25); also see G. Kofler, Ist der Spuk des Europäischen Steuerrechts bald vorbei?, in W. Schön/C. Heber (eds.), *Grundfragen des Europäischen Steuerrechts* (Springer, 2015), p. 1 (at p. 2).
379. See Chapter 2.2.1.
380. See B.J.M. Terra/P.J. Wattel, *European Tax Law*[6] (Kluwer, 2012), at pp. 4-5; also cf. *Report on the Problems of Different Turnover Tax Systems Applied Within the Common Market* (1953) (hereinafter: *Tinbergen* Report), at p. 15.
381. Cf. Completing the Internal Market, White Paper from the Commission to the European Council, COM(85) 310 final (14 Jun. 1985), at pp. 41-43.

budgets was still quite minor.[382] Presumably, political agreement was hence easier to achieve. At any rate, the high degree of positive integration not only strongly limits the Member States' tax sovereignty, but also reduces the relevance of the fundamental freedoms in the area of indirect taxes. The ECJ's case law on indirect taxes mainly concerns questions of how to interpret the detailed and technical rules of secondary EU law and whether the Member States have correctly implemented these requirements domestically.[383] Only a few decisions deal with the impact of the fundamental freedoms.[384]

By contrast, direct taxes have remained unaffected by positive integration to a large extent.[385] This is, on the one hand, due to the fact that the Treaties - as opposed to indirect taxes - do not include provisions that explicitly address the harmonization of direct taxes.[386] Within the ambit of Articles 115-117 TFEU, positive integration is still possible. However, considering the vast harmonization of indirect taxes, the Member States are reluctant when it comes to forfeiting parts of their sovereignty in the area of direct taxation. Due to the unanimity requirement,[387] harmonization of direct taxes is, therefore, difficult to achieve.[388] This does not mean that direct taxes remain unaffected by EU law.[389] Rather, the integration of direct taxes is greatly influenced by the ECJ's jurisprudence on conflicts between the fundamental freedoms and non-harmonized domestic tax legislation.[390] This is emphasized by the ECJ regularly pointing out that *"[a]lthough [...] direct taxation does not as such fall within the purview of the [EU], the powers retained by the Member States must nevertheless be exercised consistently with [EU] law."*[391]

382. In fact, only a few Member States even had a modern VAT/GST in the form of a non-cumulative value added tax on the credit invoice method at that time. Cf. R. de la Feria, *The EU VAT System and the Internal Market* (IBFD, 2009), at p. 49.
383. See B.J.M. Terra/P.J. Wattel, *European Tax Law*[6] (Kluwer, 2012), at pp. 36-37.
384. Judgment in *Schul I*, 15/81, EU:C:1982:135; Judgment *Schul II*, 47/84, EU:C:1985:216; Judgment in *Lease Plan*, C-390/96, EU:C:1998:206; Judgment in *Société générale des grandes sources d'eaux minérales françaises*, C-361/96, EU:C:1998:282; Judgment in *Kieffer and Thill*, C-114/96, EU:C:1997:316; Judgment in *Schmelz*, C-97/09 EU:C:2010:632; Judgment in *Crédit Lyonnais*, C-388/11, EU:C:2013:541.
385. For an overview of harmonization measures in the area of direct taxes see Ł. Adamczyk/A. Majdańska in M. Lang/P. Pistone/J. Schuch/C. Staringer (eds.), *Introduction to European Tax Law on Direct Taxation*[4] (Linde, 2015), at pp. 19-22.
386. See Y. Brauner/G. Kofler, The Interaction of Tax Treaties with International Economic Laws, in R. Vann (ed.), *Global Tax Treaty Commentaries* (IBFD, 2016), at Ch. 2.1.1.
387. See B.J.M. Terra/P.J. Wattel, *European Tax Law*[6] (Kluwer, 2012), at pp. 19 and 23-24.
388. See P. Farmer, Direct Taxation and the Fundamental Freedoms, in A. Arnull/D. Chalmers (eds.), *The Oxford Handbook on European Union Law* (Oxford University Press, 2015), p. 809 (at p. 810); B.J.M. Terra/P.J. Wattel, *European Tax Law*[6] (Kluwer, 2012), at p. 209.
389. See S. van Thiel, *Free Movement of Persons and Income Tax Law: The European Court in Search of Principles* (IBFD, 2002), at pp. 21-25 and pp. 153-163.
390. For an Austrian perspective see, for example, G. Kofler, Wer hat das Sagen im Steuerrecht - EuGH (Teil 2), 19 *ÖStZ* 8 (2006), p. 154 (at pp. 154 et seq.); also cf. A. Cordewener, *Europäische Grundfreiheiten und nationales Steuerrecht* (Dr Otto Schmidt, 2002), at pp. 28-32; J. Englisch, 33 *Intertax* 8-9 (2005), at pp. 310 et seq.; M. Lang, Wohin geht das Internationale Steuerrecht?, 14 *IStR* 9 (2005), p. 289 (at pp. 289 et seq.).
391. Judgment in *Schumacker*, C-279/93, EU:C:1995:31, at para. 21; Judgment in *Safir*, C-118/96, EU:C:1998:170, at para. 21; Judgment in *Eurowings*, C-294/97, EU:C:1999:524, at para. 32; Judgment in *Vestergaard*, C-55/98, EU:C:1999:533, at para. 15; Judgment in *De Coster*,

The relevance of the fundamental freedoms for direct taxation was addressed by the ECJ for the first time in the *Avoir Fiscal* case.[392] Since then, the case law on direct taxation has rapidly evolved[393] and has had a tremendous effect on traditional pillars of domestic legislation on cross-border situations.[394] This development, *inter alia*, resulted in increasing scepticism.[395] Due to the massive impact on the Member States'

C-17/00, EU:C:2001:651, at para. 25; Judgment in *FKP Scorpio Konzertproduktionen*, C-290/04, EU:C:2006:630, at para. 30; Judgment in *Lakebrink and Peters-Lakebrink*, C-182/06, EU:C:2007:452, at para. 14; Judgment in *Strojírny Prostějov*, C-53/13, EU:C:2014:2011, at para. 23; also see, for example, Judgment in *Wielockx*, C-80/94, EU:C:1995:271, at para. 16; Judgment in *Asscher*, C-107/94, EU:C:1996:251, at para. 36; Judgment in *Futura Participations and Singer*, C-250/95, EU:C:1997:239, at para. 19; Judgment in *Imperial Chemical Industries* (hereinafter: *ICI*), C-264/96, EU:C:1998:370, at para. 19; Judgment in *Royal Bank of Scotland*, C-311/97, EU:C:1999:216, at para. 19; Judgment in *Gschwind*, C-391/97, EU:C:1999:409, at para. 20; Judgment in *Saint-Gobain*, C-307/97, EU:C:1999:438, at para. 57; Judgment in *Baars*, C-251/98, EU:C:2000:22, at para. 17; Judgment in *Verkooijen*, C-35/98, EU:C:2000:294, at para. 32; Judgment in *AMID*, C-141/99, EU:C:2000:696, at para. 19; Judgment in *Metallgesellschaft and Hoechst*, C-397/98 and C-410/98, EU:C:2001:134, at para. 37; Judgment in *Gottardo*, C-55/00, EU:C:2002:16, at para. 32; Order in *Mertens*, C-431/01, EU:C:2002:492, at para. 25; Judgment in *Danner*, C-136/00, EU:C:2002:558, at para. 28; Judgment in *Lankhorst-Hohorst*, C-324/00, EU:C:2002:749, at para. 26; Judgment in *de Groot*, C-385/00, EU:C:2002:750, at para. 75; Judgment in *Skandia and Ramstedt*, C-422/01, EU:C:2003:380, at para. 25; Judgment in *de Lasteyrie du Saillant*, C-9/02, EU:C:2004:138, at para. 44; Judgment in *Manninen*, C-319/02, EU:C:2004:484, at para. 19; Judgment in *Marks & Spencer*, C-446/03, EU:C:2005:763, at para. 29; Judgment in *Keller Holding*, C-471/04, EU:C:2006:143, at para. 28; Judgment in *N*, C-470/04, EU:C:2006:525, at para. 33; Judgment in *Kerckhaert and Morres*, C-513/04, EU:C:2006:713, at para. 15; Judgment in *Test Claimants in Class IV of the ACT Group Litigation*, C-374/04, EU:C:2006:773, at para. 36; Judgment in *Cadbury Schweppes and Cadbury Schweppes Overseas*, C-196/04, EU:C:2006:544, at para. 40; Judgment in *Oy AA*, C-231/05, EU:C:2007:439, at para. 20; Judgment in *Burda*, C-284/06, EU:C:2008:365, at para. 66; Judgment in *Amurta*, C-379/05, EU:C:2007:655, at para. 16; Judgment in *Aberdeen Property Fininvest Alpha*, C-303/07, EU:C:2009:377, at para. 24; Judgment in *Damseaux*, C-128/08, EU:C:2009:471, at para. 24; Judgment in *Commission/Italy*, C-540/07, EU:C:2009:717, at para. 28; Judgment in *Commission/Spain*, C-487/08, EU:C:2010:310, at para. 37; Judgment in *Gielen*, C-440/08, EU:C:2010:148, at para. 36; Judgment in *Commission/Germany*, C-284/09, EU:C:2011:670, at para. 44; Judgment in *A*, C-48/11, EU:C:2012:485, at para. 16; Judgment in *X*, C-498/10, EU:C:2012:635, at para. 18; Judgment in *Commission/Belgium*, C-387/11, EU:C:2012:670, at para. 36; Judgment in *Commission/Belgium*, C-383/10, EU:C:2013:364, at para. 40; also cf. Judgment in *Greece/Commission*, 57/86, EU:C:1988:284, at para. 9; Judgment in *Commission/Greece*, 127/87, EU:C:1988:331, at para. 7; Judgment in *The Queen/Secretary of State for Transport, ex parte Factortame*, C-221/89, EU:C:1991:320, at para. 14; Judgment in *Commission/United Kingdom*, C-246/89, EU:C:1991:375, at para. 12.

392. Judgment in *Commission/France* (hereinafter: *Avoir Fiscal*), 270/83, EU:C:1986:37.
393. The 2015 edition of the IBFD's ECJ Direct Tax Compass, for example, lists 239 judgments that are considered to be relevant for direct taxation (see M. Cotrut [ed.], *ECJ Direct Tax Compass 2015* [IBFD, 2015]); for an overview of the CJEU cases in the area of, or of particular interest for, direct taxation also cf. http://ec.europa.eu/taxation_customs/resources/documents/common/infringements/case_law/court_cases_direct_taxation_en.pdf (last accessed: 27 Apr. 2016).
394. See G. Kofler, *Doppelbesteuerungsabkommen und Europäisches Gemeinschaftsrecht* (Linde, 2007), at p. 37; G. Kofler in W. Schön/C. Heber (eds.), *Grundfragen des Europäischen Steuerrechts* (Springer, 2015), at p. 16; B.J.M. Terra/P.J. Wattel, *European Tax Law*[6] (Kluwer, 2012), at pp. 881 et seq.
395. See, for example, K. Ahmann, Das Ertragssteuerrecht unter dem Diktat des Europäischen Gerichtshofs? Können wir uns wehren?, 93 *DStZ* 3 (2005), p. 75 (at p. 78); L. Hinnekens, European Court Goes for Robust Tax Principles for Treaty Freedoms. What About Reasonable Exceptions and Balances?, 13 *EC Tax Rev.* 2 (2004) p. 65 (at pp. 65-67); M. Wathelet, Direct taxation and EU Law: Integration or Disintegration?, 13 *EC Tax Rev.* 1 (2004), p. 2 (at p. 3).

direct tax systems, for example, the ECJ was accused of behaving *"like a bull in the china shop of direct taxation"*[396] or like the *"'Alice in the Wonderland' of fiscal legislation."*[397] The case law was partly considered rather to be destructive,[398] than to have an integrative effect.[399] It was, therefore, even red-flagged that *"Member States will not go on accepting the Court overruling them with the flimsiest arguments forever."*[400] However, in the meantime, the future of negative integration has turned out not to be that gloomy. In fact, the ECJ seems to increasingly respect the Member States' concerns.[401] Albeit being complex, partly contradictory and maybe even chaotic,[402] the evolution of the case law can generally be assessed as having positively

396. W. Vermeend, The Court of Justice of the European Communities and Direct Taxes: "Est-ce que la justice est de ce monde"?, 5 *EC Tax Rev.* 2 (1996), p. 54 (at p. 54).
397. W. Vermeend, 5 *EC Tax Rev.* 2 (1996), at p. 55.
398. Partly, this was explained by the ECJ not having sufficient specialized knowledge in the area of direct taxes. See J. Hey, Perspektiven der Unternehmensbesteuerung, 81 *StuW* 3 (2004), p. 193 (at p. 197); W. Vermeend, 5 *EC Tax Rev.* 2 (1996), at p. 54; P.J. Wattel, 31 *Legal Issues of Economic Integration* 2 (2004), at p. 82; for other reasons see B.J.M. Terra/P.J. Wattel, *European Tax Law*[6] (Kluwer, 2012), at pp. 37-38.
399. Cf. K. van Raad, The Impact of the EC Treaty's Fundamental Freedoms Provisions on EC Member States' Taxation in Border-Crossing Situations – Current State of Affairs, 4 *EC Tax Rev.* 4 (1995), p. 190 (at p. 201); D. Williams, Asscher: the European Court and the power to destroy, 6 *EC Tax Rev.* 1 (1997), p. 4 (at p. 9).
400. W. Vermeend, 5 *EC Tax Rev.* 2 (1996), at p. 55.
401. In the literature, the question was hence raised whether *"the engine of tax harmonisation [is] sputtering."* See M. Lang, Das EuGH-Urteil in der Rechtssache D. – Gerät der Motor der Steuerharmonisierung ins Stottern?, 15 *SWI* 8 (2005), p. 365 (at pp. 374-375); also cf. A. Cordewener/E. Reimer, The Future of Most-Favoured-Nation Treatment in EC Tax Law – Did the ECJ Pull the Emergency Brake Without Real Need? – Part 1, 46 *Eur. Taxn.* 6 (2006), p. 239 (at pp. 239 et seq.); A. Cordewener/E. Reimer, 46 *Eur. Taxn.* 7 (2006), at pp. 291 et seq.; G. Kofler in W. Schön/C. Heber (eds.), *Grundfragen des Europäischen Steuerrechts* (Springer, 2015), at pp. 18-21; S. Kingston, A Light in the Darkness: Recent Developments in the ECJ's Direct Tax Jurisprudence, 44 *Common Market L. Rev.* 5 (2007), p. 1321 (at pp. 1336-1343); M. Lang, Recent Case Law of the ECJ in Direct Taxation: Trends, Tensions, and Contradictions, 18 *EC Tax Rev.* 3 (2009), p. 98 (at p. 112: *"The Court has recently been more generous to the Member States compared to the 'old days'."*); M. Lang, Eine Wende in der Rechtsprechung des EuGH zu den direkten Steuern?, in M. Hebig/K. Kaiser/K. Koschmieder/M. Oblau (eds.), *Aktuelle Entwicklungsaspekte der Unternehmensbesteuerung*, Festschrift für Wilhelm H. Wacker (Erich Schmidt Verlag, 2006), p. 365 (at pp. 365-380); M. Lang, Jüngste Tendenzen in der Rechtsprechung des EuGH zur Bedeutung der Grundfreiheiten für die direkten Steuern, in M. Beusch (ed.), Steuerrecht 2007 (Schulthess, 2007), p. 5 (at pp. 5-24); M. Lang, 2005 – Eine Wende in der steuerlichen Rechtsprechung des EuGH zu den Grundfreiheiten?, in R. Mellinghof/W. Schön/H. Viskorf (eds.), *Steuerrecht im Rechtsstaat, Festschrift für Wolfgang Spindler zum 65. Geburtstag* (Dr Otto Schmidt, 2011), p. 297 (at pp. 297 et seq.).
402. Cf. P. Farmer, Tax Law and Policy in an Adolescent European Union, 61 *Bull. Intl. Taxn.* 2 (2007), p. 42 (at p. 44: *"bewildering array of concepts in the case law"*); M.J. Graetz/A.C. Warren, Income Tax Discrimination and the Political and Economic Integration of Europe, 115 *Yale L. J.* 6 (2006), p. 1186; (at p. 1243: *"labyrinth of impossibility"*); M.J. Graetz/A.C. Warren, Income Tax Discrimination: Still Stuck in the Labyrinth of Impossibility, 121 *Yale L. J.* 5 (2012), p. 1118 (at pp. 1121-1123); B.J.M. Terra/P.J. Wattel, *European Tax Law*[6] (Kluwer, 2012), at p. 37; W. Vermeend, 5 *EC Tax Rev.* 2 (1996), at p. 55 (*"'Alice in the Wonderland' of fiscal legislation"*).

promoted integration in the area of direct taxation.[403] Concerning the case law on direct taxation, the Court can meanwhile be described as "*a balancing artist between the interests of the single internal market and the [...] legitimate interests of separate Member States to protect their tax bases.*"[404]

2.2 The Convergence and the Limits of Applying the Fundamental Freedoms

The different treatment of domestic and cross-border situations is virtually inherent to direct taxation. Whereas residents are taxed on their worldwide income (universality principle), the income of non-residents is taxed only if it is earned in or derives from sources in the respective state (principle of territoriality).[405] This fundamental distinction pervades almost the entire system of rules in Member States' domestic tax law. Thus, direct tax law turns out to be a true "playground" for all kinds of non-discrimination provisions.[406] Since the TFEU contains a multiplicity of rules that prohibit a different treatment of comparable situations,[407] it was in effect only a question of time until these rules started to practically affect the domestic tax systems of Member States. The fundamental freedoms and the general prohibition of discrimination on grounds of nationality (Article 18 TFEU)[408] are the most important means in this respect.[409]

---

403. See, for example, M.J. Graetz/A.C. Warren, 121 *Yale L. J.* 5 (2012), at p. 1121; G. Kofler, *Doppelbesteuerungsabkommen und Europäisches Gemeinschaftsrecht* (Linde, 2007), at p. 42; R. Mason, Tax Discrimination and Capital Neutrality, 2 *World Tax J.* 2 (2010), p. 126 (at p. 137).
404. B.J.M. Terra/P.J. Wattel, *European Tax Law*[6] (Kluwer, 2012), at p. 37.
405. See M. Lang, *Introduction to the Law of Double Taxation Conventions*[2] (Linde, 2013), at pp. 27-28, para. 4; B.J.M. Terra/P.J. Wattel, *European Tax Law*[6] (Kluwer, 2012), at pp. 881-884.
406. G. Kofler, *Doppelbesteuerungsabkommen und Europäisches Gemeinschaftsrecht* (Linde, 2007), at p. 103.
407. See, for example, M. Bell, *Anti-Discrimination Law and the European Union* (Oxford University Press, 2002), at pp. 33-120; K. Lenaerts/P. Van Nuffel, *Constitutional Law of the European Union*[2] (Sweet & Maxwell, 2005), at pp. 124.
408. In direct tax matters, the practical relevance of Article 18 TFEU is rather low. So far, the general prohibition of non-discrimination on grounds of nationality was applied independently only in the *Schempp* case (Judgment in *Schempp*, C-403/03, EU:C:2005:446; also cf. Judgment in *Commission/Greece*, C-155/09). In the past, the ECJ assumed that Article 18 TFEU only applies independently "*on [...] rare occasions*" (Judgment in *Collins and Patricia Im- und Export/Imtrat and EMI Electrola*, C-92/92, EU:C:1993:838, at para. 17). Since the Treaty of Maastricht introduced EU citizenship (Article 20 TFEU) and the corresponding right to move and reside freely within the territory of the Member States (Article 21 TFEU), the general prohibition of non-discrimination on grounds of nationality have become more important, though. It especially applies to EU citizens who are not economically active (Judgment in *Trojani*, C-456/02, EU:C:2004:488, at para. 43; Judgment in *Bidar*, C-209/03, EU:C:2005:169, at para. 37; Judgment in *Förster*, C-158/07, EU:C:2008:630, 39).
409. Considering Article 6 TEU, the Charter of Fundamental Rights of the European Union (*OJ* C 303 [14 Dec. 2007], at pp. 1 et seq.) may also become more important in the area of taxation. Cf. D. Gutmann, Taking Human Rights Seriously: Some Introductory Words on Human Rights, Taxation and the EU, in G. Kofler/M.P. Maduro/P. Pistone (eds.), *Human Rights and Taxation in Europe and the World* (IBFD, 2011), p. 105 (at pp. 105 et seq.); P. Pistone, The EU Law Dimension of Human Rights in Tax Matters, in C. Brokelind (ed.), *Principles of Law: Function, Status and Impact in EU Tax Law* (IBFD, 2014), p. 91 (at pp. 91 et seq.).

According to the ECJ, Article 18 TFEU is a specific enunciation of the general principle of equality,[410] which is *"one of the fundamental principles of [EU] law."*[411] Unless a differentiation is objectively justified,[412] it is thus required *"that comparable situations must not be treated differently and that different situations must not be treated in the same way."*[413] However, according to the wording of Article 18 TFEU, any discrimination on grounds of nationality is prohibited *"without prejudice to any special provisions [of the Treaties]."* Thus, the general prohibition of non-discrimination on grounds of nationality applies independently only if the respective situation is not covered by a more specific non-discrimination rule of the Treaties.[414] This does not mean, though, that the fundamental freedoms incorporate a different standard of

410. Judgment in *Erpelding*, 84/87, EU:C:1988:245, at para. 39; Judgment in *Dowling*, C-85/90, EU:C:1992:402, at para. 21; Judgment in *Pastoors and Trans-Cap*, C-29/95, EU:C:1997:28, at para 14; Judgment in *Commission/Italy*, C-224/00, EU:C:2002:185, at para. 14.

411. Judgment in *Überschär*, 810/89, EU:C:1980:228, at para. 16; Judgment in *ČEZ*, C-115/08, EU:C:2009:660, at para. 89.

412. Judgment in *Ruckdeschel and others*, 117/76 and 16/77, EU:C:1977:160, at para. 7; Judgment in *Moulins and huileries de Pont-à-Mousson*, 124/76, EU:C:1977:161, at para. 17; Judgment in *Scholten-Honig*, 125/77, EU:C:1978:187, at para. 27; Judgment in *Klensch*, 201/85, EU:C:1986:439, at para. 9; Judgment in *SAFA*, C-359/89, EU:C:1991:145, at para. 23; Judgment in *Maier*, C-236/90, EU:C:1992:311, at para. 25; Judgment in *Bakers of Nailsea*, C-27/97, EU:C:1997:188, at para. 27.

413. Judgment in *Garcia Avello*, C-148/02, EU:C:2003:539, at para. 31; Judgment in *Azienda Agro-Zootecnica Franchini and Eolica di Altamura*, C-2/10, EU:C:2011:502, at para. 64; Judgment in *Hungary/Commission*, C-31/13 P, EU:C:2014:70, at para. 73; also cf. Judgment in *SFI*, C-85/97, EU:C:1998:552, at para. 30; Judgment in *Jippers and others*, C-189/01, EU:C:2001:420, at para. 128; Judgment in *Denkavit*, C-507/99, EU:C:2002:4, at para. 44; Judgment in *Omega and others*, C-122/00, EU:C:2002:161, at para. 79; Judgment in *Commission/Portugal*, C-334/03, EU:C:2005:623, at para. 24; also cf. Judgment in *Schumacker*, C-279/93, EU:C:1995:31, at para. 30; Judgment in *Wielockx*, C-80/94, EU:C:1995:271, at para. 17; Judgment in *Asscher*, C-107/94, EU:C:1996:251, at para. 40; Judgment in *Royal Bank of Scotland*, C-311/97, EU:C:1999:216, at para. 26; Judgment in *Gschwind*, C-391/97, EU:C:1999:409, at para. 21; Judgment in *Kerckhaert and Morres*, C-513/04, EU:C:2006:713, at para. 19; Judgment in *Meindl*, C-329/05, EU:C:2007:57, at para. 22; Judgment in *Talotta*, C-383/05, EU:C:2007:181, at para. 18; Judgment in *Lakebrink and Peters-Lakebrink*, C-182/06, EU:C:2007:452, at para. 27; Judgment in *Columbus Container Services*, C-298/05, EU:C:2007:754, at para. 41; Judgment in *Gielen*, C-440/08, EU:C:2010:148; at para. 38; Judgment in *Commission/Hungary*, C-253/09, EU:C:2011:795, at para. 50; Judgment in *Commission/Netherlands*, C-542/09, EU:C:2012:346, at para. 41; Judgment in *Commission/Estonia*, C-39/10, EU:C:2012:282, at para. 48; Judgment in *Banco Bilbao Vizcaya Argentaria*, C-157/10, EU:C:2011:813, at para. 41; Judgment in *Bouanich*, C-375/12, EU:C:2014:138, at para. 45.

414. Judgment in *Commission/Greece*, 305/87, EU:C:1989:218, at para. 13; Judgment in *Commission/United Kingdom*, C-246/89, EU:C:1991:375, at para. 17; Judgment in *Masgio*, C-10/90, EU:C:1991:107, at para. 12; Judgment in *Merci Convenzionali Porto di Genova*, C-179/90, EU:C:1991:464, at para. 11; Judgment in *Halliburton Services*, C-1/93, EU:C:1994:127, at para. 12; Judgment in *Skanavi and Chryssanthakopoulos*, C-193/94, EU:C:1996:70, at para. 20; Judgment in *Mora Romero*, C-131/96, EU:C:1997:317, at para. 10; Judgment in *Gilly*, C-336/96, EU:C:1998:221, at para. 37; Judgment in *Royal Bank of Scotland*, C-311/97, EU:C:1999:216, at para. 20; Judgment in *Vestergaard*, C-55/98, EU:C:1999:533, at para. 16; Judgment in *Baars*, C-251/98, EU:C:2000:22, at para. 23; Judgment in *Metallgesellschaft and Hoechst*, C-397/98 and C-410/98, EU:C:2001:134, at para. 38; Judgment in *Oteiza Olazabal*, C-100/01, EU:C:2002:712, at para. 25; Judgment in *AMOK*, C-289/02, EU:C:2003:669, at para. 25; Judgment in *Weigel*, C-387/01, EU:C:2004:256, at para. 57; Judgment in *Laval un Partneri*, C-341/05, EU:C:2007:809, at para. 54; Judgment in *Attanasio*

protection for cross-border situations than Article 18 TFEU. Within their respective ambit, Articles 45,[415] 49,[416] 56[417] and 63[418] TFEU rather implement the general prohibition of discrimination on grounds of nationality.[419,420] Domestic tax rules which are incompatible with the fundamental freedoms are consequently also incompatible

Group, C-384/08, EU:C:2010:133, at para. 37; Judgment in *Hervis Sport- és Divatkereskedelmi*, C-385/12, EU:C:2014:47, at para. 25; Judgment in *Schiebel Aircraft*, C-474/12, EU:C:2014:2139, at para. 20.

415. Judgment in *Donà/Mantero*, 13/76, EU:C:1976:115, at para. 6; Judgment in *Commission/Greece*, 305/87, EU:C:1989:218, at para. 12; Judgment in *Masgio*, C-10/90, EU:C:1991:107, at para. 13; Judgment in *Merci Convenzionali Porto di Genova*, C-179/90, EU:C:1991:464, at para. 12; Judgment in *Scholz*, C-419/92, EU:C:1994:62, at para. 6; Judgment in *Mora Romero*, C-131/96, EU:C:1997:317, at para. 11; Judgment in *Gilly*, C-336/96, EU:C:1998:221, para. 38; Judgment in *Royal Bank of Scotland*, C-311/97, EU:C:1999:216, at para. 20; Judgment in *Baars*, C-251/98, EU:C:2000:22, at para. 24; Judgment in *Metallgesellschaft and Hoechst*, C-397/98 and C-410/98, EU:C:2001:134, at para. 39; Judgment in *Oteiza Olazabal*, C-100/01, EU:C:2002:712, at paras 24-25; Judgment in *Weigel*, C-387/01, EU:C:2004:256, at paras 58-59; Judgment in *Schiebel Aircraft*, C-474/12, EU:C:2014:2139, at paras 20-21.

416. Judgment in *Reyners*, 2/74, EU:C:1974:68, at para. 16; Judgment in *Van Ameyde/UCI*, 90/76, EU:C:1977:101, at para. 27; Judgment in *Commission/Italy*, 63/86, EU:C:1988:9, at para. 12; Judgment in *Commission/Greece*, 305/87, EU:C:1989:218, at para. 12; Judgment in *Commission/United Kingdom*, C-246/89, EU:C:1991:375, at para. 18; Judgment in *Commerzbank*, C-330/91, EU:C:1993:303, at para. 21; Judgment in *Halliburton Services*, C-1/93, EU:C:1994:127, at para. 12; Judgment in *Skanavi and Chryssanthakopoulos*, C-193/94, EU:C:1996:70, at para. 21; Judgment in *Royal Bank of Scotland*, C-311/97, EU:C:1999:216, at para. 20; Judgment in *Baars*, C-251/98, EU:C:2000:22, at para. 24; Judgment in *Metallgesellschaft and Hoechst*, C-397/98 and C-410/98, EU:C:2001:134, at para. 39; Judgment in *Attanasio Group*, C-384/08, EU:C:2010:133, at para. 37; Judgment in *Hervis Sport- és Divatkereskedelmi*, C-385/12, EU:C:2014:47, at para. 25; Judgment in *Schiebel Aircraft*, C-474/12, EU:C:2014:2139, at paras 20-21.

417. Judgment in *Donà/Mantero*, 13/76, EU:C:1976:115, at para. 6; Judgment in *Van Ameyde/UCI*, 90/76, EU:C:1977:101, at para. 27; Judgment in *Commission/Italy*, 63/86, EU:C:1988:9, at para. 12; Judgment in *Commission/Greece*, 305/87, EU:C:1989:218, at para. 12; Judgment in *Commerzbank*, C-330/91, EU:C:1993:303, at para. 21; Judgment in *Royal Bank of Scotland*, C-311/97, EU:C:1999:216, at para. 20; Judgment in *Vestergaard*, C-55/98, EU:C:1999:533, at para. 17; Judgment in *AMOK*, C-289/02, EU:C:2003:669, at para. 26; Judgment in *Laval un Partneri*, C-341/05, EU:C:2007:809, at para. 55.

418. Judgment in *Cassa di Risparmio di Firenze and others*, C-222/04, EU:C:2006:8, at para. 99; Judgment in *Hollmann*, C-443/06, EU:C:2007:600, at para. 29; Judgment in *Lammers und Van Cleef*, C-105/07, EU:C:2008:24, at para. 14; Judgment in *SGI*, C-311/08, EU:C:2010:26, at paras 31-32; Judgment in *Missionswerk Werner Heukelbach*, C-25/10, EU:C:2011:65, at para. 19; Judgment in *Schröder*, C-450/09, EU:C:2011:198, at para. 29; Opinion of AG Colomer in *D*, C-376/03, EU:C:2004:663, at point 92 (FN 52).

419. On the relationship between the free movement of goods and the general prohibition of discrimination on grounds of nationality see A. Epiney in C. Calliess/M. Ruffert (eds.), *EUV/AEUV*[4] (C.H. Beck, 2011), AEUV Art. 12 MN 6; K. Spies, *Die Kapitalverkehrsfreiheit in Konkurrenz zu den anderen Grundfreiheiten* (LexisNexis, 2015), at pp. 290-291.

420. See A. Epiney in C. Calliess/M. Ruffert (eds.), *EUV/AEUV*[4] (C.H. Beck, 2011), AEUV Art. 12 MN 3 et seq.; P. Farmer/R. Lyal, *EC Tax Law* (Clarendon Press, 1994), at p. 310; E. Reimer in M. Lehner (ed.), *Grundfreiheiten im Steuerrecht der EU-Staaten* (C.H. Beck, 2000), at pp. 73-74; K. Spies, *Die Kapitalverkehrsfreiheit in Konkurrenz zu den anderen Grundfreiheiten* (LexisNexis, 2015), at p. 281; O. Thömmes, Verbote der Diskriminierung von Steuerausländern und Steuerinländern, in M. Lehner (ed.), *Steuerrecht im Europäischen Binnenmarkt*, DStJG 19 (Dr Otto Schmidt, 1996), p. 81 (at pp. 84-85); A. von Bogdandy in E. Grabitz/M. Hilf/M. Nettesheim (eds.), *Das Recht der Europäischen Union*[54] (C.H. Beck, 2014), AEUV Art. 12 MN 55 et seq.

with Article 18 TFEU[421] and, vice versa, domestic tax rules that are compatible with the fundamental freedoms are also compatible with Article 18 TFEU.[422] The fundamental freedoms and the general prohibition of non-discrimination are, therefore, essentially characterized by a uniform dogmatic concept.[423] This conclusion is teleologically substantiated insofar as all these non-discrimination provisions are legal means to implement the internal market concept.[424],[425] Considerations related to any fundamental freedom can hence be readily transposed to the interpretation of another fundamental freedom.[426] In the literature, this is commonly referred to as the convergence of the fundamental freedoms.[427]

It must nevertheless be kept in mind that each freedom protects a particular economic dimension of the internal market concept.[428] Depending on the facts of the

421. Judgment in *Commission/Greece*, 305/87, EU:C:1989:218, at para. 12; Judgment in *Commission/United Kingdom*, C-246/89, EU:C:1991:375, at para. 18; Judgment in *Commission/France*, C-334/94, EU:C:1996:90, at para. 13; Judgment in *Royal Bank of Scotland*, C-311/97, EU:C:1999:216, at para. 20; also cf. Judgment in *Donà/Mantero*, 13/76, EU:C:1976:115, at para. 19.
422. Judgment in *Van Ameyde/UCI*, 90/76, EU:C:1977:101, at para. 27; Judgment in *Höfner and Elser*, C-41/90, EU:C:1991:161, at para. 36; Judgment in *Werner*, C-112/91, EU:C:1993:27, at para. 20.
423. See G. Kofler, *Doppelbesteuerungsabkommen und Europäisches Gemeinschaftsrecht* (Linde, 2007), at pp. 45-47; F. Vanistendael, A comparative and economic approach to equality in European Taxation, in R. Gocke/D. Gosch/M. Lang (eds.), *Körperschaftsteuer, Internationales Steuerrecht, Doppelbesteuerung*, Festschrift für Franz Wassermeyer zum 65. Geburtstag (C.H. Beck, 2005), p. 523 (at p. 534).
424. Opinion 1/91, EU:C:1991:490, at para. 18.
425. See J. Englisch, 33 *Intertax* 8/9 (2005), at p. 313; J. Englisch, *Wettbewerbsgleichheit im grenzüberschreitenden Handel* (Mohr Siebeck, 2008), at pp. 194-195; G. Kofler, *Doppelbesteuerungsabkommen und Europäisches Gemeinschaftsrecht* (Linde, 2007), at pp. 46-47; F. Vanistendael in R. Gocke/D. Gosch/M. Lang (eds.), *Körperschaftsteuer, Internationales Steuerrecht, Doppelbesteuerung*, Festschrift für Franz Wassermeyer zum 65. Geburtstag (C.H. Beck, 2005), at p. 534.
426. In the literature, the ECJ's decision in the *D.* case is mentioned as an example in this respect (see G. Kofler, *Doppelbesteuerungsabkommen und Europäisches Gemeinschaftsrecht* [Linde, 2007], at p. 46 [FN 76]). The Court thereby reverted to the *Schumacker* doctrine, which was developed with respect to the freedom of workers (Judgment in *Schumacker*, C-279/93, EU:C:1995:31, at paras 31-35), when interpreting the freedom of capital (Judgment in *D*, C-376/03, EU:C:2005:424, at paras 31-38). See G. Kofler/C.P. Schindler, "Dancing with Mr D": The ECJ's Denial of Most-Favoured-Nation Treatment in the "D" case, 45 *Eur. Taxn.* 12 (2005), p. 530 (at pp. 534-535); A. Schnitger, EuGH: Vermögensteuer-Freibeträge in Holland, weil keine Vermögensteuer in Deutschland?, 13 *IStR* 22 (2004), p. 793 (at p. 801); also cf. Opinion of AG Colomer in *D.*, C-376/03, EU:C:2004:663, at points 52-58; Opinion of AG Tizzano in *SEVIC Systems*, C-411/03, EU:C:2005:762, at point 77.
427. See P. Behrens, Die Konvergenz der wirtschaftlichen Freiheiten im europäischen Gemeinschaftsrecht, 30 *EuR* 2 (1992), p. 145 (at pp. 145-162); M. Eberhartinger, Konvergenz und Neustrukturierung der Grundfreiheiten, 8 *EWS* 2 (1997), p. 43 (at pp. 43-52); A. Cordewener, *Europäische Grundfreiheiten und nationales Steuerrecht* (Dr Otto Schmidt, 2002), at pp. 103-105; J. Englisch, 33 *Intertax* 8/9 (2005), at p. 313; J. Englisch, Taxation of Cross-Border Dividends and EC Fundamental Freedoms, 38 *Intertax* 4 (2010), p. 197 (at p. 199); H.D. Jarass, Elemente einer Dogmatik der Grundfreiheiten II, 35 *EuR* 5 (2000), p. 705 (at p. 706); G. Kofler, *Doppelbesteuerungsabkommen und Europäisches Gemeinschaftsrecht* (Linde, 2007), at p. 46; K. Simader, *Withholding Taxes and the Fundamental Freedoms* (Kluwer, 2014), at pp. 50-56; also cf. P. Oliver/W. Roth, 41 *Common Market L. Rev.* 2 (2004), at pp. 439-440.
428. See A. Cordewener, *Europäische Grundfreiheiten und nationales Steuerrecht* (Dr Otto Schmidt, 2002), at p. 328; G. Kofler, *Doppelbesteuerungsabkommen und Europäisches*

case, it is therefore, possible that several freedoms may be simultaneously applicable.[429] The converging interpretation of the fundamental freedoms makes it largely expendable to determine the "preferentially" applicable free movement provision from a practical point of view,[430,431] which does not mean that it is dogmatically

Gemeinschaftsrecht (Linde, 2007), at p. 47; W. Schön, Europäische Kapitalverkehrsfreiheit und nationales Steuerrecht, in W. Schön (ed.), *Gedächtnisschrift für Brigitte Knobbe-Keuk* (Dr Otto Schmidt, 1997), p. 743 (at pp. 749-750); W. Schön, Der Kapitalverkehr mit Drittstaaten und das internationale Steuerrecht, in R. Gocke/D. Gosch/M. Lang (eds.), *Körperschaftsteuer, Internationales Steuerrecht, Doppelbesteuerung*, Festschrift für Franz Wassermeyer zum 65. Geburtstag (C.H. Beck, 2005), p. 489 (at p. 500); also cf. T. Kingreen, *Die Struktur der Grundfreiheiten des Europäischen Gemeinschaftsrechts* (Duncker & Humblot, 1999), at p. 76; K. Spies, *Die Kapitalverkehrsfreiheit in Konkurrenz zu den anderen Grundfreiheiten* (LexisNexis, 2015), at pp. 144-147.

429. Opinion of AG Alber in *Baars*, C-251/98, EU:C:2000:205, at point 14; Opinion of AG Stix-Hackl in *Centro di Musicologia Walter Stauffer*, C-386/04, EU:C:2005:785, at points 35-38; also see, for example, W.C. Haslehner, Das Konkurrenzverhältnis der Europäischen Grundfreiheiten in der Rechtsprechung des EuGH zu den direkten Steuern, 17 *IStR* 16 (2008), p. 565 (at p. 566); O.H. Jacobs, Corporation Income Tax Systems in the European Union – An Analysis of their Effects on Competition and Reform Proposals, 27 *Intertax* 8/9 (1999), p. 264 (at p. 271); G. Kofler, *Doppelbesteuerungsabkommen und Europäisches Gemeinschaftsrecht* (Linde, 2007), at pp. 945-946; W. Schön in R. Gocke/D. Gosch/M. Lang (eds.), *Körperschaftsteuer, Internationales Steuerrecht, Doppelbesteuerung*, Festschrift für Franz Wassermeyer zum 65. Geburtstag (C.H. Beck, 2005), at pp. 498-499; D. Smit, The Relationship Between the Free Movement of Capital and the Other EC Treaty Freedoms in Third Country Relationships in the Field of Direct Taxation: a Question of Exclusivity, Parallelism or Causality?, 16 *EC Tax Rev.* 6 (2007), p. 252 (at pp. 264-265); also cf. Judgment in *Svensson and Gustavsson*, C-484/93, EU:C:1995:379, at paras 7-11; Judgment in *Konle*, C-302/97, EU:C:1999:271, at para. 22; Judgment in *Canal Satélite*, C-390/99, EU:C:2002:34, at para. 29; Judgment in *Commission/Italy*, C-279/00, EU:C:2002:89, at paras 36-38; Judgment in *Commission/France*, C-334/02, EU:C:2004:129, at paras 23-25; Judgment in *Calafiori*, C-451/03, EU:C:2006:208, at paras 31-35; Judgment in *Test Claimants in Class IV of the ACT Group Litigation*, C-374/04, EU:C:2006:773, at paras 37-38; Judgment in *Test Claimants in the FII Group Litigation*, C-446/04, EU:C:2006:774, at para. 36; Judgment in *X and Passenheim-van Schoot*, C-155/08 and C-157/08, EU:C:2009:368, at para. 40; Judgment in *DMC*, C-164/12, EU:C:2014:20, at para. 31; Judgment in *Bouanich*, C-375/12, EU:C:2014:138, at paras 30-31.

430. Opinion of AG Cosmas in *Albore*, C-423/98, EU:C:2000:158, at points 38 and para. 41; also see A. Cordewener/G. Kofler/C.P. Schindler, Free Movement of Capital and Third Countries: Exploring the Outer Boundaries with *Lasertec*, *A and B* and *Holböck*, 47 *Eur. Taxn.* 8 (2007), p. 371 (at p. 373); A. Glaesner in J. Schwarze (ed.), *EU-Kommentar*[3] (Nomos, 2012), AEUV Artikel 63 at m.no 11; W.C. Haslehner, 17 *IStR* 16 (2008), at p. 570; G. Kofler, *Doppelbesteuerungsabkommen und Europäisches Gemeinschaftsrecht* (Linde, 2007), at p. 946; D. Smit, *EU Freedoms, Non-EU Countries and Company Taxation* (Kluwer, 2012), at p. 447; K. Spies, *Die Kapitalverkehrsfreiheit in Konkurrenz zu den anderen Grundfreiheiten* (LexisNexis, 2015), at pp. 170-173; also cf. P. Wattel, Test Claimants in the FII Group Litigation (FII2). Equivalence of the exemption and imputation methods. Dividends from third countries. Free movement of capital. Court of Justice, 6 *H&I* 3 (2013), p. 5 (at p. 24).

431. This is considered to be the reason why the ECJ sometimes (cf., e.g., Judgment in *Safir*, C-118/96, EU:C:1998:170, at para. 35; Judgment in *Ambry*, C-410/96, EU:C:1998:578, at para. 40; Judgment in *X and Y*, C-200/09, EU:C:1999:566, at para. 30; Judgment in *Baars*, C-251/98, EU:C:2000:205, at para. 42; Judgment in *Verkooijen*, C-35/98, EU:C:2000:294, at para. 63; Judgment in *Albore*, C-423/98, EU:C:2000:401, at para. 25; Judgment in *Metallgesellschaft and Hoechst*, C-397/98 and C-410/98, EU:C:2001:134, at para. 75; Judgment in *Danner*, C-136/00, EU:C:2002:558, at para. 58; Judgment in *Skandia and Ramstedt*, C-422/01, EU:C:2003:380, at para. 60; Judgment in *Keller Holding*, C-471/04, EU:C:2006:143, at para. 51; Judgment in *Commission/Portugal*, C-345/05, EU:C:2006:685, at para. 45; Judgment in *Commission/Sweden*, C-104/06, EU:C:2007:40, at para. 37; Judgment in *Rewe Zentralfinanz*, C-347/04,

impossible.[432] However, the delimitation becomes practically important insofar as the scope of application of the fundamental freedoms is consciously limited. For example, the freedom of movement for workers "*shall not apply to employment in the public service,*"[433] the freedom of establishment – as well as the freedom to provide services[434] – "*shall not apply, so far as any given Member State is concerned, to activities which in that State are connected, even occasionally, with the exercise of official authority,*"[435] and the free movement of capital "*shall be without prejudice to the right of Member States [...] to apply the relevant provisions of their tax law which distinguish between taxpayers who are not in the same situation with regard to their place of residence or with regard to the place where their capital is invested,*" unless such provisions "*constitute a means of arbitrary discrimination or a disguised restriction on the free movement of capital and payments.*"[436] Moreover, the free movement of capital and payments also applies in relation to third countries, whereas the other fundamental freedoms cannot be relied on in such cases.[437] Since the ambit of some fundamental freedoms is thus partially limited compared to other fundamental freedoms, the

---

EU:C:2007:194, at para. 71; Judgment in *Lammers & Van Cleeff*, C-105/07, EU:C:2008:24, at para. 35) abstains from determining the compatibility of the domestic legislation at hand in the light of a – potentially applicable – fundamental freedom, if a breach of another fundamental freedom was already found. Cf. Opinion of AG Kokott in *Bouanich*, C-265/04, EU:C:2005:479, at FN 57; Opinion of AG Stix-Hackl in *Fidium Finanz*, C-452/04, EU:C:2006:182, at points 57-60; also cf. H.-J. Aigner/U. Scheuler/M. Stefaner, General Report, in M. Lang/H.-J. Aigner/U. Scheuerle/M. Stefaner (eds.), *CFC Legislation* (Linde, 2004), p. 13 (at p. 41); D. Smit, 16 *EC Tax Rev.* 6 (2007), at p. 255.

432. See D. Gosch/J. Schönfeld, Kapitalverkehrsfreiheit und Drittstaaten – Ein (vorläufiger) Zwischenstand, 24 *IStR* 20 (2015), p. 755 (at p. 757); also cf. M. Schauer in A. Kletečka/M. Schauer (eds.), *ABGB-ON*1.01 § 6 at MN 12; also see Judgment in *Schindler*, C-275/92, EU:C:1994:119, at paras 21-30; Judgment in *Commission/Italy*, C-158/94, EU:C:1997:500, at paras 14-18; Judgment in *Karner*, C-71/02, EU:C:2004:181, at para. 47; Judgment in *Omega*, C-36/02, EU:C:2004:614, at para. 27; Judgment in *Burmanjer and others*, C-20/03, EU:C:2005:307, at paras 33-35; Judgment in *Cadbury Schweppes and Cadbury Schweppes Overseas*, C-196/04, EU:C:2006:544, at paras 32-33; Judgment in *Oy AA*, C-231/05, EU:C:2007:439, at para. 24; Judgment in *Geurts and Vogten*, C-464/05, EU:C:2007:631, at para. 16; Judgment in *Lidl Belgium*, C-414/06, EU:C:2008:278, at para. 16; Judgment in *Burda*, C-284/06, EU:C:2008:365, at para. 74; Judgment in *Aberdeen Property Fininvest Alpha*, C-303/07, EU:C:2009:377, at para. 35; Judgment in *Glaxo Wellcome*, C-182/08, EU:C:2009:559, at para. 51; Judgment in *SGI*, C-311/08, EU:C:2010:26, at paras 23-37; Judgment in *Dijkman and Dijkman-Lavaleije*, C-233/09, EU:C:2010:397, at paras 33-36; Judgment in *Josemans*, C-137/09, EU:C:2010:774, at para. 50; Judgment in *DMC*, C-164/12, EU:C:2014:20, at paras 29-38.
433. Article 45(4) TFEU.
434. Article 62 TFEU.
435. Article 51 TFEU. Moreover, according to this provision, "*[t]he European Parliament and the Council, acting in accordance with the ordinary legislative procedure, may rule that the [freedom of establishment] shall not apply to certain activities.*"
436. Article 65(1)(a) and (3) TFEU.
437. With regard to the freedom of establishment see Opinion 1/94, EU:C:1994:384, at para. 81; Order in *Lasertec*, C-492/04, EU:C:2007:273, at para. 27; Order in *A and B*, C-102/05, EU:C:2007:275, at para. 29; Judgment in *Holböck*, C-157/05, EU:C:2007:297, at para. 28; Order in *Stahlwerk Ergste Westig*, C-415/06, EU:C:2007:651, at para. 18; with regard to the free movement to provide services see Opinion 1/94, EU:C:1994:384, at para. 81; Judgment in *Fidium Finanz*, C-452/04, EU:C:2006:631, at para. 25; with regard also to the other freedoms see K. Spies, *Die Kapitalverkehrsfreiheit in Konkurrenz zu den anderen Grundfreiheiten* (LexisNexis, 2015), at pp. 343-344 (with regard to the free movement of goods), pp. 374-375 (with regard to the freedom of establishment), p. 564 (with regard to the general right of EU

question arises whether a fundamental freedom that is not limited in such a way may apply to situations that are excluded from the ambit of another fundamental freedom which would otherwise be applicable.[438]

The fundamental freedoms protect cross-border economic activities from being discriminated against through, *inter alia*, domestic legislation.[439] An economic activity may consist of various elements; for example, if the participation in a lottery requires purchasing a ticket, the prohibition of the importation of such tickets not only restricts the operation of the lottery as such, but also adversely affects the cross-border movement of tangible objects. However, according to the ECJ, the sale of tickets "*cannot be considered independently of the lottery to which they relate.*"[440] Thus, it has to be examined whether several coequal economic activities are at hand or only one economic activity which also includes elements that are not ends in themselves, but rather inevitably linked with and hence subordinated to the predominant activity.[441] On the basis of the identified economic activities it can be determined which fundamental freedoms are applicable.[442] Whether several coequal economic activities or only various elements of one economic activity are at hand is difficult to determine, especially if cross-border investments are concerned. The acquisition of real estate, for example, can be considered an investment of capital, which – in a cross-border context – is covered by the free movement of capital.[443] However, if the investment ultimately

citizens to move and reside freely within the territory of the Member States), pp. 595-597 (with regard to the free movement of workers); pp. 627-628 (with regard to the freedom to provide services).

438. See W. Schön, Kapitalverkehrsfreiheit und Niederlassungsfreiheit, in T. Ackermann/J. Köndgen (eds.), *Privat- und Wirtschaftsrecht in Europa, Festschrift für Wulf-Henning Roth zum 70. Geburtstag* (C.H. Beck, 2015), p. 551 (at p. 575); K. Spies, *Die Kapitalverkehrsfreiheit in Konkurrenz zu den anderen Grundfreiheiten* (LexisNexis, 2015), at pp. 199-204.

439. However, a citizen who is not economically active may rely on Article 18 TFEU, "*where he has been lawfully resident in the host Member State for a certain time or possesses a residence permit*" (Judgment in *Trojani*, C-456/02, EU:C:2004:488, at para. 43; Judgment in *Bidar*, C-209/03, EU:C:2005:169, at para. 37; Judgment in *Förster*, C-158/07, EU:C:2008:630, at para. 39).

440. Judgment in *Schindler*, C-275/92, EU:C:1994:119, at para. 22.

441. Judgment in *Schindler*, C-275/92, EU:C:1994:119, at paras 21-30; Judgment in *Commission/Italy*, C-158/94, EU:C:1997:500, at paras 14-18; Judgment in *Karner*, C-71/02, EU:C:2004:181, at para. 47; Judgment in *Omega*, C-36/02, EU:C:2004:614, at paras 23-27; Judgment in *Burmanjer and others*, C-20/03, EU:C:2005:307, at paras 33-35; Judgment in *Josemans*, C-137/09, EU:C:2010:774, at paras 44-50; Judgment in *Football Association Premier League and others*, C-403/08 and C-429/08, EU:C:2011:631, at para. 81.

442. Since lottery activities, for example, "*are […] not activities relating to 'goods', [but] are […] to be regarded as 'services' […] within the meaning of [Article 57 TFEU]*", they "*accordingly fall within the scope of [Article 56 TFEU].*" See Judgment in *Schindler*, C-275/92, EU:C:1994:119, at paras 25-26 and para. 37.

443. Judgment in *Trummer und Mayer*, C-222/97, EU:C:1999:143, at paras 21-22; Judgment in *Konle*, C-302/97, EU:C:1999:271, at para. 22; Judgment in *Albore*, C-423/98, EU:C:2000:401, at para. 16; Judgment in *Reisch and others*, C-515/99, C-519/99 to C-524/99 and C-526/99 to C-540/99, EU:C:2002:135, at para. 30; Judgment in *Salzmann*, C-300/01, EU:C:2003:283, at para. 39; Judgment in *D.*, C-376/03, EU:C:2005:424, at para. 24; Judgment in *Blanckaert*, C-512/03, EU:C:2005:516, at para. 35; Judgment in *Burtscher*, C-213/04, EU:C:2005:731, at para. 39; Judgment in *Centro di Musicologia Walter Stauffer*, C-386/04, EU:C:2006:568, at paras 23-24; Judgment in *Elisa*, C-451/05, EU:C:2007:594, at para. 59-61; Judgment in *Hollmann*, C-443/06, EU:C:2007:600, at para. 31; Judgment in *Établissements Rimbaud*, C-72/09,

aims at setting-up a branch in the respective state, discriminatory measures also negatively affect the freedom of establishment.[444] Purchasing a shareholding in a foreign corporation can similarly be examined with regard to the freedom of establishment,[445] because the investor may thereby aim at pursuing an economic activity, and/or the free movement of capital,[446] because a direct investment is made.[447] In relation to third countries, deciding on the applicable fundamental freedoms is especially crucial, because the free movement of capital and payments is the only fundamental freedom that also covers economic activities between Member States and third countries. Since the territorial scope of the other free movement provisions is restricted to intra-EU activities, *"it is important to ensure that the interpretation of Article 63(1) TFEU as regards relations with third countries does not enable economic*

EU:C:2010:645, at para. 17; Judgment in *Commission/Portugal*, C-267/09, EU:C:2011:273, at para. 34; Order in *projektart and others*, C-476/10, EU:C:2011:422, at para. 29; Judgment in *Commission/Belgium*, C-250/08, EU:C:2011:793, at para. 31.

444. Judgment in *Commission/Greece*, 305/87, EU:C:1989:218, at para. 22; Judgment in *Konle*, C-302/97, EU:C:1999:271, at para. 22; Judgment in *Reisch and others*, C-515/99, C-519/99 to C-524/99 and C-526/99 to C-540/99, EU:C:2002:135, at para. 29; also see Opinion of AG Alber in *Baars*, C-251/98, EU:C:1999:502, at points 27-28; Opinion of AG Stix-Hackl in *Centro di Musicologia Walter Stauffer*, C-386/04, EU:C:2005:785, at point 38.

445. Judgment in *Cadbury Schweppes and Cadbury Schweppes Overseas*, C-196/04, EU:C:2006:544, at paras 31-33; Judgment in *Test Claimants in the Thin Cap Group Litigation*, C-524/04, EU:C:2007:161, at paras 27-33; Order in *A and B*, C-102/05, EU:C:2007:275, at paras 25-29; Judgment in *Oy AA*, C-231/05, EU:C:2007:439, at paras 20-24; Order in *Stahlwerk Ergste Westig*, C-415/06, EU:C:2007:651, at paras 14-16; Judgment in *Burda*, C-284/06, EU:C:2008:365, at paras 68-75; Judgment in *Aberdeen Property Fininvest Alpha*, C-303/07, EU:C:2009:377, at paras 32-36; Judgment in *SGI*, C-311/08, EU:C:2010:26, at paras 28-37.

446. Judgment in *Glaxo Wellcome*, C-182/08, EU:C:2009:559, at paras 36-52; Judgment in *Test Claimants in the FII Group Litigation*, C-35/11, EU:C:2012:707, at paras 102-104; Judgment in *Itelcar*, C-282/12, EU:C:2013:629, at paras 14-25; Judgment in *Emerging Markets Series of DFA Investment Trust Company*, C-190/12, EU:C:2014:249, at paras 23-35; Judgment in *Kronos International*, C-47/12, EU:C:2014:2200, at paras 29-55.

447. Although the relation between the freedom of establishment and the free movement of capital and payments is specifically dealt with by Articles 49, 55 and 65(2) TFEU, a clear demarcation cannot be derived from these provisions. Article 49 TFEU stipulates that the freedom of establishment is *"subject to the provisions of the Chapter relating to capital."* Similarly, Article 55 TFEU provides that *"Member States shall accord nationals of the other Member States the same treatment as their own nationals as regards participation in the capital of companies or firms within the meaning of Article 54, without prejudice to the application of the other provisions of the Treaties."* According to Article 65(2) TFEU, on the other hand, the provisions of the Chapter relating to capital and payments *"shall be without prejudice to the applicability of restrictions on the right of establishment which are compatible with the Treaties."* These reciprocal reservations (see Opinion of AG Stix-Hackl in *Centro di Musicologia Walter Stauffer*, C-386/04, EU:C:2005:785, at point 35) are considered to indicate that both fundamental freedoms may apply simultaneously (see Opinion of AG Kokott in *Bouanich*, C-265/04, EU:C:2005:479, at point 71; also see S. Hindelang, *The Free Movement of Capital and Foreign Direct Investment* (Oxford University Press, 2009), at pp. 88-89; G. Kofler, *Doppelbesteuerungsabkommen und Europäisches Gemeinschaftsrecht* (Linde, 2007), at pp. 944-947; D. Smit, 16 *EC Tax Rev.* 6 (2007), at p. 255-257; D. Smit, *EU Freedoms, Non-EU Countries and Company Taxation* (Kluwer, 2012), at pp. 450-453; also cf. K. Spies, *Die Kapitalverkehrsfreiheit in Konkurrenz zu den anderen Grundfreiheiten* (LexisNexis, 2015), at pp. 378-381).

operators who do not fall within the limits of the territorial scope of [these freedoms] to profit from [the free movement of capital]."[448]

In principle, every national measure that negatively affects the movement of capital or payments between Member States and third countries may be examined in terms of its compatibility with the free movement of capital and payments. It has to be kept in mind, however, that there has to be a reason why Article 63 TFEU also applies in relation to third countries, whereas the other fundamental freedoms cannot be relied upon in such cases.[449] If the free movement of capital and payments is the only fundamental freedom to be considered in a certain case solely because the territorial scope of another potentially applicable fundamental freedom is limited to intra-EU situations, it has to be determined whether it is in fact in line with the objective underlying the liberalization of capital flows in relation to third countries to "*enable economic operators who do not fall within the limits of the territorial scope of [the other fundamental freedoms] to profit from [the free movement of capital].*"[450] Must Article 63 TFEU, for example, enable a third country investor to take full advantage of the internal market if this investor purchases all the shares of a company established and resident in a Member State in order to take up an economic activity within the EU? Or would that be contrary to the fact that the freedom of establishment is limited to intra-EU situations?

The ECJ has taken the view that Member States are not in breach of the free movement of capital if the national measure concerned only applies "*to those shareholdings which enable the holder to exert a definite influence on the decisions of the company concerned and to determine its activities.*"[451] Although such shareholdings are in principle covered by the freedom of establishment,[452] a third-country investor

448. Judgment in *Test Claimants in the FII Group Litigation*, C-35/11, EU:C:2012:707, at para. 100; also see Judgment in *Emerging Markets Series of DFA Investment Trust Company*, C-190/12, EU:C:2014:249, at para. 31; Judgment in *Kronos International*, C-47/12, EU:C:2014:2200, at para. 53.

449. See K. Spies, *Die Kapitalverkehrsfreiheit in Konkurrenz zu den anderen Grundfreiheiten* (LexisNexis, 2015), at p. 203; also cf. D. Thym, Freizügigkeit in Europa als Modell?, 46 *EuR* 4 (2011), p. 487 (at p. 496).

450. Judgment in *Test Claimants in the FII Group Litigation*, C-35/11, EU:C:2012:707, at para. 100; also see Judgment in *Emerging Markets Series of DFA Investment Trust Company*, C-190/12, EU:C:2014:249, at para. 31; Judgment in *Kronos International*, C-47/12, EU:C:2014:2200, at para. 53.

451. Judgment in *Test Claimants in the FII Group Litigation*, C-35/11, EU:C:2012:707, at para. 98; also see Judgment in *Itelcar*, C-282/12, EU:C:2013:629, at para. 17; Judgment in *Hervis Sport- és Divatkereskedelmi*, C-385/12, EU:C:2014:47; at para. 22; Judgment in *Emerging Markets Series of DFA Investment Trust Company*, C-190/12, EU:C:2014:249, at para. 27.

452. Judgment in *Baars*, C-251/98, EU:C:2000:205, at para. 22; Judgment in *Überseering*, C-208/00, EU:C:2002:632, at para. 77; Judgment in *X and Y*, C-436/00, EU:C:2002:704, at para. 37; Judgment in *N.*, C-470/04, EU:C:2006:525, at para. 27; Judgment in *Cadbury Schweppes and Cadbury Schweppes Overseas*, C-196/04, EU:C:2006:544, at para. 31; Judgment in *Test Claimants in the Thin Cap Group Litigation*, C-524/04, EU:C:2007:161, at para. 27; Judgment in *Rewe Zentralfinanz*, C-347/04, EU:C:2007:194, at paras 22 and 70; Judgment in *Oy AA*, C-231/05, EU:C:2007:439, at para. 20; Judgment in *Commission/Germany*, C-112/05, EU:C:2007:623, at para. 13; Judgment in *Columbus Container Services*, C-298/05, EU:C:2007:754, at para. 29; Judgment in *Heinrich Bauer Verlag*, C-360/06, EU:C:2008:531, at para. 27; Judgment in *Truck Center*, C-282/07, EU:C:2008:762, at para. 25; Judgment in *Glaxo Wellcome*, C-182/08,

cannot rely upon Article 49 TFEU due to its limited territorial scope. According to the Court, a third-country investor should also not be able to rely upon the free movement of capital if the shareholding enables the third-country investor to exert a definite influence on the decisions of the company concerned and to determine its activities.[453] By contrast, if such an investor purchases a shareholding that does not suffice to exert a definite influence on the decisions of the company concerned and to determine its activities, the freedom of establishment is not applicable. This is not only due to the third-country context; even in an intra-EU situation Article 49 TFEU would not be applicable.[454] In such a case, the third-country investor can thus rely upon the free movement of capital.[455]

Parts of the ECJ's case law hence suggest that the facts of the case are decisive for determining which fundamental freedom is to be applied preferentially.[456] Such an approach would have the result that the standstill clause in Article 64(1) TFEU would become largely meaningless,[457] because the direct investments mentioned in it are

EU:C:2009:559, at para. 47; Judgment in *Filipiak*, C-314/08, EU:C:2009:719, at para. 52; Judgment in *X*, C-87/13, EU:C:2014:2459, at para. 21.

453. Order in *KBC Bank and Beleggen, Risicokapitaal, Beheer*, C-439/07 and C-499/07, EU:C:2009:339, at paras 67-74; but see Judgment in *Test Claimants in the FII Group Litigation*, C-35/11, EU:C:2012:707, at para. 104; Judgment in *Itelcar*, C-282/12, EU:C:2013:629, at paras 14-25; Judgment in *Emerging Markets Series of DFA Investment Trust Company*, C-190/12, EU:C:2014:249, at paras 23-35; Judgment in *Kronos International*, C-47/12, EU:C:2014:2200, at paras 38-55.

454. Judgment in *Glaxo Wellcome*, C-182/08, EU:C:2009:559, at paras 36-52; also cf. Judgment in *Überseering*, C-208/00, EU:C:2002:632, at para. 77.

455. Judgment in *Haribo Lakritzen Hans Riegel*, C-436/08 and C-437/08, EU:C:2011:61, paras 36-38; Judgment in *Beker*, C-168/11, EU:C:2013:117, at paras 29-31.

456. See J. Englisch, Einige Schlussfolgerungen zur Grundfreiheitskompatibilität des § 1 AStG – zugleich Anmerkung zum Urteil des EuGH in der Rs. SGI, 19 *IStR* 4 (2010), p. 139 (at p. 139); M. Lang, Der Anwendungsbereich der Grundfreiheiten – Maßgeblichkeit des Sachverhalts oder der nationalen Rechtsvorschrift, in M. Lang/C. Weinzierl (eds.), *Europäisches Steuerrecht, Festschrift für Friedrich Rödler zum 60. Geburtstag* (Linde, 2010), p. 521 (at pp. 524-530); M. Lang, Kapitalverkehrsfreiheit, Steuerrecht und Drittstaaten, 88 *StuW* 3 (2011), p. 209 (at p. 215); N. Zorn, EG-Grundfreiheiten und dritte Länder, in P. Quantschnigg/W. Wiesner/G. Mayr (eds.), *Steuern im Gemeinschaftsrecht, Festschrift für Wolfgang Nolz* (LexisNexis, 2008), p. 211 (at pp. 216-218); N. Zorn, Nochmals: Kapitalverkehrsfreiheit für Drittstaatendividenden Eine Reaktion auf den Beitrag von Dietmar Völker in IStR 2009, 705 ff., 19 *IStR* 6 (2010), p. 190 (at pp. 191-192); this view seems to be supported by the ECJ in the following decisions: Judgment in *Burda*, C-284/06, EU:C:2008:365, at paras 68-75; Order in *KBC Bank and Beleggen, Risicokapitaal, Beheer*, C-439/07 and C-499/07, EU:C:2009:339, at para. 71; Judgment in *Aberdeen Property Fininvest Alpha*, C-303/07, EU:C:2009:377, at paras 32-36; Judgment in *SGI*, C-311/08, EU:C:2010:26, at paras 28-37; Judgment in *Haribo Lakritzen Hans Riegel*, C-436/08 and C-437/08, EU:C:2011:61, paras 36-38; Judgment in *Accor*, C-310/09, EU:C:2011:581, at paras 29-38; Judgment in *Beker*, C-168/11, EU:C:2013:117, at para. 29; Judgment in *Bouanich*, C-375/12, EU:C:2014:138, at para. 30.

457. See A. Cordewener/G. Kofler/C.P. Schindler, Free Movement of Capital, Third Country Relationships and National Tax Law: An Emerging Issue Before the ECJ, 47 *Eur. Taxn.* 3 (2007), p. 107 (at pp. 113); A. Cordewener/G. Kofler/C.P. Schindler, 47 *Eur. Taxn.* 8 (2007), p. 373; G. Kofler, *Doppelbesteuerungsabkommen und Europäisches Gemeinschaftsrecht* (Linde, 2007), at p. 949; P. Plansky, The Impact of the Fundamental Freedoms on Tax Treaties with Third Countries, in M. Lang/J. Schuch/C. Staringer (eds.), *Tax Treaty Law and EC Law* (Kluwer, 2007), p. 293 (at pp. 311-312); also see Opinion of AG Stix-Hackl in *Fidium Finanz*, C-452/04, EU:C:2006:182, at point 74; also cf. Judgment in *Test Claimants in the FII Group Litigation*, C-35/11, EU:C:2012:707, at para. 101.

considered to generally coincide with activities that would be protected by either the freedom of establishment or the freedom to provide services in intra-EU settings.[458] It could be argued, though, that a direct investment includes *"[i]nvestments of all kinds by natural persons or commercial, industrial or financial undertakings, and which serve to establish or to maintain lasting and direct links between the person providing the capital and the entrepreneur to whom or the undertaking to which the capital is made available in order to carry on an economic activity."*[459] With regard to shareholdings, for example, *"the objective of establishing or maintaining lasting economic links presupposes that the shares held by the shareholder enable [her], either pursuant to the provisions of the national laws relating to companies limited by shares or in some other way, to participate effectively in the management of that company or in its control."*[460] By contrast, the freedom of establishment only applies if the shareholding *"enable[s] the holder to exert a definite influence on the decisions of the company concerned and to determine its activities."*[461] As AG Geelhoed pointed out, a direct investment is, therefore, not necessarily covered by the freedom of establishment.[462] Still, the

458. See S. Hindelang, *The Free Movement of Capital and Foreign Direct Investment* (Oxford University Press, 2009), at p. 85.
459. Annex I to Council Directive 88/361/EEC of 24 June 1988 for the implementation of Article 67 of the Treaty, *OJ* L 178 (8 Jul. 1988), p. 5 (at p. 11); also see Judgment in *Commission/Portugal*, C-367/98, EU:C:2002:326, at paras 37-38; Judgment in *Commission/France*, C-483/99, EU:C:2002:327, at paras 36-37; Judgment in *Commission/Belgium*, C-503/99, EU:C:2002:328, at paras 37-38; Judgment in *Commission/Spain*, C-463/00, EU:C:2003:272, at paras 52-53; Judgment in *Commission/United Kingdom*, C-98/01, EU:C:2003:273, at paras 39-40; Judgment in *Associazione Azionariato Diffuso dell'AEM and others*, C-464/04, EU:C:2005:805, at para. 20; Judgment in *Test Claimants in the FII Group Litigation*, C-446/04, EU:C:2006:774, at paras 178-180; Judgment in *Holböck*, C-157/05, EU:C:2007:297, at paras 33-34; Judgment in *Commission/Germany*, C-112/05, EU:C:2007:623, at para. 18; Judgment in *Federconsumatori and others*, C-463/04, EU:C:2007:752, at para. 20; Judgment in *Commission/Italy*, C-326/07, EU:C:2009:193, at para. 35; Judgment in *Commission/Portugal*, C-543/08, EU:C:2010:669, at para. 42.
460. Judgment in *Associazione Azionariato Diffuso dell'AEM and others*, C-464/04, EU:C:2005:805, at para. 20; Judgment in *Test Claimants in the FII Group Litigation*, C-446/04, EU:C:2006:774, at para. 182; Judgment in *Holböck*, C-157/05, EU:C:2007:297, at para. 35; Judgment in *Commission/Germany*, C-112/05, EU:C:2007:623, at para. 18; Judgment in *Federconsumatori and others*, C-463/04, EU:C:2007:752, at para. 20; Judgment in *Orange European Smallcap Fund*, C-194/06, EU:C:2008:289, at para. 101.
461. Judgment in *Test Claimants in the FII Group Litigation*, C-35/11, EU:C:2012:707, at para. 98; also see Judgment in *Itelcar*, C-282/12, EU:C:2013:629, at para. 17; Judgment in *Hervis Sport- és Divatkereskedelmi*, C-385/12, EU:C:2014:47; at para. 22; Judgment in *Emerging Markets Series of DFA Investment Trust Company*, C-190/12, EU:C:2014:249, at para. 27.
462. Opinion of AG Geelhoed in *Test Claimants in the FII Group Litigation*, C-446/04, EU:C:2006:240, at point 119; also see N. Zorn in P. Quantschnigg/W. Wiesner/G. Mayr (eds.), *Steuern im Gemeinschaftsrecht* (LexisNexis, 2008), at p. 222; also cf. D. Smit, Capital Movements and Third Countries: The Significance of the Standstill-Clause Ex-Article 57(1) of the EC Treaty in the Field of Direct Taxation, 15 *EC Tax Rev.* 4 (2006), p. 203 (at p. 206); S. Hindelang, *The Free Movement of Capital and Foreign Direct Investment* (Oxford University Press, 2009), at p. 86 (*"there can be capital movements that qualify as establishments but not at the same time as direct investment"*); G. Kofler, Kapitalverkehrsfreiheit, Kontrollbeteiligungen und Drittstaaten, 4 *taxlex* 8 (2008), p. 326 (at p. 328); also cf., although ambiguous, D. Smit, *EU Freedoms, Non-EU Countries and Company Taxation* (Kluwer, 2012), at p. 67 (*"Whether an investor can effectively participate in the management and control of a company [...] differs from the test whether a definite influence exists under the freedom of establishment only in terms of the intensity, but not in substance."*); but see W.C. Haslehner, 17 *IStR* 16 (2008), at p. 575.

practical importance of Article 64(1) TFEU would be rather minor,[463] if the facts of the case are decisive for identifying the prevailing fundamental freedom in a third-country case. In the literature, it is additionally pointed out that such an approach would lead to the "counterintuitive" result that the EU law protection of a third-country investment is inversely proportional to the size of such an investment.[464] Moreover, it might be quite difficult to determine whether a certain situation should be covered by one or the other fundamental freedom. If a third-country investor, for example, bought real estate located in a Member State, the applicable fundamental freedom would depend on its intended future use. Unless the subjective intentions of the purchaser were known, it would not be possible to identify the applicable fundamental freedoms by solely focusing on the facts of the case.[465]

Given these shortcomings of relying on the facts of the case, in some parts of the literature it is argued that the national measure concerned should be decisive.[466] In some judgments, the Court indeed considers the purpose of the respective legislation.[467] In several decisions relating to shareholdings, the ECJ even refers exclusively to

463. In the literature, it is partly even assumed – albeit for other reasons – that the application of Article 64(1) TFEU is almost illusory in the field of direct taxation in any case. See D. Smit, 15 *EC Tax Rev.* 4 (2006), at p. 212.

464. See A. Cordewener/G. Kofler/C.P. Schindler, 47 *Eur. Taxn.* 3 (2007), at pp. 113-114; G. Kofler, 4 *Taxlex* 8 (2008), at p. 328; G. Kofler, *Doppelbesteuerungsabkommen und Europäisches Gemeinschaftsrecht* (Linde, 2007), at p. 949; W. Schön in T. Ackermann/J. Köndgen (eds.), *Privat- und Wirtschaftsrecht in Europa, Festschrift für Wulf-Henning Roth zum 70. Geburtstag* (C.H. Beck, 2015), at p. 576; but see M. Lang, 88 *StuW* 3 (2011), at p. 214.

465. Opinion of AG Cosmas in *Albore*, C-423/98, EU:C:2000:158, at points 40-41; also see U. Haferkamp, *Die Kapitalverkehrsfreiheit im System der Grundfreiheiten des EG-Vertrages* (Nomos, 2003), at pp. 195-196; K. Spies, *Die Kapitalverkehrsfreiheit in Konkurrenz zu den anderen Grundfreiheiten* (LexisNexis, 2015), at pp. 194 and 230-232.

466. See A. Cordewener/G. Kofler/C.P. Schindler, 47 *Eur. Taxn.* 3 (2007), at p. 114; A. Cordewener/G. Kofler/C.P. Schindler, 47 *Eur. Taxn.* 8 (2007), at pp. 372-374; J. Hey, Germany I: *Kronos International, Magdeburger Mühlenwerke, Commission vs. Germany* I-III, in M. Lang/P. Pistone/J. Schuch/C. Staringer (eds.), *ECJ – Recent Developments in Direct Taxation 2012* (Linde, 2013), p. 53 (at pp. 60-61); S. Köhler/M. Tippelhofer, Kapitalverkehrsfreiheit auch in Drittstaatenfällen?, 16 *IStR* 18 (2007), p. 645 (at p. 646); R. Lyal, Free Movement of Capital and Non-Member Countries – Consequences for Direct Taxation, in D. Weber (ed.), *The Influence of European Tax Law on Direct Taxation* (Kluwer, 2007), p. 17 (at p. 21); J. Mühlehner, Kontrollbeteiligungen und Kapitalverkehrsfreiheit im Verhältnis zu Drittstaaten, 17 *SWI* 11 (2007), p. 523 (at pp. 523-524); J. Mühlehner, Zur Anwendbarkeit der Kapitalverkehrsfreiheit auf Portfolioinvestitionen in Drittstaaten, 18 *SWI* 3 (2008), p. 102 (at pp. 102-104); H. Rehm/J. Nagler, Verwaltung verweigert faktisch Anwendung von Art. EGV Artikel 56 EG gegenüber Drittstaaten, 16 *IStR* 19 (2007), p. 700 (at pp. 701-702); J. Schönfeld, EuGH konkretisiert Anwendung der Kapitalverkehrsfreiheit im Verhältnis zu Drittstaaten: Mögliche Konsequenzen und offene Fragen aus steuerlicher Sicht, 60 *DB* 2 (2007), p. 80 (at p. 82); W.C. Haslehner, Die Kapitalverkehrsfreiheit gegenüber Drittstaaten am Beispiel ausländischer Beteiligungserträge, 3 *taxlex* 6a (2007), p. 286 (at pp. 289); W.C. Haslehner, 17 *IStR* 16 (2008), at pp. 574-575; D. Völker, Kapitalverkehrsfreiheit für Drittstaatendividenden – Widerspruch zur BFH-Rechtsprechung oder Bestätigung des BFH durch den EuGH-Beschluss vom 4. 6. 2009?, 18 *IStR* 20 (2009), p. 705 (at p. 708); W. Schön in T. Ackermann/J. Köndgen (eds.), *Privat- und Wirtschaftsrecht in Europa, Festschrift für Wulf-Henning Roth zum 70. Geburtstag* (C.H. Beck, 2015), at pp. 576-578; K. Spies, *Die Kapitalverkehrsfreiheit in Konkurrenz zu den anderen Grundfreiheiten* (LexisNexis, 2015), at p. 197; also cf. G. Kofler, 4 *taxlex* 8 (2008), at pp. 329-330.

467. Judgment in *Fidium Finanz*, C-452/04, EU:C:2006:631, at paras 43-50; Judgment in *Holböck*, C-157/05, EU:C:2007:297, at para. 22; Judgment in *Glaxo Wellcome*, C-182/08, EU:C:2009:559,

the legislative purpose:[468] "*Where it is apparent from the purpose of [the] national legislation [concerned] that it can only apply to those shareholdings which enable the holder to exert a definite influence on the decisions of the company concerned and to determine its activities,*"[469] the freedom of establishment prevails over the free movement of capital. With regard to capital movements between Member States and third countries this means that "*neither Article 49 TFEU nor Article 63 TFEU may be relied upon,*"[470] because the ambit of the preferentially applicable Article 49 TFEU is restricted to intra-EU situations. By contrast, national legislation that also covers "*shareholdings acquired solely with the intention of making a financial investment without any intention to influence the management and control of the undertaking must be examined exclusively in light of the free movement of capital.*"[471]

It should be kept in mind that the purpose and the scope of the national legislation must not be equated.[472] It is not convincing to exclusively rely on the scope of the national legislation concerned.[473] If, for example, a third-country investor purchases majority shareholdings in several companies resident in different Member States, which enable this investor to exert a definite influence on the decisions of these companies and to determine their activities, the national legislation of all these Member States might have a restrictive effect that is limited to third-country investments. The

at paras 36-52; Judgment in *Test Claimants in the FII Group Litigation*, C-35/11, EU:C:2012:707, at paras 102-104; Judgment in *Itelcar*, C-282/12, EU:C:2013:629, at para. 14-25; Judgment in *Emerging Markets Series of DFA Investment Trust Company*, C-190/12, EU:C:2014:249, at paras 23-35; Judgment in *Kronos International*, C-47/12, EU:C:2014:2200, at paras 29-55.

468. But see Judgment in *Beker*, C-168/11, EU:C:2013:117, at para. 29.

469. Judgment in *Test Claimants in the FII Group Litigation*, C-35/11, EU:C:2012:707, at para. 98; also see Judgment in *Itelcar*, C-282/12, EU:C:2013:629, at para. 17; Judgment in *Hervis Sport- és Divatkereskedelmi*, C-385/12, EU:C:2014:47; at paras 22-28; Judgment in *Emerging Markets Series of DFA Investment Trust Company*, C-190/12, EU:C:2014:249, at para. 27; Judgment in *Kronos International*, C-47/12, EU:C:2014:2200, at para. 31.

470. Judgment in *Test Claimants in the FII Group Litigation*, C-35/11, EU:C:2012:707, at para. 98; Judgment in *Emerging Markets Series of DFA Investment Trust Company*, C-190/12, EU:C:2014:249, at para. 27; also see Judgment in *Itelcar*, C-282/12, EU:C:2013:629, at para. 17.

471. Judgment in *Test Claimants in the FII Group Litigation*, C-35/11, EU:C:2012:707, at para. 92; Judgment in *Emerging Markets Series of DFA Investment Trust Company*, C-190/12, EU:C:2014:249, at para. 28; Judgment in *Kronos International*, C-47/12, EU:C:2014:2200, at para. 32; also see Judgment in *Itelcar*, C-282/12, EU:C:2013:629, at para. 18.

472. See W. Schön in T. Ackermann/J. Köndgen (eds.), *Privat- und Wirtschaftsrecht in Europa, Festschrift für Wulf-Henning Roth zum 70. Geburtstag* (C.H. Beck, 2015), at p. 576; but see M. Lang, 88 *StuW* 3 (2011), at p. 578.

473. See M. Lang in M. Lang/C. Weinzierl (eds.), *Europäisches Steuerrecht, Festschrift für Friedrich Rödler zum 60. Geburtstag* (Linde, 2010), at pp. 527-528; M. Lang, 88 *StuW* 3 (2011), at p. 215; M. O'Brien, Case C-452/04, Fidium Finanz AG v. Bundesanstalt für Finanzdienstleistungsaufsicht, judgment of the Court of Justice (Grand Chamber) of 3 October 2006, [2006] ECR I-9521, 44 *Common Market L. Rev.* 5 (2007), p. 1483 (at p. 1499); W. Schön in T. Ackermann/J. Köndgen (eds.), *Privat- und Wirtschaftsrecht in Europa, Festschrift für Wulf-Henning Roth zum 70. Geburtstag* (C.H. Beck, 2015), at p. 578; D. Smit, *EU Freedoms, Non-EU Countries and Company Taxation* (Kluwer, 2012), at pp. 475-476; N. Zorn in P. Quantschnigg/W. Wiesner/G. Mayr (eds.), *Steuern im Gemeinschaftsrecht, Festschrift für Wolfgang Nolz* (LexisNexis, 2008), at p. 216; also cf. D. Weber, Fidium Finanz AG v Bundesanstalt fur Finanzdienstleistungsaufsicht: the ECJ gives the wrong answer about the applicability of the free movement of capital between the EC Member States and non-member countries, 52 *British Tax Rev.* 6 (2007), p. 670 (at pp. 672-674).

third-country investor could, however, rely upon the free movement of capital only with regard to the investments in those Member States having restrictive national legislation which applies irrespective of the size of the shareholdings. On the other hand, Article 63 TFEU could not be relied upon by this investor with regard to those Member States having restrictive national legislation which requires that the shareholding enables the investor to exert a definite influence on the decisions of the company concerned and to determine its activities. This does not seem convincing, especially if it is assumed that the fundamental freedoms are supposed to have a uniform protective effect within the entire EU. If the prevailing fundamental freedom had to be solely determined based on whether the national legislation concerned is restricted to majority shareholdings or not, the protective effect of the free movement of capital would be different in every Member State, although the third-country investor relying upon the free movement of capital carries out the same economic activity in each Member State.

However, solely relying on the purpose of the national measure at stake also raises concerns. After all, the intention of the legislator is often hardly identifiable. A certain tax measure may even serve several purposes.[474] Similarly to the facts of the case and the ambit of the national provision concerned, the purpose of the legislation alone hence does not seem to lead to results which are fully convincing. Given this situation, it is no surprise that the ECJ's case law on the delimitation of the fundamental freedoms is still ambiguous.[475] It nevertheless shows that the scope of protection of a particular fundamental freedom might be more limited than its wording suggests. This can particularly be the case if its ambit is partially wider as compared to other fundamental freedoms.

2.3 The Different Kinds of Obstacles to Free Movement

2.3.1 The Discrimination of Cross-Border Economic Transactions

Contrary to a general principle of equality, the fundamental freedoms – at least according to the wording of the respective provisions of the TFEU – only prohibit a different treatment that is based on certain criteria.[476] Domestic legislation that employs such a prohibited criterion (e.g., nationality) causes direct or overt discrimination.[477] If the fundamental freedoms were to be understood very formally,

474. See K. Spies, *Die Kapitalverkehrsfreiheit in Konkurrenz zu den anderen Grundfreiheiten* (LexisNexis, 2015), at pp. 251-256; also cf. W. Schön in T. Ackermann/J. Köndgen (eds.), *Privat- und Wirtschaftsrecht in Europa, Festschrift für Wulf-Henning Roth zum 70. Geburtstag* (C.H. Beck, 2015), at p. 576.
475. See K. Spies, *Die Kapitalverkehrsfreiheit in Konkurrenz zu den anderen Grundfreiheiten* (LexisNexis, 2015), at pp. 197-199 and 410-412.
476. See J. Englisch, *Wettbewerbsgleichheit im grenzüberschreitenden Handel* (Mohr Siebeck, 2008), at p. 284; also cf. Opinion of AG Kokott in *Bouanich*, C-265/04, EU:C:2005:479, at point 31.
477. See, for example, T. Kingreen, *Die Struktur der Grundfreiheiten des Europäischen Gemeinschaftsrechts* (Duncker & Humblot, 1999), at p. 38; K. Lenaerts/P. Van Nuffel, *Constitutional Law of the European Union²* (Sweet & Maxwell, 2005), at p. 135.

discrimination based on criteria that are not referred to by the provisions of the TFEU would be permitted.[478] However, in practice, such discrimination may be equally detrimental to free movement.[479] Therefore, according to the ECJ, the fundamental freedoms "*forbid not only overt discrimination [...] but also all covert forms of discrimination which, by the application of other criteria of differentiation, lead in fact to the same result.*"[480] This does not mean that the conditions imposed by national law have to lead exactly to the same result as if a prohibited criterion was used. The ECJ instead insinuates an indirect or covert discrimination,[481] if the respective domestic provision is capable of affecting essentially foreign nationals, goods, services, capital or payments.[482] It is not necessary to statistically verify whether a domestic provision in

478. H.D. Jarass, Die Elemente einer Dogmatik der Grundfreiheiten, 30 *EuR* 3 (1995), p. 202 (at p. 213).
479. See B.J.M. Terra/P.J. Wattel, *European Tax Law*[6] (Kluwer, 2012), at p. 54; also cf. J. Englisch, 33 *Intertax* 8/9 (2005), at pp. 313-314.
480. Judgment in *Sotgiu*, 152/73, EU:C:1974:13, at para. 11; Judgment in *Commission/Luxembourg*, C-111/91, EU:C:1993:92, at para. 9; Judgment in *Germany/Commission*, C-156/98, EU:C:2000:467, at para. 83; Judgment in *Ferlini*, C-411/98, EU:C:2000:530, at para. 57; Judgment in *Meindl*, C-329/05, EU:C:2007:57, at para. 21; Judgment in *Talotta*, C-383/05, EU:C:2007:181, at para. 17; Judgment in *Hartmann*, C-212/05, EU:C:2007:437, at para. 29; Judgment in *Geven*, C-213/05, EU:C:2007:438, at para. 18; Judgment in *Geurts and Vogten*, C-464/05, EU:C:2007:631, at para. 20; Judgment in *Gielen*, C-440/08, EU:C:2010:148, at para. 37; Judgment in *Schmelz*, C-97/09, EU:C:2010:632, at para. 48; Judgment in *Hervis Sport- és Divatkereskedelmi*, C-385/12, EU:C:2014:47, at para. 30; Judgment in *Sopora*, C-512/13, EU:C:2015:108, at para. 23; Judgment in *Schulz-Delzers and Schulz*, C-240/10, EU:C:2011:591, at para. 34; also see Judgment in *Pinna*, 41/84, EU:C:1986:1, at para. 23; Judgment in *Allué and Coonan*, 33/88, EU:C:1989:222, at para. 11; Judgment in *URSSAF*, C-27/91, EU:C:1991:441, at para. 10; Judgment in *Scholz*, C-419/92, EU:C:1994:62, at para. 7; Judgment in *O'Flynn*, C-237/94, EU:C:1996:206, at para. 17.
481. The ECJ seems to use the terms indirect and covert discrimination interchangeably. See at Judgment in *O'Flynn*, C-237/94, EU:C:1996:206, at paras 17 and 23; Judgment in *Asscher*, C-107/94, EU:C:1996:251, at paras 36, 39 and 49; Judgment in *Clean Car Autoservice*, C-350/96, EU:C:1998:205, at paras 27 and 30; Judgment in *Kocak*, C-102/98, EU:C:2000:119, at paras 27 and 30; 39, 45 and 52; Judgment in *Graf*, C-190/98, EU:C:2000:49, at paras 14 and 18; Judgment in *Österreichischer Gewerkschaftsbund*, C-195/98, EU:C:2000:655, at paras 39 and 41; Judgment in *Örs*, C-211/98, EU:C:2000:119, at paras 39 and 45; Judgment in *de Groot*, C-385/00, EU:C:2002:750, at paras 75 and 114; Judgment in *Conijn*, C-346/04, EU:C:2006:445, at paras 15 and 25; Judgment in *Talotta*, C-383/05, EU:C:2007:181, at paras 17 and 32; Judgment in *Geurts and Vogten*, C-464/05, EU:C:2007:631, at paras 20 and 22; Judgment in *Gielen*, C-440/08, EU:C:2010:148, at paras 37 and 48; Judgment in *Hervis Sport- és Divatkereskedelmi*, C-385/12, EU:C:2014:47, at paras 30 and 41; Judgment in *Sopora*, C-512/13, EU:C:2015:108, at paras 23 and 34.
482. For the varying phrasing see, for example, Judgment in *O'Flynn*, C-237/94, EU:C:1996:206, at para. 18; also see Judgment in *Boussac*, 22/80, EU:C:1980:251, at para. 10 ("*principally*"); Judgment in *Roviello*, 20/85, EU:C:1988:283, at para. 15 ("*essentially*"); Judgment in *Biehl*, 175/88, EU:C:1990:186, at para. 14 ("*in particular*"); Judgment in *Factortame*, C-221/89, EU:C:1991:320, at para. 32 ("*in most cases*"); Judgment in *Commerzbank*, C-330/91, EU:C:1993:303, at para. 15 ("*more particularly*"); Judgment in *Mund & Fester*, C-398/92, EU:C:1994:52, at para. 16 ("*the great majority*"); Judgment in *Schumacker*, C-279/93, EU:C:1995:31, at para. 28 ("*mainly*");

fact adversely affects predominantly cross-border situations;[483] the mere capability of having such an effect is sufficient.[484]

With regard to direct taxation, the development of the concept of indirect or covert discrimination was crucial insofar as direct tax provisions usually do not refer to the nationality but rather the residence of a person.[485] Assuming that resident persons are typically nationals of their residence state whereas non-resident persons are typically nationals of another Member State,[486] the ECJ concludes that *"there is a risk that [the criterion of residence] will work in particular against taxpayers who are nationals of other Member States."*[487] Therefore, domestic tax provisions which refer to the residence of the taxpayer potentially lead to indirect or covert discrimination. This may even be the case, if a taxpayer is discriminated against by the Member State whose nationality she holds, because she is resident in another Member State.[488] According to the ECJ, the fundamental freedoms *"cannot be interpreted in such a way as to exclude a given Member State's own nationals from the benefit of [EU] law where by reason of their conduct they are, with regard to their Member State of origin, in a situation which may be regarded as equivalent to that of any other person enjoying the rights and*

483. See P. Farmer, The Court's Case Law on Taxation: A Castle Built on Shifting Sands?, 12 *EC Tax Rev.* 2 (2003), p. 75 (at p. 76); J. Wouters, The Principle of Non-discrimination in European Community Law, 8 *EC Tax Rev.* 2 (1999), p. 98 (at pp. 103-104); T. Eilmansberger, Zur Reichweite der Grundfreiheiten des Binnenmarktes (1. Teil), 121 *JBl* 6 (1999), p. 345 (at pp. 349-350).

484. Judgment in *O'Flynn*, C-237/94, EU:C:1996:206, at para. 21.

485. See P. Farmer/R. Lyal, *EC Tax Law* (Clarendon Press, 1994), at p. 312; M. Gammie/G. Brannan, EC Law Strikes at the UK Corporation Tax – The Death Knell of UK Imputation?, 23 *Intertax* 8/9 (1995), p. 389 (at p. 396); B. Knobbe-Keuk, Restrictions on the Fundamental Freedoms Enshrined in the EC Treaty by Discriminatory Tax Provisions – Ban and Justification – 3 *EC Tax Rev.* 3 (1994), p. 74 (at p. 76); M. O'Brien, Taxation and the Third Country Dimension of Free Movement of Capital in EU Law: the ECJ's Rulings and Unresolved Issues, 53 *British Tax Rev.* 6 (2008), p. 628 (at pp. 635-636); M. Sedlaczek, Capital and Payments: The Prohibition of Discrimination and Restrictions, 40 *Eur. Taxn.* 1 (2000), p. 13 (at p. 22).

486. Judgment in *Asscher*, C-107/94, EU:C:1996:251, at para. 38; Judgment in *Commission/Germany*, C-269/07, EU:C:2009:527, at paras 57-58; Judgment in *Gielen*, C-440/08, EU:C:2010:148, at para. 42; also see M. Gammie, The Role of the European Court of Justice in the Development of Direct Taxation in the European Union, 57 *Bull. Intl. Taxn.* 3 (2003), p. 86 (at p. 88).

487. Judgment in *Biehl*, 175/88, EU:C:1990:186, at para. 14; also see Judgment in *Bachmann*, C-204/90, EU:C:1992:35, at para. 9; Judgment in *Commerzbank*, C-330/91, EU:C:1993:303, at para. 15; Judgment in *Schumacker*, C-279/93, EU:C:1995:31, at para. 28; Judgment in *Commission/Luxembourg*, C-151/94, EU:C:1995:357, at para. 15; Judgment in *Asscher*, C-107/94, EU:C:1996:251, at para. 38; Judgment in *Zurstrassen*, C-87/99, EU:C:2000:251, at para. 19; Judgment in *Commission/Germany*, C-269/07, EU:C:2009:527, at paras 57-58; Judgment in *Gielen*, C-440/08, EU:C:2010:148, at paras 42 and 48.

488. In the literature, such a situation is occasionally referred to as "reverse discrimination." See, for example, M. Dahlberg, *Direct Taxation in Relation to the Freedom of Establishment and the Free Movement of Capital* (Kluwer Law International, 2005), at p. 69; P. Farmer, 12 *EC Tax Rev.* 2 (2003), at p. 77; L. Hinnekens, The Search for the Framework Conditions of the Fundamental EC Treaty Principles as Applied by the European Court to Member States' Direct Taxation, 11 *EC Tax Rev.* 3 (2002), p. 112 (at p. 114); K. Lenaerts/P. Van Nuffel, *Constitutional Law of the European Union*[2] (Sweet & Maxwell, 2005), at p. 137; A. Tryfonidou, *Reverse Discrimination in EC Law* (Kluwer, 2009), at pp. 13-18.

liberties guaranteed by the Treaty."[489] If the fundamental freedoms' scope of protection was limited to discrimination of foreign nationals, goods, services, capital and payments, such a reasoning would not be convincing.[490] However, the ECJ does not focus on the wording of the relevant provisions of the TFEU, but on the underlying concept of an internal market. With regard to the free movement of persons, for example, the ECJ held that "*[t]he provisions of the Treaty relating to the free movement of persons are [...] intended to facilitate the pursuit by [EU] citizens of occupational activities of all kinds throughout the [EU], and preclude national legislation which might place [EU] citizens at a disadvantage when they wish to extend their activities beyond the territory of a single Member State,*"[491] even if the national legislation cannot be considered to result in direct or indirect discrimination on grounds of nationality.[492] This means, however, that the fundamental freedoms do not exclusively prohibit direct and indirect discrimination based on the criteria mentioned in the respective provision of the TFEU, but aim at generally avoiding unfavourable treatment of cross-border transactions as against purely domestic transactions.[493]

If the fundamental freedoms are to prohibit discrimination of cross-border economic transactions, it should not matter which of the Member States involved causes the discrimination. The protective effect of the fundamental freedoms would be rendered largely meaningless if only the "host state" or "state of destination" was addressed, whereas the "home state" or "state of origin" would be able to impede its

489. Judgment in *Asscher*, C-107/94, EU:C:1996:251, at para. 32; also see Judgment in *Knoors*, 115/78, EU:C:1979:31, at para. 24; Judgment in *Bouchoucha*, C-61/89, EU:C:1990:343, at para. 13; Judgment in *Kraus*, C-19/92, EU:C:1993:125, at para. 15.
490. See A. Cordewener, *Europäische Grundfreiheiten und nationales Steuerrecht* (Dr Otto Schmidt, 2002), at pp. 121; G. Kofler, *Doppelbesteuerungsabkommen und Europäisches Gemeinschaftsrecht* (Linde, 2007), at p. 69; P. Stanley, C-107/94, Asscher v. Staatssecretaris van Financien. Judgment of 27 Jun. 1996. Fifth Chamber. [1996] ECR I-3089, 34 *Common Market L. Rev.* 3 (1997), p. 713 (at p. 718); also cf. E. Keeling, A First Reaction to *Asscher*, 2 *EC Tax J.* 1 (1997), p. 33 (at p. 36).
491. Judgment in *Stanton*, 143/87, EU:C:1988:378, at para. 13; Judgment in *Wolf*, 154 and 155/87, EU:C:1988:379, at para. 13; Judgment in *Singh*, C-370/90, EU:C:1992:296, at para. 16; Judgment in *Bosman*, C-415/93, EU:C:1995:463, at para. 94; Judgment in *Terhoeve*, C-18/95, EU:C:1999:22, at para. 37; also see Judgment in *Graf*, C-190/98, EU:C:2000:49, at para. 21; Judgment in *Sehrer*, C-302/98, EU:C:2000:322, at para. 32; Judgment in *de Groot*, C-385/00, EU:C:2002:750, at para. 77; Judgment in *Schilling and Fleck-Schilling*, C-209/01, EU:C:2003:610, at para. 24; Judgment in *Weigel*, C-387/01, EU:C:2004:256, at para. 52; Judgment in *Commission/Denmark*, C-464/02, EU:C:2005:546, at para. 34; Judgment in *Ritter-Colais*, C-152/03, EU:C:2006:123, at para. 33; Judgment in *Kranemann*, C-109/04, EU:C:2005:187, at para. 25; Judgment in *Turpeinen*, C-520/04, EU:C:2006:703, at para. 14; Judgment in *Lyyski*, C-40/05, EU:C:2007:10, at para. 35; Judgment in *Commission/Germany*, C-152/05, EU:C:2008:17, at para. 21; Judgment in *Renneberg*, C-527/06, EU:C:2008:566, at para. 43; Judgment in *Schmelz*, C-97/09, EU:C:2010:632, at para. 46; Judgment in *Casteels*, C-379/09, EU:C:2011:131, at para. 21; Judgment in *Radziejewski*, C-461/11, EU:C:2012:704, at para. 29; Judgment in *Commission/Belgium*, C-317/14, EU:C:2015:63, at para. 22.
492. Judgment in *Stanton*, 143/87, EU:C:1988:378, at para. 9; Judgment in *Wolf*, 154 and 155/87, EU:C:1988:379, at para. 9.
493. See A. Cordewener, *Europäische Grundfreiheiten und nationales Steuerrecht* (Dr Otto Schmidt, 2002), at pp. 200 et seq.; J. Englisch, *Dividendenbesteuerung* (Dr Otto Schmidt, 2005), at pp. 235-240; P. Farmer, 12 *EC Tax Rev.* 2 (2003), at p. 77; G. Kofler, *Doppelbesteuerungsabkommen und Europäisches Gemeinschaftsrecht* (Linde, 2007), at p. 69.

own economic actors from engaging in a cross-border economic transaction.[494] Partly, this is also explicitly reflected by the relevant provisions of the TFEU. According to Articles 28, 30 and 35 TFEU, for example, the free movement of goods covers imports as well as exports.[495] Moreover, it can be inferred from Article 65(1)(a) TFEU that Article 63 TFEU, *inter alia*, covers potential discrimination of "*taxpayers who are not in the same situation [...] with regard to the place where their capital is invested.*" Since the fundamental freedoms require a cross-border element,[496] this wording refers to a situation where the "home state" or "state of origin" provides for a different treatment of cross-border (outbound) investments and purely domestic investments.[497] Although Articles 18, 21, 45, 49 and 56 TFEU might be less clear as regards obstacles to free movement that are induced by the "home state" or "state of origin," the respective wording allows for an interpretation that such discrimination is also covered by these provisions. Article 21 TFEU, for example, grants EU citizens "*the right to move and reside freely within the territory of the Member States,*" which means that it would run counter to this provision if a Member State made it impossible for its citizens to move to another Member State. Against this background, it is consistent that the ECJ considers the fundamental freedoms to apply irrespective of which Member State is responsible for the unfavourable treatment of a cross-border economic transaction.[498]

494. See A. Cordewener, The Prohibitions of Discrimination and Restriction Within the Framework of the Fully Integrated Internal Market, in F. Vanistendael (ed.), *EU Freedoms and Taxation* (IBFD, 2006), p. 1 (at p. 9); G. Kofler, *Doppelbesteuerungsabkommen und Europäisches Gemeinschaftsrecht* (Linde, 2007), at pp. 70 et seq.
495. See A. Cordewener, *Europäische Grundfreiheiten und nationales Steuerrecht* (Dr Otto Schmidt, 2002), at p. 111.
496. Judgment in *Debauve*, 52/79, EU:C:1980:83, at para. 9; Judgment *Höfner and Elser*, C-41/90, EU:C:1991:161, at para. 37; Judgment in *López Brea and Hidalgo Palacios*, C-330/90 and C-331/90, EU:C:1992:39, at para. 7; Judgment in *Steen*, C-332/90, EU:C:1992:40, at para. 9; Judgment in *Petit*, C-153/91, EU:C:1992:354, at para. 8; Judgment in *Aubertin*, C-29/94 to C-35/94, EU:C:1995:39, at para. 9; Judgment in *USSL n° 47 di Biella*, C-134/95, EU:C:1997:16, at para. 19; Judgment in *Ueckert and Jacquet*, C-64/96 and C-65/96, EU:C:1997:285, at para. 16; Judgment in *Kapasakalis*, C-225/95, EU:C:1998:332, at para. 22; also cf. N. Shuibhne, Free Movement of Persons and the Wholly Internal Rule: Time to Move On?, 39 *Common Market L. Rev.* 4 (2002), p. 731 (at pp. 731 et seq.).
497. See A. Cordewener in F. Vanistendael (ed.), *EU Freedoms and Taxation* (IBFD, 2006), at p. 10.
498. Judgment in *Daily Mail and General Trust*, 81/87, EU:C:1988:456, at para. 16; Judgment in *Masgio*, C-10/90, EU:C:1991:107, at para. 18; Judgment in *Imperial Chemical Industries*, C-264/96, EU:C:1998:370, at para. 21; Judgment in *X and Y*, C-200/98, EU:C:1999:566, at para. 26; Judgment in *Baars*, C-251/98, EU:C:2000:205, at para. 28; Judgment in *Verkooijen*, C-35/98, EU:C:2000:294, at para. 34; Judgment in *AMID*, C-141/99, EU:C:2000:696, at para. 21; Judgment in *Smits and Peerbooms*, C-157/99, EU:C:2001:404, at para. 61; Judgment in *De Groot*, C-385/00, EU:C:2002:750, at paras 78-79; Judgment in *Bosal*, C-168/01, EU:C:2003:479, at para. 27; Judgment in *De Lasteyrie du Saillant*, C-9/02, EU:C:2004:138, at para. 42; Judgment in *Weidert and Paulus*, C-242/03, EU:C:2004:465, at para. 13; Judgment in *Lenz*, C-315/02, EU:C:2004:446, at para. 20; Judgment in *Manninen*, C-319/02, EU:C:2004:484, at para. 22; Judgment in *Marks & Spencer*, C-446/03, EU:C:2005:763, at para. 31; Judgment in *N*, C-470/04, EU:C:2006:525, at para. 35; Judgment in *Cadbury Schweppes and Cadbury Schweppes Overseas*, C-196/04, EU:C:2006:544, at para. 42; Judgment in *Columbus Container Services*, C-298/05, EU:C:2007:754, at para. 33; Judgment in *Heinrich Bauer Verlag*, C-360/06, EU:C:2008:531, at para. 26; Judgment in *Krankenheim Ruhesitz am Wannsee-Seniorenheimstatt*, C-157/07, EU:C:2008:588, at para. 29; Judgment in *Filipiak*, C-314/08, EU:C:2009:719, at para. 60; Judgment in *SGI*, C-311/08, EU:C:2010:26, at para. 39; Judgment in *CIBA*, C-96/08, EU:C:2010:185, at para. 18; Judgment in *Accor*, C-310/09, EU:C:2011:581, at para. 40;

Moreover, focusing generally on obstacles to cross-border transactions than specifically on discrimination based on the criteria mentioned in the TFEU enables – and even requires – the ECJ to also apply the fundamental freedoms if the domestic measure not (only) affects the "active" market participant, but (also) the "passive" market participant.[499] Since supply and demand are the two interacting factors of an economic relationship, adverse effects on the demand side would – at least indirectly – also affect the supply side and hence the economic transaction as a whole.[500] Therefore, the ECJ persuasively regards recipients of goods,[501] services,[502] capital and payments[503] equally protected by the fundamental freedoms as employers[504] and (sub-)subsidiaries.[505]

Due to these developments in the ECJ's case law, the appreciation of the fundamental freedoms has evolved from a rather limited prohibition of unfavourable treatment of foreign nationals to a general non-discrimination principle regarding

Judgment in *National Grid Indus*, C-371/10, EU:C:2011:785, at para. 35; Judgment in *Argenta Spaarbank*, C-350/11, EU:C:2013:447, at para. 20; Judgment in *Bouanich*, C-375/12, EU:C:2014:138, at para. 57; Judgment in *Nordea Bank Danmark*, C-48/13, EU:C:2014:2087, at para. 18; Judgment in *Finanzamt Linz*, C-66/14, EU:C:2015:661, at para. 26.

499. See A. Cordewener, *Europäische Grundfreiheiten und nationales Steuerrecht* (Dr Otto Schmidt, 2002), at pp. 234-243; A. Cordewener in F. Vanistendael (ed.), *EU Freedoms and Taxation* (IBFD, 2006), at pp. 18-21.

500. See A. Cordewener, *Europäische Grundfreiheiten und nationales Steuerrecht* (Dr Otto Schmidt, 2002), at pp. 235.

501. Judgment in *Schul I*, 15/81, EU:C:1982:135, at para. 40; Judgment in *Commission/France*, 18/84, EU:C:1985:175, at paras 15-16; Judgment in *Humblot*, 112/84, EU:C:1985:185, at para. 15; Judgment in *GB-INNO-BM*, 362/88, EU:C:1990:102, at para. 8; Judgment in *Decker*, C-120/95, EU:C:1998:167, at para. 36

502. Judgment in *Luisi and Carbone*, 286/82 and 26/83, EU:C:1984:35, at para. 10; Judgment in *Cowan*, 186/87, EU:C:1989:47, at para. 15; Judgment in *Vander Elst*, C-43/93, EU:C:1994:310, at para. 13; Judgment in *Bachmann*, C-204/90, EU:C:1992:35, at para. 31; Judgment in *Commission/Belgium*, C-300/90, EU:C:1992:37, at para. 22; Judgment in *Kohll*, C-158/96, EU:C:1998:171, at para. 35; Judgment in *Ciola*, C-224/97, EU:C:1999:252, at para. 11; Judgment in *Eurowings*, C-294/97, EU:C:1999:524, at para. 34; Judgment in *Danner*, C-136/00, EU:C:2002:558, at para. 31; Judgment in *FKP Scorpio Konzertproduktionen*, C-290/04, EU:C:2006:630, at para. 32; Judgment in *Commission/Denmark*, C-150/04, EU:C:2007:69, at para. 40.

503. Article 63 TFEU protects the cross-border movement of capital and payments and does not focus on the persons involved in the economic transaction. Due to this object-oriented character of Article 63 TFEU (see, for example, S. Hindelang, *The Free Movement of Capital and Foreign Direct Investment* [Oxford University Press, 2009], at pp. 42-43; P. Pistone, The Impact of European Law on the Relations with Third Countries in the Field of Direct Taxation, 34 *Intertax* 5 [2006], p. 234 [at p. 235]), the transferor as well as the transferee of capital or payments can rely on the free movement of capital and payments. See S. Hindelang, *The Free Movement of Capital and Foreign Direct Investment* (Oxford University Press, 2009), at pp. 204-205; with regard to the free movement of capital also see Judgment in *Sandoz*, C-439/97, EU:C:1999:456, at para. 19; Judgment in *Verkooijen*, C-35/98, EU:C:2000:294, at para. 35; Judgment in *Commission/France*, C-334/02, EU:C:2004:129, at para. 24; Judgment in *Weidert and Paulus*, C-242/03, EU:C:2004:465, at para. 14; Judgment in *Lenz*, C-315/02, EU:C:2004:446, at para. 21; Judgment in *Manninen*, C-319/02, EU:C:2004:484, at para. 23.

504. Judgment in *Clean Car Autoservice*, C-350/96, EU:C:1998:205, at para. 20-25.

505. Judgment in *Metallgesellschaft and Hoechst*, C-397/98 and C-410/98, EU:C:2001:134, at para. 41; Judgment in *Lankhorst-Hohorst*, C-324/00, EU:C:2002:749, at para. 27.

cross-border economic transactions.[506] As AG Poiares Maduro puts it, the non-discrimination principle which forms the basis of the fundamental freedoms "*is no longer linked to the criterion of nationality. It is based on the use of the right to freedom of movement. What is called in question in the national measure concerned is that it imposes a specific disadvantage on operators desirous of moving or establishing themselves within the [EU]. It is therefore a matter of pursuing discrimination against [EU] nationals wishing to assert their rights derived from the freedoms of movement.*"[507] Since double taxation is a problem typically associated with cross-border transactions,[508] this development build the base for the discussions regarding the compatibility of double taxation with the fundamental freedoms.[509]

2.3.2 The Restriction of Cross-Border Economic Transactions

2.3.2.1 "Double Burdens" and "Double Hurdles"

The internal market concept is not only impaired by national measures that impose obstacles by disadvantaging cross-border economic transactions compared to purely domestic ones. Free movement is equally hampered, for example, if the Member States provide for different standards with regard to the same economic activity. In contrast to a purely domestic transaction, all these different standards have to be met in a

506. See A. Cordewener, Deutsche Unernehmensbesteuerung und europäische Grundfreiheiten - Grundzüge des materiellen und formellen Rechtsschutzsystems der EG, 42 *DStR* 1-2 (2004), p. 6 (at p. 8); G. Kofler, *Doppelbesteuerungsabkommen und Europäisches Gemeinschaftsrecht* (Linde, 2007), at p. 80; L. Brosens, Thin Capitalization Rules and EU law, 13 *EC Tax Rev.* 4 (2004), p. 188 (at pp. 191-192); J. Englisch, 33 *Intertax* 8/9 (2005), at p. 314; J. Kokott, Die Bedeutung der europarechtlichen Diskriminierungsverbote und Grunfreiheiten für das Steuerrecht der EU-Mitgliedstaaten, in M. Lehner (ed.), *Grundfreiheiten im Steuerrecht der EU-Staaten* (C.H. Beck, 2000), p. 1 (at pp. 12-13); A. Rädler, Most-favoured nation principle and internal market - Some afterthoughts to case D., in S. van Thiel (ed.), *The European Union's prohibition of discrimination, most-favoured-nation treatment and tax treaties: opinions and materials* (CFE, 2006), p. 64 (at pp. 64-65); W. Schön, Neutrality and Territoriality - Competing or Converging Concepts in European Tax Law?, 69 *Bull. Intl. Taxn.* 4/5 (2015), p. 271 (at p. 273); W. Schön, Neutralität und Territorialität - Gegensätze oder Grundsätze des Europäischen Steuerrechts?, in W. Schön/C. Heber (eds.), Grundfragen des Europäischen Steuerrechts (Springer, 2015), p. 109 (at p. 114).
507. Opinion of AG Poiares Maduro in *Marks & Spencer*, C-446/03, EU:C:2005:201, at point 28.
508. See G. Kofler, *Doppelbesteuerungsabkommen und Europäisches Gemeinschaftsrecht* (Linde, 2007), at p. 155; G. Kofler in A. Rust (ed.), *Double Taxation Within the European Union* (Kluwer, 2011), at p. 106; W. Hellerstein/G. Kofler/R. Mason, Constitutional Restraints on Corporate Tax Integration, 62 *Tax L. Rev.* 1 (2008), p. 1 (at p. 7); V. Heydt, Juridical Double Taxation: *Kerckhaert and Morres*, in W. Haslehner/G. Kofler/A. Rust (eds.), *Landmark Decisions of the ECJ in Direct Taxation* (Kluwer, 2015), p. 181 (at p. 181); also cf. J. Englisch, 33 *Intertax* 8/9 (2005), at p. 323; W. Schön, 11 *EWS* 7 (2001), at p. 290; but see B.J.M. Terra/P.J. Wattel, *European Tax Law*[6] (Kluwer, 2012), at p. 1046; E. Traversa/C. Helleputte in M. Lang/P. Melz/E. Kristoffersson (eds.), *Value Added Tax and Direct Taxation* (IBFD, 2009), at p. 340 ("*juridical double taxation is rare in the national context*"); P. Wattel in G. Maisto (ed.), *Taxation of Intercompany Dividends under Tax Treaties and EU Law* (IBFD, 2012), at p. 44.
509. See Chapter 4.1.3.

cross-border context.[510] This can lead to a competitive disadvantage of economic actors operating cross-border as opposed to domestic competitors.[511] In the literature such situations are designated as "double hurdles"[512] or "double burdens."[513] The most prominent example used to illustrate such a constellation is the *Cassis de Dijon* case:[514] According to former German law, potable spirits that have a wine-spirit content of less than 32% were precluded from being marketed in Germany. Foreign liqueurs which had been lawfully produced and marketed in another Member State could thus be imported but not put into circulation in Germany. If a company wanted to market potable spirits in Germany that were imported from another Member State, it not only had to meet the legal requirements of the Member State of export, but also the German standards. The ECJ was asked whether the German legislation was a measure having equivalent effects to quantitative restrictions on imports as covered by Article 34 TFEU (ex-Article 30 EEC Treaty). In the *Dassonville* judgment, the Court had already stressed that "*[a]ll trading rules enacted by Member States which are capable of hindering, directly or indirectly, actually or potentially, intra-Community trade are to be considered as measures having an effect equivalent to quantitative restrictions.*"[515] Following this understanding of "measures having an equivalent effect," the German rule was, although applying equally to domestic and foreign potable spirits, found to conflict with the free movement of goods.[516]

510. In the literature, it is partly argued that double burdens can also be considered to be discrimination. If a Member State required that certain standards have to be met and did not allow for the recognition of qualifications, proofs or guarantees acquired in another Member State, different situations would be treated in the same way (see, e.g., M. Lang, *Die Rechtsprechung des EuGH zu den direkten Steuern* [Peter Lang, 2007], at pp. 37-38; M. Lang, Die Rechtsprechung des EuGH zu den direkten Steuern – Planungssicherheit für die nationalen Gesetzgeber?, in A. Wagner/V. Wedl [eds.], *Bilanz und Perspektiven zum europäischen Recht* [ÖGB Verlag, 2007], p. 113 [at p. 120]; K. Daxkobler, *Die grundfreiheitliche Rechtsprechung des EuGH* [Linde, 2015], at p. 89; also cf. Opinion of AG Lenz in *Futura Participations and Singer*, C-250/95, EU:C:1996:420, at point 34; P. Farmer, 12 *EC Tax Rev.* 2 [2003], at p. 79; G. Kofler, *Doppelbesteuerungsabkommen und Europäisches Gemeinschaftsrecht* [Linde, 2007], at pp. 97-101). This would lead to discrimination of cross-border situations, which would be specifically impaired (see J. Englisch, Zur Dogmatik der Grundfreiheiten des EGV und ihren ertragsteuerlichen Implikationen, 80 *StuW* 1 [2003], p. 88 [at pp. 89-90]; J. Englisch, 33 *Intertax* 8-9 [2005], at pp. 315-316; J. Englisch, *Dividendenbesteuerung* [Dr Otto Schmidt, 2005], at pp. 247-250; J. Schönfeld, *Hinzurechnungsbesteuerung und Europäisches Gemeinschaftsrecht* [Dr Otto Schmidt, 2005], at pp. 66 et seq.).
511. See E. Spaventa, From Gebhard to Carpenter: Towards a (Non-)Economic European Constitution, 41 *Common Market L. Rev.* 3 (2004), p. 743 (at p. 761).
512. See R. Lyal, Non-discrimination and Direct Tax in Community Law, 12 *EC Tax Rev.* 2 (2003), p. 68 (at p. 68); T. Eilmansberger, 121 *JBl* 6 (1999), at p. 350.
513. See A. Cordewener in F. Vanistendael (ed.), *EU Freedoms and Taxation* (IBFD, 2006), at p. 36; G. Kofler/R. Mason, Double Taxation: A European "Switch in Time?", 14 *Colum. J. Eur. L.* 1 (2007), p. 63 (at p. 69); G. Kofler/R. Mason, *Kerckhaert & Morres*: A European "Switch in Time?", in S. van Thiel (ed.), *The Internal Market and Direct Taxation: Is the European Court of Justice Taking a New Approach?* (CFE Brochure on European Taxation, 2007), p. 176 (at pp. 183-184 ["*dual burden*"] and 185-186 ["*double burden*"]); P. Oliver/W. Roth, 41 *Common Market L. Rev.* 2 (2004), at pp. 415.
514. Judgment in *Rewe*, 120/78, EU:C:1979:42.
515. Judgment in *Dassonville*, 8/74, EU:C:1974:85, at para. 5.
516. Judgment in *Rewe*, 120/78, EU:C:1979:42, at paras 8-15.

The approach taken in *Cassis de Dijon* was developed and became more sophisticated in the context of the free movement of goods,[517] but was later transferred to the other fundamental freedoms as well.[518] With respect to the free movement of workers,[519] the freedom of movement for services,[520] and the freedom of establishment,[521] the problem of double burdens particularly arises if certain requirements have to be fulfilled in order to be legally allowed to provide certain services (e.g., legal services)[522] or to pursue a certain career (e.g., as a lawyer)[523] in a Member State. The ECJ has made clear that national rules laying down such requirements may conflict with the fundamental freedoms if no account is taken of the knowledge, qualifications, proofs and guarantees already acquired by the person concerned in another Member State.[524]

The *Futura Participations* case shows that double burdens may also arise in the area of taxes:[525] According to former Luxembourg law, residents as well as non-residents were only allowed to deduct a loss carry-forward if proper accounts had been kept during the financial year in which the losses were incurred. Since these accounts had to comply with the relevant Luxembourg rules, a non-resident company was not able to rely on the accounts that were kept in compliance with the tax accounting rules of its residence state in order to carry-forward losses attributable to a Luxembourg

517. Judgment in *Dassonville*, 8/74, EU:C:1974:85; Judgment in *Rewe*, 120/78, EU:C:1979:42; Judgment in *Keck and Mithouard*, C-267/91 and C-268/91, EU:C:1993:905.
518. Judgment in *Choquet*, 16/78, EU:C:1978:210; Judgment in *Kraus*, C-19/92, EU:C:1993:172; Judgment in *Gebhard*, C-55/94, EU:C:1995:411; Judgment in *Pfeiffer*, C-255/97, EU:C:1999:240; Judgment in *Mac Quen*, C-108/96, EU:C:2001:67; Judgment in *Gräbner*, C-294/00, EU:C:2002:442.
519. Judgment in *Fernández de Bobadilla*, C-234/97, EU:C:1999:367; Judgment in *Sehrer*, C-302/98; EU:C:2000:322.
520. Judgment in *Webb*, 279/80, EU:C:1981:314; Judgment in *Stichting Collectieve Antennevoorziening Gouda*, C-288/89, EU:C:1991:323; Judgment in *Säger*, C-76/90, EU:C:1991:331; Judgment in *De Agostini and TV-Shop*, C-34/95, EU:C:1997:344; Judgment in *Vander Elst*, C-43/93, EU:C:1994:310; Judgment in *Guiot*, C-272/94, EU:C:1996:147; Judgment in *Arblade*, C-369/96 and C-376/96, EU:C:1999:575; Judgment in *Corsten*, C-58/98, EU:C:2000:527.
521. Judgment in *Thieffry*, 71/76, EU:C:1977:65; Judgment in *Vlassopoulou*, C-340/89, EU:C:1991:193; Judgment in *Kemmler*, C-53/95, EU:C:1996:58. Concerning the freedom of establishment, another example mentioned in the literature is the *Überseering* case (see G. Kofler, *Doppelbesteuerungsabkommen und Europäisches Gemeinschaftsrecht* [Linde, 2007], at pp. 97-98; also cf. A. Cordewener in F. Vanistendael [ed.], *EU Freedoms and Taxation* [IBFD, 2006], at p. 37): According to some Member States' domestic law, a company's legal capacity is determined by reference to the law applicable in the place where its actual centre of administration is established. A company incorporated under another Member State's law may thus be denied legal capacity if it transfers its actual center of administration to such a Member State. The ECJ came to the conclusion that it is not in line with the freedom of establishment to disregard the fact that the company was legally incorporated in another Member State. See Judgment in *Überseering*, C-208/00, EU:C:2002:632.
522. Judgment in *Gebhard*, C-55/94, EU:C:1995:411.
523. Judgment in *Vlassopoulou*, C-340/89, EU:C:1991:193.
524. Judgment in *Thieffry*, 71/76, EU:C:1977:65, at para. 19; Judgment in *Choquet*, 16/78, EU:C:1978:210, at para. 8; Judgment in *Webb*, 279/80, EU:C:1981:314, at para. 20; Judgment in *Vlassopoulou*, C-340/89, EU:C:1991:193 at para. 15; Judgment in *Gebhard*, C-55/94, EU:C:1995:411, at para. 38; Judgment in *Fernández de Bobadilla*, C-234/97, EU:C:1999:367, at paras 31-34.
525. Judgment in *Futura Participations and Singer*, C-250/95, EU:C:1997:239.

permanent establishment, which meant that the company had to "*keep, in addition to its own accounts which must comply with the tax accounting rules applicable in the Member State in which it has its seat, separate accounts for its branch's activities complying with the tax accounting rules applicable in the State in which its branch is established.*"[526] The ECJ held that the fundamental freedoms preclude Member States from requiring non-residents to keep separate accounts without considering the accounts that are already kept in the residence state.[527]

Based on the ECJ's jurisprudence on double burdens, it has been argued that Member States generally have to take into consideration taxes that are paid in another Member State in order to avoid double taxation, which can also be considered to be a double burden.[528] With regard to VAT, the ECJ actually decided that certain effects of double taxation have to be avoided:[529] Before 1993,[530] cross-border dealings between private persons could be subject to double taxation if the transferor had already paid VAT upon the acquisition of a good and the transferee had to pay VAT upon the importation of the good. Relying on the prohibition of imposing "*directly or indirectly, on the products of other Member States any internal taxation of any kind in excess of that imposed directly or indirectly on similar domestic products*" in Article 110 TFEU (ex-Article 95 EEC Treaty) and the objective of establishing an internal market, the ECJ held that the Member State of destination had to credit "*the residual part of the value-added tax of the Member State of exportation which is still contained in the value*

526. Judgment in *Futura Participations and Singer*, C-250/95, EU:C:1997:239, at para. 26.
527. According to the ECJ, "*[t]he Member State concerned may, however, require the non-resident taxpayer to demonstrate clearly and precisely that the amount of the losses which he claims to have incurred corresponds, under its domestic rules governing the calculation of income and losses which were applicable in the financial year concerned, to the amount of the losses actually incurred in that State by the taxpayer*" (Judgment in *Futura Participations and Singer*, C-250/95, EU:C:1997:239, at para. 43). To this end critically M.A.C. Anido/C. Carrero, Accounting, the Permanent Establishment and EC Law: The *Futura Participations* Case, 8 *EC Tax Rev.* 1 (1999), p. 24 (at pp. 24-38); A. Cordewener, *Europäische Grundfreiheiten und nationales Steuerrecht* (Dr Otto Schmidt, 2002), at pp. 637-638; V. Hatzopoulos, Case C-250/95, Futura Participations SA & Singer v. Administration des Contributions (Luxembourg), Judgment of 15 May 1997, [1997] ECR I-2471, 35 *Common Market L. Rev.* 2 (1998), p. 493 (at pp. 512-513); G. Toifl, Neue EuGH-Entscheidung zur Betriebsstättendiskriminierung, 7 *SWI* 7 (1997), p. 311 (at pp. 319-320).
528. See F. Vanistendael, The ECJ at the Crossroads: Balancing Tax Sovereignty Against the Imperatives of the Single Market, 46 *Eur. Taxn.* 9 (2006), p. 413 (at p. 418); F. Vanistendael, Does the ECJ have the Power of Interpretation to Build a Tax System Compatible with the Fundamental Freedoms?, 17 *EC Tax Rev.* 2 (2008), p. 52 (at pp. 62-63); with further references G. Kofler/R. Mason, 14 *Colum. J. Eur. L.* 1 (2007), at p. 73 (FN 59).
529. Judgment in *Schul I*, 15/81, EU:C:1982:135, at paras 31-40; Judgment in *Drexl*, 299/86, EU:C:1988:103, at paras 9-13; Judgment in *Commission/Italy*, 120/88, EU:C:1991:74, at para. 6; Judgment in *Commission/Spain*, C-119/89, EU:C:1991:75, at para. 6; Judgment in *Commission/ Greece*, C-159/89, EU:C:1991:77, at para. 7; also cf. Judgment in *Schul II*, 47/84, EU:C:1985:216; Judgment in *Bergeres-Becque*, 39/85, EU:C:1986:36; for a detailed analysis see G. Kofler, *Doppelbesteuerungsabkommen und Europäisches Gemeinschaftsrecht* (Linde, 2007), at pp. 193 et seq.
530. Since 1 Jan. 1993, with regard to intra-EU trade, the concepts of exportation and importation have been replaced by the concepts of intra-EU acquisition of goods and the exemption of intra-EU supplies (see Council Directive 91/680/EEC of 16 Dec. 1991 supplement the common system of value added tax and amending Directive 77/388/EEC with a view to the abolition of fiscal frontiers, *OJ* L 376 [31 Dec. 1991]).

of the product when it is imported. The amount of this reduction may not, however, be greater than the amount of value-added tax actually paid in the Member State of exportation."[531] However, according to the ECJ, this approach "*is not based on a general principle prohibiting tax cumulation but on Article 95 [EEC Treaty]*"[532] and thus "*cannot be applied to charges regulated by independent national legislation.*"[533] This line of case law hence seems to be limited to taxes whose contours are harmonized.[534] Nevertheless, in the literature it was pointed out that in the *Lindfors* case[535] the ECJ might have changed its position in this respect.[536]

Despite severe criticism in the literature,[537] the ECJ has nevertheless consistently held that the fundamental freedoms cannot be relied upon in order to counter juridical

531. Judgment in *Schul I*, 15/81, EU:C:1982:135, at para. 34.
532. Judgment in *ORO Amsterdam Beheer en Concerto*, 165/88, EU:C:1989:608, at para. 18.
533. Judgment in *Scharbatke*, C-72/92, EU:C:1993:858, at para. 15; Judgment in *Nygård*, C-234/99, EU:C:2002:244, at para. 38; also cf. Judgment in *Cura Anlagen*, C-451/99, EU:C:2002:195, at para. 40.
534. See Opinion of AG Tesauro in *Scharbatke*, C-72/92, EU:C:1993:195, at point 4; J. Baßler, Zu den "Steuerspezifika" der Grundfreiheiten des EG-Vertrages, 14 *IStR* 23 (2005), p. 822 (at pp. 825-826); A. Cordewener, *Europäische Grundfreiheiten und nationales Steuerrecht* (Dr Otto Schmidt, 2002), at pp. 867 and 881; P. Farmer/R. Lyal, *EC Tax Law* (Clarendon Press, 1994), at p. 63; G. Kofler, *Doppelbesteuerungsabkommen und Europäisches Gemeinschaftsrecht* (Linde, 2007), at pp. 200-202; G. Kofler/R. Mason, 14 *Colum. J. Eur. L.* 1 (2007), at p. 71; G. Kofler/R. Mason in S. van Thiel (ed.), *The Internal Market and Direct Taxation: Is the European Court of Justice Taking a New Approach?* (CFE Brochure on European Taxation, 2007), at p. 184; G. Kofler in A. Rust (ed.), *Double Taxation Within the European Union* (Kluwer, 2011), at pp. 110-111; D. Weber, In Search of a (New) Equilibrium Between Tax Sovereignty and the Freedom of Movement Within the EC, 34 *Intertax* 12 (2006), p. 585 (at p. 592); D. Weber, *In Search of a (New) Equilibrium Between Tax Sovereignty and the Freedom of Movement Within the EC* (Kluwer, 2006), at p. 20; critically J. Englisch in H. Schaumburg/J. Englisch (eds.), *Europäisches Steuerrecht* (2015), at MN 6.65-6.66.
535. Judgment in *Lindfors*, C-365/02, EU:C:2004:449.
536. See J. Baßler, 14 *IStR* 23 (2005), at p. 826; G. Kofler, *Doppelbesteuerungsabkommen und Europäisches Gemeinschaftsrecht* (Linde, 2007), at pp. 203-205; G. Kofler/R. Mason, 14 *Colum. J. Eur. L.* 1 (2007), at p. 71; G. Kofler/R. Mason in S. van Thiel (ed.), *The Internal Market and Direct Taxation: Is the European Court of Justice Taking a New Approach?* (CFE Brochure on European Taxation, 2007), at pp. 184-185; G. Kofler in A. Rust (ed.), *Double Taxation Within the European Union* (Kluwer, 2011), at p. 111; also cf. Chapter 4.1.2.2.
537. See G. Kofler, *Doppelbesteuerungsabkommen und Europäisches Gemeinschaftsrecht* (Linde, 2007), at pp. 154-264; G. Kofler in A. Rust (ed.), *Double Taxation Within the European Union* (Kluwer, 2011), at pp. 123-133; G. Kofler/R. Mason, 14 *Colum. J. Eur. L.* 1 (2007), at pp. 79-96; G. Kofler/R. Mason in S. van Thiel (ed.), *The Internal Market and Direct Taxation: Is the European Court of Justice Taking a New Approach?* (CFE Brochure on European Taxation, 2007), at pp. 198-215; M. Lehner in M. Lang/J. Schuch/C. Staringer (eds.), *Tax Treaty Law and EC Law* (Kluwer, 2007), at pp. 20-23; A. Rust, How European Law Could Solve Double Taxation, in A. Rust (ed.), *Double Taxation Within the European Union* (Kluwer, 2011), p. 137 (at p. 138); J. Schönfeld, 83 *StuW* 1 (2006), at pp. 80-82; S. van Thiel, Avoiding a Double Burden Within the European Union: Comments on Kofler and Rust's Analysis, in A. Rust (ed.), *Double Taxation Within the European Union* (Kluwer, 2011), p. 167 (at pp. 174-183); M. Wathelet, Tax Sovereignty of the Member States and the European Court of Justice: New Trends or Confirmation?, in L. Hinnekens/P. Hinnekens (eds.), *A Vision of Taxes Within and Outside Europe, Festschrift in Honor of Prof. Dr. Frans Vanistendael* (Kluwer, 2008), p. 905 (at p. 916); but also see P. Farmer, EC Law and National Rules on Direct Taxation: A Phoney War?, *7 EC Tax Rev.* 1 (1998), p. 13 (at pp. 13 et seq.); M. Lang, Treaty Override und Gemeinschaftsrecht, in M. Lehner (ed.), *Reden zum Andenken an Klaus Vogel* (C.H. Beck, 2010), p. 59 (at pp. 74-81); K. Lenaerts, "United in Diversity" – also *In Fiscalibus*?, in L. Hinnekens/P. Hinnekens

double taxation of income[538] or the double levying of inheritance taxes[539] or special payroll levies.[540] According to the ECJ, the elimination of double taxation is indeed among the objectives of the EU.[541] However, double taxation results "*from the exercise in parallel by two Member States of their fiscal sovereignty. [...] [EU law] does not lay down any general criteria for the attribution of areas of competence between the Member States in relation to the elimination of double taxation within the [EU].*"[542] This means that Member States may take measures to prevent double taxation. However, "*the Member States [...] are not obliged [...] to adapt their own tax systems to the different systems of tax of the other Member States in order, inter alia, to eliminate the double taxation arising from the exercise in parallel by those Member States of their fiscal sovereignty.*"[543]

The difference between the issue of double taxation and the ECJ's case law on other forms of double burdens can be seen in the object and purpose of the rules concerned.[544] If, for example, a certain standard has to be met before an imported product is allowed to be marketed in a Member State in order to guarantee that it is not

(eds.), *A Vision of Taxes Within and Outside Europe, Festschrift in Honor of Prof. Dr. Frans Vanistendael* (Kluwer, 2008), p. 617 (at pp. 628-629); K. Lenaerts, Die Entwicklung der Rechtsprechung des Gerichtshofs der Europäischen Gemeinschaften auf dem Gebiet der direkten Besteuerung, 44 *EuR* 6 (2009), p. 728 (at pp. 737-741); P. Wattel, 12 *EC Tax Rev.* 4 (2003), at p. 199; P. Wattel, Passing the Buck Around: Who is Responsible for Double Taxation? – Comments on Profs. Kofler and Rust's Analysis, in A. Rust (ed.), *Double Taxation Within the European Union* (Kluwer, 2011), p. 157 (at pp. 157 et seq.); D. Weber, 34 *Intertax* 12 (2006), at pp. 591-593; D. Weber, *In Search of a (New) Equilibrium Between Tax Sovereignty and the Freedom of Movement Within the EC* (Kluwer, 2006), at pp. 18-21; also cf. S. Douma, The Three Ds of Direct Tax Jurisdiction: Disparity, Discrimination and Double Taxation, 46 *Eur. Taxn.* 11 (2006), p. 522 (at p. 532); W. Schön, 69 *Bull. Intl. Taxn.* 4/5 (2015), at pp. 274-276; W. Schön in W. Schön/C. Heber (eds.), *Grundfragen des Europäischen Steuerrechts* (Springer, 2015), at pp. 116-119; W. Schön, Doppelbesteuerung und EU-Recht, in W. Wassermeyer (ed.), *Doppelbesteuerung, Festgabe zum 75. Geburtstag von Prof. Dr. Dr. h.c. Franz Wassermeyer* (C.H. Beck, 2015), p. 7 (at pp. 8-9).

538. Judgment in *Kerckhaert and Morres*, C-513/04, EU:C:2006:603; Judgment in *Damseaux*, C-128/08, EU:C:2009:471; Order in *Levy and Sebbag*, C-540/11, EU:C:2012:581; also see Judgment of the EFTA-Court in *Seabrokers AS v. Staten v/Skattedirektoratet*, E-7/07.
539. Judgment in *Block*, C-67/08, EU:C:2009:92.
540. Judgment in *CIBA*, C-96/08, EU:C:2010:185.
541. Judgment in *Gilly*, C-336/96, EU:C:1998:221, at para. 16; Judgment in *Bouanich*, C-265/04, EU:C:2006:51, at para. 49; Judgment in *Damseaux*, C-128/08, EU:C:2009:471, at para. 28.
542. Judgment in *Kerckhaert and Morres*, C-513/04, EU:C:2006:603, at paras 20-23; Judgment in *CIBA*, C-96/08, EU:C:2010:185 at paras 25-27; also see Judgment in *Block*, C-67/08, EU:C:2009:92, at paras 28–30; Judgment in *Damseaux*, C-128/08, EU:C:2009:471, at paras 30 and 33.
543. Judgment in *Block*, C-67/08, EU:C:2009:92, at para. 31; Judgment in *CIBA*, C-96/08, EU:C:2010:185 at para. 28; also cf. Judgment in *Columbus Container Services*, C-298/05, EU:C:2007:754, at para. 51.
544. Cf. G. Kofler in A. Rust (ed.), *Double Taxation Within the European Union* (Kluwer, 2011), at p. 124; E. Reimer, Taxation – An Area Without Mutual Recognition, in I. Richelle/W. Schön/E. Traversa (eds.), *Allocating Taxing Powers Within the European Union* (Springer, 2013), p. 197 (at p. 204); E. Reimer in H. Schaumburg/J. Englisch (eds.), *Europäisches Steuerrecht* (2015), at MN 7.181; D. Weber, 34 *Intertax* 12 (2006), at pp. 591-592; D. Weber, *In Search of a (New) Equilibrium Between Tax Sovereignty and the Freedom of Movement Within the EC* (Kluwer, 2006), at pp. 18-21; also cf. J. Englisch, *Dividendenbesteuerung* (Dr Otto Schmidt, 2005), at p. 245; J. Englisch, *Wettbewerbsgleichheit im grenzüberschreitenden Handel* (Mohr Siebeck, 2008), at pp. 329-331.

detrimental to consumer health or safety, a national measure does not have to require examinations that were already conducted in the Member State of exportation which provides for similar rules. The re-examination in the importing Member State would not contribute to the achievement of the underlying objective, but rather impose a redundant burden on the free movement of goods. On the other hand, the main purpose of taxation is to generate revenue for the state.[545] But the fact that a cross-border transaction has already been subjected to tax in one Member State does not add anything to another Member State's budget.[546] Nevertheless, since tax rules also pursue other objectives than increasing public funds,[547] it would be premature – especially in view of the *Futura Participations* case – to conclude that the ECJ's case law on double burdens is meaningless with regard to taxation.[548]

2.3.2.2 "Neutral Rules" and "Even-Handed Rules"

Another category of impediments to free movement that are in part regarded as not being "covered" by the ECJ's non-discrimination approach are national measures that cause *"an absolute burden to cross-border situations."*[549] This concerns "neutral rules"[550] or "even handed rules"[551] that are indistinctly applicable, do not expressly create distinctions on the basis of the exercise of freedom of movement and are neutral in their effects as regards the nationality of the persons affected, but nevertheless restrict access to economic activities in another Member State.[552] Concerning the

545. See R. Seer in K. Tipke/J. Lang, *Steuerrecht*[22] (Dr Otto Schmidt, 2015), at § 1 para. 6; F.P. Sutter, *Das EG-Beihilfenverbot und sein Durchführungsverbot in Steuersachen* (Linde, 2005), at p. 21; also cf. J. Englisch, *Aufteilung der Besteuerungsbefugnisse – Ein Rechtfertigungsgrund für die Einschränkung von EG-Grundfreiheiten* (Institut "Finanzen und Steuern" e.V., 2008), at p. 132.
546. See J. Snell, Non-Discriminatory Tax Obstacles in Community Law, 56 *Intl. & Comp. L. Q.* 2 (2007), p. 339 (at p. 365) (*"The collection of revenue by one State in no way protects the revenue interest of another."*); R. Szudoczky, *The Sources of EU law and Their Relationships: Lessons for the Field of Taxation* (IBFD, 2014), at p. 352 (*"Evidently, the collection of tax revenue by one State will not fill up the pocket of the other State."*); also cf. P. Farmer in A. Arnull/D. Chalmers (eds.), *The Oxford Handbook on European Union Law* (Oxford University Press, 2015), at p. 815; G. Kofler in A. Rust (ed.), *Double Taxation Within the European Union* (Kluwer, 2011), at p. 124.
547. See, for example, R. Luja, *Assessment and Recovery of Tax Incentives in the EC and the WTO: A View on State Aids, Trade Subsidies and Direct Taxation* (Intersentia, 2003), at pp. 5-8; for an compilation of Austrian tax rules which implement(ed.) non-fiscal goals see H.G. Ruppe, *Das Abgabenrecht als Lenkungsinstrument der Gesellschaft und Wirtschaft und seine Schranken in den Grundrechten,* 8. ÖJT, Band I/A (Manz, 1982), at pp. 14 et seq.; for a historical overview see R. Wernsmann, *Verhaltenslenkung in einem rationale Steuersystem* (Mohr Siebeck, 2005), at pp. 19 et seq.
548. For cases in which this jurisprudence might be of relevance see E. Reimer in I. Richelle/W. Schön/E. Traversa (eds.), *Allocating Taxing Powers Within the European Union* (Springer, 2013), at pp. 204-213.
549. A. Cordewener in F. Vanistendael (ed.), *EU Freedoms and Taxation* (IBFD, 2006), at p. 35; also see G. Kofler, *Doppelbesteuerungsabkommen und Europäisches Gemeinschaftsrecht* (Linde, 2007), at pp. 93-95.
550. Opinion of AG Fennelly in *Graf,* C-190/98, EU:C:2000:49, at point 24.
551. P. Farmer, 12 *EC Tax Rev.* 2 (2003), at p. 79.
552. Opinion of AG Fennelly in *Graf,* C-190/98, EU:C:2000:49, at points 24-28.

freedom of establishment, a prominent example are provisions that prevent economic operators – typically members of a liberal profession – from having more than one place of professional establishment. Economic operators who already have a place of professional establishment in a Member State are thus precluded from setting up and maintaining more than one place of work within the EU. According to the ECJ, this is not in line with the freedom of establishment.[553] With regard to the freedom of movement for services, the *Alpine Investments* case[554] is often cited:[555] A former Netherlands rule prohibited a practice known as "cold calling," i.e., contacting individuals by telephone without their prior consent in order to offer them various services. Since it also precluded Netherlands companies from contacting potential customers in other Member States, the ECJ considered the provision to directly affect access to the market in services in the other Member States and thus to constitute a restriction on the freedom of movement of services.[556] In respect of the free movement of workers, the *Bosman* case[557] is a popular example that is commonly mentioned in the literature.[558] It concerned the transfer of a professional footballer from a Belgian to a French club, whereupon a transfer fee had to be paid to the transferring club. According to the ECJ, such a requirement of a monetary compensation directly affects the player's access to the employment market in other Member States and thus constitutes an obstacle to the free movement of workers.[559]

This line of case law is the consequence of the approach taken in *Dassonville*,[560] which has led the ECJ to scrutinize all national measures that are "*liable to hinder or make less attractive the exercise of fundamental freedoms guaranteed by the Treaty.*"[561] In the literature, it was hence inferred that the fundamental freedoms also include a non-restriction component, which is an absolute concept that does not require any

553. Judgment in *Klopp*, 107/93, EU:C:1984:270; Judgment in *Commission/France*, 96/85, EU:C:1986:189; Judgment in *Commission/Luxembourg*, C-351/90, EU:C:1992:266; Judgment in *Ramrath*, C-106/91, EU:C:1992:230.
554. Judgment in *Alpine Investments*, C-384/93, EU:C:1995:126.
555. See, for example, C. Barnard, *The Substantive Law of the EU*[4] (Oxford University Press, 2013), at p. 386; P. Craig/G. De Búrca, *EU Law*[4] (Oxford University Press, 2008), at pp. 832-833.
556. Judgment in *Alpine Investments*, C-384/93, EU:C:1995:126, at paras 38-39.
557. Judgment in *Bosman*, C-415/93, EU:C:1995:463.
558. See, for example, P. Craig/G. De Búrca, *EU Law*[4] (Oxford University Press, 2008), at pp. 760-761.
559. Judgment in *Bosman*, C-415/93, EU:C:1995:463, at paras 103-104.
560. Judgment in *Dassonville*, 8/74, EU:C:1974:85, at para. 5.
561. Judgment in *Gebhard*, C-55/94, EU:C:1995:411, at para. 37; Judgment in *Mac Quen*, C-108/96, EU:C:2001:67, at para. 26; Judgment in *Centros*, C-212/97, EU:C:1999:126, at para. 34; Judgment in *Gräbner*, C-294/00, EU:C:2002:442, at para. 39; Judgment in *Inspire Art*, C-167/01, EU:C:2003:512, at para. 133; Judgment in *Contse*, C-234/03, EU:C:2005:644, at para. 25; Judgment in *Commission/Greece*, C-65/05, EU:C:2006:673, at para. 49; Judgment in *Commission/Germany*, C-152/05, EU:C:2008:17, at para. 26; Judgment in *Commission/Hungary*, C-253/09, EU:C:2011:795, at para. 69; Judgment in *Commission/Spain*, C-269/09, EU:C:2012:439, at para. 62; also see Judgment in *Säger*, C-76/90, EU:C:1991:331, at para. 12; Judgment in *Kraus*, C-19/92, EU:C:1993:125, at para. 32; Judgment in *Konstantinidis*, C-168/91, EU:C:1993:115, at para. 15; Judgment in *Vander Elst*, C-43/93, EU:C:1994:310, at para. 14; Judgment in *Guiot*, C-272/94, EU:C:1996:147, at para. 10; Judgment in *Reisebüro Broede*, C-3/95, EU:C:1996:487, at para. 25; Judgment in *SCI Parodi*, C-222/95, EU:C:1997:230, at para. 18; Judgment in *Syndesmos*, C-398/95, EU:C:1997:282, at para. 16; Judgment in *Arblade*, C-369/96 and C-376/96, EU:C:1999:575, at para. 33; Judgment in *Corsten*, C-58/98,

tertium comparationis.[562] If a cross-border activity is made subject to a burden caused by a national measure, the fundamental freedoms are thus impaired.[563] However, this means that almost any national provision that establishes rules or imposes obligations on economic actors could be characterized as a restriction of free movement.[564] With regard to taxation, for example, double taxation would not even be required in order to be able to invoke the fundamental freedoms. Rather, the mere fact that a tax is levied in a cross-border situation would be liable to make the exercise of the fundamental freedoms less attractive.[565,566] Blatantly, such an understanding would be quite far-reaching.[567] It is possibly for this reason that the ECJ started to narrow down what is known as the *Dassonville* formulation[568] in as early as the

EU:C:2000:527, at para. 33; Judgment in *Mazzoleni and ISA*, C-165/98, EU:C:2001:162, at para. 22; Judgment in *Analir*, C-205/99, EU:C:2001:107, at para. 21; Judgment in *Nasiopoulos*, C-575/11, EU:C:2013:430, at para. 21.

562. See, for example, A. Schnitger, *Die Grenzen der Einwirkungen der Grundfreiheiten des EG-Vertrages auf das Ertragsteuerrecht* (IDW, 2006), at p. 171; contra J. Englisch, 80 *StuW* 1 (2003), at pp. 89-90; J. Englisch, *Dividendenbesteuerung* (Dr Otto Schmidt, 2005), at pp. 241 et seq.
563. See A. Cordewener in F. Vanistendael (ed.), *EU Freedoms and Taxation* (IBFD, 2006), at p. 27.
564. See K. Banks, The Application of the Fundamental Freedoms to Member State Tax Measures: Guarding Against Protectionism or Second-Guessing National Policy Choices?, 33 *Eur. L. Rev.* 4 (2008), p. 482 (at p. 485).
565. See, for example, A. Cordewener, *Europäische Grundfreiheiten und nationales Steuerrecht* (Dr Otto Schmidt, 2002), at p. 289; J. Englisch, 33 *Intertax* 8/9 (2005), at p. 316; P. Farmer/R. Lyal, *EC Tax Law* (Clarendon Press, 1994), at p. 328; G. Kofler, *Doppelbesteuerungsabkommen und Europäisches Gemeinschaftsrecht* (Linde, 2007), at p. 122; E. Reimer in H. Schaumburg/J. Englisch (eds.), *Europäisches Steuerrecht* (2015), at MN 7.191; B.J.M. Terra/P.J. Wattel, *European Tax Law*[6] (Kluwer, 2012), at pp. 56 and 84; also see Opinion of AG Kokott in *X*, C-686/13, EU:C:2015:31, at point 40.
566. This seems to be the position taken by the ECJ in the *Sea-Land Service and Nedlloyd Lijnen* case, where it was held that "*the VTS system at issue in the main proceedings, in that it requires the payment of a tariff by sea-going vessels longer than 41 metres, is liable to impede or render less attractive the provision of those services and therefore constitutes a restriction on their free circulation*" (Judgment in *Sea-Land Service and Nedlloyd Lijnen*, C-430/99 and C-431/99, EU:C:2002:364). Cf. K. Banks, 33 *Eur. L. Rev.* 4 (2008), at p. 495; B.J.M. Terra/P.J. Wattel, *European Tax Law*[6] (Kluwer, 2012), at pp. 87-89.
567. See L. Hinnekens, The Search for the Framework Conditions of the Fundamental EC Treaty Principles as Applied by the European Court to Member States' Direct Taxation, 11 *EC Tax Rev.* 3 (2002), p. 112 (at p. 117) ("*Saying that there are no intra-Community tax borders or that there should not be any under the Single Market concept, is going a bridge too far.*"); also cf. P. Farmer, 7 *EC Tax Rev.* 1 (1998), at p. 27; R. Lyal, 12 *EC Tax Rev.* 2 (2003), at p. 74; Opinion of AG Mischo in *Pfeiffer*, C-255/97, EU:C:1998:338, at point 58 ("*One must not arrive at a situation where Member States are required to justify as 'imperative requirements' all kinds of provisions of their legislation, for instance rates of corporate taxation or their rates of VAT, which are higher than elsewhere, the necessity to use the national language in relationships with administrative authorities or the principle that a registered trademark or a business name used previously has a priority, whenever an operator claims that such a provision makes its right of establishment less attractive.*"); also cf. Judgment in *Mobistar and Belgacom Mobile*, C-544/03 and C-545/03, EU:C:2005:518, at paras 27-35.
568. See, for example, R. Barents, New Developments in Measures Having Equivalent Effect, 18 *Common Market L. Rev.* 3 (1981), p. 271 (at p. 271); M. Isenbaert, *EC Law and the Sovereignty of the Member States in Direct Taxation* (Kluwer, 2010), at p. 242; D. Edward/R. Lane, *European Union Law* (Edward Elgar, 2013), at MN 10.26; R. Szudoczky, *The Sources of EU law and Their Relationships: Lessons for the Field of Taxation* (IBFD, 2014), at p. 147 and pp. 270-274.

1990s.[569] Since then, the ECJ has recurrently held that the fundamental freedoms do not prohibit a national measure if its effects are "*too uncertain and indirect to warrant the conclusion that [...] [it] is liable to hinder trade between Member States.*"[570] As there was still an increasing tendency to invoke the *Dassonville* formulation, the ECJ felt the need "*to re-examine and clarify its case law.*"[571] In the *Keck* decision, it was thus decided that non-discriminatory national provisions restricting or prohibiting certain selling arrangements are not liable to hinder trade between Member States, whereas product-related requirements are, even if applied in a non-discriminatory way, capable of making the free movement of goods less attractive.[572]

Although the *Keck* decision has faced criticism[573] and is "*undoubtedly difficult to transpose into the context of the other freedoms of movement,*"[574] it demonstrates that the non-restriction approach has limits. In the literature, it is argued that the decisive question is whether and when a national measure *specifically* places a burden on the establishment and proper functioning of the internal market.[575] The underlying reason why the ECJ formally distinguishes between product-related rules and selling arrangements is the assumption that such rules have a different effect with regard to the establishment and functioning of the internal market.[576] However, the standard that has to be applied in order to determine whether the effects of a national measure cause an undue barrier to free movement is blurred. For example, it cannot be presumed *a priori* that neutral national commercial regulations, rules governing pay scales,

569. One could argue that it started even earlier. However, this earlier line of case law seems to be inconsistent. See Opinion of AG Tesauro in *Hünermund*, C-292/92, EU:C:1993:863, at points 10 et seq.
570. Judgment in *Krantz*, 69/88, EU:C:1990:97, at para. 11; Judgment in *CMC Motorradcenter*, C-93/92, EU:C:1993:838, at para. 12; also see Judgment in *Peralta*, C-379/92, EU:C:1994:296, at para. 24; Judgment in *Semerano Casa Uno*, C-418/93 et al, EU:C:1996:242, at para. 32; Judgment in *ED*, C-412/97, EU:C:1999:324, at para. 11; Judgment in *BASF*, C-44/98, EU:C:1999:440, at paras 16 and 21; Judgment in *Graf*, C-190/98, EU:C:2000:49, at para. 25; also cf. Judgment in *Rocher*, C-126/91, EU:C:1993:191, at para. 21 ("*rules having merely hypothetical effect on intra-Community trade*"); Judgment in *Grogan*, C-159/90, C-159/90, EU:C:1991:378, at para. 24 ("*too tenuous [...] to be capable of being regarded as a restriction*").
571. Judgment in *Keck and Mithouard*, C-267/91 and C-268/91, EU:C:1993:905, at para. 14.
572. Judgment in *Keck and Mithouard*, C-267/91 and C-268/91, EU:C:1993:905, at paras 15–16; Judgment in *Hünermund*, C-292/92, EU:C:1993:932, at para. 21; Judgment in *Deutscher Apothekerverband*, C-322/01, EU:C:2003:664, at paras 67-68; Judgment in *Mars*, C-470/93, EU:C:1995:224, at paras 12-13; Judgment in *Morellato*, C-416/00, EU:C:2003:475, at paras 28-31.
573. See, for example, Opinion of AG Bot in *Commission/Italy*, C-110/05, EU:C:2008:386, at points 77-84.
574. Opinion of AG Poiares Maduro in *Alfa Vita Vassilopoulos*, C-158/04 and C-159/04, EU:C:2006:212, at point 50; also cf. K. Steinke, *Die Übertragbarkeit der* Keck-*Rechtsprechung des EuGH auf die Niederlassungsfreiheit* (Peter Lang, 2009), at pp. 179 et seq.
575. See A. Cordewener, *Europäische Grundfreiheiten und nationales Steuerrecht* (Dr Otto Schmidt, 2002), at pp. 264 et seq.; A. Cordewener in F. Vanistendael (ed.), *EU Freedoms and Taxation* (IBFD, 2006), at pp. 34-35; T. Eilmansberger, Zur Reichweite der Grundfreiheiten des Binnenmarktes (2. Teil), 121 *JBl* 7 (1999), p. 434 (at p. 438); J. Englisch, 80 *StuW* 1 (2003), at p. 89.
576. Opinion of AG Fennelly in *Graf*, C-190/98, EU:C:1999:423, at point 19; also cf. P. Oliver/W. Roth, 41 *Common Market L. Rev.* 2 (2004), at pp. 413; S. Weatherill, After *Keck*: Some Thoughts on How to Clarify the Clarification, 33 *Common Market L. Rev.* 5 (1996), p. 885 (at pp. 889-894); critically regarding this assumption J. Englisch, 33 *Intertax* 8/9 (2005), at p. 316.

working hours or social protection or the levying of taxes per se have such an effect.[577] With regard to the issue of double taxation, on the other hand, it seems to be evident that cross-border transactions are specifically impaired,[578] although issues of multiple tax burdens may also arise in a domestic context if and insofar as intra-state bodies enjoy a certain fiscal autonomy.[579] The reason why the ECJ is nevertheless reluctant to conclude that double taxation is an infringement of the fundamental freedoms is that EU law "*does not lay down any general criteria for the attribution of areas of competence between the Member States in relation to the elimination of double taxation within the [EU].*"[580] Notwithstanding the criticism expressed in the literature,[581] it is not likely that the ECJ is going to revise this line of case law.

2.3.3 The Impediments for Free Movement Resulting from Disparities

Although the *Dassonville* formulation might suggest otherwise, it can be inferred from the ECJ's case law that the fundamental freedoms cannot be relied upon to challenge any national measure that establishes rules concerning or imposes obligations on economic actors.[582] Differences between the legal systems of two or more different

577. Opinion of AG Fennelly in *Graf*, C-190/98, EU:C:1999:423, at point 32; Opinion of AG Mischo in *Mac Quen*, C-108/96, EU:C:2000:131, at point 44.
578. See J. Englisch, *Dividendenbesteuerung* (Dr Otto Schmidt, 2005), at pp. 253-254; J. Englisch, 33 *Intertax* 8/9 (2005), at p. 323.
579. On the corresponding situation in the US see, for example, A. Cordewener, *Europäische Grundfreiheiten und nationales Steuerrecht* (Dr Otto Schmidt, 2002), at pp. 871-876; G. Kofler, *Doppelbesteuerungsabkommen und Europäisches Gemeinschaftsrecht* (Linde, 2007), at pp. 221-231; G. Kofler/R. Mason, 14 *Colum. J. Eur. L.* 1 (2007), at pp.83-96; G. Kofler/R. Mason in S. van Thiel (ed.), *The Internal Market and Direct Taxation: Is the European Court of Justice Taking a New Approach?* (CFE Brochure on European Taxation, 2007), at pp. 205-213; for an Austrian perspective see M. Lang/L. Paterno, Die Vermeidung der Doppelbesteuerung in der föderalen Struktur Österreichs, 1 *Spektrum der Rechtswissenschaften* 1 (2011), p. 76 (at pp. 76 et seq.); M. Lang/L. Paterno, Internationales Steuerrecht und Besteuerung im Bundesstaat, 21 *SWI* 12 (2011), p. 520 (at pp. 520 et seq.).
580. Judgment in *Kerckhaert and Morres*, C-513/04, EU:C:2006:603, at paras 20-23; Judgment in *CIBA*, C-96/08, EU:C:2010:185 at paras 25-27; also see Judgment in *Block*, C-67/08, EU:C:2009:92, at paras 28-30; Judgment in *Damseaux*, C-128/08, EU:C:2009:471, at paras 30 and 33.
581. See A. Rust in A. Rust (ed.), *Double Taxation Within the European Union* (Kluwer, 2011), at p. 138; also see G. Kofler, *Doppelbesteuerungsabkommen und Europäisches Gemeinschaftsrecht* (Linde, 2007), at pp. 177-264; G. Kofler/R. Mason, 14 *Colum. J. Eur. L.* 1 (2007), at pp. 79-96; G. Kofler/R. Mason in S. van Thiel (ed.), *The Internal Market and Direct Taxation: Is the European Court of Justice Taking a New Approach?* (CFE Brochure on European Taxation, 2007), at pp. 198-215; G. Kofler in A. Rust (ed.), *Double Taxation Within the European Union* (Kluwer, 2011), at pp. 123-133; S. van Thiel in A. Rust (ed.), *Double Taxation Within the European Union* (Kluwer, 2011), at pp. 174-183; M. Wathelet in L. Hinnekens/P. Hinnekens (eds.), *A Vision of Taxes Within and Outside Europe, Festschrift in Honor of Prof. Dr. Frans Vanistendael* (Kluwer, 2008), at p. 916.
582. Cf. Opinion of AG Fennelly in *Graf*, C-190/98, EU:C:2000:49, at point 32; J. Englisch, *Dividendenbesteuerung* (Dr Otto Schmidt, 2005), at pp. 241-242; T. Kingreen, *Die Struktur der Grundfreiheiten des Europäischen Gemeinschaftsrechts* (Duncker & Humblot, 1999), at pp. 104-105.

Member States, for example, although harming cross-border movement,[583] do not per se constitute discrimination or a restriction of cross-border economic transactions.[584] In fact, in the *Cassis de Dijon* decision the ECJ already held that "*[o]bstacles to movement within the Community resulting from disparities between the national laws relating to the marketing of the products in question must be accepted in so far as those provisions may be recognized as being necessary in order to satisfy mandatory requirements.*"[585] With regard to taxation, it is settled case law that the "*Treaty offers no guarantee to a citizen of the Union that transferring his residence to a Member State other than that in which he previously resided will be neutral as regards taxation. Given the disparities in the tax legislation of the Member States, such a transfer may be to the citizen's advantage or not, according to circumstances.*"[586] The fundamental freedoms hence cannot serve as a basis to challenge different tax policy decisions of the Member States, such as the determination of tax rates[587] or the determination of profits, income, expenditure, deductions and exemptions.[588] Insofar as harmonizing measures have not

583. See S. Douma, 46 *Eur. Taxn.* 11 (2006), at p. 524; J. Englisch, *Wettbewerbsgleichheit im grenzüberschreitenden Handel* (Mohr Siebeck, 2008), at p. 244; also cf. Communication from the Commission to the Council, the European Parliament and the Economic and Social Committee, Towards an Internal Market without tax obstacles, COM (2001) 582 final (23 Oct. 2001), at p. 11 ("*he multiplicity of tax laws, conventions and practices entails substantial compliance costs and represents in itself a barrier to cross-border economic activity*").
584. Judgment in *Walt Wilhelm*, 14/68, EU:C:1969:4, at para. 13; Judgment in *Kenny*, 1/78, EU:C:1978:163, at para. 18; Judgment in *Van Dam*, 185/78 to 204/78, EU:C:1979:177, at para. 10; Judgment in *Oebel*, 155/80, EU:C:1981:177, at para. 9; Judgment in *Wood and Cowie*, C-251/90 and C-252/90, EU:C:1992:198, at para. 19; Judgment in *Peralta*, C-379/92, EU:C:1994:296, at para. 48; Judgment in *Alpine Investments*, C-384/93, EU:C:1995:126, at para. 27; Judgment in *Perfili*, C-177/94, EU:C:1996:24, at para. 17; Judgment in *Reisebüro Broede*, C-3/95, EU:C:1996:487, at para. 42; Judgment in *Läärä*, C-124/97, EU:C:1999:435, at para. 36; Judgment in *Wouters*, C-309/99, EU:C:2002:98, at para. 108; Judgment in *Mac Quen*, C-108/96, EU:C:2001:67, at para. 33; Judgment in *Gräbner*, C-294/00, EU:C:2002:442, at para. 46; Judgment in *Anomar*, C-6/01, EU:C:2003:446, at para. 80; Judgment in *Milk Marque and National Farmers' Union*, C-137/00, EU:C:2003:429, at para. 124; Judgment in *Schempp*, C-403/03, EU:C:2005:446, at para. 34.
585. Judgment in *Rewe*, 120/78, EU:C:1979:42, at para. 8.
586. Judgment in *Block*, C-67/08, EU:C:2009:92, at para. 35; also see Judgment in *Hervein*, C-393/99 and C-394/99, EU:C:2002:182, at para. 51; Judgment in *Weigel*, C-387/01, EU:C:2004:256, at para. 55; Judgment in *Lindfors*, C-365/02, EU:C:2004:449, at para. 34; Judgment in *Schempp*, C-403/03, EU:C:2005:446, at para. 45; Judgment in *Alevizos*, C-392/05, EU:C:2007:251, at para. 76; Judgment in *Renneberg*, C-527/06, EU:C:2008:566, at para. 40; Judgment in *Schulz-Delzers and Schulz*, C-240/10, EU:C:2011:591, at para. 42; Judgment in *National Grid Indus*, C-371/10, EU:C:2011:785, at para. 62.
587. Judgment in *Gilly*, C-336/96, EU:C:1998:221, at para. 47; Judgment in *de Groot*, C-385/00, EU:C:2002:750, at para. 86. With regard to the problem of "excessive tax rates" see A. Cordewener, *Europäische Grundfreiheiten und nationales Steuerrecht* (Dr Otto Schmidt, 2002), at pp. 855-856; L. Hinnekens, Non-discrimination in EC Income Tax Law: Painting in the Colours of a Chameleon-Like Principle, 36 *Eur. Taxn.* 9 (1996), p. 286 (at pp. 299-300); A. Schnitger, *Die Grenzen der Einwirkungen der Grundfreiheiten des EG-Vertrages auf das Ertragsteuerrecht* (IDW, 2006), at pp. 250-252.
588. Judgment in *Futura Participations and Singer*, C-250/95, EU:C:1997:239, at para. 33.

been taken,[589] the Member States are thus free to take choices of economic policy irrespective of other Member States' decisions.[590]

As opposed to discrimination or a restriction that is caused by the rules of a single jurisdiction, the fundamental freedoms cannot remedy impediments of the internal market that are due to the interplay of differing rules in various jurisdictions.[591] Such disparities can be identified by imagining that the Member States involved have exactly the same legal system. If the disadvantage of the cross-border transaction compared to a purely domestic transaction disappears in the course of this intellectual pastime,[592] it is a result of the legislative differences between the legal systems.[593] According to the ECJ, such disparities do not fall within the scope of the fundamental freedoms, "*so long as they affect all persons subject to them in accordance with objective criteria and*

---

589. Opinion of AG Geelhoed in *Test Claimants in Class IV of the ACT Group Litigation*, C-374/04, EU:C:2006:139, at point 47.

590. Judgment in *Columbus Container Services*, C-298/05, EU:C:2007:754, at para. 51; Judgment in *Block*, C-67/08, EU:C:2009:92, at para. 31; Judgment in *CIBA*, C-96/08, EU:C:2010:185, at para. 28; Judgment in *Commission/Hungary*, C-253/09, EU:C:2011:795, at para. 83; Judgment in *Banco Bilbao Vizcaya Argentaria*, C-157/10, EU:C:2011:813, at para. 39; Judgment in *X*, C-302/12, EU:C:2013:756, at para. 29; Judgment in *Sparkasse Allgäu*, C-522/14, EU:C:2016:253, at para. 31.

591. Judgment in *Walt Wilhelm*, 14/68, EU:C:1969:4, at para. 13; Judgment in *Kenny*, 1/78, EU:C:1978:163, at para. 18; Judgment in *Van Dam*, 185/78 to 204/78, EU:C:1979:177, at para. 10; Judgment in *Oebel*, 155/80, EU:C:1981:177, at para. 9; Judgment in *Wood and Cowie*, C-251/90 and C-252/90, EU:C:1992:198, at para. 19; Judgment in *Peralta*, C-379/92, EU:C:1994:296, at para. 48; Judgment in *Alpine Investments*, C-384/93, EU:C:1995:126, at para. 27; Judgment in *Perfili*, C-177/94, EU:C:1996:24, at para. 17; Judgment in *Reisebüro Broede*, C-3/95, EU:C:1996:487, at para. 42; Judgment in *Läärä*, C-124/97, EU:C:1999:435, at para. 36; Judgment in *Wouters*, C-309/99, EU:C:2002:98, at para. 108; Judgment in *Mac Quen*, C-108/96, EU:C:2001:67, at para. 33; Judgment in *Gräbner*, C-294/00, EU:C:2002:442, at para. 46; Judgment in *Anomar*, C-6/01, EU:C:2003:446, at para. 80; Judgment in *Milk Marque and National Farmers' Union*, C-137/00, EU:C:2003:429, at para. 124; Judgment in *Schempp*, C-403/03, EU:C:2005:446, at para. 34.

592. According to AG Geelhoed (see Opinion of AG Geelhoed in *Test Claimants in Class IV of the ACT Group Litigation*, C-374/04, EU:C:2006:139, at points 48-54; Opinion of AG Geelhoed in *Test Claimants in the Thin Cap Group Litigation*, C-524/04, EU:C:2006:436, at point 53) and parts of the literature (see B.J.M. Terra/P.J. Wattel, *European Tax Law*[6] [Kluwer, 2012], at pp. 94-96; P.J. Wattel, 12 *EC Tax Rev.* 4 [2003], at pp. 198-200), disparities have to be distinguished from a dislocation of the tax base (contra S. Douma, 46 *Eur. Taxn.* 11 [2006], at pp. 532-533). In a cross-border situation, such disadvantageous tax effects may occur even if the national tax systems of all Member States were exactly the same in design and content. The disadvantage may result from either the same tax base being simultaneously used by different, unharmonized and uncoordinated jurisdictions or the separation of positive and negative parts of the income in different jurisdictions, which makes a compensation impossible (see B.J.M. Terra/P.J. Wattel, *European Tax Law*[6] [Kluwer, 2012], at p. 95). If it cannot be determined which jurisdiction is to be blamed, because the rules concerned likewise apply to cross-border and purely domestic transactions, the disadvantage results from a dislocation of the tax base. However, the concept of a dislocation has not found its way into the ECJ's case law.

593. See G. Kofler, *Doppelbesteuerungsabkommen und Europäisches Gemeinschaftsrecht* (Linde, 2007), at pp. 124-125; G. Kofler in A. Rust (ed.), *Double Taxation Within the European Union* (Kluwer, 2011), at p. 99; B.J.M. Terra/P.J. Wattel, *European Tax Law*[6] (Kluwer, 2012), at p. 94; contra D. Weber, 34 *Intertax* 12 (2006), p. 588 (FN 17); D. Weber, *In Search of a (New) Equilibrium Between Tax Sovereignty and the Freedom of Movement Within the EC* (Kluwer, 2006), at p. 12 (FN 17). This approach is similar to the "internal consistency test" as applied by the US Supreme Court. See R. Mason, 49 *Bost. Coll. L. Rev.* 4 (2008), at pp. 1277 et seq.

without regard to their nationality."[594] Thus, disparities apparently do not generally remain unaffected by the fundamental freedoms. In fact, it should not be surprising that a domestic provision which clashes with a national measure of another Member State and is hence jointly responsible for a disparity causes an infringement of the fundamental freedoms, if it - considered separately - also leads to discrimination or a restriction.[595] In view of discrimination or a restriction the disparity becomes negligible. However, it is less clear how to determine whether divergences existing between the various Member States affect all persons subject to them in accordance with objective criteria and what the outcome would be if this requirement were not fulfilled.

Since disadvantages resulting from disparities cannot be remedied by means of the fundamental freedoms, Member States do not infringe EU law if they determine, in a double taxation convention, the connecting factors for the purposes of allocating powers of taxation.[596] Differentiations that merely result from the fact that, in a tax treaty between two Member States, the taxing rights for the income of a taxpayer are assigned to one Member State, whereas the taxing rights for the income of another taxpayer are assigned to the other Member State cannot be regarded as constituting discrimination prohibited by the fundamental freedoms. As AG Colomer held in his Opinion in *Gilly*, "*[t]here is no doubt that, once the State which is to tax the income from*

594. Judgment in *Perfili*, C-177/94, EU:C:1996:24, at para. 17; Judgment in *Schempp*, C-403/03, EU:C:2005:446, at para. 34; also see Judgment in *Walt Wilhelm*, 14/68, EU:C:1969:4, at para. 13; Judgment in *Kenny*, 1/78, EU:C:1978:163, at para. 18; Judgment in *Milk Marque and National Farmers' Union*, C-137/00, EU:C:2003:429, at para. 124; also cf. W. Schön in J. Pelka (ed.), *Europa- und verfassungsrechtliche Grenzen der Unternehmensbesteuerung*, DStJG 30 (Dr Otto Schmidt, 2000), at p. 211; W. Schön, 9 *EC Tax Rev.* 2 (2000), at p. 98.
595. Cf. R. Mason, 49 *Bost. Coll. L. Rev.* 4 (2008), at pp. 1319-1320.
596. Judgment in *Gilly*, C-336/96, EU:C:1998:221, at para. 24 and para. 30; Judgment in *Saint-Gobain*, C-307/97, EU:C:1999:438, at para. 56; Judgment in *de Groot*, C-385/00, EU:C:2002:750, at para. 93; Judgment in *D.*, C-376/03, EU:C:2005:424, at para. 52; Judgment in *van Hilten-van der Heijden*, C-513/03, EU:C:2006:131, at para. 47; Judgment in *N*, C-470/04, EU:C:2006:525, at para. 44; Judgment in *Test Claimants in Class IV of the ACT Group Litigation*, C-374/04, EU:C:2006:773, at para. 52; Judgment in *Commission/Italy*, C-540/07, EU:C:2009:717, at para. 29; Judgment in *Test Claimants in the Thin Cap Group Litigation*, EU:C:2007:161, at para. 49; Judgment in *Oy AA*, C-231/05, EU:C:2007:439, at para. 52; Judgment in *Amurta*, C-379/05, EU:C:2007:655, at para. 17; Judgment in *Orange European Smallcap Fund*, C-194/06, EU:C:2008:289, at para. 32; Judgment in *Burda*, C-284/06, EU:C:2008:365, at para. 87; Judgment in *Truck Center*, C-282/07, EU:C:2008:762, at para. 22; Judgment in *Cobelfret*, C-138/07, EU:C:2009:82, at para 56; Judgment in *Commission/Netherlands*, C-521/07, EU:C:2009:360, at para. 34; Judgment in *Aberdeen Property Fininvest Alpha*, C-303/07, EU:C:2009:377, at para. 25; Judgment in *Damseaux*, C-128/08, EU:C:2009:471, at para. 30; Judgment in *Commission/Italy*, C-540/07, EU:C:2009:717, at para. 29; Judgment in *Commission/Spain*, C-487/08, EU:C:2010:310, at para. 38; Judgment in *Commission/Germany*, C-284/09, EU:C:2011:670, at para. 46; Judgment in *National Grid Indus*, C-371/10, EU:C:2011:785, at para. 45; Judgment in *Banco Bilbao Vizcaya Argentaria*, C-157/10, EU:C:2011:813, at para. 31; Judgment in *Commission/Spain*, C-269/09, EU:C:2012:439, at para. 77; Judgment in *Argenta Spaarbank*, C-350/11, EU:C:2013:447, at para. 50; Judgment in *DMC*, C-164/12, EU:C:2014:20, at para. 47; Judgment in *Nordea Bank Danmark*, C-48/13, EU:C:2014:2087, at para. 27; Judgment in *Grünewald*, C-559/13, EU:C:2015:109, at para. 40; Judgment in *Commission/Germany*, EU:C:2015:230, at para. 57; with regard to the Agreement between the European Community and its Member States, of the one part, and the Swiss Confederation, of the other, on the free movement of persons, *OJ* L 114 (30 Apr. 2002), at pp. 6-63 also see Judgment in *Bukovansky*, C-241/14, EU:C:2015:766, at para. 45.

employment has been determined, the tax payable will vary depending on which State it is. In Mrs Gilly's case, the tax she pays in Germany on the income from her employment is more than she would pay if she received the income in France or if, although received in Germany, it were taxable in France. However, that difference does not arise from the taxation criteria in the Franco-German Convention, but from German tax law, which specifies a higher rate of tax on such income than the rate in France, while in addition the tax systems and the progressive nature of the tax differ considerably in the two States."[597] The decision of Member States on how to allocate taxing rights among one another, hence, cannot be challenged by means of the fundamental freedoms, because "*the question of a state's taxation rights under a tax treaty is a question of 'allocation not discrimination'.*"[598]

2.4 Comparability

2.4.1 *The Function of the Comparability Analysis in the ECJ's Tax Jurisprudence*

The restriction-based approach of the ECJ has not yet gained much importance in the area of taxes.[599] In the literature, it is argued that even the few decisions which are said to concern restrictive tax measures have been based on a discrimination analysis.[600] In

597. Opinion of AG Colomer in *Gilly*, C-336/96, EU:C:1997:556, at points 46-47; also cf. Judgment in *Gilly*, C-336/96, EU:C:1998:221, at para. 34.

598. D. Hughes, Gilly and the Big Picture, 52 *Bull. Intl. Taxn.* 8/9 (1998), p. 329 (at p. 331); also see A. Cordewener, *Europäische Grundfreiheiten und nationales Steuerrecht* (Dr Otto Schmidt, 2002), at p. 598; D. Hohenwarter, The Allocation of Taxing Rights in the Light of the Fundamental Freedoms of EC Law, in M. Lang/J. Schuch/C. Staringer (eds.), *Tax Treaty Law and EC Law* (Kluwer, 2007), p. 83 (at p. 115); G. Kofler, *Doppelbesteuerungsabkommen und Europäisches Gemeinschaftsrecht* (Linde, 2007), at p. 542; also cf. D. Hughes, Withholding taxes and the most favoured nation clause, 51 *Bull. Intl. Taxn.* 3 (1997), p. 126 (at p. 130).

599. Cf. G. Kofler, Most-Favoured-Nation Treatment in Direct Taxation: Does EC Law Provide for Community MFN in Bilateral Double Taxation Treaties?, 5 *Hous. Bus. & Tax L. J.* 1 (2005), p. 1 (at pp. 23-24); S. van Thiel, The Future of the Principle of Non-Discrimination in the EU: Towards a Right to Most Favored Nation Treatment and a Prohibition of Double Burdens?, in R.S. Avi-Yonah/J.R. Hines Jr./M. Lang (eds.), *Comparative Fiscal Federalism* (Kluwer, 2007), p. 331 (at p. 394).

600. See J. Englisch, 38 *Intertax* 4 (2010), at pp. 202-203; P. Farmer, 12 *EC Tax Rev.* 2 (2003), at p. 81; M. Lang, Kapitalverkehrsfreiheit und Doppelbesteuerungsabkommen, in E. Lechner/C. Staringer/M. Tumpel (eds.), *Kapitalverkehrsfreiheit und Steuerrecht* (Linde, 2000), p. 181 (at pp. 189-191); M. Lang, *Die Rechtsprechung des EuGH zu den direkten Steuern* (Peter Lang, 2007), at pp. 34-39; M. Lang, 18 *EC Tax Rev.* 3 (2009), at p. 99; M. Lang in M. Hebig/K. Kaiser/K. Koschmieder/M. Oblau (eds.), *FS Wilhelm H. Wacker* (Erich Schmidt Verlag, 2006), at pp. 366-369; M. Lang in M. Beusch (ed.), *Steuerrecht 2007* (Schulthess, 2007), at pp. 7-10; M. Lang in R. Mellinghof/W. Schön/H. Viskorf (eds.), *Steuerrecht im Rechtsstaat, Festschrift für Wolfgang Spindler zum 65. Geburtstag* (Dr Otto Schmidt, 2011), at p. 300; R. Lyal, 12 *EC Tax Rev.* 2 (2003), at p. 74; also cf. N. Bammens, *The Principle of Non-Discrimination in International and European Tax Law* (IBFD, 2012), at pp. 542-566.

Futura Participations,[601] for example, non-residents were required to keep proper accounts compliant with the relevant Luxembourg rules with regard to domestic permanent establishments, just like residents, although a non-resident may be able to rely on the accounts that are kept in compliance with the tax accounting rules of its residence state.[602] It can hence be argued that, with regard to the accounting requirement, non-residents are not comparable to residents, i.e., under the Luxembourg rules different situations were treated in the same way.[603] This understanding would be in line with the ECJ's case law according to which "*comparable situations must not be treated differently and [...] different situations must not be treated in the same way.*"[604]

601. Further examples mentioned in the literature are the decisions in *Deutsche Shell* (Judgment in *Deutsche Shell*, C-293/06, EU:C:2008:129; see W.C. Haslehner, *Das Betriebstättendiskriminierungsverbot im Internationalen Steuerrecht* [Linde, 2010], at p. 148; W.C. Haslehner, EuGH-Urteil *Deutsche Shell GmbH* (Rs. C-293/06): Das gemeinschaftsrechtliche Ende der *Symmetriethese*?, 18 *SWI* 4 [2008], p. 161 [at p. 165]; contra D. Hohenwarter, *Verlustverwertung im Konzern* [LexisNexis, 2009], at p. 287; M. Lang, 18 *EC Tax Rev.* 3 (2009), at pp. 98-100; M. Lang in R. Mellinghof/W. Schön/H. Viskorf [eds.], *Steuerrecht im Rechtsstaat, Festschrift für Wolfgang Spindler zum 65. Geburtstag* [Dr Otto Schmidt, 2011], at p. 315; K. Lenaerts, Federalism and the Rule of Law: Perspectives from the European Court of Justice, 33 *Fordham Intl. L. J.* 5 [2010], p. 1338 [at p. 1365]) and *Commission/Belgium* (Judgment in *Commission/Belgium*, C-433/04, EU:C:2006:702; cf. N. Bammens, *The Principle of Non-Discrimination in International and European Tax Law* (IBFD, 2012), at pp. 559-562).
602. Judgment in *Futura Participations and Singer*, C-250/95, EU:C:1997:239.
603. See M. Lang, *Die Rechtsprechung des EuGH zu den direkten Steuern* (Peter Lang, 2007), at pp. 37-38; M. Lang, Direct Taxation: Is the ECJ Heading in a New Direction?, 46 *Eur. Taxn.* 9 (2006), p. 421 (at p. 422); M. Lang in M. Hebig/K. Kaiser/K. Koschmieder/M. Oblau (eds.), *FS Wilhelm H. Wacker* (Erich Schmidt Verlag, 2006), at p. 368; M. Lang in M. Beusch (ed.), *Steuerrecht 2007* (Schulthess, 2007), at pp. 8-9; M. Lang in R. Mellinghof/W. Schön/H. Viskorf (eds.), *Steuerrecht im Rechtsstaat, Festschrift für Wolfgang Spindler zum 65. Geburtstag* (Dr Otto Schmidt, 2011), at p. 304; also cf. J. Schönfeld, *Hinzurechnungsbesteuerung und Europäisches Gemeinschaftsrecht* (Dr Otto Schmidt, 2005), at pp. 71-73.
604. Judgment in *Garcia Avello*, C-148/02, EU:C:2003:539, at para. 31; Judgment in *Azienda Agro-Zootecnica Franchini and Eolica di Altamura*, C-2/10, EU:C:2011:502, at para. 64; Judgment in *Hungary/Commission*, C-31/13 P, EU:C:2014:70, at para. 73; also cf. Judgment in *SFI*, C-85/97, EU:C:1998:552, at para. 30; Judgment in *Jippers and others*, C-189/01, EU:C:2001:420, at para. 128; Judgment in *Denkavit*, C-507/99, EU:C:2002:4, at para. 44; Judgment in *Omega and others*, C-122/00, EU:C:2002:161, at para. 79; Judgment in *Commission/Portugal*, C-334/03, EU:C:2005:623, at para. 24; also cf. Judgment in *Schumacker*, C-279/93, EU:C:1995:31, at para. 30; Judgment in *Wielockx*, C-80/94, EU:C:1995:271, at para. 17; Judgment in *Asscher*, C-107/94, EU:C:1996:251, at para. 40; Judgment in *Royal Bank of Scotland*, C-311/97, EU:C:1999:216, at para. 26; Judgment in *Gschwind*, C-391/97, EU:C:1999:409, at para. 21; Judgment in *Kerckhaert and Morres*, C-513/04, EU:C:2006:713, at para. 19; Judgment in *Meindl*, C-329/05, EU:C:2007:57, at para. 22; Judgment in *Talotta*, C-383/05, EU:C:2007:181, at para. 18; Judgment in *Lakebrink and Peters-Lakebrink*, C-182/06, EU:C:2007:452, at para. 27; Judgment in *Columbus Container Services*, C-298/05, EU:C:2007:754, at para. 41; Judgment in Gielen, C-440/08, EU:C:2010:148; at para. 38; Judgment in *Commission/Hungary*, C-253/09, EU:C:2011:795, at para. 50; Judgment in *Commission/Netherlands*, C-542/09, EU:C:2012:346, at para. 41; Judgment in *Commission/Estonia*, C-39/10, EU:C:2012:282, at para. 48; Judgment in *Banco Bilbao Vizcaya Argentaria*, C-157/10, EU:C:2011:813, at para. 41; Judgment in *Bouanich*, C-375/12, EU:C:2014:138, at para. 45.

Despite the developments in the case law regarding the restriction-based approach, the comparability assessment is thus still of major importance in the ECJ's direct tax jurisprudence. Thereby, the cross-border transaction is in general compared with a purely domestic transaction. Depending on the particular situation, on the one hand, a resident who operates cross-border may be compared to another resident whose activities are restricted to the home state.[605] On the other hand, a non-resident making use of the fundamental freedoms may be compared to a resident of the host state.[606] Determining whether a particular tax system is discriminatory depends to a large extent on the choice of the comparator.[607] The difficulty is that no two situations are entirely alike or entirely different.[608] With regard to some aspects, two situations may be alike, whereas they are not with regard to others.[609] Therefore, consistent criteria are needed to decide which attributes have to be considered in order to determine whether comparability exists or not.[610] In the literature, however, it is indicated that the ECJ's case law does not meet this requirement.[611] The Court's approaches instead range from focusing on the legal situation,[612] the factual

605. See, for example, Judgment in *Bachmann*, C-204/90, EU:C:1992:35; Judgment in *Halliburton Services*, C-1/93, EU:C:1994:127; Judgment in *Baxter*, C-254/97, EU:C:1999:368; Judgment in *Eurowings*, C-294/97, EU:C:1999:524; Judgment in *Vestergaard*, C-55/98, EU:C:1999:533; Judgment in *X and Y*, C-200/98, EU:C:1999:566; Judgment in *Baars*, C-251/98, EU:C:2000:22; Judgment in *Zurstrassen*, C-87/99, EU:C:2000:251; Judgment in *Verkooijen*, C-35/98, EU:C:2000:294; Judgment in *AMID*, C-141/99, EU:C:2000:696; Judgment in *Lankhorst-Hohorst*, C-324/00, EU:C:2002:749; Judgment in *De Groot*, C-385/00, EU:C:2002:750; Judgment in *Bosal*, C-168/01, EU:C:2003:479.

606. See, for example, Judgment in *Avoir Fiscal*, 270/83, EU:C:1986:37; Judgment in *Commerzbank*, C-330/91, EU:C:1993:303; Judgment in *Schumacker*, C-279/93, EU:C:1995:31; Judgment in *Asscher*, C-107/94, EU:C:1996:251; Judgment in *Wielockx*, C-80/94, EU:C:1995:271; Judgment in *Futura Participations and Singer*, C-250/95, EU:C:1997:239; Judgment in *Gilly*, C-336/96, EU:C:1998:221; Judgment in *Royal Bank of Scotland*, C-311/97, EU:C:1999:216; Judgment in *Gschwind*, C-391/97, EU:C:1999:409; Judgment in *Saint-Gobain*, C-307/97, EU:C:1999:438; Judgment in *Metallgesellschaft and Hoechst*, C-397/98 and C-410/98, EU:C:2001:134; Judgment in *Gerritse*, C-234/01, EU:C:2003:340.

607. See K. Lenaerts, 33 *Fordham Intl. L. J.* 5 (2010), at p. 1363; R. Mason, Flunking the ECJ's Tax Discrimination Test, 46 *Colum. J. Transnatl. L.* 1 (2007), p. 72 (at p. 78); also cf. Opinion of AG Sharpston in *Deutsche Shell*, C-293/06, EU:C:2007:660, at point 35.

608. See, for example, P. Westen, The Empty Idea of Equality, 95 *Harv. L. Rev.* 3 (1982), p. 537 (at p. 544).

609. See H. Kelsen, *Reine Rechtslehre*[2] (Deuticke, 1960), at p. 256; M. Pöschl, *Gleichheit vor dem Gesetz* (Springer, 2008), at pp. 154-155.

610. See R. Mason, 46 *Colum. J. Transnatl. L.* 1 (2007), at p. 102.

611. See, for example, R. Mason, 46 *Colum. J. Transnatl. L.* 1 (2007), at p. 102; J. Englisch in K. Tipke/J. Lang, *Steuerrecht*[22] (Dr Otto Schmidt, 2015), at § 4 para. 86; E. Reimer in H. Schaumburg/J. Englisch (eds.), *Europäisches Steuerrecht* (2015), at p. 207, at MN 7.130.

612. Judgment in *Avoir Fiscal*, 270/83, EU:C:1986:37, at paras 19-20; Judgment in *Royal Bank of Scotland*, C-311/97, EU:C:1999:216, at paras 24-31; Judgment in *Saint-Gobain*, C-307/97, EU:C:1999:438, at paras 47-48; Judgment in *D*, C-376/03, EU:C:2005:424, at paras 58-61; Judgment in *Test Claimants in Class IV of the ACT Group Litigation*, C-374/04, EU:C:2006:773, at para. 68; Judgment in *Eckelkamp*, C-11/07, EU:C:2008:489, at paras 62-63; critically J. Englisch, 38 *Intertax* 4 (2010), at pp. 212.

circumstances[613] or both,[614] to concentrating on the objective of the particular measure[615] or even simply refraining from revealing the yardstick used.[616]

The ECJ's ostensible inconstancy is particularly problematic, because a lack of comparability seems to prevent the Court from scrutinizing the respective domestic measure in depth.[617] This is due to the fact that the ECJ's usual pattern of examining a potentially discriminatory tax measure which is covered by the ambit of the fundamental freedoms basically consists of three steps.[618] It must thus be ascertained: (1) whether the cross-border situation is discriminated against vis-à-vis a comparable domestic situation, (2) if so, whether this discrimination is justified by a legitimate aim, and (3) if so, whether the national measure is proportionate.[619] If these steps were strictly separated from each other,[620] the level of scrutiny would depend on whether comparable situations are at hand or not.[621] Denying comparability would in fact mean that there are no constraints whatsoever on how different the situations that formed the

613. Judgment in *Schumacker*, C-279/93, EU:C:1995:31, at paras 31-38; Judgment in *Wielockx*, C-80/94, EU:C:1995:271, at paras 18-22; Judgment in *Gilly*, C-336/96, EU:C:1998:221, at paras 49-50; Judgment in *Gschwind*, C-391/97, EU:C:1999:409, at paras 28-30; Judgment in *Zurstrassen*, C-87/99, EU:C:2000:251, at paras 21-23; Judgment in *Lakebrink and Peters-Lakebrink*, C-182/06, EU:C:2007:452, at paras 28-34; Judgment in *Renneberg*, C-527/06, EU:C:2008:566, at paras 59-68; critically M. Lang, Ist die Schumacker-Rechtsprechung am Ende? 51 *Recht der Internationalen Wirtschaft* 5 (2005), p. 336 (at pp. 336 et seq.).

614. Order in *Mertens*, C-431/01, EU:C:2002:492, at para. 32.

615. Judgment in *Oy AA*, C-231/05, EU:C:2007:439, at para. 38; Judgment in *Société Papillon*, C-418/07, EU:C:2008:659, at para. 27-30; Judgment in *X Holding*, C-337/08, EU:C:2010:89, at paras 20-24; Judgment in *Comission/Estonia*, C-39/10, EU:C:2012:282, at para. 51; Judgment in *X*, C-87/13, EU:C:2014:2459, at para. 27-32; Judgment in *Q*, C-133/13, EU:C:2014:2460, at paras 22-27; critically J. Englisch, 38 *Intertax* 4 (2010), at pp. 202-204; J. Englisch, 33 *Intertax* 5 (2005), at p. 210; J. Englisch, 33 *Intertax* 8/9 (2005), at p. 320; G. Kofler, *Doppelbesteuerungsabkommen und Europäisches Gemeinschaftsrecht* (Linde, 2007), at p. 998.

616. Judgment in *Verkooijen*, C-35/98, EU:C:2000:294; Judgment in *Ritter-Colais*, C-152/03, EU:C:2006:123; Judgment in *Lidl Belgium*, C-414/06, EU:C:2008:278; Judgment in *Krankenheim Ruhesitz am Wannsee-Seniorenheimstatt*, C-157/07, EU:C:2008:588; Judgment in *Argenta Spaarbank*, C-350/11, EU:C:2013:447.

617. Cf. Opinion of AG Kokott in *Nordea Bank Danmark*, C-48/13, EU:C:2014:153, at point 27.

618. From the case law of the ECJ, one could of course deduce even more steps. See, for example, B.J.M. Terra/P.J. Wattel, *European Tax Law*[6] (Kluwer, 2012), at pp. 59-63 ("*The rule of reason test – in its most extensive configuration,* i.e. *in the field of free movement of goods – consists of eight step*").

619. See, for example, G. Kofler, *Doppelbesteuerungsabkommen und Europäisches Gemeinschaftsrecht* (Linde, 2007), at pp. 51-52; R. Szudoczky, *The Sources of EU law and Their Relationships: Lessons for the Field of Taxation* (IBFD, 2014), at pp. 469-470; B.J.M. Terra/P.J. Wattel, *European Tax Law*[6] (Kluwer, 2012), at p. 64; P.J. Wattel, Forum: Interaction of State Aid, Free Movement, Policy Competition and Abuse Control in Direct Tax Matters, 5 *World Tax J.* 1 (2013), p. 128 (at p. 130); also cf. D. Hohenwarter, *Verlustverwertung im Konzern* (LexisNexis, 2009), at p. 53.

620. See N. Bammens, *The Principle of Non-Discrimination in International and European Tax Law* (IBFD, 2012), at pp. 988-990; also cf. L. De Broe/N. Bammens, Truck Center Belgian Withholding Tax on Interest Payments to Non-resident Companies Does Not Violate EC Law: A Critical Look at the ECJ's Judgment in Truck Center, 18 *EC Tax Rev.* 3 (2009), p. 131 (at p. 133).

621. See M. Lang, *Die Rechtsprechung des EuGH zu den direkten Steuern* (Peter Lang, 2007), at p. 105; also cf. M. Lang in M. Hebig/K. Kaiser/K. Koschmieder/M. Oblau (eds.), *FS Wilhelm H. Wacker* (Erich Schmidt Verlag, 2006), at p. 369.

basis of the comparison may be treated.[622] In *Truck Center*, for example, the Court held that "*the difference in treatment between companies receiving income from capital, established by the tax legislation at issue in the main proceedings, consisting in the application of different taxation arrangements to companies established in Belgium and to those established in another Member State, relates to situations which are not objectively comparable.*"[623] The ECJ pointed out that the different treatment of interest paid to non-resident companies, which were subject to a withholding tax to be retained by the resident payor, as compared to interest paid to resident companies, which did not trigger an obligation to retain a tax at source, "*reflect[s] the difference in the situations in which those companies find themselves with regard to recovery of the tax. While resident recipient companies are directly subject to the supervision of the Belgian tax authorities, which can ensure compulsory recovery of taxes, that is not the case with regard to non-resident recipient companies inasmuch as, in their case, recovery of the tax requires the assistance of the tax authorities of the other Member State.*"[624] The Court did not enlarge upon the multilateral recovery assistance treaty that was applicable in this case.[625] This implies that a non-resident recipient is regarded as not comparable to a resident recipient with regard to tax recovery, irrespective of whether the other Member State's tax authorities have a legal obligation to provide for mutual assistance or not.[626]

By contrast, with regard to the payment debtor, which is obliged to levy a withholding tax only in the case of a non-resident recipient, the ECJ did not question the comparability,[627] but rather held that "*the obligation to withhold tax at source, in that it entails an additional administrative burden and related liability risks, that restriction can be justified by the need to ensure the effective collection of tax.*"[628,629]

622. See M. Lang, 46 *Eur. Taxn.* 9 (2006), at p. 422; M. Lang, 18 *EC Tax Rev.* 3 (2009), at pp. 100-101; M. Lang in M. Hebig/K. Kaiser/K. Koschmieder/M. Oblau (eds.), *FS Wilhelm H. Wacker* (Erich Schmidt Verlag, 2006), at p. 369; K. Simader, Die Zulässigkeit der Erhebung von Quellensteuern aus gemeinschaftsrechtlicher Sicht, in M. Lang/J. Schuch/C. Staringer (eds.), *Quellensteuern* (Linde, 2010), p. 13 (at p. 28); K. Simader, *Withholding Taxes and the Fundamental Freedoms* (Kluwer, 2014), at p. 135; also cf. R. Lyal, 12 *EC Tax Rev.* 2 (2003), at p. 68.
623. Judgment in *Truck Center*, C-282/07, EU:C:2008:762, at para. 41.
624. Judgment in *Truck Center*, C-282/07, EU:C:2008:762, at paras 47-48.
625. For further references see Opinion of AG Kokott in *Truck Center*, C-282/07, EU:C:2008:513, at point 42 (FN 27).
626. See M. Lang, 18 *EC Tax Rev.* 3 (2009), at p. 100; K. Simader, *Withholding Taxes and the Fundamental Freedoms* (Kluwer, 2014), at p. 132; T. Kühbacher, Die Rs "Truck Center SA" - Neues zur Abzugsbesteuerung des § 99 EStG?, 62 *ÖStZ* 9 (2009), p. 224 (at p. 227); L. De Broe/N. Bammens, 18 *EC Tax Rev.* 3 (2009), at p. 135.
627. Judgment in *FKP Scorpio Konzertproduktionen*, C-290/04, EU:C:2006:630, at paras 33-34; Judgment in *Commission/Belgium*, C-433/04, EU:C:2006:702, at paras 30-32; Judgment in *X*, C-498/10, EU:C:2012:635, at paras 28-32; Judgment in *Strojírny Prostějov and ACO Industries Tábor*, C-53/13 and C-80/13, EU:C:2014:2011, at paras 37-42.
628. Judgment in *X*, C-498/10, EU:C:2012:635, at para. 53; also cf. Judgment in *FKP Scorpio Konzertproduktionen*, C-290/04, EU:C:2006:630, at paras 35-36; Judgment in *Brisal and KBC Finance Ireland*, C-18/15, EU:C:2016:549, at paras 21-22.
629. According to the ECJ, however, this conclusion "*was based, both in FKP Scorpio Konzertproduktionen (EU:C:2006:630) and in X (EU:C:2012:635), on the fact that the service providers at issue in those cases provided occasional services in a Member State other than that in which they were established, and remained there for only a short period of time.*" If the non-resident service provider acts through a branch in the Member State of the service recipient, a withholding tax

Notwithstanding the fact that proportionality was ultimately affirmed,[630] that comparable situations were assumed to be at hand enabled and required the Court to also examine whether the withholding tax obligation constituted an appropriate means of ensuring effective tax collection of the tax due and did not go beyond what is necessary to achieve that aim. Due to the supposed lack of comparability of resident and non-resident payment creditors, this level of scrutiny is not accomplished when the perspective of the payment creditor is focused on,[631] and in particular "*the Court does not relate the proportionality of the measure (as expressed by the feasibility of its alternative, that is, the mutual assistance procedure) to the degree of difference existing between the situations.*"[632]

Another example is the jurisprudence on losses of foreign permanent establishments. In *Lidl Belgium*, the ECJ did not even address the question of whether foreign permanent establishments are actually comparable to domestic permanent establishments if a double taxation convention prohibits the Member State of the head office to tax the profits attributable to the foreign permanent establishment. The Court instead held that not taking into account losses of a foreign permanent establishment involves a restriction on the freedom of establishment, which is nevertheless justified by the need to preserve the allocation of the power to impose taxes between the Member States concerned and the need to prevent the danger that losses may be taken into account twice.[633] It was, therefore, "*necessary to examine whether the tax regime at issue in the main proceedings goes beyond what is necessary to attain the objectives pursued.*"[634] This would be the case "*where a non-resident subsidiary has exhausted the possibilities for having the losses incurred in the Member State where it is situated taken into account for the accounting period concerned and also for previous accounting periods and where there is no possibility for that subsidiary's losses to be taken into account in that State for future periods.*"[635]

In *Timac Agro*, on the other hand, the ECJ did not care about the proportionality of the German tax system, which – since 1999 – does not allow taking into account losses from foreign permanent establishments if profits attributable to such a

obligation "*is not appropriate to ensure the effective collection of income tax.*" See Judgment in *Strojírny Prostějov and ACO Industries Tábor*, C-53/13 and C-80/13, EU:C:2014:2011, at paras 48-53; also see K. Spies, Quellensteuern auf dem Prüfstand des EuGH, 67 *ÖStZ* 21 (2014), p. 531 (at pp. 531 et seq.); J. Holthaus, EU-Rechtswidrigkeit bei Vergütungen an EU-Unternehmen mit Zweigniederlassung im Tätigkeitsstaat, 3 *ISR* 8 (2014), p. 280 (at pp. 280-282); also cf. D. Nerudová, The Czech Republic: Preliminary ruling referred by the Czech Supreme Administrative Court – joint cases: Aco Industries (C-80/13) and Strojírny Prostějov, a.s. (C-53/14), in M. Lang/P. Pistone/J. Schuch/C. Staringer/A. Storck (eds.), *ECJ – Recent Developments in Direct Taxation 2013* (Linde, 2014), p. 25 (at pp. 25 et seq.).

630. Judgment in *FKP Scorpio Konzertproduktionen*, C-290/04, EU:C:2006:630, at paras 37-38; Judgment in *X*, C-498/10, EU:C:2012:635, at paras 44-52.
631. Cf. J. Englisch, Truck Center: withholding tax on intercompany interest derived by non-resident companies compatible with freedom of establishment, 2 *H&I* 2 (2009), p. 43 (at pp. 48-50).
632. L. De Broe/N. Bammens, 18 *EC Tax Rev.* 3 (2009), at p. 135.
633. Judgment in *Lidl Belgium*, C-414/06, EU:C:2008:278, at paras 26-37.
634. Judgment in *Lidl Belgium*, C-414/06, EU:C:2008:278, at para. 44.
635. Judgment in *Lidl Belgium*, C-414/06, EU:C:2008:278, at para. 47 and para. 51.

permanent establishment cannot be taxed in Germany due to a double taxation convention. The reason is that, according to the Court, "*the situation of a permanent establishment situated in Austria is not comparable to that of a permanent establishment situated in Germany in relation to measures laid down by the Federal Republic of Germany in order to prevent or mitigate the double taxation of a resident company's profits[,] [...] since the Federal Republic of Germany does not exercise any tax powers over the profits of such a permanent establishment.*"[636] Whether the proportionality of the domestic tax system is assessed thus depends on whether comparability is – at least implicitly – assumed (*Lidl Belgium*) or rejected (*Timac Agro*).[637]

The denial of comparability also raises the question whether equal treatment of resident and non-resident income recipients would infringe the fundamental freedoms. After all, according to the ECJ's case law, "*different situations must not be treated in the same way.*"[638] However, the difficulty of such a reasoning is that it would have to be decided how different Member States have to treat different situations.[639,640] Does it mean that non-resident income recipients who – for whatever reason – would prefer to be taxed by withholding rather than by assessment can rely on the lack of comparability with resident income recipients if the latter are subject to tax assessment?[641] Similar issues also arise – at least theoretically – with regard to other decisions that were based on non-comparability. In *X Holding*, for example, the ECJ held that "*[p]ermanent establishments situated in another Member State and non-resident subsidiaries are not in a comparable situation with regard to the allocation of the power*

636. Judgment in *Timac Agro Deutschland*, C-388/14; EU:C:2015:829, at para. 65.

637. Cf. D. Eisendle, Grenzüberschreitende Verlustverrechnung im Jahre 11 nach Marks & Spencer – Status quo der EuGH-Rechtsprechung zur Berücksichtigung von Auslandsverlusten kraft Unionsrecht, 5 *ISR* 2 (2016), p. 37 (at pp. 38-39).

638. Judgment in *Garcia Avello*, C-148/02, EU:C:2003:539, at para. 31; Judgment in *Azienda Agro-Zootecnica Franchini and Eolica di Altamura*, C-2/10, EU:C:2011:502, at para. 64; Judgment in *Hungary/Commission*, C-31/13 P, EU:C:2014:70, at para. 73; also cf. Judgment in *SFI*, C-85/97, EU:C:1998:552, at para. 30; Judgment in *Jippers and others*, C-189/01, EU:C:2001:420, at para. 128; Judgment in *Denkavit*, C-507/99, EU:C:2002:4, at para. 44; Judgment in *Omega and others*, C-122/00, EU:C:2002:161, at para. 79; Judgment in *Commission/Portugal*, C-334/03, EU:C:2005:623, at para. 24; also cf. Judgment in *Schumacker*, C-279/93, EU:C:1995:31, at para. 30; Judgment in *Wielockx*, C-80/94, EU:C:1995:271, at para. 17; Judgment in *Asscher*, C-107/94, EU:C:1996:251, at para. 40; Judgment in *Royal Bank of Scotland*, C-311/97, EU:C:1999:216, at para. 26; Judgment in *Gschwind*, C-391/97, EU:C:1999:409, at para. 21; Judgment in *Kerckhaert and Morres*, C-513/04, EU:C:2006:713, at para. 19; Judgment in *Meindl*, C-329/05, EU:C:2007:57, at para. 22; Judgment in *Talotta*, C-383/05, EU:C:2007:181, at para. 18; Judgment in *Lakebrink and Peters-Lakebrink*, C-182/06, EU:C:2007:452, at para. 27; Judgment in *Columbus Container Services*, C-298/05, EU:C:2007:754, at para. 41; Judgment in Gielen, C-440/08, EU:C:2010:148; at para. 38; Judgment in *Commission/Hungary*, C-253/09, EU:C:2011:795, at para. 50; Judgment in *Commission/Netherlands*, C-542/09, EU:C:2012:346, at para. 41; Judgment in *Commission/Estonia*, C-39/10, EU:C:2012:282, at para. 48; Judgment in *Banco Bilbao Vizcaya Argentaria*, C-157/10, EU:C:2011:813, at para. 41; Judgment in *Bouanich*, C-375/12, EU:C:2014:138, at para. 45.

639. See K. Spies, EuGH zu Währungsverlusten bei ausländischen Tochtergesellschaften: Keine Abzugspflicht(?), 26 *ecolex* 8 (2015), p. 700 (at p. 702).

640. This might explain why the ECJ is reluctant to invoke this "*often repeated but rarely used*" approach (M. Lang, 18 *EC Tax Rev.* 3 [2009], at p. 99; also see K. Spies, 26 *ecolex* 8 [2015], at p. 702).

641. See K. Simader, *Withholding Taxes and the Fundamental Freedoms* (Kluwer, 2014), at p. 138.

of taxation as provided for in an agreement such as the Double Taxation Agreement, and in particular in Articles 7(1) and 23(2) thereof. Whereas a subsidiary, as an independent legal person, is subject to unlimited tax liability in the State party to such an agreement in which that subsidiary is established, the same does not apply in the case of a permanent establishment situated in another Member State, which remains in principle and in part subject to the fiscal jurisdiction of the Member State of origin."[642] Due to this lack of comparability, "*the Member State of origin is not obliged to apply the same tax scheme to non-resident subsidiaries as that which it applies to foreign permanent establishments.*"[643] Although the ECJ held that the Member State of origin „*is not obliged*" to apply equal treatment, it could be argued that such an equal treatment of different situations even constitutes an infringement of the fundamental freedoms. However, that would mean a Member State that allows for a temporary offset of foreign permanent establishment losses, which was the case in *X Holding*, is basically not allowed to apply that arrangement to non-resident subsidiaries.

This is apparently not what the ECJ has in mind. In *Timac Agro*, for example, the Court held that "*a permanent establishment situated in another Member State is not, in principle, in a situation comparable to that of a resident permanent establishment in relation to measures laid down by a Member State in order to prevent or mitigate the double taxation of a resident company's profits.*"[644] Hence, the fundamental freedoms do not preclude Member States from not taking into account foreign permanent establishment losses of domestic companies "*where, under a double taxation convention, the exclusive power to tax the profits of that establishment lies with the Member State in which the establishment is situated.*"[645] This does not mean, however, that Member States are prohibited from treating losses from domestic and foreign permanent establishments in the same way. The Court held that "*by permitting the deduction of losses incurred by a permanent establishment situated in Austria, the Federal Republic of Germany granted a tax advantage to the resident company to which that permanent establishment belonged, in the same way as if that permanent establishment had been situated in Germany, and, therefore, equated it with a resident permanent establishment so far as concerns the deduction of losses.*"[646] Thus, apparently, losses of foreign permanent establishments may be treated in the same way as losses of domestic foreign permanent establishments, although "*permanent establishments situated in a Member State other than the Member State concerned are not in a situation comparable to that of resident permanent establishments in relation to measures laid down by that Member State in order to prevent or mitigate the double taxation of a resident company's profits.*"[647]

---

642. Judgment in *X Holding*, C-337/08, EU:C:2010:89, at para. 38; also cf. Judgment in *Bosal*, C-168/01, EU:C:2003:479, at para. 32; but cf. Judgment in *CLT-UFA*, C-253/03, EU:C:2006:129, at paras 14-15 and para. 30; critically D. Hohenwarter-Mayr, Die Rs. *X Holding* – ein weiterer Teil im Puzzle der grenzüberschreitenden Gruppenbesteuerung, 20 *SWI* 4 (2010), p. 163 (at pp. 170-172).
643. Judgment in *X Holding*, C-337/08, EU:C:2010:89, at para. 40.
644. Judgment in *Timac Agro Deutschland*, C-388/14; EU:C:2015:829, at para. 65.
645. Judgment in *Timac Agro Deutschland*, C-388/14; EU:C:2015:829, at para. 66.
646. Judgment in *Timac Agro Deutschland*, C-388/14; EU:C:2015:829, at para. 28.
647. Judgment in *Timac Agro Deutschland*, C-388/14; EU:C:2015:829, at para. 27.

These issues would not arise if the ECJ had assumed comparability and had based its decision on the justification and proportionality analysis instead. The decisions in *Truck Center* and *Scorpio* notably illustrate that arguments raised at the level of comparability and justification are used interchangeable.[648] In *Truck Center*, the ECJ could have also – just as in *Scorpio* – considered the situations to be comparable, but the different treatment as justified by the need to ensure the effective collection of income tax. This would have led to the question whether a withholding tax is a proportionate means of ensuring this objective, especially in view of the opportunities provided for by the multilateral recovery assistance treaty.[649] AG Kokott followed a similar, albeit unorthodox, approach in her Opinion in *Truck Center*, by emphasizing that "*[f]or a finding of non-discrimination, it is not sufficient to point out that [...] citizens and foreign nationals are not in the same situation. It is also necessary to demonstrate that the difference in their respective situations is capable of justifying the difference in treatment. In other words, the difference in treatment must relate and be proportionate to the difference in their respective situations.*"[650] Parts of the literature have criticized this rationale. It was argued that such an approach is "*rather odd,*"[651] "*unpredictable in its outcome*"[652] and "*impractical.*"[653] Considerations of proportionality should not affect the question of comparability, but rather remain a separate step of the ECJ's analysis.[654] However, it can be argued that it is not about merging "*three separate steps into one amalgamate analysis.*"[655] Denying comparability is – as the ECJ's case law proves – simply not always sufficient to determine that a different

648. Cf. M. Lang, 15 *SWI* 8 (2005), at p. 369; M. Lang, Das EuGH-Urteil in der Rechtssache Schempp – Wächst der steuerpolitische Spielraum der Mitgliedsstaaten?, 15 *SWI* 9 (2005), p. 411 (at p. 413); M. Lang, 46 *Eur. Taxn.* 9 (2006), at pp. 421-422; M. Lang/A. Jettmar, Steuerrecht und Sozial(versicherungs)recht – Anmerkungen zum Schlussantrag in der Rs. Blanckaert –, *Internationale Wirtschaftsbriefe*, Fach 11, Gruppe 2, Nr. 15 (2005), p. 741 (at p. 742); M. Lang/J. Lüdicke/M. Reich, Beteiligungen im Privatvermögen: Die Besteuerung des Wegzugs aus Österreich und Deutschland in die Schweiz – Teil II, 17 *IStR* 20 (2008), p. 709 (at p. 712); M. Lang in M. Hebig/K. Kaiser/K. Koschmieder/M. Oblau (eds.), *FS Wilhelm H. Wacker* (Erich Schmidt Verlag, 2006), at p. 368; M. Lang in M. Beusch (ed.), *Steuerrecht 2007* (Schulthess, 2007), at pp. 9-10; M. Lang, 18 *EC Tax Rev.* 3 (2009), at p. 100; also cf. A. Cordewener, *Europäische Grundfreiheiten und nationales Steuerrecht* (Dr Otto Schmidt, 2002), at pp. 162-174; M. Lang, Die Bindung der Doppelbesteuerungsabkommen an die Grundfreiheiten des EU-Rechts, in W. Gassner/M. Lang/E. Lechner (eds.), *Doppelbesteuerungsabkommen und EU-Recht* (Linde, 1996), p. 25 (at p. 37).
649. Cf. L. De Broe, Are We Heading Towards an Internal Market Without Dividend Withholding Tax but With Interest and Royalty Withholding Tax? Some Observations on Advocate General's Kokott Opinion in Truck Center, 18 *EC Tax Rev.* 1 (2009), p. 2 (at p. 2 [FN 4]); D. Hohenwarter/F. Koppensteiner, Die Erhebung von Quellensteuern im Verhältnis zu Drittstaaten aus gemeinschaftsrechtlicher Sicht, in M. Lang/J. Schuch/C. Staringer (eds.), *Quellensteuern* (Linde, 2010), p. 67 (at pp. 97-98); K. Simader, *Withholding Taxes and the Fundamental Freedoms* (Kluwer, 2014), at pp. 135-137.
650. Opinion of AG Kokott in *Truck Center*, C-282/07, EU:C:2008:513, at point 37; also see Opinion of AG Maduro in *Huber*, C-524/06, EU:C:2008:194, at point 7.
651. J. Englisch, 38 *Intertax* 4 (2010), at p. 204.
652. L. De Broe/N. Bammens, 18 *EC Tax Rev.* 3 (2009), at p. 136.
653. N. Bammens, *The Principle of Non-Discrimination in International and European Tax Law* (IBFD, 2012), at p. 989.
654. See L. De Broe/N. Bammens, 18 *EC Tax Rev.* 3 (2009), at p. 133; N. Bammens, *The Principle of Non-Discrimination in International and European Tax Law* (IBFD, 2012), at p. 990.
655. L. De Broe/N. Bammens, 18 *EC Tax Rev.* 3 (2009), at p. 136.

treatment of the cross-border and the purely domestic situation compared therewith is in line with the fundamental freedoms.[656] Indeed, a lack of comparability releases the Member State concerned from justifying the national measure at stake,[657] because different situations must not – but, depending upon a justification and a proportionality analysis, nevertheless may[658] – be treated in the same way.[659] Since the ECJ's case law

656. Similarly, accepting comparability is not always sufficient to determine that the equal treatment of the cross-border and the purely domestic situation being compared to it is in line with the fundamental freedoms.
657. Cf. G. Kofler, *Doppelbesteuerungsabkommen und Europäisches Gemeinschaftsrecht* (Linde, 2007), at pp. 991-992.
658. If two situations are comparable, it does not mean that they have to be treated in the same way by all means. In such a situation, the ECJ rather examines whether a differentiating national measure pursues a legitimate objective in the public interest, is appropriate to ensuring the attainment of that objective, and does not go beyond what is necessary to attain it (see Judgment in *Futura Participations and Singer*, C-250/95, EU:C:1997:239, at para. 26; Judgment in *de Lasteyrie du Saillant*, C-9/02, EU:C:2004:138, at para. 49; Judgment in *SEVIC Systems*, C-411/03, EU:C:2005:762, at para. 23; Judgment in *Marks & Spencer*, C-446/03, EU:C:2005:763, at para. 35; Judgment in *N*, C-470/04, EU:C:2006:525, at para. 40; Judgment in *Cadbury Schweppes and Cadbury Schweppes Overseas*, C-196/04, EU:C:2006:544, at para. 47; Judgment in *Test Claimants in the Thin Cap Group Litigation*, C-524/04, EU:C:2007:161, at para. 64; Judgment in *Oy AA*, C-231/05, EU:C:2007:439, at para. 44; Judgment in *Lidl Belgium*, C-414/06, EU:C:2008:278, at para. 27; Judgment in *Lammers und Van Cleef*, C-105/07, EU:C:2008:24, at para. 25; Judgment in *Krankenheim Ruhesitz am Wannsee-Seniorenheimstatt*, C-157/07, EU:C:2008:588, at para. 40; Judgment in *Papillon*, C-418/07, EU:C:2008:659, at para. 33; Judgment in *Persche*, C-318/07, EU:C:2009:33, at para. 52; Judgment in *X and Passenheim-van Schoot*, C-155/08 and C-157/08, EU:C:2009:368, at para. 47; Judgment in *SGI*, C-311/08, EU:C:2010:26, at para. 56; Judgment in *Haribo Lakritzen Hans Riegel*, C-436/08 and C-437/08, EU:C:2011:61, para. 122; Judgment in *Philips Electronics*, C-18/11, EU:C:2012:532, at para. 22; Judgment in *Argenta Spaarbank*, C-350/11, EU:C:2013:447, at para. 35; Judgment in *Imfeld and Garcet*, C-303/12, EU:C:2013:822, at para. 64; Judgment in *Bouanich*, C-375/12, EU:C:2014:138, at para. 65; Judgment in *Nordea Bank Danmark*, C-48/13, EU:C:2014:2087, at para. 25). The same approach has to be applied if two situations are not comparable, i.e., equal treatment is acceptable, if it can be justified and resists the proportionality test. Consequently, denying comparability simply reveals that the pair of situations being compared do not have to be treated in the same way, but may be treated in the same way if such an equal treatment is justified. Similarly, accepting comparability reveals that the two situations do not have to be treated differently, but may be treated differently if such a different treatment is justified. In any case, the differences or similarities in treatment have to be proportionate in relation to the differences or similarities of the situations at hand. Cf. K. Simader, *Withholding Taxes and the Fundamental Freedoms* (Kluwer, 2014), at pp. 135-137; M. Lang, Marks and Spencer – More Questions than Answers: An Analysis of the Opinion Delivered by Advocate General Maduro, 14 *EC Tax Rev.* 2 (2005), p. 95 (at p. 96); M. Lang, 46 *Eur. Taxn.* 9 (2006), at p. 422; M. Lang, 18 *EC Tax Rev.* 3 (2009), at p. 100; M. Lang in M. Beusch (ed.), *Steuerrecht 2007* (Schulthess, 2007), at p. 10; R. Lyal, 12 *EC Tax Rev.* 2 (2003), at pp. 68 et seq.
659. In *Blanckaert*, the ECJ even held that a potentially restrictive tax measure "*can be justified […] by the objective difference between the [situations compared with each other].*" See Judgment in *Blanckaert*, C-512/03, EU:C:2005:516, at para. 50; also cf. Judgment in *Eckelkamp*, C-11/07, EU:C:2008:489, at para. 61 ("*In that respect, it must be stated first that, contrary to the Belgian Government's contention, which is set out in paragraph 47 of the present judgment, that difference in treatment cannot be justified on the ground that it concerns situations which are not objectively comparable.*"); Judgment in *Jäger*, C-256/06, EU:C:2008:20, at para. 43 ("*In that respect, it must be stated, first, that the difference in the amount of tax paid according to whether the inheritance consists only of agricultural land and forestry situated in Germany or consists also of such an asset situated in another Member State cannot be justified on the ground that it concerns situations which are not objectively comparable.*"); Judgment in *Arens-Sikken*, C-43/07, EU:C:2008:490, at para. 54 ("*In that respect, it must be stated that, contrary to the*

suggests that the arguments raised at the level of comparability and justification can to a certain extent be used interchangeably,[660] denying comparability does not render the proportionality analysis superfluous.[661] Otherwise, the blurred lines between the comparability analysis and the justification analysis could lead to different levels of scrutiny, depending on whether the Court considers the same arguments in the context of the comparability or the justification analysis.

However, such an approach raises the question whether a comparability analysis is still needed. As AG Kokott pointed out in her Opinion in *Nordea Bank Danmark*, *"it seems [...] that the time has come to dispense with [the comparability analysis]. First, not only is a demarcation with examining a ground of justification not possible but also*

Netherlands Government's contention, that difference in treatment cannot be justified on the ground that it concerns situations which are not objectively comparable."); Judgment in *Groupe Steria*, C-386/14, EU:C:2015:524, at para. 21-22 (*"In order for that difference in treatment to be compatible with the provisions of the Treaty on the freedom of establishment, it must relate to situations which are not objectively comparable or be justified by an overriding reason in the general interest [...].The fact that the dividends received by a parent company which enjoy full tax exemption come from subsidiaries that are part of the tax-integrated group to which the parent company concerned also belongs does not amount to an objective difference in the situation of parent companies that would justify the difference in treatment identified [...]."*); Judgment in *Miljoen*, C-10/14, C-14/14 and C-17/14, EU:C:2015:608, at para. 73 (*"Accordingly, in circumstances such as those at issue in the main proceedings, the different treatment of resident taxpayers liable to pay income tax or corporation tax and non-resident taxpayers who are subject to a withholding tax in respect of dividends cannot be justified by a difference in their situations which is relevant to the application of Article 65(1)(a) TFEU."*).

660. Cf. M. Lang, 15 *SWI* 8 (2005), at p. 369; M. Lang, 15 *SWI* 9 (2005), at p. 413; M. Lang, 46 *Eur. Taxn.* 9 (2006), at pp. 421-422; M. Lang/A. Jettmar, *Internationale Wirtschaftsbriefe*, Fach 11, Gruppe 2, Nr. 15 (2005), at p. 742; M. Lang/J. Lüdicke/M. Reich, 17 *IStR* 20 (2008), at p. 712; M. Lang in M. Hebig/K. Kaiser/K. Koschmieder/M. Oblau (eds.), *FS Wilhelm H. Wacker* (Erich Schmidt Verlag, 2006), at p. 368; M. Lang in M. Beusch (ed.), *Steuerrecht 2007* (Schulthess, 2007), at pp. 9-10; M. Lang, 18 *EC Tax Rev.* 3 (2009), at p. 100; also cf. A. Cordewener, *Europäische Grundfreiheiten und nationales Steuerrecht* (Dr Otto Schmidt, 2002), at pp. 162-174; M. Lang in W. Gassner/M. Lang/E. Lechner (eds.), *Doppelbesteuerungsabkommen und EU-Recht* (Linde, 1996), at p. 37; for a different view see N. Bammens, *The Principle of Non-Discrimination in International and European Tax Law* (IBFD, 2012), at p. 1073 (*"[T]here is a fundamental difference between these concepts, namely that justification grounds are inherent in the comparative attribute. As a result, they cannot be relied upon in the comparability analysis, as elements that are inherent in the comparative attribute should be disregarded in such context. However, these arguments reflect valid policy concerns which Member States are allowed to safeguard. For this reason, they may justify discriminatory taxation."*); with regard to the non-discrimination provision of Article 14 ECHR see, for example, I. Cameron, *An Introduction to the European Convention on Human Rights*[6] (Iustus Förlag, 2011), at p. 158 (*"Determining whether situations are 'relevantly similar' is really the same thing as determining whether an objective and reasonable justification exists for distinguishing between them"*); F. Jacobs/R. White/C. Ovey, *The European Convention on Human Rights*[5] (Oxford University Press, 2010), at p. 559 (*"[T]he issue of whether the compared groups are truly in analogous situations can sometimes only be answered by considering whether their differential treatment can be justified"*).

661. See M. Lang/J. Lüdicke/M. Reich, Beteiligungen im Privatvermögen: Die Besteuerung des Wegzugs aus Österreich und Deutschland in die Schweiz – Teil II, 17 *IStR* 20 (2008), p. 709 (at p. 712); P. Wattel, Non-Discrimination *á la Cour*: The ECJ's (Lack of) Comparability Analysis in Direct Tax Cases, 55 *Eur. Taxn.* 12 (2015), p. 542 (at p. 553: *"If [the cross-border situation and the domestic situation] are not comparable, then that is not yet the end of the analysis, as still, the Court is competent to test whether the difference in tax treatment is proportionate to the difference in fiscal position."*); also cf. J. Englisch, 38 *Intertax* 4 (2010), at p. 204.

there are not any readily apparent criteria for determining those cases in which situations must be said not to be objectively comparable in the first place. Secondly, such a finding also made it impossible to strike an appropriate balance between the fundamental freedom and the reason for the difference in treatment in the case concerned."[662] Indeed, abandoning the previous approach with regard to comparability may be a way to ensure that the ECJ's case law becomes more consistent and comprehensible. This does not necessarily imply a shift from the non-discrimination approach to the restriction-based approach in the Court's tax jurisprudence. In the literature it is in fact convincingly argued that a standard of comparison is in any case required in order to identify a restriction.[663] Hence, the ECJ should still reveal which situations are being compared with each other - and why - when examining a potentially discriminatory or restrictive tax measure. Based on this comparison, it should be demonstrated whether the differences or similarities in treatment reflect the differences or similarities of the situations at hand in an appropriate and reasonable way.[664]

Another possibility to rectify the current unsatisfactory situation is to completely disregard the legal situation in the particular Member State within the comparability analysis, but to only take it into account at the level of justification. Comparability could, for example, be determined by relying on "*the objective [...]* inherent *to the fundamental freedoms. [...] [C]omparability of situations should therefore be assumed, as a rule, if there exists a certain degree of substitutability* between *the cross-border transaction at issue and similar but purely internal transactions."*[665] However, it would require a substantial change in the ECJ's case law to adopt such an approach. Whether the Court is willing to take such a step is rather questionable.

2.4.2 The Spectrum of Comparability

The comparisons that can be drawn in order to determine whether a domestic measure is in breach of the fundamental freedoms are manifold. Typically, the ECJ compares the cross-border transaction with a purely domestic transaction. In the literature, this is

662. Opinion of AG Kokott in *Nordea Bank Dankmark*, C-48/13, EU:C:2014:153, at point 22.
663. See J. Englisch, *Dividendenbesteuerung* (Dr Otto Schmidt, 2005), at p. 248; M. Lang, Europarechtliche Aspekte der Besteuerung von Erbschaften, in D. Birk (ed.), *Steuern auf Erbschaft und Vermögen*, DStJG 22 (Dr Otto Schmidt, 1999), p. 255 (at pp. 261-263); M. Lang E. Lechner/C. Staringer/M. Tumpel (eds.), *Kapitalverkehrsfreiheit und Steuerrecht* (Linde, 2000), at pp. 189-191; M. Lang, *Die Rechtsprechung des EuGH zu den direkten Steuern* (Peter Lang, 2007), at pp. 34-39; M. Lang, 18 *EC Tax Rev.* 3 (2009), at p. 99; M. Lang in M. Hebig/K. Kaiser/K. Koschmieder/M. Oblau (eds.), *FS Wilhelm H. Wacker* (Erich Schmidt Verlag, 2006), at pp. 366-369; M. Lang in M. Beusch (ed.), *Steuerrecht 2007* (Schulthess, 2007), at pp. 7-10; M. Lang in A. Wagner/V. Wedl (eds.), Bilanz und Perspektiven zum europäischen Recht (ÖGB Verlag, 2007), at p. 120; R. Lyal, 12 *EC Tax Rev.* 2 (2003), at p. 74.
664. Cf. K. Simader, *Withholding Taxes and the Fundamental Freedoms* (Kluwer, 2014), at pp. 135-137; M. Lang, 14 *EC Tax Rev.* 2 (2005), at p. 96; M. Lang, 46 *Eur. Taxn.* 9 (2006), at p. 422; M. Lang, 18 *EC Tax Rev.* 3 (2009), at p. 100; M. Lang in M. Beusch (ed.), *Steuerrecht 2007* (Schulthess, 2007), at p. 10; R. Lyal, 12 *EC Tax Rev.* 2 (2003), at pp. 68 et seq.
665. J. Englisch, 38 *Intertax* 4 (2010), at p. 203; also see J. Englisch, *Wettbewerbsgleichheit im grenzüberschreitenden Handel* (Mohr Siebeck, 2008), at pp. 285-298.

generally referred to as "vertical comparability."[666] From the host state perspective, on the one hand, resident taxpayers may be compared to non-resident taxpayers; a comparison may be drawn, for example, between residents and non-residents with a permanent establishment in the host state,[667] between resident workers and non-resident frontier workers,[668] even if the non-resident is a national of the host state,[669] as well as between residents and non-residents who do not carry out an employment and do not have a permanent establishment in the host state, but simply earn income originating from the host state.[670] From the home state perspective, on the other hand, a resident taxpayer who operates cross-border may be compared to another resident whose activities are restricted to the home state; a comparison may be drawn, for example, between residents with a domestic permanent establishment and residents with a foreign permanent establishment,[671] between resident parent companies with resident subsidiaries and resident parent companies with non-resident subsidiaries,[672] between residents working solely in the home state and residents who also work in other Member States,[673] as well as between residents whose income originates exclusively from sources in the home state and residents whose income also originates from sources in other Member States.[674]

666. See, for example, D. Hohenwarter, *Verlustverwertung im Konzern* (LexisNexis, 2009), at pp. 25 and 81-87; M. Lang, Jüngste Tendenzen zur "horizontalen" Vergleichbarkeitsprüfung in der steuerlichen Rechtsprechung des EuGH zu den Grundfreiheiten, 21 *SWI* 4 (2011), p. 154 (at p. 154); M. Lang, Totgesagte leben länger: Horizontale Vergleichbarkeit und die Verwirklichung des Binnenmarkts, 26 *SWI* 3 (2016), p. 118 (at p. 118); M. Lang, There's Life in the Old Dog Yet: Horizontal Comparability and the Establishment of the Internal Market, in R. Avi-Yonah/M. Lang (eds.), *Fiscal Federalism* (2016), forthcoming; F. Rosenberger/V. Loidl/H. Moshammer, Grundfreiheitsprüfung des EuGH, 87 *SWK* 20 (2012), p. 936 (at p. 936); K. Simader, *Withholding Taxes and the Fundamental Freedoms* (Kluwer, 2014), at p. 157.

667. Judgment in *Avoir Fiscal*, 270/83, EU:C:1986:37; Judgment in *Commerzbank*, C-330/91, EU:C:1993:303; Judgment in *Futura Participations and Singer*, C-250/95, EU:C:1997:239; Judgment in *Royal Bank of Scotland*, C-311/97, EU:C:1999:216; Judgment in *Saint-Gobain*, C-307/97, EU:C:1999:438; Judgment in *CLT-UFA*, C-253/03, EU:C:2006:129.

668. Judgment in *Schumacker*, C-279/93, EU:C:1995:31; Judgment in *Gschwind*, C-391/97, EU:C:1999:409; Judgment in *Zurstrassen*, C-87/99, EU:C:2000:251; Judgment in *Schröder*, C-450/09, EU:C:2011:198; Judgment in *Schulz-Delzers and Schulz*, C-240/10, EU:C:2011:591; Judgment in *Ettwein*, C-425/11, EU:C:2013:121.

669. Judgment in *Asscher*, C-107/94, EU:C:1996:251; Judgment in *Gilly*, C-336/96, EU:C:1998:221.

670. Judgment in *Gerritse*, C-234/01, EU:C:2003:340; Judgment in *Conijn*, C-346/04, EU:C:2006:445; Judgment in *FKP Scorpio Konzertproduktionen*, C-290/04, EU:C:2006:630; Judgment in *Gielen*, C-440/08, EU:C:2010:148.

671. Judgment in *AMID*, C-141/99, EU:C:2000:696; Judgment in *Columbus Container Services*, C-298/05, EU:C:2007:754; Judgment in *Lidl Belgium*, C-414/06, EU:C:2008:278; Judgment in *Krankenheim Ruhesitz am Wannsee-Seniorenheimstatt*, C-157/07, EU:C:2008:588.

672. Judgment in *ICI*, C-264/96, EU:C:1998:370; Judgment in *Bosal*, C-168/01, EU:C:2003:479; Judgment in *Marks & Spencer*, C-446/03, EU:C:2005:763; Judgment in *Rewe Zentralfinanz*, C-347/04, EU:C:2007:194; Judgment in *Oy AA*, C-231/05, EU:C:2007:439; Judgment in *Papillon*, C-418/07, EU:C:2008:659; Judgment in *X Holding*, C-337/08, EU:C:2010:89.

673. Judgment in *De Groot*, C-385/00, EU:C:2002:750; Judgment in *Jundt*, C-281/06, EU:C:2007:816.

674. Judgment in *Verkooijen*, C-35/98, EU:C:2000:294; Judgment in *Manninen*, C-319/02, EU:C:2004:484; Judgment in *Lenz*, C-315/02, EU:C:2004:446; Judgment in *Meilicke and others*, C-292/04, EU:C:2007:132; Judgment in *Kerckhaert and Morres*, C-513/04, EU:C:2006:603; Judgment in *Damseaux*, C-128/08, EU:C:2009:471.

Whereas a vertical comparison is generally accepted as a tenable benchmark to establish whether a national measure leads to discrimination or not, it is disputed whether EU law also calls for "horizontal comparability," i.e., a comparison between two cross-border situations.[675] An argument in favour of such kinds of comparisons may be derived from Article 18 TFEU, which prohibits *"any discrimination on grounds of nationality."*[676] According to this wording, discrimination of nationals of different Member States may also be covered. Considering the uniform dogmatic concept underlying the fundamental freedoms as well as the general prohibition of non-discrimination,[677] this would mean that Member States not only have to refrain from treating residents and non-residents differently, but must also provide for equal treatment of non-residents from different Member States.[678]

Such an understanding may also be supported by Article 350 TFEU, according to which *"[t]he provisions of the Treaties shall not preclude the existence or completion of regional unions between Belgium and Luxembourg, or between Belgium, Luxembourg and the Netherlands, to the extent that the objectives of these regional unions are not attained by application of the Treaties."* If such agreements between the Benelux countries have to be immunized from the application of EU law, it may be argued that in all other cases the Member States are not entitled to grant specific benefits to nationals of a particular Member State or a particular group of Member States.[679]

675. For further references, with regard to the effect of "horizontal comparability" as a most-favoured nation treatment, see G. Kofler, 5 *Hous. Bus. & Tax L. J.* 1 (2005), at pp. 10-11 (FN 35-39); G. Kofler/C.P. Schindler, 45 *Eur. Taxn.* 12 (2005), at p. 532 (FN 15-19); G. Kofler, *Doppelbesteuerungsabkommen und Europäisches Gemeinschaftsrecht* (Linde, 2007), at pp. 764-808 (with regard to "inbound most-favoured nation treatment"; see especially FN 29-31) and at pp. 808-816 (with regard to "outbound most-favoured nation treatment").
676. See S. De Ceulaer, Community Most-Favoured-Nation Treatment: One Step Closer to the Multilateralization of Income Tax Treaties in the European Union?, 57 *Bull. Intl. Taxn.* 10 (2003), p. 493 (at pp. 495-496); J. Englisch in A. Cordewener/S. Enchelmaier/C.P. Schindler (eds.), *Meistbegünstigung im Steuerrecht der EU-Staaten* (C.H. Beck, 2006), at p. 170; G. Kofler, 5 *Hous. Bus. & Tax L. J.* 1 (2005), at pp. 62-65; J. Schuch, Werden die Doppelbesteuerungsabkommen durch EU-Recht zu Meistbegünstigungsklauseln?, in W. Gassner/M. Lang/E. Lechner (eds.), *Doppelbesteuerungsabkommen und EU-Recht* (Linde, 1996), p. 99 (at pp. 116-122); R. van der Linde, Some thoughts on most-favoured-nation treatment within the European Community legal order in pursuance of the *D* case, 13 *EC Tax Rev.* 1 (2004), p. 10 (at p. 13); D. Weber/E. Spierts, The "*D.* Case": Most-Favoured-Nation Treatment and Compensation of Legal Costs Before the European Court of Justice, 44 *Eur. Taxn.* 2 (2004), p. 65 (at p. 68); H. Weggenmann, EG-rechtliche Aspekte steuerlicher Meistbegünstigung im Abkommensrecht, 12 *IStR* 19 (2003), p. 677 (at pp. 679-680); also cf. Opinion of AG Colomer in *D.*, C-376/03, EU:C:2005:424, at point 97.
677. See Chapter 3.2.2.
678. See N. Dautzenberg, *Unternehmensbesteuerung im EG-Binnenmarkt* (Josef Eul Verlag, 1997), at pp. 660-662; J. Schuch in W. Gassner/M. Lang/E. Lechner (eds.), *Doppelbesteuerungsabkommen und EU-Recht* (Linde, 1996), at pp. 134-135; J. Schuch, Europa auf dem Weg zum multilateralen Doppelbesteuerungsabkommen, in W. Gassner/B. Gröhs/M. Lang (eds.), *Zukunftsaufgaben der Wirtschaftsprüfung* (Orac, 1997), p. 327 (at pp. 332-333); also cf. M. Lang, Die Zukunft des Internationalen Steuerrechts in Europa, in W. Gassner/H. Hemetsberger-Koller/M. Lang/J. Sasseville/K. Vogel (eds.), *Die Zukunft des Internationalen Steuerrechts* (Linde, 1999), p. 71 (at p. 80).
679. See A. Cordewener/E. Reimer, The Future of Most-Favoured-Nation Treatment in EC Tax Law – Did the ECJ Pull the Emergency Brake without Real Need? – Part 1, 46 *Eur. Taxn.* 6 (2006), p. 239 (at p. 246); G. Kofler, Generalanwalt zur Kapitalverkehrsfreiheit und Meistbegünstigung

The issue of horizontal comparability already arose in *Avoir Fiscal*. The French Government argued, among other things, that the disadvantage arising from not granting the shareholder's tax credit to branches of foreign companies "*may be easily avoided by setting up a subsidiary in France.*"[680] The ECJ rejected this argument by referring to Article 49 TFEU, which "*expressly leaves traders free to choose the appropriate legal form in which to pursue their activities in another Member State and that freedom of choice must not be limited by discriminatory tax provisions.*"[681] In the literature, it was thus partly assumed that the fundamental freedoms require Member States to provide for equal treatment of non-residents with domestic subsidiaries and non-residents with domestic permanent establishments.[682] However, this kind of different treatment of subsidiaries and permanent establishments by the host state, which was also emphasized in *Saint-Gobain*,[683] is inextricably linked with a different treatment of non-resident taxpayers (the non-resident company with a permanent establishment) and resident taxpayers (the resident subsidiary).[684] Although this was also the case in *CLT-UFA*,[685] the ECJ held that – due to the circumstances of the case – "*German subsidiaries and branches of companies having their seat in Luxembourg are in a situation in which they can be compared objectively.*"[686] Albeit the Court seems to be willing to compare the tax treatment of non-residents with a foreign permanent

bei DBA-Anwendung, 17 *ÖStZ* 23 (2004), p. 558 (at p. 560, FN 20); G. Kofler, 5 *Hous. Bus. & Tax L. J.* 1 (2005), at pp. 62-64; A. Rädler, Most-Favourite-Nation-Treatment in Direct Taxation – Some New Aspects, 13 *SWI* 8 (2003), p. 360 (at p. 361); C. Tietje, Die Meistbegünstigungsverpflichtung im Gemeinschaftsrecht, 30 *EuR* 4 (1995), p. 398 (at pp. 406-407); S. van Thiel, The Principle of Non-discrimination in the EU and the Right to Most-Favoured Nation Treatment in Tax Treaties, in S. van Thiel (ed.), *The European Union's Prohibition of Discrimination, Most-Favoured-Nation Treatment and Tax Treaties: Opinions and Materials* (2006), p. 119 (at pp. 130-131); contra J. Englisch in A. Cordewener/S. Enchelmaier/C.P. Schindler (eds.), *Meistbegünstigung im Steuerrecht der EU-Staaten* (C.H. Beck, 2006), at p. 183 (FN 129).

680. Judgment in *Avoir Fiscal*, 270/83, EU:C:1986:37, at para. 17.
681. Judgment in *Avoir Fiscal*, 270/83, EU:C:1986:37, at para. 22.
682. See N. Dautzenberg, *Unternehmensbesteuerung im EG-Binnenmarkt* (Josef Eul Verlag, 1997), at p. 60; N. Dautzenberg, Das EG-rechtliche Gleichbehandlungsgebot für Betriebsstätten und Tochterkapitalgesellschaften, 12 *EWS* 6 (2001), p. 270 (at pp. 270-277); also cf. W. Schön, Freie Wahl zwischen Zweigniederlassung und Tochtergesellschaft – ein Grundsatz des Europäischen Unternehmensrechts, 11 *EWS* 7 (2000), p. 281 (at pp. 283-285); R. Paetsch, *Grenzüberschreitende Verlustberücksichtigung im Europäischen Binnenmarkt* (Eul Verlag, 2004), at pp. 106-108.
683. Judgment in *Saint-Gobain*, C-307/97, EU:C:1999:438, at para. 42.
684. See K. Daxkobler, *Die grundfreiheitliche Rechtsprechung des EuGH* (Linde, 2015), at p. 136; D. Hohenwarter, *Verlustverwertung im Konzern* (LexisNexis, 2009), at p. 105; also cf. Opinion of AG Maduro in *Marks & Spencer*, C-446/03, EU:C:2005:201, at points 43-49.
685. See D. Hohenwarter, *Verlustverwertung im Konzern* (LexisNexis, 2009), at pp. 105-106; A. Schnitger, The *CLT-UFA* Case and the "Principle of Neutrality of Legal Form", 44 *Eur. Taxn.* 12 (2004), p. 522 (at pp. 524-525); A. Schnitger, Möglichkeit zur Präzisierung des europarechtlichen Prinzips der Rechtsformwahlfreiheit und Körperschaftsteuerguthaben für Betriebsstätten ausländischer Kapitalgesellschaften gemäß § 37 KStG – Vorlagenfrage an den EuGH in der Rs. CLT-UFA, 13 *IStR* 23 (2004), p. 821 (at pp. 823-825); also cf. K. Aarnio, Treatment of Permanent Establishments and Subsidiaries under EC Law: Towards a Uniform Concept of Secondary Establishment in European Tax Law?, 15 *EC Tax Rev.* 1 (2006), p. 18 (at p. 26); A. Cordewener, *Europäische Grundfreiheiten und nationales Steuerrecht* (Dr Otto Schmidt, 2002), at pp. 834-835.
686. Judgment in *CLT-UFA*, C-253/03, EU:C:2006:129, at para. 30.

establishment and non-residents with a foreign subsidiary under certain circumstances,[687] it is doubtful whether this "horizontal comparison" has an autonomous meaning transcending the host state's obligation to provide for equal treatment of non-residents with a domestic permanent establishment and residents.[688] In any case, it cannot be inferred from *CLT-UFA* that there is an EU law principle to provide for equal treatment of different legal form, particularly subsidiaries and permanent establishments. The ECJ has instead made it unmistakably clear, albeit only for the home state perspective, that "*the Member States are at liberty to determine the conditions and the level of taxation for different types of establishments chosen by national companies or partnerships operating abroad, on condition that those companies or partnerships are not treated in a manner that is discriminatory in comparison with comparable national establishments.*"[689]

Apart from this discussion, the question whether the fundamental freedoms also call for horizontal comparability tends to be equated with the issue of most-favoured nation treatment, i.e., "*treatment accorded by the granting State to the beneficiary State, or to persons or things in a determined relationship with that State, not less favourable than treatment extended by the granting State to a third State or to persons or things in the same relationship with that third State.*"[690] From an EU law perspective, the most prominent debate centres on the differences between the various bilateral double taxation conventions Member States have concluded among each other and with third countries. These differences may result in a situation whereby one Member State grants a certain beneficial treatment to a resident of another Member State, but – due to a different tax treaty – not to a resident of a third Member State.[691] The ECJ has already dealt with this issue from the host state perspective: In *D.*, a resident and national of Germany, who owned property in the Netherlands, was refused to claim a basic allowance for wealth tax purposes, which he would have been entitled to if he were a resident of Belgium.[692] In contrast to the double taxation convention between Germany

687. See M. Lang, Gemeinschaftsrechtliche Verpflichtung zur Rechtsformneutralität im Steuerrecht?, 15 *IStR* 12 (2006), p. 397 (at pp. 397 et seq.).
688. See D. Hohenwarter, *Verlustverwertung im Konzern* (LexisNexis, 2009), at p. 110; also see K. Aarnio, 15 *EC Tax Rev.* 1 (2006), at p. 26; in this respect also cf. Judgment in *Avoir Fiscal*, 270/83, EU:C:1986:37, at para. 15 ("*It thus appears that the two submissions put forward by the Commission, namely that concerning discrimination in French law against branches and agencies of insurance companies established in other Member States vis-à-vis companies established in France and that concerning the restriction of the freedom of foreign insurance companies to establish branches and agencies, are closely linked. They must therefore be considered together.*"); Judgment in *Saint-Gobain*, C-307/97, EU:C:1999:438, at para. 43 ("*The difference in treatment to which branches of non-resident companies are subject in comparison with resident companies as well as the restriction of the freedom to choose the form of secondary establishment must be regarded as constituting a single composite infringement of Articles 52 and 58 of the Treaty.*").
689. Judgment in *Columbus Container Services*, C-298/05, EU:C:2007:754, at para. 53; also see in *KBC Bank and Beleggen, Risicokapitaal, Beheer*, C-439/07 and C-499/07, EU:C:2009:339, at para. 80; Judgment in *X Holding*, C-337/08, EU:C:2010:89, at para. 40.
690. Report of the International Law Commission on the work of its thirtieth session, 8 May–28 Jul. 1978, Document A/33/10, at p. 21.
691. See G. Kofler, 5 *Hous. Bus. & Tax L. J.* 1 (2005), at p. 6.
692. Judgment in *D.*, C-376/03, EU:C:2005:424.

and the Netherlands, the treaty between Belgium and the Netherlands included a non-discrimination provision, according to which "*[i]ndividuals who are residents of one of the States shall benefit in the other State from the same personal allowances, reliefs and deductions on account of civil status or family responsibilities which the last-mentioned State grants to its own residents.*"[693] Therefore, the ECJ had to deal with, among other issues, the question whether a Member State is precluded "*from according, pursuant to a bilateral convention for the avoidance of double taxation, only to residents of the other State party to the convention the allowance which it grants to its own residents, without extending the allowance to residents of the other Member States.*"[694] Whereas AG Colomer answered this question in the affirmative,[695] the ECJ held that "*[i]t is to be remembered that, in order to avoid the same income and assets being taxed in both the Netherlands and Belgium, Article 24 of the Belgium-Netherlands Convention allocates powers of taxation between those two Member States and Article 25(3) lays down a rule under which natural persons resident in one of those two States are entitled in the other to the personal allowances which are granted by it to its own residents. The fact that those reciprocal rights and obligations apply only to persons resident in one of the two Contracting Member States is an inherent consequence of bilateral double taxation conventions. It follows that a taxable person resident in Belgium is not in the same situation as a taxable person resident outside Belgium so far as concerns wealth tax on real property situated in the Netherlands. A rule such as that laid down in Article 25(3) of the Belgium-Netherlands Convention cannot be regarded as a benefit separable from the remainder of the Convention, but is an integral part thereof and contributes to its overall balance.*"[696]

This reasoning was heavily criticized in the literature,[697] especially because of its circularity.[698] The Court considers two non-residents as not being comparable, because they are subject to two different double taxation conventions deviating from one another, although it is precisely the difference between those two tax treaties that is

693. Article 25(3) of the Belgium-Netherlands Income and Capital Tax Treaty (1970); also cf. D. Weber/E. Spierts, 44 *Eur. Taxn.* 2 (2004), at pp. 67-68.
694. Judgment in *D.*, C-376/03, EU:C:2005:424, at para. 46.
695. Opinion of AG Colomer in *D.*, C-376/03, EU:C:2004:663, at points 72-106.
696. Judgment in *D.*, C-376/03, EU:C:2005:424, at paras 60-62.
697. See, for example, M. Lang, 15 *SWI* 8 (2005), at pp. 365 et seq.; G. Kofler, Das Ende vom Anfang der gemeinschaftsrechtlichen Meistbegünstigung, 58 *ÖStZ* 19 (2005), p. 432 (at pp. 435-438); G. Kofler/C.P. Schindler, 45 *Eur. Taxn.* 12 (2005), at pp. 537-539; S. van Thiel, A Slip of the European Court in the D case (C-376/03): Denial of the Most-Favoured-Nation Treatment Because of Absence of Similarity?, 33 *Intertax* 10 (2005), p. 454 (at pp. 454-457); D. Weber, 33 *Intertax* 10 (2005), at pp. 429-444.
698. See A. Cordewener/E. Reimer, 46 *Eur. Taxn.* 7 (2006), at pp. 293-294 and p. 302; A. Cordewener in A. Cordewener/S. Enchelmaier/C.P. Schindler (eds.), *Meistbegünstigung im Steuerrecht der EU-Staaten* (C.H. Beck, 2006), at p. 224; S. Enchelmair, Meistbegünstigung im EG-Recht – Allgemein Grundsätze, in A. Cordewener/S. Enchelmaier/C.P. Schindler (eds.), *Meistbegünstigung im Steuerrecht der EU-Staaten* (C.H. Beck, 2006), p. 93 (at p. 118); J.E. Gudmundsson, European Tax Law in the Relations with EFTA Countries, 34 *Intertax* 2 (2006), p. 58 (at p. 81); D. Hohenwarter in M. Lang/J. Schuch/C. Staringer (eds.), *Tax Treaty Law and EC Law* (Kluwer, 2007), at p. 119; M.C. Pimentel, "D"istortion of the Common Market? Analysis and Future Perspectives of the MFN Clause Within EC Law, 34 *Intertax* 10 (2006), p. 485 (at p. 491); S. van Thiel, 33 *Intertax* 10 (2005), at p. 455; G. Kofler, 58 *ÖStZ* 19 (2005), at pp. 436-437.

said to effect an infringement of the fundamental freedoms. With respect to provisions of diverging double taxation conventions, two non-residents would hence never be in a comparable situation.[699]

Despite the severe criticism, the ECJ adhered to the *D.* reasoning in *Test Claimants in Class IV of the ACT Group Litigation.*[700] Although the question whether double taxation conventions may include provisions that can be "*regarded as a benefit separable from the remainder of the Convention,*" are thus not "*an integral part thereof*" and do not "*contribute to its overall balance*" remains unanswered,[701] it can be assumed that there is little scope for horizontal comparisons with regard to benefits granted by the host state through a double tax treaty.[702] This might be different when it comes to the perspective of the home state.[703] In this scenario, the question is whether a resident that invests or operates in another Member State may rely on a more beneficial double taxation convention with a third Member State.[704] In contrast to the *D.* case and the *Test Claimants in Class IV of the ACT Group Litigation* case, which concerned non-residents, residents are covered by the personal scope of all double taxation conventions concluded by their residence state. Therefore, the comparability of two residents cannot be denied just because only one of them is entitled to the benefits of a particular double taxation convention.[705] However, the ECJ emphasized that the provisions of a tax treaty establish "*reciprocal rights and obligations*" and unless a specific benefit is "*separable from the remainder of the Convention,*" it "*is an integral part thereof and contributes to its overall balance.*"[706] This is equally true for benefits the residence state has agreed upon in a double taxation convention. In the

699. Cf. E.C.C.M. Kemmeren, Pending Cases Filed by Dutch Courts I: The Van Dijk and Bujura Cases, in M. Lang/ J. Schuch/C. Staringer (eds.), *ECJ – Recent Developments in Direct Taxation* (Linde, 2006), p. 219 (at pp. 250-251).
700. Judgment in *Test Claimants in Class IV of the ACT Group Litigation*, C-374/04, EU:C:2006:773, at paras 82-94.
701. See M. Lang, 15 *SWI* 8 (2005), at p. 371.
702. See G. Kofler/C.P. Schindler, 45 *Eur. Taxn.* 12 (2005), at pp. 538-539; G. Kofler, *Doppelbesteuerungsabkommen und Europäisches Gemeinschaftsrecht* (Linde, 2007), at pp. 796-800; J. Schuch, Critical Notes on the European Court of Justice's D. Case Decision on Most Favoured-Nation Treatment under Tax Treaties, 15 *EC Tax Rev.* 1 (2006), p. 6 (at p. 7); J. Schuch, Marktintegration durch Meistbegünstigung im EG-Steuerrecht, in A. Cordewener/S. Enchelmaier/C.P. Schindler (eds.), *Meistbegünstigung im Steuerrecht der EU-Staaten* (C.H. Beck, 2006), at p. 151 (at pp. 158-159); also cf. D. Hohenwarter in M. Lang/J. Schuch/C. Staringer (eds.), *Tax Treaty Law and EC Law* (Kluwer, 2007), at pp. 119-120; but see H. van den Hurk/J. Korving, The "*D*" Case Against the Netherlands and the ECJ's Decision – Is There Still a Future for MFN Treatment?, 60 *Bull. Intl. Taxn.* 8 (2006), p. 365 (at pp. 371-373); also cf. E.C.C.M. Kemmeren in M. Lang/ J. Schuch/C. Staringer (eds.), *ECJ – Recent Developments in Direct Taxation* (Linde, 2006), at pp. 256-257.
703. See T. Rödder/J. Schönfeld, Meistbegünstigung und EG-Recht: Anmerkung zu EuGH vom 5. 7. 2005, C-376/03 ("D"), IStR 2005, 483, 14 *IStR* 15 (2005), p. 523 (at pp. 525-526).
704. See G. Kofler, *Doppelbesteuerungsabkommen und Europäisches Gemeinschaftsrecht* (Linde, 2007), at p. 808; T. Rödder/J. Schönfeld, 14 *IStR* 15 (2005), at pp. 525-526.
705. See G. Kofler, *Doppelbesteuerungsabkommen und Europäisches Gemeinschaftsrecht* (Linde, 2007), at p. 811.
706. Judgment in *D.*, C-376/03, EU:C:2005:424, at paras 61-62; Judgment in *Test Claimants in Class IV of the ACT Group Litigation*, C-374/04, EU:C:2006:773, at paras 88 and 91.

literature, it has hence been pointed out that, hence, the ECJ's reasoning in *D.* and in *Test Claimants in Class IV of the ACT Group Litigation* is transferable to the home state perspective as well.[707]

This issue was recently addressed in *Riskin and Timmermans*.[708] Belgian residents received dividends from a Polish company that were subject to Polish withholding tax. According to the applicable double taxation convention, this foreign tax can only be credited against the tax payable in Belgium if the capital and property that had generated the dividends concerned were applied in Belgium in the conduct of a professional activity.[709] As this was not the case in *Riskin and Timmermans*, the Belgian tax authority denied the credit of the Polish withholding tax.[710] The taxpayers argued that other double taxation conventions concluded by Belgium with third countries do not contain such a requirement. If they had received dividends from companies established in one of these third countries, a possible foreign withholding tax would have been credited against Belgium income tax. Due to a preliminary ruling request by the Belgian Court of First Instance, the ECJ had to decide whether it is in line with the free movement of capital that Belgium residents are treated differently depending on whether they receive dividends from Polish company or from a company established in a third country. Following its reasoning in *D.*, the Court decided that "*[t]he fact that the benefit in question is granted only to Belgian residents falling within the scope of that convention cannot be classified as a benefit that is separable from that convention, given that [...] that benefit is an integral part of the convention rules and contributes to the overall balance of mutual relations between the two contracting States to that convention. In those circumstances, Belgian residents, [...] who receive dividends from Member States, such as the Republic of Poland, and who, in order to benefit from tax deducted at source being allowed as a credit against Belgian tax, must satisfy the condition laid down in Article 285 of the CIR 1992, are not in a situation that is objectively comparable to that of Belgian residents who receive dividends from a third State with which the Kingdom of Belgium has concluded a bilateral double taxation convention providing for an unconditional right to such a set-off.*"[711] The scholarly assumption has thus turned out to be true.

707. See E.C.C.M. Kemmeren in M. Lang/ J. Schuch/C. Staringer (eds.), *ECJ – Recent Developments in Direct Taxation* (Linde, 2006), at pp. 257-27; G. Kofler, *Doppelbesteuerungsabkommen und Europäisches Gemeinschaftsrecht* (Linde, 2007), at pp. 811-812; M. Schilcher, Exemption Method and Community Law, in M. Lang/J. Schuch/C. Staringer (eds.), *Tax Treaty Law and EC Law* (Kluwer, 2007), p. 151 (at pp. 182-183); also cf. M. Lang, 15 *SWI* 8 (2005), at p. 373; A. Schnitger, § 20 Abs. 2 und 3 AStG a.F. vor dem EuGH – Meistbegünstigung "Reloaded," 87 *FR* 21 (2005), p. 1079 (at p. 1082); but see T. Rödder/J. Schönfeld, 14 *IStR* 15 (2005), at p. 526.
708. Judgment in *Riskin and Timmermans*, C-176/15, EU:C:2016:488.
709. According to Article 23(1)(b) of the Belgium-Poland double taxation convention, "*the Polish tax levied on [dividends not exempt from Belgian tax according to subparagraph (c)] shall be allowed as a credit against Belgian tax relating to such income.*" However, this tax credit is "*[s]ubject to the provisions of Belgian law regarding the deduction from Belgian tax of taxes paid abroad.*" Under Article 285 of the Belgian Income Tax Code, a tax credit requires that the respective "*capital and property are applied in Belgium in the conduct of a professional activity.*" See Judgment in *Riskin and Timmermans*, C-176/15, EU:C:2016:488, at paras 3-9.
710. Judgment in *Riskin and Timmermans*, C-176/15, EU:C:2016:488, at paras 13 and 18.
711. Judgment in *Riskin and Timmermans*, C-176/15, EU:C:2016:488, at paras 34-35.

Although the ECJ has ultimately denied comparability, the *D.* case, the *Test Claimants in Class IV of the ACT Group Litigation* case and the *Riskin and Timmermans* case indicate that a horizontal comparison may nevertheless be relevant in order to determine whether a national measure is in line with the fundamental freedoms or not.[712] Otherwise, the Court could simply have rejected considering "*whether, as regards the measures at issue, the non-resident companies concerned are in an objectively comparable situation.*"[713] In fact, the possibility of a horizontal comparability has been recalled from time to time in several cases,[714] without the ultimate decision being based exclusively on such a comparison, though. The *Columbus Container Services* case would have been predestined to apply a horizontal comparison.[715] It concerned German residents holding shares in a Belgian limited partnership. The economic activity of this partnership centred on the management of designated passive income and – due to a special tax regime for coordination centres – the Belgian taxation amounted to less than 30% of the profit actually achieved by the partnership. This triggered a German rule, according to which the tax exemption provided for in the double taxation convention between Belgium and Germany had to be denied. Instead, the partners resident in Germany were taxed on the profits derived from the partnership's trading results and the amount of tax paid in Belgium was set off against those profits. The taxation of the partners thereby corresponded to the taxation they would have suffered if the partnership had been governed by German law and had its registered office in Germany.[716] Hence, no discrimination could be said to exist by way of a vertical comparison, whereas a horizontal comparison shows that the German rule differentiated between income stemming from a partnership located in a "low tax jurisdiction" and income stemming from another foreign partnership located in a Member State where the level of taxation is higher than the threshold provided for by

---

712. See G. Kofler, *Doppelbesteuerungsabkommen und Europäisches Gemeinschaftsrecht* (Linde, 2007), at pp. 805-806; G. Kofler, "Horzontal Discrimination" in European Tax Law, in I. Richelle/W. Schön/E. Traversa (eds.), *Allocating Taxing Powers Within the European Union* (Springer, 2013), p. 187 (at p. 214); M. Lang, 15 *SWI* 8 (2005), at pp. 370-372; M. Lang, 18 *EC Tax Rev.* 3 (2009), at p. 104; M. Lang, 21 *SWI* 4 (2011), at p. 156; also cf. A. Cordewener/E. Reimer, 46 *Eur. Taxn.* 7 (2006), at pp. 293-294; A. de Graaf/G. Janssen, The Implications of the Judgment in the *D* Case: The Perspective of Two Non-believers, 14 *EC Tax Rev.* 4 (2005), p. 173 (at p. 184); J.E. Gudmundsson, 34 *Intertax* 2 (2006), at pp. 81-83; G. Kofler, 58 *ÖStZ* 19 (2005), at pp. 435-437; G. Kofler/C.P. Schindler, 45 *Eur. Taxn.* 12 (2005), at p. 537.
713. Judgment in *Test Claimants in Class IV of the ACT Group Litigation*, C-374/04, EU:C:2006:773, at para. 83.
714. Judgment in *Cadbury Schweppes and Cadbury Schweppes Overseas*, C-196/04, EU:C:2006:544, at paras 43-44; Judgment in *A.*, C-101/05, EU:C:2007:804, at paras 41-42; Judgment in *Orange European Smallcap Fund*, C-194/06, EU:C:2008:289, at para. 61; Judgment in *Commission/ Netherlands*, C-521/07, EU:C:2009:360, at para. 43; Judgment in *Haribo Lakritzen Hans Riegel*, C-436/08 and C-437/08, EU:C:2011:61, at para. 52; also see M. Lang, 21 *SWI* 4 (2011), at pp. 154 et seq.
715. Judgment in *Columbus Container Services*, C-298/05, EU:C:2007:754; also cf. J. Calderón/A. Baez, The *Columbus Container Services* ECJ Case and Its Consequences: A Lost Opportunity to Shed Light on the Scope of the Non-discrimination Principle, 37 *Intertax* 4 (2009), p. 212 (at p. 215); CFE, Opinion Statement of the CFE ECJ Task Force on ECJ, *Columbus Container Services BVBA & Co v. Finanzamt Bielefeld-Innenstadt*, 6 Dec. 2007, C-298/05 – April 2008, 48 *Eur. Taxn.* 10 (2008), p. 541 (at p. 542).
716. Judgment in *Columbus Container Services*, C-298/05, EU:C:2007:754, at para. 39 and para. 49.

the German tax legislation.[717] However, the ECJ did not attach much importance to this argument, because Member States are not "*obliged to adapt their own tax systems to the different systems of tax of the other Member States in order to guarantee that a company or partnership that has chosen to establish itself in a given Member State is taxed, at national level, in the same way as a company or partnership that has chosen to establish itself in another Member State.*"[718] Due to this rather brief reasoning, it is unclear whether the idea of horizontal comparability was generally rejected,[719] whether the two cross-border situations were considered to not be comparable in this particular case or whether the different treatment was considered to be justified and proportional.

In *Sopora*, however, the ECJ has explicitly confirmed the basic admissibility of a horizontal comparability:[720] According to Netherlands national law, certain reimbursements paid to workers may be exempt from Netherlands wage tax if they are granted to offset "extraterritorial expenses," i.e., expenses a worker incurs because she is staying outside her country of origin. The remuneration for extraterritorial expenses is deemed to be 30% of the worker's employment income, irrespective of the costs that are actually incurred. If the actual amount of extraterritorial costs incurred is higher, then this higher amount can be remunerated tax free. Since incoming workers are in any case not treated less favourably than employees resident in the Netherlands, a vertical comparison leads to the result that no discrimination is at hand. However, only those workers are eligible for this flat-rate rule who have resided within a distance of more than 150 kilometres from the Dutch border for more than eighteen months during a twenty-four-month period preceding their recruitment in the Netherlands.[721] Therefore, residents of particular (parts of) Member States are excluded, whereas residents of all other Member States can benefit from this flat-tax rule. The ECJ held that "*having regard to the wording of Article 45(2) TFEU, which seeks to abolish all discrimination based on nationality 'between workers of the Member States', read in the light of Article 26 TFEU, the view must be taken that that freedom also prohibits discrimination between non-resident workers if such discrimination leads to nationals of certain Member States being unduly favoured in comparison with others.*"[722] Although the ECJ

717. Opinion of AG Mengozzi in *Columbus Container Services*, C-298/05, EU:C:2007:197, at points 107-156.
718. Judgment in *Columbus Container Services*, C-298/05, EU:C:2007:754, at para. 39 and para. 51.
719. But see R. Migglautsch, Rs Columbus Container Services – Doppelbesteuerungsabkommen und Gemeinschaftsrecht, 19 *ecolex* 3 (2008), p. 265 (at p. 267).
720. Judgment in *Sopora*, C-512/13, EU:C:2015:108.
721. See E.C.C.M. Kemmeren, *Sopora*: A Welcome Landmark Decision on Horizontal Comparison, 24 *EC Tax Rev.* 4 (2015), p. 178 (at p. 178); G. Kofler in I. Richelle/W. Schön/E. Traversa (eds.), *Allocating Taxing Powers Within the European Union* (Springer, 2013), at pp. 209-210; M. Lang, 26 *SWI* 3 (2016), at p. 124; M. Lang in R. Avi-Yonah/M. Lang (eds.), *Fiscal Federalism* (2016), forthcoming; D. Smit, The 150km Requirement under the Dutch 30% Wage Tax Facility C-512/03 (Sopora), in M. Lang/P. Pistone/J. Schuch/C. Staringer/A. Storck (eds.), *ECJ – Recent Developments in Direct Taxation 2013* (Linde, 2014), p. 131 (at pp. 133-134); G. Meussen, Horizontal Discrimination and EU Law: The Sopora Case, 54 *Eur. Taxn.* 7 (2014), p. 322 (at pp. 322-323).
722. Judgment in *Sopora*, C-512/13, EU:C:2015:108, at para. 25.

ultimately deemed the flat-rate rule to be non-discriminatory,[723] unless the referring court ascertained that it "*systematically gives rise to a net overcompensation in respect of the extraterritorial expenses actually incurred,*"[724] it was made clear that the free movement of workers prohibits discrimination based on a vertical as well as a horizontal differentiation. Considering the convergence of the fundamental freedoms and the fact that the ECJ has interpreted Article 45(2) TFEU "*in the light of Article 26 TFEU*" it can be reasonably, but not without any doubt, assumed that the same is true for the other freedoms.[725]

---

723. The Court pointed out that "*the examination of the legislation at issue in the main proceedings must take account of the objective pursued by that legislation of facilitating the free movement of workers residing in other Member States who have accepted employment in the Netherlands and who are, by virtue of that fact, liable to incur additional expenses, by making the benefit of the flat-rate rule available to those workers and not to workers who have been resident for a long time in the Netherlands*" (Judgment in *Sopora*, C-512/13, EU:C:2015:108, at para. 26) and that it is "*an inherent aspect of the granting, on a flat-rate basis, of a tax advantage which is deemed to cover situations in which the material conditions governing entitlement to that advantage have been satisfied beyond doubt that there will be other situations in which, for a variety of reasons, those conditions have also been satisfied, with those situations also giving rise to a right to that advantage on production of appropriate proof*" (Judgment in *Sopora*, C-512/13, EU:C:2015:108, at para. 32). Moreover, "*Member States cannot be denied the possibility of attaining legitimate objectives through the introduction of rules which are easily managed and supervised by the competent authorities*" (Judgment in *Sopora*, C-512/13, EU:C:2015:108, at para. 36). This argument is typically brought forward in order to substantiate the proportionality of a national measure, which requires that a justification has already been identified (Judgment in *Commission/Italy*, C-110/05, EU:C:2009:66, at para. 60 [justified by "*the need to ensure road safety*"] and para. 67; Judgment in *Josemans*, C-137/09, EU:C:2010:774, at para. 69 [justified by "*the objective of combating drug tourism and the accompanying public nuisance*"] and para. 82; Judgment in *Commission/Spain*, C-400/08, EU:C:2011:172, at para. 118 [justified by "*the objectives relating to town and country planning, environmental protection and consumer protection*"] and para. 124). However, in *Sopora*, the Court hence inferred that "*[t]he mere fact that limits are set concerning the distance in relation to the workers' place of residence and concerning the ceiling of the exemption granted, taking as the starting point the Netherlands border and the taxable base, respectively, even though, as the referring court states, this is necessarily approximate in nature, cannot therefore, in itself, amount to indirect discrimination or an impediment to the free movement of workers. This is a* fortiori *so where, as in the present case, the flat-rate rule operates in favour of the workers who benefit from it, in that it reduces significantly the administrative steps which those workers must undertake in order to obtain the exemption for the reimbursement of extraterritorial expenses*" (Judgment in *Sopora*, C-512/13, EU:C:2015:108, at para. 34).
724. Judgment in *Sopora*, C-512/13, EU:C:2015:108, at para. 36.
725. See CFE ECJ Task Force, Opinion Statement ECJ-TF 3/2015 on the decision of the European Court of Justice in Case C-512/13, C.G. Sopora, on "horizontal discrimination," at pp. 6-7; I. De Groot, Sopora. Horizontal Discrimination. Most favoured Nation Treatment. Dutch 30% Ruling for Foreign Employees with a Specific Expertise is Not Contrary to EU Law Unless it Systematically Leads to Clear Overcompensation, 8 *H&I* 6.175 (2015), p. 5 (at p. 10); E.C.C.M. Kemmeren, 24 *EC Tax Rev.* 4 (2015), at pp. 182-183; G. Kofler in I. Richelle/W. Schön/E. Traversa (eds.), *Allocating Taxing Powers Within the European Union* (Springer, 2013), at pp. 211-212; M. Lang, 26 *SWI* 3 (2016), at pp. 129-130; M. Lang in R. Avi-Yonah/M. Lang (eds.), *Fiscal Federalism* (2016), forthcoming; also cf. Opinion of AG Léger in *Cadbury Schweppes and Cadbury Schweppes Overseas*, C-196/04, EU:C:2006:278, at points 79-80; Opinion of AG Mengozzi in *Columbus Container Services*, C-298/05, EU:C:2007:197, at points 117-118; Opinion of AG Kokott in *Sopora*, C-512/13, EU:C:2014:2375, at point 28;

2.4.3 *The Influence of the Legal Situation in Other Member States*

Comparability is typically established from the perspective of one Member State.[726] At first glance, it seems to be the ECJ's position that the legal situation in another Member State is to be disregarded, i.e., "*the Member States [...] are not obliged [...] to adapt their own tax systems to the different systems of tax of the other Member States.*"[727] However, the Court has insinuated in *Manninen* that another Member State's legislation might be relevant under certain circumstances. The ECJ held that "*the Finnish tax legislation is designed to prevent double taxation of company profits by granting to a shareholder who receives dividends a tax advantage linked to the taking into account of the corporation tax due from the company distributing the dividends. It is true that, in relation to such legislation, the situation of persons fully taxable in Finland might differ according to the place where they invested their capital. That would be the case in particular where the tax legislation of the Member State in which the investments were made already eliminated the risk of double taxation of company profits distributed in the form of dividends, by, for example, subjecting to corporation tax only such profits by the company concerned as were not distributed.*"[728] Thus, a Member State is not necessarily obliged to grant a tax advantage that is meant to eliminate economic double taxation if this objective is already achieved through measures taken by another Member State.[729]

A similar approach was taken by the ECJ in *De Groot, Beker* and *Imfeld and Garcet*. Thus, a Member State may be released from its obligation to take account of its resident taxpayers' personal and family circumstances,[730] "*if it finds that, even in the*

726. See J. Englisch, Fiscal Cohesion in the Taxation of Cross-Border Dividends (Part Two), 44 *Eur. Taxn.* 8 (2004), p. 355 (at p. 359); B. Knobbe-Keuk, 3 *EC Tax Rev.* 3 (1994), at pp. 77-78; J. Schuch, Bilateral Tax Treaties Multilateralized by the EC Treaty, in M. Lang/H. Loukota/A.J. Rädler/J. Schuch/G. Toifl/C. Urtz/F. Wassermeyer/M. Züger (eds.), *Multilateral Tax Treaties* (Linde, 1997), p. 33 (at p. 40); J. Schuch, EC Law Requires Multilateral Tax Treaty, 7 *EC Tax Rev.* 1 (1998), p. 29 (at p. 31); also cf. D. Birk, Besteuerungsgleichheit in der Europäischen Union, in M. Lehner (ed.), *Steuerrecht im Europäischen Binnenmarkt*, DStJG 19 (Dr Otto Schmidt, 1996), p. 63 (at p. 77); J. Englisch, *Dividendenbesteuerung* (Dr Otto Schmidt, 2005), at p. 240; E. Reimer in M. Lehner (ed.), *Grundfreiheiten im Steuerrecht der EU-Staaten* (C.H. Beck, 2000), at p. 50.

727. Judgment in *Columbus Container Services*, C-298/05, EU:C:2007:754, at para. 51; Judgment in *Block*, C-67/08, EU:C:2009:92, at para. 31; Judgment in *Commission/Hungary*, C-253/09, EU:C:2011:795, at para. 83; Judgment in *Banco Bilbao Vizcaya Argentaria*, C-157/10, EU:C:2011:813, at para. 39; Judgment in *X*, C-302/12, EU:C:2013:756, at para. 29; also cf. Judgment in *Deutsche Shell*, C-293/06, EU:C:2008:129, at paras 42-43; Judgment in *Krankenheim Ruhesitz am Wannsee-Seniorenheimstatt*, C-157/07, EU:C:2008:588, at para. 49; Judgment in *CIBA*, C-96/08, EU:C:2010:185 at para. 28.

728. Judgment in *Manninen*, C-319/02, EU:C:2004:484, at paras 33-34.

729. See J. Englisch, Europarechtskonforme Dividendenbesteuerung – "Aims and effects"?, 51 *RIW* 3 (2005), p. 187 (at p. 192); J. Englisch, 33 *Intertax* 5 (2005), at p. 211; G. Kofler, *Doppelbesteuerungsabkommen und Europäisches Gemeinschaftsrecht* (Linde, 2007), at p. 1021; A. Schnitger, Grenzüberschreitende Körperschaftsteueranrechnung und Neuausrichtung der Kohärenz nach dem EuGH-Urteil in der Rs. Manninen, 86 *FR* 24 (2004), p. 1357 (at p. 1358).

730. Judgment in *Schumacker*, C-279/93, EU:C:1995:31, at para. 32; also see Judgment in *Gschwind*, C-391/97, EU:C:1999:409, at para. 22; Judgment in *Zurstrassen*, C-87/99, EU:C:2000:251, at para. 21; Judgment in *de Groot*, C-385/00, EU:C:2002:750, at para. 90; Judgment in *Gerritse*, C-234/01, EU:C:2003:340, at para. 43; Judgment in *Wallentin*, C-169/03, EU:C:2004:403, at para. 15; Judgment in *D.*, C-376/03, EU:C:2005:424, at para. 27; Judgment in *Turpeinen*,

absence of a convention, one or more of the States of employment, with respect to the income taxed by them, grant advantages based on the personal and family circumstances of taxpayers who do not reside in the territory of those States but receive taxable income there."[731] Similarly to *Manninen*, it can be argued that a resident who is granted advantages based on her personal and family circumstances in another Member State is hence not comparable to another resident who does not benefit from such a foreign legislation.[732]

This line of reasoning recalls the ECJ's approach with regard to double burdens.[733] Although not explicitly stated, in *Futura Participations*,[734] for example, the Court assumed that, with regard to the Luxembourgian accounting requirement, non-residents are not comparable to residents if non-residents also have to keep accounts in compliance with the tax accounting rules of their own residence state, which may also be relied upon for the purposes of the Luxembourg legislation.[735] The double-burden line of case law boils down to the fact that if certain requirements have to be met before an activity or a transaction is allowed to take place in a Member State, account has to be taken of another Member State's standards imposed on and complied with by the person invoking the fundamental freedoms, insofar as these foreign standards likewise contribute to the achievement of the objective underlying the first-mentioned Member State's requirements. Otherwise, different situations would be treated equally. If this understanding is taken for granted, it seems consistent to apply a similar approach with regard to national measures that do not impose a burden, but rather have a positive impact on the taxpayer. In a cross-border scenario, the underlying objective of such a benefit may be equally achieved by national measures taken by another Member State. With regard to the object and purpose of the respective

C-520/04, EU:C:2006:703, at para. 27; Judgment in *Meindl*, C-329/05, EU:C:2007:57, at para. 23; Judgment in *Talotta*, C-383/05, EU:C:2007:181, at para. 19; Judgment in *Lakebrink and Peters-Lakebrink*, C-182/06, EU:C:2007:452, at paras 28-31; Judgment in *Renneberg*, C-527/06, EU:C:2008:566, at paras 59-61; Judgment in *Commission/Spain*, C-562/07, EU:C:2009:614, at para. 46; Judgment in *Commission/Belgium*, C-250/08, EU:C:2011:793, at para. 55; Judgment in *Gielen*, C-440/08, EU:C:2010:148, at paras 43-44; Judgment in *Commission/Hungary*, C-253/09, EU:C:2011:795, at para. 55; Judgment in *Schröder*, C-450/09, EU:C:2011:198, at para. 37; Judgment in *Commission/Estonia*, C-39/10, EU:C:2012:282, at para. 49; Judgment in *Beker*, C-168/11, EU:C:2013:117, at para. 43; Judgment in Ettwein, C-425/11, EU:C:2013:121, at para. 46; Judgment in *Imfeld and Garcet*, C-303/12, EU:C:2013:822, at para. 44; Judgment in *Grünewald*, C-559/13, EU:C:2015:109, at para. 25; Judgment in *Hirvonen*, C-623/13, EU:C:2015:765, at para. 31; Judgment in *Kieback*, C-9/14, EU:C:2015:406, at para. 22.

731. Judgment in *De Groot*, C-385/00, EU:C:2002:750, at para. 100; also see Judgment in *Beker*, C-168/11, EU:C:2013:117, at para. 56; Judgment in *Imfeld and Garcet*, C-303/12, EU:C:2013:822, at para. 69.
732. Critically in this respect J. Englisch, *Aufteilung der Besteuerungsbefugnisse – Ein Rechtfertigungsgrund für die Einschränkung von EG-Grundfreiheiten* (Institut "Finanzen und Steuern" e.V., 2008), at p. 25.
733. Cf. K. Daxkobler, *Die grundfreiheitliche Rechtsprechung des EuGH* (Linde, 2015), at p. 150.
734. Judgment in *Futura Participations and Singer*, C-250/95, EU:C:1997:239.
735. See M. Lang, *Die Rechtsprechung des EuGH zu den direkten Steuern* (Peter Lang, 2007), at pp. 37-38; M. Lang, Direct Taxation: Is the ECJ Heading in a New Direction?, 46 *Eur. Taxn.* 9 (2006), p. 421 (at p. 422); M. Lang in M. Hebig/K. Kaiser/K. Koschmieder/M. Oblau (eds.), *FS Wilhelm H. Wacker* (Erich Schmidt Verlag, 2006), at p. 368; M. Lang in M. Beusch (ed.), *Steuerrecht 2007* (Schulthess, 2007), at pp. 8-9; also cf. J. Schönfeld, *Hinzurechnungsbesteuerung und Europäisches Gemeinschaftsrecht* (Dr Otto Schmidt, 2005), at pp. 71-73.

legislation, taxpayers who are granted a similar benefit by another Member State may be regarded as being in a different situation than taxpayers who have not been entitled to such a beneficial treatment.

Still, the ECJ's approach in *Manninen* is heavily criticized in the literature.[736] According to some scholars, the Court's approach would imply that a supranational perspective on discrimination has to be taken, meaning that not only does the tax burden in the Member State the legislation of which is under scrutiny have to be taken into account, but the repercussions of all other Member States' tax order on the overall, supranational tax burden also have to be considered.[737] Thus, the differences between forbidden discrimination and restrictions, on the one hand, and acceptable tax disparities between unharmonized tax systems, on the other hand, would be blurred.[738] In addition, such an approach is considered to contradict the prohibition of cross-border compensation as established by the ECJ in a series of judgments,[739] according to which "*[a]ny tax advantage resulting for providers of services from the low taxation to which they are subject in the Member State in which they are established cannot be used by another Member State to justify less favourable treatment in tax matters given to recipients of services established in the latter State.*"[740] In a way, this contradiction also becomes evident when comparing the ECJ's decisions in *Amurta* and in *Manninen*.[741] In *Manninen*, concerning the tax treatment of dividends in the residence state of the shareholder, the Court took into consideration the legal situation in the source state,[742] whereas in *Amurta*, concerning the tax treatment of dividends in the source state, a different approach was taken.[743] Among other issues, the question was raised whether a Member State may refrain from granting foreign shareholders

736. See J. Englisch, 44 *Eur. Taxn.* 8 (2004), at pp. 358-361; J. Englisch, Europarechtswidrigkeit des finnischen Körperschaftsteueranrechnungsverfahrens, 13 *IStR* 19 (2004), p. 680 (at pp. 684-685); J. Englisch, *Dividendenbesteuerung* (Dr Otto Schmidt, 2005), at pp. 269-272; J. Englisch, 33 *Intertax* 5 (2005), at pp. 207-213; J. Englisch, 51 *RIW* 3 (2005), at pp. 191-194; also cf. A. Cordewener, Körperschaftsteueranrechnung für Gebietsfremde versus Kapitalverkehrsfreiheit – Zum Gutachten des EFTA-Gerichtshofs in Sachen Fokus Bank ASA, 87 *FR* 7 (2005), p. 345 (at pp. 351-356); D. Weber, 34 *Intertax* 12 (2006), pp. 597-598; D. Weber, *In Search of a (New) Equilibrium Between Tax Sovereignty and the Freedom of Movement Within the EC* (Kluwer, 2006), at pp. 29-31.

737. See J. Englisch, 33 *Intertax* 5 (2005), at p. 210.

738. See J. Englisch, 13 *IStR* 19 (2004), at p. 686; J. Englisch, 33 *Intertax* 5 (2005), at pp. 211-212; J. Englisch, 51 *RIW* 3 (2005), at p. 193; G. Kofler, *Doppelbesteuerungsabkommen und Europäisches Gemeinschaftsrecht* (Linde, 2007), at p. 1024.

739. See J. Englisch, 13 *IStR* 19 (2004), at p. 686; J. Englisch, 33 *Intertax* 5 (2005), at p. 211; J. Englisch, 51 *RIW* 3 (2005), at p. 192; J. Englisch, *Dividendenbesteuerung* (Dr Otto Schmidt, 2005), at pp. 299-300; G. Kofler, *Doppelbesteuerungsabkommen und Europäisches Gemeinschaftsrecht* (Linde, 2007), at p. 1024.

740. Judgment in *Avoir Fiscal*, 270/83, EU:C:1986:37, at para. 21; Judgment in *Asscher*, C-107/94, EU:C:1996:251, at para. 53; Judgment in *Saint-Gobain*, C-307/97, EU:C:1999:438, at para. 53; Judgment in *Eurowings Luftverkehr*, C-294/97, EU:C:1999:524, at para. 44; Judgment in *Verkooijen*, C-35/98, EU:C:2000:294, at para. 61; Judgment in *Danner*, C-136/00, EU:C:2002:558, at para. 56; Judgment in *De Groot*, C-385/00, EU:C:2002:750, at para. 97.

741. Cf. W. Schön, 69 *Bull. Intl. Taxn.* 4/5 (2015), at pp. 289-290; W. Schön in W. Schön/C. Heber (eds.), *Grundfragen des Europäischen Steuerrechts* (Springer, 2015), at pp. 151-153.

742. Judgment in *Manninen*, C-319/02, EU:C:2004:484, at paras 33-34.

743. See M. Lang, ECJ Case Law on Cross-Border Dividend Taxation – Recent Developments, 17 *EC Tax. Rev.* 2 (2008), p. 67 (at p. 72).

receiving dividends from domestic companies an exemption from withholding tax, which is provided for in the case of domestic shareholders if the residence state of the foreign shareholder unilaterally grants a full tax credit and thus offsets the withholding tax levied by the source state of the dividends.[744] The Court held that "*with regard to the objective of prevention of economic double taxation, [companies established in another Member State] are in a comparable situation to that of recipient companies established in the Netherlands or which have a permanent establishment there which holds the shares in the distributing company, the Kingdom of the Netherlands is under a duty to ensure that, under the procedures laid down by its national law to prevent or mitigate a series of liabilities to tax or economic double taxation, recipient companies established in another Member State are subject to the same treatment as recipient companies established in the Netherlands. Accordingly, the Kingdom of the Netherlands cannot rely on the existence of a tax advantage granted unilaterally by another Member State in order to escape its obligations under the Treaty.*"[745]

Given the apparent inconsistency in the case law, the critique is understandable, but not entirely warranted. According to the ECJ's case law, a supranational perspective may only be taken if certain conditions are fulfilled. Taking into account a taxpayer's personal and family circumstances, for example, "*is [in principle] a matter for the State of residence.*"[746] This can be different, if the residence state "*finds that [...] one or more of the States of employment, with respect to the income taxed by them, grant advantages based on the personal and family circumstances of taxpayers who do not reside in the territory of those States but receive taxable income there.*"[747] Still, if "*the tax legislation at issue [...] does not establish any correlation between the tax advantages*

744. For remarks on the possible neutralization through a double taxation convention see Chapter 4.1.3.2.4.

745. Judgment in *Amurta*, C-379/05, EU:C:2007:655, at paras 76-78; also cf. Judgment in *Eckelkamp*, C-11/07, EU:C:2008:489, at para. 69; Judgment in *Arens-Sikken*, C-43/07, EU:C:2008:490, at para. 66; Judgment in *Commission/Spain*, C-487/08, EU:C:2010:310, at para. 66; Judgment in *Imfeld and Garcet*, C-303/12, EU:C:2013:822, at para. 61; Judgment in *Miljoen*, C-10/14, C-14/14 and C-17/14, EU:C:2015:608, at para. 77.

746. Judgment in *Schumacker*, C-279/93, EU:C:1995:31, at para. 32; also see Judgment in *Gschwind*, C-391/97, EU:C:1999:409, at para. 22; Judgment in *Zurstrassen*, C-87/99, EU:C:2000:251, at para. 21; Judgment in *De Groot*, C-385/00, EU:C:2002:750, at para. 90; Judgment in *Gerritse*, C-234/01, EU:C:2003:340, at para. 43; Judgment in *Wallentin*, C-169/03, EU:C:2004:403, at para. 15; Judgment in *D.*, C-376/03, EU:C:2005:424, at para. 27; Judgment in *Turpeinen*, C-520/04, EU:C:2006:703, at para. 27; Judgment in *Meindl*, C-329/05, EU:C:2007:57, at para. 23; Judgment in *Talotta*, C-383/05, EU:C:2007:181, at para. 19; Judgment in *Lakebrink and Peters-Lakebrink*, C-182/06, EU:C:2007:452, at paras 28-31; Judgment in *Renneberg*, C-527/06, EU:C:2008:566, at paras 59-61; Judgment in *Commission/Spain*, C-562/07, EU:C:2009:614, at para. 46; Judgment in *Commission/Belgium*, C-250/08, EU:C:2011:793, at para. 55; Judgment in *Gielen*, C-440/08, EU:C:2010:148, at paras 43-44; Judgment in *Commission/Hungary*, C-253/09, EU:C:2011:795, at para. 55; Judgment in *Schröder*, C-450/09, EU:C:2011:198, at para. 37; Judgment in *Commission/Estonia*, C-39/10, EU:C:2012:282, at para. 49; Judgment in *Beker*, C-168/11, EU:C:2013:117, at para. 43; Judgment in Ettwein, C-425/11, EU:C:2013:121, at para. 46; Judgment in *Imfeld and Garcet*, C-303/12, EU:C:2013:822, at para. 44; Judgment in *Grünewald*, C-559/13, EU:C:2015:109, at para. 25; Judgment in *Hirvonen*, C-623/13, EU:C:2015:765, at para. 31; Judgment in *Kieback*, C-9/14, EU:C:2015:406, at para. 22.

747. Judgment in *De Groot*, C-385/00, EU:C:2002:750, at para. 100; also see Judgment in *Beker*, C-168/11, EU:C:2013:117, at para. 56; Judgment in *Imfeld and Garcet*, C-303/12, EU:C:2013:822, at para. 69.

which it grants to the residents of the Member State concerned and the tax advantages for which they may qualify in connection with their taxation in another Member State,"[748] the respective Member State "*cannot rely on the existence of a tax advantage granted unilaterally by another Member State in order to escape its obligations under the Treaty.*"[749] Thus, the legal situation in another Member State can only be taken into account if the Member State's legislation is legally linked to the foreign tax system.[750] Admittedly, it is unclear under which circumstances such a cross-border linkage is sufficient to ensure that the demands of the fundamental freedoms are met. The ECJ's decisions on the prohibition of cross-border compensation suggest that it is not possible to immunize a restrictive domestic measure by linking it with *any* tax advantage granted by another Member State.[751]

With respect to the comparability analysis, *Schempp* is the only case so far where the ECJ has ultimately accepted a different treatment of cross-border and purely domestic situations by one Member State because of the different legal situation in another Member State. The Court held that it does not constitute discrimination if the deductibility of maintenance payments by a German taxpayer to a recipient resident in Austria is conditional on the taxation of those payments in that other Member State, because "*the payment of maintenance to a recipient resident in Germany cannot be compared to the payment of maintenance to a recipient resident in Austria. The recipient is subject in each of those two cases, as regards taxation of the maintenance payments, to a different tax system.*"[752] Whereas Germany permits a deduction of maintenance payments on the side of the taxpayer responsible for paying the maintenance allowance and taxes these amounts as income on the side of the recipient of these payments, Austria considers maintenance payments to be irrelevant for tax purposes, i.e., such payments are neither deductible by the payor nor subject to tax at the level of the payee. The Court apparently deemed the (non-)deductibility of maintenance payments at the level of the payor to be sufficiently interconnected with the (non-)taxability of those payments at the level of the payee[753] so that a cross-border

748. Judgment in *Imfeld and Garcet*, C-303/12, EU:C:2013:822, at para. 73.
749. Judgment in *Amurta*, C-379/05, EU:C:2007:655, at para. 78; Judgment in *Miljoen*, C-10/14, C-14/14 and C-17/14, EU:C:2015:608, at para. 77; also see Judgment in *Eckelkamp*, C-11/07, EU:C:2008:489, at para. 69; Judgment in *Arens-Sikken*, C-43/07, EU:C:2008:490, at para. 66; Judgment in *Commission/Spain*, C-487/08, EU:C:2010:310, at para. 66; Judgment in *Imfeld and Garcet*, C-303/12, EU:C:2013:822, at para. 61.
750. Cf. G. Kofler, *Doppelbesteuerungsabkommen und Europäisches Gemeinschaftsrecht* (Linde, 2007), at pp. 1024-1025.
751. Judgment in *Avoir Fiscal*, 270/83, EU:C:1986:37, at para. 21; Judgment in *Asscher*, C-107/94, EU:C:1996:251, at para. 53; Judgment in *Saint-Gobain*, C-307/97, EU:C:1999:438, at para. 53; Judgment in *Eurowings Luftverkehr*, C-294/97, EU:C:1999:524, at para. 44; Judgment in *Verkooijen*, C-35/98, EU:C:2000:294, at para. 61; Judgment in *Danner*, C-136/00, EU:C:2002:558, at para. 56; Judgment in *De Groot*, C-385/00, EU:C:2002:750, at para. 97.
752. Judgment in *Schempp*, C-403/03, EU:C:2005:446, at paras 29-36.
753. This view can be criticized, though, when taking into consideration that Germany does not tax non-residents receiving maintenance payments from German residents and, moreover, would even be restricted in taxing those payments due to the double taxation convention concluded with Austria. See M. Lang, 15 *SWI* 9 (2005), at pp. 413-415; also see K. Daxkobler, *Die grundfreiheitliche Rechtsprechung des EuGH* (Linde, 2015), at p. 282.

payment which does not trigger a tax in the other jurisdiction is not comparable to a domestic payment the recipient of which is subjected to tax on it.[754,755]

The ECJ's case law hence provides for indications that the legal situation in another Member State might be relevant when determining the compatibility of a Member State's legislation with the fundamental freedoms. This approach should not be criticized because the ECJ takes a supranational perspective. If a Member State decides to make its tax system dependent on the legal situation in another Member State, it is the respective national measure itself which requires the Court to take such a perspective. However, if this approach was already applied in the comparability analysis, there would be "*no more room for a weighing and balancing of the conflicting EC and national policies,*" as it would take place within a proportionality analysis.[756] Denying comparability does not render the proportionality analysis superfluous,[757] especially because the arguments raised at the level of comparability and justification are to a great extent interchangeable.[758] In order to make sure that the proportionality

754. Cf. Opinion of AG Geelhoed in *Schempp*, C-403/03, EU:C:2005:62, at point 30 ("*[T]here is a logical and systematic relationship between permitting a deduction of maintenance payments on the side of the taxpayer responsible for paying the maintenance allowance and the taxability of these amounts as income on the side of the recipient of these payments. The amounts concerned are, in principle, subject to income tax within the same system. The situation of Mr Schempp, by contrast, is characterised by the fact that the tax legislation of two Member States is involved. In this situation there is no systematic link between the fiscal treatment of Mr Schempp's income and his former spouse's income.*").

755. If two situations are not comparable, the question arises whether they might nevertheless be treated equally. Concerning the *Schempp* case, one might wonder whether it is in line with the fundamental freedoms that an Austrian resident who is obliged to pay maintenance to a German resident is not allowed to deduct those payments, while they are, at the same time, subject to tax at the level of the German recipient.

756. J. Englisch, 33 *Intertax* 5 (2005), at p. 210; also see J. Englisch, 51 *RIW* 3 (2005), at pp. 191-192; J. Englisch, 38 *Intertax* 4 (2010), at pp. 203-204.

757. See M. Lang/J. Lüdicke/M. Reich, 17 *IStR* 20 (2008), at p. 712; P. Wattel, 55 *Eur. Taxn.* 12 (2015), at p. 553 ("*If [the cross-border situation and the domestic situation] are not comparable, then that is not yet the end of the analysis, as still, the Court is competent to test whether the difference in tax treatment is proportionate to the difference in fiscal position.*"); also cf. J. Englisch, 38 *Intertax* 4 (2010), at p. 204.

758. Cf. M. Lang, 15 *SWI* 8 (2005), at p. 369; M. Lang, 15 *SWI* 9 (2005), at p. 413; M. Lang, 46 *Eur. Taxn.* 9 (2006), at pp. 421-422; M. Lang/A. Jettmar, *Internationale Wirtschaftsbriefe*, Fach 11, Gruppe 2, Nr. 15 (2005), at p. 742; M. Lang/J. Lüdicke/M. Reich, 17 *IStR* 20 (2008), at p. 712; M. Lang in M. Hebig/K. Kaiser/K. Koschmieder/M. Oblau (eds.), *FS Wilhelm H. Wacker* (Erich Schmidt Verlag, 2006), at p. 368; M. Lang in M. Beusch (ed.), *Steuerrecht 2007* (Schulthess, 2007), at pp. 9-10; M. Lang, 18 *EC Tax Rev.* 3 (2009), at p. 100; also cf. A. Cordewener, *Europäische Grundfreiheiten und nationales Steuerrecht* (Dr Otto Schmidt, 2002), at pp. 162-174; M. Lang in W. Gassner/M. Lang/E. Lechner (eds.), *Doppelbesteuerungsabkommen und EU-Recht* (Linde, 1996), at p. 37; for a different view see N. Bammens, *The Principle of Non-Discrimination in International and European Tax Law* (IBFD, 2012), at p. 1073 ("*[T]here is a fundamental difference between these concepts, namely that justification grounds are inherent in the comparative attribute. As a result, they cannot be relied upon in the comparability analysis, as elements that are inherent in the comparative attribute should be disregarded in such context. However, these arguments reflect valid policy concerns which Member States are allowed to safeguard. For this reason, they may justify discriminatory taxation.*"); with regard to the non-discrimination provision of Article 14 ECHR see, for example, I. Cameron, *An Introduction to the European Convention on Human Rights*[6] (Iustus Förlag, 2011), at p. 158 ("*Determining whether situations are 'relevantly similar' is really the same thing as determining whether an objective and reasonable justification exists for distinguishing between them*"); F.

of a national measure which is legally linked with the foreign tax treatment is analysed, the legal situation in another Member State should hence be considered when determining whether the scrutinized measure is justified or not.

2.5 Justification Grounds

2.5.1 Written and Unwritten Justification Grounds

Interferences with the fundamental freedoms are not invariably prohibited. The TFEU instead provides for explicit reasons that justify discrimination and restrictions of the fundamental freedoms. According to Article 36 TFEU, for example, the free movement of goods "*shall not preclude prohibitions or restrictions on imports, exports or goods in transit justified on grounds of public morality, public policy or public security; the protection of health and life of humans, animals or plants; the protection of national treasures possessing artistic, historic or archaeological value; or the protection of industrial and commercial property.*" Similar, albeit fewer grounds of justification can be found in Article 45(3) TFEU on the free movement of workers ("*public policy, public security or public health*"), in Article 52(1) TFEU on the freedom of establishment and - due to Article 62 TFEU - on the freedom to provide services ("*public policy, public security or public health*") as well as in Article 65(1)(b) TFEU on the free movement of capital and payments ("*public policy or public security*"). Concerning tax measures, however, these written justification grounds are hardly of importance.[759] With regard to capital movements between Member States and third countries, Member States may at best rely on Article 65(4) TFEU, according to which - under certain circumstances - "*restrictive tax measures adopted by a Member State concerning one or more third countries are to be considered compatible with the Treaties in so far as they are justified by one of the objectives of the Union and compatible with the proper functioning of the internal market.*"

Jacobs/R. White/C. Ovey, *The European Convention on Human Rights*[5] (Oxford University Press, 2010), at p. 559 ("*[T]he issue of whether the compared groups are truly in analogous situations can sometimes only be answered by considering whether their differential treatment can be justified*").

759. See V.E. Englmair, The Relevance of the Fundamental Freedoms for Direct Taxation, in M. Lang/P. Pistone/J. Schuch/C. Staringer (eds.), *Introduction to European Tax Law on Direct Taxation*[4] (Linde, 2015), p. 53 (at p. 75); H. Hahn, Gemeinschaftsrecht und Recht der direkten Steuern - Teil III, 93 *DStZ* 15 (2005), p. 507 (at p. 507); also cf. A. Cordewener, *Europäische Grundfreiheiten und nationales Steuerrecht* (Dr Otto Schmidt, 2002), at p. 926; A. Cordewener/G. Kofler/S. van Thiel, The Clash Between European Freedoms and National Direct Tax Law: Public Interest Defences Available to the Member States, 46 *Common Market L. Rev.* 6 (2009), p. 1951 (at p. 1953); L. Hinnekens, Basis and Scope of Public Interest Justification of National Tax Measures Infringing Fundamental Treaty Freedoms, in F. Vanistendael (ed.), *EU Freedoms and Taxation* (IBFD, 2006), p. 73 (at p. 78); M. Lang, *Die Rechtsprechung des EuGH zu den direkten Steuern* (Peter Lang, 2007), at p. 47; K. Simader, *Withholding Taxes and the Fundamental Freedoms* (Kluwer, 2014), at p. 181; but see D. Smit/B. Kiekebeld, *EC Free Movement of Capital, Income Taxation and Third Countries: Four Selected Issues* (Kluwer, 2008), at p. 99.

The justification grounds explicitly mentioned in the TFEU are hardly suitable to justify discriminatory or restrictive tax measures from a practical point of view. Moreover, the ECJ is of the opinion that such provisions "*must be interpreted strictly,*" because they constitute a derogation from the basic rule that all obstacles to the fundamental freedoms must be eliminated.[760] However, the Court also accepts unwritten justification grounds that are not explicitly mentioned in the TFEU.[761] According to the "rule of reason,"[762] as summarized by the ECJ in *Gebhard*, "*national measures liable to hinder or make less attractive the exercise of fundamental freedoms guaranteed by the Treaty must fulfil four conditions: they must be applied in a non-discriminatory manner; they must be justified by imperative requirements in the general interest; they must be suitable for securing the attainment of the objective which they pursue; and they must not go beyond what is necessary in order to attain it.*"[763]

Due to the first requirement, it was partly assumed that only non-discriminatory restrictions can be justified by imperative requirements in the general interest.[764] However, according to AG Alber, this would mean that a "*difference in treatment could never be justified by imperative requirements in the general interest, which is a contradiction in itself because justification on such grounds is expressly permitted.*"[765] Moreover, it is argued that even non-discriminatory restrictions implicitly require a discrimination analysis. Limiting the rule of reason to non-discriminatory restrictions

760. Judgment in *Bauhuis*, 46/76, EU:C:1977:6, at para 12; Judgment in *Commission/Ireland*, 113/80, EU:C:1981:139, at para. 7; also cf. Judgment in *ERT/DEP*, C-260/89, EU:C:1991:254, at para. 24.
761. A first indication can already be found in the *Dassonville* judgment, according to which a Member State may "*take measures to prevent unfair practices […], it is however subject to the condition that these measures should be reasonable*" (Judgment in *Dassonville*, 8/74, EU:C:1974:82, at para. 6). However, the *Cassis de Dijon* case is commonly considered to be the hour of birth of the rule of reason (see, for example, A.A.M. Schrauwen, In Defence of Public Interest: The Rule of Reason, in A.A.M. Schrauwen [ed.], *Rule of Reason* [Europa Law Publishing, 2005], p. 1 [at p. 5]). The ECJ's judgment clarified that "*[o]bstacles to movement within the Community resulting from disparities between the national laws relating to the marketing of the products in question must be accepted in so far as those provisions may be recognized as being necessary in order to satisfy mandatory requirements relating in particular to the effectiveness of fiscal supervision, the protection of public health, the fairness of commercial transactions and the defence of the consumer*" (Judgment in *Rewe*, 120/78, EU:C:1979:42, at para. 8).
762. With further references see A. Cordewener, *Europäische Grundfreiheiten und nationales Steuerrecht* (Dr Otto Schmidt, 2002), at p. 61 (FN 95).
763. Judgment in *Gebhard*, C-55/94, EU:C:1995:411, at para. 37; also see Judgment in *Reisebüro Broede*, C-3/95, EU:C:1996:487, at para. 28; Judgment in *Centros*, C-212/97, EU:C:1999:126, at para. 34; Judgment in *Haim*, C-424/97, EU:C:2000:357, at para. 57; Judgment in *MacQuen*, C-108/96, EU:C:2001:67, at para. 26; Judgment in *Gräbner*, C-294/00, EU:C:2002:442, at para. 39; Judgment in *Inspire Art*, C-167/01, EU:C:2003:512, at para. 133; Judgment in *Contse*, C-234/03, EU:C:2005:664, at para. 25; Judgment in *Colegio de Ingenieros de Caminos, Canales y Puertos*, C-330/03, EU:C:2006:45, at para. 30; Judgment in *Commission/Greece*, C-65/05, EU:C:2006:673, at para. 49; Judgment in *Corporación Dermoestética*, C-500/06, EU:C:2008:421, at para. 35.
764. See L. Hinnekens in F. Vanistendael (ed.), *EU Freedoms and Taxation* (IBFD, 2006), at p. 83; J. Wouters, The Principle of Non-discrimination in European Community law, 8 *EC Tax Rev.* 2 (1999), p. 98 (at p. 104).
765. Opinion of AG Alber in *Bosal*, C-168/01, EU:C:2002:528, at point 40.

would thus not be convincing.[766] It was hence concluded that national measures leading to overt discrimination are excluded from the rule of reason, i.e., Member States may rely on unwritten grounds of justification only with regard to covert discrimination and non-discriminatory restrictions.[767] This understanding is also supported by some ECJ judgments.[768] However, considering the blurred lines between overt and covert discrimination as well as restrictions, such a distinction seems impractical and hence not comprehensible.[769] In the literature, it is additionally pointed out that the ECJ is not consistent in its jurisprudence and at times accepted unwritten justification grounds even if the national measure at stake led to overt discrimination based on nationality, i.e., the rule of reason does apply - or at least should be applied - irrespective of whether the national measure leads to overt or covert discrimination or to a non-discriminatory restriction.[770]

2.5.2 Justification Grounds in the ECJ's Tax Jurisprudence

The rule of reason requires, *inter alia*, that the restrictive tax measure is justified by imperative requirements in the general interest. Thereby, the objectives of EU law have to be taken into account. The promotion of research and development, for example, may in principle be suitable to justify a national measure which refuses the benefit of

766. Cf. M. Lang, *Die Rechtsprechung des EuGH zu den direkten Steuern* (Peter Lang, 2007), at pp. 47-48.
767. See D. Hohenwarter, *Verlustverwertung im Konzern* (LexisNexis, 2009), at p. 113; G. Kofler, *Doppelbesteuerungsabkommen und Europäisches Gemeinschaftsrecht* (Linde, 2007), at p. 108; G. Kofler, Wer hat das Sagen im Steuerrecht - EuGH (Teil 1), 19 *ÖStZ* 6 (2006), p. 106 (at p. 111); L. Hinnekens, The Search for the Framework Conditions of the Fundamental EC Treaty Principles as Applied by the European Court to Member States' Direct Taxation, 11 *EC Tax Rev.* 3 (2002), p. 112 (at p. 114); L.A. Denys, The ECJ Case Law on Cross-Border Dividends Revisited, 47 *Eur. Taxn.* 5 (2007), p. 221 (at pp. 221-222); S. Kingston, 44 *Common Market L. Rev.* 5 (2007), at pp. 1328-1329; M. Tumpel, Europarechtliche Besteuerungsmaßstäbe für die grenzüberschreitende Organisation und Finanzierung von Unternehmen, in J. Pelka (ed.), *Europa- und verfassungsrechtliche Grenzen der Unternehmensbesteuerung*, DStJG 30 (Dr Otto Schmidt, 2000), p. 321 (at pp. 324-326); for criticism see T. Kingreen, *Die Struktur der Grundfreiheiten des Europäischen Gemeinschaftsrechts* (Duncker & Humblot, 1999), at pp. 120-121; also see Opinion of AG Alber in *Bosal*, C-168/01, EU:C:2002:528, at para. 41.
768. Cf. Judgment in *Bond van Adverteerders*, 352/85, EU:C:1988:196, at para. 32; Judgment in *Stichting Collectieve Antennevoorziening Gouda*, C-288/89, EU:C:1991:323, at para. 11; Judgment in *Royal Bank of Scotland*, C-311/97, EU:C:1999:216, at para. 32; Judgment in *Ciola*, C-224/97, EU:C:1999:212, at para. 16; Judgment in *Läärä and others*, C-124/97, EU:C:1999:435, at para. 31.
769. See A. Cordewener, Deutsche Unternehmensbesteuerung und europäische Grundfreiheiten - Grundzüge des materiellen und formellen Rechtsschutzsystems der EG, 42 *DStR* 1-2 (2004), p. 6 (at pp. 8-9); D. Hohenwarter, *Verlustverwertung im Konzern* (LexisNexis, 2009), at p. 114; G. Kofler, *Doppelbesteuerungsabkommen und Europäisches Gemeinschaftsrecht* (Linde, 2007), at p. 108; R. Lyal, 12 *EC Tax Rev.* 2 (2003), at p. 74; similarly also J. Englisch, *Dividendenbesteuerung* (Dr Otto Schmidt, 2005), at pp. 273-277.
770. With a reference to *Avoir Fiscal* (Judgment in *Avoir Fiscal*, 270/83, EU:C:1986:37) see M. Lang, *Die Rechtsprechung des EuGH zu den direkten Steuern* (Peter Lang, 2007), at p. 48; K. Simader, *Withholding Taxes and the Fundamental Freedoms* (Kluwer, 2014), at pp. 182-183; with further references to *Svensson and Gustavsson* (Judgment in *Svensson and Gustavsson*, C-484/93, EU:C:1995:379) and *Baars* (Judgment in *Baars*, C-251/98, EU:C:2000:22) see D. Hohenwarter, *Verlustverwertung im Konzern* (LexisNexis, 2009), at pp. 113-114.

a tax credit for any research not carried out in the Member State concerned. However, according to the ECJ, such legislation is directly contrary to the objective of EU policy in the field of research and development as emphasized in Article 179 TFEU,[771] according to which "*[t]he Union shall have the objective of strengthening its scientific and technological bases by achieving a European research area in which researchers, scientific knowledge and technology circulate freely, and encouraging it to become more competitive.*" For the same reason, aims of a purely economic nature are not accepted as overriding reasons in the public interest.[772] If the promotion of the national economy constituted a justification ground, the objective of establishing an internal market would be thwarted.

Even if the objectives of EU law are not directly impaired, it is not sufficient to put forward considerations that can be depicted to be in the public interest. Preventing a loss of tax revenue, for example, may be considered as being in the general interest of a Member State. However, the ECJ has rejected the prevention of a diminution of tax receipts as an overriding reason in the public interest.[773] If such a reasoning were successful, almost any restrictive tax measure would be justifiable.[774] For similar

771. Judgment in *Laboratoires Fournier*, C-39/04, EU:C:2005:161; at para. 23; Judgment in *Jundt*, C-281/06, EU:C:2007:816, at para. 43; Judgment in *Commission/Austria*, C-10/10, EU:C:2011:399, at para. 37.
772. Judgment in *Bond van Adverteerders*, 352/85, EU:C:1988:196, at para. 34; Judgment in *Stichting Collectieve Antennevoorziening Gouda*, C-288/89, EU:C:1991:323, at para. 11; Judgment in *Decker*, C-120/95, EU:C:1998:167, at para. 39; Judgment in *Kohll*, C-158/96, EU:C:1998:171, at para. 41; Judgment in *Syndesmos ton en Elladi Touristikon kai Taxidiotikon Grafeion*, C-398/95, EU:C:1997:282, at para. 23; Judgment in *Müller-Fauré and van Riet*, C-385/99, EU:C:2003:270, at para. 72; Judgment in *Verkooijen*, C-35/98, EU:C:2000:294, at para. 48; Judgment in *Commission/Portugal*, C-171/08, EU:C:2010:412, at para. 71; see, however, J. Snell, Economic Aims as Justification for Restrictions on Free Movement, in A.A.M. Schrauwen (ed.), *Rule of Reason* (Europa Law Publishing, 2005), p. 35 (at pp. 35 et seq.).
773. Judgment in *Imperial Chemical Industries*, C-264/96, EU:C:1998:370, at para. 28; Judgment in *Saint-Gobain*, C-307/97, EU:C:1999:438, at para. 50; Judgment in *Verkooijen*, C-35/98, EU:C:2000:294, at para. 59; Judgment in *Metallgesellschaft and others*, C-397/98 and C-410/98, EU:C:2001:134, at para. 59; Judgment in *Danner*, C-136/00, EU:C:2002:558, at para. 56; Judgment in *De Groot*, C-385/00, EU:C:2002:750, at para. 103; Judgment in *X and Y*, C-436/00, EU:C:2002:704, para. 50; Judgment in *Bosal*, C-168/01, EU:C:2003:479, at para. 42; Judgment in *Skandia and Ramstedt*, C-422/01, EU:C:2003:380, at para. 53; Judgment in *De Lasteyrie du Saillant*, C-9/02, EU:C:2004:138, at para. 60; Judgment in *Lenz*, C-315/02, EU:C:2004:446, at para. 40; Judgment in *Manninen*, C-319/02, EU:C:2004:484, at para. 49; Judgment in *Marks & Spencer*, C-446/03, EU:C:2005:763, at para. 44; Judgment in *Meilicke and others*, C-292/04, EU:C:2007:132, at para. 30; Judgment in *Centro di Musicologia Walter Stauffer*, C-386/04, EU:C:2006:568, at para. 59; Judgment in *Schwarz and Gootjes-Schwarz*, C-76/05, EU:C:2007:492, at para. 77; Judgment in *Commission/Germany*, C-318/05, EU:C:2007:495, at para. 95; Judgment in *Orange European Smallcap Fund*, C-194/06, EU:C:2008:289, at para. 84; Judgment in *Persche*, C-318/07, EU:C:2009:33, at para. 46; Judgment in *Commission/Austria*, C-10/10, EU:C:2011:399, at para. 40; Judgment in *Tankreederei I*, C-287/10, EU:C:2010:827, at para. 27; Judgment in *Glaxo Wellcome*, C-182/08, EU:C:2009:559, at para. 82; Judgment in *CIBA*, C-96/08, EU:C:2010:185, at para. 48; Judgment in *Commission/Portugal*, C-20/09, EU:C:2011:214, at paras 64-65; Judgment in *Hervis Sport- és Divatkereskedelmi*, C-385/12, EU:C:2014:47, at para. 44.
774. See M. Poulsen, Freedom of Establishment and the Balanced Allocation of Tax Jurisdiction, 40 *Intertax* 3 (2012), p. 200 (at p. 201); also cf. K. Simader, *Withholding Taxes and the Fundamental Freedoms* (Kluwer, 2014), at p. 185.

reasons, compensatory advantages,[775] foreign low taxation,[776] a lack of harmonization,[777] administrative simplifications,[778] a lack of reciprocity,[779] the taxpayer's possibility to choose alternative arrangements in order to avoid discrimination[780] and the existence of discretionary power for the tax authorities[781] have not been accepted as overriding reasons in the public interest. By contrast, Member States successfully invoked the need to protect the coherence of the tax system - also referred to as fiscal cohesion -,[782] the principle of territoriality,[783] the preservation of the balanced allocation of the power to impose taxes,[784] the prevention of a double use of

775. Judgment in *Avoir Fiscal*, 270/83, EU:C:1986:37, at para. 21; Judgment in *Commerzbank*, C-330/91, EU:C:1993:303, at paras 16-17; Judgment in *Asscher*, C-107/94, EU:C:1996:251, at paras 51-54; Judgment in *Saint-Gobain*, C-307/97, EU:C:1999:438, at paras 51-53; Judgment in *Verkooijen*, C-35/98, EU:C:2000:294, at para. 61; Judgment in *AMID*, C-141/99, EU:C:2000:696, at paras 25-27; Judgment in *De Groot*, C-385/00, EU:C:2002:750, at para. 97; Judgment in *Lenz*, C-315/02, EU:C:2004:446, at para. 43; Judgment in *Lakebrink and Peters-Lakebrink*, C-182/06, EU:C:2007:452, at para. 24.
776. Judgment in *Eurowings*, C-294/97, EU:C:1999:524, at paras 43-45; Judgment in *Danner*, C-136/00, EU:C:2002:558, at paras 53-56; Judgment in *Lenz*, C-315/02, EU:C:2004:446, at para. 43; Judgment in *Skandia and Ramstedt*, C-422/01, EU:C:2003:380, at para. 52; Judgment in *Cadbury Schweppes and Cadbury Schweppes Overseas*, C-196/04, EU:C:2006:544, at para. 49; Judgment in *SIAT*, C-318/10, EU:C:2012:415, at para. 39.
777. Judgment in *Avoir Fiscal*, 270/83, EU:C:1986:37, at para. 24; Judgment in *Bachmann*, C-204/90, EU:C:1992:35, at paras 10-11.
778. Judgment in *Halliburton*, C-1/93, EU:C:1994:127, at paras 21-22; Judgment in *Schumacker*, C-279/93, EU:C:1995:31, at paras 43-47; Judgment in Commission/France, C-334/02, EU:C:2004:129, at para. 29; Judgment in *Centro di Musicologia Walter Stauffer*, C-386/04, EU:C:2006:568, at para. 48; Judgment in *Jäger*, C-256/06, EU:C:2008:20, at para. 53-54; Judgment in *Erny*, C-172/11, EU:C:2012:399, at paras 47-48.
779. Judgment in *Avoir Fiscal*, 270/83, EU:C:1986:37, at para. 26.
780. Judgment in *Avoir Fiscal*, 270/83, EU:C:1986:37, at para. 22.
781. Judgment in *Commission/Belgium*, C-80/92, EU:C:1994:118, at para. 20; Judgment in *Commission/Luxembourg*, C-151/94, EU:C:1995:357, at para. 18; Judgment in *Commission/France*, C-160/99, EU:C:2000:410, at para. 23; also cf. Judgment in *Schumacker*, C-279/93, EU:C:1995:31, at paras 53-54; Judgment in *Leur-Bloem*, C-28/95, EU:C:1997:369, at para. 44.
782. Judgment in *Bachmann*, C-204/90, EU:C:1992:35, at para. 27; Judgment in *Commission/Belgium*, C-300/90, EU:C:1992:37, at para. 20; Judgment in *Krankenheim Ruhesitz am Wannsee-Seniorenheimstatt*, C-157/07, EU:C:2008:588, at para. 43; Judgment in *Papillon*, C-418/07, EU:C:2008:659, at paras 50-51; Judgment in *Commission/Belgium*, C-250/08, EU:C:2011:793, at paras 69-77; Judgment in *Commission/Hungary*, C-253/09, EU:C:2011:795, at paras 70-78; Judgment in *Test Claimants in the FII Group Litigation*, C-35/11, EU:C:2012:707, at paras 57-59; Judgment in *K.*, C-322/11, EU:C:2013:716, at paras 64-71.
783. Judgment in *Futura Participations and Singer*, C-250/95, EU:C:1997:239, at para. 22; Judgment in *Centro Equestre da Lezíria Grande*, C-345/04, EU:C:2007:96, at para. 22; Judgment in *N.*, C-470/04, EU:C:2006:525, at para. 46; Judgment in *Commission/Germany*, C-591/13, EU:C:2015:230, at paras 65-69; Judgment in *Verder LabTec*, C-657/13, EU:C:2015:331, at para. 43; critically W. Schön, 69 *Bull. Intl. Taxn.* 4/5 (2015), at p. 284; W. Schön in W. Schön/C. Heber (eds.), *Grundfragen des Europäischen Steuerrechts* (Springer, 2015), at p. 140.
784. Judgment in *Marks & Spencer*, C-446/03, EU:C:2005:763, at paras 43-46 and 51; Judgment in *N.*, C-470/04, EU:C:2006:525, at paras 42-47; Judgment in *Oy AA*, C-231/05, EU:C:2007:439, at paras 53 and 60; Judgment in *Lidl Belgium*, C-414/06, EU:C:2008:278, at paras 31-34 and 37; Judgment in *Glaxo Wellcome*, C-182/08, EU:C:2009:559, at paras 82-88; Judgment in *SGI*, C-311/08, EU:C:2010:26, at paras 60-64 and 69; Judgment in *SIAT*, C-318/10, EU:C:2012:415, at paras 45-48; Judgment in *National Grid Indus*, C-371/10, EU:C:2011:785, at paras 45-49; Judgment in *X Holding*, C-337/08, EU:C:2010:89, at paras 27-33; Judgment in *K.*, C-322/11, EU:C:2013:716, at paras 50-55 and 71; Judgment in *Verder LabTec*, C-657/13, EU:C:2015:331, at para. 47.

losses,[785] the prevention of tax abuse, avoidance and evasion[786] as well as the need to ensure effective fiscal supervision and collection of taxes[787] in order to justify domestic tax measures which were found to constitute a restriction of the fundamental freedoms.

It is sometimes difficult to draw the line between acceptable and unacceptable justification grounds. Contrasting the justification ground of fiscal cohesion and the rejected consideration of compensatory advantages is particularly illustrative in this respect: The concept of fiscal cohesion was accepted as a justification ground for the first time in *Bachmann*[788] and *Commission/Belgium*.[789] According to Belgian law at that time, contributions to voluntary pension or sickness insurance plans could only be deducted from the taxable income if they were paid to Belgian insurance companies. It was argued that the non-deductibility of premium payments to foreign insurance companies is justified, because benefits paid to the insured person by a foreign insurance company do not constitute taxable income, whereas similar payments received from Belgian insurance companies were subject to tax in Belgium in the hands of the recipient.[790] The ECJ accepted this reasoning by stating that "*it is not possible to ensure the cohesion of such a tax system by means of measures which are less restrictive than those at issue in the main proceedings, and that the consequences of any other measure ensuring the recovery by the State concerned of the tax due under its legislation on sums payable by insurers pursuant to the contracts concluded with them would ultimately be similar to those resulting from the non-deductibility of contributions.*"[791] In essence, the different treatment of premium payments to Belgian and to foreign insurance companies was considered to be justified, because the disadvantage of not

785. Judgment in *Marks & Spencer*, C-446/03, EU:C:2005:763, at para. 47; Judgment in *Rewe Zentralfinanz*, C-347/04, EU:C:2007:194, at paras 45-46; Judgment in *Lidl Belgium*, C-414/06, EU:C:2008:278, at paras 35-36; but see Judgment in *Philips Electronics*, C-18/11, EU:C:2012:532, at para. 28.
786. Judgment in *Emsland-Stärke*, C-110/99, EU:C:2000:695, at paras 46-59; Judgment in *Marks & Spencer*, C-446/03, EU:C:2005:763, at paras 49-50; Judgment in *Halifax and others*, C-255/02, EU:C:2006:121, at paras 67-86; Judgment in *Cadbury Schweppes and Cadbury Schweppes Overseas*, C-196/04, EU:C:2006:544, at paras 48-71; Judgment in *Oy AA*, C-231/05, EU:C:2007:439, at para. 60; Judgment in *SGI*, C-311/08, EU:C:2010:26, at paras 65-69; Judgment in *SIAT*, C-318/10, EU:C:2012:415, at para. 48; Judgment in *Itelcar*, C-282/12, EU:C:2013:629, at para. 35.
787. Judgment in *FKP Scorpio Konzertproduktionen*, C-290/04, EU:C:2006:630, at para. 36; Judgment in *X*, C-498/10, EU:C:2012:635, at paras 39-53; for further information see K. Simader, *Withholding Taxes and the Fundamental Freedoms* (Kluwer, 2014), at pp. 220-237.
788. Judgment in *Bachmann*, C-204/90, EU:C:1992:35.
789. Judgment in *Commission/Belgium*, C-300/90, EU:C:1992:37.
790. Judgment in *Bachmann*, C-204/90, EU:C:1992:35, at para. 10; Judgment in *Commission/ Belgium*, C-300/90, EU:C:1992:37, at para. 8.
791. Judgment in *Bachmann*, C-204/90, EU:C:1992:35, at para. 27; also see Judgment in *Commission/Belgium*, C-300/90, EU:C:1992:37, at para. 20; critically A. Cordewener, *Europäische Grundfreiheiten und nationales Steuerrecht* (Dr Otto Schmidt, 2002), at pp. 449-451; B. Knobbe-Keuk, Restrictions on the Fundamental Freedoms Enshrined in the EC Treaty by Discriminatory Tax Provisions, 3 *EC Tax Rev.* 3 (1994), p. 74 (at pp. 80-81); P.J. Wattel, The EC Court's Attempts to Reconcile the Treaty Freedoms with International Tax Law, 33 *Common Market L. Rev.* 2 (1996), p. 223 (at pp. 240-243).

being able to deduct premium payments to foreign insurance companies was compensated by the advantage of not being taxed upon receiving benefits from the foreign insurance company.

At first glance, this is in contradiction to the ECJ not accepting compensatory advantages as a justification. Considering the further jurisprudence of the Court, it becomes clear, however, that the justification ground of fiscal cohesion requires that there is a sufficiently close link between the disadvantage and the advantage.[792] Thereby, the concept of fiscal cohesion performs an important corrective function.[793] If the ECJ analysed the legal consequences of a particular tax measure regardless of its function and position within the tax system of the Member State concerned, unjustified privileges would be created. Member States would be required to extend favourable tax rules to cross-border situations without being able to apply directly connected tax measures that provide for corresponding tax burdens, i.e., the "free mover" mutates into a "free rider."[794] By referring to fiscal cohesion, the perspective is hence changed from looking only at a particular element of the tax system to a broader, more systematic view, which allows the Court to also take into account correlating elements of the same tax system.[795]

2.5.3 The Blurred Boundaries Between the Principle of Territoriality, the Balanced Allocation of Taxing Powers and the Concept of Fiscal Cohesion

Not only is the line between accepted and rejected grounds of justification to a certain extent hardly determinable, but also the boundaries within the circle of justification grounds which have been accepted by the ECJ are blurred. This is particularly the case with regard to the principle of territoriality, the balanced allocation of the power to

792. See, for example, J. Englisch, *Dividendenbesteuerung* (Dr Otto Schmidt, 2005), at pp. 295-296; D. Hohenwarter, *Verlustverwertung im Konzern* (LexisNexis, 2009), at p. 120; G. Kofler, *Doppelbesteuerungsabkommen und Europäisches Gemeinschaftsrecht* (Linde, 2007), at pp. 114-115; M. Lang, *Die Rechtsprechung des EuGH zu den direkten Steuern* (Peter Lang, 2007), at pp. 54-55; K. Simader, *Withholding Taxes and the Fundamental Freedoms* (Kluwer, 2014), at p. 194.

793. Opinion of AG Maduro in *Marks & Spencer*, C-446/04, EU:C:2005:201, at point 66.

794. See A. Cordewener/M. Dahlberg/P. Pistone/E. Reimer/C. Romano, The Tax Treatment of Foreign Losses: *Ritter, M & S,* and the Way Ahead (Part Two), 44 *Eur. Taxn.* 5 (2004), p. 218 (at p. 221); J. Englisch, 44 *Eur. Taxn.* 8 (2004), at pp. 356-357; W.C. Haslehner, "Consistency" and Fundamental Freedoms: The Case of Direct Taxation, 50 *Common Market L. Rev.* 3 (2013), p. 737 (at p. 753, FN 43); G. Kofler, *Doppelbesteuerungsabkommen und Europäisches Gemeinschaftsrecht* (Linde, 2007), at pp. 113-114; W. Schön, 69 *Bull. Intl. Taxn.* 4/5 (2015), at p. 279; W. Schön in W. Schön/C. Heber (eds.), *Grundfragen des Europäischen Steuerrechts* (Springer, 2015), at p. 127.

795. See J. Englisch, 44 *Eur. Taxn.* 8 (2004), at p. 357; D. Hohenwarter, *Verlustverwertung im Konzern* (LexisNexis, 2009), at p. 120; G. Kofler, *Doppelbesteuerungsabkommen und Europäisches Gemeinschaftsrecht* (Linde, 2007), at pp. 113-114; J. Lang/J. Englisch, A European Legal Tax Order Based on Ability to Pay, in A. Amatucci (ed.), *International Tax Law* (Kluwer, 2012), p. 261 (at p. 308).

impose taxes and the principle of fiscal cohesion.[796] With regard to the principle of territoriality, it is even disputed whether it is in itself a public interest defense that justifies unequal treatment in specific cross-border situations.[797] In fact, although the ECJ has held that "*the purpose of that principle is to establish, in the application of Community law, the need to take into account the limits on the Member States' powers of taxation,*"[798] the principle of territoriality has never been explicitly referred to as an independent justification ground. In *Futura Participations*, for example, no justification was needed, because the Court did not consider it to be discriminatory if, "*for the purpose of calculating the basis of assessment for non-resident taxpayers, only profits and losses arising from their Luxembourg activities are taken into account in calculating the tax payable by them in that State. [...] Such a system, which is in conformity with the fiscal principle of territoriality, cannot be regarded as entailing any discrimination, overt or covert, prohibited by the Treaty.*"[799] In *Marks & Spencer*, the ECJ also referred to the principle of territoriality, without using it as a justification ground, though. Thus, "*it must be accepted that by taxing resident companies on their worldwide profits and non-resident companies solely on the profits from their activities in that State, the parent company's Member State is acting in accordance with the principle of territoriality enshrined in international tax law and recognised by Community law.*"[800] Nevertheless, the residence state of a parent company cannot justify restricting group relief to losses incurred by resident subsidiaries solely because profits of non-resident subsidiaries are not taxed in that state.[801] Moreover, the principle of territoriality has been mentioned by the ECJ in its jurisprudence on "exit taxes." However, the particular regimes at hand have eventually been considered justified due to the need to preserve a balanced allocation of taxing powers.[802]

Based on the vague meaning of the principle of territoriality in the ECJ's jurisprudence, some authors conclude that territoriality is a sub-principle to preserve

796. See P.J. Wattel, Fiscal Cohesion, Fiscal Territoriality and Preservation of the (Balanced) Allocation of Taxing Power; What is the Difference, in D. Weber (ed.), *The Influence of European Law on Direct Taxation* (Kluwer, 2007), p. 139 (at pp. 139 et seq.); also cf. P. Farmer, 61 *Bull. Intl. Taxn.* 2 (2007), at p. 44 ("*For example, fiscal coherence, non-comparability, territoriality and balanced allocation of taxing powers are all mainly concerned with the notion of symmetry between taxation and reliefs.*").

797. See W. Schön, 69 *Bull. Intl. Taxn.* 4/5 (2015), p. 284; W. Schön in W. Schön/C. Heber (eds.), *Grundfragen des Europäischen Steuerrechts* (Springer, 2015), at p. 140; but also see K. Daxkobler, *Die grundfreiheitliche Rechtsprechung des EuGH* (Linde, 2015), at p. 233.

798. Judgment in *Rewe Zentralfinanz*, C-374/04, EU:C:2007:194, at para. 69; also see Judgment in *Busley and Cibrian Fernandez*, C-35/08, EU:C:2009:625, at para. 30.

799. Judgment in *Futura Participations and Singer*, C-250/95, EU:C:1997:239, at paras 21-22.

800. Judgment in *Marks & Spencer*, C-446/03, EU:C:2005:763, at para. 39.

801. Judgment in *Marks & Spencer*, C-446/03, EU:C:2005:763, at para. 40; also cf. Judgment in *Bosal*, C-168/01, EU:C:2003:479, at paras 37-38; Judgment in *Manninen*, C-319/02, EU:C:2004:484, at paras 38-39; Judgment in *Rewe Zentralfinanz*, C-347/03, EU:C:2007:194, at paras 68-69; Judgment in *Keller Holding*, C-471/04, EU:C:2006:143, at para. 44; Judgment in *Commission/Belgium*, C-250/08, EU:C:2011:793, at paras 46-48.

802. Judgment in *N*, C-470/04, EU:C:2006:525, at paras 41-47; Judgment in *National Grid Indus*, C-371/10, EU:C:2011:785, at para. 46; Judgment in *DMC*, C-164/12, EU:C:2014:20, at para. 49; Judgment in *Commission/Germany*, C-591/13, EU:C:2015:230, at paras 64-65; Judgment in *Verder LabTec*, C-657/13, EU:C:2015:331, at paras 40-47.

the balanced allocation of the power to impose taxes,[803] whereas others believe that it is to be regarded as a particular form of coherence.[804] Considering that, according to the ECJ, the concept of fiscal cohesion and the need to preserve the balanced allocation of taxing powers may coincide,[805] these conflicting views are not surprising. Indeed, both justification grounds have been converged by the ECJ over time,[806] which does not necessarily mean that they are fully interchangeable.[807] The need to safeguard the balanced allocation between the Member States of the power to tax may, on the one hand, be accepted by the Court, *"in particular, where the system in question is designed to prevent conduct capable of jeopardising the right of a Member State to exercise its powers of taxation in relation to activities carried out in its territory."*[808] The concept of

803. See D. Hohenwarter, *Verlustverwertung im Konzern* (LexisNexis, 2009), at pp. 133-136; also see K. Daxkobler, *Die grundfreiheitliche Rechtsprechung des EuGH* (Linde, 2015), at p. 235.
804. See A. Cordewener/M. Dahlberg/P. Pistone/E. Reimer/C. Romano, 44 *Eur. Taxn.* 5 (2004), at p. 221; also cf. P. Arginelli, The Discriminatory Taxation of Permanent Establishments by the Host State in the European Union: a Too Much Separate Entity Approach, 35 *Intertax* 2 (2007), p. 82 (at pp. 92-96); M. Helminen, Freedom of Establishment and Oy AA, 47 *Eur. Taxn.* 11 (2007), p. 490 (at p. 495: *"The territoriality principle closely relates to the coherence principle."*); S. van Thiel, *Free Movement of Persons and Income Tax Law: The European Court in Search of Principles* (IBFD, 2002), at p. 578; also cf. M. Poulsen, 40 *Intertax* 3 (2012), p. 202 (*"In reality, this argument is, however, closely linked with the coherence justification"*); for a dissenting opinion see J. Englisch, *Aufteilung der Besteuerungsbefugnisse – Ein Rechtfertigungsgrund für die Einschränkung von EG-Grundfreiheiten* (Institut "Finanzen und Steuern" e.V., 2008), at p. 47.
805. Judgment in *National Grid Indus*, C-371/10, EU:C:2011:785, at para. 80; Judgment in *K.*, C-322/11, EU:C:2013:716, at para. 72; also see Opinion of AG Kokott in *N*, C-470/04, EU:C:2006:217, at point 106; Opinion of AG Kokott in *National Grid Indus*, C-371/10, EU:C:2011:563, at point 99.
806. See D. Weber, An Analysis of the Past, Current and Future of the Coherence of the Tax System as Justification, 24 *EC Tax Rev.* 1 (2015), p. 43 (at pp. 48 and 53).
807. See A. Cordewener/G. Kofler/S. van Thiel, 46 *Common Market L. Rev.* 6 (2009), at p. 1974 (*"Coherence can only be a justification if there is a systemic direct link within the same tax system between the tax advantage and a subsequent charge. Territoriality and balanced allocation of tax jurisdiction, on the other hand, concern the systemic coherence between the tax systems of two Member States."*), pp. 1975-1976 (*"To be distinguished from the coherence justification (concerning the coherence of the tax system of one Member State), is the agreed coherence between the tax systems of two Member States reflected in rules on the allocation of tax jurisdiction, which in itself can be an acceptable justification, because the agreement with another Member State may eliminate the disadvantage for the cross-border situation."*) and p. 1976 (FN 127: *"[W]e cannot accept the suggestion that coherence and balanced allocation of tax jurisdiction are the same; [...] The first is an autonomous revenue protection argument that comes with discrimination, but is acceptable only in the case of a systemic coherence in the tax system of one Member State. The second is an 'agreed allocation of tax jurisdiction' argument that involves the tax systems of two Member States and that ensures that the initial discriminatory effect of the tax measure of one Member State is neutralized by the agreed action undertaken by the other Member State."*); D. Weber, 24 *EC Tax Rev.* 1 (2015), p. 54 (*"The balanced allocation in the case law of the Court relates to the justifications of the division of the power to tax between two Member States (and here, the fiscal territoriality does play a role), the coherence justification can fulfil a function in situations in which the coherence of a tax system is not endangered by a breach of the fiscal territoriality as such, but another internal cohesion of the tax system of one Member State is lost."*).
808. Judgment in *Commission/Germany*, C-284/09, EU:C:2011:670, at para. 77; Judgment in *Santander Asset Management SGIIC*, C-338/11 to C-347/11, EU:C:2012:286, at para. 47; Judgment in *Emerging Markets Series of DFA Investment Trust Company*, C-190/12, EU:C:2014:249, at para. 98; Judgment in *SIAT*, C-318/10, EU:C:2012:415, at para. 45; Judgment

fiscal cohesion may, on the other hand, be relied upon as a justification ground "*where a direct link is established between a tax advantage and the offsetting of that advantage by a particular tax levy.*"[809]

In *National Grid Indus* – and later on in *K.*[810] as well as in *Timac Agro*[811] –, the ECJ has confirmed that the requirements of coherence of the tax system and the balanced allocation of powers of taxation coincide under certain circumstances.[812] According to the Netherlands law at that time, the transfer of a company's place of effective management to another Member State triggered the taxation of unrealized capital gains at the time of the transfer if the company ceases to derive profits from the business taxable in the Netherlands. Since the transfer of a company's place of effective management within the Netherlands did not lead to the taxation of unrealized capital gains, the ECJ found the Netherlands legislation to constitute a restriction that is in

---

in *Beker*, C-168/11, EU:C:2013:117, at para. 57; Judgment in Argenta Spaarbank, C-350/11, EU:C:2013:447, at para. 53; Judgment in *Commission/Belgium*, C-387/11, EU:C:2012:670, at para. 75; Judgment in *Bouanich*, C-375/12, EU:C:2014:138, at para. 81; Judgment in *Emerging Markets Series of DFA Investment Trust Company*, C-190/12, EU:C:2014:249, at para. 98; also see Judgment in *Rewe Zentralfinanz*, C-347/04, EU:C:2007:194, at para. 42; Judgment in *Oy AA*, C-231/05, EU:C:2007:439, at para. 54; Judgment in *Amurta*, C-379/05, EU:C:2007:655, at para. 58; Judgment in *Lidl Belgium*, C-414/06, EU:C:2008:278, at para. 52; Judgment in *Aberdeen Property Fininvest Alpha*, C-303/07, EU:C:2009:377, at para. 66; Judgment in *SGI*, C-311/08, EU:C:2010:26, at para. 60; Judgment in *National Grid Indus*, C-371/10, EU:C:2011:785, at para. 46; Judgment in *A Oy*, C-123/11, EU:C:2013:84, at para. 41; Judgment in *Imfeld and Garcet*, C-303/12, EU:C:2013:822, at para. 75; Judgment in *van Caster and van Caster*, C-326/12, EU:C:2014:2269, at para. 41.

809. Opinion of AG Kokott in *Nordea Bank Danmark*, C-48/13, EU:C:2014:153; at point 43; also see Judgment in *Verkooijen*, C-35/98, EU:C:2000:294, at para. 57; Judgment in *Bosal*, C-168/01, EU:C:2003:479, at para. 29; Judgment in *Schilling and Fleck-Schilling*, C-209/01, EU:C:2003:610, at para. 41; Judgment in *Weidert and Paulus*, C-242/03, EU:C:2004:465, at para. 22; Judgment in *Manninen*, C-319/02, EU:C:2004:484, at para. 42; Judgment in *Keller Holding*, C-471/04, EU:C:2006:143, at para. 40; Judgment in *Centro di Musicologia Walter Stauffer*, C-386/04, EU:C:2006:568, at para. 53; Judgment in *Commission/Portugal*, C-345/05, EU:C:2006:685, at para. 29; Judgment in *Test Claimants in the FII Group Litigation*, C-446/04, EU:C:2006:774, at para. 178; Judgment in *Meilicke and others*, C-292/04, EU:C:2007:132, at para. 28; Judgment in *Test Claimants in the Thin Cap Group Litigation*, C-524/04, EU:C:2007:161, at para. 68; Judgment in *Rewe Zentralfinanz*, C-347/04, EU:C:2007:194, at para. 62; Judgment in *Hollmann*, C-443/06, EU:C:2007:600, at para. 56; Judgment in *Amurta*, C-379/05, EU:C:2007:655, at para. 46; Judgment in *Jundt*, C-281/06, EU:C:2007:816, at para. 68; Judgment in *Heinrich Bauer Verlag*, C-360/06, EU:C:2008:531, at para. 37; Judgment in *Papillon*, C-418/07, EU:C:2008:659, at para. 44; Judgment in *Glaxo Wellcome*, C-182/08, EU:C:2009:559, at para. 79; Judgment in *Commission/Spain*, C-562/07, EU:C:2009:614, at para. 61; Judgment in *Presidente del Consiglio dei Ministri*, C-169/08, EU:C:2009:709, at para. 47; Judgment in *Commission/Belgium*, C-250/08, EU:C:2011:793, at para. 71; Judgment in *Santander Asset Management SGIIC*, C-338/11 to C-347/11, EU:C:2012:286, at para. 51; Judgment in *DI. VI. Finanziaria di Diego della Valle & C.*, C-380/11, EU:C:2012:552, at para. 47; Judgment in *Test Claimants in the FII Group Litigation*, C-35/11, EU:C:2012:707, at para. 58; Judgment in *Welte*, C-181/12, EU:C:2013:662, at para. 59; Judgment in *K*, C-322/11, EU:C:2013:716, at para. 66; Judgment in *Bouanich*, C-375/12, EU:C:2014:138, at para. 69; Judgment in *Grünewald*, C-559/13, EU:C:2015:109, at para. 48; Judgment in *Groupe Steria*, C-386/14, EU:C:2015:524, at para. 31; Judgment in *Finanzamt Linz*, C-66/14, EU:C:2015:661, at para. 44.

810. Judgment in *K.*, C-322/11, EU:C:2013:716, at para. 72.

811. Judgment in *Timac Agro Deutschland*, C-388/14; EU:C:2015:829, at para. 47.

812. Judgment in *National Grid Indus*, C-371/10, EU:C:2011:785, at para. 80.

principle prohibited by the freedom of establishment. However, according to settled case law, "*[t]he transfer of the place of effective management of a company of one Member State to another Member State cannot mean that the Member State of origin has to abandon its right to tax a capital gain which arose within the ambit of its powers of taxation before the transfer [...]. [A] Member State is entitled, [in accordance with the principle of fiscal territoriality linked to a temporal component, namely the taxpayer's residence for tax purposes within national territory during the period in which the capital gains arise,] to charge tax on those gains at the time when the taxpayer leaves the country [...]. Such a measure is intended to prevent situations capable of jeopardising the right of the Member State of origin to exercise its powers of taxation in relation to activities carried on in its territory, and may therefore be justified on grounds connected with the preservation of the allocation of powers of taxation between the Member States.*"[813] In addition, the ECJ also considered that the Netherlands legislation at hand could potentially be justified by the objective of maintaining the coherence of the tax system, because there is a direct link "*between, on the one hand, the tax advantage represented by the exemption allowed to unrealised capital gains relating to assets as long as a company obtains profits taxable in the Netherlands and, on the other, the offsetting of that advantage by a charge to tax determined at the time when that company ceases to obtain such profits.*"[814] The Netherlands legislation was nevertheless held disproportionate, because "*national legislation offering a company transferring its place of effective management to another Member State the choice between, first, immediate payment of the amount of tax, which creates a disadvantage for that company in terms of cash flow but frees it from subsequent administrative burdens, and, secondly, deferred payment of the amount of tax, possibly together with interest in accordance with the applicable national legislation, which necessarily involves an administrative burden for the company in connection with tracing the transferred assets, would constitute a measure which, while being appropriate for ensuring the balanced allocation of powers of taxation between the Member States, would be less harmful to freedom of establishment than the measure at issue in the main proceedings.*"[815]

Until *National Grid Indus* was decided, the concept of fiscal cohesion had not been decisive with regard to exit tax regimes, but it had nevertheless been addressed by the Court. In *X and Y*, for example, the ECJ pointed out that "*insofar as the Kingdom of Sweden has concluded double-taxation conventions with other Member States, there is no fiscal coherence in relation to any one taxpayer in establishing a strict correlation between the deferral of capital gains tax and the final taxation of the gain.*"[816] Despite

813. Judgment in *National Grid Indus*, C-371/10, EU:C:2011:785, at para. 46; also see Judgment in *Commission/Spain*, C-269/09, EU:C:2012:439, at para. 78; Judgment in *N*, C-470/04, EU:C:2006:525, at para. 46; Judgment in *DMC*, C-164/12, EU:C:2014:20, at para. 49; Judgment in *Commission/Germany*, C-591/13, EU:C:2015:230, at para. 65; also cf. Judgment in *Test Claimants in Class IV of the ACT Group Litigation*, C-374/04, EU:C:2006:773, at para. 59; Judgment in *Glaxo Wellcome*, C-182/08, EU:C:2009:559, at para. 83; Judgment in *Commission/Germany*, C-284/09, EU:C:2011:670, at para. 76; Judgment in Commission/Belgium, C-387/11, EU:C:2012:670, at para. 78.
814. Judgment in *National Grid Indus*, C-371/10, EU:C:2011:785, at para. 82.
815. Judgment in *National Grid Indus*, C-371/10, EU:C:2011:785, at para. 73.
816. Judgment in *X and Y*, C-436/00, EU:C:2002:704, at para. 53.

this reference to the case law on "macro-coherence,"[817] the concept of fiscal cohesion was not explicitly rejected as a justification ground.[818] The Court instead held that "*[i]n any event, refusal of deferral of taxation on type A and type B share transfers, as provided for by the national provision at issue here, is not necessary and proportionate to the objective it pursues. [...] [I]n contrast to that giving rise to the judgments cited above in* Bachmann *and* Commission v Belgium *(see* Bachmann, *paragraph 28, and* Commission v Belgium, *paragraph 20), the coherence of the tax system can be safeguarded by measures which are less restrictive or less prejudicial to freedom of establishment, relating specifically to the risk of a definitive departure of the taxpayer, in respect of all types of share transfers entailing the same objective risk.*"[819] By contrast, the concept of fiscal cohesion was explicitly rejected by the ECJ in *De Lasteyrie du Saillant.*[820] However, this is due to the fact that the scrutinized provision of French law "*does not [...] appear to be aimed at ensuring generally that increases in value are to be taxed, in the case where a taxpayer transfers his tax residence outside France, in so far as the increases in value in question are acquired during the latter's stay on French territory. That finding is supported by the fact that the tax system at issue in the main proceedings allows exoneration in respect of all taxation to which increases in value, where realised, have been subject in the country to which the taxpayer transferred his tax residence. Such taxation might have the consequence that realised increases in value, including the part of them acquired during the taxpayer's stay in France, are entirely taxed in that country. In those circumstances, the premiss on which the Netherlands Government's argument concerning fiscal coherence is based does not hold true having regard to the aim pursued by the tax system laid down by Article 167a of the CGI. Therefore, justification for such a system based on an objective of fiscal coherence, which, moreover, the French Government has not argued, cannot be accepted.*"[821] Thus, the concept of fiscal cohesion was not considered an acceptable justification ground, because the tax legislation in question did not have the purpose of safeguarding fiscal cohesion.[822] Starting with this decision in *De Lasteyrie du Saillant*, the ECJ has in fact regularly pointed out that "*an argument based on the need to safeguard the cohesion of a tax system must be examined in the light of the objective pursued by the tax legislation in question.*"[823] Therefore, it cannot be inferred from *De Lasteyrie du Saillant* that the

817. For the origin of this term see P.J. Wattel, 33 *Common Market L. Rev.* 2 (1996), at p. 238 ("*macro-cohesion*"); P.M. Manninen/R. Rytöhonka, ECJ: Finnish Income Tax Regime on the Deductibility of Pension Insurance Contributions Violates the Freedom to Provide Services, 43 *Eur. Taxn.* 2 (2003), p. 55 (at p. 56: "*macro-coherence*").
818. Opinion of AG Kokott in *N.*, C-470/04, EU:C:2006:217, at point 105.
819. Judgment in *X and Y*, C-436/00, EU:C:2002:704, at paras 57 and 59.
820. Judgment in *De Lasteyrie du Saillant*, C-9/02, EU:C:2004:138.
821. Judgment in *De Lasteyrie du Saillant*, C-9/02, EU:C:2004:138, at paras 65-67.
822. See D. Weber, 24 *EC Tax Rev.* 1 (2015), at p. 49.
823. Judgment in *Manninen*, C-319/02, EU:C:2004:484, at para. 43; Judgment in *Meilicke and others*, C-292/04, EU:C:2007:132, at para. 27; Judgment in *Amurta*, C-379/05, EU:C:2007:655, at para. 47; also see Judgment in *Deutsche Shell*, C-293/06, EU:C:2008:129, at para. 39; Judgment in *Papillon*, C-418/07, EU:C:2008:659, at para. 44; Judgment in *Aberdeen Property Fininvest Alpha*, C-303/07, EU:C:2009:377, at para. 72; Judgment in *Glaxo Wellcome*, C-182/08, EU:C:2009:559, at para. 79; Judgment in *Presidente del Consiglio dei Ministri*, C-169/08, EU:C:2009:709, at para. 47; Judgment in *CIBA*, C-96/08, EU:C:2010:185, at para. 47; Judgment

concept of fiscal cohesion was generally rejected by the ECJ with regard to exit tax regimes. On the contrary, the decision in *X and Y* has already indicated that exit tax regimes might be justified on the basis of fiscal cohesion. This was also recognized by AG Kokott in her opinion in *N.*[824] The Court nevertheless based its subsequent decision solely on the need to preserve the balanced allocation of taxing powers.[825] Taking the prior case law on exit taxation into account, particularly the decision in *X and Y*, the ECJ's approach in *National Grid Indus* should still not be considered to be a big surprise.

The Court's jurisprudence on cross-border loss compensation is another line of case law in which both the concept of fiscal cohesion and the need to preserve the balanced allocation of taxing rights are of importance.[826] In *Deutsche Shell*, for example, a German company was refused to take currency losses resulting from the repatriation of the start-up capital of an Italian permanent establishment into consideration in the corporate tax assessment in Germany. It was argued, *inter alia*, that "*taking account of the currency loss for the purposes of calculating Deutsche Shell's basis of assessment in Germany would lead to a non-coherent tax system, since any exchange rate gain obtained in a comparable situation would not be taken into account. Thus, the detriment resulting from the failure to take account of a currency loss is the corollary to the advantage resulting from the fact that an exchange rate gain would also be excluded from the basis of assessment.*"[827] However, the ECJ rejected fiscal cohesion as a justification, due to a lack of a direct link between the currency loss that actually accrued and a potential currency gain which could have accrued in the event of a different development of the exchange rate:[828] "*The failure to take account of a currency loss in order to calculate Deutsche Shell's basis of assessment for the 1992 financial year is not offset by any tax advantage in the Member State where that company has its registered office or in the Member State where its permanent establishment is situated.*" The Court had to deal with a similar issue in *K.* Due to former Finnish tax legislation, a Finnish resident was refused deduction of losses resulting from the sale of a French immovable property in Finland. Unlike its decision in *Deutsche Shell*, however, the ECJ considered the legislation at hand to be justified, *inter alia*, due to the need to ensure the cohesion of the Finnish tax system, because "*a direct link [...] exists, in the case of the same taxpayer and the same tax, between, on the one hand, the tax advantage*

in *Dijkman and Dijkman-Lavaleije*, C-233/09, EU:C:2010:397, at para. 55; Judgment in *Commission/Portugal*, C-493/09, EU:C:2011:635, at para. 36; Judgment in *Commission/Germany*, C-284/09, EU:C:2011:670, at para. 86; Judgment in *Commission/Spain*, C-269/09, EU:C:2012:439, at para. 85; Judgment in *Test Claimants in the FII Group Litigation*, C-35/11, EU:C:2012:707, at para. 58; Judgment in *Santander Asset Management SGIIC*, C-338/11, EU:C:2012:286, at para. 51; Judgment in *Argenta Spaarbank*, C-350/11, EU:C:2013:447, at para. 42; Judgment in *K.*, C-322/11, EU:C:2013:716, at para. 66; Judgment in *Emerging Markets Series of DFA Investment Trust Company*, EU:C:2014:249, at para. 92; Judgment in *Bouanich*, C-375/12, EU:C:2014:138, at para. 69; Judgment in *Grünewald*, C-559/13, EU:C:2015:109, at para. 48.

824. Opinion of AG Kokott in *N.*, C-470/04, EU:C:2006:217, at paras 105-108.
825. Judgment in *N.*, C-470/04, EU:C:2006:525, at paras 41-47.
826. Judgment in *Timac Agro Deutschland*, C-388/14; EU:C:2015:829, at paras 34-41.
827. Judgment in *Deutsche Shell*, C-293/06, EU:C:2008:129, at para. 34.
828. Judgment in *Deutsche Shell*, C-293/06, EU:C:2008:129, at para. 40.

granted, namely the taking into account of losses generated by a capital investment, and, on the other, the taxation of returns on that investment."[829]

In the literature it is pointed out that the different outcome in *Deutsche Shell* and in *K.* might be due to the "nature" of the respective losses.[830] According to settled case law, it is disproportionate to deny the deductibility of foreign losses in the residence state if the taxpayer has exhausted the possibilities available in the Member State in which the source of the loss is located of having the losses taken into account.[831] In *K.*, the losses resulting from the sale of the French immovable property could not be taken into consideration in France because, according to French law, losses on immoveable property incurred in France on an immoveable property situated in that Member State can never be deducted either from overall income or from a gain realized on the sale of another asset.[832] The ECJ hence concluded that "*a taxpayer such as K cannot be regarded, irrespective of the considerations of fact set out by the referring court, to have exhausted the possibilities available in the Member State in which the property is situated of having the losses taken into account. Since the Member State in which the property is situated does not provide for the possibility of losses incurred on the sale of the property being taken into account, such a possibility has never existed.*"[833] By contrast, in *Deutsche Shell*, it was not possible to deduct the currency loss in the state of the permanent establishment because from an Italian perspective the currency loss did not arise in the first place, since the accounting records in that Member State drawn up in the national currency could not show the currency depreciation of the start-up capital.[834]

Even if it is assumed that the currency loss in *Deutsche Shell* had to be taken into account by the residence state because the taxpayer has exhausted the legally existent, but factually non-existent possibilities available in the Member State of the permanent establishment,[835] the conflict with the ECJ's approach in *K.* regarding the concept of fiscal cohesion would remain. Whether the taxpayer has exhausted the possibilities of having the losses taken into account in the Member State in which the source of the loss is located is a question of proportionality. However, the Court did not address the issue of proportionality in *Deutsche Shell* due to a lack of justification. It, therefore, seems that the ECJ has become more generous in the assessment of whether a direct link exists or not. If this is indeed the case, the ECJ's prior decisions on cross-border loss compensation in which the need to preserve the balanced allocation of taxing powers has been accepted as a justification for the non-recognition of foreign losses by the residence state could potentially also have been decided on the basis of this more liberal approach with regard to the concept of fiscal cohesion. This seems to be the

829. Judgment in *K.*, C-322/11, EU:C:2013:716, at para. 69.
830. See D. Blum/E. Huisman, Die Rechtssache *K*: Neues zum Finalitätskriterium in der grenzüberschreitenden Verlustverrechnung, 24 *SWI* 9 (2014), p. 433 (at pp. 443-444).
831. Judgment in *Marks & Spencer*, C-446/03, EU:C:2005:763, at para. 55; Judgment in *Lidl Belgium*, C-414/06, EU:C:2008:278, at para. 47; Judgment in *A Oy*, C-123/11, EU:C:2013:84, at para. 49; Judgment in *K.*, C-322/11, EU:C:2013:716, at para. 75.
832. Opinion of AG Mengozzi in *K.*, C-322/11, EU:C:2013:183, at point 32.
833. Judgment in *K.*, C-322/11, EU:C:2013:716, at paras 76-77.
834. Judgment in *Deutsche Shell*, C-293/06, EU:C:2008:129, at para. 52.
835. See D. Blum/E. Huisman, 24 *SWI* 9 (2014), at pp. 443-444.

position of AG Kokott, who argues that "*the ground of justification called 'preservation of the allocation of the power to impose taxes between Member States' is simply an expression of other recognised grounds of justification, specifically with regard to the delimitation of Member States' fiscal sovereignty. [...] [T]he idea that the profits and losses arising from an activity must not be taken into account separately is simply an expression of the ground of justification of preservation of the coherence of a tax system.*"[836]

Albeit the concept of fiscal cohesion and the need to preserve the balanced allocation of taxing powers overlap to an increasing extent,[837] it is still premature to conclude that one of the two justification grounds renders the other meaningless. After all, there is a series of decisions that did not concern exit taxation or cross-border loss compensation and in which the ECJ has dealt with and/or accepted exclusively either the concept of fiscal cohesion or the need to preserve the balanced allocation of taxing powers. On the one hand, the decisions in *Bachmann*,[838] *Commission/Belgium* (C-300/90),[839] *Commission/Belgium* (C-250/08),[840] *Commission/Hungary*[841] and – at least to a certain extent – *Test Claimants in the FII Group Litigation*[842] were decided solely on the basis of the concept of fiscal cohesion. However, it may be asked whether those cases could have also been based on the need to preserve the balanced allocation of taxing powers. With regard to *Bachmann* and *Commission/Belgium*, for example, the ECJ pointed out in *X and Y* that the problem relating to the coherence of the tax system in those cases originated from the fact that "*payments were likely to evade taxation by the Member State which granted the tax advantage because they were made by third parties outside that Member State, that is to say in the country where those third parties were established.*"[843] Thus, it might be argued that a system, such as in *Bachmann* and in *Commission/Belgium*, according to which contributions to foreign insurance companies whose correlating payments do not constitute taxable income in the hands of the recipient are not deductible, "*is designed to prevent conduct capable of jeopardising the*

836. Opinion of AG Kokott in *Nordea Bank Danmark*, C-48/13, EU:C:2014:153, at points 42-43; also see W. Schön, 69 *Bull. Intl. Taxn.* 4/5 (2015), p. 285; W. Schön in W. Schön/C. Heber (eds.), *Grundfragen des Europäischen Steuerrechts* (Springer, 2015), at pp. 140-142; but see D. Weber, 24 *EC Tax Rev.* 1 (2015), at p. 54.
837. See M. Schaper, The Need to Prevent Abusive Practices and Fraus as a Composite Justification, 23 *EC Tax Rev.* 4 (2014), p. 220 (at p. 224); D. Weber, 24 *EC Tax Rev.* 1 (2015), at p. 48; also see B.J.M. Terra/P.J. Wattel, *European Tax Law*[6] (Kluwer, 2012), at p. 896 ("*Apparently, there is little difference between the two concepts.*"); also cf. P. Farmer, Tax Law and Policy in an Adolescent European Union, 61 *Bull. Intl. Taxn.* 2 (2007), p. 42 (at p. 44: "*For example, fiscal coherence, non-comparability, territoriality and balanced allocation of taxing powers are all mainly concerned with the notion of symmetry between taxation and reliefs.*").
838. Judgment in *Bachmann*, C-204/90, EU:C:1992:35.
839. Judgment in *Commission/Belgium*, C-300/90, EU:C:1992:37.
840. Judgment in *Commission/Belgium*, C-250/08, EU:C:2011:793.
841. Judgment in *Commission/Hungary*, C-253/09, EU:C:2011:795.
842. Judgment in *Test Claimants in the FII Group Litigation*, C-35/11, EU:C:2012:707.
843. Judgment in *X and Y*, C-436/00, EU:C:2002:704, at para. 58.

right of a Member State to exercise its powers of taxation in relation to activities carried out in its territory"[844] and may, therefore, also be justified due to the need to preserve the balanced allocation of taxing powers.

On the other hand, whereas fiscal cohesion was at the same time rejected by the ECJ, the need to preserve the balanced allocation of taxing powers was accepted as a justification ground in *Glaxo Wellcome*[845] and in the Court's jurisprudence on the compatibility of transfer pricing adjustments under the arm's length standard with the fundamental freedoms.[846] The Court first refused to accept the concept of fiscal cohesion in *Lankhorst-Hohorst*. According to the former German thin capitalization rules, interest payments by a domestic subsidiary to its domestic parent company were fully deductible at the level of the corporate taxpayer, while interest payments to a foreign parent company exceeding specific thresholds were regarded as non-deductible profit distributions. The argument of the German government that these rules were fully in line with the arm's length standard under Article 9 OECD MC was not sufficient to invoke the concept of fiscal cohesion as a justification, because "*there is no [...] direct link where, as in the present case, the subsidiary of a non-resident parent company suffers less favourable tax treatment and the German Government has not pointed to any tax advantage to offset such treatment.*"[847]

A more promising reasoning was brought forward in *Test Claimants in the Thin Cap Group Litigation*. In contrast to the German rules on thin capitalization, the UK legislation on cross-border shareholder loans only provided for the re-characterization of interest payments on intra-group loans if and insofar as the loan agreement did not comply with the arm's length standard. The double taxation conventions applicable in the case at hand, moreover, ensured that a compensatory advantage was granted by the parent company's country of residence, i.e., any increase in taxable profits in the UK was offset by a corresponding reduction in the taxable profits of the lender in the state in which it is resident. The ECJ did not reject this rationale at the outset, but pointed out that "*even if it were to be accepted that a tax advantage granted in the State*

844. Judgment in *Aberdeen Property Fininvest Alpha*, C-303/07, EU:C:2009:377, at para. 66; Judgment in *SGI*, C-311/08, EU:C:2010:26, at para. 60; Judgment in *Commission/Germany*, C-284/09, EU:C:2011:670, at para. 77; Judgment in *Santander Asset Management SGIIC*, C-338/11 to C-347/11, EU:C:2012:286, at para. 47; Judgment in *SIAT*, C-318/10, EU:C:2012:415, at para. 45; Judgment in *Commission/Belgium*, C-387/11, EU:C:2012:670, at para. 75; Judgment in *Beker*, C-168/11, EU:C:2013:117, at para. 57; Judgment in *Argenta Spaarbank*, C-350/11, EU:C:2013:447, at para. 53; Judgment in *Imfeld and Garcet*, C-303/12, EU:C:2013:822, at para. 75; Judgment in *Bouanich*, C-375/12, EU:C:2014:138, at para. 81; Judgment in *Emerging Markets Series of DFA Investment Trust Company*, C-190/12, EU:C:2014:249, at para. 98; Judgment in *van Caster and van Caster*, C-326/12, EU:C:2014:2269, at para. 41; also see in *Rewe Zentralfinanz*, C-347/04, EU:C:2007:194, at para. 42; Judgment in *Oy AA*, C-231/05, EU:C:2007:439, at para. 54; Judgment in *Amurta*, C-379/05, EU:C:2007:655, at para. 58; Judgment in *Lidl Belgium*, C-414/06, EU:C:2008:278, at para. 52; Judgment in *National Grid Indus*, C-371/10, EU:C:2011:785, at para. 46; Judgment in *A Oy*, C-123/11, EU:C:2013:84, at para. 41.

845. Judgment in *Glaxo Wellcome*, C-182/08, EU:C:2009:559, paras 82-88.

846. Judgment in *Lankhorst-Hohorst*, C-324/00, EU:C:2002:749, at paras 39-42; Judgment in *Test Claimants in the Thin Cap Group Litigation*, C-524/04, EU:C:2007:161, at paras 66-70 and 75; Judgment in *SGI*, C-311/08, EU:C:2010:26, at paras 60-69.

847. Judgment in *Lankhorst-Hohorst*, C-324/00, EU:C:2002:749, at para. 42.

in which the lending company is resident might be capable of offsetting the charge to tax arising for the borrowing company from the application of the legislation of the State in which it is resident, the Governments which have submitted observations have not shown that, by virtue of the application of the legislation in force in the United Kingdom, coupled with the DTCs concluded by that Member State, any upward adjustment to the taxable profits of the borrowing company to which the re-characterisation of interest paid to a related non-resident company may give rise is offset by the grant of a tax advantage to the latter company in the State in which it is resident."[848] While the concept of fiscal cohesion was hence not sufficient to justify the national measure at hand, the Court found the legislation under question to be "*able to prevent practices the sole purpose of which is to avoid the tax that would normally be payable on profits generated by activities undertaken in the national territory.*"[849] The need to preserve the balanced allocation of taxing powers was thereby mentioned in the context of the justification ground of prevention of abusive practices, which requires that "*the specific objective of such a restriction must be to prevent conduct involving the creation of wholly artificial arrangements which do not reflect economic reality, with a view to escaping the tax normally due on the profits generated by activities carried out on national territory. […] [T]he type of conduct described in the preceding paragraph is such as to undermine the right of the Member States to exercise their tax jurisdiction in relation to the activities carried out in their territory and thus to jeopardise a balanced allocation between Member States of the power to impose taxes.*"[850]

The approach taken in *Test Claimants in the Thin Cap Group Litigation* was refined by the ECJ in *SGI* as well as in *Glaxo Wellcome.*[851] In *SGI*, on the one hand, the Court had to deal with the Belgian transfer pricing rules, which provided for the adjustment of "unusual or gratuitous advantages" granted by a domestic company to a related foreign party. In the case at issue, for example, the taxpayer had, among other things, extended a zero-interest loan to a group company based in Luxembourg. Since an unrelated party would not grant such a loan free of interest, a notional interest calculated at an annual rate of 5% was added to the taxpayer's profits. Without any reference to the concept of fiscal cohesion, the Court held that "*national legislation which is not specifically designed to exclude from the tax advantage it confers such purely artificial arrangements – devoid of economic reality, created with the aim of escaping the tax normally due on the profits generated by activities carried out on national territory – may nevertheless be regarded as justified by the objective of preventing tax avoidance, taken together with that of preserving the balanced allocation of the power to impose taxes between the Member States.*"[852] In *Glaxo Wellcome*, on the other hand, a complex rule in the context of the former full imputation taxation system

848. Judgment in *Test Claimants in the Thin Cap Group Litigation*, C-524/04, EU:C:2007:161, at para. 69.
849. Judgment in *Test Claimants in the Thin Cap Group Litigation*, C-524/04, EU:C:2007:161, at para. 77.
850. Judgment in *Test Claimants in the Thin Cap Group Litigation*, C-524/04, EU:C:2007:161, at paras 74-75.
851. Also see Judgment in *SIAT*, C-318/10, EU:C:2012:415, paras 36-48.
852. Judgment in *SGI*, C-311/08, EU:C:2010:26, at para. 66.

in Germany was put to the test.[853] Since there was no direct link between the tax advantage concerned and the offsetting of that advantage by a particular tax levy, the German legislation could not be justified by the need to preserve the coherence of the full imputation tax system.[854] However, the German legislation was still "*capable of achieving the objective of maintaining a balanced allocation of the power to impose taxes between the Member States and of preventing wholly artificial arrangements which do not reflect economic reality and whose only purpose is to obtain a tax advantage.*"[855]

---

853. According to this legislation, a German resident shareholder who received a dividend from a company established in the same state was allowed, by means of a tax credit, to deduct from taxable income the amount of the tax which the distributing company has already paid on its profits. Thereby, profits distributed by resident companies were subject to tax once in the hands of the companies and only gave rise to tax for the final shareholder in so far as her income tax or its corporation tax exceeded the tax credit to which she/it was entitled. In addition, reductions in profits resulting from the depreciation of the underlying shares, which in principle corresponds to the amount of the profits distributed (Opinion of AG Bot in *Glaxo Wellcome*, C-182/08, EU:C:2009:438, at point 25) were also deductible. Non-resident shareholders, on the other hand, were not taxable on the profits that they received following a distribution of dividends by a resident company or a disposal of shares which they hold in that company. Therefore, they could not claim a tax credit attached thereto. However, it was possible to circumvent that legislation – in order to enable foreign shareholders who are not taxable in Germany to obtain that tax advantage – through selling the holding in the German resident company to a resident shareholder who is entitled to a tax credit in respect of imminent distributions of dividends at a price higher than its nominal value. If this surcharge was equal to the tax credit which is, in principle, allowed in respect of the company's distribution of dividends and which the foreign shareholder is not entitled to claim: (1) the foreign seller was able to make a capital gain, which was not taxed in Germany, and, at the same time, (2) the German buyer could, contrary to what would have been the case with the original shareholder, obtain the tax credit upon a distribution of profits as well as deduct the resulting losses on the partial reduction in value of the shares (Opinion of AG Bot in *Glaxo Wellcome*, C-182/08, EU:C:2009:438, at points 99-100). In order to combat this practice the new shareholder was denied deduction of the losses on the partial reduction in value of the acquired shares in a resident company to the extent of an amount that is equal to the difference between the acquisition price paid by the resident shareholder and the nominal value of the shares. The German legislation was based on the perception that such an amount represents, at least in part, the tax credit wrongly granted to the former shareholder. However, since the new German resident shareholders, with regard to the losses resulting from a reduction in value of the shares held in a resident company, were considered to be in a comparable situation, whether the shares are acquired from a resident or acquired from a non-resident, it had to be determined whether it was justified to limit the deduction only in those situations in which the shares were acquired from a non-resident (Judgment in *Glaxo Wellcome*, C-182/08, EU:C:2009:559, at paras 71-75).

854. The ECJ held "*that the disadvantages resulting from the legislation at issue in the main proceedings are suffered directly by the resident shareholder who has acquired those shares from a non-resident. For that resident shareholder, the impossibility of deducting from his taxable profits the losses related to the reduction in the value of the shares held in the resident company, where the reduction in value of the shares results from the distribution of the profits, is not offset by any tax advantage. The argument that the profit made by the non-resident who has sold the shares to the resident shareholder is not subject to taxation in Germany is irrelevant with regard to the resident shareholder who suffers the disadvantage*" (Judgment in *Glaxo Wellcome*, C-182/08, EU:C:2009:559, at paras 76-81).

855. According to the ECJ, "*[t]ransactions other than the distribution of dividends, which allow the non-resident shareholder to obtain the same result from an economic point of view as if he had been granted the tax credit in respect of the corporation tax paid by the company in which he holds the shares, could [...] undermine the ability of the Member State where that company*

The decisions in *Glaxo Wellcome* and in *SGI* suggest that the need to preserve the balanced allocation of taxing powers allows for a justification even if the restrictive legislation at hand does not enable the Member State concerned to successfully invoke the concept of fiscal cohesion due to a lack of a sufficiently close link between a tax advantage and the offsetting of that advantage by a particular tax levy. However, both decisions were rendered a couple of years ago: *Glaxo Wellcome* in 2009 and *SGI* in 2010. Considering the different approaches in *Deutsche Shell*, which was decided in 2008, and *K.*, which was decided in 2013, it cannot be excluded that the ECJ will generally be more generous with regard to the concept of fiscal cohesion in the future. Moreover, it has to be kept in mind that in *Glaxo Wellcome* as well as in *SGI* the need to preserve the balanced allocation of taxing powers has been considered together with, on the one hand, the need to prevent wholly artificial arrangements[856] and, on the other hand, the need to prevent tax avoidance.[857] It is, therefore, questionable whether the ECJ considered the need to preserve the balanced allocation of taxing powers as a truly independent justification ground in these cases.[858] In *Itelcar*, for example, the Court had to deal with the Portuguese thin capitalization rules, according to which interest was not deductible insofar as it related to the amount the overall debt owed by a person taxable in Portugal to an entity not resident in Portuguese territory or in another Member State of the EU, with which that person has "special relations," exceeded

---

resides to exercise its right to tax a profit generated by an economic activity undertaken in its territory" (Judgment in *Glaxo Wellcome*, C-182/08, EU:C:2009:559, at para. 84). If the price of the shares included an amount equal to the tax credit, which could not be claimed by the seller, "*the grant of a tax credit or the refund of an amount equal to that tax credit to the new resident shareholder would result in indirectly granting the non-resident shareholder a tax credit for the tax charged to the company. Such consequences would not just reduce the Federal Republic of Germany's tax revenues but would mean that, by indirectly granting the non-resident a financial advantage equal to the tax credit for the tax charged on the profits of a resident company, the profits normally taxable in that company's Member State of residence would be transferred to the Member State with jurisdiction to tax the profits made by the non-resident, thus jeopardising a balanced allocation of the power to impose taxes between the Member States*" (Judgment in *Glaxo Wellcome*, C-182/08, EU:C:2009:559, at paras 86-87). Moreover, "*[b]y restricting the right of the new shareholder to deduct from his taxable profits the losses resulting from the reduction in value of the shares concerned, to the extent that they do not exceed the 'blocked amount', the legislation at issue in the main proceedings is capable of preventing practices which have no objective other than to obtain for the non-resident shareholder a tax credit for the corporation tax paid by the resident company. [...] Consequently, such legislation is capable of achieving the objective of maintaining a balanced allocation of the power to impose taxes between the Member States and of preventing wholly artificial arrangements which do not reflect economic reality and whose only purpose is to obtain a tax advantage*" (Judgment in *Glaxo Wellcome*, C-182/08, EU:C:2009:559, at paras 91-92).

856. Judgment in *Glaxo Wellcome*, C-182/08, EU:C:2009:559, at paras 89-92.
857. Judgment in *SGI*, C-311/08, EU:C:2010:26, at para. 65-69; also see Judgment in *Oy AA*, C-231/05, EU:C:2007:439, at para. 60.
858. The need to preserve the balanced allocation of taxing powers has been explicitly considered as the sole justification ground in *X Holding* (Judgment in *X Holding*, C-337/08, EU:C:2010:89, at paras 25-33; with critical remarks see Opinion Statement of the CFE on *X Holding* (C-337/08), 51 *Eur. Taxn.* 4 [2011], p. 150 [at pp. 150-151]; S. van Thiel/M. Vascega, *X Holding*: Why Ulysses Should Stop Listening to the Siren, 50 *Eur. Taxn.* 8 [2010], p. 334 [at pp. 335-339]) as well as in some decisions on exit tax regimes (see, for example, Judgment in *N.*, C-470/04, EU:C:2006:525, at paras 41-47; Judgment in *DMC*, C-164/12, EU:C:2014:20, at paras 44-58; Judgment in *Verder LabTec*, C-657/13, EU:C:2015:331, at paras 40-47).

double the amount of the creditor's holding in the debtor's equity capital. The legislation is similar to, although not completely coinciding with, that in *Test Claimants in the Thin Cap Group Litigation* and in *SGI*, insofar as the Portuguese legislation provided for the possibility to demonstrate that the debtor could have obtained the same level of credit, on similar terms, from an independent entity. In contrast to *Test Claimants in the Thin Cap Group Litigation* and to *SGI*, however, the need to preserve the balanced allocation of taxing powers is not even mentioned in the ECJ's decision. Rather, the Court considered the Portuguese legislation justified, but disproportionate,[859] due to the objective of combatting tax evasion and avoidance.[860] Comparing *Test Claimants in the Thin Cap Group Litigation* and *SGI* with *Itelcar*, it thus seems possible to argue, as AG Kokott does, that "*preventing the transfer of income from one Member State to another by means of fictitious or fraudulent arrangements is simply a special instance of the recognised ground of justification of preventing tax avoidance. It is settled case-law that a national provision restricting freedom of establishment may be justified where it specifically targets wholly artificial arrangements designed to circumvent the legislation of the Member State concerned. 'Preservation of the allocation of the power to impose taxes between Member States', for its part, is concerned not with preventing a taxable person from avoiding taxation altogether, but with preventing him from moving taxable revenue to another Member State by means of artificial arrangements. The Court itself recognises this connection when it has occasion to consider the two grounds of justification together.*"[861]

2.6 Proportionality

According to the "rule of reason," as summarized by the ECJ in *Gebhard*, national measures that lead to a different treatment of cross-border and purely domestic situations do not only need to be justified by imperative requirements in the general interest in order to be compatible with the fundamental freedoms but "*they must be suitable for securing the attainment of the objective which they pursue; and they must not go beyond what is necessary in order to attain it.*"[862] The ECJ is referring here to the

859. Judgment in *Itelcar*, C-282/12, EU:C:2013:629, at paras 40-44.
860. Judgment in *Itelcar*, C-282/12, EU:C:2013:629, at para. 35.
861. Opinion of AG Kokott in *Nordea Bank Danmark*, C-48/13, EU:C:2014:153, at point 44; also see S. Heidenbauer, Die Vermeidung der Steuerumgehung und die ausgewogene *Aufteilung* der Besteuerungsbefugnis im Lichte der Rs. *SGI*, 21 *SWI* 2 (2011), p. 67 (at p. 71: "*Da die Verschiebung von Steuersubstrat in diesem Zusammenhang ein bloßer Reflex der missbräuchlichen Gestaltung ist, versteht sich auch der Rechtfertigungsgrund der Wahrung der ausgewogenen* Aufteilung *der Besteuerungsbefugnis nur als Ausfluss der Vermeidung der Steuerumgehung; er entfaltet keine eigenständige Bedeutung.*"); but see D. Hohenwarter, 20 *SWI* 2 (2011), at p. 168.
862. Judgment in *Gebhard*, C-55/94, EU:C:1995:411, at para. 37; also see Judgment in *Kraus*, C-19/92, EU:C:1993:125, at para. 32; Judgment in *Reisebüro Broede*, C-3/95, EU:C:1996:487, at para. 28; Judgment in *Centros*, C-212/97, EU:C:1999:126, at para. 34; Judgment in *Haim*, C-424/97, EU:C:2000:357, at para. 57; Judgment in *MacQuen*, C-108/96, EU:C:2001:67, at para. 26; Judgment in *Gräbner*, C-294/00, EU:C:2002:442, at para. 39; Judgment in *Inspire Art*, C-167/01, EU:C:2003:512, at para. 133; Judgment in *Contse*, C-234/03, EU:C:2005:664, at para. 25; Judgment in *Colegio de Ingenieros de Caminos, Canales y Puertos*, C-330/03, EU:C:2006:45,

principle of proportionality, which is considered to be the most important general principle of EU law[863] developed by the Court.[864]

Since it was mentioned for the first time in *Fédéchar*,[865] the principle of proportionality has been consistently held to be one of the general principles of EU law.[866] In general, it can be described as a standard that prescribes how to balance two conflicting rights, interests or policies in order to determine which of the two should prevail over the other in the circumstances of a given case.[867] When determining the compatibility of Member States' legislative acts with the fundamental freedoms, for example, the internal market's objective of unrestrained free movement and the legitimate objective in the public interest pursued by a Member State by a particular measure have to be balanced.[868] In order to do this, the ECJ applies an approach that is reminiscent of

at para. 30; Judgment in *Commission/Greece*, C-65/05, EU:C:2006:673, at para. 49; Judgment in *Corporación Dermoestética*, C-500/06, EU:C:2008:421, at para. 35; Judgment in *Berlington Hungary and others*, C-98/14, EU:C:2015:386, at para. 64.

863. On the background of such general principles of EU law, see T. Tridimas, *The General Principles of EU Law*[2] (Oxford University Press, 2006), at pp. 7-11.

864. See A. Cordewener, *Europäische Grundfreiheiten und nationales Steuerrecht* (Dr Otto Schmidt, 2002), at p. 71.

865. Judgment in *Fédéchar*, 8/55, EU:C:1956:11, at p. 299.

866. Judgment in *Schräder*, 265/87, EU:C:1989:303, at para. 21; Judgment in *Fedesa*, 331/88, EU:C:1990:391, at para. 13; Judgment in *British American Tobacco (Investments) and Imperial Tobacco*, C-491/01, EU:C:2002:741, at para. 122; Judgment in *Arnold André*, C-434/02, EU:C:2004:800, at para. 45; Judgment in *Swedish Match*, C-210/03, EU:C:2004:802, at para. 47; Judgment in *ABNA and others*, C-453/03, C-11/04, C-12/04 and C-194/04, EU:C:2005:741, at para. 68; Judgment in *IATA and ELFAA*, C-344/04, EU:C:2006:10, at para. 79; Judgment in *Agrarproduktion Staebelow*, C-504/04, EU:C:2006:30, at para. 35; Judgment in *Dokter and others*, C-28/05, EU:C:2006:408, at para. 79; Judgment in *Laserdisken*, C-479/04, EU:C:2006:549, at para. 53; Judgment in *Germany / Parliament and Council*, C-380/03, EU:C:2006:772, at para. 144; Judgment in *Piek*, C-384/05, EU:C:2007:21, at para. 34; Judgment in *Maatschap Schonewille-Prins*, C-45/05, EU:C:2007:296, at para. 45; Judgment in *Geuting*, C-375/05, EU:C:2007:574, at para. 45; Judgment in *Cementbouw Handel & Industrie / Commission*, C-202/06 P, EU:C:2007:814, at para. 52; Judgment in *Promusicae*, C-275/06, EU:C:2008:54, at para. 68; Judgment in *Militzer & Münch*, C-230/06, EU:C:2008:186, at para. 47; Judgment in *Michaniki*, C-213/07, EU:C:2008:731, at para. 48; Judgment in *Agrana Zucker*, C-33/08, EU:C:2009:367, at para. 31; Judgment in *S.P.C.M. and others*, C-558/07, EU:C:2009:430, at para. 41; Judgment in *Vodafone and others*, C-58/08, EU:C:2010:321, at para. 51; Judgment in *Afton Chemical*, C-343/09, EU:C:2010:419, at para. 45; Judgment in *Etimine*, C-15/10, EU:C:2011:504, at para. 124; but see J. Englisch, VAT and General Principles of EU Law, in D. Weber (ed.), *Traditional and Alternative Routes to European Tax Integration* (IBFD, 2010), p. 231 (at p. 237: "*A legal principle is characterized by its relative nature and its susceptibility to weighing and balancing against conflicting interests, as opposed to a legal rule, according to the predominant opinion of scholars of legal theory. By contrast, the "principle of proportionality" is in reality a rule prescribing how such conflicts should be solved in a rational way.*").

867. See J. Englisch in D. Weber (ed.), *Traditional and Alternative Routes to European Tax Integration* (IBFD, 2010), at p. 237; M. Holoubek, Zur Begründung des Verhältnismäßigkeitsgrundsatzes – verwaltungs-, verfassungs- und gemeinschaftsrechtliche Aspekte, in S. Griller/K. Korinek/M. Potacs (eds.), *Grundfragen und aktuelle Probleme des öffentlichen Rechts*, Festschrift für Heinz Peter Rill zum 60. Geburtstag (Orac, 1995), p. 97 (at pp. 119-120); R. Szudoczky, *The Sources of EU law and Their Relationships: Lessons for the Field of Taxation* (IBFD, 2014), at p. 117; A. Zalasiński, Proportionality of Anti-Avoidance and Anti-Abuse Measures in the ECJ's Direct Tax Case Law, 35 *Intertax* 5 (2007), p. 310 (at p. 312).

868. Judgment in *Council of the City of Stoke-on-Trent and Norwich City Council/B & Q Plc*, C-169/91, EU:C:1992:519, at para. 15 ("*Appraising the proportionality of national rules which pursue a*

German administrative and constitutional law traditions.[869] Thus, a three-pronged test has to be applied:[870] (1) is a certain national measure suitable to achieve or at least promote the alleged aim of a certain legitimate national interest? (suitability); (2) is there another national measure available that is equally effective in promoting the aim, but which is less burdensome for the addressee? (necessity); and (3) does the national measure, even though there is no other effective means, have an excessive impact on the addressee's own interests? (adequacy or appropriateness; proportionality *stricto sensu*).[871]

With regard to discriminatory measures taken by Member States, the ECJ does not always adopt this approach to the full extent.[872] Typically, the Court only refers to the first two aspects of the test (suitability and necessity), whereas no reference to the requirement of adequacy (proportionality *stricto sensu*) is made.[873] In the literature, it is partly assumed that the adequacy of the national measure is nevertheless taken into account implicitly.[874] Other scholars are of the opinion that the criterion of adequacy is suspect to the ECJ,[875] because it is directly related to the delicate issue of the institutional balance at the EU level[876] and hence not always considered.[877] However,

---

legitimate aim under Community law involves weighing the national interest in attaining that aim against the Community interest in ensuring the free movement of goods"); also see R. Szudoczky, *The Sources of EU law and Their Relationships: Lessons for the Field of Taxation* (IBFD, 2014), at p. 117 and p. 121; also cf. G. de Búrca, The Principle of Proportionality and its Application in EC Law, in A. Barav/D.A. Wyatt (eds.), *Yearbook of European Law 1993* (Clarendon Press, 1994), p. 105 (at p. 146).

869. See A. Cordewener, *Europäische Grundfreiheiten und nationales Steuerrecht* (Dr Otto Schmidt, 2002), at p. 74; N. Emiliou, *The Principle of Proportionality in European Law* (Kluwer, 1996), at p. 134; J. Englisch in D. Weber (ed.), *Traditional and Alternative Routes to European Tax Integration* (IBFD, 2010), at p. 235.

870. See F.G. Jacobs, Recent Developments in the Principle of Proportionality in European Community Law, in E. Ellis (ed.), *The Principle of Proportionality in the Laws of Europe* (Hart Publishing, 1999), p. 1 (at p. 1).

871. For this definition see A. Cordewener/M. Dahlberg/P. Pistone/E. Reimer/C. Romano, 44 *Eur. Taxn.* 5 (2004), at p. 223.

872. The three-pronged test seems to be applied, for example, in the following decisions: Judgment in *Commission/Denmark*, C-192/01, EU:C:2003:492, at para. 45; Judgment in *Commission/ France*, C-24/00, EU:C:2004:70, at para. 52; Judgment in *Commission/Austria*, C-150/00, EU:C:2004:237, at para. 88; Judgment in *Commission/Spain*, C-88/07, EU:C:2009:123, at para. 88; Judgment in *Commission/Germany*, C-319/05, EU:C:2007:678, at para. 87.

873. With regard to the ECJ's direct tax jurisprudence see, for example, Judgment in *Futura Participations and Singer*, C-250/95, EU:C:1997:239, at para. 26; Judgment in *De Lasteyrie du Saillant*, C-9/02, EU:C:2004:138, at para. 49; Judgment in *Marks & Spencer*, C-446/03, EU:C:2005:763, at para. 35; Judgment in *Lidl Belgium*, C-414/06, EU:C:2008:278, at para. 27; Judgment in *Aberdeen Property Fininvest Alpha*, C-303/07, EU:C:2009:377, at para. 57; Judgment in *Finanzamt Linz*, C-66/14, EU:C:2015:661, at para. 39.

874. See J. Englisch in H. Schaumburg/J. Englisch (eds.), *Europäisches Steuerrecht* (Dr Otto Schmidt, 2015), at m.no 7.206 (FN 1).

875. See J. Englisch in D. Weber (ed.), *Traditional and Alternative Routes to European Tax Integration* (IBFD, 2010), at p. 236.

876. Cf. A. von Bogdandy, The European Union as a Human Rights Organization? Human Rights and the Core of the European Union, 37 *Common Market L. Rev.* 6 (2000), p. 1307 (at pp. 1325-1327).

877. See J. Englisch in D. Weber (ed.), *Traditional and Alternative Routes to European Tax Integration* (IBFD, 2010), at p. 236; J. Englisch in H. Schaumburg/J. Englisch (eds.), *Europäisches Steuerrecht* (Dr Otto Schmidt, 2015), at m.no 7.206.

the proportionality test *stricto sensu* fulfils an important function: By asking about the suitability, only those national measures will fail to meet the proportionality test that do not have a causal relationship with the identified imperative requirements in the general interest.[878] Only in extreme cases will this rather low standard not be met,[879,880] because basically the national measure has to be "*manifestly inappropriate having regard to the objective which the competent institution intends to pursue.*"[881] Determining the necessity of a national measure, on the other hand, is a much greater hurdle.[882] For this purpose, the equally effective alternatives to the measure adopted by the Member State have to be identified.[883] In case such alternatives can be found, necessity only exists if the measure adopted by the Member State is the least restrictive with regard to the addressee's interest.[884] However, in neither of those two steps is the internal market's objective of unrestrained free movement contrasted with the legitimate objective in the public interest pursued by a Member State with a particular measure. As AG Poiares Maduro has put it, "*the greater the degree of detriment to the principle of free movement [...], the greater must be the importance of satisfying the public interest on which the Member State relies.*"[885] Whereas the suitability test is solely focused on whether the national measure is suitable to achieve or at least promote the Member State's legitimate objective, the necessity test looks for less restrictive measures that equally ensure the attainment of the objective pursued.[886] However, in conducting this test the conflicting interests of EU law and of the Member State concerned are not weighed.[887] Hence, the question whether the national measure,

878. See A. Cordewener, *Europäische Grundfreiheiten und nationales Steuerrecht* (Dr Otto Schmidt, 2002), at pp. 86-87; J. Englisch, *Wettbewerbsgleichheit im grenzüberschreitenden Handel* (Mohr Siebeck, 2008), at pp. 353-354; A. Schnitger, *Die Grenzen der Einwirkungen der Grundfreiheiten des EG-Vertrages auf das Ertragsteuerrecht* (IDW, 2006), at p. 399.
879. See J. Englisch, *Dividendenbesteuerung* (Dr Otto Schmidt, 2005), at p. 285; J. Englisch in H. Schaumburg/J. Englisch (eds.), *Europäisches Steuerrecht* (Dr Otto Schmidt, 2015), at m.no 7.205.
880. See, for example, Judgment in *Commission/Greece*, C-155/09, EU:C:2011:22, at paras 54-55; Judgment in *Missionswerk Werner Heukelbach*, C-25/10, EU:C:2011:65, at paras 35-36.
881. Judgment in *Schräder*, 265/87, EU:C:1989:303, at para. 22; Judgment in *Fedesa*, 331/88, EU:C:1990:391, at para. 14; Judgment in *Alliance for National Health and others*, C-154/04 and C-155/04, EU:C:2005:449, at para. 52.
882. See J. Englisch in H. Schaumburg/J. Englisch (eds.), *Europäisches Steuerrecht* (Dr Otto Schmidt, 2015), at m.no 7.205; L. Flynn, Coming of Age: The Free Movement of Capital Case Law 1993-2002 (2002), 39 *Common Market L. Rev.* 4 (2002), p. 773 (at p. 801).
883. See A. Schnitger, *Die Grenzen der Einwirkungen der Grundfreiheiten des EG-Vertrages auf das Ertragsteuerrecht* (IDW, 2006), at p. 399.
884. See A. Cordewener, *Europäische Grundfreiheiten und nationales Steuerrecht* (Dr Otto Schmidt, 2002), at p. 88; G. de Búrca in A. Barav/D.A. Wyatt (eds.), *Yearbook of European Law 1993* (Clarendon Press, 1994), at p. 113.
885. Opinion of AG Poiares Maduro in *Ahokainen and Leppik*, C-434/04, EU:C:2006:462, at point 26.
886. See A. Cordewener, *Europäische Grundfreiheiten und nationales Steuerrecht* (Dr Otto Schmidt, 2002), at p. 91.
887. See J. Englisch, *Dividendenbesteuerung* (Dr Otto Schmidt, 2005), at p. 285; J. Englisch, *Wettbewerbsgleichheit im grenzüberschreitenden Handel* (Mohr Siebeck, 2008), at pp. 354-355; J. Englisch in H. Schaumburg/J. Englisch (eds.), *Europäisches Steuerrecht* (Dr Otto Schmidt, 2015), at m.no 7.206; B. Strassburger, *Die Dogmatik der EU-Grundfreiheiten* (Mohr Siebeck, 2012), at pp. 136-137.

even though there is no other and less restrictive effective means of achieving the legitimate public aim, has an excessive impact on the addressee's own interests constitutes an essential element of the proportionality scrutiny.[888]

Such a far-reaching proportionality test may nevertheless be criticized. On the one hand, the balancing of legitimate interests is the prerogative of the democratically elected legislator which can be reviewed, but must not be replaced, by a court.[889] Hence, after applying the proportionality test *stricto sensu*, the Member State concerned should not be bereft of any leeway.[890] On the other hand, applying the proportionality test is subject to judicial valuation and is hence to a certain extent subjective.[891] In order not to become unpredictable,[892] it is thus all the more important that the ECJ provides detailed and thorough reasons as part of the proportionality analysis. However, this is not always the case. In *Truck Center*[893] and *Schempp*,[894] for example, the Court regarded the cross-border and the domestic situation as not being comparable and, hence, abstained from explicitly addressing the issue of proportionality. Member States may, therefore, be tempted to conclude that there are no constraints whatsoever on how different the situations that formed the basis of the comparison in these cases may be treated.[895] Indeed, a lack of comparability releases the Member State concerned from justifying the national measure at stake, because different situations must not - but, depending upon a justification and a proportionality analysis, nevertheless may - be treated in the same way. However, the arguments raised at the level of comparability and justification are to a certain extent interchangeable.[896] As the ECJ held in *Blanckaert*, a national rule which provides for less favourable tax treatment of cross-border situations "*can be justified [...] by the objective difference between the [situations compared with each other].*"[897] A lack of

888. See J. Englisch in D. Weber (ed.), *Traditional and Alternative Routes to European Tax Integration* (IBFD, 2010), at p. 236.
889. See J. Englisch, 33 *Intertax* 8/9 (2005), at p. 328; B. Strassburger, *Die Dogmatik der EU-Grundfreiheiten* (Mohr Siebeck, 2012), at p. 137; also cf. A. Cordewener, *Europäische Grundfreiheiten und nationales Steuerrecht* (Dr Otto Schmidt, 2002), at p. 90.
890. Cf. J. Englisch in D. Weber (ed.), *Traditional and Alternative Routes to European Tax Integration* (IBFD, 2010), at p. 236.
891. See T. Kingreen, *Die Struktur der Grundfreiheiten des Europäischen Gemeinschaftsrechts* (Duncker & Humblot, 1999), at p. 173; K. Simader, *Withholding Taxes and the Fundamental Freedoms* (Kluwer, 2014), at p. 290; also see D. Hohenwarter, *Verlustverwertung im Konzern* (LexisNexis, 2009), at p. 115; with regard to the Austrian constitutional equality principle see M. Pöschl, Über Gleichheit und Verhältnismäßigkeit, 119 *JBl* 7 (1997), p. 413 (at p. 432).
892. See F.P. Sutter, Pauschales Verbot grenzüberschreitenden Verlustabzugs - Verstoß gegen Niederlassungsfreiheit, 17 *EuZW* 3 (2006), p. 85 (at p. 87).
893. Judgment in *Truck Center*, C-282/07, EU:C:2008:762, at paras 41-48.
894. Judgment in *Schempp*, C-403/03, EU:C:2005:446, at paras 29-36.
895. See M. Lang, 46 *Eur. Taxn.* 9 (2006), at p. 422; M. Lang, 18 *EC Tax Rev.* 3 (2009), at pp. 100-101; M. Lang in M. Hebig/K. Kaiser/K. Koschmieder/M. Oblau (eds.), *FS Wilhelm H. Wacker* (Erich Schmidt Verlag, 2006), at p. 369; K. Simader in M. Lang/J. Schuch/C. Staringer (eds.), *Quellensteuern* (Linde, 2010), p. 13 (at p. 28); K. Simader, *Withholding Taxes and the Fundamental Freedoms* (Kluwer, 2014), at p. 135; also cf. R. Lyal, 12 *EC Tax Rev.* 2 (2003), at p. 68.
896. Cf. G. Kofler, *Doppelbesteuerungsabkommen und Europäisches Gemeinschaftsrecht* (Linde, 2007), at pp. 991-992.
897. Judgment in *Blanckaert*, C-512/03, EU:C:2005:516, at para. 50; also cf. Judgment in *Eckelkamp*, C-11/07, EU:C:2008:489, at para. 61 ("*In that respect, it must be stated first that, contrary to the*

comparability thus releases the Member State concerned from justifying the national measure at stake, but it does not render the proportionality analysis superfluous.[898] Even if two situations are not comparable, it still has to be demonstrated whether the differences or similarities in treatment reflect the differences or similarities of the situations at hand in an appropriate and reasonable way. Otherwise, the blurred lines between the comparability analysis and the justification analysis could lead to different levels of scrutiny, depending on whether the Court considers interchangeable arguments in the context of the comparability or the justification analysis.

3 THE SCOPE OF PROTECTION OF THE STATE AID PROVISIONS

3.1 The Relevance of the State Aid Provisions in Tax Law

The main purpose of taxation is to generate revenue for the state.[899] However, national tax systems are also commonly used to implement non-fiscal goals.[900] Tax incentives (or disincentives) may be introduced, for example, to facilitate research and development activities, to foster environmental-friendly investments, to stimulate economic

Belgian Government's contention, which is set out in paragraph 47 of the present judgment, that difference in treatment cannot be justified on the ground that it concerns situations which are not objectively comparable."); Judgment in *Jäger*, C-256/06, EU:C:2008:20, at para. 43 ("*In that respect, it must be stated, first, that the difference in the amount of tax paid according to whether the inheritance consists only of agricultural land and forestry situated in Germany or consists also of such an asset situated in another Member State cannot be justified on the ground that it concerns situations which are not objectively comparable.*"); Judgment in *Arens-Sikken*, C-43/07, EU:C:2008:490, at para. 54 ("*In that respect, it must be stated that, contrary to the Netherlands Government's contention, that difference in treatment cannot be justified on the ground that it concerns situations which are not objectively comparable.*"); Judgment in *Groupe Steria*, C-386/14, EU:C:2015:524, at paras 21-22 ("*In order for that difference in treatment to be compatible with the provisions of the Treaty on the freedom of establishment, it must relate to situations which are not objectively comparable or be justified by an overriding reason in the general interest […].The fact that the dividends received by a parent company which enjoy full tax exemption come from subsidiaries that are part of the tax-integrated group to which the parent company concerned also belongs does not amount to an objective difference in the situation of parent companies that would justify the difference in treatment identified […].*"); Judgment in *Miljoen*, C-10/14, C-14/14 and C-17/14, EU:C:2015:608, at para. 73 ("*Accordingly, in circumstances such as those at issue in the main proceedings, the different treatment of resident taxpayers liable to pay income tax or corporation tax and non-resident taxpayers who are subject to a withholding tax in respect of dividends cannot be justified by a difference in their situations which is relevant to the application of Article 65(1)(a) TFEU.*").

898. See M. Lang/J. Lüdicke/M. Reich, 17 *IStR* 20 (2008), at p. 712; P. Wattel, 55 *Eur. Taxn.* 12 (2015), at p. 553 ("*If [the cross-border situation and the domestic situation] are not comparable, then that is not yet the end of the analysis, as still, the Court is competent to test whether the difference in tax treatment is proportionate to the difference in fiscal position.*"); also cf. J. Englisch, 38 *Intertax* 4 (2010), at p. 204.
899. See R. Seer in K. Tipke/J. Lang, *Steuerrecht*[22] (Dr Otto Schmidt, 2015), at § 1 para. 6; F.P. Sutter, *Das EG-Beihilfenverbot und sein Durchführungsverbot in Steuersachen* (Linde, 2005), at p. 21; also cf. J. Englisch, *Aufteilung der Besteuerungsbefugnisse – Ein Rechtfertigungsgrund für die Einschränkung von EG-Grundfreiheiten* (Institut "Finanzen und Steuern" e.V., 2008), at p. 132.
900. For a historical overview see R. Wernsmann, *Verhaltenslenkung in einem rationale Steuersystem* (Mohr Siebeck, 2005), at pp. 19 et seq.

growth in underdeveloped regions or industries, to promote charitable initiatives, to strengthen the international activities of domestic companies, to attract foreign investments or to correct what is considered to be "market failure."[901] Whether such attempts to exploit the tax system in order to further general or specific socio-, economic- or culture-political aims are economically reasonable is subject to controversial discussions.[902] From a legal perspective, restrictions to national-governmental interventions in the market-based economy of the EU follow, *inter alia*, from Articles 107-109 TFEU. In order to maintain a level playing field and to ensure an efficient allocation of resources within the internal market it is determined that "*any aid granted by a Member State or through State resources in any form whatsoever which distorts or threatens to distort competition by favouring certain undertakings or the production of certain goods shall, in so far as it affects trade between Member States, be incompatible with the internal market.*" Although there is no definition of the term "aid," this wording already indicates that the potential scope of this provision is very broad; after all, it covers "*aid [...] in any form whatsoever.*" If the State aid rules were dependent on the form of the aid, Member States could easily circumvent the prohibition.[903] It is, therefore, understandable that the ECJ has come to the conclusion that "*[t]he concept of aid is [...] wider than that of a subsidy because it embraces not only positive benefits, such as subsidies themselves, but also interventions which, in various forms, mitigate the charges which are normally included in the budget of an undertaking and which, without, therefore, being subsidies in the strict meaning of the word, are similar in character and have the same effect.*"[904] The fiscal nature of a measure taken by a

901. See, for example, R. Luja, *Assessment and Recovery of Tax Incentives in the EC and the WTO: A View on State Aids, Trade Subsidies and Direct Taxation* (Intersentia, 2003), at pp. 5-8; for a compilation of Austrian tax rules which implement (ed.) non-fiscal goals see H. Ruppe, *Das Abgabenrecht als Lenkungsinstrument der Gesellschaft und Wirtschaft und seine Schranken in den Grundrechten*, 8. ÖJT, Band I/A (Manz, 1982), at pp. 14 et seq.
902. See, for example, S.S. Surrey, Tax Incentives as a Device for Implementing Government Policy: A Comparison with Direct Government Expenditures, 83 *Harv. L. Rev.* 4 (1970), p. 705 (at pp. 705 et seq.); S.S. Surrey, Steueranreize als ein Instrument der staatlichen Politik, 58 *StuW* 4 (1981), p. 359 (at pp. 359-377); K. Tipke, *Die Steuerrechtsordnung*[2] (Dr Otto Schmidt, 2000), at pp. 340-347.
903. See F.P. Sutter, The Influence of the European State Aid Rules on National Tax Policy, in K. Andersson/E. Eberhartinger/L. Oxelheim (eds.), *National Tax Policy in Europe* (Springer, 2007), p. 121 (at p. 122).
904. Judgment in *De gezamenlijke Steenkolenmijnen in Limburg*, 30/59, EU:C:1961:2, at p. 19; also Judgment in *Banco Exterior de España*, C-387/92, EU:C:1994:100, at para. 13; cf. Judgment in *Ecotrade*, C-200/97, EU:C:1998:579, at para. 34; Judgment in *Italy/Commission*, C-6/97, EU:C:1999:251, at para. 15; Judgment in *Piaggio*, C-295/97, EU:C:1999:313, at para. 34; Judgment in *Commission/Portugal*, C-404/97, EU:C:2000:345, at para. 44; Judgment in *Germany/Commission*, C-156/98, EU:C:2000:367, at para. 25; Judgment in *Banks*, C-390/98, EU:C:2001:456, at para. 30; Judgment in *Adria-Wien Pipeline and Wietersdorfer & Peggauer Zementwerke*, C-143/99, EU:C:2001:598, at para. 38; Judgment in *Italy/Commission*, C-310/99, EU:C:2002:143, at para. 51; Judgment in *Ferring*, C-53/00, EU:C:2001:627, at para. 15; Judgment in *Belgium/Commission*, C-5/01, EU:C:2002:754, at para. 32; Judgment in *Freskot*, C-355/00, EU:C:2003:298, at para. 83; Judgment in *SIM 2 Multimedia v. Commission*, C-399/00, EU:C:2003:252, at para. 35; Judgment in Spain/Commission, C-501/00, EU:C:2004:438, at para. 90; Judgment in *Chronopost/Ufex and others*, C-83/01 P, EU:C:2003:388, at para. 65; Judgment in *GIL Insurance and others*, C-308/01, EU:C:2004:252, at para. 69; Judgment in *Heiser*, C-172/03, EU:C:2005:130, at para. 36; Judgment in *Cassa di Risparmio di Firenze*,

Member State is, therefore, not sufficient to exclude it from the ambit of Articles 107-109 TFEU.[905] Tax benefits may also constitute State aid, because the beneficiaries are put in a better position than competitors who are not eligible to claim the tax benefit and hence have to pay the full amount of taxes.[906] Therefore, the ECJ's well-known statement on the impact of the fundamental freedoms on direct taxation is transferable to the area of EU State aid law:[907] "*[D]irect taxation falls within the competence of the Member States, although it is settled case-law that they must exercise that competence consistently with Community law [...] and therefore avoid taking, in that context, any measures capable of constituting State aid incompatible with the common market.*"

Although it is generally accepted that national tax systems are not safeguarded from being examined in order to establish whether they are in line with Articles 107-109 TFEU, up to the 1990s, the State aid provisions did not play a major role in tax practice.[908] In the *Ruding* Report, which was published in 1992, however, concerns were expressed "*about the tendency of Member States to introduce special tax regimes designed to attract internationally mobile business. [...] [T]here is a danger that such schemes will lead to tax atrophy in particular sectors.*"[909] This point was picked up by the European Commission in 1996[910] and led to an initiative that aimed at tackling harmful tax competition within the EU.[911] As a result, the "Code of conduct for business taxation" was adopted by the Council in 1998;[912] it is a non-binding political declaration of the Member States to eliminate domestic tax measures and refrain from

C-222/04, EU:C:2006:8, at para. 131; Judgment in *Enirisorse*, C-237/04, EU:C:2006:197, at para. 42; Judgment in *Air Liquide Industries Belgium*, C-393/04, EU:C:2006:403, at para. 29; Judgment in *Paint Graphos*, C-78/08, EU:C:2011:550, at para. 45; Judgment in *Presidente del Consiglio dei Ministri*, C-169/08, EU:C:2009:709, at para. 56; Judgment in *Commission and Spain/Government of Gibraltar and United Kingdom*, C-106/09 P and C-107/09 P, EU:C:2011:732, at para. 71; Judgment in *Seydaland Vereinigte Agrarbetriebe*, C-239/09, EU:C:2010:778, at para. 30; Judgment in *France Télécom/Commission*, C-81/10 P, EU:C:2011:811, at para. 16; Judgment in *Frucona Košice/Commission*, C-73/11 P, EU:C:2013:32, at para. 69; Judgment in *France/Commission*, C-559/12 P, EU:C:2014:217, at para. 94; Judgment in *Eventech*, C-518/13, EU:C:2015:9, at para. 33; Judgment in OTP Bank, C-672/13, EU:C:2015:185, at para. 40; Judgment in *Kernkraftwerke Lippe-Ems*, C-5/14, EU:C:2015:354, at para. 71; Judgment in *BVVG*, C-39/14, EU:C:2015:470, at para. 26.

905. Judgment in *Italy/Commission*, 173/73, EU:C:1974:71, at para. 13.
906. Judgment in *Banco Exterior de España*, C-387/92, EU:C:1994:100, at para. 14; Judgment in *Italy/Commission*, C-66/02, EU:C:2005:768, at para. 78; Judgment in *Cassa di Risparmio di Firenze*, C-222/04, EU:C:2006:8, at para. 132; Judgment in *Air Liquide Industries Belgium*, C-393/04 and C-41/05, EU:C:2006:403, at para. 30.
907. Judgment in *Spain/Commission*, C-501/00, EU:C:2004:438, at para. 123.
908. See F.P. Sutter, *Das EG-Beihilfenverbot und sein Durchführungsverbot in Steuersachen* (Linde, 2005), at pp. 24-25.
909. *Ruding* Report, at p. 201.
910. Taxation in the European Union, SEC(96) 487 final (20 March 1996); see also Taxation in the European Union, Report on the development of tax systems, COM(96) 546 final (22 Oct. 1996), at pp. 5-6 and 9-10.
911. Communication from the Commission to the Council, Towards tax co-operation in the European Union, COM(97) 495 final (1 Oct. 1997); Communication from the Commission to the Council and the European Parliament, A package to tackle harmful tax competition in the European Union, COM(97) 564 final (5 Nov. 1997).
912. Resolution of the Council and the representatives of the Governments of the Member States, meeting within the Council of 1 Dec. 1997 on a code of conduct for business taxation (hereinafter: Code of Conduct), *OJ* C 2 (6 Jan. 1998), at pp. 2 et seq.

introducing new provisions that are to be considered harmful.[913] Backed by this political mandate, the European Commission also intensified the work on the application of the State aid rules to tax measures. With the resulting Notice that was published in 1998, a fully-fledged description of the European Commission's approach with regard to tax incentives was presented.[914] Since then, it has become common practice to liaise the proceedings against harmful tax competition under the Code of conduct with investigations regarding the compatibility of the scrutinized national tax rules with Article 107 TFEU.[915] It is probably due to this "dramatic change" of the European Commission's policy[916] that "*[t]he European Union has woken up to State aid possibly contained in national direct tax measures.*"[917]

The more important the State aid provisions become, the narrower the Member States' latitude with regard to national tax policy gets.[918] This is especially due to the procedural concept of Article 108 TFEU, according to which the European Commission, on the one hand, "*shall, in cooperation with Member States, keep under constant review all systems of aid existing in those States.*" As stated in Article 1(b)(i) State Aid Procedure Regulation,[919] existing aid in particular comprises, without prejudice to explicitly mentioned special provisions, "*all aid which existed prior to the entry into force of the TFEU in the respective Member States, that is to say, aid schemes and individual aid which were put into effect before, and are still applicable after, the entry into force of the TFEU in the respective Member States.*" The European Commission's

913. For the content and the impact of the Code of Conduct see, for example, J. Mössner in M. Lang/J. Schuch/C. Staringer (eds.), *Soft Law in der Praxis* (Linde, 2005), at pp. 136-144.
914. Commission notice on the application of the State aid rules to measures relating to direct business taxation, *OJ* C 384 (10 Dec. 1998), at pp. 3 et seq.
915. Communication from the Commission to the Council, Towards tax co-operation in the European Union, COM(97) 495 final (1 Oct. 1997), at p. 13 ("*The Council notes that some, although not all, of the tax measures covered by this code fall within the scope of the provisions on state aid in Articles 92-94 of the EC Treaty. It further notes that the implementation of the code should in practice reduce the need for Community intervention under the state aid rules in the tax field. Without prejudice to Community law, it requests the Commission to provide guidance on the application of the state aid rules to fiscal aids and to commit itself to their rigorous application, taking into account negative effects of aid that are brought to light in the application of this code.*"); also cf. Taxation in the European Union, Report on the development of tax systems, COM(96) 546 final (22 Oct. 1996), at Article 6.10; also see W. Schön, Taxation and State Aid Law in the European Union, 36 *Common Market L. Rev.* 5 (1999), p. 911 (at p. 912); W. Schön, State Aid in the Area of Taxation, in L. Hancher/T. Ottervanger/P.J. Slot (eds.), *EU State Aids* (Sweet & Maxwell, 2012), p. 321 (at p. 323).
916. C. Pinto, EC State Aid Rules and Tax Incentives: A U-Turn in Commission Policy? (Part I), 39 *Eur. Taxn.* 8 (1999), p. 295 (at p. 295).
917. P.J. Wattel, Forum: Interaction of State Aid, Free Movement, Policy Competition and Abuse Control in Direct Tax Matters, 5 *World Tax J.* 1 (2013), p. 128 (at p. 128).
918. Cf. F.P. Sutter in K. Andersson/E. Eberhartinger/L. Oxelheim (eds.), *National Tax Policy in Europe*, at p. 146 and p. 149.
919. Council Regulation (EU) 2015/1589 of 13 Jul. 2015 laying down detailed rules for the application of Article 108 of the Treaty on the Functioning of the European Union (codification), *OJ* L 248 (24 Sep. 2015), p. 9 (at pp. 9-29) (hereinafter: State Aid Procedure Regulation); for the previous version see Council Regulation (EC) No 659/1999 of 22 Mar. 1999 laying down detailed rules for the application of Article 108 of the treaty on the functioning of the European Union, *OJ* L 83 (27 Mar. 1999), p. 1 (at p. 3), lastly amended by Council Regulation (EU) No 734/2013 of 22 Jul. 2013 amending Regulation (EC) No. 659/1999 laying down detailed rules for the application of Article 93 of the EC Treaty, *OJ* L 204 (31 Jul. 2014), p. 15.

review of such existing aid may, however, only lead to legal consequences *ex nunc.*[920] On the other hand, with regard to projected national measures that constitute new aid, defined as "*all aid, that is to say, aid schemes and individual aid, which is not existing aid, including alterations to existing aid,*" Article 108(3) TFEU mandates the Member States to notify the European Commission in advance and "*in sufficient time to enable it to submit its comments, of any plans to grant or alter aid.*" If such aid is authorized by way of a decision or at least no objections are raised by the European Commission within a certain period of time, after being enacted by the respective Member State, they become into existing aid,[921] which may be subject to re-evaluation in the future. In the case of doubts as to the compatibility of new aid with the internal market, however, a formal investigation procedure has to be initiated. This contradictory procedure may either lead to a (positive) decision authorizing the notified measure (Article 9(2) State Aid Procedure Regulation), which may be subject to certain conditions and obligations (Article 9(4) State Aid Procedure Regulation), or to a negative decision (Article 9(5) State Aid Procedure Regulation), i.e., the notified measure must not be put into effect.[922]

Not least because of the European Commission's prominent position within this monitoring process, it is asserted in the literature that the State aid provisions lead to a "*tax legislation under the prerogative of supranational approval.*"[923] Some scholars criticize the fact that the European Commission, by issuing various regulations, communications, recommendations, guidelines, notices and supplementary information sheets in order to illustrate its position,[924] assumes a "*creeping normative role,*" despite deficient democratic legitimation.[925] Thus, "*State aid law has become an*

920. See, for example, M. Lang, *Die Auswirkungen des gemeinschaftsrechtlichen Beihilferechts auf das Steuerrecht*, 17. ÖJT, Band IV/1 (Manz, 2009), at p. 56; M. Schütte, Procedural Aspects of EU State aid Law and Practice, in E. Szyszczak (ed.), *Research Handbook on European State Aid Law* (Edward Elgar Publishing, 2011), p. 354 (at p. 348); P.J. Slot, Administrative Procedure, in L. Hancher/T. Ottervanger/P.J. Slot (eds.), *EU State Aids* (Sweet & Maxwell, 2012), p. 945 (at p. 959, MN 25-019); F.P. Sutter, *Das EG-Beihilfenverbot und sein Durchführungsverbot in Steuersachen* (Linde, 2005), at p. 158; F.P. Sutter in H. Mayer/K. Stöger (eds.), *EUV/AEUV* (Manz, 2014), Article 108 AEUV, MN 1.
921. According to Article 1(b)(ii) State Aid Procedure Regulation, existing aid also means "*authorised aid, that is to say, aid schemes and individual aid which have been authorised by the Commission or by the Council.*"
922. On the procedure with regard to new aid see, for example, P.J. Slot in L. Hancher/T. Ottervanger/P.J. Slot (eds.), *EU State Aids* (Sweet & Maxwell, 2012), at pp. 953 et seq.; F.P. Sutter, *Das EG-Beihilfenverbot und sein Durchführungsverbot in Steuersachen* (Linde, 2005), at pp. 159 et seq.
923. H. Kube, *National Tax Law and the Transnational Control of State Aids* (EU Working Paper LAW No. 2001/9), at p. 29, who translated the equivalent German statement of V. Götz, Steuervergünstigungen als Gegenstand der europäischen Beihilfenaufsicht, in P. Kirchhof/M. Lehner/A. Raupach/M. Rodi (eds.), *Staaten und Steuern*, Festschrift für Klaus Vogel zum 70. Geburtstag (C.F. Müller, 2000), p. 579 (at p. 583); for a relativizing perspective see F.P. Sutter in H. Mayer/K. Stöger (eds.), *EUV/AEUV* (Manz, 2014), Article 107 AEUV, MN 100.
924. For an overview see M. Schweda, § 14 General Principles, in M. Heidenhain (ed.), *European State Aid Law* (C.H. Beck, 2010), p. 151 (at MN 10); F.P. Sutter in H. Mayer/K. Stöger (eds.), *EUV/AEUV* (Manz, 2014), Article 107 AEUV, MN 115-119.
925. F. Nanetti/G. Mameli, The Creeping Normative Role of the EC Commission in the twin-Track Struggle Against State Aids and Harmful Tax Competition, 11 *EC Tax Rev.* 4 (2002), p. 185 (at pp. 189-191); also see J. Englisch, Das Beihilfenverbot im Steuerrecht, in H. Schaumburg/J.

all-purpose tool to camouflage policy-making."[926] The criticism passed on the quasi-legislative actions of the European Commission relates primarily to the discretionary power resulting from Article 107(3) TFEU, according to which certain aids "*may be considered to be compatible with the internal market.*"[927] This is due to the fact that the judicial review of the European Commission's exercise of its discretion is limited. The ECJ only verifies "*whether the Commission complied with the relevant rules governing procedure and the statement of reasons, whether the facts on which the contested finding was based have been accurately stated and whether there has been any manifest error of assessment or a misuse of powers.*"[928] Apart from that, however, the European Commission's decisions are fully subject to judicial supervision.[929]

With regard to the introduction of new tax incentives or exemptions, it is not uncommon that Member States are remiss in notifying the European Commission, because the potential State aid character of such a national measure is neglected.[930] Such a failure of notification may have dramatic results. In such a case, the European

---

Englisch (eds.), *Europäisches Steuerrecht* (Dr Otto Schmidt, 2015), p. 411 (at pp. 413-414, at MN 9.3); also cf. A. Fantozzi, The Applicability of State Aid Rules to Tax Competition Measures: A Process of de Facto Harmonization in the Tax Field?, in W. Schön (ed.), Tax Competition in Europe (IBFD, 2003), p. 121 (at pp. 121-132); for an opposing view see P. Rossi-Maccanico, The Specificity Criterion in Fiscal Aid Review: Proposals for State Aid Control of Direct Business Tax Measures, 16 *EC Tax Rev.* 2 (2007), p. 90 (at p. 103); for a differentiated view see F.P. Sutter in K. Andersson/E. Eberhartinger/L. Oxelheim (eds.), *National Tax Policy in Europe*, at pp. 146-150.

926. C. Koenig, Where is State Aid Law heading to?, 13 *Eur. St. Aid L. Q.* 4 (2014), p. 611 (at p. 611).
927. According to the ECJ, the exercise of the European Commission's discretion has to involve "*economic and social assessments which must be made in a Community context*" (Judgment in *Philip Morris/Commission*, 730/79, EU:C:1980:209, at para. 24; Judgment in *Deufil/ Commission*, 310/85, EU:C:1987:96, at para. 18; Judgment in *France/Commission*, 301/87, EU:C:1990:67, at para. 49; Judgment in *Italy/Commission*, 303/88, EU:C:1991:136, at para. 34; Judgment in *Matra*, C-225/91, EU:C:1993:239, at para. 24; Judgment in *Italy/Commission*, C-372/97, EU:C:2004:234, at para. 83; Judgment in *Spain/Commission*, C-113/00, EU:C:2002:507, at para. 67; Judgment in *Spain/Commission*, C-114/00, EU:C:2002:508, at para. 81; Judgment in *Spain/Commission*, C-351/98, EU:C:2002:530, at para. 74; Judgment in *Greece/Commission*, C-278/00, EU:C:2004:239, at para. 97; Judgment in *Holland Malt/ Commission*, C-464/09 P, EU:C.2010:733, at para. 23). The European Commission has to keep in mind that national tax measures, which "*contravene other provisions of the Treaty, cannot [...] be declared by the Commission to be compatible with the common market,*" because the State aid procedure "*must never produce a result which is contrary to the specific provisions of the Treaty*" (Judgment in *Germany/Commission*, C-156/98, EU:C:2000:467, at para. 78; also see Judgment in *Commission/Italy*, 73/79, EU:C:1980:129, at para. 11; Judgment in *Matra*, C-225/91, EU:C:1991:460, at para. 41).
928. Judgment in *Belgium/Commission*, C-56/93, EU:C:1996:64, at para. 11; also see Judgment in *Matra*, C-225/91, EU:C:1993:239, at para. 25; Judgment in *Italy and SIM 2 Multimedia / Commission*, C-328/99 and C-399/00, EU:C:2003:252, at para. 39; Judgment in *Chronopost and La Poste / UFEX and others*, C-341/06 P and C-342/06 P, EU:C:2008:375, at para. 143.
929. See, for example, H.C.H. Hofmann/A. Morini, Judicial Review of Commission Decisions in State Aid, in E. Szyszczak (ed.), *Research Handbook on European State Aid Law* (Edward Elgar Publishing, 2011), p. 354 (at p. 354 et seq.); L. Flynn/T. Ottervanger, Judicial Protection, in L. Hancher/T. Ottervanger/P.J. Slot (eds.), *EU State Aids* (Sweet & Maxwell, 2012), p. 1022 (at pp. 1029 et seq.); U. Soltész, § 43 Scope of Judicial Review, in M. Heidenhain (ed.), *European State Aid Law* (C.H. Beck, 2010), p. 752 (at pp. 752 et seq.).
930. See J. Englisch in H. Schaumburg/J. Englisch (eds.), *Europäisches Steuerrecht* (Dr Otto Schmidt, 2015), at pp. 465-466, at MN 9.60; M. Lang, Seminar J: Steuerrecht, Grundfreiheiten und Beihilfeverbot, 19 *IStR* 15 (2010), p. 570 (at p. 570).

Commission can, according to Article 12 State Aid Procedure Regulation, start a formal investigation procedure on its own initiative, which may ultimately lead to a negative decision. According to the ECJ, *"the logical consequence of [aid] being found unlawful [...] [is] an order for the recovery of [it]."*[931] This is due to the standstill clause of Article 108(3) last sentence TFEU and Article 3 State Aid Procedure Regulation, according to which Member States may not put into effect notifiable measures until the European Commission has taken, or is deemed to have taken, a decision authorizing such aid. If unnotified measures are thus considered to be unlawful aid, the European Commission must, subject to a limitation period of ten years,[932] *"decide that the Member State concerned shall take all necessary measures to recover the aid from the beneficiary."*[933] The amount to be recovered from the beneficiaries not only includes the value of the unlawful aid that had been granted, but also includes interest.[934] Due to the danger of having to pay back all the sums received (or saved) as well as additional interest, the consequences for recipients of unlawful aid grants are far-reaching. This is insofar paradoxical as it is not the individual beneficiary but the Member State concerned that is responsible for the failure to notify the respective measure.[935]

It is not only the European Commission that can act if an unnotified national measure potentially constitutes unlawful aid. The supervision of Member States' legislative behaviour in EU State aid law is characterized by a *"triangle of power."*[936] This is due to the fact that the standstill clause of Article 108(3) last sentence TFEU is,

931. Judgment in *Comitato "Venezia vuole vivere" and others*, C-71/09 P, C-73/09 P and C-76/09 P, EU:C:2011:368, at para. 181; also see Judgment in *Belgium/Commission*, 142/87, EU:C:1990:125, at para. 66; Judgment in *Commission/Greece*, C-183/91, EU:C:1999:233, at para. 16; Judgment in *Commission/Portugal*, C-404/97, EU:C:2000:345, at para. 38; Judgment in *Italy and SIM 2 Multimedia/Commission*, C-328/99 and C-399/00, EU:C:2003:252, at para. 53; Judgment in *Commission/Spain*, C-404/00, EU:C:2003:373, at para. 44; Judgment in *Italy/Commission*, C-66/02, EU:C:2005:768, at para. 113; Judgment in *Commission/Italy*, C-99/02, EU:C:2004:207, at para. 15; Judgment in *Commission/Council*, C-110/02, EU:C:2004:395, at para. 41; Judgment in *Unicredito Italiano*, C-148/04, EU:C:2005:774, at para. 113; Judgment in *CELF and ministre de la Culture and de la Communication*, C-1/09, EU:C:2010:136, at para. 54; C-331/09, at para. 54; Judgment in *Commission/Slovakia*, C-507/08, EU:C:2010:802, at para. 42; Judgment in *Commission/Poland*, C-331/09, EU:C:2011:250, at para. 54; Judgment in *Commission/Italy*, C-496/09, EU:C:2011:740, at para. 87; C-529/09, at para. 90; Judgment in *Residex Capital IV*, C-275/10, EU:C:2011:814, at para. 20; Judgment in Mediaset, C-403/10 P, EU:C:2011:533, at para. 29; Judgment in *Commission/Spain*, C-529/09, EU:C:2013:31, at para. 90; Judgment in *OTP Bank*, C-672/13, EU:C:2015:185, at para. 70; Judgment in *Commission/France*, C-63/14, EU:C:2015:458, at para. 44.
932. Article 17(1) State Aid Procedure Regulation.
933. Article 16(1) State Aid Procedure Regulation.
934. Article 16(2) State Aid Procedure Regulation.
935. See Z. Chojnacka, Das Verbot der Durchführung von formell rechtswidrigen Beihilfenmaßnahmen und seine tatsächliche Effektivität – Ein Versuch der Veranschaulichung der Wirkungsweise primärrechtlicher Verfahrensvorschriften anhand der Odyssee im Fall der Energieabgabenvergütung, in I. Eisenberger/I. Golden/K. Lachmayer/G. Marx/D. Tomasovsky (eds.), *Norm und Normvorstellung*, Festschrift für Bernd-Christian Funk zum 60. Geburtstag (Springer, 2003), p. 31 (at p. 46: "*Anomalie*"); F.P. Sutter in K. Andersson/E. Eberhartinger/L. Oxelheim (eds.), *National Tax Policy in Europe*, at p. 148 ("*the ironical sanction mechanism of the EC State aid regime*").
936. F.P. Sutter, The *Adria Wien Pipeline* Case and the State Aid Provisions of the EC Treaty in Tax Matters, 41 *Eur. Taxn.* 7 (2001), p. 239 (at p. 247); F.P. Sutter in K. Andersson/E. Eberhartinger/L. Oxelheim (eds.), *National Tax Policy in Europe*, at p. 138.

in contrast to Article 107(1) TFEU,[937] directly applicable.[938] Therefore, every national administrative authority or court applying an unnotified national provision must assess whether it constitutes aid in the sense of Article 107(1) TFEU.[939] In the case of doubts, a national court may – or must, if it is a court of last instance[940] – request the ECJ to give a preliminary ruling pursuant to Article 267 TFEU. If a national administrative authority or court considers the national provision concerned to constitute State aid, it has to respect the "blocking effect" of the standstill clause and may not grant any benefits on the grounds of the national measure that has been identified as State aid. Besides the legislative authority, the executive level hence establishes a second safety net against unlawful aid grants,[941] which is, however, rather coarsely meshed with regard to tax measures. Typically, the legislator's hand is to a considerable extent led by the tax administration. It is, therefore, not to be commonly expected that the tax authorities can prevent unlawful aid grants based on legislation that has been largely influenced by themselves.[942] National courts, on the other hand, are rather willing to pick up on an infringement of EU State aid rules. However, it may take years before a national court declares a tax provision to constitute State aid. In the literature, the precise modalities how – and to what extent – national administrative authorities and

937. Judgment in *Steinike and Weinlig*, 78/76, EU:C:1977:52, at para. 8; Judgment in *Adria-Wien Pipeline and Wietersdorfer & Peggauer Zementwerke*, C-143/99, EU:C:2001:598, at para. 30.
938. Judgment in *Costa/E.N.E.L.*, 6/64, EU:C:1964:34, at p. 596; Judgment in *Lorenz GmbH / Bundesrepublik Deutschland and others*, 120/73, EU:C:1973:152, at para. 8; Judgment in *Fédération nationale du commerce extérieur des produits alimentaires and others / France*, C-354/90, EU:C:1991:440, at para. 11; Judgment in *Adria-Wien Pipeline and Wietersdorfer & Peggauer Zementwerke*, C-143/99, EU:C:2001:598, at para. 26.
939. National administrative authorities and courts have no jurisdiction to rule on the compatibility of aid with the internal market, but may only interpret and apply the concept of aid contained in Article 107 TFEU in order to determine, for example, whether a national measure that has been introduced without notifying the European Commission ought to have been subject to the preliminary examination procedure provided for in Article 108(3) TFEU. In the words of the ECJ, "*national courts must offer to individuals entitled to rely on disregard of the obligation of notification the certain prospect that all appropriate conclusions will be drawn, in accordance with national law, with regard to both the validity of the acts giving effect to the aid and the recovery of financial support granted in disregard of that provision or possible interim measures.*" See Judgment in *Transalpine Ölleitung in Österreich*, C-368/04, EU:C:2006:644, at para. 47; also see Judgment in *Adria-Wien Pipeline and Wietersdorfer & Peggauer Zementwerke*, C-143/99, EU:C:2001:598, at paras 26 and 27; also see P. Adriaanse/T. Ottervanger, Recovery of Unlawful Aid, in L. Hancher/T. Ottervanger/P.J. Slot (eds.), *EU State Aids* (Sweet & Maxwell, 2012), p. 999 (at p. 1020, MN 26-021); P. Nebbia, State Aid and the Role of National Courts, in E. Szyszczak (ed.), *Research Handbook on European State Aid Law* (Edward Elgar Publishing, 2011), p. 390 (at pp. 390 et seq.); H. Niemeyer, § 44 Proceedings Before National Courts, in M. Heidenhain (ed.), *European State Aid Law* (C.H. Beck, 2010), p. 767 (at MN 24 et seq.); for the European Commission's opinion see Commission notice on the enforcement of State aid law by national courts, *OJ* C 85 (9 Apr. 2009), p. 1 (at pp. 6 et seq).
940. See Article 267(3) TFEU: "*Where any such question is raised in a case pending before a court or tribunal of a Member State against whose decisions there is no judicial remedy under national law, that court or tribunal shall bring the matter before the Court.*"
941. See F.P. Sutter in K. Andersson/E. Eberhartinger/L. Oxelheim (eds.), *National Tax Policy in Europe*, at p. 138.
942. Cf. M. Lang, *Die Auswirkungen des gemeinschaftsrechtlichen Beihilferechts auf das Steuerrecht*, 17. ÖJT, Band IV/1 (Manz, 2009), at p. 8.

courts have to recover the aid from the beneficiaries are hence intensively discussed,[943] particularly if a decision on the compatibility of the respective national measure with the internal market has not yet been rendered, the final determination on that matter being the responsibility of the European Commission.[944] Another controversial issue is whether - and if so, to what extent - procedural remedies have to be granted to taxpayers in order to be able to claim a preferential tax treatment of competitors before national courts.[945] Since unprivileged competitors have the greatest interest in terminating distortive effects on competition by virtue of a national measure, this may be of particular importance for the future meaning of Articles 107-109 TFEU in the area of taxation.[946]

The multiplicity of players in the State aid arena may lead to more and more tax provisions turning out to constitute unlawful aid in the future. Considering the numerous contentious issues, it can be reasonably assumed that the EU State aid rules'

943. See P. Adriaanse/T. Ottervanger in L. Hancher/T. Ottervanger/P.J. Slot (eds.), *EU State Aids* (Sweet & Maxwell, 2012), at p. 1021, MN 26-022; M. Lang, *Die Auswirkungen des gemeinschaftsrechtlichen Beihilferechts auf das Steuerrecht*, 17. ÖJT, Band IV/1 (Manz, 2009), at pp. 74-80; P. Nebbia in E. Szyszczak (ed.), *Research Handbook on European State Aid Law* (Edward Elgar Publishing, 2011), at pp. 393-398; T. Jestaedt/T. Loest, § 53 Rückforderung formell rechtskräftiger Beihilfen, in M. Heidenhain (ed.), *Handbuch des Europäischen Beihilfenrechts* (C.H. Beck, 2003), p. 929 (at pp. 929 et seq.); F.P. Sutter in H. Mayer/K. Stöger (eds.), *EUV/AEUV* (Manz, 2014), Article 108 AEUV, MN 125-126.

944. Judgment in *Fédération nationale du commerce extérieur des produits alimentaires and others*, C-354/90, EU:C:1991:440, at para. 14; Judgment in *SFEI and others*, C-39/94, EU:C:1996:285, at para. 42; Judgment in *Adria-Wien Pipeline and Wietersdorfer & Peggauer Zementwerke*, C-143/99, EU:C:2001:598, at para. 29.

945. See W. Arnold, Konkurrentenklage und Abgabenverfahrensrecht, in M. Holoubek/M. Lang (eds.), *Abgabenverfahrensrecht und Gemeinschaftsrecht* (Linde, 2006), p. 403 (at pp. 403-456); J. Englisch, Die negative Konkurrentenklage im Unternehmenssteuerrecht, 85 *StuW* 1 (2008), p. 43 (at pp. 53-57); M. Köhler, Private Enforcement of State Aid Law - Problems of Guaranteeing EU Rights by Means of National (Procedural) Law, 11 *Eur. St. Aid L. Q.* 2 (2012), p. 369 (at pp. 369 et seq.); T. Lampert, Dezentrale Beihilfenaufsicht durch Konkurrentenklagen vor den nationalen Gerichten der Mitgliedstaaten, 12 *EWS* 8 (2001), p. 357 (at pp. 361-364); M. Lang, *Die Auswirkungen des gemeinschaftsrechtlichen Beihilferechts auf das Steuerrecht*, 17. ÖJT, Band IV/1 (Manz, 2009), at pp. 95-99; M. Mamut, *Konkurrentenschutz im Abgabenrecht* (2010), at pp. 107 et seq. and at pp. 141-144; L. Paterno, State Aid and Fiscal Protectionism in the European Union from the Perspective of Competitors, 65 *Bull. Intl. Taxn.* 6 (2011), p. 343 (at pp. 343 et seq.); U. Soltész, Der Rechtsschutz des Konkurrenten gegen gemeinschaftswidrige Beihilfen vor nationalen Gerichten, 12 *EuZW* 7 (2001), p. 202 (at pp. 204 et seq.); F.P. Sutter in H. Mayer/K. Stöger (eds.), *EUV/AEUV* (Manz, 2014), Article 108 AEUV, MN 127 et seq.

946. See M. Lang, *Die Auswirkungen des gemeinschaftsrechtlichen Beihilferechts auf das Steuerrecht*, 17. ÖJT, Band IV/1 (Manz, 2009), at p. 96 ("*Die Effektivität des Beihilferechts steht und fällt [...] damit, dass auch der nicht begünstigte Konkurrent Initiativen setzt und seine Position auch im Verfahren durchsetzen kann.*"); C. Staringer in *Die Auswirkungen des gemeinschaftsrechtlichen Beihilfenrechts auf das Steuerrecht, Referate und Diskussionsbeiträge*, 17. ÖJT, Band IV/2 (Manz, 2009), at p. 146 ("*[D]ie Frage der Rechtsdurchsetzung von Beihilferechtsverstößen durch den Konkurrenten und [...] das 'Drohpotenzial' für eine Behilferückforderung [werden] [...] über den Sieg oder die Niederlage des Beihilferechts in der Rechtsentwicklung entscheiden [...].*").

potential has not yet been tapped in its entirety.[947] Taxpayers benefitting from a preferential tax regime hence have to adjust to the sword of Damocles that is hanging over their heads.[948]

3.2 Tax Benefits as Obstacles to Undistorted Competition

3.2.1 Aid in Any Form Whatsoever

In order for Article 107 TFEU to be applicable, the existence of an "*aid*" is required. However, there is no legal definition of this term. According to the case law of the ECJ, a State measure constitutes aid, if "*the recipient undertaking receives an economic advantage which it would not have obtained under normal market conditions.*"[949] It is obvious that a subsidy granted by a Member State to a single enterprise or a certain group of enterprises constitutes an economic advantage. With regard to taxes, however, it is quite the opposite, as the taxpayer is in general funding the Member State and not the other way round.[950] Still, an economic advantage may exist if certain enterprises have to pay less taxes than others.[951] Accordingly, the budgetary restraint of the state to levy taxes is insofar covered by Article 107(1) TFEU, as "*[t]he concept of aid is [...] wider than that of a subsidy because it embraces not only positive benefits, such as subsidies themselves, but also interventions which, in various forms, mitigate the charges which are normally included in the budget of an undertaking and which, without, therefore, being subsidies in the strict meaning of the word, are similar in character and have the same effect.*"[952]

947. See C. HJI Panayi, State Aid and Tax: the Third Way?, 32 *Intertax* 6/7 (2004), p. 283 (at p. 306: "*Art. 87 [...] has the potential to develop into a powerful weapon at the disposal of the Commission; well capable of re-opening the debate for tax harmonization.*").

948. Cf. C. Staringer in *Die Auswirkungen des gemeinschaftsrechtlichen Beihilfenrechts auf das Steuerrecht, Referate und Diskussionsbeiträge*, 17. ÖJT, Band IV/2 (Manz, 2009), at p. 146 ("*Drohpotenzial*").

949. Judgment in *SEFI and others*, C-39/94, EU:C:1996:285, at para. 60; Judgment in *Spain/ Commission*, C-342/96, EU:C:1999:210, at para. 41; Judgment in *DM Transport*, C-256/97, EU:C:1999:332, at para. 22.

950. See W. Schön, 36 *Common Market L. Rev.* 5 (1999), at pp. 919-920; W. Schön in L. Hancher/T. Ottervanger/P.J. Slot (eds.), *EU State Aids* (Sweet & Maxwell, 2012), at pp. 328-329.

951. Judgment in *Banco Exterior de España*, C-387/92, EU:C:1994:100, at para. 14; Judgment in *Italy/Commission*, C-66/02, EU:C:2005:768, at para. 78; Judgment in *Cassa di Risparmio di Firenze*, C-222/04, EU:C:2006:8, at para. 132; Judgment in *Air Liquide Industries Belgium*, C-393/04 and C-41/05, EU:C:2006:403, at para. 30.

952. Judgment in *De gezamenlijke Steenkolenmijnen in Limburg*, 30/59, EU:C:1961:2, at p. 19; also Judgment in *Banco Exterior de España*, C-387/92, EU:C:1994:100, at para. 13; cf. Judgment in *Ecotrade*, C-200/97, EU:C:1998:579, at para. 34; Judgment in *Italy/Commission*, C-6/97, EU:C:1999:251, at para. 15; Judgment in *Piaggio*, C-295/97, EU:C:1999:313, at para. 34; Judgment in *Commission/Portugal*, C-404/97, EU:C:2000:345, at para. 44; Judgment in *Germany/Commission*, C-156/98, EU:C:2000:367, at para. 25; Judgment in *Banks*, C-390/98, EU:C:2001:456, at para. 30; Judgment in *Adria-Wien Pipeline and Wietersdorfer & Peggauer Zementwerke*, C-143/99, EU:C:2001:598, at para. 38; Judgment in *Italy/Commission*, C-310/99, EU:C:2002:143, at para. 51; Judgment in *Ferring*, C-53/00, EU:C:2001:627, at para. 15; Judgment in *Belgium/Commission*, C-5/01, EU:C:2002:754, at para. 32; Judgment in *Freskot*, C-355/00, EU:C:2003:298, at para. 83; Judgment in *SIM 2 Multimedia v. Commission*, C-399/00,

The ECJ's position is understandable. If the State aid rules were dependent on the form of the aid,[953] Member States could easily circumvent the mandated prohibition.[954] Consequently, Article 107 TFEU "*does not distinguish between the measures of State intervention concerned by reference to their causes or aims but defines them in relation to their effects.*"[955] Hence, it should also not make a difference whether certain undertakings are tax exempt or whether the taxable event is defined so narrowly that no exception is needed. Since the effect can be exactly the same, the different legal technique should, from a teleological perspective,[956] not influence the State aid

EU:C:2003:252, at para. 35; Judgment in Spain/Commission, C-501/00, EU:C:2004:438, at para. 90; Judgment in *Chronopost/Ufex and others*, C-83/01 P, EU:C:2003:388, at para. 65; Judgment in *GIL Insurance and others*, C-308/01, EU:C:2004:252, at para. 69; Judgment in *Heiser*, C-172/03, EU:C:2005:130, at para. 36; Judgment in *Cassa di Risparmio di Firenze*, C-222/04, EU:C:2006:8, at para. 131; Judgment in *Enirisorse*, C-237/04, EU:C:2006:197, at para. 42; Judgment in *Air Liquide Industries Belgium*, C-393/04, EU:C:2006:403, at para. 29; Judgment in *Paint Graphos*, C-78/08, EU:C:2011:550, at para. 45; Judgment in *Presidente del Consiglio dei Ministri*, C-169/08, EU:C:2009:709, at para. 56; Judgment in *Commission and Spain/Government of Gibraltar and United Kingdom*, C-106/09 P and C-107/09 P, EU:C:2011:732, at para. 71; Judgment in *Seydaland Vereinigte Agrarbetriebe*, C-239/09, EU:C:2010:778, at para. 30; Judgment in *France Télécom/Commission*, C-81/10 P, EU:C:2011:811, at para. 16; Judgment in *Frucona Košice/Commission*, C-73/11 P, EU:C:2013:32, at para. 69; Judgment in *France/Commission*, C-559/12 P, EU:C:2014:217, at para. 94; Judgment in *Eventech*, C-518/13, EU:C:2015:9, at para. 33; Judgment in OTP Bank, C-672/13, EU:C:2015:185, at para. 40; Judgment in *Kernkraftwerke Lippe-Ems*, C-5/14, EU:C:2015:354, at para. 71; Judgment in *BVVG*, C-39/14, EU:C:2015:470, at para. 26.

953. The "legal form" is likewise irrelevant for the question whether the national measure constitutes State aid or not. In general, it does not matter whether the State support is provided through "*tax provisions of a legislative, regulatory or administrative nature [or] through the practices of the tax authorities.*" See Commission notice on the application of the State aid rules to measures relating to direct business taxation, *OJ* C 384 (10 Dec. 1998), at p. 4, MN 10.
954. See F.P. Sutter in K. Andersson/E. Eberhartinger/L. Oxelheim (eds.), *National Tax Policy in Europe* (Springer, 2007), at p. 122.
955. Judgment in *Italy/Commission*, 173/73, EU:C:1974:71, at para. 13; Judgment in *Belgium/Commission*, C-56/93, EU:C:1996:64, at para. 79; Judgment in *France/Commission*, C-241/94, EU:C:1996:353, at para. 20; Judgment in *Belgium/Commission*, C-75/97, EU:C:1999:311, at para. 25; Judgment in *Spain/Commission*, C-480/98, EU:C:2000:559, at para. 16; Judgment in *Netherlands/Commission*, C-382/99, EU:C:2002:363, at para. 61; Judgment in *Spain/Commission*, C-409/00, EU:C:2003:92, at para. 46; Judgment in *GEMO SA*, C-126/01, EU:C:2003:622, at para. 34; Judgment *Netherlands/Commission*, C-159/01, EU:C:2004:246, at para. 51; Judgment in *Heiser*, C-172/03, EU:C:2005:130, at para. 46; Judgment in *British Aggregates/Commission*, C-487/06 P, EU:C:2008:757, at para. 85; Judgment in *Paint Graphos and others*, C-78/08 to C-80/08, EU:C:2011:550, at para. 68; Judgment *Commission/Netherlands*, C-279/08 P, EU:C:2011:551, at para. 70; Judgment in *Comitato "Venezia vuole vivere" and others/Commission*, C-71/09 P, C-73/09 P and C-76/09 P, EU:C:2011:368, at para. 94; Judgment in *Commission and Spain/Government of Gibraltar and United Kingdom*, C-106/09 P and C-107/09 P, EU:C:2011:732, at para. 87; Judgment in *France Télécom/Commission*, C-81/10 P, EU:C:2011:811, at para. 17; Judgment in *Commission/EDF*, C-124/10 P, EU:C:2012:318, at para. 77; Judgment in *Bouygues and Bouygues Télécom / Commission and others*, C-399/10 P and C-401/10 P, EU:C:2013:175, at para. 81; Judgment in *3M Italia*, C-417/10, EU:C:2012:184, at para. 36; Judgment in *BVVG*, C-39/14, EU:C:2015:470, at para. 52.
956. See J. Englisch, Steuerliche Sonderbelastung als verbotene Beihilfe – eine unionsrechtliche Achillesferse der Kernbrennstoffsteuer, 89 *StuW* 4 (2012), p. 318 (at pp. 323-324); also see A. Cordewener, Die asymmetrische Belastung von Wirtschaftssektoren im Lichte aktueller Entwicklungen des EU-Beihilfeverbots – ein Problem für die Kernbrennstoffsteuer, 5 *Ubg* 9 (2012), p. 607 (at pp. 610-611); A. Cordewener, Asymmetrical Tax Burdens and EU State Aid Control, 21 *EC Tax Rev.* 6 (2012), p. 288 (at p. 289).

analysis.[957] This conclusion has been challenged, though, by pointing out that, in contrast to Article 107(1) TFEU, the corresponding provision in Article 4(c) ECSC Treaty explicitly differentiated between "*subsidies or aids granted by States, or special charges imposed by States, in any form whatsoever.*"[958] The ECJ has hence inferred that "*an aid consists of a mitigation of the charges which are normally included in the budget of an undertaking, taking account of the nature or general scheme of the system of charges in question [...], whereas a special charge is, on the contrary, an additional charge over and above those normal charges. It follows that a single measure cannot at the same time constitute both an aid and a special charge within the meaning of Article 4(c) of the ECSC Treaty.*"[959] Since the ban on "special charges" has not been included in the EC Treaty or in Article 107(1) TFEU, some scholars argue that special charges are not covered by the TFEU's State aid prohibition.[960] It is, therefore, partly called for an analogous application of Article 107(1) TFEU.[961] Other parts of the literature, however, have countered that the wording of Article 4(c) ECSC Treaty not only differentiates between aids and special charges, but also separately addresses subsidies. Since it is undisputed that subsidies are covered by current EU State aid law, it can be argued that the wording of Article 4(c) ECSC Treaty was simply more precise, whereas Article 107(1) TFEU only mentions the generic term "aid."[962] Most notably, however, Article 4(c) ECSC Treaty contains a mere enumeration of governmental instruments of political intervention, whereas Article 107(1) TFEU mentions additional restrictive requirements, such as the favouring of certain undertakings or the production of certain goods, the (potential) distortion of competition or the adverse effect on trade between Member States. Therefore, the current EU State aid rules, in contrast to Article 4(c) ECSC Treaty, do not require clearly differentiating between the various techniques of governmental preferential treatment. Since it cannot, moreover, be reconstructed

957. See M. Lang, 11 *Eur. St. Aid L. Q.* 2 (2012), at p. 411; M. Lang, 60 *British Tax Rev.* 3 (2015), at pp. 392-393; M. Lang, 24 *IStR* 11 (2015), at pp. 370-371; also see Opinion of AG Kokott in *Presidente del Consiglio dei Ministri*, C-169/08, EU:C:2009:420, at point 128: "*[I]t is immaterial what legal mechanism is used. The tax benefit may be based on the fact that the legislature has expressly exempted some undertakings from the tax in question, to which they would otherwise be subject. Likewise the tax benefit may arise from the fact that a tax law is asymmetrically formulated in relation to its factual elements or its scope, so that some undertakings are caught as taxpayers while others are not.*"

958. A similar wording can be found in Article 67(3) ECSC Treaty, which addresses the reduction of differentials in costs of production "*by granting a special advantage to, or by imposing special burdens on, coal or steel enterprises.*"

959. Judgment in Banks, C-390/98, EU:C:2001:456, at paras 33-34.

960. See P. Rossi-Maccanico, State Aid Review of Member States' Measures Relating to Direct Business Taxation, 3 *Eur. St. Aid L. Q.* 2 (2004), p. 229 (at pp. 240-241); W. Schön in L. Hancher/T. Ottervanger/P.J. Slot (eds.), *EU State Aids* (Sweet & Maxwell, 2012), at pp. 334-335; F.P. Sutter, *Das EG-Beihilfenverbot und sein Durchführungsverbot in Steuersachen* (Linde, 2005), at pp. 123-124; with a different view see J. Englisch in H. Schaumburg/J. Englisch (eds.), *Europäisches Steuerrecht* (Dr Otto Schmidt, 2015), at p. 421, at MN 9.14.

961. See W. Schön in ÖJT (ed.), *Die Auswirkungen des gemeinschaftsrechtlichen Beihilferechts auf das Steuerrecht*, Referate und Diskussionsbeiträge, Band IV/2 (Manz, 2010), at pp. 36-37; W. Schön, Special Charges – A Gap in European Competition Law?, 5 *Eur. St. Aid L. Q.* 3 (2006), p. 495 (at pp. 495-496); W. Schön in L. Hancher/T. Ottervanger/P.J. Slot (eds.), *EU State Aids* (Sweet & Maxwell, 2012), at pp. 334-335.

962. J. Englisch, 89 *StuW* 4 (2012), at p. 322.

why the explicit ban on special charges has not been included in the EC Treaty, the *argumentum e contrario* is not considered to be compelling.[963]

Meanwhile, the ECJ has clarified that it cannot be excluded *a priori* that taxes on only certain undertakings are covered by Article 107(1) TFEU. Special charges may constitute State aid, at least if the taxpayers concerned are directly competing with undertakings not covered by the special tax and the relevant charge aims at influencing the competitive situation.[964] This is consistent with the ECJ regularly pointing out that "*classification as aid requires that all the conditions set out in that provision are fulfilled.*"[965] Thus, the characteristics of aid simply reflect the (other) legal elements of Article 107(1) TFEU. Only if there is an economic advantage can there be a "*favouring [of] certain undertakings or the production of certain goods*" and only if the economic advantage would not have been obtainable under normal market conditions, is there an "*aid granted by a Member State or through State resources [...] which distorts or threatens to distort competition.*" Thus, the term "aid" technically has no autonomous meaning within the State aid assessment.[966] By mentioning "*aid [...] in any form whatsoever,*" the extensive scope of Article 107(1) TFEU is being expressed.[967]

3.2.2 *Granting by a Member State or Through State Resources*

Article 107(1) TFEU only covers aid "*granted by a Member State or through State resources.*" Neither private patronage by ecclesiastical or charitable associations, trade unions, employer's federations or other institutions in the private sector,[968] nor contributions based on EU law and granted through EU budgetary funds can hence constitute State aid.[969] However, unlawful State aid may not only be granted by federal, regional or local public authorities.[970] Instead, according to the ECJ, "*[t]he distinction between aid granted by the State and aid granted through State resources serves to bring within the definition of aid not only aid granted directly by the State, but also aid*

963. J. Englisch, 89 *StuW* 4 (2012), at p. 322.
964. Judgment in *Ferring*, C-53/00, EU:C:2001:627, at paras 19-28; Judgment in *Laboratoires Boiron*, C-526/04, EU:C:2006:528, at paras 36-39.
965. Judgment in *GEMO SA*, C-126/01, EU:C:2003:622, at para. 21; Judgment in *Altmark Trans and Regierungspräsidium Magdeburg*, C-280/00, EU:C:2003:415, at para. 74; also see Opinion of AG Kokott in *UTECA*, C-222/07, EU:C:2008:468, at point 122.
966. See F.P. Sutter, *Das EG-Beihilfenverbot und sein Durchführungsverbot in Steuersachen* (Linde, 2005), at pp. 40-41.
967. See F.P. Sutter in H. Mayer/K. Stöger (eds.), *EUV/AEUV* (Manz, 2014), Article 107 AEUV, MN 20.
968. See M. Heidenhain, § 4 The Concept of State Aid, in M. Heidenhain (ed.), *European State Aid Law* (C.H. Beck, 2010), p. 22 (at MN 29); F.P. Sutter in H. Mayer/K. Stöger (eds.), *EUV/AEUV* (Manz, 2014), Article 107 AEUV, MN 24.
969. See, for example, C.-D. Ehlermann/M. Goyette, The Interface Between EU State Aid Control and the WTO Disciplines on Subsidies, 5 *Eur. St. Aid L. Q.* 4 (2006), p. 695 (at p. 695, FN 1); C. Koenig/M. Scholz, Die Förderung transeuropäischer Netzinfrastrukturen, 14 *EWS* 5 (2003), p. 223 (at p. 225); C. Koenig/J. Kühling, Reform des EG-Beihilfenrechts aus der Perspektive des mitgliedstaatlichen Systemwettbewerbs, 10 *EuZW* 17 (1999), p. 517 (at p. 519); C. Koenig/J. Paul in R. Streinz (ed.), *EUV/AEUV*[2] (C.H. Beck, 2012), at Art. 107 AEUV para. 64.
970. Judgment in *Germany/Commission*, 248/84, EU:C:1985:437, at para. 17; Judgment in *Portugal/ Commission*, C-88/03, EU:C:2006:511 at para. 60.

granted by public or private bodies designated or established by the State."[971] To qualify as an advantage granted by a Member State or through State resources, it is sufficient that the resources "*constantly remain under public control, and [are] therefore available to the competent national authorities.*"[972]

Aid granted through state resources typically leads to a reduction of the Member State's budget. However, this does not mean that a direct transfer of state resources is needed.[973] On the one hand, abstaining from levying taxes "*is equivalent to consumption of State resources in the form of fiscal expenditure.*"[974] Although tax benefits prevent the Member State's budget from increasing, instead of reducing it, the overall result is the same. It does not in fact make a vital difference whether a Member State does not tax certain undertakings from the outset or whether the taxes of such economic operators are refunded *ex post*.[975] On the other hand, benefits granted by the state may stimulate investments. Overall, granting aid may, therefore, indirectly even increase the Member State's tax revenue.[976] According to the ECJ, it is not possible, however, to balance the shortfall of tax revenue resulting from a tax benefit and the positive indirect effects on the Member State's budget.[977] For similar reasons, it need not necessarily constitute aid granted through state resources if a national measure leads to a decrease in tax revenue. After all, this might only be a concomitant phenomenon of a non-fiscal measure. In *Sloman Neptun*, for example, the ECJ held that "*[t]he system at issue does not seek, through its object and general structure, to create an advantage which would constitute an additional burden for the State or the abovementioned bodies, but only to alter in favour of shipping undertakings the*

971. Judgment in *Sloman Neptun*, C-72/91 and C-73/91, EU:C:1993:97, at para. 19; Judgment in *Kirsammer-Hack*, C-189/91, EU:C:1993:907, at para. 16; Judgment in *Ecotrade*, C-200/97, EU:C:1998:579, at para. 35; Judgment in *Piaggio*, C-295/97, EU:C:1999:313, at para. 35; Judgment in *PreussenElektra*, C-379/98, EU:C:2001:160, at para. 58; Judgment in *UTECA*, C-222/07, EU:C:2009:124, at para. 43; Judgment *Commission/Netherlands*, C-279/08 P, EU:C:2011:551, at para. 105; also see Judgment in *Van der Kooy*, 67, 68 and 70/85, EU:C:1988:38, at para. 35.
972. Judgment in *France/Ladbroke Racing and Commission*, C-83/98 P, EU:C:2000:248, at para. 50; Judgment in *France/Commission*, C-482/99, EU:C:2002:294, at para. 37; Judgment in *Italy and SIM 2 Multimedia/Commission*, C-328/99 and C-399/00, EU:C:2003:252, at para. 33; Judgment in *Greece/Commission*, C-278/00, EU:C:2004:239, at para. 52; Judgment in *SIM 2 Multimedia v. Commission*, C-399/00, EU:C:2003:252, at para. 33; Judgment in *Doux Élevage and Coopérative agricole UKL-ARREE*, C-677/11, EU:C:2013:348, at para. 35; Judgment in *Vent De Colère and others*, C-262/12, EU:C:2013:851, at para. 21.
973. Judgment in *Banco Exterior de España*, C-387/92, EU:C:1994:100, at para. 14; Judgment in *Italy/Commission*, C-66/02, EU:C:2005:768, at para. 78; Judgment in *Cassa di Risparmio di Firenze*, C-222/04, EU:C:2006:8, at para. 132; Judgment in *Air Liquide Industries Belgium*, C-393/04 and C-41/05, EU:C:2006:403, at para. 30; Judgment *Belgium/Commission*, C-182/03 and C-217/03, EU:C:2006:416, at para. 87.
974. Judgment *Ecotrade/Altiforni e Ferriere di Servola*, C-200/97, EU:C:1998:579, at para. 35; also see Commission notice on the application of the State aid rules to measures relating to direct business taxation, *OJ* C 384 (10 December 1998), at p. 4, MN 10.
975. See F.P. Sutter, *Das EG-Beihilfenverbot und sein Durchführungsverbot in Steuersachen* (Linde, 2005), at p. 72; also see M. Lang, Tax Rulings and State Aid Law, 60 *British Tax Rev.* 3 (2015), p. 391 (at p. 392); M. Lang, Tax Rulings und Beihilferecht, 24 *IStR* 11 (2015), p. 369 (at p. 370).
976. See W. Schön in L. Hancher/T. Ottervanger/P.J. Slot (eds.), *EU State Aids* (Sweet & Maxwell, 2012), at pp. 331.
977. Judgment *Belgium/Commission*, C-182/03 and C-217/03, EU:C:2006:416, at paras 128-129.

framework within which contractual relations are formed between those undertakings and their employees. The consequences arising from this, in so far as they relate to the difference in the basis for the calculation of social security contributions [...] and to the potential loss of tax revenue because of the low rates of pay [...] are inherent in the system and are not a means of granting a particular advantage to the undertakings concerned."[978]

Moreover, despite the opposite wording of Article 107(1) TFEU, it is not only required that the alleged aid is granted through State resources, but also that it is granted by the Member State, i.e., it has to be imputable to the State.[979] Therefore, it is irrelevant whether the national measure was adopted by the central power, by a state in a federation, by a regional or local authority[980] or by public or private bodies designated or established by the State.[981] From a practical point of view, this criterion is mainly important in order to delimit State aid and Union aid.[982] If, for example, a Member State is obliged by secondary law to implement a certain measure without having any discretion, the resulting effects are not attributable to the Member State.[983] This is not the case, however, if secondary law was implemented in an inaccurate way.[984] Moreover, even if a rule of secondary rule is optional, but upon implementation

978. Judgment in *Sloman Neptun*, C-72/91 and C-73/91, EU:C:1993:97, at para. 21; also see Judgment in *Van Tiggele*, 82/77, EU:C:1978:10, at paras 24-25; Judgment in *Kirsammer-Hack*, C-189/91, EU:C:1993:907, at paras 16-18; Judgment in *Ecotrade*, C-200/97, EU:C:1998:579, at paras 35-36; Judgment in *PreussenElektra*, C-379/98, EU:C:2001:160, at para. 62; critically M.M. Slotboom, State Aid in Community Law: A Broad or a Narrow Definition, 20 *Eur. L. Rev.* (1995), p. 289 (at pp. 295-301).

979. Judgment in *Van der Kooy*, 67, 68 and 70/85, EU:C:1988:38, at para. 28; Judgment in *France/Commission*, C-482/99, EU:C:2002:294, at para. 24; Judgment in *GEMO SA*, C-126/01, EU:C:2003:622, at para. 24; Judgment in *Pearle and others*, C-345/02, EU:C:2004:448, at para. 35; Judgment in *Belgium/Commission*, C-182/03 and C-217/03, EU:C:2006:416, at para. 127; Judgment *Commission/Netherlands*, C-279/08 P, EU:C:2011:551, at para. 103; Judgment in *Doux Élevage and Coopérative agricole UKL-ARREE*, C-677/11, EU:C:2013:348, at para. 27; also see J. Englisch, 22 *EC Tax Rev.* 1 (2013), at pp. 14-15; J. Englisch in A. Rust/C. Micheau (eds.), *State Aid and Tax Law* (Kluwer, 2013), at pp. 78-79.

980. Judgment in *Germany/Commission*, 248/84, EU:C:1985:437, at para. 17; Judgment in *Portugal/Commission*, C-88/03, EU:C:2006:511 at para. 60.

981. Judgment in *Van der Kooy*, 67, 68 and 70/85, EU:C:1988:38, at para. 35; Judgment in *Sloman Neptun*, C-72/91 and C-73/91, EU:C:1993:97, at para. 19; Judgment in *Doux Élevage and Coopérative agricole UKL-ARREE*, C-677/11, EU:C:2013:348, at para. 26.

982. See J. Englisch in H. Schaumburg/J. Englisch (eds.), *Europäisches Steuerrecht* (Dr Otto Schmidt, 2015), at p. 448, at MN 9.39; on the term "Union aid" see, for example, J. Englisch, Zur Bedeutung des gemeinschaftsrechtlichen Gleichheitssatzes im Recht der Gemeinschaftsbeihilfen, 44 *EuR* 4 (2009), p. 488 (at p. 488); M. Haidenhein, § 3 General Principles, in M. Heidenhain (ed.), *European State Aid Law* (C.H. Beck, 2010), p. 13 (at MN 16).

983. Judgment in *Puffer*, C-460/07, EU:C:2009:254, at paras 67-71; also see Judgment in *Bettati/Safety Hi-Tech*, C-341/95, EU:C:1998:353, at para. 74; also see European Commission, Commission Notice on the notion of State Aid as referred to in Article 107(1) of the Treaty on the Functioning of the European Union, *OJ* C 262 (19 Jul. 2016), at para. 44; with regard to VAT also see B. Terra, Value Added Tax and State Aid Law in the EU, 40 *Intertax* 2 (2012), p. 101 (at p. 109), who, however, considers such a measure to be "*justified by the nature or general scheme of the VAT system.*"

984. See J. Englisch in H. Schaumburg/J. Englisch (eds.), *Europäisches Steuerrecht* (Dr Otto Schmidt, 2015), at p. 448, at MN 9.39; also cf. C. Koenig/M. Busch, Gemeinschaftsrechtliche Anforderungen an eine Umsatzsteuerbefreiung für Postdienstleistungen (§ 4 Nr. 11b UStG), 20 *EWS* 12 (2009), p. 510 (at pp. 514-515).

inherently leads to negative effects on competition and intra-EU trade, such effects need not necessarily be attributable to the transposing Member State.[985]

3.2.3 Distortions of Competition and Adverse Effects on Trade Between Member States

The State aid rules only cover aid "*which distorts or threatens to distort competition*" and only "*in so far as it affects trade between Member States.*" According to the ECJ, "*competition is distorted where a measure mitigates the burden imposed on a beneficiary undertaking and thereby strengthens its position as regards competing undertakings.*"[986] It is not necessary that there is a direct competitive relation between the undertakings or the products concerned.[987] In *Heiser*, for example, the Court held that "*aid [...], which is intended to release an undertaking from costs which it would normally have had to bear in its day-to-day management or normal activities, distorts the conditions of competition.*"[988] Moreover, the magnitude of the advantage is irrelevant.[989] Consequently, the requirements for evidence that competition is distorted or is threatened to be distorted are not very demanding.[990] Particularly for tax purposes, it is in general sufficient that a financial advantage is granted to an undertaking in a liberalized economic sector where there is, or could be, competition in order to determine that the aid has a real or potential effect on competition and on trade between Member States.[991]

The wording of Article 107(1) TFEU, however, does not reveal whether the State aid prohibition concerns aid which distorts or threatens to distort competition either on

985. See J. Englisch in H. Schaumburg/J. Englisch (eds.), *Europäisches Steuerrecht* (Dr Otto Schmidt, 2015), at p. 448, at MN 9.39; J. Englisch, 22 *EC Tax Rev.* 1 (2013), at pp. 15-16; J. Englisch in A. Rust/C. Micheau (eds.), *State Aid and Tax Law* (Kluwer, 2013), at pp. 80-81; with a less nuanced view see European Commission, Commission Notice on the notion of State Aid as referred to in Article 107(1) of the Treaty on the Functioning of the European Union, *OJ* C 262 (19 Jul. 2016), at para. 45-46.
986. Judgment in *Belgium/Commission*, C-182/03 and C-217/03, EU:C:2006:416, at para. 131; Order in *Greece/Commission*, C-431/14 P-R, EU:C:2014:2418, at para. 30.
987. See M. Lang, *Die Auswirkungen des gemeinschaftsrechtlichen Beihilferechts auf das Steuerrecht*, 17. ÖJT, Band IV/1 (Manz, 2009), at p. 50; F.P. Sutter, 41 *Eur. Taxn.* 7 (2001), at p. 243; F.P. Sutter in H. Mayer/K. Stöger (eds.), *EUV/AEUV* (Manz, 2014), Article 107 AEUV, MN 48; also cf. Judgment *Exécutif régional wallon/Commission*, 62/87 and 72/87, EU:C:1988:132, at paras 14-15.
988. Judgment in *Heiser*, C-172/03, EU:C:2005:130, at para. 36.
989. See Commission notice on the application of the State aid rules to measures relating to direct business taxation, *OJ* C 384 (10 Dec. 1998), at p. 4.
990. Opinion of AG Kokott in *Comitato "Venezia vuole vivere" and others*, C-71/09 P, C-73/09 P and C-76/09 P, EU:C:2010:771, at para. 162.
991. Judgment in *Spain/Commission*, C-351/98, EU:C:2002:530, at para. 58; Judgment in *Spain/Commission*, C-409/00, EU:C:2003:92, at para. 75; Judgment in *Unicredito Italiano*, C-148/04, EU:C:2005:774, at para. 57; also see European Commission, Commission Notice on the notion of State Aid as referred to in Article 107(1) of the Treaty on the Functioning of the European Union, *OJ* C 262 (19 Jul. 2016), at para. 187.

the national or the European market.[992] The ECJ does apparently not require a distortion of competition at the national level. In *Heiser*, for example, the Court followed, in contrast to the opinion previously expressed by AG Mischo,[993] the view of the Austrian Supreme Administrative Court, according to which "*it is not inconceivable that orthodontists in Austria might be in competition with orthodontists in other EU Member States. [Therefore,] a rule excluding the reduction of deductions inherent in the system of VAT and expressly provided for by Article 20 of the Sixth Directive [...] constitutes an advantage granted using State resources which strengthens the position of the undertakings on which it is conferred compared with other competing undertakings, which cannot make such deductions.*"[994]

The extensive interpretation of the requirement that an aid has to distort or threaten to distort competition at an intra-EU level makes it difficult to distinguish it from the requirement that trade between Member States needs to be affected. Similarly to the Court's understanding of distorted competition,[995] it has regularly been pointed out that intra-European trade "*must be regarded as affected [...], when aid granted by a Member State strengthens the position of an undertaking compared with other undertakings competing in intra-European trade.*"[996] It is thereby not necessary that the privileged undertaking is not directly involved in cross-border trade, because the

992. See F.P. Sutter, *Das EG-Beihilfenverbot und sein Durchführungsverbot in Steuersachen* (Linde, 2005), at p. 130; F.P. Sutter in H. Mayer/K. Stöger (eds.), *EUV/AEUV* (Manz, 2014), Article 107 AEUV, MN 48.
993. Opinion of AG Mischo in *Adria-Wien Pipeline and Wietersdorfer & Peggauer Zementwerke*, C-143/99, EU:C:2001:250, at point 78: "*I cannot accept the argument that a higher tax on undertakings in the tertiary sector creates an inverse advantage for undertakings in the primary and secondary sectors, as those undertakings are not in competition. (Taxing dental surgeons at a higher rate does not provide any advantage for bicycle manufacturers)*"; for a different view see Opinion of AG Darmon in *Sloman Neptun*, C-72/91 and C-73/91, EU:C:1992:130, at point 61: "*Although it is not incorrect, that concept is ambiguous, in my view, so far as aid is concerned since discrimination necessarily implies the existence of undertakings or products in an identical situation, and therefore in competition, which are excluded from the benefit of the contested measure. In this case, aid may, as I see it, be restricted de facto to certain undertakings or to certain products when there are no competing undertakings or products in the Member State in question. Nevertheless, by derogating from the normal application of the system concerned, the aid distorts competition to the detriment of undertakings established in other Member States. It is unnecessary, in my view, to identify 'discrimination' within the Member State in question, which would involve establishing the existence of competing products or undertakings. Once again all that is required, it seems to me, is that the measure should be in the nature of a derogation.*"
994. Judgment in *Heiser*, C-172/03, EU:C:2005:130, at paras 21-22.
995. Judgment in *Belgium/Commission*, C-182/03 and C-217/03, EU:C:2006:416, at para. 131; Order in *Greece/Commission*, C-431/14 P-R, EU:C:2014:2418, at para. 30.
996. Judgment in *Trapeza Eurobank Ergasias*, C-690/13, EU:C:2015:235, at para. 24; also see Judgment in *Philip Morris*, 730/79, EU:C:1980:209, at para. 11; Judgment in *Italy/Commission*, C-66/02, EU:C:2005:768, at para. 115; Judgment in *Unicredito Italiano*, C-148/04, EU:C:2005:774, at para. 56; Judgment in *Cassa di Risparmio di Firenze*, C-222/04, EU:C:2006:8, at para. 141; Judgment in *Commission/Italy and Wam*, C-494/06 P, EU:C:2009:272, at para. 52; Judgment in *Paint Graphos and others*, C-78/08, EU:C:2011:550, at para. 79; Judgment in *Libert and others*, C-197/11, EU:C:2013:288, at para. 77; Judgment in *Eventech*, C-518/13, EU:C:2015:9, at para. 66; Judgment in *OTP Bank*, C-672/13, EU:C:2015:185, at para. 55; Judgment in Trapeza Eurobank Ergasias, C-690/13, EU:C:2015:235, at para. 24; also cf. Judgment in *France/Commission*, 259/85, EU:C:1987:478, at para. 24.

advantageous treatment may impede foreign competitors from entering the domestic market.[997] Moreover, there is no threshold or percentage below which the Court may consider that trade between Member States is not affected. The relatively small amount of aid or the relatively small size of the receiving undertaking does not as such exclude the possibility that trade between Member States might be affected.[998] Therefore, the requirements placed on the proof that trade between Member States is affected are again very modest.[999] In certain cases, it is even sufficient that the European Commission sets out "*the very circumstances in which the aid is granted [in order to] show that the aid is capable of affecting trade between Member States.*"[1000]

Overall, one cannot avoid getting the impression that the ECJ's approaches with regard to the requirements of distorted competition and affected intra-European trade are to a large extent similar.[1001] In fact, the ECJ usually does not address those requirements separately.[1002] For this reason, the EGC has probably held that both requirements are "*as a general rule inextricably linked.*"[1003] Since both requirements are, moreover, applied very generously by the European Commission as well as by the CJEU, parts of the literature even consider them to be virtually irrelevant[1004] or at least of ancillary importance.[1005]

---

997. Judgment in *France/Commission*, 102/87, EU:C:1988:391, at para. 19; Judgment in *Italy/Commission*, C-305/89, EU:C:1991:142, at para. 26; Judgment in *Spain/Commission*, C-278/92, C-279/92 and C-280/92, EU:C:1994:325, at para. 40; Judgment in *Altmark Trans and Regierungspräsidium Magdeburg*, C-280/00, EU:C:2003:415, at para. 78.
998. Judgment in *France/Commission*, 259/85, EU:C:1987:478, at para. 24; Judgment in *Belgium/Commission*, 142/87, EU:C:1990:125, at para. 43; Judgment in *Spain/Commission*, C-278/92, C-279/92 and C-280/92, EU:C:1994:325, at para. 42; Judgment in *Altmark Trans and Regierungspräsidium Magdeburg*, C-280/00, EU:C:2003:415, at para. 81.
999. See M. Heidenhain, § 4 The Concept of State Aid, in M. Heidenhain (ed.), *European State Aid Law* (C.H. Beck, 2010), p. 22 (at MN 80); F.P. Sutter, *Das EG-Beihilfenverbot und sein Durchführungsverbot in Steuersachen* (Linde, 2005), at p. 138.
1000. Judgment in *Netherlands and Leeuwarder Papierwarenfabriek/Commission*, 296 and 318/82, EU:C:1985:113, at para. 24; Judgment in *Germany and others/Commission*, C-329/93, C-62/95 and C-63/95, at para. 52.
1001. See C. Quigley, *European State Aid Law and Policy, Third Edition* (Hart Publishing, 2015),11 at pp. 82-83.
1002. Judgment in *Belgium/Commission*, 234/84, EU:C:1986:302, at para. 19; Judgment *Exécutif régional wallon/Commission*, 62/87 and 72/87, EU:C:1988:132, at para. 18; Judgment in *Italy/Commission*, 303/88, EU:C:1991:136, at para. 26; Judgment in *Italy/Commission*, C-305/89, EU:C:1991:142, at para. 26.
1003. Judgment in *Regione Autonoma Friuli-Venezia Giulia/Commission*, T-288/97, EU:T:2001:115, at para. 41; Judgment in *Alzetta and others/Commission*, T-298/97, T-312/97, T-313/97, T-315/97, T-600/97 to T-607/97, T-1/98, T-3/98 to T-23/98, EU:T:2000:151, at para. 81; Judgment in *EDF/Commission*, T-156/04, EU:T:2009:505, at para. 135; Judgment in *Westfälisch-Lippischer Sparkassen- und Giroverband/Commission*, T-457/09, EU:T:2014:683, at para. 249; Judgment in *Hellenic Republic/Commission*, T-233/11, EU:T:2015:948, at para. 165; Judgment in *Aughinish Alumnia/Commission*, T-50/06 and T-69/06, EU:T:2016:227, at para. 113; also see C. Nowak, Die Entwicklung des EG-Beihilfenkontrollrechts in den Jahren 2001 und 2002, 14 *EuZW* 13 (2003), p. 389 (at p. 396).
1004. M. Lang, *Die Auswirkungen des gemeinschaftsrechtlichen Beihilferechts auf das Steuerrecht*, 17. ÖJT, Band IV/1 (Manz, 2009), at p. 50.
1005. J. Englisch in H. Schaumburg/J. Englisch (eds.), *Europäisches Steuerrecht* (Dr Otto Schmidt, 2015), at p. 449, at MN 9.41.

3.3 Comparability

3.3.1 *Different Treatment*

The major dispute with regard to potential fiscal aid revolves around the identification of a selective advantage as required by Article 107(1) TFEU, which only applies if *certain* undertakings or the production of *certain* goods are *favoured*. The term "*favouring*" indicates that there needs to be a preferential treatment of a group of undertakings or products. To determine whether this is the case calls for a comparison, because in general "*no advantage can be identified without a comparator first being found as a benchmark for treatment.*"[1006] According to the ECJ, a national measure allegedly causing preferential tax treatment is covered by Article 107(1) TFEU if the budgetary restraint of the state to levy taxes "*mitigate[s] the charges which are normally included in the budget of an undertaking.*"[1007] Thus, "*the very existence of an advantage may be established only when compared with 'normal' taxation.*"[1008] Since there is no autonomous general description of a "normal" tax system,[1009] a tax measure can only be identified as State aid if it causes a deviation from the common tax regime that has

1006. M. Ross, State aid and National Courts: Definitions and Other Problems – A Case of Premature Emancipation?, 37 *Common Market L. Rev.* 2 (2000), p. 401 (at p. 407).

1007. Judgment in *De gezamenlijke Steenkolenmijnen in Limburg*, 30/59, EU:C:1961:2, at p. 19; Judgment in *Banco Exterior de España*, C-387/92, EU:C:1994:100, at para. 13; cf. Judgment in *Ecotrade*, C-200/97, EU:C:1998:579, at para. 34; Judgment in *Italy/Commission*, C-6/97, EU:C:1999:251, at para. 15; Judgment in *Piaggio*, C-295/97, EU:C:1999:313, at para. 34; Judgment in *Commission/Portugal*, C-404/97, EU:C:2000:345, at para. 44; Judgment in *Germany/Commission*, C-156/98, EU:C:2000:367, at para. 25; Judgment in *Banks*, C-390/98, EU:C:2001:456, at para. 30; Judgment in *Adria-Wien Pipeline and Wietersdorfer & Peggauer Zementwerke*, C-143/99, EU:C:2001:598, at para. 38; Judgment in *Italy/Commission*, C-310/99, EU:C:2002:143, at para. 51; Judgment in *Ferring*, C-53/00, EU:C:2001:627, at para. 15; Judgment in *Belgium/Commission*, C-5/01, EU:C:2002:754, at para. 32; Judgment in *Freskot*, C-355/00, EU:C:2003:298, at para. 83; Judgment in *SIM 2 Multimedia v. Commission*, C-399/00, EU:C:2003:252, at para. 35; Judgment in Spain/Commission, C-501/00, EU:C:2004:438, at para. 90; Judgment in *Chronopost/Ufex and others*, C-83/01 P, EU:C:2003:388, at para. 65; Judgment in *GIL Insurance and others*, C-308/01, EU:C:2004:252, at para. 69; Judgment in *Heiser*, C-172/03, EU:C:2005:130, at para. 36; Judgment in *Cassa di Risparmio di Firenze*, C-222/04, EU:C:2006:8, at para. 131; Judgment in *Enirisorse*, C-237/04, EU:C:2006:197, at para. 42; Judgment in *Air Liquide Industries Belgium*, C-393/04, EU:C:2006:403, at para. 29; Judgment in *Paint Graphos*, C-78/08, EU:C:2011:550, at para. 45; Judgment in *Presidente del Consiglio dei Ministri*, C-169/08, EU:C:2009:709, at para. 56; Judgment in *Commission and Spain/Government of Gibraltar and United Kingdom*, C-106/09 P and C-107/09 P, EU:C:2011:732, at para. 71; Judgment in *Seydaland Vereinigte Agrarbetriebe*, C-239/09, EU:C:2010:778, at para. 30; Judgment in *France Télécom/Commission*, C-81/10 P, EU:C:2011:811, at para. 16; Judgment in *Frucona Košice/Commission*, C-73/11 P, EU:C:2013:32, at para. 69; Judgment in *France/Commission*, C-559/12 P, EU:C:2014:217, at para. 94; Judgment in *Eventech*, C-518/13, EU:C:2015:9, at para. 33; Judgment in OTP Bank, C-672/13, EU:C:2015:185, at para. 40; Judgment in *Kernkraftwerke Lippe-Ems*, C-5/14, EU:C:2015:354, at para. 71; Judgment in *BVVG*, C-39/14, EU:C:2015:470, at para. 26.

1008. Judgment in *Portugal/Commission*, C-88/03, EU:C:2006:511, at para. 56; Judgment in *Commission and Spain/Government of Gibraltar and United Kingdom*, C-106/09 P and C-107/09 P, EU:C:2011:732, at para. 90;

1009. See W. Schön, 36 *Common Market L. Rev.* 5 (1999), at p. 932; W. Schön in L. Hancher/T. Ottervanger/P.J. Slot (eds.), *EU State Aids* (Sweet & Maxwell, 2012), at p. 339.

been established by the very same Member State.[1010] Therefore, "*it is necessary to begin by identifying and examining the common or 'normal' regime applicable in the Member State concerned [,] [...] [i]n order to classify a domestic tax measure as 'selective'.*"[1011]

It is by no means obvious how to identify the general rule and the exception.[1012] It is all the more deplorable that "*neither the Commission nor the Court of Justice has succeeded in determining precisely what is covered by the term 'derogation from the norm' or what constitutes the 'norm' or 'a general system'.*"[1013] Partly, it is argued that a tax measure deviates from the common tax regime if the enterprises covered by a rule outnumber the enterprises which are excluded from its scope.[1014] AG Jääskinen, for example, was in doubt about whether the planned corporate tax reform of Gibraltar constituted State aid, because, "*as far as its economic effects are concerned, the Gibraltar regime appears rather to be designed to grant 'selective disadvantages' since*

1010. See W. Schön, 36 *Common Market L. Rev.* 5 (1999), at pp. 923-924; W. Schön in L. Hancher/T. Ottervanger/P.J. Slot (eds.), *EU State Aids* (Sweet & Maxwell, 2012), at p. 339; R. Szudoczky, *The Sources of EU law and Their Relationships: Lessons for the Field of Taxation* (IBFD, 2014), at p. 494; C. Quigley, *European State Aid Law and Policy, Third Edition* (Hart Publishing, 2015), at p. 9; also see Opinion of AG Jääskinen in *Commission and Spain/Government of Gibraltar and United Kingdom*, C-106/09 P and C-107/09 P, EU:C:2011:215, at point 175 ("*Inasmuch as European Union law does not have any default tax system, the reference framework must remain the national reference framework*"); also cf. Judgment in *Spain/ Commission*, C-73/03, EU:C:2004:711, at para. 28.

1011. Judgment in *Paint Graphos and others*, C-78/08 to C-80/08, EU:C:2011:550, at para. 49; Judgment in *P*, C-6/12, EU:C:2013:525, at para. 19; Judgment in *Ministerio de Defensa and Navantia*, C-522/13, EU:C:2014:2262, at para. 35.

1012. See W. Schön, 36 *Common Market L. Rev.* 5 (1999), at p. 930; W. Schön in L. Hancher/T. Ottervanger/P.J. Slot (eds.), *EU State Aids* (Sweet & Maxwell, 2012), at p. 339; R. Szudoczky, *The Sources of EU law and Their Relationships: Lessons for the Field of Taxation* (IBFD, 2014), at p. 495; also see Opinion of AG Jääskinen in *Commission and Spain / Government of Gibraltar and United Kingdom*, C-106/09 P and C-107/09 P, EU:C:2011:215, at point 184; also cf. M. Lang, 24 *ÖStZ* 24 (2011), at p. 596; M. Lang, 11 *Eur. St. Aid L. Q.* 2 (2012), at pp. 418-419; M. Lang in P. Pistone (ed.), *Legal Remedies in European Tax Law* (IBFD, 2009), at pp. 269-270; M. Lang, 27 *ÖStZ* 11 (2014), at pp. 278-280; M. Lang, Europäisches Beihilfenrecht und Besteuerung – am Beispiel des § 8c KStG, in J. Lüdicke (ed.), *Praxis und Zukunft des Internationalen Steuerrechts* (Dr Otto Schmidt, 2012), p. 85 (at pp. 93-96); M. Lang in I. Richelle/W. Schön/E. Traversa (eds.), *Allocating Taxing Powers Within the European Union* (Springer, 2013), at p. 34.

1013. Opinion of AG Jääskinen in *Commission and Spain / Government of Gibraltar and United Kingdom*, C-106/09 P and C-107/09 P, EU:C:2011:215, at point 184; also see J. Englisch in H. Schaumburg/J. Englisch (eds.), *Europäisches Steuerrecht* (Dr Otto Schmidt, 2015), at p. 432, at MN 9.22 and at p. 438, at MN 9.28; R. Ismer/S. Piotrowski, The Selectivity of Tax Measures: A Tale of Two Consistencies, 43 *Intertax* 10 (2015), p. 559 (at p. 561); also cf. A. Bartosch, Is There a Need for a Rule of Reason in European State Aid Law? Or How to Arrive at a Coherent Concept of Material Selectivity?, 47 *Common Market L. Rev.* 3 (2010), p. 729 (at pp. 741-742); A. Biondi, State Aid is Falling Down, Falling Down: An Analysis of the Case Law on the Notion of Aid, 50 *Common Market L. Rev.* 6 (2013), p. 1719 (at p. 1719: "*the EU Courts are showing signs of mental fatigue in determining the criteria that need to be fulfilled in order for a measure to be classified as aid. The case law from Luxembourg is thus extremely convoluted and complex.*").

1014. See R. Luja, Group Taxation, Sectoral Tax Benefits and De Facto Selectivity in State Aid Review, 8 *Eur. St. Aid L. Q.* 4 (2009), p. 473 (at p. 483); also see R. Luja, Revisiting the Balance Between Aid, Selectivity and Selective Aid in Respect of Taxes and Special Levies, 9 *Eur. St. Aid L. Q.* 1 (2010) p. 161 (at pp. 161 et seq.).

less than 1% of companies are actually taxed."[1015] However, it has to be kept in mind that the wording of Article 107(1) TFEU does not require that the majority of undertakings or productions of goods is treated less beneficially. It rather applies if a national measure favours *certain* undertakings or the production of *certain* goods. Moreover, from a teleological perspective, competition might also be distorted if the majority is favoured, while only a minority is treated disadvantageously. In addition, given the Member States' obligation to notify the European Commission about any plans to grant or alter aid, it would be necessary to seriously predict in advance how many persons or real life situations will be covered under a certain rule.[1016] From a practical perspective, this seems hardly possible. Even if it was, the number of taxpayers or real life situations covered by a rule may change over time. Hence, what may be the "normal" rule at one point in time could be the "exception" at another point in time.[1017] It is, therefore, convincing that the ECJ remained unimpressed that only 1% of corporate taxpayers would have been affected by the planned corporate tax reform in Gibraltar.[1018]

Another way to identify the general rule and the exception would be to look at the wording of the law. If it is explicitly stated that rule A should apply, unless certain conditions are fulfilled, which would trigger rule B, it could be argued that rule B is an exception to rule A, because it only applies in certain cases. However, the same result could be reached by phrasing the law in a different way so that rule B should apply, unless certain conditions are fulfilled, which would trigger rule A. This can be illustrated by the following example:[1019] "*The corporate tax rate is 30 % (rule A). If a corporation has fewer than 10 employees the rate is reduced to 20 % (rule B).*" The same result can be reached by phrasing the law in another way: "*The corporate tax rate is 20 % (rule B). If a corporation has 10 or more employees the rate is increased to 30 % (rate A).*" If the wording of the law was decisive, it would only be a matter of legal technique whether rule A or rule B is considered to be the general rule or the exception.[1020] Such

1015. Opinion of AG Jääskinen in *Commission and Spain/Government of Gibraltar and United Kingdom*, C-106/09 P and C-107/09 P, EU:C:2011:215, at point 239.
1016. See M. Lang in P. Pistone (ed.), *Legal Remedies in European Tax Law* (IBFD, 2009), at p. 269; M. Lang, *Die Auswirkungen des gemeinschaftsrechtlichen Beihilferechts auf das Steuerrecht*, 17. ÖJT, Band IV/1 (Manz, 2009), at p. 25; M. Lang, 24 *ÖStZ* 24 (2011), at p. 596; M. Lang, 19 *IStR* 15 (2010), at p. 577 (FN 69); M. Lang in J. Lüdicke (ed.), *Praxis und Zukunft des Internationalen Steuerrechts* (Dr Otto Schmidt, 2012), at p. 96; M. Lang, 11 *Eur. St. Aid L. Q.* 2 (2012), at p. 419; M. Lang in I. Richelle/W. Schön/E. Traversa (eds.), *Allocating Taxing Powers Within the European Union* (Springer, 2013), at p. 33; R. Szudoczky, *The Sources of EU law and Their Relationships: Lessons for the Field of Taxation* (IBFD, 2014), at p. 497.
1017. See M. Lang, 60 *British Tax Rev.* 3 (2015), at p. 393; M. Lang, 24 *IStR* 11 (2015), at pp. 370-371; M. Lang in P. Pistone (ed.), *Legal Remedies in European Tax Law* (IBFD, 2009), at p. 269.
1018. See M. Lang, 24 *ÖStZ* 24 (2011), at p. 596.
1019. See M. Lang in P. Pistone (ed.), *Legal Remedies in European Tax Law* (IBFD, 2009), at p. 269.
1020. See M. Lang, *Die Auswirkungen des gemeinschaftsrechtlichen Beihilferechts auf das Steuerrecht*, 17. ÖJT, Band IV/1 (Manz, 2009), at p. 25; M. Lang, 19 *IStR* 15 (2010), at p. 576; M. Lang in P. Pistone (ed.), *Legal Remedies in European Tax Law* (IBFD, 2009), at p. 269; M. Lang, 24 *ÖStZ* 24 (2011), at p. 596; M. Lang, 11 *Eur. St. Aid L. Q.* 2 (2012), at p. 419; M. Lang in J. Lüdicke (ed.), *Praxis und Zukunft des Internationalen Steuerrechts* (Dr Otto Schmidt, 2012), at p. 96; M. Lang, 60 *British Tax Rev.* 3 (2015), at p. 393; M. Lang, 24 *IStR* 11 (2015), at p. 370; F.P. Sutter, Beihilfen im materiellen Steuerrecht – Steuergesetze und Verwaltungshandeln der

an approach would not be in line with Article 107(1) TFEU, which "*defines State interventions on the basis of their effects, and thus independently of the techniques used.*"[1021]

Hence, there has to be another indicator to identify unlawful fiscal aid. According to the ECJ's more recent jurisprudence, the State aid analysis is not primarily about whether a national measure constitutes an exception to a general rule,[1022] but whether it causes a different treatment of economic operators that are in a comparable factual and legal situation.[1023] Thus, a derogation from the reference framework can be shown "*by demonstrating that the measure [...] differentiates between economic operators who [...] are in a comparable factual and legal situation.*"[1024] This does not make the analysis much easier, because it remains unclear which attributes are to be considered in order to determine whether comparability exists or not. No two situations are entirely alike or entirely different.[1025] With regard to some aspects, two situations may be alike, although they are not with regard to others.[1026] Which aspects are decisive is contingent upon the context and to a certain extent also a matter of the merits.[1027]

Some scholars argue that the yardstick that has to be used for the comparison has to be inferred from Article 107 TFEU. Since this provision prohibits unequal treatment that may cause distortions of competition, the intensity of competitive relationships between undertakings or the production of certain goods is considered to be pivotal when determining comparability.[1028] This approach is subject to criticism. It is argued that it would ignore the cross-border dimension of the State aid rules in tax matters.[1029]

Steuerbehörden im Spannungsfeld zum EG-Beihilfenverbot, in Studiengesellschaft für Wirtschaft und Recht (ed.), *Beihilfenrecht* (Linde, 2004), p. 37 (at pp. 42-43).

1021. Judgment in *British Aggregates/Commission*, C-487/06 P, EU:C:2008:757, at para. 89; Judgment *Commission/Netherlands*, C-279/08 P, EU:C:2011:551, at para. 51; Judgment in *Commission and Spain/Government of Gibraltar and United Kingdom*, C-106/09 P and C-107/09 P, EU:C:2011:732, at para. 87; Judgment *Kernkraftwerke Lippe-Ems*, C-5/14, EU:C:2015:354, at para. 75; Judgment in *Commission/MOL*, C-15/14 P, EU:C:2015:362, at para. 86.
1022. See R. Lyal, Transfer Pricing Rules and State Aid, 38 *Fordham Intl. L. J.* 4 (2015), p. 1017 (at p. 1035): "*The question, what is the rule and what the exception is in reality of no importance.*"
1023. Opinion of AG Kokott in *Finanzamt Linz*, C-66/14, EU:C:2015:242, at point 88.
1024. Judgment in *Paint Graphos and others*, C-78/08 to C-80/08, EU:C:2011:550, at para. 49; Judgment in *P*, C-6/12, EU:C:2013:525, at para. 19; Judgment in *Ministerio de Defensa and Navantia*, C-522/13, EU:C:2014:2262, at para. 35.
1025. See, for example, P. Westen, 95 *Harv. L. Rev.* 3 (1982), at p. 544.
1026. See H. Kelsen, *Reine Rechtslehre*² (Deuticke, 1960), at p. 256.
1027. See M. Pöschl, *Gleichheit vor dem Gesetz* (Springer, 2008), at p. 179; also see M. Lang, *Die Auswirkungen des gemeinschaftsrechtlichen Beihilferechts auf das Steuerrecht*, 17. ÖJT, Band IV/1 (Manz, 2009), at p. 26.
1028. See M. Lang in P. Pistone (ed.), *Legal Remedies in European Tax Law* (IBFD, 2009), at p. 270; M. Lang, *Die Auswirkungen des gemeinschaftsrechtlichen Beihilferechts auf das Steuerrecht*, 17. ÖJT, Band IV/1 (Manz, 2009), at p. 26; M. Lang in ÖJT (ed.), *Die Auswirkungen des gemeinschaftsrechtlichen Beihilferechts auf das Steuerrecht*, Referate und Diskussionsbeiträge, Band IV/2 (Manz, 2010), at p. 69; M. Lang, 24 *ÖStZ* 24 (2011), at p. 598; M. Lang, 19 *IStR* 15 (2010), at p. 578; M. Lang in J. Lüdicke (ed.), *Praxis und Zukunft des Internationalen Steuerrechts* (Dr Otto Schmidt, 2012), at p. 99; M. Lang, 11 *Eur. St. Aid L. Q.* 2 (2012), at p. 420; M. Lang in I. Richelle/W. Schön/E. Traversa (eds.), *Allocating Taxing Powers Within the European Union* (Springer, 2013), at p. 36; also see C. Micheau, 17 *EC Tax Rev.* 6 (2008), at p. 283.
1029. See J. Englisch in H. Schaumburg/J. Englisch (eds.), *Europäisches Steuerrecht* (Dr Otto Schmidt, 2015), at pp. 443-444, at MN 9.32.

If, for example, undertakings supplying services or engaging in trade were subjected in their residence state to an energy tax, whereas undertakings that produce goods were exempt, Article 107(1) TFEU would not apply if there was a lack of a competitive relationship between those two business sectors.[1030] Whether the tax exemption has a distorting effect on cross-border competition or negatively affects trade between Member States in the sense of Article 107(1) TFEU would be irrelevant, particularly because non-resident undertakings would not be affected by the tax anyway. Such a result is considered to be unconvincing, especially if the legislator has actually intended to impact the competitive relations between domestic and foreign undertakings involved in production.[1031] But how would a tax that affects neither domestic nor foreign undertakings involved in production distort or threaten to distort competition among them? If it did not, the special charge would not constitute State aid, because it would not distort competition, whether between different sectors or between domestic and foreign undertakings of the same sector. In contrast, would cross-border competition instead not be distorted if domestic production undertakings are subject to an energy tax, whereas foreign undertakings involved in production do not suffer this burden, because their residence state does not levy an energy tax? If yes, does Article 107(1) TFEU also prohibit the Member States from introducing taxes that are not levied in other Member States? To the extent that the tax concerned falls within the competence of the Member States, such a prohibition would not be convincing.[1032] According to the ECJ, the Member States must rather exercise their competence "*consistently with Community law [...] and therefore avoid taking, in that context, any measures capable of constituting State aid incompatible with the common market.*"[1033] An energy tax might hence constitute State aid if domestic undertakings are taxed whereas foreign competitors with domestic energy-producing facilities are not subject to the very same tax.

Still, if the competitive relationship between undertakings or the production of goods were exclusively decisive, almost all tax measures would need to be justified. Sole proprietors are, for example, competing with corporations. Therefore, the fact that corporations are subject to a flat tax rate, whereas individuals are subject to a progressive tax rate would require a justification in order not to constitute State aid. As such a result is quite far-reaching,[1034] it is not surprising that opponents of this

1030. Nikolaus Zorn mentions another example to illustrate that a comparability analysis based on the competitive relationship is not convincing: If there was only one car-producing company in a Member State, a tax benefit for the car-producing sector would not constitute State aid, because there is no competitor in the domestic market (N. Zorn in ÖJT [ed.], *Die Auswirkungen des gemeinschaftsrechtlichen Beihilferechts auf das Steuerrecht*, Referate und Diskussionsbeiträge, Band IV/2 [Manz, 2010], at p. 71). However, this conclusion is based on the assumption that the car-producing sector is not in a competitive relationship with any other sector. Whether this is actually true, is questionable.

1031. See W. Schön in ÖJT (ed.), *Die Auswirkungen des gemeinschaftsrechtlichen Beihilferechts auf das Steuerrecht*, Referate und Diskussionsbeiträge, Band IV/2 (Manz, 2010), at p. 31.

1032. See J. Hey, EU-Beihilfen und Steuervergünstigungen – Gemeinsamkeiten und Unterschiede, 92 *StuW* 4 (2015), p. 331 (at p. 335).

1033. Judgment in *Spain/Commission*, C-501/00, EU:C:2004:438, at para. 123.

1034. Cf. J. Hey, 92 *StuW* 4 (2015), at p. 335; for a similar discussion with regard to the fundamental freedoms' impact on direct taxation see L. Hinnekens, 11 *EC Tax Rev.* 3 (2002), at p. 117

approach argue for an alternative solution. To this end, based on the ECJ's jurisprudence,[1035] the fundamental principles underlying the respective tax are deemed to be decisive for the comparability analysis.[1036] Regulatory taxes, for example, are meant to further non-fiscal objectives. When establishing the benchmark for the State aid analysis, hence, the underlying principles to achieve those objectives have to be considered.[1037] With regard to environmental taxes, for example, this might be the polluter pays principle.[1038] Thus, if a Member State introduces an energy tax on natural gas and electricity due to ecological considerations, granting undertakings manufacturing goods – in contrast to undertakings supplying services – a rebate of energy taxes in order to preserve the competitiveness of the manufacturing sector has to be considered to be a derogation from the general system,[1039] because "*[e]nergy*

("*Saying that there are no intra-Community tax borders or that there should not be any under the Single Market concept, is going a bridge too far.*"); also cf. P. Farmer, 7 *EC Tax Rev.* 1 (1998), at p. 27; R. Lyal, 12 *EC Tax Rev.* 2 (2003), at p. 74; Opinion of AG Mischo in *Pfeiffer*, C-255/97, EU:C:1998:338, at point 58 ("*One must not arrive at a situation where Member States are required to justify as 'imperative requirements' all kinds of provisions of their legislation, for instance rates of corporate taxation or their rates of VAT, which are higher than elsewhere, the necessity to use the national language in relationships with administrative authorities or the principle that a registered trademark or a business name used previously has a priority, whenever an operator claims that such a provision makes its right of establishment less attractive.*"); also cf. Judgment in *Mobistar and Belgacom Mobile*, C-544/03 and C-545/03, EU:C:2005:518, at paras 27-35.

1035. The ECJ sometimes assesses the comparability on the basis of the "*objective assigned to the tax system of the Member State.*" See Judgment in *Heiser*, C-172/03, EU:C:2005:130, at para. 40; Judgment in *Portugal/Commission*, C-88/03, EU:C:2006:511, at para. 54; Judgment in *Paint Graphos and others*, C-78/08 to C-80/08, EU:C:2011:550, at para. 49; Judgment in *P.*, C-6/12, EU:C:2013:525, at para. 19; also see Judgment in *GIL Insurance and others*, C-308/01, EU:C:2004:252, at para. 68; Judgment in *Ministerio de Defensa and Navantia*, C-522/13, EU:C:2014:2262, at para. 35.

1036. See K. Drüen, Die Sanierungsklausel des § 8c KStG als europarechtswidrige Beihilfe, 49 *DStR* 7 (2011), p. 289 (at p. 291); J. Englisch in H. Schaumburg/J. Englisch (eds.), *Europäisches Steuerrecht* (Dr Otto Schmidt, 2015), at p. 425, at MN 9.17; J. Englisch, 22 *EC Tax Rev.* 1 (2013), at p. 11; J. Englisch in A. Rust/C. Micheau (eds.), *State Aid and Tax Law* (Kluwer, 2013), at p. 72.

1037. See J. Englisch, 22 *EC Tax Rev.* 1 (2013), at p. 11 (FN 19); J. Englisch in A. Rust/C. Micheau (eds.), *State Aid and Tax Law* (Kluwer, 2013), at p. 73 (FN 19); also cf. H. Drabbe, The Test of Selectivity in State Aid Litigation: The Relevance of Drawing Internal and External Comparisons to Identify the Reference Framework, in A. Rust/C. Micheau (eds.), *State Aid and Tax Law* (Kluwer, 2013), p. 87 (at pp. 101-102: "*[O]ne should draw a distinction between, on the one hand, the objectives attributed to a particular tax regime and which are extrinsic to it (i.e., social policy, environmental, international competitiveness objectives) and, on the other hand, the mechanisms inherent in the tax system itself and which are necessary for the achievement of such objectives (e.g, the progressive nature of taxation. Only the latter can be taken into consideration for the purpose of this justification.*"); P. Rossi-Maccanico, 3 *Eur. St. Aid L. Q.* 2 (2004), at p. 243 ("*It seems that comparison of the situations in the light of the objective pursued by a measure shows that there is no express limitation to the internal objectives of the tax system. The external objectives have been consistently taken as reference by the Court8 to expand the notion of inherent objective of a tax system to include external objectives that are absorbed by the tax system as guiding principles, even when they are not necessary to the existence of a tax system.*").

1038. See W. Schön in L. Hancher/T. Ottervanger/P.J. Slot (eds.), *EU State Aids* (Sweet & Maxwell, 2012), at p. 345 (FN 161).

1039. See W. Schön in L. Hancher/T. Ottervanger/P.J. Slot (eds.), *EU State Aids* (Sweet & Maxwell, 2012), at p. 345.

consumption by each of those sectors is equally damaging to the environment."[1040] Direct taxes within the EU, on the other hand, are considered to be generally based on the taxpayers' ability to pay.[1041] With regard to direct taxation, the benchmark is hence deemed to result from all direct tax measures implementing this principle.[1042] Those principles seem to coincide with what the ECJ calls "*the nature [and/or] general scheme of the [tax] system,*"[1043] "*the basic or guiding principles of [the] tax system*"[1044] or "*the logic of the tax system.*"[1045,1046] Against this background, the alternative approach suggested in the literature can be described – in the words of AG Léger – in the

1040. Judgment in *Adria-Wien Pipeline and Wietersdorfer & Peggauer Zementwerke*, C-143/99, EU:C:2001:598, at para. 52.
1041. See K.A. Frick, *Einkommensteuerliche Steuervergünstigungen und Beihilfeverbot nach dem EG-Vertrag* (Pro Universitate Verlag, 1994), at p. 39; K. Tipke, Über "richtiges Steuerrecht," 65 *StuW* 3 (1988), p. 262 (at pp. 270-271); J. Englisch, Ability to Pay, in C. Brokelind (ed.), *Principles of Law: Function, Status and Impact in EU Tax Law* (IBFD, 2014), p. 439 (at p. 453: "*Altogether, there is a strong but certainly not uniform tendency among Member States of the European Union to consider ability to pay as a constitutionally relevant standard of equality of taxation.*"); J. Hey in K. Tipke/J. Lang, *Steuerrecht*[22] (Dr Otto Schmidt, 2015), at § 3 paras 40-41.
1042. See J. Englisch in C. Brokelind (ed.), *Principles of Law: Function, Status and Impact in EU Tax Law* (IBFD, 2014), at pp. 459-460; W. Schön, 36 *Common Market L. Rev.* 5 (1999), at p. 926; W. Schön in ÖJT (ed.), *Die Auswirkungen des gemeinschaftsrechtlichen Beihilferechts auf das Steuerrecht*, Referate und Diskussionsbeiträge, Band IV/2 (Manz, 2010), at p. 33; W. Schön in L. Hancher/T. Ottervanger/P.J. Slot (eds.), *EU State Aids* (Sweet & Maxwell, 2012), at pp. 342-343; R. Szudoczky, *The Sources of EU law and Their Relationships: Lessons for the Field of Taxation* (IBFD, 2014), at pp. 506-507; also cf. K. Drüen, 49 *DStR* 7 (2011), at p. 291; O. Ehrmann, Beihilferechtliche Zulässigkeit des § 8c Abs. 1a KStG, 49 *DStR* 1 (2011), p. 5 (at pp. 7-8).
1043. Judgment in *Italy/Commission*, 173/73, EU:C:1974:71, at para. 15; Judgment in *Belgium/Commission*, C-75/97, EU:C:1999:311, at para. 33; Judgment in *France/Commission*, C-251/97, EU:C:1999:480, at para. 36; Judgment in *Italy/Commission*, C-310/99, EU:C:2002:143, at para. 51; Judgment in *Banks*, C-390/98, EU:C:2001:456, at para. 33; Judgment in *Adria-Wien Pipeline and Wietersdorfer & Peggauer Zementwerke*, C-143/99, EU:C:2001:598, at para. 42; Judgment in *Spain/Commission*, C-351/98, EU:C:2002:530, at para. 42; Judgment in *GIL Insurance and others*, C-308/01, EU:C:2004:252, at para. 72; Judgment in *Freskot*, C-355/00, EU:C:2003:298, at para. 86; Judgment *Netherlands/Commission*, C-159/01, EU:C:2004:246, at para. 42; Judgment in *Heiser*, C-172/03, EU:C:2005:130, at para. 43; Judgment in *AEM*, C-128/03 and C-129/03, EU:C:2005:224, at para. 39; Judgment in *British Aggregates/Commission*, C-487/06 P, EU:C:2008:757, at para. 129; Judgment in *Paint Graphos and others*, C-78/08 to C-80/08, EU:C:2011:550, at para. 76; Judgment *Commission/Netherlands*, C-279/08 P, EU:C:2011:551, at para. 62; Judgment in *Commission and Spain/Government of Gibraltar and United Kingdom*, C-106/09 P and C-107/09 P, EU:C:2011:732, at para. 146; Judgment in *BNP Paribas and BNL/Commission*, C-452/10 P, EU:C:2012:366, at para. 101; Judgment in *P*, C-6/12, EU:C:2013:525, at para. 22; Judgment in *Commission/MOL*, C-15/14 P, EU:C:2015:362, at para. 61.
1044. Judgment in *Portugal/Commission*, C-88/03, EU:C:2006:511, at para. 81; Judgment in *Paint Graphos and others*, C-78/08 to C-80/08, EU:C:2011:550, at para. 65 and para. 69; Judgment in *P*, C-6/12, EU:C:2013:525, at para. 22; Judgment in *Ministerio de Defensa and Navantia*, C-522/13, EU:C:2014:2262, at para. 43.
1045. Judgment in *Spain/Commission*, C-501/00, EU:C:2004:438, at para. 122; also see Judgment in *BNP Paribas and BNL/Commission*, C-452/10 P, EU:C:2012:366, at paras 137-138.
1046. See J. Englisch in H. Schaumburg/J. Englisch (eds.), *Europäisches Steuerrecht* (Dr Otto Schmidt, 2015), at p. 444, at MN 9.33.

following way: "*[A] measure constitutes a derogation where it does not apply to all the undertakings which, in view of the nature and the scheme of the system, are capable of benefiting from it.*" [1047]

However, irrespective of whether "*the nature [and/or] general scheme of the [tax] system,*" "*the basic or guiding principles of [the] tax system*" or "*the logic of the tax system*" is considered to be decisive, it has to be established what the nature, the general scheme or the logic of the tax system is or what its fundamental, basic or guiding principles are. Since an independent European approach cannot be inferred due to a lack of harmonization,[1048] it is difficult - if not impossible[1049] - to establish a uniform concept of taxation principles for purposes of State aid law.[1050] With regard to the ability-to-pay principle, for example, it is pointed out in the literature that "*there is [no] consensus in any form among the Member State on the implementation of the principle of ability to pay in national tax systems.*"[1051] If the ability-to-pay principle was hence considered decisive for establishing the common or "normal" direct tax regime applicable in a Member State,[1052] the individual Member State's domestic understanding of the ability-to-pay principle would be pivotal.[1053] However, unless this principle is considered to be predetermined by natural law, its contours have to be inferred from the existing legal provisions.[1054] Therefore, the wording, the history, the systematic embedment as well as the objective of a national measure allegedly causing State aid

1047. Opinion of AG Léger in *Belgium/Commission*, C-182/03 and C-217/03, EU:C:2006:89, at point 293; also see H. Drabbe in A. Rust/C. Micheau (eds.), *State Aid and Tax Law* (Kluwer, 2013), at p. 96; J. Englisch in H. Schaumburg/J. Englisch (eds.), *Europäisches Steuerrecht* (Dr Otto Schmidt, 2015), at pp. 442-443, at MN 9.32; R. Szudoczky, *The Sources of EU law and Their Relationships: Lessons for the Field of Taxation* (IBFD, 2014), at p. 559.

1048. This does not mean that EU law does not include some features that are also considered to form the basis of the "ability-to-pay" principle. See J. Englisch in C. Brokelind (ed.), *Principles of Law: Function, Status and Impact in EU Tax Law* (IBFD, 2014), at pp. 448-451.

1049. See F. Engelen/A. Gunn, Towards a Theoretical Assessment Framework, in A. Rust/C. Micheau (eds.), *State Aid and Tax Law* (Kluwer, 2013), p. 137 (at p. 141: "*We [...] reject the notion that there could exist a framework of reference for assessing the existence of an advantage* outside *the actual tax system of the Member State itself*").

1050. See J. Englisch in C. Brokelind (ed.), *Principles of Law: Function, Status and Impact in EU Tax Law* (IBFD, 2014), at p. 456 ("*Assuming that ability to pay is indeed a constitutionally relevant and enforceable standard of equal and equitable taxation at Union level, the consequences of such an acknowledgement are currently still limited. This is due to the fact that so far, hardly any secondary Union law exists concerning the harmonization of direct taxation, beyond mere coordination of selected aspects of national tax systems.*"); J. Lang/J. Englisch in A. Amatucci (ed.), International Tax Law (Kluwer, 2012), at p. 285 ("*[T]here does not exist one single cross-border concept of ability-to-pay valid for all Member States – this could only be installed by way of legal harmonization. Instead, the principle of ability to pay rooted in each on of the Member States' constitutional and taxing traditions must open its respective window towards a cross-border outlook.*").

1051. F. Vanistendael, 23 *EC Tax Rev.* 3 (2014), at p. 121.

1052. Critically M. Lang, *Die Auswirkungen des gemeinschaftsrechtlichen Beihilferechts auf das Steuerrecht*, 17. ÖJT, Band IV/1 (Manz, 2009), at p. 28; F.P. Sutter, *Das EG-Beihilfenverbot und sein Durchführungsverbot in Steuersachen* (Linde, 2005), at pp. 107-109.

1053. See K. Drüen, 49 *DStR* 7 (2011), at p. 292 ("*[E]s [geht] allein um die Analyse des nationalen Steuersystems*").

1054. See N. Zorn, VfGH prüft bisherige Liebhabereipraxis, 70 *SWK* 19 (1995), A 417 (at A 420); also cf. H. Ruppe, Die Leistungsfähigkeit des Steuerrechts - Die österreichische Perspektive, 88 *StuW* 4 (2011), p. 372 (at p. 375).

has to be taken into account as well in order to determine whether it specifies or whether it deviates from the fundamental principles underlying, or the inherent logic in, the respective Member State's tax system. It is hence convincing that the ECJ not only takes into account the *"objective assigned to the tax system of the Member State,"*[1055] but also refers to *"the objective of the measure in question."*[1056] The Court thereby makes *"a distinction [...] between, on the one hand, the objectives attributed to a particular tax regime, which are extrinsic to it, and, on the other hand, the mechanisms inherent in the tax system itself, which are necessary for the achievement of such objectives."*[1057] Whether a tax provision implements the nature, the general scheme or the logic of the tax system or has another function is thus not easy to determine as very often various possibilities exist to achieve a certain objective and, in addition, almost any tax regime is full of exceptions.[1058] Income taxes, for example, are typically assessed on an annual basis.[1059] This limitation of the taxable period would disadvantage taxpayers with fluctuating income if there were no possibility to link two taxable periods. If a taxpayer earned a profit of 100 in year two, taxes would have to be paid irrespective of whether there was a corresponding loss in year one. In order to avoid such consequences resulting from the limitation of the taxable period, many jurisdictions provide for a loss carry-forward. Some scholars consider such an inter-periodical component to be a fundamental principle of income taxation.[1060] However, linking two taxable periods may be considered inappropriate under certain

1055. Judgment in *Heiser*, C-172/03, EU:C:2005:130, at para. 40; Judgment in *Portugal/Commission*, C-88/03, EU:C:2006:511, at para. 54; Judgment in *Paint Graphos and others*, C-78/08 to C-80/08, EU:C:2011:550, at para. 49; Judgment in *P*, C-6/12, EU:C:2013:525, at para. 19; also see Judgment in *Ministerio de Defensa and Navantia*, C-522/13, EU:C:2014:2262, at para. 35; see also Judgment in *GIL Insurance and others*, C-308/01, EU:C:2004:252, at para. 68.

1056. Judgment in *Adria-Wien Pipeline and Wietersdorfer & Peggauer Zementwerke*, C-143/99, EU:C:2001:598, at para. 41; Judgment *Commission/Netherlands*, C-279/08 P, EU:C:2011:551, at para. 62; also see Judgment in *Mediaset*, C-403/10 P, EU:C:2011:533, at para. 36; Judgment in *Commission/MOL*, C-15/14 P, EU:C:2015:362, at para. 59; Judgment in *Eventech*, C-518/13, EU:C:2015:9, at para. 55.

1057. Judgment in *Portugal/Commission*, C-88/03, EU:C:2006:511, at para. 81; Judgment in *Ministerio de Defensa and Navantia*, C-522/13, EU:C:2014:2262, at para. 43; also see Judgment in *Paint Graphos and others*, C-78/08 to C-80/08, EU:C:2011:550, at para. 69.

1058. With regard to the ability-to-pay principle see J. Englisch in H. Schaumburg/J. Englisch (eds.), *Europäisches Steuerrecht* (Dr Otto Schmidt, 2015), at p. 440, at MN 9.29; M. Lang, *Die Auswirkungen des gemeinschaftsrechtlichen Beihilferechts auf das Steuerrecht*, 17. ÖJT, Band IV/1 (Manz, 2009), at p. 28; W. Schön in ÖJT (ed.), *Die Auswirkungen des gemeinschaftsrechtlichen Beihilferechts auf das Steuerrecht*, Referate und Diskussionsbeiträge, Band IV/2 (Manz, 2010), at p. 33; W. Schön, 36 *Common Market L. Rev.* 5 (1999), at p. 927; W. Schön in L. Hancher/T. Ottervanger/P.J. Slot (eds.), *EU State Aids* (Sweet & Maxwell, 2012), at pp. 343-344; with regard to the inherent logic of a tax system see F.P. Sutter, *Das EG-Beihilfenverbot und sein Durchführungsverbot in Steuersachen* (Linde, 2005), at pp. 109-118.

1059. See V. Thuronyi, The Concept of Income, 46 *Tax L. Rev.* 1 (1990), p. 45 (at p. 65).

1060. See, for example, H. Berg/R. Schmich, Die Beschränkung des Verlustabzuges im Karlsruher Entwurf zum Einkommensteuergesetz, 40 *DStR* 9 (2002), p. 346 (at p. 347); J. Hackmann, Lebenseinkommensbesteuerung durch interperiodischen Progressionsausgleich, 57 *StuW* 4 (1980), p. 318 (at p. 318); J. Hey in K. Tipke/J. Lang, *Steuerrecht*[22] (Dr Otto Schmidt, 2015), at § 8 para. 44; R. Ismer, Prinzipien der Einkünfteermittlung – Periodizitätsprinzip, in J. Hey (ed.), *Einkünfteermittlung*, DStjG 34 (Dr Otto Schmidt, 2011), p. 91 (at p. 108); H. Kube, Die intertemporale Verlustverrechnung – Verfassungsrechtlicher Rahmen und legislativer Gestaltungsraum, 49 *DStR* 38 (2011), p. 1781 (at p. 1785); J. Lang, *Die Bemessungsgrundlage der*

circumstances. In Germany, for example, the possibility for corporations to carry forward losses is restricted in order to limit the trafficking of loss carry-forwards through purchasing and selling shares in companies.[1061] What does this restriction say about the nature, the general scheme or the logic of the German tax system? According to the European Commission, the intention of this restriction is "*to prevent companies which change ownership from carrying forward their losses.*"[1062] However, companies which do not change ownership can carry forward losses without any restriction. Are companies which do not change ownership hence favoured vis-à-vis companies which do change ownership?

The European Commission identified "*the German corporate income tax system in its present form, and in particular the rules on tax loss carry-forward for companies subject to change in their shareholding*" as the reference system.[1063] As the German rules provide for an exception to this reference system by allowing a loss carry-forward if there is a change in the shareholding of a company in difficulties, the European Commission suspected Germany of granting unlawful State aid. It argued that "*all companies which change ownership are, in the light of the objective of the tax system, in a comparable factual and legal situation,*"[1064] taking into account that "*the objective of the corporate income tax system is to generate revenue for the budget*" and the restriction to carrying forward losses "*is intended to prevent companies which change ownership from carrying forward their losses.*"[1065] The European Commission further concluded that the exception to the restriction to carrying forward losses "*was introduced to support ailing companies during the financial and economic crisis.*"[1066] Since such an objective is "*extrinsic to the tax system,*" it "*cannot be relied upon to justify a measure*

Einkommensteuer (Dr Otto Schmidt, 1988), at pp. 188-190; C. Mönikes, *Die Verlustverrechnungsbeschränkungen des Einkommensteuergesetzes im Lichte der Verfassung* (Shaker Verlag, 2006), at p. 32.

1061. See § 8c German CITA.
1062. Commission Decision of 26 Jan. 2011 on State aid C 7/10 (ex CP 250/09 and NN 5/10) implemented by Germany - Scheme for the carry-forward of tax losses in the case of restructuring of companies in difficulty (*Sanierungsklausel*), *OJ* L 235 (10 Sep. 2011), at para. 71.
1063. Commission Decision of 26 Jan. 2011 on State aid C 7/10 (ex CP 250/09 and NN 5/10) implemented by Germany - Scheme for the carry-forward of tax losses in the case of restructuring of companies in difficulty (*Sanierungsklausel*), *OJ* L 235 (10 Sep. 2011), p. 26 (at para. 66); also see Judgment in *GFKL Financial Services AG*, T-620/11, EU:T:2016:59, at paras 111-126; Judgment in *Heitkamp Bauholding GmbH*, T-287/11, EU:T:2016:60, at paras 103-109.
1064. See Judgment in *GFKL Financial Services AG*, T-620/11, EU:T:2016:59, at paras 136-142; Judgment in *Heitkamp Bauholding GmbH*, T-287/11, EU:T:2016:60, at paras 128-134.
1065. Commission Decision of 26 Jan. 2011 on State aid C 7/10 (ex CP 250/09 and NN 5/10) implemented by Germany - Scheme for the carry-forward of tax losses in the case of restructuring of companies in difficulty (*Sanierungsklausel*), *OJ* L 235 (10 Sep. 2011), at para. 71.
1066. Commission Decision of 26 Jan. 2011 on State aid C 7/10 (ex CP 250/09 and NN 5/10) implemented by Germany - Scheme for the carry-forward of tax losses in the case of restructuring of companies in difficulty (*Sanierungsklausel*), *OJ* L 235 (10 Sep. 2011), at paras 87-88; Judgment in *GFKL Financial Services AG*, T-620/11, EU:T:2016:59, at paras 158-159; Judgment in *Heitkamp Bauholding GmbH*, T-287/11, EU:T:2016:60, at paras 164-165.

by the nature and the overall structure of the tax system."[1067] However, if allowing a company in difficulties to carry forward losses constitutes State aid, the question arises whether Article 107(1) TFEU also prohibits Germany from providing for a loss carry-forward for companies which do not change ownership. It could be argued that companies which do change ownership and companies which do not change ownership are not comparable in the light of the objective of the German tax system, which is – according to the European Commission – "*to generate revenue for the budget*" and "*to prevent companies which change ownership from carrying forward their losses.*"[1068] However, if the maximization of the Member State's budget were decisive, it would not be convincing to allow companies which do not change ownership to carry forward losses, because this would in fact not increase Germany's budget. To exclusively focus on the objective of preventing certain companies from carrying forward losses is also unconvincing, because the German system would then be partly immunized from being scrutinized since specific objectives are introduced for specific groups of taxpayers.[1069] Hence, the fact that the German system provides for a loss carry-forward for companies which do not change ownership also has to be taken into account. This was disregarded by the European Commission, which is why its decision is heavily criticized by German scholars.[1070] It is argued that the "correct" reference system would have been the possibility of carrying forward losses, which derives from the ability-to-pay principle.[1071] However, whether the ability-to-pay principle actually requires the German legislator to provide for a loss carry-forward may also be questioned. Whereas some scholars consider such an inter-periodical component to be a fundamental principle of income taxation,[1072] others argue that it is an exception to

1067. Commission Decision of 26 Jan. 2011 on State aid C 7/10 (ex CP 250/09 and NN 5/10) implemented by Germany – Scheme for the carry-forward of tax losses in the case of restructuring of companies in difficulty (*Sanierungsklausel*), *OJ* L 235 (10 Sep. 2011), at para. 89.

1068. Commission Decision of 26 Jan. 2011 on State aid C 7/10 (ex CP 250/09 and NN 5/10) implemented by Germany – Scheme for the carry-forward of tax losses in the case of restructuring of companies in difficulty (*Sanierungsklausel*), *OJ* L 235 (10 Sep. 2011), at para. 71.

1069. Cf. H. Drabbe in A. Rust/C. Micheau (eds.), *State Aid and Tax Law* (Kluwer, 2013), at p. 96; J. Englisch in H. Schaumburg/J. Englisch (eds.), *Europäisches Steuerrecht* (Dr Otto Schmidt, 2015), at pp. 442-443, at MN 9.32.

1070. See K. Drüen, 49 *DStR* 7 (2011), at pp. 291-292; H. Jochum, Systemfragen zu Mantelkauf und Sanierungsklausel, 93 *FR* 11 (2011), p. 497 (at p. 498); C. Marquart, Die Möglichkeit der Verlustverrechnung als selektive Begünstigung sanierungsbedürftiger Unternehmen?, 20 *IStR* 12 (2011), p. 445 (at pp. 448-449).

1071. See K. Drüen, 49 *DStR* 7 (2011), at p. 291; also see Action brought on 2 Dec. 2011 – *ATMvision v. European Commission*, T-627/11; Action brought on 2 Dec. 2011 – *Sky Deutschland and Sky Deutschland Fernsehen v. Commission*, T-626/11.

1072. See, for example, H. Berg/R. Schmich, 40 *DStR* 9 (2002), at p. 347; J. Hackmann, 57 *StuW* 4 (1980), at p. 318; J. Hey in K. Tipke/J. Lang, *Steuerrecht*[22] (Dr Otto Schmidt, 2015), at § 8 para. 44; R. Ismer in J. Hey (ed.), *Einkünfteermittlung*, DStjG 34 (Dr Otto Schmidt, 2011), at p. 108; H. Kube, 49 *DStR* 38 (2011), at p. 1785; J. Lang, *Die Bemessungsgrundlage der Einkommensteuer* (Dr Otto Schmidt, 1988), at pp. 188-190; C. Mönikes, *Die Verlustverrechnungsbeschränkungen des Einkommensteuergesetzes im Lichte der Verfassung* (Shaker Verlag, 2006), at p. 32.

the principle of periodicity.[1073] It would thus also be arguable that the principle of periodicity is the "correct" reference framework,[1074] which would confirm the European Commission's approach.

This example illustrates that assessing comparability for the purposes of EU State aid law is a sophisticated task. Like many other legal questions, it requires an in-depth analysis of the national measure concerned and its role in and influence on the Member State's tax system at stake. This is confirmed by the ECJ, in conceding that classifying a domestic tax measure as selective "*presupposes not only familiarity with the content of the provisions of relevant law but also requires examination of their scope on the basis of administrative and judicial practice and of information relating to the ambit* ratione personae *of those provisions.*"[1075] However, the ECJ cannot interpret domestic law autonomously. With regard to preliminary ruling procedures, for example, it is settled case law that "*the interpretation of national rules is a matter for the national courts and not the Court of Justice.*"[1076] In order to be able to adopt a position the ECJ hence has to rely on either the referring court,[1077] which has to submit all the information

1073. Cf. F. Dötsch, Zur (Nicht-)Vererblichkeit des Verlustabzugs nach § ESTG § 10d EStG, 46 *DStR* 14 (2008), p. 641 (at p. 642); P. Kirchhof, Der verfassungsrechtliche Auftrag zur Besteuerung nach der finanziellen Leistungsfähigkeit, 62 *StuW* 4 (1985), p. 319 (at p. 322); P. Kirchhof in P. Kirchhof/H. Söhn/R. Mellinghoff (eds.), *EStG*[121] (C.F. Müler, 2002), at § 2 paras A 136-A 137; P. Kirchhof in P. Kirchhof (ed.), *EStG*[12] (Dr Otto Schmidt, 2013), § 2 paras 18-20 and 120-120a; D. Schneider, Vertikale Gerechtigkeit wider Rechtsformneutralität und Lebenseinkommensbesteuerung, in T. Siegel/P. Kirchhof/D. Schneeloch/U. Schramm (eds.), *Steuertheorie, Steuerpolitik und Steuerpraxis*, Festschrift für Peter Bareis zum 65. Geburtstag (Schäffer-Pschel, 2005), p. 275 (at pp. 284-287); C.-H. Witt, Keine Vererblichkeit von Verlustvoträgen - Der Beschluss des Großen Senats und seine Folgen, 63 *BB* 23 (2008), p. 1199 (at p. 1201); also cf. W. Schick, *Der Verlustrücktrag* (C.H. Beck, 1976), at pp. 13-21.

1074. See M. Lang in J. Lüdicke (ed.), *Praxis und Zukunft des Internationalen Steuerrechts* (Dr Otto Schmidt, 2012), at p. 94.

1075. Judgment in *P*, C-6/12, EU:C:2013:525, at para. 20.

1076. Judgment in *Vanacker and Lesage*, C-37/92, EU:C:1993:836, at para. 7; Judgment in *Wilson*, C-506/04, EU:C:206:587, at para. 34; with regard to State aid see especially Judgment in *Unión General de Trabajadores de la Rioja*, C-428/06 to C-434/06, EU:C:2008:488, at para. 144; Judgment in *Iglesias Gutiérrez*, C-352/14 and C-353/14, EU:C:2015:691, at para. 21; also see Judgment in *Placanica*, C-338/04, EU:C:2007:133, at para. 36; Judgment in *Gerdin*, C-448/08, EU:C:2008:616, at para. 54; Judgment in *Liga Portuguesa de Futebol Profissional and Bwin International*, C-42/07, EU:C:2009:519, at para. 37; Judgment in *Sjöberg*, C-447/08, EU:C:2010:415, at para. 54; Judgment in *Varzim Sol*, C-25/11, EU:C:2012:94, at para. 27; Judgment in *Almos Agrárkülkereskedelmi*, C-337/13, EU:C:2014:328, at para. 18; also see Judgment in *Dickinger and Ömer*, C-347/09, EU:C:2011:582, at para. 51; Judgment in *Pfleger and others*, C-390/12, EU:C:2014:281, at para. 47; Judgment in *Berlington Hungary and others*, C-98/14, EU:C:2015:386, at para. 57 ("*The identification of the objectives in fact pursued by the national legislation is, in the context of a case referred to the Court under Article 267 TFEU, within the jurisdiction of the referring court.*").

1077. The *Kernkraftwerke Lippe-Ems*-decision is an illustrative example in this respect. It was argued that a German excise duty on nuclear fuel constitutes State aid, because energy sources other than nuclear fuel used for the production of electricity are not taxed. The ECJ was not convinced by this argument, since "*it is not apparent from the material available to the Court that - regardless of the fact that the energy sector in Germany is, from a tax perspective, according to the information provided by that court, heavily regulated and subject to measures of State intervention - it is possible, in the light of the effects of that degree of regulation and those measures, to identify a tax regime which has as its objective the taxation of energy sources used to produce electricity or energy sources used to produce electricity which do not contribute to CO^2 emissions*'. However, as the Court deemed itself not to be in a position to give a final

necessary for such a classification[1078] and/or – especially when it comes to infringement procedures or actions for annulment – the arguments raised by: (1) the European Commission (and/or the General Court), which has *"to prove that [the national measure] creates differences between undertakings which [...] are in a comparable factual and legal situation,"*[1079] (2) the government or Member State concerned, which has *"to show that it is actually justified by the nature and general scheme of the system in question,"*[1080] and (3) the arguments raised by other intervening Member States.

Thus, assessing whether a national measure differentiates between economic operators who are in a comparable factual and legal situation is no different from answering any other legal question. Almost always there will be arguments in favour and against such a comparability. Since the ECJ has to base its decision on the persuasiveness of the arguments raised by the intervening parties, it is not surprising that the Court's judgments can be debated. However, the disputes in the literature are not primarily due to the different approaches suggested. The different results are rather based on a different appraisal of the same arguments, which are structured in a different way. The approach focusing on the fundamental principles underlying the respective tax considers "the nature and the scheme of the tax system" at the level of comparability. There is hence no need to ask whether a national measure, *"although conferring an advantage on its recipient, were justified by the nature or general scheme of the system of which it is part."*[1081,1082] By contrast, the approach focusing on the competitive relationship allows for the very same arguments, but at the level of justification.[1083] It is the ECJ itself that gives grounds for these differing, but –

ruling on this issue, this conclusion was subjected *"to verfication by the referring court."* See Judgment *Kernkraftwerke Lippe-Ems*, C-5/14, EU:C:2015:354, at para. 77.

1078. Judgment in *P.*, C-6/12, EU:C:2013:525, at para. 21; also cf. Judgment in *Freskot*, C-355/00, EU:C:2003:298, at para. 87; Judgment in *AEM*, C-128/03 and C-129/03, EU:C:2005:224, at para. 48; Judgment *Kernkraftwerke Lippe-Ems*, C-5/14, EU:C:2015:354, at para. 77.

1079. Judgment *Commission/Netherlands*, C-279/08 P, EU:C:2011:551, at para. 62; also see Judgment in *Commission/MOL*, C-15/14 P, EU:C:2015:362, at para. 59.

1080. Judgment *Netherlands/Commission*, C-159/01, EU:C:2004:246, at para. 43; Judgment *Commission/Netherlands*, C-279/08 P, EU:C:2011:551, at para. 62 and para. 77; Judgment in *Commission and Spain/Government of Gibraltar and United Kingdom*, C-106/09 P and C-107/09 P, EU:C:2011:732, at para. 146; Judgment in *BNP Paribas and BNL/Commission*, C-452/10 P, EU:C:2012:366, at para. 121.

1081. Judgment in *Heiser*, C-172/03, EU:C:2005:130, at para. 43.

1082. See J. Englisch in H. Schaumburg/J. Englisch (eds.), *Europäisches Steuerrecht* (Dr Otto Schmidt, 2015), at p. 444, at MN 9.32; W. Schön in ÖJT (ed.), *Die Auswirkungen des gemeinschaftsrechtlichen Beihilferechts auf das Steuerrecht*, Referate und Diskussionsbeiträge, Band IV/2 (Manz, 2010), at p. 30.

1083. See M. Lang, 11 *Eur. St. Aid L. Q.* 2 (2012), at p. 420: *"The establishment of unequal treatment between companies in a comparable situation, however, does not necessarily constitute State aid[.] [...] A measure may, according to the ECJ, be justified by the nature and the inner structure of the tax system"*; M. Lang in P. Pistone (ed.), *Legal Remedies in European Tax Law* (IBFD, 2009), at p. 270: *"If two situations have been found comparable, a different treatment is only acceptable if there is a justification for it. The ECJ mentions the nature and the overall structure of the tax system in that context"*; M. Lang, *Die Auswirkungen des gemeinschaftsrechtlichen Beihilferechts auf das Steuerrecht*, 17. ÖJT, Band IV/1 (Manz, 2009), at pp. 26-27 and M. Lang, 24 *ÖStZ* 24 (2011), at p. 598 and M. Lang in J. Lüdicke (ed.), *Praxis und Zukunft des Internationalen Steuerrechts* (Dr Otto Schmidt, 2012), at pp. 99-100: *"Ist einmal die unterschiedliche Behandlung von Unternehmen erwiesen, die sich in einer vergleichbaren Situation*

pertaining to the outcome – almost superimposable approaches.[1084] On the one hand, a national measure only has to fulfil the condition of selectivity, if it "*is such as to favour 'certain undertakings or the production of certain goods' in comparison with others which, in the light of the objective pursued by the system in question, are in a comparable legal and factual situation.*"[1085] On the other hand, the ECJ has emphasized that a national measure which "*is justified by the nature or general scheme of the system of which it is part does not fulfil that condition of selectivity.*"[1086] This illustrates that the arguments raised at the level of comparability and justification are used interchangeably.[1087] The scholarly discussions thus reveal that different approaches impair the exchange of legal arguments. The lack of dogmatic rigour does, therefore, not compellingly mean that the ECJ misinterprets the law, but that its decisions lack transparency.

3.3.2 Preferential Treatment

For Article 107(1) TFEU to be applicable, it is not sufficient to assert that certain undertakings or the production of certain goods is treated differently compared to

befinden, ist dies alleine – der Judikatur zufolge – noch nicht schädlich[.] [...] Eine Maßnahme kann nach Auffassung des EuGH durch die Natur und den inneren Aufbau des Steuersystems gerechtfertigt sein."

1084. See W. Schön in ÖJT (ed.), *Die Auswirkungen des gemeinschaftsrechtlichen Beihilferechts auf das Steuerrecht*, Referate und Diskussionsbeiträge, Band IV/2 (Manz, 2010), at p. 30.

1085. Judgment in *Heiser*, C-172/03, EU:C:2005:130, at para. 40; also see Judgment in *Portugal/Commission*, C-88/03, EU:C:2006:511, at para. 54; also cf. Judgment in *GIL Insurance and others*, C-308/01, EU:C:2004:252, at para. 68; Judgment in *Paint Graphos and others*, C-78/08 to C-80/08, EU:C:2011:550, at para. 49; Judgment in *P*, C-6/12, EU:C:2013:525, at para. 19; Judgment in *Ministerio de Defensa and Navantia*, C-522/13, EU:C:2014:2262, at para. 35.

1086. Judgment in *Adria-Wien Pipeline and Wietersdorfer & Peggauer Zementwerke*, C-143/99, EU:C:2001:598, at para. 42; Judgment in *P*, C-6/12, EU:C:2013:525, at para. 22; also see Judgment in *Italy/Commission*, 173/73, EU:C:1974:71, at para. 15; Judgment in *Belgium/Commission*, C-75/97, EU:C:1999:311, at para. 33; Judgment in *France/Commission*, C-251/97, EU:C:1999:480, at para. 36; Judgment in *Italy/Commission*, C-310/99, EU:C:2002:143, at para. 51; Judgment in *Spain/Commission*, C-351/98, EU:C:2002:530, at para. 42; Judgment in *GIL Insurance and others*, C-308/01, EU:C:2004:252, at para. 72; Judgment in *Freskot*, C-355/00, EU:C:2003:298, at para. 86; Judgment *Netherlands/Commission*, C-159/01, EU:C:2004:246, at para. 42; Judgment in *Heiser*, C-172/03, EU:C:2005:130, at para. 43; Judgment in *AEM*, C-128/03 and C-129/03, EU:C:2005:224, at para. 39; Judgment in *Paint Graphos and others*, C-78/08 to C-80/08, EU:C:2011:550, at para. 76; Judgment *Commission/Netherlands*, C-279/08 P, EU:C:2011:551, at para. 62; Judgment in *Commission and Spain/Government of Gibraltar and United Kingdom*, C-106/09 P and C-107/09 P, EU:C:2011:732, at para. 145; Judgment in *BNP Paribas and BNL/Commission*, C-452/10 P, EU:C:2012:366, at para. 101.

1087. See R. Szudoczky, *The Sources of EU Law and Their Relationships: Lessons for the Field of Taxation* (IBFD, 2014), at p. 597; also cf. M. Prek/S. Lefèvre, 11 *Eur. St. Aid L. Q.* 2 (2012), at p. 342; P. Rossi-Maccanico, The Point on Selectivity in State Aid Review of Business Tax Measures, in P. Pistone (ed.), *Legal Remedies in European Tax Law* (IBFD, 2009), p. 223 (at p. 231); also see F.P. Sutter in Studiengesellschaft für Wirtschaft und Recht (ed.), *Beihilfenrecht* (Linde, 2004), at p. 42; F.P. Sutter, *Das EG-Beihilfenverbot und sein Durchführungsverbot in Steuersachen* (Linde, 2005), at p. 96, who points out that thus the ECJ's State aid analysis is tautological; also cf. J. Englisch in H. Schaumburg/J. Englisch (eds.), *Europäisches Steuerrecht* (Dr Otto Schmidt, 2015), at p. 444, at MN 9.32, who considers the ECJ's approach to be redundant.

others. A national measure which leads to such a differentiation may only constitute State aid if it also leads to a preferential treatment. Not only national measures that directly address and thereby privilege certain undertakings or the production of certain goods may lead to such a preferential treatment, but – as can be inferred from Article 107(2)(a) TFEU[1088] – also national measures that only indirectly lead to an economic advantage of economic operators.[1089] A subsidy, for example, that is granted to gasoline stations in order to counteract certain competitive disadvantages resulting from their location near the border renders it unnecessary to invoke the contractual obligation of oil companies supplying the gasoline stations to compensate such disadvantages. Therefore, such a national measure indirectly privileges oil companies "*since its effect was to mitigate the burdens which would normally have affected the budget of companies anxious to maintain their market position in the light of developments in the domestic and international markets.*"[1090] Accordingly, tax reliefs or incentives for individual consumers,[1091] employees[1092] or investors[1093] may also be covered by Article 107(1) TFEU if such measures collaterally effect the favouring of certain undertakings or the production of certain goods.[1094]

Different treatment normally, but not necessarily, means that a group of taxpayers is treated more beneficially than another one. This is due to the fact that a national measure does not constitute State aid simply because it aims at favouring certain undertakings or the production of certain goods, but Article 107(1) TFEU rather requires looking at its effects.[1095] National measures can only be regarded as

1088. Judgment *Mediaset/Commission*, C-403/10 P, EU:C:2011:533, at para. 81.
1089. Judgment in *Germany/Commission*, C-156/98, EU:C:2000:467, at paras 22-28; Judgment in *Netherlands/Commission*, C-382/99, EU:C:2002:363, at paras 60-66; Judgment in *Mediaset*, C-403/10 P, EU:C:2011:533, at paras 73-77.
1090. Judgment in *Netherlands/Commission*, C-382/99, EU:C:2002:363, at para. 66.
1091. Judgment *Mediaset/Commission*, C-403/10 P, EU:C:2011:533, at para. 81.
1092. Judgment in *De gezamenlijke Steenkolenmijnen in Limburg*, 30/59, EU:C:1961:2.
1093. Judgment of 4 Mar. 2009, *Associazione italiana del risparmio gestito and Fineco Asset Management/Commission*, T-445/05, EU:T:2009:50, at paras 139-146.
1094. See J. Englisch in H. Schaumburg/J. Englisch (eds.), *Europäisches Steuerrecht* (Dr Otto Schmidt, 2015), at p. 418, at MN 9.10.
1095. Judgment in *Italy/Commission*, 173/73, EU:C:1974:71, at para. 13; Judgment in *Deufil/Commission*, 310/85, EU:C:1987:96, at para. 8; Judgment in *Belgium/Commission*, C-56/93, EU:C:1996:64, at para. 79; Judgment in *France/Commission*, C-241/94, EU:C:1996:353, at para. 20; Judgment in *Belgium/Commission*, C-75/97, EU:C:1999:311, at para. 25; Judgment in *Spain/Commission*, C-480/98, EU:C:2000:559, at para. 16; Judgment in *Netherlands/Commission*, C-382/99, EU:C:2002:363, at para. 61; Judgment in *Spain/Commission*, C-409/00, EU:C:2003:92, at para. 46; Judgment in *GEMO*, C-126/01, EU:C:2003:622, at para. 34; Judgment in *Netherlands/Commission*, C-159/01, EU:C:2004:246, at para. 51; Judgment in *Heiser*, C-172/03, EU:C:2005:130, at para. 46; Judgment in *British Aggregates/Commission*, C-487/06 P, EU:C:2008:757, at para. 85; Judgment in *Comitato "Venezia vuole vivere" and others/Commission*, C-71/09 P, C-73/09 P and C-76/09 P, EU:C:2011:368, at para. 94; Judgment in *Paint Graphos and others*, C-78/08 to C-80/08, EU:C:2011:550, at para. 68; Judgment *Commission/Netherlands*, C-279/08 P, EU:C:2011:551, at para. 70; Judgment in *Commission and Spain/Government of Gibraltar and United Kingdom*, C-106/09 P and C-107/09 P, EU:C:2011:732, at para. 87; Judgment in *France Télécom/Commission*, C-81/10 P, EU:C:2011:811, at para. 17; Judgment in *Commission/EDF*, C-124/10 P, EU:C:2012:318, at para. 77; Judgment in *Bouygues and Bouygues Télécom / Commission and others*, C-399/10 P and C-401/10 P, EU:C:2013:175, at para. 81; Judgment in *3M Italia*, C-417/10, EU:C:2012:184, at para. 36; Judgment in *BVVG*, C-39/14, EU:C:2015:470, at para. 52.

promotional if, for example, the Member State does not receive an appropriate consideration from the alleged beneficiary. Otherwise, the economic value granted by the Member State only serves as a remuneration for the recipient's quid pro quo.[1096] Whether the consideration received by the Member State is appropriate depends on what would have been agreed upon under the same or comparable market conditions between two unaffiliated private undertakings.[1097] Insofar as there is a transfer of equivalent economic values, the Member State's business partner is not favoured and, consequently, Article 107(1) TFEU does not apply.[1098] Moreover, what is known as, as the case may be, "private investor test," "market economy investor principle," "private creditor test" or "private vendor test" follows from the principle of equal treatment,[1099] according to which, *inter alia, "the public and private sectors are to be treated equally."*[1100] Thus, a Member State cannot be blamed for market-compliant behaviour.[1101] If a private undertaking had acted in the same way, the Member State cannot be accused of having distorted or threatened to distort competition in a way that affects intra-European trade.[1102] Therefore, in the case of having market-compliant effects, a national measure does not constitute State aid, due to a lack of a preferential treatment as well as lack of a distortion of competition affecting intra-European trade.

Albeit the underlying idea seems plausible, a comparison with a non-governmental market operator shows weaknesses, especially with regard to tax measures.[1103] On the one hand, the practical experience in the area of transfer pricing reveals how difficult it is to assess what would have been agreed upon under the same or comparable market conditions between two unaffiliated private undertakings.[1104]

1096. See F.P. Sutter, *Das EG-Beihilfenverbot und sein Durchführungsverbot in Steuersachen* (Linde, 2005), at p. 85; F.P. Sutter in H. Mayer/K. Stöger (eds.), *EUV/AEUV* (Manz, 2014), Article 107 AEUV, MN 35.

1097. Judgment in *Belgium/Commission*, 234/84, EU:C:1986:302, at paras 14-18; Judgment in *Belgium/Commission*, 142/87, EU:C:1990:125, at paras 25-29; Judgment in *Italy/Commission*, C-305/89, EU:C:1991:142, at paras 18-19; Judgment in *Italy/Commission*, C-261/89, EU:C:1991:367, at para. 8; Judgment in *Spain/Commission*, C-342/96, EU:C:1999:210, at para. 46; Judgment in *Spain/Commission*, C-42/93, EU:C:1994:326, at paras 13-14; Judgment in *DM Transport*, C-256/97, EU:C:1999:332, at paras 23-24; Judgment in *France/Commission*, C-482/99, EU:C:2002:294, at paras 69-70; Judgment in *Italy and SIM 2 Multimedia/Commission*, C-328/99 and C-399/00, EU:C:2003:252, at para. 38; Judgment in *Commission/EDF*, C-124/10 P, EU:C:2012:318, at para. 78; also see M. Heidenhain, § 4 The Concept of State Aid, in M. Heidenhain (ed.), *European State Aid Law* (C.H. Beck, 2010), at MN 2.

1098. See M. Mamut, Privatinvestorgrundsatz und Steuerbeihilfen, in T. Jaeger (ed.), *Jahrbuch Beihilferecht 09* (NWV, 2009), p. 329 (at pp. 344-345).

1099. The European Commission merges these principles and tests under the notion of "market economy operator test." See European Commission, Commission Notice on the notion of State Aid as referred to in Article 107(1) of the Treaty on the Functioning of the European Union, *OJ* C 262 (19 July 2016), at paras 73-75.

1100. Judgment in *France/Commission*, C-482/99, EU:C:2002:294, at para. 69; Judgment in *Italy and SIM 2 Multimedia/Commission*, C-328/99 and C-399/00, EU:C:2003:252, at para. 37; also see Judgment *Italy/Commission*, 303/88, EU:C:1991:136, at para. 20.

1101. See. W.C. Haslehner, Die Anwendbarkeit des Privatinvestortests bei Steuerbeihilfen, in T. Jaeger/B. Rumersdorfer (ed.), *Jahrbuch Beihilferecht 11* (NWV, 2011), p. 273 (at p. 276).

1102. See M. Mamut in T. Jaeger (ed.), *Jahrbuch Beihilferecht 09* (NWV, 2009), at p. 333.

1103. See M. Mamut in T. Jaeger (ed.), *Jahrbuch Beihilferecht 09* (NWV, 2009), at pp. 336-338.

1104. See L.E. Schoueri, Arm's Length: Beyond the Guidelines of the OECD, 69 *Bull. Intl. Taxn.* 12 (2015), p. 690 (at pp. 699-700).

On the other hand, there is no "market" in the area of taxation.[1105] It cannot be determined whether a non-governmental market operator would also have abstained from levying a tax under normal market conditions.[1106] Therefore, in tax matters, the various principles and tests may only be invoked if it is actually possible to compare a Member State with a normal market operator in tax matters.[1107] This could be the case, for example, if a tax claim is waived or reduced for a private enterprise in financial difficulties.[1108] If a Member State does not want to frustrate the reorganization of a private undertaking in financial troubles by insisting on levying the full amount of taxes, a tax relief could be granted that puts the fiscus on an equal footing with all other creditors, which are also prepared - for example, within the framework of a judicial insolvency proceeding - to waive parts of their debt claims. Therefore, it could be argued that, by granting such a tax relief, the Member State behaves like a non-governmental market operator,[1109] albeit, however, the origins of a tax claim and a contractual debt claim are different insofar as there is no quid pro quo in taxes.[1110]

Furthermore, if a State acted exclusively like a non-governmental market operator aiming at maximizing profits purely based on economic principles, the availability of services of general economic interest, which ought to be provided irrespective of the specific situation or the degree of economic profitability,[1111] would be severely limited. There is hence no point in a comparison with a non-governmental operator if a Member State remunerates private undertakings in order to make sure that such services of general economic interest are publicly available.[1112] According to the ECJ, such a remuneration does not constitute State aid, if it "*must be regarded as compensation for the services provided by the recipient undertakings in order to discharge public service obligations, so that those undertakings do not enjoy a real financial advantage and the measure thus does not have the effect of putting them in a more favourable competitive*

1105. See W. Schön, 36 *Common Market L. Rev.* 5 (1999), at p. 923; W. Schön in L. Hancher/T. Ottervanger/P.J. Slot (eds.), *EU State Aids* (Sweet & Maxwell, 2012), at p. 337; critically W.C. Haslehner in T. Jaeger/B. Rumersdorfer (ed.), *Jahrbuch Beihilferecht 11* (NWV, 2011), at p. 284.

1106. See T. Jaeger, *Behilfen durch Steuern und parafiskalische Abgaben* (NWV, 2006), at pp. 175-176, para. 195.

1107. See W. Schön in L. Hancher/T. Ottervanger/P.J. Slot (eds.), *EU State Aids* (Sweet & Maxwell, 2012), at p. 337; W. Schön, *Max Planck Institute for Tax Law and Public Finance Working Paper 2015-14* (December 2015), at p. 3; for a sceptical view see M. Mamut in T. Jaeger (ed.), *Jahrbuch Beihilferecht 09* (NWV, 2009), at pp. 341-342.

1108. Judgment in *DM Transport*, C-256/97, EU:C:1999:332, at paras 24-25. Another example in the ECJ's jurisprudence concerns the reduction of tax claims against an enterprise which is wholly owned by the respective Member State (Judgment in *Commission/EDF*, C-124/10 P, EU:C:2012:318).

1109. See M. Gruber, *Die Sanierung im Unternehmenssteuerrecht* (LexisNexis, 2014), at pp. 285-286; also see Judgment in *HAMSA*, T-152/99, EU:T:2002:188, at paras 166 et seq.; also cf. Judgment in *Ecotrade*, C-200/97, EU:C:1998:579, at para. 36.

1110. See M. Mamut in T. Jaeger (ed.), *Jahrbuch Beihilferecht 09* (NWV, 2009), at p. 342.

1111. For this definition see Judgment in *Corbeau*, C-320/91, EU:C:1993:198, in at para. 15; Judgment in *Ambulanz Glöckner*, C-475/99, EU:C:2001:577, at para. 55.

1112. See W.C. Haslehner, Steuerbeihilfen für die Daseinsvorsorge - Alte Probleme und neue Entwicklungen zum gemeinwirtschaftlichen Ausgleich, in T. Jaeger/B. Rumersdorfer (ed.), *Jahrbuch Beihilferecht 10* (NWV, 2010), p. 343 (at p. 347).

position than the undertakings competing with them."[1113] If, for example, a private undertaking is compensated by a Member State for the additional costs arising from also providing passenger train transportation in difficult accessible regions, which would otherwise not have access to this kind of public transport, it can be argued that the compensation only puts this service provider on an equal footing with competitors who do not provide services in those regions and hence do not have to bear the resulting costs.[1114] According to the case law of the ECJ, Member States are thus particularly enabled to compensate, in an objective and transparent manner, the additional costs incurred by an undertaking in the discharge of clearly defined public service obligations.[1115] Albeit the ECJ has not yet mentioned the necessity of a synallagmatic link between the tax relief and the provision of public services, it is argued that there needs to be "*a strong nexus between the tax advantage granted and the obligations imposed, which [...] moreover [have to be] clearly defined.*"[1116] Otherwise, the tax relief cannot be considered to be a compensation for providing services of general economic interest, but may nevertheless be justified under Articles 107(2) and 107(3) TFEU.[1117] It is hence disputed whether tax measures – in contrast to parafiscal duties – are actually a suitable means to provide for such a compensation.[1118]

3.3.3 Selective Treatment

If a group of undertakings, the production of a group of goods or the supply of a group of services are not only treated differently, but are in fact treated more beneficially compared to others, the national measure concerned might constitute State aid. However, some ECJ judgments suggest that a preferential treatment of groups of taxpayers which are in a comparable factual and legal situation is not prohibited in general. Rather, "*the criteria forming the basis of assessment which are adopted by a tax system must also, in order to be capable of being recognised as conferring selective advantages, be such as to characterise the recipient undertakings, by virtue of the properties which are specific to them, as a privileged category, thus permitting such a regime to be described as favouring 'certain' undertakings or the production of 'certain'*

1113. Judgment in *Altmark Trans and Regierungspräsidium Magdeburg*, C-280/00, EU:C:2003:415, at para. 87; also see Judgment in *Ferring*, C-53/00, EU:C:2001:627, at para. 27; Judgment in *Enirisorse*, C-34/01 to C-38/01, EU:C:2003:640, at para. 31; Judgment in *Servizi Ausiliari Dottori Commercialisti*, C-451/03, EU:C:2006:208, at para. 60; Judgment in *Essent Netwerk Noord and others*, C-206/06, EU:C:2008:413, at para. 80; Judgment in *Commission/Deutsche Post*, C-399/08 P, EU:C:2010.481, at para. 41.
1114. Judgment in *Ferring*, C-53/00, EU:C:2001:627, at para. 27.
1115. On the conditions that have to be satisfied see Judgment in *Altmark Trans and Regierungspräsidium Magdeburg*, C-280/00, EU:C:2003:415, at paras 88-93.
1116. Opinion of AG Jacobs in *GEMO*, C-126/01, EU:C:2002:273, at point 128; also see M. Mamut in T. Jaeger (ed.), *Jahrbuch Beihilferecht 09* (NWV, 2009), at p. 343.
1117. Opinion of AG Jacobs in *GEMO*, C-126/01, EU:C:2002:273, at points 118 et seq.
1118. See W.C. Haslehner in T. Jaeger/B. Rumersdorfer (ed.), *Jahrbuch Beihilferecht 10* (NWV, 2010), at pp. 355-359; T. Jaeger, *Behilfen durch Steuern und parafiskalische Abgaben* (NWV, 2006), at pp. 128-129, para. 137; M. Mamut in T. Jaeger (ed.), *Jahrbuch Beihilferecht 09* (NWV, 2009), at pp. 346-349.

goods within the meaning of Article [107(1) TFEU]."[1119] Thus, a differentiation could only be considered selective if the taxpayers which are – considering the effects of the national measure – treated more beneficially than others can be regarded, by virtue of the properties which are specific to them, as a group of "*certain undertakings or the production of certain goods.*"[1120]

The ECJ tends to interpret the selectivity criterion quite extensively.[1121] A group of *certain* undertakings may, for example, be identified by the common characteristic of primarily operating in the production of goods[1122] or of having exporting activities and making certain investments.[1123] Even "*large industrial undertakings engaged in trade between the Member States*"[1124] and "*offshore companies, which by their nature have no employees and do not occupy business premises*"[1125] share specific features characterizing them as "*certain undertakings.*" It thus seems reasonable to conclude that a preferential treatment "*is always selective.*"[1126]

However, in *Gibraltar*, the ECJ confirmed that not every kind of differentiation leads to a selective advantage: "*The advantages alleged by the Commission resulting from measures applicable without distinction to all economic operators, namely the requirement to make a profit, which would benefit unprofitable operators, and those resulting from the capping of tax, which would benefit very profitable operators, do not mean that the tax regime under consideration can be regarded as entailing selective effects. Those effects are not such that they favour 'certain undertakings' or 'the production of certain goods' within the meaning of Article 87(1) EC, but are merely the consequence of the random event that the undertaking in question is unprofitable or very profitable during the period of assessment.*"[1127] In fact, if every kind of differentiation

1119. Judgment in *Commission and Spain/Government of Gibraltar and United Kingdom*, C-106/09 P and C-107/09 P, EU:C:2011:732, at para. 104; also cf. Judgment in *Commission/MOL*, C-15/14 P, EU:C:2015:362, at para. 59: "*It must be observed at the outset that, as the Advocate General stated in point 47 of his Opinion, the requirement as to selectivity under Article 107(1) TFEU must be clearly distinguished from the concomitant detection of an economic advantage, in that, where the Commission has identified an advantage, understood in a broad sense, as arising directly or indirectly from a particular measure, it is also required to establish that that advantage specifically benefits one or more undertakings.*"

1120. Opinion of AG Kokott in *Finanzamt Linz*, C-66/14, EU:C:2015:242, at points 84-85 and 105; differently Opinion of AG Wathelet in *Commission/World Duty Free Group, Banco Santander and Santusa Holding*, C-20/15 P and C-21/15 P, EU:C:2016:624, at paras 10, 78-110; also see R. Ismer/S. Piotrowski, 43 *Intertax* 10 (2015), at pp. 562-563.

1121. Opinion of AG Kokott in *Finanzamt Linz*, C-66/14, EU:C:2015:242, at point 112; also see F.P. Sutter in H. Mayer/K. Stöger (eds.), *EUV/AEUV* (Manz, 2014), Article 107 AEUV, MN 41.

1122. Judgment in *Adria-Wien Pipeline and Wietersdorfer & Peggauer Zementwerke*, C-143/99, EU:C:2001:598, at para. 49.

1123. Judgment in *Spain/Commission*, C-501/00, EU:C:2004:438, at para. 120.

1124. Judgment in *Commission/Netherlands*, C-279/08 P, EU:C:2011:551, at para. 63.

1125. Judgment in *Commission and Spain/Government of Gibraltar and United Kingdom*, C-106/09 P and C-107/09 P, EU:C:2011:732, at para. 106.

1126. R. Szudoczky, *The Sources of EU Law and Their Relationships: Lessons for the Field of Taxation* (IBFD, 2014), at pp. 580-581; also see M. Prek/S. Lefèvre, 11 *Eur. St. Aid L. Q.* 2 [2012], at p. 337; also cf. M.V. Ezcurra, 41 *Intertax* 6/7 [2013], at pp. 343-344; P.C. Van der Vegt, BNP Paribas. State aid incompatible with the common market. General Court, 4 *H&I* 5 (2011), p. 95 (at p. 122).

1127. Judgment in *Commission and Spain/Government of Gibraltar and United Kingdom*, C-106/09 P and C-107/09 P, EU:C:2011:732, at para. 83.

had to be regarded as selective, the State aid rules would have an even more dramatic impact on tax law than hitherto expected. The Member States' latitude with regard to national tax policy would be seriously hampered.[1128] As this would harbour "*the risk of adversely affecting the division of competences between the Member States and the European Union, laid down in Articles 2 to 6 TFEU, and the division of internal competences between the European Parliament and the Council, laid down in Article 14 TFEU, on the one hand, and the Commission, laid down in Article 17 TFEU, on the other,*"[1129] AG Kokotts argued for a "*careful handling [of] [...] [t]he criterion relating to the selectivity of a national provision [...]. If the provision concerns neither one or more individually identifiable sectors capable of being defined by reference to their economic activity, nor individually identifiable undertakings, as the wording of Article 107(1) TFEU requires, then the provision in question cannot in principle be assumed to be selective.*"[1130]

However, in *World Duty* the ECJ held that "*the imposition of [...] a [...] requirement to identify a particular category of undertakings, additional to the analytical method applicable to selectivity in tax matters [...], which essentially involves ascertaining whether the exclusion of certain operators from the benefit of a tax advantage that arises from a measure derogating from an ordinary tax system constitutes discrimination with respect to those operators, cannot be inferred from the Court's case-law [...]. All that matters [...] is the fact that the measure, irrespective of its form or the legislative means used, should have the effect of placing the recipient undertakings in a position that is more favourable than that of other undertakings, although all those undertakings are in a comparable factual and legal situation in the light of the objective pursued by the tax system concerned.*"[1131] It is thus not necessary that the taxpayers which are – considering the effects of the national measure – treated more beneficially than others can be regarded, by virtue of the properties which are specific to them, as a group of "*certain undertakings or the production of certain goods.*"[1132]

Such an understanding implies that the term "*certain*" should not be overrated.[1133] This also seems to be the position of AG Wathelet who argues that "*the identification of undertakings with specific characteristics would be an extremely*

1128. Cf. F.P. Sutter in K. Andersson/E. Eberhartinger/L. Oxelheim (eds.), *National Tax Policy in Europe*, at p. 146 and p. 149.
1129. By contrast, AG Wathelet argues that interpreting the selectivity criterion in a broad sense would "*not jeopardise the institutional balance between the Commission and the Member States but reflects the will of the constituent power as expressed in the wording of Article 107(1) TFEU*" (Opinion of AG Wathelet in *Commission/World Duty Free Group, Banco Santander and Santusa Holding*, C-20/15 P and C-21/15 P, EU:C:2016:624, at point 92 [FN 69]).
1130. Opinion of AG Kokott in *Finanzamt Linz*, C-66/14, EU:C:2015:242, at points 113-115; also cf. L. De Broe, The State Aid Review Against Aggressive Tax Planning: "Always Look a Gift Horse in the Mouth," 24 *EC Tax Rev.* 6 (2015), p. 290 (at p. 291).
1131. Judgment in *Commission/World Duty Free Group, Banco Santander and Santusa Holding*, C-20/15 P and C-21/15 P, EU:C:2016:981, at paras 71 and 79.
1132. Opinion of AG Kokott in *Finanzamt Linz*, C-66/14, EU:C:2015:242, at points 84-85 and 105.
1133. Apparently, it could also be replaced by the term "*some,*" i.e., it would be sufficient that there is a "*favouring of [some] undertakings or the production of [some] goods.*"

imprecise, not to say arbitrary, exercise that would create legal uncertainty."[1134] Moreover, according to AG Wathelet, the wording of Article 107 TFEU does not suggest that the "*terms 'favouring certain undertakings or the production of certain goods' require the identification of a category of undertakings which exhibit specific characteristics and are exclusively favoured by the measure at issue."*[1135] However, rejecting AG Kokott's understanding solely by referring to the wording of Article 107(1) TFEU is not convincing. This provision explicitly applies to "*certain*" undertakings or the production of "*certain*" goods. If Article 107(1) TFEU only requires determining whether "*the undertakings benefiting from a tax measure enjoy a tax advantage to which they would not be entitled under the normal tax regime and which cannot be claimed by undertakings performing similar operations,"*[1136] the question arises why it was considered to be necessary to include the word "certain," particularly because the requirement to make a comparison already derives from the fact that Article 107(1) TFEU requires a "*favouring*" of certain undertakings or the production of certain goods.

Still, if the Court followed AG Kokott's approach, the crucial question would have been how to distinguish between properties of preferentially treated undertakings that allow characterizing them as a group of "certain undertakings" and properties which are irrelevant from a State aid law perspective. Although it is argued that this would be "*an extremely imprecise, not to say arbitrary, exercise,"*[1137] it is in fact possible to identify properties of preferentially treated undertakings that allow characterizing them as a group of "certain undertakings" by means of legal interpretation. From the wording of Articles 107(2)(c) and 107(3)(a) TFEU, for example, it can be inferred that a tax benefit which is limited to a certain geographic area will normally be selective.[1138] Moreover, the wording of Article 107(3)(c) TFEU suggests that a selective treatment may also result from a benefit that is only granted to undertakings or the production of goods characterized by "*certain economic activities,*" such as undertakings of a particular industrial sector.[1139] It thus seems that the Treaties contain some evidence as to what commonalities of a group of undertakings may result in such a group being identifiable as a group of "*certain undertakings.*" From a systematic perspective, other provisions may hence also help to determine characteristics that may be relevant when

1134. Opinion of AG Wathelet in *Commission/World Duty Free Group, Banco Santander and Santusa Holding*, C-20/15 P and C-21/15 P, EU:C:2016:624, at point 84.
1135. Cf. Opinion of AG Wathelet in *Commission/World Duty Free Group, Banco Santander and Santusa Holding*, C-20/15 P and C-21/15 P, EU:C:2016:624, at point 84.
1136. Opinion of AG Wathelet in *Commission/World Duty Free Group, Banco Santander and Santusa Holding*, C-20/15 P and C-21/15 P, EU:C:2016:624, at para. 92. AG Wathelet seems to dismiss this consideration as "*an excessively formalistic and restrictive approach*" (Opinion of AG Wathelet in *Commission/World Duty Free Group, Banco Santander and Santusa Holding*, C-20/15 P and C-21/15 P, EU:C:2016:624, at para. 85).
1137. Opinion of AG Wathelet in *Commission/World Duty Free Group, Banco Santander and Santusa Holding*, C-20/15 P and C-21/15 P, EU:C:2016:624, at point 84.
1138. Judgment in *Portugal/Commission*, C-88/03, EU:C:2006:511, at para. 60; Judgment in *Comitato "Venezia vuole vivere" and others/Commission*, C-71/09 P, C-73/09 P and C-76/09 P, EU:C:2011:368, at para. 96; also see T. Jestaedt in L. Hancher/T. Ottervanger/P.J. Slot (eds.), *EU State Aids* (Sweet & Maxwell, 2012), p. 783 (at p. 784, m.no 21-002); F.P. Sutter in K. Andersson/E. Eberhartinger/L. Oxelheim (eds.), *National Tax Policy in Europe*, at p. 130; critically C. Arhold, 17 *EuZW* 23 (2006), at pp. 717 et seq.
1139. Judgment in *Italy/Commission*, 173/73, EU:C:1974:71, at para. 15.

interpreting the term "certain" in Article 107(1) TFEU, especially those which explicitly or implicitly deal with or emphasize the necessity not to treat explicitly specified groups of persons or transactions less beneficially than others. In fact, the Treaties contain a whole set of rules that deal with objectionable differentiations. A number of provisions, for example, deal with the different treatment of men and women.[1140] This might be an explanation for the ECJ, in *Commission/Italy*, having accepted the European Commission's argument that a greater reduction in employers' contributions to the Italian sickness insurance scheme for female employees than for male employees leads to a selective benefit for "*certain Italian industries employing large number of female employees, such as, in particular, those in the textile, clothing, footwear and leather-goods sector.*"[1141]

However, since the ECJ has - at least for now - taken a more liberal approach in *World Duty*,[1142] one cannot but agree with Wolfgang Schön that this could potentially "*transform state aid control in the field of taxation into a wide-reaching anti-discrimination prohibition streamlining national legislation.*"[1143] Taking into account the development of the Court's case law in the area of the fundamental freedoms, it is not impossible that this "trend" of interpreting the State aid provisions in a rather broad way might only be of a temporary nature and some day in the future scholars will conclude that "*[t]he Court has recently been more generous to the Member States compared to the 'old days'.*"[1144] This could be the case, for example, if the Court attached - compared to its previous jurisprudence - more value to the fact that Article 107(1) TFEU only covers aid "*which distorts or threatens to distort competition,*" "*in so far as it affects trade between Member States*" or if the Member States were given more leeway when it comes to justifying selective advantages. For now, however, almost any kind of differentiation in the Member States' tax system is at risk of being blamed as unlawful State aid.

1140. See Articles 2 and 3(3) TEU as well as Articles 8, 10, 19(1), 153(1)(i) and 157 TFEU.

1141. Judgment in *Commission/Italy*, 203/82, EU:C:1983:218, at para. 4.

1142. Judgment in *Commission/World Duty Free Group, Banco Santander and Santusa Holding*, C-20/15 P and C-21/15 P, EU:C:2016:981.

1143. W. Schön in I. Richelle/W. Schön/E. Traversa (eds.), *State Aid Law and Business Taxation* (Springer, 2016), at p. 19.

1144. M. Lang, 18 *EC Tax Rev.* 3 (2009), at p. 112; also see M. Lang, 15 *SWI* 8 (2005), at pp. 374-375; also cf. A. Cordewener/E. Reimer, 46 *Eur. Taxn.* 6 (2006), at pp. 239 et seq.; A. Cordewener/E. Reimer, 46 *Eur. Taxn.* 7 (2006), at pp. 291 et seq.; G. Kofler in W. Schön/C. Heber (eds.), *Grundfragen des Europäischen Steuerrechts* (Springer, 2015), at pp. 18-21; S. Kingston, 44 *Common Market L. Rev.* 5 (2007), at pp. 1336-1343; M. Lang in M. Hebig/K. Kaiser/K. Koschmieder/M. Oblau (eds.), *Aktuelle Entwicklungsaspekte der Unternehmensbesteuerung*, Festschrift für Wilhelm H. Wacker (Erich Schmidt Verlag, 2006), at pp. 365-380; M. Lang in M. Beusch (ed.), Steuerrecht 2007 (Schulthess, 2007), at pp. 5-24; M. Lang, in R. Mellinghof/W. Schön/H. Viskorf (eds.), *Steuerrecht im Rechtsstaat, Festschrift für Wolfgang Spindler zum 65. Geburtstag* (Dr Otto Schmidt, 2011), at pp. 297 et seq.

3.4 Exceptions and Justification Grounds

3.4.1 De Jure *Exceptions and Discretionary Exceptions*

As can be inferred from Articles 107(2) and 107(3) TFEU, "*the basic prohibition of State aid is neither absolute nor unconditional.*"[1145] On the one hand, Article 107(2) TFEU explicitly declares certain types of aid as to be "*compatible with the internal market.*" Although these types of aid are de jure declared compatible with the internal market, the European Commission still insists on being notified if a Member State intends to grant this kind of aid.[1146] With regard to those types of aid which are listed in Article 107(3) TFEU, on the other hand, it is left to the European Commission's discretion to approve their compatibility with the internal market. When deciding on the compatibility of an aid mentioned in Article 107(3) TFEU, the European Commission has to base its discretionary decision on "*economic and social assessments which must be made in a Community context.*"[1147] Moreover, it has to keep in mind that national tax measures, which "*contravene other provisions of the Treaty, cannot […] be declared by the Commission to be compatible with the common market,*" because the State aid procedure "*must never produce a result which is contrary to the specific provisions of the Treaty.*"[1148] The room for discretion is extremely wide, because the judicial review is limited to verifying "*whether the Commission complied with the relevant rules governing procedure and the statement of reasons, whether the facts on which the contested*

1145. Judgment in *Adria-Wien Pipeline and Wietersdorfer & Peggauer Zementwerke*, C-143/99, EU:C:2001:598, at para. 30; also see Judgment in *Ianelli/Meroni*, 74/76, EU:C:1977:51, at para. 11; Judgment in *Steinike & Weinlig*, 78/76, EU:C:1977:52, at para. 8; Judgment in *France/Commission*, 301/87, EU:C:1990:67, at para. 15; Judgment in *Compagnie commerciale de l'Ouest/Receveur principal des douanes de La Pallice-Port*, C-78/90, C-79/90, C-80/90, C-81/90, C-82/90 and C-83/90, EU:C:1992:118, at para. 33; Judgment in *Sanders Adour and Guyomarc'h Orthez/Directeur des services fiscaux des Pyrénées-Atlantiques*, C-149/91 and C-150/91, EU:C:1992:261, at para. 25; Judgment in *Lornoy and others/Belgian State*, C-17/91, EU:C:1992:514, at para. 29; Judgment in *Claeys*, C-114/91, EU:C:1992:516, at para. 22; Judgment in *Demoor and others/Belgian State*, C-144/91 and C-145/91, EU:C:1992:518, at para. 25; Judgment in *CELBI/Fazenda Pública*, C-266/91, EU:C:1993:334; at para. 22; Judgment in *Scharbatke/Germany*, C-72/92, EU:C:1993:858, at para. 19; Judgment in *SEFI and others*, C-39/94, EU:C:1996:285, at para. 36.

1146. See F.P. Sutter in H. Mayer/K. Stöger (eds.), *EUV/AEUV* (Manz, 2014), Article 107 AEUV, MN 88; critically T. Eilmansberger, Zur Reichweite des Durchführungsverbots nach Art 93 Abs 3 EGV, 10 *ecolex* 3 (1999), p. 212 (at pp. 212 et seq.).

1147. Judgment in *Philip Morris/Commission*, 730/79, EU:C:1980:209, at para. 24; Judgment in *Deufil/Commission*, 310/85, EU:C:1987:96, at para. 18; Judgment in *France/Commission*, 301/87, EU:C:1990:67, at para. 49; Judgment in *Italy/Commission*, 303/88, EU:C:1991:136, at para. 34; Judgment in *Matra*, C-225/91, EU:C:1993:239, at para. 24; Judgment in *Italy/Commission*, C-372/97, EU:C:2004:234, at para. 83; Judgment in *Spain/Commission*, C-113/00, EU:C:2002:507, at para. 67; Judgment in *Spain/Commission*, C-114/00, EU:C:2002:508, at para. 81; Judgment in *Spain/Commission*, C-351/98, EU:C:2002:530, at para. 74; Judgment in *Greece/Commission*, C-278/00, EU:C:2004:239, at para. 97; Judgment in *Holland Malt/Commission*, C-464/09 P, EU:C.2010:733, at para. 23.

1148. Judgment in *Germany/Commission*, C-156/98, EU:C:2000:467, at para. 78; also see Judgment in *Commission/Italy*, 73/79, EU:C:1980:129, at para. 11; Judgment in *Matra*, C-225/91, EU:C:1991:460, at para. 41.

finding was based have been accurately stated and whether there has been any manifest error of assessment or a misuse of powers."[1149]

Since Article 107(1) TFEU declares any State aid to be "*incompatible with the internal market,*" whereas Articles 107(2) and 107(3) TFEU include certain types of aid which shall or may be considered to "*be compatible with the internal market,*" the State aid rules lead to a normative conflict. The wording does not explicitly reveal the relationship between Article 107(1) TFEU, on the one hand, and Articles 107(2) and 107(3) TFEU, on the other hand. However, a national measure that fulfils the requirements of Article 107(1) TFEU constitutes State aid and is hence in general "*incompatible with the internal market.*" Such an aid nevertheless is or may be "*compatible with the internal market,*" if it additionally fulfils the requirements of Article 107(2) or 107(3) TFEU. Thus, the normative conflict can be solved by the principle *lex specialis derogat legi generali*. If an aid is covered by Article 107(2) or 107(3) TFEU, the legal consequences of Article 107(1) TFEU are or may be negated.

As Articles 107(2) and 107(3) TFEU presuppose the existence of an "*aid,*" these provisions also contain indications that are helpful for the interpretation of Article 107(1) TFEU. According to Article 107(2)(a) TFEU, for example, "*aid having a social character, granted to individual consumers, provided that such aid is granted without discrimination related to the origin of the products concerned [...] shall be compatible with the internal market.*" Since Article 107(1) TFEU only applies if certain undertakings or the production of certain goods are favoured, aid granted to individual consumers does not constitute unlawful State aid.[1150] Thus, it can be inferred from Article 107(2)(a) TFEU that also national measures that only *indirectly* lead to an economic advantage of economic operators may constitute State aid.[1151] Furthermore, as the wording of Articles 107(2)(c) and 107(3)(a) TFEU indicates, a tax benefit that is limited to a certain geographic area may also constitute State aid.[1152] The wording of Article 107(3)(c) TFEU, in addition, suggests that a benefit that is only granted to undertakings or the production of goods characterized by "*certain economic activities,*" such as undertakings of a particular industrial sector,[1153] is likely to be covered by Article 107(1) TFEU.

1149. Judgment in *Belgium/Commission*, C-56/93, EU:C:1996:64, at para. 11; Judgment in *Italy and SIM 2 Multimedia/Commission*, C-328/99 and C-399/00, EU:C:2003:252, at para. 39; Judgment in *Chronopost and La Poste / UFEX and others*, C-341/06 P and C-342/06 P, EU:C:2008:375, at para. 143.
1150. See W. Cremer in C. Calliess/M. Ruffert (eds.), *EUV/AEUV*[4] (C.H. Beck, 2011), AEUV Art. 107 MN 25.
1151. Judgment in *Germany/Commission*, C-156/98, EU:C:2000:467, at paras 22-28; Judgment in *Netherlands/Commission*, C-382/99, EU:C:2002:363, at paras 60-66; Judgment in *Mediaset*, C-403/10 P, EU:C:2011:533, at paras 73-77.
1152. Judgment in *Portugal/Commission*, C-88/03, EU:C:2006:511, at para. 60; Judgment in *Comitato "Venezia vuole vivere" and others/Commission*, C-71/09 P, C-73/09 P and C-76/09 P, EU:C:2011:368, at para. 96; also see T. Jestaedt in L. Hancher/T. Ottervanger/P.J. Slot (eds.), *EU State Aids* (Sweet & Maxwell, 2012), p. 783 (at p. 784, m.no 21-002); F.P. Sutter in K. Andersson/E. Eberhartinger/L. Oxelheim (eds.), *National Tax Policy in Europe*, at p. 130; critically C. Arhold, 17 *EuZW* 23 (2006), at pp. 717 et seq.
1153. Judgment in *Italy/Commission*, 173/73, EU:C:1974:71, at para. 15.

3.4.2 *Justification by Means of the Mechanisms Inherent in the Tax System*

According to the ECJ, a selective advantage which prima facie constitutes State aid may be justified *"by the nature [and/or] general scheme of the [tax] system"*[1154] if it results directly from *"the basic or guiding principles of [the] tax system"*[1155] or if the measure is consonant with *"the logic of the tax system."*[1156] In order to determine whether this is the case *"a distinction must be made between, on the one hand, the objectives attributed to a particular tax regime and which are extrinsic to it and, on the other, the mechanisms inherent in the tax system itself which are necessary for the achievement of such objectives."*[1157] Selective advantages may be justified by means of the mechanisms inherent in the tax system. By contrast, it is unclear whether objectives which are extrinsic to the tax system may also serve as a justification.[1158]

However, referring to the mechanisms inherent in the tax system as a justification ground is confusing, because the ECJ already takes into account the objectives of the tax system when determining whether a national measure *"is such as to favour 'certain undertakings or the production of certain goods' in comparison with others which [...] are in a comparable legal and factual situation."*[1159] With good cause, the Court's

1154. Judgment in *Italy/Commission*, 173/73, EU:C:1974:71, at para. 15; Judgment in *Belgium/Commission*, C-75/97, EU:C:1999:311, at para. 33; Judgment in *France/Commission*, C-251/97, EU:C:1999:480, at para. 36; Judgment in *Italy/Commission*, C-310/99, EU:C:2002:143, at para. 51; Judgment in *Banks*, C-390/98, EU:C:2001:456, at para. 33; Judgment in *Adria-Wien Pipeline and Wietersdorfer & Peggauer Zementwerke*, C-143/99, EU:C:2001:598, at para. 42; Judgment in *Spain/Commission*, C-351/98, EU:C:2002:530, at para. 42; Judgment in *GIL Insurance and others*, C-308/01, EU:C:2004:252, at para. 72; Judgment in *Freskot*, C-355/00, EU:C:2003:298, at para. 86; Judgment *Netherlands/Commission*, C-159/01, EU:C:2004:246, at para. 42; Judgment in *Heiser*, C-172/03, EU:C:2005:130, at para. 43; Judgment in *AEM*, C-128/03 and C-129/03, EU:C:2005:224, at para. 39; Judgment in *British Aggregates/Commission*, C-487/06 P, EU:C:2008:757, at para. 129; Judgment in *Paint Graphos and others*, C-78/08 to C-80/08, EU:C:2011:550, at para. 76; Judgment *Commission/Netherlands*, C-279/08 P, EU:C:2011:551, at para. 62; Judgment in *Commission and Spain/Government of Gibraltar and United Kingdom*, C-106/09 P and C-107/09 P, EU:C:2011:732, at para. 146; Judgment in *BNP Paribas and BNL/Commission*, C-452/10 P, EU:C:2012:366, at para. 101; Judgment in *P*, C-6/12, EU:C:2013:525, at para. 22; Judgment in *Commission/MOL*, C-15/14 P, EU:C:2015:362, at para. 61.

1155. Judgment in *Portugal/Commission*, C-88/03, EU:C:2006:511, at para. 81; Judgment in *Paint Graphos and others*, C-78/08 to C-80/08, EU:C:2011:550, at para. 65 and para. 69; Judgment in *P*, C-6/12, EU:C:2013:525, at para. 22; Judgment in *Ministerio de Defensa and Navantia*, C-522/13, EU:C:2014:2262, at para. 43.

1156. Judgment in *Spain/Commission*, C-501/00, EU:C:2004:438, at para. 122; also see Judgment in *BNP Paribas and BNL/Commission*, C-452/10 P, EU:C:2012:366, at paras 137-138.

1157. Judgment in *Paint Graphos and others*, C-78/08, EU:C:2011:550, at para. 69; Judgment in *Ministerio de Defensa and Navantia*, C-522/13, EU:C:2014:2262, at para. 43; also see Judgment in *Portugal/Commission*, C-88/03, EU:C:2006:511, at para. 81.

1158. See R. Szudoczky, *The Sources of EU Law and Their Relationships: Lessons for the Field of Taxation* (IBFD, 2014), at p. 615; but see Opinion of AG Geelhoed in *Portugal/Commission*, C-88/03, EU:C:2005:618, at point 76: *"In this respect, a distinction has been drawn between the 'external' objectives of a tax scheme – for example, social or regional objectives – which fall outside the scope of the justification, and the objectives 'inherent in the tax system itself' – for example, efficiency in tax collection and progressive taxation."*

1159. Judgment in *Heiser*, C-172/03, EU:C:2005:130, at para. 40; also see Judgment in *Portugal/Commission*, C-88/03, EU:C:2006:511, at para. 54; also cf. Judgment in *GIL Insurance and others*, C-308/01, EU:C:2004:252, at para. 68; Judgment in *Paint Graphos and others*, C-78/08

approach is, therefore, described as "tautological"[1160] and "redundant,"[1161] because the same arguments are considered at the level of comparability and at the level of justification.[1162,1163] With regard to infringement procedures and actions for annulment, this redundancy is probably due to the ECJ's division of responsibilities.[1164] On the one hand, the European Commission has "*to prove that [the national measure] creates differences between undertakings which [...] are in a comparable factual and legal situation.*"[1165] The Member State concerned, on the other hand, has "*to show that [the national measure] is actually justified by the nature and general scheme of the system in question.*"[1166] The ECJ hence does not distinguish between arguments that may only be raised at the level of comparability and other arguments that may only be

---

to C-80/08, EU:C:2011:550, at para. 49; Judgment in *P*, C-6/12, EU:C:2013:525, at para. 19; Judgment in *Ministerio de Defensa and Navantia*, C-522/13, EU:C:2014:2262, at para. 35.

1160. F.P. Sutter in Studiengesellschaft für Wirtschaft und Recht (ed.), *Beihilfenrecht* (Linde, 2004), at p. 42; F.P. Sutter in M. Lang/J. Schuch/C. Staringer (eds.), *Die abkommensrechtliche Verteilung der Besteuerungsrechte zwischen Ansässigkeits- und Quellenstaat* (Linde, 2005), at p. 92; F.P. Sutter, *Das EG-Beihilfenverbot und sein Durchführungsverbot in Steuersachen* (Linde, 2005), at p. 96.

1161. J. Englisch in H. Schaumburg/J. Englisch (eds.), *Europäisches Steuerrecht* (Dr Otto Schmidt, 2015), at p. 444, at MN 9.32; W.C. Haslehner, Materielle Selektivität von Steuerbeihilfen im Lichte des *Gibraltar*-Urteils des EuGH, in T. Jaeger/B. Haslinger (ed.), *Jahrbuch Beihilferecht 12* (NWV, 2012), p. 301 (at p. 320).

1162. See R. Szudoczky, *The Sources of EU Law and Their Relationships: Lessons for the Field of Taxation* (IBFD, 2014), at p. 597; also cf. M. Prek/S. Lefèvre, 11 *Eur. St. Aid L. Q.* 2 (2012), at p. 342; P. Rossi-Maccanico in P. Pistone (ed.), *Legal Remedies in European Tax Law* (IBFD, 2009), p. 223 (at p. 231).

1163. It is not a specific of State aid law that the boundaries between comparability and justification are blurred. A similar issue also arises, for example, with regard to the concept of fiscal cohesion as a justification for prima facie obstacles to the fundamental freedoms. It may be relied upon as a justification ground "*where a direct link is established between a tax advantage and the offsetting of that advantage by a particular tax levy*" (Opinion of AG Kokott in *Nordea Bank Danmark*, C-48/13, EU:C:2014:153; at point 43; also see Judgment in *Verkooijen*, C-35/98, EU:C:2000:294, at para. 57; Judgment in *Bosal*, C-168/01, EU:C:2003:479, at para. 29; Judgment in *Schilling and Fleck-Schilling*, C-209/01, EU:C:2003:610, at para. 41; Judgment in *Manninen*, C-319/02, EU:C:2004:484, at para. 42; Judgment in *Keller Holding*, C-471/04, EU:C:2006:143, at para. 40; Judgment in *Test Claimants in the Thin Cap Group Litigation*, C-524/04, EU:C:2007:161, at para. 68; Judgment in *Rewe Zentralfinanz*, C-347/04, EU:C:2007:194, at para. 62; Judgment in *Papillon*, C-418/07, EU:C:2008:659, at para. 44; Judgment in *Glaxo Wellcome*, C-182/08, EU:C:2009:559, at para. 79; Judgment in *DI. VI. Finanziaria di Diego della Valle & C.*, C-380/11, EU:C:2012:552, at para. 47; Judgment in *Welte*, C-181/12, EU:C:2013:662, at para. 59). However, if a tax advantage that is limited to purely domestic situations is fully offset by an interrelated tax levy, the cross-border situation is not disadvantaged (cf. G. Kofler, *Doppelbesteuerungsabkommen und Europäisches Gemeinschaftsrecht* [Linde, 2007], at p. 114; also see K. Daxkobler, *Die grundfreiheitliche Rechtsprechung des EuGH* [Linde, 2015], at pp. 226-230). This is why AG Geelhoed concluded that "*the 'fiscal cohesion defence' was in fact conceptually indistinct from that of determining whether national legislation is discriminatory. In the vast majority of cases, therefore, one could indeed question whether the defence of 'fiscal cohesion' really has any useful separate function*" (Opinion of AG Geelhoed in *Test Claimants in the Thin Cap Group Litigation*, C-524/04, EU:C:2006:436, at point 90).

1164. Cf. R. Lyal, 38 *Fordham Intl. L. J.* 4 (2015), at p. 1033.

1165. Judgment *Commission/Netherlands*, C-279/08 P, EU:C:2011:551, at para. 62; also see Judgment in *Commission/MOL*, C-15/14 P, EU:C:2015:362, at para. 59.

1166. Judgment *Netherlands/Commission*, C-159/01, EU:C:2004:246, at para. 43; Judgment *Commission/Netherlands*, C-279/08 P, EU:C:2011:551, at para. 62 and para. 77; Judgment in

raised at the level of justification. The Court rather separates the arguments raised by the European Commission and the arguments raised by the Member State concerned. If the European Commission's arguments are not convincing in itself, the ECJ cannot declare a national measure to constitute State aid, because it has not been proven that it creates differences between undertakings which are in a comparable factual and legal situation.[1167] But if those arguments are convincing enough as such, it is up to the Member State to put forward arguments against the reasoning of the European Commission. If the arguments in favour of the Member State prevail, the ECJ considers the selective advantage to be justified.[1168]

3.4.3 *Justification by Means of Objectives Extrinsic to the Tax System*

Whether policy objectives which are extrinsic to the tax system should also be able to serve as a justification for State aid purposes is disputed. The ECJ has held that such "external" policy objectives do not constitute justification grounds for purposes of Article 107 TFEU. In *British Aggregates*, for example, the Court held that "*the need to take account of requirements relating to environmental protection, however legitimate, cannot justify the exclusion of selective measures, even specific ones such as environmental levies, from the scope of Article 87(1) EC [...] as account may in any event usefully be taken of the environmental objectives when the compatibility of the State aid measure with the common market is being assessed pursuant to Article 87(3) EC.*"[1169] Some scholars argue in a similar vein that, in general, there is no necessity to allow for a justification based on "external" policy objectives, because it would undermine the prerogative of the European Commission to declare the aids mentioned in Article 107(3) TFEU to be compatible with the internal market.[1170] However, due to the extensive interference with the Member States' sovereignty connected therewith, this kind of justification is considered to be appropriate if the national measure concerned is de facto selective,[1171] i.e., "*although the formal criteria for the application of the*

Commission and Spain/Government of Gibraltar and United Kingdom, C-106/09 P and C-107/09 P, EU:C:2011:732, at para. 146; Judgment in *BNP Paribas and BNL/Commission*, C-452/10 P, EU:C:2012:366, at para. 121.

1167. Cf. Judgment in *3M Italia*, C-417/10, EU:C:2012:184, at paras 41-42; Judgment in *Paint Graphos*, C-78/08, EU:C:2011:550, at paras 54-63.

1168. Judgment in *Tiercé Ladbroke/Commission*, C-353/95 P, EU:C:1997:596, at para. 35; Judgment in *GIL Insurance and others*, C-308/01, EU:C:2004:252, at paras 73-78; also cf. Judgment in *AEM*, C-128/03 and C-129/03, EU:C:2005:224, at para. 43.

1169. Judgment in *British Aggregates/Commission*, C-487/06 P, EU:C:2008:757, at para. 92; also see Judgment in *Spain/Commission*, C-409/00, EU:C:2003:92, at paras 53-54; Judgment *Commission/Netherlands*, C-279/08 P, EU:C:2011:551, at para. 75.

1170. See J. Englisch in H. Schaumburg/J. Englisch (eds.), *Europäisches Steuerrecht* (Dr Otto Schmidt, 2015), at p. 444, at MN 9.33; also cf. R. Ismer/S. Piotrowski, 43 *Intertax* 10 (2015), at p. 564.

1171. See J. Englisch in H. Schaumburg/J. Englisch (eds.), *Europäisches Steuerrecht* (Dr Otto Schmidt, 2015), at p. 442, at m.no 9.31 and at pp. 444-445, at MN 9.33; J. Englisch, 22 *EC Tax Rev.* 1 (2013), at p. 11; J. Englisch in A. Rust/C. Micheau (eds.), *State Aid and Tax Law* (Kluwer, 2013), at p. 73; similarly C. Micheau, 17 *EC Tax Rev.* 6 (2008), at p. 282.

measure are formulated in general and objective terms, the structure of the measure is such that its effects significantly favour a particular group of undertakings."[1172]

It is questionable whether such a strict distinction between de jure and de facto selectivity is feasible. A similar view is held with regard to the fundamental freedoms, according to which national measures leading to overt discrimination are excluded from the rule of reason, i.e., Member States may rely on "unwritten" grounds of justification only with regard to covert discrimination and non-discriminatory restrictions.[1173] The problem with such an approach is that it is often difficult to determine whether a national measure leads to overt or covert discrimination or to a non-discriminatory restriction, which is why such a distinction is considered to be impractical and hence not comprehensible.[1174] However, it may be similarly challenging to distinguish between de jure and de facto selectivity. Moreover, many tax measures are generally granted by way of general norms which are not de jure selective, but may nevertheless favour economic operators over others in practice.[1175] Hence, even if "external" justification grounds were only acceptable for de facto selective national measures, they would play a major role with regard to taxes.

The policy objectives of a national measure are taken into account either way. If it is not possible to justify selective tax advantages due to policy objectives which are extrinsic to the tax system, it would still have to be determined whether the national measure pursues an objective which is extrinsic to a particular tax regime or whether it implements the mechanisms inherent in the tax system. Depending on the context, however, one and the same objective might once be considered to be system-inherent and some other time it might be extrinsic to the particular tax system. In *Kernkraftwerke Lippe-Ems*, for example, the ECJ confirmed that Article 107(1) TFEU does not prohibit a Member State from levying "*a duty on the use of nuclear fuel for the commercial production of electricity with a view to raising revenue intended, inter alia, to contribute, in the context of fiscal consolidation and in accordance with the*

1172. European Commission, Commission Notice on the notion of State Aid as referred to in Article 107(1) of the Treaty on the Functioning of the European Union, *OJ* C 262 (19 Jul. 2016), at para. 121; for a different understanding see R. Ismer/S. Piotrowski, 43 *Intertax* 10 (2015), at pp. 566-569.

1173. See D. Hohenwarter, *Verlustverwertung im Konzern* (LexisNexis, 2009), at p. 113; G. Kofler, *Doppelbesteuerungsabkommen und Europäisches Gemeinschaftsrecht* (Linde, 2007), at p. 108; G. Kofler, 19 *ÖStZ* 6 (2006), at p. 111; L. Hinnekens, 11 *EC Tax Rev.* 3 (2002), at p. 114; L.A. Denys, 47 *Eur. Taxn.* 5 (2007), at pp. 221-222; S. Kingston, 44 *Common Market L. Rev.* 5 (2007), at pp. 1328-1329; M. Tumpel in J. Pelka (ed.), *Europa- und verfassungsrechtliche Grenzen der Unternehmensbesteuerung*, DStJG 30 (Dr Otto Schmidt, 2000), at pp. 324-326; for criticism see T. Kingreen, *Die Struktur der Grundfreiheiten des Europäischen Gemeinschaftsrechts* (Duncker & Humblot, 1999), at pp. 120-121; also see Opinion of AG Alber in *Bosal*, C-168/01, EU:C:2002:528, at para. 41.

1174. See A. Cordewener, Deutsche Unternehmensbesteuerung und europäische Grundfreiheiten - Grundzüge des materiellen und formellen Rechtsschutzsystems der EG, 42 *DStR* 1-2 (2004), p. 6 (at pp. 8-9); D. Hohenwarter, *Verlustverwertung im Konzern* (LexisNexis, 2009), at p. 114; G. Kofler, *Doppelbesteuerungsabkommen und Europäisches Gemeinschaftsrecht* (Linde, 2007), at p. 108; R. Lyal, 12 *EC Tax Rev.* 2 (2003), at p. 74; similarly also J. Englisch, *Dividendenbesteuerung* (Dr Otto Schmidt, 2005), at pp. 273-277.

1175. See C. Micheau, Tax Selectivity in European Law of State Aid: Legal Assessment and Alternative Approaches, 40 *Eur. L. Rev.* 3 (2015), p. 323 (at p. 325).

polluter-pays principle, to a reduction in the burden entailed for the Federal budget by the rehabilitation required at the Asse II mining site, where radioactive waste from the use of nuclear fuel is stored." The reason is that "*methods of producing electricity, other than that based on nuclear fuel, [...] are not, in the light of the objective pursued by [the rules introduced by KernbrStG], in a factual and legal situation that is comparable to that of the production method based on nuclear fuel, as only that method generates radioactive waste arising from the use of such fuel.*"[1176] Presumably, Germany could have reached the same economic and financial effects by introducing a tax disincentive for operators of nuclear power stations within its income tax system instead of introducing an excise duty on nuclear fuels. However, whereas the polluter-pays principle is intrinsic to a special levy on nuclear fuels, it is extrinsic to the income tax system. Despite the supposed coinciding effects, a different tax burden for producers of electricity using nuclear fuels, on the one hand, and producers of electricity using other forms of energy sources, on the other hand, could not be justified by the lack of comparability of these two groups, because not only the objective of the tax disincentive but also – and indeed primarily – "*the nature [and/or] general scheme of the [tax] system*"[1177] which results directly from "*the basic or guiding principles of [the] tax system*"[1178] or from "*the logic of the tax system*"[1179] has to be taken into account.

Although the different legislative technique does not necessarily affect the final outcome, it is not uncommon that special levies with a very specific scope are subject to a less intense level of scrutiny than specific exceptions from taxes with a very broad scope.[1180] This does not mean that a national measure can avoid from being scrutinized

1176. Judgment in *Kernkraftwerke Lippe-Ems*, C-5/14, EU:C:2015:354, at paras 78-79.

1177. Judgment in *Italy/Commission*, 173/73, EU:C:1974:71, at para. 15; Judgment in *Belgium/Commission*, C-75/97, EU:C:1999:311, at para. 33; Judgment in *France/Commission*, C-251/97, EU:C:1999:480, at para. 36; Judgment in *Italy/Commission*, C-310/99, EU:C:2002:143, at para. 51; Judgment in *Banks*, C-390/98, EU:C:2001:456, at para. 33; Judgment in *Adria-Wien Pipeline and Wietersdorfer & Peggauer Zementwerke*, C-143/99, EU:C:2001:598, at para. 42; Judgment in *Spain/Commission*, C-351/98, EU:C:2002:530, at para. 42; Judgment in *GIL Insurance and others*, C-308/01, EU:C:2004:252, at para. 72; Judgment in *Freskot*, C-355/00, EU:C:2003:298, at para. 86; Judgment *Netherlands/Commission*, C-159/01, EU:C:2004:246, at para. 42; Judgment in *Heiser*, C-172/03, EU:C:2005:130, at para. 43; Judgment in *AEM*, C-128/03 and C-129/03, EU:C:2005:224, at para. 39; Judgment in *British Aggregates/Commission*, C-487/06 P, EU:C:2008:757, at para. 129; Judgment in *Paint Graphos and others*, C-78/08 to C-80/08, EU:C:2011:550, at para. 76; Judgment *Commission/Netherlands*, C-279/08 P, EU:C:2011:551, at para. 62; Judgment in *Commission and Spain/Government of Gibraltar and United Kingdom*, C-106/09 P and C-107/09 P, EU:C:2011:732, at para. 146; Judgment in *BNP Paribas and BNL/Commission*, C-452/10 P, EU:C:2012:366, at para. 101; Judgment in *P*, C-6/12, EU:C:2013:525, at para. 22; Judgment in *Commission/MOL*, C-15/14 P, EU:C:2015:362, at para. 61.

1178. Judgment in *Portugal/Commission*, C-88/03, EU:C:2006:511, at para. 81; Judgment in *Paint Graphos and others*, C-78/08 to C-80/08, EU:C:2011:550, at para. 65 and para. 69; Judgment in *P*, C-6/12, EU:C:2013:525, at para. 22; Judgment in *Ministerio de Defensa and Navantia*, C-522/13, EU:C:2014:2262, at para. 43.

1179. Judgment in *Spain/Commission*, C-501/00, EU:C:2004:438, at para. 122; also see Judgment in *BNP Paribas and BNL/Commission*, C-452/10 P, EU:C:2012:366, at paras 137-138.

1180. With regard to the jurisprudence of the Austrian Constitutional Court see M. Achatz, Die Auswahl von Besteuerungsgegenständen – verfassungsrechtliche Aspekte, 15 *ÖStZ* 21 (2002), p. 534 (at pp. 534-541); H. Ruppe, Verfassungsrechtliche Vorgaben für Umweltabgaben, in E. Bernat/E. Böhler/A. Weilinger (eds.), *Zum Recht der Wirtschaft, Festschrift Heinz Krejci*

by the European Commission and the CJEU by labelling it an independent tax. Rather, it has to be determined whether a tax actually has an autonomous character or whether it is in fact based on the same principles as another tax, which could mean that both of them have to be considered collectively.[1181] However, since the legal evaluation should not be based on the legislative technique,[1182] it would go too far to generally deny the possibility of justifying selective advantages within a broad tax system by referring to the externality of the national measure's objective if the same economic and financial effect could also be reached by levying a special tax which in itself is deemed to establish an independent tax system that is based on the very same objectives. However, if one follows this approach, the question arises which objectives are legitimate from a State aid law perspective in order to serve as a justification for selective tax advantages.

In general, (not) levying taxes cannot per se be considered to infringe either the fundamental freedoms or Article 107(1) TFEU.[1183] Insofar as "*taxation falls within the competence of the Member States*"[1184] it is up to the Member States to decide on the object and the conceptual design of a tax,[1185] unless specific aims of EU law are violated,[1186] which would be the case, for example, if a Member State, in conflict with Article 30 TFEU, were to levy customs duties on imports and exports. Apart from that, Member States enjoy a wide discretion. In *Kernkraftwerke Lippe-Ems*, for example, the duty under scrutiny was deemed to be based on the idea of equivalency of costs. According to the ECJ, a duty on the use of nuclear fuel for the commercial production of electricity cannot be considered to be a selective measure if the resultant revenue is intended to cover the costs that originate from the radioactive waste that is only

(Verlag Österreich, 2001), p. 2079 (at pp. 2087-2088); C. Staringer/S. Denk, Verfassungsrechtliche Zulässigkeit der Stabilitätsabgabe, 26 *ÖZW* 3 (2012), p. 70 (at p. 75); with regard to the State aid law analysis also cf. W. Schön in L. Hancher/T. Ottervanger/P.J. Slot (eds.), *EU State Aids* (Sweet & Maxwell, 2012), at pp. 344-346.

1181. Cf. J. Englisch in H. Schaumburg/J. Englisch (eds.), *Europäisches Steuerrecht* (Dr Otto Schmidt, 2015), at p. 439, at m.no 9.29; W. Schön in L. Hancher/T. Ottervanger/P.J. Slot (eds.), *EU State Aids* (Sweet & Maxwell, 2012), at p. 342.

1182. With regard to the jurisprudence of the Austrian Constitutional Court see C. Staringer, Rechtsfragen der Zulässigkeit von "Handymastensteuern," in M. Achatz/T. Ehrke-Rabel/J. Heinrich/R. Leitner/O. Taucher (eds.), *Steuerrecht Verfassungsrecht Europarecht*, Festschrift Hans-Georg Ruppe (Facultas, 2007), p. 573 (at p. 587); also cf. H. Ruppe in E. Bernat/E. Böhler/A. Weilinger (eds.), *Zum Recht der Wirtschaft, Festschrift Heinz Krejci* (Verlag Österreich, 2001), at pp. 2087.

1183. Cf. J. Englisch in H. Schaumburg/J. Englisch (eds.), *Europäisches Steuerrecht* (Dr Otto Schmidt, 2015), at p. 438, at m.no 9.28.

1184. Judgment in *Spain/Commission*, C-501/00, EU:C:2004:438, at para. 123; Judgment in *Commission and Spain/Government of Gibraltar and United Kingdom*, C-106/09 P and C-107/09 P, EU:C:2011:732, at para. 37.

1185. Judgment in *Commission and Spain/Government of Gibraltar and United Kingdom*, C-106/09 P and C-107/09 P, EU:C:2011:732, at para. 97: "*It is true that, in the absence of European Union rules governing the matter, it falls within the competence of the Member States, or of infra-State bodies having fiscal autonomy, to designate bases of assessment and to spread the tax burden across the different factors of production and economic sectors.*"

1186. See W. Schön, Der freie Warenverkehr, die Steuerhoheit der Mitgliedstaaten und der Systemgedanke im europäischen Steuerrecht, Teil II, 36 *EuR* 3 (2001), p. 341 (at p. 357); also see W.C. Haslehner in T. Jaeger/B. Haslinger (ed.), *Jahrbuch Beihilferecht 12* (NWV, 2012), at pp. 321-322.

generated by those electricity producers that use nuclear fuel.[1187] Since the legislative technique should not affect the State aid analysis, a national measure that is not implementing a mechanism inherent in the tax system in which it is embedded should hence, in general, be justifiable if it is equally based on the principle of equivalence of costs. The decision in *AEM* is another example for the Court's acceptance of considerations of equivalence. An increased charge for access to and use of the national electricity transmission system required only of undertakings generating and distributing electricity from hydroelectric or geothermal installations was considered to be attributable to the nature and general scheme of the system of charges in question, because this surcharge was intended to offset certain advantages "*created for those undertakings by the liberalization of the market in electricity following the implementation of Directive 96/92.*"[1188] Thus, a different treatment of undertakings might be justified by the nature and general scheme of the tax system if it is based on the principle of equivalence of benefits.

However, it is much more difficult to demonstrate that a national measure within a tax system that is based on, for example, the ability-to-pay principle actually implements the idea of equivalence. Against this background, it can also be alleged that different effects of regulatory taxes are considered to be acceptable,[1189] although the ECJ is reluctant to consider national measures that insert regulatory elements into a non-regulatory tax to be justified due to the underlying policy consideration that is extrinsic to the tax system concerned.[1190]

By all means, the logic underlying a certain tax or a particular national measure has to be implemented consistently. In *Gibraltar*, for example, the ECJ held that even a whole tax system can be selective if it, "*instead of laying down general rules applying to all undertakings from which a derogation is made for certain undertakings, achieves the same result by adjusting and combining the tax rules in such a way that their very application results in a different tax burden for different undertakings.*"[1191] The Court identified the differentiating effect of the planned corporate tax reform in Gibraltar, which led to a preferential treatment of offshore companies, by referring to its objective.[1192] Since it was aimed to "*introduce a general system of taxation for all*

1187. Judgment in *Kernkraftwerke Lippe-Ems*, C-5/14, EU:C:2015:354, at paras 78-79.
1188. Judgment in *AEM*, C-128/03 and C-129/03, EU:C:2005:224, at paras 40, 43 and – for a description of the advantages – 20.
1189. See J. Englisch in H. Schaumburg/J. Englisch (eds.), *Europäisches Steuerrecht* (Dr Otto Schmidt, 2015), at pp. 425-426, at MN 9.17; W. Schön in L. Hancher/T. Ottervanger/P.J. Slot (eds.), *EU State Aids* (Sweet & Maxwell, 2012), at pp. 344-345.
1190. With regard to ecological policy considerations see, for example, Judgment in *Adria-Wien Pipeline and Wietersdorfer & Peggauer Zementwerke*, C-143/99, EU:C:2001:598, at paras 52-53; with regard to environmental policy considerations see, for example, Judgment *Netherlands/Commission*, C-159/01, EU:C:2004:246, at paras 40-48; Judgment *Commission/Netherlands*, C-279/08 P, EU:C:2011:551, at para. 76; with regard to employment policy considerations see, for example, Judgment in *Belgium/Commission*, C-75/97, EU:C:1999:311, at paras 37-39.
1191. Judgment in *Commission and Spain/Government of Gibraltar and United Kingdom*, C-106/09 P and C-107/09 P, EU:C:2011:732, at para. 93.
1192. Critically in this respect J. Temple Lang, The Gibraltar State Aid and Taxation Judgment – A "Methodological Revolution"?, 11 *Eur. St. Aid L. Q.* 4 (2012), p. 805 (at p. 808); also cf. R. Ismer/S. Piotrowski, 43 *Intertax* 10 (2015), at p. 569.

companies established in Gibraltar[,] […] it is apparent that the regime at issue, by combining [various features], even though they are founded on criteria that are in themselves of a general nature, in practice discriminates between companies which are in a comparable situation with regard to the objective of the proposed tax reform."[1193] Thus, the alleged objective of the planned corporate tax reform in Gibraltar was legitimate.

Whereas national measures that are alien to the tax system concerned are typically suspicious from a State aid law point of view, different tax burdens that simply result from a coherent realization and application of the logic, principles and aims on which the tax system is based are not problematic.[1194] However, if the economic and financial effect of a national measure that is alien to the tax system in which it is implemented could also be reached by levying a special tax which in itself is deemed to establish an independent tax system that is sacrosanct from an State aid law perspective, the national measure should be considered to be justified.

3.5 Proportionality

In order to be compatible with the fundamental freedoms, national measures that lead to a different treatment of cross-border and purely domestic situations must be justified by more than imperative requirements in the general interest. According to established case law, the ECJ rather also regularly requires that such measures must be proportionate.[1195] By contrast, it took until 2011 for the Court to explicitly refer to the principle of proportionality with regard to its jurisprudence on Article 107(1) TFEU. According to the relevant decision in *Paint Graphos*, "*in order for tax exemptions such as those at issue in the main proceedings to be justified by the nature or general scheme of the tax system of the Member State concerned, it is also necessary to ensure that those exemptions are consistent with the principle of proportionality and do not go beyond what is necessary, in that the legitimate objective being pursued could not be attained by less far-reaching measures.*"[1196] Thus, a national measure may only be justified by the nature and general scheme of the tax system if there is no alternative that is equally effective in promoting the pursued aim, but which is less burdensome for the addressee. Additionally, by referring to the national measure's consistency "*with the*

1193. Judgment in *Commission and Spain/Government of Gibraltar and United Kingdom*, C-106/09 P and C-107/09 P, EU:C:2011:732, at para. 102.
1194. See J. Englisch in H. Schaumburg/J. Englisch (eds.), *Europäisches Steuerrecht* (Dr Otto Schmidt, 2015), at pp. 425-426 and pp. 433-435, at MN 9.17 and MN 9.23; W. Schön, 36 *Common Market L. Rev.* 5 (1999), at p. 926; W. Schön in L. Hancher/T. Ottervanger/P.J. Slot (eds.), *EU State Aids* (Sweet & Maxwell, 2012), at p. 343; F.P. Sutter, *Das EG-Beihilfenverbot und sein Durchführungsverbot in Steuersachen* (Linde, 2005), at p. 109; R. Szudoczky, *The Sources of EU law and Their Relationships: Lessons for the Field of Taxation* (IBFD, 2014), at pp. 506-507.
1195. See Chapter 3.2.6.
1196. Judgment in *Paint Graphos and others*, C-78/08, EU:C:2011:550, at para. 75.

logic and general scheme of the tax system,"[1197] the ECJ implicitly requires the national measure to be suitable to achieve or at least promote the alleged objective.[1198]

As the principle of proportionality has been consistently held to be one of the general principles of EU law,[1199] it should not come as a surprise that it also affects the ECJ's State aid law analysis. In fact, indications for its relevance can already be found in decisions preceding *Paint Graphos*.[1200] In *Adria-Wien Pipeline*, for example, the Court held that "*ecological considerations underlying the national legislation at issue do not justify treating the consumption of natural gas or electricity by undertakings supplying services differently than the consumption of such energy by undertakings manufacturing goods. Energy consumption by each of those sectors is equally damaging to the environment.*"[1201] Thus, limiting the energy tax rebate to the manufacturing sector was not considered to be suitable to achieve the environmental objective of the national legislation, because the energy consumption by the favoured sector was equally damaging to the environment. In *Portugal/Commission*, the ECJ similarly pointed out that "*[m]easures such as those at issue, which apply to all economic operators without any distinction as to their financial circumstances, cannot be regarded as ensuring that for the purpose of redistribution the criterion of ability to pay is observed. Although it is true that the disadvantages related to the insularity of the Azores*

1197. Judgment in *Paint Graphos and others*, C-78/08, EU:C:2011:550, at paras 73-74.

1198. See R. Szudoczky, *The Sources of EU Law and Their Relationships: Lessons for the Field of Taxation* (IBFD, 2014), at p. 643; also cf. G. Mathisen, Consistency and Coherence as Conditions for Justification of Member State Measures Restricting Free Movement, 47 *Common Market L. Rev.* 4 (2010), p. 1021 (at p. 1026 and at pp. 1038-1039).

1199. Judgment in *Schräder*, 265/87, EU:C:1989:303, at para. 21; Judgment in *Fedesa*, 331/88, EU:C:1990:391, at para. 13; Judgment in *British American Tobacco (Investments) and Imperial Tobacco*, C-491/01, EU:C:2002:741, at para. 122; Judgment in *Arnold André*, C-434/02, EU:C:2004:800, at para. 45; Judgment in *Swedish Match*, C-210/03, EU:C:2004:802, at para. 47; Judgment in *ABNA and others*, C-453/03, C-11/04, C-12/04 and C-194/04, EU:C:2005:741, at para. 68; Judgment in *IATA and ELFAA*, C-344/04, EU:C:2006:10, at para. 79; Judgment in *Agrarproduktion Staebelow*, C-504/04, EU:C:2006:30, at para. 35; Judgment in *Dokter and others*, C-28/05, EU:C:2006:408, at para. 79; Judgment in *Laserdisken*, C-479/04, EU:C:2006:549, at para. 53; Judgment in *Germany / Parliament and Council*, C-380/03, EU:C:2006:772, at para. 144; Judgment in *Piek*, C-384/05, EU:C:2007:21, at para. 34; Judgment in *Maatschap Schonewille-Prins*, C-45/05, EU:C:2007:296, at para. 45; Judgment in *Geuting*, C-375/05, EU:C:2007:574, at para. 45; Judgment in *Cementbouw Handel & Industrie / Commission*, C-202/06 P, EU:C:2007:814, at para. 52; Judgment in *Promusicae*, C-275/06, EU:C:2008:54, at para. 68; Judgment in *Militzer & Münch*, C-230/06, EU:C:2008:186, at para. 47; Judgment in *Michaniki*, C-213/07, EU:C:2008:731, at para. 48; Judgment in *Agrana Zucker*, C-33/08, EU:C:2009:367, at para. 31; Judgment in *S.P.C.M. and others*, C-558/07, EU:C:2009:430, at para. 41; Judgment in *Vodafone and others*, C-58/08, EU:C:2010:321, at para. 51; Judgment in *Afton Chemical*, C-343/09, EU:C:2010:419, at para. 45; Judgment in *Etimine*, C-15/10, EU:C:2011:504, at para. 124; but see J. Englisch in D. Weber (ed.), *Traditional and Alternative Routes to European Tax Integration* (IBFD, 2010), at p. 237 ("*A legal principle is characterized by its relative nature and its susceptibility to weighing and balancing against conflicting interests, as opposed to a legal rule, according to the predominant opinion of scholars of legal theory. By contrast, the 'principle of proportionality' is in reality a rule prescribing how such conflicts should be solved in a rational way.*").

1200. See R. Szudoczky, *The Sources of EU Law and Their Relationships: Lessons for the Field of Taxation* (IBFD, 2014), at pp. 640-641.

1201. Judgment in *Adria-Wien Pipeline and Wietersdorfer & Peggauer Zementwerke*, C-143/99, EU:C:2001:598, at para. 52.

might, in principle, be suffered by all economic operators regardless of their financial circumstances, the mere fact that the regional tax system is conceived in such a way as to ensure the correction of such inequalities does not allow the conclusion to be drawn that every tax advantage granted by the authorities of the autonomous region concerned is justified by the nature and overall structure of the national tax system. [...] [T]he Portuguese Government has not shown that the adoption by the Autonomous Region of the Azores of the measures at issue was necessary for the functioning and effectiveness of the general tax system."[1202]

If the logic and fundamental principles underlying the respective tax are deemed to be decisive for the comparability analysis,[1203] it is understandable that the ECJ has almost never explicitly referred to the principle of proportionality. In order to answer the question whether a national measure specifies or whether it deviates from the fundamental principles underlying or the inherent logic of the respective Member State's tax system, an in-depth analysis of the national measure concerned and its role in and influence on the Member State's tax system at stake is required. Thereby, it has to be determined whether the scrutinized tax measure consistently and coherently implements the alleged logic and principles of the tax system in which it is embedded. However, if this is to be done at the level of comparability, there is not much room left for additional proportionality considerations. The Court's approach with regard to the State aid rules thus approximates its approach with regard to the fundamental freedoms in that it involves a comparability, a justification and a proportionality analysis.[1204] However, the borderlines between these steps are even less clearly established than in the Court's jurisprudence on the fundamental freedoms.

4 THE CONVERGENCE OF THE ECJ'S APPROACHES WITH REGARD TO THE FUNDAMENTAL FREEDOMS AND THE STATE AID PROVISIONS

Although at first glance the State aid provisions do not seem to have much in common with the fundamental freedoms – particularly since the two regimes are clearly separated[1205] – a closer examination reveals that the ECJ's approach with regard to these two sets of rules are quite similar. Considering that they both serve the same purpose (i.e., promoting, as a means of negative integration, the implementation of the internal market),[1206] this is not as surprising as one might initially think. After all, either

1202. Judgment in *Portugal/Commission*, C-88/03, EU:C:2006:511, at paras 82-83.

1203. See K. Drüen, 49 *DStR* 7 (2011), at p. 291; J. Englisch in H. Schaumburg/J. Englisch (eds.), *Europäisches Steuerrecht* (Dr Otto Schmidt, 2015), at p. 425, at MN 9.17; J. Englisch, 22 *EC Tax Rev.* 1 (2013), at p. 11; J. Englisch in A. Rust/C. Micheau (eds.), *State Aid and Tax Law* (Kluwer, 2013), at p. 72.

1204. See Chapter 3.3.

1205. See R. Szudoczky, *The Sources of EU Law and Their Relationships: Lessons for the Field of Taxation* (IBFD, 2014), at p. 468.

1206. Judgment in *Hansen*, 91/78, EU:C:1979:65, at para. 9; Judgment in *Commission/France*, 18/84, EU:C:1985/175, at para. 13; also see C. Micheau, Fundamental Freedoms and State Aid Rules under EU Law: The Example of Taxation, 52 *Eur. Taxn.* 5 (2012), p. 210 (at p. 211); M. O'Brien, Company Taxation, State Aid and Fundamental Freedoms: is the Next Step Enhanced Co-operation?, 30 *Eur. L. Rev.* 2 (2005), p. 209 (at p. 231); R. Szudoczky, *The Sources of EU*

regime protects a particular dimension of the internal market concept.[1207] On the one hand, according to Article 26(2) TFEU, the internal market "*shall comprise an area without internal frontiers in which the free movement of goods, persons, services and capital is ensured in accordance with the provisions of the Treaties.*" To abolish obstacles to the free movement of goods, persons, services and capital, the fundamental freedoms ought to eliminate the compartmentalizing effect of the Member States' legal systems.[1208] On the other hand, the internal market concept reflects the EU economic policy perception of "*an open market economy with free competition, favouring an efficient allocation of resources.*"[1209,1210] To ensure an efficient allocation of resources, a level playing field within the internal market has to be provided for.[1211] Since the Treaty of Lisbon, this is emphasized in a protocol annexed to the Treaties that clarifies that the "*internal market [...] includes a system ensuring that competition is not distorted.*"[1212] To implement this dimension of the internal market concept, distortions induced by the market participants,[1213] by the Member States,[1214] or by differences between the Member States' legal systems[1215] have to be avoided. From a tax perspective, the State aid rules (Articles 107-109 TFEU) are the most relevant means to implement this aspect of the internal market.[1216] According to the ECJ, "*the Treaty rules on State aid [...] are the expression of one of the essential tasks with which the European Community is entrusted under Article 2 EC, namely the establishment of a common market and the promotion of a high degree of competitiveness and convergence of economic performance.*"[1217]

Law and Their Relationships: Lessons for the Field of Taxation (IBFD, 2014), at p. 469; P.J. Wattel, 5 *World Tax J.* 1 (2013), at p. 129; P.J. Wattel, Some Fringe Areas of EU State Aid Law in Direct Tax Matters, in D. Weber (ed.), *EU Income Tax Law: Issues for the Years Ahead* (IBFD, 2013), p. 139 (at p. 139).

1207. See Chapter 3.1.

1208. See, for example, A. Cordewener, *Europäische Grundfreiheiten und nationales Steuerrecht* (Dr Otto Schmidt, 2002), at p. 352; G. Kofler, *Doppelbesteuerungsabkommen und Europäisches Gemeinschaftsrecht* (Linde, 2007), at p. 51; B. Strassburger, *Die Dogmatik der EU-Grundfreiheiten* (Mohr Siebeck, 2012), at p. 10.

1209. Article 120 TFEU.

1210. See, for example, D. Hanf in J. Pelkmans/D. Hanf/M. Chang (eds.), *The EU Internal Market in Comparative Perspective* (Peter Lang, 2008), at p. 77; W. Schön in J. Pelka (ed.), *Europa- und verfassungsrechtliche Grenzen der Unternehmensbesteuerung*, DStJG 30 (Dr Otto Schmidt, 2000), at pp. 191-195; W. Schön, 9 *EC Tax Rev.* 2 (2000), at p. 91; W. Schön in I. Richelle/W. Schön/E. Traversa (eds.), *Allocating Taxing Powers Within the European Union* (Springer, 2013), at p. 93; J. Schönfeld, *Hinzurechnungsbesteuerung und Europäisches Gemeinschaftsrecht* (Dr Otto Schmidt, 2005), at pp. 16-18; J.H.H. Weiler, 100 *Yale L. J.* 8 (1991), at pp. 2477-2478; B. Strassburger, *Die Dogmatik der EU-Grundfreiheiten* (Mohr Siebeck, 2012), at p. 8.

1211. Cf. J. Pelkmans/P. Robson, 26 *JCMS* 3 (1987), p. 181 (at p. 183); W. Schön in J. Pelka (ed.), *Europa- und verfassungsrechtliche Grenzen der Unternehmensbesteuerung*, DStJG 30 (Dr Otto Schmidt, 2000), at p. 194.

1212. Protocol (No 27) on the Internal Market and Competition, *OJ* C 326 (26 Oct. 2012), p. 47 (at p. 309).

1213. Articles 101-102.

1214. Articles 106-107.

1215. Article 116.

1216. See P. Pistone/R. Szudoczy in M. Lang/P. Pistone/J. Schuch/C. Staringer (eds.), *Introduction to European Tax Law on Direct Taxation*[4] (Linde, 2015), at p. 28.

1217. Judgment in *Commission/Greece*, C-369/07, EU:C:2009:428, at paras 118-119.

Since the State aid provisions and the fundamental freedoms protect different dimensions of the internal market concept, the two regimes not only have different scopes of application,[1218] but also provide for different criteria for identifying impediments of the internal market, and this naturally influences the methodological approaches with regard to the two set of rules. The ECJ's usual pattern of examining a potentially discriminatory tax measure which is covered by the ambit of the fundamental freedoms basically consists of three steps.[1219] It must thus be ascertained: (1) whether the cross-border situation is discriminated against vis-à-vis a comparable domestic situation, and (2) if so, whether this discrimination is justified by a legitimate aim, and (3) if so, whether the national measure is proportionate.[1220] On the other hand, in order to decide whether a national measure constitutes State aid within the meaning of Article 107(1) TFEU, the ECJ as well as the European Commission usually examine: (1) whether a selective advantage has been conferred on the recipient, (2) which has been financed by the State or through State resources, (3) if so, whether trade between Member States is thereby affected in a way that competition is distorted or threatens to be distorted, and (4) if so, whether the national measure is nevertheless justified by the nature or general scheme of the tax system.[1221]

1218. See F. Vanistendael, Fiscal Support Measures and Harmful Tax Competition, 9 *EC Tax Rev.* 3 (2000), p. 152 (at pp. 155-156).

1219. From the case law of the ECJ, one could of course deduce more steps. See, for example, B.J.M. Terra/P.J. Wattel, *European Tax Law*[6] (Kluwer, 2012), at pp. 59-63 ("*The rule of reason test – in its most extensive configuration,* i.e. *in the field of free movement of goods – consists of eight steps*").

1220. See, for example, G. Kofler, *Doppelbesteuerungsabkommen und Europäisches Gemeinschaftsrecht* (Linde, 2007), at pp. 51-52; R. Szudoczky, *The Sources of EU Law and Their Relationships: Lessons for the Field of Taxation* (IBFD, 2014), at pp. 469-470; B.J.M. Terra/P.J. Wattel, *European Tax Law*[6] (Kluwer, 2012), at p. 64; P.J. Wattel, 5 *World Tax J.* 1 (2013), at p. 130; P.J. Wattel in D. Weber (ed.), *EU Income Tax Law: Issues for the Years Ahead* (IBFD, 2013), at pp. 140-141; also cf. D. Hohenwarter, *Verlustverwertung im Konzern* (LexisNexis, 2009), at p. 53.

1221. In detail, it is unclear whether the approaches of the ECJ and the European Commission are in fact congruent. According to the Court, "*for a measure to be categorised as State aid within the meaning of the Treaty, [...] four cumulative conditions [...] must be fulfilled. First, there must be an intervention by the State or through State resources; second, the intervention must be liable to affect trade between Member States; third, it must confer an advantage on the recipient; fourth, it must distort or threaten to distort competition*" (Judgment in *Presidente del Consiglio dei Ministri*, C-169/08, EU:C:2009:709, at para. 52; also see Judgment in *Altmark Trans and Regierungspräsidium Magdeburg*, C-280/00, EU:C:2003:415, at para. 75; Judgment in *Pearle and others*, C-345/02, EU:C:2004:448, at para. 33; Judgment in *Heiser*, C-172/03, EU:C:2005:130, at para. 27; Judgment in *Enirisorse*, C-237/04, EU:C:2006:197, at para. 38-39; Judgment in *Commission/Deutsche Post*, C-399/08 P, EU:C:2010:481, at para. 39; Judgment in *Doux Élevage and Coopérative agricole UKL-ARREE*, C-677/11, EU:C:2013:348, at para. 25; Judgment in *Trapeza Eurobank Ergasias*, C-690/13, EU:C:2015:235, at para. 17; Judgment in *BVVG*, C-39/14, EU:C:2015:470, at para. 24). The European Commission, on the other hand, emphasizes that "*[f]irstly, the measure must confer on recipients an advantage which relieves them of charges that are normally borne from their budgets[;] [...] [s]econdly, the advantage must be granted by the State or through State resources[;] [...] [t]hirdly, the measure must affect competition and trade between Member States[;] [...] [l]astly, the measure must be specific or selective in that it favours 'certain undertakings or the production of certain goods'[;] [...] [h]owever, the selective nature of a measure may be justified by 'the nature or general scheme of the system'*" (Commission notice on the application of the State aid rules to measures relating to direct business taxation, *OJ* C 384 [10 Dec. 1998], p. 3 [at p. 4]). In the literature,

Despite the ostensible differences between the two examination patterns, both approaches comprise a comparative element. When examining the compatibility of a national measure with the fundamental freedoms, the cross-border situation is in general contrasted with a purely domestic situation.[1222] Thereby, the legal situation,[1223]

there are also disputes concerning the individual criteria that have to be examined. There are, for example, different views on whether a differentiation has to be made between the existence of an "advantage" and the examination of "selectivity" (for a view advocating this see, for example, J. Englisch in H. Schaumburg/J. Englisch [eds.], *Europäisches Steuerrecht* [Dr Otto Schmidt, 2015], at pp. 438-439, at MN 9.28; H. López, General Thought on Selectivity and Consequences of a Broad Concept of State Aid in Tax Matters, 9 *Eur. St. Aid L. Q.* 4 [2010], p. 807 [at pp. 808-810]; R. Luja, 9 *Eur. St. Aid L. Q.* 1 [2010], at pp. 161 et seq.; R. Luja, The Selectivity Test: The Concept of Sectoral Aid, in A. Rust/C. Micheau [eds.], *State Aid and Tax Law* [Kluwer, 2013], p. 107 [at p. 111]; J. Luts, Compatibility of IP Box Regimes with EU State Aid Rules and Code of Conduct, 23 *EC Tax Rev.* 5 [2014], p. 258 [at p. 269]; C. Micheau, Tax Selectivity in State Aid Review: a Debatable Case Practice, 17 *EC Tax Rev.* 6 [2008], p. 276 [at pp. 280-281]; P. Rossi-Maccanico, The Gibraltar Judgment and the Point on Selectivity in Fiscal Aids, 18 *EC Tax Rev.* 2 [2009], p. 67 [at p. 71]; W. Schön, Die Auswirkungen des gemeinschaftsrechtlichen Beihilferechts auf das Steuerrecht, in ÖJT [ed.], *Die Auswirkungen des gemeinschaftsrechtlichen Beihilferechts auf das Steuerrecht*, Referate und Diskussionsbeiträge, Band IV/2 [Manz, 2010], p. 21 [at pp. 28-31]; W. Schön in L. Hancher/T. Ottervanger/P.J. Slot [eds.], *EU State Aids* [Sweet & Maxwell, 2012], at pp. 351-352; C. Quigley, *European State Aid Law and Policy, Third Edition* [Hart Publishing, 2015], at pp. 5-6; also cf. V.H. Guerrero, Defining the Balance Between Free Competition and Tax Sovereignty in EC and WTO Law: The "due respect" to the General Tax System, 5 *German L. J.* 1 [2004], p. 87 [at p. 91]; K. Lenaerts, State Aid and Direct Taxation, in H. Kanninen/N. Korjus/A. Rosas [eds.], *EU Competition Law in Context: Essays in Honour of Virpi Tiili* [Hart Publishing, 2009], p. 291 [at pp. 294 et seq.]; also see Opinion of AG Jääskinen in *Commission and Spain/Government of Gibraltar and United Kingdom*, C-106/09 P and C-107/09 P, EU:C:2011:215, at point 158; also cf. Opinion of AG Kokott in *Presidente del Consiglio dei Ministri*, C-169/08, EU:C:2009:420, at points 125-130; Opinion of AG Jääskinen in *Paint Graphos and others*, C-78/08 to C-80/08, EU:C:2010:411, at points 71 and 79; for an opposing view see, for example, M. Lang, 19 *IStR* 15 [2010], at p. 577; M. Lang, State Aid and Taxation: Selectivity and Comparability Analysis, in I. Richelle/W. Schön/E. Traversa [eds.], *Allocating Taxing Powers Within the European Union* [Springer, 2013], p. 27 [at pp. 27-29]; M. Lang, Das Gibraltar-Urteil des EuGH: Neue beihilferechtliche Vorgaben für das Steuerrecht?, 24 *ÖStZ* 24 [2011], p. 593 [at p. 597]; M. Lang, Die Firmenwertabschreibung als selektive Beihilfe?, 27 *ÖStZ* 11 [2014], p. 277 [at p. 280]; also see M.V. Ezcurra, State Aids and Energy Taxes: Towards a Coherent Reference Framework, 41 *Intertax* 6/7 [2013], p. 340 [at p. 343]; R. Szudoczky, *The Sources of EU Law and Their Relationships: Lessons for the Field of Taxation* [IBFD, 2014], at pp. 578-581; also cf. M. Prek/S. Lefèvre, The Requirement of Selectivity in the Recent Case-Law of the Court of Justice, 11 *Eur. St. Aid L. Q.* 2 [2012], p. 335 [at pp. 337-338]).

1222. On the question of "horizontal comparability," i.e., comparing two cross-border situations, see Chapter 3.2.4.2.

1223. Judgment in *Avoir Fiscal*, 270/83, EU:C:1986:37, at paras 19-20; Judgment in *Royal Bank of Scotland*, C-311/97, EU:C:1999:216, at paras 24-31; Judgment in *Saint-Gobain*, C-307/97, EU:C:1999:438, at paras 47-48; Judgment in *D.*, C-376/03, EU:C:2005:424, at paras 58-61; Judgment in *Test Claimants in Class IV of the ACT Group Litigation*, C-374/04, EU:C:2006:773, at para. 68; Judgment in *Eckelkamp*, C-11/07, EU:C:2008:489, at paras 62-63; critically J. Englisch, 38 *Intertax* 4 (2010), at pp. 212.

the factual circumstances[1224] - or both[1225] - and/or the objective of the particular measure[1226] is/are taken into account. Within the EU State aid law analysis, on the other hand, it has to be determined whether certain undertakings are favoured "*in comparison with other undertakings which are in a legal and factual situation that is comparable in the light of the objective pursued by the measure in question.*"[1227] Although the comparability analysis for purposes of Article 107(1) TFEU still appears to be vaguer, it apparently shares common features with the approach taken with regard to the fundamental freedoms.[1228]

Moreover, irrespective of whether a national measure prima facie infringes the fundamental freedoms and/or the State aid rules, it may be immunized under certain conditions. Both regimes provide for explicit reasons that immunize either impediments of the fundamental freedoms or national measures constituting State aid in the sense of Article 107(1) TFEU. With regard to the fundamental freedoms, for example, the freedom of movement for workers "*shall not apply to employment in the public service,*"[1229] the freedom of establishment - as well as the freedom to provide services[1230] - "*shall not apply, so far as any given Member State is concerned, to activities which in that State are connected, even occasionally, with the exercise of*

1224. Judgment in *Schumacker*, C-279/93, EU:C:1995:31, at paras 31-38; Judgment in *Wielockx*, C-80/94, EU:C:1995:271, at paras 18-22; Judgment in *Gilly*, C-336/96, EU:C:1998:221, at paras 49-50; Judgment in *Gschwind*, C-391/97, EU:C:1999:409, at paras 28-30; Judgment in *Zurstrassen*, C-87/99, EU:C:2000:251, at paras 21-23; Judgment in *Lakebrink and Peters-Lakebrink*, C-182/06, EU:C:2007:452, at paras 28-34; Judgment in *Renneberg*, C-527/06, EU:C:2008:566, at paras 59-68; critically M. Lang, 51 *RIW* 5 (2005), at pp. 336 et seq.

1225. Order in *Mertens*, C-431/01, EU:C:2002:492, at para. 32.

1226. Judgment in *Oy AA*, C-231/05, EU:C:2007:439, at para. 38; Judgment in *Société Papillon*, C-418/07, EU:C:2008:659, at paras 27-30; Judgment in *X Holding*, C-337/08, EU:C:2010:89, at paras 20-24; Judgment in *Comission/Estonia*, C-39/10, EU:C:2012:282, at para. 51; Judgment in *X.*, C-87/13, EU:C:2014:2459, at paras 27-32; Judgment in *Q*, C-133/13, EU:C:2014:2460, at paras 22-27; critically J. Englisch, 38 *Intertax* 4 (2010), at pp. 202-204; J. Englisch, 33 *Intertax* 5 (2005), at p. 210; J. Englisch, 33 *Intertax* 8/9 (2005), at p. 320; G. Kofler, *Doppelbesteuerungsabkommen und Europäisches Gemeinschaftsrecht* (Linde, 2007), at p. 998.

1227. Judgment in *Adria-Wien Pipeline and Wietersdorfer & Peggauer Zementwerke*, C-143/99, EU:C:2001:598, at para. 38; see also Judgment in *GIL Insurance and others*, C-308/01, EU:C:2004:252, at para. 68; Judgment in *Spain/Commission*, C-409/00, EU:C:2003:92, at para. 47; Judgment in *Heiser*, C-172/03, EU:C:2005:130, at para. 40; Judgment in *Portugal/Commission*, C-88/03, EU:C:2006:511, at para. 54; Judgment in *Unión General de Trabajadores de la Rioja*, C-428/06 to C-434/06, EU:C:2008:488, at para. 46; Judgment in *British Aggregates/Commission*, C-487/06 P, EU:C:2008:757, at para. 82; Judgment in *Presidente del Consiglio dei Ministri*, C-169/08, EU:C:2009:709, at para. 61; Judgment in *Paint Graphos and others*, C-78/08 to C-80/08, EU:C:2011:550, at para. 49; Judgment in *P.*, C-6/12, EU:C:2013:525, at para. 19; Judgment in *Ministerio de Defensa and Navantia*, C-522/13, EU:C:2014:2262, at para. 35.

1228. See M. Lang, 19 *IStR* 15 (2010), at pp. 575-577; M. Lang, Selectivity as a Criterion to Determine Whether a Tax Measure Constitutes State Aid, in P. Pistone (ed.), *Legal Remedies in European Tax Law* (IBFD, 2009), p. 269 (at p. 270); R. Szudoczky, *The Sources of EU Law and Their Relationships: Lessons for the Field of Taxation* (IBFD, 2014), at p. 471; P.J. Wattel, 5 *World Tax J.* 1 (2013), at p. 130; P.J. Wattel in D. Weber (ed.), *EU Income Tax Law: Issues for the Years Ahead* (IBFD, 2013), at p. 141; also cf. P. Rossi-Maccanico, Fiscal Aid Review and Cross-Border Tax Distortions, 40 *Intertax* 2 (2012), p. 92 (at pp. 99-100).

1229. Article 45(4) TFEU.

1230. Article 62 TFEU.

official authority,"[1231] and the free movement of capital "*shall be without prejudice to the right of Member States [...] to apply the relevant provisions of their tax law which distinguish between taxpayers who are not in the same situation with regard to their place of residence or with regard to the place where their capital is invested,*" unless such provisions "*constitute a means of arbitrary discrimination or a disguised restriction on the free movement of capital and payments.*"[1232] Furthermore, the TFEU also provides for explicit reasons that justify discrimination and restrictions of the fundamental freedoms. According to Article 36 TFEU, for example, the free movement of goods "*shall not preclude prohibitions or restrictions on imports, exports or goods in transit justified on grounds of public morality, public policy or public security; the protection of health and life of humans, animals or plants; the protection of national treasures possessing artistic, historic or archaeological value; or the protection of industrial and commercial property.*" Similar, albeit fewer grounds of justification can be found in Article 45(3) TFEU on the free movement of workers ("*public policy, public security or public health*"), in Article 52(1) TFEU on the freedom of establishment and – due to Article 62 TFEU – on the freedom to provide services ("*public policy, public security or public health*") as well as in Article 65(1)(b) TFEU on the free movement of capital and payments ("*public policy or public security*"). The State aid rules also provide for certain aid measures that are, on the one hand, *ipso iure* considered compatible with the internal market (Article 107(2) TFEU) or, on the other hand, may be declared compatible with the internal market by the European Commission (Article 107(3) TFEU).

In addition, unwritten justifications have been developed by the ECJ both in the area of the fundamental freedoms as well as the State aid rules. According to the "rule of reason,"[1233] prima facie infringements of the fundamental freedoms can be "*justified by imperative requirements in the general interest.*"[1234] Based thereon, in the direct tax jurisprudence, so far, Member States successfully invoked the need to protect the coherence of the tax system – also referred to as fiscal cohesion –,[1235] the principle of

1231. Article 51 TFEU. Moreover, according to this provision, "*[t]he European Parliament and the Council, acting in accordance with the ordinary legislative procedure, may rule that the [freedom of establishment] shall not apply to certain activities.*"
1232. Article 65(1)(a) and (3) TFEU.
1233. Cf. A. Cordewener, *Europäische Grundfreiheiten und nationales Steuerrecht* (Dr Otto Schmidt, 2002), at p. 61 (FN 95).
1234. Judgment in *Gebhard*, C-55/94, EU:C:1995:411, at para. 37; Judgment in *Reisebüro Broede*, C-3/95, EU:C:1996:487, at para. 28; Judgment in *Centros*, C-212/97, EU:C:1999:126, at para. 34; Judgment in *Inspire Art*, C-167/01, EU:C:2003:512, at para. 133; Judgment in *Gambelli*, C-243/01, EU:C:2003:597, at para. 65; Judgment in *Contse*, C-234/03, EU:C:2005:664, at para. 25; Judgment in *Commission/Belgium*, C-522/04, EU:C:2007:405, at para. 47; see also Judgment in *Haim*, C-424/97, EU:C:2000:357, at para. 57; Judgment in *MacQuen*, C-108/96, EU:C:2001:67, at para. 26; Judgment in *Gräbner*, C-294/00, EU:C:2002:442, at para. 39; Judgment in *Colegio*, C-330/03, EU:C:2006:45, at para. 30; Judgment in *Commission/Greece*, C-65/05, EU:C:2006:673, at para. 49; Judgment in *Corporación Dermoestética*, C-500/06, EU:C:2008:421, at para. 35.
1235. Judgment in *Bachmann*, C-204/90, EU:C:1992:35, at para. 27; Judgment in *Commission/Belgium*, C-300/90, EU:C:1992:37, at para. 20; Judgment in *Krankenheim Ruhesitz am Wannsee-Seniorenheimstatt*, C-157/07, EU:C:2008:588, at para. 43; Judgment in *Papillon*, C-418/07, EU:C:2008:659, at paras 50-51; Judgment in *Commission/Belgium*, C-250/08,

territoriality,[1236] the preservation of the balanced allocation of the power to impose taxes,[1237] the prevention of a double use of losses,[1238] the prevention of tax abuse, avoidance and evasion[1239] as well as the need to ensure effective fiscal supervision and collection of taxes[1240] in order to justify domestic tax measures which were found, prima facie, to constitute a restriction of the fundamental freedoms. With regard to the State aid rules, the ECJ accepts unwritten justifications as well.[1241] According to the case law of the Court, a tax measure "*which, although conferring an advantage on its recipient, is justified by the nature or general scheme of the system of which it is part does not fulfil the condition of selectivity,*"[1242] and thus "*may be justified if the Member State*

EU:C:2011:793, at paras 69-77; Judgment in *Commission/Hungary*, C-253/09, EU:C:2011:795, at paras 70-78; Judgment in *Test Claimants in the FII Group Litigation*, C-35/11, EU:C:2012:707, at paras 57-59; Judgment in *K*, C-322/11, EU:C:2013:716, at paras 64-71.

1236. Judgment in *Futura Participations and Singer*, C-250/95, EU:C:1997:239, at para. 22; Judgment in *Centro Equestre da Lezíria Grande*, C-345/04, EU:C:2007:96, at para. 22; Judgment in *N.*, C-470/04, EU:C:2006:525, at para. 46; Judgment in *Commission/Germany*, C-591/13, EU:C:2015:230, at paras 65-69; Judgment in *Verder LabTec*, C-657/13, EU:C:2015:331, at para. 43; critically W. Schön, 69 *Bull. Intl. Taxn.* 4/5 (2015), at p. 284; W. Schön in W. Schön/C. Heber (eds.), *Grundfragen des Europäischen Steuerrechts* (Springer, 2015), at p. 140.

1237. Judgment in *Marks & Spencer*, C-446/03, EU:C:2005:763, at paras 43-46 and 51; Judgment in *N.*, C-470/04, EU:C:2006:525, at paras 42-47; Judgment in *Oy AA*, C-231/05, EU:C:2007:439, at paras 53 and 60; Judgment in *Lidl Belgium*, C-414/06, EU:C:2008:278, at paras 31-34 and 37; Judgment in *Glaxo Wellcome*, C-182/08, EU:C:2009:559, at paras 82-88; Judgment in *SGI*, C-311/08, EU:C:2010:26, at paras 60-64 and 69; Judgment in *SIAT*, C-318/10, EU:C:2012:415, at paras 45-48; Judgment in *National Grid Indus*, C-371/10, EU:C:2011:785, at paras 45-49; Judgment in *X Holding*, C-337/08, EU:C:2010:89, at paras 27-33; Judgment in *K.*, C-322/11, EU:C:2013:716, at paras 50-55 and 71; Judgment in *Verder LabTec*, C-657/13, EU:C:2015:331, at para. 47.

1238. Judgment in *Marks & Spencer*, C-446/03, EU:C:2005:763, at para. 47; Judgment in *Rewe Zentralfinanz*, C-347/04, EU:C:2007:194, at paras 45-46; Judgment in *Lidl Belgium*, C-414/06, EU:C:2008:278, at paras 35-36; but see Judgment in *Philips Electronics*, C-18/11, EU:C:2012:532, at para. 28.

1239. Judgment in *Emsland-Stärke*, C-110/99, EU:C:2000:695, at paras 46-59; Judgment in *Marks & Spencer*, C-446/03, EU:C:2005:763, at paras 49-50; Judgment in *Halifax and others*, C-255/02, EU:C:2006:121, at paras 67-86; Judgment in *Cadbury Schweppes and Cadbury Schweppes Overseas*, C-196/04, EU:C:2006:544, at paras 48-71; Judgment in *Oy AA*, C-231/05, EU:C:2007:439, at para. 60; Judgment in *SGI*, C-311/08, EU:C:2010:26, at paras 65-69; Judgment in *SIAT*, C-318/10, EU:C:2012:415, at para. 48; Judgment in *Itelcar*, C-282/12, EU:C:2013:629, at para. 35.

1240. Judgment in *FKP Scorpio Konzertproduktionen*, C-290/04, EU:C:2006:630, at para. 36; Judgment in *X.*, C-498/10, EU:C:2012:635, at paras 39-53; for further information see K. Simader, *Withholding Taxes and the Fundamental Freedoms* (Kluwer, 2014), at pp. 220-237.

1241. See K. Lenaerts in H. Kanninen/N. Korjus/A. Rosas (eds.), *EU Competition Law in Context: Essays in Honour of Virpi Tiili* (Hart Publishing, 2009), at p. 302 ("*Just as the ECJ recognises that tax restrictions to free movement may be justified as mandatory requirements of general interest, it recognises equally a tax measure forbidden in principle by Article 87(1) EC may be justified – and this beyond the exemptions provided for in Article 87(2) and (3) EC – by the nature or overall structure of the tax system.*").

1242. Judgment in *Adria-Wien Pipeline and Wietersdorfer & Peggauer Zementwerke*, C-143/99, EU:C:2001:598, at para. 42; Judgment in *P.*, C-6/12, EU:C:2013:525, at para. 22; see also Judgment in *Italy/Commission*, 173/73, EU:C:1974:71, at para. 15; Judgment in *Belgium/Commission*, C-75/97, EU:C:1999:311, at para. 33; Judgment in *Banks*, C-390/98, EU:C:2001:456, at para. 34; Judgment in *GIL Insurance and others*, C-308/01, EU:C:2004:252, at para. 72; Judgment in *Heiser*, C-172/03, EU:C:2005:130, at para. 43; Judgment in *British Aggregates/Commission*, C-487/06 P, EU:C:2008:757, at para. 88; Judgment in *British*

concerned can show that that measure results directly from the basic or guiding principles of its tax system."[1243] Hence, the ECJ's approaches with regard to the fundamental freedoms and the State aid rules converge insofar as unwritten grounds of justification have emerged.[1244]

What is more, according to the "rule of reason," as summarized by the ECJ in *Gebhard*, national measures that lead to a different treatment of cross-border and purely domestic situations need not only be justified by imperative requirements in the general interest in order to be compatible with the fundamental freedoms. Rather, *"they must be suitable for securing the attainment of the objective which they pursue; and they must not go beyond what is necessary in order to attain it."*[1245] Thereby, the ECJ refers to the principle of proportionality, which was mentioned for the first time in *Fédéchar*.[1246] Since then, the principle of proportionality has been consistently held to be one of the general principles of EU law.[1247] It is hence not surprising that this

---

Aggregates/Commission, C-487/06 P, EU:C:2008:757, at para. 88; Judgment in *Paint Graphos and others*, C-78/08, EU:C:2011:550, at para. 64.

1243. Judgment in *Paint Graphos and others*, C-78/08, EU:C:2011:550, at para. 65; Judgment in *P.*, C-6/12, EU:C:2013:525, at para 22; see also Judgment in *Portugal/Commission*, C-88/03, EU:C:2006:511, at para. 81; Judgment in *Ministerio de Defensa and Navantia*, C-522/13, EU:C:2014:2262, at para. 43.

1244. See R. Szudoczky, *The Sources of EU Law and Their Relationships: Lessons for the Field of Taxation* (IBFD, 2014), at pp. 471-472; P.J. Wattel, 5 *World Tax J.* 1 (2013), at p. 130; P.J. Wattel in D. Weber (ed.), *EU Income Tax Law: Issues for the Years Ahead* (IBFD, 2013), at p. 141; also cf. P. Rossi-Maccanico, 40 *Intertax* 2 (2012), at pp. 99-100.

1245. Judgment in *Gebhard*, C-55/94, EU:C:1995:411, at para. 37; see also Judgment in *Kraus*, C-19/92, EU:C:1993:125, at para. 32; Judgment in *Reisebüro Broede*, C-3/95, EU:C:1996:487, at para. 28; Judgment in *Centros*, C-212/97, EU:C:1999:126, at para. 34; Judgment in *Haim*, C-424/97, EU:C:2000:357, at para. 57; Judgment in *MacQuen*, C-108/96, EU:C:2001:67, at para. 26; Judgment in *Gräbner*, C-294/00, EU:C:2002:442, at para. 39; Judgment in *Inspire Art*, C-167/01, EU:C:2003:512, at para. 133; Judgment in *Contse*, C-234/03, EU:C:2005:664, at para. 25; Judgment in *Colegio de Ingenieros de Caminos, Canales y Puertos*, C-330/03, EU:C:2006:45, at para. 30; Judgment in *Commission/Greece*, C-65/05, EU:C:2006:673, at para. 49; Judgment in *Corporación Dermoestética*, C-500/06, EU:C:2008:421, at para. 35.

1246. Judgment in *Fédéchar*, 8/55, EU:C:1956:11, at p. 299.

1247. Judgment in *Schräder*, 265/87, EU:C:1989:303, at para. 21; Judgment in *Fedesa*, 331/88, EU:C:1990:391, at para. 13; Judgment in *British American Tobacco (Investments) and Imperial Tobacco*, C-491/01, EU:C:2002:741, at para. 122; Judgment in *Arnold André*, C-434/02, EU:C:2004:800, at para. 45; Judgment in *Swedish Match*, C-210/03, EU:C:2004:802, at para. 47; Judgment in *ABNA and others*, C-453/03, C-11/04, C-12/04 and C-194/04, EU:C:2005:741, at para. 68; Judgment in *IATA and ELFAA*, C-344/04, EU:C:2006:10, at para. 79; Judgment in *Agrarproduktion Staebelow*, C-504/04, EU:C:2006:30, at para. 35; Judgment in *Dokter and others*, C-28/05, EU:C:2006:408, at para. 79; Judgment in *Laserdisken*, C-479/04, EU:C:2006:549, at para. 53; Judgment in *Germany / Parliament and Council*, C-380/03, EU:C:2006:772, at para. 144; Judgment in *Piek*, C-384/05, EU:C:2007:21, at para. 34; Judgment in *Maatschap Schonewille-Prins*, C-45/05, EU:C:2007:296, at para. 45; Judgment in *Geuting*, C-375/05, EU:C:2007:574, at para. 45; Judgment in *Cementbouw Handel & Industrie / Commission*, C-202/06 P, EU:C:2007:814, at para. 52; Judgment in *Promusicae*, C-275/06, EU:C:2008:54, at para. 68; Judgment in *Militzer & Münch*, C-230/06, EU:C:2008:186, at para. 47; Judgment in *Michaniki*, C-213/07, EU:C:2008:731, at para. 48; Judgment in *Agrana Zucker*, C-33/08, EU:C:2009:367, at para. 31; Judgment in *S.P.C.M. and others*, C-558/07, EU:C:2009:430, at para. 41; Judgment in *Vodafone and others*, C-58/08, EU:C:2010:321, at para. 51; Judgment in *Afton Chemical*, C-343/09, EU:C:2010:419, at para. 45; Judgment in *Etimine*, C-15/10, EU:C:2011:504, at para. 124; but see J. Englisch in D. Weber (ed.), *Traditional and Alternative Routes to European Tax Integration* (IBFD, 2010), at

principle has finally expanded into the ECJ's State aid law jurisprudence as well: In *Paint Graphos*, the Court held that "*in order for tax exemptions such as those at issue in the main proceedings to be justified by the nature or general scheme of the tax system of the Member State concerned, it is also necessary to ensure that those exemptions are consistent with the principle of proportionality and do not go beyond what is necessary, in that the legitimate objective being pursued could not be attained by less far-reaching measures.*"[1248] Thus, with regard to the EU State aid law analysis, the ECJ also seems to apply the last step of the "rule of reason" as originally developed in the area of the fundamental freedoms.[1249]

Overall, it can, therefore, be concluded that the Court's approaches with regard to the fundamental freedoms and the State aid rules have converged to a certain extent. Although not applied consistently, both approaches involve a comparability, a justification and a proportionality analysis.[1250] However, the convergence of the examination patterns should not be confused with congruency of the legal analysis.[1251] With regard to the comparability test, for example, the fundamental freedoms prohibit differential treatment based on nationality or any similar factor, whereas Article 107(1) TFEU precludes a differential treatment "*which distorts or threatens to distort competition [...], in so far as it affects trade between Member States.*" Hence, comparability in the context of the fundamental freedom analysis is exclusively based on *inter*state distinctions. In contrast, the State aid rules also, but not only, allow *intra*state comparisons.[1252]

The yardsticks and valuations need not fully coincide either. With regard to the fundamental freedoms, for example, the ECJ has held that "*[i]t is for each Member State to ensure that individuals obtain reparation for damage caused to them by non-compliance with Community law, whichever public authority is responsible for the breach and whichever public authority is in principle, under the law of the Member State concerned, responsible for making reparation. A Member State cannot, therefore, plead the distribution of powers and responsibilities between the bodies which exist in its national legal order in order to free itself from liability on that basis.*"[1253] The Court's

p. 237 ("*A legal principle is characterized by its relative nature and its susceptibility to weighing and balancing against conflicting interests, as opposed to a legal rule, according to the predominant opinion of scholars of legal theory. By contrast, the 'principle of proportionality' is in reality a rule prescribing how such conflicts should be solved in a rational way.*").

1248. Judgment in *Paint Graphos and others*, C-78/08, EU:C:2011:550, at para. 75.
1249. See P.J. Wattel, 5 *World Tax J.* 1 (2013), at p. 134; P.J. Wattel in D. Weber (ed.), *EU Income Tax Law: Issues for the Years Ahead* (IBFD, 2013), at p. 147; P.J. Wattel, Comparing Criteria: State Aid, Free Movement, Harmful Tax Competition and Market Distorting Disparities, in I. Richelle/W. Schön/E. Traversa (eds.), *Allocating Taxing Powers Within the European Union* (Springer, 2013), p. 59 (at p. 68).
1250. See R. Szudoczky, *The Sources of EU Law and Their Relationships: Lessons for the Field of Taxation* (IBFD, 2014), at p. 472.
1251. Cf. M. Lang, 19 *IStR* 15 (2010), at p. 578.
1252. See P.J. Wattel, 5 *World Tax J.* 1 (2013), at p. 129; P.J. Wattel in D. Weber (ed.), *EU Income Tax Law: Issues for the Years Ahead* (IBFD, 2013), at p. 140; also see R. Szudoczky, *The Sources of EU Law and Their Relationships: Lessons for the Field of Taxation* (IBFD, 2014), at p. 524.
1253. Judgment in *Konle*, C-302/97, EU:C:1999:271, at para. 62; also see Judgment in *Haim*, C-424/97, EU:C:2000:357, at paras 27-28.

approach pertaining to federal tax systems with regard to EU State aid law, on the other hand, is more sophisticated: As the wording of Articles 107(2)(c) and 107(3)(a) TFEU indicates, if a tax benefit is limited to a certain geographic area, it will normally be selective and qualify as State aid, if all other requirements are fulfilled as well.[1254] In principle, this does not change if the national measure was adopted by a state in a federation or by a regional authority and not by the federal or central power.[1255] Otherwise, Member States could circumvent the prohibition to grant State aid by shifting taxing powers to sub-national bodies.[1256] However, as AG Kokott pointed out, "*[i]f the limited territorial application of local tax rules alone were to give grounds for the selectivity of a measure, the autonomy which the national Constitution accords the local or regional authority would be very questionable.*"[1257] It is hence necessary to balance the freedom of Member States to allocate taxing powers to regional or local authorities, which is explicitly addressed in Article 4(2) TEU,[1258] and the interests of the internal market concept.[1259] To this end, the ECJ distinguishes between systems of symmetrical and asymmetrical distribution of tax competences.[1260] If all the local authorities at the same level (regions, districts or others) have the autonomous power to enact tax measures (symmetrical distribution of tax competences), the Court seems to generally negate selectivity.[1261] If, on the other hand, only certain regional or local authorities have such an autonomous power (asymmetrical distribution of tax competences), the accusation of having granted regional State aid may only be successfully refuted if the sub-national body is "sufficiently autonomous" from an institutional, procedural, economic and financial point of view, i.e.: (1) it has, from a constitutional point of view, a political and administrative status separate from that of the central government, (2) the central government must not be able to directly intervene as regards the

1254. Judgment in *Portugal/Commission*, C-88/03, EU:C:2006:511, at para. 60; Judgment in *Comitato "Venezia vuole vivere" and others/Commission*, C-71/09 P, C-73/09 P and C-76/09 P, EU:C:2011:368, at para. 96; also see T. Jestaedt, Regional Aid, in L. Hancher/T. Ottervanger/ P.J. Slot (eds.), *EU State Aids* (Sweet & Maxwell, 2012), p. 783 (at p. 784, m.no 21-002); F.P. Sutter in K. Andersson/E. Eberhartinger/L. Oxelheim (eds.), *National Tax Policy in Europe*, at p. 130; critically C. Arhold, Steuerhoheit auf regionaler oder lokaler Ebene und der europäische Beihilfenbegriff – wie weit reicht das Konzept von der regionalen Selektivität, 17 *EuZW* 23 (2006), p. 717 (at pp. 717 et seq.).

1255. Judgment in *Germany/Commission*, 248/84, EU:C:1985:437, at para. 17; Judgment in *Portugal/Commission*, C-88/03, EU:C:2006:511 at para. 60; also see K. Lenaerts in H. Kanninen/N. Korjus/A. Rosas (eds.), *EU Competition Law in Context: Essays in Honour of Virpi Tiili* (Hart Publishing, 2009), at p. 300.

1256. See M. Lang, 19 *IStR* 15 (2010), p. 574; F.P. Sutter in K. Andersson/E. Eberhartinger/L. Oxelheim (eds.), *National Tax Policy in Europe*, at pp. 130-131.

1257. Opinion of AG Kokott in *Unión General de Trabajadores de la Rioja*, C-428/06 to C-434/06, EU:C:2008:262, at point 56.

1258. With regard to this provision also cf. Judgment in *Sayn-Wittgenstein*, C-208/09, EU:C:2010:806, at paras 81-95.

1259. See E. Traversa, The Selectivity Test: The Concept of "Regional Aid," in A. Rust/C. Micheau (eds.), *State Aid and Tax Law* (Kluwer, 2013), p. 119 (at p. 121); also cf. C. Arhold, 17 *EuZW* 23 (2006), at p. 720.

1260. Judgment in *Portugal/Commission*, C-88/03, EU:C:2006:511, at para. 48; also see M. Lang, 19 *IStR* 15 (2010), at p. 574.

1261. Judgment in *Portugal/Commission*, C-88/03, EU:C:2006:511, at para. 64; also see C. Arhold, 17 *EuZW* 23 (2006), at p. 719.

content of the regional or local authority's decision, and (3) the financial consequences of the decision taken at the regional or local level for undertakings in the respective region must not be offset by aid or subsidies from other regions or the central government.[1262]

Parts of the literature point out that another difference between the two set of rules is that the State aid rules address *positive* discrimination, whereas the fundamental freedoms focus on *negative* discrimination.[1263] Considering that the fundamental freedoms protect cross-border situations from being treated *worse* than comparable domestic situations and the State aid rules are aimed at restricting the *favouring* of certain undertakings or the production of certain goods, this seems plausible. However, to the extent a comparison is required in order to determine a violation of the fundamental freedoms and/or State aid law, positive and negative discrimination are two sides of the same coin. If taxpayer A is treated worse than taxpayer B, taxpayer B is necessarily treated more favourably than taxpayer A.[1264] The fundamental freedoms and the State aid rules are thus based on the same underlying principle, i.e., the principle of equal treatment.[1265] The yardsticks for determining whether two situations are comparable or not and whether different or equal treatment is justified and proportionate may differ,[1266] not least because the two set of rules protect different dimensions of the internal market concept.[1267] Since both regimes ultimately aim at promoting the implementation of the internal market, it could be considered to examine the ECJ's case law with regard to the other regime when examining the compatibility of a national measure either with the fundamental freedoms or with the EU State aid rules. AG Kokott seems to go even further by emphasizing that in order "*to*

1262. Judgment in *Portugal/Commission*, C-88/03, EU:C:2006:511, at para. 67; Judgment in *Unión General de Trabajadores de la Rioja*, C-428/06 to C-434/06, para. 51; also see F.P. Sutter in H. Mayer/K. Stöger (eds.), *EUV/AEUV* (Manz, 2014), Article 108 AEUV, MN 65.

1263. See P.J. Wattel, 5 *World Tax J.* 1 (2013), at p. 129; P.J. Wattel in D. Weber (ed.), *EU Income Tax Law: Issues for the Years Ahead* (IBFD, 2013), at p. 140.

1264. Cf. P. Nicolaides, Fiscal Aid in the EC – A Critical Review of Current Practice, 24 *World Competition* 3 (2001), p. 319 (at p. 326: "*If one of the fundamental freedoms is restricted, say the right of establishment, then some EU companies are being treated less favourably than others. It follows from this that some companies are treated more favourably than others and this conclusion may be sufficient for the selectivity criterion of Article 87(1) to apply.*").

1265. See M. Lang, *Die Auswirkungen des gemeinschaftsrechtlichen Beihilferechts auf das Steuerrecht*, 17. ÖJT, Band IV/1 (Manz, 2009), at p. 26; M. Lang, 19 *IStR* 15 (2010), p. 577; M. Lang, State Aid and Taxation: Recent Trends in the Case Law of the ECJ, 11 *Eur. St. Aid L. Q.* 2 (2012), p. 411 (at p. 420); K. Lenaerts in H. Kanninen/N. Korjus/A. Rosas (eds.), *EU Competition Law in Context: Essays in Honour of Virpi Tiili* (Hart Publishing, 2009), at p. 299; M. Prek/S. Lefèvre, 11 *Eur. St. Aid L. Q.* 2 (2012), at p. 336; R. Szudoczky, *The Sources of EU Law and Their Relationships: Lessons for the Field of Taxation* (IBFD, 2014), at p. 523; also see Opinion of AG Cosmas in *Tiercé Ladbroke*, C-353/95, EU:C:1997:233, at point 30; with a different, but perhaps only more nuanced view see J. Englisch in H. Schaumburg/J. Englisch (eds.), *Europäisches Steuerrecht* (Dr Otto Schmidt, 2015), at p. 443, at MN 9.32.

1266. See, for example, M. Lang, *Die Auswirkungen des gemeinschaftsrechtlichen Beihilferechts auf das Steuerrecht*, 17. ÖJT, Band IV/1 (Manz, 2009), at p. 26.

1267. H. Kube, Die Gleichheitsdogmatik des europäischen Wettbewerbsrechts - zur Beihilfenkontrolle staatlicher Ausgleichsleistungen, 39 *EuR* 2 (2004), p. 230 (at pp. 248-249).

avoid conflicting assessments as between the law of State aid and the law of fundamental freedoms, the same criteria must be applied in both cases."[1268]

Against this background, the EU law compatibility of double taxation and double non-taxation should not be analysed isolated from one another. Rather, the convergence of the ECJ's approaches with regard to the fundamental freedoms and the State aid rules suggest that arguments which have been raised with regard to one set of rules should also be taken into account when applying the other set or rules. Thereby, it has to be taken into account that the impact of the fundamental freedoms on the phenomenon of double taxation has already been thoroughly examined in the literature as well as by the ECJ.[1269] By contrast, the State aid rules' potential to address the phenomenon of double non-taxation has so far only been touched upon. Considering the already mentioned convergence, it is time to examine whether it is possible to extract arguments from the ECJ's jurisprudence on the compatibility of double taxation with the fundamental freedoms that may speak in favour of or against double non-taxation constituting (un-)lawful State aid.

1268. Opinion of AG Kokott in *Presidente del Consiglio dei Ministri*, C-169/08, EU:C:2009:420, at point 134; also see also cf. P. Rossi-Maccanico, 40 *Intertax* 2 (2012), at pp. 99-100 ("*In principle, there is no reason not to follow similar criteria than the ones developed by the CJ in reviewing tax discriminations or restrictions hindering the exercise of fundamental freedoms in the internal market, when reviewing tax preferences under state aid rules*").
1269. See Chapter 4.1.3.

CHAPTER 4

The Impact of EU Law on Double (Non-)Taxation

1 DOUBLE TAXATION IN THE LIGHT OF EU LAW

1.1 The Challenge of Tackling Double Taxation by Means of Primary EU Law

States can levy taxes by virtue of their sovereignty. From a public international law perspective, there are hardly any limits to the taxation rights of sovereign states, provided that there is a personal and/or a material nexus of the taxable event to the taxing jurisdiction.[1270] Since there is also no explicit or customary international law prohibition of double taxation,[1271] the same event may be taxed in two or even more states. Within the EU, this kind of double or multiple taxation is not only economically problematic,[1272] but also suspect from a legal perspective. After all, tax overlaps resulting from the coexistence of national tax systems negatively affect the functioning

1270. See, for example, G. Kofler, *Doppelbesteuerungsabkommen und Europäisches Gemeinschaftsrecht* (Linde, 2007), at p. 131; G. Kofler in A. Rust (ed.), *Double Taxation within the European Union* (Kluwer, 2011), at p. 104; K. Vogel, 59 *StuW* 2 (1982), at p. 112; K. Vogel/A. Rust in E. Reimer/A. Rust (eds.), *Klaus Vogel on Double Taxation Conventions, Fourth Edition* (Kluwer, 2015), Introduction at MN 8.

1271. See K. Vogel, *Der räumliche Anwendungsbereich der Verwaltungsrechtsnorm* (Alfred Metzner Verlag, 1965), at pp. 351-352; K. Vogel, 59 *StuW* 2 (1982), at p. 112; K. Vogel/A. Rust in E. Reimer/A. Rust (eds.), *Klaus Vogel on Double Taxation Conventions, Fourth Edition* (Kluwer, 2015), Introduction, at MN 9.

1272. Opinion of AG Colomer in *D*, C-376/03, EU:C:2004:663, at point 85 ("*the fact that a taxable event might be taxed twice is the most serious obstacle there can be to people and their capital crossing [...] borders*").

of the internal market.[1273] As (inter-state) double taxation[1274] is a problem specific to cross-border transactions,[1275] it seems opportune to inquire whether the fundamental freedoms can be relied upon by taxpayers in order to get relief from double taxation.[1276] Such an analysis is challenging,[1277] because, on the one hand, double taxation may be due to a disparity, which does not fall within the scope of the fundamental freedoms, *"so long as they affect all persons subject to them in accordance with objective criteria and without regard to their nationality."*[1278] If, for example, a hybrid financial instrument is treated as debt in the residence state and as equity in the source state, the amount paid by the debtor is not deductible in the source state, but still has to be subjected to tax by the creditor in the residence state.[1279] On the other hand, double taxation might persist even if all Member States had the same (non-discriminatory) tax

1273. Judgment in *Kerckhaert and Morres*, C-513/04, EU:C:2006:603, at para. 21; Judgment in *Columbus Container Services*, C-298/05, EU:C:2007:754, at para. 44; Judgment in *Block*, C-67/08, EU:C:2009:92, at para. 29; Judgment in *Damseaux*, C-128/08, EU:C:2009:471, at para. 22; Judgment in *CIBA*, C-96/08, EU:C:2010:185 at para. 26.
1274. Double taxation may also occur within one and the same state if the fiscal competence is not centralized, but the administrative units (e.g., regions, provinces, cantons or federal states) may autonomously decide on imposing taxes. On double taxation within the US see, for example, A. Cordewener, *Europäische Grundfreiheiten und nationales Steuerrecht* (Dr Otto Schmidt, 2002), at pp. 871-876; G. Kofler, *Doppelbesteuerungsabkommen und Europäisches Gemeinschaftsrecht* (Linde, 2007), at pp. 221-231; G. Kofler/R. Mason, 14 *Colum. J. Eur. L.* 1 (2007), at pp. 83-91; G. Kofler/R. Mason in S. van Thiel (ed.), *The Internal Market and Direct Taxation: Is the European Court of Justice Taking a New Approach?* (CFE Brochure on European Taxation, 2007), at pp. 205-213.
1275. See G. Kofler, *Doppelbesteuerungsabkommen und Europäisches Gemeinschaftsrecht* (Linde, 2007), at p. 155; G. Kofler in A. Rust (ed.), *Double Taxation Within the European Union* (Kluwer, 2011), at p. 106; W. Hellerstein/G. Kofler/R. Mason, 62 *Tax L. Rev.* 1 (2008), at p. 7; V. Heydt in W. Haslehner/G. Kofler/A. Rust (eds.), *Landmark Decisions of the ECJ in Direct Taxation* (Kluwer, 2015), at p. 181; also cf. J. Englisch, 33 *Intertax* 8/9 (2005), at p. 323; W. Schön, 11 *EWS* 7 (2001), at p. 290; but see B.J.M. Terra/P.J. Wattel, *European Tax Law*[6] (Kluwer, 2012), at p. 1046; E. Traversa/C. Helleputte in M. Lang/P. Melz/E. Kristoffersson (eds.), *Value Added Tax and Direct Taxation* (IBFD, 2009), at p. 340 (*"juridical double taxation is rare in the national context"*); P. Wattel in G. Maisto (ed.), *Taxation of Intercompany Dividends under Tax Treaties and EU Law* (IBFD, 2012), at p. 44.
1276. In the literature, it is emphasized that this question *"is nearly as old as the EC Treaty itself"* (G. Kofler in A. Rust [ed.], *Double Taxation Within the European Union* [Kluwer, 2011], at p. 104; also see G. Kofler, *Doppelbesteuerungsabkommen und Europäisches Gemeinschaftsrecht* [Linde, 2007], at p. 154).
1277. See L. Hinnekens, *AMID*: The Wrong Bridge or a Bridge Too Far? An Analysis of a Recent Decision of the European Court of Justice, 41 *Eur. Taxn.* 6 (2001), p. 206 (at p. 208: *"Does unresolved double taxation, like any other tax hindrance to the freedom of establishment, constitute a violation of Article 43 EC? It is one of today's trickiest issues concerning the scope of the prohibition of national tax practices based on the fundamental freedoms, specifically of the freedom of establishment and free movement of persons by home State tax measures."*).
1278. Judgment in *Perfili*, C-177/94, EU:C:1996:24, at para. 17; Judgment in *Schempp*, C-403/03, EU:C:2005:446, at para. 34; see also Judgment in *Walt Wilhelm*, 14/68, EU:C:1969:4, at para. 13; Judgment in *Kenny*, 1/78, EU:C:1978:163, at para. 18; Judgment in *Milk Marque and National Farmers' Union*, C-137/00, EU:C:2003:429, at para. 124.
1279. See, for example, O. Remacle/S. Nonnenkamp, Economic Double Taxation as an Obstacle to Cross-Border Investments, in A. Rust (ed.), *Double Taxation Within the European Union* (Kluwer, 2011), p. 17 (at pp. 33-34); for other examples see G. Fibbe/A. de Graaf, Is Double Taxation Arising from Autonomous Tax Classification of Foreign Entities Incompatible with EC Law?, in H.P.A.M. van Arendonk/F.A. Engelen/S. Jansen (eds.), *A Tax Globalist, Essays in Honour of Maarten J. Ellis* (IBFD, 2005), p. 237 (at pp. 237-238 and pp. 253-254); G. Kofler,

system.[1280] If, for example, all Member States subjected taxpayers with a domicile or habitual abode in their territory to unlimited tax liability, a taxpayer with domiciles in more than one Member State would be faced with double or even multiple taxation.[1281] It is, therefore, not possible to identify *the* Member State responsible for the over-taxation, "*i.e., no one tax jurisdiction is to blame for the tax disadvantage.*"[1282]

Either way, impediments of the fundamental freedoms resulting from double taxation "*should be distinguished from discrimination, as they result not from the rules of just one tax jurisdiction, but from the co-existence of two separate tax jurisdictions.*"[1283] This does not necessarily mean that such restrictions are untouchable from an EU law perspective. On the one hand, with regard to restrictions that result from more than one Member State providing for regulatory standards with regard to the same economic activity, for example, the ECJ held that the relevant domestic rules, although applying equally to domestic and cross-border situations, may conflict with the fundamental freedoms.[1284] The decision in *Futura Participations* shows that tax law is no exception to this line of case law.[1285] It may therefore be argued that double

Doppelbesteuerungsabkommen und Europäisches Gemeinschaftsrecht (Linde, 2007), at p. 909; R. Obser, § 8a KStG im Inbound-Sachverhalt – eine EG-rechtliche Beurteilung, 14 *IStR* 23 (2005), p. 799 (at pp. 801-802).

1280. See G. Kofler, *Doppelbesteuerungsabkommen und Europäisches Gemeinschaftsrecht* (Linde, 2007), at pp. 154-155; G. Kofler in A. Rust (ed.), *Double Taxation Within the European Union* (Kluwer, 2011), at p. 106; also see Opinion of AG Geelhoed in *Test Claimants in Class IV of the ACT Group Litigation*, C-374/04, EU:C:2006:139, at point 48: "*A [...] restrictive consequence of the fact that direct tax systems are national is the necessity to divide tax jurisdiction over the income of cross-border economic operators (dislocation of tax base). [...] However, unlike disparities, they would continue to exist even if national tax systems were exactly the same in design and content.*"

1281. For another example see M. Lang, *Introduction to the Law of Double Taxation Conventions*[2] (Linde, 2013), at paras 6-7; K. Vogel/A. Rust in E. Reimer/A. Rust (eds.), *Klaus Vogel on Double Taxation Conventions, Fourth Edition* (Kluwer, 2015), Introduction at MN 3.

1282. Opinion of AG Geelhoed in *Test Claimants in Class IV of the ACT Group Litigation*, C-374/04, EU:C:2006:139, at point 48.

1283. Opinion of AG Geelhoed in *Test Claimants in Class IV of the ACT Group Litigation*, C-374/04, EU:C:2006:139, at point 48.

1284. Judgment in *Dassonville*, 8/74, EU:C:1974:85; Judgment in *Thieffry*, 71/76, EU:C:1977:65; Judgment in *Choquet*, 16/78, EU:C:1978:210; Judgment in *Rewe*, 120/78, EU:C:1979:42; Judgment in *Webb*, 279/80, EU:C:1981:314; Judgment in *Vlassopoulou*, C-340/89, EU:C:1991:193; Judgment in *Stichting Collectieve Antennevoorziening Gouda*, C-288/89, EU:C:1991:323; Judgment in *Säger*, C-76/90, EU:C:1991:331; Judgment in *Kraus*, C-19/92, EU:C:1993:172; Judgment in *Keck and Mithouard*, C-267/91 and C-268/91, EU:C:1993:905; Judgment in *Vander Elst*, C-43/93, EU:C:1994:310; Judgment in *Gebhard*, C-55/94, EU:C:1995:411; Judgment in *Kemmler*, C-53/95, EU:C:1996:58; Judgment in *Guiot*, C-272/94, EU:C:1996:147; Judgment in *De Agostini and TV-Shop*, C-34/95, EU:C:1997:344; Judgment in *Pfeiffer*, C-255/97, EU:C:1999:240; Judgment in *Fernández de Bobadilla*, C-234/97, EU:C:1999:367; Judgment in *Arblade*, C-369/96 and C-376/96, EU:C:1999:575; Judgment in *Sehrer*, C-302/98; EU:C:2000:322; Judgment in *Corsten*, C-58/98, EU:C:2000:527; Judgment in *Mac Quen*, C-108/96, EU:C:2001:67; Judgment in *Gräbner*, C-294/00, EU:C:2002:442.

1285. According to former Luxembourg law, residents as well as non-residents were only allowed to deduct a loss carry-forward if proper accounts had been kept during the financial year in which the losses were incurred. Since these accounts had to comply with the relevant Luxembourg rules, a non-resident company was not able to rely on the accounts that were kept in compliance with the tax accounting rules of its residence state in order to carry-forward losses attributable to a Luxembourg permanent establishment, which meant that the company had to "*keep, in addition to its own accounts which must comply with the tax*

taxation should also be regarded as an infringement of the fundamental freedoms, because the resultant distortion of the internal market is comparable to the effects of "double burdens" or "double hurdles" arising from regulatory measures.[1286] On the other hand, with regard to double taxation resulting from disparities, it is settled case law that disparities only remain unaffected by the fundamental freedoms if "*they affect all persons subject to them in accordance with objective criteria and without regard to their nationality.*"[1287] Thus, it seems that the ECJ has left the possibility open to tackle disparities by means of the fundamental freedoms. Either way, the question would then not be *whether* Member States have to avoid double taxation, but *how* they have to avoid it.[1288]

---

accounting rules applicable in the Member State in which it has its seat, separate accounts for its branch's activities complying with the tax accounting rules applicable in the State in which its branch is established" (Judgment in *Futura Participations and Singer*, C-250/95, EU:C:1997:239, at para. 26). The ECJ held that the fundamental freedoms preclude Member States from demanding non-residents to keep separate accounts without considering the accounts that are already kept in the residence state. According to the ECJ, "*[t]he Member State concerned may, however, require the non-resident taxpayer to demonstrate clearly and precisely that the amount of the losses which he claims to have incurred corresponds, under its domestic rules governing the calculation of income and losses which were applicable in the financial year concerned, to the amount of the losses actually incurred in that State by the taxpayer*" (Judgment in *Futura Participations and Singer*, C-250/95, EU:C:1997:239, at para. 43). To this end critically A. Cordewener, *Europäische Grundfreiheiten und nationales Steuerrecht* (Dr Otto Schmidt, 2002), at pp. 637-638; G. Toifl, 7 *SWI* 7 (1997), at pp. 319-320.

1286. See A. Cordewener, *Europäische Grundfreiheiten und nationales Steuerrecht* (Dr Otto Schmidt, 2002), at pp. 876-877; J. Schönfeld in H. Flick/F. Wassemeyer/H. Baumhoff/J. Schönfeld (eds.), *Außensteuerrecht*[57] (Dr Otto Schmidt, 2005), Vor § 34c EStG at m.no 3; F. Vanistendael, 46 *Eur. Taxn.* 9 (2006), at p. 418; F. Vanistendael, 17 *EC Tax Rev.* 2 (2008), p. 52 (at pp. 62-63); S. van Thiel, Removal of Income Tax Barriers to Market Integration in the European Union: Litigation by the Community Citizen Instead of Harmonization by the Community Legislature?, 12 *EC Tax Rev.* 1 (2003), p. 4 (at p. 10); also cf. N. Herzig, Besteuerung der Unternehmen in Europa – Harmonisierung im Wettbewerb der Systeme, in M. Lehner (ed.), *Steuerrecht im Europäischen Binnenmarkt*, DStJG 19 (Dr Otto Schmidt, 1996), p. 121 (at pp. 139-140); F.C. de Hosson, The Slow and Lonesome Death of the Arbitration Convention, 31 *Intertax* 12 (2003), p. 482 (at p. 483); R. Obser, § 8a KStG im Inbound-Sachverhalt – eine EG-rechtliche Beurteilung, 14 *IStR* 23 (2005), p. 799 (at pp. 800-801); J. Schönfeld, 83 *StuW* 1 (2006), at p. 80; W. Schön, 11 *EWS* 7 (2001), at p. 290; A. Schnitger, *Die Grenzen der Einwirkungen der Grundfreiheiten des EG-Vertrages auf das Ertragsteuerrecht* (IDW, 2006), at pp. 258-260; J. Malherbe/M. Wathelet, Pending Cases Filed by Belgian Courts: The Kerckhaert-Morres Case Pending Cases involving Belgium: The Belgian Coordination Centres Cases, *Commission v. Belgium*, *Commission v. Belgium* Pending Cases Filed by French Courts: The Denkavit Case, in M. Lang/J. Schuch/C. Staringer (eds.), *ECJ – Recent Developments in Direct Taxation* (Linde, 2006), p. 29 (at p. 55); M. Lehner in M. Lang/J. Schuch/C. Staringer (eds.), *Tax Treaty Law and EC Law* (Linde, 2007), at pp. 20-22; but see H. Hahn, Grenzüberschreitende Berücksichtigung von Betriebsstättenverlusten? – Bemerkungen zu einer neu entfachten Diskussion, 11 *IStR* 20 (2002), p. 681 (at p. 686); M. Lang in M. Lehner (ed.), *Reden zum Andenken an Klaus Vogel* (C.H. Beck, 2010), at p. 75; M. Lang, 22 *IStR* 16 (2013), at p. 369; P. Farmer, 7 *EC Tax Rev.* 1 (1998), at pp. 13 et seq.; P. Wattel, 12 *EC Tax Rev.* 4 (2003), at p. 199.

1287. Judgment in *Perfili*, C-177/94, EU:C:1996:24, at para. 17; Judgment in *Schempp*, C-403/03, EU:C:2005:446, at para. 34; see also Judgment in *Walt Wilhelm*, 14/68, EU:C:1969:4, at para. 13; Judgment in *Kenny*, 1/78, EU:C:1978:163, at para. 18; Judgment in *Milk Marque and National Farmers' Union*, C-137/00, EU:C:2003:429, at para. 124.

1288. See V. Heydt, Einfluss des Gemeinschaftsrechts auf die Doppelbesteuerung, in W. Haarmann (ed.), *Auslegung und Anwendung von Doppelbesteuerungsabkommen* (Dr Otto Schmidt,

1.2 Double Taxation and Positive Integration

1.2.1 Secondary EU Law as a Tool to Legally Enforce the Primary EU Law's Aim of Avoiding Double Taxation

Already at an early stage, the ECJ recognized that "*the abolition of [the effects of double taxation] is doubtless desirable in the interests of the freedom of movement of goods.*"[1289] However, according to the respective decision in *Statens Control*, this does not change the fact that "*the EEC Treaty contains no provision prohibiting effects of double taxation*" which may occur, for example, if exported precious metals are subject to a charge imposed in order to cover the costs of its supervision both in the exporting and the importing state. The abolition of such effects can rather "*only result from the harmonization of the national systems under Article 99 or possibly Article 100 of the Treaty. At present, Community law does not however contain any rules which prevent a Member State from also including, in the application of a system of taxation intended to finance the control of precious metal, products intended for export. For the same reason, the fact that a system of taxation is arranged so that the same quantity of metal marketed on the national territory can be included only once for the purpose of establishing the basis of assessment to the levy intended to finance the control of precious metal is not such as to make the application of the same tax to exported products appear discriminatory when the procedures for the control and for the taxation of imports in other States are not within the influence of the exporting State.*"[1290]

Although the ECJ clearly stated that there is no general prohibition of double taxation in primary EU law, the Court did not consider itself to be prevented from obliging the Member States to avoid double taxation in the area of harmonized VAT by relying on the prohibition of imposing "*directly or indirectly, on the products of other Member States any internal taxation of any kind in excess of that imposed directly or indirectly on similar domestic products*" in Article 110 TFEU (ex-Article 95 EEC Treaty) and the objective of establishing an internal market: Before 1993,[1291] cross-border dealings between private persons could be subject to double taxation, if "*a private individual imports goods from another Member State without a tax exemption since such goods already attract value-added tax in that Member State unless relief is granted on exportation, as is done if the exporter is a taxable person.*"[1292] The obligation to

2004), p. 32 (at p. 53); G. Kofler, *Doppelbesteuerungsabkommen und Europäisches Gemeinschaftsrecht* (Linde, 2007), at p. 29 and p. 132.

1289. Judgment in *Statens Kontrol*, 142/77, EU:C:1978:144, at para. 34; also see Judgment in *Nygård*, C-234/99, EU:C:2002:244, at para. 38.

1290. Judgment in *Statens Kontrol*, 142/77, EU:C:1978:144, at paras 33-36.

1291. Since 1 Jan. 1993, with regard to intra-EU trade, the concepts of exportation and importation have been replaced by the concepts of intra-EU acquisition of goods and the exemption of intra-EU supplies (see Council Directive 91/680/EEC of 16 Dec. 1991 supplement the common system of value added tax and amending Directive 77/388/EEC with a view to the abolition of fiscal frontiers, *OJ* L 376 [31 Dec. 1991]).

1292. Judgment in *Drexl*, 299/86, EU:C:1988:103, at para. 10; also cf. Judgment in *Ministère public / Profant*, 249/84, EU:C:1985:393, at para. 17: "*the overlapping of taxes involved in the levying of value-added tax on the importation of goods on which value-added tax had already been paid in the exporting Member State and was not refunded.*"

subject the importation of goods to VAT already followed from Articles 2(2) and 7 Sixth VAT Directive.[1293] Since, in addition, only taxable persons were authorized to deduct input VAT,[1294] double taxation seemed to be the result of implementing the requirements of secondary EU law. In *Schul I*, the ECJ had hence not only been asked whether *"the charging by a Member State of turnover tax on the importation of goods from another Member State which are supplied by a private person [must] be regarded as internal taxation[,] [within the meaning of Article 95 of the Treaty,] in excess of that imposed on similar domestic products if no turnover tax is charged on the supply of goods which are already in that Member State if they are supplied by a private person,"* but also, in case this question should be answered in the affirmative, whether the Sixth VAT Directive itself *"is incompatible with the Treaty and therefore invalid in so far as that provision requires Member States to subject the importation of goods from other Member States to value-added tax without making any exception for goods supplied by private persons which, when supplied within the Member State concerned, would not be subject to that tax."*[1295]

In contrast to AG Rozès,[1296] the ECJ held that the Member State of destination had to credit *"the residual part of the value-added tax of the Member State of exportation which is still contained in the value of the product when it is imported. The amount of this reduction may not, however, be greater than the amount of value-added tax actually paid in the Member State of exportation."*[1297] As the Court thereby relied on Article 95 EEC Treaty and the objective of establishing an internal market, it was speculated whether the same conclusions could be drawn with regard to other taxes, such as income taxes[1298] or inheritance taxes.[1299] However, the decision could also be perceived as to imply that the obligation to credit the VAT which had already been paid in

1293. Sixth Council Directive of 17 May 1977 on the harmonization of the laws of the Member States relating to turnover taxes - Common system of value added tax: uniform basis of assessment (77/388/EEC), *OJ* L 145 (13 Jun. 1977), at pp. 3 and 5.
1294. Article 17 Sixth Council Directive of 17 May 1977 on the harmonization of the laws of the Member States relating to turnover taxes - Common system of value added tax: uniform basis of assessment (77/388/EEC), *OJ* L 145 (13 Jun. 1977), at pp. 13-14; also see Judgment in *Schul I*, 15/81, EU:C:1982:135, at para. 15: *"[A]lthough deliveries for export are themselves exempt from value-added tax, whether carried out by taxable persons or private persons, only taxable persons are authorized to exercise the right to deduct."*
1295. Judgment in *Schul I*, 15/81, EU:C:1982:135, at p. 1413.
1296. Opinion of AG Rozès in *Schul I*, 15/81, EU:C:1981:304, at point 5.
1297. Judgment in *Schul I*, 15/81, EU:C:1982:135, at para. 34; also see Judgment in *Bergeres-Becque*, 39/85, EU:C:1986:36, at paras 5-9; Judgment in *Drexl*, 299/86, EU:C:1988:103, at para. 11; also cf. Judgment in *Schul II*, 47/84, EU:C:1985:216, at paras 15-17; Judgment in *Ministère public / Profant*, 249/84, EU:C:1985:393, at paras 23-28; Judgment in *Commission/Italy*, 120/88, EU:C:1991:74, at para. 6; Judgment in *Commission/Spain*, C-119/89, EU:C:1991:75, at para. 6; Judgment in *Commission/Greece*, C-159/89, EU:C:1991:77, at para. 7.
1298. See S. van Thiel, *Free Movement of Persons and Income Tax Law: The European Court in Search of Principles* (IBFD, 2002), at p. 315; S. van Thiel, 12 *EC Tax Rev.* 1 (2003), at p. 10; S. van Thiel/C. Achilles, Die Beseitigung ertragsteuerlicher Hindernisse im Binnenmarkt: Eine Darstellung der Einflüsse der Rechtsprechung des EuGH auf die Ertragsbesteuerung in der Europäischen Union (Teil I), 12 *IStR* 15 (2003), p. 530 (at p. 534).
1299. See F. Fraberger, Erbschaftssteuerabkommen und Gemeinschaftsrecht, in D. Aigner/H. Aigner/K. Fellner/F. Fraberger/J. Heinrich/G. Konezny/H. Loukota/F.P. Sutter/U. Zehetner/M. Züger, *Erbschaftssteuern und Doppelbesteuerungsabkommen* (Linde, 2002), p. 211 (at pp. 237-238).

the Member State of exportation[1300] does not primarily result from the EEC Treaty, but rather from the Sixth VAT Directive interpreted in the light of the EEC Treaty. After all, the Court emphasized that "*there are no grounds for considering [Article 2(2) Sixth VAT Directive] [...] to be invalid. It is simply necessary to define the scope of that provision and interpret it in a manner consistent with the requirements of the treaty.*"[1301] The ECJ hence concluded that Article 2(2) Sixth VAT Directive "*must be interpreted as not constituting an obstacle to the obligation under Article 95 of the Treaty to take into account, for the purpose of applying value-added tax to imports of products from another Member State supplied by a private person where no such tax is levied on the supply of similar products by a private person within the territory of the Member State of importation, the residual part of the value-added tax paid in the Member State of exportation contained in the value of the product when it is imported.*"[1302,1303]

The wording of the decision indeed suggests that Article 2(2) Sixth VAT Directive does simply not prevent Member States from crediting foreign VAT ("*must be interpreted as not constituting an obstacle*"). The subsequent case law, however, points toward a different understanding of the *Schul I* decision. In *Profant*, for example, the ECJ enlarged upon Article 14(2) Sixth VAT Directive, which, *inter alia*, provides that "*the Commission shall submit to the Council at the earliest opportunity proposals designed to lay down Community tax rules clarifying the scope of the exemptions referred to in paragraph 1 and detailed rules for their implementation. Until the entry into force of these rules, Member States may [...] adapt their national provisions to minimize distortion of competition and in particular the non-imposition or double imposition of value added tax within the Community*":[1304] According to former Belgian law, the temporary importation of means of transport "*imported by natural persons normally resident in another country for their personal use*" was exempted from VAT. For purposes of this exemption, persons who worked in Belgium, but who returned at least once a month to another country where their family home is situated or where, if they have no family home, they are entered in the population registers, were treated as having their normal residence abroad. In the case of married persons, the matrimonial

1300. See A. Cordewener, *Europäische Grundfreiheiten und nationales Steuerrecht* (Dr Otto Schmidt, 2002), at pp. 867 (FN 171); V. Heydt in W. Haarmann (ed.), *Auslegung und Anwendung von Doppelbesteuerungsabkommen* (Dr Otto Schmidt, 2004), at pp. 42-46; 41-42; G. Kofler, *Doppelbesteuerungsabkommen und Europäisches Gemeinschaftsrecht* (Linde, 2007), at pp. 199-200.

1301. Judgment in *Schul I*, 15/81, EU:C:1982:135, at para. 43.

1302. Judgment in *Schul I*, 15/81, EU:C:1982:135, at para. 44.

1303. In the literature, it is disputed whether the ECJ has teleologically reduced the scope of Article 2(2) Sixth VAT Directive so that the importation of goods may only be subjected to VAT insofar as the resultant tax exceeds the VAT that had already been paid in the Member State of exportation (see S. Vogenauer, *Die Auslegung von Gesetzen in England und auf dem Kontinent* [Mohr Siebeck, 2001], at p. 382), whether it has "*filled the gap left unfilled by the legislature*" (G. Slynn, They Call it "Teleological," 7 *Denning L. J.* 7 (1992), p. 225 [at p. 234]), or whether the Court's approach resulted in *contra legem* interpretation of the Sixth VAT Directive (see R. Szudoczky, *The Sources of EU Law and Their Relationships: Lessons for the Field of Taxation* [IBFD, 2014], at pp. 408-409).

1304. Sixth Council Directive of 17 May 1977 on the harmonization of the laws of the Member States relating to turnover taxes – Common system of value added tax: uniform basis of assessment (77/388/EEC), *OJ* L 145 (13 June 1977), at pp. 11-12.

home was deemed to be the family home.[1305] The exemption was thus granted to Luxembourg students in respect of their motor vehicles registered in Luxembourg who were normally resident in Luxembourg and attended an educational establishment in Belgium. However, if two cross-border commuting Luxembourg students who lived together in a students' room in Belgium married, the VAT exemption was no longer applicable. If the motor vehicle had been bought and subjected to VAT in Luxembourg, denying the exemption from Belgian VAT resulted in double taxation. Although Article 14(1)(c) Sixth VAT Directive obliged the Member States to exempt the "*temporary importation*" of goods from VAT, it was unclear what temporary importation actually means. It was hence assumed that Article 14(2) Sixth VAT Directive allowed Belgium to continue to apply its domestic provisions until "*Community tax rules clarifying the scope of the exemptions referred to in paragraph 1 and detailed rules for their implementation*" are laid down.[1306] However, the ECJ pointed out "*that according to Article 14 the national provisions in question are to be maintained in force 'on matters related to' the exemptions provided for by the Community rules and are to be adapted to minimize cases of double imposition of value-added tax within the Community. Those requirements must in turn be viewed in the light of one of the objectives of the harmonization of value-added tax which is, as stated in the third recital in the preamble to the Sixth Directive, to make further progress in the effective removal of restrictions on the movement of persons and goods and the integration of national economies. Those considerations show that the authorities of the Member States do not enjoy a complete discretion in implementing the exemptions under Article 14 of the Sixth Council Directive, for they have to observe the fundamental objectives of the harmonization of value-added tax such as, in particular, to facilitate the free movement of persons and goods and to prevent cases of double taxation. It follows that in applying their national provisions on exemptions from value-added tax to motor vehicles used by students from another Member State the tax authorities of a Member State are required to apply the concept of temporary importation in such a way as to avoid derogating, by taxing their vehicles twice, from the freedom of nationals of Member States to pursue their studies in the Member State of their choice.*"[1307]

In later judgments it was confirmed what the decision in *Profant* already suggested – that "*the provisions of the Directive must be interpreted in the light of the fundamental aims of the endeavour to harmonize VAT, in particular [...] the prevention of double taxation.*"[1308] If the decision in *Schul I* is read in the light of this consideration, the Court could have found the Member States' obligation to credit foreign VAT simply

1305. Judgment in *Ministère public / Profant*, 249/84, EU:C:1985:393, at para. 5.
1306. Judgment in *Ministère public / Profant*, 249/84, EU:C:1985:393, at para. 23.
1307. Judgment in *Ministère public / Profant*, 249/84, EU:C:1985:393, at paras 24-26.
1308. Judgment in *Klattner / Elliniko Dimosio*, C-389/95, EU:C:1997:258, at para. 25; see also Judgment in *Ministère public / Profant*, 249/84, EU:C:1985:393, at para. 25; Judgment in *Ledoux*, 127/86, EU:C:1988:366, at para. 11; Judgment in *Ryborg*, C-297/89, EU:C:1991:160, at para. 13.

by interpreting Article 2(2) Sixth VAT Directive in the light of the Directive's aim to prevent double taxation. This would explain why it was held in *Scharbatke* that "*although under the system of value added tax (VAT) and on the basis of the harmonization rules in this field the VAT paid in the exporting Member State must be taken into account, as stated in the judgment in Case 15/81 Schul v Inspecteur der Invoerrechten en Accijnzen [1982] ECR 1409, that solution cannot be applied to charges regulated by independent national legislation.*"[1309] Since the Treaties do not contain a general prohibition of double taxation,[1310] there is no legal guidance on how to avoid double taxation with respect to unharmonized taxes. Even with regard to the Sixth VAT Directive, the Court emphasized that double taxation cannot always be avoided, because "*the Community system of VAT is the result of a gradual harmonization of national legislation pursuant to Articles 99 and 100 of the Treaty. The Court has consistently held that this harmonization, as brought about by successive directives and in particular by the Sixth Directive, is still only partial. The harmonization is designed in particular to preclude double taxation, so that the deduction of input tax at each stage of taxation is an integral part of the system of VAT. That objective has not yet been achieved, however, as is clear from Article 32 of the Sixth Directive, and nowhere in the common system of value-added tax, as it stands at present, are to be found the necessary bases for determining and laying down detailed rules for applying a common system of taxation enabling double taxation to be avoided in trade in second-hand goods. Until the Community legislature has taken action, it is therefore necessary to continue to apply Article 32 of the Sixth Directive, which merely authorizes Member States that apply a special system of VAT to second-hand goods to retain that system but does not impose on them any obligation to introduce such a system if none exists.*"[1311] The Court's approach in *Schul I* is hence limited. It requires that the provisions of secondary EU law can be interpreted in a way that double taxation is avoided.[1312] Secondary EU law may thus serve as a tool to legally enforce the primary EU law's aim of avoiding double taxation.[1313] However, it cannot ensure that double taxation is avoided in each and every case.

1309. Judgment in *Scharbatke*, C-72/92, EU:C:1993:858, at para. 15; also see Opinion of AG Stix-Hackl in *Lindfors*, C-365/02, EU:C:2004:130, at point 69: "*Furthermore, the prohibition on double taxation raised by the Commission – which [...] constitutes an objective of harmonisation in the field of value added tax – does not apply automatically to all types of tax.*"
1310. Judgment in *Statens Kontrol*, 142/77, EU:C:1978:144, at para. 33; Judgment in *Nygård*, C-234/99, EU:C:2002:244, at para. 38.
1311. Judgment in *ORO Amsterdam Beheer en Concerto*, 165/88, EU:C:1989:608, at paras 21-24; also cf. Judgment in *Eurodenthal*, C-240/05, EU:C:2006:763, at paras 50-57.
1312. Cf. A. Cordewener, *Europäische Grundfreiheiten und nationales Steuerrecht* (Dr Otto Schmidt, 2002), at p. 867; also cf. W. Schön, 36 *EuR* 3 (2001), at p. 353 (FN 177); P. Farmer/R. Lyal, *EC Tax Law* (Clarendon Press, 1994), at p. 63.
1313. See J. Baßler, 14 *IStR* 23 (2005), at p. 825; G. Kofler, *Doppelbesteuerungsabkommen und Europäisches Gemeinschaftsrecht* (Linde, 2007), at p. 202; also cf. A. Cordewener, *Europäische Grundfreiheiten und nationales Steuerrecht* (Dr Otto Schmidt, 2002), at p. 881.

1.2.2 The Lindfors Decision: Has the ECJ Changed Its Position on Double Taxation with Regard to Non-harmonized Taxes?

Although the *Schul I* approach seems to be limited to harmonized taxes,[1314] the *Lindfors* decision gave reason to ask whether the ECJ has changed its position.[1315] Before a vehicle was registered or brought into use, Finland required the importer or the manufacturer, if the vehicle was manufactured inland, to pay a car tax ("*Autovero*"), which is not covered by any secondary EU law legislation.[1316] With regard to the import of a vehicle, the European Commission argued that the Finnish car tax would lead to double taxation, if "*tax has already been charged on the registration of the vehicle and its bringing into use in the State of origin,*" which would compromise "*the fundamental right to freedom of movement enshrined in Article 18 EC for citizens of the Union.*"[1317] AG Stix-Hackl dismissed this plea by pointing out that "*the prohibition on double taxation raised by the Commission – which [...] constitutes an objective of harmonisation in the field of value added tax – does not apply automatically to all types of tax. [...] [A]s Community law stands with regard to motor vehicle registration taxes – such as the Autovero – consequences of the lack of harmonisation in this area such as double taxation have to be accepted; at best that could be prevented by voluntary measures of the Member States.*"[1318] The ECJ, on the other hand, emphasized that "*any disadvantage, by comparison with the situation in which [a citizen of the Union that transferring his activities to a Member State other than that in which he previously resided] carried on activities prior to that transfer*" may be "*contrary to Article 18 EC [Treaty],*" if "*the legislation concerned does not place that citizen at a disadvantage as compared with those already subject to such a tax.*"[1319] However, it was left to the national court to ascertain whether the tax reduction which was granted to "*Union citizens exercising their right to freedom of movement in connection with a transfer of residence to Finland [...] and [...] other provisions of national law [are] capable of ensuring that, as regards that tax, Ms Lindfors is not placed in a less favourable position than that of citizens who have been permanently resident in Finland. Should the national court find that such a*

1314. See M. Achatz in P. Kirchhof/H. Nieskens (eds.), *Festschrift für Wolfram Reiss zum 65. Geburtstag* (Dr Otto Schmidt, 2008), at pp. 176-177.
1315. See J. Baßler, 14 *IStR* 23 (2005), at p. 826; G. Kofler, *Doppelbesteuerungsabkommen und Europäisches Gemeinschaftsrecht* (Linde, 2007), at pp. 203-205; G. Kofler/R. Mason, 14 *Colum. J. Eur. L.* 1 (2007), at p. 71; G. Kofler/R. Mason in S. van Thiel (ed.), *The Internal Market and Direct Taxation: Is the European Court of Justice Taking a New Approach?* (CFE Brochure on European Taxation, 2007), at p. 184; G. Kofler in A. Rust (ed.), *Double Taxation Within the European Union* (Kluwer, 2011), at p. 111.
1316. Judgment in *Lindfors*, C-365/02, EU:C:2004:449, at paras 24-30 and para. 36.
1317. Judgment in *Lindfors*, C-365/02, EU:C:2004:449, at para. 23.
1318. Opinion of AG Stix-Hackl in *Lindfors*, C-365/02, EU:C:2004:130, at point 69-71.
1319. Judgment in *Lindfors*, C-365/02, EU:C:2004:449, at para. 34; also see Judgment in *Herrvein and others*, C-393/99 and C-394/99, EU:C:2002:182, at para. 51; Judgment in *Weigel*, C-387/01, EU:C:2004:256; at para. 55; Judgment in *Alevizos*, C-392/05, EU:C:2007:251, at para. 76.

less favourable situation exists, it will have to examine whether that difference in treatment is justified by objective considerations independent of the residence of the persons concerned and proportionate to the legitimate aim pursued by national law."[1320]

In the literature, it was argued that the "*less favourable position*" the ECJ referred to in *Lindfors* can only arise if the Union citizen who imported a vehicle into Finland already had to pay a car tax in the Member State of exportation. Thus, unless there is a proportionate justification, Article 18 EC Treaty would be infringed, if the Finnish rules - particularly the tax reduction granted by Finland upon importation of a vehicle by a Union citizen - did not fully compensate for the car tax the Union citizen had paid in the Member State of exportation. As the Finnish car tax was not a harmonized tax, the *Lindfors* case was considered to indicate the Court's willingness to also apply the *Schul I* approach to unharmonized taxes.[1321] However, it is doubtful whether this is what the ECJ actually had in mind.

In *Alevizos*, the Court had to deal with a Greek excise duty and special vehicle registration tax levied on the permanent import into Greece of a private motor vehicle. Just as in the *Lindfors* case, this tax not only potentially led to double taxation.[1322] Instead, the Court also held that "*on the assumption that the taxes at issue in the main proceedings do not come within the scope of Article 1(1) of Directive 83/183, it is necessary to assess the effect that the application of those taxes has on the right of a Community national such as Mr Alevizos to freedom of movement, as enshrined in Articles 18 EC and 39 EC.*"[1323] Following its judgment in *Lindfors*, the ECJ held that "*the EC Treaty offers no guarantee to a worker that transferring his activities to a Member State other than that in which he previously resided will be neutral as regards taxation. Given the disparities in the tax legislation of the Member States, such a transfer may be to the worker's advantage in terms of indirect taxation or not, according to circumstance. It follows that, in principle, any disadvantage, by comparison with the situation in which that worker carried on activities prior to that transfer, is not contrary to Article 39 EC, provided, however, that the legislation concerned does not place that worker at a disadvantage as compared with those already subject to such a tax.*"[1324] However, in contrast to - but nevertheless referring to - the *Lindfors* decision, the Court explicitly pointed out that, "*[a]gainst that background, the compatibility of the taxes at issue in the main proceedings with Article 39 EC will depend, particularly, on the level of those taxes and on their detailed rules of application [...]. In the present case, it will be for the national court to determine whether the national provisions governing the taxes at issue in the main proceedings are based on objective criteria and ensure, in particular as*

1320. Judgment in *Lindfors*, C-365/02, EU:C:2004:449, at paras 34-35.
1321. See J. Baßler, 14 *IStR* 23 (2005), at p. 826; G. Kofler, *Doppelbesteuerungsabkommen und Europäisches Gemeinschaftsrecht* (Linde, 2007), at pp. 204-205.
1322. Judgment in *Alevizos*, C-392/05, EU:C:2007:251, at para. 39; also see Opinion of AG Kokott in *Alevizos*, C-392/05, EU:C:2007:60, at point 37.
1323. Judgment in *Alevizos*, C-392/05, EU:C:2007:251, at para. 65.
1324. Judgment in *Alevizos*, C-392/05, EU:C:2007:251, at para. 76.

regards the account to be taken of the actual depreciation of the vehicle subject to tax [...] that Mr Alevizos is not placed in a less favourable position than that of workers who have been permanently resident in Greece (see, to that effect, Lindfors, paragraph 35)."[1325] Thereby, the ECJ refers to previous decisions, in which it was clarified that "*[i]n the context of a system of registration duty, criteria such as engine type, engine capacity and a classification based on environmental considerations constitute objective criteria. They may thus be used in such a system. On the other hand, there is no requirement that the amount of the duty be linked to the price of the vehicle. However, a registration duty must not burden products originating from other Member States more heavily than similar national products. A new vehicle in respect of which registration duty has been paid [...] loses, with time, part of its market value. With the depreciation in value, the amount of registration duty included in the residual value of the vehicle also diminishes. Since it is a used vehicle, it can be sold only for a percentage of its initial value, which contains the residual amount of the registration duty.*" Hence, if an imported motor vehicle "*of the same model, age, mileage and other characteristics, bought second-hand in another Member State [...], will [...] attract the full rate of registration duty for that category of vehicle[,] [t]he duty is [...] a heavier burden on imported used vehicles than on similar used vehicles already registered in [that Member State] which have already borne that duty at an earlier stage. Thus, although the purpose of and reason for the registration are environmental in nature and unrelated to the market value of the vehicle, the consequence of the first paragraph of Article 90 EC is that account must be taken of the depreciation of used vehicles when they are being taxed, since that duty is characterised by the fact that it is charged only once when the vehicle is first registered for use in the Member State concerned and is thus incorporated in that value.*"[1326]

Against this background, it is reasonable to assume that in *Lindfors* as well the Court did not refer to the potential double taxation that could have arisen, because Finland did not credit the car tax the Union citizen had paid in the Member State of exportation. Most likely, the ECJ rather instructed the national court to determine whether the Finnish car tax was based on objective criteria and to ensure, in particular as regards the account to be taken of the actual depreciation of the vehicle subject to tax,[1327] that "*Ms Lindfors is not placed in a less favourable position than that of citizens who have been permanently resident in Finland.*"[1328]

1325. Judgment in *Alevizos*, C-392/05, EU:C:2007:251, at paras 77-78.

1326. Judgment in *Nádasdi*, C-290/05 and C-333/05, EU:C:2006:652, at paras 52-56; also see Judgment in *Commission/Denmark*, 47/88, EU:C:1990:449, at paras 18-22; Judgment in *Weigel*, C-387/01, EU:C:2004:256, at para. 70.

1327. Judgment in *Alevizos*, C-392/05, EU:C:2007:251, at para. 78, where the ECJ referred to Judgment in *Commission/Denmark*, 47/88, EU:C:1990:449, at paras 19-22; Judgment in *Weigel*, C-387/01, EU:C:2004:256, at para. 70; Judgment in *Nádasdi*, C-290/05 and C-333/05, EU:C:2006:652, at paras 47 and 51-57.

1328. Judgment in *Lindfors*, C-365/02, EU:C:2004:449, at para. 35.

1.3 Double Taxation and the Fundamental Freedoms

1.3.1 Juridical Double Taxation

1.3.1.1 The ECJ's Dilemma and Suggested Solutions

Despite its increasing significance with regard to other taxes, the issue of double taxation is typically still associated with direct taxes. Considering the pertinent literature, it is striking that particular attention is given to the question whether juridical double taxation, i.e., "*the imposition of comparable taxes in two (or more) States on the same taxpayer in respect of the same subject matter and for identical periods,*"[1329] is a problem to be resolved by EU law.[1330] Although it is emphasized in the literature that this question "*is nearly as old as the EC Treaty itself,*"[1331] it was not until 2006 that the ECJ, for the first time, explicitly took a stand on the issue:[1332] In *Kerckhaert and Morres*, a Belgium-resident married couple received dividends from a company established in France. The dividends were not only subject to a (treaty-reduced) 15% withholding tax due to the limited tax liability of both individuals in France. Instead taxes also had to be paid at a rate of 25% in Belgium on the residual amount of the distributed dividends.[1333] For lack of a possibility to credit the French withholding tax,[1334] the Belgian shareholders' tax

1329. Commentary on the 1992-2014 OECD MC, Introduction para. 1; see also Commentary on the 1963-1977 OECD MC, Articles 23(A) and 23(B) para. 1.
1330. For detailed references see G. Kofler, *Doppelbesteuerungsabkommen und Europäisches Gemeinschaftsrecht* (Linde, 2007), at pp. 154-167.
1331. G. Kofler in A. Rust (ed.), *Double Taxation Within the European Union* (Kluwer, 2011), at p. 104; also see G. Kofler, *Doppelbesteuerungsabkommen und Europäisches Gemeinschaftsrecht* (Linde, 2007), at p. 154; also cf. Y. Brauner/G. Kofler in R. Vann (ed.), *Global Tax Treaty Commentaries* (IBFD, 2016), at Chapter 2.2.2.1.
1332. For prior cases that also – at least indirectly – concerned the issue of juridical double taxation see V. Heydt in W. Haarmann (ed.), *Auslegung und Anwendung von Doppelbesteuerungsabkommen* (Dr Otto Schmidt, 2004), at pp. 42-46; G. Kofler, 16 *SWI* 2 (2006), at pp. 66-67; G. Kofler, *Doppelbesteuerungsabkommen und Europäisches Gemeinschaftsrecht* (Linde, 2007), at pp. 180-193.
1333. See J. Malherbe/M. Wathelet in M. Lang/J. Schuch/C. Staringer (eds.), *ECJ – Recent Developments in Direct Taxation* (Linde, 2006), at p. 53; P. Smet/H. Laloo, ECJ to Rule on Taxation of Inbound Dividends in Belgium, 45 *Eur. Taxn.* 4 (2005), p. 158 (at pp. 158-159).
1334. According to Article 19(A)(1) of the relevant double taxation convention between Belgium and France, a credit was only available "*under the conditions laid down in Belgian law.*" When the treaty was concluded, Belgian domestic law provided for a foreign tax credit. However, with regard to individuals, the relevant provisions were limited in 1988. Since the double taxation convention referred to Belgian domestic law, Belgian courts concluded that a foreign tax credit is neither available under domestic nor under double tax treaty law. See M. Quaghebeur, ECJ to Examine Belgian Treatment of Inbound Dividend, 37 *Tax Notes Intl.* 9 (28 Feb. 2005), p. 739 (at p. 741); M. Quaghebeur, *Kerckhaert-Morres v. Belgian State*: The Wrong Battle?, 52 *British Tax Rev.* 2 (2007), p. 121 (at p. 129); P. Smet/H. Laloo, 45 *Eur. Taxn.* 4 (2005), at p. 159.

burden[1335] was higher in the cross-border situation than in a comparable domestic situation:[1336]

		Dividend Distribution Within Belgium	Dividend Distribution from France to Belgium
	Gross Amount of Dividend Distribution	100.00	100.00
-	French Withholding Tax (15%)	–	(15.00)
	Tax Base in Belgium	100.00	85.00
-	Belgian Income Tax (25%)	(25.00)	(21.25)
	Total Amount of Taxes	25.00	36.25
	Net Amount of Dividend	75.00	63.75

1335. Considering the after-tax result, in the specific case of *Kerckhaert and Morres*, however, the cross-border dividend distribution was more beneficial than in a purely domestic situation, because due to the double taxation convention between Belgium and France a Belgian dividend recipient was entitled to the *avoir fiscal*, i.e. an amount of 50% of the underlying corporation tax was paid to the shareholder in addition to the dividend payment and, for tax purposes, was treated in the same way as the dividend. Consequently, Belgian shareholders receiving dividends from a French company ended up with a higher payment than in a purely domestic situation (see Opinion of AG Geelhoed in *Kerckhaert and Morres*, C-514/04, EU:C:2006:242, at points 25-26; also see V. Heydt in W. Haslehner/G. Kofler/A. Rust [eds.], *Landmark Decisions of the ECJ in Direct Taxation* [Kluwer, 2015], at p. 183; R. Mason, 49 *Bost. Coll. L. Rev.* 4 [2008], at p. 1296 [FN 107]; P. Smet/H. Laloo, 45 *Eur. Taxn.* 4 [2005], at p. 158).

		Dividend Distribution Within Belgium	Dividend Distribution from France to Belgium
	Gross Amount of Dividend Distribution	100.00	100.00
+	French *Avoir Fiscal*	–	50.00
	Tax Base in France	–	150.00
-	French Withholding Tax (15%)	–	(22.50)
	Tax Base in Belgium	100.00	127.50
-	Belgian Income Tax (25%)	(25.00)	(31.88)
	Total Amount of Taxes	25.00	54.38
	Net Amount of Dividend	75.00	95.62

1336. See G. Kofler, *Doppelbesteuerungsabkommen und Europäisches Gemeinschaftsrecht* (Linde, 2007), at p. 168; H.M. Liebman/O. Rousselle, Discriminatory Treatment of Dividends in The European Union: Is the End Near?, 39 *Tax Notes Intl.* 2 (11 Jul. 2005), p. 143 (at p. 145); R. Mason, 49 *Bost. Coll. L. Rev.* 4 (2008), at p. 1297 (FN 109); M. Quaghebeur, 37 *Tax Notes Intl.* 9 (28 February 2005), at p. 739.

The Belgian dividend recipients argued that cross-border dividend distributions differ from purely domestic ones, probably having in mind the taxes that had to be paid in France.[1337] According to the ECJ's case law, not only must "*comparable situations [...] not be treated differently,*" but also "*different situations must not be treated in the same way.*"[1338] Thus, Belgium should not be allowed to subject foreign dividends to the same tax treatment as domestic dividends. However, the ECJ did not accept this argument, because "*in respect of the tax legislation of his State of residence, the position of a shareholder receiving dividends is not necessarily altered [...] merely by the fact that he receives those dividends from a company established in another Member State, which, in exercising its fiscal sovereignty, makes those dividends subject to a deduction at source by way of income tax.*"[1339] Since it was hence not to be criticized that "*the Belgian tax legislation does not make any distinction between dividends from companies established in Belgium and dividends from companies established in another Member State,*" the Court concluded – following AG Geelhoed's Opinion[1340] – that "*the adverse consequences which might arise from the application of an income tax system such as the Belgian system at issue in the main proceedings result from the exercise in parallel by two Member States of their fiscal sovereignty. [...] Community law, in its current state and in a situation such as that in the main proceedings, does not lay down any general criteria for the attribution of areas of competence between the Member States in relation to the elimination of double taxation within the Community.*"[1341] Hence, insofar as "*no uniform or harmonisation measure designed to eliminate double taxation has as yet been adopted at Community law level,*" "*it is for the Member States to take the measures*

1337. Cf. A. Rust in A. Rust (ed.), *Double Taxation Within the European Union* (Kluwer, 2011), at p. 141.
1338. Judgment in *Garcia Avello*, C-148/02, EU:C:2003:539, at para. 31; Judgment in *Azienda Agro-Zootecnica Franchini and Eolica di Altamura*, C-2/10, EU:C:2011:502, at para. 64; Judgment in *Hungary/Commission*, C-31/13 P, EU:C:2014:70, at para. 73; also cf. Judgment in *SFI*, C-85/97, EU:C:1998:552, at para. 30; Judgment in *Jippers and others*, C-189/01, EU:C:2001:420, at para. 128; Judgment in *Denkavit*, C-507/99, EU:C:2002:4, at para. 44; Judgment in *Omega and others*, C-122/00, EU:C:2002:161, at para. 79; Judgment in *Commission/Portugal*, C-334/03, EU:C:2005:623, at para. 24; also cf. Judgment in *Schumacker*, C-279/93, EU:C:1995:31, at para. 30; Judgment in *Wielockx*, C-80/94, EU:C:1995:271, at para. 17; Judgment in *Asscher*, C-107/94, EU:C:1996:251, at para. 40; Judgment in *Royal Bank of Scotland*, C-311/97, EU:C:1999:216, at para. 26; Judgment in *Gschwind*, C-391/97, EU:C:1999:409, at para. 21; Judgment in *Kerckhaert and Morres*, C-513/04, EU:C:2006:713, at para. 19; Judgment in *Meindl*, C-329/05, EU:C:2007:57, at para. 22; Judgment in *Talotta*, C-383/05, EU:C:2007:181, at para. 18; Judgment in *Lakebrink and Peters-Lakebrink*, C-182/06, EU:C:2007:452, at para. 27; Judgment in *Columbus Container Services*, C-298/05, EU:C:2007:754, at para. 41; Judgment in Gielen, C-440/08, EU:C:2010:148; at para. 38; Judgment in *Commission/Hungary*, C-253/09, EU:C:2011:795, at para. 50; Judgment in *Commission/Netherlands*, C-542/09, EU:C:2012:346, at para. 41; Judgment in *Commission/Estonia*, C-39/10, EU:C:2012:282, at para. 48; Judgment in *Banco Bilbao Vizcaya Argentaria*, C-157/10, EU:C:2011:813, at para. 41; Judgment in *Bouanich*, C-375/12, EU:C:2014:138, at para. 45.
1339. Judgment in *Kerckhaert and Morres*, C-513/04, EU:C:2006:713, at para. 19.
1340. Opinion of AG Geelhoed in *Kerckhaert and Morres*, C-514/04, EU:C:2006:242, at points 30-36; also see Opinion of AG Geelhoed in *Test Claimants in Class IV of the ACT Group Litigation*, C-374/04, EU:C:2006:139, at points 48 et seq.
1341. Judgment in *Kerckhaert and Morres*, C-513/04, EU:C:2006:713, at paras 20 and 22.

necessary to prevent situations such as that at issue in the main proceedings by applying, in particular, the apportionment criteria followed in international tax practice."[1342]

Whereas some scholars were positive toward the ECJ's approach in *Kerckhaert and Morres*,[1343] others considered it unsatisfactory that taxpayers cannot rely on the fundamental freedoms to defend themselves from juridical double taxation[1344] and hence put forward proposals how to overcome the ECJ's main problem, which is to identify the Member State that should be made responsible for, and hence obliged to avoid, juridical double taxation.

First, it is sometimes argued that the taxpayer's Member State of residence should (always) be obliged to avoid juridical double taxation by at least crediting the taxes paid in another Member State,[1345] because not only is "source country entitlement" – in the words of AG Geelhoed – "*the generally accepted rule of taxation priority [under international tax law] [...]: that is, priority of taxation right over source country income lies with the source State,*"[1346] but this should rather also be inferable from the ECJ's decisions in *Cassis de Dijon*,[1347] *Schumacker*[1348] and *Marks & Spencer*.[1349] However, since the fundamental freedoms likewise address the "home state" or "state of origin"

1342. Judgment in *Kerckhaert and Morres*, C-513/04, EU:C:2006:713, at paras 22-23.
1343. See M. Lang in M. Lehner (ed.), *Reden zum Andenken an Klaus Vogel* (C.H. Beck, 2010), p. 59 (at pp. 74-81); K. Lenaerts in L. Hinnekens/P. Hinnekens (eds.), *A Vision of Taxes Within and Outside Europe, Festschrift in Honor of Prof. Dr. Frans Vanistendael* (Kluwer, 2008), at pp. 628-629; K. Lenaerts, 44 *EuR* 6 (2009), at pp. 737-741; P. Wattel, 12 *EC Tax Rev.* 4 (2003), at p. 199; P. Wattel in A. Rust (ed.), *Double Taxation Within the European Union* (Kluwer, 2011), at pp. 157 et seq.; D. Weber, 34 *Intertax* 12 (2006), at pp. 591-593; D. Weber, *In Search of a (New) Equilibrium Between Tax Sovereignty and the Freedom of Movement Within the EC* (Kluwer, 2006), at pp. 18-21; also cf. S. Douma, 46 *Eur. Taxn.* 11 (2006), at p. 532; W. Schön, 69 *Bull. Intl. Taxn.* 4/5 (2015), at pp. 274-276; W. Schön in W. Schön/C. Heber (eds.), *Grundfragen des Europäischen Steuerrechts* (Springer, 2015), at pp. 116-119; W. Schön in W. Wassermeyer (ed.), *Doppelbesteuerung, Festgabe zum 75. Geburtstag von Prof. Dr. Dr. h.c. Franz Wassermeyer* (C.H. Beck, 2015), at pp. 8-9.
1344. See A. Rust in A. Rust (ed.), *Double Taxation Within the European Union* (Kluwer, 2011), at p. 138; also see G. Kofler, *Doppelbesteuerungsabkommen und Europäisches Gemeinschaftsrecht* (Linde, 2007), at pp. 177-264; G. Kofler/R. Mason, 14 *Colum. J. Eur. L.* 1 (2007), at pp. 79-96; G. Kofler/R. Mason in S. van Thiel (ed.), *The Internal Market and Direct Taxation: Is the European Court of Justice Taking a New Approach?* (CFE Brochure on European Taxation, 2007), at pp. 198-215; G. Kofler in A. Rust (ed.), *Double Taxation Within the European Union* (Kluwer, 2011), at pp. 123-133; S. van Thiel in A. Rust (ed.), *Double Taxation Within the European Union* (Kluwer, 2011), at pp. 174-183; M. Wathelet in L. Hinnekens/P. Hinnekens (eds.), *A Vision of Taxes Within and Outside Europe, Festschrift in Honor of Prof. Dr. Frans Vanistendael* (Kluwer, 2008), at p. 916.
1345. See J. Schönfeld, The Cadbury Schweppes Case: Are the Days of the United Kingdom's CFC Legislation Numbered?, 44 *Eur. Taxn.* 10 (2004), p. 441 (at p. 443); J. Schönfeld, *Hinzurechnungsbesteuerung und Europäisches Gemeinschaftsrecht* (Dr Otto Schmidt, 2005), at pp. 86-87; J. Schönfeld, 83 *StuW* 1 (2006), at p. 81; J. Schönfeld in H. Flick/F. Wassemeyer/H. Baumhoff/J. Schönfeld (eds.), *Außensteuerrecht*[57] (Dr Otto Schmidt, 2005), Vor § 34c EStG at m.no 3; also cf. J. Englisch, 33 *Intertax* 8-9 (2005), at pp. 324-325, referring to the rare cases in which the Member State involved have not concluded a double taxation convention.
1346. Opinion of AG Geelhoed in *Test Claimants in Class IV of the ACT Group Litigation*, C-374/04, EU:C:2006:139, at point 51.
1347. Judgment in *Rewe*, 120/78, EU:C:1979:42.
1348. Judgment in *Schumacker*, C-279/93, EU:C:1995:31.
1349. Judgment in *Marks & Spencer*, C-446/03, EU:C:2005:763.

and the "host state" or "state of destination," there is no "*generally accepted rule of taxation priority*" in EU law.[1350] The "mutual recognition approach," which was established in *Cassis de Dijon*, further developed and refined in the context of the free movement of goods[1351] and later on transferred to the other fundamental freedoms as well,[1352] does not change this situation. This approach is also not exclusively applied to the "home state" or "state of origin," but applies with regard to the "host state" or "state of destination" as well.[1353] Applying this approach in the area of direct taxes would imply that the Member State that taxes first receives all the revenue, while other Member States, which would in principle also provide for taxation, go away empty-handed ("*first-come-first-tax*").[1354] With regard to regulatory measures, such as health or safety standards, such a result is acceptable. If a certain standard has to be met before an imported product is allowed to be marketed in a Member State in order to guarantee that it is not detrimental to consumer health or safety, a national measure does not have to require examinations that were already conducted in the Member State of exportation which provides for similar rules. The re-examination in the importing Member State would not contribute to the achievement of the underlying objective, but rather impose a redundant burden on the free movement of goods. By contrast, the main purpose of taxation is to generate revenue for the state[1355] and it does not add anything to the budget of a Member State if a cross-border transaction has already been subjected to tax in another Member State.[1356]

Moreover, with regard to the *Schumacker* decision, it is indeed correct that, since then, the ECJ has regularly pointed out "*that in principle the overall taxation of taxpayers, taking account of their personal and family circumstances, is a matter for the*

1350. See A. Cordewener, *Europäische Grundfreiheiten und nationales Steuerrecht* (Dr Otto Schmidt, 2002), at pp. 880-881; J. Englisch, *Dividendenbesteuerung* (Dr Otto Schmidt, 2005), at pp. 256-257; G. Kofler, *Doppelbesteuerungsabkommen und Europäisches Gemeinschaftsrecht* (Linde, 2007), at p. 240; for other critical remarks see A. Rust in A. Rust (ed.), *Double Taxation Within the European Union* (Kluwer, 2011), at pp. 143-144.

1351. Judgment in *Dassonville*, 8/74, EU:C:1974:85; Judgment in *Rewe*, 120/78, EU:C:1979:42; Judgment in *Keck and Mithouard*, C-267/91 and C-268/91, EU:C:1993:905.

1352. Judgment in *Choquet*, 16/78, EU:C:1978:210; Judgment in *Kraus*, C-19/92, EU:C:1993:172; Judgment in *Gebhard*, C-55/94, EU:C:1995:411; Judgment in *Pfeiffer*, C-255/97, EU:C:1999:240; Judgment in *Mac Quen*, C-108/96, EU:C:2001:67; Judgment in *Gräbner*, C-294/00, EU:C:2002:442.

1353. See J. Englisch, *Dividendenbesteuerung* (Dr Otto Schmidt, 2005), at p. 257.

1354. Critically in this respect G. Kofler, *Doppelbesteuerungsabkommen und Europäisches Gemeinschaftsrecht* (Linde, 2007), at p. 244, also referring to Justice Goldberg's dissenting opinion in *General Motors Crop. v. Washington*, 377 U.S. (1964), p. 436 (at p. 458).

1355. See R. Seer in K. Tipke/J. Lang, *Steuerrecht*[22] (Dr Otto Schmidt, 2015), at § 1 para. 6; F.P. Sutter, *Das EG-Beihilfenverbot und sein Durchführungsverbot in Steuersachen* (Linde, 2005), at p. 21; also cf. J. Englisch, *Aufteilung der Besteuerungsbefugnisse - Ein Rechtfertigungsgrund für die Einschränkung von EG-Grundfreiheiten* (Institut "Finanzen und Steuern" e.V., 2008), at p. 132.

1356. See J. Snell, 56 *Intl. & Comp. L. Q.* 2 (2007), at p. 365 ("*The collection of revenue by one State in no way protects the revenue interest of another.*"); R. Szudoczky, *The Sources of EU Law and Their Relationships: Lessons for the Field of Taxation* (IBFD, 2014), at p. 352 ("*Evidently, the collection of tax revenue by one State will not fill up the pocket of the other State.*"); also cf. G. Kofler in A. Rust (ed.), *Double Taxation Within the European Union* (Kluwer, 2011), at p. 124.

State of residence."[1357] But the same line of case law shows that, under certain circumstances, the "host state" or "state of destination" has to step into the breach.[1358] For the same reason, it cannot be deduced from *Marks & Spencer* that it is *always* for the Member State of residence to avoid juridical double taxation, because this state is obliged to take into account foreign losses if the possibilities of having such losses taken into account in the other state concerned have been exhausted - which would mean that there is a "final loss" - and no possibility for the foreign losses to be taken into account for future period exists.[1359] After all, in *Lakebrink*[1360] and *Renneberg*[1361] it was actually the other way round; the "host state" or "state of destination" had to allow the deduction of losses incurred in the "home state" or "state of origin." The ECJ's case law hence rather indicates that determining the Member State accountable for eliminating restrictions on cross-border movement is a decision that has to be made on a case-by-case basis.[1362]

Second, it was suggested to hold all Member States involved jointly and severally liable for the excessive burden suffered by the cross-border situation.[1363] However, this

1357. Judgment in *Schumacker*, C-279/93, EU:C:1995:31, at para. 32; also see Judgment in *Gschwind*, C-391/97, EU:C:1999:409, at para. 22; Judgment in *Zurstrassen*, C-87/99, EU:C:2000:251, at para. 21; Judgment in *de Groot*, C-385/00, EU:C:2002:750, at para. 90; Judgment in *Gerritse*, C-234/01, EU:C:2003:340, at para. 43; Judgment in *Wallentin*, C-169/03, EU:C:2004:403, at para. 15; Judgment in *D.*, C-376/03, EU:C:2005:424, at para. 27; Judgment in *Turpeinen*, C-520/04, EU:C:2006:703, at para. 27; Judgment in *Meindl*, C-329/05, EU:C:2007:57, at para. 23; Judgment in *Talotta*, C-383/05, EU:C:2007:181, at para. 19; Judgment in *Lakebrink and Peters-Lakebrink*, C-182/06, EU:C:2007:452, at paras 28-31; Judgment in *Renneberg*, C-527/06, EU:C:2008:566, at paras 59-61; Judgment in *Commission/Spain*, C-562/07, EU:C:2009:614, at para. 46; Judgment in *Commission/Belgium*, C-250/08, EU:C:2011:793, at para. 55; Judgment in *Gielen*, C-440/08, EU:C:2010:148, at paras 43-44; Judgment in *Commission/Hungary*, C-253/09, EU:C:2011:795, at para. 55; Judgment in *Schröder*, C-450/09, EU:C:2011:198, at para. 37; Judgment in *Commission/Estonia*, C-39/10, EU:C:2012:282, at para. 49; Judgment in *Beker*, C-168/11, EU:C:2013:117, at para. 43; Judgment in Ettwein, C-425/11, EU:C:2013:121, at para. 46; Judgment in *Imfeld and Garcet*, C-303/12, EU:C:2013:822, at para. 44; Judgment in *Grünewald*, C-559/13, EU:C:2015:109, at para. 25; Judgment in Hirvonen, C-623/13, EU:C:2015:765, at para. 31; Judgment in Kieback, C-9/14, EU:C:2015:406, at para. 22.

1358. Judgment in *Schumacker*, C-279/93, EU:C:1995:31; Judgment in *Wielockx*, C-80/94, EU:C:1995:271; Judgment in *Asscher*, C-107/94, EU:C:1996:251; Judgment in *Gschwind*, C-391/97, EU:C:1999:409; Judgment in *De Groot*, C-385/00, EU:C:2002:750; Judgment in *Wallentin*, C-169/03, EU:C:2004:403.

1359. Judgment in *Marks & Spencer*, C-446/03, EU:C:2005:763, at para. 55.

1360. Judgment in *Lakebrink and Peters-Lakebrink*, C-182/06, EU:C:2007:452.

1361. Judgment in *Renneberg*, C-527/06, EU:C:2008:566.

1362. See W. Schön in W. Schön (ed.), *Gedächtnisschrift für Brigitte Knobbe-Keuk* (Dr Otto Schmidt, 1997), at p. 762; also see G. Kofler, *Doppelbesteuerungsabkommen und Europäisches Gemeinschaftsrecht* (Linde, 2007), at p. 240.

1363. See P. Farmer in A. Arnull/D. Chalmers (eds.), *The Oxford Handbook on European Union Law* (Oxford University Press, 2015), at p. 815; V. Heydt in W. Haslehner/G. Kofler/A. Rust (eds.), *Landmark Decisions of the ECJ in Direct Taxation* (Kluwer, 2015), at pp. 189-190; G. Kofler/R. Mason, 14 *Colum. J. Eur. L.* 1 (2007), at p. 81; G. Kofler/R. Mason in S. van Thiel (ed.), *The Internal Market and Direct Taxation: Is the European Court of Justice Taking a New Approach?* (CFE Brochure on European Taxation, 2007), at pp. 201-202; G. Kofler in A. Rust (ed.), *Double Taxation Within the European Union* (Kluwer, 2011), at p. 129; H. Loukota/H. Jirousek, Doppelbesteuerung und Gemeinschaftsrecht, 17 *SWI* 1 (2007), p. 295 (at pp. 300-301); S. van Thiel, Income tax Payments and Social Security Contributions from a Community Law Point of View: How the European Court of Justice Should Streamline Its Approach in the Interest of

approach would have the strange effect that taxpayers may choose which Member State has to (at least partially) abstain from taxing by filing a return where it seems most attractive to them.[1364] Member States could indeed avoid such an outcome by bi- or multilaterally agreeing on how to avoid juridical double taxation.[1365] Still, until such an agreement has been reached, the behaviour of taxpayers could seriously influence the negotiating position of the Member States if one or more Member States is more often called on to do away with juridical double taxation than others.

Third, another approach would be to analogously apply the provisions of the Parent-Subsidiary Directive,[1366] the Merger Directive,[1367] the Interest and Royalty

---

the Internal Market, in M. Lang (ed.), *Double Taxation Conventions and Social Security Conventions* (Linde, 2006), p. 37 (at pp. 103-104); S. van Thiel, Why the European Court of Justice Should Interpret Directly Applicable Community Law as a Right to Most-Favoured Nation Treatment and a Prohibition of Double Taxation, in D. Weber (ed.), *The Influence of European Law on Direct Taxation* (Kluwer, 2007), p. 75 (at pp. 126-127); S. van Thiel, The Future of the Principle of Non-Discrimination in the EU: Towards a Right to Most Favored Nation Treatment and a Prohibition of Double Burdens?, in R.S. Avi-Yonah/J.R. Hines Jr./M. Lang (eds.), *Comparative Fiscal Federalism* (Kluwer, 2007), p. 331 (at pp. 391-392); S. van Thiel in A. Rust (ed.), *Double Taxation Within the European Union* (Kluwer, 2011), at pp. 180-181.

1364. See J. Hey, 81 *StuW* 3 (2004), at p. 198; G. Kofler, *Doppelbesteuerungsabkommen und Europäisches Gemeinschaftsrecht* (Linde, 2007), at pp. 239, 244 and 263; M. Lehner, The Influence of EU Law on Tax Treaties from a German Perspective, 54 *Bull. Intl. Taxn.* 8 (2000), p. 461 (at p. 465); for a critical view also cf. W. Schön, 69 *Bull. Intl. Taxn.* 4/5 (2015), at p. 275 (FN 41); W. Schön in W. Schön/C. Heber (eds.), *Grundfragen des Europäischen Steuerrechts* (Springer, 2015), at p. 117 (FN 37); W. Schön in W. Wassermeyer (ed.), *Doppelbesteuerung, Festgabe zum 75. Geburtstag von Prof. Dr. Dr. h.c. Franz Wassermeyer* (C.H. Beck, 2015), at pp. 8-9; for a different position, arguing that in the absence of harmonization neither Member State could be held responsible, see R. van der Linde, 13 *EC Tax Rev.* 1 (2004), at p. 14; E. Reimer in M. Lehner (ed.) *Grundfreiheiten im Steuerrecht der EU-Staaten* (C.H. Beck, 2000), at p. 58; also see P. Farmer, 7 *EC Tax Rev.* 1 (1998), at p. 27.

1365. See G. Kofler/R. Mason, 14 *Colum. J. Eur. L.* 1 (2007), at p. 81; G. Kofler/R. Mason in S. van Thiel (ed.), *The Internal Market and Direct Taxation: Is the European Court of Justice Taking a New Approach?* (CFE Brochure on European Taxation, 2007), at p. 202; G. Kofler in A. Rust (ed.), *Double Taxation Within the European Union* (Kluwer, 2011), at p. 129; S. van Thiel in A. Rust (ed.), *Double Taxation Within the European Union* (Kluwer, 2011), at p. 181; also cf. the Commission's view in the European Parliament's Notice to Members on Petition 626/2000 by Mr Klaus Schuler (German), Concerning the Dual Taxation of an Inheritance, PE 331.802/REV (25 Jan. 2007), at p. 6.

1366. Council Directive 2011/96/EU of 30 Nov. 2011 on the common system of taxation applicable in the case of parent companies and subsidiaries of different Member States, *OJ* L 345 (29 Dec. 2011), p. 8 (at pp. 8-16), as amended by: (1) Council Directive 2013/13/EU of 13 May 2013 adapting certain directives in the field of taxation, by reason of the accession of the Republic of Croatia, *OJ* L 141 (28 May 2013), p. 30 (at pp. 30-31), (2) Council Directive 2014/86/EU of 8 Jul. 2014 amending Directive 2011/96/EU on the common system of taxation applicable in the case of parent companies and subsidiaries of different Member States, *OJ* L 219 (25 Jul. 2014), p. 40 (at pp. 40-41) and (3) Council Directive (EU) 2015/121 of 27 Jan. 2015 amending Directive 2011/96/EU on the common system of taxation applicable in the case of parent companies and subsidiaries of different Member States, OJ L 21 (28 Jan. 2015), p. 1 (at pp. 1-3).

1367. Council Directive 2009/133/EC of 19 Oct. 2009 on the common system of taxation applicable to mergers, divisions, partial divisions, transfers of assets and exchanges of shares concerning companies of different Member States and to the transfer of the registered office of an SE or SCE between Member States, *OJ* L 310 (25 Nov. 2009), p. 34 (at pp. 34-46), as amended by (1)

Directive[1368] and – until it is fully repealed – the Savings Directive.[1369] Indeed, the ECJ does not restrict itself by only referring to the wording in order to interpret the law, but rather takes a teleological approach and also considers the history, the context, the systematics and the objective(s) of the legislation.[1370] However, the direct tax directives cannot be analogously applied in order to solve *all* cases of juridical double taxation.[1371] Instead, it has to be shown that in the light of the particular directive's objectives and the primary law's general principle of equality,[1372] according to which "*comparable situations must not be treated differently and that different situations must not be treated in the same way,*"[1373] the individual case should be covered by the

Council Directive 2013/13/EU of 13 May 2013 adapting certain directives in the field of taxation, by reason of the accession of the Republic of Croatia, *OJ* L 141 (28 May 2013), p. 30 (at pp. 30-31).

1368. Council Directive 2003/49/EC of 3 Jun. 2003 on a common system of taxation applicable to interest and royalty payments made between associated companies of different Member States, *OJ* L 157 (26 Jun. 2003), p. 49 (at pp. 49-54), as amended by: (1) Council Directive 2004/66/EC of 26 Apr. 2004 adapting Directives 1999/45/EC, 2002/83/EC, 2003/37/EC and 2003/59/EC of the European Parliament and of the Council and Council Directives 77/388/EEC, 91/414/EEC, 96/26/EC, 2003/48/EC and 2003/49/EC, in the fields of free movement of goods, freedom to provide services, agriculture, transport policy and taxation, by reason of the accession of the Czech Republic, Estonia, Cyprus, Latvia, Lithuania, Hungary, Malta, Poland, Slovenia and Slovakia, OJ L 168 (1 May 2004), p. 35 (at p. 35), (2) Council Directive 2004/76/EC of 29.4.2004 amending Directive 2003/49/EC as regards the possibility for certain Member States to apply transitional periods for the application of a common system of taxation applicable to interest and royalty payments made between associated companies of different Member States, OJ L 157 (30 Apr. 2004), p. 106 (at pp. 106-113) and (3) Council Directive 2013/13/EU of 13 May 2013 adapting certain directives in the field of taxation, by reason of the accession of the Republic of Croatia, *OJ* L 141 (28 May 2013), p. 30 (at pp. 30-31).

1369. Council Directive 2003/48/EC of 3 Jun. 2003 on taxation of savings income in the form of interest payments, *OJ* L 157 (26 Jun. 2003), p. 38 (at pp. 38-48), repealed by Council Directive (EU) 2015/2060 of 10 Nov. 2015 repealing Directive 2003/48/EC on taxation of savings income in the form of interest payments, *OJ* L 301 (2015), p. 1 (at pp. 1-4).

1370. For further references, especially with regard to an analogous application of the law, see R.F. van Brederode/T. O'Shea, Legal Interpretation of Tax Law: The European Union, in R.F. van Brederode/R. Krever (eds.), *Legal Interpretation of Tax Law* (Kluwer, 2014), p. 107 (at p. 119); S. Vogenauer, *Die Auslegung von Gesetzen in England und auf dem Kontinent* (Mohr Siebeck, 2001) at pp. 361-373.

1371. See A. Rust in A. Rust (ed.), *Double Taxation Within the European Union* (Kluwer, 2011), at pp. 144-148.

1372. Judgment in *Dowling*, C-85/90, EU:C:1992:402, at para. 21; Judgment in *Pastoors and Trans-Cap*, C-29/95, EU:C:1997:28, at para 14; Judgment in *Commission / Italy*, C-224/00, EU:C:2002:185, at para. 14.

1373. Judgment in *Garcia Avello*, C-148/02, EU:C:2003:539, at para. 31; Judgment in *Azienda Agro-Zootecnica Franchini and Eolica di Altamura*, C-2/10, EU:C:2011:502, at para. 64; Judgment in *Hungary/Commission*, C-31/13 P, EU:C:2014:70, at para. 73; also cf. Judgment in *SFI*, C-85/97, EU:C:1998:552, at para. 30; Judgment in *Jippers and others*, C-189/01, EU:C:2001:420, at para. 128; Judgment in *Denkavit*, C-507/99, EU:C:2002:4, at para. 44; Judgment in *Omega and others*, C-122/00, EU:C:2002:161, at para. 79; Judgment in *Commission/Portugal*, C-334/03, EU:C:2005:623, at para. 24; also cf. Judgment in *Schumacker*, C-279/93, EU:C:1995:31, at para. 30; Judgment in *Wielockx*, C-80/94, EU:C:1995:271, at para. 17; Judgment in *Asscher*, C-107/94, EU:C:1996:251, at para. 40; Judgment in *Royal Bank of Scotland*, C-311/97, EU:C:1999:216, at para. 26; Judgment in *Gschwind*, C-391/97, EU:C:1999:409, at para. 21; Judgment in *Kerckhaert and Morres*, C-513/04, EU:C:2006:713, at para. 19; Judgment in *Meindl*, C-329/05, EU:C:2007:57, at para. 22; Judgment in *Talotta*, C-383/05, EU:C:2007:181, at para. 18; Judgment in *Lakebrink and Peters-Lakebrink*, C-182/06, EU:C:2007:452, at para. 27; Judgment in *Columbus Container Services*, C-298/05,

harmonizing measure, although the wording suggests differently.[1374] The ECJ is rather conservative in this respect.[1375] In *Gaz de France*, for example, the question was raised whether the former Parent-Subsidiary Directive[1376] can be analogously applied to a cross-border dividend distribution received by a company having a legal form that is not mentioned in the annex to the Parent-Subsidiary Directive. The Court initially held that such an analogy "*could meet the objectives of Directive 90/435, as highlighted in the third recital in the preamble thereto, since it would imply an extension of the scope of that directive to a larger number of companies and would thus contribute to removing the disadvantage affecting cooperation between companies of different Member States in comparison with cooperation between companies of the same Member State and would facilitate the grouping together of companies at Community level.*"[1377] However, for various reasons,[1378] the ECJ concluded that "*since the legal forms under French law covered by Directive 90/435 are exhaustively listed in point (f) of the Annex thereto, the extension of the scope of that directive by analogy to other forms of company, [...] even if they were comparable, would not be admissible.*"[1379] Analogously applying the provision of the direct tax directives hence seems to be of only limited help to overcome juridical double taxation within the EU.

Fourth, in the literature, it is contemplated to identify the Member State responsible for juridical double taxation by examining whether a Member State's tax system is internally consistent. Two suggestions have been made in this regard: On the one hand, a Member State's tax system is only deemed to be consistent if it allows another Member State to claim a primary taxing right when the latter state was (hypothetically) in the position of the former.[1380] According to this approach, it would be inconsistent

EU:C:2007:754, at para. 41; Judgment in *Gielen*, C-440/08, EU:C:2010:148; at para. 38; Judgment in *Commission/Hungary*, C-253/09, EU:C:2011:795, at para. 50; Judgment in *Commission/Netherlands*, C-542/09, EU:C:2012:346, at para. 41; Judgment in *Commission/Estonia*, C-39/10, EU:C:2012:282, at para. 48; Judgment in *Banco Bilbao Vizcaya Argentaria*, C-157/10, EU:C:2011:813, at para. 41; Judgment in *Bouanich*, C-375/12, EU:C:2014:138, at para. 45.

1374. See A. Cordewener, *Europäische Grundfreiheiten und nationales Steuerrecht* (Dr Otto Schmidt, 2002), at pp. 882; G. Kofler, *Doppelbesteuerungsabkommen und Europäisches Gemeinschaftsrecht* (Linde, 2007), at p. 242.
1375. See A. Rust in A. Rust (ed.), *Double Taxation Within the European Union* (Kluwer, 2011), at p. 148.
1376. Council Directive 90/435/EEC of 23 Jul. 1990 on the common system of taxation applicable in the case of parent companies and subsidiaries of different Member States, *OJ* L 225 (20 Aug. 1990), p. 6 (at pp. 6-9).
1377. Judgment in *Gaz de France - Berliner Investissement*, C-247/08, EU:C:2009:600, at para. 35.
1378. For an analysis of this case see G.F. Boulogne/W.W. Geursen, *Gaz de France*: Dividends to Companies Not Listed in the Parent-Subsidiary Directive Are Not Exempt, 50 *Eur. Taxn.* 4 (2010), p. 129 (at pp. 129-140); H. Hahn, Von kleinen Aktiengesellschaften, sociétés par actions simplifiées und anderen Raritäten – der Anwendungsbereich der Mutter-Tochter-Richtlinie nach "Gaz de France," 21 *EWS* 5 (2010), p. 176 (at pp. 176-181).
1379. Judgment in *Gaz de France - Berliner Investissement*, C-247/08, EU:C:2009:600, at para. 43; also cf. Judgment in *Aberdeen Property Fininvest Alpha*, C-303/07, EU:C:2009:377, at paras 26-28.
1380. See A. Rust in A. Rust (ed.), *Double Taxation Within the European Union* (Kluwer, 2011), at pp. 153-154; critically W. Schön, 69 *Bull. Intl. Taxn.* 4/5 (2015), at p. 275 (FN 41); W. Schön

if Member State A, on the one hand, decided to tax non-residents receiving dividends from domestic companies and, on the other hand, also wants to tax residents receiving dividends from foreign companies. In the latter case, it is up to the distributing company's residence state to tax the non-resident dividend recipient in the same way as Member State A does. Of course, it could similarly be argued that if Member State A imposes a tax on residents receiving dividends from foreign companies, it would be inconsistent to also tax non-residents receiving dividends from domestic companies, because, in the latter case, it is up to the other Member State to tax resident dividend recipients in the same way as Member State A does. It is indeed true that many Member States "*are willing to grant a tax credit unilaterally*" to their residents being subject to juridical double taxation.[1381] However, unless such a unilateral tax credit can be legally enforced, which is not the case in all Member States (at least not with regard to all types of income), this circumstance does not mean that the Member State's tax claims on income received by non-residents should be the benchmark for examining the tax system's consistency. After all, a Member State might also grant unilateral relief from juridical double taxation for non-residents.[1382]

On the other hand, but quite similar to the idea of consistency just described, it is suggested to adopt the US Supreme Court's "internal consistency test."[1383] This approach requires assuming "*that all member states apply tax law identical to the defendant member state's*"[1384] or, in other words, to hypothetically apply "*the challenged state's law in both a source and a resident capacity.*"[1385] If this intellectual pastime shows that, for example, a cross-border dividend distribution suffers a higher tax burden than a comparable domestic dividend distribution, the Member State's tax system would be internally inconsistent, because if this tax system was "*adopted by all the Member States, cross-border dividends would* always *bear more tax than domestic dividends.*" Applying the "internal consistency test" to the facts of the *Kerckhaert and Morres* case, for example, would supposedly reveal "*the structural flaws inherent in*

in W. Schön/C. Heber (eds.), *Grundfragen des Europäischen Steuerrechts* (Springer, 2015), at pp. 117-118 (FN 37); P. Wattel in A. Rust (ed.), *Double Taxation Within the European Union* (Kluwer, 2011), at p. 166.

1381. A. Rust in A. Rust (ed.), *Double Taxation Within the European Union* (Kluwer, 2011), at p. 154.

1382. With regard to Austria see, for example, G. Stoll, *BAO Kommentar, Band I* (Orac, 1994), at p. 509.

1383. See G. Kofler/R. Mason, 14 *Colum. J. Eur. L.* 1 (2007), at pp. 83-98; G. Kofler/R. Mason in S. van Thiel (ed.), *The Internal Market and Direct Taxation: Is the European Court of Justice Taking a New Approach?* (CFE Brochure on European Taxation, 2007), at pp. 205-219; G. Kofler, *Doppelbesteuerungsabkommen und Europäisches Gemeinschaftsrecht* (Linde, 2007), at pp. 221-231; R. Mason, 49 *Bost. Coll. L. Rev.* 4 (2008), at pp. 1309-1319; R. Mason/M.S. Knoll, What Is Tax Discrimination?, 121 *Yale L. J.* 5 (2011-2012), p. 1014 (at pp. 1106-1114).

1384. R. Mason, 49 *Bost. Coll. L. Rev.* 4 (2008), at p. 1309; critically W. Haslehner, 50 *Common Market L. Rev.* 3 (2013), at pp. 741-742.

1385. G. Kofler/R. Mason, 14 *Colum. J. Eur. L.* 1 (2007), at p. 91; G. Kofler/R. Mason in S. van Thiel (ed.), *The Internal Market and Direct Taxation: Is the European Court of Justice Taking a New Approach?* (CFE Brochure on European Taxation, 2007), at p. 214 (at FN 214).

Belgian taxation of cross-border dividends," if it is assumed that "*Belgium would levy a typical 15% withholding tax on outbound dividends*":[1386]

		Dividend Distribution Within Belgium	*Dividend Distribution from France to Belgium*
	Gross Amount of Dividend Distribution	100.00	100.00
-	French (= Belgian) Withholding Tax (15%)	–	(15.00)
	Tax Base in Belgium	100.00	85.00
-	Belgian Income Tax (25%)	(25.00)	(21.25)
	Total Amount of Taxes	25.00	36.25
	Net Amount of Dividend	75.00	63.75

However, one has to be aware that the "internal consistency test" is "*not about double taxation*";[1387] at least not primarily. It rather "*provides a reliable way to rule out the possibility that a disparity caused a tax disadvantage.*"[1388] If all Member States adopted the same tax system, "*there would be no disparities. Thus, any cross-border tax disadvantage that remains after application of the [internal consistency test] cannot be due to tax disparities.*"[1389] The "internal consistency test" is hence not about sorting out which Member State is responsible for eliminating a cross-border tax disadvantage, in general, or double taxation, in particular, but is a method – but not a standard[1390] – to determine whether the cross-border tax disadvantage results from *discrimination* that can be potentially challenged due to the inconsistency of *one* Member State's tax system or from a *disparity* created by the interaction of *several* Member States' tax systems which cannot be challenged under the fundamental freedoms. This means that if the "internal consistency test" shows that there is no disparity, the ECJ could still "*find that internally inconsistent member state tax laws were justified for public policy reasons, or it could find that the cross-border and internal situations were so dissimilar that the member state was not required to treat them the same. As a result, although a failure of internal consistency tends to suggest discrimination, it is not sufficient to establish a violation of EC law. Thus, rather than constituting a per se violation of the EC Treaty, a failure of internal consistency should be understood to create a rebuttable*

1386. G. Kofler/R. Mason, 14 *Colum. J. Eur. L.* 1 (2007), at p. 92-93; G. Kofler/R. Mason in S. van Thiel (ed.), *The Internal Market and Direct Taxation: Is the European Court of Justice Taking a New Approach?* (CFE Brochure on European Taxation, 2007), at p. 215.
1387. M.S. Knoll/R. Mason, *Wynne*: It's Not About Double Taxation, 57 *State Tax Notes* 7 (16 Feb. 2015), p. 413 (at p. 420); also cf. M.S. Knoll/R. Mason, *Comptroller v. Wynne*: Internal Consistency, a National Marketplace, and Limits on State Sovereignty to Tax, 163 *University of Pennsylvania Law Rev. Online* (2015), p. 267 (at pp. 281-283).
1388. R. Mason, 49 *Bost. Coll. L. Rev.* 4 (2008), at p. 1282.
1389. R. Mason, 49 *Bost. Coll. L. Rev.* 4 (2008), at p. 1310; also see G. Kofler/R. Mason, 14 *Colum. J. Eur. L.* 1 (2007), at p. 93.
1390. See R. Mason, 49 *Bost. Coll. L. Rev.* 4 (2008), at pp. 1300, 1309-1310 and 1319-1321.

presumption of discrimination."[1391] The "internal consistency test" is hence not meant to complement the Court's analysis, but rather to replace the previous – and still upheld – approach for identifying discriminatory tax provision. Therefore, for the time being, invoking this approach does not fully solve the ECJ's dilemma. After all, even if the "internal consistency test" were to be applied – which, according to some scholars, would clash with the Court's jurisprudence on fiscal cohesion[1392] – the Member State responsible for the juridical double taxation would remain unidentifiable if the tax systems of all Member States involved were internally consistent. Similarly, if, for example, all Member States taxed residents receiving dividends from foreign companies at a rate of 25 % and also provided for a 15 % withholding tax on dividends paid by domestic companies to foreign shareholders, no Member States' tax system is internal coherent. In such a situation, the "internal consistency test" would hence simply confirm that the Member States involved are likewise responsible for the juridical double taxation.

Fifth, according to the ECJ, *"in the allocation of fiscal jurisdiction, it [is not] unreasonable for the Member States to base their agreements on international practice and the model convention drawn up by the OECD."*[1393] Based on this jurisprudence, one may argue that *"nothing precludes an interpretation the EC Treaty, so far as possible, in accordance with an OECD model convention."*[1394] However, the OECD MC provides for several options and equivalent alternatives. It is, for example, left to the contracting states to decide on the rate of source taxation for dividends and interest.[1395] Whether the residence state has to grant relief from double taxation through the credit or the exemption method – except for passive income – also remains unsettled.[1396] It is hence not possible to infer clear guidance from the OECD MC on how to eliminate juridical double taxation in each and every case.[1397] Moreover, not all Member States are members of the OECD as well;[1398] and even if they were, they would not be legally

1391. R. Mason, 49 *Bost. Coll. L. Rev.* 4 (2008), at p. 1311.
1392. See W. Haslehner, 50 *Common Market L. Rev.* 3 (2013), at pp. 741-742.
1393. Judgment in *Gilly*, C-336/96, EU:C:1998:221, at para. 16; also see Judgment in *van Hilten-van der Heijden*, C-513/03, EU:C:2006:131, at para. 48; Judgment in *N*, C-470/04, EU:C:2006:525, at para. 45; Judgment in *Lidl Belgium*, C-414/06, EU:C:2008:278, at para. 22.
1394. Opinion of AG Mischo in *Lankhorst-Hohorst*, C-324/00, EU:C:2002:545, at point 81; also see V. Heydt, Juristische Doppelbesteuerung als ungelöstes Problem: Kann der EuGH Klarheit schaffen?, 21 *SWI* 9 (2011), p. 371 (at p. 373); G. Kofler, *Doppelbesteuerungsabkommen und Europäisches Gemeinschaftsrecht* (Linde, 2007), at p. 249; T. Kühbacher, Doppelbesteuerung und Unionsrecht: letzter Akt einer (un)endlichen Geschichte, 20 *SWI* 7 (2010), p. 308 (at p. 312); A. Rust in A. Rust (ed.), *Double Taxation Within the European Union* (Kluwer, 2011), at p. 149; also cf. A. Cordewener, *Europäische Grundfreiheiten und nationales Steuerrecht* (Dr Otto Schmidt, 2002), at p. 887; G. Fibbe/A. de Graaf in H.P.A.M. van Arendonk/F.A. Engelen/S. Jansen (eds.), *A Tax Globalist, Essays in Honour of Maarten J. Ellis* (IBFD, 2005), at p. 258 (FN 58); A. Schnitger, *Die Grenzen der Einwirkungen der Grundfreiheiten des EG-Vertrages auf das Ertragsteuerrecht* (IDW, 2006), at p. 266.
1395. Articles 10 and 11 OECD MC.
1396. Articles 23 A and 23 B OECD MC.
1397. See G. Kofler, *Doppelbesteuerungsabkommen und Europäisches Gemeinschaftsrecht* (Linde, 2007), at p. 250; A. Rust in A. Rust (ed.), *Double Taxation Within the European Union* (Kluwer, 2011), at pp. 149-150.
1398. Bulgaria, Croatia, Cyprus, Estonia, Latvia, Lithuania, Malta, Romania have not joined the OECD yet.

required to follow the suggestions of the OECD MC.[1399] It is, therefore, not surprising that the bilateral double taxation conventions concluded by the Member States include numerous deviations from the corresponding rules in the OECD MC. These differences show that the OECD MC might indeed be considered to be a "*common European standard,*"[1400] but neither does it constitute customary international law[1401] nor is it legally binding from an EU law perspective.[1402] If the ECJ nevertheless consulted the provisions of the OECD MC in order to avoid juridical double taxation which is not solved by an existing double taxation convention anyway, it would have to create an autonomous "vocabulary of concepts."[1403] This could be geared to the OECD MC, but also would have to be superimposed on existing treaties, because juridical double taxation could persist despite the existence of a bilateral tax treaty due to: (1) a varying evaluation of the facts of the case, (2) a diverging interpretation of the rules of the double taxation convention or (3) the disparities between the domestic tax systems of the contracting states.[1404] Moreover, it is questionable whether the Treaties provide a

1399. According to Article 5 OECD Convention, "*the Organisation may: (a) take decisions which, except as otherwise provided, shall be binding on all the Members; (b) make recommendations to Members; and (c) enter into agreements with Members, non-member States and international organisations.*" Whereas decisions lead to an obligation of the Member countries to act in a certain way (see H.J. Hahn/A. Weber, *Die OECD, Organisation für Wirtschaftliche Zusammenarbeit und Entwicklung* [Nomos, 1976], at pp. 95 et seq.; H. J. Hahn, Die Organisation für Wirtschaftliche Zusammenarbeit und Entwicklung (OECD), Entstehung und Rechtsordnung, 22 *ZaöRV* [1962] at pp. 78 et seq.), it is for the Member countries to decide upon the implementation of recommendations (see Article 18(b) OECD, Rules of Procedure of the Organisation [2013] [hereinafter OECD Procedural Rules]; also see G. Dahm, Die völkerrechtliche Verbindlichkeit von Empfehlungen internationaler Organisationen, 12 *DÖV* 10 [1959], p. 361 [at pp. 361 et seq.]; A. Elkin, The Organisation for European Economic Co-Operation, Its Structure and Powers, in B. Landheer/W.H. Carter [eds)], *European Yearbook*, Vol. IV [Nijhoff, 1958], p. 96 [at pp. 131-133]; A.J. Van den Tempel, *Beseitigung der Doppelbesteuerung* [Internationales Steuerdokumentationsbüro, 1967], at pp. 23-24). The OECD MC is a recommendation of the OECD Council. According to Article 18(b) OECD Procedural Rules, it "*shall be submitted to the Members for consideration in order that they may, if they consider it opportune, provide for their implementation.*" The Member countries are hence not legally obliged to adopt the provisions of the OECD MC.

1400. M. Lehner, 54 *Bull. Intl. Taxn.* 8 (2000), at p. 465; also see G. Kofler, *Doppelbesteuerungsabkommen und Europäisches Gemeinschaftsrecht* (Linde, 2007), at p. 251; also cf. F. Vanistendael, 46 *Eur. Taxn.* 9 (2006), at p. 419 ("the international norm").

1401. See M. Lang in W. Gassner/M. Lang/E. Lechner (eds.), *Doppelbesteuerungsabkommen und EU-Recht* (Linde, 1996), at pp. 35-36; but see R.S. Avi-Yonah, International Tax as International Law, 57 *Tax L. Rev.* 4 (2004), p. 483 (pp. 483 et seq.), who argues that some rules of the OECD MC have become part of customary international law due to their widespread use in bilateral tax treaties.

1402. See G. Kofler, *Doppelbesteuerungsabkommen und Europäisches Gemeinschaftsrecht* (Linde, 2007), at pp. 250-251.

1403. G. Kofler, *Doppelbesteuerungsabkommen und Europäisches Gemeinschaftsrecht* (Linde, 2007), at pp. 255-257.

1404. See OECD, *The Application of the OECD Model Tax Convention to Partnerships*, Issues in International Taxation No. 6 (OECD, 1999), at para. 94 et seq.; also see H. Loukota in W. Gassner/M. Lang (eds.), *30 Jahre Steuerrecht an der Wirtschaftsuniversität Wien* (Orac, 1998), at p. 269; H. Loukota in R. Beiser/S. Kirchmayr/G. Mayr/N. Zorn (eds.), *Ertragsteuern in Wissenschaft und Praxis*, Festschrift Werner Doralt (LexisNexis, 2007), at pp. 280-282; H. Loukota, 9 *SWI* 2, (1999), at pp. 70-77; J. Schuch/J. Bauer in W. Gassner/M. Lang/E. Lechner (eds.), *Personengesellschaften im Recht der Doppelbesteuerungsabkommen* (Linde, 2000), at p. 31.

proper basis for such a far-reaching interpretation.[1405] According to the ECJ, "*the interpretation of national law and any assessment of the facts in the case is a matter for the national court.*"[1406] Thus, the ECJ cannot solve those situations of juridical double taxation that result from a varying evaluation of the facts of the case or a diverging interpretation of the rules of the double taxation convention.

Sixth, it is suggested to rely on the existing double taxation conventions in order to identify the Member State responsible for a remaining juridical double taxation. Such an approach could at least solve those situations in which juridical double taxation was not avoided, because the contracting states interpret the provisions of an existing bilateral tax treaty differently. In such a case, it would have to be determined which of the two different interpretations - or whether even an interpretation deviating from both contracting states' understanding - is correct.[1407] However, according to the ECJ, it has "*no jurisdiction [...] to rule on the interpretation of provisions other than those of Community law.*"[1408] By relying on Article 273 TFEU, Member States could only voluntarily decide to grant the ECJ jurisdiction in any dispute regarding the interpretation of a bilateral double taxation convention. Thus, it is possible to appeal to the ECJ if there is a "*dispute between Member States which relates to the subject matter of the Treaties,*" which "*is submitted to it under a special agreement between the parties.*" Given that double taxation was explicitly mentioned in Article 293 second indent EC Treaty, it was concluded in the past that double taxation "*relates to the subject matter of the Treaties.*"[1409] Although this provision has been abolished through the Treaty of

1405. Cf. A. Rust in A. Rust (ed.), *Double Taxation Within the European Union* (Kluwer, 2011), at p. 150.

1406. Judgment in *Badischer Winzerkeller*, C-264/04, EU:C:2006:402, at para. 43; also see Judgment in *Grünewald*, C-559/13, EU:C:2015:109, at para. 32; with regard to the facts of the case also see Judgment in *Öhlschläger / Hauptzollamt Emmerich*, 104/77, EU:C:1978:69, at para. 4; Judgment in *Denkavit Futtermittel*, 36/79, EU:C:1979:258, at para. 12; Judgment in *AGS Assedic Pas-de-Calais / Dumon and Froment*, C-235/95, EU:C:1998:365, at para. 25; Judgment in *Salgoil / Ministero del commercio con l'estero*, 13/68, EU:C:1968:54, at p. 459; Judgment in *Van der Hulst / Produktschap voor Siergewassen*, 51/74, EU:C:1975:9, at para. 12; Judgment *Lirussi*, C-175/98 and C-177/98, EU:C:1999:486, at paras 37-38; Judgment in *RAR*, C-282/00, EU:C:2003:277, at paras 46-47; Judgment in *Gauweiler and others*, C-62/14, EU:C:2015:400, at para. 15; with regard to the interpretation of domestic provisions also see Judgment in *Vanacker and Lesage*, C-37/92, EU:C:1993:836, at para. 7; Judgment in *X*, C-60/02, EU:C:2004:10, at para. 58; Judgment in *Wilson*, C-506/04, EU:C:2006:587, at para. 34; Judgment in *Krzysztof Peśla*, C-345/08, EU:C:2009:771, at paras 64-65; Judgment in *Winner Wetten*, C-409/06, EU:C:2010:503, at para. 35.

1407. See G. Kofler, *Doppelbesteuerungsabkommen und Europäisches Gemeinschaftsrecht* (Linde, 2007), at pp. 257 and 262-263.

1408. Judgment in *AMID*, C-141/99, EU:C:2000:696, at para. 18; also cf. Order in *Generalstaatsanwaltschaft and others/Hartmann*, C-162/98, EU:C:1998:539, at paras 8-12; Opinion of AG Kokott in *Bouanich*, C-265/04, EU:C:2005:479, at point 53 (FN 47).

1409. See M. Züger, Der EuGH als Schiedsgericht im neuen DBA Österreich-Deutschland, 9 *SWI* 1 (1999), p. 19 (at p. 22); M. Züger, Mutual Agreement and Arbitration Procedure in a Multilateral Tax Treaty, in M. Lang/H. Loukota/A.J. Rädler/J. Schuch/G. Toifl/C. Urtz/F. Wassermeyer/M. Züger, *Multilateral Tax Treaties* (Linde, 1997), p. 155 (at p. 177); M. Züger, Das Schiedsverfahren nach dem neuen DBA Österreich-Deutschland, in W. Gassner/M. Lang/E. Lechner (eds.), *Das neue Doppelbesteuerungsabkommen Österreich-Deutschland* (Linde, 1999), p. 245 (at p. 249); M. Züger, Der Einfluß des Schiedsverfahrens vor dem EuGH auf das Abgabenrecht, in M. Holoubek/M. Lang (eds.), *Das EuGH-Verfahren in Steuersachen*

Lisbon, there are good reasons to assume that this is still the case.[1410] However, Article 273 TFEU not only requires that the "*dispute between Member States [...] relates to the subject matter of the Treaties,*" but also that it is submitted to the ECJ "*under a special agreement between the parties.*" At present, such special agreements are quite rare in practice.[1411] For tax purposes, the only example is Article 25(5) of the double taxation convention between Austria and Germany. According to this provision, upon application of a person covered by this provision, any difficulty or doubt arising as to the interpretation or application of the convention[1412] which cannot be removed by the competent authorities by the use of the mutual agreement procedure within a period of three years from the date of initiation of the procedure must be referred to arbitration proceedings before the ECJ pursuant to Article 239 EC Treaty (now-Article 273 TFEU) by the contracting states.[1413] However, unless such a special agreement provides for a legal basis to call in the ECJ or it changes its position, it is not possible to admonish a Member State for misinterpreting a double taxation convention by invoking the fundamental freedoms.[1414]

Still, it might be contemplated to rely on the existing double taxation conventions in order to provide relief from juridical double taxation resulting from a Member State unilaterally deviating from what has been agreed upon in the double tax convention. By introducing such a "treaty override," a Member State precludes juridical double taxation to be avoided by the double taxation convention. This Member State can hence be identified as being responsible for juridical double taxation not being avoided[1415] or, in other words, "*if there exists such a treaty between two Member States,*

(Linde, 2000), p. 301 (at p. 305); also see I. Kerschner/F. Koppensteiner/C. Seydl, Österreich erhebt aufgrund einer DBA-Streitigkeit erstmals Klage beim EuGH, 26 *SWI* 3 (2016), p. 134 (at pp. 137-138).

1410. See, for example, E.C.C.M. Kemmeren, 17 *EC Tax Rev.* 4 [2008], at pp. 156-158.

1411. See U. Karpenstein in E. Grabitz/M. Hilf/M. Nettesheim (eds.), *Das Recht der Europäischen Union*[57] (C.H. Beck, 2015), Art. 273 AEUV at para. 3.

1412. It can be inferred from Article 344 TFEU that questions about the interpretation or application of a public international law contract can be considered to constitute a "*dispute between Member States*" as required by Article 273 TFEU. See M. Züger in W. Gassner/M. Lang/E. Lechner (eds.), *Das neue Doppelbesteuerungsabkommen Österreich-Deutschland* (Linde, 1999), at p. 249; M. Züger in M. Holoubek/M. Lang (eds.), *Das EuGH-Verfahren in Steuersachen* (Linde, 2000), at p. 305; also see I. Kerschner/F. Koppensteiner/C. Seydl, 26 *SWI* 3 (2016), at p. 137.

1413. Unofficial translation by the IBFD.

1414. Concerning the procedural problems which would arise, if this were possible, see J. Hey, 81 *StuW* 3 (2004), at p. 198; G. Kofler, *Doppelbesteuerungsabkommen und Europäisches Gemeinschaftsrecht* (Linde, 2007), at pp. 257-258 and 262-263.

1415. See A. Cordewener, *Europäische Grundfreiheiten und nationales Steuerrecht* (Dr Otto Schmidt, 2002), at pp. 882-886; J. Englisch, *Dividendenbesteuerung* (Dr Otto Schmidt, 2005), at pp. 257-261; J. Englisch, 33 *Intertax* 8/9 (2005), at p. 324; M. Gammie, Double Taxation, Bilateral Treaties and the Fundamental Freedoms of the EC Treaty, in H. van Arendonk/F.A. Engelen/S. Jansen (eds.), *A Tax Globalist, Essays in Honour of Maarten J. Ellis* (IBFD, 2005), p. 266 (at pp. 279-280); G. Kofler, 16 *SWI* 2 (2006), at pp. 70-71; G. Kofler, *Doppelbesteuerungsabkommen und Europäisches Gemeinschaftsrecht* (Linde, 2007), at pp. 258-263 and 604-618; T. Kühbacher, 20 *SWI* 7 (2010), at p. 312; A. Rust in A. Rust (ed.), *Double Taxation Within the European Union* (Kluwer, 2011), at pp. 150-151; for a different opinion see P. Wattel in A. Rust (ed.), *Double Taxation Within the European Union* (Kluwer, 2011), at pp. 163-164.

both of them are obliged under Community law to apply and interpret its stipulations in a way that in conformity with the basic freedoms, i.e. in a way that avoids double taxation. Consequently, when one national jurisdiction fails to correctly implement the treaty provisions, it can be identified as the one that is responsible for the infringement of the basic freedoms caused by international double taxation."[1416] This EU law obligation to adhere to the provisions of a bilateral treaty concluded with another Member State can be inferred from Article 4(3) TEU,[1417] according to which "*[t]he Member States shall take any appropriate measure, general or particular, to ensure fulfilment of the obligations arising out of the Treaties or resulting from the acts of the institutions of the Union*" and "*shall facilitate the achievement of the Union's tasks and refrain from any measure which could jeopardise the attainment of the Union's objectives.*" This principle of loyalty is considered to require that bilateral tax treaties are interpreted and applied in a way that is consistent with EU law.[1418] A Member State that unilaterally deviates from the provisions of a double taxation convention is thus allegedly infringing Article 4(3) TEU.[1419]

1.3.1.2 Tax Treaty Override, Juridical Double Taxation and Primary EU Law

Despite the numerous proposals on how to overcome the dilemma that the Member State responsible for juridical double taxation has to be identified, the ECJ has adhered to the approach taken in *Kerckhaert and Morres*. In *Block*, the Court first transposed its conclusions to inheritance taxes.[1420] Although one might have hence been tempted to

1416. J. Englisch, 33 *Intertax* 8/9 (2005), at p. 324; also see J. Englisch, *Dividendenbesteuerung* (Dr Otto Schmidt, 2005), at p. 259; G. Kofler, 16 *SWI* 2 (2006), at p. 71; G. Kofler, *Doppelbesteuerungsabkommen und Europäisches Gemeinschaftsrecht* (Linde, 2007), at p. 260.

1417. See J. Englisch, 33 *Intertax* 8/9 (2005), at p. 324; J. Englisch, *Dividendenbesteuerung* (Dr Otto Schmidt, 2005), at pp. 257-258; G. Kofler, *Doppelbesteuerungsabkommen und Europäisches Gemeinschaftsrecht* (Linde, 2007), at pp. 606-607; R.H.M.J. Offermanns, Restrictions on Treaty Override Resulting from EU Law, 53 *Eur. Taxn.* 9 (2013), p. 430 (at pp. 434-435); R. Seer, Grenzen der Zulässigkeit eines treaty overridings am Beispiel der Switch-over-Klausel des § 20 AStG (Teil II), 6 *IStR* 17 (1997), p. 520 (at p. 522); R. Seer, Nationales Recht, Doppelbesteuerungsabkommen und Europarecht aus deutscher Sicht, in B. Brzezinski/J. Gluchowski/C. Kosikowski/R. Mastalski (eds.), *Księga pamiątkowa ku czci Profesora Apoloniusza Kosteckiego* (Torun, 1998), p. 201 (at pp. 213-214); for a different opinion see M. Lang in M. Lehner (ed.), *Reden zum Andenken an Klaus Vogel* (C.H. Beck, 2010), at pp. 81-86; also cf. M. Lang, Der EuGH als Interpret von Doppelbesteuerungsabkommen, in J. Lüdicke/J.M. Mössner/L. Hummel (eds.), *Das Steuerrecht der Unternehmen – Festschrift für Gerrit Frotscher zum 70. Geburtstag* (Haufe-Lexware, 2013), p. 365 (at pp. 369-370).

1418. See J. Englisch, 33 *Intertax* 8/9 (2005), at p. 324, J. Englisch, *Dividendenbesteuerung* (Dr Otto Schmidt, 2005), at p. 258 and G. Kofler, *Doppelbesteuerungsabkommen und Europäisches Gemeinschaftsrecht* (Linde, 2007), at pp. 606-607, who refer to Judgment in *Matteucci / Communauté française de Belgique*, 235/87, EU:C:1988:460, at para. 19.

1419. See R. Seer, 6 *IStR* 17 (1997), at p. 522; R. Seer in B. Brzezinski/J. Gluchowski/C. Kosikowski/R. Mastalski (eds.), *Księga pamiątkowa ku czci Profesora Apoloniusza Kosteckiego* (Torun, 1998), at p. 214; also see T. Scherer, Treaty Override und Unionsrecht – ein Versuch, 25 *IStR* 18 (2016), p. 741 (at pp. 744-745).

1420. Judgment in *Block*, C-67/08, EU:C:2009:92.

consider issues of juridical double taxation to be *acte clair* or *acte éclairé*,[1421,1422] Belgian courts in particular were still in doubt. Despite *Kerckhaert and Morres* and *Block*, the Belgian legislation's compatibility with EU law was again questioned, but from different angles, in *Damseaux*[1423] and *Levy and Sebbag*.[1424] Whereas the ECJ had already held that Belgian domestic law did not infringe the fundamental freedoms, *Damseaux* was specifically about the EU law compatibility of the Belgium-France double taxation convention,[1425] which was also confirmed by the Court.[1426] In *Levy and Sebbag*, it was argued that the "*unilateral change of the Belgian legislation is a perfect example of jeopardizing an objective of the EC Treaty, i.e. the elimination of double taxation. [...] A Member State should not be allowed to erode the* effet utile *of Community law achieved by a DTC which for many years effectively eliminates double taxation, by subsequently enacting rules in domestic tax law that lead to the contrary result.*"[1427] Relying on Article 10 EC Treaty (now-Article 4(3) TFEU) and Article 293 second indent EC Treaty, the Court was thus asked whether "*a Member State [is] acting in compliance with Community law, [...] if it undertakes, in a double taxation convention with another Member State, to eliminate the double taxation of dividends resulting from the division of the power of taxation laid down in that convention but subsequently amends its national law in such a way that such double taxation is no longer relieved*"?[1428] However, following its line of reasoning in *Kerckhaert and Morres* and *Damseaux*, the ECJ concluded that neither the principle of loyalty nor Article 293

1421. Cf. G. Kofler/V. Metzler, Block: Kein Verbot der juristischen Doppelbesteuerung im Binnenmarkt, 22 *ÖStZ* 9 (2009), p. 219 (at p. 224: "*Durch das Urteil in* Block *scheint die Frage nach dem grundfreiheitsrechtlichen Verbot einer Doppelbesteuerung zu einem vorläufigen – negativen – Abschluss gekommen zu sein. Damit scheint zugleich das Schicksal der noch anhängigen Rs* Damseaux *und* Kommission/Belgien *besiegelt. Es gilt also: Die juristische Doppelbesteuerung ist zwar potenziell eines der schwerwiegendsten Hindernisse für die Ausübung der Grundfreiheiten, ihr ist aber durch diese nicht beizukommen!*").

1422. On these concepts see A.P. Dourado, Is it *Acte Clair*? General report on the role played by *CILFIT* in direct taxation, in A.P. Dourado/R. da Palma Borges (eds.), *The Acte Clair in EC Direct Tax Law* (IBFD, 2008), p. 13 (at pp. 17 et seq.).

1423. Judgment in *Damseaux*, C-128/08, EU:C:2009:471.

1424. Order in *Levy and Sebbag*, C-540/11, EU:C:2012:581.

1425. See K. Daxkobler/E. Huisman, *Levy & Sebbag*: The ECJ Has Once Again Been Asked To Deliver Its Opinion on Juridical Double Taxation in the Internal Market, 53 *Eur. Taxn.* 8 (2013), p. 400 (at p. 402); L. De Broe, Relief of Double Taxation of Cross-Border Dividends Within the Union and the Principle of Loyal Cooperation, 21 *EC Tax Rev.* 4 (2012), p. 180 (at p. 180); L. De Broe/T. Gernay, Belgium: The Imfeld & Garcet Case and the Levy Case, in M. Lang/P. Pistone/J. Schuch/C. Staringer/A. Storck (eds.), ECJ Recent Developments in Direct Taxation 2012 (Linde, 2013), p. 9 (at p. 18); T. Kühbacher, Die Rs Damseaux: Ist juristische Doppelbesteuerung im Gemeinschaftsrecht nun endgültig erlaubt?, 22 *ÖStZ* 20 (2009), p. 496 (at pp. 496-497); G. Kofler in A. Rust (ed.), *Double Taxation Within the European Union* (Kluwer, 2011), at p. 121; M. Tippelhofer, EG-Vertrag verbietet für 2005 nicht Treaty override, 22 *IStR* 8 (2013), p. 307 (at p. 310).

1426. Judgment in *Damseaux*, C-128/08, EU:C:2009:471.

1427. L. De Broe, 21 *EC Tax Rev.* 4 (2012), at p. 181.

1428. Reference for a preliminary ruling from the Tribunal de première instance de Bruxelles (Belgium), lodged on 24 Oct. 2011 – Daniel Levy and Carine Sebbag v État Belge, SPF Finances, C-540/11, 2012/C 25/53, *OJ* C 25 (28 January 2013), p. 30 (at p. 31).

second indent EC Treaty can be relied upon in order to demonstrate that the Belgium legislation infringes the fundamental freedoms.[1429]

The basic conclusion of the ECJ's analysis is that juridical double taxation "*does not alone constitute a restriction prohibited by the Treaty.*"[1430] Although "*the abolition of [the effects of double taxation] is doubtless desirable,*"[1431] the Court considers itself incapable of blaming a particular – or even both – Member State(s) for the adverse consequences resulting from "*the exercise in parallel by two Member States of their fiscal sovereignty.*"[1432] This can be inferred from the ECJ regularly pointing out that EU law "*does not lay down any general criteria for the attribution of areas of competence between the Member States in relation to the elimination of double taxation within the Community.*"[1433] Even if this self-restriction of the Court is taken for granted,[1434] it remains unclear whether the situation is different if someone else is legally entitled to and takes the responsibility for identifying the Member State which can be held liable for the juridical double taxation. In *Columbus Container Services*, for example, the ECJ would have had a chance to clarify whether the fundamental freedoms prohibit a Member State from unilaterally deviating from what has been agreed upon in a double tax convention. However, the Court did not go into detail on this issue, but merely pointed out that it "*may not examine the relationship between a national measure [...] and the provisions of a double taxation convention [...] since that question does not fall within the scope of Community law.*"[1435]

In preliminary ruling procedures, the ECJ refuses with good cause to interpret domestic provisions or the rules of double taxation conventions.[1436] According to

1429. Order in *Levy and Sebbag*, C-540/11, EU:C:2012:581; see K. Daxkobler/E. Huisman, 53 *Eur. Taxn.* 8 [2013], at p. 405; L. De Broe/T. Gernay in M. Lang/P. Pistone/J. Schuch/C. Staringer/A. Storck [eds.], *ECJ Recent Developments in Direct Taxation 2012* [Linde, 2013], at pp. 18-19; M. Tippelhofer, 22 *IStR* 8 (2013), at pp. 311-312.
1430. Judgment in *CIBA*, C-96/08, EU:C:2010:185, at para. 29.
1431. Judgment in *Statens Kontrol*, 142/77, EU:C:1978:144, at para. 34; also see Judgment in *Nygård*, C-234/99, EU:C:2002:244, at para. 38.
1432. Judgment in *Kerckhaert and Morres*, C-513/04, EU:C:2006:603, at para. 20; Judgment in *Columbus Container Services*, C-298/05, EU:C:2007:754, at para. 43; Judgment in *CIBA*, C-96/08, EU:C:2010:185, at para. 25; Judgment in *Commission/Spain*, C-487/08, EU:C:2010:310, at para. 27.
1433. Judgment in *Kerckhaert and Morres*, C-513/04, EU:C:2006:603, at paras 20-23; Judgment in *CIBA*, C-96/08, EU:C:2010:185 at paras 25-27; see also Judgment in *Block*, C-67/08, EU:C:2009:92, at paras 28-30; Judgment in *Damseaux*, C-128/08, EU:C:2009:471, at paras 30 and 33.
1434. In the literature, it has been heavily criticized that the ECJ has applied a different approach with regard to its case law on social security law. See K. Daxkobler, *Die grundfreiheitliche Rechtsprechung des EuGH* (Linde, 2015), at pp. 136; 551-564; also cf. G. Kofler, *Doppelbesteuerungsabkommen und Europäisches Gemeinschaftsrecht* (Linde, 2007), at pp. 206-220.
1435. Judgment in *Columbus Container Services*, C-298/05, EU:C:2007:754, at para. 47; critically in this respect P. Farmer, Columbus Container Services BVBA & Co v Finanzamt Bielefeld-Innenstadt: the ECJ fails to grasp the tax competition nettle in relation to foreign income rules, 53 *British Tax Rev.* 2 (2008), p. 105 (at p. 107); also see Judgment in *Damseaux*, C-128/08, EU:C:2009:471, at para. 22.
1436. See M. Lang, 17 *EC Tax Rev.* 2 (2008), at p. 69; M. Lang, Die Zukunft der Doppelbesteuerungsabkommen im Lichte von Columbus Container, in P. Kirchhof/H. Nieskens (eds.), *Festschrift für Wolfram Reiss zum 65. Geburtstag* (Dr Otto Schmidt, 2008), p. 679 (at p. 681).

Article 267 TFEU, the Court has *"jurisdiction to give preliminary rulings concerning [...] the interpretation of the Treaties."* The interpretation of national rules, on the other hand, *"is a matter for the national courts and not the Court of Justice."*[1437] However, in *Columbus Container Services*, the referring court did not ask *whether*, but rather informed the ECJ *that* the domestic provisions are *"contrary to the [Bilateral Tax] Convention."*[1438] In essence, the Court was thus asked whether a Member State may unilaterally deviate from the provisions of a double taxation convention.[1439] This question requires the ECJ neither to interpret national law nor to examine the relationship between a national measure and the provisions of a double tax treaty, but exclusively concerns *"the interpretation of the Treaties."*[1440] Without having guidance from the Court about how to interpret EU law, it is not possible for a national court *"to draw, in compliance with its national law, the conclusions arising from the absence of implementation of"* a provision of a bilateral double taxation convention obliging the respective Member State to prevent juridical double taxation.[1441]

However, it has to be kept in mind that the ECJ cannot be called in merely because a Member State has allegedly violated public international law.[1442] Such a claim could not be based on Articles 258-260 TFEU either, because this would require arguing that the *"Member State has failed to fulfil an obligation under the Treaties"* and an obligation under public international law does not equal an obligation under the Treaties. Nor could Article 267 TFEU be relied upon, because the Court thus only has *"jurisdiction to give preliminary rulings concerning [...] the interpretation of the Treaties [or] the validity and interpretation of acts of the institutions, bodies, offices or agencies of the Union."* If the Member States want the Court to also adjudicate upon questions that do not concern *"an obligation under the Treaties"* or *"the interpretation of the Treaties,"* they have to rely on Article 273 TFEU.[1443] However, this provision not only requires that the *"dispute between Member States [...] relates to the subject matter of the Treaties,"* but also that it is submitted to the ECJ *"under a special agreement between the parties."* Unless such a special agreement provides for a legal basis to call in the ECJ, unilateral measures that deviate from the provisions of the double taxation convention cannot per se be challenged by means of a preliminary ruling or an

1437. Judgment in *Wilson*, C-506/04, EU:C:2006:587, at para. 34; also see Judgment in *Vanacker and Lesage*, C-37/92, EU:C:1993:836, at para. 7; Judgment in *X*, C-60/02, EU:C:2004:10, at para. 58; Judgment in *Badischer Winzerkeller*, C-264/04, EU:C:2006:402, at para. 43; Judgment in *Krzysztof Peśla*, C-345/08, EU:C:2009:771, at paras 64-65; Judgment in *Winner Wetten*, C-409/06, EU:C:2010:503, at para. 35.

1438. Judgment in *Columbus Container Services*, C-298/05, EU:C:2007:754, at para. 25.

1439. Cf. Opinion of AG Mengozzi in *Columbus Container Services*, C-298/05, EU:C:2007:197, at point 38: *"it is not the difference between the Federal Republic of Germany and the Kingdom of Belgium in respect of the legal and fiscal classification of Columbus which the referring court regards as involving a possible restriction on the freedoms of movement under the Treaty, but merely the replacement of the exemption method by the set-off method as regards taxation of the income and capital of a permanent establishment located abroad."*

1440. See J. Calderón/A. Baez, 37 *Intertax* 4 (2009), at pp. 218-219; K. Daxkobler, *Die grundfreiheitliche Rechtsprechung des EuGH* (Linde, 2015), at p. 186.

1441. Judgment in *Damseaux*, C-128/08, EU:C:2009:471, at para. 21.

1442. See U. Karpenstein in E. Grabitz/M. Hilf/M. Nettesheim (eds.), *Das Recht der Europäischen Union*[57] (C.H. Beck, 2015), Art. 279 AEUV at para. 12.

1443. See Chapter 4.1.3.1.1.

infringement procedure. It is hence convincing that the Court concluded in *Columbus Container Services* that it "*may not examine the relationship between a national measure [...] and the provisions of a double taxation convention [...] since that question does not fall within the scope of Community law.*"[1444]

However, a unilateral measure that deviates from the provisions of a double taxation convention not only raises the question whether public international law (and perhaps also domestic constitutional law)[1445] was violated. If such a treaty override in addition leads to juridical double taxation, it also becomes relevant from an EU law perspective. After all, "*the fact that a taxable event might be taxed twice is the most serious obstacle there can be to people and their capital crossing [...] borders.*"[1446] The ECJ may hence be asked whether the fundamental freedoms have to be interpreted as prohibiting a Member State from causing juridical double taxation by unilaterally deviating from the provisions of a double taxation convention, which would otherwise avoid the adverse consequences resulting from the exercise in parallel by two Member States of their fiscal sovereignty. It could be argued that such a Member State "*has failed to fulfil an obligation under the Treaties,*" which would allow the European Commission as well as other Member States to initiate a procedure according to Articles 258-259 TFEU. After all, Article 4(3) TEU, *inter alia*, obliges the Member States to "*take any appropriate measure, general or particular, to ensure fulfilment of the obligations arising out of the Treaties or resulting from the acts of the institutions of the Union*" and to "*facilitate the achievement of the Union's tasks and refrain from any measure which could jeopardise the attainment of the Union's objectives.*" According to the ECJ, the actual significance of this provision "*depends, in each particular case, on the provisions of the Treaties or on the rules laid down within its general framework.*"[1447] Indeed, the ECJ's jurisprudence indicates that EU law does not oblige the Member States to avoid juridical double taxation.[1448] Still, the elimination of double taxation is among the objectives of the EU.[1449] It may, therefore, be argued that by unilaterally deviating from the provisions of a double taxation convention the respective Member State has taken a "*measure which could jeopardise the attainment of the Union's objectives*" and has hence failed to fulfil its obligations resulting from Article 4(3) TEU.

1444. Judgment in *Columbus Container Services*, C-298/05, EU:C:2007:754, at para. 47; also see Judgment in *Damseaux*, C-128/08, EU:C:2009:471, at para. 22.

1445. See, for example, the decision of the German Constitutional Court from 15. Dec. 2015, 2 BvL 1/12; for an analysis of this decision see A. Cloer/T. Hagemann, Constitutionality of Treaty Override, 56 *Eur. Taxn.* 7 (2016), forthcoming; G. Kofler/A. Rust, Deutsches BVerfG zur Verfassungskonformität von -"Treaty Overrides," 26 *SWI* 3 (2016), p. 144 (at pp. 144-150); M. Lehner, Treaty Override ist nicht verfassungswidrig, 25 *IStR* 6 (2016), p. 217 (at pp. 217-220); W. Mitschke, Treaty Override verfassungsgemäß, 54 *DStR* 7 (2016), p. 359 (at pp. 376-377).

1446. Opinion of AG Colomer in *D.*, C-376/03, EU:C:2004:663, at point 85.

1447. Judgment in *Geddo / Ente Nazionale Risi*, 2/73, EU:C:1973:89, at point 4; also see Order in *Levy and Sebbag*, C-540/11, EU:C:2012:581, at para. 26.

1448. Judgment in *Statens Kontrol*, 142/77, EU:C:1978:144, at paras 33-36.

1449. Judgment in *Gilly*, C-336/96, EU:C:1998:221, at para. 16; Judgment in *Bouanich*, C-265/04, EU:C:2006:51, at para. 49; Judgment in *Damseaux*, C-128/08, EU:C:2009:471, at para. 28.

However, this was the case neither in *Columbus Container Services* nor in *Levy and Sebbag*.[1450] In *Columbus Container Services*, the German treaty override did not lead to double taxation, but "only" provided - under certain conditions - for the application of the credit method, among other ones, with regard to income attributable to a foreign permanent establishment, even if an applicable double taxation convention required Germany to apply the exemption method.[1451] Hence, compared to a purely domestic situation, the cross-border situation was not treated less favourably.[1452] The overall tax burden for cross-border profit distributions rather corresponded to the tax burden a comparable profit distribution within Germany would have triggered:

		German Permanent Establishment	*Belgian Permanent Establishment*	
			Exemption Method	*Credit Method*
	Belgian Tax Base	-	100.00	100.00
	Belgian Tax (10%)	-	10.00	10.00
	German Tax Base	100.00	0.00	100.00
-	German Tax (25%)	(25.00)	0.00	(25.00)
+	Credit for Belgian Tax	-	-	10.00
=	German Tax Burden	25.00	0.00	15.00
=	Total Tax Burden	25.00	10.00	25.00

By contrast, in *Levy and Sebbag*, the taxpayer concerned was actually subject to juridical double taxation. The dividends received from a company established in

1450. But see Y. Brauner/G. Kofler in R. Vann (ed.), *Global Tax Treaty Commentaries* (IBFD, 2016), at Chapter 2.3.1.1; G. Kofler/A. Rust, 26 *SWI* 3 (2016), at pp. 144-145.

1451. See, for example, A. Rainer/O. Thömmes, Are German CFC rules compatible with EU freedoms?, 33 *Intertax* 11 (2005), p. 554 (at p. 554); A. Schnitger, German CFC Legislation Pending Before the European Court of Justice - Abuse of the Law and Revival of the Most-Favoured-Nation-Clause?, 15 *EC Tax Rev.* 3 (2006), p. 151 (at p. 156).

1452. See G. Kofler, *Doppelbesteuerungsabkommen und Europäisches Gemeinschaftsrecht* (Linde, 2007), at pp. 610-612; Opinion of AG Mengozzi in *Columbus Container Services*, C-298/05, EU:C:2007:197, at points 77-98; also see A. Cordewener, German "Anti-avoidance" Measures versus Belgian Coordination Centres: A Long Struggle Without Survivors, in L. Hinnekens/P. Hinnekens (eds.), *A Vision of Taxes Within and Outside European Borders, Festschrift in Honor of Prof. Dr. Frans Vanistendael* (Kluwer, 2008), p. 203 (at pp. 229-230); A. Körner, Europarecht und CFC-Regelungen - Anrufung des EuGH im Verfahren "Cadbury Schweppes," 13 *IStR* 20 (2004), p. 697 (at p. 704); A. Schnitger, 15 *EC Tax Rev.* 3 (2006), at p. 157; J. Lüdicke, Pending Cases Filed by German Courts I: The Meilicke, CLT-UFA, Keller Holding, Lasertac, Rewe Zentralfinanz, Ritter-Colais, Kolumbus Container Services, and Stauffer Cases, in M. Lang/J. Schuch/C. Staringer (eds.), *ECJ Recent Developments in Direct Taxation* (Linde, 2006), p. 113 (at p. 167); A. Musil, *Deutsches Treaty Overriding und seine Vereinbarkeit mit Europäischem Gemeinschaftsrecht* (Duncker & Humblot, 2000), at pp. 117 and 122; T. Scheipers/A. Maywald, Zur Vereinbarkeit des § ASTG § 20 Abs. ASTG § 20 Absatz 2 AStG mit EG-Recht unter Berücksichtigung der Ausführungen des Generalanwalts Léger in der Rs. Cadbury Schweppes, 15 *IStR* 14 (2006), p. 472 (at p. 474).

France were not only subject to a (treaty-reduced) 15% withholding tax in France but taxes also had to be paid at a rate of 25% in Belgium on the residual amount of the distributed dividends.[1453] However, although Belgium and France had concluded a double taxation convention that was applicable in this case, double taxation was not caused by either Belgium or France unilaterally deviating from this public international law treaty. Rather, the tax credit provided for in Article 19(A)(1) of the relevant double taxation convention was only available "*under the conditions laid down in Belgian law.*" When the treaty was concluded, Belgian domestic law had provided for a foreign tax credit. However, the relevant provisions were limited in 1988. Since the double taxation convention referred to Belgian domestic law, Belgian courts concluded that a foreign tax credit is no longer available under domestic or under double tax convention law.[1454] If the avoidance of juridical double taxation within a double taxation convention is contingent on domestic law, it is up to the particular contracting state to decide whether double taxation should be avoided or not. Both would be in line with the provisions of such a double taxation convention. Therefore, in *Levy and Sebbag*, it was not possible to argue that Belgium has failed to fulfil its obligation resulting from Article 10 EC Treaty, because it did not unilaterally deviate from the provisions of the double taxation convention concluded with France.[1455]

Therefore, it still remains to be seen whether the ECJ's conclusions will be different if a unilateral treaty override really undoes the intended purpose of a double taxation convention, i.e., it results in juridical double taxation.[1456] However, while the Court did not - have to - explicitly enlarge upon this issue, AG Mengozzi emphasized that "*a (possible) conflict between rules of domestic law and rules of international law [...] in my view has nothing to do with Community law. [...] [I]t does not fall to the Court to resolve such a conflict of rules.*"[1457] It may indeed be questioned why a Member State should be prevented from unilaterally limiting the effects of a double taxation convention if it is allowed to reach a similar - but more ultimate - result by terminating the treaty altogether.[1458] Moreover, why should the avoidance of juridical double

1453. On the facts of the case see K. Daxkobler/E. Huisman, 53 *Eur. Taxn.* 8 (2013), at p. 401; L. De Broe, 21 *EC Tax Rev.* 4 (2012), at p. 180; L. De Broe/T. Gernay in M. Lang/P. Pistone/J. Schuch/C. Staringer/A. Storck (eds.), ECJ Recent Developments in Direct Taxation 2012 (Linde, 2013), at p. 17.

1454. See G. Kofler, *Doppelbesteuerungsabkommen und Europäisches Gemeinschaftsrecht* (Linde, 2007), at p. 169; M. Quaghebeur, 37 *Tax Notes Intl.* 9 (28 Feb. 2005), at p. 741; M. Quaghebeur, 52 *British Tax Rev.* 2 (2007), at p. 129; P. Smet/H. Laloo, 45 *Eur. Taxn.* 4 (2005), at p. 159; but see G. Kofler/A. Rust, 26 *SWI* 3 (2016), at pp. 144-145, who apparently do not share the interpretation of the Belgian courts.

1455. See K. Daxkobler, *Die grundfreiheitliche Rechtsprechung des EuGH* (Linde, 2015), at pp. 187-188.

1456. See A. Rust in A. Rust (ed.), *Double Taxation Within the European Union* (Kluwer, 2011), at pp. 150-151: "*That does not mean that treaty override is generally prohibited by EU law. Only if a treaty override leads to double taxation the treaty rules have to be respected as the treaty rules contain an attribution decision*"; E. Reimer, The Abolition of Article 293 EC: Comments on Hofmann's Analysis, in A. Rust (ed.), *Double Taxation Within the European Union* (Kluwer, 2011), p. 87 (at pp. 94-95); also cf. U. Forsthoff, Treaty Override und Europarecht, 15 *IStR* 15 (2006), p. 509 (at pp. 511-512).

1457. Opinion of AG Mengozzi in *Columbus Container Services*, C-298/05, EU:C:2007:197, at point 75.

1458. See P. Wattel in A. Rust (ed.), *Double Taxation Within the European Union* (Kluwer, 2011), at p. 164.

taxation by means of a double taxation convention be protected against unilateral annulment, but national measures that also avoid juridical double taxation may be limited or abolished without infringing the fundamental freedoms? In *Kerckhaert and Morres*,[1459] *Damseaux*[1460] and *Levy and Sebbag*,[1461] the latter has been considered to be permissible by the ECJ. Some authors argue that the provisions of the Member States' double taxation conventions are – in contrast to provisions of domestic law – "implementation rules" of primary EU law.[1462] At first glance, this would seem to be possible to infer from Article 293 second indent EC Treaty.[1463] After all, the ECJ held that conventions which are concluded "*on the basis of that article and within the framework defined by it [...] and also the national provisions to which the Convention refers are linked to the EEC Treaty.*"[1464] However, it is doubtful that the Member States' bilateral double taxation conventions are concluded on the basis of and within the framework defined by Article 293 second indent EC Treaty. On the one hand, the Member States' competence to conclude such conventions results from their sovereignty under public international law and does not depend upon the existence of Article 293 second indent EC Treaty.[1465] Otherwise, the abolition of this provision through the Treaty of Lisbon would have deprived the Member States of the possibility to bilaterally conclude double taxation conventions. On the other hand, Article 293 second indent EC Treaty merely stated that the "*Member States shall, so far as necessary enter into negotiations with each other with a view to securing for the benefit of their nationals [...] the abolition of double taxation within the Community.*" In view of this wording, it is unclear whether this provision referred to: (1) bilateral conventions only,[1466]

1459. Judgment in *Kerckhaert and Morres*, C-513/04, EU:C:2006:603.
1460. Judgment in *Damseaux*, C-128/08, EU:C:2009:471.
1461. Order in *Levy and Sebbag*, C-540/11, EU:C:2012:581.
1462. See G. Kofler, *Doppelbesteuerungsabkommen und Europäisches Gemeinschaftsrecht* (Linde, 2007), at pp. 257 and 493; also cf. P. Pistone, *The Impact of Community Law on Tax Treaties* (Kluwer, 2002), at pp. 77-78 ("*tax co-ordination treaties [...] can be viewed as conveyors of Community law interests and should be granted a specific position in that legal order, aside strict Community law*"); critically M. Lang in M. Lehner (ed.), *Reden zum Andenken an Klaus Vogel* (C.H. Beck, 2010), at pp. 73-74; M. Lang in J. Lüdicke/J.M. Mössner/L. Hummel (eds.), *Das Steuerrecht der Unternehmen – Festschrift für Gerrit Frotscher zum 70. Geburtstag* (Haufe-Lexware, 2013), at p. 367.
1463. See L. Hinnekens, Compatibility of Bilateral Tax Treaties with European Community Law. The Rules, 3 *EC Tax Rev.* 4 (1994), p. 146 (at p. 161); also cf. M. Lang in M. Lehner (ed.), *Reden zum Andenken an Klaus Vogel* (C.H. Beck, 2010), at pp. 73-74; M. Lang in J. Lüdicke/J.M. Mössner/L. Hummel (eds.), *Das Steuerrecht der Unternehmen – Festschrift für Gerrit Frotscher zum 70. Geburtstag* (Haufe-Lexware, 2013), at p. 367, who refers to the Hans Kelsen's reference to the "Midas touch," according to which, "*[j]ust as everything King Midas touched turned into gold, everything to which law refers becomes law*" (see H. Kelsen, *Pure Theory of Law* [University of California Press, 1967], at p. 161).
1464. Judgment in *Mund & Fester / Hatrex Internationaal Transport*, C-398/92, EU:C:1994:52, at para. 12.
1465. See M. Lang in M. Lehner (ed.), *Reden zum Andenken an Klaus Vogel* (C.H. Beck, 2010), at p. 73; M. Lang in J. Lüdicke/J.M. Mössner/L. Hummel (eds.), *Das Steuerrecht der Unternehmen – Festschrift für Gerrit Frotscher zum 70. Geburtstag* (Haufe-Lexware, 2013), at p. 368; G. Kofler, *Doppelbesteuerungsabkommen und Europäisches Gemeinschaftsrecht* (Linde, 2007), at p. 367.
1466. See J.F. Avery Jones, 7 *EC Tax Rev.* 2 (1998), p. 96; A. Cordewener/E. Reimer, 46 *Eur. Taxn.* 7 (2006), at p. 300, FN 160; M. Lehner, *Möglichkeiten zur Verbesserung des*

(2) multilateral conventions only[1467] or (3) both.[1468] Since the ECJ has repeatedly pointed out that "*apart from the Convention of 23 July 1990 on the elimination of double taxation in connection with the adjustment of profits of associated enterprises (OJ 1990 L 225, p. 10), no unifying or harmonising measure for the elimination of double taxation has yet been adopted at Community level, nor have the Member States yet concluded any multilateral convention to that effect under Article 220 of the Treaty,*"[1469] it seems that the Court does not consider bilateral conventions to be concluded on the basis of and within the framework defined by Article 293 second indent EC Treaty. However, even if Article 293 second indent EC Treaty was (also) implicitly referring to bilateral double taxation conventions, due to its abolition through the Treaty of Lisbon, it would no longer be possible to rely on this provision in order to argue that the Member States' double tax conventions are "*linked to*" EU law.

Still, there is a difference between a tax treaty override and limiting or abolishing unilateral measures aimed at the avoidance of juridical double taxation, which could be relevant for the ECJ's legal analysis. In the former case, the Member State which unilaterally deviates from the provisions of the double taxation convention violates a public international law contract,[1470] whereas in the latter case there is no EU

Verständigungsverfahrens auf der Grundlage des EWG-Vertrags (C.H. Beck, 1982), at p. 142; N. Dautzenberg, 47 *DB* 31 (1994), at p. 1543; H. Doyle, 35 *Eur. Taxn.* 1 (1995), at p. 16; H. Schaumburg, 47 *RIW* 3 (2001), at p. 169; J. Schuch, 7 *EC Tax Rev.* 1 (1998), at p. 36); F. Vanistendael, 31 *Common Market L. Rev.* 2 (1994), at p. 295; P.J. Wattel, 12 *EC Tax Rev.* 4 (2003), at p. 199; P.J. Wattel, 31 *Legal Issues of Economic Integration* 2 (2004), at p. 87.

1467. See A. de Graaf, 7 *EC Tax Rev.* 4 (1998), at p. 270; J. Englisch in A. Cordewener/S. Enchelmaier/C.P. Schindler (eds.), *Meistbegünstigung im Steuerrecht der EU-Staaten* (C.H. Beck, 2006), at p. 175, FN 83; L. Hinnekens, 7 *EC Tax Rev.* 4 (1998), at p. 250; H. Krabbe, 28 *RIW* 4 (1982), at p. 270; U. Eyles, *Das Niederlassungsrecht der Kapitalgesellschaften in der Europäischen Gemeinschaft* (Nomos, 1990), at pp. 264-265; A. Musil, *Deutsches Treaty Overriding und seine Vereinbarkeit mit Europäischem Gemeinschaftsrecht* (Duncker & Humblot, 2000), at pp. 101-103; P. Pistone, *The Impact of Community Law on Tax Treaties* (Kluwer, 2002), at pp. 71-72; T.B. Scherer in D. Birk (ed.), *Handbuch des Europäischen Steuer- und Abgabenrechts* (NWB, 1995), at § 31 para. 102; T.B Scherer, *Doppelbesteuerung und Europäisches Gemeinschaftsrecht* (C.H. Beck, 1995), at pp. 79-87; S. van Thiel, *Free Movement of Persons and Income Tax Law: The European Court in Search of Principles* (IBFD, 2002), at pp. 130-131; C. Vedder in M. Lehner/O. Thömmes/C. Vedder/A. Wiedow, *Europarecht und Internationales Steuerrecht* (C.H. Beck, 1994), at p. 9; D. Weber, 33 *Intertax* 10 (2005), at p. 436.

1468. See W. Schön, 4 *IStR* 3 (1995), at p. 119; I.E. Schwartz/W. Mölls in H. von der Groeben/J. Schwarze (eds.), *Kommentar zum Vertrag über die Europäische Union und zur Gründung der Europäischen Gemeinschaft*[6] (Nomos, 2004), at Artikel 293 EG para. 85.

1469. Judgment in *Gilly*, C-336/96, EU:C:1998:221, at para. 23; also see Judgment in *N.*, C-470/04, EU:C:2006:525, at para. 43; Judgment in *Test Claimants in Class IV of the ACT Group Litigation*, C-374/04, EU:C:2006:773, at para. 51; Judgment in *D.*, C-376/03, EU:C:2005:424, at para. 50; Judgment in *Damseaux*, C-128/08, EU:C:2009:471, at para. 28.

1470. This is also the difference between unilaterally deviating from and terminating a double taxation convention (see P. Wattel in A. Rust (ed.), *Double Taxation Within the European Union* (Kluwer, 2011), at p. 164, who emphasizes that the termination of a double taxation convention leads to the same result as unilaterally deviating from the treaty and hence concludes that neither can be considered to infringe the fundamental freedoms). While public international law fully respects a contracting state's right to withdraw from a bilateral contract, unilaterally deviating from such a contract contravenes the principle of *pacta sunt servanda*. See M. Lehner, Grundlagen des Abkommensrechts, in K. Vogel/M. Lehner (eds.), *DBA*[6] (C.H. Beck, 2015), p. 111 (at p. 251 [para. 198]); T. Stein, Völkerrecht und nationales

law[1471] or public international law[1472] obligation to uphold unilateral measures aimed at the avoidance of juridical double taxation.[1473] However, the fact that a Member State can be blamed for having violated a public international law contract need not necessarily mean that the respective Member State can also be held liable from an EU law perspective for the resulting juridical double taxation. This would require that it is legally relevant for EU law purposes that public international law has been violated. It could be argued in this respect that, according to Article 19 TEU, the Court "*shall ensure that in the interpretation and application of the Treaties the law is observed.*" Since the wording of this provision is not restricted to EU law, but rather refers to "*the law*" in general, one could claim that the ECJ must also ensure that public international law is observed, at least within the ambit of the Treaties. Such an understanding would be supported by Article 4(3) TEU, according to which, "*[p]ursuant to the principle of sincere cooperation, the Union and the Member States shall, in full mutual respect, assist each other in carrying out tasks which flow from the Treaties.*" Notwithstanding the ambiguous wording, the ECJ interprets this provision as also obliging the Member States "*to cooperate in good faith*" with one another.[1474] This does not mean that Member States are generally prohibited from unilaterally deviating from public international law contracts concluded with another Member State. Concluding such contracts is not per se a task "*which flow[s] from the Treaties.*" But Article 293 second indent EC Treaty indicates that the avoidance of juridical double taxation was at least among these tasks. However, since EU law does not oblige the Member States to address themselves to this task, the obligations of Article 4(3) TEU are only triggered if Member States voluntarily decide to avoid juridical double taxation by means of a double taxation convention. Thus, Article 4(3) TEU transforms the EU law's non-binding objective of eliminating double taxation[1475] into a legal obligation not to frustrate a legal commitment two or more Member State have voluntarily and in concert entered into.[1476] If the elimination of double taxation is still – i.e., despite Article 293 EC Treaty's abolition through the Treaty of Lisbon – among the objectives

Steuerrecht im Widerstreit?, 15 *IStR* 15 (2006), p. 505 (at p. 508); K. Vogel/A. Rust in E. Reimer/A. Rust (eds.), *Klaus Vogel on Double Taxation Conventions, Fourth Edition* (Kluwer, 2015), Introduction at MN 158.

1471. Judgment in *Kerckhaert and Morres*, C-513/04, EU:C:2006:603; Judgment in *Damseaux*, C-128/08, EU:C:2009:471; Order in *Levy and Sebbag*, C-540/11, EU:C:2012:581.

1472. See K. Vogel, *Der räumliche Anwendungsbereich der Verwaltungsrechtsnorm* (Alfred Metzner Verlag, 1965), at pp. 351-352; K. Vogel, 59 *StuW* 2 (1982), at p. 112; K. Vogel/A. Rust in E. Reimer/A. Rust (eds.), *Klaus Vogel on Double Taxation Conventions, Fourth Edition* (Kluwer, 2015), Introduction at MN 9.

1473. Cf. G. Kofler, *Doppelbesteuerungsabkommen und Europäisches Gemeinschaftsrecht* (Linde, 2007), at pp. 172-173.

1474. Judgment in *Athanasopoulos and others / Bundesanstalt für Arbeit*, C-251/89, EU:C:1991:242, at para. 57; also cf. Judgment in *Commission/France*, 42/82, EU:C:1983:88, at para. 36; Judgment in *Matteucci / Communauté française de Belgique*, 235/87, EU:C:1988:460, at para. 19.

1475. Judgment in *Gilly*, C-336/96, EU:C:1998:221, at para. 16; Judgment in *Bouanich*, C-265/04, EU:C:2006:51, at para. 49; Judgment in *Damseaux*, C-128/08, EU:C:2009:471, at para. 28.

1476. See J. Englisch, 33 *Intertax* 8/9 (2005), at p. 324.

of the EU,[1477] it is hence arguable that two Member States which voluntarily decided to conclude a double taxation convention are obliged, "*[p]ursuant to the principle of sincere cooperation,*" to "*assist each other in carrying out*" the task of avoiding juridical double taxation "*in full mutual respect.*" According to such an understanding, it would still be possible to terminate an existing double taxation convention. Since this is not a violation of public international law, the principle of sincere cooperation would not be violated, either. However, if the provisions of a double taxation convention are unilaterally deviated from, the particular Member State has failed to obey Article 4(3) TFEU. This does not per se entail an infringement of EU law.[1478,1479] After all, the actual

1477. Judgment in *Gilly*, C-336/96, EU:C:1998:221, at para. 16; Judgment in *Bouanich*, C-265/04, EU:C:2006:51, at para. 49; Judgment in *Damseaux*, C-128/08, EU:C:2009:471, at para. 28.

1478. But see T. Scheipers/A. Maywald, 15 *IStR* 14 (2006), at pp. 473-474; T. Scherer, 25 *IStR* 18 (2016), at pp. 744-745; J. Schönfeld, *Hinzurechnungsbesteuerung und Europäisches Gemeinschaftsrecht* (Dr Otto Schmidt, 2005), at p. 528; R. Seer, 6 *IStR* 17 (1997), at p. 522; R. Seer in B. Brzezinski/J. Gluchowski/C. Kosikowski/R. Mastalski (eds.), *Księga pamiątkowa ku czci Profesora Apoloniusza Kosteckiego* (Torun, 1998), at p. 214, who apparently consider every unilateral deviation from a double taxation convention to constitute an infringement of EU law.

1479. The ECJ's judgment in *Merida* might be interpreted differently, though. According to former German law, employees were granted an "interim assistance" in the event of dismissal in addition to their unemployment benefit. In a purely domestic case, the total benefit corresponded to the net salary which would have been payable to the employee in the absence of dismissal. To this end, not only social security contributions, but also the amount of taxes payable under German tax law is deducted by means of a notional calculation in order to determine the interim assistance, which – in the first year following cessation of the employment relationship – amounts to 100% of the difference between the net salary which would have been payable to the former employee as an active worker and the amount of the unemployment benefit. With regard to foreign residents, the same calculation applies. However, the notional taking into account of the German wage tax has an unfavourable effect on the cross-border situation, if the interim assistance is taxed in the foreign individual's residence state. Since Germany notionally deducts the German tax on wages, even if it were obliged to grant an exemption from taxation due to the double taxation convention with the foreign individual's residence state, the interim assistance "*is being subjected to unlawful double taxation*" (Judgment in *Merida*, C-400/02, EU:C:2004:537, at para. 11). According to the ECJ, the notional deduction of German wage tax "*puts at a disadvantage persons who [...] reside and are liable to tax in a Member State other than the Federal Republic of Germany as opposed to workers resident and liable to tax in the latter State*" (Judgment in *Merida*, C-400/02, EU:C:2004:537, at para. 24). In a purely domestic situation "*the interim assistance amounts to 100% of the difference between the basis of assessment and the amount of the unemployment benefit*" and hence "*the income of former workers residing in Germany is equivalent to that which would be paid to them as active workers*" (Judgment in *Merida*, C-400/02, EU:C:2004:537, at paras 26-27). In the cross-border situation, on the other hand, "*the notional deduction of German wage tax in determining the basis of assessment of the interim assistance does not enable the same result to be achieved*" (Judgment in *Merida*, C-400/02, EU:C:2004:537, at para. 28). This disadvantage would even persist if Germany reimbursed the tax that had to be paid in the frontier worker's residence state, because the interim assistance would still "*be of a lower amount than that corresponding to the difference between the remuneration paid during the course of active life and the unemployment benefit received by the person concerned. [...] Thus, in the case of frontier workers in Mr Merida's situation the notional application of the German wage tax prevents the payment of the interim assistance from offsetting, during the course of the first year following cessation of the employment relationship, loss of wages consequent thereon, contrary to the position in the case of workers residing in Germany*" (Judgment in *Merida*, C-400/02, EU:C:2004:537, at paras 33 and 35). In essence, the ECJ concluded that the German calculation of the interim assistance would even be unlawful if it was not subject to double taxation. The problem was thus not

significance of Article 4(3) TFEU "*depends, in each particular case, on the provisions of the Treaties or on the rules laid down within its general framework.*"[1480] Therefore, a Member State that unilaterally deviates from a double taxation convention may only be held liable under EU law if this deviation leads to a result (e.g., juridical double taxation) which is contrary to the Treaties objective of eliminating double taxation.[1481]

1.3.1.3 The Fundamental Freedom's Impact on Double Taxation Conventions

Although double taxation conventions are primarily intended to grant relief from juridical double taxation and should, therefore, not be (unilaterally) deviated from, they may as well contain rules that have a discriminatory effect. Therefore, the question arises whether rules contained in a double taxation convention may infringe the fundamental freedoms, notwithstanding that they are intended to avoid double taxation, and therefore foster the internal market's objective of free movement. It should thereby be kept in mind that double taxation conventions are the consequence

---

that the same income was (indirectly) subjected to taxation in two different Member State. This was avoided by Germany granting a reimbursement for the taxes paid in the other Member State (Opinion of AG Stix-Hackl in *Merida*, C-400/02, EU:C:2004:80, at point 15; also see K. Daxkobler, *Die grundfreiheitliche Rechtsprechung des EuGH* [Linde, 2015], at p. 186). Rather, the disadvantage resulted from the different tax rates applicable in the Member States concerned (cf. Opinion of AG Stix-Hackl in *Merida*, C-400/02, EU:C:2004:80, at points 24-25). If the frontier worker's residence state has a lower tax rate than Germany, the "*application of the notional deduction of German wage tax to frontier workers [...] in fact results in those workers losing a part of the net income which they received when they were working with the forces stationed in Germany, that part corresponding to the difference between the amount of income tax paid in France and the higher amount of German wage tax notionally deducted on calculation of the interim assistance*" (Judgment in *Merida*, C-400/02, EU:C:2004:537, at para. 34). Such a conclusion conflicts with the ECJ regularly pointing out that the "*Treaty offers no guarantee to a citizen of the Union that transferring his residence to a Member State other than that in which he previously resided will be neutral as regards taxation. Given the disparities in the tax legislation of the Member States, such a transfer may be to the citizen's advantage or not, according to circumstances*" (Judgment in *Block*, C-67/08, EU:C:2009:92, at para. 35; see also Judgment in *Hervein*, C-393/99 and C-394/99, EU:C:2002:182, at para. 51; Judgment in *Weigel*, C-387/01, EU:C:2004:256, at para. 55; Judgment in *Lindfors*, C-365/02, EU:C:2004:449, at para. 34; Judgment in *Schempp*, C-403/03, EU:C:2005:446, at para. 45; Judgment in *Alevizos*, C-392/05, EU:C:2007:251, at para. 76; Judgment in *Renneberg*, C-527/06, EU:C:2008:566, at para. 40; Judgment in *Schulz-Delzers and Schulz*, C-240/10, EU:C:2011:591, at para. 42; Judgment in *National Grid Indus*, C-371/10, EU:C:2011:785, at para. 62). Thus, the fundamental freedoms cannot be relied upon to undo disadvantages resulting from differences between the tax scales of the Member States concerned (Judgment in *Gilly*, C-336/96, EU:C:1998:221, at para. 47; also see Judgment in *De Groot*, C-385/00, EU:C:2002:750, at para. 86). However, this seeming inconsistency could be resolved, if *Merida* is understood as to mean that a Member State must not unilaterally deviate from the provisions of a bilateral double taxation convention (cf. G. Kofler, *Doppelbesteuerungsabkommen und Europäisches Gemeinschaftsrecht* [Linde, 2007], at p. 189).

1480. Judgment in *Geddo / Ente Nazionale Risi*, 2/73, EU:C:1973:89, at point 4; also see Order in *Levy and Sebbag*, C-540/11, EU:C:2012:581, at para. 26.

1481. Similarly, but not explicitly requiring actual double taxation, J. Bron, Das Treaty Override im deutschen Steuerrecht vor dem Hintergrund aktueller Entwicklungen, 16 *IStR* 12 (2007), p. 431 (at p. 435); J. Englisch, *Dividendenbesteuerung* (Dr Otto Schmidt, 2005), at pp. 258-259; J. Englisch, 33 *Intertax* 8/9 (2005), at p. 324; G. Kofler, *Doppelbesteuerungsabkommen und Europäisches Gemeinschaftsrecht* (Linde, 2007), at pp. 606-607.

of negotiations between at least[1482] two contracting states, *"in which the respective contracting parties' rights and duties are usually based on the principle of reciprocity. That means that such conventions are based on a well-defined equilibrium – also as regards the financial consequences."*[1483] While a Member State is responsible and can also be held liable for restrictions or for discrimination resulting from double taxation conventions,[1484] it is hence discussed in the literature whether the *do ut des* or quid pro quo of double taxation conventions may be successfully invoked as a justification ground.[1485]

Such a rationale had already been relied upon by the French Government in *Avoir Fiscal*: The shareholder's tax credit which was available for French resident companies was partly extended to branches of foreign companies by including additional provisions to existing double taxation conventions between France and other Member States. However, this extension was subject to a condition of reciprocity, i.e., *"foreign*

1482. A multilateral tax treaty was concluded, for example, by Denmark, Finland, Iceland, Norway and Sweden (hereinafter: Nordic Convention). See, for example, M. Helminen, *The Nordic Multilateral Tax Treaty* (IBFD, 2014); N. Mattsson, Is the multilateral Convention a Solution for the Future? Comments with Reflection to the Nordic Experience, 13 *Intertax* 9 (1985), p. 212 (at pp. 212 et seq.); on the issue of multilateral tax treaties in general see, for example, M. Lang, The Concept of a Multilateral Tax Treaty, in M. Lang/H. Loukota/A.J. Rädler/J. Schuch/G. Toifl/C. Urtz/F. Wassermeyer/M. Züger, *Multilateral Tax Treaties* (Kluwer, 1998), p. 187 (at pp. 187 et seq.); H. Loukota, Multilateral Tax Treaty Versus Bilateral Treaty Network, in M. Lang/H. Loukota/A.J. Rädler/J. Schuch/G. Toifl/C. Urtz/F. Wassermeyer/M. Züger, *Multilateral Tax Treaties* (Kluwer, 1998), p. 85 (at pp. 85 et seq.).

1483. Opinion of AG Van Gerven in *Grana-Novoa*, C-23/92, EU:C:1993:162, at point 12.

1484. Judgment in *De Groot*, C-385/00, EU:C:2002:750, at para. 110: *"Article 48 of the Treaty precludes rules such as those at issue in the main proceedings – irrespective of whether or not they are laid down in a convention for the avoidance of double taxation – whereby a taxpayer forfeits, in the calculation of the income tax payable by him in his State of residence, part of the tax-free amount of that income and of his personal tax advantages because, during the year in question, he also received income in another Member State which was taxed in that State without his personal and family circumstances being taken into account"*; Judgment in *Commission/UK*, C-466/98, at para. 53-54: *"[In] paragraphs 59 and 60 of the* Saint-Gobain *judgment [...],the Court merely held that the extension to permanent establishments of companies having their seat in a Member State other than the Federal Republic of Germany of a tax advantage provided for by a bilateral international agreement concluded by the Federal Republic of Germany with a non-member country could be decided upon unilaterally by the former without in any way affecting the rights of the non-member country arising from that agreement and without imposing any new obligations on that non-member country. That does not mean, however, that, where the infringement of Community law results directly from a provision of a bilateral international agreement concluded by a Member State after its accession to the Community, the Court is prevented from holding that that infringement exists so as not to compromise the rights which non-member countries derive from the very provision which infringes Community law"*; also see Opinion of AG Colomer in *D*, C-376/03, EU:C:2004:663, at point 94: *"Redundant though it may seem, I should point out once again that, in the light of the view taken by the participating governments, when Member States exercise their taxation powers, they must do so consistently with Community law, irrespective of the instrument used – a law, a regulation or an international or Community agreement or an agreement with a third country."*

1485. See G. Kofler, *Doppelbesteuerungsabkommen und Europäisches Gemeinschaftsrecht* (Linde, 2007), at pp. 696-697; M. Lang in W. Gassner/M. Lang/E. Lechner (eds.), *Doppelbesteuerungsabkommen und EU-Recht* (Linde, 1996), at p. 32; M. Lang, The Binding Effect of the EC Fundamental Freedoms on Tax Treaties, in W. Gassner/M. Lang/E. Lechner (eds.), *Tax Treaties and EC Law* (Kluwer, 1996), p. 15 (at p. 22).

undertakings will be allowed to benefit from the tax credit if and when the same concession is granted to French companies having secondary establishments in the other contracting Member State."[1486] The French Government argued that if the fundamental freedoms required to generally grant the shareholder's tax credit to branches of foreign companies, the balance established in those double taxation conventions would be disturbed.[1487] The ECJ rejected this argument: "*[T]he rights conferred by Article 52 of the Treaty are unconditional and a Member State cannot make respect for them subject to the contents of an agreement concluded with another Member State. In particular, that article does not permit those rights to be made subject to a condition of reciprocity imposed for the purpose of obtaining corresponding advantages in other Member States.*"[1488] Thus, it is not sufficient in order to justify a different treatment that a Member State is prepared to extend a unilateral tax benefit granted in purely domestic situations to cross-border situations via a provision incorporated in a double taxation convention that is subject to a condition of reciprocity.[1489]

Whereas *Avoir Fiscal* concerned a domestic tax benefit, the issue in *Saint-Gobain* was whether Germany has to extend the benefits provided for in the double taxation conventions with the United States and Switzerland to a permanent establishment of a French company, which was not entitled to those tax treaty benefits due to a lack of residency in at least one of the contracting states. It was, *inter alia*, argued that "*double-taxation treaties are based on the principle of reciprocity and that the balance inherent in such treaties would be disturbed if the benefit of their provisions was extended to companies established in Member States which were not parties to them.*"[1490] However, the ECJ held that "*the obligations which Community law imposes on the Federal Republic of Germany do not affect in any way those resulting from its agreements with the United States of America and the Swiss Confederation. The balance and the reciprocity of the treaties concluded by the Federal Republic of Germany with those two countries would not be called into question by a unilateral extension, on the part of the Federal Republic of Germany, of the category of recipients in Germany of the tax advantage provided for by those treaties, in this case corporation tax relief for international groups, since such an extension would not in any way affect the rights of the non-member countries which are parties to the treaties and would not impose any new obligation on them.*"[1491] Although the Court rejected the argument of reciprocity in *Saint-Gobain*, the following decision in *Gottardo* has clarified that "*[d]isturbing the balance and reciprocity of a bilateral international convention concluded between a Member State and a non-member country may, it is true, constitute an objective justification for the refusal by a Member State party to that convention to extend to nationals of other Member States the advantages which its own nationals derive from*

1486. Opinion of AG Mancini in *Avoir Fiscal*, 270/83, EU:C:1985:413, at point 7.
1487. Opinion of AG Mancini in *Avoir Fiscal*, 270/83, EU:C:1985:413, at point 12.
1488. Judgment in *Avoir Fiscal*, 270/83, EU:C:1986:37, at para. 26.
1489. See K. Daxkobler, *Die grundfreiheitliche Rechtsprechung des EuGH* (Linde, 2015), at p. 263.
1490. Judgment in *Saint-Gobain*, C-307/97, EU:C:1999:438, at para. 56.
1491. Judgment in *Saint-Gobain*, C-307/97, EU:C:1999:438, at para. 60; also see Opinion of AG Mischo in *Saint-Gobain*, C-307/97, EU:C:1999:110, at points 81-85.

that convention."[1492] At first glance, this statement seems to be the very reverse of what the ECJ said in *Saint-Gobain.*[1493] However, not only did the Court explicitly refer to this decision.[1494] Just as in *Saint-Gobain*, it also emphasized that "*[t]he unilateral extension by the Italian Republic, to workers who are nationals of other Member States, of the benefit of having insurance periods which they completed in Switzerland taken into account for the purpose of acquiring entitlement to Italian old-age benefits would in no way compromise the rights which the Swiss Confederation derives from the Italo-Swiss Convention and would not impose any new obligations on that country."*[1495] Thus, it can be reasonably assumed that in *Gottardo* the Court "*either clarified or developed further the* Saint-Gobain *reasoning to a certain extent."*[1496]

Although it is not clearly stated, the ECJ seems, albeit within the comparability analysis,[1497] to have ultimately accepted the reciprocity argument in the *D.* case:[1498] Due to a non-discrimination provision in the double taxation convention between Belgium and the Netherlands, Belgian residents who owned property in the Netherlands were entitled to claim the Netherlands basic allowance for wealth tax purposes. Since such a provision was not provided for in the double taxation convention between Germany and the Netherlands, German residents were denied the allowance. This distinction raised the question whether a Member State is precluded "*from according, pursuant to a bilateral convention for the avoidance of double taxation, only to residents of the other State party to the convention the allowance which it grants to its own residents, without extending the allowance to residents of the other Member States."*[1499] With reference to *Saint-Gobain* and *Gottardo*,[1500] AG Colomer argued that EU law requires the Netherlands to extend to German residents the benefits Belgian residents may claim due to the non-discrimination provision that was included in the double taxation convention between Belgium and the Netherlands, but not in the double taxation convention between Germany and the Netherlands,[1501] while being aware of "*the dangers which the foregoing considerations imply for the equilibrium and reciprocity which prevail in the system of double-taxation treaties*"[1502] and the fact that "*[a]n affirmative reply to the second question referred to the Court would severly fetter the complex system of bilateral agreements for the avoidance of double taxation in the*

1492. Judgment in *Gottardo*, C-55/00, EU:C:2002:16, at para. 36.
1493. See M. Lang/S. Dommes, Tax Treaty Law and EC Law – Reciprocity and the Balance of a Tax Treaty, in M. Lang/J. Schuch/C. Staringer (eds.), *Tax Treaty Law and EC Law* (Linde, 2007), p. 61 (at p. 71).
1494. Judgment in *Gottardo*, C-55/00, EU:C:2002:16, at para. 36, referring to Judgment in *Saint-Gobain*, C-307/97, EU:C:1999:438, at para. 60.
1495. Judgment in *Gottardo*, C-55/00, EU:C:2002:16, at para. 37.
1496. See M. Lang/S. Dommes in M. Lang/J. Schuch/C. Staringer (eds.), *Tax Treaty Law and EC Law* (Linde, 2007), at p.72.
1497. See G. Kofler, *Doppelbesteuerungsabkommen und Europäisches Gemeinschaftsrecht* (Linde, 2007), at pp. 696-706 (FN 50); M. Lang, 15 *SWI* 8 (2005), at p. 372.
1498. See G. Kofler, *Doppelbesteuerungsabkommen und Europäisches Gemeinschaftsrecht* (Linde, 2007), at pp. 703-704.
1499. Judgment in *D*, C-376/03, EU:C:2005:424, at para. 46.
1500. Opinion of AG Colomer in *D*, C-376/03, EU:C:2004:663, at points 90-93.
1501. Opinion of AG Colomer in *D.*, C-376/03, EU:C:2004:663, at points 94-100.
1502. Opinion of AG Colomer in *D.*, C-376/03, EU:C:2004:663, at point 101.

Community."[1503] The ECJ, however, did not agree with this opinion, but instead pointed out that "*[i]t is to be remembered that, in order to avoid the same income and assets being taxed in both the Netherlands and Belgium, Article 24 of the Belgium-Netherlands Convention allocates powers of taxation between those two Member States and Article 25(3) lays down a rule under which natural persons resident in one of those two States are entitled in the other to the personal allowances which are granted by it to its own residents. The fact that those reciprocal rights and obligations apply only to persons resident in one of the two Contracting Member States is an inherent consequence of bilateral double taxation conventions. It follows that a taxable person resident in Belgium is not in the same situation as a taxable person resident outside Belgium so far as concerns wealth tax on real property situated in the Netherlands. A rule such as that laid down in Article 25(3) of the Belgium-Netherlands Convention cannot be regarded as a benefit separable from the remainder of the Convention, but is an integral part thereof and contributes to its overall balance. Having regard to the foregoing considerations, the answer to the second question asked must be that Articles 56 EC and 58 EC do not preclude a rule laid down by a bilateral convention for the avoidance of double taxation such as the rule at issue in the main proceedings from not being extended, in a situation and in circumstances such as those in the main proceedings, to residents of a Member State which is not party to that convention.*"[1504]

In the literature, the ECJ's judgment in *D.* was not only criticized because of its circular reasoning,[1505] but also because it is hard to reconcile with the decisions in *Saint-Gobain* and *Gottardo.*[1506] By denying comparability based on the "*inherent consequence of bilateral double taxation conventions*" to grant "*reciprocal rights and obligations [...] only to persons resident in one of the two Contracting Member States,*" instead of focusing on possible justification grounds, the ECJ veils the underlying reasons for the different outcome in *D.*, on the one hand, and *Saint-Gobain*, on the other hand.[1507] In *D.*, the Court could have used the same reasoning as in *Saint-Gobain* to hold that "*the obligations which Community law imposes on the [Netherlands] do not*

1503. Opinion of AG Colomer in *D.*, C-376/03, EU:C:2004:663, at point 105.

1504. Judgment in *D.*, C-376/03, EU:C:2005:424, at paras 60-63.

1505. See A. Cordewener/E. Reimer, 46 *Eur. Taxn.* 7 (2006), at pp. 293-294 and p. 302; A. Cordewener in A. Cordewener/S. Enchelmaier/C.P. Schindler (eds.), *Meistbegünstigung im Steuerrecht der EU-Staaten* (C.H. Beck, 2006), at p. 224; S. Enchelmair in A. Cordewener/S. Enchelmaier/C.P. Schindler (eds.), *Meistbegünstigung im Steuerrecht der EU-Staaten* (C.H. Beck, 2006), p. 93 (at p. 118); J.E. Gudmundsson, 34 *Intertax* 2 (2006), at p. 81; D. Hohenwarter in M. Lang/J. Schuch/C. Staringer (eds.), *Tax Treaty Law and EC Law* (Kluwer, 2007), at p. 119; M.C. Pimentel, 34 *Intertax* 10 (2006), at p. 491; S. van Thiel, 33 *Intertax* 10 (2005), at p. 455; G. Kofler, 58 *ÖStZ* 19 (2005), at pp. 436-437.

1506. See P. Cussons/E. FitzGerald, EU Report, in IFA (ed.), *The Attribution of Profits to Permanent Establishments*, CDFI 92b (IBFD, 2006), p. 69 (at p. 71); G. Kofler, *Doppelbesteuerungsabkommen und Europäisches Gemeinschaftsrecht* (Linde, 2007), at pp. 696-706; M. Lang, 15 *SWI* 8 (2005), at pp. 372-374; M. Lang in M. Hebig/K. Kaiser/K. Koschmieder/M. Oblau (eds.), *Festschrift für Wilhelm H. Wacker* (Erich Schmidt Verlag, 2006), at pp. 370-373; M. Lang/S. Dommes in M. Lang/J. Schuch/C. Staringer (eds.), *Tax Treaty Law and EC Law* (Linde, 2007), at pp. 73-75.

1507. With regard to the factual and legal differences in the *D.* case and the *Saint-Gobain* case see M. Lang/S. Dommes in M. Lang/J. Schuch/C. Staringer (eds.), *Tax Treaty Law and EC Law* (Linde, 2007), at p. 74.

affect in any way those resulting from its agreements with [Germany] and [Belgium]. The balance and the reciprocity of the treaties concluded by the [Netherlands] with those two countries would not be called into question by a unilateral extension, on the part of the [Netherlands], [...] since such an extension would not in any way affect the rights of [Germany and Belgium] which are parties to the treaties and would not impose any new obligation on them."[1508] On the other hand, in *Saint-Gobain*, the Court could have used the same reasoning as in *D.* to deny, at least with regard to the issue of getting access to tax treaty benefits, the comparability of a non-resident with a domestic permanent establishment and a resident:[1509] The exemption from German corporate tax for dividends received by German residents from companies established in the United States and Switzerland provided for in the former double taxation convention between Germany and the United States and in the former double taxation convention between Germany and Switzerland could have been regarded as constituting part of the reciprocal rights and obligations of those tax treaties and the fact that "*those reciprocal rights and obligations apply only to persons resident in one of the two Contracting Member States is an inherent consequence of bilateral double taxation conventions. It follows that a taxable person resident in [France] is not in the same situation as a taxable person resident [in Germany] so far as concerns [the taxation of dividends received by a company resident in a treaty partner state of Germany].*"

It may be speculated whether the Court might have been guided by an argument raised by the Swedish Government in *Saint-Gobain*, according to which "*in certain extreme situations extending the scope of bilateral double-taxation treaties could lead to no tax yield being produced at all.*"[1510] Although the ECJ rejected this rationale in *Saint-Gobain*, because it "*is not relevant in the case referred since it has not been argued that there was a risk that profits would not be taxed in any country,*"[1511] it might have

1508. M. Lang/S. Dommes in M. Lang/J. Schuch/C. Staringer (eds.), *Tax Treaty Law and EC Law* (Linde, 2007), at p. 75; also cf. A. Cordewener/E. Reimer, 46 *Eur. Taxn.* 7 (2006), at p. 296; G. Kofler, *Doppelbesteuerungsabkommen und Europäisches Gemeinschaftsrecht* (Linde, 2007), at p. 706; M. Lang, 15 *SWI* 8 (2005), at p. 372; M. Lang in M. Hebig/K. Kaiser/K. Koschmieder/M. Oblau (eds.), *Festschrift für Wilhelm H. Wacker* (Erich Schmidt Verlag, 2006), at pp. 372-373; J. Schuch, 15 *EC Tax Rev.* 1 (2006), at p. 8; S. van Thiel, 33 *Intertax* 10 (2005), at pp. 455-456; D. Weber, 33 *Intertax* 10 (2005), at pp. 436-437.

1509. However, this would have raised the question of whether such an approach is in line with the position the ECJ has taken in *Avoir Fiscal*, according to which "*there is no objective difference between [companies whose registered office is in France and branches and agencies situated in France of companies whose registered office is abroad],*" because "*French tax law does not distinguish, for the purpose of determining the income liable to corporation tax, between companies having their registered office in France and branches and agencies situated in France of companies whose registered office is abroad. By virtue of Article 209 of the code général des impôts, both are liable to taxation on profits made in undertakings carried on in France, to the exclusion of profits which are made abroad or which France is entitled to tax under the terms of a double taxation agreement. Since the rules at issue place companies whose registered office is in France and branches and agencies situated in France of companies whose registered office is abroad on the same footing for the purposes of taxing their profits, those rules, cannot, without giving rise to discrimination, treat them differently in regard to the grant of an advantage related to taxation, such as shareholders' tax credits*" (Judgment in *Avoir Fiscal*, 270/83, EU:C:1986:37, at paras 19-20).

1510. Judgment in *Saint-Gobain*, C-307/97, EU:C:1999:438, at para. 62.

1511. Judgment in *Saint-Gobain*, C-307/97, EU:C:1999:438, at para. 63.

affected the Court's decision in *D.*[1512] However, as in *Saint-Gobain*, apparently, this argument was not brought forward. Neither was there a risk that no wealth tax would be levied at all in the circumstances of the *D.* case. Instead, the governments which have submitted observations and the Commission, in a more general and abstract way, referred "*to the danger which the extension of the benefits provided for by a bilateral convention to all Community residents would entail for the application of existing bilateral conventions and of those which the Member States might be prompted to conclude in the future, and to the legal uncertainty which that extension would cause.*"[1513] Moreover, the UK Government contended "*that most-favoured-nation status entails a risk of tax evasion if a taxpayer invokes the least rigorous of the anti-fraud provisions included by a Member State in its agreements with others.*"[1514] Both arguments may be considered as valid policy reasons against a general most-favoured nation principle. However, from a legal perspective, it is questionable whether these arguments justify a different treatment of comparable groups of non-residents resulting from differences in the double taxation conventions concluded by a Member State. With respect to a different treatment of domestic and cross-border situations, the ECJ had already pointed out that tax measures have to be in line with the fundamental freedoms, "*irrespective of whether or not they are laid down in a convention for the avoidance of double taxation.*"[1515] If the ECJ, in the context of Article 45(2) TFEU, "*read in the light of Article 26 TFEU,*" acknowledges that the fundamental freedoms also prohibit "*discrimination between non-resident[s] if such discrimination leads to nationals of certain Member States being unduly favoured in comparison with others,*"[1516] it should hence not make a difference whether the different treatment results, as in *Sopora*, from domestic legislation or, as in *D.*, at least indirectly, from a double taxation convention.[1517]

Admittedly, such an approach might have tremendous effects on the network of double taxation conventions concluded by the Member States.[1518] However, as AG

1512. See G. Kofler, *Doppelbesteuerungsabkommen und Europäisches Gemeinschaftsrecht* (Linde, 2007), at p. 707; M. Lang/S. Dommes in M. Lang/J. Schuch/C. Staringer (eds.), *Tax Treaty Law and EC Law* (Linde, 2007), at pp. 79-80; also cf. P. Cussons/E. FitzGerald in IFA (ed.), *The Attribution of Profits to Permanent Establishments*, CDFI 92b (IBFD, 2006), at p. 71.
1513. Judgment in *D.*, C-376/03, EU:C:2005:424, at para. 48.
1514. Opinion of AG Colomer in *D.*, C-376/03, EU:C:2004:663, at point 102.
1515. Judgment in *De Groot*, C-385/00, EU:C:2002:750, at para. 110; also see Opinion of AG Colomer in *D.*, C-376/03, EU:C:2004:663, at point 94: "*Redundant though it may seem, I should point out once again that, in the light of the view taken by the participating governments, when Member States exercise their taxation powers, they must do so consistently with Community law, irrespective of the instrument used – a law, a regulation or an international or Community agreement or an agreement with a third country*"; also cf. Judgment in *Bouanich*, C-265/04, EU:C:2006:51, at paras 50-51; Judgment in *Test Claimants in Class IV of the ACT Group Litigation*, C-374/04, EU:C:2006:773, at para. 71; Judgment in *Denkavit Internationaal and Denkavit France*, C-170/05, EU:C:2006:783, at para. 45; Judgment in *Test Claimants in the Thin Cap Group Litigation*, C-524/04, EU:C:2007:161, at para. 54; Judgment in *Amurta*, C-379/05, EU:C:2007:655, at para. 80.
1516. Judgment in *Sopora*, C-512/13, EU:C:2015:108, at para. 25.
1517. For a more nuanced view see I.M. de Groot, Member States Must Apply Most Favoured Nation Treatment under EU Law, 42 *Intertax* 6/7 (2014), p. 405 (at p. 415).
1518. See, for example, E.C.C.M. Kemmeren, 6 *EC Tax Rev.* 3 (1997), at p. 148 ("*one of the pillars of tax treaty law, the reciprocity principle, would have been demolished*"); M. Lehner, 54 *Bull.*

Colomer has rightly emphasized, "*it would not be the first time that a ruling of the Court of Justice caused upheaval in the legal systems of the Member States.*"[1519] Furthermore, the policy concerns raised by various governments and the Commission in *D.* are to be respected insofar as they can be transformed into legally valid justification grounds. The UK Government's reference, for example, to the potential risk of tax evasion may justify a different treatment if the respective measure of the Member State relying on this argument complies with the requirements the ECJ has developed in its previous jurisprudence on the need to prevent tax avoidance, tax evasion and abuse.[1520] In the literature, moreover, it is contemplated whether the concept of fiscal cohesion may be invoked by Member States in order to justify different treatment resulting from rules within double taxation conventions.[1521] This requires a direct link "*between a tax advantage and the offsetting of that advantage by a particular tax levy.*"[1522] To a certain extent, reference to the balance and reciprocity of a double taxation convention also boils down to the need to preserve fiscal cohesion.[1523] Considering that double taxation conventions are the consequence of negotiations between at least two contracting states, "*in which the respective contracting parties' rights and duties are usually based*

Intl. Taxn. 8 (2000), at p. 470 ("*Assuming that the fundamental freedoms granted most-favoured-nation treatment, this would result in the abolition of the principle of reciprocity which, however, forms the backbone of bilateral agreements*"); P.J. Wattel, 33 *Common Market L. Rev.* 2 (1996), at p. 252 ("*such a most favoured nation effect would really ruffle settled international tax law*").

1519. Opinion of AG Colomer in *D.*, C-376/03, EU:C:2004:663, at point 105.
1520. For an analysis of this jurisprudence see, for example, L. De Broe, *International Tax Planning and Prevention of Abuse* (IBFD, 2008), at pp. 799-929; J. Englisch, Verbot des Rechtsmissbrauchs – ein allgemeiner Rechtsgrundsatz des Gemeinschaftsrechts?, 86 *StuW* 1 (2009), p. 3 (at pp. 3-22); M. Lang, *Cadbury Schweppes'* Line of Case Law from the Member States' Perspective, in R. de la Feria/S. Vogenauer (eds.), *Prohibition of Abuse of Law* (Hart, 2011), p. 435 (at pp. 435-458); M. Lang/S. Heidenbauer, Wholly Artificial Arrangements, in L. Hinnekens/P. Hinnekens (eds.), *A Vision of Taxes Within and Outside European Borders, Festschrift in Honor of Prof. Dr. Frans Vanistendael* (Kluwer, 2008), p. 597 (at pp. 597-616); W. Schön, Rechtsmissbrauch und Europäisches Steuerrecht, in P. Kirchhof/H. Nieskens (eds.), *Festschrift für Wolfram Reiss zum 65. Geburtstag* (Dr Otto Schmidt, 2008), p. 571 (at pp. 571-596); D. Weber, *Tax Avoidance and the EC Treaty Freedoms* (Kluwer, 2005).
1521. See G. Kofler, 5 *Hous. Bus. & Tax L. J.* 1 (2005), at pp. 82-85; M. Lang in W. Gassner/M. Lang/E. Lechner (eds.), *Doppelbesteuerungsabkommen und EU-Recht* (Linde, 1996), at pp. 38-42; M. Lang in W. Gassner/M. Lang/E. Lechner (eds.), *Tax Treaties and EC Law* (Kluwer, 1996), at pp. 27-30; D. Weber/E. Spierts, 44 *Eur. Taxn.* 2 (2004), at p. 69.
1522. Opinion of AG Kokott in *Nordea Bank Danmark*, C-48/13, EU:C:2014:153; at point 43; also see Judgment in *Verkooijen*, C-35/98, EU:C:2000:294, at para. 57; Judgment in *Bosal*, C-168/01, EU:C:2003:479, at para. 29; Judgment in *Schilling and Fleck-Schilling*, C-209/01, EU:C:2003:610, at para. 41; Judgment in *Manninen*, C-319/02, EU:C:2004:484, at para. 42; Judgment in *Keller Holding*, C-471/04, EU:C:2006:143, at para. 40; Judgment in *Test Claimants in the Thin Cap Group Litigation*, C-524/04, EU:C:2007:161, at para. 68; Judgment in *Rewe Zentralfinanz*, C-347/04, EU:C:2007:194, at para. 62; Judgment in *Papillon*, C-418/07, EU:C:2008:659, at para. 44; Judgment in *Glaxo Wellcome*, C-182/08, EU:C:2009:559, at para. 79; Judgment in *DI. VI. Finanziaria di Diego della Valle & C.*, C-380/11, EU:C:2012:552, at para. 47; Judgment in *Welte*, C-181/12, EU:C:2013:662, at para. 59.
1523. See G. Kofler, 5 *Hous. Bus. & Tax L. J.* 1 (2005), at p. 83.

on the principle of reciprocity,"[1524] all treaty rules are somehow interrelated.[1525] Thus, neither provision of a double taxation convention could *"be regarded as a benefit separable from the remainder of the Convention,"*[1526] which would mean that each and every double taxation convention has to be considered as a coherent tax system. Such an argument is based on the assumption that the granting of tax treaty benefits to residents of a treaty partner but not to residents of other Member States can be justified by the fact that the respective treaty partner made up for any of those benefits by granting a corresponding tax advantage during the treaty negotiations.[1527] However, according to the ECJ's case law, the concept of fiscal cohesion requires that a concrete tax disadvantage is compensated for by a corresponding tax advantage, with the result that the taxpayer concerned suffers no discrimination.[1528] Thus, it would not be sufficient to refer to the *do ut des* or quid pro quo of double taxation conventions in order to invoke the concept of fiscal cohesion, but rather it has to be established for each and every tax treaty benefit individually whether it is offset by a sufficiently linked disadvantage or not.[1529] If, for example, Member State A has concluded a double taxation convention with Member State B that provides for a maximum withholding tax rate of 15% with regard to dividends whereas a double taxation convention concluded by that Member State with Member State C provides for a maximum

1524. Opinion of AG Van Gerven in *Grana-Novoa*, C-23/92, EU:C:1993:162, at point 12.
1525. See M. Lang in W. Gassner/M. Lang/E. Lechner (eds.), *Doppelbesteuerungsabkommen und EU-Recht* (Linde, 1996), at pp. 33; M. Lang in W. Gassner/M. Lang/E. Lechner (eds.), *Tax Treaties and EC Law* (Kluwer, 1996), at p. 23.
1526. Judgment in *D.*, C-376/03, EU:C:2005:424, at para. 62.
1527. See G. Kofler, 5 *Hous. Bus. & Tax L. J.* 1 (2005), at p. 84.
1528. Judgment in *Verkooijen*, C-35/98, EU:C:2000:294, at para. 57; Judgment in *Bosal*, C-168/01, EU:C:2003:479, at para. 29; Judgment in *Schilling and Fleck-Schilling*, C-209/01, EU:C:2003:610, at para. 41; Judgment in *Weidert and Paulus*, C-242/03, EU:C:2004:465, at para. 22; Judgment in *Manninen*, C-319/02, EU:C:2004:484, at para. 42; Judgment in *Keller Holding*, C-471/04, EU:C:2006:143, at para. 40; Judgment in *Centro di Musicologia Walter Stauffer*, C-386/04, EU:C:2006:568, at para. 53; Judgment in *Commission/Portugal*, C-345/05, EU:C:2006:685, at para. 29; Judgment in *Test Claimants in the FII Group Litigation*, C-446/04, EU:C:2006:774, at para. 178; Judgment in *Meilicke and others*, C-292/04, EU:C:2007:132, at para. 28; Judgment in *Test Claimants in the Thin Cap Group Litigation*, C-524/04, EU:C:2007:161, at para. 68; Judgment in *Rewe Zentralfinanz*, C-347/04, EU:C:2007:194, at para. 62; Judgment in *Hollmann*, C-443/06, EU:C:2007:600, at para. 56; Judgment in *Amurta*, C-379/05, EU:C:2007:655, at para. 46; Judgment in *Jundt*, C-281/06, EU:C:2007:816, at para. 68; Judgment in *Heinrich Bauer Verlag*, C-360/06, EU:C:2008:531, at para. 37; Judgment in *Papillon*, C-418/07, EU:C:2008:659, at para. 44; Judgment in *Glaxo Wellcome*, C-182/08, EU:C:2009:559, at para. 79; Judgment in *Commission/Spain*, C-562/07, EU:C:2009:614, at para. 61; Judgment in *Presidente del Consiglio dei Ministri*, C-169/08, EU:C:2009:709, at para. 47; Judgment in *Commission/Belgium*, C-250/08, EU:C:2011:793, at para. 71; Judgment in *Santander Asset Management SGIIC*, C-338/11 to C-347/11, EU:C:2012:286, at para. 51; Judgment in *DI. VI. Finanziaria di Diego della Valle & C.*, C-380/11, EU:C:2012:552, at para. 47; Judgment in *Test Claimants in the FII Group Litigation*, C-35/11, EU:C:2012:707, at para. 58; Judgment in *Welte*, C-181/12, EU:C:2013:662, at para. 59; Judgment in *K.*, C-322/11, EU:C:2013:716, at para. 66; Judgment in *Bouanich*, C-375/12, EU:C:2014:138, at para. 69; Judgment in *Grünewald*, C-559/13, EU:C:2015:109, at para. 48; Judgment in *Groupe Steria*, C-386/14, EU:C:2015:524, at para. 31; Judgment in *Finanzamt Linz*, C-66/14, EU:C:2015:661, at para. 44; also see K. Daxkobler, *Die grundfreiheitliche Rechtsprechung des EuGH* (Linde, 2015), at pp. 226-230.
1529. Cf. G. Kofler, 5 *Hous. Bus. & Tax L. J.* 1 (2005), at pp. 84-85; D. Weber/E. Spierts, 44 *Eur. Taxn.* 2 (2004), at p. 69.

withholding tax rate of 10%, residents of Member State B may argue that they are discriminated against by Member State A as compared to residents of Member State C, because of the different maximum withholding tax rates provided for in the double taxation conventions.[1530] However, Member State A may object that the tax disadvantage of a higher maximum withholding tax rate in the double taxation convention concluded with Member State B is neutralized by the residence state's obligation to grant a credit for the withholding tax levied in Member State A.[1531]

Although this rationale implies that there would be no discrimination in the first place and hence no justification would be needed,[1532] the underlying thought corresponds to the idea of fiscal cohesion.[1533] At first glance, it could be argued that the legal situation in another Member State is typically not taken into account by the ECJ.[1534] However, since the credit method explicitly refers to the taxation in the other contracting state, this legal linking requires the Court to consider the effects of the double taxation convention in the respective other contracting state as well. In fact, such an approach would not even be a novelty. Rather, a thorough analysis of the ECJ's jurisprudence shows that the obligations of double taxation conventions are partly taken into account by the Court in order to determine whether the prima facie discriminatory effect of a Member States' domestic legislation may be neutralized due to the impact of a double taxation convention.

1530. For similar examples see J. Schuch in W. Gassner/M. Lang/E. Lechner (eds.), *Doppelbesteuerungsabkommen und EU-Recht* (Linde, 1996), at pp. 102-104; J. Schuch in W. Gassner/B. Gröhs/M. Lang (eds.), *Zukunftsaufgaben der Wirtschaftsprüfung* (Orac, 1997), at pp. 332-333; O. Thömmes in M. Lehner (ed.), *Steuerrecht im Europäischen Binnenmarkt*, DStJG 19 (Dr Otto Schmidt, 1996), at p. 101; S. van Thiel, *Free Movement of Persons and Income Tax Law: The European Court in Search of Principles* (IBFD, 2002), at p. 514; H. Weggenmann, 12 *IStR* 19 (2003), at pp. 680-684; S. de Ceulaer, 57 *Bull. Intl. Taxn.* 10 (2003), at pp. 499-501; also cf. M. Helminen, The Future of Source State Dividend Withholding Taxes in Finland and the European Union, 48 *Eur. Taxn.* 7 (2008), p. 354 (at p. 356: "*One cannot conclude, for example, that it would be in accordance with the EC Treaty to apply different dividend withholding tax rates to residents of different Member States.*").

1531. See G. Kofler, 5 *Hous. Bus. & Tax L. J.* 1 (2005), at pp. 74-78; G. Kofler, 17 *ÖStZ* 23 (2004), at pp. 561-562; M. Tumpel in J. Pelka (ed.), *Europa- und verfassungsrechtliche Grenzen der Unternehmensbesteuerung*, DStJG 30 (Dr Otto Schmidt, 2000), at p. 344; R. van der Linde, 13 *EC Tax Rev.* 1 (2004), at p. 14; F. Wassermeyer, Does the EC Treaty Force the Member States to Conclude a Multilateral Tax Treaty?, in M. Lang/H. Loukota/A.J. Rädler/J. Schuch/G. Toifl/C. Urtz/F. Wassermeyer/M. Züger (eds.), *Multilateral Tax Treaties* (Linde, 1997), p. 15 (at p. 24).

1532. See G. Kofler, Tax Treaty "Neutralization" of Source State Discrimination under the EU Fundamental Freedoms?, 65 *Bull. Intl. Taxn.* 12 (2011), p. 684 (at p. 685).

1533. AG Geelhoed, for example, identified several decisions of the ECJ, in which "*assessment of the applicability of the 'fiscal cohesion defence' was in fact conceptually indistinct from that of determining whether national legislation is discriminatory*" (Opinion of AG Geelhoed in *Test Claimants in the Thin Cap Group Litigation*, C-524/04, EU:C:2006:436, at point 90); also see K. Daxkobler, *Die grundfreiheitliche Rechtsprechung des EuGH* (Linde, 2015), at pp. 227-228; D. Smit/B. Kiekebeld, *EC Free Movement of Capital* (Kluwer, 2008), at pp. 104-105.

1534. See, among other authors, J. Englisch, *Dividendenbesteuerung* (Dr Otto Schmidt, 2005), at p. 240; G. Kofler, *Doppelbesteuerungsabkommen und Europäisches Gemeinschaftsrecht* (Linde, 2007), at pp. 564-565; M. Lang, *Die Rechtsprechung des EuGH zu den direkten Steuern* (Peter Lang, 2007), at pp. 75-80.

1.3.1.4 *The Compensation for Discriminatory Effects by Means of a Double Taxation Convention*

By concluding a double taxation convention, the contracting states commit themselves to relinquishing or restricting their taxing rights in order to eliminate double taxation. The effects of double taxation conventions can hence be pictured as *"a stencil that is placed over the pattern of domestic law and covers over certain parts."*[1535] In those cases in which the domestic tax liabilities are covered by this imaginary stencil, the imposition of taxes is restricted or eliminated.[1536] Since the effects of domestic tax law are thus suppressed, the question arises whether double taxation conventions may also remedy the discriminatory effect of a domestic tax measure if the latter is considered separately.[1537]

The ECJ had to deal with this issue in *Bouanich*:[1538] According to former Swedish law, the repurchase of shares by a Swedish company from a shareholder resident in Sweden was taxed as a capital gain, i.e., for a private individual a tax rate of 30 % was charged on the proceeds of sale less the acquisition costs. If, however, the shareholder was not domiciled or permanently resident in Sweden, the payment made to that person was treated as a dividend distribution, i.e., a tax of 30 % was levied on the gross amount of the payment due to a lack of deductibility of the acquisition costs.[1539] If this kind of different treatment caused by domestic legislation was considered to infringe the fundamental freedoms, the Swedish Administrative Court of Appeal in Sundsvall raised the question whether the result would change due to the fact that *"the double taxation agreement between the Member State in which the limited company is resident and the Member State in which the shareholder is resident provides that there is to be a lower rate of taxation than that applied to a share repurchase payment made to a shareholder in the first Member State, and a shareholder in the second Member State, with reference to the commentaries on the OECD Model Tax Convention, is also permitted a deduction corresponding to the nominal value of the repurchased shares."*[1540]

1535. See K. Vogel/A. Rust in E. Reimer/A. Rust (eds.), *Klaus Vogel on Double Taxation Conventions*[4] (Kluwer, 2015), Introduction at MN 68.
1536. See M. Lang, *Introduction to the Law of Double Taxation Conventions*[2] (Linde, 2013), at m.no 45.
1537. See G. Kofler, *Doppelbesteuerungsabkommen und Europäisches Gemeinschaftsrecht* (Linde, 2007), at p. 555 and pp. 558-559.
1538. Judgment in *Bouanich*, C-265/04, EU:C:2006:51; for an analysis of this judgment see C. Brokelind, The ECJ *Bouanich* Case: The Capital Gains and Dividend Classification of Share Buy-Backs in Swedish Tax Law, 6 *Eur. Taxn.* 6 (2006), p. 268 (at pp. 268-274); S. Dommes/S. Heidenbauer, Schwedische Besteuerung von Aktienrückkäufen verstößt gegen Kapitalverkehrsfreiheit – Urteil in der Rs. Bouanich, 16 *SWI* 3 (2006), p. 126 (at pp. 126 et seq.).
1539. On the Swedish legislation see, for example, C. Brokelind, 6 *Eur. Taxn.* 6 (2006), at pp. 268-270; B. Wiman, Pending Cases Filed by Swedish Courts: The Skatteverket v A, Skatteverket v A and B, and Bouanich Cases, in M. Lang/J. Schuch/C. Staringer (eds.), *ECJ – Recent Developments in Direct Taxation* (Linde, 2006), p. 297 (at pp. 305-306).
1540. Judgment in *Bouanich*, C-265/04, EU:C:2006:51, at para. 21; for critical remarks on the interpretation of the double taxation convention by the Swedish Administrative Court of Appeal in Sundsvall see S. Dommes/S. Heidenbauer, 16 *SWI* 3 (2006), at pp. 128-129.

After having found the Swedish domestic legislation to be prima facie incompatible with the free movement of capital,[1541] the ECJ dismissed the Commission's argument – which was based on *Avoir Fiscal*[1542] and *Saint-Gobain*[1543] – that the "*observance of Community law cannot depend on the content of the double taxation agreement concluded between two Member States.*"[1544] To consider double taxation conventions as being generally irrelevant when determining the compatibility of a Member State's legislation with the fundamental freedoms would ignore the fact that, "*[o]nce these agreements have been ratified by the national parliament, they form part of the national law on direct taxation, in the same way as purely domestic provisions.*"[1545] Therefore, the double taxation convention between France and Sweden, which was applicable in the *Bouanich* case, must be taken "*into account in order to give an interpretation of Community law that is relevant to the national court.*"[1546] However, in order to determine whether this tax treaty ensures in practice the elimination of all disadvantages for non-resident shareholders, "*it is necessary to know the cost of acquisition of those shares as well as their nominal value.*"[1547] Nevertheless, "*the assessment and finding of the facts in a case are not matters for the Court of Justice but for the national court [...]. It is therefore a matter for the national court to determine in the proceedings before it whether the fact that non-resident shareholders are permitted to deduct the nominal value and are liable to a maximum tax rate of 15% amounts to treatment that is no less favourable than that afforded to resident shareholders, who have the right to deduct the cost of acquisition and are taxed at a rate of 30%.*"[1548]

1541. Judgment in *Bouanich*, C-265/04, EU:C:2006:51, at paras 28-43.
1542. Judgment in *Avoir Fiscal*, 270/83, EU:C:1986:37, at para. 26.
1543. Judgment in *Saint-Gobain*, C-307/97, EU:C:1999:438, at paras 54-63.
1544. Opinion of AG Kokott in *Bouanich*, C-265/04, EU:C:2005:479, at point 44 (FN 36); also see Judgment in *Bouanich*, C-265/04, EU:C:2006:51, at para. 46.
1545. Opinion of AG Mischo in *Saint-Gobain*, C-307/97, EU:C:1999:110, at point 77; also cf. Opinion of AG Lenz in *Futura Participations and Singer*, C-250/95, EU:C:1996:420, at point 74: "*Like other provisions of domestic law, double-taxation conventions as elements of domestic law must not contravene the requirements of EC law*"; also see M. Lang in W. Gassner/M. Lang/E. Lechner (eds.), *Doppelbesteuerungsabkommen und EU-Recht* (Linde, 1996), at p. 27 and p. 30; M. Petritz/J. Schuch, Die Verteilung der Besteuerungsrechte zwischen Ansässigkeits- und Quellenstaat aus dem Blickwinkel der gemeinschaftsrechtliche Grundfreiheiten, in W. Gassner/M. Lang/J. Schuch/C. Staringer (eds.), *Die Verteilung der Besteuerungsrechte zwischen Ansässigkeits- und Quellenstaat im Recht der Doppelbesteuerungsabkommen* (Linde, 2005), p. 123 (at pp. 125-126).
1546. Judgment in *Bouanich*, C-265/04, EU:C:2006:51, at para. 51; also see Judgment in *Denkavit Internationaal and Denkavit France*, C-170/05, EU:C:2006:783, at para. 45; Judgment in *Test Claimants in the Thin Cap Group Litigation*, C-524/04, EU:C:2007:161, at para. 54; Judgment in *Amurta*, C-379/05, EU:C:2007:655, at para. 80; also see Opinion of AG Geelhoed in *Test Claimants in Class IV of the ACT Group Litigation*, C-374/04, EU:C:2006:139, at points 70-73; Opinion of AG Geelhoed in *Denkavit Internationaal and Denkavit France*, C-170/05, EU:C:2006:266, at point 33; Opinion of AG Geelhoed in *Test Claimants in the Thin Cap Group Litigation*, C-524/04, EU:C:2006:436, at points 56 and 69; also cf. Judgment in *De Groot*, C-385/00, EU:C:2002:750, at para. 99; Judgment in *Manninen*, C-319/02, EU:C:2004:484, at para. 21; Judgment in *Test Claimants in Class IV of the ACT Group Litigation*, C-374/04, EU:C:2006:773, at para. 71; Judgment in *Beker*, C-168/11, EU:C:2013:117, at para. 56; Judgment in *Imfeld and Garcet*, C-303/12, EU:C:2013:822, at para. 69.
1547. Judgment in *Bouanich*, C-265/04, EU:C:2006:51, at para. 53; also see Opinion of AG Kokott in *Bouanich*, C-265/04, EU:C:2005:479, at points 53-69.
1548. Judgment in *Bouanich*, C-265/04, EU:C:2006:51, at paras 54-55.

It can be inferred from *Bouanich* that from an EU law perspective it is "*open to a Member State to ensure the fulfilment of its obligations under the Treaty free movement provisions by means of provisions contained in a DTC.*"[1549] This understanding corresponds to the Member States' possibilities of how to adopt, within the framework of their national legal system, all the measures necessary to ensure that an EU directive is fully effective, in accordance with the objective that it pursues.[1550] According to Article 288(3) TFEU, "*[a] directive shall be binding, as to the result to be achieved, upon each Member State to which it is addressed, but shall leave to the national authorities the choice of form and methods.*" Therefore, a Member State may also adopt the requirements of an EU directive by means of a double taxation convention[1551] if this form and method of implementation ensures the result to be achieved by the particular directive.[1552] If, for example, a Member State has concluded double taxation conventions with all other Member States, all of which provide for the exemption method with respect to (non-deductible) dividend payments that are covered by the Parent-Subsidiary Directive, the requirements of Article 4(1) Parent-Subsidiary Directive would be met. Moreover, considering *Bouanich*, there would be no conflict with the fundamental freedoms either, even if remaining domestic tax law did not provide for a tax exemption of cross-border inbound dividend distributions as compared to comparable dividend distributions in the same Member State.

The result might be different, however, if the discriminatory effect of a Member State's domestic legislation is not neutralized by the same Member State's obligations under a double taxation convention alone, but only when the overall impact of the tax treaty is considered. Generally, the ECJ does not take into account the tax treatment in

1549. Opinion of AG Geelhoed in *Test Claimants in Class IV of the ACT Group Litigation*, C-374/04, EU:C:2006:139, at point 70; also see E.C.C.M. Kemmeren, ECJ should not unbundle integrated tax systems!, 17 *EC Tax Rev.* 1 (2008), p. 4 (at p. 5); G. Kofler, Bouanich: Diskriminierende Bemessungsgrundlage und Doppelbesteuerungsabkommen, 19 *ÖStZ* 13 (2006), p. 290 (at p. 292); G. Kofler, *Doppelbesteuerungsabkommen und Europäisches Gemeinschaftsrecht* (Linde, 2007), at p. 564.

1550. On the obligation to domestically implement EU directives see Judgment in *Royer*, 48/75, EU:C:1976:57, at para. 73; Judgment in *Commission/Italy*, C-336/97, EU:C:1999:314, at para. 19; Judgment in *Commission/France*, C-97/00, EU:C:2001:149, at para. 9; Judgment in *Commission/Sweden*, C-478/99, EU:C:2002:281, at para. 15; Judgment in *Commission/France*, C-233/00; EU:C:2003:371, at para. 75; Judgment in *Commission/Italy*, C-456/03, EU:C:2005:388, at para. 50; Judgment in *Commission/Germany*, C-531/03, EU:C:2005:159, at para. 16; Judgment in *Kofoed*, C-321/05, EU:C:2007:408, at para. 41; also see G. Kofler in H. Schaumburg/J. Englisch (eds.), *Europäisches Steuerrecht* (Dr Otto Schmidt, 2015), at m.no 13.9-13.11; G. Kofler, Auslegung und Anwendung des harmonisierten Steuerrechts, 3 *ISR* 4 (2014), p. 126 (at p. 129).

1551. With regard to Article 4(2) Parent-Subsidiary Directive see G. Kofler, *Mutter-Tochter-Richtlinie – Kommentar* (LexisNexis, 2011), Artikel 4 at paras 36-37.

1552. Judgment in *Royer*, 48/75, EU:C:1976:57, at para. 73; Judgment in *Commission/France*, C-233/00, EU:C:2003:371, at para. 76; Judgment in *Commission/France*, C-296/01, EU:C:2003:626, at para. 55; Judgment in *Commission/Italy*, C-456/03, EU:C:2005:388, at para. 51; Judgment in *Commission/Luxembourg*, C-32/05, EU:C:2006:749, at para. 34; Judgment in *Kofoed*, C-321/05, EU:C:2007:408, at para. 43; Judgment in *Danske Svineproducenter*, C-491/06, EU:C:2008.263, at para. 27; Order in *KBC Bank and Beleggen, Risicokapitaal, Beheer*, C-439/07 and C-499/07, EU:C:2009:339, at paras 49-50; Judgment in *Flachglas Torgau*, C-204/09, EU:C:2012:71, at para. 60; Judgment in *Commission/Poland*, C-29/14, EU:C:2015:379, at para. 38.

another country.[1553] Member States must provide for non-discriminatory treatment in their legal system, irrespective of the legal circumstances of the same taxable activity in other Member States.[1554] Even before *Bouanich* was decided, it had nevertheless been speculated in the literature whether the discriminatory effect of a Member State's domestic legislation may be neutralized by another Member State's obligation, due to a double taxation convention, to compensate for the resultant disadvantage.[1555] Initially, such a view was rejected by the EFTA Court in the *Fokus Bank* decision.[1556] According to former Norwegian domestic legislation, outbound dividend distributions were subject to a 15% withholding tax to be levied by the distributing company, whereas no such tax was triggered by intra-Norwegian dividend payments.[1557] However, the double taxation conventions concluded between the Netherlands, on the one hand, and Germany as well as the UK, on the other hand, provided for the avoidance of juridical double taxation by means of a tax credit, the amount of which, in principle, corresponds to the withholding tax levied by the other contracting state. Therefore, the question was raised whether Germany's and the UK's obligation to credit the Norwegian withholding tax on outbound dividends is legally significant for the examination of the Norwegian tax system's compliance with the EEA Agreement.[1558] The Norwegian State's representatives argued "*that the total tax on a foreign shareholder's dividends must be taken into account when comparing it to the situation of a Norwegian shareholder, including tax credits that the former may be granted in its home state. [...] [T]he investment choice of potential foreign shareholders is not adversely affected by the Norwegian legislation since the grant of tax credits in their home states keeps the overall*

1553. See Chapter 3.2.4.3. and Chapter 4.1.3.2.4.

1554. See A. Cordewener, *Europäische Grundfreiheiten und nationales Steuerrecht* (Dr Otto Schmidt, 2002), at pp. 828-831; J. Englisch, *Dividendenbesteuerung* (Dr Otto Schmidt, 2005), at p. 240; G. Kofler, *Doppelbesteuerungsabkommen und Europäisches Gemeinschaftsrecht* (Linde, 2007), at pp. 564-566.

1555. See G. Kofler, 5 *Hous. Bus. & Tax L. J.* 1 (2005), at pp. 74-78; G. Kofler, 17 *ÖStZ* 23 (2004), at pp. 561-562; B. Larking, Fokus Bank: The End of Withholding Tax as we Know It?, 14 *EC Tax Rev.* 2 (2005), p. 69 (at pp. 74-75); M. Tumpel in J. Pelka (ed.), *Europa- und verfassungsrechtliche Grenzen der Unternehmensbesteuerung*, DStJG 30 (Dr Otto Schmidt, 2000), at p. 344; R. van der Linde, 13 *EC Tax Rev.* 1 (2004), at p. 14; F. Wassermeyer in M. Lang/H. Loukota/A.J. Rädler/J. Schuch/G. Toifl/C. Urtz/F. Wassermeyer/M. Züger (eds.), *Multilateral Tax Treaties* (Linde, 1997), p. 15 (at p. 24).

1556. Judgment of the EFTA Court in *Fokus Bank*, E-1/04 (23 Nov. 2004); for an analysis of the judgment see A. Bullen, Norwegian Withholding Tax Contrary to Rules on Free Movement of Capital in EEA Agreement, *45 Eur. Taxn.* 2 (2005), p. 75 (at pp. 75-77); G. Kofler, EFTA-Gerichtshof: Besteuerung von "Auswärtsausschüttungen" unter der EWR-Kapitalverkehrsfreiheit, 18 *ÖStZ* 7 (2005), p. 143 (at pp. 143 et seq.); G. Kofler, *Doppelbesteuerungsabkommen und Europäisches Gemeinschaftsrecht* (Linde, 2007), at pp. 572-582; B. Larking, 14 *EC Tax Rev.* 2 (2005), at pp. 69-77; K. Simader, *Withholding Taxes and the Fundamental Freedoms* (Kluwer, 2014), at pp. 239-241; F. Zimmer, EFTA Court Strikes Down Norwegian Withholding Tax on Dividends, 36 *Tax Notes Intl. 10* (6 Dec. 2004), p. 840 (at pp. 840-843).

1557. Moreover, non-resident taxpayers were not able to claim the imputation tax credit that was granted to resident shareholders in order to avoid economic double taxation. On this issue see, for example, G. Kofler, *Doppelbesteuerungsabkommen und Europäisches Gemeinschaftsrecht* (Linde, 2007), at pp. 576-581; K. Simader, *Withholding Taxes and the Fundamental Freedoms* (Kluwer, 2014), at pp. 239-240.

1558. Judgment of the EFTA Court in *Fokus Bank*, E-1/04 (23 Nov. 2004), at para. 7.

tax burden constant."[1559] However, the EFTA Court rejected this argument:[1560] "*In that respect, it suffices to state that a restriction and discrimination, such as that resulting from the tax legislation at issue, can not be offset by advantages which shareholders may obtain in their countries of residence. As a general rule, and supposing that tax advantages do in fact exist, unfavourable tax treatment contrary to a fundamental freedom cannot be justified by the existence of such tax advantages [...]. A Contracting Party cannot shift its obligation to comply with the EEA Agreement to another Contracting Party by relying on the latter to make good for discrimination and disadvantages caused by the former's legislation. Likewise, the principle of legal certainty would require that the granting, or not, of an imputation tax credit to a non-resident shareholder, may not depend on whether a tax credit is granted in his or her state of residence in respect of dividend payments.*"

In contrast to the EFTA Court, the ECJ took a more liberal approach:[1561] In *Denkavit*,[1562] the ECJ had to deal with the former French legislation according to which the payment of dividends by a resident subsidiary to a non-resident parent company was subject to a withholding tax, whereas no such tax was levied upon the distribution of dividends by a resident subsidiary to a resident parent company. However, the double taxation convention between France and the Netherlands, which was applicable in the case concerned, provided for the credit method with regard to dividends. Therefore, a non-resident parent company of a French subsidiary was, in principle, authorized to offset the withholding tax levied by France against its tax liability in the Netherlands. From an overall perspective, it could be argued that a non-resident taxpayer is not adversely affected if the withholding tax levied by the source state reduces the tax liability in the residence state. Following previous judgments,[1563] the ECJ considered the applicable double taxation convention as part of the relevant legal framework, which has to be taken into account when assessing a discriminatory

1559. Judgment of the EFTA Court in *Fokus Bank*, E-1/04 (23 Nov. 2004), at para. 36; for the same reasoning see J. Englisch, 33 *Intertax* 5 (2005), at p. 210.
1560. Judgment of the EFTA Court in *Fokus Bank*, E-1/04 (23 Nov. 2004), at para. 37; also see T. Leegaard/A. Valat, Imputation Tax Credit under Free Movement of Capital (Art. 40 EEA Agreement), 44 *Eur. Taxn.* 4 (2004), p. 207 (at p. 210); critically G. Kofler, Einige Überlegungen gegen die DBA-Irrelevanzthese im Fokus Bank-Urteil, 18 *ÖStZ 8* (2005), p. 169 (at pp. 171-172); F. Zimmer, 36 *Tax Notes Intl. 10* (2004), at pp. 842-843; Opinion of AG Geelhoed in *Test Claimants in Class IV of the ACT Group Litigation*, C-374/04, EU:C:2006:139, at point 71 (FN 83).
1561. See K. Simader, *Withholding Taxes and the Fundamental Freedoms* (Kluwer, 2014), at p. 241.
1562. For an analysis of the judgment see E. Biebl, EuGH-Entscheidung Denkavit und ihre Folgen für die österreichische Quellenbesteuerung, 17 *SWI* 2 (2007), p. 65 (at pp. 65 et seq.); J. Delaurière, Does Denkavit Signal the End of Withholding Tax?, 45 *Tax Notes Intl.* 4 (2007), p. 303 (at pp. 303-311); T. Pons, The *Denkavit Internationaal* Case and Its Consequences: The Limit between Distortion and Discrimination?, 47 *Eur. Taxn.* 5 (2007), p. 214 (at pp. 214-220); A. Rainer, EC Tax Scene: ECJ Rules French Withholding Tax on Outbound Dividends Violates EC Treaty, 35 *Intertax* 2 (2007), p. 134 (at pp. 134-136); K. Simader, *Withholding Taxes and the Fundamental Freedoms* (Kluwer, 2014), at pp. 241-245; F. Vanistendael, *Denkavit Internationaal*: The Balance Between Fiscal Sovereignty and the Fundamental Freedoms?, 47 *Eur. Taxn.* 5 (2007), p. 210 (at pp. 210-211).
1563. Judgment in *Manninen*, C-319/02, EU:C:2004:484, at para. 21; Judgment in *Bouanich*, C-265/04, EU:C:2006:51, at para. 51; Judgment in *Test Claimants in Class IV of the ACT Group Litigation*, C-374/04, EU:C:2006:773, at para. 71.

treatment by the source state.[1564] However, since the Netherlands domestic legislation provided for a tax exemption with respect to foreign-source dividends, the tax credit provided for in the France-Netherlands double taxation convention did not improve the overall situation of the taxpayer concerned.[1565] Therefore, "*the combined application of the Franco-Netherlands Convention and the relevant Netherlands legislation does not serve to overcome the effects of the restriction on freedom of establishment*" that results from the French legislation by imposing a liability to tax on dividends paid to a non-resident parent company while allowing resident parent companies almost full exemption from such a tax.[1566] Although the Court hence seemed to be open to considering the effects of the double taxation convention, in fact, the discrimination resulting from the French legislation was not neutralized.[1567]

In *Amurta*,[1568] the ECJ has refined its position concerning the neutralization of discrimination resulting from a withholding tax obligation in the source state by the residence state. According to former Netherlands law, certain outbound dividends were subject to a withholding tax, while no such tax was imposed on comparable resident recipients of a dividend payment.[1569] It was, *inter alia*, argued that such a different treatment is justified by reasons relating to the cohesion of the tax system, "*since it is guaranteed under the DTC that dividend tax withheld in respect of an outbound dividend is deductible from the corporation tax due from the recipient company in Portugal.*"[1570] Although this argument was rejected,[1571] the ECJ has confirmed that "*it cannot be excluded that a Member State may succeed in ensuring compliance with its obligations under the Treaty through the conclusion of a convention for the avoidance of double taxation with another Member State [...]. However, [...] [i]t is [...] for the national court to establish whether account should be taken, in the main proceedings, of the DTC, and, if so, to determine whether that convention enables the*

1564. Judgment in *Denkavit Internationaal and Denkavit France*, C-170/05, EU:C:2006:783, at para. 45.
1565. See M. Helminen, 48 *Eur. Taxn.* 7 (2008), at p. 355; K. Simader, *Withholding Taxes and the Fundamental Freedoms* (Kluwer, 2014), at pp. 242-245.
1566. Judgment in *Denkavit Internationaal and Denkavit France*, C-170/05, EU:C:2006:783, at paras 46-56.
1567. See L.A. Denys, 47 *Eur. Taxn.* 5 (2007), at p. 231; E.C.C.M. Kemmeren, 17 *EC Tax Rev.* 1 (2008), at p. 6; G. Kofler/M. Tumpel, Amurta: Diskriminierende Quellenbesteuerung und Anrechnungsmethode, 21 *ÖStZ* 3 (2008), p. 54 (at p. 56); K. Simader in M. Lang/J. Schuch/C. Staringer (eds.), *Quellensteuern* (Linde, 2010), at p. 41; K. Simader, *Withholding Taxes and the Fundamental Freedoms* (Kluwer, 2014), at p. 251.
1568. For an analysis of the judgment see J. Bellingwout, *Amurta*: A Tribute to (the Late) Advocate General Geelhoed, 48 *Eur. Taxn.* 3 (2008), p. 124 (at pp. 126-132); E. Biebl, EuGH in der Rs. *Amurta*: Einschränkung der Kapitalverkehrsfreiheit durch Quellen-steuer auf Outbound-Dividenden, 18 *SWI* 1 (2008), p. 29 (at pp. 29 et seq.); J. Englisch, Quellensteuerabzug bei Dividenden, die an eine ausländische Empfängergesellschaft ausgeschüttet werden, 16 *IStR* 23 (2007), p. 854 (at pp. 858-860); G. Kofler/M. Tumpel, 21 *ÖStZ* 3 (2008), at pp. 54 et seq.; A. Rainer, Quellensteuerabzug bei Dividenden, die an eine ausländische Empfängergesellschaft ausgeschüttet werden, 16 *IStR* (2007), p. 854 (at pp. 860-861); K. Simader, *Withholding Taxes and the Fundamental Freedoms* (Kluwer, 2014), at pp. 245-247.
1569. Judgment in *Amurta*, C-379/05, EU:C:2007:655, at paras 26-27.
1570. Judgment in *Amurta*, C-379/05, EU:C:2007:655, at para. 45 and paras 69-72.
1571. Judgment in *Amurta*, C-379/05, EU:C:2007:655, at para. 52 and paras 81-83.

effects of the restriction on the free movement of capital identified in the context of the reply to the first question, in paragraph 28 of this judgment, to be neutralised."[1572]

From *Denkavit* and *Amurta* one can infer that the ECJ, in principle, accepts a neutralization of the discriminatory effect of a Member State's domestic legislation by another Member State's obligation, due to a double taxation convention, to compensate for the resulting disadvantage.[1573] The Court has by now emphasized that "*[i]t is [...] necessary for that purpose that application of the double taxation convention allow the effects of the difference in treatment under national legislation to be compensated for. The difference in treatment between dividends distributed to companies established in other Member States and those distributed to resident companies does not totally disappear unless the tax withheld at source under national legislation can be set off against the tax due in the other Member State in the full amount of the difference in treatment arising under the national legislation.*"[1574] If the income is not sufficiently taxed in the residence state of the taxpayer, for example, because of a domestic tax exemption,[1575] differences in the taxable base (net taxation vs gross taxation),[1576] a limitation of the creditable amount (full credit vs ordinary credit),[1577] or due to overall losses,[1578] the residence state may not be able to neutralize the source state's discrimination.[1579] However, it may be argued that even in such situations a neutralization of the discriminatory effect of the source state's domestic legislation is possible. This would require that the residence state grant a refund with regard to[1580] or a

1572. Judgment in *Amurta*, C-379/05, EU:C:2007:655, at paras 79-83; also see Judgment in *Commission/Italy*, C-540/07, EU:C:2009:717, at para. 36; Judgment in *Commission/Spain*, C-487/08, EU:C:2010:310, at para. 58; Judgment in *Secilpar*, C-199/10, EU:C:2010:706, at paras 39-41; Judgment in *Commission/Germany*, C-284/09, EU:C:2011:670, at para. 62; Judgment in *Miljoen*, C-10/14, C-14/14 and C-17/14, EU:C:2015:608, at paras 78-80.

1573. See M. Helminen, 48 *Eur. Taxn.* 7 (2008), at p. 355; G. Kofler, 65 *Bull. Intl. Taxn.* 12 (2011), at p. 685; K. Simader, *Withholding Taxes and the Fundamental Freedoms* (Kluwer, 2014), at p. 247.

1574. Judgment in *Commission/Italy*, C-540/07, EU:C:2009:717, at para. 37; also see Judgment in *Commission/Spain*, C-487/08, EU:C:2010:310, at para. 59; Judgment in *Secilpar*, C-199/10, EU:C:2010:706, at para. 40; Judgment in *Commission/Germany*, C-284/09, EU:C:2011:670, at para. 63; Judgment in *Miljoen*, C-10/14, C-14/14 and C-17/14, EU:C:2015:608, at para. 79.

1575. Judgment in *Denkavit Internationaal and Denkavit France*, C-170/05, EU:C:2006:783, at paras 46-47.

1576. See A. Fortuin, *Commission v. Spain*. Failure to fulfil obligations. Dividends distributed to resident and non-resident companies. Court of Justice, 3 *H&I* 9 (2010), p. 61 (at p. 62).

1577. See G. Kofler, 65 *Bull. Intl. Taxn.* 12 (2011), at pp. 688-689; K. Simader, *Withholding Taxes and the Fundamental Freedoms* (Kluwer, 2014), at pp. 252-255; also see Opinion of AG Mengozzi in *Amurta*, C-379/05, EU:C:2007:323, at points 87-89.

1578. See T. Pons, The *Denkavit Internationaal* Case and Its Consequences: The Limit Between Distortion and Discrimination?, 47 *Eur. Taxn.* 5 (2007), p. 214 (at p. 218).

1579. Judgment in *Commission/Italy*, C-540/07, EU:C:2009:717, at para. 38; Judgment in *Commission/Spain*, C-487/08, EU:C:2010:310, at para. 62; Judgment in *Commission/Germany*, C-284/09, EU:C:2011:670, at para. 68; Judgment in *Miljoen*, C-10/14, C-14/14 and C-17/14, EU:C:2015:608, at para. 86.

1580. See E. Biebl, 18 *SWI* 1 (2008), pp. 33-34; J. Englisch, 38 *Intertax* 4 (2010), at p. 219; M. Lang, Zum Seminar G: Verbietet das Gemeinschaftsrecht die Erhebung von Quellensteuern?, 18 *IStR* 15 (2009), p. 539 (at p. 540); K. Simader in M. Lang/J. Schuch/C. Staringer (eds.), *Quellensteuern* (Linde, 2010), at p. 42; J. Bellingwout, 48 *Eur. Taxn.* 3 (2008), at p. 129; K. Simader, *Withholding Taxes and the Fundamental Freedoms* (Kluwer, 2014), at pp. 255-258.

carry-forward of[1581] taxes that are not creditable due to a lack of sufficiently taxed income.[1582] Moreover, in case the residence state only partially provides for a compensation, it is questionable whether the source state may take care of the remaining discriminatory effect,[1583] for example, by granting a refund to the extent the taxes are not creditable in or refunded by the residence state.[1584] Since the ECJ has not yet been confronted with these issues, the concrete conditions which have to be met by a Member State in order to "*succeed in ensuring compliance with its obligations under the Treaty by concluding a convention for the avoidance of double taxation with another Member State*"[1585] still remain unclear.

1.3.2 Economic Double Taxation

1.3.2.1 The (Apparent) Resemblance of Economic and Juridical Double Taxation from an EU Law Perspective

An important difference between juridical and economic double taxation is that the former phenomenon generally arises only in a cross-border context, whereas the latter frequently also occurs in a purely domestic situation.[1586] However, both phenomena have in common that they were intensively addressed by the ECJ in its jurisprudence regarding the fundamental freedoms. With regard to economic double taxation, the

1581. See G. Kofler, 18 *ÖStZ 8* (2005), at p. 172 (FN 44); G. Kofler/M. Tumpel, 21 *ÖStZ* 3 (2008), at p. 57 (FN 34); G. Kofler, 65 *Bull. Intl. Taxn.* 12 (2011), at p. 689; K. Simader, *Withholding Taxes and the Fundamental Freedoms* (Kluwer, 2014), at p. 258.
1582. See Opinion of AG Kokott in *X.*, C-498/10, EU:C:2011:870, at point 65; sceptical J. Bellingwout, 48 *Eur. Taxn.* 3 (2008), at p. 129.
1583. See J. Bellingwout, 48 *Eur. Taxn.* 3 (2008), at p. 130; W. Loukota, *EG-Grundfreiheiten und beschränkte Steuerpflicht* (Linde, 2006), at p. 276; G. Kofler, 65 *Bull. Intl. Taxn.* 12 (2011), at p. 689; D.E. Van Sprundel, An Analysis of the Netherlands Dividend Withholding Tax on Shares – No Need to Abolish This Tax Yet?, 48 *Eur. Taxn.* 12 (2008), p. 607 (at p. 614); also see VwGH 23. 9. 2010, 2008/15/0086; contra K. Simader, *Withholding Taxes and the Fundamental Freedoms* (Kluwer, 2014), at p. 251.
1584. According to s. 21(1)(1a) of the Austrian Corporate Income Tax Act, for example, certain non-resident shareholders may claim a refund of Austrian withholding tax on outbound dividends insofar as no tax treaty credit for the withholding tax is available in the residence state of the shareholder. See G. Kofler, Austria: Changes to Austria's Tax Treatment of Outbound Inter-Company Dividends, 18 *EC Tax Rev.* 6 (2009), p. 312 (at pp. 313-314); G. Kofler, 65 *Bull. Intl. Taxn.* 12 (2011), at p. 689.
1585. Judgment in *Amurta*, C-379/05, EU:C:2007:655, at para. 79; Judgment in *Commission/Italy*, C-540/07, EU:C:2009:717, at para. 36; Judgment in *Commission/Spain*, C-487/08, EU:C:2010:310, at para. 58; Judgment in *Secilpar*, C-199/10, EU:C:2010:706, at para. 39; Judgment in *Commission/Germany*, C-284/09, EU:C:2011:670, at para. 62.
1586. See G. Kofler, *Doppelbesteuerungsabkommen und Europäisches Gemeinschaftsrecht* (Linde, 2007), at p. 155; G. Kofler in A. Rust (ed.), *Double Taxation within the European Union* (Kluwer, 2011), at p. 106; W. Hellerstein/G. Kofler/R. Mason, 62 *Tax L. Rev.* 1 (2008), at p. 7; V. Heydt in W. Haslehner/G. Kofler/A. Rust (eds.), *Landmark Decisions of the ECJ in Direct Taxation* (Kluwer, 2015), at p. 181; also cf. J. Englisch, 33 *Intertax* 8/9 (2005), at p. 323; but see B.J.M. Terra/P.J. Wattel, *European Tax Law*[6] (Kluwer, 2012), at p. 1046; E. Traversa/C. Helleputte in M. Lang/P. Melz/E. Kristoffersson (eds.), *Value Added Tax and Direct Taxation* (IBFD, 2009), at p. 340 ("*juridical double taxation is rare in the national context*"); P. Wattel in G. Maisto (ed.), *Taxation of Intercompany Dividends under Tax Treaties and EU Law* (IBFD, 2012).

most illustrative example arises when profits are earned by a company and subsequently distributed to its shareholders. In the past, many Member States granted relief from economic double taxation only in the case of purely domestic dividend distributions.[1587] Unsurprisingly, it had been increasingly questioned in the literature whether domestically-aligned relief mechanisms are in line with the fundamental freedoms.[1588] The European Commission correctly highlighted that these concerns not only pertain to the shareholder's Member State of residence, but also to the Member State of the distributing company.[1589] After all, the discriminatory effect is due to the interaction of taxing both the company upon making profits and the shareholder upon receiving (parts of) this profit via a dividend distribution.

However, if relief from economic double taxation had to be granted by both the shareholder's Member State of residence and the Member State of the distributing company, the profits earned by the company and received by the shareholder via a dividend could even remain effectively untaxed.[1590] Such consequences could be avoided if only one Member State was obliged to avoid economic double taxation.[1591]

1587. See H.J. Ault, 47 *Tax L. Rev.* 2 (1992), at p. 579; P. Farmer/R. Lyal, *EC Tax Law* (Clarendon Press, 1994), at pp. 251-252; G. Kofler, *Doppelbesteuerungsabkommen und Europäisches Gemeinschaftsrecht* (Linde, 2007), at pp. 941 and 971; O.H. Jacobs, 27 *Intertax* 8/9 (1999), at pp. 271-272; S. Lodin, 7 *EC Tax Rev.* 4 (1998), at p. 229.

1588. See, for example, N. Dautzenberg, Die Ertragsbesteuerung des Kapitaleinkommens in der EU: Zur Bedeutung des Begriffs "Kapitalanlageort" in Art. 73 d EGV, 8 *EWS* 11 (1997), p. 379 (at p. 383); B. Knobbe-Keuk, Ist das deutsche Körperschaftsteueranrechnungsverfahren zu halten?, in P. Kirchhof/K. Offerhaus/H. Schöberle (eds.), *Steuerrecht Verfassungsrecht Finanzpolitik*, Festschrift für Franz Klein (Dr Otto Schmidt, 1994), p. 347 (at pp. 351-352); H. Liede/L. Hintsanen, 43 *Eur. Taxn.* 1 (2003), at pp. 31-35; S. Lodin, 7 *EC Tax Rev.* 4 (1998), at pp. 220-238; K. Ståhl, Dividend Taxation in a Free Capital Market, 6 *EC Tax Rev.* 4 (1997), p. 227 (at pp. 227-236); C. Staringer, Auslandsdividenden und Kapitalverkehrsfreiheit, 13 *ÖStZ* 2 (2000), p. 26 (pp. 27-31); C. Staringer in E. Lechner/C. Staringer/M. Tumpel (eds.), *Kapitalverkehrsfreiheit und Steuerrecht* (Linde, 2000), at pp. 99-112; W. Schön in W. Schön (ed.), *Gedächtnisschrift für Brigitte Knobbe-Keuk* (Dr Otto Schmidt, 1997), at pp. 774-776; M. Tumpel in J. Pelka (ed.), *Europa- und verfassungsrechtliche Grenzen der Unternehmensbesteuerung*, DStJG 30 (Dr Otto Schmidt, 2000), at pp. 358-361; G. Toifl, Besteuerung ausländischer Dividendeneinkünfte und Kapitalverkehrsfreiheit, 12 *SWI* 10 (2002), p. 458 (at pp. 458-466); M. Tumpel, Zweifel des Verwaltungsgerichtshofes an der Vereinbarkeit der Dividenden-besteuerung in Österreich mit der Kapitalverkehrsfreiheit, 12 *SWI* 10 (2002), p. 454 (at pp. 454-457); K. van Raad, The Impact of the EC Treaty's Fundamental Freedoms Provisions on EC Member States' Taxation in Border-Crossing Situations – Current State of Affairs, 4 *EC Tax Rev.* 4 (1995), p. 190 (at pp. 200-201); G. Toifl, Verstößt die Beschränkung der Endbesteuerung auf inländische Kapitalerträge gegen die Kapitalverkehrsfreiheit nach Art. 73b EGV?, 9 *SWI* 6 (1999), p. 255 (at pp. 255-257).

1589. Communication from the Commission to the Council, the European Parliament and the European Economic and Social Committee, *Dividend Taxation of Individuals in the Internal Market*, COM(2003) 810 final (19 Dec. 2003), at p. 20; also see J. Englisch, Fiscal Cohesion in the Taxation of Cross-Border Dividends (Part One), 44 *Eur. Taxn.* 7 (2004), p. 323 (at p. 327); J. Englisch, 33 *Intertax* 5 (2005), at p. 201; J. Englisch, 51 *RIW* 3 (2005), at pp. 187-188; C. Staringer in E. Lechner/C. Staringer/M. Tumpel (eds.), *Kapitalverkehrsfreiheit und Steuerrecht* (Linde, 2000), at p. 116.

1590. See J. Englisch, 44 *Eur. Taxn.* 8 (2004), at p. 363; W. Schön in W. Schön (ed.), *Gedächtnisschrift für Brigitte Knobbe-Keuk* (Dr Otto Schmidt, 1997), at pp. 775-776; C. Staringer in E. Lechner/C. Staringer/M. Tumpel (eds.), *Kapitalverkehrsfreiheit und Steuerrecht* (Linde, 2000), at p. 117.

1591. Cf. G. Kofler, *Doppelbesteuerungsabkommen und Europäisches Gemeinschaftsrecht* (Linde, 2007), at p. 978.

This question resembles the discussion on whether the fundamental freedoms can be invoked by a taxpayer in order to overcome the problem of juridical double taxation. It, therefore, could be concluded that economic double taxation results from the exercise in parallel by two Member States of their fiscal sovereignty and, hence, cannot be tackled by means of the fundamental freedoms.[1592] However, in contrast to its case law on juridical double taxation, the ECJ has struck a different path.

1.3.2.2 *The Obligation of the Shareholder's Member State of Residence to Avoid Bilaterally-Caused Economic Double Taxation*

Before the ECJ had to decide on the fundamental freedoms' impact on the tax treatment of foreign-source dividends in the shareholder's Member State of residence for the first time, it had already been settled case law that the fundamental freedoms are not only aimed at ensuring that foreign nationals are treated in the host Member States in the same way as nationals, but also prohibit the Member State of origin from hindering its residents from extending their business activities to cross-border situations.[1593] It was, therefore, only a matter of time before the ECJ was confronted with shareholders claiming relief from economic double taxation for foreign-source dividends by referring to the corresponding tax treatment of dividends paid by a domestic company.

The first case was referred to the Court in 2000. In *Verkooijen*, the Netherlands tax system on cross-border dividends was put to the test. Whereas domestic dividends received by individuals only had to be taxed if the received payment exceeded a certain threshold, foreign-source dividends did not qualify for this tax-exempt amount. According to the ECJ, this different treatment "*has the effect of dissuading nationals of a Member State residing in the Netherlands from investing their capital in companies which have their seat in another Member State*" and "*constitutes an obstacle to the raising of capital in the Netherlands since the dividends which such companies pay to Netherlands residents receive less favourable tax treatment than dividends distributed by a company established in the Netherlands.*"[1594] Although the Court held that such a different treatment of domestic and cross-border dividend distributions may be compatible with the fundamental freedoms, if they "*are not objectively comparable,*"[1595] it

1592. See E. Reimer, Germany, 40 *Eur. Taxn.* 1 (2000), p. 48 (at p. 50).
1593. Judgment in *Daily Mail and General Trust*, 81/87, EU:C:1988:456, at para. 16; Judgment in *Masgio*, C-10/90, EU:C:1991:107, at para. 18; Judgment in *Imperial Chemical Industries*, C-264/96, EU:C:1998:370, at para. 21; Judgment in *X and Y*, C-200/98, EU:C:1999:566, at para. 26; Judgment in *Baars*, C-251/98, EU:C:2000:205, at para. 28.
1594. Judgment in *Verkooijen*, C-35/98, EU:C:2000:294, at para. 34.
1595. Judgment in *Verkooijen*, C-35/98, EU:C:2000:294, at para. 43; Judgment in *Lenz*, C-315/02, EU:C:2004:446, at para. 27; Judgment in *Manninen*, C-319/02, EU:C:2004:484, at para. 29; Judgment in *Test Claimants in the FII Group Litigation*, C-446/04, EU:C:2006:774, at para. 46; Judgment in *Orange European Smallcap Fund*, C-194/06, EU:C:2008:289, at para. 59; Judgment in *Haribo Lakritzen Hans Riegel*, C-436/08 and C-437/08, EU:C:2011:61, at para. 58; Judgment in *Accor*, C-310/09, EU:C:2011:581, at para. 44; Judgment in *Kronos International*, C-47/12, EU:C:2014:2200, at para. 69.

did not enlarge upon the question of, implicitly presumed, comparability.[1596] This is insofar surprising as it was disputed in the literature whether domestic and cross-border dividend distributions are actually comparable. A Member State could argue, for example, that the corporate income tax of the company and the personal income tax of the shareholder complement each other.[1597] Thus, the tax on income earned by an individual through establishing a company is collected partly from the company and partly from the shareholders. If shareholders were not treated differently, depending on whether they receive domestic or cross-border dividend distributions, different situations would be treated alike. With regard to a purely domestic situation, a Member State can subject the income earned by an individual through establishing a company to corporate income tax as well as personal income tax. By contrast, in a cross-border situation, the shareholder's Member State of residence is generally limited to taxing the dividend distribution at the level of the shareholder.[1598] In order to ensure that the income earned by an individual through establishing a company is subject to the same *domestic* tax burden in the shareholder's Member State of residence, irrespective of whether the company was established in the same or in another state, the lack of a possibility to tax the income at the level of the foreign company has to be compensated for by subjecting shareholders receiving cross-border dividends to a higher tax burden than shareholders receiving dividends from a domestic company.[1599]

Although this reasoning was put forth by some Member States,[1600] the Court has never been responsive to it. It rather focussed on the underlying motive of dividend

1596. This examination pattern is insofar remarkable as the comparability analysis is usually part of assessing whether the national tax provision at issue constitutes a discriminatory restriction to the fundamental freedoms (see, for example, Judgment in *Schumacker*, C-279/93, EU:C:1995:31, at para. 30; Judgment in *Wielockx*, C-80/94, EU:C:1995:271, at para. 17; Judgment in *Asscher*, C-107/94, EU:C:1996:251, at para. 40; Judgment in *Royal Bank of Scotland*, C-311/97, EU:C:1999:216, at para. 26; Judgment in *Gschwind*, C-391/97, EU:C:1999:409, at para. 21; Order in *Mertens*, C-431/01, EU:C:2002:492, at para. 32). In its judgments on inbound dividends, however, the comparability analysis is discussed as a possible justification of such a restriction (critically J. Englisch, Kapitalertragsteuer: Unterschiedliche Besteuerung von inländischen Kapitalerträgen und von Kapitalerträgen aus einem anderen Mitgliedstaat, 13 *IStR* 15 [2004], p. 526 [at p. 527]; J. Englisch, 38 *Intertax* 4 [2010], at pp. 202-203; G. Kofler, *Doppelbesteuerungsabkommen und Europäisches Gemeinschaftsrecht* [Linde, 2007], at pp. 989-990).

1597. See C. Staringer, 13 *ÖStZ* 2 (2000), at p. 30.

1598. This limitation does not apply, though, if the profits of the company have a nexus to the shareholder's Member State of residence, which would lead to the company being subject to limited tax liability in that state. See also W. Hellerstein/G. Kofler/R. Mason, 62 *Tax L. Rev.* 1 (2008), at p. 19 (FN 101).

1599. See C. Staringer in E. Lechner/C. Staringer/M. Tumpel (eds.), *Kapitalverkehrsfreiheit und Steuerrecht* (Linde, 2000), at p. 108; also cf. J. Englisch, 13 *IStR* 15 (2004), at p. 527; J. Englisch, 51 *RIW* 3 (2005), at p. 192; J. Englisch, 33 *Intertax* 5 (2005), at p. 210; G. Kofler, *Doppelbesteuerungsabkommen und Europäisches Gemeinschaftsrecht* (Linde, 2007), at p. 1005.

1600. Judgment in *Lenz*, C-315/02, EU:C:2004:446, at para. 28; Judgment in *Manninen*, C-319/02, EU:C:2004:484, at para. 30.

relief mechanisms, which are "*designed to attenuate,*"[1601] "*to mitigate*"[1602] or "*to prevent*"[1603] "*the economic effects of double taxation of company profits arising from the taxation of company profits by way of corporation tax and the taxation of a shareholder who is a taxpayer, by way of income tax, on the same profits distributed in the form of dividends.*"[1604] As profits distributed by non-resident companies and profits distributed by domestic companies are likewise "*capable of being subjected to double taxation,*"[1605] domestic and cross-border dividend distributions are comparable from the perspective of a fully taxable shareholder.[1606]

This approach is subject to criticism.[1607] It is argued that there are at least two reasons why the Member State's legislative aims should not influence the Court's comparability analysis, but should rather "*be reserved for the justification assessment*":[1608] First, the motives underlying national tax provisions might be quite complex and maybe even ambiguous, if not conflicting. Within the justification analysis, the resultant legal uncertainty could be considerably reduced, because "*there exists an established case law on legitimate mandatory reasons and [...] the Member State must prove that its taxation rules really serve the alleged reasons.*"[1609] However, albeit it is certainly true that it can be very difficult to objectively identify a national measure's aim(s), this challenge does not become any less by shifting it from the comparability to the justification analysis; or *vice versa*. Either way, identifying a national measure's objective is not – or should not be – a matter for the ECJ. With regard to preliminary

1601. Judgment in *Lenz*, C-315/02, EU:C:2004:446, at para. 30.
1602. Judgment in *Test Claimants in the FII Group Litigation*, C-446/04, EU:C:2006:774, at para. 62; Judgment in *Haribo Lakritzen Hans Riegel*, C-436/08 and C-437/08, EU:C:2011:61, at para. 59; Judgment in *Accor*, C-310/09, EU:C:2011:581, at para. 45.
1603. Judgment in *Manninen*, C-319/02, EU:C:2004:484, at para. 33; Judgment in *Test Claimants in the FII Group Litigation*, C-446/04, EU:C:2006:774, at para. 62; Judgment in *Meilicke and others*, C-292/04, EU:C:2007:132, at para. 21; Judgment in *Haribo Lakritzen Hans Riegel*, C-436/08 and C-437/08, EU:C:2011:61, at para. 59; Judgment in *Accor*, C-310/09, EU:C:2011:581, at para. 45.
1604. Judgment in *Lenz*, C-315/02, EU:C:2004:446, at para. 30.
1605. Judgment in *Manninen*, C-319/02, EU:C:2004:484, at para. 35; also see Judgment in *Lenz*, C-315/02, EU:C:2004:446, at para. 31; Judgment in *Haribo Lakritzen Hans Riegel*, C-436/08 and C-437/08, EU:C:2011:61, at para. 59.
1606. Judgment in *Lenz*, C-315/02, EU:C:2004:446, at paras 32-33; Judgment in *Manninen*, C-319/02, EU:C:2004:484, at paras 36-37; Judgment in *Test Claimants in the FII Group Litigation*, C-446/04, EU:C:2006:774, at para. 62; Judgment in *Orange European Smallcap Fund*, C-194/06, EU:C:2008:289, at para. 40; Judgment in *Haribo Lakritzen Hans Riegel*, C-436/08 and C-437/08, EU:C:2011:61, at para. 59; Judgment in *Meilicke and others*, C-262/09, EU:C:2011:438, at para. 30; Judgment in *Accor*, C-310/09, EU:C:2011:581, at para. 45; Judgment in *Santander Asset Management SGIIC*, C-338/11 to C-347/11, EU:C:2012:286, at para. 42; Judgment in *Test Claimants in the FII Group Litigation*, C-35/11, EU:C:2012:707, at para. 37; Judgment in *Emerging Markets Series of DFA Investment Trust Company*, C-190/12, EU:C:2014:249, at para. 58; also cf. Judgment in *Masco Denmark and Damixa*, C-593/14, EU:C:2016:984, at para. 31.
1607. See J. Englisch, 13 *IStR* 15 (2004), at p. 527; J. Englisch, *Dividendenbesteuerung* (Dr Otto Schmidt, 2005), at p. 343; J. Englisch, 38 *Intertax* 4 (2010), at pp. 202-204; J. Englisch, 33 *Intertax* 5 (2005), at pp. 208-210; J. Englisch, 33 *Intertax* 8/9 (2005), at pp. 320-321; G. Kofler, *Doppelbesteuerungsabkommen und Europäisches Gemeinschaftsrecht* (Linde, 2007), at p. 998.
1608. J. Englisch, 38 *Intertax* 4 (2010), at p. 203; also see J. Englisch, 13 *IStR* 15 (2004), at p. 527; J. Englisch, 33 *Intertax* 5 (2005), at p. 210; J. Englisch, 33 *Intertax* 8/9 (2005), at p. 320.
1609. J. Englisch, 33 *Intertax* 5 (2005), at p. 210.

ruling procedures, it is settled case law that "*[t]he identification of the objectives in fact pursued by the national legislation is, in the context of a case referred to the Court under Article 267 TFEU, within the jurisdiction of the referring court.*"[1610] If the necessary information is not submitted by the national court, the ECJ might indeed still rely on the arguments raised by the European Commission, by the Member State concerned and by other intervening parties. However, unless the referring court which is called to interpret national law reveals the underlying motives of the scrutinized measure, there is always the danger that they "*might be misconceived by the ECJ.*"[1611] This is especially the case if the Court autonomously determines a scrutinized measure's objective by, for example, relying on "*[t]he documents before the Court.*"[1612] Still, correctly identifying a national measure's objective may pose problems, irrespective of whether it is done within the comparability or the justification analysis.

Second, a comparability analysis that is based on the scrutinized measure's objective increases the Member States' leeway to introduce differentiating provisions. The different treatment of domestic and cross-border situations would "*always have to be accepted insofar as it serves the – legitimate – objective of the national legislator,*"[1613] because domestic and cross-border situations could no longer be considered to be comparable. But if there is no comparability, "*then, unlike in the context of considering a ground of justification, there is no examination of the proportionality of the difference in treatment of domestic and cross-border situations.*"[1614] For lack of comparability there is hence no room for a weighing and balancing of the internal market's objective of unrestrained free movement and the objective pursued by a Member State with a particular measure.[1615] This means that there are no constraints whatsoever on how different the situations that formed the basis of the comparison may be treated.[1616] Against this background, the ECJ should indeed refrain from its previous approach. Alternatively, the Court could follow AG Kokott, who emphasized that "*[f]or a finding of non-discrimination, it is not sufficient to point out that [...] citizens and foreign nationals are not in the same situation. It is also necessary to demonstrate that the difference in their respective situations is capable of justifying the difference in treatment. In other words, the difference in treatment must relate and be proportionate to the*

1610. Judgment in *Berlington Hungary and others*, C-98/14, EU:C:2015:386, at para. 57; also see Judgment in *Vanacker and Lesage*, C-37/92, EU:C:1993:836, at para. 7; Judgment in *X.*, C-60/02, EU:C:2004:10, at para. 58; Judgment in *Wilson*, C-506/04, EU:C:2006:587, at para. 34; Judgment in *Badischer Winzerkeller*, C-264/04, EU:C:2006:402, at para. 43; Judgment in *Krzysztof Peśla*, C-345/08, EU:C:2009:771, at paras 64-65; Judgment in *Winner Wetten*, C-409/06, EU:C:2010:503, at para. 35.
1611. J. Englisch, 38 *Intertax* 4 (2010), at p. 203.
1612. Judgment in *Lenz*, C-315/02, EU:C:2004:446, at para. 30.
1613. J. Englisch, 38 *Intertax* 4 (2010), at p. 203.
1614. Opinion of AG Kokott in *Nordea Bank Danmark*, C-48/13, EU:C:2014:153, at point 27.
1615. See J. Englisch, 33 *Intertax* 5 (2005), at p. 210.
1616. See M. Lang, 46 *Eur. Taxn.* 9 (2006), at p. 422; M. Lang, 18 *EC Tax Rev.* 3 (2009), at pp. 100-101; M. Lang in M. Hebig/K. Kaiser/K. Koschmieder/M. Oblau (eds.), *FS Wilhelm H. Wacker* (Erich Schmidt Verlag, 2006), at p. 369; K. Simader in M. Lang/J. Schuch/C. Staringer (eds.), *Quellensteuern* (Linde, 2010), at p. 28; K. Simader, *Withholding Taxes and the Fundamental Freedoms* (Kluwer, 2014), at p. 135; also cf. R. Lyal, 12 *EC Tax Rev.* 2 (2003), at p. 68.

difference in their respective situations."[1617] However, parts of the literature consider this approach to be "*rather odd,*"[1618] "*unpredictable in its outcome*"[1619] and "*impractical.*"[1620] It is hence suggested to completely disregard the legal situation in the particular Member State within the comparability analysis, but to only take it into account at the level of justification.[1621] Instead, comparability could, for example, be determined by relying on "*the objective [...]* inherent *to the fundamental freedoms. [...] [C]omparability of situations should therefore be assumed, as a rule, if there exists a certain degree of substitutability* between *the cross-border transaction at issue and similar but purely internal transactions.*"[1622] Despite this criticism, the basic conclusion that domestic- and foreign-source dividends are comparable coincides with the dominant view in the literature.[1623]

However, the comparability analysis is not the only controversial aspect within the discussion on whether foreign-source dividends also have to be granted relief from economic double taxation. Rather, it has regularly been pointed out that the interaction of company and shareholder taxation could be seen as a coherent whole.[1624] Indeed, there is no legal obligation to treat companies as independent taxpayers. Member States could also abstain from levying a corporate income tax and instead proportionally attribute the income of a company to its shareholders; as is typically done with respect to partnerships.[1625] However, many states consider this to be impractical from an economic as well as an administrative perspective.[1626] Still, against this background,

1617. Opinion of AG Kokott in *Truck Center*, C-282/07, EU:C:2008:513, at point 37; also see Opinion of AG Maduro in *Huber*, C-524/06, EU:C:2008:194, at point 7.
1618. J. Englisch, 38 *Intertax* 4 (2010), at p. 204.
1619. L. De Broe/N. Bammens, 18 *EC Tax Rev.* 3 (2009), at p. 136.
1620. N. Bammens, *The Principle of Non-Discrimination in International and European Tax Law* (IBFD, 2012), at p. 989.
1621. See J. Englisch, 13 *IStR* 15 (2004), at p. 527; J. Englisch, 33 *Intertax* 5 (2005), at p. 210; J. Englisch, 33 *Intertax* 8/9 (2005), at p. 320; J. Englisch, 38 *Intertax* 4 (2010), at p. 203.
1622. J. Englisch, 38 *Intertax* 4 (2010), at p. 203; also see J. Englisch, *Wettbewerbsgleichheit im grenzüberschreitenden Handel* (Mohr Siebeck, 2008), at pp. 285-298.
1623. See D. Witzel, Die europarechtlichen Anforderungen an die Besteuerung von Auslandsdividenden - Der Fall "Schmid" -, 11 *IStR* 22 (2002), p. 758 (at p. 760); J. Englisch, 44 *Eur. Taxn.* 7 (2004), at p. 325; also cf. C. Staringer, 13 *ÖStZ* 2 (2000), at p. 28; C. Staringer in E. Lechner/C. Staringer/M. Tumpel (eds.), *Kapitalverkehrsfreiheit und Steuerrecht* (Linde, 2000), at pp. 103-104. According to some authors, however, the comparability could also depend on the tax system of the foreign companies Member State of residence. See W. Schön in W. Schön (ed.), *Gedächtnisschrift für Brigitte Knobbe-Keuk* (Dr Otto Schmidt, 1997), at pp. 775-776; M. Tumpel in J. Pelka (ed.), *Europa- und verfassungsrechtliche Grenzen der Unternehmensbesteuerung*, DStJG 30 (Dr Otto Schmidt, 2000), at p. 358.
1624. See M.J. Graetz/C. Warren, Dividend Taxation in Europe: When the ECJ Makes Tax Policy, 44 *Common Market L. Rev.* 6 (2007), p. 1577 (at pp. 1596-1598); C. Staringer, 13 *ÖStZ* 2 (2000), at p. 30; C. Staringer in E. Lechner/C. Staringer/M. Tumpel (eds.), *Kapitalverkehrsfreiheit und Steuerrecht* (Linde, 2000), at p. 110; D. Weber, 34 *Intertax* 12 (2006), pp. 597-598; D. Weber, *In Search of a (New) Equilibrium Between Tax Sovereignty and the Freedom of Movement Within the EC* (Kluwer, 2006), at p. 30.
1625. See D. Gutmann, General Report, in D. Gutmann (ed.), *Corporate Income Tax Subjects* (IBFD, 2016), p. 1 (at p. 1); M. Lang/C. Staringer, General Report, in IFA (ed.), *Qualification of Taxable Entities and Treaty Protection*, CDFI 99B (Sdu, 2014), p. 17 (at pp. 26-27).
1626. See J. Hey in I. Ebling (ed.), *Besteuerung von Einkommen*, DStJG 24 (Dr Otto Schmidt, 2001), at pp. 217-218; H. Ruppe, *Die Steuerliche Doppelbelastung der Körperschaftsgewinne* (Jupiter-Verlag, 1967), pp. 133-134.

it could be argued that the corporate tax on the profits of the company merely serves as a pre-payment of the shareholder's income tax.[1627] Consequently, the taxation of distributed profits at the level of the shareholder should accommodate the difference between a lower corporate income tax rate and a higher personal income tax rate.[1628] From this perspective, the corporate income tax and the shareholder's income tax on distributed profits could be considered to be systematically interconnected. However, the ECJ typically recognizes such correlations of different provisions within a Member State's tax system only if "*a direct link is established between a tax advantage and the offsetting of that advantage by a particular tax levy.*"[1629]

Originally, the ECJ only accepted the principle of fiscal cohesion as a justification ground if "*a direct link existed, in the case of one and the same taxpayer, between the grant of a tax advantage and the offsetting of that advantage by a fiscal levy, both of which related to the same tax. Where there is no such direct link, because, for example, one is dealing with different taxes or the tax treatment of different taxpayers, the argument based on the coherence of the tax system cannot be relied upon.*"[1630] Thus, the asserted link between the taxation of a company's profit and of the subsequently distributed amount at the level of the shareholder would not be sufficient to justify a different treatment of domestic and cross-border profit distributions, because both different taxes and different taxpayers are involved. While this was indeed the ECJ's rationale for not accepting fiscal cohesion as a justification ground in *Verkooijen*,[1631] the Court additionally emphasized in *Lenz* that "*the Austrian tax legislation does not make the obtaining of the tax advantages at issue enjoyed by Austrian residents on their domestic revenue from capital dependent upon the taxation of the companies' profits by way of corporation tax.*"[1632] The latter extension may have been inspired by the Opinion of AG Kokott in *Manninen*, which was published a couple of months before *Lenz* was decided. Thus, "*strict adherence to the criterion of the same taxpayer may have arbitrary consequences in some circumstances [...]. In principle, the double taxation of corporate profits can be avoided in a number of ways. The corporation tax*

1627. Opinion of AG Geelhoed in *Test Claimants in the FII Group Litigation*, C-446/04, EU:C:2006:240, at point 5; also see M. Lang, 17 *EC Tax Rev.* 2 (2008), at p. 72; D. Weber, 34 *Intertax* 12 (2006), p. 597; D. Weber, *In Search of a (New) Equilibrium Between Tax Sovereignty and the Freedom of Movement Within the EC* (Kluwer, 2006), at p. 30.
1628. See C. Staringer, 13 *ÖStZ* 2 (2000), at p. 30.
1629. Opinion of AG Kokott in *Nordea Bank Danmark*, C-48/13, EU:C:2014:153; at point 43; also see Judgment in *Verkooijen*, C-35/98, EU:C:2000:294, at para. 57; Judgment in *Bosal*, C-168/01, EU:C:2003:479, at para. 29; Judgment in *Schilling and Fleck-Schilling*, C-209/01, EU:C:2003:610, at para. 41; Judgment in *Manninen*, C-319/02, EU:C:2004:484, at para. 42; Judgment in *Keller Holding*, C-471/04, EU:C:2006:143, at para. 40; Judgment in *Test Claimants in the Thin Cap Group Litigation*, C-524/04, EU:C:2007:161, at para. 68; Judgment in *Rewe Zentralfinanz*, C-347/04, EU:C:2007:194, at para. 62; Judgment in *Papillon*, C-418/07, EU:C:2008:659, at para. 44; Judgment in *Glaxo Wellcome*, C-182/08, EU:C:2009:559, at para. 79; Judgment in *DI. VI. Finanziaria di Diego della Valle & C.*, C-380/11, EU:C:2012:552, at para. 47; Judgment in *Welte*, C-181/12, EU:C:2013:662, at para. 59.
1630. Judgment in *Bosal*, C-168/01, EU:C:2003:479, at paras 29-30; also see Judgment in *Baars*, C-251/98, EU:C:2000:22, at para. 40; Judgment in *de Groot*, C-385/00, EU:C:2002:750, at para. 73; Judgment in *Schilling and Fleck-Schilling*, C-209/01, EU:C:2003:610, at para. 41.
1631. Judgment in *Verkooijen*, C-35/98, EU:C:2000:294, at para. 57.
1632. Judgment in *Lenz*, C-315/02, EU:C:2004:446, at para. 30.

can be fully offset when taxing the dividend (as with the Finnish model for domestic dividends) or the dividend can be exempted from income tax. In that case the one and only taxation occurs entirely at company level. However, the opposite is also conceivable, namely that only the undertaking's retained profits are subjected to corporation tax. Then the shareholder receives his dividend from untaxed income; it is taxed for the first time when he is assessed for income tax. Finally, taxes can be levied partly on the undertaking and partly on the recipient of the dividend, as under the half income tax method or what the Commission terms schedular systems. In the dispute in the main proceedings, in fact, only part of Mr Manninen's dividend is taxed in Finland; the other part consists of withholding tax retained by the undertaking in Sweden at the time of distribution. These examples show that it is relatively unimportant who is ultimately credited with the once-only tax payment – the undertaking or the shareholder – at least as long as the same tax rates are applied at both levels. In the case of the Finnish set-off model, one could also take the view, as does the referring court, that the undertaking ultimately pays a kind of advance dividend tax on behalf of the shareholder, in so far as it deducts corporation tax on corporate earnings that are subsequently distributed as dividends. These considerations suggest that, exceptionally, a link justifying the tax cohesion argument may exist if a charge on one taxpayer is offset by a relief for another. The preconditions for this are that:

- *the tax is levied, if not on the same taxpayer then at least on the same income or the same economic process; and*
- *the legal configuration of the system ensures that the advantage accrues to the one taxpayer only if the disadvantage to the other is real and in the same amount.*"[1633]

Even if the ECJ had already followed this more generous approach in *Verkooijen* and *Lenz*, it would not have been possible to successfully rely on the principle of fiscal cohesion. After all, the tax systems scrutinized in these cases did not provide for an *exact* correspondence between the tax burden on the company's profit and the tax advantage granted to the recipient of the subsequent distribution, but rather for a lump-sum relief from economic double taxation.[1634] In *Manninen*, on the other hand, the disputed Finnish imputation system would have met these requirements:[1635] Dividends distributed by Finnish or foreign quoted companies that were received by individual shareholders resident in Finland were taxed as revenue from capital at a rate of 29%. This tax rate corresponded to the corporate income tax rate levied on profits

1633. Opinion of AG Kokott in *Manninen*, C-319/02, EU:C:2004:164, at points 57-61.

1634. See J. Englisch, Europarechtswidrigkeit des finnischen Körperschaftsteueranrechnungsverfahrens, 13 *IStR* 19 (2004), p. 680 (at p. 685); J. Englisch, 33 *Intertax* 5 (2005), at p. 206; J. Englisch, 38 *Intertax* 4 (2010), at p. 207; W. Hellerstein/G. Kofler/R. Mason, 62 *Tax L. Rev.* 1 (2008), at p. 23; G. Kofler, *Doppelbesteuerungsabkommen und Europäisches Gemeinschaftsrecht* (Linde, 2007), at pp. 116 and 1012; B.J.M. Terra/P.J. Wattel, *European Tax Law*[6] (Kluwer, 2012), at p. 1051; also see Opinion of AG Kokott in *Manninen*, C-319/02, EU:C:2004:164, at points 62-63; also cf. M. Lang, 17 *EC Tax Rev.* 2 (2008), at p. 70.

1635. Opinion of AG Kokott in *Manninen*, C-319/02, EU:C:2004:164, at point 64.

earned by a Finnish resident company. In order to avoid economic double taxation of such revenue on the distribution of dividends, shareholders were entitled to a tax credit equal to $^{29}/_{71}$ ths of the amount of the dividends they received during the relevant tax period. Together with the amount of dividends received, this tax credit formed the tax base for the income tax levied on revenue from capital. As a result, the effective tax rate on profits earned by a Finnish resident company and distributed as a dividend to a Finnish resident shareholder was 29%. By contrast, a Finnish shareholder who received dividends from a Swedish company was not granted a tax credit for the underlying Swedish corporate income tax. If potential withholding taxes are ignored, the total amount of taxes on cross-border profit distributions was thus higher than in a purely domestic situation:[1636]

		Finnish Dividends	*Swedish Dividends*
	Corporate Income Tax Base	100.00	100.00
-	Corporate Income Tax (29%)	(29.00)	(29.00)
=	Dividend	71.00	71.00
+	Tax Credit	29.00	-
=	Shareholder Income Tax Base	100.00	71.00
-	Shareholder Income Tax (29%)	(29.00)	(20.59)
+	Tax Credit	29.00	-
=	Finnish Income Tax	0.00	20.59
	Total Tax on Underlying Profit	29.00	49.59
	Net Dividend	71.00	50.41

Since the Finnish tax credit is only granted if and to the extent the distributed profits were subjected to domestic corporate income tax, it was argued that, "*unlike in the case of the tax system examined in Verkooijen, there is [...] a direct link between the taxation of the company's profits and the tax credit granted to the shareholder receiving the dividends. [...] [I]f a tax credit were to be granted to the recipients of dividends paid by a Swedish company to shareholders who were fully taxable in Finland, the authorities of that Member State would be obliged to grant a tax advantage in relation to corporation tax that was not levied by that State, thereby threatening the cohesion of the national tax system.*"[1637] By conditionally accepting this argument,[1638] the ECJ implicitly suggested

1636. Opinion of AG Kokott in *Manninen*, C-319/02, EU:C:2004:164, at points 6-12; also see L. Hintsanen/K. Pettersson, The Implications of the ECJ Holding the Denial of Finnish Imputation Credits in Cross-Border Situations to Be Incompatible with the EC Treaty in the *Manninen* Case, 45 *Eur. Taxn.* 4 (2005), p. 130 (at pp. 130-131); H. Liede/L. Hintsanen, 43 *Eur. Taxn.* 1 (2003), at pp. 31-32; G. Kofler, Manninen: Kapitalverkehrsfreiheit verpflichtet zur grenzüberschreitenden Anrechnung ausländischer Körperschaftsteuer, 17 *ÖStZ* 24 (2004), p. 582 (at pp. 583-584); G. Kofler, *Doppelbesteuerungsabkommen und Europäisches Gemeinschaftsrecht* (Linde, 2007), at pp. 983-984; L. Mutén, ECJ Advocate General Issues Opinion on Finland's Imputation System, 33 *Tax Notes Intl.* 13 (29 Mar. 2004), p. 1154 (at pp. 1154-1155).

1637. Judgment in *Manninen*, C-319/02, EU:C:2004:484, at paras 40-41.

1638. Judgment in *Manninen*, C-319/02, EU:C:2004:484, at para. 45.

that a direct link may also exist within a Member State's tax system if different taxes and different taxpayers are involved.[1639] Still, the Court did not consider the Finnish system to be justified, because limiting the tax credit to dividends distributed by domestic companies "*does not appear to be necessary in order to preserve the cohesion of the Finnish tax system.*"[1640] The reason for this conclusion was that "*an argument based on the need to safeguard the cohesion of a tax system must be examined in the light of the objective pursued by the tax legislation in question.*"[1641] Since the ECJ considered the Finnish tax system to be "*designed to prevent double taxation of company profits distributed to shareholders,*"[1642] it concluded that "*the cohesion of that tax system is assured as long as the correlation between the tax advantage granted in favour of the shareholder and the tax due by way of corporation tax is maintained. Therefore, in a case such as that at issue in the main proceedings, the granting to a shareholder who is fully taxable in Finland and who holds shares in a company established in Sweden of a tax credit calculated by reference to the corporation tax owed by that company in Sweden would not threaten the cohesion of the Finnish tax system and would constitute a measure less restrictive of the free movement of capital than that laid down by the Finnish tax legislation.*"[1643]

1639. See J. Englisch, 13 *IStR* 19 (2004), at p. 685; J. Englisch, 33 *Intertax* 5 (2005), at p. 206; J. Englisch, 33 *Intertax* 8/9 (2005), at pp. 333-334; J. Englisch, 38 *Intertax* 4 (2010), at p. 207; G. Kofler, 17 *ÖStZ* 24 (2004), at p. 585; M. Lang, 17 *EC Tax Rev.* 2 (2008), at p. 69; D. Weber, 24 *EC Tax Rev.* 1 (2015), at pp. 51-52; also cf. M.J. Graetz/C. Warren, 44 *Common Market L. Rev.* 6 (2007), at p. 1598; W. Hellerstein/G. Kofler/R. Mason, 62 *Tax L. Rev.* 1 (2008), at p. 23; F. Vanistendael, Cohesion: the phoenix rises from his ashes, 14 *EC Tax Rev.* 5 (2005), p. 208 (at pp. 219-220); with doubts G. Kofler, Einige Überlegungen zur steuerlichen Kohärenz nach dem Urteil des EuGH in der Rs Manninen, 18 *ÖStZ* 1/2 (2005), p. 26 (at p. 28) and G. Kofler, *Doppelbesteuerungsabkommen und Europäisches Gemeinschaftsrecht* (Linde, 2007), at p. 1014, who points out that the ECJ has emphasized that "*[t]he end result of such a system is that dividends are no longer taxed in the hands of the shareholder*" (Judgment in *Manninen*, C-319/02, EU:C:2004:484, at para. 20). Thus, the Court may have acted on the assumption that the Finnish tax system effectively provided for only one level of taxation.

1640. Judgment in *Manninen*, C-319/02, EU:C:2004:484, at para. 45; also see Judgment in *Meilicke and others*, C-292/04, EU:C:2007:132, at para. 28.

1641. Judgment in *Manninen*, C-319/02, EU:C:2004:484, at para. 43; Judgment in *Meilicke and others*, C-292/04, EU:C:2007:132, at para. 27; Judgment in *Amurta*, C-379/05, EU:C:2007:655, at para. 47; also see Judgment in *Deutsche Shell*, C-293/06, EU:C:2008:129, at para. 39; Judgment in *Papillon*, C-418/07, EU:C:2008:659, at para. 44; Judgment in *Aberdeen Property Fininvest Alpha*, C-303/07, EU:C:2009:377, at para. 72; Judgment in *Glaxo Wellcome*, C-182/08, EU:C:2009:559, at para. 79; Judgment in *Presidente del Consiglio dei Ministri*, C-169/08, EU:C:2009:709, at para. 47; Judgment in *CIBA*, C-96/08, EU:C:2010:185, at para. 47; Judgment in *Dijkman and Dijkman-Lavaleije*, C-233/09, EU:C:2010:397, at para. 55; Judgment in *Commission/Portugal*, C-493/09, EU:C:2011:635, at para. 36; Judgment in *Commission/Germany*, C-284/09, EU:C:2011:670, at para. 86; Judgment in *Commission/Spain*, C-269/09, EU:C:2012:439, at para. 85; Judgment in *Test Claimants in the FII Group Litigation*, C-35/11, EU:C:2012:707, at para. 58; Judgment in *Santander Asset Management SGIIC*, C-338/11, EU:C:2012:286, at para. 51; Judgment in *Argenta Spaarbank*, C-350/11, EU:C:2013:447, at para. 42; Judgment in *K*, C-322/11, EU:C:2013:716, at para. 66; Judgment in *Emerging Markets Series of DFA Investment Trust Company*, EU:C:2014:249, at para. 92; Judgment in *Bouanich*, C-375/12, EU:C:2014:138, at para. 69; Judgment in *Grünewald*, C-559/13, EU:C:2015:109, at para. 48.

1642. Judgment in *Manninen*, C-319/02, EU:C:2004:484, at paras 33 and 44.

1643. Judgment in *Manninen*, C-319/02, EU:C:2004:484, at para. 46; also see Judgment in *Meilicke and others*, C-292/04, EU:C:2007:132, at para. 29.

With regard to the calculation of such a foreign tax credit, the Court stressed that "*the tax actually paid by the company established in that other Member State*" has to be taken into account.[1644] This gave reason for speculations about whether the Member States have to ensure that the aggregate transnational tax burden of profits earned by a company in one Member State and distributed to shareholders in another Member State does not exceed the total tax burden that would have arisen in the shareholder's residence state in a purely domestic situation.[1645] Such an approach would have been contradictory to the ECJ's regularly pointing out that the fundamental freedoms do not enable a taxpayer to claim that the tax burden on the cross-border situation should correspond to the tax burden a comparable domestic situation would have to face in the tax jurisdiction that has the lowest tax burden of all tax jurisdictions involved.[1646] However, in *Test Claimants in the FII Group Litigation*, the ECJ clarified that "*when the profits underlying foreign-sourced dividends are subject in the Member State of the company making the distribution to a lower level of tax than the tax levied in the Member State of the recipient company, the latter Member State must grant an overall tax credit corresponding to the tax paid by the company making the distribution in the Member State in which it is resident. Where, conversely, those profits are subject in the Member State of the company making the distribution to a higher level of tax than the tax levied by the Member State of the company receiving them, the latter Member State is obliged to grant a tax credit only up to the limit of the amount of corporation tax for which the company receiving the dividends is liable. It is not required to repay the difference, that is to say, the amount paid in the Member State of the company making the distribution which is greater than the amount of tax payable in the Member State of the company receiving it.*"[1647] Thus, a Member State that avoids economic double taxation of profit distributions in a purely domestic situation is obliged to grant equivalent relief in cross-border situations. However, from an internal market perspective, double taxation only occurs if the taxes of two or more states overlap in such a manner that the cross-border situation bears a higher tax burden than a comparable domestic situation would have to face in the tax jurisdiction that has the highest tax burden of all tax jurisdictions involved.[1648] Due to the principle of fiscal cohesion, it is hence (only) justified that the amount of a foreign tax credit may be lower than in a

1644. Judgment in *Manninen*, C-319/02, EU:C:2004:484, at para. 54.
1645. See J. Englisch, 13 *IStR* 19 (2004), at p. 685.
1646. Judgment in *Gilly*, C-336/96, EU:C:1998:221, at para. 47; Judgment in *Hervein*, C-393/99 and C-394/99, EU:C:2002:182, at para. 51; Judgment in *De Groot*, C-385/00, EU:C:2002:750, at para. 86; Judgment in *Weigel*, C-387/01, EU:C:2004:256, at para. 55; Judgment in *Lindfors*, C-365/02, EU:C:2004:449, at para. 34; Judgment in *Schempp*, C-403/03, EU:C:2005:446, at para. 45; Judgment in *Alevizos*, C-392/05, EU:C:2007:251, at para. 76; Judgment in *Renneberg*, C-527/06, EU:C:2008:566, at para. 40; Judgment in *Block*, C-67/08, EU:C:2009:92, at para. 35; Judgment in *Schulz-Delzers and Schulz*, C-240/10, EU:C:2011:591, at para. 42; Judgment in *National Grid Indus*, C-371/10, EU:C:2011:785, at para. 62.
1647. Judgment in *Test Claimants in the FII Group Litigation*, C-446/04, EU:C:2006:774, at paras 51-52.
1648. See Chapter 1.

purely domestic situation if the distributing company's Member State of residence provides for a lower corporate income tax rate than the Member State of the shareholder.[1649]

1.3.2.3 The Obligation of the Distributing Company's Member State of Residence to Avoid Unilaterally-Caused Economic Double Taxation

Given the ECJ's jurisprudence on the tax treatment of foreign-source dividends (inbound situation), one is tempted to assume that the Court's considerations are transferable to the tax treatment of dividends distributed to foreign shareholders (outbound situation) as well.[1650] If the Member State of the distributing company provides for a system designed to grant full or partial relief from economic double taxation in the case of domestic situations, it would seem consistent to assume that non-resident dividend recipients are comparable to resident dividend recipients, because "*both [...] are capable of being the subject of double taxation.*"[1651] This was in fact the position taken by the EFTA Court in *Fokus Bank* regarding the Norwegian imputation tax credit,[1652] which was granted to resident but not to non-resident shareholders.[1653] According to the EFTA Court, "*[t]he purpose of the tax credit mechanism set up by Norwegian tax law is to avoid economic double taxation [...]. That purpose can only be achieved if all the shareholders are given the benefit of an imputation credit, irrespective of their places of residence. Economic double taxation of the same assets will create the same undesirable effect, regardless of the shareholders' places of residence. In that respect, residents and non-residents are in a comparable situation.*"[1654]

However, the ECJ took a different approach. According to the Court, "*in the context of measures laid down by a Member State in order to prevent or mitigate the imposition of a series of charges to tax on, or the double taxation of, profits distributed*

1649. See J. Englisch, 13 *IStR* 19 (2004), at p. 685; G. Kofler, *Doppelbesteuerungsabkommen und Europäisches Gemeinschaftsrecht* (Linde, 2007), at pp. 1026-1027.

1650. See M.J. Graetz/C. Warren, 44 *Common Market L. Rev.* 6 (2007), at p. 1599; also cf. Communication from the Commission to the Council, the European Parliament and the European Economic and Social Committee, *Dividend taxation of individuals in the Internal Market*, COM(2003) 810 final (19 Dec. 2003), at p. 20 ("*The Commission believes that analysis of this case law leads to fundamental conclusions about the design of dividend taxation systems: Member States cannot levy higher taxes on inbound dividends than on domestic dividends. Likewise, they cannot levy higher taxes on outbound dividends than on domestic dividends.*").

1651. Cf. Judgment in *Lenz*, C-315/02, EU:C:2004:446, at paras 30-32; also see Judgment in *Manninen*, C-319/02, EU:C:2004:484, at para. 36.

1652. See B. Larking, 14 *EC Tax Rev.* 2 (2005), at p. 72.

1653. On the Norwegian system at that time see A. Bullen, *45 Eur. Taxn.* 2 (2005), at p. 75; K. Eicker/F. Breuer, EWR-Kapitalverkehrsfreiheit: Grenzüberschreitende Anrechnung von Körperschaftsteuer (Quellensteuer); Verfahrensrechte ausländischer Anteilseigner in den EWR/EFTA-Mitgliedstaaten, 14 *IStR* 2 (2005), p. 55 (at p. 60); G. Kofler, 18 *ÖStZ* 7 (2005), at p. 144; G. Kofler, *Doppelbesteuerungsabkommen und Europäisches Gemeinschaftsrecht* (Linde, 2007), at pp. 1037-1038; B. Larking, 14 *EC Tax Rev.* 2 (2005), at p. 69; F. Zimmer, 36 *Tax Notes Intl.* 10 (6 Dec. 2004), at p. 840.

1654. Judgment of the EFTA Court in *Fokus Bank*, E-1/04 (23 Nov. 2004), at para. 30.

by a resident company, resident shareholders receiving dividends are not necessarily in a situation which is comparable to that of shareholders receiving dividends who are resident in another Member State [...]. However, as soon as a Member State, either unilaterally or by way of a convention, imposes a charge to tax on the income, not only of resident shareholders, but also of non-resident shareholders, from dividends which they receive from a resident company, the situation of those non-resident shareholders becomes comparable to that of resident shareholders."[1655] If this approach were applied consistently, a Member State could treat dividend distributions to non-residents less beneficially than in a purely domestic context by imposing a charge to tax only on dividends received by non-residents, while dividends received by residents are not subjected to tax. However, this is apparently not what the ECJ has in mind. In *Commission/Spain*, for example, Spanish resident companies were entitled to deduct from their taxable income the whole amount of a gross dividend received if it was distributed by another Spanish resident company and if the recipient, for a continuous period of at least one year, had a direct or indirect shareholding of 5% or more in the capital of the distributing company. Thus, intra-Spain dividend distributions remained effectively untaxed at the level of the receiving company. By contrast, dividends distributed by Spanish resident companies and received by non-resident companies were subject to a withholding tax, unless the recipient had a direct shareholding of at least 20%, which must have been held without interruption for one year preceding the day on which the distributed profits fell due. Although Spain hence imposed a charge to tax only on dividends received by non-residents, while dividends received by residents were not subjected to tax, the ECJ held that "*the Kingdom of Spain chose to exercise its power of taxation over dividends distributed to companies established in other Member States. Non-resident recipients of those dividends thus find themselves in a situation comparable to that of resident companies as regards the risk of economic double taxation of dividends distributed by resident companies, so that non-resident recipients cannot be treated differently from resident recipients.*"[1656]

Comparability thus only indirectly depends on whether the distributing company's Member State of residence, "*either unilaterally or by way of a convention, imposes a charge to tax on the income, not only of resident shareholders, but also of non-resident shareholders, from dividends which they receive from a resident company.*"[1657] The

1655. Judgment in *Denkavit Internationaal and Denkavit France*, C-170/05, EU:C:2006:783, at paras 34-35; also see Judgment in *Test Claimants in Class IV of the ACT Group Litigation*, C-374/04, EU:C:2006:773, at paras 56-68; Judgment in *Amurta*, C-379/05, EU:C:2007:655, at paras 37-38; Judgment in *Aberdeen Property Fininvest Alpha*, C-303/07, EU:C:2009:377, at paras 42-43; Judgment in *Commission/Italy*, C-540/07, EU:C:2009:717, at paras 51-52; Judgment in *Commission/Spain*, C-487/08, EU:C:2010:310, at paras 50-51; Order in *Secilpar*, C-199/10, EU:C:2010:706, at paras 36-37; Judgment in *Commission/Germany*, C-284/09, EU:C:2011:670, at paras 55-56; Order in *Amorim Energia*, C-38/11, EU:C:2012:358, at paras 57-58; Order in *Tate & Lyle Investments*, C-384/11, EU:C:2012:463, at para. 31; Judgment in *Commission/Belgium*, C-387/11, EU:C:2012:670, at paras 48-49; also cf. Judgment in *Orange European Smallcap Fund*, C-194/06, EU:C:2008:289, at para. 79.

1656. Judgment in *Commission/Spain*, C-487/08, EU:C:2010:310, at para. 53.

1657. Judgment in *Denkavit Internationaal and Denkavit France*, C-170/05, EU:C:2006:783, at paras 34-35; also see Judgment in *Test Claimants in Class IV of the ACT Group Litigation*, C-374/04, EU:C:2006:773, at paras 56-68; Judgment in *Amurta*, C-379/05, EU:C:2007:655, at paras

actual yardstick for establishing comparability is whether "*it is solely because of the exercise by that State of its taxing powers that, irrespective of any taxation in another Member State, a risk of a series of charges to tax may arise.*"[1658] If a Member State does not tax dividends received by non-resident shareholders, there is no need to enlarge upon the issue of whether there is a different treatment between resident and non-resident shareholders, because there is no unilaterally-induced economic double taxation in any case.

By using such an approach the ECJ not only takes a different stance depending on whether the tax treatment of inbound or outbound profit distributions is at stake but it also fails to address discrimination that may arise if dividends distributed by resident companies and received by non-resident individuals are not taxed, whereas resident individual shareholders may claim a refund to the extent the amount of the tax credit exceeds the amount of income tax which would have to be paid without the imputation system.[1659] Such a different treatment could result in discrimination if the Member State which implemented an imputation system for resident shareholders has decided to exercise "*its right to tax*" in such a way that the effective tax rate on the profits "*generated through an economic activity undertaken on its territory*" corresponds with the shareholder's income tax rate.[1660] In such a case, the effective tax rate on profits

37-38; Judgment in *Aberdeen Property Fininvest Alpha*, C-303/07, EU:C:2009:377, at paras 42-43; Judgment in *Commission/Italy*, C-540/07, EU:C:2009:717, at paras 51-52; Judgment in *Commission/Spain*, C-487/08, EU:C:2010:310, at paras 50-51; Order in *Secilpar*, C-199/10, EU:C:2010:706, at paras 36-37; Judgment in *Commission/Germany*, C-284/09, EU:C:2011:670, at paras 55-56; Order in *Amorim Energia*, C-38/11, EU:C:2012:358, at paras 57-58; Order in *Tate & Lyle Investments*, C-384/11, EU:C:2012:463, at para. 31; Judgment in *Commission/Belgium*, C-387/11, EU:C:2012:670, at paras 48-49; also cf. Judgment in *Orange European Smallcap Fund*, C-194/06, EU:C:2008:289, at para. 79.

1658. Judgment in *Test Claimants in Class IV of the ACT Group Litigation*, C-374/04, EU:C:2006:773, at para. 70; also see Judgment in *Amurta*, C-379/05, EU:C:2007:655, at para. 39; Judgment in *Commission/Italy*, C-540/07, EU:C:2009:717, at para. 53; Judgment in *Commission/Spain*, C-487/08, EU:C:2010:310, at para. 50; Judgment in *Commission/Germany*, C-284/09, EU:C:2011:670, at para. 57; Judgment in *Commission/Belgium*, C-387/11, EU:C:2012:670, at para. 50; Judgment in *Emerging Markets Series of DFA Investment Trust Company*, C-190/12, EU:C:2014:249, at para. 59.

1659. See J. Englisch, *Dividendenbesteuerung* (Dr Otto Schmidt, 2005), at p. 208; J. Englisch, Dividend Taxation: Outbound and Inbound (*Verkooijen* and *ACT Group Litigation*), in W. Haslehner/G. Kofler/A. Rust (eds.), *Landmark Decisions of the ECJ in Direct Taxation* (Kluwer, 2015), p. 41 (at p. 56); also see A. Cordewener, 87 *FR* 7 (2005), at p. 358; J. Hey, Vorrecht des Quellenstaates und binnenmarktkonforme Besteuerung von Kapitalgesellschaften in der Europäischen Union, in W. Spindler/K. Tipke/T. Rödder (eds.), *Steuerzentrierte Rechtsberatung*, Festschrift für Harald Schaumburg zum 65. Geburtstag (Dr Otto Schmidt, 2009), p. 767 (at p. 784, FN 93); G. Kofler, *Doppelbesteuerungsabkommen und Europäisches Gemeinschaftsrecht* (Linde, 2007), at p. 1058; M. Mössner/D. Kellersmann, Freiheit des Kapitalverkehrs in der EU und das deutsche Körperschaftsteueranrechnungsverfahren, 87 *DStZ* 14 (1999), p. 505 (at p. 513); A. Schnitger, Körperschaftsteueranrechnung für beschränkt Steuerpflichtige nach der Entscheidung des EFTA-Gerichtshofs in der Rs. Fokus Bank – Ein zweischneidiges Schwert, 87 *FR* 7 (2005), p. 360 (at pp. 360-361).

1660. Cf. J. Englisch, 38 *Intertax* 4 (2010), at pp. 213-217 ("*[I]f a Member State has voluntarily surrendered the concept of definitive taxation at company level by implementing an imputation system for resident shareholders, which effectively converts the corporation tax into a mere prepayment of the shareholder's income tax, why should that Member State still be permitted to claim 'source country entitlement' to the revenue generated by taxing corporate profits? It would thereby betray its own judgment that such revenue is only an interim one, to be replaced*

earned by a resident company and distributed to a resident shareholder could be lower than on profits earned by a resident company and distributed to a non-resident shareholder. In the former case, the effective tax rate corresponds to the income tax rate of the shareholder. By contrast, in the latter case, it corresponds to the corporate tax rate. Hence, if the corporate tax rate is higher than the shareholder's individual tax rate, the overall tax burden on profits generated by a resident company and distributed to a resident shareholder is lower than on profits generated by a resident company and distributed to a non-resident shareholder.[1661] With regard to highly integrated imputation systems, the ECJ should hence not only look at one tax subject, i.e., how the shareholder is treated, but should rather focus on the tax object, i.e., the tax treatment of the profits earned by the resident company and subsequently distributed to the shareholder.

The Court has actually indicated that it might be willing to accept such an object-oriented approach, which considers the tax consequences of more than one tax subject, although not within the comparability but the justification analysis. Member States have repeatedly argued that the assessment of whether profits earned by a resident company and distributed to either non-resident or resident companies may be treated differently also depends on the tax treatment of those profits when they are passed on to the shareholders of the receiving company.[1662] Relief from economic double taxation may be limited to resident companies receiving dividends, because the shareholders of such companies are typically taxed in the distributing company's Member State of residence when the dividends are passed on to them. By contrast, shareholders of non-resident companies can usually not be taxed by the distributing company's Member State of residence.[1663] The ECJ has countered, however, that it

by the revenue subsequently generated from taxing the profi t distribution at shareholder level."); and J. Englisch in W. Haslehner/G. Kofler/A. Rust (eds.), *Landmark Decisions of the ECJ in Direct Taxation* (Kluwer, 2015), at p. 56 ("*Such a Member State has chosen to ultimately tax the profits generated by corporate activities on its territory only in the hands of the shareholders.*").

1661. Admittedly, residents and non-residents are typically treated differently, in that residents are subject to tax with their worldwide income, whereas non-residents are only subject to tax on income that has a certain nexus to the respective state's territory (see Judgment of the EFTA Court in *Fokus Bank*, E-1/04 [23 Nov. 2004], at para. 29; also cf. M. Mössner/D. Kellersmann, 87 *DStZ* 14 [1999], at p. 513). Within a progressive tax scale, the effective tax rate on profits generated by a resident company and distributed to a resident shareholder thus depends on the amount of the shareholder's worldwide income, whereas in a cross-border context only – if any – the non-resident shareholder's domestic-source income is taken into account. In order not to discriminate against profits generated by a resident company and distributed to a non-resident shareholder the calculation of the tax credit or refund of corporate tax initially levied on the subsequently distributed profits would, therefore, have to be based on the fiction that the non-resident was a resident shareholder.

1662. Judgment in *Aberdeen Property Fininvest Alpha*, C-303/07, EU:C:2009:377, at para. 61; Judgment in *Commission/Italy*, C-540/07, EU:C:2009:717, at paras 24 and 56; Judgment in *Commission/Germany*, C-284/09, EU:C:2011:670, at paras 59 and 84; Judgment in *Santander Asset Management SGIIC*, C-338/11 to C-347/11, EU:C:2012:286, at para. 25; Judgment in *Commission/Belgium*, C-387/11, EU:C:2012:670, at para. 58; Judgment in *Emerging Markets Series of DFA Investment Trust Company*, C-190/12, EU:C:2014:249, at paras 62-63.

1663. Judgment in *Commission/Italy*, C-540/07, EU:C:2009:717, at para. 24 ("*In the case in which the shareholder is a non-resident company, which will normally distribute the dividends to non-resident natural persons, there is no taxation of natural persons.*").

could easily be that the shareholders of a non-resident company which receives dividends from a resident company are taxed by the latter company's Member State of residence.[1664] Moreover, "*comparing the tax burden on dividends paid to non-resident companies with the overall tax burden on dividends where a resident company in receipt of dividends redistributes them to its resident shareholders amounts to comparing systems and situations which are not comparable, namely, on the one hand, natural persons in receipt of national dividends and their income tax arrangements and, on the other, capital companies in receipt of dividends leaving the country and the withholding tax levied by the [distributing company's Member State of residence].*"[1665] The Member States thus cannot rely on the tax consequences connected with a re-distribution of profits earned by a domestic company and distributed to either non-resident or resident companies in order to show that these situations are not comparable. Neither can a Member State successfully rely on this argument in order to justify such a different treatment.[1666] However, in *Aberdeen Property Fininvest Alpha* and subsequent judgments the ECJ has given the impression that this might be different if the relief mechanism is subject to the conditions that: (1) the dividends have to be re-distributed and (2) may be taxed in that state in the hands of the shareholders to whom the profits are passed on.[1667] Thus, the ECJ apparently would have accepted such a justification if those conditions had been fulfilled. However, the different treatment of profits earned by a resident company and distributed either to a non-resident or a resident shareholder would probably still be problematic, because an immediate relief associated with postponed taxation of ultimate shareholders leads to a cash-flow advantage as compared to preliminary taxation combined with subsequent non-taxation of re-distributions.[1668]

1.3.2.4 The Avoidance of Double Non-Taxation Through Linking the Member States' (Dividend) Taxation Systems

The ECJ's approach with regard to the tax treatment of non-resident shareholders differs substantially from its jurisprudence on the tax treatment of dividends distributed by non-resident companies and received by resident shareholders. In essence, the Court's comparability analysis depends on whether the tax system of the distributing company's or of the shareholder's Member State of residence is at stake. In the former

1664. Judgment in *Commission/Germany*, C-284/09, EU:C:2011:670, at para. 60; Judgment in *Emerging Markets Series of DFA Investment Trust Company*, C-190/12, EU:C:2014:249, at para. 94.
1665. Judgment in *Commission/Germany*, C-284/09, EU:C:2011:670, at para. 60; also see Judgment in *Commission/Italy*, C-540/07, EU:C:2009:717, at para. 43.
1666. Judgment in *Commission/Italy*, C-540/07, EU:C:2009:717, at para. 56.
1667. Judgment in *Aberdeen Property Fininvest Alpha*, C-303/07, EU:C:2009:377, at para. 73; Judgment in *Commission/Germany*, C-284/09, EU:C:2011:670, at para. 87; Judgment in *Santander Asset Management SGIIC*, C-338/11 to C-347/11, EU:C:2012:286, at paras 30-31; Judgment in *Emerging Markets Series of DFA Investment Trust Company*, C-190/12, EU:C:2014:249, at paras 62 and 93.
1668. See J. Englisch, 38 *Intertax* 4 (2010), at p. 204; J. Englisch in W. Haslehner/G. Kofler/A. Rust (eds.), *Landmark Decisions of the ECJ in Direct Taxation* (Kluwer, 2015), at pp. 58-59.

case, it is required that economic double taxation may arise within *one and the same* Member State's tax system.[1669] By contrast, in the latter case, comparability is assumed if economic double taxation may be caused by *two* Member States' tax systems.[1670] According to the Court, these different approaches are necessary for three reasons, none of which are entirely convincing:[1671] First, if the Member State of the distributing company was obliged to avoid economic double taxation caused by its and another Member State's tax system, this "*would mean in point of fact that that State would be obliged to abandon its right to tax a profit generated through an economic activity undertaken on its territory.*"[1672] But does the shareholder's Member State of residence not also have a right to tax a profit indirectly generated by a resident shareholder through engaging in an economic activity undertaken on another Member State's territory via a foreign company? It is at least undisputed that there is neither a general international law nor an EU law prohibition to tax dividends distributed by non-resident companies and received by resident shareholders. Moreover, the shareholder's Member State of residence may only subject the underlying profits of non-resident companies to corporate income tax if there is a sufficient nexus to its territory. Resident companies, on the other hand, are subject to unlimited tax liability with their worldwide income. Other than the foreign distributing company's income subject to limited tax liability, the shareholder's Member State of residence does not impose a tax on the profits earned by a foreign company. Thus, it could be argued that dividends distributed by non-resident companies are only comparable to dividends distributed by resident companies to the extent the shareholder's Member State of residence may tax

1669. See G. Kofler, 65 *Bull Intl. Taxn.* 12 (2011), at p. 684; G. Kofler, Indirect Credit versus Exemption: Double Taxation Relief for Intercompany Distributions, 66 *Bull. Intl. Taxn.* 2 (2012), p. 77 (at p. 77, FN 7); also cf. M. Tenore, Taxation of Cross-Border Dividends in the European, 19 *EC Tax Rev.* 2 (2010), p. 74 (at p. 77: "*[T]he analysis of the ECJ was limited to the tax treatment in the UK; that is the Host State; the ECJ did not consider any possible economic double taxation which might have arisen as a consequence of taxes (if any) levied in the Home State in the hands of the parent company resident therein.*").

1670. See L.A. Denys, 47 *Eur. Taxn.* 5 (2007), at p. 232; J. Englisch, 38 *Intertax* 4 (2010), at pp. 216-217; J. Englisch in W. Haslehner/G. Kofler/A. Rust (eds.), *Landmark Decisions of the ECJ in Direct Taxation* (Kluwer, 2015), at p. 45; also cf. M. Gammie, Non-Discrimination and the Taxation of Cross-Border Dividends, 2 *World Tax J.* 2 (2010), p. 162 (at pp. 171-172); F. Vanistendael, 47 *Eur. Taxn.* 5 (2007), at p. 212; P. Wattel in G. Maisto (ed.), *Taxation of Intercompany Dividends under Tax Treaties and EU Law* (IBFD, 2012), at p. 42.

1671. See N. Bammens, *The Principle of Non-Discrimination in International and European Tax Law* (IBFD, 2012), at pp. 776-778; J. Englisch, 38 *Intertax* 4 (2010), at pp. 213-217; J. Englisch in W. Haslehner/G. Kofler/A. Rust (eds.), *Landmark Decisions of the ECJ in Direct Taxation* (Kluwer, 2015), at pp. 55-57; also cf. W. Schön, 69 *Bull. Intl. Taxn.* 4/5 (2015), at pp. 289-290; W. Schön in W. Schön/C. Heber (eds.), *Grundfragen des Europäischen Steuerrechts* (Springer, 2015), at pp. 151-153; but see S. van Thiel, The Direct Income Tax Case Law of the European Court of Justice: Past Trends and Future Developments, 62 *Tax L. Rev.* 1 (2008), p. 143 (at pp. 165-167).

1672. Judgment in *Test Claimants in Class IV of the ACT Group Litigation*, C-374/04, EU:C:2006:773, at para. 59; also see Judgment in *Glaxo Wellcome*, C-182/08, EU:C:2009:559, at para. 83; Judgment in *Commission/Germany*, C-284/09, EU:C:2011:670, at para. 80; Order in *Tate & Lyle Investments*, C-384/11, EU:C:2012:463, at para. 30; Judgment in *Commission/Belgium*, C-387/11, EU:C:2012:670, at para. 78; also cf. Judgment in *Oy AA*, C-231/05, EU:C:2007:439, at para. 56.

the underlying profits.[1673] Therefore, the ECJ could have found dividends distributed by resident and non-resident companies not to be comparable, because obliging the shareholder's Member State of residence to avoid economic double taxation caused by its and another Member State's tax system "*would mean in point of fact that that State would be obliged to abandon its right to tax*" a dividend received by its residents. Of course, neither should the residence state of the distributing company be prevented from taxing profits earned by this company. Thus, the Court could be understood as meaning that the source state has the primary right to tax.[1674] However, such a prioritization of overlapping taxing rights contradicts the ECJ's jurisprudence on juridical double taxation,[1675] according to which EU law "*does not lay down any general criteria for the attribution of areas of competence between the Member States in relation to the elimination of double taxation within the [EU].*"[1676]

Second, according to the ECJ, "*as regards a procedure for preventing or mitigating economic double taxation by the grant of a tax advantage to the ultimate shareholder, it must be pointed out that it is usually the Member State in which the latter is resident that is best placed to determine the shareholder's ability to pay tax.*"[1677] It is indeed settled case law that "*a non-resident's personal ability to pay tax, determined by reference to his aggregate income and his personal and family circumstances, is more easy to assess at the place where his personal and financial interests are centred. In general, that is the place where he has his usual abode.*"[1678] However, not only is this line of case law highly disputed[1679] but it is also difficult to understand why the Member State that "*is*

1673. Cf. C. Staringer in E. Lechner/C. Staringer/M. Tumpel (eds.), *Kapitalverkehrsfreiheit und Steuerrecht* (Linde, 2000), at p. 108; also cf. J. Englisch, 13 *IStR* 15 (2004), at p. 527; J. Englisch, 51 *RIW* 3 (2005), at p. 192; J. Englisch, 33 *Intertax* 5 (2005), at p. 210; G. Kofler, *Doppelbesteuerungsabkommen und Europäisches Gemeinschaftsrecht* (Linde, 2007), at p. 1005.

1674. See J. Hey in W. Spindler/K. Tipke/T. Rödder (eds.), *Steuerzentrierte Rechtsberatung*, Festschrift für Harald Schaumburg zum 65. Geburtstag (Dr Otto Schmidt, 2009), at p. 776.

1675. See N. Bammens, *The Principle of Non-Discrimination in International and European Tax Law* (IBFD, 2012), at pp. 776-777; J. Englisch, 38 *Intertax* 4 (2010), at p. 214.

1676. Judgment in *Kerckhaert and Morres*, C-513/04, EU:C:2006:603, at paras 20-23; Judgment in *CIBA*, C-96/08, EU:C:2010:185 at paras 25-27; see also Judgment in *Block*, C-67/08, EU:C:2009:92, at paras 28-30; Judgment in *Damseaux*, C-128/08, EU:C:2009:471, at paras 30 and 33.

1677. Judgment in *Test Claimants in Class IV of the ACT Group Litigation*, C-374/04, EU:C:2006:773, at para. 60.

1678. Judgment in *Schumacker*, C-279/93, EU:C:1995:31, at para. 32; Judgment in *Gschwind*, C-391/97, EU:C:1999:409, at para. 22; Judgment in *Zurstrassen*, C-87/99, EU:C:2000:251, at para. 21; Judgment in *De Groot*, C-385/00, EU:C:2002:750, at para. 66; Judgment in *Gerritse*, C-234/01, EU:C:2003:340, at para. 43; Judgment in *Wallentin*, C-169/03, EU:C:2004:403, at para. 15; Judgment in *Meindl*, C-329/05, EU:C:2007:57, at para. 23; Judgment in *Commission/Spain*, C-562/07, EU:C:2009:614, at para. 46; Judgment in *Commission/Belgium*, C-250/08, EU:C:2011:793, at para. 55; Judgment in *Commission/Hungary*, C-253/09, EU:C:2011:795, at para. 55; Judgment in *Schröder*, C-450/09, EU:C:2011:198, at para. 37; Judgment in *Commission/Estonia*, C-39/10, EU:C:2012:282, at para. 49; Judgment in *Grünewald*, C-559/13, EU:C:2015:109, at para. 25; Judgment in *Hirvonen*, C-623/13, EU:C:2015:765, at para. 31; Judgment in *Kieback*, C-9/14, EU:C:2015:406, at para. 22.

1679. See, for example, K. Daxkobler, *Die grundfreiheitliche Rechtsprechung des EuGH* (Linde, 2015), at pp. 195-220; M. Lang, 51 *RIW* 5 (2005), at pp. 336-344; H. Niesten, Growing Impetus for Harmonization of Personal and Family Allowances: Current State of Affairs of the Schumacker-Doctrine after Imfeld and Garcet, 24 *EC Tax Rev.* 4 (2015), p. 185 (at pp.

best placed" to determine a taxpayer's ability to pay should also be primarily responsible for preventing or mitigating economic double taxation.[1680] Imputation systems, for example, require determining the exact amount of corporate income tax borne by the distributed profits. This can be done much more easily by the distributing company's Member State of residence.[1681]

Third, the Court refers to Article 4(1) Parent-Subsidiary Directive, which "*[l]ikewise [...] requires the Member State of the parent company which receives profits distributed by a subsidiary which is resident in another Member State, and not the latter State, to avoid a series of charges to tax, either by refraining from taxing such profits or by taxing such profits while authorising that parent company to deduct from the amount of tax due that fraction of the corporation tax paid by the subsidiary which relates to those profits and, if appropriate, the amount of the withholding tax levied by the Member State in which the subsidiary is resident.*"[1682] It is unclear why the Parent-Subsidiary Directive should matter when interpreting the fundamental freedoms if it is not even applicable.[1683] Even if it was, Article 7(2) Parent-Subsidiary Directive would have to be taken into account.[1684] Thus, "*[t]his Directive shall not affect the application of domestic or agreement-based provisions designed to eliminate or lessen economic double taxation of dividends, in particular provisions relating to the payment of tax credits to the recipients of dividends.*"[1685] The requirements of the Parent-Subsidiary Directive can thus not serve as a guideline for determining the comparability of situations.[1686]

194-195); B. Peeters, Mobility of EU Citizens and Family Taxation: A Hard to Reconcile Combination, 23 *EC Tax Rev.* 3 (2014), p. 118 (at pp. 119-120); K. van Raad, Non-residents: Personal Allowances. Deduction of Personal Expenses and Tax Rates, 2 *World Tax J.* 2 (2010), p. 154 (at pp. 154-161); P.J. Wattel, Progressive Taxation of Non-Residents and Intra-EC Allocation of Personal Allowances: Why *Schumacker*, *Asscher*, *Gilly* and *Gschwind* Do Not Suffice, 40 Eur. Taxn. 6 (2000), p. 210 (at pp. 210-223); P.J. Wattel, 31 *Legal Issues of Economic Integration* 2 (2004), at pp. 84-87.

1680. Cf. G. Kofler, *Doppelbesteuerungsabkommen und Europäisches Gemeinschaftsrecht* (Linde, 2007), at p. 1043; but see M. Tenore, 19 *EC Tax Rev.* 2 (2010), at p. 83 ("*The ECJ case law has affirmed that [...] the Home State is, in principle, in a better position to ascertain the overall ability to pay of the taxpayer and consequently to take care of the elimination of economic double taxation*").

1681. See J. Englisch, 38 *Intertax* 4 (2010), at p. 216; J. Englisch in W. Haslehner/G. Kofler/A. Rust (eds.), *Landmark Decisions of the ECJ in Direct Taxation* (Kluwer, 2015), at pp. 56-57; also see N. Bammens, *The Principle of Non-Discrimination in International and European Tax Law* (IBFD, 2012), at p. 777.

1682. Judgment in *Test Claimants in Class IV of the ACT Group Litigation*, C-374/04, EU:C:2006:773, at para. 60; also cf. Judgment in *Burda*, C-284/06, EU:C:2008:365, at paras 89-90.

1683. Cf. N. Bammens, *The Principle of Non-Discrimination in International and European Tax Law* (IBFD, 2012), at p. 777.

1684. See J. Englisch, 38 *Intertax* 4 (2010), at p. 216; J. Englisch in W. Haslehner/G. Kofler/A. Rust (eds.), *Landmark Decisions of the ECJ in Direct Taxation* (Kluwer, 2015), at p. 57; also see N. Bammens, *The Principle of Non-Discrimination in International and European Tax Law* (IBFD, 2012), at pp. 777-778.

1685. The ECJ has already confirmed that this provision entitles Member States to derogate from the requirements of the Parent-Subsidiary Directive under certain circumstances. Judgment in *Océ van der Grinten*, C-58/01, EU:C:2003:495, at paras 80-89.

1686. J. Englisch, 38 *Intertax* 4 (2010), at p. 216.

Overall, the ECJ's explanation why only the shareholder's but not the distributing company's Member State of residence is obliged to eliminate or mitigate the effects of economic double taxation caused by both Member States' tax systems in a similar way as this Member State avoids or attenuates the effects of economic double taxation caused exclusively by its own tax system is thus not convincing.[1687] This raises the question whether the ECJ should instead have argued that *all* Member States providing for relief mechanisms "*designed to attenuate,*"[1688] "*to mitigate*"[1689] or "*to prevent*"[1690] "*the economic effects of double taxation of company profits arising from the taxation of company profits by way of corporation tax and the taxation of a shareholder who is a taxpayer, by way of income tax, on the same profits distributed in the form of dividends,*"[1691] are obliged to extend such mechanisms to cross-border situations as well,[1692] because profits distributed by non-resident companies and profits distributed by domestic companies are likewise "*capable of being subjected to double taxation.*"[1693] This implies that the distributing company's Member State of residence would also be obliged to extend possible relief mechanisms to cross-border situations. However, if relief from economic double taxation had to be granted by both the shareholder's Member State of residence and the Member State of the distributing company, this could lead to double non-taxation, because the overall tax burden on profits earned by a company established in one Member State and received by a shareholder resident in another Member State via a dividend could be less than in the comparable purely domestic situations.[1694] The ECJ is well aware of this potential result, which may even arise although the Court interprets the fundamental freedoms as only obliging the shareholder's Member State of residence to avoid the effects of economic double taxation caused by both Member States' tax systems in a similar way as it avoids or

1687. See N. Bammens, *The Principle of Non-Discrimination in International and European Tax Law* (IBFD, 2012), at pp. 776-778; J. Englisch, 38 *Intertax* 4 (2010), at pp. 213-217; J. Englisch in W. Haslehner/G. Kofler/A. Rust (eds.), *Landmark Decisions of the ECJ in Direct Taxation* (Kluwer, 2015), at pp. 55-57; M.J. Graetz/C. Warren, 44 *Common Market L. Rev.* 6 (2007), at p. 1611; also cf. W. Schön, 69 *Bull. Intl. Taxn.* 4/5 (2015), at pp. 289-290; W. Schön in W. Schön/C. Heber (eds.), *Grundfragen des Europäischen Steuerrechts* (Springer, 2015), at pp. 151-153; but see S. van Thiel, 62 *Tax L. Rev.* 1 (2008), at pp. 165-167.

1688. Judgment in *Lenz*, C-315/02, EU:C:2004:446, at para. 30.

1689. Judgment in *Test Claimants in the FII Group Litigation*, C-446/04, EU:C:2006:774, at para. 62; Judgment in *Haribo Lakritzen Hans Riegel*, C-436/08 and C-437/08, EU:C:2011:61, at para. 59; Judgment in *Accor*, C-310/09, EU:C:2011:581, at para. 45.

1690. Judgment in *Manninen*, C-319/02, EU:C:2004:484, at para. 33; Judgment in *Test Claimants in the FII Group Litigation*, C-446/04, EU:C:2006:774, at para. 62; Judgment in *Meilicke and others*, C-292/04, EU:C:2007:132, at para. 21; Judgment in *Haribo Lakritzen Hans Riegel*, C-436/08 and C-437/08, EU:C:2011:61, at para. 59; Judgment in *Accor*, C-310/09, EU:C:2011:581, at para. 45.

1691. Judgment in *Lenz*, C-315/02, EU:C:2004:446, at para. 30.

1692. Cf. J. Englisch in W. Haslehner/G. Kofler/A. Rust (eds.), *Landmark Decisions of the ECJ in Direct Taxation* (Kluwer, 2015), at p. 57.

1693. Judgment in *Manninen*, C-319/02, EU:C:2004:484, at para. 35; also see Judgment in *Lenz*, C-315/02, EU:C:2004:446, at para. 31; Judgment in *Haribo Lakritzen Hans Riegel*, C-436/08 and C-437/08, EU:C:2011:61, at para. 59.

1694. Cf. J. Englisch, 44 *Eur. Taxn.* 8 (2004), at p. 363; W. Schön in W. Schön (ed.), *Gedächtnisschrift für Brigitte Knobbe-Keuk* (Dr Otto Schmidt, 1997), at pp. 775-776; C. Staringer in E. Lechner/C. Staringer/M. Tumpel (eds.), *Kapitalverkehrsfreiheit und Steuerrecht* (Linde, 2000), at p. 117; also cf. A. Schnitger, 86 *FR* 24 (2004), at p. 1358.

attenuates the effects of economic double taxation caused exclusively by its own tax system. After all, the other Member State may voluntarily ensure that profits distributed by resident companies are not subject to economic double taxation, which would otherwise be caused by both Member States' tax systems. In *Manninen*, the Court hence pointed out that the shareholder's Member State of residence does not have to extend domestic-oriented imputation systems to cross-border situations, if "*the tax legislation of the Member State in which the investments were made already eliminated the risk of double taxation of company profits distributed in the form of dividends, by, for example, subjecting to corporation tax only such profits by the company concerned as were not distributed.*"[1695]

According to the ECJ's decision in *Lenz*, this caveat apparently only applies if the tax legislation of the shareholder's Member State of residence establishes a direct link between the taxation of the distributing company's profits and the relief granted to the shareholder receiving the dividends.[1696,1697] This is in line with the approach taken by the ECJ in *Imfeld and Garcet*:[1698] According to settled case law, "*in principle the overall taxation of taxpayers, taking account of their personal and family circumstances, is a matter for the State of residence.*"[1699] However, a Member State may be released from its obligation to take account of its resident taxpayers' personal and family circumstances, "*if it finds that [...] one or more of the States of employment, with respect to the income taxed by them, grant advantages based on the personal and family*

1695. Judgment in *Manninen*, C-319/02, EU:C:2004:484, at para. 34.
1696. Judgment in *Lenz*, C-315/02, EU:C:2004:446, at para. 42.
1697. However, whether such a link exists is usually – and should be – examined within the justification and not the comparability analysis. See J. Englisch, 13 *IStR* 19 (2004), at pp. 684-685; G. Kofler, *Doppelbesteuerungsabkommen und Europäisches Gemeinschaftsrecht* (Linde, 2007), at pp. 996-998; also cf. J. Englisch, 38 *Intertax* 4 (2010), at p. 203; J. Englisch, 13 *IStR* 15 (2004), at p. 527; J. Englisch, 33 *Intertax* 5 (2005), at p. 210; J. Englisch, 33 *Intertax* 8/9 (2005), at p. 320.
1698. Judgment in *Imfeld and Garcet*, C-303/12, EU:C:2013:822; for a detailed analysis of this judgment see L. Cerioni, Guido Imfeld and *Nathalie Garcet v. Belgian State*: a continuation of the Schumacker doctrine?, 59 *British Tax Rev.* 2 (2014), p. 128 (at pp. 128-135); H. Niesten, 24 *EC Tax Rev.* 4 (2015), at pp. 185-201; also see B. Peeters, 23 *EC Tax Rev.* 3 (2014), at pp. 118-120.
1699. Judgment in *Schumacker*, C-279/93, EU:C:1995:31, at para. 32; also see Judgment in *Gschwind*, C-391/97, EU:C:1999:409, at para. 22; Judgment in *Zurstrassen*, C-87/99, EU:C:2000:251, at para. 21; Judgment in *de Groot*, C-385/00, EU:C:2002:750, at para. 90; Judgment in *Gerritse*, C-234/01, EU:C:2003:340, at para. 43; Judgment in *Wallentin*, C-169/03, EU:C:2004:403, at para. 15; Judgment in *D.*, C-376/03, EU:C:2005:424, at para. 27; Judgment in *Turpeinen*, C-520/04, EU:C:2006:703, at para. 27; Judgment in *Meindl*, C-329/05, EU:C:2007:57, at para. 23; Judgment in *Talotta*, C-383/05, EU:C:2007:181, at para. 19; Judgment in *Lakebrink and Peters-Lakebrink*, C-182/06, EU:C:2007:452, at paras 28-31; Judgment in *Renneberg*, C-527/06, EU:C:2008:566, at paras 59-61; Judgment in *Commission/Spain*, C-562/07, EU:C:2009:614, at para. 46; Judgment in *Commission/Belgium*, C-250/08, EU:C:2011:793, at para. 55; Judgment in *Gielen*, C-440/08, EU:C:2010:148, at paras 43-44; Judgment in *Commission/Hungary*, C-253/09, EU:C:2011:795, at para. 55; Judgment in *Schröder*, C-450/09, EU:C:2011:198, at para. 37; Judgment in *Commission/Estonia*, C-39/10, EU:C:2012:282, at para. 49; Judgment in *Beker*, C-168/11, EU:C:2013:117, at para. 43; Judgment in Ettwein, C-425/11, EU:C:2013:121, at para. 46; Judgment in *Imfeld and Garcet*, C-303/12, EU:C:2013:822, at para. 44; Judgment in *Grünewald*, C-559/13, EU:C:2015:109, at para. 25; Judgment in Hirvonen, C-623/13, EU:C:2015:765, at para. 31; Judgment in Kieback, C-9/14, EU:C:2015:406, at para. 22.

circumstances of taxpayers who do not reside in the territory of those States but receive taxable income there."[1700] Based on this jurisprudence, the Belgian government argued that a taxpayer may be deprived of claiming a tax-free income allowance for dependent children in its residence state if the personal and family circumstances are taken into account in another Member State, so that the residence state is released from any obligation in that regard.[1701] The Court did not accept this argument, because "*[t]he tax legislation at issue in the main proceedings establishes a tax advantage for couples in the form, in particular, of a supplementary tax-free income allowance for dependent children, which is set off against the income of the member of the couple who earns the greater part of their income, but fails to take any account whatsoever of the fact that, after exercising the freedoms guaranteed by the Treaty, he may be in a position of not earning income as an individual in Belgium, with the direct and automatic consequence that the couple then loses the entire benefit of that advantage.*" Thus, according to the ECJ, the denial of the tax-free income allowance was not per se problematic, it was rather "*the automatic nature of that loss which is contrary to freedom of establishment.*"[1702]

For the same reason, it was not possible to justify the Belgian legislation, either. The Court, once again, confirmed that a taxpayer's Member State of residence is no longer responsible for granting "*to the taxpayer the personal and family allowances to which he is entitled, [if] that State [...] finds that [...] one or more of the States of employment, with respect to the income taxed by them, grant advantages based on the personal and family circumstances of taxpayers who do not reside in the territory of those States but earn taxable income there.*"[1703] However, this requirement was not met in *Imfeld and Garcet*, because "*the tax legislation at issue in the main proceedings does not establish any correlation between the tax advantages which it grants to the residents*

1700. Judgment in *De Groot*, C-385/00, EU:C:2002:750, at para. 100; see also Judgment in *Beker*, C-168/11, EU:C:2013:117, at para. 56; Judgment in *Imfeld and Garcet*, C-303/12, EU:C:2013:822, at para. 69.
1701. Judgment in *Imfeld and Garcet*, C-303/12, EU:C:2013:822, at para. 58.
1702. Judgment in *Imfeld and Garcet*, C-303/12, EU:C:2013:822, at para. 62; also see Opinion of AG Cruz Villalón in *Imfeld and Garcet*, C-303/12, EU:C:2013:402, at point 75 ("*it cannot be considered that the grant of that tax advantage in Germany may, in some way, compensate for the loss of the tax advantage registered by the applicants in the main proceedings in Belgium. The grant of the 'Freibetrag für Kinder' is, in fact, a purely short-term circumstance which may change at any time, since the Federal Republic of Germany may inter alia withdraw or reduce the amount of that advantage without that having any effect on the conditions for granting the 'supplementary allowance for dependent children' in Belgium. The compatibility of the Belgian tax legislation with EU law cannot depend on such circumstances*"); also cf. L. Cerioni, 59 *British Tax Rev.* 2 (2014), at p. 132 ("*Belgium could restrict Belgian relief where Germany gives relief, but only where Belgium's legislation recognises this.*") and at p. 134 ("*Imfeld suggests in even clearer terms than de Groot that the CJEU would also follow this approach in assessing the existence of a restriction but only when* either *a double tax convention allocates the personal deductions-granting obligation between the two contracting Member States* or *national laws are unilaterally correlated with each other (which are the only cases where* all *personal and family-related deductions could be granted once*"); H. Niesten, 24 *EC Tax Rev.* 4 (2015), at p. 192.
1703. Judgment in *Imfeld and Garcet*, C-303/12, EU:C:2013:822, at para. 69; also see Judgment in *De Groot*, C-385/00, EU:C:2002:750, at paras 99-100; Judgment in *Beker*, C-168/11, EU:C:2013:117, at para. 56.

of the Member State concerned and the tax advantages for which they may qualify in connection with their taxation in another Member State. The applicants in the main proceedings failed to benefit from the supplementary tax-free income allowance for dependent children, not because they benefited from an equivalent advantage in Germany, but only because the benefit of it was nullified by the rules for its offsetting."[1704]

Apparently, a Member State may thus restrict the granting of tax benefits to purely domestic situations if the resultant disadvantage for comparable cross-border situations is neutralized by another Member State granting an equivalent advantage.[1705] In order for such a limitation to be justified the ECJ requires the Member State which is generally compelled by the fundamental freedoms to a certain behaviour to step into the breach if the other Member State – for whatever reason – no longer provides for such a compensatory tax benefit. However, this cannot be done only by making the restriction to purely domestic situations dependent on the taxpayer receiving an equivalent advantage by another Member State. A Member State may rather also disengage itself from an obligation resulting from the fundamental freedoms by concluding a bilateral or multilateral agreement that legally obliges another Member State to assume this obligation. This was already emphasized by the ECJ in *De Groot* with regard to the basic obligation of a Member State to take account of its taxpayers' personal and family circumstances.[1706] In *Bouanich*, it was additionally clarified that such an agreement "*forms part of the legal background*" of a Member State's legal system, i.e., "*the Court of Justice must take it into account in order to give an interpretation of Community law.*"[1707] In contrast to the EFTA Court,[1708] the ECJ thus held in *Amurta* that, although the Member State of a company distributing profits to a non-resident shareholder is obliged to avoid economic double taxation caused by its own tax system in the same way as it avoids such effects in purely domestic

1704. Judgment in *Imfeld and Garcet*, C-303/12, EU:C:2013:822, at para. 73.

1705. On the question how to determine whether another Member State provides for equivalent advantages with regard to personal and family circumstances see H. Niesten, 24 *EC Tax Rev.* 4 (2015), at pp. 196-197; B. Peeters, 23 *EC Tax Rev.* 3 (2014), at pp. 119-120; also cf. K. Daxkobler, *Die grundfreiheitliche Rechtsprechung des EuGH* (Linde, 2015), at pp. 200 and 202-204; M. Lang, 51 *RIW* 5 (2005), at pp. 341-343.

1706. Judgment in *De Groot*, C-385/00, EU:C:2002:750, at para. 99; also see Judgment in *Beker*, C-168/11, EU:C:2013:117, at para. 56; Judgment in *Imfeld and Garcet*, C-303/12, EU:C:2013:822, at para. 69; also cf. Judgment in *Manninen*, C-319/02, EU:C:2004:484, at para. 21; Judgment in *Test Claimants in Class IV of the ACT Group Litigation*, C-374/04, EU:C:2006:773, at para. 71.

1707. Judgment in *Bouanich*, C-265/04, EU:C:2006:51, at para. 51; also see Judgment in *Denkavit Internationaal and Denkavit France*, C-170/05, EU:C:2006:783, at para. 45; Judgment in *Test Claimants in the Thin Cap Group Litigation*, C-524/04, EU:C:2007:161, at para. 54; Judgment in *Amurta*, C-379/05, EU:C:2007:655, at para. 80.

1708. Judgment of the EFTA Court in *Fokus Bank*, E-1/04 (23 Nov. 2004), at para. 37 ("*A Contracting Party cannot shift its obligation to comply with the EEA Agreement to another Contracting Party by relying on the latter to make good for discrimination and disadvantages caused by the former's legislation. Likewise, the principle of legal certainty would require that the granting, or not, of an imputation tax credit to a non-resident shareholder, may not depend on whether a tax credit is granted in his or her state of residence in respect of dividend payments.*").

situations,[1709] "*it cannot be excluded that a Member State may succeed in ensuring compliance with its obligations under the Treaty through the conclusion of a convention for the avoidance of double taxation with another Member State [...]. However, [...] [i]t is [...] for the national court to establish whether account should be taken, in the main proceedings, of the DTC, and, if so, to determine whether that convention enables the effects of the restriction on the free movement of capital identified in the context of the reply to the first question, in paragraph 28 of this judgment, to be neutralised.*"[1710]

It is remarkable that, in contrast to *De Groot*, the ECJ held in *Amurta* that a Member State "*may not rely on the existence of a full tax credit granted unilaterally by another Member State to a recipient company established in the latter Member State in order to escape the obligation to prevent economic double taxation of dividends resulting from the exercise of its power to tax in a situation where the first Member State prevents economic double taxation of dividends distributed to companies established in its territory.*"[1711] In principle, it is convincing that the ECJ does not take into account the tax treatment in other Member States.[1712] Neither do the Treaties oblige the Member States "*to adapt their own tax systems to the different systems of tax of the other Member States,*"[1713] nor can a Member State "*rely on the existence of a tax advantage granted unilaterally by another Member State in order to escape its obligations under the Treaty.*"[1714] However, if a provision of a Member State's tax system explicitly refers to the tax treatment in another Member State, the Member State's tax law referred to also becomes "*part of the legal background*" of the referring Member State's legal

1709. See Chapter 4.1.3.2.3.

1710. Judgment in *Amurta*, C-379/05, EU:C:2007:655, at paras 79-83; also see Judgment in *Commission/Italy*, C-540/07, EU:C:2009:717, at para. 36; Judgment in *Commission/Spain*, C-487/08, EU:C:2010:310, at para. 58; Judgment in *Secilpar*, C-199/10, EU:C:2010:706, at paras 39-41; Judgment in *Commission/Germany*, C-284/09, EU:C:2011:670, at para. 62; Judgment in *Miljoen*, C-10/14, C-14/14 and C-17/14, EU:C:2015:608, at paras 78-80.

1711. Judgment in *Amurta*, C-379/05, EU:C:2007:655, at para. 84; also see Judgment in *Commission/Spain*, C-487/08, EU:C:2010:310, at para. 66; Judgment in *Miljoen*, C-10/14, C-14/14 and C-17/14, EU:C:2015:608, at paras 77 and 82.

1712. See G. Kofler, *Doppelbesteuerungsabkommen und Europäisches Gemeinschaftsrecht* (Linde, 2007), at pp. 564-566.

1713. Judgment in *Columbus Container Services*, C-298/05, EU:C:2007:754, at para. 51; Judgment in *Block*, C-67/08, EU:C:2009:92, at para. 31; Judgment in *Commission/Hungary*, C-253/09, EU:C:2011:795, at para. 83; Judgment in *Banco Bilbao Vizcaya Argentaria*, C-157/10, EU:C:2011:813, at para. 39; Judgment in *X*, C-302/12, EU:C:2013:756, at para. 29; also cf. Judgment in *Deutsche Shell*, C-293/06, EU:C:2008:129, at para. 42-43; Judgment in *Krankenheim Ruhesitz am Wannsee-Seniorenheimstatt*, C-157/07, EU:C:2008:588, at para. 49; Judgment in *CIBA*, C-96/08, EU:C:2010:185 at para. 28.

1714. Judgment in *Amurta*, C-379/05, EU:C:2007:655, at para. 78; Judgment in *Miljoen*, C-10/14, C-14/14 and C-17/14, EU:C:2015:608, at para. 77; also see Judgment in *Eckelkamp*, C-11/07, EU:C:2008:489, at para. 69; Judgment in *Arens-Sikken*, C-43/07, EU:C:2008:490, at para. 66; Judgment in *Commission/Spain*, C-487/08, EU:C:2010:310, at para. 66; Judgment in *Imfeld and Garcet*, C-303/12, EU:C:2013:822, at para. 61; also see Judgment in *Eurowings*, C-294/97, EU:C:1999:524, at paras 43-45; Judgment in *Verkooijen*, C-35/98, EU:C:2000:294, at para. 61; Judgment in *Danner*, C-136/00, EU:C:2002:558, at paras 53-56; Judgment in *Lenz*, C-315/02, EU:C:2004:446, at para. 43; Judgment in *Skandia and Ramstedt*, C-422/01, EU:C:2003:380, at para. 52; Judgment in *Cadbury Schweppes and Cadbury Schweppes Overseas*, C-196/04, EU:C:2006:544, at para. 49; Judgment in *SIAT*, C-318/10, EU:C:2012:415, at para. 39.

system.[1715] If such a legal link with another Member State's tax systems existed, disregarding the other Member State's tax system would misconstrue the referring Member State's legal framework. However, determining whether a Member State's tax system is in line with the fundamental freedoms requires taking into account the *entire* legal framework of this Member State. Moreover, it would be contradictory if a Member State could deny its taxpayers to fully take into account their personal and family circumstances as long as this limitation is legally conditioned on another Member State unilaterally allowing for the very same circumstances, but the same Member State may not refuse non-resident shareholders to claim a domestic relief from unilaterally-caused economic double taxation as long as this restriction is legally contingent upon their Member State of residence unilaterally neutralizing the otherwise resultant disadvantage.[1716]

If it is thus taken for granted that another Member State's tax system is relevant when scrutinizing the legislation of a Member State explicitly referring to a foreign tax treatment, it becomes clear that it is not fully convincing – at least from a tax policy perspective – to argue that the fundamental freedoms require both the shareholder's Member State of residence and the Member State of the distributing company to grant relief from economic double taxation caused by the interaction of their tax systems in the same way as they grant relief from economic double taxation caused only by their own tax system.[1717] After all, it would be possible for both Member States to condition the respective relief mechanisms on the other Member State not granting an equivalent relief. As such a bidirectional linkage would be circular,[1718] the Court would have to face the same dilemma that also arises with respect to juridical double taxation, which is to identify the Member State that should be made responsible for and hence obliged to avoid double taxation.[1719] Although the detrimental effects on cross-border dividend distributions would have remained, it would thus at least have been more consistent to stick to the same approach as applied with regard to juridical double taxation.[1720] Thus, the Court could have declared economic double taxation caused by different tax systems to "*result from the exercise in parallel by two Member States of their fiscal sovereignty*" and since EU law, "*in its current state [...], does not lay down any general criteria for the attribution of areas of competence between the Member States in relation*

1715. See M. Lang, *Die Rechtsprechung des EuGH zu den direkten Steuern* (Peter Lang, 2007), at p. 79.

1716. See E. Kemmeren, 17 *EC Tax Rev.* 1 (2008), at p. 9; M. Schwenke, Kapitalertragsteuer bei Streubesitzdividenden gemeinschaftswidrig?, 17 *IStR* 13 (2008), p. 473 (at p. 477); B.J.M. Terra/P.J. Wattel, *European Tax Law*[6] (Kluwer, 2012), at p. 908.

1717. Cf. J. Englisch in W. Haslehner/G. Kofler/A. Rust (eds.), *Landmark Decisions of the ECJ in Direct Taxation* (Kluwer, 2015), at p. 57.

1718. Cf. K. Dziurdź, "Circularly Linked" Rules Countering Deduction and Non-Inclusion Schemes: Some Thoughts on a Tie-Breaker Test, 67 *Bull. Intl. Taxn.* 6 (2013), p. 306 (at pp. 306-310).

1719. See Chapter 4.1.3.1.1. Whether relief from economic double taxation has to be granted by the shareholder's or by the distributing company's Member State of residence would then depend on which Member State's relief mechanism is scrutinized by the ECJ first. Such a result would not be convincing. Cf. J. Englisch, 33 *Intertax* 5 (2005), at p. 212; J. Englisch, 51 *RIW* 3 (2005), at p. 193.

1720. See P. Wattel in G. Maisto (ed.), *Taxation of Intercompany Dividends under Tax Treaties and EU Law* (IBFD, 2012), at p. 44.

to the elimination of double taxation within the Community [...] it is for the Member States to take the measures necessary to prevent situations such as that at issue in the main proceedings by applying, in particular, the apportionment criteria followed in international tax practice."[1721,1722]

1.4 Double Taxation and the Limits of the Fundamental Freedoms

With regard to juridical double taxation, the Court has surrendered to identifying the Member State that should be made responsible for and hence obliged to avoid juridical double taxation. Therefore, it concluded that neither Member State is obliged to avoid or mitigate the effects of juridical double taxation. By contrast, according to the ECJ, Member States that avoid or mitigate economic double taxation exclusively caused by their own tax system in a purely domestic context are obliged to provide for the same relief in cross-border situations. However, if profits are earned by a company resident in one Member State and distributed to a shareholder resident in another Member State, double taxation may occur for various reasons. It might be caused by: (1) the tax system of the distributing company's Member State of residence if the company is taxed when the profits are earned and the non-resident shareholder is taxed when the (after-tax) profits are distributed, (2) the tax system of the shareholder's Member State of residence if the distributing company is subject to limited tax liability in that Member State, because its profits have a nexus to that state's territory, and the same (after-tax) profits are also taxed as part of the resident shareholder's worldwide income or (3) both Member State's tax systems if the distributing company's Member State of residence (only) taxes the profits when they are earned and the shareholder's Member State of residence (only) taxes the profits when they are distributed. In the last-mentioned case, the resultant economic double taxation is different from the double imposition of taxes on profits earned by a *resident* company and distributed to its *resident* shareholders, in that no Member State alone can be held responsible for it. Hence, the ECJ is confronted with the same problem that occurs when a taxpayer is subject to juridical double taxation, i.e., "*the imposition of comparable taxes in two (or more) States on the same taxpayer in respect of the same subject matter and for identical periods.*"[1723]

Unlike its jurisprudence on juridical double taxation, the Court did not hesitate to exclusively hold the shareholder's Member State of residence responsible for eliminating or mitigating the effects of economic double taxation caused by both Member

1721. Judgment in *Kerckhaert and Morres*, C-513/04, EU:C:2006:713, at paras 20 and 22-23; Judgment in *CIBA*, C-96/08, EU:C:2010:185 at paras 25-27; see also Judgment in *Block*, C-67/08, EU:C:2009:92, at paras 28-30; Judgment in *Damseaux*, C-128/08, EU:C:2009:471, at paras 30 and 33.

1722. See J. Englisch, 38 *Intertax* 4 (2010), at p. 217; also cf. W. Schön, 69 *Bull. Intl. Taxn.* 4/5 (2015), at p. 290; D. Weber, 34 *Intertax* 12 (2006), at p. 598; D. Weber, *In Search of a (New) Equilibrium Between Tax Sovereignty and the Freedom of Movement Within the EC* (Kluwer, 2006), at pp. 30-31; also cf. W. Schön in W. Schön/C. Heber (eds.), *Grundfragen des Europäischen Steuerrechts* (Springer, 2015), at pp. 153.

1723. Commentary on the 1992-2014 OECD MC, Introduction para. 1; see also Commentary on the 1963-1977 OECD MC, Article 23(A) and 23(B) para. 1.

States' tax systems in a similar way as this Member State avoids or attenuates the effects of economic double taxation caused exclusively by its own tax system. Apart from the fact that the Court's rationale why it is (only) the shareholder's and not (also) the distributing company's Member State of residence is not convincing,[1724] one may wonder why it is not transferable to the issue of juridical double taxation as well. Perhaps, the reason is that juridical double taxation is considered to be a phenomenon that generally arises only in a cross-border context, whereas economic double taxation may also occur in a purely domestic situation.[1725] After all, the ECJ has emphasized that profits distributed by resident and non-resident companies are likewise "*capable of being subjected to [economic] double taxation.*"[1726] Therefore, domestic and cross-border dividend distributions are considered to be comparable from the perspective of a fully taxable shareholder.[1727] By contrast, it is generally assumed that there is typically no domestic counterpart for juridical double taxation, unless the fiscal competence within a Member State is not centralized, but the administrative units (e.g., regions, provinces, cantons or federal states) may autonomously decide on imposing direct taxes.[1728] Apart from the latter case, it could hence be argued that only

1724. See N. Bammens, *The Principle of Non-Discrimination in International and European Tax Law* (IBFD, 2012), at pp. 776-778; J. Englisch, 38 *Intertax* 4 (2010), at pp. 213-217; J. Englisch in W. Haslehner/G. Kofler/A. Rust (eds.), *Landmark Decisions of the ECJ in Direct Taxation* (Kluwer, 2015), at pp. 55-57; M.J. Graetz/C. Warren, 44 *Common Market L. Rev.* 6 (2007), at p. 1611; also cf. W. Schön, 69 *Bull. Intl. Taxn.* 4/5 (2015), at pp. 289-290; W. Schön in W. Schön/C. Heber (eds.), *Grundfragen des Europäischen Steuerrechts* (Springer, 2015), at pp. 151-153; but see S. van Thiel, 62 *Tax L. Rev.* 1 (2008), at pp. 165-167.

1725. See G. Kofler, *Doppelbesteuerungsabkommen und Europäisches Gemeinschaftsrecht* (Linde, 2007), at p. 155; G. Kofler in A. Rust (ed.), *Double Taxation Within the European Union* (Kluwer, 2011), at p. 106; W. Hellerstein/G. Kofler/R. Mason, 62 *Tax L. Rev.* 1 (2008), at p. 7; V. Heydt in W. Haslehner/G. Kofler/A. Rust (eds.), *Landmark Decisions of the ECJ in Direct Taxation* (Kluwer, 2015), at p. 181; also cf. J. Englisch, 33 *Intertax* 8/9 (2005), at p. 323; but see B.J.M. Terra/P.J. Wattel, *European Tax Law*[6] (Kluwer, 2012), at p. 1046; P. Wattel in G. Maisto (ed.), *Taxation of Intercompany Dividends under Tax Treaties and EU Law* (IBFD, 2012), at pp. 44-45, who argues that "*for some reason many people think that juridical double taxation does not exist domestically. That is only the case, precisely,* because *it is invariably prevented in internal situations.*" Since "both *forms of double taxation exist both* domestically *and in cross-border situations [...] [e]ither* both *economic double taxation and juridical double taxation result 'from the exercise in parallel by two Member States of their fiscal sovereignty',* or both *economic double taxation and juridical double taxation are discriminatory because both foreign dividends and domestic dividends are subjected to tax in the hands of the shareholder and should therefore be treated alike.*"

1726. Judgment in *Manninen*, C-319/02, EU:C:2004:484, at para. 35; also see Judgment in *Lenz*, C-315/02, EU:C:2004:446, at para. 31; Judgment in *Haribo Lakritzen Hans Riegel*, C-436/08 and C-437/08, EU:C:2011:61, at para. 59.

1727. Judgment in *Lenz*, C-315/02, EU:C:2004:446, at paras 32-33; Judgment in *Manninen*, C-319/02, EU:C:2004:484, at paras 36-37; Judgment in *Test Claimants in the FII Group Litigation*, C-446/04, EU:C:2006:774, at para. 62; Judgment in *Orange European Smallcap Fund*, C-194/06, EU:C:2008:289, at para. 40; Judgment in *Haribo Lakritzen Hans Riegel*, C-436/08 and C-437/08, EU:C:2011:61, at para. 59; Judgment in *Meilicke and others*, C-262/09, EU:C:2011:438, at para. 30; Judgment in *Accor*, C-310/09, EU:C:2011:581, at para. 45; Judgment in *Santander Asset Management SGIIC*, C-338/11 to C-347/11, EU:C:2012:286, at para. 42; Judgment in *Test Claimants in the FII Group Litigation*, C-35/11, EU:C:2012:707, at para. 37; Judgment in *Emerging Markets Series of DFA Investment Trust Company*, C-190/12, EU:C:2014:249, at para. 58.

1728. See, for example, M. Lang/L. Paterno, 1 *Spektrum der Rechtswissenschaften* 1 (2011), at p. 78.

cross-border situations are *"capable of being subjected to [juridical] double taxation."* Since a Member State hence does not need to provide for relief from juridical double taxation in purely domestic situations, the fundamental freedoms cannot oblige Member States to extend non-existing relief mechanisms to cross-border situations.

If this is in fact the reason why juridical double taxation is considered to differ from economic double taxation, a Member State may escape its obligation to extend a domestically-aligned shareholder imputation mechanism to dividends distributed by non-resident companies by changing its domestic system. Instead of levying, for example, a 29% corporate income tax on a company's profit which – after the profits being distributed – can be proportionally credited against the shareholder's 29% income tax on dividends, Finland could have levied a 29% income tax and deem a company's profit to be directly and proportionally attributable to the shareholders.[1729] Thus, economic double taxation would no longer exist in a domestic context. Consequently, in *Manninen*, the Court could not have obliged Finland to grant its resident shareholders relief from economic double taxation caused by the taxation of the distributing company's profits in another Member State and the taxation of the dividends at the shareholder level. Admittedly, it could be argued that such a system is also *"designed to attenuate,"*[1730] *"to mitigate"*[1731] or *"to prevent"*[1732] *"the economic effects of double taxation of company profits arising from the taxation of company profits by way of corporation tax and the taxation of a shareholder who is a taxpayer, by way of income tax, on the same profits distributed in the form of dividends,"*[1733] which would mean that economic double taxation also has to be avoided in cross-border situations. However, according to such an understanding, the same would be true with regard to juridical double taxation. If, for example, a Member State wanted dividends received by individual shareholders to be subject to an effective tax rate of 30%, it could require such shareholders to pay a 30% tax on all dividends received within a year or it could commit companies to withhold a tax of 15% upon the distribution of profits and additionally require the taxpayer to pay another 15% tax when filing the tax return. By not introducing the latter system, the Member State avoids *"the imposition of comparable taxes in two (or more) States on the same taxpayer in respect of the same subject matter and for identical periods."*[1734] Indeed, one could counter that the latter system cannot be perceived as leading to juridical double taxation, because the tax burden remains unchanged irrespective of which system is used. However, this is also

1729. Cf. D. Weber, 34 *Intertax* 12 (2006), p. 598; D. Weber, *In Search of a (New) Equilibrium Between Tax Sovereignty and the Freedom of Movement Within the EC* (Kluwer, 2006), at p. 30.
1730. Judgment in *Lenz*, C-315/02, EU:C:2004:446, at para. 30.
1731. Judgment in *Test Claimants in the FII Group Litigation*, C-446/04, EU:C:2006:774, at para. 62; Judgment in *Haribo Lakritzen Hans Riegel*, C-436/08 and C-437/08, EU:C:2011:61, at para. 59; Judgment in *Accor*, C-310/09, EU:C:2011:581, at para. 45.
1732. Judgment in *Manninen*, C-319/02, EU:C:2004:484, at para. 33; Judgment in *Test Claimants in the FII Group Litigation*, C-446/04, EU:C:2006:774, at para. 62; Judgment in *Meilicke and others*, C-292/04, EU:C:2007:132, at para. 21; Judgment in *Haribo Lakritzen Hans Riegel*, C-436/08 and C-437/08, EU:C:2011:61, at para. 59; Judgment in *Accor*, C-310/09, EU:C:2011:581, at para. 45.
1733. Judgment in *Lenz*, C-315/02, EU:C:2004:446, at para. 30.
1734. Commentary on the 1992-2014 OECD MC, Introduction para. 1; see also Commentary on the 1963-1977 OECD MC, Article 23(A) and 23(B) para. 1.

true with regard to the taxation of distributed profits. If a Member State wanted profits earned by a company and distributed to the shareholders to be effectively taxed at a rate of 30%, it either could levy a 30% corporate income tax on a company's profit which – after the profits being distributed – can be proportionally credited against the shareholder's 30% income tax on dividends or it could only levy a 30% income tax and deem a company's profit to be directly and proportionally attributable to the shareholders.[1735]

There is also another reason why it is not surprising that the ECJ is heavily criticized for differentiating between juridical and economic double taxation. Despite the OECD's varying definitions,[1736] the underlying problem of juridical and economic double taxation is the same if double taxation is perceived as a situational and relative phenomenon.[1737] Whether a taxpayer, a certain item of income, a transaction or an activity is subject to "double taxation" thus depends on the tax burden suffered by a comparable taxpayer, a comparable item of income, a comparable transaction or a comparable activity.[1738] When applying the fundamental freedoms, for example, the ECJ typically compares the cross-border situation with a purely domestic situation. Hence, from an internal market perspective, double taxation is at hand if the cross-border situation bears a higher tax burden than a comparable domestic situation would have to face in the tax jurisdiction that has the highest tax burden of all tax jurisdictions involved.[1739] This would be the case, for example, if Member State A as well as Member State B provided for imputation systems in order to ensure that the effective tax rate on

1735. In fact, there are of course endless possibilities to reach the ultimate aim of subjecting profits earned by a company and distributed to the shareholders to an effective tax rate of 30%.

1736. Whereas juridical double taxation is defined as "*the imposition of comparable taxes in two (or more) States on the same taxpayer in respect of the same subject matter and for identical periods*" (see Commentary on the 1992-2014 OECD MC, Introduction para. 1; see also Commentary on the 1963-1977 OECD MC, Article 23(A) and 23(B) para. 1), economic double taxation is considered to result from the "*taxation of the same income in the hands of different persons*" (see Commentary on the 1977-2014 OECD MC, Article 9 para. 5; see also Commentary on the 1963 OECD MC, Article 23(A) and 23(B) para. 2).

1737. Cf. R.A. Musgrave, *The Theory of Public Finance* (McGraw-Hill, 1959), at p. 163 ("*The only meaningful way in which the terms* double taxation *or* under-taxation *can be used in connection with equity is to indicate discrimination for or against particular taxpayers in terms of a given index of equality.*").

1738. See Chapter 1.2.2.

1739. With regard to direct taxation see G. Kofler, *Doppelbesteuerungsabkommen und Europäisches Gemeinschaftsrecht* (Linde, 2007), at p. 235; J. Englisch, 33 *Intertax* 8/9 (2005), at p. 325 (FN 151); J. Englisch in A. Cordewener/S. Enchelmaier/C.P. Schindler (eds.), *Meistbegünstigung im Steuerrecht der EU-Staaten* (C.H. Beck, 2006), at p. 176; L. Fischer/P. Warneke, *Grundlagen der Internationalen Betriebswirtschaftlichen Steuerlehre*[2] (Erich Schmidt Verlag, 1974), at p. 41; E. Reimer in M. Lehner (ed.), *Grundfreiheiten im Steuerrecht der EU-Staaten* (C.H. Beck, 2000), at pp. 57-58; J. Schönfeld in H. Flick/F. Wassemeyer/H. Baumhoff/J. Schönfeld (eds.), *Außensteuerrecht*[57] (Dr Otto Schmidt, 2005), Vor § 34c EStG at m.no 2; J. Schönfeld, 83 *StuW* 1 (2006), at pp. 80-82; Y. Brauner, 56 *Tax L. Rev.* 2 (2002), at pp. 309-310 ("*Ideally, no item of income should avoid any country's claim for taxation, and no item of income should be subject to taxation at a level (rate) higher than that of either of the competing countries (what is normally called 'double taxation'). [...] [T]he tax [...] ideally should not amount in total to a rate higher than the highest of the rates, but not more than that.*"); with regard to indirect taxation see J. Englisch, *Wettbewerbsgleichheit im grenzüberschreitenden Handel* (Mohr Siebeck, 2008), at p. 788.

profits earned by *resident* companies and distributed to *resident* shareholders corresponds to the respective shareholder's average income tax rate within the respective tax period, but do not grant equivalent relief in cross-border situations. If both Member States provided for a corporate income tax rate of 25% and the average income tax rate of a taxpayer was 50%, profits earned by a resident company and distributed to such a resident shareholder would be subject to an effective tax rate of 50%, whereas profits that are distributed cross-border would suffer from an effective tax rate of 62.5%:

		Member State A	*Member State B*	*Cross-Border Dividend*
	Corporate Income Tax Base	100.00	100.00	100.00
-	Corporate Income Tax (25%)	(25.00)	(25.00)	(25.00)
=	Dividend	75.00	75.00	75.00
+	Tax Credit	25.00	25.00	–
=	Shareholder Income Tax Base	100.00	100.00	75.00
-	Shareholder Income Tax (50%)	(50.00)	(50.00)	(37.50)
+	Tax Credit	25.00	25.00	–
=	Income Tax	25.00	25.00	37.50
	Total Tax on Underlying Profit	50.00	50.00	62.50

In such a case, according to the ECJ, the shareholder's Member State of residence would be obliged to extend its domestically-aligned imputation system to the cross-border situation. A Member State that provides for a relief mechanism, which is "*designed to attenuate,*"[1740] "*to mitigate*"[1741] or "*to prevent*"[1742] "*the economic effects of double taxation of company profits arising from the taxation of company profits by way of corporation tax and the taxation of a shareholder who is a taxpayer, by way of income tax, on the same profits distributed in the form of dividends,*"[1743] has to grant equivalent relief in cross-border situations, because profits distributed by non-resident companies and profits distributed by domestic companies are likewise "*capable of being subjected*

1740. Judgment in *Lenz*, C-315/02, EU:C:2004:446, at para. 30.
1741. Judgment in *Test Claimants in the FII Group Litigation*, C-446/04, EU:C:2006:774, at para. 62; Judgment in *Haribo Lakritzen Hans Riegel*, C-436/08 and C-437/08, EU:C:2011:61, at para. 59; Judgment in *Accor*, C-310/09, EU:C:2011:581, at para. 45.
1742. Judgment in *Manninen*, C-319/02, EU:C:2004:484, at para. 33; Judgment in *Test Claimants in the FII Group Litigation*, C-446/04, EU:C:2006:774, at para. 62; Judgment in *Meilicke and others*, C-292/04, EU:C:2007:132, at para. 21; Judgment in *Haribo Lakritzen Hans Riegel*, C-436/08 and C-437/08, EU:C:2011:61, at para. 59; Judgment in *Accor*, C-310/09, EU:C:2011:581, at para. 45.
1743. Judgment in *Lenz*, C-315/02, EU:C:2004:446, at para. 30.

to double taxation."[1744] Thus, the ECJ assumes that purely domestic as well as cross-border situations would be "*subjected to double taxation*" if both Member State A and Member State B abolished their imputation systems. However, if double taxation is perceived as a situational and relative phenomenon, this is by no means obvious. Without any relief mechanism, intra-state and cross-border profit distributions would likewise suffer from an effective tax burden of 62.5%. But if the cross-border situation does not bear a higher tax burden than a comparable domestic situation, why does the Court still assume that there is double taxation?

Obviously, it is for the same reason that it is generally considered to be desirable to provide for an integration of corporate and shareholder income taxes. Without such an integration, it would make a huge difference whether a business is organized as a sole proprietorship, a partnership or a corporation, because direct tax systems are typically affected by a dualism of business taxation. Thus, profits earned via a sole proprietorship or a partnership are directly attributable to the individual acting as a sole proprietor or a partner within a partnership. The effective tax burden of such profits hence results from the effective tax rate of the individual. By contrast, profits earned by corporations are initially subject to corporate income tax. If the after-tax profit is subsequently distributed, it is again taxed at the level of the shareholder as a dividend. Without a relief mechanism, the effective tax burden of profits earned via a corporation would be composed of the effective tax burden of the corporate profits plus the effective tax burden of the distributed (after-tax) profits. The different legal form cannot justify such a different treatment of business profits per se.[1745] The integration of corporate and shareholder income taxes is hence meant to at least mitigate the different tax burdens resulting from the dualism of business taxation.[1746] However, from this it follows that, from a purely domestic perspective, the term "economic double taxation" involves a comparison of the tax burdens resulting from the use of different legal forms when organizing a business.[1747] By contrast, determining whether

1744. Judgment in *Manninen*, C-319/02, EU:C:2004:484, at para. 35; also see Judgment in *Lenz*, C-315/02, EU:C:2004:446, at para. 31; Judgment in *Haribo Lakritzen Hans Riegel*, C-436/08 and C-437/08, EU:C:2011:61, at para. 59.

1745. See J. Lang in I. Ebling (ed.), *Besteuerung von Einkommen*, DStJG 24 (Dr Otto Schmidt, 2001), at pp. 98-100; J. Hennrichs, 79 *StuW* 3 (2002), p. 201 (at p. 202); J. Hennrichs/U. Lehmann, 84 *StuW* 1 (2007), at p. 17; J. Hey in I. Ebling (ed.), *Besteuerung von Einkommen*, DStJG 24 (Dr Otto Schmidt, 2001), at pp. 166-167; M. Jachmann, *Steuergesetzgebung zwischen Gleichheit und wirtschaftlicher Freiheit* (Boorberg, 2000), at pp. 60-66.

1746. See J. Hey in I. Ebling (ed.), *Besteuerung von Einkommen*, DStJG 24 (Dr Otto Schmidt, 2001), at pp. 157-181; M. Jachmann, *Steuergesetzgebung zwischen Gleichheit und wirtschaftlicher Freiheit* (Boorberg, 2000), at pp. 61-66; M. Jachmann in J. Pelka (ed.), *Europa- und verfassungsrechtliche Grenzen der Unternehmensbesteuerung, DStJG 23* (Dr Otto Schmidt, 2000), at pp. 17-22; W. Schön, 77 *StuW* 2 (2000), at p. 152; S. Sieker in S.F. Seeger (ed.), *Perspektiven der Unternehmensbesteuerung*, DStJG 25 (Dr Otto Schmidt, 2002), at p. 176; also cf. J. Englisch, *Dividendenbesteuerung* (Dr Otto Schmidt, 2005), at pp. 130-131; J. Heinrich in M. Achatz/T. Ehrke-Rabel/J. Heinrich/R. Leitner/O. Taucher (eds.), *Steuerrecht Verfassungsrecht Europarecht, Festschrift für Hans Georg Ruppe* (Facultas, 2007), at pp. 203-211; J. Lang in S. Widmann (ed.), *Besteuerung der GmbH und ihrer Gesellschafter*, DStJG 20 (Dr Otto Schmidt, 1997), at pp. 70-71.

1747. Cf. H. Ruppe, *Die Steuerliche Doppelbelastung der Körperschaftsgewinne* (Jupiter-Verlag, 1967), pp. 139-140.

a cross-border situation is subject to double taxation requires a comparison with the tax burden of a comparable domestic situation. Given the different content of the term "double taxation," it is misleading to argue that Member States avoiding or mitigating economic double taxation exclusively caused by their own tax system in a purely domestic context are obliged to provide for the same relief in cross-border situations. Thereby, the ECJ pretends that economic double taxation in a purely domestic situation is the same as in a cross-border situation. However, in order to prove that this is the case, one has to focus on the comparison that is relied on to identify double taxation in the first place.[1748] The actual question thus is whether a Member State that mitigates the diverging tax effects of organizing a business as an individual enterprise, a partnership or a corporation in a domestic context is obliged to also avoid or mitigate the diverging tax effects of domestic and cross-border business activities.

The answer to this question depends on the particular legislation under scrutiny. If a resident shareholder receiving dividends from a resident corporation benefits from an imputation credit, a tax exemption, a reduced tax rate or a diminished tax base, whereas such a benefit is not available for cross-border dividend distributions, the domestic situation is treated differently than a purely domestic situation. Unless there is a reason to assume that intra-state or cross-border profit distributions are not comparable, such a different treatment needs to be justified. If the benefit granted in a purely domestic situation is contingent upon the distributed profits having been subject to *domestic* corporate income tax,[1749] there is a direct link between the intra-state taxation of the distributing company's profits and the tax benefit granted to the shareholder receiving the dividends.[1750] Such a legal link proves that the tax benefit is effectively intended to ensure that profits earned by a company and distributed to its shareholder are subjected to a certain *domestic* tax burden. The different treatment could thus be justified by the need to protect the coherence of the tax system. However, focusing on whether a legal link exists or not is too formalistic, especially because introducing such a link is a waltz. Considering the ECJ's case law, it is not only about whether two legal provisions are legally linked, but also whether "*a direct link is established between a tax advantage and the offsetting of that advantage by a particular tax levy.*"[1751] Thus, a Member State may only rely on the concept of fiscal cohesion if

1748. See R.A. Musgrave, *The Theory of Public Finance* (McGraw-Hill, 1959), at p. 163: "*The only meaningful way in which the terms* double taxation *or* under-taxation *can be used in connection with equity is to indicate discrimination for or against particular taxpayers in terms of a given index of equality. It is this index that must be decided upon* first *to prove that double taxation or undertaxation occurs, rather than the reverse order.*"

1749. In order for such a link to be proportional an imputation credit would also have to be granted to the extent the profits distributed by a foreign corporation were subject to corporate income tax in the shareholder's Member State of residence. Such an understanding corresponds with the ECJ's approach with regard to outbound dividends. See Chapter 4.1.3.2.4.

1750. The lack of such a legal link was emphasized by the ECJ in *Lenz* (Judgment in *Lenz*, C-315/02, EU:C:2004:446, at para. 30).

1751. Opinion of AG Kokott in *Nordea Bank Danmark*, C-48/13, EU:C:2014:153; at point 43; also see Judgment in *Verkooijen*, C-35/98, EU:C:2000:294, at para. 57; Judgment in *Bosal*, C-168/01, EU:C:2003:479, at para. 29; Judgment in *Schilling and Fleck-Schilling*, C-209/01, EU:C:2003:610, at para. 41; Judgment in *Weidert and Paulus*, C-242/03, EU:C:2004:465, at para. 22; Judgment in *Manninen*, C-319/02, EU:C:2004:484, at para. 42; Judgment in *Keller*

the tax benefit granted to shareholders receiving dividends fully compensates for the corporate income tax that had to be paid by the distributing company when the profits were earned.[1752] Although the Finnish legislation provided for such an exact correspondence between the corporate income tax paid by the distributing company and the tax benefit granted to the shareholder, the ECJ held in *Manninen* that limiting the imputation system to intra-state dividend distributions "*does not appear to be necessary in order to preserve the cohesion of the Finnish tax system.*"[1753] The reason why the Finnish system was considered not to be proportional was that the Court equated the mitigation of diverging tax effects resulting from organizing a business as either an individual enterprise, a partnership or a corporation with the avoidance or attenuation of diverging tax effects resulting from engaging in either domestic or cross-border business activities.[1754] If the Court had not been misguided by the term "double

Holding, C-471/04, EU:C:2006:143, at para. 40; Judgment in *Centro di Musicologia Walter Stauffer*, C-386/04, EU:C:2006:568, at para. 53; Judgment in *Commission/Portugal*, C-345/05, EU:C:2006:685, at para. 29; Judgment in *Test Claimants in the FII Group Litigation*, C-446/04, EU:C:2006:774, at para. 178; Judgment in *Meilicke and others*, C-292/04, EU:C:2007:132, at para. 28; Judgment in *Test Claimants in the Thin Cap Group Litigation*, C-524/04, EU:C:2007:161, at para. 68; Judgment in *Rewe Zentralfinanz*, C-347/04, EU:C:2007:194, at para. 62; Judgment in *Hollmann*, C-443/06, EU:C:2007:600, at para. 56; Judgment in *Amurta*, C-379/05, EU:C:2007:655, at para. 46; Judgment in *Jundt*, C-281/06, EU:C:2007:816, at para. 68; Judgment in *Heinrich Bauer Verlag*, C-360/06, EU:C:2008:531, at para. 37; Judgment in *Papillon*, C-418/07, EU:C:2008:659, at para. 44; Judgment in *Glaxo Wellcome*, C-182/08, EU:C:2009:559, at para. 79; Judgment in *Commission/Spain*, C-562/07, EU:C:2009:614, at para. 61; Judgment in *Presidente del Consiglio dei Ministri*, C-169/08, EU:C:2009:709, at para. 47; Judgment in *Commission/Belgium*, C-250/08, EU:C:2011:793, at para. 71; Judgment in *Santander Asset Management SGIIC*, C-338/11 to C-347/11, EU:C:2012:286, at para. 51; Judgment in *DI. VI. Finanziaria di Diego della Valle & C.*, C-380/11, EU:C:2012:552, at para. 47; Judgment in *Test Claimants in the FII Group Litigation*, C-35/11, EU:C:2012:707, at para. 58; Judgment in *Welte*, C-181/12, EU:C:2013:662, at para. 59; Judgment in *K.*, C-322/11, EU:C:2013:716, at para. 66; Judgment in *Bouanich*, C-375/12, EU:C:2014:138, at para. 69; Judgment in *Grünewald*, C-559/13, EU:C:2015:109, at para. 48; Judgment in *Groupe Steria*, C-386/14, EU:C:2015:524, at para. 31; Judgment in *Finanzamt Linz*, C-66/14, EU:C:2015:661, at para. 44.

1752. Opinion of AG Kokott in *Manninen*, C-319/02, EU:C:2004:164, at points 62-63; also see J. Englisch, 13 *IStR* 19 (2004), at p. 685; J. Englisch, 33 *Intertax* 5 (2005), at p. 206; J. Englisch, 38 *Intertax* 4 (2010), at p. 207; G. Kofler, *Doppelbesteuerungsabkommen und Europäisches Gemeinschaftsrecht* (Linde, 2007), at pp. 116 and 1012; B.J.M. Terra/P.J. Wattel, *European Tax Law*[6] (Kluwer, 2012), at p. 1051; also cf. W. Hellerstein/G. Kofler/R. Mason, 62 *Tax L. Rev.* 1 (2008), at p. 23; M. Lang, 17 *EC Tax Rev.* 2 (2008), at p. 70; critically J. Englisch, 44 *Eur. Taxn.* 8 (2004), at p. 361.

1753. Judgment in *Manninen*, C-319/02, EU:C:2004:484, at para. 45.

1754. This can be inferred from the ECJ assuming that "*the Finnish tax legislation is designed to prevent double taxation of company profits by granting to a shareholder who receives dividends a tax advantage linked to the taking into account of the corporation tax due from the company distributing the dividends.*" Since the Finnish system "*takes account of the corporation tax owed by a company in order to prevent double taxation of the profits distributed, shareholders who are fully taxable in Finland find themselves in a comparable situation, whether they receive dividends from a company established in that Member State or from a company established in Sweden,*" because "*both dividends distributed by a company established in Finland and those paid by a company established in Sweden are, apart from the tax credit, capable of being subjected to double taxation.*" Judgment in *Manninen*, C-319/02, EU:C:2004:484, at paras 33-36.

taxation,"[1755] it would have needed to make much more effort in order to explain why it is disproportionate not to grant an imputation credit for profits distributed by a non-resident company. Had the shareholder receiving such a dividend not invested in a foreign corporation, but instead participated in a foreign partnership or acted as a sole proprietor, the profits earned abroad would have been fully subject to unlimited tax liability in the taxpayer's Member State of residence. If such a Member State also granted an imputation credit for foreign corporate income tax, the domestic effective tax burden of business profits would be very different depending on whether a cross-border business activity is organized as a sole proprietorship, a foreign partnership or a foreign corporation. Such a result is not in line with the aim of integrating corporate and shareholder income taxes, which is to at least mitigate the different tax burdens resulting from the dualism of business taxation.

Of course, from the taxpayer's perspective, it does not make a difference where corporate income tax has to be paid. However, the very same issue arises if a business activity is organized as a sole proprietorship. If, for example, a sole proprietor earned income via a foreign permanent establishment, the resultant tax burden would also be higher than if the income was earned via a domestic permanent establishment. Irrespective of whether it is about juridical or economic double taxation, the higher tax burden suffered in a cross-border situation always results "*from the exercise in parallel by two Member States of their fiscal sovereignty.*"[1756] As long as EU law "*does not lay down any general criteria for the attribution of areas of competence between the Member States in relation to the elimination of double taxation within the [EU],*"[1757] such an outcome is undoubtedly problematic from an internal market perspective. However, according to the ECJ, unless there is a "*uniform or harmonisation measure designed to eliminate double taxation [...] adopted at Community law level,*"[1758] "*it is for the Member States to determine whether, and to what extent, [...] double taxation [...] is to be avoided and, for that purpose, to establish, either unilaterally or through double taxation conventions concluded with other Member States, procedures intended to prevent or mitigate such [...] double taxation.*"[1759]

1755. See R.A. Musgrave, *The Theory of Public Finance* (McGraw-Hill, 1959), at p. 163 ("*the concept of double taxation as taxing a thing more than once is fallacious*").

1756. Judgment in *Kerckhaert and Morres*, C-513/04, EU:C:2006:603, at para. 20; Judgment in *Columbus Container Services*, C-298/05, EU:C:2007:754, at para. 43; Judgment in *CIBA*, C-96/08, EU:C:2010:185, at para. 25; Judgment in *Commission/Spain*, C-487/08, EU:C:2010:310, at para. 27.

1757. Judgment in *Kerckhaert and Morres*, C-513/04, EU:C:2006:603, at paras 20-23; Judgment in *CIBA*, C-96/08, EU:C:2010:185 at paras 25-27; see also Judgment in *Block*, C-67/08, EU:C:2009:92, at paras 28-30; Judgment in *Damseaux*, C-128/08, EU:C:2009:471, at paras 30 and 33.

1758. Judgment in *Kerckhaert and Morres*, C-513/04, EU:C:2006:713, at para. 22; Judgment in *Columbus Container Services*, C-298/05, EU:C:2007:754, at para. 45; Judgment in *Block*, C-67/08, EU:C:2009:92, at para. 30; Judgment in *CIBA*, C-96/08, EU:C:2010:185, at para. 27.

1759. Judgment in *Amurta*, C-379/05, EU:C:2007:655, at para. 24; Judgment in *Les Vergers du Vieux Tauves*, C-48/07, EU:C:2008:758, at para. 46; Judgment in *Aberdeen Property Fininvest Alpha*, C-303/07, EU:C:2009:377, at para. 28; Judgment in *Gaz de France - Berliner Investissement*, C-247/08, EU:C:2009:600, at para. 37; Judgment in *Commission/Italy*, C-540/07, EU:C:2009:717, at para. 31; Judgment in *Commission/Germany*, C-284/09, EU:C:2011:670, at para. 48; also see Judgment in *Kerckhaert and Morres*, C-513/04, EU:C:2006:713, at para. 23;

2 DOUBLE NON-TAXATION IN THE LIGHT OF EU LAW

2.1 The Challenge of Tackling Double Non-Taxation by Means of Primary EU Law

In the past, from a single taxpayer's business perspective, making use of legal possibilities to reduce the effective tax burden did not seem to involve any major drawbacks. Since the media as well as non-governmental organizations have increasingly unmasked the tax planning schemes used by multinational corporations to reduce taxation on income,[1760] it is clear that this is not true; at least not anymore. The Starbucks tax controversy is a vivid example which illustrates that today multinational corporations "*may face significant reputational risk if their effective tax rate is viewed as being too low*":[1761] In 2012, the media exposed the fact that the amount of taxes paid in the UK by the US-based globally operating coffee company Starbucks dramatically clashed with the company's actual economic performance.[1762] These reports unleashed intense public indignation, including sit-ins and threats of boycotting UK Starbucks

Judgment in *Test Claimants in Class IV of the ACT Group Litigation*, C-374/04, EU:C:2006:773, at para. 54; Judgment in *Test Claimants in the Thin Cap Group Litigation*, C-524/04, EU:C:2007:161, at para. 49; Judgment in *Cobelfret*, C-138/07, EU:C:2009:82, at para 56; Judgment in *Damseaux*, C-128/08, EU:C:2009:471, at para. 30; Judgment in *Commission/Spain*, C-487/08, EU:C:2010:310, at para. 31; Judgment in *Banco Bilbao Vizcaya Argentaria*, C-157/10, EU:C:2011:813, at para. 31.

1760. See, for example, B. Barrow, Amazon faces probes after "not paying a penny in company tax in Britain for two years," *The Daily Mail* (5 Apr. 2012); T. Bergin, Special Report: How Starbucks Avoids UK Taxes, *Reuters* (15 Oct. 2012); T. Bergin, Fast Food, Tax Lite, *Reuters* (15 Oct. 2012); P. Campbell, Facebook's UK Tax Bill was Less than It Pays Its Average Worker: Company Paid Just £238,000 to the Taxman in 2011 Despite UK Revenue Being £175 million, *The Daily Mail* (10 Oct. 2012); C. Duhigg/D. Kocieniewski, How Apples Sidesteps Billions in Taxes, *The New York Times* (28 Apr. 2012); J. Drucker, Google 2.4% Rate Shows How $60 Billion Is Lost to Tax Loopholes, *Bloomberg* (21 Oct. 2010); J. Drucker, Dodging Repatriation Tax Lets U.S. Companies Bring Home Cash, *Bloomberg* (29 Dec. 2010); J. Drucker, Google Revenues Sheltered in No-Tax Bermuda Soar to $10 Billion, *Bloomberg* (10 Dec. 2012); D. Egan, Does a Company's Responsibility to Society Start with Paying Its Taxes?, *The Guardian* (9 Sep. 2011); S. Pfeifer [?], He Put a Dent in Tax Evasion, *Los Angeles Times* (26 Oct. 2009); R. Sutherland, Amazon, Google, and the Sordid Reality of Tax Avoidance, *The Daily Mail* (6 Apr. 2012); R. Sutherland, Apple "made £6bn" in UK... But Paid Only £10m in Tax, *The Daily Mail* (8 Apr. 2012); M. Warman, Google Pays Just £6m UK Tax, *The Telegraph* (8 Aug. 2012); R. Waters, Microsoft's Foreign Tax Planning under Scrutiny, *Financial Times* (7 Jun. 2011). See also David Kocieniewski's series called "But Nobody Pays That" in *The New York Times*, for which he was awarded a Pulitzer Price for explanatory journalism in 2013; similar series are "Tax Gap" in *The Guardian* and "The Great Corporate Tax Dodge" in *Bloomberg*.

1761. OECD, *Action Plan on Base Erosion and Profit Shifting* (OECD, 2013), at p. 8; also see OECD, *Addressing Base Erosion and Profit Shifting* (OECD, 2013), at p. 30.

1762. See T. Bergin, Special Report: How Starbucks Avoids UK taxes, *Reuters* (15 Oct. 2012); for a technical analysis of Starbuck's tax structure see E.D. Kleinbard, Through a Latte Darkly: Starbuck's Stateless Income Planning, 139 *Tax Notes* (24 Jun. 2013), p. 1515 (at pp. 1519-1531).

stores.[1763,1764] Politics reacted immediately. In less than a month, the House of Commons' Committee of Public Accounts convened a hearing to review the UK corporate tax planning not only of Starbucks, but of Amazon and Google as well.[1765] Although these companies were not accused of having acted illegally but of having acted immorally,[1766] the public pressure was so intense that Starbucks pledged to voluntarily pay GBP 20 million in UK corporate tax in 2013 and 2014, irrespective of its actual business results.[1767]

From an EU law perspective, the main issue is not that taxpayers engaging in complex international tax planning structures risk losing popularity among consumers. It is rather about the resultant distorting effect on competition. The increasing public pressure to pay a "*fair share of taxes,*"[1768] on the one hand, may be much higher for

1763. See P. Campbell, Starbucks Facing Boycott Over Tax, *Daily Mail* (16 Oct. 2012); J. Thompson/V. Houlder, Starbucks Faces Boycott Calls Over Tax Affairs, *Financial Times* (17 Oct. 2012); S. Neville/Z. Wood/S. Bowers, UK Uncut Targets Starbucks Over Tax, *The Guardian* (18 Oct. 2012); S. Neville/S. Malik, Starbucks Wakes Up and Smells the Stench of Tax Avoidance Controversy, *The Guardian* (12 Nov. 2012); R. Escobales/T. McVeigh, Starbucks Hit by UK Uncut Protests as Tax Row Boils Over, *The Guardian* (8 Dec. 2012).

1764. As the media reports concerned Starbucks' UK tax bill, the tax controversy triggered far less interest in other countries. In Germany, for example, it was not until 2014 that comedians picked up the increasing attention paid to Starbuck's tax strategies in the UK and launched the "Star Bucket Challenge" in order to also draw German society's attention to the issue of multinational corporations not paying "enough" taxes. The idea was based on a very successful social media campaign called the "Ice Bucket Challenge" (see N. McCarthy, Ice Bucket Challenge: ALS Wikipedia Page Views Increase 18-Fold, *Forbes* [8 Sep. 2014]; E. Steel, "Ice Bucket Challenge" Donations for A.L.S. Research Top $41 Million, *New York Times* [21 Aug. 2014]). People were thereby encouraged to be filmed having a bucket of ice water poured on their heads and then nominating others to do the same in order to promote awareness of the disease amyotrophic lateral sclerosis (ALS). In a similar vein, the German comedians suggested posting videos online where customers spill a cup of Starbucks coffee on themselves after having realized that Starbucks forgot to put taxes in it. Although this campaign was far less successful than the archetype, it still caused Austrian and German media to increasingly report on current developments within the BEPS project (see D. Segler, Auf zur Starbucket-Challenge, *Frankfurter Rundschau* [29 Oct. 2014]; A. Sator, Starbucks: Kaffee ohne Steuern schmeckt nicht, *DerStandard* [4 Nov. 2014]; G. Kucera, Aktionismus gegen Steuerflucht, *Wiener Zeitung* [3 Nov. 2014]; E. Past, Steueroasen: #Starbucketchallenge fordert Gerechtigkeit + Video, *Wirtschaftsblatt* [5 Nov. 2014]).

1765. See T. Bergin, Starbucks, Amazon and Google to Face MPs Over Tax, *Reuters* (12 Nov. 2012); T. Bergin, UK Lawmakers Slam Starbucks, Amazon and Google on Tax, *Reuters* (12 Nov. 2012); S. Hoggart, A Highly Taxing Session for the Men from Amazon, Google and Starbucks, *The Guardian* (12 Nov. 2012); R. Murphy, Amazon, Google and Starbucks are Struggling to Defend Their Tax Avoidance, *The Guardian* (13 Nov. 2012).

1766. See UK House of Commons Committee of Public Accounts, HM Revenue & Customs: Annual Report and Accounts 2011-2012, Nineteenth Report of Session 2012-2013, HC 716 (3 Dec. 2012), at p. 60 ("*We are not accusing you of being illegal; we are accusing you of being immoral.*").

1767. See V. Houlder/J. Pickard/L. Lucas/B. Jopson, Starbucks to pay £20m UK Corporate Tax, *Financial Times* (6 Dec. 2012); S. Neville/J. Treanor, Starbucks to pay £20m in Tax Over Next Two Years After Customer Revolt, *The Guardian* (6 Dec. 2012); L. Pollak, The Marketing Smackdown and that Very Odd Voluntary Tax "payment," *Financial Times Alphaville* (13 Dec. 2012).

1768. G20 Leaders' Declaration, Saint Petersburg Summit, (5-6 Sep. 2013), at para. 50; J. Alumnia in European Commission Press Release, *State Aid: Commission Investigates Transfer Pricing Arrangements on Corporate Taxation of Apple (Ireland) Starbucks (Netherlands) and Fiat Finance and Trade (Luxembourg)*, IP/14/663 (11 Jun. 2014), at p. 1; European Commission,

businesses that are well-known among consumers than for others. By giving in to this pressure, the former may be put at a disadvantage with their competitors.[1769] On the other hand, competition may also be harmed because taxpayers only operating in a Member State's domestic market may have difficulties in competing with multinational enterprises "*that have the ability to shift their profits across borders to avoid or reduce tax.*"[1770] This kind of distortion of competition could be avoided by means of secondary EU law or legislative changes of Member States' domestic laws that aim at eliminating the possibilities for taxpayers to reduce the effective tax burden by engaging in cross-border tax planning. However, to the extent tax laws remain unharmonized there will always be the danger of inconsistencies resulting from the interaction of deviating tax systems. Therefore, the question arises whether primary EU law, in particular the State aid rules, can resolve resultant distortions of competition.

The tax planning structures in question are typically set up to strictly comply with the legal requirements and are hence conceptually different from abusive tax schemes.[1771] They may, for example, benefit from preferential regimes enacted by a single state[1772] and/or exploit inconsistencies resulting from the interaction of domestic

Statement by Vice President Alumnia on Opening of In-Depth Investigation into Possible State Aid Granted by Luxembourg to Amazon, Statement/14/303 (7 Oct. 2014), at p. 2; also see M. Vestager in European Commission Press Release, *Commission Decides Selective Tax Advantages Fort Fiat in Luxembourg and Starbucks in the Netherlands are Illegal under EU State Aid Rules*, IP/15/5580 (21 Oct. 2015), at p. 1; also cf. R. Lyal, 38 *Fordham Intl. L. J.* 4 (2015), at p. 1018; S.A. Stevens, The Duty of Countries and Enterprises to Pay Their Fair Share, 42 *Intertax* 11 (2014), p. 702 (at p. 702).

1769. See OECD, *Action Plan on Base Erosion and Profit Shifting* (OECD, 2013), at p. 8.

1770. OECD, *Action Plan on Base Erosion and Profit Shifting* (OECD, 2013), at p. 8; also see OECD, *Addressing Base Erosion and Profit Shifting* (OECD, 2013), at pp. 8, 39 and 50; G. Osborne/P. Moscovici/W. Schäuble, We are determined that multinationals will not avoid tax, *Financial Times* (16 Feb. 2013): "*Some multinationals are exploiting the transfer pricing or treaty rules to shift profits to places with no or low taxation, allowing them to pay as little as 5 per cent in corporate taxes while smaller businesses are paying up to 30 per cent. This distorts competition, giving larger companies an advantage over smaller, more domestic companies. In this difficult economic climate, it cannot be right that larger companies can avoid paying tax, with families and small businesses ending up paying more*"; also cf. European Commission Press Release, *Commission Decides Selective Tax Advantages Fort Fiat in Luxembourg and Starbucks in the Netherlands are Illegal under EU State Aid Rules*, IP/15/5580 (21 Oct. 2015), at p. 1 ("*Tax rulings cannot use methodologies, no matter how complex, to establish transfer prices with no economic justification and which unduly shift profits to reduce the taxes paid by the company. It would give that company an unfair competitive advantage over other companies (typically SMEs) that are taxed on their actual profits because they pay market prices for the goods and services they use.*").

1771. See M. Boyle, 50 *British Tax Rev.* 5 (2005), at p. 528; T. Ehrke-Rabel/G. Kofler, 22 *ÖStZ* 19 (2009), at pp. 470 et seq.; G. Kofler in R. Hüttemann (ed.), *Gestaltungsfreiheit und Gestaltungsmissbrauch im Steuerrecht*, DStjG 34 (Dr Otto Schmidt, 2010), at p. 232; G. Kofler/H. Kofler in G. Brähler/C. Lösel (eds.), *Deutsches und internationales Steuerrecht – Gegenwart und Zukunft, Festschrift Djanani* (Gabler, 2008), at pp. 382-383; D. Rosenbloom, 53 *Tax L. Rev.* 137 (2000), at p. 143. see also OECD, *Action Plan on Base Erosion and Profit Shifting* (OECD 2013), at p. 15.

1772. See OECD, *Countering Harmful Tax Practices More Effectively, Taking into Account Transparency and Substance, Action 5: 2015 Final Report* (OECD, 2015), at p. 19 ("*In order for a regime to be considered preferential, it must offer some form of tax preference in comparison with the general principles of taxation in the relevant country.*").

tax systems, including rules adopted in accordance with international standards to relieve double taxation, that provide opportunities to eliminate or significantly reduce the effective tax burden on the profit of a group of companies.[1773] Examining whether preferential regimes enacted by a single state are compatible with the State aid rules is among the ECJ's day-to-day business. By contrast, the compatibility of double non-taxation caused by a taxpayer exploiting gaps in the interaction of different tax systems and/or double taxation conventions with Article 107 TFEU raises the same question that troubles the Court, scholars and practitioners when dealing with the issue of whether double taxation is reconcilable with the fundamental freedoms:[1774] Which Member State should be made responsible for the tax burden being too low?

Applying the State aid rules to situations of double non-taxation also entails another challenge. Whereas the fundamental freedoms typically require a comparison between the cross-border and the domestic situation,[1775] the State aid rules only apply if there is a preferential treatment of certain economic operators which are in a comparable situation with non-privileged economic operators.[1776] Although the ECJ tends to interpret this comparability criterion quite generously,[1777] it is questionable whether a preferential treatment of domestic situations vis-à-vis cross-border

1773. See OECD, *Action Plan on Base Erosion and Profit Shifting* (OECD 2013), at p. 10 ("*BEPS relates chiefly to instances where the interaction of different tax rules leads to double non-taxation or less than single taxation. It also relates to arrangements that achieve no or low taxation by shifting profits away from the jurisdictions where the activities creating those profits take place. No or low taxation is not per se a cause of concern, but it becomes so when it is associated with practices that artificially segregate taxable income from the activities that generate it. In other words, what creates tax policy concerns is that, due to gaps in the interaction of different tax systems, and in some cases because of the application of bilateral tax treaties, income from cross-border activities may go untaxed anywhere, or be only unduly lowly taxed.*").

1774. See R. Luja, *EU State Aid Law and National Tax Rulings*, IP/A/TAXE/2015-02, PE 563.453 (October 2015), at pp. 9, 13 and 15; R. Luja, 76 *Tax Notes Intl.* 4 (27 Oct. 2014), at pp. 353-354; R. Luja, 60 *British Tax Rev.* 3 (2015), at p. 387; R. Szudoczky/J.L. van de Streek, Revisiting the Dutch Interest Box under the EU State Aid Rules and the Code of Conduct: When a "Disparity" Is Selective and Harmful, 38 *Intertax* 5 (2010), p. 260 (at p. 272); R. Szudoczky in I. Richelle/W. Schön/E. Traversa (eds.), *Allocating Taxing Powers within the European Union* (Springer, 2013), at pp. 177-179.

1775. See Chapter 3.2.4.1.

1776. See, for example, Judgment in *Adria-Wien Pipeline and Wietersdorfer & Peggauer Zementwerke*, C-143/99, EU:C:2001:598, at para. 38; Judgment in *GIL Insurance and others*, C-308/01, EU:C:2004:252, at para. 68; Judgment in *Spain/Commission*, C-409/00, EU:C:2003:92, at para. 47; Judgment in *Heiser*, C-172/03, EU:C:2005:130, at para. 40; Judgment in *Portugal/Commission*, C-88/03, EU:C:2006:511, at para. 54; Judgment in *Unión General de Trabajadores de la Rioja*, C-428/06 to C-434/06, EU:C:2008:488, at para. 46; Judgment in *British Aggregates/Commission*, C-487/06 P, EU:C:2008:757, at para. 82; Judgment in *Presidente del Consiglio dei Ministri*, C-169/08, EU:C:2009:709, at para. 61; Judgment in *Paint Graphos and others*, C-78/08 to C-80/08, EU:C:2011:550, at para. 49; Judgment in *P*, C-6/12, EU:C:2013:525, at para. 19; Judgment in *Ministerio de Defensa and Navantia*, C-522/13, EU:C:2014:2262, at para. 35.

1777. See Chapter 3.3.3.3.

situations – or *vice versa* – is sufficient to prove that *certain* undertakings or the production of *certain* goods are *favoured*.[1778] The recent jurisprudence suggests that it is.[1779]

However, to the extent these difficulties cannot be successfully overcome, double non-taxation may still be tackled by means of uni- or bilateral measures. In fact, the OECD,[1780] *inter alia*, suggests that specific and targeted rules denying certain benefits[1781] in the case of double non-taxation should be introduced at a domestic and a double tax treaty level. Within the EU, the Anti-Tax Avoidance Directive has picked up this suggestion and obliges the Member States to introduce such rules.[1782] A number of Member States had already seized the OECD's suggestion before the Anti-Tax Avoidance Directive was adopted and introduced rules that specifically address cross-border tax planning structures. Pursuant to some of these rules, for example, the domestic tax treatment of an entity, instrument or transfer involving a foreign country is linked to the tax treatment in the foreign country, thus eliminating the possibility for mismatches.[1783] However, due to the fact that such structures require a cross-border situation, the result of such rules is that benefits which are granted in purely domestic situations are denied in a cross-border situation. This leads to the question whether such a different treatment of domestic and cross-border situations constitutes

1778. For a view which tends to support selectivity see R. Luja, *EU State Aid Law and National Tax Rulings*, IP/A/TAXE/2015-02, PE 563.453 (October 2015), at p. 11; F.P. Sutter, Drei und mehr Normhypothesen zur beihilfenrechtlichen Einordnung des österreichischen unilateralen Entlastungssystems zur Vermeidung der Doppelbesteuerung, in J. Bauer/E. Burgstaller/K. Haslinger/J. Herdin/I. Hofbauer/M. Lang/H. Loukota/W. Loukota/M. Schilcher/J. Schuch/C. Staringer/F.P. Sutter/U. Zieseritsch (eds.), *Unilaterale Maßnahmen zur Vermeidung der Doppelbesteuerung* (Linde, 2004), p. 249 (at p. 265); F.P. Sutter, 14 *SWI* 1 (2004), at p. 10; R. Szudoczky in I. Richelle/W. Schön/E. Traversa (eds.), *Allocating Taxing Powers Within the European Union* (Springer, 2013), at pp. 173-177; also see Opinion of AG Wathelet in *Commission/World Duty Free Group, Banco Santander and Santusa Holding*, C-20/15 P and C-21/15 P, EU:C:2016:624, at point 137; for a view which tends to deny selectivity see R. Luja, Tax Treaties and State Aid: Some Thoughts, 44 *Eur. Taxn.* 4 (2004), p. 234 (at p. 234); F. Engelen, State Aid and Restrictions on Free Movement: Two Sides of the Same Coin?, 52 *Eur. Taxn.* 5 (2012), p. 204 (at pp. 208-209).

1779. Judgment in *Commission/World Duty Free Group, Banco Santander and Santusa Holding*, C-20/15 P and C-21/15 P, EU:C:2016:981.

1780. OECD, *Neutralising the Effects of Hybrid Mismatch Arrangements, Action 2: 2015 Final Report* (OECD, 2015), at pp. 13-131; OECD, *Preventing the Granting of Treaty Benefits in Inappropriate Circumstances, Action 6: 2015 Final Report* (OECD, 2015), at pp. 17-90; OECD, *Designing Effective Controlled Foreign Company Rules, Action 3: 2015 Final Report* (OECD, 2015); OECD, *Limiting Base Erosion Involving Interest Deductions and Other Financial Payments, Action 4: 2015 Final Report* (OECD, 2015).

1781. Examples that already exist in some Member States are the deduction for an expense or specific payments, the compensation of losses, the exemption for certain categories of income or a foreign tax credit. See OECD, *Hybrid Mismatch Arrangements: Policy and Compliance Issues* (OECD, 2012), at pp. 15-21.

1782. Council Directive (EU) 2016/1164 of 12 Jul. 2016 laying down rules against tax avoidance practices that directly affect the functioning of the internal market, *OJ* L 193 (19 Jul. 2016), p. 1 (at pp. 1-14) as changed by Council Directive (EU) 2017/952 of 29 May 2017 amending Directive (EU) 2016/1164 as regards hybrid mismatches with third countries, OJ L 144 (7 Jun. 2017), p. 1 (at pp. 1-11).

1783. See OECD, *Neutralising the Effects of Hybrid Mismatch Arrangements, Action 2: 2015 Final Report* (OECD, 2015), at pp. 13-131; also see OECD, *Hybrid Mismatch Arrangements: Policy and Compliance Issues* (OECD, 2012), at p. 14.

discrimination incompatible with the fundamental freedoms.[1784] Given this potential conflict of uni- or bilateral measures with primary EU law, Member States should also consider alternatives in order to limit situations of double non-taxation. The ECJ's case law shows, for example, that secondary EU law might serve as a tool to legally enforce the primary EU law's aim of avoiding double taxation.[1785] Therefore, the suggestion could be put forward to likewise examine whether secondary EU law may also be relied upon in order to avoid cross-border situations from being treated more beneficially than purely domestic situations.

2.2 Double Non-Taxation and Positive Integration

2.2.1 Specific Provisions Aimed at Avoiding Double Non-Taxation

2.2.1.1 Double Non-Taxation and the VAT Directive

Like double taxation, double non-taxation is not an exclusive problem of income taxes.[1786] With regard to VAT, for example, the relevance of non-taxation was already reflected in Article 9(3) Sixth VAT Directive. Thus, "*[i]n order to avoid double taxation, non-taxation or the distortion of competition the Member States may, with regard to the supply of services referred to in 2(e) and the hiring out of movable tangible property consider: (a) the place of supply of services, which under this Article would be situated*

1784. With regard to the proposals made in the BEPS project see P. Baker, 61 *British Tax Rev.* 3 (2015), at pp. 408-416; J. Bates/D.M. Berman/R. Gani/D. Gutmann/T. Imamura/G. Klugman/A. Rust, 41 *Intertax* 6/7 (2013), at pp. 403-404; F. Debelva/D. Scornos/J. Van den Berghen/P. Van Braband, 24 *EC Tax Rev.* 3 (2015), at pp. 132-143; R. de Bour/O. Marres, 43 *Intertax* 1 (2015), at pp. 33-35; E.C.C.M. Kemmeren, 23 *EC Tax Rev.* 4 (2014), at pp. 191-193; S. Douma, 61 *British Tax Rev.* 3 (2015), at pp. 370-377; A.P. Dourado, 43 *Intertax* 1 (2015), at pp. 54-56; J. Englisch, 61 *British Tax Rev.* 3 (2015), at pp. 285-307; M. Helminen, 61 *British Tax Rev.* 3 (2015), at pp. 325-339; C. HJI Panayi, 70 *Bull. Intl. Taxn.* (2016), at pp. 96-112; C. Marchgraber, 54 *Eur. Taxn.* 4 (2014), at pp. 139-141; E. Pinetz in M. Lang/P. Pistone/A. Rust/J. Schuch/C. Staringer (eds.), *Base Erosion and Profit Shifting* (Linde, 2016), at pp. 294-296; P. Pistone/R. Julien/F. Cannas in M. Lang/P. Pistone/A. Rust/J. Schuch/C. Staringer (eds.), *Base Erosion and Profit Shifting* (Linde, 2016), at pp. 166-210; A. Rust, 61 *British Tax Rev.* 3 (2015), at pp. 308-324; A. Rust in W. Schön/C. Heber (eds.), Grundfragen des Europäischen Steuerrechts (Springer, 2015), at pp. 89-106; W. Schön, 61 *British Tax Rev.* 3 (2015), at pp. 420-428; R. Streinz, 61 *British Tax Rev.* 3 (2015), at pp. 429-442; R. Szudoczky/P. Koch in M. Lang/P. Pistone/A. Rust/J. Schuch/C. Staringer (eds.), *Base Erosion and Profit Shifting* (Linde, 2016), at pp. 239-244; E. Traversa, 58 *British Tax Rev.* 5 (2013), at pp. 615-619; A. Zalasiński, 61 *British Tax Rev.* 3 (2015), at pp. 444-448.

1785. See Chapter 4.1.2.1.

1786. See G. Bizioli in M. Lang/P. Melz/E. Kristoffersson (ed.), T. Ecker (ass. ed.), *Value Added Tax and Direct Taxation* (IBFD, 2009), at pp. 403-407; T. Ecker, *A VAT/GST Model Convention* (IBFD, 2013), at pp. 27-47; J. Englisch, *Wettbewerbsgleichheit im grenzüberschreitenden Handel* (Mohr Siebeck, 2008), at pp. 763-769; N. Eriksen/K. Haydl in M. Lang/P. Melz/E. Kristoffersson (ed.), T. Ecker (ass. ed.), *Value Added Tax and Direct Taxation* (IBFD, 2009), at p. 1153; R. Millar in M. Lang/P. Melz/E. Kristoffersson (ed.), T. Ecker (ass. ed.), *Value Added Tax and Direct Taxation* (IBFD, 2009), at pp. 418-436; P. Rendahl in M. Lang/P. Melz/E. Kristoffersson (ed.), T. Ecker (ass. ed.), *Value Added Tax and Direct Taxation* (IBFD, 2009), at p. 1126; A.A. Verstraeten in M. Lang/P. Melz/E. Kristoffersson (ed.), T. Ecker (ass. ed.), *Value Added Tax and Direct Taxation* (IBFD, 2009), at p. 376.

within the territory of the country, as being situated outside the Community where the effective use and enjoyment of the services take place outside the Community; (b) the place of supply of services, which under this Article would be situated outside the Community, as being within the territory of the country where the effective use and enjoyment of the services take place within the territory of the country."[1787]

Initially, the place of supply of services within the EU VAT system was generally based on this concept of effective use and enjoyment.[1788] Since VAT is a tax on consumption (expenditure) that should accordingly be levied in the country where consumption takes place,[1789] it was supposed that services are most likely consumed at the place of effective use and enjoyment.[1790] However, given the increase in cross-border economic activities as well as the development of new forms of services due to technological advancements, it was recognized "*that systematically defining the place of consumption as the place of taxation could lead to some serious practical problems.*"[1791] In order to avoid "*difficulties of interpretation which might arise from notions such as the place of utilization or exploitation of the services*"[1792] the concept of effective use and enjoyment has hence been more and more replaced by a detailed set of rules based on various presumptions with regard to the place of consumption ("proxies").[1793] However, although these sophisticated place-of-supply rules aim at avoiding, "*first, conflicts of jurisdiction which may result in double taxation, and, secondly, non-taxation,*"[1794] such conflicts may still occur with regard to transactions where third

1787. Sixth Council Directive of 17 May 1977 on the harmonization of the laws of the Member States relating to turnover taxes – Common system of value added tax: uniform basis of assessment (77/388/EEC), *OJ* L 145 (13 June 1977), at p. 6.

1788. Article 6(3) of the Second Council Directive of 11 Apr. 1967 on the harmonization of legislation of Member States concerning turnover taxes – Structure and procedures for application of the common system of value added tax (67/228/EEC), 10 *OJ* 71 (14 Apr. 1967), p. 1303 (at p. 1305).

1789. See, for example, OECD, *International VAT/GST Guidelines* (OECD, 2014), at p. 7 ("*as a tax on consumption, the revenue should accrue to the jurisdiction where the final consumption takes place*").

1790. Cf. T. Ecker, Place of Effective Use and Enjoyment of Services – EU History Repeats Itself, 23 *Intl. VAT Monitor* 6 (2012), p. 407 (at p. 407).

1791. Proposal for a Council Directive amending Directive 77/388/EEC as regards the place of supply of services, COM(2003) 822 final (23 Dec. 2003), at p. 2; also cf. Judgment in *Hamann*, 51/88, EU:C:1989:189, at para. 18, according to which, for certain services, "*it is difficult, if not impossible, to determine the place of their utilization [...][,] [s]ince they may easily cross frontiers [...]. [...] [I]n each case a practical criterion must be laid down for VAT charging*"; also see Judgment in *ARO Lease*, C-190/95, EU:C:1997:374, at para. 14; Judgment in *Lease Plan Luxembourg*, C-390/96, EU:C:1998:206, at para. 23.

1792. Proposal for a sixth Council Directive on the harmonization of Member States concerning turnover taxes, COM(73) 950 (20 Jun. 1973), *Bulletin of the European Communities*, Supplement 11/73, at p. 11.

1793. See T. Ecker, 23 *Intl. VAT Monitor* 6 (2012), at p. 408; B. Terra/J. Kajus/O. Henkow, The Place of Supply, in B. Terra/J. Kajus (eds.), *A Guide to the Recast VAT Directive* (IBFD, 2015), at Chapter 5.7.4, citing the VAT Committee's Working Paper No. 633.

1794. Judgment in *Kollektivavtalsstiftelsen TRR Trygghetsråde*, C-291/07, EU:C:2008:609, at para. 24; Judgment in *Athesia Druck*, C-1/08, EU:C:2009:108, at para. 20; also see Judgment in *Berkholz*, 168/84, EU:C:1985:299, at para. 14; Judgment in *Dudda*, C-327/94, EU:C:1996:355, at para. 20; Judgment in *Linthorst, Pouwels en Scheres*, C-167/95, EU:C:1997:105, at para. 10; Judgment in *Commission/France*, C-429/97, EU:C:2001:54, at para. 41; Judgment in *SPI*, C-108/00, EU:C:2001:173, at para. 15; Judgment in *RAL (Channel Islands) and others*,

countries are involved.[1795] Non-Member States are not bound to follow the rules of secondary EU law and may hence apply different place-of-supply rules.[1796] In order to avoid double taxation, non-taxation and distortions of competition resulting from the application of deviating place-of-supply rules by a Member State and a third country, Member States have been granted the option to unilaterally deviate from the standard place-of-supply rules laid down by the VAT Directive and to instead tax services at the place where they are effectively used and enjoyed.[1797]

This option does not allow the Member States to arbitrarily shift the place of supply of services from one state to another. On the one hand, it only applies if a third country is involved in a cross-border supply of services. A Member State can, therefore, only shift "*the place of supply from a member State of the European Union to the place outside the European Union where the service is effectively used and enjoyed or from a place outside the European Union to the Member State where the service is effectively used and enjoyed.*"[1798] On the other hand, Member States may not deviate from all, but only from some place-of-supply rules. In the Sixth VAT Directive, for example, the option was limited to what are known as "distance services" as mentioned in Article 9(2)(e) Sixth VAT Directive as well as the hiring out of movable tangible property. This limitation was maintained when the Sixth VAT Directive was recast.[1799,1800] As from 1

C-452/03, EU:C:2005:289, at para. 23; Judgment in *Levob Verzekeringen and OV Bank*, C-41/04, EU:C:2005:649, at para. 32; Judgment in *Gillan Beach*, C-114/05, EU:C:2006:169, at para. 14; Judgment in *Aktiebolaget NN*, C-111/05, EU:C:2007:195, at para. 43; Judgment in *Commission/Germany*, C-401/06, EU:C:2007:759, at para. 29; Judgment in *EGN*, C-377/08, EU:C:2009:42, at para. 27; Judgment in *RCI Europe*, C-37/08, EU:C:2009:507, at para. 20; Judgment in *ADV Allround*, C-218/10, EU:C:2012:35, at para. 27; Judgment in *Welmory*, C-605/12, EU:C:2014:2298, at para. 42; Judgment in *SMK*, C-97/14, EU:C:2015:290, at para. 32; Judgment in *WebMindLicenses*, C-419/14, EU:C:2015:832, at para. 41.

1795. See E. Traversa/C. Helleputte in M. Lang/P. Melz/E. Kristoffersson (ed.), T. Ecker (ass. ed.), *Value Added Tax and Direct Taxation* (IBFD, 2009), at pp. 355-356.

1796. With regard to VAT, the application of different proxies to establish the place of consumption is a typical reason for double taxation or non-taxation. See T. Ecker in M. Lang/P. Melz/E. Kristoffersson (ed.), T. Ecker (ass. ed.), *Value Added Tax and Direct Taxation* (IBFD, 2009), at p. 1270; T. Ecker, *A VAT/GST Model Convention* (IBFD, 2013), at p. 40; N.P. Eriksen, 33 *Intertax* 4 (2005), at p. 168; R. Millar in R. Krever/D. White (eds.), *GST in Retrospect and Prospect* (Thomson Reuters, 2007), at p. 325; R. Millar in M. Lang/P. Melz/E. Kristoffersson (ed.), T. Ecker (ass. ed.), *Value Added Tax and Direct Taxation* (IBFD, 2009), at p. 430; also see OECD, *The Application of Consumption Taxes to the International Trade in Services and Intangibles, Progress Report and Draft Principles* (OECD, 2005), at p. 3; Consultation paper Introduction of a mechanism for eliminating double imposition of VAT in individual cases, Taxud/D1/ ... (5 Jan. 2007), at pp. 2-3; also cf. H.G. Ruppe in IFA (ed.), *International Problems in the Field of General Sales Taxes on Sales of Goods and Services, CDFI 68b* (IBFD, 1983), at p. 121.

1797. See B. Terra/J. Kajus/O. Henkow in B. Terra/J. Kajus (eds.), *A Guide to the Recast VAT Directive* (IBFD, 2015), at Chapter 5.7.4, citing the VAT Committee's Working Paper No. 633.

1798. T. Ecker, 23 *Intl. VAT Monitor* 6 (2012), at p. 407; also cf. G. Echevarría Zubeldia, Legal Uncertainty of the EU Effective-Use-and-Enjoyment Criterion, 23 *Intl. VAT Monitor* 4 (2012), p. 228 (at p. 228); B. Terra, *The Place of Supply in European VAT* (Kluwer, 1998), at p. 221.

1799. Council Directive 2006/112/EC of 28 Nov. 2006 on the common system of value added tax, OJ L 347 (11 Dec. 2006), at p. 19 (hereinafter: VAT Directive).

1800. The scope of the provision on the place of effective use and enjoyment of services was nevertheless indirectly broadened, because the list of "distance services" was enhanced. In contrast to the Sixth VAT Directive, the option hence also applied to "*the provision of access to, and of transport or transmission through, natural gas and electricity distribution systems*

January 2010, however, the option's scope has been considerably extended.[1801] Since 1 January 2015, the option – now incorporated in Article 59a VAT Directive – applies to all place-of-supply rules on B2B and B2C transactions, except for services covered by Articles 46-55 and 57 VAT Directive.[1802]

The possibility of Member States to unilaterally deviate from the standard place-of-supply rules is heavily criticized in the literature.[1803] The respective option is compared to "*using a steamroller to crack nuts.*"[1804] This is due to the fact that, on the one hand, it is not only "*very difficult to determine where the actual use and enjoyment of a service takes place.*"[1805] Relying on such a criterion could rather also "*lead to some serious practical problems*"[1806] due to "*difficulties of interpretation.*"[1807] This becomes particularly apparent if one considers that the situation at the time the place of supply of services within the EU VAT system was generally based on the concept of effective

---

and the provision of other services directly linked thereto; [...] telecommunications services; [...] radio and television broadcasting services; [...] [and] electronically supplied services," unless the latter were rendered to non-taxable persons (see Articles 56(1) and 58 VAT Directive). Moreover, according to Article 59 VAT Directive, "*Member States shall apply Article 58(b) to telecommunications services supplied to non-taxable persons who are established in a Member State, or who have their permanent address or usually reside in a Member State, by a taxable person who has established his business outside the Community or has a fixed establishment there from which the services are supplied, or who, in the absence of such a place of business or fixed establishment, has his permanent address or usually resides outside the Community. [...] Until 31 December 2006, Member States shall apply Article 58(b) to radio and television broadcasting services, as referred to in point (j) of Article 56(1), supplied to non-taxable persons who are established in a Member State, or who have their permanent address or usually reside in a Member State, by a taxable person who has established his business outside the Community or who has a fixed establishment there from which the services are supplied, or who, in the absence of such a place of business or fixed establishment, has his permanent address or usually resides outside the Community.*"

1801. Council Directive 2008/8/EC of 12 Feb. 2008 amending Directive 2006/112/EC as regards the place of supply of services, OJ L 44 (20 Feb. 2008), p. 11 (at p. 15).

1802. Council Directive 2006/112/EC of 28 Nov. 2006 on the common system of value added tax, *OJ* L 347 (11 Dec. 2006), as amended by Council Directive 2008/8/EC of 12 Feb. 2008 amending Directive 2006/112/EC as regards the place of supply of services, *OJ* L 44 (20 Feb. 2008), at p. 18.

1803. See G. Echevarría Zubeldia, 23 *Intl. VAT Monitor* 4 (2012), at pp. 228-229; T. Ecker, 23 *Intl. VAT Monitor* 6 (2012), at pp. 407-410; B. Terra/J. Kajus/O. Henkow in B. Terra/J. Kajus (eds.), *A Guide to the Recast VAT Directive* (IBFD, 2015), at Chapter 5.7.4.

1804. B. Terra/J. Kajus/O. Henkow in B. Terra/J. Kajus (eds.), *A Guide to the Recast VAT Directive* (IBFD, 2015), at Chapter 5.7.4; also see B. Terra, European Proposals for New Rules Regarding the Place of Supply of Services, in R. Krever/D. White (eds.), *GST in Retrospect and Prospect* (Thomson Reuters, 2007), p. 369 (at p. 383).

1805. European Commission, *Consultation Paper VAT – the Place of Supply of Services to Non-Taxable Persons* (2005), at p. 6; also see Judgment in *Hamann*, 51/88, EU:C:1989:189, at para. 18, according to which, for certain services, "*it is difficult, if not impossible, to determine the place of their utilization [...][,] [s]ince they may easily cross frontiers [...]. [...] [I]n each case a practical criterion must be laid down for VAT charging.*"

1806. Proposal for a Council Directive amending Directive 77/388/EEC as regards the place of supply of services, COM(2003) 822 final (23 Dec. 2003), at p. 2; also see OECD, *Applying Value Added Taxes to Cross-border Supplies of Services and Intangibles, Emerging Concepts of Defining Place of Taxation* (OECD, 2008), at p. 4 ("*[T]here is agreement that defining place of taxation under a 'pure consumption' test would, in most cases, be impractical*").

1807. Proposal for a sixth Council Directive on the harmonization of Member States concerning turnover taxes, COM(73) 950 (20 June 1973), *Bulletin of the European Communities*, Supplement 11/73, at p. 11; also see T. Ecker, 23 *Intl. VAT Monitor* 6 (2012), at pp. 408-409.

use and enjoyment.[1808] Not least because of the interpretative leeway resulting from the term *"effective use and enjoyment,"* *"there really existed nine separate and different systems of VAT, rather than a single Community system."*[1809] However, while the Second VAT Directive generally based the place of supply of services within the EU VAT system on the concept of effective use and enjoyment, it is questionable whether Article 59a VAT Directive allows Member States to unilaterally deviate from the standard place-of-supply rules irrespective of whether applying the standard place-of-supply rules would lead to *"double taxation, non-taxation or distortion of competition"* or not.[1810] Doubts arise in particular, because it would not have been necessary to incorporate the passage *"In order to prevent double taxation, non-taxation or distortion of competition"* into the wording of Article 59a VAT Directive, if the provision does not require double taxation, non-taxation or a distortion of competition anyway. If it is assumed that the EU legislator meant this part of the wording to have a constitutive effect, it is arguable that Member States may only deem the place of supply to be where the service is effectively used and enjoyed if the application of the standard place-of-supply rules led to double taxation, non-taxation or a distortion of competition. Such an interpretation would also be in line with the VAT Directive's aim of avoiding both double taxation and non-taxation, which is expressed several times in the preamble.[1811] If exercising the option incorporated in Article 59a VAT Directive was not contingent upon the standard place-of-supply rules actually leading to double taxation, non-taxation or a distortion of competition, Member States may not always avoid but rather even – knowingly or unknowingly – cause double taxation, non-taxation or a distortion of competition by unilaterally deviating from the standard place-of-supply rules. However, according to the ECJ, double taxation resulting from the taxation of *"a supply of services in another Member State when it has already lawfully been subject to VAT in the State of the supplier of the services"* is *"contrary to the principle of fiscal neutrality inherent in the common system of VAT."*[1812] Interpreting Article 59a VAT

1808. Article 6(3) of the Second Council Directive of 11 Apr. 1967 on the harmonization of legislation of Member States concerning turnover taxes – Structure and procedures for application of the common system of value added tax (67/228/EEC), 10 *OJ* 71 (14 Apr. 1967), p. 1305.

1809. A.J. Easson, *Taxation in the European Community* (The Athlone Press, 1993), at p. 101; also cf. R. de la Feria, *The EU VAT System and the Internal Market* (IBFD, 2009), at pp. 53-54.

1810. According to the European Commission, *"[t]he exercise of this option by Member States does not depend on the tax treatment that the services are subject to outside the Community. The fact that a service may be taxed in a third country under its national rules would for example not prevent a Member State from taxing that service if it is effectively used and enjoyed on its territory."* See B. Terra/J. Kajus/O. Henkow in B. Terra/J. Kajus (eds.), *A Guide to the Recast VAT Directive* (IBFD, 2015), at Chapter 5.7.4, citing the VAT Committee's Working Paper No. 633.

1811. Council Directive 2006/112/EC of 28 Nov. 2006 on the common system of value added tax, OJ L 347 (11 Dec. 2006), as amended by Council Directive 2008/8/EC of 12 Feb. 2008 amending Directive 2006/112/EC as regards the place of supply of services, *OJ* L 44 (20 Feb. 2008), at pp. 2 (*"to avoid double taxation or non taxation"*), 3 (*"to avoid double taxation"*), 4 (*"with a view to preventing double taxation"*) and 5 (*"address the problem of double taxation of cross-border transactions"*).

1812. Judgment in *Cookies World*, C-155/01, EU:C:2003:449, at para. 60; also cf. Judgment in *Kühne*, 50/88, EU:C:1989:262, at para. 10; Judgment in *Mohsche*, C-193/91, EU:C:1993:203, at para. 9; Judgment in *Commission/Italy*, C-45/95, EU:C:1997:315, at para. 15; Judgment in

Directive as requiring actual double taxation, non-taxation or a distortion of competition would hence also give consideration to the principle of fiscal neutrality. Moreover, from a practical perspective, such an understanding would dramatically decrease the risk "*that the discretionary powers of each individual Member State to apply the use and enjoyment override for all or some supplies will result in a rather muddled allocation of the place of supply of services.*"[1813]

Even if the ECJ shared this understanding of Article 59a VAT Directive, it would still be questionable whether double taxation or double non-taxation could be successfully avoided in each and every case by relying on the place of effective use and enjoyment of services instead of applying the standard place-of-supply rules. It has to be kept in mind that this criterion is "*a concept of EU Law.*"[1814] Member States are, therefore, not at liberty to use any criterion to determine the place of effective use and enjoyment of services. Since it is for the ECJ to interpret Article 59a VAT Directive, the criteria used by Member States can rather be scrutinized by the Court.[1815] In *Athesia Druck*, for example, it was concluded that Article 9(3)(b) Sixth VAT Directive is to be understood as to mean that "*[t]he country within which the effective use and enjoyment of the services take place, [...] is to be understood, with regard to advertising services, as referring to the country from which the advertising material is disseminated.*"[1816] It is hence only possible to avoid double taxation or non-taxation either by shifting "*the place of supply from a member State of the European Union to the place outside the European Union,*"[1817] if the place of effective use and enjoyment is actually outside the European Union, or by shifting "*the place of supply [...] from a place outside the European Union to the Member State,*"[1818] if the place of effective use and enjoyment is actually in this Member State. Hence, the potential of invoking Article 59a VAT Directive in order to avoid double taxation, non-taxation or a distortion of competition is more limited than one might expect at first glance. This provision nevertheless confirms that – at least certain provisions of – the VAT Directive also aim(s) at avoiding double non-taxation.[1819]

Bakcsi, C-415/98, EU:C:2001:136, at para. 46; Judgment in *HE*, C-25/03, EU:C:2005:241, at para. 71; Order in *Salus*, C-18/05 and C-155/05, EU:C:2006:447, at para. 29; Judgment in *Puffer*, C-460/07, EU:C:2009:254, at paras 45-46; Judgment in *Swiss Re Germany Holding*, C-242/08, EU:C:2009:647, at para. 63; Judgment in *Klub*, C-153/11, EU:C:2012:163, at para. 42; Judgment in *X*, C-334/10, EU:C:2012:473, at para. 33; Judgment in *Rodopi-M 91*, C-259/12, EU:C:2013:414, at para. 36; Judgment in *NLB Leasing*, C-209/14, EU:C:2015:440, at para. 40.

1813. B. Terra in R. Krever/D. White (eds.), *GST in Retrospect and Prospect* (Thomson Reuters, 2007), at pp. 383-384; B. Terra/J. Kajus/O. Henkow in B. Terra/J. Kajus (eds.), *A Guide to the Recast VAT Directive* (IBFD, 2015), at Chapter 5.7.4; also see T. Ecker, 23 *Intl. VAT Monitor* 6 (2012), at p. 409.

1814. F. Annacondia/W. van der Corput, EU Place-of-Supply Rules from 2010 – VAT Committee Guidelines, 21 *Intl. VAT Monitor* 3 (2010); T. Ecker, 23 *Intl. VAT Monitor* 6 (2012), at p. 410; also see B. Terra/J. Kajus/O. Henkow in B. Terra/J. Kajus (eds.), *A Guide to the Recast VAT Directive* (IBFD, 2015), at Chapter 5.7.4, citing the VAT Committee's Working Paper No. 633.

1815. See T. Ecker, 23 *Intl. VAT Monitor* 6 (2012), at p. 410.

1816. Judgment in *Athesia Druck*, C-1/08, EU:C:2009:108, at para. 29.

1817. T. Ecker, 23 *Intl. VAT Monitor* 6 (2012), at p. 407.

1818. T. Ecker, 23 *Intl. VAT Monitor* 6 (2012), at p. 407.

1819. Judgment in *Berkholz*, 168/84, EU:C:1985:299, at para. 14; Judgment in *Dudda*, C-327/94, EU:C:1996:355, at para. 20; Judgment in *Linthorst, Pouwels en Scheres*, C-167/95,

2.2.1.2 Double Non-Taxation and the Parent-Subsidiary Directive

The 2014 Amendment of the Parent-Subsidiary Directive

Although the European VAT system has – at least partly – explicitly dealt with (double) non-taxation since the adoption of the Sixth VAT Directive 1977,[1820] it took until 2014 for this issue to find its way into a directive on direct taxation. Back then, the Parent-Subsidiary Directive was amended to ensure that it does "*not lead to situations of double non-taxation and, therefore, generate unintended tax benefits for groups of parent companies and subsidiaries of different Member States when compared to groups of companies of the same Member State.*"[1821] These unintended tax benefits may arise if a group of companies exploits the fact that hybrid financial instruments may be treated as debt in the Member State of the distributing company and as equity in the Member State of the receiving company. Thereby it would be possible to obtain a double tax benefit[1822] if the amount paid by the debtor was deductible as interest in the source state, but at the same time exempted as a dividend at the level of the creditor in the residence state due to the requirements of the Parent-Subsidiary Directive.

In 2010, the EU Code of Conduct Group already emphasized that "*[i]n as far as payments under a hybrid loan arrangement are qualified as a tax deductible expense for the debtor in the arrangement, Member States shall not exempt such payments as profit distributions under a participation exemption.*"[1823] The possible problem with this

EU:C:1997:105, at para. 10; Judgment in *Commission/France*, C-429/97, EU:C:2001:54, at para. 41; Judgment in *SPI*, C-108/00, EU:C:2001:173, at para. 15; Judgment in *RAL (Channel Islands) and others*, C-452/03, EU:C:2005:289, at para. 23; Judgment in *Levob Verzekeringen and OV Bank*, C-41/04, EU:C:2005:649, at para. 32; Judgment in *Gillan Beach*, C-114/05, EU:C:2006:169, at para. 14; Judgment in *Aktiebolaget NN*, C-111/05, EU:C:2007:195, at para. 43; Judgment in *Commission/Germany*, C-401/06, EU:C:2007:759, at para. 29; Judgment in *Kollektivavtalsstiftelsen TRR Trygghetsråde*, C-291/07, EU:C:2008:609, at para. 24; Judgment in *EGN*, C-377/08, EU:C:2009:42, at para. 27; Judgment in *Athesia Druck*, C-1/08, EU:C:2009:108, at para. 20; Judgment in *RCI Europe*, C-37/08, EU:C:2009:507, at para. 20; Judgment in *ADV Allround*, C-218/10, EU:C:2012:35, at para. 27; Judgment in *Welmory*, C-605/12, EU:C:2014:2298, at para. 42; Judgment in *SMK*, C-97/14, EU:C:2015:290, at para. 32; Judgment in *WebMindLicenses*, C-419/14, EU:C:2015:832, at para. 41.

1820. Sixth Council Directive of 17 May 1977 on the harmonization of the laws of the Member States relating to turnover taxes – Common system of value added tax: uniform basis of assessment (77/388/EEC), *OJ* L 145 (13 Jun. 1977), at p. 6.

1821. Council Directive 2014/86/EU of 8 Jul. 2014 amending Directive 2011/96/EU on the common system of taxation applicable in the case of parent companies and subsidiaries of different Member States, *OJ* L 219 (25 Jul. 2014), p. 40 (at p. 40).

1822. Some scholars also refer to "double dip" in this context (see, for example, S. Bendlinger, *Steueroasen und Offshore-Strukturen* [Linde, 2013], at pp. 230-231; T. Polivanova-Rosenauer, 10 *taxlex* 3 [2014], at p. 108; W. Wiesner, 21 *RWZ* 1 [2011], at p. 4; see also J. Bundgaard, 50 *Eur. Taxn.* 11 [2010], at p. 490, who distinguishes, though, between "*real double-dip structures and deduction/non-inclusion structures*").

1823. The first report of the Code of Conduct Group that dealt with this issue (Doc. 10033/10 LIMITE FISC 47 [25 May 2010]) is only partially accessible to the public. The relevant paragraph has been deleted (para. 31). However, this sentence is literally cited by a later report (see Doc. 16766/10 LIMITE FISC 139 [22 Nov. 2010], at para. 17) and also by the European Commission (see Proposal for a Council Directive amending Directive 2011/96/EU on the common system of taxation applicable in the case of parent companies and subsidiaries in different Member States, COM[2013] 814 final [25 Nov. 2013], at p. 2 [FN 5]).

suggestion was, however, that Article 4(1) Parent-Subsidiary Directive - before the 2014 amendment - obliged Member States either to refrain from taxing distributed profits that "*a parent company or its permanent establishment, by virtue of the association of the parent company with its subsidiary, receives*" or to "*tax such profits while authorising the parent company and the permanent establishment to deduct from the amount of tax due that fraction of the corporation tax related to those profits and paid by the subsidiary and any lower-tier subsidiary, subject to the condition that at each tier a company and its lower-tier subsidiary fall within the definitions laid down in Article 2 and meet the requirements provided for in Article 3, up to the limit of the amount of the corresponding tax due.*" Since this wording suggests that Member States either have to tax distributed profits while granting an indirect tax credit or have to refrain from taxing distributed profits irrespective of how the distribution is treated in the Member State of the distributing company, cross-border tax arbitrage using hybrid financing was assumed to be in line with the Parent-Subsidiary Directive.[1824]

Despite the arguments supporting the view that the previous version of the Parent-Subsidiary Directive did not necessarily cover profit distributions that lead to a deduction at the level of the subsidiary,[1825] the European Commission released a proposal for a council directive amending the Parent-Subsidiary Directive[1826] which, *inter alia,* aimed at "*ensuring that the application of the directive does not inadvertently prevent effective action against double non-taxation in the area of hybrid loan structures.*"[1827] To achieve this it was suggested to limit the scope of the exemption method

1824. Communication from the Commission to the European Parliament and the Council, An Action Plan to strengthen the fight against tax fraud and tax evasion, COM(2012) 722 final (6 Dec. 2012), at p. 7; Commission Staff Working Document, Impact Assessment, SWD(2013) 474 final (25 Nov. 2013), at p. 6; Commission Staff Working Document, Executive Summary of the Impact Assessment, SWD(2013) 473 final (25 Nov. 2011), at p. 2; Proposal for a Council Directive amending Directive 2011/96/EU on the common system of taxation applicable in the case of parent companies and subsidiaries of different Member States, COM(2013) 814 final (25 Nov. 2013), at pp. 2-3; European Parliament, Report on the proposal for a Council directive amending Directive 2011/96/EU on the common system of taxation applicable in the case of parent companies and subsidiaries of different Member States, PE 526.302v02-00 (24 Mar. 2014), at p. 11; also see M. Desens, Kritische Bestandsaufnahme zu den geplanten Änderungen in § 8b KStG, 51 *DStR*, Beihefter zu Heft 4 (2013), p. 13 (at p. 22); S. Kudert/C. Kahlenberg, Extension of the Domestic Correspondence Principle, 54 *Eur. Taxn.* 1 (2014), p. 40 (at p. 44); also cf. G. Kofler, Hybrid Loans in the Parent-Subsidiary-Directive, in P. Valente (ed.), *Elusione Fiscale Internazionale* (IPSOA [Kluwer], 2014), p. 682 (at pp. 687-688).

1825. See also with further references, C. Marchgraber, 54 *Eur. Taxn.* 4 (2014), at pp. 138-139.

1826. Proposal for a Council Directive amending Directive 2011/96/EU on the common system of taxation applicable in the case of parent companies and subsidiaries of different Member States, COM(2013) 814 final (25 Nov. 2013); for an analysis of this proposal see P.R. Listl, Anmerkungen zum Entwurf der Änderung der EU Mutter-Tochter-Richtlinie vom 25. 11. 2013, 23 *IStR* 12 (2014), at pp. 448 et seq.; C. Marchgraber, 54 *Eur. Taxn.* 4 (2014), at pp. 133 et seq.; H. van den Hurk, Proposed Amended Parent-Subsidiary Directive Reveals the European Commission's Lack of Vision, 68 *Bull. Intl. Taxn.* 9 (2014), at pp. 488 et seq.; D. Weber, Comments, 7 *H&I* 3.47 (2014), p. 47 (at pp. 47 et seq.).

1827. Communication from the Commission to the European Parliament and the Council, An Action Plan to strengthen the fight against tax fraud and tax evasion, COM(2012) 722 final (6 Dec. 2012), at p. 9; Proposal for a Council Directive amending Directive 2011/96/EU on the common system of taxation applicable in the case of parent companies and subsidiaries of different Member States, COM(2013) 814 final (25 Nov. 2013), at p. 3.

by changing Article 4(1)(a) Parent-Subsidiary Directive, so that a tax exemption will be provided only "*to the extent that such profits are not deductible by the subsidiary of the parent company.*"[1828] The European Commission assumed that the realization of this proposal would have obliged the Member States to tax distributed profits their resident parent companies or permanent establishments of other Member State's parent companies within their territory receive from a subsidiary resident in another Member State.[1829] However, this assumption was challenged in the literature. It was argued that a realization of the European Commission's proposal would only have limited the scope of Article 4(1)(a) Parent-Subsidiary Directive, because the wording of the European Commission's proposal does not suggest that the Member States are obliged to tax distributed profits to the extent that such profits are deductible by the subsidiary.[1830]

Apparently, these doubts were shared by the European Parliament's Committee on Legal Affairs as well as by the Greek Presidency, which both suggested slightly amending the European Commission's proposal in order to clarify this issue. According to the proposal of the European Parliament's Committee on Legal Affairs, Member States must "*refrain from taxing such profits, but only to the extent that such profits are not deductible by the subsidiary of the parent company.*"[1831] The Greek Presidency's proposal was even more explicit by stating that the Member State of a parent company or its permanent establishment must "*refrain from taxing such profits to the extent that such profits are not deductible by the subsidiary, and tax such profits to the extent that such profits are deductible by the subsidiary.*"[1832] Some Member States – in particular

1828. Proposal for a Council Directive amending Directive 2011/96/EU on the common system of taxation applicable in the case of parent companies and subsidiaries of different Member States, COM(2013) 814 final (25 Nov. 2013), at p. 9.

1829. Proposal for a Council Directive amending Directive 2011/96/EU on the common system of taxation applicable in the case of parent companies and subsidiaries of different Member States, COM(2013) 814 final (25 Nov. 2013), at p. 6 ("*The obligation to tax is limited only the portion of hybrid financial payments which is deductible in the source Member State.*") and at p. 7 ("*Under the proposed amendment, the Member State of the parent company and the Member State of its permanent establishment deny the benefits of the tax exemption to distributions of profits that are deductible by the subsidiary of the parent company.*"); European Commission Press Release of 25 Nov. 2013, *Tackling Tax Avoidance: Commission tightens key EU corporate tax rules*, IP/13/1149 ("*Under the proposal, if a hybrid loan payment is tax deductible in the subsidiary's Member State, then it must be taxed by the Member State where the parent company is established.*").

1830. See C. Marchgraber, 54 *Eur. Taxn.* 4 (2014), at pp. 135-136; D. Weber, 7 *H&I* 3.47 (2014), at p. 56.

1831. European Parliament, Draft Opinion of the Committee on Legal Affairs for the Committee on Economic and Monetary Affairs on the proposal for a Council directive amending Directive 2011/96/EU on the common system of taxation applicable in the case of parent companies and subsidiaries of different Member States, PE 526.293v01-00, JURI_PA(2014)526293 (10 Jan. 2014), at pp. 5-6; European Parliament, Opinion of the Committee on Legal Affairs for the Committee on Economic and Monetary Affairs on the proposal for a Council directive amending Directive 2011/96/EU on the common system of taxation applicable in the case of parent companies and subsidiaries of different Member States, PE 526.293v02-00, JURI_AD(2014)526293 (12 Feb. 2014), at pp. 5-6.

1832. See Doc. 7961/14 LIMITE FISC 54 (20 Mar. 2014), at p. 4; Doc. 8757/1/14 REV 1 LIMITE FISC 69 (9 Apr. 2014), at p. 3; Doc. 8757/14 LIMITE FISC 69 (9 Apr. 2014), at p. 4; Doc. 8836/14 LIMITE FISC 70 (11 Apr. 2014), at p. 5.

Sweden and Malta – raised concerns regarding the amendments envisaged by the Greek Presidency.[1833] Sweden's reluctance to agree on the proposed amendments was due to its national treatment of certain types of investment companies,[1834] whereas Malta objected to a wording which clearly states an obligation to tax.[1835] After the European Commission agreed to clarify that "*the case raised by Sweden would not fall within the scope of the Directive as defined in the Presidency compromise*" by entering a statement in the Council Minutes, Sweden and subsequently also Malta lifted their reservations.[1836] Thus, it was possible to reach a political agreement on the Greek Presidency's compromise text paired with a number of statements to be made in the Council Minutes.[1837] Since the 2014 amendment, Article 4(1)(a) Parent-Subsidiary Directive thus stipulates that the Member State of a parent company and the Member State of its permanent establishment receiving distributed profits from a subsidiary within the EU must "*refrain from taxing such profits to the extent that such profits are not deductible by the subsidiary, and tax such profits to the extent that such profits are deductible by the subsidiary.*"

The (Non-)Deductibility Requirement

In order to avoid mismatches in the tax treatment of intra-EU cross-border profit distributions paid by subsidiary companies to their parent companies, one has to determine whether such a mismatch actually exists. To this end, the amended Article 4(1)(a) Parent-Subsidiary Directive requires that the payments are deductible "*by the subsidiary.*" Therefore, the tax treatment in the Member State of the parent company and in the Member State of its permanent establishment depends upon the tax treatment in the Member State where the subsidiary is considered to be resident (Article 2(a)(ii) Parent-Subsidiary Directive).[1838] According to the wording of Article 4(1)(a) Parent-Subsidiary Directive, it is irrelevant why the payments are deductible by

1833. See Doc. 9193/14 LIMITE FISC 74 (28 Apr. 2014), at para. 5; Doc. 9397/14 FISC 78 (30 April 2014), at paras 5-6.

1834. Cf. E. Nilsson, Sweden – Corporate Taxation s. 12, *Country Analyses IBFD* (accessed 5 May 2015).

1835. See Doc. 9926/14 FISC 80 ECOFIN 493 (19 May 2014), at paras 6-8; see also A. Vroom, Malta and the Hybrid Loan Amendment to the EU Parent-Subsidiary Directive, 55 *Eur. Taxn.* 2 (2015), p. 102 (at pp. 102-104).

1836. Doc. 10419/14 FISC 92 ECOFIN 529 (3 Jun. 2014), at para. 9.

1837. See Doc. 11291/14 FISC 104 ECOFIN 706 (27 Jun. 2014), at para. 4; for the corresponding statements of the Council and the European Commission see Doc. 10419/14 FISC 92 ECOFIN 529 (3 Jun. 2014), at p. 9; Doc. 11291/14 ADD 1 FISC 104 ECOFIN 706 (27 Jun. 2014), at p. 3; Doc. 11684/14 ADD 1 PV/CONS 39 ECOFIN 739 (23 Jul. 2014), at p. 3.

1838. If the subsidiary is a dual EU-resident company, the Member State of the parent company and its permanent establishment will have to consider the tax treatment in both Member States where the subsidiary is resident for tax purposes. The same is true if the subsidiary has a permanent establishment in another Member State that considers the profit distribution to be a deductible interest payment attributable to the permanent establishment. Double non-taxation would already be avoided in such situations, though, if the residence state of the subsidiary – as defined by a double taxation convention – did not consider the profit distribution to be a deductible interest payment and at the same time did not exempt the profits of the subsidiary due to a double taxation convention concluded with the other residence state of a dual EU-resident company or with the Member State of the subsidiary's permanent establishment.

the subsidiary. The tax exemption has to be refused irrespective of whether the deductibility in the Member State of the subsidiary is due to a divergent characterization of the underlying financial instrument or whether dividend distributions are deductible by the subsidiary for some other reason.[1839] This is perfectly in line with the objective of "*avoiding situations of double non-taxation deriving from mismatches in the tax treatment of profit distributions between Member States.*"[1840] The 2014 amendment not only addresses mismatches in the characterization of financial instruments as either equity or debt, but refers to a divergent treatment of profit distributions. Whether the mismatch stems from a classification conflict in respect of the underlying financial instrument is, therefore, irrelevant.[1841]

The wording of Article 4(1)(a) Parent-Subsidiary Directive suggests that it has to be determined whether the profit distribution is treated as a deductible business expense in the Member State of the subsidiary. However, considering the objective of avoiding double non-taxation, it should not make any difference whether the dividend payment reduces the tax base of the subsidiary or whether a tax credit or a bonus is granted upon the distribution of profits that has the same economic effect. Whether double non-taxation is avoided or not would otherwise be contingent upon the legal technique used by the Member State of the subsidiary. The wording allows for an interpretation according to which every tax incentive that is triggered by the distribution of profits is to be considered to lead to a (partial) deductibility of the distributed profits. However, the Member State of the parent company and the Member State of its permanent establishment are obliged to tax distributed profits only "*to the extent*" of the deduction claimed by the subsidiary. It is hence not sufficient that the tax incentive is triggered by the profit distribution. Rather, its extent also has to be directly

1839. In Brazil, for example, legal entities are allowed to pay remuneration to their shareholders in the form of what the law characterizes as *juros sobre capital próprio*, which is a form of compensation made to shareholders in consideration solely to their equity holdings in the entity, and is determined based on the amount of current and accumulated profits of such entity (see, for example, C.C. de Ulhôa Canto/P.V. de Ulhôa Canto, National Report Brazil, in IFA [ed.], *New Tendencies in Tax Treatment of Cross-Border Interest of Corporations, CDFI XCIIIb* [IBFD, 2008], p. 151 [at p. 160]; R.M. Bispo, Cross-Border Intra-Group Hybrid Finance: A Comparative Analysis of the Legal Approach Adopted by Brazil, the United Kingdom and the United States, 67 *Bull. Intl. Taxn.* 11 [2013], p. 364 [at p. 373]). If a Member State introduced a similar regime, it would probably be covered by the 2014 amendment.

1840. Council Directive 2014/86/EU of 8 Jul. 2014 amending Directive 2011/96/EU on the common system of taxation applicable in the case of parent companies and subsidiaries of different Member States, *OJ* L 219 (25 Jul. 2014), at p. 40.

1841. For a similar discussion in Austria see S. Kirchmayr/G. Kofler, Beteiligungsertragsbefreiung und internationale Steuerarbitrage, *GES* 9 (2011), p. 449 (at pp. 451-452); S. Lang, Gewinnanteile aus internationalen Schachtelbeteiligungen am Beispiel Brasiliens, 23 *SWI* 3 (2013), p. 95 (at p. 96); C. Marchgraber/E. Titz, Die Wirkungsweise des § 10 Abs 7 KStG im System der Beteiligungsertragsbefreiung, 24 *ÖStZ* 15/16 (2011), p. 373 (at p. 374); C. Marchgraber, Dividendenbesteuerung und internationale Steuerarbitrage, in M. Lang/C. Marchgraber/A. Rust/J. Schuch/C. Staringer (eds.), *Dividenden im Konzern* (Linde, 2016), p. 95 (at pp. 103-104); M. Stefaner, Wann greift die Besteuerung von grenzüberschreitenden Beteiligungserträgen gemäß § 10 Abs 7 KStG?, 22 *SWI* 6 (2012), p. 276 (at p. 278); M. Stefaner, Genussrechte im Konzernsteuerrecht, in M. Schragl/M. Stefaner (eds.), *Handbuch Genussrechte*[2] (Linde, 2013), p. 253 (at pp. 280-281); see also EAS 3211 (11 May 2011); for a similar discussion in Germany see M. Desens, 51 *DStR*, Beihefter zu Heft 4 (2013), at p. 19; S. Kudert/C. Kahlenberg, 54 *Eur. Taxn.* 1 (2014), at p. 41.

dependent on the amount of the distributed profits. As a result, a tax exemption only is to be granted if the subsidiary cannot claim a tax incentive that is triggered by the profit distribution and the extent of which is directly dependent on the amount of the distributed profits. Therefore, notional interest deduction regimes, for example, do not release the Member State of the parent company and the Member State of its permanent establishment from their obligation to refrain from taxing intra-EU cross-border profit distributions or to grant an indirect tax credit.[1842] Although such regimes provide for a notional interest deduction on equity, the deduction is normally not triggered by the distribution of profits. Moreover, the deductible amount is typically calculated annually on the basis of the company's adjusted equity as it appears in the balance sheet of the preceding accounting period.[1843]

According to the wording of Article 4(1)(a) Parent-Subsidiary Directive, the Member States have to refuse the tax exemption for distributed profits to the extent that such profits are deduct*ible* by the subsidiary. It might, therefore, be argued that it is irrelevant whether the subsidiary has actually claimed the deduction. The mere entitlement to it would hence be sufficient to refuse the tax exemption.[1844] However, it has to be kept in mind that the objective of the 2014 amendment is to avoid situations of double non-taxation.[1845] This requires that the subsidiary is not only entitled to, but also effectively claims a corresponding deduction; only then is the tax burden on the distributed profits effectively reduced.[1846] Furthermore, even if the subsidiary intended

1842. Similarly G. Kofler in P. Valente (ed.), *Elusione Fiscale Internazionale* (IPSOA [Kluwer], 2014), at p. 685. For the corresponding discussion in Austria and Germany see J. Becker/T. Loose, Zur geplanten Ausdehnung des materiellen Korrespondenzprinzips auf hybride Finanzierungen, 21 *IStR* 19 (2012), p. 758 (at p. 759); M. Desens, 51 *DStR*, Beihefter zu Heft 4 (2013), at p. 20; M. Desens, Ist die neue Korrespondenzregel in der Mutter-Tochter-Richtlinie mit dem primären Unionsrecht vereinbar?, 23 *IStR* 22 (2014), p. 825 (at p. 827); M.L. Haisch/M. Helios/D. Niedling, JStG 2013 – Geplante Änderungen im Finanzierungsbereich, 65 *DB* 37 (2012), p. 2060 (at p. 2061); M.L. Haisch/M. Helios/D. Niedling, AmtshilfeRLUmsG: Änderungen im Finanzierungsbereich, 66 *DB* 26/27 (2013), p. 1444 (at p. 1445); S. Kudert/C. Kahlenberg, 54 *Eur. Taxn.* 1 (2014), at p. 42; C. Marchgraber in M. Lang/C.Marchgraber/A. Rust/J. Schuch/C. Staringer (eds.), *Dividenden im Konzern* (Linde, 2016), at pp. 105-106.

1843. See, for example, A. Haelterman/H. Verstraete, The "Notional Interest Deduction" in Belgium, 62 *Bull. Intl. Taxn.* 8 (2008), at pp. 362 et seq.; F. Leone/E. Zanotti, Notional Interest Deduction Regime Introduced, 52 *Eur. Taxn.* 8 (2012), at pp. 432 et seq.

1844. See F. Schiefer, Maßnahmen zur Bekämpfung hybrider Finanzierungsinstrumente, 61 *IWB* 10 (2015), p. 352 (at pp. 355-356); also cf. E. Strimitzer/M. Vock in P. Quantschnigg/B. Renner/G. Schellmann/R. Stöger/M. Vock (eds.), *Die Körperschaftsteuer (KStG 1988)*[27] (LexisNexis, 2015), at § 10 para. 372.

1845. This is also affirmed by the European Commission's statement in the Council Minutes, according to which "*the proposed amendments to Article 4.1 (a) of the Parent Subsidiary directive are not intended to be applicable if there is no double non-taxation or if their application would lead to double taxation of the profit distributions between parent and subsidiary companies.*" See Doc. 10419/14 FISC 92 ECOFIN 529 (3 Jun. 2014), at p. 9; Doc. 11291/14 ADD 1 FISC 104 ECOFIN 706 (27 Jun. 2014), at p. 3; Doc. 11684/14 ADD 1 PV/CONS 39 ECOFIN 739 (23 Jul. 2014), at p. 3.

1846. See G. Kofler, "Hybride Finanzinstrumente" in der Mutter-Tochter-Richtlinie, 9 *Zeitschrift für Finanzmarktrecht* 5 (2014), p. 214 (at p. 217, FN 45); for a similar discussion in Austria see C. Marchgraber in M. Lang/C.Marchgraber/A. Rust/J. Schuch/C. Staringer (eds.), *Dividenden im Konzern* (Linde, 2016), at pp. 104-105; E. Strimitzer/M. Vock in P. Quantschnigg/B. Renner/G. Schellmann/R. Stöger/M. Vock (eds.), *Die Körperschaftsteuer (KStG 1988)*[24] (LexisNexis, 2014), § 10 MN 372; M. Stefaner, Besteuerung von Beteiligungserträgen gemäß

to claim a deduction, the extent of deductible expenses might be limited, for example, due to thin capitalization rules, general interest barriers or rules denying the deduction of interest related to tax-exempt dividends.[1847] Even in the case of a mismatch in the characterization of a financial instrument as either equity or debt, such legislative limitations on the deductibility of business expenses would oblige the Member State of the parent company and its permanent establishment to either grant an indirect tax credit or refrain from taxing the resultant payments to the extent that the payments are not deductible by the subsidiary.

The Obligation to Tax

Until the 2014 amendment, the Parent-Subsidiary Directive did not oblige Member States to tax distributed profits. The Member States were free either to refrain from taxing distributed profits received by a resident parent company or a domestic permanent establishment of another Member State's parent company or to tax such profits while granting an indirect tax credit. However, the first option of completely refraining from taxation is now limited. To the extent that profit distributions are deductible by the subsidiary the Member State of the parent company and the Member State of its permanent establishment are obliged to tax such profits. Article 4(1) Parent-Subsidiary Directive no longer provides for the possibility of refraining from taxation in such a case, because both Article 4(1)(a) and Article 4(1)(b) Parent-Subsidiary Directive stipulate that "*the Member State of the parent company and the Member State of its permanent establishment shall [...] tax such profits [...].*"

The wording does not specify, however, what the Member States have to do in order to satisfy the obligation to "*tax [distributed] profits to the extent that such profits are deductible by the subsidiary.*"[1848] If it were taken literally, one could even argue that the Member States are obliged to introduce a specific kind of tax on such distributed profits. However, such a reading would not be convincing. Although not explicitly mentioned, there are good reasons to conclude that Article 4(1)(a), as well as Article 4(1)(b), Parent-Subsidiary Directive refers to a corporate income tax to be levied on such profit distributions. First, the objective of the Parent-Subsidiary Directive is to avoid juridical and economic double taxation of a certain type of income - namely dividends and other profit distributions - paid by subsidiary companies to their parent companies.[1849] Second, Article 4(1)(b) Parent-Subsidiary Directive explicitly refers to "*the corporation tax*" related to the distributed profits. However, concluding that the 2014 amendment hence imposes a legal obligation on the Member States to introduce

§ 10 Abs 7 KStG auch bei fehlendem Abzug im Ausland?, 22 *SWI* 10 (2012), p. 443 (at pp. 444-445); for practical problems resulting from such an understanding see J. Becker/T. Loose, 21 *IStR* 19 (2012), at pp. 759-761; M.L. Haisch/M. Helios/D. Niedling, *DB* 26/27 (2013), p. 1444 (at p. 1445); P.R. Listl, 23 *IStR* 12 (2014), at p. 451.

1847. For further references see J. Hey, Base Erosion and Profit Shifting and Interest Expenditure, 68 *Bull. Intl. Taxn.* 6/7 (2014), p. 332 (at pp. 335-336).

1848. See G. Kofler in P. Valente (ed.), *Elusione Fiscale Internazionale* (IPSOA [Kluwer], 2014), at p. 686.

1849. See Council Directive 2011/96/EU of 30 Nov. 2011 on the common system of taxation applicable in the case of parent companies and subsidiaries of different Member States, *OJ* L 345 (29 Dec. 2011), at p. 1.

a corporate income tax would not be convincing, either. After all, the obligation to tax only applies within the scope of the Parent-Subsidiary Directive[1850] and it only covers distributions of profits received by a company of a Member State or by intra-EU permanent establishments of companies of a Member State.

In order to qualify as a "company of a Member State" the entity, *inter alia*, has to be "*subject to one of the taxes listed in Annex I, Part B, without the possibility of an option or of being exempt, or to any other tax which may be substituted for any of those taxes.*" If a Member State abolished all taxes referred to in Article 2(a)(iii) Parent-Subsidiary Directive, profits distributed or dividends received by companies established and resident in that Member State would, in principle, no longer be covered by the Parent-Subsidiary Directive.[1851]

Similarly, Article 2(b) Parent-Subsidiary Directive states that a fixed place of business situated in a Member State through which the business of a company of another Member State is wholly or partly carried on qualifies as a permanent establishment only "*in so far as the profits of that place of business are subject to tax in the Member State in which it is situated by virtue of the relevant bilateral tax treaty or, in the absence of such a treaty, by virtue of national law.*" The wording of this provision is misleading,[1852] as double taxation conventions typically do not create tax obligations

1850. But see G. van Gelder/B. Niels, Recent Developments in Hybrid Financial Instruments, 16 *Derivatives & Financial Instruments* 5 (2014), p. 219 (at p. 223: "*It is unclear whether the obligation for Member States to comply with this rule is limited to those situations where the Parent-Subsidiary Directive (2011/96) applies or whether the scope of this rule should be applied more broadly.*").

1851. Companies that are not subject to corporate income tax in the Member State where they were established – this criterion is reflected by Article 2(a)(i) Parent-Subsidiary Directive (see G. Kofler, *Mutter-Tochter-Richtlinie – Kommentar* [LexisNexis, 2011], Artikel 2 at para. 14) – would be covered by the Parent-Subsidiary Directive, though, if such companies were subject to tax in another Member State (see, for example, G. Fibbe, The Different Translations of the Term "company" in the Merger Directive and the Parent-Subsidiary Directive: a Babylonian Confusion of Tongues?, 15 *EC Tax Rev.* 2 [2006], p. 95 [at pp. 99-100]; M. Tenore, 38 *Intertax* 4 [2010], at pp. 235-236; B.J.M. Terra/P.J. Wattel, *European Tax Law*[6] [Kluwer, 2012], at pp. 608-609). However, this does not mean the 2014 amendment addresses both the Member State where the company was established and the Member State where the company is subject to tax (Article 2(a)(iii) Parent-Subsidiary Directive). If a Member State did not have a corporate income tax, it would not be convincing to consider this Member State to be "*the Member State of the parent company*" as stated in Article 4(1) Parent-Subsidiary Directive. Since Article 2(a)(ii) Parent-Subsidiary Directive stipulates that a company of a Member State only exists if "*according to the tax laws of a Member State it is considered to be resident in that Member State,*" the term "*the Member State of the parent company*" rather seems to refer to the Member States in which the company is resident for tax purposes (see also with further arguments supporting such an understanding, P. Farmer/R. Lyal, *EC Tax Law* [Clarendon Press, 1994], at p. 266; G. Kofler/H. Kofler, Betriebsstätten in der Mutter-Tochter-Richtlinie, in P. Quantschnigg/W. Wiesner/G. Mayr [eds.], *Steuern im Gemeinschaftsrecht, Festschrift für Wolfgang Nolz* [LexisNexis, 2008], p. 53 [at pp. 66-67]; G. Kofler, *Mutter-Tochter-Richtlinie – Kommentar* [LexisNexis, 2011], Artikel 2 at para. 15; G. Maisto, The 2003 amendments to the EC Parent-Subsidiary Directive: what's next?, 13 *EC Tax Rev.* 4 [2004], p. 164 [at p. 166]).

1852. See S. Bendlinger, Änderung der Mutter-Tochter-Richtlinie der EU, 14 *SWI* 6 (2004), p. 277 (at p. 280); J. Englisch/A. Schütze, The Implementation of the EC Parent-Subsidiary Directive in Germany – Recent Developments and Unresolved Issues, 45 *Eur. Taxn.* 11 (2005), p. 488 (at p. 491); L. Jesse, Richtlinien-Umsetzungsgesetz – EURLUmsG: Anpassung des § 43b EStG

but rather allocate taxing rights between the contracting states.[1853] Whether profits are subject to tax or not is in general contingent upon domestic law. According to parts of the literature, the subject-to-tax requirement is in fact aimed at avoiding the benefits of the Parent-Subsidiary Directive being improperly claimed in situations where the parent company and the subsidiary are resident in the same Member State.[1854] In such a situation, the Parent-Subsidiary Directive only applies if the holding in the capital of the subsidiary is attributable to a parent company's permanent establishment situated in another Member State.[1855] If there was no subject-to-tax requirement, the interposition of a permanent establishment in another Member State where it is not subject to tax would have the effect that the benefits of the Parent-Subsidiary Directive can be claimed without facing taxation in the Member State where the permanent establishment is situated.[1856] Following this reasoning, the subject-to-tax requirement should be interpreted in a way that the profits have to be subject to tax according to the domestic law of the state of the permanent establishment *and* the taxing right of the state of the permanent establishment may not be (fully) restricted by a double taxation convention.[1857]

If a Member State does not have a corporate income tax regime, it would not be affected by the 2014 amendment of the Parent-Subsidiary Directive. Such a Member State would not be obliged to introduce a corporate income tax. It is, therefore, reasonable to conclude that Article 4(1) Parent-Subsidiary Directive merely determines that Member States are not allowed to refrain from taxing distributed profits to the extent that such profits are deductible by the subsidiary.[1858] In addition, the 2014 amendment does not require that a parent company has to effectively pay taxes on the distributed profits received in the period the distribution takes place. This is, on the one hand, supported by the fact that it is in line with Article 4(1) Parent-Subsidiary Directive to tax distributed profits to the extent that such profits are deductible by the subsidiary while at the same time authorizing the parent company and its permanent establishment receiving such profits "*to deduct from the amount of tax due that fraction of the corporation tax related to those profits and paid by the subsidiary and any*

(Kapitalertragsteuerbefreiung) an die geänderte Mutter-Tochter-Richtlinie, 14 *IStR* 5 (2005), p. 151 (at p. 155); G. Kofler, *Mutter-Tochter-Richtlinie – Kommentar* (LexisNexis, 2011), Artikel 2 at para. 39.

1853. See, for example, M. Lang, *Introduction to the Law of Double Taxation Conventions*[2] (Linde, 2013), at paras 44-46; also cf. K. Vogel/A. Rust in E. Reimer/A. Rust (eds.), *Klaus Vogel on Double Taxation Conventions, Fourth Edition* (Kluwer, 2015), Introduction at MN 51-53.

1854. See G. Kofler, *Mutter-Tochter-Richtlinie – Kommentar* (LexisNexis, 2011), Artikel 2 at para. 39; G. *Kofler*/H. *Kofler* in P. Quantschnigg/W. Wiesner/G. Mayr (eds.), *Steuern im Gemeinschaftsrecht, FS Nolz* (LexisNexis, 2008), at p. 63.

1855. See Article 1(1)(d) Parent-Subsidiary Directive.

1856. See *supra* n. 47.

1857. See G. Maisto, 13 *EC Tax Rev.* 4 (2004), p. 164 (at p. 170); see also J. Englisch/A. Schütze, 45 *Eur. Taxn.* 11 (2005), at p. 491.

1858. In *Cobelfret* and *KBC Bank and Beleggen, Risicokapitaal, Beheer*, the ECJ pointed out that "*there is nothing in the scheme or purpose of Directive 90/435 to suggest that there is any significant difference between the concepts of 'refraining from taxing' and 'exempting' the profits received by the parent company*" (Judgment in *Cobelfret*, C-138/07, EU:C:2009:82, at para. 43; Judgment in *KBC Bank and Beleggen, Risicokapitaal, Beheer*, C-439/07 and C-499/07, EU:C:2009:339, at para. 41).

lower-tier subsidiary, subject to the condition that at each tier a company and its lower-tier subsidiary fall within the definitions laid down in Article 2 and meet the requirements provided for in Article 3, up to the limit of the amount of the corresponding tax due." Thus, Article 4(1) Parent-Subsidiary implicitly accepts that an indirect tax credit can reduce the amount of tax due to zero. On the other hand, it also has to be kept in mind that the ECJ held "*that, even if the dividends received by the parent company are not subject to corporation tax for the tax year in the course of which those dividends were distributed, that reduction of losses of the parent company may have the effect that the parent company is subject indirectly to taxation on those dividends in subsequent tax years when its results are positive.*"[1859] Thus, distributed profits have to be considered to be taxed also if, for example, they lead to a reduction of the parent company's loss carry-forward.[1860]

The Aim of Avoiding Double Non-Taxation

The 2014 amendment not only changed the wording of Article 4(1)(a) Parent-Subsidiary Directive in order to oblige the Member States not to refrain from taxing distributed profits to the extent that such profits are deductible by the subsidiary. It also clarified that "*[t]he benefits of Directive 2011/96/EU should not lead to situations of double non-taxation and, therefore, generate unintended tax benefits for groups of parent companies and subsidiaries of different Member States when compared to groups of companies of the same Member State.*"[1861] Like the VAT Directive, the Parent-Subsidiary Directive hence also aims at the avoidance of double non-taxation.

2.2.2 The Avoidance of Double (Non-)Taxation by Means of Secondary EU Law

Not only does secondary EU law contain certain provisions that specifically aim at avoiding double taxation or double non-taxation. According to the ECJ's case law, possible risks of double taxation or double non-taxation generally have to be considered when interpreting secondary EU law.[1862] In *RAL*, for example, the Court

1859. Judgment in *Cobelfret*, EU:C:2009:82, at para. 40; see also Judgment in *KBC Bank and Beleggen, Risicokapitaal, Beheer*, EU:C:2009:339, at para. 40.

1860. Similarly G. Kofler in P. Valente (ed.), *Elusione Fiscale Internazionale* (IPSOA [Kluwer], 2014), at p. 686. In the literature, it is argued that the obligation to refrain from taxing distributed profits covered by the Parent-Subsidiary Directive does not even tolerate taking into account such profits when calculating the amount of tax on the remaining income of the parent company in the case of a progressive corporate tax scale (see M. Tumpel, *Harmonisierung der direkten Unternehmensbesteuerung in der EU* [Verlag Österreich, 1994], at p. 271). If this opinion were followed, exemption with progression of distributed profits would perhaps be sufficient in order to comply with the obligation to tax as introduced by the 2014 amendment.

1861. Council Directive 2014/86/EU of 8 Jul. 2014 amending Directive 2011/96/EU on the common system of taxation applicable in the case of parent companies and subsidiaries of different Member States, *OJ* L 219 (25. Jul. 2014), at p. 40.

1862. See E. Traversa/C. Helleputte in M. Lang/P. Melz/E. Kristoffersson (ed.), T. Ecker (ass. ed.), *Value Added Tax and Direct Taxation* (IBFD, 2009), at p. 131; also cf. B. Terra, *The Place of Supply in European VAT* (Kluwer, 1998), at pp. 122, 137-138; K. Spies in M. Lang/P.

concluded that services linked to the operation of slot gaming machines relate to entertainment activities. Hence, according to Article 9(2)(c) Sixth VAT Directive, the place of supply "*shall be the place where those services are physically carried out.*" One of the reasons why the ECJ came to this conclusion was that it "*leads to a rational solution from the point of view of taxation.*"[1863] Had the ECJ decided that the services are covered by Article 9(1) Sixth VAT Directive, the place of supply would have been outside the EU, because the supplier had established its business in Guernsey. In the literature, it is assumed that such services were not subject to VAT in Guernsey. If this was actually the case, the latter outcome would have resulted in non-taxation.[1864] Parts of the literature thus assume that "*[t]he argument of achieving a* 'rational result' *seems to refer to the avoidance of non-taxation.*"[1865,1866]

The *RBS Deutschland Holding* case is another example where there was a danger of double non-taxation. However, in contrast to *RAL*, this outcome resulted from a different interpretation and implementation of the VAT Directive in Germany and the UK: Cars acquired by a UK company were sold to a company established in Germany and leased back under a "master lease agreement." According to this agreement, the UK lessee was liable to pay the German lessor the full residual value of the cars on the expiry of the lease, unless the lessor sold the cars to a third person. In the latter case, the lessee would have been – depending on the circumstances – entitled to or liable for the difference between the sales prices of the cars and their residual value. Additionally, both companies entered into a "put option agreement," according to which the lessor was granted an option to require the lessee to buy back the leased cars. Under UK domestic VAT law, the lease transactions were treated as supplies of services. The place of supply was hence deemed to be in Germany, where the supplier's business was established. According to German domestic VAT law, however, the lease transactions were treated as supplies of goods. The place of supply was thus deemed to be in the UK where the goods were located when the supplies took place. Consequently, VAT

Pistone/A. Rust/J. Schuch/C. Staringer/D. Raponi (eds.), *CJEU – Recent Developments in Value Added Tax 2015* (Linde, 2016), at pp. 156-160.

1863. Judgment in *RAL (Channel Islands) and others*, C-452/03, EU:C:2005:289, at para. 33; on this terminology also see Judgment in *Berkholz*, 168/84, EU:C:1985:299, at para. 17; Judgment in *Faaborg-Gelting Linien*, C-231/94, EU:C:1996:184, at para. 16; also see Judgment in *DFDS*, C-260/95, EU:C:1997:77, at para. 19; Judgment in *ARO Lease*, C-190/95, EU:C:1997:374, at para. 15; Judgment in *Lease Plan Luxembourg*, C-390/96, EU:C:1998:206, at para. 24; Judgment in *Welmory*, C-605/12, EU:C:2014:2298, at para. 53.

1864. See E. Traversa/C. Helleputte in M. Lang/P. Melz/E. Kristoffersson (eds.), *Value Added Tax and Direct Taxation* (IBFD, 2009), at p. 357; also see K. Spies in M. Lang/P. Pistone/A. Rust/J. Schuch/C. Staringer/D. Raponi (eds.), *CJEU – Recent Developments in Value Added Tax 2015* (Linde, 2016), at pp. 157-158.

1865. K. Spies in M. Lang/P. Pistone/A. Rust/J. Schuch/C. Staringer/D. Raponi (eds.), *CJEU – Recent Developments in Value Added Tax 2015* (Linde, 2016), at p. 158.

1866. If double non-taxation is perceived as a situational and relative phenomenon (see Chapter 1. 2.3), the *RAL* case did not necessarily lead to the cross-border situation bearing a lesser tax burden than a comparable domestic situation would have to face in the tax jurisdiction that has the lowest tax burden of all tax jurisdictions involved. Whether there actually was a danger of double non-taxation depends on how services linked to the operation of slot gaming machines would have been treated if they had been physically carried out in Guernsey. If they had remained untaxed as well, double non-taxation would not have been an issue in *RAL*.

was paid neither in Germany nor in the UK. This prompted the Commissioners for HMRC to deny the lessor deduction of the input VAT charged to it when the cars were originally purchased from the lessee. However, the Court of Session of Scotland (First Division, Inner House) felt uncertain whether this is in line with the Sixth VAT Directive. The ECJ confirmed that these concerns were legitimate. Although the Court emphasized that *"it may seem inconsistent,"* it concluded that denying input VAT deduction in such a case conflicts with the Sixth VAT Directive: *"[T]he fact that a Member State has not collected output VAT because of the manner in which it has categorised a commercial transaction cannot deny a taxable person the right to deduct input VAT paid in another Member State."*[1867]

According to the ECJ, the *"inconsistent"* result that a taxable person may deduct input VAT without having paid output VAT was not due to an abusive behaviour by the companies involved.[1868] In the words of AG Mazák, *"where a taxable person makes use of an 'anomaly' or inconsistency in the VAT system such as that at issue, which is, however, due to that system itself or, more particularly, caused by differences in the application of that system in the Member States concerned, not every 'use' made of that possibility by a taxable person may automatically be deemed to be constitutive of an 'abuse'."*[1869] This does not mean that the ECJ considered the resultant double non-taxation to be in line with the Sixth VAT Directive. On the contrary, according to settled case law, such a result contradicts the place-of-supply rules' aim of avoiding, *"first, conflicts of jurisdiction which may result in double taxation, and, secondly, non-taxation."*[1870] Yet, the ECJ did not enlarge upon whether the lease transactions at stake constituted a supply of goods – as supposed by Germany – or a supply of services – as

1867. Judgment in *RBS Deutschland Holding*, C-277/09, EU:C:2010:810, at paras 42-44.
1868. See R. Korf, Neues zum Missbrauch – Anmerkungen zu den EuGH-Urteilen RBS Deutschland Holdings und Weald Leasing Ltd, 20 *IStR* 4 (2011), p. 146 (at pp. 146-149); P. Piantavigna, Tax Abuse in European Union law: A Theory, 20 *EC Tax Rev.* 3 (2011), p. 134 (at p. 143); M. Poulsen, Treaty/Directive Shopping and Abuse of EU Law, 41 *Intertax* 4 (2013), p. 230 (at pp. 243-244); C. Wächter, Rechtsmissbrauch und Qualifikationskonflikt im Umsatzsteuerrecht, 49 *DStR* 2 (2011), p. 49 (at pp. 50-51); critically T. Rosembuj, Hybrid Entities Why Not Tax Pass-throughs as Corporations, 40 *Intertax* 5 (2012), p. 298 (at pp. 317-318).
1869. Opinion of AG Mazák in *RBS Deutschland Holding*, C-277/09, EU:C:2010:566, at point 76.
1870. Judgment in *Kollektivavtalsstiftelsen TRR Trygghetsråde*, C-291/07, EU:C:2008:609, at para. 24; Judgment in *Athesia Druck*, C-1/08, EU:C:2009:108, at para. 20; also see Judgment in *Berkholz*, 168/84, EU:C:1985:299, at para. 14; Judgment in *Dudda*, C-327/94, EU:C:1996:355, at para. 20; Judgment in *Linthorst, Pouwels en Scheres*, C-167/95, EU:C:1997:105, at para. 10; Judgment in *Commission/France*, C-429/97, EU:C:2001:54, at para. 41; Judgment in *SPI*, C-108/00, EU:C:2001:173, at para. 15; Judgment in *RAL (Channel Islands) and others*, C-452/03, EU:C:2005:289, at para. 23; Judgment in *Levob Verzekeringen and OV Bank*, C-41/04, EU:C:2005:649, at para. 32; Judgment in *Gillan Beach*, C-114/05, EU:C:2006:169, at para. 14; Judgment in *Aktiebolaget NN*, C-111/05, EU:C:2007:195, at para. 43; Judgment in *Commission/Germany*, C-401/06, EU:C:2007:759, at para. 29; Judgment in *EGN*, C-377/08, EU:C:2009:42, at para. 27; Judgment in *RCI Europe*, C-37/08, EU:C:2009:507, at para. 20; Judgment in *ADV Allround*, C-218/10, EU:C:2012:35, at para. 27; Judgment in *Welmory*, C-605/12, EU:C:2014:2298, at para. 42; Judgment in *SMK*, C-97/14, EU:C:2015:290, at para. 32; Judgment in *WebMindLicenses*, C-419/14, EU:C:2015:832, at para. 41.

supposed by the UK – under the rules of the Sixth VAT Directive,[1871] because this question has "*not been raised*" by the referring court.[1872]

While there is hence no decision which clearly proves that the ECJ considers possible risks of double non-taxation when interpreting secondary EU law, there are a couple of judgments which emphasize that "*the provisions of the Directive must be interpreted in the light of the fundamental aims of the endeavour to harmonize VAT, in particular [...] the prevention of double taxation.*"[1873] The *Schul I* decision shows that the Court is prepared to rely on interpretative artifices in order to accommodate the objective of preventing double taxation.[1874] Article 2(2) Sixth VAT Directive required Member States to subject the importation of goods to VAT. Although the wording of this provision did not include any reference to the tax treatment in the Member State of export, the ECJ concluded that "*in so far as [...] an imported product supplied by a private person may not lawfully benefit from a remission of tax on exportation and so remains burdened upon importation with part of the value-added tax paid in the Member State of exportation the amount of value-added tax payable on importation must be reduced by the residual part of the value-added tax of the Member State of exportation which is still contained in the value of the product when it is imported.*"[1875] Given the wording of Article 2(2) Sixth VAT Directive, some scholars argue that the Court's approach resulted in a *contra legem* interpretation of the Sixth VAT Directive.[1876] However, it is also discussed whether the ECJ has either teleologically reduced the scope of Article 2(2) Sixth VAT Directive so that the importation of goods may only be subjected to VAT insofar as the resultant tax exceeds the VAT that had already been

1871. But also cf. Judgment in *Faaborg-Gelting Linien / Finanzamt Flensburg*, C-231/94, EU:C:1996:184.
1872. Opinion of AG Mazák in *RBS Deutschland Holding*, C-277/09, EU:C:2010:566, at points 32-33; also see M. Lang in M. Achatz/M. Tumpel (eds.), *Umsatzsteuer und Internationales Steuerrecht* (Linde, 2012), at pp. 24-25; S. Pfeiffer, *VAT Grouping from a European Perspective* (IBFD, 2015), at p. 190 (FN 961); K. Spies in M. Lang/P. Pistone/A. Rust/J. Schuch/C. Staringer/D. Raponi (eds.), *CJEU – Recent Developments in Value Added Tax 2015* (Linde, 2016), at p. 158 (FN 135); C. Wächter, 49 *DStR* 2 (2011), at p. 51.
1873. Judgment in *Klattner / Elliniko Dimosio*, C-389/95, EU:C:1997:258, at para. 25; see also Judgment in *Ministère public / Profant*, 249/84, EU:C:1985:393, at para. 25; Judgment in *Ledoux*, 127/86, EU:C:1988:366, at para. 11; Judgment in *Ryborg*, C-297/89, EU:C:1991:160, at para. 13.
1874. For similar issues with regard to the compatibility of secondary EU law with primary EU law see R. Szudoczky, The Influence of Primary Law on the Interpretation of Secondary Law in the Field of EU Citizenship and Direct Taxation: "Whatever works" ..., in D. Weber (ed.), *Traditional and Alternative Routes to European Tax Integration* (IBFD, 2010), p. 191 (at pp. 200-215); R. Szudoczky, *The Sources of EU law and Their Relationships: Lessons for the Field of Taxation* (IBFD, 2014), at pp. 233-252.
1875. Judgment in *Schul I*, 15/81, EU:C:1982:135, at para. 34; also see Judgment in *Bergeres-Becque*, 39/85, EU:C:1986:36, at paras 5-9; Judgment in *Drexl*, 299/86, EU:C:1988:103, at para. 11; also cf. Judgment in *Schul II*, 47/84, EU:C:1985:216, at paras 15-17; Judgment in *Ministère public / Profant*, 249/84, EU:C:1985:393, at paras 23-28; Judgment in *Commission/Italy*, 120/88, EU:C:1991:74, at para. 6; Judgment in *Commission/Spain*, C-119/89, EU:C:1991:75, at para. 6; Judgment in *Commission/Greece*, C-159/89, EU:C:1991:77, at para. 7.
1876. See R. Szudoczky, *The Sources of EU law and Their Relationships: Lessons for the Field of Taxation* (IBFD, 2014), at pp. 408-409.

paid in the Member State of exportation[1877] or whether it has "*filled the gap left unfilled by the legislature.*"[1878] Irrespective of the ECJ's ambiguous methodological approach, the *Schul I* decision raises a fundamental question: Why is it possible to rely on secondary EU law in order to avoid situations of double taxation (and/or double non-taxation), even if such situations are not specifically dealt with by the particular provisions?

In *Schul I*, the ECJ not only had to deal with the issue of potential double taxation, but was also asked whether Article 2(2) Sixth VAT Directive "*is incompatible with the Treaty and therefore invalid in so far as that provision requires Member States to subject the importation of goods from other Member States to value-added tax without making any exception for goods supplied by private persons which, when supplied within the Member State concerned, would not be subject to that tax.*"[1879] According to the Court, "*there are no grounds for considering [Article 2(2) Sixth VAT Directive] [...] to be invalid. It is simply necessary to define the scope of that provision and interpret it in a manner consistent with the requirements of the treaty*'.[1880] This approach corresponds to the ECJ regularly pointing out that, "*[a]ccording to a general principle of interpretation, a provision must be interpreted, as far as possible, in such a way as not to detract from its validity.*"[1881] For this reason, "*if the wording of secondary Community law is open to more than one interpretation, preference should be given to the interpretation which renders the provision consistent with the EC Treaty rather than to the interpretation which leads to its being incompatible with the Treaty.*"[1882] In doubt, secondary EU law thus has to be interpreted in a way that avoids conflicts not only with the

1877. See S. Vogenauer, *Die Auslegung von Gesetzen in England und auf dem Kontinent* (Mohr Siebeck, 2001), at p. 382.
1878. G. Slynn, 7 *Denning L. J.* 7 (1992), at p. 234.
1879. Judgment in *Schul I*, 15/81, EU:C:1982:135, at p. 1413.
1880. Judgment in *Schul I*, 15/81, EU:C:1982:135, at para. 43.
1881. Judgment in *Italy/Commission*, C-403/99, EU:C:2001:507, at para. 37; also see Judgment in *Schwebda and Bayer CropScience*, C-361/06, EU:C:2008:296, at para. 49; Judgment in *Sturgeon and others*, C-402/07 and C-432/07, EU:C:2009:716, at para. 47; Judgment in *Chatzi*, C-149/10, EU:C:2010:534, at para. 43; Judgment in *McDonagh*, C-12/11, EU:C:2013:43, at para. 44; Judgment in *Réexamen Commission/Strack*, C-579/12 RX-II, EU:C:2013:570, at para. 40; Judgment in *Parliament/Council*, C-317/13 and C-679/13, EU:C:2015:223, at para. 49; Judgment in *Parliament/Council*, C-540/13, EU:C:2015:224, at para. 39; Judgment in *Parliament/Council*, C-595/14, EU:C:2015:847, at para. 41; Judgment in *N.*, C-601/15 PPU, EU:C:2016:84, at para. 48.
1882. Judgment in *Ordre des barreaux francophones and germanophone and others*, C-305/05, EU:C:2007:383, at para. 28; also see Judgment in *Commission/Council*, 218/82, EU:C:1983:369, at para. 15; Judgment in *Klensch and others*, 201/85 and 202/85, EU:C:1986:439, at para. 21; Judgment in *Commission/Germany*, 205/84, EU:C:1986:463, at para. 62; Judgment in *Rauh*, C-314/89, EU:C:1991:143, at para. 17; Judgment in *Neu and others/Secrétaire d'État à l'Agriculture et à la Viticulture*, C-90/90 and C-91/90, EU:C:1991:303, at para. 12; Judgment in *Dr. Tretter*, C-90/92, EU:C:1993:264, at para. 11; Judgment in *Herbrink*, C-98/91, EU:C:1994:24, at para. 9; Judgment in *Spain/Commission*, C-135/93, EU:C:1995:201, at para. 37; Judgment in *Commission/France*, C-434/97, EU:C:2000:98, at para. 21; Judgment in *Schilling and Nehring*, C-63/00, EU:C:2002:296, at para. 24; Judgment in *Sturgeon and others*, C-402/07 and C-432/07, EU:C:2009:716, at para. 47; also cf. Judgment in *Wachauf*, 5/88, EU:C:1989:321, at para. 22; Judgment in *Socridis*, C-166/98, EU:C:1999:316, at para. 19; Judgment in *Chatzi*, C-149/10, EU:C:2010:534, at para. 43.

fundamental freedoms,[1883] but also "*with primary law as a whole, including the principle of equal treatment, which requires that comparable situations must not be treated differently and that different situations must not be treated in the same way unless such treatment is objectively justified.*"[1884] If double taxation is perceived as a situational and relative phenomenon,[1885] it is consistent with this line of jurisprudence to interpret secondary EU law, in the case of doubt, in a way so as to avoid that the free movement requirement of the internal market concept is impaired by secondary EU law causing cross-border situations to be subject to a higher tax burden than comparable domestic situations. Such an approach likewise accommodates the principle of equal treatment and the free movement requirement of the internal market concept. On similar grounds, the potential danger of double non-taxation should be taken into account when interpreting secondary EU law. Indeed, the EU legislator does not run the risk of infringing Article 107 TFEU, because "*the condition of intervention by the State is not met*"[1886] if selective advantages derive from secondary EU law, which the Member States are bound to transpose in their national law.[1887] However, as the internal market concept generally aims at ensuring that competition is not distorted,[1888] it is consistent to interpret secondary EU law, in the case of doubt, in a way so as to avoid distortions of competition, which may also arise if secondary EU law causes double non-taxation.

By perceiving double taxation and double non-taxation as situational and relative phenomena,[1889] it thus becomes apparent how secondary EU law might serve as a tool to avoid double taxation as well as double non-taxation. It is a severe obstacle for the free movement requirement of the internal market concept if the taxes of two or more

1883. Judgment in *Verband Sozialer Wettbewerb/Clinique Laboratories and Estée Lauder*, C-315/92, EU:C:1994:34, at para. 12; Judgment in *Bristol-Myers Squibb and others/Paranova*, C-427/93, C-429/93 and C-436/93, EU:C:1996:282 at para. 27; Judgment in *Phytheron International/Bourdon*, C-352/95, EU:C:1997:170, at para. 18; also cf. Judgment in *Rewe-Zentrale*, 37/83, EU:C:1984:89, at para. 18; Judgment in *Denkavit Nederland*, 15/83, EU:C:1983:183, at para. 15; Judgment in *Meyhui*, C-51/93, EU:C:1994:312, at para. 11; Judgment in *Kieffer and Thill*, C-114/96, EU:C:1997:316, at para. 27; Judgment in *Bettati/Safety Hi-Tech*, C-341/95, EU:C:1998:353, at para. 61; Judgment in *Schwarzkopf*, C-169/99, EU:C:2001:439, at para. 37; Judgment in *Ravil*, C-469/00, EU:C:2003:295, at para. 86; Judgment in *Consorzio del Prosciutto di Parma and Salumificio S. Rita*, C-108/01, EU:C:2003:296, at para. 54; Judgment in *Arnold André*, C-434/02, EU:C:2004:800, at para. 57; Judgment in *Swedish Match*, C-210/03, EU:C:2004:802, at para. 59; Judgment in *Alliance for Natural Health and others*, C-154/04 and C-155/04, EU:C:2005:449, at para. 47; Judgment in *Schmelz*, C-97/09, EU:C:2010:632, at para. 50.

1884. Judgment in *Sturgeon and others*, C-402/07 and C-432/07, EU:C:2009:716, at para. 47; also see Judgment in *Chatzi*, C-149/10, EU:C:2010:534, at para. 43; also cf. Judgment in *McDonagh*, C-12/11, EU:C:2013:43, at para. 44; Judgment in *Réexamen Commission/Strack*, C-579/12 RX-II, EU:C:2013:570, at para. 40; Judgment in *N.*, C-601/15 PPU, EU:C:2016:84, at para. 48.

1885. See Chapter 1.2.2.

1886. Judgment in *Puffer*, C-460/07, EU:C:2009:254, at para. 70; also see Judgment in *Bettati/Safety Hi-Tech*, C-341/95, EU:C:1998:353, at para. 74; also see European Commission, Commission Notice on the notion of State Aid as referred to in Article 107(1) of the Treaty on the Functioning of the European Union, *OJ* C 262 (19 Jul. 2016), at para. 44.

1887. For requirements arising due to the principle of equal treatment see, however, J. Englisch, 44 *EuR* 4 (2009), at pp. 490-513.

1888. See Chapter 3.1.1.

1889. See Chapter 1.2.

states overlap in such a manner that cross-border situations bear a higher tax burden than comparable domestic situations. Therefore, the ECJ has – at least in the past – even considered the abolition of double taxation to be included among the objectives of EU law.[1890] If secondary EU law caused double taxation, it would conflict with this objective. Double non-taxation, on the other hand, is considered to harm competition and economic efficiency.[1891] Based on this assumption, it can be argued that secondary EU law causing double non-taxation conflicts with the internal market concept's aim of ensuring that competition is not distorted. Since the ECJ is keen to avoid conflicts between primary and secondary EU law by adopting a reconciling interpretation of provisions of secondary EU law in light of primary EU law,[1892] it should hence also take into account whether a certain interpretation may cause double taxation or double non-taxation. However, this principle or technique of "*in dubio pro communitate*"[1893] is not only applicable if a certain interpretation of secondary EU law runs the risk of creating a conflict with primary EU law by causing double taxation or double non-taxation. It may also be applied if various arguments speak in favour of different interpretations of a provision of secondary EU law, neither of which would per se lead to an infringement of the Treaties. To the extent secondary EU law is intended to materialize the EU's aim of establishing and ensuring the functioning of the internal market, it must be interpreted in the light of those provisions of the Treaties which reflect the internal market concept's main characteristics of abolishing obstacles to free movement and ensuring undistorted competition.[1894] Thus, secondary EU law cannot avoid all situations of double taxation or double non-taxation. Still, the principle or technique of "*in dubio pro communitate*" may turn the balance if various arguments speak in favour of different interpretations of a provision of secondary EU law. In doubt, secondary EU law should be interpreted in a way that avoids double taxation as well as double non-taxation.

1890. Judgment in *Gilly*, C-336/96, EU:C:1998:221, at para. 16; also see Judgment in *Bouanich*, C-265/04, EU:C:2006:51, at para. 49; Judgment in *Damseaux*, C-128/08, EU:C:2009:471, at para. 28; Order in *Levy and Sebbag*, C-540/11, EU:C:2012:581, at para. 27.
1891. OECD, *Action Plan on Base Erosion and Profit Shifting* (OECD, 2013), at p. 15.
1892. See G. Kofler, Das Verhältnis zwischen primärem und sekundärem Unionsrecht im direkten Steuerrecht, in M. Lang/Ch. Weinzierl (eds.), *Europäisches Steuerrecht, Festschrift für Friedrich Rödler* (Linde, 2010), p. 433 (at p. 436); G. Kofler/M. Tenore, Fundamental Freedoms and Directives in the Area of Direct Taxation, in D. Weber (ed.), *Traditional and Alternative Routes to European Tax Integration* (IBFD, 2010), p. 311 (at p. 316); R. Szudoczky, *The Sources of EU law and Their Relationships: Lessons for the Field of Taxation* (IBFD, 2014), at pp. 231-232; S. Vogenauer, *Die Auslegung von Gesetzen in England und auf dem Kontinent* (Mohr Siebeck, 2001), at pp. 352 and 387-388.
1893. K. Mortelmans, The Relationship Between the Treaty Rules and Community Measures for the Establishment and Functioning of the Internal Market – Towards a Concordance Rule, 39 *Common Market L. Rev.* 6 (2002), p. 1303 (at p. 1325); also see R. Szudoczky in D. Weber (ed.), *Traditional and Alternative Routes to European Tax Integration* (IBFD, 2010), at p. 192; R. Szudoczky, *The Sources of EU Law and Their Relationships: Lessons for the Field of Taxation* (IBFD, 2014), at pp. 231-323.
1894. Cf. Judgment in *Torrekens*, 28/68, EU:C:1969:17, at para. 10; Judgment in *Duffy*, 34/69, EU:C:1969:71, at paras 5-7; also cf. Judgment in *CILFIT*, 283/81, EU:C:1982:335, at para. 20 ("*[E]very provision of Community law must be placed in its context and interpreted in the light of the provisions of Community law as a whole*") and Judgment in *Dürbeck*, C-389/93, EU:C:1995:174, at para. 38.

2.3 Double Non-Taxation and the State Aid Rules

2.3.1 The Unilaterally-Directed Effect of the State Aid Rules

From an internal market perspective, double non-taxation should be perceived as a situational and relative phenomenon. Whether a cross-border situation is subject to double non-taxation depends on the tax burden the respective comparable domestic situation would have to face in the individual Member States that are involved.[1895] If it is true that competition and economic efficiency is harmed by cross-border transactions sustaining a lesser tax burden than comparable domestic transactions,[1896] the question arises whether the Treaties' provisions dealing with undistorted competition prohibit such a preferential treatment of cross-border situations.[1897]

From a tax perspective, the State aid rules are the most relevant means to implement the competition aspect of the internal market concept.[1898] According to the ECJ, Article 107(1) TFEU requires that the charges which are normally included in the budget of an undertaking are mitigated.[1899] Since there is no autonomous general

---

1895. Cf. Y.Brauner, 16 *Florida Tax Rev.* 2 (2014), at p. 79 (*"double non-taxation," that is, taxation of circumstances of transactions at a level that is lower than they would have faced in a purely domestic setting."*).

1896. OECD, *Action Plan on Base Erosion and Profit Shifting* (OECD, 2013), at p. 15.

1897. Cf. W. in I. Richelle/W. Schön/E. Traversa (eds.), *Allocating Taxing Powers Within the European Union* (Springer, 2013), 133-160; R. Luja, 76 *Tax Notes Intl.* 4 (27 Oct. 2014), at pp. 353-356; R. Luja, IP/A/TAXE/2015-02, PE 563.453 (October 2015), at pp. 14-15; R. Luja, 60 *British Tax Rev.* 3 (2015), at pp. 379-390; P. Rossi-Maccanico, 75 *Tax Notes Intl.* 10 (8 Sep. 2014), at pp. 857-868; P. Rossi-Maccanico, 24 *EC Tax Rev.* 2 (2015), at pp. 63-77; D.S. Smit, 25 *EC Tax Rev.* 2 (2016), at pp. 110-112; R. Szudoczky in I. Richelle/W. Schön/E. Traversa (eds.), *Allocating Taxing Powers Within the European Union* (Springer, 2013), 163-183; A. Taferner/ J.W. Kuipers, 56 *Eur. Taxn.* 4 (2016), at pp. 142-143.

1898. See P. Pistone/R. Szudoczy in M. Lang/P. Pistone/J. Schuch/C. Staringer (eds.), *Introduction to European Tax Law on Direct Taxation*[4] (Linde, 2015), at p. 28.

1899. Judgment in *De gezamenlijke Steenkolenmijnen in Limburg*, 30/59, EU:C:1961:2, at p. 19; Judgment in *Banco Exterior de España*, C-387/92, EU:C:1994:100, at para. 13; Judgment in *Ecotrade*, C-200/97, EU:C:1998:579, at para. 34; Judgment in *Italy/Commission*, C-6/97, EU:C:1999:251, at para. 15; Judgment in *Piaggio*, C-295/97, EU:C:1999:313, at para. 34; Judgment in *Commission/Portugal*, C-404/97, EU:C:2000:345, at para. 44; Judgment in *Germany/Commission*, C-156/98, EU:C:2000:367, at para. 25; Judgment in *Banks*, C-390/98, EU:C:2001:456, at para. 30; Judgment in *Adria-Wien Pipeline and Wietersdorfer & Peggauer Zementwerke*, C-143/99, EU:C:2001:598, at para. 38; Judgment in *Italy/Commission*, C-310/ 99, EU:C:2002:143, at para. 51; Judgment in *Ferring*, C-53/00, EU:C:2001:627, at para. 15; Judgment in *Belgium/Commission*, C-5/01, EU:C:2002:754, at para. 32; Judgment in *Freskot*, C-355/00, EU:C:2003:298, at para. 83; Judgment in *SIM 2 Multimedia v. Commission*, C-399/00, EU:C:2003:252, at para. 35; Judgment in Spain/Commission, C-501/00, EU:C:2004:438, at para. 90; Judgment in *Chronopost/Ufex and others*, C-83/01 P, EU:C:2003:388, at para. 65; Judgment in *GIL Insurance and others*, C-308/01, EU:C:2004:252, at para. 69; Judgment in *Heiser*, C-172/03, EU:C:2005:130, at para. 36; Judgment in *Cassa di Risparmio di Firenze*, C-222/04, EU:C:2006:8, at para. 131; Judgment in *Enirisorse*, C-237/04, EU:C:2006:197, at para. 42; Judgment in *Air Liquide Industries Belgium*, C-393/04, EU:C:2006:403, at para. 29; Judgment in *Paint Graphos*, C-78/08, EU:C:2011:550, at para. 45; Judgment in *Presidente del Consiglio dei Ministri*, C-169/08, EU:C:2009:709, at para. 56; Judgment in *Commission and Spain/Government of Gibraltar and United Kingdom*, C-106/09 P and C-107/09 P, EU:C:2011:732, at para. 71; Judgment in *Seydaland Vereinigte Agrarbetriebe*, C-239/09, EU:C:2010:778, at para. 30; Judgment in *France Télécom/Commission*,

description of a "normal" tax system,[1900] a tax measure can only be identified as State aid if it causes a deviation from the common tax regime that has been established by the very same Member State.[1901] However, double non-taxation is not always caused by a single tax measure embedded in the common tax regime of a single Member State, but rather often results, for example, from the interaction of deviating domestic tax systems of different Member States[1902] or a different application of a double taxation convention.[1903] In parts of the literature it is, therefore, argued that "*double non-taxation [...] can and should be addressed within the EU, but not via State aid[,] [...] as mismatches resulting from genuine disparities cannot be attributed to a single Member State.*"[1904]

C-81/10 P, EU:C:2011:811, at para. 16; Judgment in *Frucona Košice/Commission*, C-73/11 P, EU:C:2013:32, at para. 69; Judgment in *France/Commission*, C-559/12 P, EU:C:2014:217, at para. 94; Judgment in *Eventech*, C-518/13, EU:C:2015:9, at para. 33; Judgment in OTP Bank, C-672/13, EU:C:2015:185, at para. 40; Judgment in *Kernkraftwerke Lippe-Ems*, C-5/14, EU:C:2015:354, at para. 71; Judgment in *BVVG*, C-39/14, EU:C:2015:470, at para. 26.

1900. See W. Schön, 36 *Common Market L. Rev.* 5 (1999), at p. 932; W. Schön in L. Hancher/T. Ottervanger/P.J. Slot (eds.), *EU State Aids* (Sweet & Maxwell, 2012), at p. 339.

1901. See W. Schön, 36 *Common Market L. Rev.* 5 (1999), at pp. 923-924; W. Schön in L. Hancher/T. Ottervanger/P.J. Slot (eds.), *EU State Aids* (Sweet & Maxwell, 2012), at p. 339; R. Szudoczky, *The Sources of EU law and Their Relationships: Lessons for the Field of Taxation* (IBFD, 2014), at p. 494; C. Quigley, *European State Aid Law and Policy, Third Edition* (Hart Publishing, 2015), at p. 9; also see Opinion of AG Jääskinen in *Commission and Spain/Government of Gibraltar and United Kingdom*, C-106/09 P and C-107/09 P, EU:C:2011:215, at point 175 ("*Inasmuch as European Union law does not have any default tax system, the reference framework must remain the national reference framework*"); also cf. Judgment in *Spain/Commission*, C-73/03, EU:C:2004:711, at para. 28.

1902. Financial instruments, for example, are traditionally divided into equity and debt. A wide variety of instruments, however, incorporate elements of both equity and debt and are, therefore, referred to as hybrid financial instruments (see, for example, J.A. Duncan in IFA [ed.], *Tax Treatment of Hybrid Financial Instruments in Cross-Border Transactions*, CDFI 85a [SDU, 2000], at pp. 24 et seq.; M. Helminen, *The Dividend Concept in International Tax Law* [Kluwer, 1999], at pp. 251 et seq.; M. Helminen 58 *Bull. Intl. Taxn.* 2 [2004], at pp. 56 et seq.). As such instruments usually cannot be clearly classified as either equity or debt the classification may vary in different jurisdictions. From a tax planning perspective, this mismatch in treatment can be exploited by using a hybrid instrument that is treated as debt in the source state and as equity in the residence state. Thereby, it is possible to obtain a double tax benefit, since the amount paid by the debtor is deductible as interest in the source state and might be exempt as a dividend at the level of the creditor in the residence state due to a dividend exemption system (see C. Marchgraber, 54 *Eur. Taxn.* 4 [2014], at pp. 134-135; C. Marchgraber, 70 *Bull. Intl. Taxn.* 3 [2016], at p. 124).

1903. With regard to short-term assignments of an employee, for example, the Supreme Court of the employee's residence state may consider the "user" in the other contracting state to be the employer according to Article 15(2)(b) OECD MC. Thus, the employee's remuneration may be taxed in the other contracting state under Article 15(1) OECD MC. If the Supreme Court of the other contracting state, in contrast, considered the "formal employer" in the residence state to also be the employer for purposes of Article 15(2)(b) OECD MC, it would consider the employee's remuneration to be taxable only in the residence state under Article 15(2) OECD MC. But for Article 23 A(4) OECD MC (for an analysis of this provision and further references see C. Marchgraber, Conflicts of Qualification and Interpretation: How Should Developing Countries React?, 44 *Intertax* 4 [2016], p. 307 [at pp. 312-313]; C. Marchgraber, Vermeidung doppelter Nichtbesteuerung im DBA-Recht, in M. Lang/C. Marchgraber/A. Rust/J. Schuch/C. Staringer [eds.], *Niedrigbesteuerung im Unternehmenssteuerrecht* [Linde, 2016], p. 95 [at p. 111, FN 64]), the remuneration of the employee would remain untaxed.

1904. R. Luja, 60 *British Tax Rev.* 3 (2015), at p. 387; also see R. Luja, 76 *Tax Notes Intl.* 4 (27 Oct. 2014), at pp. 353-354; R. Luja, IP/A/TAXE/2015-02, PE 563.453 (October 2015), at pp. 14-17; A. Taferner/J.W. Kuipers, 56 *Eur. Taxn.* 4 (2016), at p. 142 ("*Double non-taxation does not*

This conclusion strikingly reminds one of the ECJ's main reason not to interpret the fundamental freedoms as prohibiting double taxation, which is that "*no one tax jurisdiction is to blame for the tax disadvantage.*"[1905] However, this does not mean that the fundamental freedoms generally do not apply to situations of double taxation. The resultant tax disadvantage only remains invulnerable if the particular provisions of the involved Member States do not per se lead to discrimination.[1906] In *Amid*, for example, the ECJ had to deal with the *Velasquez* doctrine, which was developed by Belgian courts in the 1980s.[1907] Thus, a Belgian company had to set off losses suffered in Belgium against profits earned via a permanent establishment in Luxembourg, although these profits were exempt from Belgian tax according to the double taxation convention between Belgium and Luxembourg. Since it was not possible to take into account the losses in Luxembourg either, the refusal of a loss carry-forward in Belgium resulted in double taxation, because essentially the profits earned via the permanent establishment were effectively taxed in Belgium as well as in Luxembourg.[1908] According to the ECJ, the Belgian system violated the freedom of establishment. However, the reason was not that the taxpayer was subject to double taxation, but rather that the Belgian tax system was discriminatory, because losses could have been deducted from taxable income if the permanent establishment had been located in Belgium.[1909]

[...] result from the tax system of one country, but from how the systems of several countries relate to each other. This is not a problem of state aid, but of lack of harmonization"); also cf. L. De Broe, The State Aid Review Against Aggressive Tax Planning: "Always Look a Gift Horse in the Mouth," 24 *EC Tax Rev.* 6 (2015), p. 290 (at p. 293: "*the state aid review should not be used as a means [...] to address mismatches and the doulbe non-taxation following from disparities in the tax legislations of two or more Member States*"); P. Pistone/R. Szudoczy in M. Lang/P. Pistone/J. Schuch/C. Staringer (eds.), *Introduction to European Tax Law on Direct Taxation*[4] (Linde, 2015), at pp. 31-32 ("*an advantage which results from disparities between the tax systems is outside the scope of the State aid rules*"); D.S. Smit, 25 *EC Tax Rev.* 2 (2016), at p. 112 ("*removing international disparities [...] should in my view be done through legislation instead of through application of the European state aid rules*").

1905. Opinion of AG Geelhoed in *Test Claimants in Class IV of the ACT Group Litigation*, C-374/04, EU:C:2006:139, at point 48.

1906. See W. Haslehner in I. Richelle/W. Schön/E. Traversa (eds.), *Allocating Taxing Powers Within the European Union* (Springer, 2013), at p. 137.

1907. See P. Goris, The *Velasquez* Doctrine: An Example of International Juridical Double Taxation, 36 *Eur. Taxn.* 10 (1996), p. 327 (at pp. 327-328); L. Hinnekens, *AMID*: The Wrong Bridge or a Bridge Too Far? An Analysis of a Recent Decision of the European Court of Justice, 41 *Eur. Taxn.* 6 (2001), p. 206 (at pp. 206-207); J. Van Steenwinckel/J. Van Vaeck, European Court of Justice 14 Dec. 2000, C-141/99, 10 *EC Tax Rev.* 2 (2001), p. 98 (at p. 100); for further references see A. Cordewener, *Europäische Grundfreiheiten und nationales Steuerrecht* (Dr Otto Schmidt, 2002), at p. 784.

1908. See A. Cordewener, *Europäische Grundfreiheiten und nationales Steuerrecht* (Dr Otto Schmidt, 2002), at pp. 796 and 859-860; G. Kofler, *Doppelbesteuerungsabkommen und Europäisches Gemeinschaftsrecht* (Linde, 2007), at pp. 182-183; also cf. L. Hinnekens, 41 *Eur. Taxn.* 6 (2001), at p. 208; M. Züger, Neue internationale Steuerfälle vor dem EuGH, 10 *SWI* 3 (2000), p. 133 (at p. 136).

1909. Judgment in *AMID*, C-141/99, EU:C:2000:696, at paras 27-33; critically J.F. Avery Jones, A Comment on "AMID: The Wrong Bridge or a Bridge Too Far"? 41 *Eur. Taxn.* 13 (2001), p. 251 (at p. 251); W. Bernhard, Einkünfte aus ausländischen Betriebsstätten im Lichte des Europarechts, 10 *IStR* 12 (2001), p. 366 (at pp. 366-368); M. Dassesse, The ECJ's Decision in *AMID* and its Implications for Belgian Companies, 55 *Bull. Intl. Taxn.* 6 (2001), p. 254 (at pp. 254-257); L. Hinnekens, 41 *Eur. Taxn.* 6 (2001), at pp. 206-210; J. Van Steenwinckel/J. Van

Not only *Amid*, but other decisions as well[1910] prove that double taxation should not hastily be considered to be a problem which is not covered by the fundamental freedoms. Only if the applicable rules of the involved Member States' tax systems are entirely non-discriminatory, is the fundamental freedoms' potential maxed out. This should also be kept in mind when it is examined whether double non-taxation may be addressed by the State aid rules. Before concluding that this is not possible, because the cause for double non-taxation cannot be attributed to a single Member State, it has to be made sure that the applicable rules of the involved Member States' tax systems do not themselves constitute State aid.[1911] Of course, this cannot be done in an abstract and blanket way. As the ECJ has pointed out, analysing whether a national measure constitutes State aid "*presupposes not only familiarity with the content of the provisions of relevant law but also requires examination of their scope on the basis of administrative and judicial practice and of information relating to the ambit* ratione personae *of those provisions.*"[1912] Applying State aid law thus requires an in-depth analysis of the national measure concerned and its role in and influence on the affected Member State's tax system. It is virtually impossible to provide a thorough State aid law analysis of all domestic provisions of the Member States' tax systems which might be jointly responsible for double non-taxation. Still, due to some prominent investigations by the European Commission regarding tax planning schemes of multinational enterprises,[1913] scholars have started to look for arguments which might be relevant for such

Vaeck, 10 *EC Tax Rev.* 2 (2001), at pp. 98-101; for a detailed analysis of this judgment see A. Cordewener, *Europäische Grundfreiheiten und nationales Steuerrecht* (Dr Otto Schmidt, 2002), at pp. 782-801.

1910. See G. Kofler, *Doppelbesteuerungsabkommen und Europäisches Gemeinschaftsrecht* (Linde, 2007), at pp. 183-193; also see K. Daxkobler, *Die grundfreiheitliche Rechtsprechung des EuGH* (Linde, 2015), at pp. 172-173.

1911. See W. Haslehner in I. Richelle/W. Schön/E. Traversa (eds.), *Allocating Taxing Powers within the European Union* (Springer, 2013), at p. 137.

1912. Judgment in *P.*, C-6/12, EU:C:2013:525, at para. 20.

1913. European Commission Press Release, *State aid: Commission orders Luxembourg to deliver information on tax practices*, IP/14/309 (24 March 2014); European Commission Press Release, *State Aid: Commission Investigates Transfer Pricing Arrangements on Corporate Taxation of Apple (Ireland) Starbucks (Netherlands) and Fiat Finance and Trade (Luxembourg)*, IP/14/663 (11 Jun. 2014), at p. 2; European Commission, *Statement by Vice President Alumnia on Opening of Three Investigations on Transfer Pricing Arrangements on Corporate Taxation by Apple (Ireland), Starbucks (Netherlands) and Fiat Finance and Trade (Luxembourg)*, Statement/14/190 (11 Jun. 2014); European Commission, State aid SA. 38375 (2014/NN) (ex 2014/CP) – Luxembourg *Alleged aid to FFT*, C(2014) 3627 final (11 Jun. 2014); European Commission, State aid SA.38374 (2014/C) (ex 2014/NN) (ex 2014/CP) – Netherlands Alleged aid to Starbucks, C(2014) 3626 final (11 Jun. 2014); European Commission, State aid SA.38373 (2014/C) (ex 2014/NN) (ex 2014/CP) – Ireland *Alleged aid to Apple*, C(2014) 3606 final (11 Jun. 2014); European Commission, *Statement by Vice President Almunia on Opening of Indepth Investigation into Possible State Aid Granted by Luxembourg to Amazon*, Statement/14/303 (7 Oct. 2014); European Commission Press Release, *State Aid: Commission Investigates Transfer Pricing Arrangements on Corporate Taxation of Amazon in Luxembourg*, IP/14/1105 (7 Oct. 2014); European Commission, State aid SA.38944 (2014/C) – Luxembourg Alleged aid to Amazon by way of a tax ruling, C(2014) 7156 final (7 Oct. 2014); European Commission, State aid SA.37667 (2015/C ex 2015/NN) – Belgium - Excess profit tax ruling system in Belgium – Art. 185§2 b) CIR92, C(2015) 563 final (3 Feb. 2015); European Commission, *Statement by Commissioner Vestager on Commission State Aid Decisions Regarding Illegal Tax Advantages Granted by Luxembourg (Fiat) and the Netherlands*

an analysis, thereby specifically focusing on unilateral and bilateral measures that are commonly associated with double non-taxation:[1914] (1) uni- and bilateral measures which grant relief from juridical double taxation; (2) downward adjustments of profits due to transfer pricing rules and (3) participation exemption regimes.

2.3.2 Thoughts on the State Aid Law Compatibility of Selected Measures Commonly Associated with Double Non-Taxation

2.3.2.1 Relief from Juridical Double Taxation and State Aid Law

The term "double non-taxation" is often used in order to describe an (allegedly) inadvertent result of applying double taxation conventions.[1915] Such a treaty may, for example, prevent one of the contracting states from taxing a certain item of income, but may not provide for a corresponding obligation for the other contracting state to tax this item of income domestically.[1916] This could lead to an item of income remaining

---

(Starbucks) and On the Optical Disk Drives Cartel, Statement/15/5881 (21 Oct. 2015); European Commission Press Release, *Commission Decides Selective Tax Advantages for Fiat in Luxembourg and Starbucks in the Netherlands are Illegal under EU State Aid Rules*, IP/15/5880 (21 Oct. 2015); Commission Decision of 21.10.2015 on State Aid SA.38374 (2014/C ex 2014/NN) implemented by the Netherlands to Starbucks, C(2015) 7143 final (21 Oct. 2015); Commission Decision of 21.10.2015 on State Aid SA.38375 (2014/C ex 2014/NN) which Luxembourg granted to Fiat, C(2015) 7152 final (21 Oct. 2015); European Commission Press Release, *State Aid: Commission Opens Formal Investigation into Luxembourg's Tax Treatment of McDonald's*, IP/15/6221 (3 Dec. 2015); European Commission, State aid SA. 38945 (2015/C) (ex 2015/NN) – Luxembourg Alleged aid to McDonald's, C(2015) 8343 final (3 Dec. 2015); European Commission Press Release, *State Aid: Commission Concludes Belgian "Excess Profit" Tax Scheme Illegal; Around €700 Million to be Recovered from 35 Multinational Companies*, IP/16/42 (11 Jan. 2016); Commission Decision of 11.1.2016 on the Excess Profit Exemption State Aid Scheme SA.37667 (2015/C) (ex 2015/NN) implemented by Belgium, C(2015) 9837 final (11 Jan. 2016).

1914. See A. Gunn/J. Luts, Tax Rulings, APAs and State Aid: Legal Issues, 24 *EC Tax Rev.* 2 (2015), p. 119 (at pp. 119-125); W. Haslehner in I. Richelle/W. Schön/E. Traversa (eds.), *Allocating Taxing Powers Within the European Union* (Springer, 2013), at pp. 135-143; R. Luja, 76 *Tax Notes Intl.* 4 (27 Oct. 2014), at pp. 353-356; R. Luja, IP/A/TAXE/2015-02, PE 563.453 (October 2015), at pp. 12-19; R. Luja, 60 *British Tax Rev.* 3 (2015), at pp. 383-389; R. Lyal, 38 *Fordham Intl. L. J.* 4 (2015), at pp. 1028-1043; P. Rossi-Maccanico, 75 *Tax Notes Intl.* 10 (8 Sep. 2014), at pp. 857-868; P. Rossi-Maccanico, 24 *EC Tax Rev.* 2 (2015), at pp. 63-77; D.S. Smit, 25 *EC Tax Rev.* 2 (2016), at pp. 110-112; R. Szudoczky in I. Richelle/W. Schön/E. Traversa (eds.), *Allocating Taxing Powers Within the European Union* (Springer, 2013), at pp. 169-179; A. Taferner/J.W. Kuipers, 56 *Eur. Taxn.* 4 (2016), at pp. 136-144; also cf. M. Lang, 60 *British Tax Rev.* 3 (2015), pp. 394-395; M. Lang, 24 *IStR* 11 (2015), at pp. 371-372; N. Robins/S. Shamsi, The European Commission's State Aid Clampdown: The End of "Selective" Tax Rulings?, 18 *Derivatives and Financial Instruments* 1 (2016).

1915. Cf. G. Frotscher, *Internationales Steuerrecht*[4] (C.H. Beck, 2015), at p. 7, at § 1 MN 19; F. Haase, *Internationales und Europäisches Steuerrecht*[4] (C.F. Müller, 2014), at p. 16, at § 1 para. 37; V. Kluge, *Das Internationale Steuerrecht*[4] (C.H. Beck, 2000), at p. 929, at S.334; E. Traversa/C. Helleputte in M. Lang/P. Melz/E. Kristoffersson (eds.), *Value Added Tax and Direct Taxation* (IBFD, 2009), at p. 340; U. Wolff, 13 *IStR* 16 (2004), at p. 542; also cf. M. Lang, 25 *SWI* 5 (2015), at pp. 198 et seq.

1916. See M. Lang, 11 *IStR* 18 (2002), at pp. 611-612); M. Lang in IFA (ed.), *Double Non-Taxation*, CDFI 89a (SDU, 2004), at p. 83; M. Lang in W. Haarmann (ed.), *Auslegung und Anwendung von Doppelbesteuerungsabkommen* (Dr Otto Schmidt, 2004), at p. 92.

untaxed, because one contracting state is restricted from taxing it by the double taxation convention, while the other contracting state does not domestically exercise the taxing right assigned to it by the very same double taxation convention.[1917] However, double taxation conventions may even lead to double non-taxation if an item of income is taxable according to both contracting states' domestic tax laws. After all, the courts or the competent authorities of the contracting states may come to different conclusions when applying and interpreting the double taxation convention.[1918] According to the OECD, this may be due to: (1) a varying evaluation of the facts of the case, (2) a diverging interpretation of the rules of the double taxation convention or (3) the disparities between the domestic tax systems of the contracting states.[1919] Double taxation conventions may hence lead to double non-taxation if both contracting states

1917. The McDonald's case is an illustrative example of such a situation (see European Commission Press Release, *State Aid: Commission Opens Formal Investigation into Luxembourg's Tax Treatment of McDonald's*, IP/15/6221 [3 Dec. 2015]; European Commission, State aid SA. 38945 (2015/C) (ex 2015/NN) – Luxembourg Alleged aid to McDonald's, C(2015) 8343 final [3 Dec. 2015]; also see R. Szudoczky in I. Richelle/W. Schön/E. Traversa [eds.], *Allocating Taxing Powers Within the European Union* [Springer, 2013], at pp. 171-173): For the right to use the McDonald's brand and associated services, franchisees operating in Europe and Russia have to pay royalties to a company in Luxembourg, which is designated as responsible for McDonald's strategic decision-making. As the royalties are internally transferred to a US branch of the Luxembourg company, the question arises whether Luxembourg has a taxing right for the royalties according to the double taxation convention concluded with the US. The tax authorities in Luxembourg assumed that the royalties are attributable to a US permanent establishment and therefore Luxembourg has to apply the exemption method according to Articles 7 and 25(2)(a) of the double taxation convention concluded with the US (European Commission, State aid SA. 38945 (2015/C) (ex 2015/NN) – Luxembourg Alleged aid to McDonald's, C(2015) 8343 final [3 Dec. 2015], at p. 10, at para. 41). Under US law, however, the US branch did not undertake sufficient business or trade in the US in order for the Luxembourg company to be subject to limited tax liability in the US (European Commission, State aid SA. 38945 (2015/C) (ex 2015/NN) – Luxembourg Alleged aid to McDonald's, C(2015) 8343 final [3 Dec. 2015], at p. 11, at para. 46). Therefore, the royalties are taxed neither in Luxembourg due to the double taxation convention nor in the US due to US domestic law (European Commission, State aid SA. 38945 (2015/C) (ex 2015/NN) – Luxembourg Alleged aid to McDonald's, C(2015) 8343 final [3 Dec. 2015], at p. 19, at para. 85).

1918. This can be illustrated by the following example (see C. Marchgraber in M. Lang/C. Marchgraber/A. Rust/J. Schuch/C. Staringer [eds.], *Niedrigbesteuerung im Unternehmenssteuerrecht* [Linde, 2016], at p. 111 [FN 64]): With regard to short-term assignments of an employee, the Supreme Court of the employee's residence state may consider the "user" in the other contracting state to be the employer according to Article 15(2)(b) OECD MC. Thus, the employee's remuneration may be taxed in the other contracting state under Article 15(1) OECD MC. If the Supreme Court of the other contracting state, in contrast, considered the "formal employer" in the residence state to also be the employer for purposes of Article 15(2)(b) OECD MC, it would consider the employee's remuneration to be taxable only in the residence state due to Article 15(2) OECD MC. But for Article 23 A(4) OECD MC (for an analysis of this provision and further references see C. Marchgraber, 44 *Intertax* 4 [2016], at pp. 312-313; C. Marchgraber in M. Lang/C. Marchgraber/A. Rust/J. Schuch/C. Staringer [eds.], *Niedrigbesteuerung im Unternehmenssteuerrecht* [Linde, 2016], at p. 111 [FN 64]), the remuneration of the employee would remain untaxed.

1919. See OECD, *The Application of the OECD Model Tax Convention to Partnerships*, Issues in International Taxation No. 6 (OECD, 1999), at MN 94 et seq.; also see H. Loukota in W. Gassner/M. Lang (eds.), *Besteuerung und Bilanzierung international tätiger Unternehmen*, 30 Jahre Steuerrecht an der Wirtschaftsuniversität Wien (Orac, 1998), at p. 269; H. Loukota in R. Beiser/S. Kirchmayr/G. Mayr/N. Zorn (eds.), *Ertragsteuern in Wissenschaft und Praxis*, Festschrift für Werner Doralt (LexisNexis, 2007), at pp. 280 et seq.; H. Loukota, 9 *SWI* 2

refrain from levying taxes according to their domestic tax laws due to the (different application of the) bilateral double taxation convention.

Given these possible outcomes, scholars have started to discuss whether it may constitute State aid if the benefits of a double taxation convention are not made dependent on the other contracting state domestically exercising the taxing right allegedly assigned to it.[1920] More fundamentally, however, it may even be asked whether granting uni- or bilateral relief from juridical double taxation does per se constitute State aid. With regard to international trade law, a similar question was already raised in the 1970s by the US requesting the establishment of a panel of experts to examine whether certain income tax practices maintained by Belgium,[1921] France[1922] and the Netherlands[1923] – together with the "DISC case"[1924] commonly referred to as the "tax legislation cases"[1925] – violated Article XVI(4) GATT 1947.[1926] It was, *inter alia*, argued that the Netherlands granted a form of subsidy on export sales by uni- or bilaterally providing relief from juridical double taxation. According to the representatives of the US, these relief mechanisms meant that "*the Netherlands, at least in practice, followed the territoriality principle of taxation and that, as a result, did not tax the export sales income of foreign branches or foreign sales subsidiaries of domestic manufacturing firms. [...] This system of remitting or exempting taxation of profits from export sales by foreign branches or subsidiaries created a distortion in conditions of international competition in that it afforded a remission or exemption of direct taxes in violation of the Netherlands' commitment as a contracting party under Article XVI:4.*

(1999), at pp. 70 et seq.; J. Schuch/J. Bauer in W. Gassner/M. Lang/E. Lechner (eds.), *Personengesellschaften im Recht der Doppelbesteuerungsabkommen* (Linde, 2000), at p. 31.

1920. See W. Haslehner in I. Richelle/W. Schön/E. Traversa (eds.), *Allocating Taxing Powers Within the European Union* (Springer, 2013), at pp. 135-143; R. Szudoczky in I. Richelle/W. Schön/E. Traversa (eds.), *Allocating Taxing Powers Within the European Union* (Springer, 2013), at pp. 169-179; also see F.P. Sutter in J. Bauer/E. Burgstaller/K. Haslinger/J. Herdin/I. Hofbauer/M. Lang/H. Loukota/W. Loukota/M. Schilcher/J. Schuch/C. Staringer/F.P. Sutter/U. Zieseritsch (eds.), *Unilaterale Maßnahmen zur Vermeidung der Doppelbesteuerung* (Linde, 2004), at p. 265; F.P. Sutter, 14 *SWI* 1 (2004), at p. 270.

1921. Report of the Panel presented to the Council of Representatives on 12 Nov. 1976, *Income Tax Practices Maintained by Belgium*, L/4424 – 23S/127 (2 Nov. 1976).

1922. Report of the Panel presented to the Council of Representatives on 12 Nov. 1976, *Income Tax Practices Maintained by the Netherlands*, L/4425 – 23S/137 (2 Nov. 1976).

1923. Report of the Panel presented to the Council of Representatives on 12 Nov. 1976, *Income Tax Practices Maintained by France*, L/4423 – 23S/114 (2 Nov. 1976).

1924. Report of the Panel presented to the Council of Representatives on 12 Nov. 1976, *United States Tax Legislation (DISC)*, L/4422 – 23S/98 (2 Nov. 1976).

1925. See, for example, V. Bobek/L. Hauptman/S. Beloglavec, National Report Slovenia, in J. Herdin/I. Hofbauer (eds.), *WTO and Direct Taxation* (Linde, 2005), p. 611 (at p. 635); V.H. Guerrero, Defining the Balance Between Free Competition and Tax Sovereignty in EC and WTO Law: The Due Respect to the General Tax System, 5 *German L. J.* 1 (2004), p. 87 (at p. 95, FN 37); L. Hintsanen, National Report Finland, in J. Herdin/I. Hofbauer (eds.), *WTO and Direct Taxation* (Linde, 2005), p. 257 (at p. 275); G.C. Hufbauer, Tax Discipline in the WTO, 4 *Journal of World Trade* 4 (2010), p. 763 (at p. 768); J.M. Lang/R.B. Stack/S. Charnovitz/J.T. Brady, What Tax Lawyers Should Know About Trade Law, 29 *Tax Mgt. Intl. J.* 10 (2000), p. 566 (at p. 570); W. Schön, World Trade Organization Law and Tax Law, 58 *Bull. Intl. Taxn.* 7 (2002), p. 283 (at p. 295, FN 99); K.E. Sørensen, Direct Taxation and the WTO Agreements, 42 *Eur. Taxn.* 6 (2002), p. 206 (at p. 208); F.P. Sutter, 14 *SWI* 1 (2004), at p. 7.

1926. The General Agreement on Tariffs and Trade, 55 *U.N.T.S.* 194 (30 Oct. 1947).

The relative tax burden on the sale of products for export as against domestic sales was lower as a result of the remission of taxes on a portion of export sales income."[1927] The panel of experts basically followed this argument and concluded "*that the particular application of the world-wide principle by the Netherlands, in conjunction with the qualified exemption in respect of foreign income, allowed some part of export activities belonging to an economic process originating in the country, to be outside the scope of the Netherlands' taxes. In this way the Netherlands has foregone revenue from this source and created a possibility of a pecuniary benefit to exports in those cases where income and corporation tax provisions were significantly more liberal in foreign countries. [...] [The] practices [...] constituted a subsidy on exports because the above-mentioned benefits to exports did not apply to domestic activities for the internal market.*"[1928]

The controversies triggered by the decisions in the "tax legislation cases" prolonged the adoption of the corresponding reports until 1981. In order to clarify that the panel decisions should not be overestimated, a declaration was adopted, which stated that the reports were accepted "*on the understanding that with respect to these cases, and in general, economic processes (including transactions involving exported goods) located outside the territorial limits of the exporting country need not to be subject to taxation by the exporting country [...]. Furthermore Article XVI:4 does not prohibit the adoption of measures to avoid double taxation of foreign source income.*"[1929] The discomfort triggered by the "tax legislation cases" was hence not short-lived, but even in the long term influenced the further development of international trade law: Since the WTO was created through the Marrakesh Agreement,[1930] rules for the regulation of subsidies are to be found in the SCM Agreement.[1931] Thereby, it has been clarified that WTO Member States should not be limited "*from taking measures to avoid the double taxation of foreign-source income earned by its enterprises or the enterprises of another Member.*"[1932] With regard to this carve-out clause, the Appellate Body held in the ETI dispute[1933] that "*one of the widely recognized methods of avoiding double taxation is the tax exemption method. Under this method, States may exempt income from taxation to avoid double taxation, irrespective of whether or not another State taxes the exempt*

1927. Report of the Panel presented to the Council of Representatives on 12 Nov. 1976, *Income Tax Practices Maintained by the Netherlands*, L/4425 - 23S/137 (2 Nov. 1976), at para. 14.

1928. Report of the Panel presented to the Council of Representatives on 12 Nov. 1976, *Income Tax Practices Maintained by the Netherlands*, L/4425 - 23S/137 (2 Nov. 1976), at paras 34-35.

1929. GATT Council, *Tax Legislation*, L/5271 - 28S/114 (18 Dec. 1981).

1930. Marrakesh Agreement Establishing the World Trade Organization (15 Apr. 1994), 1867 *U.N.T.S.* 154 (1995).

1931. Agreement on Subsidies and Countervailing Measures (15 Apr. 1994), 1869 *U.N.T.S.* 14 (1999).

1932. See Footnote 59 to the SCM Agreement.

1933. See, for example, R. Luja, *Assessment and Recovery of Tax Incentives and the WTO* (Intersentia, 2003), at pp. 156-166; C. Micheau, *State Aid, Subsidy and Tax Incentives under EU and WTO Law* (Kluwer, 2014), at pp. 138-147; V. Pejkov, Changes in the Legal Order of the United States after the FSC and ETI Decisions and Conformity with WTO Law of the New Regulations, in J. Herdin-Winter/I. Hofbauer (eds.), *The Relevance of WTO Law for Tax Matters* (Linde, 2006), p. 333 (at pp. 344-348); K.E. Sørensen, 42 *Eur. Taxn.* 6 (2002), at pp. 210-211.

income. The avoidance of double taxation is not an exact science. Indeed, the income exempted from taxation in the State of residence of the taxpayer might not be subject to a corresponding, or any, tax in a 'foreign' State. Yet, this does not necessarily mean that the measure is not taken to avoid double taxation of foreign-source income. Thus, [...] measures falling under footnote 59 are not required to be perfectly tailored to the actual double tax burden. However, the fact that measures falling under footnote 59 to the SCM Agreement may grant a tax exemption even for income that is not taxed in another jurisdiction does not mean that such tax exemptions may be granted, under the fifth sentence of footnote 59, for any income. Footnote 59 prescribes that the income benefitting from a double taxation-avoidance measure must be 'foreign-source' and [...] that means that the income must have links with a 'foreign' State such that it could properly be subjected to tax in that State, as well as in the Member taking the double taxation-avoidance measure." [1934] Thus, according to the Appellate Body in the ETI dispute, uni- or bilateral mechanisms granting relief from juridical double taxation do not infringe WTO law, as long as the relief is limited to income that has a sufficient nexus with another state so that it might be susceptible to being subject to double taxation.

Although mechanisms that grant relief from juridical double taxation have to a large extent been whitewashed for WTO law purposes, the corresponding background shows that it is by no means obvious that a Member State which uni- or bilaterally provides relief from juridical double taxation may not be accused of granting State aid. More than a decade ago, a scholarly discussion already took place on whether State aid could result from a Member State providing for different mechanisms in order to avoid juridical double taxation.[1935] There might, for example, be a unilateral relief mechanism according to which foreign-source income remains tax exempt, whereas bilateral relief mechanisms may only provide for a credit of the foreign taxes.[1936] The same issue

1934. Report of the Appellate Body, United States – Tax Treatment for "Foreign Sales Corporations," WT/DS108/AB/RW (14 Jan. 2002), at paras 146-147.

1935. See F.P. Sutter in J. Bauer/E. Burgstaller/K. Haslinger/J. Herdin/I. Hofbauer/M. Lang/H. Loukota/W. Loukota/M. Schilcher/J. Schuch/C. Staringer/F.P. Sutter/U. Zieseritsch (eds.), *Unilaterale Maßnahmen zur Vermeidung der Doppelbesteuerung* (Linde, 2004), at pp. 249-279; F.P. Sutter, 14 *SWI* 1 (2004), at pp. 4-13; F.P. Sutter in M. Lang/J. Schuch/C. Staringer (eds.), *Die abkommensrechtliche Verteilung der Besteuerungsrechte zwischen Ansässigkeits- und Quellenstaat* (Linde, 2005), at pp. 83-122; R. Luja, 44 *Eur. Taxn.* 4 (2004), at pp. 234-238; also cf. Commission Decision of 17 Feb. 2003 on aid scheme C54/2001 (ex NN55/2000) Ireland – Foreign Income (2003/601/EC), *OJ* L 204 (13 Aug. 2003), p. 51 (at pp. 51-59); European Commission, *Report on the Implementation of the Commission Notice on the Application of the State Aid Rules to Measures Relating to Direct Business Taxation*, C(2004) 434 (9 Feb. 2004), at para. 16.

1936. See W. Haslehner in I. Richelle/W. Schön/E. Traversa (eds.), *Allocating Taxing Powers Within the European Union* (Springer, 2013), at p. 139 ("*one has to decide whether the right reference framework to analyse double taxation relief measures consists of [...] domestic law rules on foreign income (unilateral relief provisions)*"); R. Luja, 44 *Eur. Taxn.* 4 (2004), at p. 235 ("*A tax treaty may entitle a taxpayer to a different level of relief. Suppose the unilateral relief method for certain income is the tax credit method. Do we then have a selective benefit when the tax treaty provides for an exemption?*"); R. Szudoczky in I. Richelle/W. Schön/E. Traversa (eds.), *Allocating Taxing Powers Within the European Union* (Springer, 2013), at p. 173 ("*Within the corporate tax system we have to look at the provisions on unilateral double taxation relief, as they are the general rules compared to which the double taxation relief*

arises if some double taxation conventions only incorporate the credit method, whereas others also include the exemption method.[1937,1938] Considering the ECJ's decision in *D.*,[1939] it might be argued that "*differences in the level of relief are part of the nature and general scheme of a tax system if we take account of the Member States' sovereignty (not) to conclude tax treaties and the negotiation process and the mutual give-and-take of budgetary benefits that are an integral part thereof.*"[1940] However, even if one accepted such a reasoning, it would still remain unclear whether it is in line with Article 107 TFEU that within one and the same relief mechanism a distinction is drawn between various types of income.[1941] A double taxation convention might, for example,

---

mechanism under a tax treaty may constitute a derogation."); also see F.P. Sutter in M. Lang/J. Schuch/C. Staringer (eds.), *Die abkommensrechtliche Verteilung der Besteuerungsrechte zwischen Ansässigkeits- und Quellenstaat* (Linde, 2005), at pp. 103-104; also cf. Commission Decision of 17 Feb. 2003 on aid scheme C54/2001 (ex NN55/2000) Ireland – Foreign Income (2003/601/EC), *OJ* L 204 (13 Aug. 2003), p. 51 (at pp. 51-59); European Commission, *Report on the Implementation of the Commission Notice on the Application of the State Aid Rules to Measures Relating to Direct Business Taxation*, C(2004) 434 (9 Feb. 2004), at para. 16.

1937. See W. Haslehner in I. Richelle/W. Schön/E. Traversa (eds.), *Allocating Taxing Powers Within the European Union* (Springer, 2013), at p. 139 ("*one has to decide whether the right reference framework to analyse double taxation relief measures consists of […] the tax treaty network of a Member State as a whole*"); R. Luja, 44 *Eur. Taxn.* 4 (2004), at p. 235 ("*Can we speak of a selective benefit if there are differences between tax treaties concluded by an EU Member State? For instance, EU Member State A (Member State A) agrees with Member State B to grant a tax exemption for profits from a PE abroad, while, hypothetically, agreeing upon a tax credit with Member State C.*"); R. Szudoczky in I. Richelle/W. Schön/E. Traversa (eds.), *Allocating Taxing Powers Within the European Union* (Springer, 2013), at p. 173 (FN 41: "*Another question in connection with double tax relief mechanisms is whether the fact that different treaties provide for different methods could be considered as a different treatment of comparable situations which grants selective advantage to certain enterprises.*").

1938. Parts of the literature argue that such differences could be justified, because "*a finding of state aid should not depend on the vagaries of tax rate changes by other countries […]. [I]t is reasonable to make the existence of equivalent tax rates a necessary simplifying assumption for purposes of assessing the validity of the relief provisions. Any advantage accruing to the taxpayer as a consequence of a tax rate mismatch would then not be attributed to the residence state and could be ignored. Such approach would notably coincide with the Court of Justice's view on tax system disparities in the context of the fundamental freedoms*" (W. Haslehner in I. Richelle/W. Schön/E. Traversa [eds.], *Allocating Taxing Powers Within the European Union* [Springer, 2013], at p. 142; also cf. R. Szudoczky in I. Richelle/W. Schön/E. Traversa [eds.], *Allocating Taxing Powers Within the European Union* [Springer, 2013], at pp. 174-175: "*The fact that different treaties provide for different methods of relieving double taxation could be explained by the fact that treaties are the result of a negotiation process which is conducted in the specific economic and legal context of a bilateral relationship and which involves a give-and-take process of mutual benefits and concessions.*").

1939. Judgment in *D.*, C-376/03, EU:C:2005:424.

1940. R. Luja, 44 *Eur. Taxn.* 4 (2004), at p. 235; also cf. F.P. Sutter in M. Lang/J. Schuch/C. Staringer (eds.), *Die abkommensrechtliche Verteilung der Besteuerungsrechte zwischen Ansässigkeits- und Quellenstaat* (Linde, 2005), at pp. 113-115; critically W. Haslehner in I. Richelle/W. Schön/E. Traversa (eds.), *Allocating Taxing Powers Within the European Union* (Springer, 2013), at p. 140; R. Szudoczky in I. Richelle/W. Schön/E. Traversa (eds.), *Allocating Taxing Powers Within the European Union* (Springer, 2013), at p. 174.

1941. W. Haslehner in I. Richelle/W. Schön/E. Traversa (eds.), *Allocating Taxing Powers Within the European Union* (Springer, 2013), at p. 139 ("*one has to decide whether the right reference framework to analyse double taxation relief measures consists of […] the provisions applied to particular foreign income under an individual treaty*"); R. Luja, 44 *Eur. Taxn.* 4 (2004), at p. 235 ("*It is possible that selective benefits are introduced within the general framework of double taxation relief. For instance, Member State A agreed upon a tax credit with Member State C for*

provide for the credit method with regard to business profits as covered by Article 7 OECD MC, but for the exemption method with regard to income earned due to rendering professional services or other activities of an independent character as covered by Article 14 UN MC.[1942,1943]

Given the WTO "tax legislation cases," it should first be examined whether granting uni- or bilateral relief from juridical double taxation per se constitutes State aid. Such measures could be perceived as causing a deviation from the common tax regime that has been established by the very same Member State. After all, levying no or less *domestic* tax on foreign income seems to conflict with the universality principle that is implemented by many domestic tax law systems. Thus, if a sufficient personal connection exists between the taxable person and the state, the person's worldwide income should be taxed.[1944] This problem could also be phrased in a comparative way:

PE income in their tax treaty. However, for a specific sector of industry a tax exemption would be agreed upon. If such theoretical provision were included in a tax treaty, it could indeed give rise to State aid."); also see F.P. Sutter in M. Lang/J. Schuch/C. Staringer (eds.), *Die abkommensrechtliche Verteilung der Besteuerungsrechte zwischen Ansässigkeits- und Quellenstaat* (Linde, 2005), at pp. 106-113.

1942. Such a differentiation can, for example, be found in the double taxation convention between Austria and Liechtenstein. The Austrian Constitutional Court has already held that this is in line with the Austrian constitutional principle of equality. See VfGH 23. 6. 2014, SV 2/2013, AT:VFGH:2014:SV2.2013; also see D. Aigner/G. Kofler/M. Tumpel, Zu den verfassungsrechtlichen Bedenken gegen Art 14 des österreichisch-liechtensteinischen Doppelbesteuerungsabkommens, 4 *Spektrum der Rechtswissenschaften* 1 (2014), p. 1 (at pp. 1-40); R. Beiser, Die Befreiungs- und Anrechnungsmethode im Licht des Gleichheitssatzes, 24 *SWI* 2 (2014), p. 52 (at pp. 52-57); A. Binder/V. Wöhrer, SWI-Jahrestagung: Privilegierung von Freiberuflern im DBA Liechtenstein verfassungsrechtlich problematisch, 24 *SWI* 1 (2014), p. 10 (at pp. 10-14); H. Jirousek, Ist Artikel 14 DBA-Liechtenstein verfassungswidrig?, 27 *ÖStZ* 3 (2014), p. 64 (at pp. 64-67); M. Lang, Doppelbesteuerungsabkommen und Gleichheitssatz, 24 *SWI* 2 (2014), p. 58 (at pp. 58-74); M. Lang, Die Konsequenzen des VfGH-Erkenntnisses zum DBA Liechtenstein, 24 *SWI* 9 (2014), p. 402 (at pp. 402-409); H. Loukota, DBA Liechtenstein auf dem Prüfstand des Verfassungsgerichtshofs, 24 *SWI* 1 (2014), p. 2 (at pp. 2-9); C. Staringer, DBA-Politik und Verfassungsrecht, 24 *SWI* 3 (2014), p. 90 (at pp. 90-102); F.P. Sutter, Verfassungsrechtliche Schranken der Differenzierung zwischen Anrechnungs- und Freistellungsmethode in einem DBA, 23 *SWI* 12 (2013), p. 514 (at pp. 514-520).

1943. In parts of the literature it is argued that, "*[a]s long as differences in the outcome of tax treaty negotiations between contracting states are considered to be a natural phenomenon, the differences in the level of double taxation relief should be considered part of the general national tax system for State aid purposes*" (R. Luja, 44 *Eur. Taxn.* 4 [2004], at p. 235).

1944. See W. Haslehner in I. Richelle/W. Schön/E. Traversa (eds.), *Allocating Taxing Powers Within the European Union* (Springer, 2013), at p. 139 ("*one has to decide whether the right reference framework to analyse double taxation relief measures consists of [...] domestic law applying to domestic income*"); R. Luja, 44 *Eur. Taxn.* 4 (2004), at p. 234 ("*Taking the national tax regime as a reference, a tax relief resulting from a tax treaty would lead to a benefit in the strictest sense: a benefit that, without doubt, is provided out of state resources (i.e. the tax normally collected). I would like to point out that from a State aid point of view the presence of a benefit is to be determined by making a comparison with the tax normally due by a certain taxpayer in a certain country. The fact that in cases of double taxation there may, on balance, be no actual benefit, because two states would have fully taxed the same part of a tax base had there be no form of relief, is irrelevant from a State aid perspective. As for the other elements of the State aid definition, I agree that the granting of relief may affect trade within the European Union and distort competition.*"); F.P. Sutter, 14 *SWI* 1 (2004), at p. 7 and F.P. Sutter in J. Bauer/E. Burgstaller/K. Haslinger/J. Herdin/I. Hofbauer/M. Lang/H. Loukota/W. Loukota/M. Schilcher/J. Schuch/C. Staringer/F.P. Sutter/U. Zieseritsch (eds.), *Unilaterale Maßnahmen zur Vermeidung der Doppelbesteuerung* (Linde, 2004), at p. 261 ("*Was ist die*

Granting relief from juridical double taxation leads to a different treatment of residents earning income domestically and residents earning foreign income.[1945] Whereas the former have to pay the full amount of *domestic* taxes in their residence state, the latter do not have to pay or at least pay less *domestic* tax there.

In the literature, a lot of effort is made to prevent tax measures that grant relief from juridical double taxation from being suspected of constituting State aid. Some scholars argue that "*tax provisions which are advantageous for foreign investors are not 'aid' at all to the extent that they only strive to reduce or compensate the disadvantageous effects of double taxation. Thus, any tax exemption or which simply provides compensation for taxes the investor has to pay at home does not grant the taxpayer a 'favour' but puts him on equal footing with domestic taxpayers or investors.*"[1946] Such an approach presumes that *foreign* taxes already have to be taken into account when examining whether a *domestic* tax system might potentially be covered by Article 107 TFEU. It is doubtful that the ECJ would refrain from thoroughly examining the State aid law compatibility of tax measures that grant relief from juridical double taxation due to an argument based on such a supranational perspective. After all, according to settled case law, "*the fact that a Member State seeks to approximate, by unilateral measures, the conditions of competition in a particular sector of the economy to those prevailing in other Member States cannot deprive the measures in question of their character as aid.*"[1947]

However, a similar argument could be used in order to challenge the comparability of taxpayers earning income domestically and taxpayers earning foreign income. Since only the latter can be subject to juridical double taxation, it is argued in the literature that they are not comparable to the former "*in light of the objectives of a tax*

steuerliche 'Normalbelastung' – die Besteuerungssituation bei Existenz eines DBA oder bei Fehlen eines DBA?"); also see F.P. Sutter in M. Lang/J. Schuch/C. Staringer (eds.), *Die abkommensrechtliche Verteilung der Besteuerungsrechte zwischen Ansässigkeits- und Quellenstaat* (Linde, 2005), at pp. 89-91 and 100-101.

1945. See W. Haslehner in I. Richelle/W. Schön/E. Traversa (eds.), *Allocating Taxing Powers Within the European Union* (Springer, 2013), at p. 139 ("*The related question under the comparability approach is whether a resident taxpayer with foreign income that is exempt under the provisions of a tax treaty is comparable to [...] a resident taxpayer with domestic income*"); also cf. R. Szudoczky in I. Richelle/W. Schön/E. Traversa (eds.), *Allocating Taxing Powers Within the European Union* (Springer, 2013), at p. 176.

1946. W. Schön, 36 *Common Market L. Rev.* 5 (1999), at p. 935; also see W. Schön in L. Hancher/T. Ottervanger/P.J. Slot (eds.), *EU State Aids* (Sweet & Maxwell, 2012), at p. 350; also cf. F.P. Sutter in J. Bauer/E. Burgstaller/K. Haslinger/J. Herdin/I. Hofbauer/M. Lang/H. Loukota/W. Loukota/M. Schilcher/J. Schuch/C. Staringer/F.P. Sutter/U. Zieseritsch (eds.), *Unilaterale Maßnahmen zur Vermeidung der Doppelbesteuerung* (Linde, 2004), at p. 261; F.P. Sutter in M. Lang/J. Schuch/C. Staringer (eds.), *Die abkommensrechtliche Verteilung der Besteuerungsrechte zwischen Ansässigkeits- und Quellenstaat* (Linde, 2005), at p. 101.

1947. Judgment in *Italy/Commission*, C-372/97, EU:C:2004:234, at para. 67; also see Judgment in Commission/France, 6 and 11-69, EU:C:1969:68, at paras 20-21; Judgment in *Italy/Commission*, C-6/97, EU:C:1999:251, at para. 21; Judgment in *Italy/Commission*, C-298/00 P, EU:C:2004:240, at para. 61; Judgment in *Heiser*, C-172/03, EU:C:2005:130, at para. 54; Judgment in *Comitato "Venezia vuole vivere" and others/Commission*, C-71/09 P, C-73/09 P and C-76/09 P, EU:C:2011:368, at para. 95.

system that is based on the ability-to-pay principle."[1948] Against the background of the case law with regard to the fundamental freedoms, such a lack of comparability might prevent the ECJ from scrutinizing the proportionality of the domestic measure.[1949] If this were the case, this argument should not be raised at the comparability but at the justification level. The European Commission, for example, considers tax measures that grant relief from juridical double taxation to be justified by the nature and general scheme of the system, because *"[e]ach firm is supposed to pay tax once only. It is therefore inherent in the logic of the tax system that taxes paid in the State in which the firm is resident for tax purposes should be taken into account."*[1950] Indeed, it would not be convincing to conclude that granting relief from juridical double taxation constitutes State aid. In essence, this would mean that Member States are to a large extent precluded from taking measures to avoid *"the most serious obstacle there can be to people and their capital crossing [...] borders."*[1951] This would be contrary to the ECJ's conclusion that *"it is for the Member States to take [such] measures."*[1952]

Still, although there are good reasons to conclude that it is justified from a State aid law perspective to provide for uni- and bilateral measures that grant relief from juridical double taxation, it is questionable whether such measures *"are consistent with the principle of proportionality and do not go beyond what is necessary, in that the legitimate objective being pursued could not be attained by less far-reaching measures."*[1953] Parts of the literature emphasize that *"[a]pplying a double tax relief rule to an item of income which has not been taxed and thus enabling it to remain untaxed appears to be inconsistent with the rule's own objective."*[1954] It could, therefore, be argued that, in order to be proportionate, the ambit of tax measures that are intended to grant relief from juridical double taxation has to be restricted to situations of *actual*

1948. W. Haslehner in I. Richelle/W. Schön/E. Traversa (eds.), *Allocating Taxing Powers Within the European Union* (Springer, 2013), at p. 140.
1949. See Chapter 3.2.4.1.
1950. Commission notice on the application of the State aid rules to measures relating to direct business taxation, *OJ* C 384 (10 Dec. 1998), at p. 7; also see European Commission, Commission Notice on the notion of State Aid as referred to in Article 107(1) of the Treaty on the Functioning of the European Union, *OJ* C 262 (19 July 2016), at para. 139; also see F.P. Sutter in J. Bauer/E. Burgstaller/K. Haslinger/J. Herdin/I. Hofbauer/M. Lang/H. Loukota/W. Loukota/M. Schilcher/J. Schuch/C. Staringer/F.P. Sutter/U. Zieseritsch (eds.), *Unilaterale Maßnahmen zur Vermeidung der Doppelbesteuerung* (Linde, 2004), at pp. 269-270; F.P. Sutter, 14 *SWI* 1 (2004), at pp. 11-13; also cf. R. Luja, 44 *Eur. Taxn.* 4 (2004), at pp. 234 and 237; R. Szudoczky in I. Richelle/W. Schön/E. Traversa (eds.), *Allocating Taxing Powers Within the European Union* (Springer, 2013), at p. 167.
1951. Opinion of AG Colomer in *D*, C-376/03, EU:C:2004:663, at point 85.
1952. Judgment in *Kerckhaert and Morres*, C-513/04, EU:C:2006:713, at paras 20 and 22-23; Judgment in *CIBA*, C-96/08, EU:C:2010:185 at paras 25-27; see also Judgment in *Block*, C-67/08, EU:C:2009:92, at paras 28-30; Judgment in *Damseaux*, C-128/08, EU:C:2009:471, at paras 30 and 33.
1953. Judgment in *Paint Graphos and others*, C-78/08, EU:C:2011:550, at para. 75.
1954. R. Szudoczky in I. Richelle/W. Schön/E. Traversa (eds.), *Allocating Taxing Powers Within the European Union* (Springer, 2013), at p. 175; also see W. Haslehner in I. Richelle/W. Schön/E. Traversa (eds.), *Allocating Taxing Powers Within the European Union* (Springer, 2013), at p. 142.

double taxation.[1955] This would mean that a Member State which provides for relief from juridical double taxation can be accused of granting State aid if the respective measures do not include a subject-to-tax clause.[1956] Such a conclusion has some drawbacks, though: First, it should be kept in mind that the other contracting state adds to the resultant double non-taxation as well. It, therefore, also needs to be examined whether this state's domestic tax system is in line with Article 107 TFEU. Typically, for example, non-residents are subject to limited tax liability if they earn income in a Member State through a domestically located permanent establishment. With regard to construction sites, however, some Member States only deem a permanent establishment to exist if a certain time threshold is exceeded.[1957] This could lead to double non-taxation if the domestic time period is longer than the corresponding time period provided for in the double taxation convention concluded with the construction site operator's Member State of residence. Even if there were a permanent establishment according to the double taxation convention, the longer time period under domestic law could lead to the respective Member State not exercising its taxing right

1955. See F.P. Sutter, 14 *SWI* 1 (2004), at p. 13; F.P. Sutter in J. Bauer/E. Burgstaller/K. Haslinger/J. Herdin/I. Hofbauer/M. Lang/H. Loukota/W. Loukota/M. Schilcher/J. Schuch/C. Staringer/F.P. Sutter/U. Zieseritsch (eds.), *Unilaterale Maßnahmen zur Vermeidung der Doppelbesteuerung* (Linde, 2004), at p. 270; F.P. Sutter in M. Lang/J. Schuch/C. Staringer (eds.), *Die abkommensrechtliche Verteilung der Besteuerungsrechte zwischen Ansässigkeits- und Quellenstaat* (Linde, 2005), at p. 118; also see W. Haslehner in I. Richelle/W. Schön/E. Traversa (eds.), *Allocating Taxing Powers within the European Union* (Springer, 2013), at p. 142.

1956. According to such a clause, the taxing right of a contracting state is restricted by the double taxation convention only if the other contracting state domestically exercises the taxing right assigned to it. The forms and wordings of subject-to-tax clauses contained in the various bilateral double taxation conventions are manifold (see M. Lang in IFA [ed.], *Double Non-Taxation*, CDFI 89a [SDU, 2004], at p. 105). According to the literature, one criterion in order to categorize such rules is whether the subject-to-tax clause only applies to a certain distributive rule (specific subject-to-tax clause) or whether it applies to all categories of income covered by the double taxation convention (general subject-to-tax clause) (see M. Schilcher, Subject-to-tax-Klauseln in der österreichischen Abkommenspraxis [Linde, 2004], at p. 53; also see E. Burgstaller/M. Schilcher, Subject-to-Tax Clauses in Tax Treaties, 44 *Eur. Taxn.* 6 [2004], p. 266 [at p. 275]; M. Lampe, General Subject-To-Tax Clauses in Recent Tax Treaties, 39 *Eur. Taxn.* 4/5 [1999], p. 183 [at p. 184]; M. Schilcher, Die tatsächliche Besteuerung als maßgebendes Kriterium für die Festlegung des Quellenstaates nach den Doppelbesteuerungsabkommen ("Subject-to-tax-Klauseln"), in W. Gassner/M. Lang/J. Schuch/C. Staringer [eds.], *Die Verteilung der Besteuerungsrechte zwischen Ansässigkeits- und Quellenstaat im Recht der Doppelbesteuerungsabkommen* [Linde, 2005], p. 353 [at p. 361]). Another distinctive characteristic could be whether the subject-to-tax clause focusses on double non-taxation resulting from the source state's lack of exercising the taxing right assigned to it by the double taxation convention or whether it aims at preventing double non-taxation caused by the absence of taxation in the residence state (see M. Lang in IFA [ed.], *Double Non-Taxation*, CDFI 89a [SDU, 2004], at pp. 105-106).

1957. In Austria, for example, the construction site has to last for more than six months. See S. Bendlinger/D. Herbrich, Die Betriebsstättenfrist bei Bauausführungen und Montagen, 10 *SWI* 12 (2000), p. 562 (at pp. 562-575); G. Stoll, *BAO Kommentar* (Orac, 1994), at p. 399; also cf. M. Tumpel, Die Betriebsstätte gem § 29 BAO – Ein Begriff von zentraler Bedeutung und komplexem Inhalt, in M. Tanzer (ed.), *Die BAO im 21. Jahrhundert, Festschrift für Gerold Stoll zum 80. Geburtstag* (LexisNexis, 2005), p. 77 (at pp. 89-90).

domestically.[1958] If the domestic rules do not provide for such a time threshold with regard to other kinds of potential permanent establishments, such as offices, branches or places of extraction of natural resources, the State aid law compatibility of such a domestic tax system could be challenged.[1959] After all, the different treatment of construction sites and other kinds of potential permanent establishments could be regarded as State aid for the foreign construction sector. If this were the case, it would be questionable whether the construction site operator's Member State of residence can also be accused of granting State aid by providing for relief from juridical double taxation although there is no actual taxation in the Member State where the construction site is located. In essence, this would imply that one Member State may be obliged to neutralize distortions of competition caused by another Member State.

Second, even if the respective other state's tax system is fully in line with Article 107 TFEU, it could be argued that the State aid analysis of a Member State's tax system should not depend on what another Member State's tax system looks like. If, for example, a Member State levied a tax of 0.01 % on a non-resident taxpayer earning a certain item of income sourced in that state, the taxpayer's Member State of residence would not grant State aid by granting relief from juridical double taxation through exempting the foreign-source income. By contrast, the latter Member State would grant State aid if the former Member State's tax rate on such an item of income was 0 %. Maybe this uncomfortable result was one of the reasons why the Appellate Body in the ETI dispute held that tax measures intended to grant relief from juridical double taxation "*are not required to be perfectly tailored to the actual double tax burden.*"[1960]

Third, double non-taxation might also result from a diverging interpretation of the rules of the double taxation convention. An item of income might, for example, be taxable according to both contracting states' domestic laws, but might still remain untaxed, because both contracting states consider themselves to be precluded from taxing by the double taxation convention. In such cases, it is unclear which Member State should be required to include a subject-to-tax clause. If both Member States considered themselves to be precluded from taxation only if the item of income concerned is actually taxed in the other contracting state, the outcome would be ambiguous. Unless the issue is resolved by way of a mutual agreement procedure, there are two possible solutions to this situation of circular cross references: Either double non-taxation remains, because both contracting states take the position that the other contracting state may tax, or the subject-to-tax clauses lead to double taxation, because

1958. See, for example, M. Görl in K. Vogel/M. Lehner (eds.), *Doppelbesteuerungsabkommen*[6] (C.H. Beck, 2015), at Artikel 5 para. 79; A. Pickering, *Tax Treaty Policy Framework and Country Model, Papers on Selected Topics in Negotiation of Tax Treaties for Developing Countries*, Paper No. 2-N (May 2013), at p. 19.

1959. Cf. R. Luja, 44 *Eur. Taxn.* 4 (2004), at p. 235; F.P. Sutter in M. Lang/J. Schuch/C. Staringer (eds.), *Die abkommensrechtliche Verteilung der Besteuerungsrechte zwischen Ansässigkeits- und Quellenstaat* (Linde, 2005), at p. 108.

1960. Report of the Appellate Body, United States – Tax Treatment for "Foreign Sales Corporations," WT/DS108/AB/RW (14 Jan. 2002), at para. 146.

both contracting states conclude that the limits otherwise imposed by the double taxation convention are lifted.[1961] Neither outcome is satisfying from an internal market perspective.

2.3.2.2 *Transfer Pricing Adjustments and State Aid Law*

Whereas the State aid law compatibility of double taxation conventions is almost exclusively discussed in the scholarly literature, a more prominent and even more disputed issue is whether the Member States' transfer pricing rules are in line with Article 107 TFEU.[1962] These rules are based on the fact that enterprises are generally taxed separately, irrespective of whether they are legally, commercially and/or financially interconnected.[1963] However, if different enterprises are somehow associated with one another, their relationship may permit (or force) them to establish special conditions for economic transactions taking place between them.[1964] As the prices paid or received for such transactions influence the amount of profits each enterprise has to declare for commercial and tax law purposes, associated enterprises may consciously exploit this possibility in order to manipulate their commercial and taxable result.[1965] From a mere tax revenue perspective, this does not give rise to major concerns as long as the enterprises involved are all subject to unlimited tax liability in the same state, because then "*the profits of [all] involved companies are subject to domestic corporate tax.*"[1966] But if the associated enterprises are residents of different states, related-party transactions may be used to influence the amount of profits which have to be declared

1961. See C. Marchgraber, 23 *EC Tax Rev.* 5 (2014), at p. 299.
1962. See L. De Broe, 24 *EC Tax Rev.* 6 (2015), at pp. 290-293; K. Dirix, Harmful Tax Competition: Six Belgian Tax Incentives under the Microscope, 22 *EC Tax Rev.* 5 (2013), p. 233 (at pp. 248-249); A. Gunn/J. Luts, 24 *EC Tax Rev.* 2 (2015), at pp. 119-125; W. Haslehner in I. Richelle/W. Schön/E. Traversa (eds.), *Allocating Taxing Powers Within the European Union* (Springer, 2013), at pp. 144-159; M. Lang, 60 *British Tax Rev.* 3 (2015), at pp. 394-395; M. Lang, 24 *IStR* 11 (2015), at pp. 371-372; R. Luja, 76 *Tax Notes Intl.* 4 (27 Oct. 2014), at pp. 354-355; R. Luja, IP/A/TAXE/2015-02, PE 563.453 (October 2015), at pp. 12-14; R. Luja, 60 *British Tax Rev.* 3 (2015), at pp. 383-386; R. Lyal, 38 *Fordham Intl. L. J.* 4 (2015), at pp. 1028-1043; N. Robins/S. Shamsi, 18 *Derivatives and Financial Instruments* 1 (2016); P. Rossi-Maccanico, 75 *Tax Notes Intl.* 10 (8 Sep. 2014), at p. 866; P. Rossi-Maccanico, 24 *EC Tax Rev.* 2 (2015), at pp. 68-70; R. Szudoczky in I. Richelle/W. Schön/E. Traversa (eds.), *Allocating Taxing Powers Within the European Union* (Springer, 2013), at pp. 179-182; A. Taferner/J.W. Kuipers, 56 *Eur. Taxn.* 4 (2016), at pp. 136-144.
1963. See J. Wittendorf, *Transfer Pricing and the Arm's Length Principle in International Tax Law* (Kluwer, 2010), at pp. 5-8; also cf. OECD, *Transfer Pricing Guidelines for Multinational Enterprises and Tax Administrations* (OECD, 2010), at pp. 17-18, at para. 5.
1964. See at A. Bullen, *Arm's Length Transaction Structures* (IBFD, 2011), p. 3; P. Rossi-Maccanico, 24 *EC Tax Rev.* 2 (2015), at p. 74; B.J.M. Terra/P.J. Wattel, *European Tax Law*[6] (Kluwer, 2012), at p. 704; also see Commission Decision of 16 Oct. 2002 on the State aid scheme C 49/2001 (ex NN 46/2000) – Coordination Centres – implemented by Luxembourg (2003/501/EC), *OJ* L 170 (9 Jul. 2003), p. 20 (at p. 21, at para. 18).
1965. See R.S. Avi-Yonah, The Rise and Fall of Arm's Length: A Study in the Evolution of U.S. International Taxation, 15 *Virginia Tax Rev.* 1 (1995), p. 89 (at p. 90); B.J.M. Terra/P.J. Wattel, *European Tax Law*[6] (Kluwer, 2012), at p. 704.
1966. W. Schön in I. Richelle/W. Schön/E. Traversa (eds.), *Allocating Taxing Powers Within the European Union* (Springer, 2013), at p. 81; also see J. Monsenego, *Introduction to Transfer Pricing* (Kluwer, 2015), at p. 5.

in the countries involved.[1967] Many states have thus enacted transfer pricing rules that aim at reducing the effects of such transactions on the involved states' tax revenue.[1968] Most commonly, these rules are based on the arm's length principle.[1969] Thus, the profits of the associated enterprises are adjusted if they do not reflect "*the conditions which would have obtained between independent enterprises in comparable transactions and comparable circumstances.*"[1970] Associated enterprises are hence taxed as if they conducted business like an independent enterprise.[1971]

According to the OECD, a major reason "*why OECD member countries and other countries have adopted the arm's length principle [...] is that the arm's length principle provides broad parity of tax treatment for members of MNE groups and independent enterprises. Because the arm's length principle puts associated and independent enterprises on a more equal footing for tax purposes, it avoids the creation of tax advantages or disadvantages that would otherwise distort the relative competitive positions of either type of entity.*"[1972] Given the above-mentioned possibility of distortions of competition, the question arises whether it constitutes State aid if a Member State does not have transfer pricing rules or if these rules do not successfully avoid or at least mitigate distortions of competition.[1973] The European Commission, for example, argues that "*the arm's length principle [...] is [...] a general principle of equal treatment in taxation falling within the application of Article 107(1) of the Treaty, which binds the Member [...]. The arm's length principle therefore necessarily forms part of the [...] assessment under Article 107(1) of the Treaty of tax measures granted to group companies,*

1967. See J. Monsenego, *Introduction to Transfer Pricing* (Kluwer, 2015), at pp. 3-7.
1968. See, for example, R.S. Avi-Yonah, 15 *Virginia Tax Rev.* 1 (1995), at p. 90; E.J. Bartelsman/R.M.W.J. Beetsma, Why pay more? Corporate tax avoidance through transfer pricing in OECD countries, 87 *Journal of Public Economics* 9-10 (2003), p. 2225 (at pp. 2225-2227); K.A. Clausing, Multinational Firm Tax Avoidance and Tax Policy, 62 *National Tax J.* 4 (2009), p. 703 (at pp. 703-705); J.G. Gravelle, Tax Havens: International Avoidance and Evasion, 62 *National Tax J.* 4 (2009), p. 727 (at pp. 733-734); C. Keuschnigg/M.P. Devereux, *The Distorting Arm's Length Principle*, Oxford University Centre for Business Taxation, Working Paper 09/10 (9 Jul. 2009), at p. 1; J. Roin, Can the Income Tax be Saved? The Promise and Pitfalls of Adopting Worldwide Formulary Apportionment, 61 *Tax L. Rev.* 3 (2008), p. 169 (at pp. 171 and 182-185); W. Schön, Transfer Pricing - Business Incentives, International Taxation and Corporate Law, in K.A. Konrad/W. Schön (eds.), *Fundamentals of International Transfer Pricing in Law and Economics* (Springer, 2012), p. 47 (at p. 53); W. Schön, International Tax Coordination for a Second-Best World (Part III), 2 *World Tax J.* 3 (2010), p. 227 (at p. 230).
1969. See W. Schön in K.A. Konrad/W. Schön (eds.), *Fundamentals of International Transfer Pricing in Law and Economics* (Springer, 2012), at p. 53; also see OECD, *Multi-Country Analysis of Existing Transfer Pricing Simplification Measures* (OECD, 2011), at p. 9, at para. 16 ("*All 33 respondent countries indicate that their legislation establishes a general obligation to comply with the arm's length principle ('ALP').*").
1970. OECD, *Transfer Pricing Guidelines for Multinational Enterprises and Tax Administrations* (OECD, 2010), at p. 33, at para. 1.6.
1971. Cf. G. Kofler, The BEPS Action Plan and Transfer Pricing: The Arm's Length Standard Under Pressure?, 58 *British Tax Rev.* 5 (2013), p. 646 (at p. 646).
1972. OECD, *Transfer Pricing Guidelines for Multinational Enterprises and Tax Administrations* (OECD, 2010), at p. 34, at para. 1.8.
1973. See A. Taferner/J.W. Kuipers, 56 *Eur. Taxn.* 4 (2016), at pp. 138-139.

independently of whether a Member State has incorporated this principle into its national legal system and in what form."[1974]

A Member State may only be accused of violating Article 107(1) TFEU if a group of taxpayers is treated differently than a comparable group of taxpayers. From a single entity's perspective, not having transfer pricing rules does not lead to a different, but rather a congruent, tax treatment of independent and associated enterprises. Not having transfer pricing rules – in other words – does not lead to a deviation from the common tax regime that has been established by the very same Member State.[1975] However, according to the ECJ, EU law contains a general principle of equality.[1976] Thus, it is not only required "*that comparable situations must not be treated differently,*" but also "*that different situations must not be treated in the same way.*"[1977] Based on this general principle of equality, it could be argued that independent and

1974. Commission Decision of 11.1.2016 on the Excess Profit Exemption State Aid Scheme SA.37667 (2015/C) (ex 2015/NN) implemented by Belgium, C(2015) 9837 final (11 Jan. 2016), at p. 34, at para. 150; Commission Decision of 21.10.2015 on State Aid SA.38375 (2014/C ex 2014/NN) which Luxembourg granted to Fiat, C(2015) 7152 final (21 Oct. 2015), at p. 48, at para. 228; Commission Decision of 21.10.2015 on State Aid SA.38374 (2014/C ex 2014/NN) implemented by the Netherlands to Starbucks, C(2015) 7143 final (21 Oct. 2015), at pp. 62-63, at para. 264.

1975. See Chapter 3.3.3.3.

1976. Judgment in *Überschär*, 810/89, EU:C:1980:228, at para. 16; Judgment in *ČEZ*, C-115/08, EU:C:2009:660, at para. 89.

1977. Judgment in *Garcia Avello*, C-148/02, EU:C:2003:539, at para. 31; Judgment in *Azienda Agro-Zootecnica Franchini and Eolica di Altamura*, C-2/10, EU:C:2011:502, at para. 64; Judgment in *Hungary/Commission*, C-31/13 P, EU:C:2014:70, at para. 73; also cf. Judgment in *SFI*, C-85/97, EU:C:1998:552, at para. 30; Judgment in *Jippers and others*, C-189/01, EU:C:2001:420, at para. 128; Judgment in *Denkavit*, C-507/99, EU:C:2002:4, at para. 44; Judgment in *Omega and others*, C-122/00, EU:C:2002:161, at para. 79; Judgment in *Commission/Portugal*, C-334/03, EU:C:2005:623, at para. 24; also cf. Judgment in *Schumacker*, C-279/93, EU:C:1995:31, at para. 30; Judgment in *Wielockx*, C-80/94, EU:C:1995:271, at para. 17; Judgment in *Asscher*, C-107/94, EU:C:1996:251, at para. 40; Judgment in *Royal Bank of Scotland*, C-311/97, EU:C:1999:216, at para. 26; Judgment in *Gschwind*, C-391/97, EU:C:1999:409, at para. 21; Judgment in *Kerckhaert and Morres*, C-513/04, EU:C:2006:713, at para. 19; Judgment in *Meindl*, C-329/05, EU:C:2007:57, at para. 22; Judgment in *Talotta*, C-383/05, EU:C:2007:181, at para. 18; Judgment in *Lakebrink and Peters-Lakebrink*, C-182/06, EU:C:2007:452, at para. 27; Judgment in *Columbus Container Services*, C-298/05, EU:C:2007:754, at para. 41; Judgment in *Gielen*, C-440/08, EU:C:2010:148; at para. 38; Judgment in *Commission/Hungary*, C-253/09, EU:C:2011:795, at para. 50; Judgment in *Commission/Netherlands*, C-542/09, EU:C:2012:346, at para. 41; Judgment in *Commission/Estonia*, C-39/10, EU:C:2012:282, at para. 48; Judgment in *Banco Bilbao Vizcaya Argentaria*, C-157/10, EU:C:2011:813, at para. 41; Judgment in *Bouanich*, C-375/12, EU:C:2014:138, at para. 45.

associated enterprises are not comparable[1978] and hence have to be treated differently, because (only) the latter may establish conditions for economic transactions taking place between them which do not correspond to what independent enterprises would have agreed on. With regard to debt financing activities between associated enterprises, for example, the European Commission argued that "*related companies are not in a legal and factual situation comparable to that of unrelated companies. The reason is that related companies, unlike unrelated companies, are not engaged in a merely commercial transaction when they try to obtain loan or equity financing within the group. The parent and the subsidiary share the same interests, which is not the case in a commercial transaction with a third-party provider of finance, where each party tries to maximise its profits at the expense of the other.*"[1979] However, it is yet unclear whether Article 107(1) TFEU has to be interpreted in the light of the general principle of equality. Even with regard to the fundamental freedoms, the ECJ hardly ever relies on the "*often repeated but rarely used*" approach that "*different situations must not be treated in the same way.*"[1980]

Even if the State aid rules in principle also prohibited different situations from being treated alike, it would still have to be proven that a Member State thereby actually favours certain undertakings or the production of certain goods. Since "*no advantage can be identified without a comparator first being found as a benchmark for treatment,*"[1981] this requires identifying the proper pair of comparison. At first glance, one may be tempted to compare the tax treatment of a group of companies as a whole with the tax treatment of an independent company. However, aside from group

1978. See R. Luja, State Aid Benchmarking and Tax Rulings: Can We Keep It Simple?, in I. Richelle/W. Schön/E. Traversa (eds.), *Allocating Taxing Powers Within the European Union* (Springer, 2013), p. 111 (at p. 114).

1979. Commission Decision of 8 Jul. 2009 on the groepsrentebox scheme which the Netherlands is planning to implement (C 4/07 (ex N 465/06)), *OJ* L 288 (4 Nov. 2009), at p. 37, para. 103; also see Commission Decision of 28 Oct. 2009 on State aid C 10/07 (ex NN 13/07) implemented by Hungary for tax deductions for intra-group interest, *OJ* L 42 (17 Feb. 2010), p. 3 (at p. 15, para. 111).

1980. M. Lang, 18 *EC Tax Rev.* 3 (2009), at p. 99; also see K. Spies, 26 *ecolex* 8 (2015), at p. 702.

1981. M. Ross, 37 *Common Market L. Rev.* 2 (2000), at p. 407.

taxation systems, the Member States typically treat each company as a single taxable person, irrespective of whether it is part of a group or not.[1982] Although a group of

1982. Parts of the literature nevertheless take into account the group of companies as a whole. In order to show that transfer pricing rules should not subjected to a State aid law anlaysis, it is argued that transfer pricing "*may be a zero sum game*" (L. De Broe, 24 *EC Tax Rev.* 6 [2015], at p. 292), if the effects of transfer pricing legislation on all associated enterprises are taken into account (see W. Haslehner in I. Richelle/W. Schön/E. Traversa [eds.], *Allocating Taxing Powers Within the European Union* [Springer, 2013], at pp. 158-159: "*[S]tate aid law [...] applies to the undertaking as a whole, which is the multinational enterprise. [...] If the relevant subject for state aid purposes is the multinational enterprise as a whole, no aid can thus arise despite the application of rules that are not in line with the arm's length standard*"; also cf. W. Schön in I. Richelle/W. Schön/E. Traversa [eds.], *Allocating Taxing Powers Within the European Union* [Springer, 2013], at pp. 84-87). However, unless Member States have legally linked their transfer pricing rules, it is doubtful whether such an argument would be accepted by the ECJ. In *SGI*, for example, the Court emphasized that "*the tax burden borne by the recipient company in a domestic situation cannot be likened to the taxation, in a cross-border situation, of the company granting the advantage in question*" (Judgment in *SGI*, C-311/08, EU:C:2010:26, at para. 52). The European Commission also argues that "*[t]he conduct of other Member States, and in particular the possibility that they might take account of the advantage conferred by a Member States in an attempt to reduce or cancel its effects, does not in any way detract from the reality of that advantage*" (Commission Decision of 16 Oct. 2002 on the State aid scheme C 49/2001 (ex NN 46/2000) – Coordination Centres – implemented by Luxembourg (2003/501/EC), *OJ* L 170 [9 Jul. 2003], at p. 25, at para. 48). However, even if a group of companies could be considered to be a whole for tax purposes, it remains unclear which Member State should be held responsible for the resultant distortion of competition in a cross-border situation. The European Commission, for example, blames the Member State that allows for downward adjustments although there is no corresponding upward adjustment in the respective other Member State. But it would be likewise possible to argue that the respective other Member State infringes the State aid rules by not applying a corresponding upward adjustment, although its domestic tax system provides for transfer pricing rules which would enable the profits of associated enterprises to be increased if they are not at arm's length (cf. W. Haslehner in I. Richelle/W. Schön/E. Traversa [eds.], *Allocating Taxing Powers Within the European Union* [Springer, 2013], at p. 158). In fact, in various State aid procedures, the European Commission accuses Ireland (European Commission, State aid SA.38373 (2014/C) (ex 2014/NN) (ex 2014/CP) – Ireland *Alleged aid to Apple*, C(2014) 3606 final [11 Jun. 2014]), the Netherlands (European Commission, State aid SA.38374 (2014/C) (ex 2014/NN) (ex 2014/CP) – Netherlands Alleged aid to Starbucks, C(2014) 3626 final [11 Jun. 2014]), and Luxembourg (European Commission, State aid SA. 38375 (2014/NN) (ex 2014/CP) – Luxembourg *Alleged aid to FFT*, C(2014) 3627 final (11 Jun. 2014); Commission Decision of 21.10.2015 on State Aid SA.38375 (2014/C ex 2014/NN) which Luxembourg granted to Fiat, C(2015) 7152 final (21 Oct. 2015); European Commission, State aid SA.38944 (2014/C) – Luxembourg Alleged aid to Amazon by way of a tax ruling, C(2014) 7156 final [7 October 2014]) of granting State aid, because the transfer pricing adjustments made with respect to associated enterprises resident in the respective Member States should have increased their profits to a greater extent than it was actually done. Against this background, the situation strikingly recalls the ECJ's main reason not to interpret the fundamental freedoms as prohibiting double taxation, which is that "*no one tax jurisdiction is to blame for the tax disadvantage*" (Opinion of AG Geelhoed in *Test Claimants in Class IV of the ACT Group Litigation*, C-374/04, EU:C:2006:139, at point 48). Given the associated challenge, it could be argued that the State aid analysis of a Member State's transfer pricing rules should not depend on what another state's tax system looks like (cf. W. Haslehner in I. Richelle/W. Schön/E. Traversa [eds.], *Allocating Taxing Powers Within the European Union* [Springer, 2013], at p. 158; R. Luja, *EU State Aid Law and National Tax Rulings*, IP/A/TAXE/2015-02, PE 563.453 [October 2015], at p. 13; R. Luja, 60 *British Tax Rev.* 3 [2015], at pp. 385-386). This would be in line with the ECJ's case law on the fundamental freedoms, according to which another Member State's tax system should not be taken into account, unless there is a direct link between the tax systems of two Member States (see Chapter 4.1.3.2.4.). If a Member State's

companies may be regarded as an economic unit[1983] and even a single undertaking for State aid purposes,[1984] it thus does not seem apt to compare an independent enterprise with a whole group of companies.[1985] Rather, the tax treatment of an individual enterprise which is part of a group of companies should be compared with an independent enterprise. This also seems to be the position of the European Commission.[1986] However, from a single entity's perspective, transactions with an associated enterprise which are not at arm's length may improve, but may also worsen the tax situation as compared to an independent enterprise which is bound to accept market-compliant conditions. Hence, not having transfer pricing rules does not generally favour (or disadvantage) associated enterprises as compared to independent enterprises. Still, whether this argument is sufficient to refute the State aid accusation is debatable.[1987] According to AG Kokott, for example, the possibility that a rule may lead

---

transfer pricing rules hence aim at avoiding "*the creation of tax advantages or disadvantages that would otherwise distort the relative competitive positions of [members of MNE groups and independent enterprises]*" (OECD, *Transfer Pricing Guidelines for Multinational Enterprises and Tax Administrations* [OECD, 2010], at p. 34, at para. 1.8; also cf. H. Lamon, Belgium, in IFA [ed.], *Cross-Border Business Restructuring*, CDFI 96a [IBFD, 2011], p. 127 [at p. 134: "*The rationale for downward adjustment is that the taxpayer is able to demonstrate that the adjusted profits correctly reflect what they would have been had the transaction been at arm's length.*"]), whereas another Member State does not care about such distortions of competition or does not agree on the first Member State's interpretation of the arm's length principle, the resultant double taxation or double non-taxation could be perceived as a disparity (see L. De Broe, 24 *EC Tax Rev.* 6 [2015], at p. 291 ["*Mismatches resulting from interpretation differences of the OECD TPG between two or more Member States [...] are the result of disparities in the tax legislation of different Member States and are therefore, as a matter of principle, not suitable of being challenged by the State aid rules.*"]). No single Member State could be blamed for the problems that thereby arise. If double taxation or double non-taxation results from two Member States not agreeing on the "correct" arm's length price, this could be different. However, it would require that it is possible to determine the "correct" arm's length price (see A. Taferner/J.W. Kuipers, 56 *Eur. Taxn.* 4 [2016], at p. 142). Since "*transfer pricing is not an exact science but does require the exercise of judgment on the part of both the tax administration and taxpayer*" (OECD, *Transfer Pricing Guidelines for Multinational Enterprises and Tax Administrations* [OECD, 2010], at p. 36, at para. 1.13.), this seems rather doubtful.

1983. Judgment in *Cassa di Risparmio di Firenze and others*, C-222/04, EU:C:2006:8, at para. 110; Judgment in *AceaElectrabel Produzione*, C-480/09 P, EU:C:2010:787, at paras 46-70; also see Commission Decision of 11.1.2016 on the Excess Profit Exemption State Aid Scheme SA.37667 (2015/C) (ex 2015/NN) implemented by Belgium, C(2015) 9837 final (11 Jan. 2016), at p. 43, at para. 184.

1984. Judgment in *Intermills*, 323/82, EU:C:1984:345, at para. 11; also see European Commission, Commission Notice on the notion of State Aid as referred to in Article 107(1) of the Treaty on the Functioning of the European Union, *OJ* C 262 (19 Jul. 2016), at para. 11; Commission Decision of 11.1.2016 on the Excess Profit Exemption State Aid Scheme SA.37667 (2015/C) (ex 2015/NN) implemented by Belgium, C(2015) 9837 final (11 Jan. 2016), at p. 43, at para. 184.

1985. In cross-border situations, such a comparison would additionally lead to the problem that a cross-border group of companies is subject to several Member States' tax systems. This would require considering and scrutinizing all involved Member States' tax systems simultaneously, although they might not be legally interconnected and might even be very different.

1986. Commission Decision of 8 Jul. 2009 on the groepsrentebox scheme which the Netherlands is planning to implement (C 4/07 (ex N 465/06)), *OJ* L 288 (4 Nov. 2009), p. 26 (at p. 24, paras 80-81).

1987. Cf. M. Lang, 27 *ÖStZ* 11 (2014), at p. 288.

to advantages as well as disadvantages "*does nothing to alter the fact that, in [the former cases], a tax advantage [is] none the less*" granted.[1988]

However, even if Member States were not obliged to enact transfer pricing rules in the first place,[1989] this would not mean that EU law can be disregarded if such legislation is introduced voluntarily. The European Commission, for example, argues that transfer pricing rules may lead to a more favourable treatment of associated enterprises as compared to independent enterprises. Some Member States, for example, also apply transfer pricing adjustments if the arm's length principle leads to the conclusion that the profits of an associated enterprise are too high. In a State aid procedure against Belgium, the European Commission argues that downward adjustments of a group company's profits constitute State aid, unless they are accompanied by a corresponding upward adjustment of the profits of the other associated enterprise which is also part of the respective transaction. The reason is that in general a corporate income tax system, such as the Belgian one, "*takes the corporate accounting profit as a starting point.*"[1990] If a Member State decreases the profits of an associated enterprise in the case of non-arm's length transactions with another associated enterprise, it allegedly allows "*the beneficiaries to reduce their tax base and the amount of tax paid in comparison with a situation where those adjustments would not take place and all profits registered in the accounts of the beneficiaries would be taken into account.*"[1991]

1988. Opinion of AG Kokott in *Finanzamt Linz*, C-66/14, EU:C:2015:242, at point 37.

1989. See R. Luja, 76 *Tax Notes Intl.* 4 (27 Oct. 2014), at p. 355 ("*In theory, a country could be lacking effective antiabuse rules and may be forced to accept contracts at face value without any arm's-length testing. This would obviously go against anything BEPS and harmful tax competition projects stand for, but in such a hypothetical case, state aid rules would not have an effect.*"); P.J. Wattel, The Cat and the Pigeons: Some General Comments on (TP) Tax Rulings and State Aid After the Starbucks and Fiat Decisions, in I. Richelle/W. Schön/E. Traversa (eds.), *Allocating Taxing Powers Within the European Union* (Springer, 2013), p. 185 (at p. 186).

1990. European Commission, State aid SA.37667 (2015/C ex 2015/NN) – Belgium - Excess profit tax ruling system in Belgium – Art. 185§2 b) CIR92, C(2015) 563 final (3 Feb. 2015), at p. 17, at para. 58; Commission Decision of 11.1.2016 on the Excess Profit Exemption State Aid Scheme SA.37667 (2015/C) (ex 2015/NN) implemented by Belgium, C(2015) 9837 final (11 Jan. 2016), at p. 26, at paras 121-122; but see R. Lyal, 38 *Fordham Intl. L. J.* 4 (2015), at p. 1040 ("*In relation to rulings on transfer pricing [...] the identification of the reference system seems straightforward. It is quite simply the taxation of independent companies. They are taxed on their revenue less costs, both sides of the equation being fixed by the market. For related companies the answer is no different: they are taxed on revenue less costs, on both sides the elements that are not fixed by the market must be verified and where necessary substituted by a price that corresponds to the price that would be charged in a market transaction.*"); also cf. Judgment in *Belgium/Commission*, C-182/03 and C-217/03, EU:C:2006:416, at para. 95 ("*In order to decide whether a method of assessment of taxable income such as that laid down under the regime for coordination centres confers an advantage on them, it is necessary, as the Commission suggests at point 95 of the contested decision, to compare that regime with the ordinary tax system, based on the difference between profits and outgoings of an undertaking carrying on its activities in conditions of free competition.*").

1991. European Commission, State aid SA.37667 (2015/C ex 2015/NN) – Belgium - Excess profit tax ruling system in Belgium – Art. 185§2 b) CIR92, C(2015) 563 final (3 Feb. 2015), at pp. 17-18,

The European Commission's reasoning is, *inter alia*, based on a comparison of the tax treatment of a stand-alone company and a company which is associated with other (foreign) companies.[1992] Thus, it is implicitly assumed that applying transfer pricing rules to intra-group transactions may constitute State aid if they lead to a reduction of the *individual* associated enterprise's profits as compared to the calculation of the profits of an independent enterprise.[1993] It is doubtful, though, that such a different treatment actually violates Article 107 TFEU.[1994] According to the OECD, transfer pricing rules that are based on the arm's length principle aim at providing "*broad parity of tax treatment for members of MNE groups and independent enterprises.*"[1995] If this is true,[1996] the individual associated enterprise is not granted a beneficial treatment as compared to an independent enterprise by subjecting it to transfer pricing rules, but such legislation rather tries to ensure equal treatment.[1997] Moreover, according to the OECD, transfer pricing rules are considered to avoid "*the*

at para. 63; Commission Decision of 11.1.2016 on the Excess Profit Exemption State Aid Scheme SA.37667 (2015/C) (ex 2015/NN) implemented by Belgium, C(2015) 9837 final (11 Jan. 2016), at p. 28, at para. 133.

1992. European Commission, State aid SA.37667 (2015/C ex 2015/NN) – Belgium - Excess profit tax ruling system in Belgium – Art. 185§2 b) CIR92, C(2015) 563 final (3 Feb. 2015), at pp. 18-19, at para. 67 and at p. 23, at para. 85; Commission Decision of 11.1.2016 on the Excess Profit Exemption State Aid Scheme SA.37667 (2015/C) (ex 2015/NN) implemented by Belgium, C(2015) 9837 final (11 Jan. 2016), at pp. 29-30, at para. 138; also cf. W. Haslehner in I. Richelle/W. Schön/E. Traversa (eds.), *Allocating Taxing Powers Within the European Union* (Springer, 2013), at p. 155.

1993. But see W. Haslehner in I. Richelle/W. Schön/E. Traversa (eds.), *Allocating Taxing Powers Within the European Union* (Springer, 2013), at p. 152, according to whom the European Commission's view is that "*a tax system that calculates taxable profits to consist of the result of receipts minus costs as achieved in a free market (i.e. based on such market prices), must in turn apply measures to ensure that a comparable measure of profit is applied to companies that do not (necessarily) transact at market prices.*"

1994. Cf. W. Haslehner in I. Richelle/W. Schön/E. Traversa (eds.), *Allocating Taxing Powers Within the European Union* (Springer, 2013), at p. 153.

1995. OECD, *Transfer Pricing Guidelines for Multinational Enterprises and Tax Administrations* (OECD, 2010), at p. 34, at para. 1.8; also see Commission Decision of 11.1.2016 on the Excess Profit Exemption State Aid Scheme SA.37667 (2015/C) (ex 2015/NN) implemented by Belgium, C(2015) 9837 final (11 Jan. 2016), at pp. 33-34, at para. 148.

1996. For critical remarks see W. Schön in I. Richelle/W. Schön/E. Traversa (eds.), *Allocating Taxing Powers Within the European Union* (Springer, 2013), at pp. 93-97.

1997. See H. Hamaekers, The Arm's Length Principle and the Role of Comparables, 46 *Bull. Intl. Taxn.* 12 (1992), p. 602 (at p. 603: "*Taxpayers with a controlling interest in a company are placed in the same position as other taxpayers through application of the arm's length principle which neutralizes the advantage of the former.*"); W. Schön in I. Richelle/W. Schön/E. Traversa (eds.), *Allocating Taxing Powers Within the European Union* (Springer, 2013), at p. 96 ("*[T]he arm's-length standard is [...] a legal [...] concept, trying to grant equal treatment to group companies and independent companies.*"); A. Taferner/J.W. Kuipers, 56 *Eur. Taxn.* 4 (2016), at p. 138 ("*The aim of transfer pricing rules is [...] to establish a level playing field between stand-alone and group companies.*"); R.J.S. Tavares/B.N. Bogenschneider/M. Pankiv, The Intersection of EU State Aid and U.S. Tax Deferral: A Spectacle of Fireworks, Smoke, and Mirrors, 19 *Florida Tax Rev.* 3 (2016), p. 121 (at p. 174).

creation of tax advantages or disadvantages that would otherwise distort the relative competitive positions of [members of MNE groups and independent enterprises]."[1998] If this is true as well, transfer pricing rules do not grant tax advantages, but rather neutralize non-tax advantages. Such legislation thus avoids or at least mitigates distortions of competition.[1999] But if distortion of competition is not caused but rather tackled by the transfer pricing rules, it would be counterintuitive if this was prohibited by Article 107 TFEU.

If transfer pricing rules hence do not constitute State aid because they only apply to associated but not to independent enterprises, they would still be suspicious from an EU law perspective for another reason. The *SGI* decision, for example, shows that a Member State's legislation constitutes a restriction of the fundamental freedoms if transfer pricing adjustments can only be triggered by cross-border dealings between associated enterprises, whereas dealings between two resident associated enterprises remain untouched. The case concerned the Belgian transfer pricing rules, which provided for the adjustment of "unusual or gratuitous advantages" granted by a domestic company to a related foreign company. In the circumstances at issue, the taxpayer had, *inter alia*, extended a zero-interest loan to a group company based in Luxembourg. Since an unrelated party would not grant such a loan free of interest, a notional interest calculated at an annual rate of 5% was added to the taxpayer's profits. Since such an adjustment would not have been made if the company granting the loan had been resident in Belgium, the cross-border situation was treated less favourably than a comparable domestic situation.[2000] According to the ECJ, such a different treatment is justified, but in order to be proportionate as well the taxpayer, "*on each occasion on which there is a suspicion that a transaction goes beyond what the company concerned would have agreed under fully competitive conditions,*" must be "*given an opportunity, without being subject to undue administrative constraints, to provide evidence of any commercial justification that there may have been for the transaction*" and "*the corrective tax measure must be confined to the part which exceeds what would have been agreed if the companies did not have a relationship of interdependence.*"[2001]

In contrast to the facts of the case in *SGI*, transfer pricing rules may also lead to a more favourable treatment of cross-border situations as compared to domestic situations that are not subject to such legislation. This could be the case, for example, if the profits of an associated enterprise are adjusted downwards in order to correct the result of a non-arm's length transaction with a foreign associated enterprise. According to the European Commission, such a downward adjustment of an enterprise's profits may be problematic from a State aid point of view if it "*only applies to [...] entities of multinational groups*" and hence "*is [not] applicable to entities of a purely [domestic]*

1998. OECD, *Transfer Pricing Guidelines for Multinational Enterprises and Tax Administrations* (OECD, 2010), at p. 34, at para. 1.8.
1999. Cf. R. Beiser, Die Wegzugsbesteuerung und das arm's length-Prinzip im Licht der Rechtsprechung "Hughes de Lasteyrie du Saillant," 17 *ÖStZ* 13 (2004), p. 282 (at p. 286); G. Kofler, *Doppelbesteuerungsabkommen und Europäisches Gemeinschaftsrecht* (Linde, 2007), at p. 897.
2000. Judgment in *SGI*, C-311/08, EU:C:2010:26, at paras 42-55.
2001. Judgment in *SGI*, C-311/08, EU:C:2010:26, at paras 71-72.

group."[2002] Thus, the European Commission compares the tax treatment of an individual enterprise which is part of a domestic group of companies with the tax treatment of an individual enterprise which is part of a cross-border group of companies.[2003] If this comparison is applied consistently, transfer pricing rules that only apply to cross-border situations would generally run the risk of constituting State aid. Either the individual enterprise which is part of a cross-border group is favoured due to a downward adjustment of its profits or the individual enterprise which is part of a domestic group is favoured due to a lack of an upward adjustment of its profits.

Depending on the respective domestic tax system,[2004] it may be argued that enterprises which are part of either a domestic or a foreign group of companies are not comparable[2005] or that a different treatment is justified. If downward profit adjustments, for example, are considered to aim at avoiding double taxation,[2006] cross-border intra-group activities could be seen as not being comparable with domestic intra-group activities. However, according to the European Commission, both types of entities "*should be subject to tax [...] on the total amount of their profits. As mentioned above, the calculation of the taxable profits starts from the profits as they are registered in the accounts and the Commission does not see why a derogation to that principle would be warranted for [...] entities of multinational groups of associated companies. The fact that multinationals – contrary to [...] standalone companies [...] – are the only ones whose revenues can originate in cross-border activities and be subject to international double taxation does not, in light of the objective of the tax system, put the [...] entity of such a multinational group in a different legal and factual situation.*"[2007]

2002. European Commission, State aid SA.37667 (2015/C ex 2015/NN) – Belgium - Excess profit tax ruling system in Belgium – Art. 185§2 b) CIR92, C(2015) 563 final (3 Feb. 2015), at p. 23, at para. 85; Commission Decision of 11.1.2016 on the Excess Profit Exemption State Aid Scheme SA.37667 (2015/C) (ex 2015/NN) implemented by Belgium, C(2015) 9837 final (11 Jan. 2016), at pp. 29-30, at para. 138.

2003. Also cf. Commission Decision of 5 Sep. 2002 on the aid scheme implemented by Germany for control and coordination centres, *OJ* L 177 (16 Jul. 2003), p. 17 (at p. 20, para. 32).

2004. See R. Luja, 60 *British Tax Rev.* 3 (2015), at p. 386 and R. Szudoczky in I. Richelle/W. Schön/E. Traversa (eds.), *Allocating Taxing Powers Within the European Union* (Springer, 2013), at pp. 181-182, who take into account the different objectives that might be associated with transfer pricing rules.

2005. See W. Haslehner in I. Richelle/W. Schön/E. Traversa (eds.), *Allocating Taxing Powers Within the European Union* (Springer, 2013), at p. 153, who argues that "*[i]n the absence of a need to allocate profits properly to taxpayers in line with an agreed allocation of taxing rights vis-à-vis other countries, there is no reason to require transfer pricing adjustments in the case of purely domestic transactions, which is entirely logical and consistent.*"

2006. See, for example, A. Fross, Earnings Stripping and Thin Cap Rules: Maintaining an Arm's Length Distance, 53 *Eur. Taxn.* 10 (2013), p. 507 (at p. 509); J. Wittendorf, *Transfer Pricing and the Arm's Length Principle in International Tax Law* (Kluwer, 2010), at pp. 146-147; with further references G. Kofler in E. Reimer/A. Rust (eds.), *Klaus Vogel on Double Taxation Conventions, Fourth Edition* (Kluwer, 2015), at Article 9 para. 7.

2007. European Commission, State aid SA.37667 (2015/C ex 2015/NN) – Belgium - Excess profit tax ruling system in Belgium – Art. 185§2 b) CIR92, C(2015) 563 final (3 Feb. 2015), at pp. 18-19, at para. 67.

Even if the cross-border and the domestic situation were hence supposed to be comparable, one could still argue that it is justified to limit the ambit of transfer pricing rules to cross-border situations in order to avoid double taxation. However, according to the European Commission, downward profit adjustments are only considered to be in line with Article 107 TFEU if the residence state of the other associated enterprise applies "*an upward correction of the tax base to restore the tax base at the level it would have had, had the prises been set at market conditions.*"[2008] If downward profit adjustments aim at the avoidance of double taxation, they should only be applied in "*an actual situation of double taxation.*"[2009]

Given that the European Commission's reasoning is based on a comparison of the tax treatment of an individual enterprise that is part of a cross-border group and the tax treatment of an individual enterprise that is part of a domestic group, the same considerations should also apply with regard to upward profit adjustments. If transfer pricing rules do not apply in purely domestic situations, an associated enterprise that is part of a domestic group is favoured insofar as its profits are not subject to upward adjustments, whereas the profits of an associated enterprise that is part of a cross-border group are increased in the case of non-arm's length transactions. By arguing that downward profit adjustments lead to a favourable treatment of associated enterprises that are part of a cross-border group, which is subject to transfer pricing rules, the European Commission implicitly assumes that upward adjustments of an associated enterprise's profits lead to a favourable treatment of associated enterprises that are part of a domestic group which is not subject to transfer pricing rules. Of course, it could be argued that upward profit adjustments aim at the avoidance of double non-taxation and it is thus justified to only apply them in cross-border situations. However, in view of the European Commission's reasoning with regard to downward profit adjustments, one may counter that they should accordingly only be applied in an actual situation of double non-taxation.

Overall, the European Commission's approach would leave the Member States three options in order to make sure that their transfer pricing rules do not violate Article 107 TFEU. First, transfer pricing rules could be completely abandoned. However, this seems to be neither probable nor desirable – and maybe not even in line with State aid

2008. European Commission, State aid SA.37667 (2015/C ex 2015/NN) – Belgium - Excess profit tax ruling system in Belgium – Art. 185§2 b) CIR92, C(2015) 563 final (3 Feb. 2015), at p. 17, at para. 59 (also cf. at p. 17, at para. 62 and at p. 18 at para. 68 and at p. 24, at paras 91-92).
2009. European Commission, State aid SA.37667 (2015/C ex 2015/NN) – Belgium - Excess profit tax ruling system in Belgium – Art. 185§2 b) CIR92, C(2015) 563 final (3 Feb. 2015), at p. 17, at para. 68 and at p. 24, at para. 91; Commission Decision of 11.1.2016 on the Excess Profit Exemption State Aid Scheme SA.37667 (2015/C) (ex 2015/NN) implemented by Belgium, C(2015) 9837 final (11 Jan. 2016), at pp. 40-42, at paras 172-178; also cf. K. Dirix, 22 *EC Tax Rev.* 5 (2013), at pp. 248-249; W. Haslehner in I. Richelle/W. Schön/E. Traversa (eds.), *Allocating Taxing Powers Within the European Union* (Springer, 2013), at p. 157 ("*A unilateral downward adjustment that cannot be expected to be matched by a corresponding upward adjustment by another jurisdiction is thus likely to fall foul of state aid rules.*").

law – unless another legal framework is adopted that replaces the transfer pricing rules.[2010] Second, the Member States could make their transfer pricing rules dependent on whether there is an actual situation of double taxation or double non-taxation. However, if all Member States incorporated such a condition, the outcome would be ambiguous, because whether there is an actual situation of double taxation or double non-taxation depends on whether the respective other Member State applies its transfer pricing rules or not. But the respective other Member State's transfer pricing rules would also depend on whether there is an actual situation of double taxation or double non-taxation. Unless this problem of circularly-linked rules can be resolved by way of a mutual agreement or an arbitration procedure,[2011] it might be that neither Member State applies its transfer pricing rules due to a lack of actual double taxation or double non-taxation. Since this also seems to be an insufficient result, the ambit of transfer pricing rules could, third, be extended so as to also apply in domestic situations.[2012] The ECJ's case law on the compatibility of thin capitalization rules[2013] and transfer pricing rules[2014] with the fundamental freedoms has also had such an effect.[2015] Although *"tax base protective measures"* might make no sense in a purely

2010. The Member States' transfer pricing rules could, for example, be replaced by a consolidated profit calculation method based on a uniform principle in which the profits are allocated to the various entities of a group according to a specific key and taxed according to the applicable rates in the various Member States. The European Commission's proposal on a Common Consolidated Corporate Tax Base (Proposal for a Council Directive on a Common Consolidated Corporate Tax Base (CCCTB), COM(2011) 121/4 [2011], at pp. 49-55) is based on such a mechanism. On the issue of profit allocation see, for example, M. Petutschnig, Sharing the Benefits of the EU's *Common Consolidated Corporate Tax Base* within Corporate Groups, 7 *World Tax J.* 2 (2015), p. 241 (at pp. 241-263); B.J.M. Terra/P.J. Wattel, *European Tax Law*[6] (Kluwer, 2012), at pp. 810-812; also cf. M.P. Devereux/S. Loretz, The Effects of EU Formula Apportionment on Corporate Tax Revenues, 29 *Fiscal Studies* 1 (2008), p. 1 (at pp. 1-33); S. Mayer, *Formulary Apportionment for the Internal Market* (IBFD, 2009); C.E. McLure/J.M. Weiner, Deciding whether the European Union should adopt formula apportionment of company income, in S. Cnossen (ed.), *Taxing Capital Income in the European Union* (Oxford University Press, 2000), p. 243 (at pp. 243-292); C.E. McLure, Replacing Separate Entity Accounting and the Arm's Length Principle with Formulary Apportionment, 56 *Bull. Intl. Taxn.* 12 (2002), p. 586 (at pp. 586-599); A. Russo, Formulary Apportionment for Europe: An Analysis and A Proposal, 33 *Intertax* 1 (2005), p. 2 (at pp. 2-31); J.M. Weiner/J. Mintz, An Exploration of Formula Apportionment in the European Union, 42 *Eur. Taxn.* 8 (2002), p. 346 (at pp. 346-351); J.M. Weiner, Formula One. The race to find a common formula to apportion the EU tax base, 17 *EC Tax Rev.* 3 (2008), p. 100 (at pp. 100-110); P. Weninger, *Formulary Apportionment in the EU* (Intersentia, 2009).

2011. See, for example, P. Plansky, The EU Arbitration Convention, in M. Lang/P. Pistone/J. Schuch/C. Staringer (eds.), *Introduction to European Tax Law on Direct Taxation*[4] (Linde, 2015), p. 257 (at pp. 257-269).

2012. In fact, most domestic tax systems already include measures which are similar to transfer pricing rules, such as hidden profit distributions. For the Austrian system see, for example, G. Ressler/B. Stürzlinger in M. Lang/A. Rust/J. Schuch/C. Staringer (eds.), *KStG*[2] (Linde, 2016), at § 8 paras 96-99.

2013. Judgment in *Lankhorst-Hohorst*, C-324/00, EU:C:2002:749; Judgment in *Test Claimants in the Thin Cap Group Litigation*, C-524/04, EU:C:2007:161; Judgment in *Itelcar*, C-282/12, EU:C:2013:629.

2014. Judgment in *SGI*, C-311/08, EU:C:2010:26.

2015. See B.J.M. Terra/P.J. Wattel, *European Tax Law*[6] (Kluwer, 2012), at p. 731.

domestic situation,[2016] such a development could still be reasonable. Through applying transfer pricing rules to associated enterprises that are part of a domestic group it could, for example, be avoided that profits are artificially shifted to an entity which is in a loss position in order to achieve a liquidity advantage.[2017]

2.3.2.3 Participation Exemption Regimes and State Aid Law

Another interesting question which has been raised in the literature is whether participation exemption regimes that are typically available for corporations constitute State aid.[2018] There are different reasons why such legislation could be perceived as violating Article 107 TFEU. First, a Member State may thereby grant a tax exemption to corporations receiving dividends from their subsidiaries, whereas sole proprietors who receive dividends from a corporation in which they hold shares have to pay taxes. It could be argued that this leads to a differentiation "*between economic operators who [...] are in a comparable factual and legal situation.*"[2019] If the competitive relationship between undertakings or the production of goods were decisive for the comparability analysis,[2020] the different treatment of sole proprietors and competing corporations would have to be justified. Similarly, if the fundamental principles underlying the respective tax were decisive for the comparability analysis,[2021] it would have to be explained why it is in line with "*the nature [and/or] general scheme of the [tax]*

2016. B.J.M. Terra/P.J. Wattel, *European Tax Law*[6] (Kluwer, 2012), at p. 736; also see Opinion of AG Geelhoed in *Test Claimants in the Thin Cap Group Litigation*, C-524/04, EU:C:2006:436, at point 68.
2017. See W. Schön in I. Richelle/W. Schön/E. Traversa (eds.), *Allocating Taxing Powers Within the European Union* (Springer, 2013), at p. 81.
2018. See R. Szudoczky in I. Richelle/W. Schön/E. Traversa (eds.), *Allocating Taxing Powers Within the European Union* (Springer, 2013), at pp. 166-168.
2019. Judgment in *Paint Graphos and others*, C-78/08 to C-80/08, EU:C:2011:550, at para. 49; Judgment in *P*, C-6/12, EU:C:2013:525, at para. 19; Judgment in *Ministerio de Defensa and Navantia*, C-522/13, EU:C:2014:2262, at para. 35.
2020. See M. Lang in P. Pistone (ed.), *Legal Remedies in European Tax Law* (IBFD, 2009), at p. 270; M. Lang, *Die Auswirkungen des gemeinschaftsrechtlichen Beihilferechts auf das Steuerrecht*, 17. ÖJT, Band IV/1 (Manz, 2009), at p. 26; M. Lang in ÖJT (ed.), *Die Auswirkungen des gemeinschaftsrechtlichen Beihilferechts auf das Steuerrecht*, Referate und Diskussionsbeiträge, Band IV/2 (Manz, 2010), at p. 69; M. Lang, 24 *ÖStZ* 24 (2011), at p. 598; M. Lang, 19 *IStR* 15 (2010), at p. 578; M. Lang in J. Lüdicke (ed.), *Praxis und Zukunft des Internationalen Steuerrechts* (Dr Otto Schmidt, 2012), at p. 99; M. Lang, 11 *Eur. St. Aid L. Q.* 2 (2012), at p. 420; also see C. Micheau, 17 *EC Tax Rev.* 6 (2008), at p. 283.
2021. See K. Drüen, 49 *DStR* 7 (2011), at p. 291; J. Englisch in H. Schaumburg/J. Englisch (eds.), *Europäisches Steuerrecht* (Dr Otto Schmidt, 2015), at p. 425, at MN 9.17; J. Englisch, 22 *EC Tax Rev.* 1 (2013), at p. 11; J. Englisch in A. Rust/C. Micheau (eds.), *State Aid and Tax Law* (Kluwer, 2013), at p. 72.

system,"[2022] *"the basic or guiding principles of [the] tax system"*[2023] or *"the logic of the tax system"*[2024] to grant a participation exemption to corporations but not to sole proprietors.

It may be argued that legal and natural persons are not comparable or that a difference in treatment is justified, because they *"each have their own tax laws, the provisions of which [...] differ widely when it comes to the determination of the basis of assessment."*[2025] However, the determination of the basis of assessment for dividends might be very similar for sole proprietors and corporations. In Austria, for example, the determination of a corporation's taxable income basically follows the rules for individuals.[2026] With regard to the determination of the basis of assessment for dividends, there may hence be only minor differences between a sole proprietor and a corporation. But it also has to be kept in mind that *"there is a fundamental factual difference between the two groups inasmuch as only legal persons, subject to corporation tax, have shareholders who share in the company's income and are themselves subject to tax on their earnings."*[2027] This difference could be decisive for the State aid analysis, depending on how economic double taxation is avoided by the respective tax system. A Member State may, for example, decide to collect the tax on corporate profits partly from the company and partly from the shareholders. To this end, income derived by a corporation is initially subject to corporate income tax. If the after-tax profit is subsequently distributed, it is again taxed at the level of the shareholder as a dividend. In order to avoid an excessive tax burden, many Member States have incorporated schedular systems that provide for a reduced tax rate or a diminished tax base in the

2022. Judgment in *Italy/Commission*, 173/73, EU:C:1974:71, at para. 15; Judgment in *Belgium/Commission*, C-75/97, EU:C:1999:311, at para. 33; Judgment in *France/Commission*, C-251/97, EU:C:1999:480, at para. 36; Judgment in *Italy/Commission*, C-310/99, EU:C:2002:143, at para. 51; Judgment in *Banks*, C-390/98, EU:C:2001:456, at para. 33; Judgment in *Adria-Wien Pipeline and Wietersdorfer & Peggauer Zementwerke*, C-143/99, EU:C:2001:598, at para. 42; Judgment in *Spain/Commission*, C-351/98, EU:C:2002:530, at para. 42; Judgment in *GIL Insurance and others*, C-308/01, EU:C:2004:252, at para. 72; Judgment in *Freskot*, C-355/00, EU:C:2003:298, at para. 86; Judgment *Netherlands/Commission*, C-159/01, EU:C:2004:246, at para. 42; Judgment in *Heiser*, C-172/03, EU:C:2005:130, at para. 43; Judgment in *AEM*, C-128/03 and C-129/03, EU:C:2005:224, at para. 39; Judgment in *British Aggregates/Commission*, C-487/06 P, EU:C:2008:757, at para. 129; Judgment in *Paint Graphos and others*, C-78/08 to C-80/08, EU:C:2011:550, at para. 76; Judgment *Commission/Netherlands*, C-279/08 P, EU:C:2011:551, at para. 62; Judgment in *Commission and Spain/Government of Gibraltar and United Kingdom*, C-106/09 P and C-107/09 P, EU:C:2011:732, at para. 146; Judgment in *BNP Paribas and BNL/Commission*, C-452/10 P, EU:C:2012:366, at para. 101; Judgment in *P*, C-6/12, EU:C:2013:525, at para. 22; Judgment in *Commission/MOL*, C-15/14 P, EU:C:2015:362, at para. 61.

2023. Judgment in *Portugal/Commission*, C-88/03, EU:C:2006:511, at para. 81; Judgment in *Paint Graphos and others*, C-78/08 to C-80/08, EU:C:2011:550, at para. 65 and para. 69; Judgment in *P.*, C-6/12, EU:C:2013:525, at para. 22; Judgment in *Ministerio de Defensa and Navantia*, C-522/13, EU:C:2014:2262, at para. 43.

2024. Judgment in *Spain/Commission*, C-501/00, EU:C:2004:438, at para. 122; also see Judgment in *BNP Paribas and BNL/Commission*, C-452/10 P, EU:C:2012:366, at paras 137-138.

2025. Opinion of AG Kokott in *Finanzamt Linz*, C-66/14, EU:C:2015:242, at point 92; also see M. Lang, 27 *ÖStZ* 11 (2014), at pp. 284-285.

2026. See K. Ubelhoer/S. Pfeiffer/E. Huisman/E. Schaffer, *Introduction to Austrian Tax Law* (Facultas, 2014), at p. 47.

2027. Opinion of AG Kokott in *Finanzamt Linz*, C-66/14, EU:C:2015:242, at point 92.

case of dividend income of individuals.[2028] However, corporate profits would still be excessively burdened if an individual holds shares in a corporation that again holds shares in another corporation which earns the profits. Without a participation exemption regime, such profits would be subject to corporate income tax twice. If a Member State can successfully prove that the corporate income tax for corporations and the personal income tax for their individual shareholders complement each other,[2029] it may also argue that the State aid analysis of participation exemption regimes should not only focus on how the individual or corporate shareholder is treated but the overall tax burden on the underlying profits should also be taken into account. Given the different outcomes from an object-oriented point of view, objections to a different tax treatment of profits earned by a company and subsequently distributed either to an individual or a corporate shareholder could thereby be dispelled.

Second, a participation exemption regime might not only be restricted to corporate shareholders, but typically requires certain other conditions to be met as well. In Germany, for example, 95% of all dividends received by a corporation remain effectively tax exempt, unless the receiving company holds less than 10% in the capital of the distributing company.[2030] Since this restriction applies irrespective of whether the profits are distributed by a domestic or a foreign company, it is in general considered to be unproblematic from the perspective of the fundamental freedoms.[2031] However, the German participation exemption regime might still be objectionable under EU law, because it leads to a favourable treatment of corporations that hold a sufficient participation in the capital of another company as compared to minority corporate shareholders. Such a different treatment cannot be justified by the objective of the German legislation of avoiding economic double taxation.[2032] Profit distributions may after all be subject to economic double taxation irrespective of whether they are received by a corporation that holds at least or less than 10% in the capital of the distributing company.[2033] It also seems insufficient to argue that the commercial commitment is all the more intense, the higher the holding in the capital of the distributing company is.[2034] Although this might be true in general, it remains unclear why economic double taxation is acceptable in the case of a less intense commercial

2028. See J. Englisch, 33 *Intertax* 5 (2005), at p. 200; G. Kofler, *Doppelbesteuerungsabkommen und Europäisches Gemeinschaftsrecht* (Linde, 2007), at pp. 938-940.

2029. See C. Staringer, 13 *ÖStZ* 2 (2000), at p. 30.

2030. See T. Hagemann/C. Kahlenberg, Tax Liability on Dividends from Portfolio Investments: Amendments under the Act on the Implementation of the ECJ Decision in Case C-284/09, 53 *Eur. Taxn.* 11 (2013), p. 575 (at pp. 575-578).

2031. See D. Gosch in D. Gosch (ed.), *Körperschaftsteuergesetz*³ (Beck, 2015), at § 8b para 287a.

2032. For a discussion of the objective of the German participation exemption regime see, for example, D. Gosch in D. Gosch (ed.), *Körperschaftsteuergesetz*³ (Beck, 2015), at § 8b para 1; A. Herlinghaus in T. Rödder/A. Herlinghaus/R. Neumann (eds.), *Körperschaftsteuergesetz* (Dr Otto Schmidt, 2015), at § 8b paras 4-6; A. Schnitger in A. Schnitger/O. Fehrenbacher (eds.), KStG (Springer, 2012), at § 8b para. 6.

2033. See M. Desens, 51 *DStR*, Beihefter zu Heft 4 (2013), at p. 14; D. Gosch in D. Gosch (ed.), *Körperschaftsteuergesetz*³ (Beck, 2015), at § 8b para 287b; A. Herlinghaus in T. Rödder/A. Herlinghaus/R. Neumann (eds.), *Körperschaftsteuergesetz* (2015), at § 8b para. 84.

2034. Cf. M.L. Haisch/M. Helios, Steuerpflicht von Streubesitzdividenden in der Direkt-und Fondsanlage, 66 *DB* 14 (2013), p. 724 (at p. 724).

commitment.[2035] Hence, the example of the German participation exemption regime shows that certain conditions of participation exemption regimes might be critical from a State aid law perspective.

Third, participation exemption regimes could generally be perceived as derogating *"from the normal rule according to which profits are liable to tax."*[2036] This reasoning is implicitly based on a comparison between companies receiving tax-exempt dividends from their subsidiaries and companies earning other kind of income which does not benefit from such an exemption. However, it is argued that these situations are not comparable; and even if they were, the different treatment would be justified, because participation exemption regimes aim at avoiding economic double taxation. Since companies that earn other kinds of income are not exposed to such double taxation, a different treatment is considered to be in line with Article 107 TFEU.[2037] Again, however, one may wonder whether the ambit of participation exemption regimes that are intended to grant relief from economic double taxation has to be restricted to situations of *actual* double taxation in order to be proportionate.[2038] If, for example, the distributed profits have never been subject to corporate income tax at the level of the distributing company, there is no need to avoid the non-existent economic double taxation. In a purely domestic situation, this could be the case, for example, if the distributing company benefits from an individual tax exemption, because it pursues charitable objectives. In a cross-border context, on the other hand, economic double taxation may already be avoided by the distributing company's Member State of residence by, for example, granting a deduction for dividend distributions or by refunding the corporate tax underlying the distributed profits.[2039] In addition, the missing necessity to avoid economic double taxation could also result from a deviating classification of the profit distribution. If, for example, a group of companies used a hybrid financial instrument that is treated as debt in the Member State of the financed company and as equity in the Member State of the financing company, the amount paid by the debtor would be deductible as interest in the source state, but would at the same time qualify for the participation exemption regime in the receiving company's Member State of residence.

There might be good reasons to apply a participation exemption regime, although the distributed profits have never been subject to corporate income tax at the level of the distributing company. If the lack of taxation is, for example, due to the distributing

2035. See A. Herlinghaus, Rechtsfragen zur Steuerpflicht von Streubesitzdividenden gem. § 8b Abs. 4 KStG n.F., 95 *FR* 12 (2013), p. 529 (at p. 533); A. Herlinghaus in T. Rödder/A. Herlinghaus/R. Neumann (eds.), *Körperschaftsteuergesetz* (2015), at § 8b para. 84; J. Intemann, Die Neuregelung zur Steuerpflicht von Streubesitzdividenden, 68 *BB* 21 (2013), p. 1239 (at pp. 1239-1240).

2036. R. Szudoczky in I. Richelle/W. Schön/E. Traversa (eds.), *Allocating Taxing Powers Within the European Union* (Springer, 2013), at p. 167.

2037. See R. Szudoczky in I. Richelle/W. Schön/E. Traversa (eds.), *Allocating Taxing Powers Within the European Union* (Springer, 2013), at p. 167.

2038. See R. Szudoczky in I. Richelle/W. Schön/E. Traversa (eds.), *Allocating Taxing Powers Within the European Union* (Springer, 2013), at p. 168.

2039. See J. Englisch, *Dividendenbesteuerung* (Dr Otto Schmidt, 2005), at p. 89; B.J.M. Terra/P.J. Wattel, *European Tax Law*[6] (Kluwer, 2012), at p. 226.

company's charitable status, not granting a tax exemption for distributed profits might undo the objective that is pursued by granting the individual tax exemption to the charitable company in the first place.[2040] Applying the participation exemption regime could thus be justified for the same reasons the tax exemption that is available for charitable companies does not constitute State aid.[2041] By contrast, if economic double taxation is already avoided by the distributing company's Member State of residence, one should also examine whether this Member State's tax system is compatible with Article 107 TFEU. Even if this were the case, it could be argued that the State aid analysis of a Member State's tax system should not depend on what another state's tax system looks like. This would be in line with the ECJ's case law on the fundamental freedoms, according to which another Member State's tax system should not be taken into account, unless there is a direct link between the tax systems of two Member States.[2042] Therefore, if a payment is, for example, considered to be deductible interest by the paying company's Member State of residence and a tax-exempt dividend by the receiving company's Member State of residence, the resultant double non-taxation could be perceived as a disparity, unless the respective domestic rules are linked. Overall, participation exemption regimes that are not explicitly restricted to situations of actual double taxation should hence not hastily be labelled as constituting State aid.

2.4 Double Non-Taxation and the Limits of the State Aid Rules

The ECJ's jurisprudence on the compatibility of tax measures with State aid law is still in its infancy. Similar to the fundamental freedoms, Article 107 TFEU has the potential of putting traditional pillars of the Member State's tax systems into question.[2043] However, the State aid rules may encounter their limits if distortions of competition do not result from the rules of just one tax jurisdiction, but from the co-existence of several separate tax jurisdictions. For the EU primary law evaluation of double non-taxation, it is still unclear where these limits are. The fact that Article 107(1) TFEU only applies if *certain* undertakings or the production of *certain* goods are favoured seems to be the least challenge. Due to the ECJ's previous case law,[2044] this condition of selectivity was partly understood as requiring that taxpayers which are treated more beneficially than others can be regarded, by virtue of the properties which are specific to them, as a

2040. With regard to the Austrian participation exemption regime see, for example, K. Fürnsinn/C. Massoner in M. Lang/A. Rust/J. Schuch/C. Staringer (eds.), *KStG*[2] (Linde, 2016), at § 10 para. 23; S. Kirchmayr in M. Achatz/S. Kirchmayr (eds.), *KStG* (Facultas, 2011), at § 10 para 6; E. Strimitzer/M. Vock in P. Quantschnigg/B. Renner/G. Schellmann/R. Stöger/M. Vock (eds.), *Die Körperschaftsteuer*[27] (LexisNexis, 2015), at § 10 para. 28.

2041. Cf. Judgment in *Paint Graphos and others*, C-78/08 to C-80/08, EU:C:2011:550.

2042. See Chapter 4.1.3.2.4.

2043. Cf. C. HJI Panayi, 32 *Intertax* 6/7 (2004), at p. 306 ("*Art. 87 [...] has the potential to develop into a powerful weapon at the disposal of the Commission; well capable of re-opening the debate for tax harmonization.*").

2044. Judgment in *Commission and Spain/Government of Gibraltar and United Kingdom*, C-106/09 P and C-107/09 P, EU:C:2011:732, at para. 104; also cf. Judgment in *Commission/MOL*, C-15/14 P, EU:C:2015:362, at para. 59.

group of "*certain undertakings or the production of certain goods.*"[2045] This lead to a discussion on whether the fact that there is a cross-border context is already sufficient "*to characterise the recipient undertakings, by virtue of the properties which are specific to them, as a privileged category.*"[2046,2047] However, since the Court's judgment in *World Duty*, this debate seems to be obsolete, because "*a [...] requirement to identify a particular category of undertakings, additional to the analytical method applicable to selectivity in tax matters [...], which essentially involves ascertaining whether the exclusion of certain operators from the benefit of a tax advantage that arises from a measure derogating from an ordinary tax system constitutes discrimination with respect to those operators, cannot be inferred from the Court's case-law.*"[2048]

An issue which could more likely lead to the efficacy of the State aid rules being confined is that the European Commission has to decide whether the aid presumably resulting from double non-taxation has to be recovered.[2049] Such a recovery requires determining "*as accurately as possible from whom the aid is to be recovered.*"[2050] However, the beneficiary of double non-taxation may not always be clearly identifiable. This becomes particularly apparent in the case of hybrid mismatch arrangements.[2051] If, for example, a hybrid financial instrument was treated as debt in the debtor' Member State of residence and as equity in the investor's Member State of residence, the amount paid by the debtor to the investor would be deductible as interest in the source state, but at the same time could be exempted as a dividend at the level of the investor in its residence state. Since such a double tax benefit does typically not

2045. Opinion of AG Kokott in *Finanzamt Linz*, C-66/14, EU:C:2015:242, at points 84-85 and 105; with a different opinion see R. Ismer/S. Piotrowski, 43 *Intertax* 10 (2015), at pp. 562-563.
2046. Judgment in *Commission and Spain/Government of Gibraltar and United Kingdom*, C-106/09 P and C-107/09 P, EU:C:2011:732, at para. 104.
2047. For a view which tends to support selectivity see R. Luja, *EU State Aid Law and National Tax Rulings*, IP/A/TAXE/2015-02, PE 563.453 (October 2015), at p. 11; F.P. Sutter in J. Bauer/E. Burgstaller/K. Haslinger/J. Herdin/I. Hofbauer/M. Lang/H. Loukota/W. Loukota/M. Schilcher/J. Schuch/C. Staringer/F.P. Sutter/U. Zieseritsch (eds.), *Unilaterale Maßnahmen zur Vermeidung der Doppelbesteuerung* (Linde, 2004), at p. 265; F.P. Sutter, 14 *SWI* 1 (2004), at p. 10; R. Szudoczky in I. Richelle/W. Schön/E. Traversa (eds.), *Allocating Taxing Powers Within the European Union* (Springer, 2013), at pp. 173-177; for a view which tends to deny selectivity R. Luja, 44 *Eur. Taxn.* 4 (2004), at p. 234; F. Engelen, 52 *Eur. Taxn.* 5 (2012), at pp. 208-209.
2048. Judgment in *Commission/World Duty Free Group, Banco Santander and Santusa Holding*, C-20/15 P and C-21/15 P, EU:C:2016:981, at paras 71 and 79.
2049. If unnotified measures are considered to be unlawful aid, the European Commission shall, subject to a limitation period of ten years (Article 17[1] State Aid Procedure Regulation), "*decide that the Member State concerned shall take all necessary measures to recover the aid from the beneficiary ('recovery decision')*" (Article 16[1] State Aid Procedure Regulation). The amount to be recovered from the beneficiaries not only includes the value of the unlawful aid that had been granted, but must also include interest (Article 16[2] State Aid Procedure Regulation).
2050. Opinion of AG Van Gerven in *Italy/Commission*, C-303/88, EU:C:1990:352, at p. I-1466.
2051. According to the OECD, such tax planning structures are supposed to exploit "*differences in the tax treatment of instruments, entities or transfers between two or more countries*" and "*often lead to 'double non-taxation' that may not be intended by either country*" (OECD, *Hybrid Mismatch Arrangements: Tax Policy and Compliance Issues* [OECD, 2012], at para. 3).

arise in a purely domestic context,[2052] using a hybrid financial instrument for the purpose of cross-border tax arbitrage leads to double non-taxation.

From a State aid perspective, it can hardly be challenged that the coaction of the deviating tax systems leads to favourable treatment of the cross-border situation as compared to purely domestic situations.[2053] Nevertheless, considered individually, neither the investor nor the debtor in their respective Member State of residence receive an advantage as compared to an investor or a debtor in a purely domestic situation. This does not definitely mean that Article 107(1) TFEU is not applicable. It rather has to be examined whether the investor and the debtor have to be regarded as an economic unit[2054] and thus possibly as a single undertaking for State aid purposes.[2055] This calls for an examination whether the separate entities are legally associated and also have "*other functional, economic and organic links.*"[2056] Even if separate entities cannot be regarded as a single undertaking, it may be argued that, due to the wording of Article 107 TFEU, an advantage can also be attributed to various undertakings. Such an understanding seems to be in line with the ECJ pointing out that there might be more than one beneficiary of an aid.[2057] With regard to double non-taxation resulting from the use of a hybrid financial instrument, for example, both the investor and the debtor could be regarded as the recipients of the aid. However, if the European Commission requires recovery of the aid, such an understanding would not only raise the question of how to attribute the full amount of aid to each individual undertaking. Prior to that, it rather needs to be determined what the economic value of the benefit received actually is.[2058]

Given the involvement of more than one Member State, it is unclear which Member State's tax system should be primarily relied on in order to calculate the

2052. Some scholars also refer to "double dip" in this context (see, for example, S. Bendlinger, *Steueroasen und Offshore-Strukturen* [Linde, 2013], at pp. 230-231; T. Polivanova-Rosenauer, 10 *taxlex* 3 [2014], at p. 108; W. Wiesner, 21 *RWZ* 1 [2011], at p. 4; see also J. Bundgaard, 50 *Eur. Taxn.* 11 [2010], at p. 490, who distinguishes, though, between "*real double-dip structures and deduction/non-inclusion structures*").

2053. R. Szudoczky in I. Richelle/W. Schön/E. Traversa (eds.), *Allocating Taxing Powers Within the European Union* (Springer, 2013), at p. 167: "*Double non-taxation is evidently an advantage for the purposes of Article 107(1) TFEU.*"

2054. Judgment in *Cassa di Risparmio di Firenze and others*, C-222/04, EU:C:2006:8, at para. 110; Judgment in *AceaElectrabel Produzione*, C-480/09 P, EU:C:2010:787, at paras 46-70.

2055. Judgment in *Intermills*, 323/82, EU:C:1984:345, at para. 11; also see European Commission, Commission Notice on the notion of State Aid as referred to in Article 107(1) of the Treaty on the Functioning of the European Union, *OJ* C 262 (19 Jul. 2016), at para. 11.

2056. European Commission, Commission Notice on the notion of State Aid as referred to in Article 107(1) of the Treaty on the Functioning of the European Union, *OJ* C 262 (19 Jul. 2016), at para. 11; also see Judgment in *AceaElectrabel Produzione*, C-480/09 P, EU:C:2010:787, at para. 51 ("*What may reveal that it is possible to exercise functions relating to control, direction and financial support – going beyond the simple placing of capital by an investor – and illustrate the existence of organic and functional links between an entity owning a controlling shareholding in a company and the controlled company itself, is the fact that members of the management committee and the controlling body of that entity are appointed to the equivalent bodies of the controlled company*").

2057. Judgment in *Residex Capital IV*, C-275/10, EU:C:2011:814, at para. 43.

2058. See Opinion of AG Jääskinen in *Commission and Spain/Government of Gibraltar and United Kingdom*, C-106/09 P and C-107/09 P, EU:C:2011:215, at point 160; also see F. Engelen/A. Gunn in A. Rust/C. Micheau (eds.), *State Aid and Tax Law* (Kluwer, 2013), at p. 140; C.

amount of aid which has been granted jointly by the Member States involved. For the same reason, double non-taxation not only raises practical difficulties if it is considered to constitute unlawful aid which has to be recovered but it would also have to be determined which Member State should be obliged to stop applying its tax measure which is jointly responsible for double non-taxation. Given the comparable discussion regarding how to identify the Member State responsible for double taxation, several solutions could be contemplated: First, according to the ECJ, "*in the allocation of fiscal jurisdiction, it [is not] unreasonable for the Member States to base their agreements on international practice and the model convention drawn up by the OECD.*"[2059] Based on this jurisprudence, some scholars point out that "*nothing precludes an interpretation the EC Treaty, so far as possible, in accordance with an OECD model convention.*"[2060] With regard to direct taxes, one might hence be tempted to argue that double non-taxation should always be avoided by the residence state. This would correspond to the OECD's approach with regard to double non-taxation resulting from a different application of double taxation conventions due to a varying evaluation of the facts of the case or a diverging interpretation of the rules contained therein. To avoid such kind of double non-taxation, Article 23 A(4) OECD MC was incorporated into the OECD MC in the course of its amendment in the year 2000.[2061] Thus, "*[t]he provisions of paragraph 1 shall not apply to income derived or capital owned by a resident of a Contracting State where the other Contracting State applies the provisions of this Convention to exempt such income or capital from tax or applies the provisions of paragraph 2 of Article 10 or 11 to such income.*" The residence state may hence not grant an exemption if the other contracting state considers itself to be fully or partially restricted from taxing an item of income or capital by the double taxation convention due to a different interpretation of the double taxation convention or a divergent evaluation of the facts of the case.[2062]

Quigley, *European State Aid Law and Policy, Third Edition* (Hart Publishing, 2015), at p. 590; W. Schön, *Max Planck Institute for Tax Law and Public Finance Working Paper 2015-14* (December 2015), at p. 9.

2059. Judgment in *Gilly*, C-336/96, EU:C:1998:221, at para. 16; also see Judgment in *van Hilten-van der Heijden*, C-513/03, EU:C:2006:131, at para. 48; Judgment in *N.*, C-470/04, EU:C:2006:525, at para. 45; Judgment in *Lidl Belgium*, C-414/06, EU:C:2008:278, at para. 22.

2060. Opinion of AG Mischo in *Lankhorst-Hohorst*, C-324/00, EU:C:2002:545, at point 81; also see V. Heydt, 21 *SWI* 9 (2011), at p. 373; G. Kofler, *Doppelbesteuerungsabkommen und Europäisches Gemeinschaftsrecht* (Linde, 2007), at p. 249; T. Kühbacher, 20 *SWI* 7 (2010), at p. 312; A. Rust in A. Rust (ed.), *Double Taxation Within the European Union* (Kluwer, 2011), at p. 149; also cf. A. Cordewener, *Europäische Grundfreiheiten und nationales Steuerrecht* (Dr Otto Schmidt, 2002), at p. 887; G. Fibbe/A. de Graaf in H.P.A.M. van Arendonk/F. A. Engelen/S. Jansen (eds.), *A Tax Globalist, Essays in Honour of Maarten J. Ellis* (IBFD, 2005), at p. 258 (FN 58); A. Schnitger, *Die Grenzen der Einwirkungen der Grundfreiheiten des EG-Vertrages auf das Ertragsteuerrecht* (IDW, 2006), at p. 266.

2061. Commentary on Article 23 A and 23 B of the OECD MC 2000-2012, at para. 56.1; also see OECD, *The Application of the OECD Model Tax Convention to Partnerships*, Issues in International Taxation No. 6 (OECD, 1999), at para. 113; also cf. H. Krabbe, 9 *IStR* 7 (2000), at pp. 196 et seq.; K. Vogel, 54 *Bull. Intl. Taxn.* 3 (2000), at pp. 98-99.

2062. For an analysis of this provision see C. Marchgraber, 44 *Intertax* 4 [2016], at pp. 312-313; C. Marchgraber in M. Lang/C. Marchgraber/A. Rust/J. Schuch/C. Staringer [eds.], *Niedrigbesteuerung im Unternehmenssteuerrecht* [Linde, 2016], at pp. 108-112.

However, even if one disregards that not all Member States are members of the OECD as well[2063] and that the OECD MC is not legally binding,[2064] it would not be convincing to infer from the existence of Article 23 A(4) OECD MC that there is something like an internationally and generally accepted priority rule which could be relied on for State aid law purposes. Not all Member States' tax treaties contain a provision similar to Article 23 A(4) OECD MC, nor is this provision out of the question from a tax policy perspective. Within the UN Committee of Experts on International Cooperation in Tax Matters,[2065] for example, it is disputed whether Article 23 A(4) OECD MC should be incorporated into the UN MC as well.[2066] The Committee members apparently do not agree on whether "*including paragraph 4 of Article 23A of the OECD Model in the UN Model [is] desirable*" or whether it would be "*detrimental to the interests of the source state.*"[2067] There are good reasons to be sceptical.[2068] By concluding a double taxation convention, both contracting states commit themselves to relinquishing, completely or partially, the imposition of taxes in specific situations. With respect to the residence state, double taxation is typically avoided through either exempting certain income or capital from taxation or granting a tax credit equal to the income or capital tax paid in the other contracting state. The other contracting state's taxing rights are also limited by a double taxation convention. Either the provisions of

2063. Bulgaria, Croatia, Cyprus, Estonia, Latvia, Lithuania, Malta, Romania have not joined the OECD yet.

2064. According to Article 5 OECD Convention, "*the Organisation may: (a) take decisions which, except as otherwise provided, shall be binding on all the Members; (b) make recommendations to Members; and (c) enter into agreements with Members, non-member States and international organisations.*" Whereas decisions lead to an obligation of the Member countries to act in a certain way (see H.J. Hahn/A. Weber, *Die OECD, Organisation für Wirtschaftliche Zusammenarbeit und Entwicklung* [Nomos, 1976], at pp. 95 et seq.; H.J. Hahn, 22 *ZaöRV* [1962] at pp. 78 et seq.), it is for the Member countries to decide upon the implementation of recommendations (see Article 18(b) OECD, Rules of Procedure of the Organisation [2013] [hereinafter OECD Procedural Rules]; also see G. Dahm, Die völkerrechtliche Verbindlichkeit von Empfehlungen internationaler Organisationen, 12 *DÖV* 10 [1959], p. 361 [at pp. 361 et seq.]; A. Elkin in B. Landheer/W.H. Carter [eds.], *European Yearbook*, Vol. IV [Nijhoff, 1958], at pp. 131-133; A.J. Van den Tempel, *Beseitigung der Doppelbesteuerung* [Internationales Steuerdokumentationsbüro, 1967], at pp. 23-24). The OECD MC is a recommendation of the OECD Council. According to Article 18(b) OECD Procedural Rules, it "*shall be submitted to the Members for consideration in order that they may, if they consider it opportune, provide for their implementation.*" The Member countries are hence not legally obliged to adopt the provisions of the OECD MC.

2065. On the function of this group of experts see V. Daurer, *Tax Treaties and Developing Countries* (Kluwer, 2013), at pp. 58-62; M. Lennard, The Purpose and Current Status of the United Nations Tax Work, 13 *Asia-Pacific Tax Bull.* 1 (2008), p. 23 (at pp. 24-25).

2066. In 2011 (see Inclusion of Article 23A (4) of the OECD Model in Article 23A of the UN Model, E/C.18/2011/CRP.2/Add.3; Report on the seventh session of the Committee of Experts on International Cooperation in Tax Matters, E/2011/45-E/C.18/2011/6, at MN 63-65), it was decided to abstain from adopting this provision, but to provide, in the Commentary on Article 23 UN MC, for the option to include a provision which is similar to Article 23 A(4) OECD MC but adapted to accommodate the differences of the UN MC. See Commentary on Article 23 of the UN MC 2011, at para. 19.

2067. Inclusion of Article 23A (4) of the OECD Model in Article 23A of the UN Model, E/C.18/2011/CRP.2/Add.3, at MN 23; Comments on Article 23A(4) of OECD Model, E/C.18/2014/CRP.16, at MN 8-9.

2068. See C. Marchgraber, 44 *Intertax* 4 (2016), at pp. 313-314.

a double taxation convention mandate that this state's tax must not exceed a certain rate or its taxing right is even entirely removed, i.e., the income or capital may only be taxed in the residence state. However, if both contracting states abstain from taxing in certain situations in order to avoid additional tax burdens resulting from the interaction of different states' tax systems,[2069] it is by no means obvious which of the two contracting states should be entitled to recapture its taxing right if a conflict of interpretation leads to the result that both contracting states consider themselves to be restricted from taxation.[2070] Article 23 A(4) OECD MC stipulates that, in such a case, the residence state is exclusively entitled to fill up the tax vacuum created by the conflict of interpretation. Another equally convincing approach would be to solely authorize the other contracting state to avoid double non-taxation by refraining from granting the benefits of the double taxation convention.[2071] Ultimately, however, both alternatives create an imbalance insofar as only one of the contracting states is entitled to avoid double non-taxation although both contracting states have equally committed themselves to relinquishing, completely or partially, the imposition of taxes in specific situations by concluding the double taxation convention in the first place.

Not only is it hence unconvincing to infer from Article 23 A(4) OECD MC that double non-taxation should, as a matter of principle, always be avoided by the residence state. Such an approach would rather also be incomprehensible. In a triangular situation, for example, there might not be a single residence state. If, for example, a hybrid financial instrument leads to a payment to a dual-resident company, both the Member State in which the company has its seat and the Member State in which the company's place of effective management is located can be regarded as the residence state.[2072] Moreover, double non-taxation is a phenomenon which may also occur in the area of indirect taxes, such as VAT,[2073] which do not necessarily rely on the concepts of residence and source. Simply obliging the Member State of residence to avoid double non-taxation would thus be an inept solution.

Second, it could be considered to analogously apply provisions of secondary EU law which aim at avoiding double non-taxation. According to Article 4(1)

2069. See Commentary on the Introduction to the OECD MC 1963-2014, at para. 1 at seq.

2070. The most balanced solution to solve conflicts of interpretation would probably be to initiate a mutual agreement procedure followed by a binding arbitration procedure. Double taxation as well as double non-taxation would thereby be avoided in the same way, whereas both Article 23 A(4) OECD MC and the proposed alternative would automatically avoid double non-taxation, but would not solve conflicts of interpretation which lead to double taxation.

2071. Whether it is up to the residence state or the other contracting state to recapture its taxing right could even be made dependent on the item of income or capital concerned.

2072. Cf. C. Marchgraber, 70 *Bull. Intl. Taxn.* 3 (2016), at p. 127.

2073. See G. Bizioli in M. Lang/P. Melz/E. Kristoffersson (ed.), T. Ecker (ass. ed.), *Value Added Tax and Direct Taxation* (IBFD, 2009), at pp. 403-407; T. Ecker, *A VAT/GST Model Convention* (IBFD, 2013), at pp. 27-47; J. Englisch, *Wettbewerbsgleichheit im grenzüberschreitenden Handel* (Mohr Siebeck, 2008), at pp. 763-769; N. Eriksen/K. Haydl in M. Lang/P. Melz/E. Kristoffersson (ed.), T. Ecker (ass. ed.), *Value Added Tax and Direct Taxation* (IBFD, 2009), at p. 1153; R. Millar in M. Lang/P. Melz/E. Kristoffersson (ed.), T. Ecker (ass. ed.), *Value Added Tax and Direct Taxation* (IBFD, 2009), at pp. 418-436; P. Rendahl in M. Lang/P. Melz/E. Kristoffersson (ed.), T. Ecker (ass. ed.), *Value Added Tax and Direct Taxation* (IBFD, 2009), at p. 1126; A.A. Verstraeten in M. Lang/P. Melz/E. Kristoffersson (ed.), T. Ecker (ass. ed.), *Value Added Tax and Direct Taxation* (IBFD, 2009), at p. 376.

Parent-Subsidiary Directive, for example, Member States are obliged to "*tax [distributed] profits to the extent that such profits are deductible by the subsidiary.*" However, this obligation to tax only applies within the ambit of the Parent-Subsidiary Directive.[2074] Hybrid financial instruments would thus still lead to double non-taxation if some Member States refrained from extending this predetermined rule to other situations which are not covered by the Parent-Subsidiary Directive. Even if an analogous application of Article 4(1) Parent-Subsidiary were possible – which is by no means obvious –,[2075] such an approach would only be of very limited help to overcome double non-taxation within the EU. After all, there are only a few secondary EU law provisions that deal with double non-taxation.

Third, in the literature, it is contemplated to identify the Member State responsible for juridical double taxation by examining whether a Member State's tax system is internally consistent.[2076] To this end, it has to be assumed "*that all member states apply tax law identical to the defendant member state's*"[2077] or, in other words, to hypothetically apply "*the challenged state's law in both a source and a resident capacity.*"[2078] Only if double taxation disappeared in this intellectual pastime would the respective Member State's tax system be internally consistent. With regard to double non-taxation, it could also be checked whether cross-border situations would still suffer a lower tax burden than comparable domestic situations if the respective Member State's tax system was adopted by all other Member States as well. However, even if the ECJ applied such an "internal consistency test," it would not offer a comprehensive solution to the phenomenon of double non-taxation. On the one hand, this test only "*provides a reliable way to rule out the possibility that a disparity caused a tax disadvantage.*"[2079] It is hence of no help if the tax systems of all Member States involved are internally consistent. On the other hand, double non-taxation also arises, for example, if two Member States come to different conclusions when applying and interpreting their common double taxation convention or if two Member States rely on

2074. But see G. van Gelder/B. Niels, 16 *Derivatives & Financial Instruments* 5 (2014), at p. 223 ("*It is unclear whether the obligation for Member States to comply with this rule is limited to those situations where the Parent-Subsidiary Directive (2011/96) applies or whether the scope of this rule should be applied more broadly.*").

2075. See Chapter 4.2.2.2.

2076. See G. Kofler/R. Mason, 14 *Colum. J. Eur. L.* 1 (2007), at pp. 83-98; G. Kofler/R. Mason in S. Van Thiel (ed.), *The Internal Market and Direct Taxation: Is the European Court of Justice Taking a New Approach?* (CFE Brochure on European Taxation, 2007), at pp. 205-219; G. Kofler, *Doppelbesteuerungsabkommen und Europäisches Gemeinschaftsrecht* (Linde, 2007), at p. 221-231; R. Mason, 49 *Bost. Coll. L. Rev.* 4 (2008), at pp. 1309-1319; R. Mason/M.S. Knoll, 121 *Yale L. J.* 5 (2011-2012), at pp. 1106-1114; also cf. A. Rust in A. Rust (ed.), *Double Taxation Within the European Union* (Kluwer, 2011), at pp. 153-154; critically W. Schön, 69 *Bull. Intl. Taxn.* 4/5 (2015), at p. 275 (FN 41); W. Schön in W. Schön/C. Heber (eds.), *Grundfragen des Europäischen Steuerrechts* (Springer, 2015), at pp. 117-118 (FN 37); P. Wattel in A. Rust (ed.), *Double Taxation Within the European Union* (Kluwer, 2011), at p. 166.

2077. R. Mason, 49 *Bost. Coll. L. Rev.* 4 (2008), at p. 1309; critically W. Haslehner, 50 *Common Market L. Rev.* 3 (2013), at pp. 741-742.

2078. G. Kofler/R. Mason, 14 *Colum. J. Eur. L.* 1 (2007), at p. 91; G. Kofler/R. Mason in S. Van Thiel (ed.), *The Internal Market and Direct Taxation: Is the European Court of Justice Taking a New Approach?* (CFE Brochure on European Taxation, 2007), at p. 214 (at FN 214).

2079. R. Mason, 49 *Bost. Coll. L. Rev.* 4 (2008), at p. 1282.

different arm's length prices when applying their, in other respects superimposable, transfer pricing rules. In such cases, the "internal consistency test" would be improper to identify the Member State that should be primarily obliged to do away double non-taxation.

Fourth, if two Member States applied the same rules, but come to different conclusions due to a diverging interpretation,[2080] it is theoretically possible to blame one of them for having caused double non-taxation by figuring out which of the two interpretations is correct and which one is wrong.[2081] If – and insofar as – an advantage that arises from a Member State's misinterpreting the law constituted State aid,[2082] the resultant double non-taxation should also be imputable to this Member State. However, the ECJ has "*no jurisdiction [...] to rule on the interpretation of provisions other than those of Community law.*"[2083] Only by relying on Article 273 TFEU, may Member States voluntarily decide to grant the ECJ jurisdiction in any dispute regarding the interpretation of a bilateral double taxation convention.[2084] Apart from that, "*the interpretation of national rules is a matter for the national courts and not the Court of Justice.*"[2085] If a diverging interpretation of the same rule results from a different jurisprudence of the involved Member States' Supreme Courts, it is hence not possible for the ECJ to subscribe to the decision of either court.

Overall, it thus becomes apparent that the attempt to apply Article 107 TFEU to double non-taxation not only raises practical questions of how and from whom to recover tax advantages linked therewith. Instead, one also has to rise to the same challenge that has prompted the ECJ to consider juridical double taxation as a problem

2080. Such a situation could occur, for example, if two Member States refrain from levying taxes according to their domestic tax laws due to a different interpretation and application of their common double taxation convention.

2081. Cf. See G. Kofler, *Doppelbesteuerungsabkommen und Europäisches Gemeinschaftsrecht* (Linde, 2007), at pp. 257 and 262-263.

2082. See C. Quigley, *European State Aid Law and Policy, Third Edition* (Hart Publishing, 2015), at pp. 106-107; also cf. Cf. M. Lang, 60 *British Tax Rev.* 3 (2015), at p. 395; M. Lang, 24 *IStR* 11 (2015), at p. 371; R. Luja, *EU State Aid Law and National Tax Rulings*, IP/A/TAXE/2015-02, PE 563.453 (October 2015), at p. 15.

2083. Judgment in *AMID*, C-141/99, EU:C:2000:696, at para. 18; also cf. Order in *Generalstaatsanwaltschaft and others/Hartmann*, C-162/98, EU:C:1998:539, at paras 8-12; Opinion of AG Kokott in *Bouanich*, C-265/04, EU:C:2005:479, at point 53 (FN 47).

2084. See Chapter 4.1.3.1.1.

2085. Judgment in *Vanacker and Lesage*, C-37/92, EU:C:1993:836, at para. 7; Judgment in *Wilson*, C-506/04, EU:C:206:587, at para. 34; with regard to State aid see especially Judgment in *Unión General de Trabajadores de la Rioja*, C-428/06 to C-434/06, EU:C:2008:488, at para. 144; Judgment in *Iglesias Gutiérrez*, C-352/14 and C-353/14, EU:C:2015:691, at para. 21; also see Judgment in *Placanica*, C-338/04, EU:C:2007:133, at para. 36; Judgment in *Gerdin*, C-448/08, EU:C:2008:616, at para. 54; Judgment in *Liga Portuguesa de Futebol Profissional and Bwin International*, C-42/07, EU:C:2009:519, at para. 37; Judgment in *Sjöberg*, C-447/08, EU:C:2010:415, at para. 54; Judgment in *Varzim Sol*, C-25/11, EU:C:2012:94, at para. 27; Judgment in *Almos Agrárkülkereskedelmi*, C-337/13, EU:C:2014:328, at para. 18; also see Judgment in *Dickinger and Ömer*, C-347/09, EU:C:2011:582, at para. 51; Judgment in *Pfleger and others*, C-390/12, EU:C:2014:281, at para. 47; Judgment in *Berlington Hungary and others*, C-98/14, EU:C:2015:386, at para. 57 ("*The identification of the objectives in fact pursued by the national legislation is, in the context of a case referred to the Court under Article 267 TFEU, within the jurisdiction of the referring court.*").

that cannot be solved by means of the fundamental freedoms.[2086] Given the case law on the fundamental freedoms, it seems reasonable to expect the Court to follow a similar reasoning towards the prevention of double non-taxation: Due to the lack of general criteria to determine which Member State is primarily required to counteract double non-taxation, it is a problem that cannot be generally solved by means of the State aid rules.[2087] Double non-taxation may only be collaterally avoided if the jointly responsible rules of the involved Member States' tax systems themselves constitute State aid.[2088] Apart from that, however, it is for the Member States, albeit not legally obliged, to take appropriate measures to avoid double non-taxation.

2086. See Chapter 4.1.3.1.1.

2087. This also seems to be the view of the European Commission. See Commission Decision of 8 Jul. 2009 on the groepsrentebox scheme which the Netherlands is planning to implement (C 4/07 (ex N 465/06)), *OJ* L 288 (4 Nov. 2009), at p. 38, paras 115-117: "*[A]ny advantage resulting from an international context owing to a low taxation rate in the Netherlands which is not mirrored by a low rate of deduction in the Netherlands but instead corresponds to a normal deduction rate abroad, is not imputable to the Netherlands. It should also be underlined that the advantage resulting from deduction at the normal rate abroad will not be financed through Dutch resources, and, in the country concerned, the deduction at the normal rate will stem only from the application of the normal tax system (and not from a specific measure departing from it). As a consequence, the Commission considers that any advantages at the level of a multinational group that would result from a cross-border situation, as described in the opening decision, are the result of tax disparities between different tax jurisdictions and should therefore be excluded from the scope of the State aid assessment.*"

2088. See Chapter 4.2.3.1.

CHAPTER 5
Concluding and Summarizing Remarks

During the past few years, the term double non-taxation has become more and more popular,[2089] especially since the initiation of the BEPS project.[2090] Despite its increasing

2089. See, for example, L. De Broe, 23 *EC Tax Rev.* 6 (2014), at pp. 310 et seq.; M. Helminen, 53 *Eur. Taxn.* 7 (2013), at pp. 306 et seq.; C. Kahlenberg, 43 *Intertax* 3 (2015), at pp. 218 et seq.; C. Marchgraber, 23 *EC Tax Rev.* 5 (2014), at pp. 293 et seq.; P. Rossi-Maccanico, 75 *Tax Notes Intl.* 10 (8 Sep. 2014), at pp. 862-867; D.S. Smit, 25 *EC Tax Rev.* 2 (2016), at pp. 109-112; A. Ting, 59 *British Tax Rev.* 1 (2014), at pp. 40 et seq.; A. Van de Vijver, 24 *EC Tax Rev.* 5 (2015), at pp. 240 et seq.; also see I. Jankowiak, *Doppelte Nichtbesteuerung im Internationalen Steuerrecht* (C.H. Beck, 2009); M. Lang, 25 *SWI* 5 (2015), at pp. 198 et seq., who even uses the term "triple non-taxation"; A. Wiesemann, *Entstehung und Vermeidung systembedingter doppelter Nicht- und Minderbesteuerung in Outbound-Konstellationen* (Nomos, 2014).

2090. See OECD, *Addressing Base Erosion and Profit Shifting* (OECD, 2013), at p. 34 ("*The interaction of domestic tax systems sometimes leads to an overlap, which means that an item of income can be taxed by more than one jurisdiction thus resulting in double taxation. The interaction can also leave gaps, which result in an item of income not being taxed anywhere thus resulting in so called 'double non-taxation'.*"); OECD, *Action Plan on Base Erosion and Profit Shifting* (OECD, 2013), at p. 10 ("*BEPS relates chiefly to instances where the interaction of different tax rules leads to double non-taxation or less than single taxation.*"); OECD, *OECD/G20 Base Erosion and Profit Shifting Project, Explanatory Statement, 2014 Deliverables* (OECD, 2014), at p. 3 ("*Beyond securing revenues by realigning taxation with economic activities and value creation, the OECD/G20 BEPS Project aims to create a single set of consensus-based international tax rules to address BEPS, and hence to protect tax bases while offering increased certainty and predictability to taxpayers. A key focus of this work is to eliminate double non-taxation.*"); OECD, *OECD/G20 Base Erosion and Profit Shifting Project, Explanatory Statement, 2015 Final Reports* (OECD, 2014), at para. 3 ("*BEPS can result in double non-taxation but addressing BEPS should not result in double taxation.*"); OECD, *OECD/G20 Base Erosion and Profit Shifting Project, Preventing the Granting of Treaty Benefits in Inappropriate Circumstances, Action 6: 2015 Final Report* (OECD, 2015), at p. 10, p. 13 and p. 91 ("*tax treaties are not intended to be used to generate double non-taxation*"); with regard to the European Commission's use of this term see Staff working paper, The internal market: factual examples of double non-taxation cases, Consultation document, TAXUD D1 D(2012) (29 Feb. 2012); Summary report of the responses received on the public consultation on factual examples and possible ways to tackle double non-taxation cases, TAXUD D1 D(2012) (5 Jul. 2012); Commission Recommendation of 6. 12. 2012 on aggressive tax planning, C(2012) 8806 final (6 Dec. 2012), at pp. 2 and 3; Communication from the Commission to the European Parliament and the Council, A Fair and Efficient Corporate Tax System in the

prominence, hardly any attempts have been made to summarize the content of this term in a memorable definition.[2091] Typically, certain tax planning structures are put forward as examples of situations which are considered to remain double non-taxed. Although this is a practical approach in order to get an idea of what double non-taxation could be, it has not yet led to an internationally accepted understanding of this phenomenon. From an EU law perspective, this is not too surprising. Neither the European Treaties nor any provision of secondary EU law explicitly uses this term. De jure, it is hence inexistent. This should not belie the fact that double non-taxation is nevertheless considered to be a legally relevant phenomenon – just as double taxation. Partly, it is assumed that both double taxation and double non-taxation are *"incompatible with the internal market."*[2092] However, it remains unclear what the underlying problem actually ought to be.

With regard to double taxation, it is argued that the imposition of comparable taxes in two (or more) Member States on the same business activity is a severe obstacle for the free movement requirement of the internal market concept.[2093] However, as every form of taxation somehow hinders economic activities,[2094] it could even be argued that the mere fact that a tax is levied in a cross-border situation would be liable

---

European Union: 5 Key Areas for Action, COM(2015) 302 final (17 Jun. 2015), at p. 9; Commission Recommendation of 28. 1. 2016 on the implementation of measures against tax treaty abuse, COM(2016) 271 final (28 Jan. 2016), at p. 2; M. Vestager in European Commission Press Release, *State aid: Commission opens formal investigation into Luxembourg's tax treatment of McDonald's*, IP/15/6221 (3 Dec. 2015), at p. 1; European Commission Press Release, *State Aid: Commission Concludes Belgian "Excess Profit" Tax Scheme Illegal; Around € 700 Million to be Recovered from 35 Multinational Companies*, IP/16/42 (11 Jan. 2016), at p. 2.

2091. See H. Hahn, 12 *IStR* 13 (2003), at pp. 446-448; I. Jankowiak, *Doppelte Nichtbesteuerung im Internationalen Steuerrecht* (C.H. Beck, 2009), at pp. 32-33; M. Schilcher, *Subject-to-tax-Klauseln in der österreichischen Abkommenspraxis* (Linde 2004), at p. 17; J. Rogers-Glabush, *IBFD International Tax Glossary*[7] (IBFD, 2015), at p. 157 (*"A term used to describe the situation that results when income is not taxed either in the state of source or in the state of the recipient's residence."*).

2092. Opinion of the Economic and Social Committee on Taxation in the European Union, Report on the development of tax systems (SEC[96] 487 final and COM[96] 546 final), *OJ* C 296 (29 Sep. 1997), at p. 43; also see Taxation in the European Union, SEC(96) 487 final (20 Mar. 1996), at p. 13 ("*[t]he Single Market is clearly not compatible with either double taxation of the same taxable base or no taxation at all*"); Commission Recommendation of 6 Dec. 2012 on aggressive tax planning, C(2012) 8806 final (6 Dec. 2012), at p. 2 ("*[t]he Single Market is clearly not compatible with either double taxation [...] or no taxation at all*").

2093. Answer given by Mr Bolkestein on behalf of the Commission in order to answer the written question E-2287/99 by Karin Riis-Jørgensen (ELDR) to the Commission regarding "Right to freedom of movement and Danish tax rules," *OJ* C 225 E (8 Aug. 2000), p. 87 (at p. 88 "*the [...] Member States are bound by the EC Treaty principle of free movement within the Community to avoid and eliminate double taxation*"); for further references see G. Kofler, *Doppelbesteuerungsabkommen und Europäisches Gemeinschaftsrecht* (Linde, 2007), at pp. 160-162.

2094. See B.J.M. Terra/P.J. Wattel, *European Tax Law*[6] (Kluwer, 2012), at p. 84.

to make the exercise of the fundamental freedoms less attractive.[2095,2096] Therefore, it is not sufficient that double taxation is inconsistent with the idea of free movement in order to come to the conclusion that it violates EU law. Similarly, it has not yet been explained why it should be incompatible with EU law if a certain item of income, a transaction or an activity remains untaxed. However, taking into account the various examples which are typically used to illustrate situations of double taxation and double non-taxation, it becomes apparent that they share a common characteristic: in almost all cases, the cross-border situation sustains a higher (double taxation) or a lesser (double non-taxation) tax burden than the comparable domestic situation. If this is considered to be problematic, it is reasonable to perceive double taxation and double non-taxation as situational and relative phenomena. Whether a cross-border situation is subject to double taxation or double non-taxation thus depends on the tax burden the respective comparable domestic situation would have to face in the individual Member States which are involved.[2097]

While double taxation is considered to be a problem that has been known and dealt with in the literature and by the ECJ for quite some time,[2098] double non-taxation seems to be a very recent phenomenon. In fact, however, it is far from new that the interaction of the diverse domestic tax systems, including rules adopted in accordance with international standards to relieve double taxation, can be exploited by taxpayers in order to significantly reduce their tax burden.[2099] For quite some time, this has raised concerns from an EU tax policy perspective.[2100] In fact, it has been emphasized repeatedly that it is not in line with the internal market concept that certain income

2095. See, for example, A. Cordewener, *Europäische Grundfreiheiten und nationales Steuerrecht* (Dr Otto Schmidt, 2002), at p. 289; J. Englisch, 33 *Intertax* 8/9 (2005), at p. 316; P. Farmer/R. Lyal, *EC Tax Law* (Clarendon Press, 1994), at p. 328; G. Kofler, *Doppelbesteuerungsabkommen und Europäisches Gemeinschaftsrecht* (Linde, 2007), at p. 122; E. Reimer in H. Schaumburg/J. Englisch (eds.), *Europäisches Steuerrecht* (2015), at MN 7.191; B.J.M. Terra/P.J. Wattel, *European Tax Law*[6] (Kluwer, 2012), at pp. 56 and 84; also see Opinion of AG Kokott in *X*, C-686/13, EU:C:2015:31, at point 40.

2096. This seems to be the position taken by the ECJ in the *Sea-Land Service and Nedlloyd Lijnen* case, where it was held that "*the VTS system at issue in the main proceedings, in that it requires the payment of a tariff by sea-going vessels longer than 41 metres, is liable to impede or render less attractive the provision of those services and therefore constitutes a restriction on their free circulation*" (Judgment in *Sea-Land Service and Nedlloyd Lijnen*, C-430/99 and C-431/99, EU:C:2002:364). Cf. K. Banks, 33 *Eur. L. Rev.* 4 (2008), at p. 495; B.J.M. Terra/P.J. Wattel, *European Tax Law*[6] (Kluwer, 2012), at pp. 87-89.

2097. See Chapter 1.

2098. See Chapter 2.1.2. and Chapter 4.1.

2099. See, for example, J.F. Kennedy, Special Message to the Congress on Taxation (20 Apr. 1961) ("*Recently more and more enterprises organized abroad by American firms have arranged their corporate structures – aided by artificial arrangements between parent and subsidiary regarding intercompany pricing, the transfer of patent licensing rights, the shifting of management fees, and similar practices which maximize the accumulation of profits in the tax haven – so as to exploit the multiplicity of foreign tax systems and international agreements in order to reduce sharply or eliminate completely their tax liabilities both at home and abroad.*"); also cf. J. Scott Wilkie, 62 *Canadian Tax J.* 2 (2014), at p. 458 ("*The catchy BEPS acronym may be unique, but the undercurrents of base erosion and profit shifting have been present, for those who would notice, for quite some time.*").

2100. See Chapter 2.

remains untaxed accidentally.[2101] Still, it was not until the beginning of the global financial crisis in 2007 that states realized that "*too little attention has been paid to the problems of double non-taxation.*"[2102] This was not only due to the fact that the ensuing economic slowdown put enormous pressure on countries' budgets. Rather, the media as well as non-governmental organizations have also started to pay increasing attention to the tax planning schemes used by multinational corporations.[2103] Due to the

2101. Communication from the Commission to the Council, "Making the Most of the Internal Market": Strategic Programme, COM(93) 632 final (22 Dec. 1993), at p. 35; Taxation in the European Union, Report on the developments of tax systems, COM(96) 546 final (22 Oct. 1996), at p. 3; Taxation in the European Union, SEC(96) 487 final (20 Mar. 1996), at p. 6; Commission Staff Working Paper, The 1996 Single Market Review, SEC(96) 2378 (16 Dec. 1996), at p. 50 and at p. 54; Tax co-ordination in the European Union, Working Paper, Economic Affairs Series, ECON 125 EN (European Parliament, 2000), at p. 22; Communication from the Commission to the Council, the European Parliament and the Economic and Social Committee, Tax Policy in the European Union - Priorities for the years ahead, COM(2001) 260 final (23 May 2001), *OJ* C 284 (10 Oct. 2001), at pp. 24-25; Communication from the Commission to the Council, the European Parliament and the Economic and Social Committee, Co-ordinating Member States' direct tax systems in the Internal Market, COM(2006) 823 final (19 Dec. 2006), at p. 4 and at p. 6; Communication from the Commission to the Council, the European Parliament and the Economic and Social Committee, The application of anti-abuse measures in the area of direct taxation - within the EU and in relation to third countries, COM(2007) 785 final (10 Dec. 2007), at p. 6; see also Opinion of the European Economic and Social Committee on the Impact of the territoriality of tax law on industrial change (2008/C 120/14), *OJ* C 120 (16 May 2008), at p. 51; Annex Growth-Friendly Tax Policies in Member States and better Tax Coordination in the EU to the Communication from the Commission to the Council, the European Parliament, the Economic and Social Committee and the Committee of Regions, Annual Growth Survey 2012, COM(2011) 815 final, Vol. 5/5 - Annex IV (23 Nov. 2011), at pp. 9-11; Staff working paper, The internal market: factual examples of double non-taxation cases, Consultation document, TAXUD D1 D(2012) (29 Feb. 2012), at p. 4; Summary report of the responses received on the public consultation on factual examples and possible ways to tackle double non-taxation cases, TAXUD D1 D(2012) (5 Jul. 2012), at p. 2.
2102. H.J. Ault, 70 *Tax Notes Intl.* 12 (2013), at p. 1199.
2103. See, for example, B. Barrow, Amazon Faces Probes After "not paying a penny in company tax in Britain for two years," *The Daily Mail* (5 Apr. 2012); T. Bergin, Special Report: How Starbucks Avoids UK taxes, *Reuters* (15 Oct. 2012); T. Bergin, Fast Food, Tax Lite, *Reuters* (15 Oct. 2012); P. Campbell, Facebook's UK Tax Bill was Less than It Pays Its Average Worker: Company Paid Just £238,000 to the Taxman in 2011 Despite UK Revenue Being £175 Million, *The Daily Mail* (10 Oct. 2012); C. Duhigg/D. Kocieniewski, How Apples Sidesteps Billions in Taxes, *The New York Times* (28 Apr. 2012); J. Drucker, Google 2.4% Rate Shows How $60 Billion Is Lost to Tax Loopholes, *Bloomberg* (21 Oct. 2010); J. Drucker, Dodging Repatriation Tax Lets U.S. Companies Bring Home Cash, *Bloomberg* (29 Dec. 2010); J. Drucker, Google Revenues Sheltered in No-Tax Bermuda Soar to $10 Billion, *Bloomberg* (10 Dec. 2012); D. Egan, Does a Company's Responsibility to Society Start with Paying Its Taxes?, *The Guardian* (9 Sep. 2011); S. Pfeifer, He Put a Dent in Tax Evasion, *Los Angeles Times* (26 Oct. 2009); R. Sutherland, Amazon, Google, and the Sordid Reality of Tax Avoidance, *The Daily Mail* (6 Apr. 2012); R. Sutherland, Apple "made £6bn" in UK... But Paid Only £10m in Tax, *The Daily Mail* (8 Apr. 2012); M. Warman, Google Pays Just £6m UK Tax, *The Telegraph* (8 Aug. 2012); R. Waters, Microsoft's Foreign Tax Planning under Scrutiny, *Financial Times* (7 Jun. 2011). See also David Kocieniewski's series called "But Nobody Pays That" in *The New York Times*, for which he was awarded a Pulitzer Price for explanatory journalism in 2013; similar series are "Tax Gap" in *The Guardian* and "The Great Corporate Tax Dodge" in *Bloomberg*.

financial and public pressure, political steps have become inevitable.[2104,2105] However, double non-taxation still is a rather abstract and widely unknown phenomenon. A proper response hence first requires gathering information. To this end, the OECD[2106] and the European Commission[2107] have started corresponding initiatives. Based on the collected material, both institutions have presented strategies to curtail double non-taxation.[2108,2109] The OECD is thereby taking the lead, while the European Commission

2104. Cf. H. Ault, 70 *Tax Notes Intl.* 12 (2013), at p. 1196; Y. Brauner, 6 *World Tax J.* 1 (2014), at p. 10; Y.Brauner, 16 *Florida Tax Rev.* 2 (2014), at pp. 57-58; P. Essers, 68 *Bull. Intl. Taxn.* 2 (2014), at pp. 55-56; A. de Graaf/P. de Haan/M. de Wilde, 42 *Intertax* 5 (2014), at pp. 312-314; M. Herksen, 14 *Transfer Pricing Intl. J.* 8 (2013), at p. 4; M. Plowgian, 65 *The Tax Executive* 4 (2013), at p. 255.

2105. See G20 Leaders Declaration (19 Jun. 2012), at para 48 ("*We reiterate the need to prevent base erosion and profit shifting and we will follow with attention the ongoing work of the OECD in this area.*"); G20 Final Communiqué, Meeting of Finance Ministers and Central Bank Governors (4-5 Nov. 2012), at para. 21 ("*We also welcome the work that the OECD is undertaking into the problem of base erosion and profit shifting and look forward to a report about progress of the work at our next meeting.*"); G8 Communiqué (18 Jun. 2013), at p. 1 and paras 23-29; see also G8 Lough Erne Declaration (18 Jun. 2013).

2106. In 2010, the OECD created the Aggressive Tax Planning Steering Group in order to "*strengthen international co-operation on countering aggressive tax planning amongst tax administrations and tax policy makers so as to improve the design and implementation of tax laws in an international context*" (OECD, *Directory of Bodies* [OECD, 2012], at p. 276). Based, *inter alia*, on the work of this steering group, the OECD published several reports dealing with various aspects of aggressive tax planning. See OECD, *Addressing Tax Risks Involving Bank Losses* (OECD, 2010); OECD, *Corporate Loss Utilisation Through Aggressive Tax Planning* (OECD, 2011); OECD, *Tackling Aggressive Tax Planning Through Improved Transparency and Disclosure* (OECD, 2011); OECD, *Hybrid Mismatch Arrangements: Tax Policy and Compliance Issues* (OECD, 2012); OECD, *Aggressive Tax Planning Based on After-Tax Hedging* (OECD, 2013).

2107. Staff working paper, The Internal Market: Factual Examples of Double Non-taxation Cases, Consultation document, TAXUD D1 D(2012) (29 Feb. 2012).

2108. With regard to the OECD particularly see OECD, *Addressing Base Erosion and Profit Shifting* (OECD, 2013); OECD, *Action Plan on Base Erosion and Profit Shifting* (OECD, 2013).

2109. With regard to the EU see Communication from the Commission to the European Parliament and the Council on concrete ways to reinforce the fight against tax fraud and tax evasion, including in relation to third countries, COM(2012) 351 final (27 Jun. 2012); Commission Recommendation regarding measures intended to encourage third countries to apply minimum standards of good governance in tax matters, C(2012) 8805 final (6 Dec. 2012); Commission recommendation on aggressive tax planning, C(2012) 8806 final (6 Dec. 2012); Commission Decision on setting up a Commission Expert Group to be known as the Platform for Tax Good Governance, Aggressive Tax Planning and Double Taxation, C(2013) 2236 final (23 Apr. 2013); Commission Decision of 17 Jun. 2015 establishing the Commission Expert Group "Platform for Tax Good Governance, Aggressive Tax Planning and Double Taxation" and replacing Decision C(2013)2236, C(2015) 4095 final (17 Jun. 2015); Communication from the Commission to the European Parliament and the Council, A Fair and Efficient Corporate Tax System in the European Union: 5 Key Areas for Action, COM(2015) 302 final (17 Jun. 2015); Communication from the Commission to the European Parliament and the Council, Anti-Tax Avoidance Package: Next steps towards delivering effective taxation and greater tax transparency in the EU, COM(2016) 23 final (18 Jan. 2016); Commission Recommendation of 28.1.2016 on the implementation of measures against tax treaty abuse, C(2016) 271 final (28 Jan. 2016); Commission Staff Working Document Accompanying the document Communication from the Commission to the European Parliament and the Council – Anti Tax Avoidance Package: Next Steps towards delivering effective taxation and greater tax transparency in the EU, SWD(2016) 6 final (28 Jan. 2016); Study on Structures of Aggressive Tax Planning and Indicators, Taxation Papers, Working Paper n. 61-2015 (European Union, 2016); Council Directive (EU) 2016/1164 of 12 Jul. 2016 laying down rules against tax avoidance practices that directly affect the functioning of the internal market, *OJ* L 193 (19 Jul. 2016), p.

is primarily anxious to ensure "*a coordination [...] of Member States' approach to external base erosion threats*"[2110] in order to avoid that "*the unilateral and divergent implementation of BEPS by each Member State [...] fragment[s] the Single Market by creating national policy clashes, distortions and tax obstacles for businesses in the EU*" and "*create[s] new loopholes and mismatches that could be exploited by companies seeking to avoid taxation.*"[2111] Partly, however, the proposals and recommendations of the European Commission deviate from or even transcend the results prepared by the OECD.[2112] At first glance, one could assume that these deviations are due to the fact that the legislative changes envisaged by the OECD can only be successfully implemented by Member States if they meet the requirements of EU law.[2113] After all, it is emphasized that "*[c]ertain factors which are unique to the EU need to be taken into account in developing effective solutions. These include the unique elements of the Single Market and the single currency area. The Treaties require that the fundamental freedoms – including the freedom of establishment – be respected. Reforms must therefore be tailored for the EU context and fix inconsistencies on an EU-wide basis.*"[2114] However, a thorough analysis of whether the OECD's recommendations in the BEPS

1 (at pp. 1-14) as changed by Council Directive (EU) 2017/952 of 29 May 2017 amending Directive (EU) 2016/1164 as regards hybrid mismatches with third countries, OJ L 144 (7 Jun. 2017), p. 1 (at pp. 1-11).

2110. Commission Staff Working Document Accompanying the document Communication from the Commission to the European Parliament and the Council – Anti Tax Avoidance Package: Next Steps towards delivering effective taxation and greater tax transparency in the EU, SWD(2016) 6 final (28 Jan. 2016), at p. 5.

2111. Proposal for a Council Directive laying down rules against tax avoidance practices that directly affect the functioning of the internal market, COM(2016) 26 final (28 Jan. 2016), at p. 3.

2112. See S. Benz/J. Böhmer, Das Anti Tax Avoidance Package (ATA-Paket) der EU-Kommission zur Umsetzung der BEPS-Maßnahmen in der EU, 69 *DB* 6 (2016), p. 307 (at pp. 307-314); S. Eilers/F. Oppel, BEPS erreicht die EU: Das Anti Tax Avoidance Package der EU-Kommission, 25 *IStR* 8 (2016), p. 312 (at pp. 312-319); J. Lüdicke/F. Oppel, Kommissions-Entwurf einer Anti-BEPS-Richtlinie: Grundlegende Änderungen und Verschärfungen des deutschen Rechts, 69 *DB* 10 (2016), p. 549 (at pp. 549-555); G. Rautenstrauch, Richtlinienentwürfe zur Umsetzung des BEPS-Projekts – Die EU-Kommission legt vor, 69 *DB* 6 (2016), p. M5 (at p. M5).

2113. See OECD, *Designing Effective Controlled Foreign Company Rules, Action 3: 2015 Final Report* (OECD, 2015), at p. 10 ("*In particular, this report recognises that the recommendations must be sufficiently adaptable to comply with EU law, and it sets out possible design options that could be implemented by EU Member States.*"); OECD, *Preventing the Granting of Treaty Benefits in Inappropriate Circumstances, Action 6: 2015 Final Report* (OECD, 2015), at pp. 14 ("*some countries may have [...] concerns based on EU law that prevent them from adopting the exact wording of the model provisions that are recommended in this report*"), 19 ("*It is also recognised that the LOB rule will need to be adapted to reflect certain constraints or policy choices concerning other aspects of a bilateral tax treaty between two Contracting States (e.g. constitutional restrictions or concerns based on EU law or policy choices concerning the treatment of collective investment vehicles)*"); also cf. E.C.C.M. Kemmeren, 23 *EC Tax Rev.* 4 (2014), at pp. 190-191; C. HJI Panayi, 70 *Bull. Intl. Taxn.* (2016), at p. 96.

2114. Communication from the Commission to the European Parliament and the Council, A Fair and Efficient Corporate Tax System in the European Union: 5 Key Areas for Action, COM(2015) 302 final (17 Jun. 2015), at p. 6.

project are in line with EU law is missing, although scholars increasingly identify potential conflicts between the recommended anti-BEPS measures and EU law,[2115] especially the fundamental freedoms.[2116]

Since the OECD and the European Commission take the view that general anti-avoidance rules as well as specific and targeted rules denying certain benefits in the case of double non-taxation should be introduced at a domestic and a double tax treaty level, the focus on the fundamental freedoms is not surprising. The BEPS project almost exclusively deals with double non-taxation in an international context. The envisaged rules would thus - at least indirectly - lead to a different treatment of domestic and cross-border situations. Although such a different treatment potentially impairs the establishment and functioning of the internal market, one should not forget that ignoring the phenomenon of double non-taxation and not taking such measures may also be problematic from a legal perspective. After all, according to the OECD, such an outcome "*harms competition, economic efficiency, transparency and fairness.*"[2117] If this is true, double non-taxation conflicts with the EU's economic policy perception of "*an open market economy with free competition, favouring an efficient allocation of resources.*"[2118] In the literature, it is hence also discussed whether anti-BEPS measures could not only be justified, but may even be legally required in order for Member States not to infringe the Treaties' provisions dealing with

2115. See P. Baker, 61 *British Tax Rev.* 3 (2015), at pp. 408-416; P. Benéitez Régli, 56 *Eur. Taxn.* 6 (2016), at pp. 230-245; F. Debelva/D. Scornos/J. Van den Berghen/P. Van Braband, 24 *EC Tax Rev.* 3 (2015), at pp. 132-143; R. de Bour/O. Marres, 43 *Intertax* 1 (2015), at pp. 33-35; E.C.C.M. Kemmeren, 23 *EC Tax Rev.* 4 (2014), at pp. 191-193; S. Douma, 61 *British Tax Rev.* 3 (2015), at pp. 370-377; A.P. Dourado, 43 *Intertax* 1 (2015), at pp. 54-56; J. Englisch, 61 *British Tax Rev.* 3 (2015), at pp. 285-307; M. Helminen, 61 *British Tax Rev.* 3 (2015), at pp. 325-339; C. HJI Panayi, 70 *Bull. Intl. Taxn.* (2016), at pp. 96-112; C. Marchgraber, 54 *Eur. Taxn.* 4 (2014), at pp. 139-141; E. Pinetz in M. Lang/P. Pistone/A. Rust/J. Schuch/C. Staringer (eds.), *Base Erosion and Profit Shifting* (Linde, 2016), at pp. 294-296; P. Pistone/R. Julien/F. Cannas in M. Lang/P. Pistone/A. Rust/J. Schuch/C. Staringer (eds.), *Base Erosion and Profit Shifting* (Linde, 2016), at pp. 166-210; A. Rust, 61 *British Tax Rev.* 3 (2015), at pp. 308-324; A. Rust in W. Schön/C. Heber (eds.), Grundfragen des Europäischen Steuerrechts (Springer, 2015), at pp. 89-106; W. Schön, 61 *British Tax Rev.* 3 (2015), at pp. 420-428; R. Streinz, 61 *British Tax Rev.* 3 (2015), at pp. 429-442; R. Szudoczky/P. Koch in M. Lang/P. Pistone/A. Rust/J. Schuch/C. Staringer (eds.), *Base Erosion and Profit Shifting* (Linde, 2016), at pp. 239-244; E. Traversa, 58 *British Tax Rev.* 5 (2013), at pp. 615-619; A. Zalasiń ski, 61 *British Tax Rev.* 3 (2015), at pp. 444-448.
2116. For an analysis of the ECJ's jurisprudence on the fundamental freedoms see Chapter 3.2.
2117. OECD, *Action Plan on Base Erosion and Profit Shifting* (OECD, 2013), at p. 15.
2118. Article 120 TFEU.

undistorted competition,[2119] especially the State aid rules.[2120] From a more general perspective, one may even ask whether double non-taxation is compatible with Article 107 TFEU at all.

Such an analysis is challenging as double non-taxation typically does not result from the rules of just one tax jurisdiction, but from the co-existence of several separate tax jurisdictions.[2121] This is remarkably evocative of a problem that is subject to long-standing discussions in the literature on whether double taxation is reconcilable with the fundamental freedoms: Which Member State should be made responsible for the tax burden being too high (double taxation) or too low (double non-taxation)? Thus, this suggests examining whether the arguments that speak in favour of and against double taxation being prohibited by the fundamental freedoms[2122] support or rebut the view that Member States which do not avoid situations of double non-taxation may be accused of having granted State aid.[2123] However, given the case law on the fundamental freedoms' impact on double taxation, there are good reasons to expect the ECJ to follow a similar reasoning towards the prevention of double non-taxation as it does with regard to double taxation: Due to the lack of general criteria to determine which Member State is primarily required to counteract double (non-)taxation, it is a problem that cannot be generally solved by means of the fundamental freedoms or the State aid rules.

2119. Cf. W. Haslehner in I. Richelle/W. Schön/E. Traversa (eds.), *State Aid Law and Business Taxation* (Springer, 2016), 133-160; R. Luja, 76 *Tax Notes Intl.* 4 (27 Oct. 2014), at pp. 353-356; R. Luja, EU State Aid Law and National Tax Rulings: In-Depth Analysis for the TAXE Special Committee, IP/A/TAXE/2015-02, PE 563.453 (October 2015), at pp. 14-15; R. Luja, 60 *British Tax Rev.* 3 (2015), at pp. 379-390; P. Rossi-Maccanico, 75 *Tax Notes Intl.* 10 (8 Sep. 2014), at pp. 857-868; P. Rossi-Maccanico, 24 *EC Tax Rev.* 2 (2015), at pp. 63-77; D.S. Smit, 25 *EC Tax Rev.* 2 (2016), at pp. 110-112; R. Szudoczky in I. Richelle/W. Schön/E. Traversa (eds.), *State Aid Law and Business Taxation* (Springer, 2016), 163-183; A. Taferner/J.W. Kuipers, 56 *Eur. Taxn.* 4 (2016), at pp. 142-143.

2120. For an analysis of the ECJ's jurisprudence on the State aid rules see Chapter 3.3.

2121. Cf. R. Luja, 60 *British Tax Rev.* 3 (2015), at p. 387 ("*double non-taxation [...] can and should be addressed within the EU, but not via State aid[,] [...] as mismatches resulting from genuine disparities cannot be attributed to a single Member State*"); R. Luja, 76 *Tax Notes Intl.* 4 (27 Oct. 2014), at pp. 353-354; R. Luja, IP/A/TAXE/2015-02, PE 563.453 (October 2015), at pp. 14-17; A. Taferner/J.W. Kuipers, 56 *Eur. Taxn.* 4 (2016), at p. 142 ("*Double non-taxation does not [...] result from the tax system of one country, but from how the systems of several countries relate to each other. This is not a problem of state aid, but of lack of harmonization*"); also cf. L. De Broe, 24 *EC Tax Rev.* 6 (2015), at p. 293 ("*the state aid review should not be used as a means [...] to address mismatches and the double non-taxation following from disparities in the tax legislations of two or more Member States*"); P. Pistone/R. Szudoczy in M. Lang/P. Pistone/J. Schuch/C. Staringer (eds.), *Introduction to European Tax Law on Direct Taxation*[4] (Linde, 2015), at pp. 31-32 ("*an advantage which results from disparities between the tax systems is outside the scope of the State aid rules*"); D.S. Smit, 25 *EC Tax Rev.* 2 (2016), at p. 112 ("*removing international disparities [...] should in my view be done through legislation instead of through application of the European state aid rules*").

2122. See Chapter 4.1.

2123. See Chapter 4.2.

This does not mean that the State aid rules generally remain inapplicable in situations of double non-taxation. The resultant tax advantages are rather only legally invulnerable if the particular provisions of the involved Member States do not per se infringe Article 107 TFEU.[2124] Since the ECJ's jurisprudence on the compatibility of tax measures with State aid law is still in its infancy, it might easily be that traditional pillars of the Member States' tax systems which are jointly responsible for double non-taxation may be put into question in the future.[2125] Moreover, even if the State aid rules cannot be relied upon in order to oblige Member States to avoid double non-taxation, they may still voluntarily take their own measures. With regard to double taxation, the ECJ has already emphasized that insofar as "*no uniform or harmonisation measure designed to eliminate double taxation has as yet been adopted at Community law level,*" "*it is for the Member States to determine whether, and to what extent, [...] double taxation [...] is to be avoided and, for that purpose, to establish, either unilaterally or through double taxation conventions concluded with other Member States, procedures intended to prevent or mitigate such [...] double taxation.*"[2126] However, this statement should not be misunderstood. Domestic or double tax treaty provisions which aim at eliminating situations of double taxation or double non-taxation are not sacrosanct from an EU law perspective. They rather also have to be in line with the fundamental freedoms and the State aid rules. Member States should thus particularly avoid that measures which aim at preventing double taxation lead to double non-taxation and measures which aim at preventing double non-taxation lead to double taxation. Otherwise, they may, *a fortiori*, run the risk of violating EU law. Especially if such measures are taken unilaterally without being reconciled with what happens in the respective other jurisdiction, the Member State which is to blame for the resultant interference with the internal market might be clearly identifiable. So even if EU law does not oblige Member States to avoid double taxation and double non-taxation, it still requires them to closely cooperate in this respect. Thus,

2124. See W. Haslehner in I. Richelle/W. Schön/E. Traversa (eds.), *State Aid Law and Business Taxation* (Springer, 2016), 157.
2125. Cf. C. HJI Panayi, 32 *Intertax* 6/7 (2004), at p. 306 ("*Art. 87 [...] has the potential to develop into a powerful weapon at the disposal of the Commission; well capable of re-opening the debate for tax harmonization.*").
2126. Judgment in *Amurta*, C-379/05, EU:C:2007:655, at para. 24; Judgment in *Les Vergers du Vieux Tauves*, C-48/07, EU:C:2008:758, at para. 46; Judgment in *Aberdeen Property Fininvest Alpha*, C-303/07, EU:C:2009:377, at para. 28; Judgment in *Gaz de France - Berliner Investissement*, C-247/08, EU:C:2009:600, at para. 37; Judgment in *Commission/Italy*, C-540/07, EU:C:2009:717, at para. 31; Judgment in *Commission/Germany*, C-284/09, EU:C:2011:670, at para. 48; also see Judgment in *Kerckhaert and Morres*, C-513/04, EU:C:2006:713, at para. 23; Judgment in *Test Claimants in Class IV of the ACT Group Litigation*, C-374/04, EU:C:2006:773, at para. 54; Judgment in *Test Claimants in the Thin Cap Group Litigation*, C-524/04, EU:C:2007:161, at para. 49; Judgment in *Cobelfret*, C-138/07, EU:C:2009:82, at para 56; Judgment in *Damseaux*, C-128/08, EU:C:2009:471, at para. 30; Judgment in *Commission/Spain*, C-487/08, EU:C:2010:310, at para. 31; Judgment in *Banco Bilbao Vizcaya Argentaria*, C-157/10, EU:C:2011:813, at para. 31.

"*[a] coordinated approach to implementing growth-friendly tax systems and tackling cross-border problems*" is not only "*essential for a well-functioning Single Market*" from a policy perspective.[2127] There are also legal reasons which support the view that "*the appropriate way forward involves coordinated initiatives*" in the EU.[2128]

2127. Communication from the Commission to the European Parliament and the Council, Anti-Tax Avoidance Package: Next steps towards delivering effective taxation and greater tax transparency in the EU, COM(2016) 23 final (18 Jan. 2016), at pp. 2-3; Commission Staff Working Document Accompanying the document Communication from the Commission to the European Parliament and the Council – Anti Tax Avoidance Package: Next Steps towards delivering effective taxation and greater tax transparency in the EU, SWD(2016) 6 final (28 Jan. 2016), at pp. 5 and 25

2128. Proposal for a Council Directive laying down rules against tax avoidance practices that directly affect the functioning of the internal market, COM(2016) 26 final (28 Jan. 2016), at pp. 4 and 6.

Bibliography

Achatz M., Die Auswahl von Besteuerungsgegenständen – verfassungsrechtliche Aspekte, 15 *ÖStZ* 21 (2002), p. 534.

Achatz M., Der Handel mit Zahnersatz im Binnenmarkt, in Kirchhof P./Nieskens H. (eds.), *Festschrift für Wolfram Reiss zum 65. Geburtstag* (Dr Otto Schmidt, 2008), p. 169.

Achatz M./Kirchmayr S. (eds.), *KStG* (Facultas, 2011).

Adamczyk Ł./Majdańska A., The Sources of EU Law Relevant for Direct Taxation, in Lang M./Pistone P./Schuch J./Staringer C. (eds.), *Introduction to European Tax Law on Direct Taxation*[4] (Linde, 2015), p. 1.

Adriaanse P./Ottervanger T., Recovery of Unlawful Aid, in Hancher L./Ottavanger T./Slot P.J. (eds.), *EU State Aids* (Sweet & Maxwell, 2012), p. 999.

Ahmann K., Das Ertragssteuerrecht unter dem Diktat des Europäischen Gerichtshofs? Können wir uns wehren?, 93 *DStZ* 3 (2005), p. 75.

Aigner D./Kofler G./Tumpel M., Zu den verfassungsrechtlichen Bedenken gegen Art 14 des österreichisch-liechtensteinischen Doppelbesteuerungsabkommens, 4 *Spektrum der Rechtswissenschaften* 1 (2014), p. 1.

Aigner H.-J./Scheuler U./Stefaner M., General Report, in Lang M./Aigner H.-J./Scheuler U./Stefaner M. (eds.), *CFC Legislation* (Linde, 2004), p. 13.

Anido M.A.C./Carrero C., Accounting, the Permanent Establishment and EC Law: The *Futura Participations* case, 8 *EC Tax Rev.* 1 (1999), p. 24.

Annacondia F./van der Corput W., EU Place-of-Supply Rules from 2010 – VAT Committee Guidelines, 21 *Intl. VAT Monitor* 3 (2010).

Anschütz U., Harmonization of Direct Taxes in the European Economic Community, 13 *Harv. Intl. L. J.* 1 (1972), p. 1.

Arginelli P., The Discriminatory Taxation of Permanent Establishments by the Host State in the European Union: a Too Much Separate Entity Approach, 35 *Intertax* 2 (2007), p. 82.

Arhold C., Steuerhoheit auf regionaler oder lokaler Ebene und der europäische Beihilfenbegriff – wie weit reicht das Konzept von der regionalen Selektivität, 17 *EuZW* 23 (2006), p. 717.

Arnold W., Konkurrentenklage und Abgabenverfahrensrecht, in Holoubek M./Lang M. (eds.), *Abgabenverfahrensrecht und Gemeinschaftsrecht* (Linde, 2006), p. 403.

Ault H., Some Reflections on the OECD and The Sources of International Tax Principles, 70 *Tax Notes Intl.* 12 (2013), p. 1195.

Ault H.J., Corporate Integration, Tax Treaties and the Division of the International Tax Base: Principles and Practices, 47 *Tax L. Rev.* 2 (1992), p. 565.

Avery Jones J.F., A Comment on "AMID: The Wrong Bridge or a Bridge Too Far?", 41 *Eur. Taxn.* 13 (2001), p. 251.

Avery Jones J.F., Flows of Capital Between the EU and Third Countries and the Consequences of Disharmony in European International Tax Law, 7 *EC Tax Rev.* 2 (1998), p. 95.

Avi-Yonah R.S., Corporations, Society, and the State: A Defense of the Corporate Tax, 90 *Virginia L. Rev.* 5 (2004), p. 1193.

Avi-Yonah R.S., Globalization, Tax Competition, and the Fiscal Crisis of the Welfare State, 113 *Harv. L. Rev.* 7 (2000), p. 1573.

Avi-Yonah R.S., International Tax as International Law, 57 *Tax L. Rev.* 4 (2004), p. 483.

Avi-Yonah R.S., The Rise and Fall of Arm's Length: A Study in the Evolution of U.S. International Taxation, 15 *Virginia Tax Rev.* 1 (1995), p. 89.

Baker P., The BEPS Action Plan in the Light of EU Law: Treaty Abuse, 61 *British Tax Rev.* 3 (2015), p. 408.

Bammens N., *The Principle of Non-Discrimination in International and European Tax Law* (IBFD, 2012).

Banks K., The Application of the Fundamental Freedoms to Member State Tax Measures: Guarding Against Protectionism or Second-Guessing National Policy Choices?, 33 *Eur. L. Rev.* 4 (2008), p. 482.

Barents R., New Developments in Measures Having Equivalent Effect, 18 *Common Market L. Rev.* 3 (1981), p. 271.

Barents R., The Internal Market Unlimited: Some Observations on the Legal Basis of Community Legislation, 30 *Common Market L. Rev.* 1 (1993), p. 85.

Barnard C., *The Substantive Law of the EU*[4] (Oxford University Press, 2013).

Bartelsman E.J./Beetsma R.M.W.J., Why Pay More? Corporate Tax Avoidance Through Transfer Pricing in OECD countries', 87 *Journal of Public Economics* 9-10 (2003), p. 2225.

Bartosch A., Is there a Need for a Rule of Reason in European State aid law? Or How to Arrive at a Coherent Concept of Material Selectivity?, 47 *Common Market L. Rev.* 3 (2010), p. 729.

Baßler J., Zu den "Steuerspezifika" der Grundfreiheiten des EG-Vertrages, 14 *IStR* 23 (2005), p. 822.

Bates J./Berman D.M./Gani R./Gutmann D./Imamura T./Klugman G./Rust A., Limitation on Benefits Articles in Income Tax Treaties: The Current State of Play, 41 *Intertax* 6/7 (2013), p. 395.

Becker J./Loose T., Zur geplanten Ausdehnung des materiellen Korrespondenzprinzips auf hybride Finanzierungen, 21 *IStR* 19 (2012), p. 758.

Behrens P., Der Wettbewerb im Vertrag von Lissabon, 19 *EuZW* 7 (2008), p. 193.

Behrens P., Die Konvergenz der wirtschaftlichen Freiheiten im europäischen Gemeinschaftsrecht, 30 *EuR* 2 (1992), p. 145.

Beiser R., Die Befreiungs- und Anrechnungsmethode im Licht des Gleichheitssatzes, 24 *SWI* 2 (2014), p. 52.

Beiser R., Die Wegzugsbesteuerung und das arm's length-Prinzip im Licht der Rechtsprechung "Hughes de Lasteyrie du Saillant", 17 *ÖStZ* 13 (2004), p. 282.

Bell M., *Anti-Discrimination Law and the European Union* (Oxford University Press, 2002).

Bellingwout J., *Amurta*: A Tribute to (The Late) Advocate General Geelhoed, 48 *Eur. Taxn.* 3 (2008), p. 124.

Bendlinger S., *Steueroasen und Offshore-Strukturen* (Linde, 2013).

Bendlinger S., Änderung der Mutter-Tochter-Richtlinie der EU, 14 *SWI* 6 (2004), p. 277.

Bendlinger S./ Herbrich D., Die Betriebsstättenfrist bei Bauausführungen und Montagen, 10 *SWI* 12 (2000), p. 562.

Benéitez Régli P., BEPS Actions 2, 3 and 4 and the Fundamental Freedoms: Is There a Way Out?, 56 *Eur. Taxn.* 6 (2016), p. 230.

Benz S./Böhmer J., Das Anti Tax Avoidance Package (ATA-Paket) der EU-Kommission zur Umsetzung der BEPS-Maßnahmen in der EU, 69 *DB* 6 (2016), p. 307.

Berg H./Schmich R., Die Beschränkung des Verlustabzuges im Karlsruher Entwurf zum Einkommensteuergesetz, 40 *DStR* 9 (2002), p. 346.

Bernhard W., Einkünfte aus ausländischen Betriebsstätten im Lichte des Europarechts, 10 *IStR* 12 (2001), p. 366.

Biebl E., EuGH in der Rs. *Amurta*: Einschränkung der Kapitalverkehrsfreiheit durch Quellen-steuer auf Outbound-Dividenden, 18 *SWI* 1 (2008), p. 29.

Biebl E., EuGH-Entscheidung Denkavit und ihre Folgen für die österreichische Quellenbesteuerung, 17 *SWI* 2 (2007), p. 65.

Binder A./Wöhrer V., SWI-Jahrestagung: Privilegierung von Freiberuflern im DBA Liechtenstein verfassungsrechtlich problematisch, 24 *SWI* 1 (2014), p. 10.

Biondi A., State Aid is Falling Down, Falling Down: An Analysis of the Case Law on the Notion of Aid, 50 *Common Market L. Rev.* 6 (2013), p. 1719.

Birk D. (ed.), *Handbuch des Europäischen Steuer- und Abgabenrechts* (NWB, 1995).

Birk D., Besteuerungsgleichheit in der Europäischen Union, in Lehner M. (ed.), *Steuerrecht im Europäischen Binnenmarkt*, DStJG 19 (Dr Otto Schmidt, 1996), p. 63.

Bispo R.M., Cross-Border Intra-Group Hybrid Finance: A Comparative Analysis of the Legal Approach Adopted by Brazil, the United Kingdom and the United States, 67 *Bull. Intl. Taxn.* 11 (2013), p. 364.

Bizioli G., Comparative Analysis of the Causes of Double (Non-)Taxation in the Income and VAT/GST Contexts, in Lang M./Melz P./Kristoffersson E. (ed.), Ecker T. (ass. ed.), *Value Added Tax and Direct Taxation* (IBFD, 2009), p. 383.

Blum D.W./Huisman E., Die Rechtssache *K*: Neues zum Finalitätskriterium in der grenzüberschreitenden Verlustverrechnung, 24 *SWI* 9 (2014), p. 433.

Bobek V./Hauptman L./Beloglavec S., National Report Slovenia, in J. Herdin/I. Hofbauer (eds.), *WTO and Direct Taxation* (Linde, 2005), p. 611.

Bock Y., *Rechtsangleichung und Regulierung im Binnenmarkt* (Nomos, 2004).

Bolougne F./Sumrada Slavnic N., Cross-Border Restructuring and "Final Losses", 52 *Eur. Taxn.* 10 (2012), p. 486.

Bos W.J., The Changing World of European Tax Policy, 40 *Eur. Taxn.* 9 (2000), p. 409.

Boulogne G.F./ Geursen W.W., *Gaz de France*: Dividends to Companies Not Listed in the Parent-Subsidiary Directive Are Not Exempt, 50 *Eur. Taxn.* 4 (2010), p. 129.

Boyle M., Cross-Border Tax Arbitrage – Policy Choices and Political Motivations, 50 *British Tax Rev.* 5 (2005), p. 527.

Brauner Y., An International Tax Regime in Crystallization, 56 *Tax L. Rev.* 2 (2002), p. 259.

Brauner Y., BEPS: An Interim Evaluation, 6 *World Tax J.* 1 (2014), p. 10.

Brauner Y., What the BEPS?, 16 *Florida Tax Rev.* 2 (2014), p. 55.

Brauner Y./Kofler G., The Interaction of Tax Treaties with International Economic Laws, in Vann R. (ed.), *Global Tax Treaty Commentaries* (IBFD, 2016).

Brokelind C., The ECJ *Bouanich* Case: The Capital Gains and Dividend Classification of Share Buy-Backs in Swedish Tax Law, 6 *Eur. Taxn.* 6 (2006), p. 268.

Brosens L., Thin capitalization rules and EU law, 13 *EC Tax Rev.* 4 (2004), p. 188.

Brugger F., Wegzugsbesteuerung und Abkommensrecht, 17 *SWI* 11 (2007), p. 510.

Bullen A., *Arm's Length Transaction Structures* (IBFD, 2011).

Bullen A., Norwegian Withholding Tax Contrary to Rules on Free Movement of Capital in EEA Agreement, *45 Eur. Taxn.* 2 (2005), p. 75.

Bundgaard J., Classification and Treatment of Hybrid Financial Instruments and Income Derived Therefrom under EU Corporate Tax Directives – Part 2, 50 *Eur. Taxn.* 11 (2010), p. 490.

Burgstaller E./Schilcher M., Subject-to-Tax Clauses in Tax Treaties, 44 *Eur. Taxn.* 6 (2004), p. 266.

Calderón J./Baez A., The *Columbus Container Services* ECJ Case and Its Consequences: A Lost Opportunity to Shed Light on the Scope of the Non-discrimination Principle, 37 *Intertax* 4 (2009), p. 212.

Calliess C./Ruffert M. (eds.), *EUV/AEUV*[4] (C.H. Beck, 2011).

Cerioni L., Guido Imfeld and Nathalie Garcet v Belgian State: a continuation of the Schumacker doctrine?, 59 *British Tax Rev.* 2 (2014), p. 128.

Cerioni L., The Commission's Proposal for a Directive on Double Taxation Dispute Resolution Mechanisms: Overcoming the Final Hurdle of Juridical Double Taxation within the European Union, 57 *Eur. Taxn.* 5 (2017), p. 182.

CFE ECJ Task Force, Opinion Statement ECJ-TF 3/2015 on the decision of the European Court of Justice in Case C-512/13, C.G. Sopora, on "horizontal discrimination".

CFE, Opinion Statement of the CFE ECJ Task Force on ECJ, *Columbus Container Services BVBA & Co v. Finanzamt Bielefeld-Innenstadt*, 6 December 2007, C-298/05 – April 2008, 48 *Eur. Taxn.* 10 (2008), p. 541.

CFE, Opinion Statement FC 3/2016 on the European Commission's proposal for an Anti-Tax Avoidance Directive of 28 January 2016 (2016).

Chojnacka Z., Das Verbot der Durchführung von formell rechtswidrigen Beihilfenmaßnahmen und seine tatsächliche Effektivität – Ein Versuch der Veranschaulichung der Wirkungsweise primärrechtlicher Verfahrensvorschriften anhand der Odyssee im Fall der Energieabgabenvergütung, in Eisenberger I./Golden I./ Lachmayer K./Marx G./Tomasovsky D. (eds.), *Norm und Normvorstellung*, Festschrift für Bernd-Christian Funk zum 60. Geburtstag (Springer, 2003), p. 31.

Clausing K.A., Multinational Firm Tax Avoidance and Tax Policy, 62 *National Tax J.* 4 (2009), p. 703.

Cordewener A., *Europäische Grundfreiheiten und nationales Steuerrecht* (Dr Otto Schmidt, 2002).

Cordewener A., Asymmetrical Tax Burdens and EU State Aid Control, 21 *EC Tax Rev.* 6 (2012), p. 288.

Cordewener A., Case C-136/00, *Rolf Dieter Danner*, Judgment of the Court of Justice (Fifth Chamber) of 3 October 2002, (2002) ECR I-8147, 40 *Common Market L. Rev.* 4 (2003), p. 965.

Cordewener A., Company Taxation, Cross-Border Financing and Thin Capitalization in the EU Internal Market: Some Comments on *Lankhorst-Hohorst GmbH*, 43 *Eur. Taxn.* 4 (2003), p. 102.

Cordewener A., Cross-Border Loss Relief and the "Effet Utile" of EU Law: Are We Losing It?, 20 *EC Tax Rev.* 2 (2011), p. 58.

Cordewener A., Deutsche Unternehmensbesteuerung und europäische Grundfreiheiten - Grundzüge des materiellen und formellen Rechtsschutzsystems der EG, 42 *DStR* 1-2 (2004), p. 6.

Cordewener A., Die asymmetrische Belastung von Wirtschaftssektoren im Lichte aktueller Entwicklungen des EU-Beihilfeverbots – ein Problem für die Kernbrennstoffsteuer, 5 *Ubg* 9 (2012), p. 607.

Cordewener A., German "Anti-avoidance" Measures versus Belgian Coordination Centres: A Long Struggle without Survivors, in Hinnekens L./Hinnekens P. (eds.), *A Vision of Taxes Within and Outside European Borders, Festschrift in Honor of Prof. Dr. Frans Vanistendael* (Kluwer, 2008), p. 203.

Cordewener A., Körperschaftsteueranrechnung für Gebietsfremde versus Kapitalverkehrsfreiheit – Zum Gutachten des EFTA-Gerichtshofs in Sachen Fokus Bank ASA, 87 *FR* 7 (2005), p. 345.

Cordewener A., The Prohibitions of Discrimination and Restriction Within the Framework of the Fully Integrated Internal Market, in Vanistendael F. (ed.), *EU Freedoms and Taxation* (IBFD, 2006), p. 1.

Cordewener A./Dahlberg M./Pistone P./Reimer E./Romano C., The Tax Treatment of Foreign Losses: *Ritter, M & S*, and the Way Ahead (Part Two), 44 *Eur. Taxn.* 5 (2004), p. 218.

Cordewener A./Kofler G./ Schindler C.P., Free Movement of Capital and Third Countries: Exploring the Outer Boundaries with *Lasertec, A and B* and *Holböck*, 47 *Eur. Taxn.* 8 (2007), p. 371.

Cordewener A./Kofler G./Schindler C.P., Free Movement of Capital, Third Country Relationships and National Tax Law: An Emerging Issue before the ECJ, 47 *Eur. Taxn.* 3 (2007), p. 107.

Cordewener A./Kofler G./Van Thiel S., The Clash Between European Freedoms and National Direct Tax Law: Public Interest Defences Available to the Member States, 46 *Common Market L. Rev.* 6 (2009), p. 1951.

Cordewener A./Reimer E., The Future of Most-Favoured-Nation Treatment in EC Tax Law – Did the ECJ Pull the Emergency Brake without Real Need? – Part 1, 46 *Eur. Taxn.* 6 (2006), p. 239.

Cordewener A./Reimer E., The Future of Most-Favoured-Nation Treatment in EC Tax Law – Did the ECJ Pull the Emergency Brake without Real Need? – Part 2, 46 *Eur. Taxn.* 7 (2006), p. 291.

Cotrut M. (ed.), *ECJ Direct Tax Compass 2015* (IBFD, 2015).

Craig P./De Búrca G., *EU Law*[4] (Oxford University Press, 2008).

Cussons P./FitzGerald E., EU Report, in IFA (ed.), *The Attribution of Profits to Permanent Establishments*, CDFI 92b (IBFD, 2006), p. 69.

Dahlberg M., *Direct Taxation in Relation to the Freedom of Establishment and the Free Movement of Capital* (Kluwer Law International, 2005).

Dahm G., Die völkerrechtliche Verbindlichkeit von Empfehlungen internationaler Organisationen, 12 *DÖV* 10 (1959), p. 361.

Dassesse M., The ECJ's Decision in *AMID* and its Implications for Belgian Companies, 55 *Bull. Intl. Taxn.* 6 (2001), p. 254.

Daurer V., *Tax Treaties and Developing Countries* (Kluwer, 2013).

Dauses M.A., Die rechtliche Dimension des Binnenmarktes, 1 *EuZW* 1 (1990), p. 8.

Dautzenberg N., Das EG-rechtliche Gleichbehandlungsgebot für Betriebsstätten und Tochterkapitalgesellschaften, 12 *EWS* 6 (2001), p. 270.

Dautzenberg N., Die Ertragsbesteuerung des Kapitaleinkommens in der EU: Zur Bedeutung des Begriffs "Kapitalanlageort" in Art. 73 d EGV, 8 *EWS* 11 (1997), p. 379.

Dautzenberg N., Doppelbesteuerung und EG-Vertrag: Die Anrechnungsmethode als gemeinschaftsrechtlicher Mindeststandard?, 47 *DB* 31 (1994), p. 1542.

Dautzenberg N., *Unternehmensbesteuerung im EG-Binnenmarkt* (Josef Eul Verlag, 1997).

Daxkobler K./Huisman E., *Levy & Sebbag*: The ECJ Has Once Again Been Asked To Deliver Its Opinion on Juridical Double Taxation in the Internal Market, 53 *Eur. Taxn.* 8 (2013), p. 400.

de Boer R.A./ Nouwen M.F. (eds.), *The European Union's Struggle with Mismatches and Aggressive Tax Planning* (Eleven International Publishing, 2013).

de Bour R./Marres O., BEPS Action 2: Neutralizing the Effects on Hybrid Mismatch Arrangements, 43 *Intertax* 1 (2015), p. 14.

De Broe L., Are We Heading Towards an Internal Market Without Dividend Withholding Tax but with Interest and Royalty Withholding Tax? Some Observations on Advocate General's Kokott Opinion in Truck Center, 18 *EC Tax Rev.* 1 (2009), p. 2.

De Broe L., At Last, Some Output on the Fight against Double Non-taxation, 23 *EC Tax Rev.* 6 (2014), p. 310.

De Broe L., General Report, in IFA (ed.), *The Tax Treatment of Transfer of Residence by Individuals*, CDFI 87b (IBFD, 2002), p. 19.

De Broe L., Hard times for Emigration Taxes, in van Arendonk H./Engelen F.A./Jansen S. (eds.), *A Tax Globalist, Essays in Honour of Maarten J. Ellis* (IBFD, 2005), p. 210.

De Broe L., *International Tax Planning and Prevention of Abuse* (IBFD, 2008).

De Broe L., Relief of Double Taxation of Cross-border Dividends Within the Union and the Principle of Loyal Cooperation, 21 *EC Tax Rev.* 4 (2012), p. 180.

De Broe L., The State Aid Review against Aggressive Tax Planning: "Always Look a Gift Horse in the Mouth", 24 *EC Tax Rev.* 6 (2015), p. 290.
De Broe L., The State Aid Review against Aggressive Tax Planning: "Always Look a Gift Horse in the Mouth", 24 *EC Tax Rev.* 6 (2015), p. 290.
De Broe L./Bammens N., Truck Center Belgian Withholding Tax on Interest Payments to Non-resident Companies Does Not Violate EC Law: A Critical Look at the ECJ's Judgment in Truck Center, 18 *EC Tax Rev.* 3 (2009), p. 131.

De Broe L./Gernay T., Belgium: the Imfeld & Garcet case and the Levy case, in Lang M./Pistone P./Schuch J./Staringer C./Storck A. (eds.), ECJ Recent Developments in Direct Taxation 2012 (Linde, 2013), p. 9.

de Búrca G., The Principle of Proportionality and its Application in EC Law, in Barav A./Wyatt D.A. (eds.), *Yearbook of European Law 1993* (Clarendon Press, 1994), p. 105.

De Ceulaer S., Community Most-Favoured-Nation Treatment: One Step Closer to the Multilateralization of Income Tax Treaties in the European Union?, 57 *Bull. Intl. Taxn.* 10 (2003), p. 493.

de Graaf A., Avoidance of international double taxation: Community or joint policy?, 7 *EC Tax Rev.* 4 (1998), p. 258.

de Graaf A./de Haan P./de Wilde M., Fundamental Change in Countries' Corporate Tax Framework Needed to Properly Address BEPS, 42 *Intertax* 5 (2014), p. 306.

de Graaf A./Janssen G., The Implications of the Judgment in the *D* case: The Perspective of Two Non-believers, 14 *EC Tax Rev.* 4 (2005), p. 173

De Groot I., Sopora. Horizontal Discrimination. Most Favoured Nation Treatment. Dutch 30% Ruling for Foreign Employees with a Specific Expertise is not Contrary to EU Law Unless It Systematically Leads to Clear Overcompensation, 8 *H&I* 6.175 (2015), p. 5.

de Groot I.M., Member States Must Apply Most Favoured Nation Treatment under EU Law, 42 *Intertax* 6/7 (2014), p. 405.

de Hosson F.C., The Parent-Subsidiary Directive, 18 *Intertax* 10 (1990), p. 414.

de Hosson F.C., The Slow and Lonesome Death of the Arbitration Convention, 31 Intertax 12 (2003), p. 482.

de la Feria R., *The EU VAT System and the Internal Market* (IBFD, 2009).
de la Feria R., *The EU VAT System and the Internal Market* (IBFD, 2009).
de Ulhôa Canto C.C./de Ulhôa Canto P.V., National Report Brazil, in IFA (ed.), *New Tendencies in Tax Treatment of Cross-Border Interest of Corporations, CDFI XCIIIb* (IBFD, 2008), p. 151.

Debelva F./Scornos D./Van den Berghen J./Van Braband P., LOB Clauses and EU-Law Compatibility: A Debate Revived by BEPS?, 24 *EC Tax Rev.* 3 (2015), p. 132.

Deckert M.R./Lilienthal N.O., Die Rechtsetzungskompetenzen der EG im Privatrecht, 10 *EWS* 4 (1999), p. 121.

Delaurière J., Does Denkavit Signal the End of Withholding Tax?, 45 *Tax Notes Intl.* 4 (2007), p. 303.

Denys L.A., The ECJ Case Law on Cross-Border Dividends Revisited 47 *Eur. Taxn.* 5 (2007), p. 221.

Desens M., Ist die neue Korrespondenzregel in der Mutter-Tochter-Richtlinie mit dem primären Unionsrecht vereinbar?, 23 *IStR* 22 (2014), p. 825.

Desens M., Kritische Bestandsaufnahme zu den geplanten Änderungen in § 8b KStG, 51 *DStR*, Beihefter zu Heft 4 (2013), p. 13.

Devereux M.P./Loretz S., The Effects of EU Formula Apportionment on Corporate Tax Revenues, 29 *Fiscal Studies* 1 (2008), p. 1.

Dirix K., Harmful Tax Competition: Six Belgian Tax Incentives under the Microscope, 22 *EC Tax Rev.* 5 (2013), p. 233.

Dommes S./Heidenbauer S., Schwedische Besteuerung von Aktienrückkäufen verstößt gegen Kapitalverkehrsfreiheit - Urteil in der Rs. Bouanich, 16 *SWI* 3 (2006), p. 126.

Dötsch F., Zur (Nicht-)Vererblichkeit des Verlustabzugs nach § ESTG § 10d EStG, 46 *DStR* 14 (2008), p. 641.

Douma S., Limitations on Interest Deduction: an EU Law Perspective, 61 *British Tax Rev.* 3 (2015), p. 364.

Douma S., The Three Ds of Direct Tax Jurisdiction: Disparity, Discrimination and Double Taxation, 46 *Eur. Taxn.* 11 (2006), p. 522.

Dourado A.P., Aggressive Tax Planning in EU Law and in the Light of BEPS: The EC Recommendation on Aggressive Tax Planning and BEPS Actions 2 and 6, 43 *Intertax* 1 (2015), p. 42.

Dourado A.P., Is it *Acte Clair*? General report on the role played by *CILFIT* in direct taxation, in Dourado A.P./ da Palma Borges R. (eds.), *The Acte Clair in EC Direct Tax Law* (IBFD, 2008), p. 13.

Dourado A.P., The EU Anti Tax Avoidance Package: Moving Ahead of BEPS?, 44 *Intertax* 6/7 (2016), p. 440.

Doyle H., Is Article 26 of the Netherlands-United States Tax Treaty Compatible with EC Law?, 35 *Eur. Taxn.* 1 (1995), p. 14.

Drabbe H., The Test of Selectivity in State Aid Litigation: The Relevance of Drawing Internal and External Comparisons to Identify the Reference Framework, in Rust A./Micheau C. (eds.), *State Aid and Tax Law* (Kluwer, 2013), p. 87.

Drüen K., Die Sanierungsklausel des § 8c KStG als europarechtswidrige Beihilfe, 49 *DStR* 7 (2011), p. 289.

Duncan J.A., General Report, in IFA (ed.), *Tax Treatment of Hybrid Financial Instruments in Cross-Border Transactions*, CDFI 85a (SDU, 2000), p. 24.

Dziurdź K., "Circularly Linked" Rules Countering Deduction and Non-Inclusion Schemes: Some Thoughts on a Tie-Breaker Test, 67 *Bull. Intl. Taxn.* 6 (2013), p. 306.

Easson A.J., *Taxation in the European Community* (The Athlone Press, 1993).

Eberhartinger M., Konvergenz und Neustrukturierung der Grundfreiheiten, 8 *EWS* 2 (1997), p. 43.

Ebling K., *Unilaterale Maßnahmen gegen die internationale Doppelbesteuerung bei den Steuern vom Ertrag* (Dissertation Johannes Gutenberg Universität Mainz, 1970).

Echevarría Zubeldia G., Legal Uncertainty of the EU Effective-Use-and-Enjoyment Criterion, 23 *Intl. VAT Monitor* 4 (2012), p. 228.

Ecker T., *A VAT/GST Model Convention* (IBFD, 2013).

Ecker T., Place of Effective Use and Enjoyment of Services – EU History Repeats Itself, 23 *Intl. VAT Monitor* 6 (2012), p. 407.

Ecker T., Tax Treaties – A Solution to VAT/GST Double Taxation, in Lang M./Melz P./Kristoffersson E. (ed.), Ecker T. (ass. ed.), *Value Added Tax and Direct Taxation* (IBFD, 2009), p. 1269.

Ecker T./Variychuk E., VAT treaties: the Russian Federation, 2 *World J. of VAT/GST L.* 2 (2013), p. 81.

Edward D./Lane R., *European Union Law* (Edward Elgar, 2013), at MN 10.26;

Ehlermann C.-D./Goyette M., The Interface between EU State Aid Control and the WTO Disciplines on Subsidies, 5 *Eur. St. Aid L. Q.* 4 (2006), p. 695.

Ehrke-Rabel T./Kofler G., Gratwanderungen – Das Niemandsland zwischen aggressiver Steuerplanung, Missbrauch und Abgabenhinterziehung, 22 *ÖStZ* 19 (2009), p. 456.

Ehrke-Rable T., VAT grouping: the relevance of the territorial restriction in Article 11 VAT Directive, 1 *World J. of VAT Law* 1 (2012), p. 61.

Ehrmann O., Beihilferechtliche Zulässigkeit des § 8c Abs. 1a KStG, 49 *DStR* 1 (2011), p. 5.

Eicker K./Breuer F., EWR-Kapitalverkehrsfreiheit: Grenzüberschreitende Anrechnung von Körperschaftsteuer (Quellensteuer); Verfahrensrechte ausländischer Anteilseigner in den EWR/EFTA-Mitgliedstaaten, 14 *IStR* 2 (2005), p. 55.

Eilers S./Oppel F., BEPS erreicht die EU: Das Anti Tax Avoidance Package der EU-Kommission, 25 *IStR* 8 (2016), p. 312.

Eilmansberger T., Zur Reichweite der Grundfreiheiten des Binnenmarktes (1. Teil), 121 *JBl* 6 (1999), p. 345.

Eilmansberger T., Zur Reichweite der Grundfreiheiten des Binnenmarktes (2. Teil), 121 *JBl* 7 (1999), p. 434.

Eilmansberger T., Zur Reichweite des Durchführungsverbots nach Art 93 Abs 3 EGV, 10 *ecolex* 3 (1999), p. 212.

Eisendle D., Grenzüberschreitende Verlustverrechnung im Jahre 11 nach Marks & Spencer – Status quo der EuGH-Rechtsprechung zur Berücksichtigung von Auslandsverlusten kraft Unionsrecht, 5 *ISR* 2 (2016), p. 37.

Elkin A., The Organisation for European Economic Co-Operation, Its Structure and Powers, in Landheer B./Carter W.H. (eds.), *European Yearbook*, Vol. IV (Nijhoff, 1958), p. 96.

Emiliou N., *The Principle of Proportionality in European Law* (Kluwer, 1996).

Enchelmair S., Meistbegünstigung im EG-Recht – Allgemein Grundsätze, in Cordewener A./ Enchelmaier S./Schindler C.P. (eds.), *Meistbegünstigung im Steuerrecht der EU-Staaten* (C.H. Beck, 2006), p. 93.

Engelen F., State Aid and Restrictions on Free Movement: Two Sides of the Same Coin?, 52 *Eur. Taxn.* 5 (2012), p. 204.

Engelen F./Gunn A., Towards a Theoretical Assessment Framework, in Rust A./ Micheau C. (eds.), *State Aid and Tax Law* (Kluwer, 2013), p. 137.

Englisch J., Ability to Pay, in C. Brokelind (ed.), *Principles of Law: Function, Status and Impact in EU Tax Law* (IBFD, 2014), p. 439.

Englisch J., *Aufteilung der Besteuerungsbefugnisse – Ein Rechtfertigungsgrund für die Einschränkung von EG-Grundfreiheiten* (Institut "Finanzen und Steuern" e.V., 2008).

Englisch J., BEPS Action 1: Digital Economy – EU Law Implications, 61 *British Tax Rev.* 3 (2015), p. 280.

Englisch J., Das Beihilfenverbot im Steuerrecht, in H. Schaumburg/Englisch J. (eds.), *Europäisches Steuerrecht* (Dr Otto Schmidt, 2015), p. 411.

Englisch J., Development of the EU VAT System, in Lang M./Staringer C./Schuch J./Pistone P./Raponi D. (eds.), *ECJ – Recent Developments in Value Added Tax* (Linde, 2014), p. 21.

Englisch J., Dividend Taxation: Outbound and Inbound (*Verkooijen* and *ACT Group Litigation*), in Haslehner W./Kofler G./Rust A. (eds.), *Landmark Decisions of the ECJ in Direct Taxation* (Kluwer, 2015), p. 41.

Englisch J., Die negative Konkurrentenklage im Unternehmenssteuerrecht, 85 *StuW* 1 (2008), p. 43.

Englisch J., Dividend Taxation: Outbound and Inbound (*Verkooijen* and *ACT Group Litigation*), in Haslehner W.C./Kofler G./Rust A. (eds.), *Landmark Decisions of the ECJ in Direct Taxation* (Kluwer, 2015), p. 41.

Englisch J., *Dividendenbesteuerung* (Dr Otto Schmidt, 2005).

Englisch J., Einige Schlussfolgerungen zur Grundfreiheitskompatibilität des § 1 AStG – zugleich Anmerkung zum Urteil des EuGH in der Rs. SGI, 19 *IStR* 4 (2010), p. 139.

Englisch J., EU State Aid Rules Applied to Indirect Tax Measures, 22 *EC Tax Rev.* 1 (2013), p. 9.

Englisch J., Europarechtskonforme Dividendenbesteuerung – „Aims and effects"?, 51 *RIW* 3 (2005), p. 187.

Englisch J., Europarechtswidrigkeit des finnischen Körperschaftsteueranrechnungsverfahrens, 13 *IStR* 19 (2004), p. 680.

Englisch J., Fiscal Cohesion in the Taxation of Cross-Border Dividends (Part One), 44 *Eur. Taxn.* 7 (2004), p. 323.

Englisch J., Fiscal Cohesion in the Taxation of Cross-Border Dividends (Part Two), 44 *Eur. Taxn.* 8 (2004), p. 355.

Englisch J., Indirect Taxation, in Rust A./Micheau C. (eds.), *State Aid and Tax Law* (Kluwer, 2013), p. 69.

Englisch J., Kapitalertragsteuer: Unterschiedliche Besteuerung von inländischen Kapitalerträgen und von Kapitalerträgen aus einem anderen Mitgliedstaat, 13 *IStR* 15 (2004), p. 526.

Englisch J., Meistbegünstigung im EG-Steuerrecht: Der Weg ins Chaos, in Cordewener A./Enchelmaier S./Schindler C.P. (eds.), *Meistbegünstigung im Steuerrecht der EU-Staaten* (C.H. Beck, 2006), p. 163.

Englisch J., Quellensteuerabzug bei Dividenden, die an eine ausländische Empfängergesellschaft ausgeschüttet werden, 16 *IStR* 23 (2007), p. 854.

Englisch J., Shareholder Relief and EC Treaty Law – Supranational „Aims and Effects"?, 33 *Intertax* 5 (2005), p. 200.

Englisch J., Steuerliche Sonderbelastung als verbotene Beihilfe – eine unionsrechtliche Achillesferse der Kernbrennstoffsteuer, 89 *StuW* 4 (2012), p. 318.

Englisch J., Taxation of Cross-Border Dividends and EC Fundamental Freedoms, 38 *Intertax* 4 (2010), p. 197.

Englisch J., The European Treaties' Implications for Direct Taxes, 33 *Intertax* 8/9 (2005), p. 310.

Englisch J., Truck Center: withholding tax on intercompany interest derived by non-resident companies compatible with freedom of establishment, 2 *H&I* 2 (2009), p. 43.

Englisch J., VAT and General Principles of EU Law, in Weber D. (ed.), *Traditional and Alternative Routes to European Tax Integration* (IBFD, 2010), p. 231.

Englisch J., Verbot des Rechtsmissbrauchs - ein allgemeiner Rechtsgrundsatz des Gemeinschaftsrechts?, 86 *StuW* 1 (2009), p. 3.

Englisch J., *Wettbewerbsgleichheit im grenzüberschreitenden Handel* (Mohr Siebeck, 2008).

Englisch J., Zur Bedeutung des gemeinschaftsrechtlichen Gleichheitssatzes im Recht der Gemeinschaftsbeihilfen, 44 *EuR* 4 (2009), p. 488.

Englisch J., Zur Dogmatik der Grundfreiheiten des EGV und ihren ertragsteuerlichen Implikationen, 80 *StuW* 1 (2003), p. 88.

Englisch J./Schütze A., The Implementation of the EC Parent-Subsidiary Directive in Germany - Recent Developments and Unresolved Issues, 45 *Eur. Taxn.* 11 (2005), p. 488.

Englisch J./Yevgenyeva A., The "Upgraded" Strategy Against Harmful Tax Practices Under the BEPS Action Plan, 58 *British Tax Rev.* 5 (2013), p. 620.

Englmair V.E., The Relevance of the Fundamental Freedoms for Direct Taxation, in Lang M./Pistone P./Schuch J./Staringer C. (eds.), *Introduction to European Tax Law on Direct Taxation*[4] (Linde, 2015), p. 53.

Epiney A., Gemeinschaftsrechtlicher Umweltschutz und Verwirklichung des Binnenmarktes - "Harmonisierung" auch der Rechtsgrundlagen?, 47 *JZ* 11 (1992), p. 564.

Eriksen N./ Haydl K., Avoidance of VAT/GST Double (Non-)Taxation: Recommendations and Other Types of Soft Law v. Legally Binding Instruments to Allocate Taxing Rights Between States (e.g. Bilateral Tax Treaties), in Lang M./Melz P./Kristoffersson E. (ed.), Ecker T. (ass. ed.), *Value Added Tax and Direct Taxation* (IBFD, 2009), p. 1145.

Eriksen N.P., Should Tax Treaties Play a Role for Consumption Taxes?, 33 *Intertax* 4 (2005), p. 166.

Eskildsen C.B., VAT Grouping versus Freedom of Establishment, 20 *EC Tax Rev.* 3 (2011), p. 114.

Essers P., International Tax Justice between Machiavelli and Habermas, 68 *Bull. Intl. Taxn.* 2 (2014), p. 54.

Eyles U., *Das Niederlassungsrecht der Kapitalgesellschaften in der Europäischen Gemeinschaft* (Nomos, 1990).

Ezcurra M.V., State Aids and Energy Taxes: Towards a Coherent Reference Framework, 41 *Intertax* 6/7 (2013), p. 340.

F. Wassermeyer, Does the EC Treaty Force the Member States to Conclude a Multilateral Tax Treaty?, in Lang M./Loukota H./ Rädler A.J./Schuch J./Toifl G./Urtz C./Wassermeyer F./Züger M. (eds.), *Multilateral Tax Treaties* (Linde, 1997), p. 15.

Fantozzi A., The Applicability of State Aid Rules to Tax Competition Measures: A Process of de Facto Harmonization in the Tax Field?, in Schön W. (ed.), Tax Competition in Europe (IBFD, 2003), p. 121.

Farmer P., Columbus Container Services BVBA & Co v Finanzamt Bielefeld-Innenstadt: the ECJ fails to grasp the tax competition nettle in relation to foreign income rules, 53 *British Tax Rev.* 2 (2008), p. 105.

Farmer P., Direct Taxation and the Fundamental Freedoms, in Arnull A./Chalmers D. (eds.), *The Oxford Handbook on European Union Law* (Oxford University Press, 2015), p. 809.

Farmer P., EC Law and national rules on direct taxation: A phoney war?, 7 *EC Tax Rev.* 1 (1998), p. 13

Farmer P., Tax Law and Policy in an Adolescent European Union, 61 *Bull. Intl. Taxn.* 2 (2007), p. 42.

Farmer P., The Court's case law on taxation: a castle built on shifting sands?, 12 *EC Tax Rev.* 2 (2003), p. 75.

Farmer P./Lyal R., *EC Tax Law* (Clarendon Press, 1994).

Fibbe G., The different translations of the term 'company' in the Merger Directive and the Parent-Subsidiary Directive: a Babylonian confusion of tongues?, 15 *EC Tax Rev.* 2 (2006), p. 95.

Fibbe G./De Graaf A., Is double taxation arising from autonomous tax classification of foreign entities incompatible with EC law?, in Van Arendonk H.P.A.M./Engelen F.A./Jansen S. (eds.), *A Tax Globalist, Essays in honour of Maarten J. Ellis* (IBFD, 2005), p. 237.

Fischer L./Warneke P., *Grundlagen der Internationalen Betriebswirtschaftlichen Steuerlehre*[2] (Erich Schmidt Verlag, 1974).

Flick H./Wassemeyer F./Baumhoff H./Schönfeld J. (eds.), *Außensteuerrecht*[57] (Dr Otto Schmidt, 2005).

Flynn L., Coming of Age: The Free Movement of Capital Case Law 1993–2002 (2002), 39 *Common Market L. Rev.* 4 (2002), p. 773.

Flynn L./Ottervanger T., Judicial Protection, in Hancher L./Ottavanger T./Slot P.J. (eds.), *EU State Aids* (Sweet & Maxwell, 2012), p. 1022.

Forsthoff U., Treaty Override und Europarecht, 15 *IStR* 15 (2006), p. 509.

Fortuin A., Commission v Spain. Failure to fulfil obligations. Dividends distributed to resident and non-resident companies. Court of Justice, 3 *H&I* 9 (2010), p. 61.

Fraberger F., Erbschaftssteuerabkommen und Gemeinschaftsrecht, in Aigner D./Aigner H./Fellner K./Fraberger F./Heinrich J./Konezny G./Loukota H./Sutter F.P./Zehetner U./Züger M., *Erbschaftssteuern und Doppelbesteuerungsabkommen* (Linde, 2002), p. 211.

Frick K.A., *Einkommensteuerliche Steuervergünstigungen und Beihilfeverbot nach dem EG-Vertrag* (Pro Universitate Verlag, 1994).

Fross A., Earnings Stripping and Thin Cap Rules: Maintaining an Arm's Length Distance, 53 *Eur. Taxn.* 10 (2013), p. 507.

Frotscher G., *Internationales Steuerrecht*[3] (C.H. Beck, 2009).

Frotscher G., *Internationales Steuerrecht*[4] (C.H. Beck, 2015).

Furdson E., *The European Defence Community: A History* (Macmillan, 1980).

Gammie M., The Role of the European Court of Justice in the Development of Direct Taxation in the European Union, 57 *Bull. Intl. Taxn.* 3 (2003), p. 86.

Gammie M., Double taxation, bilateral treaties and the fundamental freedoms of the EC Treaty, in H. van Arendonk/F.A. Engelen/S. Jansen (eds.), *A Tax Globalist, Essays in honour of Maarten J. Ellis* (IBFD, 2005), p. 266.

Gammie M., Non-Discrimination and the Taxation of Cross-Border Dividends, 2 *World Tax J.* 2 (2010), p. 162.

Gammie M., The role of the European Court of Justice in the development of direct taxation in the European Union, 57 *Bull. Intl. Taxn.* 3 (2003), p. 86.

Gammie M./Brannan G., EC Law Strikes at the UK Corporation Tax – The Death Knell of UK Imputation?, 23 *Intertax* 8/9 (1995), p. 389.

Geiger R./Khan D./Kotzur M. (eds.), *EUV/AEUV*[5] (C.H. Beck).

Good K., Institutional Reform under the Single European Act, 3 *Am. U. J. Intl. L. Pol.* 1 (1988), p. 299.

Goris P., The *Velasquez* Doctrine: An Example of International Juridical Double Taxation, 36 *Eur. Taxn.* 10 (1996), p. 327.

Gosch D. (ed.), *Körperschaftsteuergesetz*[3] (Beck, 2015).

Gosch D./Schönfeld J., Kapitalverkehrsfreiheit und Drittstaaten – Ein (vorläufiger) Zwischenstand, 24 *IStR* 20 (2015), p. 755.

Götz V., Steuervergünstigungen als Gegenstand der europäischen Beihilfenaufsicht, in Kirchhof P./Lehner M./Raupach A./Rodi M. (eds.), *Staaten und Steuern*, Festschrift für Klaus Vogel zum 70. Geburtstag (C.F. Müller, 2000), p. 579.

Grabitz E./Hilf M./Nettesheim M. (eds.), *Das Recht der Europäischen Union*[54] (C.H. Beck, 2014).

Graetz M.J./Warren A.C., Income Tax Discrimination and the Political and Economic Integration of Europe, 115 *Yale L. J.* 6 (2006), p. 1186.

Graetz M.J./Warren A.C., Income Tax Discrimination: Still Stuck in the Labyrinth of Impossibility, 121 *Yale L. J.* 5 (2012), p. 1118.

Graetz M.J./Warren C., Dividend Taxation in Europe: When the ECJ Makes Tax Policy, 44 *Common Market L. Rev.* 6 (2007), p. 1577.

Grambeck H., Outsourcing in the EU Financial Sector – Where Are We Heading?, 20 *Intl. VAT Monitor* 6 (2009), p. 462.

Gravelle J.G., Tax Havens: International Avoidance and Evasion, 62 *National Tax J.* 4 (2009), p. 727.

Gruber M., *Die Sanierung im Unternehmenssteuerrecht* (LexisNexis, 2014).

Gudmundsson J.E., European Tax Law in the Relations with EFTA Countries, 34 *Intertax* 2 (2006), p. 58.

Guerrero V.H., Defining the Balance between Free Competition and Tax Sovereignty in EC and WTO Law: The Due Respect to the General Tax System, 5 *German L. J.* 1 (2004), p. 87.

Gunn A./Luts J., Tax Rulings, APAs and State Aid: Legal Issues, 24 *EC Tax Rev.* 2 (2015), p. 119.

Gutmann D., General Report, in Gutmann D. (ed.), *Corporate Income Tax Subjects* (IBFD, 2016), p. 1.

Gutmann D., Taking Human Rights Seriously: Some Introductory Words on Human Rights, Taxation and the EU, in Kofler G./ Maduro M.P./Pistone P. (eds.), *Human Rights and Taxation in Europe and the World* (IBFD, 2011), p. 105.

Haase F., *Internationales und Europäisches Steuerrecht*[4] (C.F. Müller, 2014).

Hackmann J., Lebenseinkommensbesteuerung durch interperiodischen Progressionsausgleich, 57 *StuW* 4 (1980), p. 318.

Haelterman A./Verstraete H., The "Notional Interest Deduction" in Belgium, 62 *Bull. Intl. Taxn.* 8 (2008), p. 362.

Haferkamp U., *Die Kapitalverkehrsfreiheit im System der Grundfreiheiten des EG-Vertrages* (Nomos, 2003).

Hagemann T./Kahlenberg C., Tax Liability on Dividends from Portfolio Investments: Amendments under the Act on the Implementation of the ECJ Decision in Case C-284/09, 53 *Eur. Taxn.* 11 (2013), p. 575.

Hahn H., Gemeinschaftsrecht und Recht der direkten Steuern - Teil III, 93 *DStZ* 15 (2005), p. 507.

Hahn H., Generalthema I des 58. IFA-Kongresses 2004 in Wien: Double-Non-Taxation Überblick über den deutschen Nationalbericht, 12 *IStR* 13 (2003), p. 446.

Hahn H., Grenzüberschreitende Berücksichtigung von Betriebsstättenverlusten? - Bemerkungen zu einer neu entfachten Diskussion, 11 *IStR* 20 (2002), p. 681.

Hahn H., Von kleinen Aktiengesellschaften, sociétés par actions simplifiées und anderen Raritäten - der Anwendungsbereich der Mutter-Tochter-Richtlinie nach „Gaz de France", 21 *EWS* 5 (2010), p. 176.

Hahn H.J./Weber A., *Die OECD, Organisation für Wirtschaftliche Zusammenarbeit und Entwicklung* (Nomos, 1976).

Hahn J., Die Organisation für Wirtschaftliche Zusammenarbeit und Entwicklung (OECD), Entstehung und Rechtsordnung, 22 *ZaöRV* (1962) p. 78.

Haisch M.L./Helios M., Steuerpflicht von Streubesitzdividenden in der Direkt- und Fondsanlage, 66 *DB* 14 (2013), p. 724.

Haisch M.L./Helios M./Niedling D., AmtshilfeRLUmsG: Änderungen im Finanzierungsbereich, 66 *DB* 26/27 (2013), p. 1444.

Haisch M.L./Helios M./Niedling D., JStG 2013 - Geplante Änderungen im Finanzierungsbereich, 65 *DB* 37 (2012), p. 2060.

Hamaekers H., The Arm's Length Principle and the Role of Comparables, 46 *Bull. Intl. Taxn.* 12 (1992), p. 602.

Hanf D., Legal Concept and Meaning of the Internal Market, in Pelkmans J./Hanf D./Chang M. (eds.), *The EU Internal Market in Comparative Perspective* (Peter Lang, 2008), p. 77.

Harris C.M., The European Community's Parent-Subsidiary Directive, 9 *Fla. J. Intl. L.* 123 (1994), p. 111.

Haslehner W., Double Taxation Relief, Transfer Pricing Adjustments and State Aid Law, in Richelle I./Schön W./Traversa E. (eds.), *State Aid Law and Business Taxation* (Springer, 2016), 133.

Haslehner W.C., "Consistency" and Fundamental Freedoms: The Case of Direct Taxation, 50 *Common Market L. Rev.* 3 (2013), p. 737.

Haslehner W.C., *Das Betriebstättendiskriminierungsverbot im Internationalen Steuerrecht* (Linde, 2010).

Haslehner W.C., Das Konkurrenzverhältnis der Europäischen Grundfreiheiten in der Rechtsprechung des EuGH zu den direkten Steuern, 17 *IStR* 16 (2008), p. 565.

Haslehner W.C., Die Anwendbarkeit des Privatinvestortests bei Steuerbeihilfen, in Jaeger T./Rumersdorfer B. (ed.), *Jahrbuch Beihilferecht 11* (NWV, 2011), p. 273.

Haslehner W.C., Die Kapitalverkehrsfreiheit gegenüber Drittstaaten am Beispiel ausländischer Beteiligungserträge, 3 *taxlex* 6a (2007), p. 286.

Haslehner W.C., EuGH-Urteil *Deutsche Shell GmbH* (Rs. C-293/06): Das gemeinschaftsrechtliche Ende der *Symmetriethese*?, 18 *SWI* 4 (2008), p. 161.

Haslehner W.C., Materielle Selektivität von Steuerbeihilfen im Lichte des *Gibraltar*-Urteils des EuGH, in Jaeger T./Haslinger B. (ed.), *Jahrbuch Beihilferecht 12* (NWV, 2012), p. 301.

Haslehner W.C., Steuerbeihilfen für die Daseinsvorsorge – Alte Probleme und neue Entwicklungen zum gemeinwirtschaftlichen Ausgleich, in Jaeger T./ Rumersdorfer B. (ed.), *Jahrbuch Beihilferecht 10* (NWV, 2010), p. 343.

Hatzopoulos V., Case C-250/95, Futura Participations SA & Singer v. Administration des Contributions (Luxembourg), Judgment of 15 May 1997, (1997) ECR I-2471, 35 *Common Market L. Rev.* 2 (1998), p. 493.

Haug-Adrion E., Die Harmonisierung der direkten Unternehmensbesteuerung in der EG, in Eisele P./Zimmermann R. (eds.) *Steuerrecht im Wandel* (Stuttgart: Schäffer Verlag, 1989), p. 267.

Heidenbauer S., Die Vermeidung der Steuerumgehung und die ausgewogene *Aufteilung* der Besteuerungsbefugnis im Lichte der Rs. *SGI*, 21 *SWI* 2 (2011), p. 67.

Heidenhain M., § 3 General Principles, in Heidenhain M. (ed.), *European State Aid Law* (C.H. Beck, 2010), p. 13.

Heidenhain M., § 4 The Concept of State Aid, in Heidenhain M. (ed.), *European State Aid Law* (C.H. Beck, 2010), p. 22.

Heinrich J., Die Rechtsformneutralität der Besteuerung – rechtspolitisches Ziel oder rechtliches Gebot?, in Achatz M./Ehrke-Rabel T./Heinrich J./Leitner R./Taucher O. (eds.), *Steuerrecht Verfassungsrecht Europarecht*, Festschrift für Hans Georg Ruppe (Facultas, 2007), p. 203.

Hellerstein W./Kofler G./Mason R., Constitutional Restraints on Corporate Tax Integration, 62 *Tax L. Rev.* 1 (2008), p. 1.

Helminen M., Classification of Cross-Border Payments on Hybrid Instruments, 58 *Bull. Intl. Taxn.* 2 (2004), p. 56.

Helminen M., EU Law Compatibility of BEPS Action 2: Neutralising the Effects of Hybrid Mismatch Arrangements, 61 *British Tax Rev.* 3 (2015), p. 325.

Helminen M., Freedom of Establishment and Oy AA, 47 *Eur. Taxn.* 11 (2007), p. 490.

Helminen M., *The Dividend Concept in International Tax Law* (Kluwer, 1999).

Helminen M., The Future of Source State Dividend Withholding Taxes in Finland and the European Union, 48 *Eur. Taxn.* 7 (2008), p. 354.

Helminen M., *The Nordic Multilateral Tax Treaty* (IBFD, 2014).

Helminen M., The Problem of Double Non-Taxation in the European Union – To What Extent Could This Be Resolved through a Multilateral EU Tax Treaty Based on the Nordic Convention?, 53 *Eur. Taxn.* 7 (2013), p. 306.

Hennrichs J., Dualismus der Unternehmensbesteuerung aus gesellschaftsrechtlicher und steuersystematischer Sicht, 79 *StuW* 3 [2002], p. 201.

Hennrichs J./Lehmann U., Rechtsformneutralität der Unternehmensbesteuerung, 84 *StuW* 1 (2007), p. 16.

Herksen M., The BEPS Action Plan – A Story of the turtle and the hare?, 14 *Transfer Pricing Intl. J.* 8 (2013), p. 4.

Herlinghaus A., Rechtsfragen zur Steuerpflicht von Streubesitzdividenden gem. § 8b Abs. 4 KStG n.F., 95 *FR* 12 (2013), p. 529.

Herzig N., Besteuerung der Unternehmen in Europa – Harmonisierung im Wettbewerb der Systeme, in Lehner M. (ed.), *Steuerrecht im Europäischen Binnenmarkt*, DStJG 19 (Dr Otto Schmidt, 1996), p. 121.

Hey J., Base Erosion and Profit Shifting and Interest Expenditure, 68 *Bull. Intl. Taxn.* 6/7 (2014), p. 332.

Hey J., Besteuerung von Unternehmensgewinnen und Rechtsformneutralität, in Ebling I. (ed.), *Besteuerung von Einkommen*, DStJG 24 (Dr Otto Schmidt, 2001), p. 155.

Hey J., EU-Beihilfen und Steuervergünstigungen – Gemeinsamkeiten und Unterschiede, 92 *StuW* 4 (2015), p. 331.

Hey J., Germany I: *Kronos International, Magdeburger Mühlenwerke, Commission vs. Germany* I-III, in Lang M./Pistone P./Schuch J./Staringer C. (eds.), *ECJ – Recent Developments in Direct Taxation 2012* (Linde, 2013), p. 53.

Hey J., Perspektiven der Unternehmensbesteuerung, 81 *StuW* 3 (2004), p. 193.

Hey J., Vorrecht des Quellenstaates und binnenmarktkonforme Besteuerung von Kapitalgesellschaften in der Europäischen Union, in Spindler W./Tipke K./ Rödder T. (eds.), *Steuerzentrierte Rechtsberatung*, Festschrift für Harald Schaumburg zum 65. Geburtstag (Dr Otto Schmidt, 2009), p. 767.

Hey J./Wendt M. (eds.), *Herrmann C./Heuer G./Raupach A., Einkommensteuer- und Körperschaftsteuergesetz, Kommentar*[265] (Dr Otto Schmidt, 2014).

Heydt V., Einfluss des Gemeinschaftsrechts auf die Doppelbesteuerung, in W. Haarmann (ed.), *Auslegung und Anwendung von Doppelbesteuerungsabkommen* (Dr Otto Schmidt, 2004), p. 32.

Heydt V., Juridical Double Taxation: *Kerckhaert and Morres*, in Haslehner W.C./Kofler G./Rust A. (eds.), *Landmark Decisions of the ECJ in Direct Taxation* (Kluwer, 2015), p. 181.

Heydt V., Juristische Doppelbesteuerung als ungelöstes Problem: Kann der EuGH Klarheit schaffen?, 21 *SWI* 9 (2011), p. 371.

Hindelang S., *The Free Movement of Capital and Foreign Direct Investment* (Oxford University Press, 2009).

Hinnekens L., *AMID*: The Wrong Bridge or a Bridge Too Far? An Analysis of a Recent Decision of the European Court of Justice, 41 *Eur. Taxn.* 6 (2001), p. 206.

Hinnekens L., Basis and scope of public interest justification of national tax measures infringing fundamental Treaty freedoms, in Vanistendael F. (ed.), *EU Freedoms and Taxation* (IBFD, 2006), p. 73.

Hinnekens L., Compatibility of Bilateral Tax Treaties with European Community Law. The Rules, 3 *EC Tax Rev.* 4 (1994), p. 146.

Hinnekens L., Different interpretations of the European Tax Arbitration Convention, 7 *EC Tax Rev.* 4 (1998), p. 247.

Hinnekens L., European Court goes for robust tax principles for treaty freedoms. What about reasonable exceptions and balances?, 13 *EC Tax Rev.* 2 (2004) p. 65.

Hinnekens L., Non-discrimination in EC income tax law: painting in the colours of a chameleon-like principle, 36 *Eur. Taxn.* 9 (1996), p. 286.

Hinnekens L., The search for the framework conditions of the fundamental EC Treaty principles as applied by the European Court to Member State' direct taxation, 11 *EC Tax Rev.* 3 (2002), p. 112.

Hinnekens L./ Schelpe D., Bachmann v. Belgium (C-204/90) and Commission v. Belgium, 28. January 1992 (C-300/90), 1 *EC Tax Rev.* 1 (1992), p. 58.

Hintsanen L., National Report Finland, in Herdin J./Hofbauer I. (eds.), *WTO and Direct Taxation* (Linde, 2005), p. 257.

Hintsanen L./Pettersson K., The Implications of the ECJ Holding the Denial of Finnish Imputation Credits in Cross-Border Situations to Be Incompatible with the EC Treaty in the *Manninen* Case, 45 *Eur. Taxn.* 4 (2005), p. 130.

HJI Panayi C., *European Union Corporate Tax Law* (Cambridge University Press, 2013).

HJI Panayi C., State Aid and Tax: the Third Way?, 32 *Intertax* 6/7 (2004), p. 283.

HJI Panayi C., The Compatibility of the OECD/G20 Base Erosion and Profit Shifting Proposals with EU Law, 70 *Bull. Intl. Taxn.* (2016), p. 95.

Hofmann H.C.H./Morini A., Judicial review of Commission Decisions in State aid, in Szyszczak E. (ed.), *Research Handbook on European State Aid Law* (Edward Elgar Publishing, 2011), p. 354.

Hohenwarter D., The Allocation of Taxing Rights in the light of the Fundamental Freedoms of EC Law, in Lang M./Schuch J./Staringer C. (eds.), *Tax Treaty Law and EC Law* (Kluwer, 2007), p. 83.

Hohenwarter D., *Verlustverwertung im Konzern* (LexisNexis, 2009).

Hohenwarter D./Koppensteiner F., Die Erhebung von Quellensteuern im Verhältnis zu Drittstaaten aus gemeinschaftsrechtlicher Sicht, in Lang M./Schuch J./Staringer C. (eds.), *Quellensteuern* (Linde, 2010), p. 67.

Hohenwarter-Mayr D., Die Rs. *X Holding* – ein weiterer Teil im Puzzle der grenzüberschreitenden Gruppenbesteuerung, 20 *SWI* 2 (2011), p. 163.

Holoubek M., Zur Begründung des Verhältnismäßigkeitsgrundsatzes – verwaltungs-, verfassungs- und gemeinschaftsrechtliche Aspekte, in Griller S./Korinek K./ Potacs M. (eds.), *Grundfragen und aktuelle Probleme des öffentlichen Rechts*, Festschrift für Heinz Peter Rill zum 60. Geburtstag (Orac, 1995), p. 97.

Holthaus J., EU-Rechtswidrigkeit bei Vergütungen an EU-Unternehmen mit Zweigniederlassung im Tätigkeitsstaat, 3 *ISR* 8 (2014), p. 280.

Hufbauer G.C., Tax Discipline in the WTO, 4 *Journal of World Trade* 4 (2010), p. 763.

Hughes D., Gilly and the Big Picture, 52 *Bull. Intl. Taxn.* 8/9 (1998), p. 329.

Hughes D., Withholding taxes and the most favoured nation clause, 51 *Bull. Intl. Taxn.* 3 (1997), p. 126.

I. Cameron, *An introduction to the European convention on human rights*[6] (Iustus Förlag, 2011).

Ilhi U./Malmer K./Schonewille P./Tuominen I., Dividend taxation in the European Union, in IFA (ed.), *Trends in company shareholder taxation: single or double taxation?*, CDFI 88a (Kluwer, 2003), p. 71.

Intemann J., Die Neuregelung zur Steuerpflicht von Streubesitzdividenden, 68 *BB* 21 (2013), p. 1239.

Isenbaert M., *EC Law and the Sovereignty of the Member States in Direct Taxation* (Kluwer, 2010), at p. 242;

Ismer R., Prinzipien der Einkünfteermittlung - Periodizitätsprinzip, in Hey J. (ed.), *Einkünfteermittlung*, DStjG 34 (Dr Otto Schmidt, 2011), p. 91.

Ismer R./S. Piotrowski, The Selectivity of Tax Measures: A Tale of Two Consistencies, 43 *Intertax* 10 (2015), p. 559.

Jachmann M., Besteuerung von Unternehmen als Gleichheitsproblem, in Pelka J. (ed.), *Europa- und verfassungsrechtliche Grenzen der Unternehmensbesteuerung*, DStJG 23 (Dr Otto Schmidt, 2000), p. 9.

Jachmann M., *Steuergesetzgebung zwischen Gleichheit und wirtschaftlicher Freiheit* (Boorberg, 2000).

Jacobs F./White R./Ovey C., *The European Convention on Human Rights*[5] (Oxford University Press, 2010).

Jacobs F.G., Recent Developments in the Principle of Proportionality in European Community Law, in Ellis E. (ed.), *The Principle of Proportionality in the Laws of Europe* (Hart Publishing, 1999), p. 1.

Jacobs O.H., Corporation Income Tax Systems in the European Union - An Analysis of their Effects on Competition and Reform Proposals, 27 *Intertax* 8/9 (1999), p. 264.

Jacobs O.H., Corporation Income Tax Systems in the European Union - An Analysis of their Effects on Competition and Reform Proposals, 27 *Intertax* 8/9 (1999), p. 264.

Jaeger T., *Behilfen durch Steuern und parafiskalische Abgaben* (NWV, 2006).

Jankowiak I., *Doppelte Nichtbesteuerung im Internationalen Steuerrecht* (C.H. Beck, 2009).

Jarass H.D., Die Elemente einer Dogmatik der Grundfreiheiten, 30 *EuR* 3 (1995), p. 202.

Jarass H.D., Elemente einer Dogmatik der Grundfreiheiten II, 35 *EuR* 5 (2000), p. 705 (at p. 706);

Jesse L., Richtlinien-Umsetzungsgesetz - EURLUmsG: Anpassung des § 43b EStG (Kapitalertragsteuerbefreiung) an die geänderte Mutter-Tochter-Richtlinie, 14 *IStR* 5 (2005), p. 151.

Jestaedt T., Regional Aid, in Hancher L./Ottavanger T./Slot P.J. (eds.), *EU State Aids* (Sweet & Maxwell, 2012), p. 783.

Jestaedt T./Loest T., § 53 Rückforderung formell rechtskräftiger Beihilfen, in Heidenhain M. (ed.), *Handbuch des Europäischen Beihilfenrechts* (C.H. Beck, 2003), p. 929.

Jiménez A.J.M., *Towards Corporate Tax Harmonization in the European Community* (1999).

Jirousek H., Ist Artikel 14 DBA-Liechtenstein verfassungswidrig?, 27 *ÖStZ* 3 (2014), p. 64.

Jochum H., Systemfragen zu Mantelkauf und Sanierungsklausel, 93 *FR* 11 (2011), p. 497.

K. Daxkobler, *Die grundfreiheitliche Rechtsprechung des EuGH* (Linde, 2015).

Kahlenberg C., Die Anti-BEPS-Richtlinie als wesentlicher Bestandteil des EU Anti Tax Avoidance Package, 26 *SWI* 4 (2016), p. 206.

Kahlenberg C., Prevention of Double Non-taxation: An Analysis of Cross-Border Financing from a German Perspective, 43 *Intertax* 3 (2015), p. 218.

Kanduth-Kristen S./Laudacher M./Lenneis C./Marschner E./Vock M. (ed.), *Jakom Einkommensteuergesetz*[9] (Linde, 2016).

Keeling E., A First Reaction to *Asscher*, 2 *EC Tax J.* 1 (1997), p. 33.

Kelsen H., *Pure Theory of Law* (University of California Press, 1967).

Kelsen H., *Reine Rechtslehre*[2] (Deuticke, 1960).

Kemmeren E.C.C.M., After repeal of Article 293 EC Treaty under the Lisbon Treaty: the EU objective of eliminating double taxation can be applied more widely, 17 *EC Tax Rev.* 4 (2008), p. 156.

Kemmeren E.C.C.M., ECJ should not unbundle integrated tax systems!, 17 *EC Tax Rev.* 1 (2008), p. 4.

Kemmeren E.C.C.M., Pending Cases Filed by Dutch Courts I: The Van Dijk and Bujura Cases, in Lang M./ Schuch J./Staringer C. (eds.), *ECJ – Recent Developments in Direct Taxation* (Linde, 2006), p. 219.

Kemmeren E.C.C.M., *Sopora*: A Welcome Landmark Decision on Horizontal Comparison, 24 *EC Tax Rev.* 4 (2015), p. 178.

Kemmeren E.C.C.M., The termination of the 'most favoured nation clause' dispute in tax treaty law and the necessity of a Euro Model Tax Convention, 6 *EC Tax Rev.* 3 (1997), p. 146.

Kemmeren E.C.C.M., Where is EU Law in the OECD BEPS Discussion?, 23 *EC Tax Rev.* 4 (2014), p. 190.

Kerschner I./Koppensteiner F./Seydl C., Österreich erhebt aufgrund einer DBA-Streitigkeit erstmals Klage beim EuGH, 26 *SWI* 3 (2016), p. 134.

Keuschnigg C./Devereux M.P., *The Distorting Arm's Length Principle*, Oxford University Centre for Business Taxation, Working Paper 09/10 (9 July 2009).

Kiekebeld B.J., *Harmful tax competition in the European Union* (Kluwer, 2004).

Kingreen T., *Die Struktur der Grundfreiheiten des Europäischen Gemeinschaftsrechts* (Duncker & Humblot, 1999).

Kingreen T., Fundamental Freedoms, in von Bogdandy A./Bast J. (eds.), *Principles of European Constitutional Law*[2] (Hart Publishing, 2009), p. 515.

Kingston S., A Light in the Darkness: Recent Developments in the ECJ's Direct Tax Jurisprudence, 44 *Common Market L. Rev.* 5 (2007), p. 1321.

Kirchhof P., Der verfassungsrechtliche Auftrag zur Besteuerung nach der finanziellen Leistungsfähigkeit, 62 *StuW* 4 (1985), p. 319.

Kirchhof P./ Söhn H./Mellinghoff R. (eds.), *EStG*[121] (C.F. Müler, 2002).

Kirchmayr S./Kofler G., Beteiligungsertragsbefreiung und internationale Steuerarbitrage, *GES* 9 (2011), p. 449.

Kleinbard E.D., Through a Latte Darkly: Starbuck's Stateless Income Planning, 139 *Tax Notes* (24 June 2013), p. 1515.

Kletečka A./Schauer M. (eds.), *ABGB-ON*$^{1.01}$.

Kluge V., *Das Internationale Steuerrecht*^{4} (C.H. Beck, 2000).

Knobbe-Keuk B., Ist das deutsche Körperschaftsteueranrechnungsverfahren zu halten?, in Kirchhof P./Offerhaus K./Schöberle H. (eds.), *Steuerrecht Verfassungsrecht Finanzpolitik*, Festschrift für Franz Klein (Dr Otto Schmidt, 1994), p. 347.

Knobbe-Keuk B., Restrictions on the Fundamental Freedoms Enshrined in the EC Treaty by Discriminatory Tax Provisions - Ban and Justification - 3 *EC Tax Rev.* 3 (1994), p. 74.

Knoll M.S./Mason R., *Comptroller v. Wynne*: Internal Consistency, a National Marketplace, and Limits on State Sovereignty to Tax, 163 *University of Pennsylvania Law Rev. Online* (2015), p. 267.

Knoll M.S./Mason R., *Wynne*: It's Not About Double Taxation, 57 *State Tax Notes* 7 (16 February 2015), p. 413.

Koenig C., Where is State Aid Law heading to?, 13 *Eur. St. Aid L. Q.* 4 (2014), p. 611.

Koenig C./Busch M., Gemeinschaftsrechtliche Anforderungen an eine Umsatzsteuerbefreiung für Postdienstleistungen (§ 4 Nr. 11b UStG), 20 *EWS* 12 (2009), p. 510.

Koenig C./Kühling J., Reform des EG-Beihilfenrechts aus der Perspektive des mitgliedstaatlichen Systemwettbewerbs, 10 *EuZW* 17 (1999), p. 517.

Koenig C./Scholz M., Die Förderung transeuropäischer Netzinfrastrukturen, 14 *EWS* 5 (2003), p. 223.

Kofler G., "Hybride Finanzinstrumente" in der Mutter-Tochter-Richtlinie, 9 *Zeitschrift für Finanzmarktrecht* 5 (2014), p. 214.

Kofler G., "Horzontal Discrimination" in European Tax Law, in Richelle I./Schön W./Traversa E. (eds.), *Allocating Taxing Powers within the European Union* (Springer, 2013), p. 187.

Kofler G., Auslegung und Anwendung des harmonisierten Steuerrechts, 3 *ISR* 4 (2014), p. 126.

Kofler G., Austria: Changes to Austria's Tax Treatment of Outbound Inter-Company Dividends, 18 *EC Tax Rev.* 6 (2009), p. 312.

Kofler G., Bouanich: Diskriminierende Bemessungsgrundlage und Doppelbesteuerungsabkommen, 19 *ÖStZ* 13 (2006), p. 290.

Kofler G., Das Ende vom Anfang der gemeinschaftsrechtlichen Meistbegünstigung, 58 *ÖStZ* 19 (2005), p. 432.

Kofler G., Das Verhältnis zwischen primärem und sekundärem Unionsrecht im direkten Steuerrecht, in Lang M./ Weinzierl Ch. (eds.), *Europäisches Steuerrecht, Festschrift für Friedrich Rödler* (Linde, 2010), p. 433.

Kofler G., *Doppelbesteuerungsabkommen und Europäisches Gemeinschaftsrecht* (Linde, 2007).

Kofler G., Double Taxation and European Union Law: Analysis of the Jurisprudence, in Rust A. (ed.), *Double Taxation within the European Union* (Kluwer, 2011).

Kofler G., EFTA-Gerichtshof: Besteuerung von "Auswärtsausschüttungen" unter der EWR-Kapitalverkehrsfreiheit, 18 *ÖStZ* 7 (2005), p. 143.

Kofler G., Einige Überlegungen gegen die DBA-Irrelevanzthese im Fokus Bank-Urteil, 18 *ÖStZ 8* (2005), p. 169.

Kofler G., Generalanwalt zur Kapitalverkehrsfreiheit und Meistbegünstigung bei DBA-Anwendung, 17 *ÖStZ* 23 (2004), p. 558.

Kofler G., Hughes de Lasteyrie du Saillant: Wegzugsbesteuerung verstößt gegen die Niederlassungsfreiheit!, 16 *ÖStZ* 11 (2003), p. 262.

Kofler G., Hybrid Loans in the Parent-Subsidiary-Directive, in P. Valente (ed.), *Elusione Fiscale Internazionale* (IPSOA (Kluwer), 2014), p. 682.

Kofler G., Indirect Credit versus Exemption: Double Taxation Relief for Intercompany Distributions, 66 *Bull. Intl. Taxn.* 2 (2012), p. 77.

Kofler G., Ist der Spuk des Europäischen Steuerrechts bald vorbei?, in Schön W./ Heber C. (eds.), *Grundfragen des Europäischen Steuerrechts* (Springer, 2015), p. 1.

Kofler G., Kapitalverkehrsfreiheit, Kontrollbeteiligungen und Drittstaaten, 4 *taxlex* 8 (2008), p. 326.

Kofler G., Manninen: Kapitalverkehrsfreiheit verpflichtet zur grenzüberschreitenden Anrechnung ausländischer Körperschaftsteuer, 17 *ÖStZ* 24 (2004), p. 582

Kofler G., Most-Favoured-Nation Treatment in Direct Taxation: Does EC Law Provide for Community MFN in Bilateral Double Taxation Treaties?, 5 *Hous. Bus. & Tax L. J.* 1 (2005), p. 1.

Kofler G., *Mutter-Tochter-Richtlinie* (LexisNexis, 2011).

Kofler G., Steuergestaltung im Europäischen und Internationalen Recht, in Hüttemann R. (ed.), *Gestaltungsfreiheit und Gestaltungsmissbrauch im Steuerrecht,* DStJG 34 (Dr Otto Schmidt, 2010), p. 213.

Kofler G., Tax Treaty "Neutralization" of Source State Discrimination under the EU Fundamental Freedoms?, 65 *Bull. Intl. Taxn.* 12 (2011), p. 684.

Kofler G., The BEPS Action Plan and Transfer Pricing: The Arm's Length Standard Under Pressure?, 58 *British Tax Rev.* 5 (2013), p. 646.

Kofler G., Wer hat das Sagen im Steuerrecht - EuGH (Teil 1), 19 *ÖStZ* 6 (2006), p. 106.

Kofler G., Wer hat das Sagen im Steuerrecht - EuGH (Teil 2), 19 *ÖStZ* 8 (2006), p. 154.

Kofler G./Kofler H., Betriebsstätten in der Mutter-Tochter-Richtlinie, in Quantschnigg P./Wiesner W./Mayr G. (eds.), *Steuern im Gemeinschaftsrecht, Festschrift für Wolfgang Nolz* (LexisNexis, 2008), p. 53.

Kofler G./Kofler H., Internationale Steuerarbitrage, in Brähler G./Lösel C. (eds.), *Deutsches und internationales Steuerrecht - Gegenwart und Zukunft, Festschrift Djanani* (Gabler, 2008), p. 381.

Kofler G./Mason R., Double Taxation: A European "Switch in Time?", 14 *Colum. J. Eur. L.* 1 (2007), p. 63.

Kofler G./Mason R., *Kerckhaert & Morres*: A European "Switch in Time?", in Van Thiel S. (ed.), *The internal market and direct taxation: Is the European Court of Justice taking a new approach?* (CFE Brochure on European Taxation, 2007), p. 176.

Kofler G./Metzler V., Block: Kein Verbot der juristischen Doppelbesteuerung im Binnenmarkt, 22 *ÖStZ* 9 (2009), p. 219.

Kofler G./Rust A., Deutsches BVerfG zur Verfassungskonformität von -"Treaty Overrides", 26 *SWI* 3 (2016), p. 144.

Kofler G./Schindler C.P., "Dancing with Mr D": The ECJ's Denial of Most-Favoured-Nation Treatment in the "D" case, 45 *Eur. Taxn.* 12 (2005), p. 530.

Kofler G./Tenore M., Fundamental Freedoms and Directives in the Area of Direct Taxation, in Weber D. (ed.), *Traditional and Alternative Routes to European Tax Integration* (IBFD, 2010), p. 311.

Kofler G./Tumpel M., Amurta: Diskriminierende Quellenbesteuerung und Anrechnungsmethode, 21 *ÖStZ* 3 (2008), p. 54.

Kogels H., Unity Divided, 21 *EC Tax Review* 3 (2012), p. 117.

Köhler M., Private Enforcement of State Aid Law – Problems of Guaranteeing EU Rights by means of National (Procedural) Law, 11 *Eur. St. Aid L. Q.* 2 (2012), p. 369.

Köhler S./Tippelhofer M., Kapitalverkehrsfreiheit auch in Drittstaatenfällen?, 16 *IStR* 18 (2007), p. 645.

Kokott J., Die Bedeutung der europarechtlichen Diskriminierungsverbote und Grunfreiheiten für das Steuerrecht der EU-Mitgliedstaaten, in Lehner M. (ed.), *Grundfreiheiten im Steuerrecht der EU-Staaten* (C.H. Beck, 2000), p. 1.

Korf R., Neues zum Missbrauch – Anmerkungen zu den EuGH-Urteilen RBS Deutschland Holdings und Weald Leasing Ltd, 20 *IStR* 4 (2011), p. 146.

Körner A., Europarecht und CFC-Regelungen - Anrufung des EuGH im Verfahren "Cadbury Schweppes", 13 *IStR* 20 (2004), p. 697.

Körner A., Europarecht und Wegzugsbesteuerung - das EuGH-Urteil "de Lasteyrie du Saillant", 13 *IStR* 12 (2004), p. 424.

Krabbe H., EG-Schiedsverfahren bei Berichtigung von Verrechnungspreisen im Konzern, 28 *RIW* 4 (1982), p. 269.

Kreile R., Zum Vorentwurt einer EG-Richtlinie über die Harmonisierung der steuerrechtlichen Gewinnermittlungsvorschriften, Supplement 18/88 to 41 *Der Betrieb* 45 (1988).

Kube H., Die Gleichheitsdogmatik des europäischen Wettbewerbsrechts - zur Beihilfenkontrolle staatlicher Ausgleichsleistungen, 39 *EuR* 2 (2004), p. 230.

Kube H., Die intertemporale Verlustverrechnung – Verfassungsrechtlicher Rahmen und legislativer Gestaltungsraum, 49 *DStR* 38 (2011), p. 1781.

Kube H., *National Tax Law and the Transnational Control of State Aids* (EU Working Paper LAW No. 2001/9).

Kudert S./Kahlenberg C., Extension of the Domestic Correspondence Principle, 54 *Eur. Taxn.* 1 (2014), p. 40.

Kühbacher T., Die Rs "Truck Center SA" - Neues zur Abzugsbesteuerung des § 99 EStG?, 62 *ÖStZ* 9 (2009), p. 224.

Kühbacher T., Die Rs Damseaux: Ist juristische Doppelbesteuerung im Gemeinschaftsrecht nun endgültig erlaubt?, 22 *ÖStZ* 20 (2009), p. 496.

Kühbacher T., Doppelbesteuerung und Unionsrecht: letzter Akt einer (un)endlichen Geschichte, 20 *SWI* 7 (2010), p. 308.

Lamon H., Belgium, in IFA (ed.), *Cross-Border Business Restructuring*, CDFI 96a (IBFD, 2011), p. 127.

Lampe M., General Subject-To-Tax Clauses in Recent Tax Treaties, 39 *Eur. Taxn.* 4/5 (1999), p. 183.

Lampert T., Dezentrale Beihilfenaufsicht durch Konkurrentenklagen vor den nationalen Gerichten der Mitgliedstaaten, 12 *EWS* 8 (2001), p. 357.

Lang J. in Widmann S. (ed.), *Besteuerung der GmbH und ihrer Gesellschafter*, DStJG 20 (Dr Otto Schmidt, 1997), p. 69.

Lang J., *Die Bemessungsgrundlage der Einkommensteuer* (Dr Otto Schmidt, 1988).

Lang J., Prinzipien und Systeme der Besteuerung von Einkommen, in Ebling I. (ed.), *Besteuerung von Einkommen,* DStJG 24 (Dr Otto Schmidt, 2001), p. 49

Lang J./Englisch J., A European Legal Tax Order Based on Ability to Pay, in A. Amatucci (ed.), *International Tax Law* (Kluwer, 2012), p. 261 (at p. 308).

Lang J.M./Stack R.B./Charnovitz S./Brady J.T., What Tax Lawyers Should Know About Trade Law, 29 *Tax Mgt. Intl. J.* 10 (2000), p. 566.

Lang M., "Aggressive Steuerplanung" - eine Analyse der Empfehlung der Europäischen Kommission, 23 *SWI* 2 (2013), p. 62.

Lang M., 2005 - Eine Wende in der steuerlichen Rechtsprechung des EuGH zu den Grundfreiheiten?, in Mellinghof R./Schön W./ Viskorf H. (eds.), *Steuerrecht im Rechtsstaat, Festschrift für Wolfgang Spindler zum 65. Geburtstag* (Dr Otto Schmidt, 2011), p. 297.

Lang M., *Cadbury Schweppes*' Line of Case Law from the Member States' Perspective, in de la Feria R./Vogenauer S. (eds.), *Prohibition of Abuse of Law* (Hart, 2011), p. 435.

Lang M., Das EuGH-Urteil in der Rechtssache D. - Gerät der Motor der Steuerharmonisierung ins Stottern?, 15 *SWI* 8 (2005), p. 365.

Lang M., Das EuGH-Urteil in der Rechtssache Schempp - Wächst der steuerpolitische Spielraum der Mitgliedsstaaten?, 15 *SWI* 9 (2005), p. 411.

Lang M., Das Gibraltar-Urteil des EuGH: Neue beihilferechtliche Vorgaben für das Steuerrecht?, 24 *ÖStZ* 24 (2011), p. 593.

Lang M., Der Anwendungsbereich der Grundfreiheiten - Maßgeblichkeit des Sachverhalts oder der nationalen Rechtsvorschrift, in Lang M./ Weinzierl C. (eds.), *Europäisches Steuerrecht, Festschrift für Friedrich Rödler zum 60. Geburtstag* (Linde, 2010), p. 521.

Lang M., Der EuGH als Interpret von Doppelbesteuerungsabkommen, in Lüdicke J./Mössner J.M./Hummel L. (eds.), *Das Steuerrecht der Unternehmen - Festschrift für Gerrit Frotscher zum 70. Geburtstag* (Haufe-Lexware, 2013), p. 365.

Lang M., *Die Auswirkungen des gemeinschaftsrechtlichen Beihilferechts auf das Steuerrecht*, 17. ÖJT, Band IV/1 (Manz, 2009).

Lang M., Die Bindung der Doppelbesteuerungsabkommen an die Grundfreiheiten des EU-Rechts, in Gassner W./Lang M./Lechner E. (eds.), *Doppelbesteuerungsabkommen und EU-Recht* (Linde, 1996), p. 25.

Lang M., Die Firmenwertabschreibung als selektive Beihilfe?, 27 *ÖStZ* 11 (2014), p. 277.

Lang M., Die gemeinschaftsrechtlichen Rahmenbedingungen für "Exit Taxes" im Lichte der Schlussanträge von GA Kokott in der Rechtssache N., 16 *SWI* 5 (2006), p. 213.

Lang M., Die Konsequenzen des VfGH-Erkenntnisses zum DBA Liechtenstein, 24 *SWI* 9 (2014), p. 402.

Lang M., Die Rechtsprechung des EuGH zu den direkten Steuern - Planungssicherheit für die nationalen Gesetzgeber?, in Wagner A./Wedl V. (eds.), *Bilanz und Perspektiven zum europäischen Recht* (ÖGB Verlag, 2007), p. 113.

Lang M., *Die Rechtsprechung des EuGH zu den direkten Steuern* (Peter Lang, 2007).

Lang M., Die Vermeidung der Doppelbesteuerung und der doppelten Nichtbesteuerung als DBA-Auslegungsmaxime?, 11 *IStR* 18 (2002), p. 609.

Lang M., Die Zukunft der Doppelbesteuerungsabkommen im Lichte von Columbus Container, in Kirchhof P./Nieskens H. (eds.), *Festschrift für Wolfram Reiss zum 65. Geburtstag* (Dr Otto Schmidt, 2008), p. 679.

Lang M., Die Zukunft des Internationalen Steuerrechts in Europa, in Gassner W./ Hemetsberger-Koller H./Lang M./Sasseville J./Vogel K. (eds.), *Die Zukunft des Internationalen Steuerrechts* (Linde, 1999), p. 71.

Lang M., Direct Taxation: Is the ECJ Heading in a New Direction?, 46 *Eur. Taxn.* 9 (2006), p. 421.

Lang M., Direkte Steuern und EU-Steuerpolitik - Wo bleiben die Visionen?, 22 *IStR* 10 (2013), p. 365.

Lang M., Doppelbesteuerungsabkommen und Gleichheitssatz, 24 *SWI* 2 (2014), p. 58.

Lang M., Dreifache Nichtbesteuerung als Ergebnis der Anwendung von Doppelbesteuerungsabkommen, 25 *SWI* 5 (2015), p. 198.

Lang M., ECJ case law on cross-border dividend taxation - recent developments, 17 *EC Tax. Rev.* 2 (2008), p. 67.

Lang M., Eine Wende in der Rechtsprechung des EuGH zu den direkten Steuern?, in Hebig M./Kaiser K./Koschmieder K./Oblau M. (eds.), *Aktuelle Entwicklungsaspekte der Unternehmensbesteuerung*, Festschrift für Wilhelm H. Wacker (Erich Schmidt Verlag, 2006), p. 365.

Lang M., Europäisches Beihilfenrecht und Besteuerung - am Beispiel des § 8c KStG, in Lüdicke J. (ed.), *Praxis und Zukunft des Internationalen Steuerrechts* (Dr Otto Schmidt, 2012), p. 85.

Lang M., Europarechtliche Aspekte der Besteuerung von Erbschaften, in Birk D. (ed.), *Steuern auf Erbschaft und Vermögen*, DStJG 22 (Dr Otto Schmidt, 1999), p. 255.

Lang M., Gemeinschaftsrechtliche Verpflichtung zur Rechtsformneutralität im Steuerrecht?, 15 *IStR* 12 (2006), p. 397.

Lang M., *General Report*, in IFA (ed.), *Double Non-Taxation*, CDFI 89a (SDU, 2004), p. 73.

Lang M., *Introduction to the Law of Double Taxation Conventions*[2] (Linde, 2013).

Lang M., Ist die Schumacker-Rechtsprechung am Ende? 51 *Recht der Internationalen Wirtschaft* 5 (2005), p. 336.

Lang M., Jüngste Tendenzen in der Rechtsprechung des EuGH zur Bedeutung der Grundfreiheiten für die direkten Steuern, in Beusch M. (ed.), Steuerrecht 2007 (Schulthess, 2007), p. 5.

Lang M., Jüngste Tendenzen zur "horizontalen" Vergleichbarkeitsprüfung in der steuerlichen Rechtsprechung des EuGH zu den Grundfreiheiten, 21 *SWI* 4 (2011), p. 154.

Lang M., Kapitalverkehrsfreiheit und Doppelbesteuerungsabkommen, in Lechner E./ Staringer C./ Tumpel M. (eds.), *Kapitalverkehrsfreiheit und Steuerrecht* (Linde, 2000), p. 181.

Lang M., Kapitalverkehrsfreiheit, Steuerrecht und Drittstaaten, 88 *StuW* 3 (2011), p. 209.

Lang M., Marks and Spencer - more questions than answers: an analysis of the Opinion delivered by Advocate General Maduro, 14 *EC Tax Rev.* 2 (2005), p. 95.

Lang M., Recent Case Law of the ECJ in Direct Taxation: Trends, Tensions, and Contradictions, 18 *EC Tax Rev.* 3 (2009), p. 98.

Lang M., Selectivity as a Criterion to Determine Whether a Tax Measure Constitutes State Aid, in Pistone P. (ed.), *Legal Remedies in European Tax Law* (IBFD, 2009), p. 269.

Lang M., Seminar J: Steuerrecht, Grundfreiheiten und Beihilfeverbot, 19 *IStR* 15 (2010), p. 570.

Lang M., State Aid and Taxation: Recent Trends in the Case Law of the ECJ, 11 *Eur. St. Aid L. Q.* 2 (2012), p. 411.

Lang M., State Aid and Taxation: Selectivity and Comparability Analysis, in Richelle I./ Schön W./Traversa E. (eds.), *Allocating Taxing Powers within the European Union* (Springer, 2013), p. 27.

Lang M., Tax Rulings and State Aid Law, 60 *British Tax Rev.* 3 (2015), p. 391.

Lang M., Tax Rulings und Beihilferecht, 24 *IStR* 11 (2015), p. 369.

Lang M., *The Application of the OECD Model Tax Convention to Partnerships – A Critical Analysis of the Report Prepared by the OECD Committee on Fiscal Affairs* (Linde, 2000).

Lang M., The Binding Effect of the EC Fundamental Freedoms on Tax Treaties, in Gassner W./Lang M./Lechner E. (eds.), *Tax Treaties and EC Law* (Kluwer, 1996), p. 15.

Lang M., The Concept of a Multilateral Tax Treaty, in Lang M./Loukota H./Rädler A.J./Schuch J./Toifl G./Urtz C./Wassermeyer F./Züger M., *Multilateral Tax Treaties* (Kluwer, 1998), p. 187.

Lang M., There's Life in the Old Dog Yet: Horizontal Comparability and the Establishment of the Internal Market, in Avi-Yonah R.S./Lang M. (eds.), *Comparative Fiscal Federalism*[2] (2016), forthcoming.

Lang M., Totgesagte leben länger: Horizontale Vergleichbarkeit und die Verwirklichung des Binnenmarkts, 26 *SWI* 3 (2016), p. 118.

Lang M., Treaty Override und Gemeinschaftsrecht, in Lehner M. (ed.), *Reden zum Andenken an Klaus Vogel* (C.H. Beck, 2010), p. 59

Lang M., Umsatzsteuer und Doppelbesteuerung, in Achatz M./Tumpel M. (eds.), *Umsatzsteuer und Internationales Steuerrecht* (Linde, 2012), p. 19.

Lang M., Vermeidung der Doppelbesteuerung und der doppelten Nichtbesteuerung als Auslegungsmaxime für Doppelbesteuerungsabkommen?, in Haarmann W. (ed.), *Auslegung und Anwendung von Doppelbesteuerungsabkommen* (Dr Otto Schmidt, 2004), p. 83.

Lang M., Wohin geht das Internationale Steuerrecht?, 14 *IStR* 9 (2005), p. 289.

Lang M., Zum Seminar G: Verbietet das Gemeinschaftsrecht die Erhebung von Quellensteuern?, 18 *IStR* 15 (2009), p. 539.

Lang M./ Dommes S., Tax Treaty Law and EC Law – Reciprocity and the Balance of a Tax Treaty, in Lang M./Schuch J./Staringer C. (eds.), *Tax Treaty Law and EC Law* (Linde, 2007), p. 61.

Lang M./Heidenbauer S., Wholly Artificial Arrangements, in Hinnekens L./Hinnekens P. (eds.), *A Vision of Taxes within and outside European Borders*, Festschrift in honor of Prof. Dr. Frans Vanistendael (Kluwer, 2008), p. 597.

Lang M./Jettmar A., Steuerrecht und Sozial(versicherungs)recht – Anmerkungen zum Schlussantrag in der Rs. Blanckaert – *Internationale Wirtschaftsbriefe*, Fach 11, Gruppe 2, Nr. 15 (2005), p. 741.

Lang M./Lüdicke J./Reich M., Beteiligungen im Privatvermögen: Die Besteuerung des Wegzugs aus Österreich und Deutschland in die Schweiz – Teil II, 17 *IStR* 20 (2008), p. 709.

Lang M./Lüdicke J./Reich M., Beteiligungen im Privatvermögen: Die Besteuerung des Wegzugs aus Österreich und Deutschland in die Schweiz – Teil II, 17 *IStR* 20 (2008), p. 709.

Lang M./Paterno L., Die Vermeidung der Doppelbesteuerung in der föderalen Struktur Österreichs, 1 *Spektrum der Rechtswissenschaften* 1 (2011), p. 76.

Lang M./Paterno L., Internationales Steuerrecht und Besteuerung im Bundesstaat, 21 *SWI* 12 (2011), p. 520.

Lang M./Rust A./Schuch J./Staringer C. (eds.), *KStG*^{2} (Linde, 2016).

Lang M./Staringer C., General Report, in IFA (ed.), *Qualification of taxable entities and treaty protection*, CDFI 99B (Sdu, 2014), p. 17.

Lang S., Gewinnanteile aus internationalen Schachtelbeteiligungen am Beispiel Brasiliens, 23 *SWI* 3 (2013), p. 95.

Larking B., Fokus Bank: the end of withholding tax as we know it?, 14 *EC Tax Rev.* 2 (2005), p. 69.

Leegaard T./Valat A., Imputation Tax Credit under Free Movement of Capital (Art. 40 EEA Agreement), 44 *Eur. Taxn.* 4 (2004), p. 207.

Lehner M., Avoidance of Double Taxation within the European Unio: Is There an Obligation under EC Law?, in Lang M./Schuch J./Staringer C. (eds.) *Tax Treaty Law and EC Law* (Linde, 2007), p. 11.

Lehner M., Grundlagen des Abkommensrechts, in Vogel K./Lehner M. (eds.), *DBA*^{6} (C.H. Beck, 2015), p. 111.

Lehner M., Limitation of the national power of taxation by the fundamental freedoms and non-discrimination clauses of the EC Treaty, 9 *EC Tax Rev.* 1 (2000), p. 5.

Lehner M., *Möglichkeiten zur Verbesserung des Verständigungsverfahrens auf der Grundlage des EWG-Vertrags* (C.H. Beck, 1982).

Lehner M., The Influence of EU Law on Tax Treaties from a German Perspective, 54 *Bull. Intl. Taxn.* 8 (2000), p. 461.

Lehner M., Treaty Override ist nicht verfassungswidrig, 25 *IStR* 6 (2016), p. 217.

Lenaerts K., "United in Diversity" – also *In Fiscalibus?*, in Hinnekens L./Hinnekens P. (eds.), *A Vision of Taxes within and outside Europe, Festschrift in honor of Prof. Dr. Frans Vanistendael* (Kluwer, 2008), p. 617.

Lenaerts K., Die Entwicklung der Rechtsprechung des Gerichtshofs der Europäischen Gemeinschaften auf dem Gebiet der direkten Besteuerung, 44 *EuR* 6 (2009), p. 728.

Lenaerts K., Federalism and the Rule of Law: Perspectives from the European Court of Justice, 33 *Fordham Intl. L. J.* 5 (2010), p. 1338.

Lenaerts K., State Aid and Direct Taxation, in Kanninen H./Korjus N./Rosas A. (eds.), *EU Competition Law in Context: Essays in Honour of Virpi Tiili* (Hart Publishing, 2009), p. 291.

Lenaerts K./Van Nuffel P., *Constitutional Law of the European Union*[2] (Sweet & Maxwell, 2005), at p. 143.

Lennard M., The Purpose and Current Status of the United Nations Tax Work, 13 *Asia-Pacific Tax Bull.* 1 (2008), p. 23.

Leone F./Zanotti E., Notional Interest Deduction Regime Introduced, 52 *Eur. Taxn.* 8 (2012), p. 432.

Liebman H.M./Rousselle O., Discriminatory Treatment of Dividends in The European Union: Is the End Near?, 39 *Tax Notes Intl.* 2 (11 July 2005), p. 143.

Liede H./Hintsanen L., Finnish Imputation System under ECJ Scrutiny, 43 *Eur. Taxn.* 1 (2003), p. 31.

Listl P.R., Anmerkungen zum Entwurf der Änderung der EU Mutter-Tochter-Richtlinie vom 25. 11. 2013, 23 *IStR* 12 (2014), p. 448.

Lodin S., The imputation systems and cross-border dividends - the need for new solutions, 7 *EC Tax Rev.* 4 (1998), p. 229.

López H., General Thought on Selectivity and Consequences of a Broad Concept of State Aid in Tax Matters, 9 *Eur. St. Aid L. Q.* 4 (2010), p. 807.

Lornsen B., *Unilaterale Maßnahmen der Bundesrepublik Deutschland zur Ausschaltung der internationalen Doppelbesteuerung bei der Einkommen- und Körperschaftsteuer* (Peter Lang, 1987).

Loukota H., DBA Liechtenstein auf dem Prüfstand des Verfassungsgerichtshofs, 24 *SWI* 1 (2014), p. 2.

Loukota H., Der Einfluss des österreichischen Ertragsteuerrechtes auf die Auslegung von Doppelbesteuerungsabkommen, in Beiser R./Kirchmayr S./Mayr G./Zorn N. (eds.), *Ertragsteuern in Wissenschaft und Praxis*, Festschrift für Werner Doralt (LexisNexis, 2007), p. 263.

Loukota H., Die Vermeidung von Besteuerungskonflikten für das international tätige Unternehmen, in Gassner W./Lang M. (eds.), *Besteuerung und Bilanzierung international tätiger Unternehmen*, 30 Jahre Steuerrecht an der Wirtschaftsuniversität Wien (Orac, 1998), p. 265.

Loukota H., Lösung internationaler Qualifikationskonflikte, 9 *SWI* 2 (1999), p. 70.

Loukota H., Multilateral Tax Treaty Versus Bilateral Treaty Network, in Lang M./Loukota H./Rädler A.J./Schuch J./Toifl G./Urtz C./Wassermeyer F./Züger M., *Multilateral Tax Treaties* (Kluwer, 1998), p. 85.

Loukota H./Jirousek H., Doppelbesteuerung und Gemeinschaftsrecht, 17 *SWI* 1 (2007), p. 295.

Loukota W., *EG-Grundfreiheiten und beschränkte Steuerpflicht* (Linde, 2006).

Lüdicke J., Pending Cases Filed by German Courts I: The Meilicke, CLT-UFA, Keller Holding, Lasertac, Rewe Zentralfinanz, Ritter-Colais, Kolumbus Container Services, and Stauffer Cases, in Lang M./Schuch J./Staringer C. (eds.), *ECJ Recent Developments in Direct Taxation* (Linde, 2006), p. 113.

Lüdicke J./Oppel F., Kommissions-Entwurf einer Anti-BEPS-Richtlinie: Grundlegende Änderungen und Verschärfungen des deutschen Rechts, 69 *DB* 10 (2016), p. 549.

Lüdicke J./Oppel F., Der Vorschlag der EU-Kommission einer Anti-BEPS-Richtlinie – ein erster Überblick, 71 *BB* 6 (2016), p. 351.

Luja R., *Assessment and Recovery of Tax Incentives in the EC and the WTO: A View on State Aids, Trade Subsidies and Direct Taxation* (Intersentia, 2003).

Luja R., EU State Aid Law and National Tax Rulings: In-Depth Analysis for the TAXE Special Committee, IP/A/TAXE/2015-02, PE 563.453 (October 2015).

Luja R., EU State Aid Rules and Their Limits, 76 *Tax Notes Intl.* 4 (27 October 2014), p. 353.

Luja R., Group Taxation, Sectoral Tax Benefits and De Facto Selectivity in State Aid Review, 8 *Eur. St. Aid L. Q.* 4 (2009), p. 473.

Luja R., Revisiting the Balance between Aid, Selectivity and Selective Aid in Respect of Taxes and Special Levies, 9 *Eur. St. Aid L. Q.* 1 (2010), p. 161.

Luja R., Tax Treaties and State Aid: Some Thoughts, 44 *Eur. Taxn.* 4 (2004), p. 234.

Luja R., State Aid Benchmarking and Tax Rulings: Can We Keep It Simple?, in Richelle I./Schön W./Traversa E. (eds.), *Allocating Taxing Powers within the European Union* (Springer, 2013), p. 111.

Luja R., The Selectivity Test: The Concept of Sectoral Aid, in Rust A./Micheau C. (eds.), *State Aid and Tax Law* (Kluwer, 2013), p. 107.

Luja R., Will the EU's State Aid Regime Survive BEPS?, 60 *British Tax Rev.* 3 (2015), p. 379.

Luts J., Compatibility of IP Box Regimes with EU State Aid Rules and Code of Conduct, 23 *EC Tax Rev.* 5 (2014), p. 258.

Lyal R., Free Movement of Capital and Non-Member Countries – Consequences for Direct Taxation, in Weber D. (ed.), *The Influence of European Tax Law on Direct Taxation* (Kluwer, 2007), p. 17.

Lyal R., Non-discrimination and direct tax in Community law, 12 *EC Tax Rev.* 2 (2003), p. 68.

Lyal R., Transfer Pricing Rules and State Aid, 38 *Fordham Intl. L. J.* 4 (2015), p. 1017.

Lynch F.M.B., Resolving the Paradox of the Monnet Plan: National and International Planning in French Reconstruction, 37 *The Economic History Review* 2 (1984), p. 229.

Maisto G., The 2003 amendments to the EC Parent-Subsidiary Directive: what's next?, 13 *EC Tax Rev.* 4 (2004), p. 164.

Malherbe J./Wathelet M., Pending Cases Filed by Belgian Courts: The Kerckhaert-Morres Case Pending Cases involving Belgium: The Belgian Coordination Centres Cases, Commission v Belgium, Commission v Belgium Pending Cases Filed by French Courts: The Denkavit Case, in Lang M./ Schuch J./Staringer C. (eds.), *ECJ – Recent Developments in Direct Taxation* (Linde, 2006), p. 29.

Malmer K., Emigration taxes and EC law, in IFA (ed.), *The tax treatment of transfer of residence by individuals*, CDFI 87b (IBFD, 2002), p. 79.

Mamut M., *Konkurrentenschutz im Abgabenrecht* (2010).

Mamut M., Privatinvestorgrundsatz und Steuerbeihilfen, in Jaeger T. (ed.), *Jahrbuch Beihilferecht 09* (NWV, 2009), p. 329.

Manninen P.M./Rytöhonka R., ECJ: Finnish Income Tax Regime on the Deductibility of Pension Insurance Contributions Violates the Freedom to Provide Services, 43 *Eur. Taxn.* 2 (2003), p. 55.

Marchgraber C., Conflicts of Qualification and Interpretation: How Should Developing Countries React?, 44 *Intertax* 4 (2016), p. 307.

Marchgraber C., Cross-Border Tax Arbitrage, the Parent-Subsidiary Directive (2011/96) and Double Tax Treaty Law, 70 *Bull. Intl. Taxn.* 3 (2016), p. 123.

Marchgraber C., Dividendenbesteuerung und internationale Steuerarbitrage, in Lang M./Marchgraber C./Rust A./Schuch J./Staringer C. (eds.), *Dividenden im Konzern* (Linde, 2016), p. 95.

Marchgraber C., Tackling Deduction and Non-Inclusion Schemes – The Proposal of the European Commission, 54 *Eur. Taxn.* 4 (2014), p. 133.

Marchgraber C., The Avoidance of Double Non-taxation in Double Tax Treaty Law: A Critical Analysis of the Subject-To-Tax Clause Recommended by the European Commission, 23 *EC Tax Rev.* 5 (2014), p. 293.

Marchgraber C., Vermeidung doppelter Nichtbesteuerung im DBA-Recht, in Lang M./Marchgraber C./Rust A./Schuch J./Staringer C. (eds.), *Niedrigbesteuerung im Unternehmenssteuerrecht* (Linde, 2016), p. 95.

Marchgraber C./Titz E., Die Wirkungsweise des § 10 Abs 7 KStG im System der Beteiligungsertragsbefreiung, 24 *ÖStZ* 15/16 (2011), p. 373.

Marquart C., Die Möglichkeit der Verlustverrechnung als selektive Begünstigung sanierungsbedürftiger Unternehmen?, 20 *IStR* 12 (2011), p. 445.

Mason R., Flunking the ECJ's Tax Discrimination Test, 46 *Colum. J. Transnatl. L.* 1 (2007), p. 72.

Mason R., Made in America for European Tax: The Internal Consistency Test, 49 *Bost. Coll. L. Rev.* 4 (2008), p. 1277.

Mason R., Tax Discrimination and Capital Neutrality, 2 *World Tax J.* 2 (2010), p. 126.

Mason R./Knoll M.S., What Is Tax Discrimination?, 121 *Yale L. J.* 5 (2011-2012), p. 1014.

Mathisen G., Consistency and Coherence as Conditions for Justification of Member State Measures Restricting Free Movement, 47 *Common Market L. Rev.* 4 (2010), p. 1021.

Mattsson N., Is the multilateral convention a solution for the future? - Comments with reflection to the Nordic experience, 13 *Intertax* 9 (1985), p. 212.

Mayer H./Stöger K. (eds.), *EUV/AEUV* (Manz, 2014).

Mayer S., *Formulary Apportionment for the Internal Market* (IBFD, 2009).

McLure C.E., Replacing Separate Entity Accounting and the Arm's Length Principle with Formulary Apportionment, 56 *Bull. Intl. Taxn.* 12 (2002), p. 586.

McLure C.E./Weiner J.M., Deciding whether the European Union should adopt formular apportionment of company income, in Cnossen S. (ed.), *Taxing Capital Income in the European Union* (Oxford University Press, 2000), p. 243.

Meerpohl J., *Die Mutter-/Tochter-Richtlinie der Europäischen Gemeinschaft und ihre Umsetzung in das Recht der Mitgliedstaaten* (Peter Lang, 1998).

Meussen G., Horizontal Discrimination and EU Law: The Sopora Case, 54 *Eur. Taxn.* 7 (2014), p. 322.

Micheau C., *State Aid, Subsidy and Tax Incentives under EU and WTO Law* (Kluwer, 2014).

Micheau C., Tax Selectivity in European Law of State Aid: Legal Assessment and Alternative Approaches, 40 *Eur. L. Rev.* 3 (2015), p. 323.

Micheau C., Tax selectivity in State aid review: a debatable case practice, 17 *EC Tax Rev.* 6 (2008), p. 276.

Migglautsch R., Rs Columbus Container Services – Doppelbesteuerungsabkommen und Gemeinschaftsrecht, 19 *ecolex* 3 (2008), p. 265.

Millar R., Cross-border Services: A Survey of the Issues, in Krever R./White D. (eds.) *GST in Retrospect and Prospect* (Thomson Reuters, 2007), p. 317.

Millar R., Intentional and Unintentional Double Non-Taxation, in Lang M./Melz P./Kristoffersson E. (ed.), Ecker T. (ass. ed.), *Value Added Tax and Direct Taxation* (IBFD, 2009), p. 409.

Millar R., *Sources of Conflict in Cross-Border Services Rules for VAT*, Sydney Law School Research Paper No. 08/14 (2008).

Mitschke W., Treaty Override verfassungsgemäß, 54 *DStR* 7 (2016), p. 359. Aarnio K., Treatment of permanent establishments and subsidiaries under EC law: towards a uniform concept of secondary establishment in European tax law?, 15 *EC Tax Rev.* 1 (2006), p. 18.

Mönikes C., *Die Verlustverrechnungsbeschränkungen des Einkommensteuergesetzes im Lichte der Verfassung* (Shaker Verlag, 2006).

Monsenego J., *Introduction to Transfer Pricing* (Kluwer, 2015).

Monti M., The climate is changing, 7 *EC Tax Rev.* 1 (1998), p. 2.

Monti M., The Single Market and beyond: challenges for tax policy in the European Union, 6 *EC Tax Rev.* 1 (1997), p. 2.

Morriss A.P./Moberg L., Cartelizing Taxes: Understanding the OECD's Campaign against "Harmful Tax Competition", 4 *Colum. J. Tax L.* 1 (2012), p. 1.

Mortelmans K., The Relationship Between the Treaty Rules and Community Measures for the Establishment and Functioning of the Internal Market – Towards a Concordance Rule, 39 *Common Market L. Rev.* 6 (2002), p. 1303.

Mössner J.M., Der Code of Conduct for Business Taxation vom 1.12.1997, in Lang M./Schuch J./Staringer C. (eds.), *Soft Law in der Praxis* (Linde, 2005), p. 136.

Mössner J.M., Die Methoden zur Vermeidung der Doppelbesteuerung – Vorzüge, Nachteile, aktuelle Probleme, in Vogel K. (ed.), *Grundfragen des Internationalen Steuerrechts* (Dr Otto Schmidt, 1985), p. 135.

Mössner M./Kellersmann D., Freiheit des Kapitalverkehrs in der EU und das deutsche Körperschaftsteueranrechnungsverfahren, 87 *DStZ* 14 (1999), p. 505.

Mudambi R., The Role of Duration in Multinational Investment Strategies, 29 *Journal of Intl. Business Studies* 2 (1998), p. 239.

Mühlehner J., Kontrollbeteiligungen und Kapitalverkehrsfreiheit im Verhältnis zu Drittstaaten, 17 *SWI* 11 (2007), p. 523.

Mühlehner J., Umsatzsteuerliche Organschaft und Niederlassungsfreiheit, 16 *SWI* 7 (2006), p. 300.

Mühlehner J., Zur Anwendbarkeit der Kapitalverkehrsfreiheit auf Portfolioinvestitionen in Drittstaaten, 18 *SWI* 3 (2008), p. 102.

Müller-Graff P., Die Rechtsangleichung zur Verwirklichung des Binnenmarktes, 24 *EuR* 2 (1989), p. 107.

Musgrave R.A., *The Theory of Public Finance* (McGraw-Hill, 1959).

Musil A., *Deutsches Treaty Overriding und seine Vereinbarkeit mit Europäischem Gemeinschaftsrecht* (Duncker & Humblot, 2000).

Mutén L., ECJ Advocate General Issues Opinion on Finland's Imputation System, 33 *Tax Notes Intl.* 13 (29 March 2004), p. 1154.

Nanetti F./Mameli G., The creeping normative role of the EC Commission in the twin-track struggle against State aids and harmful tax competition, 11 *EC Tax Rev.* 4 (2002), p. 185.

Navarro A./Parada L./Schwarz P., The Proposal for an EU Anti-avoidance Directive: Some Preliminary Thoughts, 25 *EC Tax Rev.* 3 (2016), p. 117.

Nebbia P., State aid and the role of national courts, in Szyszczak E. (ed.), *Research Handbook on European State Aid Law* (Edward Elgar Publishing, 2011), p. 390.

Nerudová D., The Czech Republic: Preliminary ruling referred by the Czech Supreme Administrative Court - joint cases: Aco Industries (C-80/13) and Strojírny Prostějov, a.s. (C-53/14), in Lang M./Pistone P./Schuch J./Staringer C./ Storck A. (eds.), *ECJ – Recent Developments in Direct Taxation 2013* (Linde, 2014), p. 25.

Nicolaides P., Fiscal Aid in the EC - A Critical Review of Current Practice, 24 *World Competition* 3 (2001), p. 319.

Niemeyer H., § 44 Proceedings before National Courts, in Heidenhain M. (ed.), *European State Aid Law* (C.H. Beck, 2010), p. 767.

Niesten H., Growing Impetus for Harmonization of Personal and Family Allowances: Current State of Affairs of the Schumacker-Doctrine after Imfeld and Garcet, 24 *EC Tax Rev.* 4 (2015), p. 185.

Nilsson E., Sweden - Corporate Taxation sec. 12, *Country Analyses IBFD* (accessed 5 May 2015).

Nowak C., Binnenmarktziel und Wirtschaftsverfassung der Europäischen Union vor und nach dem Reformvertrag von Lissabon, 44 *Europarecht* Beiheft 1 (2009), p. 129.

Nowak C., Die Entwicklung des EG-Beihilfenkontrollrechts in den Jahren 2001 und 2002, 14 *EuZW* 13 (2003), p. 389.

O'Brien M., Case C-452/04, Fidium Finanz AG v. Bundesanstalt für Finanzdienstleistungsaufsicht, judgment of the Court of Justice (Grand Chamber) of 3 October 2006, (2006) ECR I-9521, 44 *Common Market L. Rev.* 5 (2007), p. 1483.

O'Brien M., Company taxation, State aid and fundamental freedoms: is the next step enhanced co-operation?, 30 *Eur. L. Rev.* 2 (2005), p. 209.

O'Brien M., Taxation and the Third Country Dimension of Free Movement of Capital in EU Law: the ECJ's Rulings and Unresolved Issues, 53 *British Tax Rev.* 6 (2008), p. 628.

Obser R., § 8a KStG im Inbound-Sachverhalt - eine EG-rechtliche Beurteilung, 14 *IStR* 23 (2005), p. 799.

Offermanns R.H.M.J., Restrictions on Treaty Override Resulting from EU Law, 53 *Eur. Taxn.* 9 (2013), p. 430.

Oliver P./Roth W., The Internal Market and the Four Freedoms, 41 *Common Market L. Rev.* 2 (2004), p. 407.

Opinion Statement FC 3/2014 of the CFE on the Recommendation C(2012)8806 on aggressive tax planning, an EU GAAR and double non-taxation (available at http://www.cfe-eutax.org).

Opinion Statement of the CFE on *X Holding* (C-337/08), 51 *Eur. Taxn.* 4 (2011), p. 150

P. Kirchhof (ed.), *EStG*[15] (Dr Otto Schmidt, 2016).

Paetsch R., *Grenzüberschreitende Verlustberücksichtigung im Europäischen Binnenmarkt* (Eul Verlag, 2004).

Papotti R./Setti C., The ECJ Decision in *Timac Agro* (Case C-388/14): Another Properly Shaped Piece in the ECJ's Tax Loss Puzzle, 56 *Eur. Taxn.* 6 (2016), p. 246.

Paterno L., State Aid and Fiscal Protectionism in the European Union from the Perspective of Competitors, 65 *Bull. Intl. Taxn.* 6 (2011), p. 343.

Peeters B., Mobility of EU Citizens and Family Taxation: A Hard to Reconcile Combination, 23 *EC Tax Rev.* 3 (2014), p. 118.

Pejkov V., Changes in the Legal Order of the United States after the FSC and ETI Decisions and Conformity with WTO Law of the New Regulations, in J. Herdin-Winter/I. Hofbauer (eds.), *The Relevance of WTO Law for Tax Matters* (Linde, 2006), p. 333.

Pelkmans J./Robson P., The Aspirations of the White Paper, 26 *JCMS* 3 (1987), p. 181.

Pescatore P., Die "Einheitliche Europäische Akte" - Eine ernste Gefahr für den Gemeinsamen Markt, 21 *EuR* 2 (1986), p. 153.

Petritz M./Schuch J., Die Verteilung der Besteuerungsrechte zwischen Ansässigkeits- und Quellenstaat aus dem Blickwinkel der gemeinschaftsrechtliche Grundfreiheiten, in Gassner W./Lang M./Schuch J./Staringer C. (eds.), *Die Verteilung der Besteuerungsrechte zwischen Ansässigkeits- und Quellenstaat im Recht der Doppelbesteuerungsabkommen* (Linde, 2005), p. 123.

Petutschnig M., Sharing the Benefits of the EU's *Common Consolidated Corporate Tax Base* within Corporate Groups, 7 *World Tax J.* 2 (2015), p. 241.

Pfeiffer S., *VAT Grouping from a European Perspective* (IBFD, 2015).

Philipp A., *Befreiungssystem mit Progressionsvorbehalt und Anrechnungsverfahren* (Orac, 1971).

Piantavigna P., Tax Abuse in European Union law: A Theory, 20 *EC Tax Rev.* 3 (2011), p. 134.

Pickering A., *Tax Treaty Policy Framework and Country Model, Papers on Selected Topics in Negotiation of Tax Treaties for Developing Countries*, Paper No. 2-N (May 2013).

Pimentel M.C., 'D'istortion of the Common Market? Analysis and Future Perspectives of the MFN Clause Within EC Law, 34 *Intertax* 10 (2006), p. 485.

Pinetz E., Use of a Principal Purpose Test to Prevent Treaty Abuse, in Lang M./Pistone P./Rust A./Schuch J./Staringer C. (eds.), *Base Erosion and Profit Shifting* (Linde, 2016), p. 271.

Pinto C., EC State Aid Rules and Tax Incentives: A U-Turn in Commission Policy? (Part I), 39 *Eur. Taxn.* 8 (1999), p. 295.

Pinto C., *Tax Competition and EU Law* (Kluwer, 2003).

Pires M., *International Juridical Double Taxation of Income* (Kluwer, 1989).

Pistone P., Soft Tax Coordination: A Suitable Path for the OECD and the European Union to Address the Challenges of International Double (Non-)Taxation in VAT/GST Systems, in Lang M./Melz P./Kristoffersson E. (ed.), Ecker T. (ass. ed.), *Value Added Tax and Direct Taxation* (IBFD, 2009), p. 1161.

Pistone P., The EU Law Dimension of Human Rights in Tax Matters, in Brokelind C. (ed.), *Principles of Law: Function, Status and Impact in EU Tax Law* (IBFD, 2014), p. 91.

Pistone P., *The Impact of Community Law on Tax Treaties* (Kluwer, 2002).

Pistone P., The Impact of European Law on the Relations with Third Countries in the Field of Direct Taxation, 34 *Intertax* 5 (2006), p. 234.

Pistone P./Julien R./Cannas F., Can the Derivative Benefits Provision and Competent Authority Discretionary Relief Provision Render the OECD-Proposed Limitation on Benefits Clause Compatible with EU Fundamental Freedoms?, in Lang M./Pistone P./Rust A./Schuch J./Staringer C. (eds.), *Base Erosion and Profit Shifting* (Linde, 2016), p. 165-

Pistone P./Szudoczy R., The Coordination of Tax Policies in the EU, in Lang M./Pistone P./ Schuch J./Staringer C. (eds.), *Introduction to European Tax Law on Direct Taxation*[4] (Linde, 2015), p. 27.

Plansky P., The EU Arbitration Convention, in Lang M./Pistone P./Schuch J./Staringer C. (eds.), *Introduction to European Tax Law on Direct Taxation*[4] (Linde, 2015), p. 257.

Plansky P., The impact of the fundamental freedoms on tax treaties with third countries, in Lang M./Schuch J./Staringer C. (eds.), *Tax Treaty Law and EC Law* (Kluwer, 2007), p. 293.

Plowgian M., BEPS: The Shifting International Tax Landscape and What Companies Should Be Doing Now, 65 *The Tax Executive* 4 (2013), p. 255.

Polivanova-Rosenauer T., AbgÄG 2014: Abzugsverbot für Zinsen und Lizenzgebühren, 10 *taxlex* 3 (2014), p. 105.

Pons T., The *Denkavit Internationaal* Case and Its Consequences: The Limit between Distortion and Discrimination?, 47 *Eur. Taxn.* 5 (2007), p. 214.

Pöschl M., *Gleichheit vor dem Gesetz* (Springer, 2008).

Poulsen M., Freedom of Establishment and the Balanced Allocation of Tax Jurisdiction, 40 *Intertax* 3 (2012), p. 200.

Poulsen M., Treaty/Directive Shopping and Abuse of EU Law, 41 *Intertax* 4 (2013), p. 230.

Prek M./Lefèvre S., The Requirement of Selectivity in the Recent Case-Law of the Court of Justice, 11 *Eur. St. Aid L. Q.* 2 (2012), p. 335.

Quaghebeur M., ECJ to Examine Belgian Treatment of Inbound Dividend, 37 *Tax Notes Intl.* 9 (28 February 2005), p. 739.

Quaghebeur M., *Kerckhaert-Morres v Belgian State*: the wrong battle?, 52 *British Tax Rev.* 2 (2007), p. 121.

Quantschnigg P./Renner B./Schellmann G./Stöger R./Vock M. (eds.), *Die Körperschaftsteuer (KStG 1988)*[27] (LexisNexis, 2015).

Quigley C., *European State Aid Law and Policy, Third Edition* (Hart Publishing, 2015).

Rädler A., Most-favoured nation principle and internal market – Some afterthoughts to case D., in Van Thiel S. (ed.), *The European Union's prohibition of discrimination, most-favoured-nation treatment and tax treaties: opinions and materials* (CFE, 2006), p. 64.

Rädler A., Most-Favourite-Nation-Treatment in Direct Taxation - Some New Aspects, 13 *SWI* 8 (2003), p. 360.

Rainer A., EC Tax Scene: ECJ Rules French Withholding Tax on Outbound Dividends Violates EC Treaty, 35 *Intertax* 2 (2007), p. 134.

Rainer A., Quellensteuerabzug bei Dividenden, die an eine ausländische Empfängergesellschaft ausgeschüttet werden, 16 *IStR* (2007), p. 854.

Rainer A./Thömmes O., Are German CFC rules compatible with EU freedoms?, 33 *Intertax* 11 (2005), p. 554.

Rau G./Dürrwächter E. (eds.), *Umsatzsteuergesetz*[154] (Dr Otto Schmidt, 2013).

Rautenstrauch G., Richtlinienentwürfe zur Umsetzung des BEPS-Projekts – Die EU-Kommission legt vor, 69 *DB* 6 (2016), p. M5.

Rehm H./Nagler J., Verwaltung verweigert faktisch Anwendung von Art. EGV Artikel 56 EG gegenüber Drittstaaten, 16 *IStR* 19 (2007), p. 700.

Reimer E., Die Auswirkungen der Grundfreiheiten auf das Ertragsteuerrecht der Bundesrepublik Deutschland – Eine Bestandsaufnahme, in Lehner M. (ed.), *Grundfreiheiten im Steuerrecht der EU-Staaten* (C.H. Beck, 2000), p. 39.

Reimer E., Germany, 40 *Eur. Taxn.* 1 (2000), p. 48.

Reimer E., Taxation – an Area without Mutual Recognition, in Richelle I./Schön W./Traversa E. (eds.), *Allocating Taxing Powers Within the European Union* (Springer, 2013), p. 197.

Reimer E., The Abolition of Article 293 EC: Comments on Hofmann's Analysis, in Rust A. (ed.), *Double Taxation Within the European Union* (Kluwer, 2011), p. 87.

Reimer E./Rust A. (eds.), *Klaus Vogel on Double Taxation Conventions, Fourth Edition* (Kluwer, 2015).

Remacle O./Nonnenkamp S., Economic Double Taxation as an Obstacle to Cross-Border Investments, in Rust A. (ed.), *Double Taxation within the European Union* (Kluwer, 2011), p. 17.

Rendahl P., EU VAT and Double Taxation: A Fine Line between Interpretation and Application, 41 *Intertax* 8/9 (2013), p. 450.

Rendahl P., Unilateral Measures to Avoid International Double (Non-)Taxation: VAT/GST v. Direct Taxation, in Lang M./Melz P./Kristoffersson E. (ed.), Ecker T. (ass. ed.), *Value Added Tax and Direct Taxation* (IBFD, 2009), p. 1119.

Robins N./Shamsi S., The European Commission's State Aid Clampdown: The End of "Selective" Tax Rulings?, 18 *Derivatives and Financial Instruments* 1 (2016).

Rödder T./Herlinghaus A./Neumann R. (eds.), *Körperschaftsteuergesetz* (Dr Otto Schmidt, 2015).

Rödder T./Schönfeld J., Meistbegünstigung und EG-Recht: Anmerkung zu EuGH vom 5. 7. 2005, C-376/03 ("D."), IStR 2005, 483, 14 *IStR* 15 (2005), p. 523.

Rogers-Glabush J., *IBFD International Tax Glossary*[7] (IBFD, 2015).

Roin J., Can the Income Tax be Saved? The Promise and Pitfalls of Adopting Worldwide Formulary Apportionment, 61 *Tax L. Rev.* 3 (2008), p. 169.

Rosembuj T., Hybrid Entities Why Not Tax Pass-throughs as Corporations, 40 *Intertax* 5 (2012), p. 298.

Rosenberger F./Loidl V./Moshammer H., Grundfreiheitsprüfung des EuGH, 87 *SWK* 20 (2012), p. 936.

Rosenbloom D., International Tax Arbitrage and the "International Tax System", 53 *Tax L. Rev.* 137 (2000), p. 137.

Ross M., State aid and National Courts: Definitions and Other Problems - A Case of Premature Emancipation?, 37 *Common Market L. Rev.* 2 (2000), p. 401.

Rossi-Maccanico P., Fiscal Aid Review and Cross-Border Tax Distortions, 40 *Intertax* 2 (2012), p. 92.

Rossi-Maccanico P., Fiscal Aid, Tax Competition, and BEPS, 75 *Tax Notes Intl.* 10 (8 September 2014), p. 857.

Rossi-Maccanico P., Fiscal State Aids, Tax Base Erosion and Profit Shifting, 24 *EC Tax Rev.* 2 (2015), p. 63.

Rossi-Maccanico P., State Aid Review of Member States' Measures Relating to Direct Business Taxation, 3 *Eur. St. Aid L. Q.* 2 (2004), p. 229.

Rossi-Maccanico P., The Gibraltar Judgment and the Point on Selectivity in Fiscal Aids, 18 *EC Tax Rev.* 2 (2009), p. 67.

Rossi-Maccanico P., The Point on Selectivity in State Aid Review of Business Tax Measures, in Pistone P. (ed.), *Legal Remedies in European Tax Law* (IBFD, 2009), p. 223.

Rossi-Maccanico P., The specificity criterion in fiscal aid review: proposals for state aid control of direct business tax measures, 16 *EC Tax Rev.* 2 (2007), p. 90.

Ruppe H., *Das Abgabenrecht als Lenkungsinstrument der Gesellschaft und Wirtschaft und seine Schranken in den Grundrechten*, 8. ÖJT, Band I/A (Manz, 1982).

Ruppe H., *Das Abgabenrecht als Lenkungsinstrument der Gesellschaft und Wirtschaft und seine Schranken in den Grundrechten*, 8. ÖJT, Band I/A (Manz, 1982).

Ruppe H., Die Leistungsfähigkeit des Steuerrechts - Die österreichische Perspektive, 88 *StuW* 4 (2011), p. 372.

Ruppe H., *Die Steuerliche Doppelbelastung der Körperschaftsgewinne* (Jupiter-Verlag, 1967).

Ruppe H., *Die Steuerliche Doppelbelastung der Körperschaftsgewinne* (Jupiter-Verlag, 1967).

Ruppe H., General Report, in IFA (ed.), *International Problems in the Field of General Sales Taxes on Sales of Goods and Services, CDFI 68b* (IBFD, 1983), p. 109.

Ruppe H., Verfassungsrechtliche Vorgaben für Umweltabgaben, in Bernat E./Böhler E./Weilinger A. (eds.), *Zum Recht der Wirtschaft, Festschrift Heinz Krejci* (Verlag Österreich, 2001), p. 2079.

Russo A., Formulary Apportionment for Europe: An Analysis and A Proposal, 33 *Intertax* 1 (2005), p. 2.

Rust A., BEPS Action 2: 2014 Deliverable – Neutralising the Effects of Hybrid Mismatch Arrangements and its Compatibility with the Non-discrimination Provisions in Tax Treaties and the Treaty on the Functioning of the European Union, 61 *British Tax Rev.* 3 (2015), p. 308.

Rust A., Der BEPS Aktionspunkt 2 zur Neutralisierung der Effekte hybrider Gestaltungen und seine Vereinbarkeit mit den Diskriminierungsverboten der Doppelbesteuerungsabkommen und des AEUV, in Schön W./Heber C. (eds.), Grundfragen des Europäischen Steuerrechts (Springer, 2015), p. 89.

Rust A., How European Law Could Solve Double Taxation, in Rust A. (ed.), *Double Taxation within the European Union* (Kluwer, 2011), p. 137.

Schaper M., The Need to Prevent Abusive Practices and Fraus as a Composite Justification, 23 *EC Tax Rev.* 4 (2014), p. 220.

Schaumburg H., Problemfelder im internationalen Erbschaftsteuerrecht, 47 *RIW* 3 (2001), p. 161.

Schaumburg H./Englisch J. (eds.), *Europäisches Steuerrecht* (Dr Otto Schmidt, 2015).

Scheipers T./Maywald A., Zur Vereinbarkeit des § ASTG § 20 Abs. ASTG § 20 Absatz 2 AStG mit EG-Recht unter Berücksichtigung der Ausführungen des Generalanwalts Léger in der Rs. Cadbury Schweppes, 15 *IStR* 14 (2006), p. 472.

Scherer T.B., *Doppelbesteuerung und Europäisches Gemeinschaftsrecht* (C.H. Beck, 1995).

Scherer T.B., Treaty Override und Unionsrecht – ein Versuch, 25 *IStR* 18 (2016), p. 741.

Schick W., *Der Verlustrücktrag* (C.H. Beck, 1976).

Schiefer F., Maßnahmen zur Bekämpfung hybrider Finanzierungsinstrumente, 61 *IWB* 10 (2015), p. 352.

Schilcher M., Die tatsächliche Besteuerung als maßgebendes Kriterium für die Festlegung des Quellenstaates nach den Doppelbesteuerungsabkommen ("Subject-to-tax-Klauseln"), in Gassner W./Lang M./Schuch J./Staringer C. (eds.), *Die Verteilung der Besteuerungsrechte zwischen Ansässigkeits- und Quellenstaat im Recht der Doppelbesteuerungsabkommen* (Linde, 2005), p. 353.

Schilcher M., Exemption Method and Community Law, in Lang M./Schuch J./Staringer C. (eds.), *Tax Treaty Law and EC Law* (Kluwer, 2007), p. 151.

Schilcher M., *Subject-to-tax-Klauseln in der österreichischen Abkommenspraxis* (Linde 2004).

Schindler C.P., Hughes de Lasteyrie du Saillant als Ende der (deutschen) Wegzugsbesteuerung?, 13 *IStR* 9 (2004), p. 300.

Schlunk H.J., How I Learned to Stop Worrying and Love Double Taxation, 79 *Notre Dame L. Rev.* 1 (2003), p. 127.

Schneider D., Vertikale Gerechtigkeit wider Rechtsformneutralität und Lebenseinkommensbesteuerung, in Siegel T./Kirchhof P./Schneeloch D./Schramm U. (eds.), *Steuertheorie, Steuerpolitik und Steuerpraxis*, Festschrift für Peter Bareis zum 65. Geburtstag (Schäffer-Pschel, 2005), p. 275.

Schnitger A., § 20 Abs. 2 und 3 AStG a.F. vor dem EuGH - Meistbegünstigung "Reloaded", 87 *FR* 21 (2005), p. 1079.

Schnitger A., *Die Grenzen der Einwirkungen der Grundfreiheiten des EG-Vertrages auf das Ertragsteuerrecht* (IDW, 2006).

Schnitger A., EuGH: Vermögensteuer-Freibeträge in Holland, weil keine Vermögensteuer in Deutschland?, 13 *IStR* 22 (2004), p. 793.

Schnitger A., German CFC legislation pending before the European Court of Justice – abuse of the law nad revival of the most-favoured-nation-clause?, 15 *EC Tax Rev.* 3 (2006), p. 151.

Schnitger A., Grenzüberschreitende Körperschaftsteueranrechnung und Neuausrichtung der Kohärenz nach dem EuGH-Urteil in der Rs. Manninen, 86 *FR* 24 (2004), p. 1357.

Schnitger A., Körperschaftsteueranrechnung für beschränkt Steuerpflichtige nach der Entscheidung des EFTA-Gerichtshofs in der Rs. Fokus Bank - Ein zweischneidiges Schwert, 87 *FR* 7 (2005), p. 360.

Schnitger A., Möglichkeit zur Präzisierung des europarechtlichen Prinzips der Rechtsformwahlfreiheit und Körperschaftsteuerguthaben für Betriebsstätten ausländischer Kapitalgesellschaften gemäß § 37 KStG – Vorlagenfrage an den EuGH in der Rs. CLT-UFA, 13 *IStR* 23 (2004), p. 821.

Schnitger A., The *CLT-UFA* Case and the "Principle of Neutrality of Legal Form", 44 *Eur. Taxn.* 12 (2004), p. 522.

Schnitger A./ Fehrenbacher O. (eds.), KStG (Springer, 2012).

Schön W., Der "Wettbewerb" der europäischen Steuerordnungen als Rechtsproblem, in Pelka J. (ed.), *Europa- und verfassungsrechtliche Grenzen der Unternehmensbesteuerung*, DStJG 23 (Dr Otto Schmidt, 2000), p. 191.

Schön W., Der freie Warenverkehr, die Steuerhoheit der Mitgliedstaaten und der Systemgedanke im europäischen Steuerrecht, Teil II, 36 *EuR* 3 (2001), p. 341.

Schön W., Der Kapitalverkehr mit Drittstaaten und das internationale Steuerrecht, in Gocke R./Gosch D./Lang M. (eds.), *Körperschaftsteuer, Internationales Steuerrecht, Doppelbesteuerung*, Festschrift für Franz Wassermeyer zum 65. Geburtstag (C.H. Beck, 2005), p. 489.

Schön W., Die Auswirkungen des gemeinschaftsrechtlichen Beihilferechts auf das Steuerrecht, in ÖJT (ed.), *Die Auswirkungen des gemeinschaftsrechtlichen Beihilferechts auf das Steuerrecht*, Referate und Diskussionsbeiträge, Band IV/2 (Manz, 2010), p. 21.

Schön W., Die beschränkte Steuerpflicht zwischen europäischem Gemeinschaftsrecht und deutschem Verfassungsrecht, 4 *IStR* 3 (1995), p. 119.

Schön W., Doppelbesteuerung und EU-Recht, in Wassermeyer W. (ed.), *Doppelbesteuerung, Festgabe zum 75. Geburtstag von Prof. Dr. Dr. h.c. Franz Wassermeyer* (C.H. Beck, 2015), p. 7.

Schön W., Europäische Kapitalverkehrsfreiheit und nationales Steuerrecht, in Schön W. (ed.), *Gedächtnisschrift für Brigitte Knobbe-Keuk* (Dr Otto Schmidt, 1997), p. 743.

Schön W., Freie Wahl zwischen Zweigniederlassung und Tochtergesellschaft - ein Grundsatz des Europäischen Unternehmensrechts, 11 *EWS* 7 (2000), p. 281.

Schön W., International Tax Coordination for a Second-Best World (Part III), 2 *World Tax J.* 3 (2010), p. 227.

Schön W., Kapitalverkehrsfreiheit und Niederlassungsfreiheit, in Ackermann T./ Köndgen J. (eds.), *Privat- und Wirtschaftsrecht in Europa, Festschrift für Wulf-Henning Roth zum 70. Geburtstag* (C.H. Beck, 2015), p. 551.

Schön W., Neue Wege im Europäischen Steuerrecht, 9 *EuZW* 5/6 (1998), p. 129.

Schön W., Neutralität und Territorialität - Gegensätze oder Grundsätze des Europäischen Steuerrechts?, in Schön W./ Heber C. (eds.), Grundfragen des Europäischen Steuerrechts (Springer, 2015), p. 109.

Schön W., Neutrality and Territoriality - Competing or Converging Concepts in European Tax Law?, 69 *Bull. Intl. Taxn.* 4/5 (2015), p. 271.

Schön W., Rechtsmissbrauch und Europäisches Steuerrecht, in Kirchhof P./Nieskens H. (eds.), *Festschrift für Wolfram Reiss zum 65. Geburtstag* (Dr Otto Schmidt, 2008), p. 571.

Schön W., Special Charges - A Gap in European Copmetition Law?, 5 *Eur. St. Aid L. Q.* 3 (2006), p. 495.

Schön W., State Aid in the Area of Taxation, in Hancher L./Ottavanger T./Slot P.J. (eds.), *EU State Aids* (Sweet & Maxwell, 2012), p. 321.

Schön W., Tax Competition in Europe - General Report, in Schön W. (ed.), *Tax Competition in Europe* (IBFD, 2003), p. 1.

Schön W., Tax competition in Europe - the legal perspective, 9 *EC Tax Rev.* 2 (2000), p. 89.

Schön W., Tax Legislation and the Notion of Fiscal Aid - A Review of Five Years of European Jurisprudence - *Max Planck Institute for Tax Law and Public Finance Working Paper 2015-14* (December 2015).

Schön W., Tax Legislation and the Notion of Fiscal Aid: A Review of 5 Years of European Jurisprudence, in Richelle I./Schön W./Traversa E. (eds.), *State Aid Law and Business Taxation* (Springer, 2016), p. 3.

Schön W., Taxation and State Aid Law in the European Union, 36 *Common Market L. Rev.* 5 (1999), p. 911.

Schön W., Transfer Pricing - Business Incentives, International Taxation and Corporate Law, in Konrad K.A./Schön W. (eds.), *Fundamentals of International Transfer Pricing in Law and Economics* (Springer, 2012), p. 47.

Schön W., Transfer Pricing Issues of BEPS in the Light of EU Law, 61 *British Tax Rev.* 3 (2015), p. 417.

Schön W., Transfer Pricing, the Arm's Length Standard and European Union Law, in Richelle I./Schön W./Traversa E. (eds.), *Allocating Taxing Powers within the European Union* (Springer, 2013), p. 73.

Schön W., World Trade Organization Law and Tax Law, 58 *Bull. Intl. Taxn.* 7 (2002), p. 283.

Schön W., Zum Entwurf eines Steuersenkungsgesetzes, 77 *StuW* 2 (2000), p. 151.

Schönfeld J., Doppelbesteuerung und EG-Recht, 83 *StuW* 1 (2006), p. 79.

Schönfeld J., EuGH konkretisiert Anwendung der Kapitalverkehrsfreiheit im Verhältnis zu Drittstaaten: Mögliche Konsequenzen und offene Fragen aus steuerlicher Sicht, 60 *DB* 2 (2007), p. 80.

Schönfeld J., *Hinzurechnungsbesteuerung und Europäisches Gemeinschaftsrecht* (Dr Otto Schmidt, 2005).

Schönfeld J., The Cadbury Schweppes Case: Are the Days of the United Kingdom's CFC Legislation Numbered?, 44 *Eur. Taxn.* 10 (2004), p. 441.

Schoueri L.E., Arm's Length: Beyond the Guidelines of the OECD, 69 *Bull. Intl. Taxn.* 12 (2015), p. 690.

Schrauwen A.A.M., In Defence of Public Interest: The Rule of Reason, in Schrauwen A.A.M. (ed.), *Rule of Reason* (Europa Law Publishing, 2005), p. 1.

Schuch J., Bilateral Tax Treaties Multilateralized by the EC Treaty, in Lang M./Loukota H./ Rädler A.J./Schuch J./Toifl G./Urtz C./Wassermeyer F./Züger M. (eds.), *Multilateral Tax Treaties* (Linde, 1997), p. 33.

Schuch J., Critical notes on the European Court of Justice's D case decision on mostfavoured-nation treatment under tax treaties, 15 *EC Tax Rev.* 1 (2006), p. 6.

Schuch J., EC law requires multilateral tax treaty, 7 *EC Tax Rev.* 1 (1998), p. 29.

Schuch J., Europa auf dem Weg zum multilateralen Doppelbesteuerungsabkommen, in Gassner W./ Gröhs B./Lang M. (eds.), *Zukunftsaufgaben der Wirtschaftsprüfung* (Orac, 1997), p. 327.

Schuch J., Marktintegration durch Meistbegünstigung im EG-Steuerrecht, in Cordewener A./ Enchelmaier S./Schindler C.P. (eds.), *Meistbegünstigung im Steuerrecht der EU-Staaten* (C.H. Beck, 2006), at p. 151.

Schuch J., Werden die Doppelbesteuerungsabkommen durch EU-Recht zu Meistbegünstigungsklauseln?, in Gassner W./Lang M./Lechner E. (eds.), *Doppelbesteuerungsabkommen und EU-Recht* (Linde, 1996), p. 99.

Schuch J./Bauer J., Die Überlegungen des OECD-Steuerausschusses zur Lösung von Qualifikationskonflikten, in Gassner W./Lang M./Lechner E. (eds.), *Personengesellschaften im Recht der Doppelbesteuerungsabkommen* (Linde, 2000), p. 27.

Schütte M., Procedural aspects of EU State aid law and practice, in Szyszczak E. (ed.), *Research Handbook on European State Aid Law* (Edward Elgar Publishing, 2011), p. 354.

Schwarze J. (ed.), *EU-Kommentar*[3] (Nomos, 2012).

Schweda M., § 14 General Principles, in Heidenhain M. (ed.), *European State Aid Law* (C.H. Beck, 2010), p. 151.

Schwenke M., Kapitalertragsteuer bei Streubesitzdividenden gemeinschaftswidrig?, 17 *IStR* 13 (2008), p. 473.

Scott Wilkie J., Policy Forum: BEPS One Year In – Taking Stock, 62 *Canadian Tax J.* 2 (2014), p. 458.

Sedlaczek M., Capital and Payments: The Prohibition of Discrimination and Restrictions, 40 *Eur. Taxn.* 1 (2000), p. 13.

Seer R., Grenzen der Zulässigkeit eines treaty overridings am Beispiel der Switch-over-Klausel des § 20 AStG (Teil II), 6 *IStR* 17 (1997), p. 520.

Seer R., Nationales Recht, Doppelbesteuerungsabkommen und Europarecht aus deutscher Sicht, in Brzezinski B./Gluchowski J./Kosikowski C./Mastalski R. (eds.), *Księga pamiątkowa ku czci Profesora Apoloniusza Kosteckiego* (Torun, 1998), p. 201.

Seiler C., Das Steuerrecht unter dem Einfluss der Marktfreiheiten, 82 *StuW* 1 (2005), p. 25.

Shuibhne N., Free Movement of Persons and the Wholly Internal Rule: Time to Move On?, 39 *Common Market L. Rev.* 4 (2002), p. 731.

Sieker S., Möglichkeiten rechtsformneutraler Besteuerung von Einkommen, in Seeger S.F. (ed.), *Perspektiven der Unternehmensbesteuerung*, DStJG 25 (Dr Otto Schmidt, 2002), p. 145.

Simader K., Die Zulässigkeit der Erhebung von Quellensteuern aus gemeinschaftsrechtlicher Sicht, in Lang M./Schuch J./Staringer C. (eds.), *Quellensteuern* (Linde, 2010), p. 13.

Simader K., *Withholding Taxes and the Fundamental Freedoms* (Kluwer, 2014).

Slot P.J., Administrative Procedure, in Hancher L./Ottavanger T./Slot P.J. (eds.), *EU State Aids* (Sweet & Maxwell, 2012), p. 945.

Slotboom M.M., State Aid in Community Law: A Broad or a Narrow Definition, 20 *Eur. L. Rev.* (1995), p. 289.

Slynn G., They Call it 'Teleological', 7 *Denning L. J.* 7 (1992), p. 225.

Smet P./Laloo H., ECJ to Rule on Taxation of Inbound Dividends in Belgium, 45 *Eur. Taxn.* 4 (2005), p. 158.

Smit D., Capital movements and third countries: the significance of the standstill-clause ex-Article 57(1) of the EC Treaty in the field of direct taxation, 15 *EC Tax Rev.* 4 (2006), p. 203.

Smit D., Commission v UK. UK legislation allowing cross-border group relief subjet to certain conditions is compatible with EU law. Court of Justice, 8 *H&I* 4 (2015), p. 27.

Smit D., *EU Freedoms, Non-EU Countries and Company Taxation* (Kluwer, 2012).

Smit D., The 150km Requirement under the Dutch 30% Wage Tax Facility C-512/03 (Sopora), in Lang M./Pistone P./Schuch J./Staringer C./ Storck A. (eds.), *ECJ – Recent Developments in Direct Taxation 2013* (Linde, 2014), p. 131.

Smit D., The relationship between the free movement of capital and the other EC Treaty freedoms in third country relationships in the field of direct taxation: a question of exclusivity, parallelism or causality?, 16 *EC Tax Rev.* 6 (2007), p. 252.

Smit D.S., International Juridical Double Non-taxation and State Aid, 25 *EC Tax Rev.* 2 (2016), p. 109 (at pp. 109-112);

Snell J., Economic Aims as Justification for Restrictions on Free Movement, in A.A.M. Schrauwen (ed.), *Rule of Reason* (Europa Law Publishing, 2005), p. 35.

Snell J., Non-Discriminatory Tax Obstacles in Community Law, 56 *Intl. & Comp. L. Q.* 2 (2007), p. 339.

Soltész U., § 43 Scope of Judicial Review, in Heidenhain M. (ed.), *European State Aid Law* (C.H. Beck, 2010), p. 752.

Soltész U., Der Rechtsschutz des Konkurrenten gegen gemeinschaftswidrige Beihilfen vor nationalen Gerichten, 12 *EuZW* 7 (2001), p. 202.

Sørensen K.E., Direct Taxation and the WTO Agreements, 42 *Eur. Taxn.* 6 (2002), p. 206.

Spaventa E., From Gebhard to Carpenter: Towards a (Non-)Economic European Constitution, 41 *Common Market L. Rev.* 3 (2004), p. 743.

Spies K., *Die Kapitalverkehrsfreiheit in Konkurrenz zu den anderen Grundfreiheiten* (LexisNexis, 2015).

Spies K., EuGH zu Währungsverlusten bei ausländischen Tochtergesellschaften: Keine Abzugspflicht(?), 26 *ecolex* 8 (2015), p. 700.

Spies K., Quellensteuern auf dem Prüfstand des EuGH, 67 *ÖStZ* 21 (2014), p. 531.

Spies K., The CJEU's Approach in Direct Tax and VAT Law: Consistencies and Divergences, in Lang M./Pistone P./Rust A./Schuch J./Staringer C./Raponi D. (eds.), *CJEU - Recent Developments in Value Added Tax 2015* (Linde, 2016), p. 135.

Ståhl K., Dividend taxation in a free capital market, 6 *EC Tax Rev.* 4 (1997), p. 227.

Stanley P., C-107/94, Asscher v. Staatssecretaris van FInancien. Judgment of 27 June 1996. Fifth Chamber. (1996) ECR I-3089., 34 *Common Market L. Rev.* 3 (1997), p. 713.

Staringer C., Auslandsdividenden und Kapitalverkehrsfreiheit, 13 *ÖStZ* 2 (2000), p. 26.

Staringer C., BEPS - Was kommt jetzt auf uns zu?, 25 *SWI* 12 (2015), p. 575.

Staringer C., DBA-Politik und Verfassungsrecht, 24 *SWI* 3 (2014), p. 90.

Staringer C., Dividendenbesteuerung und Kapitalverkehrsfreiheit, in Lechner E./ Staringer C./Tumpel M. (eds.), *Kapitalverkehrsfreiheit und Steuerrecht* (Linde, 2000), p. 93.

Staringer C., Rechtsfragen der Zulässigkeit von "Handymastensteuern", in M. Achatz/T. Ehrke-Rabel/J. Heinrich/R. Leitner/O. Taucher (eds.), *Steuerrecht Verfassungsrecht Europarecht*, Festschrift Hans-Georg Ruppe (Facultas, 2007), p. 573.

Staringer C./ Denk S., Verfassungsrechtliche Zulässigkeit der Stabilitätsabgabe, 26 *ÖZW* 3 (2012), p. 70.

Stefaner M., Besteuerung von Beteiligungserträgen gemäß § 10 Abs 7 KStG auch bei fehlendem Abzug im Ausland?, 22 *SWI* 10 (2012), p. 443.

Stefaner M., Genussrechte im Konzernsteuerrecht, in Schragl M./Stefaner M. (eds.), *Handbuch Genussrechte*² (Linde, 2013), p. 253.

Stefaner M., Wann greift die Besteuerung von grenzüberschreitenden Beteiligungserträgen gemäß § 10 Abs 7 KStG?, 22 *SWI* 6 (2012), p. 276.

Stein T., Völkerrecht und nationales Steuerrecht im Widerstreit?, 15 *IStR* 15 (2006), p. 505.

Stevens S.A., The Duty of Countries and Enterprises to Pay Their Fair Share, 42 *Intertax* 11 (2014), p. 702.

Stoll G., *BAO Kommentar, Band I* (Orac, 1994).

Strassburger B., *Die Dogmatik der EU-Grundfreiheiten* (Mohr Siebeck, 2012).

Streinz R. (ed.), *EUV/AEUV*² (C.H. Beck, 2012).

Streinz R., Multilateral Instrument and EU Competence, 61 *British Tax Rev.* 3 (2015), p. 429.

Surrey S.S., Steueranreize als ein Instrument der staatlichen Politik, 58 *StuW* 4 (1981), p. 359.

Surrey S.S., Tax Incentives as a Device for Implementing Government Policy: A Comparison with Direct Government Expenditures, 83 *Harv. L. Rev.* 4 (1970), p. 705.

Sutter F.P., Beihilfen im materiellen Steuerrecht – Steuergesetze und Verwaltungshandeln der Steuerbehörden im Spannungsfeld zum EG-Beihilfenverbot, in Studiengesellschaft für Wirtschaft und Recht (ed.), *Beihilfenrecht* (Linde, 2004), p. 37.

Sutter F.P., *Das EG-Beihilfenverbot und sein Durchführungsverbot in Steuersachen* (Linde, 2005).

Sutter F.P., Die abkommensrechtliche Verteilung der Besteuerungsrechte zwischen Ansässigkeits- und Quellenstaat aus beihilfenrechtlicher Sicht, in Lang M./Schuch J./Staringer C. (eds.), *Die abkommensrechtliche Verteilung der Besteuerungsrechte zwischen Ansässigkeits- und Quellenstaat* (Linde, 2005), p. 83.

Sutter F.P., Die DBA-Freistellungsmethode als unzulässige Beihilfe i. S. d. Art. 87 EG?, 14 *SWI* 1 (2004), p. 4.

Sutter F.P., Drei und mehr Normhypothesen zur beihilfenrechtlichen Einordnung des österreichischen unilateralen Entlastungssystems zur Vermeidung der Doppelbesteuerung, in Bauer J. /Burgstaller E. /Haslinger K. /Herdin J. /Hofbauer I. /Lang M./Loukota H./Loukota W./Schilcher M./Schuch J./Staringer C./Sutter F.P./Zieseritsch U. (eds.), *Unilaterale Maßnahmen zur Vermeidung der Doppelbesteuerung* (Linde, 2004), p. 249.

Sutter F.P., Pauschales Verbot grenzüberschreitenden Verlustabzugs – Verstoß gegen Niederlassungsfreiheit, 17 *EuZW* 3 (2006), p. 85.

Sutter F.P., The *Adria Wien Pipeline* Case and the State Aid Provisions of the EC Treaty in Tax Matters, 41 *Eur. Taxn.* 7 (2001), p. 239.

Sutter F.P., The Influence of the European State Aid Rules on National Tax Policy, in Andersson K./Eberhartinger E./Oxelheim L. (eds.), *National Tax Policy in Europe* (Springer, 2007), p. 121.

Sutter F.P., Verfassungsrechtliche Schranken der Differenzierung zwischen Anrechnungs- und Freistellungsmethode in einem DBA, 23 *SWI* 12 (2013), p. 514.

Swinkels J., The Phenomenon of VAT Groups under EU Law and Their VAT-Saving Aspects, 21 *Intl. VAT Monitor* 1 (2010), p. 36.

Swinkels J., VAT-Saving Concepts and Interpretations, 16 *Intl. VAT Monitor* 6 (2005), p. 417.

Swinkels J., VAT-Saving Solutions and Abuse of Law, 18 *Intl. VAT Monitor* 5 (2007), p. 331.

Szudoczky R., Double Taxation Relief, Transfer Pricing Adjustments and State Aid Law: Comments, in Richelle I./Schön W./Traversa E. (eds.), *State Aid Law and Business Taxation* (Springer, 2016), 163.

Szudoczky R., The Influence of Primary Law on the Interpretation of Secondary Law in the Field of EU Citizenship and Direct Taxation: "Wathever works" ..., in Weber D. (ed.), *Traditional and Alternative Routes to European Tax Integration* (IBFD, 2010), p. 191.

Szudoczky R., *The Sources of EU law and Their Relationships: Lessons for the Field of Taxation* (IBFD, 2014).

Szudoczky R./Koch P., Limiation on Benefits: "Qualified Person" - Article X(1) and (2) of the OECD Model, in Lang M./Pistone P./Rust A./Schuch J./Staringer C. (eds.), *Base Erosion and Profit Shifting* (Linde, 2016), p. 219.

Szudoczky R./van de Streek J.L., Revisiting the Dutch Interest Box under the EU State Aid Rules and the Code of Conduct: When a 'Disparity' Is Selective and Harmful, 38 *Intertax* 5 (2010), p. 260.

Taferner A./Kuipers J.W., Tax Rulings: In Line With OECD Transfer Pricing Guidelines, but Contrary to EU State Aid Rules?, 56 *Eur. Taxn.* 4 (2016), p. 134.

Tavares R.J.S./ Bogenschneider B.N./Pankiv M., The Intersection of EU State Aid and U.S. Tax Deferral: A Spectacle of Fireworks, Smoke, and Mirrors, 19 *Florida Tax Rev.* 3 (2016), p. 121.

Temple Lang J., The Gibraltar State Aid and Taxation Judgment - A "Methodological Revoluation"?, 11 *Eur. St. Aid L. Q.* 4 (2012), p. 805.

Tenore M., Taxation of Cross-Border Dividends in the European, 19 *EC Tax Rev.* 2 (2010), p. 74.

Terra B., European Proposals for New Rules Regarding the Place of Supply of Services, in Krever R./White D. (eds.), *GST in Retrospect and Prospect* (Thomson Reuters, 2007), p. 369.

Terra B., *The Place of Supply in European VAT* (Kluwer, 1998).

Terra B., Value Added Tax and State Aid Law in the EU, 40 *Intertax* 2 (2012), p. 101.

Terra B./ Kajus J. (eds.), *A Guide to the Recast VAT Directive* (IBFD, 2015).

Terra B./ Kajus J., *Introduction to European VAT* (IBFD, 2016).

Terra B.J.M./Wattel P.J., *European Tax Law*[6] (Kluwer, 2012).

Thömmes O., Verbote der Diskriminierung von Steuerausländern und Steuerinländern, in Lehner M. (ed.), *Steuerrecht im Europäischen Binnenmarkt*, DStJG 19 (Dr Otto Schmidt, 1996), p. 81.

Thömmes O./Fuks E. (eds.) *EC Corporate Tax Law* (IBFD, 2007).

Thuronyi V., The Concept of Income, 46 *Tax L. Rev.* 1 (1990), p. 45.

Thym D., Freizügigkeit in Europa als Modell?, 46 *EuR* 4 (2011), p. 487.

Tietje C., Die Meistbegünstigungsverpflichtung im Gemeinschaftsrecht, 30 *EuR* 4 (1995), p. 398.

Tillinghast D., The Impact of the Internet on the Taxation of International Transactions, 50 *Bull. Intl. Taxn.* 11/12 (1996), p. 524.

Timmermans C.W.A., Genesis and Development of the European Communities, in Kapteyn P.J.G./McDonnell A.M./Mortelmans K.J.M./Timmermans C.W.A./ Geelhoed C.W.A. (eds.), *The Law of the European Union and the European Communities*[4] (Kluwer, 2008), p. 1.

Ting A., iTax - Apple's International Tax Structure and the Double Non-Taxation Issue, 59 *British Tax Rev.* 1 (2014), p. 40.

Tipke K., *Die Steuerrechtsordnung*[2] (Dr Otto Schmidt, 2000).

Tipke K., Über "richtiges Steuerrecht", 65 *StuW* 3 (1988), p. 262.

Tipke K./Lang J., *Steuerrecht*[22] (Dr Otto Schmidt, 2015).

Tippelhofer M., EG-Vertrag verbietet für 2005 nicht Treaty override, 22 *IStR* 8 (2013), p. 307.

Toifl G., Besteuerung ausländischer Dividendeneinkünfte und Kapitalverkehrsfreiheit, 12 *SWI* 10 (2002), p. 458.

Toifl G., Neue EuGH-Entscheidung zur Betriebsstättendiskriminierung, 7 *SWI* 7 (1997), p. 311.

Toifl G., Verstößt die Beschränkung der Endbesteuerung auf inländische Kapitalerträge gegen die Kapitalverkehrsfreiheit nach Art. 73b EGV?, 9 *SWI* 6 (1999), p. 255.

Traversa E., Interest Deductibility and the BEPS Action Plan: *nihil novi sub sole?*, 58 *British Tax Rev.* 5 (2013), p. 607.

Traversa E., The Selectivity Test: The Concept of "Regional Aid", in Rust A./Micheau C. (eds.), *State Aid and Tax Law* (Kluwer, 2013), p. 119.

Traversa E./Helleputte C., Double (Non-)Taxation in VAT and Direct Taxes: How to Achieve Some Convergence within a *Summa Divisio*? A European Perspective, in Lang M./Melz P./Kristoffersson E. (ed.), Ecker T. (ass. ed.), *Value Added Tax and Direct Taxation* (IBFD, 2009), p. 339.

Tridimas T., *The General Principles of EU Law*^{2} (Oxford University Press, 2006).

Tryfonidou A., *Reverse Discrimination in EC Law* (Kluwer, 2009).

Tumpel M., Die Betriebsstätte gem § 29 BAO – Ein Begriff von zentraler Bedeutung und komplexem Inhalt, in Tanzer M. (ed.), *Die BAO im 21. Jahrhundert, Festschrift für Gerold Stoll zum 80. Geburtstag* (LexisNexis, 2005), p. 77.

Tumpel M., Europarechtliche Besteuerungsmaßstäbe für die grenzüberschreitende Organisation und Finanzierung von Unternehmen, in Pelka J. (ed.), *Europa- und verfassungsrechtliche Grenzen der Unternehmensbesteuerung*, DStJG 30 (Dr Otto Schmidt, 2000), p. 321.

Tumpel M., Europarechtliche Besteuerungsmaßstäbe für die grenzüberschreitende Organisation und Finanzierung von Unternehmen, in Pelka J. (ed.), *Europa- und verfassungsrechtliche Grenzen der Unternehmensbesteuerung*, DStJG 30 (Dr Otto Schmidt, 2000), p. 321.

Tumpel M., *Harmonisierung der direkten Unternehmensbesteuerung in der EU* (Verlag Österreich, 1994).

Tumpel M., *Harmonisierung der direkten Unternehmensbesteuerung in der EU* (Verlag Österreich, 1994).

Tumpel M., Zweifel des Verwaltungsgerichtshofes an der Vereinbarkeit der Dividenden-besteuerung in Österreich mit der Kapitalverkehrsfreiheit, 12 *SWI* 10 (2002), p. 454.

Uebelhoer K./Pfeiffer S./Huisman E./Schaffer E., *Introduction to Austrian Tax Law* (Facultas, 2014).

van Arendonk H., Citizens and Taxation in the EU: Fifty Years after the Neumark Report, 21 *EC Tax Review* 3 (2012), p. 144.

van Arendonk H., Hughes de Lasteyrie du Saillant: crossing borders?, in van Arendonk H./Engelen F.A./Jansen S. (eds.), *A Tax Globalist, Essays in honour of Maarten J. Ellis* (IBFD, 2005), p. 181.

van Brederode R.F./O'Shea T., Legal Interpretation of Tax Law: The European Union, in van Brederode R.F./Krever R. (eds.), *Legal Interpretation of Tax Law* (Kluwer, 2014), p. 107.

Van de Vijver A., International Double (Non-)taxation: Comparative Guidance from European Legal Principles, 24 *EC Tax Rev.* 5 (2015), p. 240.

van den Hurk H., Proposed Amended Parent-Subsidiary Directive Reveals the European Commission's Lack of Vision, 68 *Bull. Intl. Taxn.* 9 (2014), p. 488.

van den Hurk H./Korving J., The "*D*" Case against the Netherlands and the ECJ's Decision – Is There Still a Future for MFN Treatment?, 60 *Bull. Intl. Taxn.* 8 (2006), p. 365.

Van den Tempel A.J., *Beseitigung der Doppelbesteuerung* (Internationales Steuerdokumentationsbüro, 1967).

van der Groeben H./Schwarze J. (eds.), *Kommentar zum Vertrag über die Europäische Union und zur Gründung der Europäischen Gemeinschaft*[6] (Nomos, 2004).

van der Linde R., Some thoughts on most-favoured-nation treatment within the European Community legal order in pursuance of the *D* case, 13 *EC Tax Rev.* 1 (2004), p. 10.

Van der Vegt P.C., BNP Paribas. State aid incompatible with the common market. General Court, 4 *H&I* 5 (2011), p. 95.

van Doesum A./van Kesteren H./van Norden G., The Internal Market and VAT: intra-group transactions of branches, subsidiaries and VAT groups, 16 *EC Tax Rev.* 1 (2007), p. 34.

van Gelder G./Niels B., Recent Developments in Hybrid Financial Instruments, 16 *Derivatives & Financial Instruments* 5 (2014), p. 219.

van Raad K., Non-residents: Personal Allowances. Deduction of Personal Expenses and Tax Rates, 2 *World Tax J.* 2 (2010), p. 154.

van Raad K., The Impact of the EC Treaty's Fundamental Freedoms Provisions on EC Member States' Taxation in Border-Crossing Situations - Current State of Affairs, 4 *EC Tax Rev.* 4 (1995), p. 190.

van Raad K., The Impact of the EC Treaty's Fundamental Freedoms Provisions on EC Member States' Taxation in Border-Crossing Situations – Current State of Affairs, 4 *EC Tax Rev.* 4 (1995), p. 190.

Van Sprundel D.E., An Analysis of the Netherlands Dividend Withholding Tax on Shares – No Need to Abolish This Tax Yet?, 48 *Eur. Taxn.* 12 (2008), p. 607.

Van Steenwinckel J./Van Vaeck J., European Court of Justice 14 December 2000, C-141/99, 10 *EC Tax Rev.* 2 (2001), p. 98.

Van Thiel S., A Slip of the European Court in the D case (C-376/03): Denial of the Most-Favoured-Nation Treatment because of Absence of Similarity?, 33 *Intertax* 10 (2005), p. 454.

Van Thiel S., Avoiding a Double Burden within the European Union: Comments on Kofler and Rust's Analysis, in Rust A. (ed.), *Double Taxation within the European Union* (Kluwer, 2011), p. 167.

Van Thiel S., *Free Movement of Persons and Income Tax Law: The European Court in Search of Principles* (IBFD, 2002).

Van Thiel S., Income tax payments and social security contributions from a Community law point of view: how the European Court of Justice should streamline its approach in the interest of the internal market, in Lang M. (ed.), *Double Taxation Conventions and Social Security Conventions* (Linde, 2006), p. 37.

Van Thiel S., Removal of income tax barriers to market integration in the European Union: litigation by the community citizen instead of harmonization by the community legislature?, 12 *EC Tax Rev.* 1 (2003), p. 4.

Van Thiel S., The Direct Income Tax Case Law of the European Court of Justice: Past Trends and Future Developments, 62 *Tax L. Rev.* 1 (2008), p. 143.

Van Thiel S., The Future of the Principle of Non-Discrimination in the EU: Towards a Right to Most Favored Nation Treatment and a Prohibition of Double Burdens?, in Avi-Yonah R.S./Hines Jr. J.R./Lang M. (eds.), *Comparative Fiscal Federalism* (Kluwer, 2007), p. 331.

Van Thiel S., The principle of non-discrimination in the EU and the right to most-favoured nation treatment in tax treaties, in Van Thiel S. (ed.), *The European Union's prohibition of discrimination, most-favoured-nation treatment and tax treaties: opinions and materials* (2006), p. 119.

Van Thiel S., Why the European Court of Justice Should Interpret Directly Applicable Community Law as a Right to Most-Favoured Nation Treatment and a Prohibition of Double Taxation, in Weber D. (ed.), *The Influence of European Law on Direct Taxation* (Kluwer, 2007), p. 75.

Van Thiel S./Achilles C., Die Beseitigung ertragsteuerlicher Hindernisse im Binnenmarkt: Eine Darstellung der Einflüsse der Rechtsprechung des EuGH auf die Ertragsbesteuerung in der Europäischen Union (Teil I), 12 *IStR* 15 (2003), p. 530.

Van Thiel S./Vascega M., *X Holding*: Why Ulysses Should Stop Listening to the Siren, 50 *Eur. Taxn.* 8 (2010), p. 334.

Vanistendael F., A comparative and economic approach to equality in European Taxation, in Gocke R./Gosch D./Lang M. (eds.), *Körperschaftsteuer – Internationales Steuerrecht – Doppelbesteuerungsabkommen*, FS Franz Wassermeyer (C.H. Beck, 2005), p. 523.

Vanistendael F., Ability to Pay in European Community Law, 23 *EC Tax Rev.* 3 (2014), p. 121.

Vanistendael F., Cohesion: the phoenix rises from his ashes, 14 *EC Tax Rev.* 5 (2005), p. 208.

Vanistendael F., *Denkavit Internationaal*: The Balance between Fiscal Sovereignty and the Fundamental Freedoms?, 47 *Eur. Taxn.* 5 (2007), p. 210.

Vanistendael F., Does the ECJ have the power of interpretation to build a tax system compatible with the fundamental freedoms?, 17 *EC Tax Rev.* 2 (2008), p. 52.

Vanistendael F., Fiscal support measures and harmful tax competition, 9 *EC Tax Rev.* 3 (2000), p. 152.

Vanistendael F., The ECJ at the Crossroads: Balancing Tax Sovereignty against the Imperatives of the Single Market, 46 *Eur. Taxn.* 9 (2006), p. 413.

Vanistendael F., The European Tax Paradox: How Less Begets More, 50 *Bull. Intl. Taxn.* 11/12 (1996), p. 531.

Vanistendael F., *The Future of Corporate Income Harmonisation in the E. C. after Ruding and Maastricht* (ZEW, 1992).

Vanistendael F., The Limits to the New Community Tax Order, 31 *Common Market L. Rev.* 2 (1994), p. 293.

Vedder C., Einwirkungen des Europarechts auf das innerstaatliche Recht und auf internationale Verträge der Mitgliedstaaten: die Regelung der Doppelbesteuerung, in Lehner M./Thömmes O./Vedder C./Wiedow A., *Europarecht und Internationales Steuerrecht* (C.H. Beck, 1994), p. 1.

VerLoren van Themaat P., The Contributions to the Establishment of the Internal Market by the Case-Law of the Court of Justice of the European Communities, in Bieber R./Dehousse R./Pinder J./Weiler J.H.H. (eds.), *1992: One European Market?* (Nomos, 1988), p. 109.

Vermeend W., The Court of Justice of the European Communities and direct taxes: 'Est-ce que la justice est de ce monde'?, 5 *EC Tax Rev.* 2 (1996), p. 54.

Verstraeten A.A., Double (non-)taxation in VAT and Direct Taxes: Which Tax is Better for Developing Countries?, in Lang M./Melz P./Kristoffersson E. (ed.), Ecker T. (ass. ed.), *Value Added Tax and Direct Taxation* (IBFD, 2009), p. 369.

Vogel K., *Der räumliche Anwendungsbereich der Verwaltungsrechtsnorm* (Alfred Metzner Verlag, 1965).

Vogel K., Doppelbesteuerungsabkommen und ihre Auslegung (I), 59 *StuW* 2 (1982), p. 111.

Vogel K., Internationales Steuerrecht, 85 *DStZ* 9 (1997), p. 269.

Vogel K./Lehner M. (eds.), *Doppelbesteuerungsabkommen*[6] (C.H. Beck, 2015).

Vogenauer S., *Die Auslegung von Gesetzen in England und auf dem Kontinent* (Mohr Siebeck, 2001), at p. 382

Völker D., Kapitalverkehrsfreiheit für Drittstaatendividenden – Widerspruch zur BFH-Rechtsprechung oder Bestätigung des BFH durch den EuGH-Beschluss vom 4. 6. 2009?, 18 *IStR* 20 (2009), p. 705.

von Bogdandy A., The European Union as a Human Rights Organization? Human Rights and the Core of the European Union, 37 *Common Market L. Rev.* 6 (2000), p. 1307.

von der Groeben H./Schwarze J. (eds.), *Kommentar zum Vertrag über die Europäische Union und zur Gründung der Europäischen Gemeinschaft*[6] (Nomos, 2004).

Vroom A., Malta and the Hybrid Loan Amendment to the EU Parent-Subsidiary Directive, 55 *Eur. Taxn.* 2 (2015), p. 102.

Vyncke K., VAT Grouping in the European Union: Purposes, Possibilities and Limitations, 18 *Intl. VAT Monitor* 4 (2007), p. 250.

Wächter C., Rechtsmissbrauch und Qualifikationskonflikt im Umsatzsteuerrecht, 49 *DStR* 2 (2011), p. 49.

Wassermeyer F./Kaeser C./Schwenke M. (eds.), *Doppelbesteuerung*[132] (C.H. Beck, 2016).

Wathelet M., Direct taxation and EU law: integration or disintegration?, 13 *EC Tax Rev.* 1 (2004), p. 2.

Wathelet M., Tax Sovereignty of the Member States and the European Court of Justice: New Trends or Confirmation?, in Hinnekens L./Hinnekens P. (eds.), *A Vision of*

Taxes within and outside Europe, Festschrift in honor of Prof. Dr. Frans Vanistendael (Kluwer, 2008), p. 905

Wattel P.J., Comparing Criteria: State Aid, Free Movement, Harmful Tax Competition and Market Distorting Disparities, in Richelle I./Schön W./Traversa E. (eds.), *Allocating Taxing Powers within the European Union* (Springer, 2013), p. 59.

Wattel P.J., Corporate tax jurisdiction in the EU with respect to branches and subsidiaries; dislocation distinguished from discrimination and disparity; a plea for territoriality, 12 *EC Tax Rev.* 4 (2003), p. 194.

Wattel P.J., Fiscal Cohesion, Fiscal Territoriality and Preservation of the (Balanced) Allocation of Taxing Power; What is the Difference, in Weber D. (ed.), *The Influence of European Law on Direct Taxation* (Kluwer, 2007), p. 139.

Wattel P.J., Forum: Interaction of State Aid, Free Movement, Policy Competition and Abuse Control in Direct Tax Matters, 5 *World Tax J.* 1 (2013), p. 128.

Wattel P.J., Non-Discrimination *á la Cour*: The ECJ's (Lack of) Comparability Analysis in Direct Tax Cases, 55 *Eur. Taxn.* 12 (2015), p. 542.

Wattel P.J., Passing the Buck Around: Who is Responsible for Double Taxation? – Comments on Profs. Kofler and Rust's Analysis, in Rust A. (ed.), *Double Taxation Within the European Union* (Kluwer, 2011), p. 157.

Wattel P.J., Progressive Taxation of Non-Residents and Intra-EC Allocation of Personal Allowances: Why *Schumacker, Asscher, Gilly* and *Gschwind* Do Not Suffice, 40 Eur. Taxn. 6 (2000), p. 210.

Wattel P.J., Red Herrings in Direct Tax Cases before the ECJ, 31 *Legal Issues of Economic Integration* 2 (2004), p. 81.

Wattel P.J., Some Fringe Areas of EU State Aid Law in Direct Tax Matters, in Weber D. (ed.), *EU Income Tax Law: Issues for the Years Ahead* (IBFD, 2013), p. 139.

Wattel P.J., Stateless Income, State Aid and the (Which?) Arm's Length Principle, 44 *Intertax* 11 (2016), p. 791.

Wattel P.J., Taxation of Intercompany Dividends and EU Law: Three Surprising Aspects of the Recent Case Law of the European Court, in Maisto G. (ed.), *Taxation of Intercompany Dividends under Tax Treaties and EU Law* (IBFD, 2012), p. 39.

Wattel P.J., Test Claimants in the FII Group Litigation (FII2). Equivalence of the exemption and imputation methods. Dividends from third countries. Free movement of capital. Court of Justice, 6 *H&I* 3 (2013), p. 5.

Wattel P.J., The Cat and the Pigeons: Some General Comments on (TP) Tax Rulings and State Aid After the Starbucks and Fiat Decisions, in Richelle I./Schön W./Traversa E. (eds.), *Allocating Taxing Powers within the European Union* (Springer, 2013), p. 185.

Wattel P.J., The EC Court's Attempts to Reconcile the Treaty Freedoms with International Tax Law, 33 *Common Market L. Rev.* 2 (1996), p. 223.

Weatherill S., After *Keck*: Some Thoughts on How to Clarify the Clarification, 33 *Common Market L. Rev.* 5 (1996), p. 885.

Weber D., An Analysis of the Past, Current and Future of the Coherence of the Tax System as Justifiation, 24 *EC Tax Rev.* 1 (2015), p. 43.

Weber D., Comments, 7 *H&I* 3.47 (2014), p. 47.

Weber D., Fidium Finanz AG v Bundesanstalt fur Finanzdienstleistungsaufsicht: the ECJ gives the wrong answer about the applicability of the free movement of capital between the EC Member States and non-member countries, 52 *British Tax Rev.* 6 (2007), p. 670.

Weber D., In Search of a (New) Equilibrium Between Tax Sovereignty and the Freedom of Movement Within the EC, 34 *Intertax* 12 (2006), p. 585.

Weber D., *In search of a (new) equilibrium between tax sovereignty and the freedom of movement within the EC* (Kluwer, 2006).

Weber D., Most-Favoured Nation Treatment under Tax Treaties Rejected in the European Community: Background and Analysis of the *D* case, 33 *Intertax* 10 (2005), p. 429.

Weber D., *Tax Avoidance and the EC Treaty Freedoms* (Kluwer, 2005).

Weber D./Spierts E., The "*D* Case": Most-Favoured-Nation Treatment and Compensation of Legal Costs before the European Court of Justice, 44 *Eur. Taxn.* 2 (2004), p. 65.

Weggenmann H., EG-rechtliche Aspekte steuerlicher Meistbegünstigung im Abkommensrecht, 12 *IStR* 19 (2003), p. 677.

Weiler J.H.H., The Transformation of Europe, 100 *Yale L. J.* 8 (1991), p. 2403.

Weiner J.M., Formula One. The race to find a common formula to apportion the EU tax base, 17 *EC Tax Rev.* 3 (2008), p. 100.

Weiner J.M./Mintz J., An Exploration of Formula Apportionment in the European Union, 42 *Eur. Taxn.* 8 (2002), p. 346.

Weninger P., *Formulary Apportionment in the EU* (Intersentia, 2009).

Wernsmann R., *Verhaltenslenkung in einem rationale Steuersystem* (Mohr Siebeck, 2005).

Westen P., The Empty Idea of Equality, 95 *Harv. L. Rev.* 3 (1982), p. 537.

Wiesemann A., *Entstehung und Vermeidung systembedingter doppelter Nicht- und Minderbesteuerung in Outbound-Konstellationen* (Nomos, 2014).

Wiesner W., Abgabenänderungsgesetz im BBG 2011 – Unternehmensbesteuerung, 21 *RWZ* 1 (2011), p. 3.

Williams D., Asscher: the European Court and the power to destroy, 6 *EC Tax Rev.* 1 (1997), p. 4.

Wiman B., Pending Cases Filed by Swedish Courts: The Skatteverket v A, Skatteverket v A and B, and Bouanich Cases, in Lang M./Schuch J./Staringer C. (eds.), *ECJ – Recent Developments in Direct Taxation* (Linde, 2006), p. 297.

Witt C.-H., Keine Vererblichkeit von Verlustvorträgen - Der Beschluss des Großen Senats und seine Folgen, 63 *BB* 23 (2008), p. 1199.

Wittendorf J., *Transfer Pricing and the Arm's Length Principle in International Tax Law* (Kluwer, 2010).

Witzel D., Die europarechtlichen Anforderungen an die Besteuerung von Auslandsdividenden - Der Fall "Schmid" -, 11 *IStR* 22 (2002), p. 758.

Wolff U., Generalthema I: Doppelte Nicht-Besteuerung, 13 *IStR* 16 (2004), p. 542.

Wouters J., The principle of non-discrimination in European Community Law, 8 *EC Tax Rev.* 2 (1999), p. 98.

Zalasiński A., Conclusion of the BEPS Multilateral Instrument and Distribution of Competences between the EU and its Member States, 61 *British Tax Rev.* 3 (2015), p. 444.

Zalasiński A., Proportionality of Anti-Avoidance and Anti-Abuse Measures in the ECJ's Direct Tax Case Law, 35 *Intertax* 5 (2007), p. 310.

Zimmer F., EFTA Court Strikes Down Norwegian Withholding Tax on Dividends, 36 *Tax Notes Intl. 10* (6 December 2004), p. 840.

Zorn N., EG-Grundfreiheiten und dritte Länder, in Quantschnigg P./ Wiesner W./Mayr G. (eds.), *Steuern im Gemeinschaftsrecht, Festschrift für Wolfgang Nolz* (LexisNexis, 2008), p. 211.

Zorn N., Nochmals: Kapitalverkehrsfreiheit für Drittstaatendividenden Eine Reaktion auf den Beitrag von Dietmar Völker in IStR 2009, 705 ff., 19 *IStR* 6 (2010), p. 190.

Zorn N., Rechtsangleichungskompetenzen des Rates der Europäischen Gemeinschaften für die Besteuerung von Unternehmen, in Pelka J. (ed.), *Europa- und verfassungsrechtliche Grenzen der Unternehmensbesteuerung,* DStJG 30 (Dr Otto Schmidt, 2000), p. 227.

Zorn N., VfGH prüft bisherige Liebhabereipraxis, 70 *SWK* 19 (1995), A 417.

Züger M., Das Schiedsverfahren nach dem neuen DBA Österreich-Deutschland, in Gassner W./Lang M./Lechner E. (eds.), *Das neue Doppelbesteuerungsabkommen Österreich-Deutschland* (Linde, 1999), p. 245.

Züger M., Der Einfluß des Schiedsverfahrens vor dem EuGH auf das Abgabenrecht, in Holoubek M./Lang M. (eds.), *Das EuGH-Verfahren in Steuersachen* (Linde, 2000), p. 301.

Züger M., Der EuGH als Schiedsgericht im neuen DBA Österreich-Deutschland, 9 *SWI* 1 (1999), p. 19.

Züger M., Mutual Agreement and Arbitration Procedure in a Multilateral Tax Treaty, in Lang M./Loukota H./Rädler A.J./Schuch J./Toifl G./Urtz C./Wassermeyer F./ Züger M., *Multilateral Tax Treaties* (Linde, 1997), p. 155.

Züger M., Neue internationale Steuerfälle vor dem EuGH, 10 *SWI* 3 (2000), p. 133.

Zuidgeest R., Cross-Border VAT Grouping, 21 *Intl. VAT Monitor* 1 (2010), p. 25.

Index

A

Ability-to-pay, 185, 188, 208, 352
  acquis communautaire, 43
Adria-Wien Pipeline, 210
Aggressive tax planning, 4, 54–56
Aid, 23, 40, 69, 315, 388
Alevizos, 233, 234
Amazon, 314
Amurta, 132, 276, 277, 301, 302
Anti-avoidance rules, 4, 55, 387
Anti-Tax Avoidance Directive (ATAD), 56, 317
Arbitration, 36, 44, 62, 249, 366
Arm's Length Principle, 356, 361, 362
ATAD. *See* Anti-Tax Avoidance Directive (ATAD)
Autonomy, 104, 220
Avoir Fiscal, 73, 122, 236, 262, 263, 272

B

Balanced allocation of taxing rights, 148
Base Erosion and Profit Shifting (BEPS), 5, 7–14, 43, 56, 381, 386, 387
Beker, 130
BEPS. *See* Base Erosion and Profit Shifting (BEPS)
Block, 44, 250, 251
Bosman, 101
Bouanich, 271–274, 301

C

Cassis de Dijon, 95, 96, 105, 238, 239
Circularly Linked Rules, 366
Code of Conduct, 39, 40, 51, 53, 162, 163, 324
Coherence, 140, 144–147, 150, 153, 216, 285, 310
Cohesion. *See* Coherence
Columbus Container Services, 127, 252–255
Common consolidated corporate tax base (CCCTB), 39
Common market. *See* Internal market
Comparability
  Fundamental Freedoms
    horizontal comparability
      Sopora, 128, 267
    vertical comparability, 120
  State aid, 178–199
Compensation, 101, 129, 132, 134, 140–142, 148–151, 192, 194, 195, 233, 269, 271, 274, 277, 281, 301, 311, 351
Competition, 2, 22–24, 28, 31, 36, 38, 40, 60, 65, 68–70, 161–163, 168, 169, 180–182, 193, 199, 212, 213, 219, 229, 314, 315, 318, 320, 322, 323, 338–340, 346, 351, 354, 356, 363, 371, 387, 388
Consistency, 209, 244–246, 377, 378

Convergence, 75–88, 129, 211–222
Credit method, 19, 255, 270, 275, 349, 350
Cross-border tax arbitrage. *See* Tax arbitrage

D

Damseaux, 251, 257
Dassonville, 95, 101–104
De Groot, 130–302
De Lasteyrie, 49, 50, 147
Denkavit, 275, 277
Deutsche Shell, 148, 149, 154
DISC cases, 346
Discrimination
  covert, 89, 90, 138, 205
  direct, 91
  indirect, 91
  negative, 221
  overt, 88–90, 138, 205
  positive, 221
Disparity, 9, 20, 31, 51, 104–108, 132, 224, 226, 245, 247, 341, 345, 371, 377
Dispute resolution, 43
Distortion, 23, 28, 35, 39, 40, 60, 67, 69, 70, 171, 175, 181, 193, 212, 226, 229, 315, 318, 320, 322, 323, 338, 346, 354, 356, 363, 371, 386
Dividend exemption, 12
Double burden, 94–100, 131, 226
Double hurdle, 94–100, 226
Double non-taxation, 1–29, 31–64, 68, 71, 222–379, 381–385, 387–389
Double taxation
  bilaterally caused, 280–290
  economic, 15, 44–48, 130, 133, 278–307, 309, 310, 312, 330, 368–371
  inter-state, 224
  intra-state, 309
  juridical, 15, 18, 19, 26, 41–44, 48, 235–280, 296, 303–306, 344–355, 377, 378
  unilaterally caused, 290–294, 303
Double Taxation Convention, 1, 41, 107, 247, 389
Double Tax Treaty, 6, 125, 253, 317, 387, 389

E

EC Multilateral Tax Convention on Income and Capital, 34
Equality, 76, 88, 242, 357, 358
ETI dispute, 347, 348, 354
Excise duty, 17, 206, 233
Exemption method, 246, 255, 273, 325, 347, 349, 350
Exit taxation, 49–51, 143, 146, 148, 150

F

Final losses, 240
Financial crisis, 3, 384
Fiscal cohesion. *See* Coherence
Fiscal supervision, 141, 217
Fokus Bank, 274, 290
Free movement, 14, 19, 20, 22, 28, 47, 65, 68–70, 79–84, 87–89, 91, 92, 94–96, 100–104, 126, 129, 136, 156, 158, 212, 216, 230, 239, 261, 272, 273, 277, 283, 288, 302, 338, 339, 382, 383
Free movement of capital, 69, 80–84, 87, 88, 126, 136, 216, 272, 277, 288, 302
Fundamental Freedoms, 6, 48, 69, 224, 383
Futura Participations, 96, 100, 109, 131, 143, 225

G

General Anti-Avoidance Rules (GAAR), 4, 387
Gibraltar, 179, 180, 196, 208, 209
Glaxo Wellcome, 151–154
Google, 314

H

Harmful tax competition. *See* Tax competition
Hybrid instrument, 12, 53
Hybrid loan, 12, 53, 324, 325
Hybrid mismatch, 11, 372

I

Imfeld and Garcet, 130, 299, 300
Inconsistency, 3, 133, 245, 315, 335, 386
In dubio pro communitate, 339
Inheritance tax, 17, 99, 228, 250
Integration, 29, 38, 45, 46, 59, 65, 70–72, 74, 75, 211, 227–234, 258, 309, 318–339
Interest and Royalty Directive, 43
Internal consistency test, 244–246, 377, 378
Internal market, 14, 31, 65, 224, 382

J

J.F. Kennedy, 3
Justification
  Fundamental Freedoms
    unwritten justification grounds, 136–138
    written justification grounds, 136–138
  State aid
    de jure exceptions, 200–201
    discretionary exceptions, 200–201
    justification by means of objectives extrinsic to the tax system, 204–209
    justification by means of the mechanisms inherent in the tax system, 202–204

K

Keck, 103
Kerckhaert and Morres, 235, 238, 244, 250, 251, 257
Kernkraftwerke Lippe-Ems, 205

L

League of Nations, 17
Lenz, 285, 286, 299
Levy and Sebbag, 251, 255–257
Lidl Belgium, 113, 114
Lindfors, 98, 232
Linking Rules, 366
Lottery Winnings, 13, 24

M

Manninen, 130–132, 285, 286, 299, 306, 311
Merger Directive, 36, 41, 241
Most-Favoured Nation (MFN), 123, 267
Multilateral Convention, 41, 43, 258

N

National Grid Indus, 145, 146, 148
Negative integration, 29, 70, 74, 211
Neumark Report, 31, 32, 41
Neutralization, 276, 277
Neutral Rules, 100–104
Non-discrimination, 76, 78, 93, 100, 116, 119, 124, 264, 283

P

Paint Graphos, 209, 210, 219
Parafiscal charge, 17
Parent-Subsidiary Directive, 36, 41, 46–48, 52, 241, 243, 273, 297, 324–333, 377
Participation exemption, 52, 53, 324, 344, 367–371
Payroll levy, 17, 99
Place-of-supply, 60, 319–323, 335
Preferential treatment, 23, 28, 171, 178, 191–193, 195, 196, 208, 316, 340
Principle of loyalty, 250, 251
Profit adjustment, 364, 365
Proportionality
  adequacy, 157
  appropriateness, 157

Fundamental Freedoms, 155, 156, 162, 199, 209, 211–219, 221, 222, 284, 352
necessity, 157, 158, 204, 370
State aid, 210–213, 215–222, 352–356, 358
suitability, 157, 158

R

RBS Deutschland Holding, 60, 61, 334
Reference system, 187, 188
Regulatory tax, 183, 208
Restriction, 66, 69, 80, 94, 95, 101–103, 105–108, 110, 112, 113, 119, 132, 136–138, 141, 145, 152, 161, 187, 205, 216, 217, 225, 230, 240, 252, 262, 275–277, 301–303, 363, 369
Riskin and Timmermans, 126, 127
Ruding Report, 35–38, 42, 47, 49, 162
Rule of Reason, 137, 138, 155, 205, 216, 218, 219

S

Saint-Gobain, 122, 263–267, 272
Savings Directive, 42, 242
Schedular system, 45, 286, 368
Schempp, 134, 159
Schul I, 228–233, 336, 337
Scorpio, 116
Segré Report, 31, 32, 41
Selectivity
de facto selectivity, 204, 205
de jure selectivity, 200, 205, 382
SGI, 152, 154, 155, 363
Sopora, 128, 267
Sovereignty, 29, 32, 39, 43, 71, 72, 99, 150, 204, 223, 237, 252, 254, 257, 280, 303, 312, 349
Special charges, 171, 172
Starbucks, 313, 314
State aid, 23, 40, 69, 315, 388
State resources, 161, 172–174, 176, 213
Subject-to-tax clause, 55, 353, 354
Subsidy, 12, 34–36, 41, 46–48, 52, 63, 113–115, 120, 122, 123, 143, 151, 161, 169, 171, 192, 221, 243, 273, 275, 297, 324–333, 346, 347, 358, 367, 370, 377

T

Tax arbitrage, 36, 51–53, 325, 373
Tax competition, 2, 36, 38, 162, 163
Tax corridor, 25
Tax evasion, 32, 54, 155, 267, 268
Tax fraud, 53, 54
Tax planning, 2–4, 11, 12, 36, 54–56, 313–315, 317, 343, 381, 382, 384
Tax policy, 3, 13, 20, 25, 31–64, 105, 163, 197, 303, 375, 383
Territoriality, 75, 140, 142–155, 217, 346
Tertium comparationis, 102
Thin capitalization, 37, 151, 154, 330, 366
Third Countries, 42, 52–54, 60, 66, 80, 82–84, 86–88, 123, 126, 136, 320
Timac Agro, 113–115, 145
Trade between Member States, 23, 70, 103, 161, 171, 175–177, 182, 199, 213, 219
Transfer pricing, 37, 151, 152, 193, 344, 355–357, 360–367, 378
Treaty override, 249–261
Truck Center, 112, 116, 159

U

Unanimity requirement, 72

V

Van den Tempel Report, 32
VAT Directive, 16, 58, 60–63, 228–231, 318, 320–324, 333–337
VAT grouping, 62, 63
Verkooijen, 280, 285–287

W

White Paper, 33
Withholding tax, 42, 52, 112, 113, 116, 126, 133, 235, 236, 245, 246, 256, 269, 270, 274–276, 286, 287, 291, 294, 297
World Duty, 197, 199, 372
WTO Law, 348

EUCOTAX Series on European Taxation

(1) Peter HJ Essers, Guido JME de Bont & Eric CCM Kemmeren (eds), *The Compatibility of Anti-Abuse Provisions in Tax Treaties with EC Law*, 1998 (ISBN 90-411-9678-1).
(2) Gerard TK Meussen (ed.), *The Principle of Equality in European Taxation*, 1999 (ISBN 90-411-9693-5).
(3) Michael Lang (ed.), *Tax Treaty Interpretation*, 2001 (ISBN 90-411-9857-1).
(4) Pasquale Pistone, *The Impact of Community Law on Tax Treaties: Issues and Solutions*, 2002 (ISBN 90-411-9860-1).
(5) René Offermanns, *The Entrepreneurship Concept in a European Comparative Tax Law Perspective*, 2002 (ISBN 90-411-9887-3).
(6) Michael Lang & Mario Züger, *Settlement of Disputes in Tax Treaty Law*, 2002 (ISBN 90-411-9904-7).
(7) Carlo Pinto, *Tax Competition and EU Law*, 2003 (ISBN 90-411-9913-6).
(8) Michael Lang, Hans-Jörgen Aigner, Ulrich Scheuerle & Markus Stefaner, *CFC Legislation, Tax Treaties and EC Law*, 2004 (ISBN 90-411-2284-2).
(9) Mattias Dahlberg, *Direct Taxation in Relation to the Freedom of Establishment and the Free Movement of Capital*, 2005 (ISBN 90-411-2363-6).
(10) Michael Lang, Judith Herdin & Ines Hofbauer, *WTO and Direct Taxation*, 2005 (ISBN 90-411-2371-7).
(11) Dennis Weber, *Tax Avoidance and the EC Tray Freedoms: A Study of the Limitations under European Law for the Prevention of Tax Avoidance*, 2005 (ISBN 90-411-2402-0).
(12) Félix Alberto Vega Borrego, *Limitations on Benefits Clauses on Double Taxation Conventions*, 2005 (ISBN 90-411-2370-9).
(13) Michael Lang, Josef Schuch & Claus Staringer, *ECJ-Recent Developments in Direct Taxation*, 2006 (ISBN 90-411-2509-4).
(14) Reuven S. Avi-Yonah, James R. Hines Jr. & Michael Lang, *Comparative Fiscal Federalism. Comparing the European Court of Justice and the US Supreme Court's Tax Jurisprudence*, 2007 (ISBN 978-90-411-2552-1).
(15) Christiana HJI Panayi, *Double Taxation, Tax Treaties, Treaty-Shopping and the European Community*, 2007 (ISBN 978-90-411-2658-0).
(16) Dennis Weber, *The Influence of European Law on Direct Taxation: Recent and Future Developments*, 2007 (ISBN 978-90-411-2667-2).
(17) Michael Lang & Pasquale Pistone, *The EU and Third Countries: Direct Taxation*, 2007 (ISBN 978-90-411-2665-8).
(18) Oskar Henkow, *Financial Activities in European VAT: A Theoretical and Legal Research of the European VAT System and Preferred Treatment of Financial Activities*, 2007 (ISBN 978-90-411-2703-7).
(19) Michael Lang (ed.), *Tax Compliance Costs for Companies in an Enlarged European Community*, 2008 (ISBN 978-90-411-2666-5).

(20) Michael Lang (ed.), *Source versus Residence. Problems Arising from the Allocation of Taxing Rights in Tax Treaty Law and Possible Alternatives,* 2008 (ISBN 978-90-411-2763-1).
(21) Ioanna Mitroyanni, *Integration Approaches to Group Taxation in the European Internal Market,* 2008 (ISBN 978-90-411-2779-2).
(22) Rolf Eicke, *Tax Planning with Holding Companies. Repatriation of US Profits from Europe:Concepts, Strategies, Structures,* 2008 (ISBN978-90-411-2794-5).
(23) Peter Essers et al. (ed.), *The Influence of IAS/IFRS on the CCCTB, Tax Accounting, Disclosure and Corporate Law Accounting Concepts: 'A Clash of Cultures',* 2008 (ISBN 978-90-411-2819-5).
(24) Tonny Schenk-Geers, *International Exchange of Information and the Protection of Taxpayers,* 2009 (ISBN 978-90-411-3142-3).
(25) Raymond Adema, *UCITS and Taxation: Towards Harmonization of the Taxation of UCITS,* 2009 (ISBN 978-90-411-2839-3).
(26) Michael Lang, Jianwen Liu & Gongliang Tang (eds), *Europe–China Tax Treaties,* 2010 (ISBN 978-90-411-3216-1).
(27) Michael Lang, Pasquale Pistone, Josef Schuch & Claus Staringer (eds), *Procedural Rules in Tax Law in the Context of European Union and Domestic Law,* 2010 (ISBN 978-90-411-3376-2).
(28) Sjaak J.J.M. Jansen, *Fiscal Sovereignty of the Member States in an Internal Market: Past and Future,* 2011 (ISBN 978-90-411-3403-5).
(29) Dennis Weber & Bruno da Silva, *From Marks & Spencer to X Holding: The Future of Cross-Border Group Taxation,* 2011 (ISBN 978-90-411-3399-1).
(30) Claus Bohn Jespersen, *Intermediation of Insurance and Financial Services in European VAT,* 2011 (ISBN 978-90-411-3732-6).
(31) Sabine Heidenbauer, *Charity Crossing Borders: The Fundamental Freedoms' Influence on Charity and Donor Taxation in Europe,* 2011 (ISBN 978-90-411-3813-2).
(32) Michael Lang, et al., *The Future of Indirect Taxation: Recent Trends in VAT and GST Systems around the World,* 2012 (ISBN 978-90-411-3797-5).
(33) Harm van den Broek, *Cross-Border Mergers within the EU: Proposals to Remove the Remaining Tax Obstacles,* 2012 (ISBN 978-90-411-3824-8).
(34) Michael Lang, et al. (eds), *Tax Treaty Case Law around the Globe – 2011,* 2012 (ISBN 978-90-411-3876-7).
(35) Dennis Weber (ed.), *CCCTB: Selected Issues,* 2012 (ISBN 978-90-411-3872-9).
(36) Daniël Smit, *EU Freedoms, Non-EU Countries and Company Taxation,* 2012 (ISBN 978-90-411-4041-8).
(37) Rita de la Feria, *VAT Exemptions: Consequences and Design Alternatives,* 2013 (ISBN 978-90-411-3276-5).
(38) Karin Simader, *Withholding Taxes and the Fundamental Freedoms,* 2013 (ISBN 978-90-411-4842-1).
(39) Madeleine Merkx, *Establishments in European VAT,* 2013 (ISBN 978-90-411-4554-3).
(40) Carla De Pietro, *Tax Treaty Override,* 2014 (ISBN 978-90-411-5406-4).

(41) G.K. Fibbe & A.J.A. Stevens (eds), *Hybrid Entities and the EU Direct Tax Directives*, 2015 (ISBN 978-90-411-5942-7).
(42) Gerard Staats, *Personal Pensions in the EU*, 2015 (ISBN 978-90-411-5953-3).
(43) Michael Lang & Ine Lejeune (eds), *VAT/GST in a Global Digital Economy*, 2015 (ISBN 978-90-411-5952-6).
(44) Massimo Basilavecchia, Lorenzo del Federico & Pietro Mastellone (eds), *Tax Implications of Environmental Disasters and Pollution*, 2015 (ISBN 978-90-411-5611-2).
(45) Cristina Trenta, *Rethinking EU VAT for P2P Distribution*, 2015 (ISBN 978-90-411-6137-6).
(46) Marie Lamensch, Edoardo Traversa & Servaas van Thiel (eds), *Value Added Tax and the Digital Economy: The 2015 EU Rules and Broader Issues*, 2016 (ISBN 978-90-411-6612-8).
(47) Raffaele Petruzzi, *Transfer Pricing Aspects of Intra-Group Financing*, 2016 (ISBN 978-90-411-6732-3).
(48) Mario Grandinetti (ed.), *Corporate Tax Base in the Light of the IAS/IFRS and EU Directive 2013/34: A Comparative Approach*, 2016 (ISBN 978-90-411-6745-3).
(49) Bruno da Silva, *The Impact of Tax Treaties and EU Law on Group Taxation Regimes*, 2016 (ISBN 978-90-411-6905-1).
(50) Michael Lang, Alfred Storck & Raffaele Petruzzi (eds), *Transfer Pricing in a Post-BEPS World*, 2016 (ISBN 978-90-411-6710-1).
(51) Marta Papis-Almansa, *Insurance in European VAT: Current and Preferred Treatment in the Light of the New Zealand and Australian GST Systems*, 2017 (ISBN 978-90-411-8360-6).
(52) Wolfgang Speckhahn, *Real Estate Investment Trusts In Europe: Europeanising Tax Regimes*, 2017 (ISBN 978-90-411-8360-6).
(53) Frank J.G. Nellen, *Information Asymmetries in EU VAT*, 2017 (ISBN 978-90-411-8837-3).
(54) Erik Ros, *EU Citizenship and Direct Taxation*, 2017 (ISBN 978-90-411-8584-6).
(55) Werner Haslehner, Georg Kofler & Alexander Rust (eds), *EU Tax Law and Policy in the 21st Century*, 2017 (ISBN 978-90-411-8815-1).
(56) Claudia Sanò, *National Legal Presumptions and European Tax Law*, 2018 (ISBN 978-90-411-6613-5).
(57) Christoph Marchgraber, *Double (Non-)Taxation and EU Law*, 2018 (ISBN 978-90-411-9410-7).

www.ingramcontent.com/pod-product-compliance
Lightning Source LLC
LaVergne TN
LVHW020003031026
849161LV00023B/838
* 9 7 8 9 0 4 1 1 9 4 1 0 7 *